THE NEW NEGRO

Alain Locke by Winold Reiss. 1925. Private Collection.

THE NEW NEGRO

▶▶▶ THE LIFE OF ◀◀◀
ALAIN LOCKE

JEFFREY C. STEWART

OXFORD
UNIVERSITY PRESS

OXFORD
UNIVERSITY PRESS

Oxford University Press is a department of the University of Oxford.
It furthers the University's objective of excellence in research, scholarship,
and education by publishing worldwide. Oxford is a registered trade mark of
Oxford University Press in the UK and certain other countries.

Published in the United States of America by Oxford University Press
198 Madison Avenue, New York, NY 10016, United States of America.

Library of Congress Cataloging-in-Publication Data
Names: Stewart, Jeffrey C., 1950–author.
Title: The new Negro : the life of Alain Locke / Jeffrey C. Stewart.
Description: New York, NY : Oxford University Press, 2018. | Includes
bibliographical references and index.
Identifiers: LCCN 2017026626 (print) | LCCN 2017026908 (ebook) |
ISBN 9780199723317 (Updf) | ISBN 9780190652852 (Epub) | ISBN 9780195089578
(hardcover : acid-free paper)
Subjects: LCSH: Locke, Alain, 1885–1954. | Locke, Alain, 1885–1954—Political
and social views. | African American philosophers—Biography. | African
American intellectuals—Biography. | African American college
teachers—Biography. | Harlem Renaissance. | African American
arts—History. | African Americans—Intellectual life. | BISAC: HISTORY /
United States / 20th Century. | HISTORY / Social History. | BIOGRAPHY &
AUTOBIOGRAPHY / Composers & Musicians.
Classification: LCC E185.97.L79 (ebook) | LCC E185.97.L79 S83 2017 (print) |
DDC 191—dc23
LC record available at https://lccn.loc.gov/2017026626

1 3 5 7 9 8 6 4 2

Printed by Edwards Brothers Malloy, United States of America

To John Wesley Blassingame (1940–2000)
scholar, mentor, and friend,
who set me on this course

CONTENTS

PART II   ENTER THE NEW NEGRO

PART III   METAMORPHOSIS

ACKNOWLEDGMENTS

This biography of Alain Locke exists because of the inspiration of a community of scholars, mentors, and friends, including Eleanor W. Traylor, E. Curmie Price, Monifa Love Asante, Anissa Ryan Stewart, Fath Davis Ruffins, Marta Reid Stewart, Julie Thacker, Gilbert Morris, Paula Lieberman, Hugo Hopping, Prudence Cumberbatch, Lois Mailou Jones, Richard Long, Carl Faber Jr., Dr. Phyllis Daen, Lawrence Lee Jones, Margaret Rose Vendryes, Patricia Hills, Claudia Tate, Richard Powell, Henry Louis Gates Jr., Rose Cherubin, Laurie Monahan, Renate Reiss, Ethelbert Miller, John S. Wright, Paul Coates, Kellie Jones, Joellen El Bashir, Arthur Fauset, Clifford L. Muse, Richard Edward Jenkins III, Melvin Oliver, Vincent Johnson, Harold Lewis, Doxey Wilkerson, Arthur Davis, Sterling Brown, Sabrina Vellucci, Marion Deshmukh, Wilburn Williams, William Banner, Charles Prudhomme, Linda Heywood, Shirley Moody-Turner, Jerry G. Watts, Robin Kelly, Stephanie Batiste, Paul Ruffins, Suzanne Preston Blier, Steven Nelson, Anna Scacchi, Meaghan Alston, Roberto Strongman, Gwendolyn DuBois Shaw, Lowery Stokes Sims, Ossie Davis, Steven Jones, Stephanie Batiste, Sass Smith, Leroy Odinga Perry, Marissa Parham, Joyce Owens, Jonathan Holloway, Nell Painter, Esme Bhan, David Musto, Evelyn Brooks Higginbotham, Peter Fitzsimmons, Arcilla Stahl, Michelle Huneven, Bruce Johnston, Lizabeth Cohen, Jamaica Kincaid, Stanley Crouch, Samella Lewis, Stephen Goldsmith, Nelson Maldonado-Torres, Helen Vendler, Gordon Teskey, Thomas Richards, Cristina Giorcelli, Azfar Hussain, Werner Sollors, Christa Clarke, Jacqueline Goggin, Bill Pencak, Maurice Natanson, Gerald Early, Celeste-Marie Bernier, Kimberly Camp, Chela Sandoval, Kathryn Coney, Alan Trachtenberg, Aida Hurtado, Isaac Julien, Camara Dia Holloway, Alvia Wardlaw, Nathan A. Scott, John Hope Franklin, A'Lelia Bundles, Robert Farris Thompson, Kobena Mercer, Judith Green, George Lipsitz, Claudine Michel, David Levering Lewis, Aida Hurtado, Ellen Cummings, Michael Winston, Thomas C. Battle, Donna M. Wells, David Driskell, Clifford Muse, Clarence Walker, Christopher McAuley, Cornel West, Jane Duran, Corey Blechman, Samella Lewis, Arnold Rampersad, Lydia Balian, Ashley Champayne, Charlotte

Becker, Robert A. Hill, Francille Wilson, W. Tjark Reiss, and many others. Special thanks go to my editor, Susan Ferber, Oxford University Press, for her unstinting support, and my agent, Marie Brown, for her guidance and fealty. I also thank the Moorland-Spingarn Research Center at Howard University, Beinecke Library at Yale University, the W. E. B. Du Bois Research Institute and the Charles Warren Center at Harvard University, the Woodrow Wilson Center, George Mason University, the Getty Foundation, the National Humanities Center, the Terra Foundation, and the University of California at Santa Barbara for support over many years of this project.

THE NEW
NEGRO

PART 1

THE EDUCATION OF ALAIN LOCKE

Mary Hawkins Locke, ca. 1921. Courtesy of the Moorland-Spingarn Research Center, Howard University.

1

A Death and a Birth

Alain Locke rose early on April 23, 1922, a cool, clear Sunday after Easter in Washington, D.C. It was also the Sunday before his mother's sixty-seventh birthday. He woke her, helped her dress, and then served breakfast. Afterward, he read to her from the Sunday edition of the *Evening Star*. Headlines announced that the secret Russian-German economic pact threatened to break up the Genoa Conference, the Pan-American Conference of Women proposed a League of Nations, and Sir Arthur Conan Doyle, the Sherlock Holmes author, was to speak in Washington as part of his nationwide tour. Only the last caught her interest—she and her son shared an interest in psychic phenomena, and Sir Conan's lecture on spiritualism was sure to be provocative and revealing. She dozed off when Alain launched into the details of his particular interest, the struggle between Germany and the Allies for trading rights with newly Communist Russia.[1] That afternoon she was "stricken," in the words of her son. He laid her down in her bed, where, at 7 P.M., she died, leaving her son of thirty-seven years alone in their home. The next day he taught his philosophy class at Howard University as usual. Only later in that day did students learn that Dr. Locke's mother had died. Others learned of her passing from Tuesday's *Evening Star*, which carried the death notice, "Locke. Sunday, April 23, 1922 at her residence, 1326 R Street NW, Mary Hawkins, beloved wife of the late Pliny Ishmael Locke and mother of Alain Leroy Locke. Last reception to friends Wednesday evening, from 6 to 8 o'clock, at her residence."[2]

A student of Locke's, poet Mae Miller Sullivan, recalls that her father, Kelly Miller, a dean at Howard University, hurried her mother that Wednesday evening saying, "Mama, get your things together. We mustn't be late for Dr. Locke's reception for his mother."[3] The Millers and other friends of the Lockes climbed the stairs to the second-story apartment on R Street to find the deceased Mary Locke propped up on the parlor couch, as though she might lean and pour tea at any moment. She was dressed exquisitely in her fine gray dress, her hair perfectly arranged. She even had gloves on. Locke invited his guests to "take tea with Mother for the last time."[4] After a short visit, most left quickly. On Thursday,

Locke had her cremated and, according to his friend Douglas Stafford, he kept "the ashes of his mother reposed in a finely embellished casket" on the White grand piano in his home.[5]

The story of Locke's "wake" for his mother became part of the folklore of Washington's middle class. On the one hand, it was common practice in the early twentieth century for the deceased to be laid in state in a bedroom to be visited by family friends. It probably did not surprise close friends that Locke had placed gloves on his dead mother's hands, since they were part of proper attire for tea in a Victorian household. On the other hand, having her seated and dressed as if alive struck most visitors as wildly eccentric. It was known that Locke and his mother were close and that the two kept pretty much to themselves. When they did entertain, it was together. Dr. Metz T. P. Lochard, a colleague and close friend, recalled many Sunday strolls and stimulating conversations with Locke and his mother, whom Lochard recalled as a refined, cultured, and well-read woman. "She had all the ways of an old English aristocrat. She was gentle, affable, kind, tolerant and indulgent. That's why Locke was so attached to her."[6] The obituary notice that Locke published in the *Crisis*, the magazine of the National Association for the Advancement of Colored People (NAACP), said Mary Hawkins Locke came from "an old Philadelphian family."[7] Hers was a well-respected family whose members had had close ties with the upper class in Philadelphia.

Such closeness between sons and mothers was not unheard of in the early twentieth-century Black community, almost as compensation for the disruption of maternal relationships under slavery. Certainly that "peculiar institution" had not allowed slave mothers to provide anything like the undivided attention Locke had enjoyed. The post-emancipation community tended to idealize mother-love, especially among the northern bourgeoisie, where two-parent family relationships symbolized class respectability and the nurturing, caretaking mother anchored Victorian families. Mother was a boy's most reliable companion, especially around the turn of the century when male mortality rates were high. It was no accident that Langston Hughes's famous poem about a boy's struggle to survive is dedicated to his mother, who consoles the son by sharing her burden with him—"Son, life for me ain't been no crystal stair."[8]

Life had been no crystal stair for Mary Locke, either. After her husband's death when Alain was six, she had taught school days and nights, and in the summer, to earn enough to support the two of them during his long educational tenure. Despite constant work, Mary had showered him with the kind of close attention, constant encouragement, and special nurturing that this tiny, physically delicate, often sickly child demanded. He, in turn, responded to this outpouring of care by taking on and living up to her dreams and high expectations. He had excelled first at Central High in Philadelphia and then again at Harvard College, where he won several scholarships and graduated Phi Beta Kappa. In his final year, he had been the first African American to be chosen as a Rhodes Scholar to

Oxford. After further study at the University of Berlin, he had returned to the United States and become a professor at Howard University.

Upon her retirement in 1915, Locke took his mother with him when he returned to Harvard for graduate study that led to his PhD in philosophy in 1918. Afterward, they lived together in his second-story apartment in Washington, D.C., and he filled her declining years with the kind of reading material and trips to museums and concerts that she had lavished on him as a child. If from her deathbed, she had surveyed the work she had done, she would have concluded it was a job well done. In turn, Locke's wake to his mother and his tribute to her in the *Crisis* testified to how much he valued her and how deeply he mourned her.[9]

Had Locke not chosen to invite members of the community to his bizarre public wake, then perhaps his relationship with his mother and her dominating role in his life would have gone unmentioned. Instead, people who knew nothing else about Locke's life and work knew of the tea with the mother propped up as if alive. Locke's obsessive attention to detail in staging the wake, down to the finery of the lace on her dress and the placing of gloves on her hands, tended to caricature his mother in the very act of honoring her, bringing his high-minded, spiritual, self-sacrificing love down to the level of common snicker and unguarded amusement. Such adulation forced the community to confront an unsettling issue. In one theatrical gesture, Locke had symbolized the problem of an entire generation of young men and women who, because of their "proper honoring of elders," felt stifled by both their parents and the Victorian fetishes of decorous living, social propriety, and group respectability. Like others of his talented generation, Locke had been unable to separate from his mother. Even death did not finally sever that cord.

Alain Locke was unknown to the general public, in part because he had devoted much of his adult life to a quiet caring for his aging mother, but also because he had failed to take on a major role as a Black intellectual, such as his forerunner at Harvard and Berlin, W. E. B. Du Bois, had done.[10] Locke had avoided involvement with the National Association for the Advancement of Colored People (NAACP), had avoided involvement with more radical organizations like Marcus Garvey's Universal Negro Improvement Association (UNIA), and especially avoided such socialist organizations as Hubert Harrison's International Colored Unity League (ICUL). He did not like civil rights movements or more accurately civil rights organizations, did not like the whole practice of protest that had already become definitive in Black political advancement in the early twentieth century. Locke was not one to be found in a march, or a riot, or demonstrating to bring about change—even of wrongs he agreed were despicable. Born and bred in Philadelphia's Black middle class, Anglophile in dress and class snobbishness, a man who seemed to represent in his learning and bearing an old world Black tradition that no one knew existed, he was a fish out of water in most situations of mass political organization because of his class consciousness and sense of distance from most Negroes. And for years he had been insulated from any criticism of this lack of public involvement in Black affairs by his caring for his mother. Now, that excuse was gone.

There was one more thing. He was a tiny, effeminate, gay man—a dandy, really, often seen walking with a cane, discreet, of course, but with just enough of a hint of a swagger, to announce to those curious that he was queer, in more ways than one, but especially in that one way that disturbed even those who supported Negro liberation. His sexual orientation made him unwelcome in some communities and feared in others as a kind of pariah. And early on he had decided that working with masses of Black people in close quarters like mass movements rushed scandal and exposure he could not afford. So, he kept his distance from the masses of Black people, the working and lower-middle classes of the race, those his mother had taught him to avoid anyway.

But Locke did something remarkable with his alienation. He decided to use art, the beautiful and the sublime that nurtured his and his friends' subjectivities in a world of hate, to subjectivize the Negro, to transform the image of the Negro from a poor relation of the American family to that of the premier creator of American culture. Rejecting the notion advanced by W. E. B. Du Bois that the political struggle for civil rights should be the focal point of Black intellectual life, Locke argued that what really made the Negro unique in America was the extent to which Black people had produced the only indelible art that America had produced. At a time when radicals argued that the rioting of Blacks in Chicago in 1919 against racial attacks by Whites was the essence of the New Negro, Locke argued that a new consciousness had emerged since World War I of positive possibility for Black people in the twentieth century despite the constraints of American segregation. At a time in the early 1920s when the popular discourse about Negroes even in liberal progressive circles was that of a tragic problem of American democracy that needed fixing, Locke created a counter-image—that of a New Negro who was reinventing himself or herself in a new century often without the help of Whites. The New Negro was a cultural giant held down by White Lilliputians and all that was needed was for this giant to throw off the intellectual strings that bound this intellect to self-pitying despair about Black people's plight in America, and assume his or her true role—as the architect of a new, more vibrant future called American culture if those in his or her path would just get out of the way.

In the 1920s, these views were radical, but Locke found a way to advance them by using Beauty to subjectivize Black people. By focusing his advocacy of the New Negro on art, literature, music, dance, and theater, arenas in which queer Black people of color like himself found sanctuary, Locke shifted the discussion of the Black experience to the creative industries that even racists admitted were mastered by Black people. The spirituals, to take his favorite example, had transformed Anglican hymns into something fundamentally American but also transformed the attitudes of Whites and Blacks who heard them. "Afro-Americans," a term he used frequently, manifested a creative genius from the moment they landed in the Americas by taking a foreign culture and making something new out of that. The enslaved were just that—temporarily bound but spiritually free people, who, despite earthly oppression, could create works of beauty, as the "sorrow songs" had shown. Those songs showed Locke, a philosopher, that a consciousness existed even in the most oppressive people who could change their perspective on their life through art. Beauty, in other words, was a source of power for it could transform the situation of Black people by transforming how they saw themselves. By focusing on Black cultural production, Locke sought to revitalize urban Black communities, elevate Black self-esteem, and create a role for himself as a leader of African-derived peoples.

Something about the death of his mother in 1922 released him to take on this daunting, Herculean task. Her death loosened the grip of her Black Victorian culture on his thinking, but it also left him with a crushing longing for the unconditional love she bestowed on him. The process was not immediate or easy. At first he was inconsolable, dogged by pangs of loneliness and anxiety that left him wandering the streets of Washington, D.C., with a faraway look in his eyes. Although he continued to teach classes, those who knew him better realized that a sharp pain lingered behind the hungry look in his eyes. One friend in particular offered herself as a kind of mother-surrogate and helped Locke through this difficult period. That woman was Georgia Douglas Johnson, a well-known Washington, D.C. poet, who was married to a prominent attorney and the Recorder of Deeds for the District of Columbia. Most important, Mrs. Johnson was the organizer of the "Saturday Nighters," an informal salon of writers who met at her home to eat, drink, and talk literature. She nurtured the controversial bright lights of literary Washington, such as Jean Toomer, one of the most experimental and respected novelist of the Harlem Renaissance period, and Richard Bruce, the enfant terrible whose drawings and short stories elaborated on the theme of male homosexuality. Johnson was able to provide a literary family for these young rebels because she identified with the generational struggle of youth to free itself from the constraints of living in aggressively assimilated, bourgeois Washington. She believed passion, however controversial, was better than cold Victorian moralism, and as she watched Locke trudge the steep hill toward Howard University every day, she felt the pain of his loss. Moreover, as a woman married to a strict Victorian twenty years her senior, a man who derided her activities with "artistes," Johnson could identify with the generational crisis Locke was undergoing.

Johnson began to help Locke to live without his mother when she wrote him, "If you should ever take sick suddenly in the night or day, just have some one in the house phone or call me. I shall be happy to come day or night regardless of the night work I'm doing. I mean this and want you to feel that you can count on

me at any time. I think your mother would like me to say this to you." At the
same time, she encouraged his dark explorations of the macabre when she continued, "Please send me a copy of the poems you read to me...especially the one
about the worms going through skulls, etc." Johnson was also experimenting in
her poetry, reaching toward the controversial issues of sexual frustration, spiritual death, and personal renewal she would tackle effectively in *An Autumn Love
Cycle* (1927). Perhaps more than Locke's other friends, Johnson sensed that an
internal struggle waged inside him between the temptation to remain a Victorian
or move forward into uncharted waters of modernism—a struggle waging in her
as well. Encouraging him to go to Europe, she recalled, "I have remembered the
expression in your eyes. I do hope that you will see many happy scenes that will
delight and draw you into forgetfulness."[11]

The next time Georgia Douglas Johnson and Locke's other friends heard from
him he was in Berlin. Locke had left New York on June 22, 1922, for Liverpool
and had gone immediately to Paris where, on walks up and down the Champs
Elysees, he recalled earlier sojourns taken there with his mother. But it was in
Berlin, where in earlier years he had studied, that Locke seized on the rewards of
living without his mother. He delved into Berlin's pulsating nightlife, its bohemian artistic community, and its perplexing double infatuation with urban modernism and rural romanticism. He emerged with a vision of a renaissance of
the modern spirit he wanted to inspire in urban America. Locke saw Europe had
changed dramatically since he and his mother had last visited in 1914. Here was
a Europe alive to African culture, as reflected in the flock of artists who daily
went to ethnological museums to study African sculpture for its lessons in
cubism and expressionism. It was in Berlin that Locke was re-exposed to modernism and began to conceive for himself a new mission—to lead a new African
American modernism that would reject the stuffy, rule-bound, repressed
Victorian culture he had grown up under and in many respects epitomized. When
he returned home that fall, Locke began to envision a new, more public role for
himself, freed from the fetters of his past and his caretaker role with his mother.

There were self-destructive temptations in this new freedom as well. For a
closeted homosexual, his mother's departure meant that he could delve into the
nightlife of Berlin—and New York—with an abandon not possible before. Was
that the path forward, simply to immerse in the sexual pursuit of young men?
Or was there something of the older tradition of discipline, self-management,
and cultural aspiration that he needed to allow him to become something more
powerful than simply a college professor on the make? Even if he turned away
from the pursuit of sex for sex's sake, the deeper problem remained: how was he
going to become influential in a Victorian world that was patriarchal and heterosexual? Locke avoided groups, especially Black grass-roots organizations and
establishment civil rights organizations like the NAACP, because of his fear that
his sexuality would be exposed. Black middle-class politics was fundamentally

patriarchal and heterosexual, revolving around social occasions where the leaders, always male, and their wives dominated the political agenda with their socially conservative narratives about "respectability" and "representativeness," and the demand that the race "put its best foot forward" to combat White discourses that Black people were fundamentally subhuman. Behaving heterosexual was part of the price of admission into these organizations, and having Locke roving around meetings with an eye out for attractive young men was an explosive situation. That Locke had published his mother's obituary in the NAACP's *Crisis* was ironic, because Locke was not a member of that organization, or a fan. Yet, the *Crisis*, edited by America's premier intellectual, W. E. B. Du Bois, was one of the very few journals in which art and culture was reviewed, discussed, and promoted seriously.

Alienated from the community surrounding bourgeois and grass-roots movements of race advancement of his time, Locke decided to create an alternative community of straight and queer people built around queer people's love of art and culture. In this work, Georgia Douglas Johnson modeled what he wished to foster as much as the Berlin gay community. His new community would be an open secret, an art movement eventually called the Harlem Renaissance, that could accept him and others like him who built a sense of belonging to one another out of the love that aesthetes and dandies like him had privately shared. His coming out—to the extent that that was possible—was to become a public player in creation of the subjectivity that would come to dominate American culture of the twentieth century. Though still closeted, still afraid of exposure and arrest, he nevertheless became a public intellectual while remaining an active homosexual. He could not build a public civil rights movement like Du Bois's to transform the material or even the political condition of the Negro, but he could build an aesthetic movement to transform the image of the Negro as a discursive sign in American culture. He could do that because he fostered a community of people who shared a belief that the Black experience of America could foster great art.

Still handicapped psychologically by his dependence on a mother figure even after his mother's death, Locke found that he could be a nurturing hero by editing and advancing the work of more creative people than himself. Even before his mother's death, he had begun to privately counsel and promote new talents like Countee Cullen, Claude McKay, Langston Hughes, Ann Spencer, and Georgia Douglas Johnson herself. After his mother's death, he would stake his claim to being an influential Black intellectual on them, defying the notion that the advancement of Black interests was mainly a political or economic undertaking. A tempered radical, Locke took what he loved—and had shared with his mother, a love of art—and turned it into an intervention—a means for a catharsis in the American soul, not the basis of propaganda for the race, as Du Bois later advocated. His really radical notion was that the Negroes had to transform their vision of themselves, to become New Negroes, and see the world with a new vision of creative possibility, if others were going to treat them differently, with more dignity and respect that the race so richly desired. Justice, he believed, would follow upon seeing, for the first time, that the Negro was beautiful. He would re-create politics by teaching a new generation of Black artists that they had a lofty mission—to march the Negro race out of the Plato's cave of American racism and allow them to see themselves through art as a great people. By subjectivizing the Negro, Locke believed the New Negro artists would change the calculus of American life and make Negroes the initiators of progressive change, not the recipients or dependents of it.

Here was that deeper irony Locke's life always conveyed—here was a man who was deeply dependent on other people who preached independence and self-determination as his aesthetic politics. He was a deeply conflicted man, who operated as a loner, who befriended but often abandoned writers, artists, and lovers out of fear of being abandoned himself. He could be selfish, untrustworthy, vindictive, and vicious, but he could also be the sweetest of persons, who devoted himself to students, helped less fortunate, often destitute artists survive, and created the rationale, along the way, for contemporary Black art and literature. Culture would be his business.

Mary would live through him, but where she had worshipped culture as an escape from the experience, he would use culture to return the artist to the Black experience of suffering and travail that America had been for generations, and transform that experience into something beautiful. He would take a dying, decorative, bourgeois culture and transform it into a new, living aesthetic that included the folk culture of the masses and drew on the African ancestral culture. Three years after his mother's death, he wrote a clarion call to the young Black writers in Philadelphia, his hometown, trying to break free as he had just done himself.

> I was taught to reverence my elders and fear God in my own village. But I hope Philadelphia youth will realize that the past can enslave more than the oppressor, and pride shackle stronger than prejudice. Vital creative thinking—inspired group living—must be done, and if necessary we must turn our backs on the past to face the future. The Negro needs background—tradition and the sense of breeding, to be sure, and it will be singularly happy if Philadelphia can break ground for the future without breaking faith with the past. But if the birth of the New Negro among us halts in the shell of conservatism, threatens to suffocate in the close air of self complacency and snugness, then the egg shell must be smashed to pieces and the living thing freed. And more of them I hope will be ugly ducklings, children too strange for the bondage of barnyard provincialism, who shall some day fly in the face of the sun and seek the open seas. For especially for the Negro, I believe in the "life to come."[12]

Locke became a "mid-wife to a generation of young writers," as he labeled himself, a catalyst for a revolution in thinking called the New Negro. The deeper truth was that he, Alain Locke, was also the New Negro, for he embodied all of its contradictions as well as its promise. Rather than lamenting his situation, his marginality, his quiet suffering, he would take what his society and his culture had given him and make something revolutionary out of it.

Locke did it out of his need for love. This need led him into dangerous yet fulfilling relationships with some of the most creative men of the twentieth century, but also drove him to something else—to try and get that love from Black people as a whole, by doing all he could to gain their approval, win their recognition, even though he could never fully experience it for fear of rejection. As such, he remained a lonely figure, but also a figure of reinvention, for his message was that all peoples, especially oppressed people, had the power to remake themselves and refuse to be what others expected them to remain.

In his mother's end was his beginning. Mary had mothered him. Now, he would mother a movement.

Circular for Opening of Sarah Shorter Hawkins store in Philadelphia, 1873. Courtesy of the Moorland-Spingarn Research Center, Howard University.

2

A Black Victorian Childhood

Alain, christened Arthur LeRoy Locke at birth, was a sickly, tiny baby. He was not expected to live. Born on September 13, 1885 (though he publicly gave his birth date as 1886), Locke contracted rheumatic fever at birth, and cried and gasped for breath during attacks.[1] That entire first year the family, especially his mother, Mary, lived with the terror that the next attack would kill him. Mary spent every possible moment with him, leaving household and shopping duties to his grandmothers. In her nurture of her son, Mary found fulfillment she lacked in her roles as teacher, wife, or daughter. He needed her and seemed strengthened by her bathing, stroking, and breastfeeding. Even after the crisis had passed, Mary remained extremely protective of her "one and only." She had nursed him back from death and she kept vigilant watch lest some new, unforeseen illness take him away. By his third year, his health had stabilized even if the economic situation of a relatively modest Black middle-class family had not.

Roy, as he was called as a child, had been born at home on South 19th Street, located at the edge of Philadelphia's Seventh Ward, a Black residential neighborhood. W. E. B. Du Bois, the sociologist hired by the University of Pennsylvania in 1897 to study living conditions in Philadelphia, described the neighborhood in which Locke was born:

> Above Eighteenth, is one of the best Negro residence sections of the city, centering about Addison street. Some undesirable elements have crept in even here...but still it remains a centre of quiet, respectable families, who own homes and live well.[2]

Locke's birthplace and two successive family residences at 1574 South 6th Street, where they moved in 1890, and 2221 South 5th Street, where they lived after 1892, represented the epitome of rental Victorian furnishings available to the "better classes" of Negroes in Philadelphia. Mary, Pliny, and the two grandmothers lived in six rooms on 19th Street. Mary tastefully decorated the second-story flat with furnishings from her mother's home and with curtains and upholstery coverings she and her mother made. A White visitor to the Locke household in

1885 would have been struck by how closely these accommodations resembled those of middle-class White Philadelphians.

Charles Shorter, Alain Locke's maternal great-grandfather, was an eighteenth-century Black success story. A hero of the War of 1812, he won the admiration of city fathers when he captured a British ship off Philadelphia's harbor and turned it over to the Americans. After the war, Shorter amassed a small fortune as a sailmaker and used much of his money to purchase books for the Library of the Free African Society founded by Absalom Jones and Richard Allen in 1787. In the aftermath of the War of 1812, a core group of Black ministers, entrepreneurs, political aspirants, educators, and artists emerged who inhabited the same social class and shared a collective vision of forging a Black community devoted to self-help, classical education, and sustainable middle-class families. This elite group comprised people like the wealthy sailmaker James Forten; ministers Richard Allen and the self-educated Absalom Jones, who founded independent African Methodist churches in Philadelphia; the political leader Robert Purvis; entrepreneur Henrietta Bowers; and Locke's paternal grandfather, Ishmael Locke, the first teacher at one of the first schools for Black youth in the United States, the Institute of Colored Youth. In Black Victorian Philadelphia, an array of churches, benevolent societies, literary and historical societies, the Home for Aged and Infirm Colored Persons, and the Frederick Douglass Memorial Hospital all attested to the ability of the Black elite and middle class to found institutions that ministered to their needs and to those of the lower class. In the process, Black Philadelphians developed a distinctive urban style. Mirroring the Quaker ideology that an enlightened life was possible on earth, the Philadelphia Black elite prided itself on its command of English and Anglo-American culture and turned that culture to its own purposes of group advancement and individual accomplishment. A sense that educated Negroes were at least the equals of their White peers in their mastery of English literature, religious doctrine, and Victorian mores and manners pervaded the Black aristocracy, as they sought to call themselves.

Ishmael Locke was a model for his grandson even though he never knew him. Born in Salem County, New Jersey, in 1820, he was a "pioneer educator," one of the most respected Black teachers in the antebellum North. Ishmael carried a letter of recommendation with him to Philadelphia in 1844 that stated, "Ishmael Locke is of good character; served as a teacher for 2 1/2 years—taught reading, writing, arithmetic, geography, and astronomy... in the school for coloured children in this town." Having a letter from the White elite of Salem was crucial to Ishmael's ability to secure employment as a teacher among the Quaker elite of Philadelphia. The letter's White signatories especially noted his "habits of the strictest morality, his personal order and decorum," and "the reputation he has obtained for intelligence and literary attainments; [both] have secured for him the confidence and esteem of our community." Another recommender noted Ishmael was "a most efficient and excellent teacher, having advanced his pupils rapidly by discipline in the school, and greatly improved their conduct and condition by the force of good example and precept."[3]

Just two years after Ishmael Locke arrived in Philadelphia, working-class Whites rioted and attacked Black churches, schools, and meetinghouses on the very avenue, Lombard Street, where Ishmael's new school stood. Hired as the first principal of the Quaker-founded Institute for Colored Youth, a teacher's college, Ishmael was charged with inculcating in rising young Blacks the gentlemanly values of the Yankee middle class, precisely those behaviors and attributes that attracted the ire of the rioting Irish working class. Black elite institutions were the prime targets of White rioters, who felt that Blacks like Ishmael were too successful at assimilating upper-class Anglo-American values and too "uppity" because of it.

Ishmael escaped attack, partly because he and his wife, Mathilda, resided in New Jersey in 1846, having purchased a home in Camden. Ishmael may have continued residing in New Jersey because of his political stature in its Black community. Certainly it was not because New Jersey was a less racist state than Pennsylvania. Both states took voting rights away from free Negroes who had voted for years because it was coupled to Democratic Party demands to establish universal suffrage for White males by eliminating property qualifications for voting. Ishmael Locke was a member of the New Jersey "Coloured Convention" that protested this disenfranchisement of Blacks and coauthor of the petition to return the vote to New Jersey's Black population. Tellingly, he argued that free Negroes deserved political representation because of their property, education, and cultivation—their assimilation of Anglo-American middle-class values. The petition read:

> Being endowed under the blessings of a beneficent Providence and favourable circumstances, with the same rationality, knowledge, and feelings, in common with the better and more favoured portions of civilized mankind, we would no longer deride you and ourselves by exhibiting the gross inconsistency, and by so far belying the universal law and the great promptings of our nature; cultivated as we claim to be, as to have you no longer suppose that we are ignorant of the important and undeniable fact that we are indeed men like yourselves.[4]

Ishmael's faith that culture and accomplishment could triumph over racism lay in the Black Victorian ideology of educated African Americans that held sway for over a century. "Victorianism" came to be the term used for a set of rules for public and private life that characterized middle-class status. On the one hand, sexual prudishness, verbal and literary censorship, and personal self-discipline signified that one was "civilized." On the other, Victorians allowed the most conspicuous display of wealth through dress and public parade. By the time of the Great Exhibition of 1851 in London, a Victorian style had crystallized into a public pedagogy of how the lower and working classes, and minorities and colonials, ought to act if they wanted to be considered middle class and civilized.

As Locke observed in his study of imperialism, Victorianism abroad created desire in the subject populations to emulate British culture to gain admission to civilization. Something like that psychology operated among Black Victorians, who inhabited London, Boston, Washington, D.C., and especially Philadelphia, where increasingly, educated free Negroes grew up imbibing the nineteenth century's Anglo-American love of class, home, and strict public behavior. Ishmael's Black Victorianism boiled down to three things: culture, education, and a commitment to the race. Black Victorianism thus had an affirmative twist, to use civilized ways to defend the race from attack and improve the lifestyle of barely free Negroes in the antebellum North.

Black Victorianism barely hid its deeper tragedy. Racism was not restrained by proof of cultural equality or performance of middle-class rituals. The vote was not restored to New Jersey's Blacks, and the citizenship rights of northern free Negroes continued to decline in the 1850s, despite numerous manifestations of self-improvement and successful social integration. Economic conditions for the tiny Black middle class worsened, due in part to increasing economic competition between Blacks and working-class Whites. Ishmael Locke experienced difficulties, forcing him to leave the job in Philadelphia in 1850, the year his first son, Pliny, was born. In 1851, another son, Phaeton, was born, but before that year was over, Ishmael had died of tuberculosis, leaving his widow to rent out the home in Camden and live with relatives in Philadelphia.

Like his grandfather, Locke would have close ties with the Yankee elite throughout his education and career, while lacking their financial security. Like his grandfather, Locke would base his appeal for freedom and justice in American life on the culture of African Americans, in part because both the masses and most of the Black elite lacked the economic resources of other middle-class Americans. But Locke would subtly resent his paternal grandfather and father because of their economic situation, while subtly favoring his maternal grandmother and mother, because they were from the entrepreneurial side of Black Victorianism. A tension resonated in Locke throughout his life between the political progression of his paternal grandfather's side of the family that was committed to race service and ignored the financial consequences and the economically relentless middle-class side of his maternal grandmother's family that was always seeking money. As an adult he often stated that he had to make Black advocacy pay. The Black Victorians had all the ingredients of an elite Anglo-American lifestyle except the most important, money, and it caused Locke a great deal of pain throughout his life.

When Locke remarked with pride years later that he came from a family that was "fanatically middle class," he alluded to the price Black Victorians like him paid for striving to be equal to Whites culturally while barely making a living as educators. Constantly scrutinizing one's dress, one's speech, and one's deportment in public meant that self-scrutiny dominated their innermost thoughts. After his mother's death, Locke recognized this internal policing as crippling to his and other Black artists' aspiration to create a distinctive voice in American culture. For most of his life, he remained a Black Philadelphian—a brilliant son of a middle-class culture with no future, who admitted his life of the mind had been shackled by an upbringing that made him "paralyzingly discrete."[5]

The one person in Roy's family seemingly not "paralyzed" was his father, Pliny Ishmael Locke, a man "of small stature and slight build," according to Christopher J. Perry, the editor of the *Philadelphia Tribune*, who called the senior Locke a born leader of men. Perry published his account of Pliny Locke's life in his column "Pencil Pusher's Points," one of the more popular items in this local Black newspaper. Told for the benefit of younger readers, the story unfolds that Pliny, after first excelling in and then teaching at his father's school, the Institute of Colored Youth, "joined the army of educators to the Southland," only to return to Philadelphia and become the first Black civil service employee in the Post Office in 1883. Subsequently he was appointed a clerk in the customs house and an inspector in the gas department. Pliny was president of local political organizations such as the Quaker City Beneficial Association and was very active in city politics, receiving a commission at the customs house.[6]

According to Perry, Pliny "was born to command, in whatever field he worked men seemed to feel a confidence in him and were content to be guided by his judgment. All of his teachers conceded to him a wonderful mind and felt that had he been at Harvard, Yale or any of the great institutions of learning, he would have been in the forefront of the strongest." But Pliny's most striking characteristic was his courage:

> To illustrate the phase of the grit and resourcefulness of the man is to tell the story of his first morning in his new charge [as a teacher at the South Chester Bourory School for Blacks]. He was as quick at perception as of action, and saw a recalcitrant spirit, who was likewise dominant. He rang the bell for order, and as quick as a flash jumped from the platform, grasped the big lad by the throat, threw him down; and then called the rest of the startled scholars to order. There was a complete hush and he let go of the refractory spirit, only to throw him out of the door a minute later. After that order was supreme in his school.[7]

As Perry observed, Pliny was "brave, even to the point of indiscretion at times." For example, while working as a bellman in a hotel one summer, Pliny wrote: "how I chafe under the regime of ignorant negroes and domineering Whites, who seem to think that every negro is a boy and a dog—Hoyt, one of the room clerks and myself have had it several times and last night the man who has the newsstand and myself had a warm time of it."[8] While a government employee in Washington, Pliny wrote to Mary that he had let a White congressman have a piece of his mind when the latter claimed Blacks ought to be grateful and acquiescent to the Republican Party after what Lincoln's party had done for them. "You can imagine how well such talk accorded with my ideas—I spoke as I felt and he seemed utterly surprised that I should do so."[9] Pliny exuded the attitude of self-assertive Black manhood characteristic of the Reconstruction Era, when Blacks fought for the right to vote and demanded equality with Whites.

The immediate problem that had faced Pliny and other graduates of his father's school in the Reconstruction period was not the right to vote but the right to work. Graduating at the top of his class in 1867, he stayed on two additional years to teach, and then, at nineteen years of age, left Philadelphia bent on carving out his own reputation as an educator. Pliny and Mary probably met at the Institute during his two-year teaching stint; he may have been Mary's teacher. When an offer came from the Freedmen's Bureau in Washington to start a school for Blacks in rural East Tennessee, he jumped at the chance. At least working in the South would be better than joining the ranks of other unemployed graduates of the Institute for Colored Youth. Although the Institute was producing excellent teachers, the school boards of Philadelphia, Camden, and other New Jersey municipalities had established very few schools for Blacks.

Pliny arrived in Tennessee at a time when the Freedmen's Bureau, created by Congress in 1865, had become a shadow of its former self. By January 1869, the combined opposition of White landowners, poor Whites, Conservatives, and the Ku Klux Klan had forced severe cutbacks in the amount of food, education, and medical attention the freedmen received. Fortunately for Pliny, his commission directed him to start his school in East Tennessee, which had escaped the Klan's reign of terror that had devastated Blacks in the plantation counties of West Tennessee.

Nevertheless, East Tennessee was not free of White hostility. As he wrote to Mary, "There are plenty of outspoken and bitter rebels and negro haters here. They hate the sight of a northern man." Pliny was appalled at the conditions under which Blacks lived where he started his school. "I am now writing in a house that people north would scarcely keep their horses in."[10] A month later he confided that his school had managed a "daily attendance of about 30 of the most uncouth, ugliest and greasiest mortals you ever beheld. I am indeed engaged in the arduous duty of instilling knowledge in the minds of true representatives of Ham or of blackness. But whether they will ever achieve renown or not I can not say."[11]

Pliny was not alone among Reconstruction-Era northern African Americans in his distaste for the Black masses, because their middle-class backgrounds made it difficult for them to identify with the aspirations, usually for literacy and for land, of the rural freedmen. The Reconstruction-era congressmen paid a price for their bias—most lost political power, because they could not hold onto their lower-class Black constituency and could not gain White loyalty. Whenever Pliny took positions of public leadership, he would either be thrown into racial conflict with Whites, who resented him because he was Black, or into class conflict with lower-class Blacks whose values, habits, and attitudes were repulsive to him. In his letters to Mary, Pliny derisively termed poor Blacks in Tennessee "kids" and seemed to resent rural Blacks as much as the "Negro hating" poor White rebels. Like most Black Victorians of his day, Pliny also disliked poor Whites. Yet the consequence of his class bias against poor Blacks was more serious since it meant he would never be able to build an enduring political base as a Black leader.

Added to race and class conflict was the regional problem of living in the South, something Pliny found especially disagreeable. He soon became ill, and in April 1869 fell from a horse, severely injuring his arm. Although he resolved to stay for two years, that May Washington notified him that his position would be terminated. After a brief return to Philadelphia, in October 1871, Pliny accepted a clerk position in the Washington office of the Freedmen's Bureau. He arrived in Washington, D.C., to find that John W. Cromwell, a classmate at the Institute for Colored Youth, had recommended him to John Langston, the noted Afro-American lawyer and dean of the Howard University Law School. Shortly after a personal interview with Dean Langston, Pliny enrolled in law school, obtained housing at the university, and settled down to work in the Bureau and as Langston's personal secretary.

Pliny's move to Washington strained relations with Mary. She felt rejected when he left Philadelphia a second time. Although she knew that law school and a government clerkship were excellent opportunities for him, she had secretly hoped he would find employment in or near Philadelphia. Moreover, his infrequent letters showed that Pliny was becoming a rogue about town, who sported a cane and kid gloves and flirted with Washington ladies. Mary began to believe that their courtship would never result in marriage.

Ironically, in September 1872, just after his letters began to open with "my dearest love," Pliny stopped writing to Mary. Mary stopped corresponding as well, which elicited from Pliny the following note:

> I see from your account that in the case of Love vs. Pride, the defendant won but owing to some mischance he failed to get damages and thus I lost the pleasure of receiving a letter. I do not blame you but I am certainly sorry that you were prevented from mailing it. Am I such an enigma and so little understood, that when flushed with joy at long-deferred success, that I am thought to be inapproachable? I have more

cause to ASK forgiveness than to grant it, for after all am I not the cause
of that seeming lack of confidence?...Did brute and beast and villain
again become synonyms with Locke?[12]

Pliny had stopped writing after he lost his job at the Freedman's Bureau. When
he did write he said that "pride would not let me open my heart to any, not even
to you, my loved—yes, dearly loved one." Although Pliny secured another clerkship in the Treasury Department, his economic situation and their courtship
remained rocky for the next three years until Mary wrote him in February 1875
that he was forgiven and that she wanted to share his sorrow as well as his success. This proud man struggled with a melancholy streak. With Mary, especially,
who was not only of a higher social class but also a fault-finding lover, Pliny felt
that he had to be a "tough-minded" success story to be accepted by her and
her mother.

Class and gender tensions dominated Pliny's long-distance courtship of Mary
Hawkins. To Pliny, Sarah Shorter Hawkins (Mary's mother) was everything he
resented about Philadelphia upper-class society. Sarah embodied the sense of
superior status through connections with wealthy Whites that characterized the
Philadelphia Black Brahmins. In fact, she did not even consider herself Negro,
preferring to term herself a free person of color. She continued her father's early
nineteenth-century strategy of entrepreneurship by opening dressmaking shops
in Philadelphia and Cape May, New Jersey, with her daughter, Mary. Sarah was
also something of an early feminist, who insisted on her daughter attending
the Institute of Colored Youth so that she could support herself and never be
dependent on a man. She taught her daughter to speak her mind forcefully even
in the presence of men, and stand up for women's rights. For example, when
Pliny wrote from Tennessee that Governor Brownlee's daughter talked too much,
she chastised him for his biased comments about women. But most important,
Sarah taught her daughter that she was a member of "society," and as such, had
a responsibility to cultivate her mind, to restrict her social contacts to people
of her "class," and to act at all times as a model of proper conduct. Pliny picked
up that Sarah was not only in a different class from his but also may have been
dismissive of him and his courtship of Mary. As he wrote Mary in 1875: "She
[Sarah] is one of the few persons in whose sight I wish to appear well yet without
a hypocritical pretense of being what I am not—without hiding all my faults
and failures. To this feeling I ascribe my utter inability to be perfectly at ease in
her society."[13]

Washington was a welcome escape from the tensions of his courtship and a
politically vibrant city at the center of Reconstruction politics. As John Mercer
Langston's secretary, Pliny attended political meetings, wrote speeches for the
future congressional representative from Virginia, and helped Langston lobby
for passage of the 1875 Supplementary Civil Rights Bill. Pliny argued strongly

for integrated schools in a letter he wrote to Mary in 1872: "I am an earnest advocate of Mixed Schools and also of Social Equality. I feel that the colored people will never be able to rival the whites till, accustomed to mingle with them, they lose that inborn feeling of inferiority and that humbling servility, which so plainly exhibit themselves whenever they come in contact with whites." He criticized as shortsighted Black schoolteacher opposition to integrated schools on the grounds that integration would mean the loss of their jobs. While Black teachers deserved "great praise," Pliny responded to Langston's criticism of segregated schools by noting, "I should not like to be called in to disprove it by citing examples of WELL CONDUCTED negro schools."[14] Pliny disliked Black schools on scientific grounds: they were inefficient, dirty, and poorly disciplined, and as a Black Brahmin, he saw himself as a leader bringing rationality and order to a largely inefficient, and often religiously oriented, educational system. Integrated schools were needed to expose Black teachers and students to modernizing tendencies in education.

Moreover, as a man in an increasingly female profession, Pliny believed Black women were not pushing the kind of manly rights he felt Blacks needed to be equal to Whites. Education, for Pliny, was not simply reading, writing, and arithmetic, but the cutting away of that "inborn feeling of inferiority...in contact with whites" from Black children. Masculinity, patriarchy, and a class-conscious lower-middle-class anger fueled his belief in a pedagogy that would liberate Blacks from the White supremacist notion that they were powerless and worthless. Unfortunately for Pliny and his generation of Black leaders, neither school integration nor Black social and cultural equality would become a reality. The wheedling down of the Civil Rights Bill of 1875 and its nullification by the Supreme Court in 1883 spelled the demise of social equality for the Black elite. Pliny's generation suffered a collective sense of bitterness and frustration captured in his statement, "Negroes seem to be born to become the footballs of the whites."[15]

Inside this nineteenth-century rationalist was a bitter man, who, after graduating at the top of his class at Howard University Law School in 1874, never practiced law because Black lawyers were little called for as Black civil rights were systematically eroded in the 1870s and 1880s. Yet except in moments when his anger boiled out from inside, these obstacles did not shake Pliny's faith that if an educated Black man competed with the White man on his own level, he would be successful. Indeed, his anger at the "recalcitrant youth" expressed both Pliny's lack of authority and his conservative middle-class belief in self-help.

After graduation from law school, Pliny could obtain only clerking jobs in Washington. When he lost his job at the Treasury Department in 1876, he struggled on shoestring jobs until he returned to his mother's house in 1879. He spent a summer looking for work and then on August 20, 1879, Pliny and Mary were secretly married. Upon being reappointed to the Treasury in 1879, Pliny returned to Washington without his new bride. After another firing and a short stint at the Freedmen's Savings Bank in 1880, Pliny returned to Philadelphia for good to take a teaching position at a Black school in South Chester. Only then, when Pliny had obtained steady employment, did the couple inform their parents of their marriage.

Perry's account of Pliny's stewardship of the South Chester School is mistaken in one particular: discipline did not reign supreme after Pliny ejected a surly student from his class. In fact, Pliny was appointed principal of the school a month later because the previous one had resigned and no one else seemed to be able to maintain discipline and authority. Over the next three years, a constant struggle ensued at the school, at which Mary began teaching in 1881.

Dissatisfied with the low pay and difficult working conditions at the South Chester School, Pliny applied for a Post Office clerkship. The Civil Service Law of 1883 required all applicants to take a written exam and undergo a rigorous personal interview, which inquired into their employment background and personal character. Pliny achieved one of the highest scores on the examination, and after the interview he was chosen over several White applicants. His selection was heralded by local and regional Black newspapers as an important achievement for a Black man and a signal that the new Civil Service laws were "democratic" in appointing Pliny to an office no other Black man had served in for more than twenty years.

The Civil Service Law was part of a national reaction by the largely Republican, Anglo-American middle class against the dominance of government jobs by Democratic Party machines, often run by the Irish working class. The Black middle class and the Irish working class had remained enemies after the riots of the 1830s and 1840s, and the Black educated elite had continued to tie its bid for upward mobility to assimilation of upper-class Yankee values. While the Civil Service Law did not help lower-class Blacks get jobs in the city, it did reward those like Pliny, who had excelled at education.

In Washington, Pliny had described the predicament of the educated Black middle class. "How well I can now realize the truth and force of the assertion that 'cursed is that man who hangs on Princes (Congressmen's) favors.'"[16] By rejecting segregation, Pliny and his free-born middle class forfeited the option of developing autonomous Black economic and political power. By alienating themselves from the Black masses, Pliny and his class failed to develop a strong constituency among the lower classes of their race. Pliny remained as "cursed" in Philadelphia as he had been in Washington: when the political climate changed in 1886, he lost his Post Office job and eventually returned to teaching.

Despite its limitations, the Post Office appointment was personally significant for Pliny. He had finally obtained a position of prestige and stable employment in his own community of Philadelphia. Alain Locke was born two years after the Post Office appointment, a sign that the young couple felt they could now provide for a family. Yet even before the Post Office appointment, Pliny was resolute in his belief that the ideology of achievement, which fueled his own education and career, would be successful. As he stated as principal speaker on the January 1, 1883, celebration of the Emancipation Proclamation:

> Our present, though possibly not all it should be, still is such to give us cause for rejoicing and making indeed a jubilee of this, our grand national holiday. [For men like Frederick Douglass and John Langston] are writing on the pages of history stern facts and not delusive fancies, refuting in their public and private lives the base and unwarranted assertions that the negro cannot rise.
>
> Vested with rights making us theoretically equal to all other men, we owe it to ourselves to see that we shall become practically so. The wide domains of laws, medicine, commerce, agriculture and all the sciences, present pleasing and inviting fields for energy, perseverance and pluck. To these let us turn our earnest endeavors, making the race which patient under suffering, great in deeds and acts. For years we have furnished the muscle; let us now add to it brains.[17]

We can only wonder what made this proud, brave, and skeptical Black thinker speak such homilies and portents of progress after witnessing so many examples of continued racism. Perhaps it was part of the Black Victorian ideology that the dire circumstances of survival had to be disguised in order that those following would not give up the struggle.

Mary Hawkins Locke, a proper Victorian lady, realized all the virtues of nineteenth-century true womanhood. Metz T. P. Lochard recalled that her graciousness, intelligence, and charm embellished her poised and reserved demeanor. As a Black woman, Mary Locke inherited a matriarchal tradition that valued both work and financial independence for women. But nineteenth-century middle-class Black women could not escape the pressure to live up to the Victorian ideal to be a lady, refined and cultured with a knowledge of art and literature, and respectable—which meant to marry, to have a beautiful home, and to give birth to a son. Mary delayed getting married until she was twenty-nine and settling down to a two-career marriage with Pliny until 1884, when he began to earn a salary from his Post Office appointment. She left her teaching position at the end of the school year in 1884 to become a full-time housewife. Little more than a year later she gave birth to her first son, Alain LeRoy Locke.

The marriage and family life Mary led was far different from what she expected when Roy was born. After Pliny was dismissed from his Post Office job, Mary, who had spent the first year at home nursing her sickly son, had to return to teaching. She was able to secure reappointment at her old school in Camden. During a family discussion, Pliny made a remarkable suggestion: he would take a janitorial job so he could work nights and care for their son during the day while she worked. The adult Alain Locke recalled this as an important factor in his childhood.

> Although I was idolized by both parents, early childhood life was un-
> usually close with my father, who changed his position from day to
> night shift in the post-office to be able to take care of me. This included
> bathing and all intimate care since father was distrustful of the old-
> fashioned ways of both grandmothers. He became my constant com-
> panion and playmate, though forced to resume daytime work when
> I was four.[18]

Locke wanted to hide that his father was a janitor, but he liked the devotion expressed by an ambitious father willing to change his work to care for his son.

Mary resented having to give up her close relationship with Roy in order to work. She was angry that she could not depend on Pliny for regular employment and that he did not take respectable work, such as a teaching job. She also resented his implicit criticism of her mother's child-rearing. Most important, she resented his displacing her as the most important person in Roy's life. As Locke recalled:

> Relations with mother were also close in spite of this unusual interest
> on the part of the father. This was not only due to their common fixa-
> tion on their "one and only," but on the fact that our physician pro-
> longed lactation by special diet so that I nursed at the breast until the
> age of three, and after weaning had to be fed milk by the spoonful.
> I would take it in no other way and it had to be whipped into bubbles;
> presumably because of being used to the aeration in breat [sic] feeding.[19]

While working, Mary returned from school twice a day to feed her son. Mary did not need much encouragement to continue breast feeding. Both parents fought for the attention of their child, which increased his initial feeling of being "adored by both parents," but also sowed tension. This young but already sensitive child felt the building conflict between the parents. "Both parents were extremely strong-willed personalities and knew not to cross one another."[20]

Locke would only be weaned after his mother gave birth to another son in 1889. After Pliny took over Roy's childcare, he potty-trained his son at the age of two. He taught him to organize his clothes, to wash, to take care of some of his own needs, and to take responsibility for informing his father when he needed attention.

Pliny did not want to give over his son's nurture to women, not even his wife. He did not want a spoiled son, a quality he already saw developing when he took over home care from Mary in 1886. He instructed Roy in self-sufficiency, explaining to the boy that his mother could not be with him because she had to work. Pliny taught Roy to read by reading aloud to him such classics as Virgil's *Aeneid* and Homer's *Ulysses* in the afternoons after the boy's early morning math exercises were concluded. Young Locke learned early that intellectual brilliance pleased both parents, but especially his father. By age four, he was already serious, so unconcerned with humor and frivolity that he later recalled that, when given the task of going downstairs on Sunday mornings to retrieve the paper, he first cut out the comics section before bringing it upstairs.[21]

Locke gives us the flavor of this boyhood:

> I was indulgently but intelligently treated. As an example, bed time routine was a ritual, my father first, this included an inspection of my clothes which had to be arranged orderly on a chair by the bedside: father intended a military school for my early boyhood training, and then my mother. No special indulgence as to sentiment; very little kissing, little or no fairy stories, no frightening talk or games. The housekeeper was dismissed by my father for frightening me by tales og [sic] the "Boogy-man."[22]

Pliny was a rationalist who believed that superstition, and indeed religion, had no place in the instruction of children. As Locke recalled, "I was unusually obedient, but never had any unreasonable conditions to put up with, since most things were explained to me beforehand."[23] Son and father took walks in the park near their home, his father explaining to him the various trees and foliage and the rudiments of botany. His father wanted him to become a doctor, but after discussion with his mother about the boy's weak health, it was agreed that he would be a teacher.

The effect of this upbringing was that Locke developed his ability for logical analysis, but generally lacked feeling. In his own recollection: "I was a self-centered, rather selfish and extremely poised child, mature enough even before my father's death to be indifferent to others and what they did or thought. I would not accept money or gifts from other people, no matter how tempting. Was trained to be extremely polite but standoffish with others." Of course, this social distance was not simply the father's doing. His mother, father, and grandmothers reinforced this atmosphere of severe restraint:

> I must have at one time, but I have no memory of having slept in anything but my own room, and scarcely have any memory of seeing any of the household undressed. Though a relatively poor family, household etiquette was extreme. Except while being bathed I have also no memory of ever being in the bathroom with anyone in the family. It was

a household where we washed interminably, and except to keep from open offense to others, I was taught to avoid kissing or being kissed by outsiders. If it happened, I would as soon as possible without being observed, find an excuse for using my handkerchief, often spitting surreptitiously into it if kissed too openly.[24]

The Locke family's phobia of contact with undesirables crystallized within the family into racial self-hate. Locke recalled that his maternal grandmother, Sarah Shorter, would rise early in the morning to wash the family clothes and then hang them to dry before the neighbors were up. In addition, when he was instructed to help her with the laundry, she chastised him from under her large floppy hat and gloves to "Stay out of the sun! You're black enough already!" Through the education of his family, Locke learned that he must do everything possible not to act Black, to deny who and what he was. Pliny's attempt to limit the influence of the grandmothers becomes understandable as an attempt to shield his son from their negative social conditioning. Pliny obsessed over cleanliness as well. Constant cleaning, bathing, and avoidance of the sun were compulsive if unsuccessful strategies to wash off the stain of Blackness and deny that being Black meant the family could never live the life of White "Proper Philadelphians," whose manners, homes, and aspirations the Lockes emulated so closely.

Denial also characterized Alain's response to the birth of his brother in April 1889. He never publicly acknowledged the birth of Arthur Locke (apparently his parents changed our Alain's name to Alan or Allen prior to this Arthur's birth; later Locke himself changed it back to Alain). In only one autobiographical reference did he admit to having a brother; in others he claimed to be his parents' "one and only," arguing that because of "the necessity of a double salary to maintain a decent standard of living, they had agreed on only one child, if the child was male."[25] Clearly the existence of a rival to his mother and father's affections was too much for Locke to bear. When Mary had to nurse this second sickly child and could no longer nurse her firstborn, Alain refused to eat for days until his frantic father discovered that whipping the milk persuaded his son to drink it. Even in a household with two grandmothers, a precocious, jealous three-year-old was too much to handle. Arthur Locke died six months after his birth.

Shortly after Arthur's death, Pliny was able to resume his full-time nurture of Alain. But around the age of four, Alain began to resist the father's overtures. Pliny sought to mold his son in his own image, and being a lieutenant in the National Guard, he wished his son to attend military school. Pliny was a skilled baseball player on one of the local Colored Baseball League teams, and one afternoon in the backyard of their new residence at 1574 South 6th Street, Pliny tried to teach his son to play catch. After several refusals by the younger Locke to cooperate, the frustrated father wound up his arm and threw the baseball at Alain, who protectively wrapped his arms around his body. Locke later recalled that even at this early age, he possessed a clear sense of those activities that suited him and those that did not; masculine sports such as baseball were not his idea of recreation, and this strong-willed son would have nothing to do with it.

Pliny began to realize that he was losing the battle for his son's gender identity. He noticed that when Mary was home over the summer, Alain spent most of his time clinging constantly to his mother's skirts and legs and, even if rather unhelpfully, joined in his mother's "feminine" activities such as sewing, making hats, and creating the decorative lace things with which she and her mother beautified their relatively modest home. Locke was not going to grow into the aggressively masculine "ladies' man" that Pliny had styled himself in Washington, and the father, obsessed with creating his child in his own image, was unable to allow the child his own identity.

The increasing tension between father and son culminated in Pliny whipping Roy for some unrecalled infraction.

> When during one of mother's absences he chastised me with the only whipping I remember ever having had; my grandmothers were strictly forbidden to discipline me (and I knew that, much to their chagrin) it was then decided (when I was somewhere between four and five) that mother was to have final authority in discipline. I either remember or was told that this was one of the few serious quarrels of their married life, and that it had been settled that way on mother's ultimatum. Both were extremely strong-willed personalities and knew not to cross one another. Both were bread[-]winners and therefore relatively independent.[26]

At the time of this incident, Mary's teaching job paid considerably more than Pliny's janitorial job. She possessed both the economic and psychological leverage to leave the relationship if Pliny did not sacrifice his authority with the child. Pliny's beating of Alain was a continuation of his attempt to control his increasingly independent son. The father vented his mounting rage at the boy for his emerging effeminacy and his bent toward the aesthetic pursuits of the mother.

Alain was already a spoiled child who let his grandmothers know, through his disrespect of their commands, that he realized they could not spank him and therefore had no real authority over him. Now Pliny lacked that authority as well. Pliny could now only propose, suggest, entreat his son; he could no longer command. As laudable as was his mother's desire to protect her son, Locke recalled his mother protectively placing her arms around him to shield him from his angry father—her act also served the selfish motive of reestablishing her primacy in her son's life.[27] Her love was greater because she would not punish him, would not limit his indulgence, and would continue to spoil him rather than rein him in.

The mother's victory made Alain identify with his mother as the power center of the family. Even more than before, he copied what she did, how she walked, how she talked, and how she viewed the world in order to acquire by imitation the power she had. He would take her side and saw the negative aspects of the family's economic situation as his father's fault. "If only he had..." complained the mother, and he picked up the tune: "If my daddy had done what he was supposed to do."[28] He sided with her because she was his protector, and even as a mature man, Alain would be drawn to and mimic the ideas of older women who served as protectors and patrons in his adult struggles against patriarchal authority. This dialogue between mother and son took place behind closed doors. An adult Locke simply refrained from mentioning his father. Locke did resent his father for not being a recognized leader, serving as a secretary to a celebrity like John Mercer Langston, rather than being an outstanding lawyer and statesman himself. Like his mother, Alain Locke wanted to be respectable, and that required superlative ancestors.

But the real source of Locke's reticence about his father before outsiders may have been rooted in the white-hot rage he felt for his father after the beating. Did not his father claim to rule by reason and not force? Had Roy not been an obedient child who, once things were explained to him, did what he was asked? How could his father, whom he idolized and loved for his strength of character and moral rationality, commit this immoral act? Afterward the son felt the arbitrariness of all moralism, that there was no just God, just simply the rule of force and power. The incident also planted deep within him a hatred of patriarchy and the kind of power Black fathers wielded over their families.

Locke sensed, but was too young to really know, that he was spanked for being different. He learned early not to reveal himself to others, to cloak his vulnerable identity so that others would not be able to punish him similarly. Locke would be teased and tormented by both Black and White schoolboys of Philadelphia. From the Whites, the harassment would leave him confused as to whether his race, his size, or his effeminacy were the cause of his being singled out for abuse. With the Black boys it would always be clearer: in him even small Black boys found someone against whom they could prove their marginal manhood with little fear of retaliation. The effeminacy, moreover, in a Black male context legitimated the violence: why not torture the little Black faggot who dared not to be masculine?

After the beating and his mother's ultimatum, Alain avoided contact with his father, especially in situations where the two were alone. That distance was made easier by Pliny's decision to return to daytime work: Pliny obtained a teaching position when a school for Blacks opened in Thurlow, Pennsylvania, in July 1890. Then, in 1891, Pliny competed for and won the post of meter inspector in the gas department, the first Black man to secure such a Custom House appointment in Philadelphia, the Black press crowed. During the first year, he did not draw a salary, but by 1892 he was appointed inspector in the gas department. Unfortunately, just at the point when Pliny was regaining his prestige in the family through professional accomplishment, he developed heart trouble and died on August 23, 1892.

Pliny's death came less than three weeks before Alain's seventh birthday, at a time when the child saw it as a victory in his rivalry for the mother. She had already shown that her loyalty was to her son and not to her husband. From the child's standpoint the spanking symbolized the father's desire to kill him; now the father had died from the blow he delivered in return.

The death freed Alain from an oppressive father but saddled him with a new burden: defining an identity separate from his mother. That task would prove more difficult for Locke:

> Of course, my father's death at six, threw me into the closest companionship with my mother, which remained, except for the separation of three years at college and four years abroad, close until her death at 71, when I was thirty six. I returned home during every vacation and when abroad my mother visited me every vacation. As a child I stopped play promptly and waited for her return every school day, and the only childhood terror I vividly remember, was about [an] accident that might have happened to her, if by chance she was late.[29]

He could live without his father, but not his mother for the next thirty-seven years.

His father's death also left Locke free to pursue his mother's interest in the aesthetic realm. Had his father lived, Alain Locke might have been pressured to pursue the scientific and rationalistic careers of medicine, law, or mathematics, but now he could immerse himself without restriction into the decorative arts, religious mysticism, and sentimental literature. As a young adolescent intellectual, he would extol the values of the Victorian society his mother lived in and represent himself as a custodian of that culture. But underneath his appearance of "respectability" was an aesthete and a dandy who rebelled against "responsible" society as a literary decadent, bohemian, and homosexual. Here were the beginnings of his rebellion against his mother's authority in his subversion of the bourgeois sentimental values she extolled. The rebellious rogue of the father lived on, inverted into the outrageous dandy barely hidden in the figure of the son.

Most important, the father lived on in Locke's later approach to race politics. The father's death removed the political temper from the family, and for the next sixteen years, not only was Locke's primary interest in aesthetics but he also actively avoided involvement in racial politics. Aesthetics would become an escape from the Black experience and the responsibility of race leadership. Only after returning from Oxford would Locke begin a career as a lecturer on race topics.

Pliny Locke's funeral took place on an oppressively humid day in August, and while reported in the Black press, it was a small affair attended by thirty of

Philadelphia's Black elite and a smattering of Whites. William Armstead, an early suitor of Mary's before her marriage to Pliny, may have helped the widow as she walked from the burial site. Back home, Mary probably closed off the upstairs bedroom where her husband had died, as was the custom of the time, and returned downstairs to prepare her son's special diet of eggs and celery.

Alain was all she had left to live for and, while her mother still lived with them, Mary's attention was focused on providing him with the support and encouragement needed to make it without a father. The next morning, she arose earlier than usual to paste up in the kitchen a phrase she had written down at the last Philadelphia Negro Improvement Association meeting: "Aim at the sky if you want to hit a tree." Fifteen years later, on the evening of his Rhodes Scholar appointment, Locke would recall this injunction to high achievement as being an instigator of his early ambition to be a success. It was a sign to this young boy that he was now the hero in this female-dominated family and that he must live up to his mother's cultural expectations.

His father was gone.

Pliny Locke, September 10, 1875. Courtesy of the Moorland-Spingarn Research Center, Howard University.

3

Child God and Black Aesthete

French philosopher Jean Paul Sartre wrote in his autobiography that if his father had lived, he would have crushed him. Allan, soon to rename himself Alain, Locke must have felt something similar about his father's death in retrospect. He never referred to his father publicly. According to his student and later friend, Robert Fennell, Locke always talked about his mother, usually to every class, but never his father. "Sometimes I wondered if he ever had a father," Fennell quipped.[1] Pliny's death allowed Locke to become a child god of a matriarchal universe that included his mother, two grandmothers, and most important, him.[2] This tiny insulated universe was crucial to nurturing his later ambitions. Locke was growing up in what historian Rayford Logan called the "nadir" in American race relations, when Blacks were pushed back into agricultural labor, slapped with segregation in education and transportation, robbed of the vote, and lynched when they protested against such travesties.[3] Bishop Henry Turner of the African Methodist Episcopal Church captured the decade's lesson to Black men when he stated, "There is no manhood future in the United States for the Negro.... He can never be a *man*—full, symmetrical, and undwarfed."[4] At home, however, bathed with the undivided love of his mother, Locke grew into adolescence with a sense that nothing could stop him from being a man, that nothing could dwarf him.

Pliny's death left his mother the head of a poor, barely middle-class family. Her measly salary of $400 a year was just scarcely enough to meet her expenses as the only employed member of the household. Grandmother Locke would follow her son to the grave in 1894, thus easing the burden on Mary, although the $25 spent on a single buggy and simple burial in the family plot was an embarrassment to this proud family. In order to save money, Mary would eventually move the family to a modest home on the all-White but less expensive Stevens Street in Camden. She would also take in boarders periodically, teach night school, and give private piano lessons in her home to make ends meet.

There was also the challenge of rearing a brilliant and precocious young child whose mind was absorbing and processing everything in his world and questioning it relentlessly. Locke told a story about his upbringing that highlights Mary's achievement in feeding his mental growth, while instilling some sense of the limits he needed to respect if he wanted to succeed in the world. Fennell recalled:

> He told the story that, one time when he was a child, he was riding on a streetcar with his mother, a trolley really, in Philadelphia. And in those days the trolleys had an overhead line. And he said that he asked his mother, "What makes the streetcar run?" And his mother replied, "The electricity." Now this was a new word for him. "Mother, what is electricity?" He told us that this was the 1000th question he had asked his mother that day. And she turned to him and said, Alain, shut up! Just surprised the hell out of us. We certainly did not expect that she would say that. And he used that example to say, "You women today don't know how to rear children." Dewey and all that mess was fashionable then.[5]

To survive, he would have to learn to control himself, to limit his demands on other people, and to study their reactions to his needs if he wanted them met.

Mary Locke's reaction to her son's constant questioning may also illuminate her fatigue. She carried a heavy financial burden in a Black Victorian world rapidly falling apart. Her family's impoverishment was part of a larger systemic decline of the old Black middle class reaching its own nadir at the turn of the century. Most of the great pre–Civil War families started by Black entrepreneurs had lost their money and power by the mid-nineteenth century, and the postwar generations of elite Blacks found themselves excluded from Philadelphia's business growth sectors.[6] Those families who did remain successful were forced to shift from community leadership to professional roles, a realm in which the Lockes had distinguished themselves already. Benjamin Tucker Tanner, a free person of color who had graduated from Allegheny College, was the most powerful African Methodist Episcopal minister in Philadelphia in the 1860s. His son, Henry Ossawa Tanner, became a painter, but after studying at the Philadelphia Academy of Fine Arts and experiencing discrimination in the city's art community, he became an expatriate in Paris. His younger sister, Mary Louise, was the mother of Sadie T. Alexander, the first Black woman to earn a PhD in America. In cases like the Tanner family, where economic decline was avoided, leadership in the Black community was sacrificed, along with close contact with the Black masses.

Mary had contact with the Black masses because she was forced to teach in segregated schools. Under Philadelphia's curious segregation rules, all students were not segregated, but Black teachers were, ironically justified as needed to ensure positions for Black teachers. Segregation increased in Philadelphia over the next decade, becoming the rule there by the 1910s. Mary had a job at the segregated Mount Vernon School in Camden, New Jersey, but she could never leave it for a job in one of the few remaining integrated schools. Having obtained her job in 1886 when she returned to work after the birth of her second son, she saw the number of pupils increase over the years as barely literate southern migrants flooded into Camden desperate for education. Mary was fulfilling the mission of her husband and father-in-law to aid "self-improvement" among ex-slaves, yet at the same time was alienated from the culture of those coming into her community. Mary was stuck in an all-Black world of education while her son advanced in White areas of educational excellence.

Not all of the old Black middle class suffered decline. Some, like Philadelphia's Minton family, thrived in the new environment, but engendered bitterness from Mary. She had known the Mintons since the early days of the Institute of Colored Youth, when Martha Minton had taught Ishmael Locke. After the Civil War, the Mintons had continued to prosper in part because Theophilus and Martha's sons had pursued lucrative medical careers. But after seeing one of the sons at a ball, Mary could not hold back her resentment. She wrote Alain, "They say Minton has transferred his youthful affections from Rose to Helen Stevens. I suppose the money is the bait and the stylish team they have is another consideration for his lordship[.] She will not relish the color of his skin, I think, however. The caterers certainly make the money."[7] Caterers was a cultural as well as an economic sign—a position of service, largely to White people, with all the deference and condescension that went with "Brown service" to elite Whites, but also a sign of finding economic opportunity in servicing Black occasions of spectacular celebration and display. To make such an accommodation to economic reality gritted against the upper-class aspirations of Mary Locke.

Mary even resented those in the Locke family who were economically secure, describing them as unsophisticated. Successful relatives, such as Harry and Lizzie Locke, were also caterers, who frequently invited Mary and her son over to dinner on the weekends, often after church on Sunday. Mary and her son seldom went, however. Harry and Lizzie Locke had cats and allowed them to walk all over the kitchen and dining room tables, something that Mary and especially Roy abhorred. Harry and Lizzie were "unrefined" and "dirty," but they were kind-hearted and often loaned her money. Varick, the father of Locke's younger cousin Ross Hawkins, a distant relative on Mary's side of the family, was also a source of tension. Varick roomed with Mary and was relatively well off. He loaned her money but complained bitterly and loudly when she was unable to pay it back. He was also sometimes drunk on weekends. Another roomer, Mr. Bush, was more redeeming. He was a loyal friend of the family and a refined schoolteacher. Though he lacked social position in Philadelphia, he was open to discussions of art and culture. His amiability, willingness to work at odd jobs, and display of fatherly interest in her son made Bush almost a surrogate husband for Mary.

Mary Locke escaped from Philadelphia's Black Victorian decline through participation in the White world of Philadelphia's genteel culture. She took watercolor lessons at the Pennsylvania Academy of Fine Arts and took Alain, who gained his early love of pictures from such visits. She also took singing lessons, and while music was a love in itself, her remarks about the singing class reveal what else she valued about such situations. "I went over Wednesday night to the singing class and liked it very much. The class is all white, but one colored man, very nice looking."[8] Although poverty forced her to move to Camden, she was able, almost as compensation, to live on the all-White block of Stevens Street. And when she went to church on Sundays, she preferred to attend Philadelphia Christ Church, the hub of Anglo-American Episcopalians in Philadelphia, rather than Black Episcopalian St. Thomas. Worship in White institutions was more "cultured" than even the refined audience at St. Thomas. Mary also became a follower of Dr. Felix Adler's Ethical Culture Society, attending lectures at the Philadelphia meeting house and enrolling Locke in classes there. She described later in life what a typical visit to the Ethical Culture Society meant to her. "I got myself ready and went to the Ethical Culture Society at the Century Club to hear Prof. Josiah Royce on 'Race Questions and Prejudices.' I went early and it was well I did for it was crowded—but such an audience! CULTURE written in every line of the faces—such an audience as you would enjoy."[9]

Culture with a capital C was more than just an elitist escape for the Black middle class. It was a vision of what constituted an ideal society. What Mary saw on the faces of those Whites at the Ethical Culture Society was a commitment to the notion that economic, social, political, and aesthetic interests of their city had shared responsibility to foster the life of the mind as well as trade, industry, and social position. Despite the decline in power of Philadelphia's upper class by the early twentieth century, its shared vision of a responsible society still held sway in such institutions as the Pennsylvania Academy of Fine Arts, the Academy of Music, the Franklin Institute, and the Free Library that were open to all regardless of race. Such cosmopolitanism extended to Mary's early upbringing of her son. She took him regularly to concerts at the Academy of Music, to lectures at the Ethical Culture Society, and to the library to read the Greek myths. Although the Black Victorians maintained such independent institutions as the Demosthenian Institute and the Negro Historical Society, they partook of all that Philadelphia had to offer. For Mary, "Culture" was a vision of enlightened living she had imbibed while growing up in Philadelphia.[10]

Nevertheless, lack of money—and a husband to supply it—exerted downward pressure on the family's social position. As Mary wrote her son after repaying a long-standing loan to a disagreeable lender, "Our financial straits have thrown us into contact with strange people."[11] Families like the Lockes who had once lived comfortably and had prided themselves on their hereditary gentility found themselves losing ground too often to Blacks they regarded as uncouth, uncivilized, and often uneducated, who had the money but lacked the breeding and good manners that their upbringing had promised them would ensure their social position. Locke grew up resenting his family's poverty. Abandonment and poverty did not deter him from having an overweening confidence in his ability to be a success and to have an exceedingly optimistic personality. Beneath that exterior lay a deep-seated anxiety about money. Throughout his life he would bristle at any reference to his early poverty and seek to create the myth of his family's wealth and prominence.

Such insecurity is perhaps illustrated by Locke's public recollection that his family owned their Camden home and his mother was a school principal, when in fact his mother rented the house and she was not a principal, as he once claimed. Like his mother, Locke harbored bitterness toward the wealthier if somewhat less sophisticated members of the Black bourgeoisie and was even more sharply critical of less fortunate Blacks. Following Mary's lead, he would strive constantly to associate himself with Whites, believing such connections were the key to elevating the family's status. As a student in Philadelphia schools, he was compulsively determined to be successful, as if such success would vindicate his family reputation. Perhaps he was right. As Sadie T. Alexander recalled, "The Lockes were not wealthy. No one believed them to be so. The chief reputation of the family came from his achievements."[12] The only area left to his family for redemption was education, and Alain Locke would be their redeemer.

Even before his father's death, Alain's dependency on his mother caused him problems when he attempted to make the transition to school. Fortunately, an observant, caring kindergarten teacher at the David Foy school helped him separate himself from his mother, mentally break out of his intense home life, and settle down to school work.

Locke recalled to his friend Douglas Stafford that this teacher was a student of Froebelian psychology, who had:

> faced him with Froebel's toy-symbols, forms which, their designer had intended, neither conveyed a denotation nor played with some set of mind. If the master of Keilhau was correct, his tools for children were sufficiently indeterminate to throw the child back onto pre-lingually developed resources. The hope is that the child may enjoy some awareness of what he is like and wants before we undertake explicitly to tell him what answers are best. Alain credited these experiences with what was his most striking personal trait, an unusual freedom from inner conflict. He was able, he felt, to distinguish between those things belonging to his temperament and earliest subconscious learning on the one hand, and on the other[,] those objective necessities in society demanding respect.[13]

Froebel, the inventor of the kindergarten, believed that children needed a year of transition between home life and formal school learning. Such a conference with the kindergarten teacher seems to have been a success. Although school was not home, Locke's earliest school experiences confirmed that in this new environment, he could maintain his individuality. He was extremely fortunate to be in such an elite Philadelphia school environment, since to a remarkable degree, his early schoolteachers indulged rather than suppressed his sense of specialness. For the rest of his stay at David Foy School, Locke was a superb student, even if his idiosyncrasy of demanding only fine-point pens with which to write somewhat unnerved his elementary schoolteachers.

By the time Locke transferred to Charles S. Close School, in the First Ward of Philadelphia, he was an excellent student. In his first year (eighth grade) at Charles Close, he received straight As in all subjects and in conduct. In the tenth grade, Locke was written up in the local newspaper as doing excellent work, especially in math. He was also the smallest student, the newspaper noted. That same year he won admittance to Central High School, the second-oldest high school in America and the jewel of the public school system in Philadelphia. He was already a star at age thirteen.

Education also provided Locke with an unconscious adolescent quest to construct a sexual identity. Rather than adolescent rebellion, he slowly opened up a new realm of emotional intimacy and sexual consciousness to people other than his mother. Schooling brought him into contact with boys, mostly White boys, first at Charles Close, and then at Central High, who accepted him, even as they thought him odd. As Locke later recalled to Douglas Stafford, "'I think those white boys must have looked at me in much the same way as ducks upon a chicken.' Race was not the only thing. How could they figure out a fellow forbidden by health from doing those things they took for granted as the only possible meaningful stuff of which to make a boy's life?"[14]

Locke's health figures in the construction of his identity as a young boy as much as his diminutive height—two factors that set him apart from the others as much as his race, he recalls. He was tiny—no more than 4'11" when fully grown, so perhaps in the height range of three and a half feet tall in junior and senior high schools. And he was weak, still suffering the after-effects of rheumatic fever, heart valves that did not work properly, so participation in sports, such as baseball and track, nascent football or rugby, was completely out. Of course, Locke did not want to participate in such sports, he said, but the sense that he envied the kind of homosocial frivolity and bodily comradeship made possible by participation in such sports lurks in his recollections. Already, because of physical predicament and mental outlook, he was an outsider; and yet, Locke turned that position into that of the perennial observer. In doing so, he created, one suspects, an intriguing, even captivating identity for himself among these young White boys. He was the boy with the wry sense of humor, the sardonic wit, the ability to make observation of others into a discourse that would allow him to stay in the mix even as he stood outside of real participation.

Locke's recollection of an incident with the "White boys" at a swimming hole shows how he was able to participate even as a virtual invalid.

> I have waded from time to time at resorts but I never swam and never wished to. But I used to go swimming with those boys. I might dangle a foot, but the most important thing was watching the clothes. A prankster, you see, could tie them into knots or make off with them. It was a filthy hole, but I sat on the bank. Besides, <u>they had to provide for me, make me necessary.</u> They couldn't understand me, but they liked me and had to have me involved.[15]

Douglass Stafford, his close friend, relates the rest of the story:

> The surface of the bank was slick with mud. He was squatted upon its crest, discovering the changing curves and shapes of moving bodies. The appearing and disappearing flesh robbed him of control. Pink, tan, and youthfully fuzzed sinews sped into and out of the murky mess. He was fairly hypnotized. His staunchest and most admired defender stood poised to dive from a coarse old plane, his dripping body gleaming in the sunlight. Alain gasped and fell in. The diver never plunged. The whole naked troop came to his rescue, begging, even before they could be sure he was alive, that he say nothing to his mother of the accident, lest he not be allowed to come with them again. "I'm sorry," he gasped, "but I'll have to tell my mother. She'll let me come back." They wrung out his clothes, dried them with theirs, and watched him head homeward for a long talk with his mother, they fearful all the while that "the chicken" would come no more.[16]

Locke's retelling of this incident to his friend Stafford decades later creates another narrative of how frail health awakened his sexual needs. The emotions catalyzed by such witnessing of the beauty of young male bodies brought forth an emotion he could not control. At the waterhole, Locke discovered emotions that were his alone. The Victorian rigid separation of public and private spheres would allow him and others to indulge and pursue emotional relationships without public rebuke. Indeed, single-sex schooling unconsciously encouraged boys such as Locke to develop powerful emotional attachments with their classmates.

From the standpoint of Locke's relationship with his mother, the challenge was to find a compromise that allowed him to have a sexual life within the context of his overwhelming—and emasculating—emotional involvement with her. The humorous splashdown carried a terrifying symbolism for this child who was dreadfully fearful of the water: the awakening of adolescent sexual emotion carried the possibility of losing the love of his life—his mother. Going home to tell her about it was key: he could not gain the one by losing the other.

Because little direct evidence has survived, the precise details of Locke's first sexual experience will probably never be available. But Locke did narrate to his friend Stafford some of his feelings about this adolescent encounter. Stafford recalled that Locke was not at all ambivalent about this first explicitly sexual experience, which took place in a neighboring cellar where a darkroom had been set up. "He could revisit the interlude more than half a century later throughout his life, without shame, embarrassment, or apology. There was, at least on his part, no clumsy adolescent fumbling of the kind that can distort later erotic attitudes. It was, he said, just as he had expected and wanted it to be. This discovery of his most secret self came when he awakened with another in an unlighted room to some part of the universe that he could sense in no other way. He had sinned against no one. Consenting equally, they had joined in a new way the total rhythm, however varied or enriched with seeming dissonance to its cadence. There was no need for slyly written notes or the awful waste of childishly concealed passion. He went straight home and told his mother. They talked sensibly about the event and what it could mean. The only surprise to him later in this was the naturalness with which he found himself this close to another besides his mother."[17]

The notion that Locke's mother would not have had any misgivings about her son having had a sexual experience with another man begs credibility. Perhaps revealing this incident, which might not be regarded as homosexuality today, but as youthful experimentation, might not upset his mother because from her standpoint it meant he was not interested in girls and hence not interested in ever leaving her for another. Still, it seems incredible that she would not have felt that her son's sexuality was being determined by someone else's—a man, who, in consummating a set of feelings was, in the terms of the day, steering him astray. Later letters from Mary to her son while he was away at school do not contain references that support the notion she had a clear and unwavering sense of his sexual identity. Like most mothers, she probably suspected something; but that they talked about it while he was in high school as a natural occurrence seems a recollection that is a reconstruction.

As Locke remarked to Stafford, so overwhelming was his intimacy with his mother and his distance from all others that he was "surprised" to find himself able to be close to anyone "besides his mother." The story of Locke's sexual intimacy with a man as an adolescent, therefore, makes plain that no matter what level of confidence he shared with his mother about what happened, any such intimacy had to accommodate to the primacy of his relationship with his mother.

As an adolescent, Locke was balancing three worlds—the world he shared with his mother, the barely visible world of his sexuality, and the very visible world of integrated education at Central High School. Founded in 1836 at Broad and Green Streets, Central High was extremely proud of its excellent faculty, most of whom were drawn from college positions, and of its curriculum, which "compared favorably with the courses of instruction in most American colleges."[18] In 1894, Dr. Robert Ellis Thompson left his chair at the University of Pennsylvania to become the principal of the school, and Central received the right to confer the bachelor of arts degree on its graduates. Thompson revolutionized the curriculum of the school, organizing the teachers and the subjects into departments along college lines. By the time Locke arrived in 1898, Central was one of the finest academic institutions in the nation.

Originally established to attract the sons of the Philadelphia elite to the public school system, Central also enabled poorer boys to rise socially through their studies.[19] Admittance was contingent not only on intelligence but also on mastering elite manners and gentlemanly behavior. Central stood for the values of Victorian manhood, for Character, Discipline, and Self-Restraint as the essential qualities of a Victorian gentleman. Students might choose whether they wanted to specialize in the classical, the Latin scientific, or the modern language course of study, but they all had to listen to Dr. Francis Brandt lecture on the fruits of Discipline, or Dr. Robert Thompson explain the transition to manhood as progress up the stem of a *Y* to a fork in the road where one branch led to a life of good, and the other to a life of evil.

Electing the classical course with a heavy load of Greek, Latin, and English composition, Locke graduated from Central with an overall average of 94.6, just barely runner-up to the class valedictorian. In addition to the numerous courses in the humanities, including electives in American literature and French, Locke took numerous electives in the sciences, including anatomy and physiology, astronomy, chemistry, and physics. His record suggests he would have succeeded admirably at his family's first career recommendation that he go to medical school. His best marks were registered in Latin composition, anatomy, architecture, chemistry, history, French, English philology, and ethics.

Locke succeeded at Central not only because he was a brilliant student but also because his family and community had trained him in the manners, behavior, and attitude of Victorianism. His intelligence and refinement made him a hit with White students at Central. When Locke in 1902 applied for two more years of graduate work at the School of Pedagogy, he was gladly accepted. When Locke later in 1903 applied for admission to Harvard, Dr. Thompson wrote an enthusiastic letter of recommendation that revealed how Central's students and teachers regarded him.

> This is his sixth year under our care.... With every year he has risen higher in the esteem and confidence of those who have been teaching him.... I presume you know that he is a colored youth and also that the nearer one is to the South, the sharper the race prejudices which divide

his people from the whites. I have known but few boys...who have not even needed to overcome this unhappy prejudice, and to attain complete popularity with their classmates. Of these Mr. Locke is a notable instance. His white classmates accepted him on perfectly equal terms, deferred to his opinion as much as to that of any of their number, and the only thing they found peculiar in him was his excessive attention to his personal cleanliness. They used to say that if Mr. Locke had to defile his hands with chalk at the blackboard, he had no peace until he got them washed. I have had the opportunity of meeting him twice a week in that class, and I have been impressed with his fineness of discrimination, his evidence of fresh thought, his admirable personal bearing, and indeed almost everything that goes to make a good teacher.[20]

Thompson's fatherly letter (and Harvard's underlining) shows Locke's success in gaining "complete popularity with 'his' classmates." But it also reveals the level of stress Locke's achievement cost him. Brought up in the rigid discipline of his Black Victorian family, he had internalized the "white normative gaze" of elite Philadelphians to such an extent that he could easily conform to their expectations. But his "excessive attention to his personal cleanliness" suggests the neurotic struggle brewing just beneath the surface of that success. Thompson's language is telling. "If Mr. Locke had to defile his hands with chalk at the blackboard, he had no peace until he got them washed." References to "dirt" or "soiling" are psychologically associated with feces; but here, interestingly, it is "chalk" Locke is trying to wash off his black body. Normally, one would assume a young hyper-assimilating African American would be trying to wash the black off; while that is still operative here, there is also the possibility of another interpretation—that he is trying to wipe the "white," that is, "chalk" off his body. Locke paid an enormous cost almost daily in Central High and the School of Pedagogy to fit in and gain the confidence of those whom he secretly found to be *soiling* his soul.

Why would Locke have such ambivalence around the people he seemed so eager to impress? It is because of the contradiction of his education. Although Locke was "everything that goes to make a good teacher," according to Thompson, Locke had no chance of being hired at a mixed school in Philadelphia, especially not at Central or the School of Pedagogy, where most of his classmates and friends eventually taught. The teacher preparation of the School of Pedagogy was a fraud for him, and the ideology of the Black Victorians that manifestation of gentlemanly culture would override racism a cruel myth. Without an extraordinary effort and a bit of luck, Locke knew he was destined, if not careful, to end up like his mother—slaving away trying to educate the very people that his education had educated him away from knowing anything about. After six years of working very hard to fit in, to show he was as White and talented as any of his "fellows," there was nothing he could do to eradicate that he was Black. And all the while he carried out his performance, he secretly resented them because given his intelligence and accomplishment, not to welcome him into their community was to *defile* him.

Nonetheless, the School of Pedagogy was crucial to Locke's future. For it was there that Locke completed his transformation from a Black Victorian into a Black Aesthete—and then began to leave even that subject formation behind. The "six years in our care" allowed him to recognize and re-create himself in the language of late nineteenth-century men of culture who had lost faith in the moral vision of Victorian society and dispense with the notion that his young classmates owed anyone anything. Locke became an expert in performing the transition from the responsible to the irresponsible lover of art by fashioning a unique "aesthetic" personality that was part serious, part humorous, always pre-cocious, and able to participate in the intellectual games as a player whose witty asides and spectacular assertions gave him a unique persona. There Locke had crafted a lifelong asset—the ability to make an enduring impression on White people who in turn would do everything they could to help him. In 1925 School of Pedagogy literature professor Hughes Mearns, with whom Locke sustained a mentoring relationship into the 1930s, wrote Locke about his first impression of him.

> I have never ceased talking about you since the day I was bowled over by a bit of your sixteen-year-old genius and asked you, with a grin of course, whether you were a rogue or a genius. You said speculatively but hesitatingly, that you did not think you had it in you to make a rogue and that, of course, therefore, nodding at the paper, it must be—if I say that it must be—that you are—well, what one says one is! It was great fun.[21]

Locke had become a rogue, a practical jokester, a trickster, at the School of Pedagogy but most important adopted the persona of the aesthete, who, his classmate and friend Albert Rowland complained, made jokes whenever they attended church or chapel together.[22] By the 1890s, the young adolescents at Central and the School of Pedagogy could no longer take seriously the dictums of the old Victorian patriarchs at the school. As these young aesthetes secretly rebelled against the patriarchal fathers of American education, Mearns served as a sympathetic uncle who encouraged their creativity, imagination, and rebellion. And the key to that rebellion was the rejection of the moral element in art and the taking seriously the religious grounding of aesthetics in a traditional moral universe. Instead of partaking of art as a means to something else, something higher, Locke and friends venerated art as an end of its own, and made the pursuit of art experiences the main concern of their lives. Locke mimicked his classmates' adoration of art of all kinds, developed a taste for noticing and commenting on the picturesque, and arranged his room at home with art, such that his rooms, like those of his classmates from elite White families, became art objects themselves. Art and nature began to substitute for religion as the source of their most important spiritual experiences. Classmate Phil Boyer wrote to Locke: "I have just returned from an hour's walk through God's own country. Is not the silent worship of His creation an excellent substitute for Sunday school?"[23]

At the School of Pedagogy, Locke mastered the language of ambiguity and indirection, of irony and wit, of pun and "signifying" that characterized this aesthetic temperament. He wrote Boyer,

> The arrival of your letter is ancient history and I do not recall the date but I do remember that it was a very welcome one and that the news concerning the increase in your protégés was as startling as it was amusing. When I think of the fact that you have the S of P on your hands there is something pitiable in your plight but remember that the hand that rocks the cradle rules the world.[24]

Boyer ably parried Locke's thrusts, writing back some months later:

> I have at last taken an evening at home and was just about to re-read my Dickens Christmas Carol when I thought of you and the length of time it has been up to me to fill a "pot of message" as you call it. Conscience stricken, I threw aside the book and like a good little youngster, am now at work. I am writing, too, because I am beginning to be filled with that "good will toward men" Christmas Spirit that extends even so far as Harvard. May you have the happiest Christmas of your life even if you are "corrupt and contented" and I am not sure but that the very fact of your being in that state will make you happier, that is, if you are undeniably there.[25]

One can see why Mearns called Locke "great fun!"

Locke was fun because he had become an expert in performing what could be called the closet. Aestheticism was at base the performance of unfulfilled same-sex love. While most of his classmates were young men infatuated with one another, the way they expressed it was in the rebellion against moralism in art. Long walks talking about art, debating the merits of one picture over another, putting down a less sophisticated classmate's taste in some banal watercolors, for example, were all part of the performance of intimacy through art appreciation— especially art appreciation and taste detached from any moral agenda. But here was also another key: most of his classmates were not having sex with other young men. Rather, they were indulged in an adolescent pastime that would, in fact, pass, or if consummated, would be done in such a way that a kiss or more was not enough to concretize into an identity as a homosexual. The problem for Locke is that he was already past that by the time he graduated from School of Pedagogy: he was not just interested in the art to have a homosocial relationship, but instead saw the pursuit of art as part of an overall romantic relationship with men who were valued because they shared that interest as well. Ultimately, Locke would have to leave School of Pedagogy not only for racial, but also sexual reasons: he could never abide by the compromise Philadelphia teaching would exact of him—to be in the closet for the rest of his life. Unlike Phil Boyer, who was a heterosexual rogue who married and settled into provincial teaching in the suburbs, Locke was a homosexual aesthete. Philadelphia never accepted Walt Whitman's homosexuality and was not about to accept the Whitman side of Locke.

Knowing that he could not stay at the School of Pedagogy despite being the peer of its aesthetes, Locke pressed all of his supporters for help in finding another mooring, as when he wrote to ask Mearns for help on his Harvard application:

> As I remember it, you were still at school when the decision was reached that I had better prepare myself for the full entrance examinations to Harvard. Quite as you predicted I have come across several instructions and regulations which I hope have other interpretations than those which I, in my ignorance of Harvard regime, can give them. Your kind offer to help in event of such little difficulties has not been forgotten but I have purposely waited until I had quite a collection of them that I might not too often and without cause impose upon your patience or encroach upon your time. Indeed even now I should feel less culpable and more the less grateful if you could let me know when an hour's talk would give you the least inconvenience.[26]

Locke's language descends to the ingratiating, but yet Mearns approved. Recalling Martin Green's observation that the English dandy-aesthete Harold Acton "moved in curves" with his arm on his hip, Locke's language moves in curves, approaching and withdrawing.[27] It is also a reminder of how observers described Booker T. Washington's way of behaving in front of White folks—indirect, not challenging, but getting what he wanted. Locke could be even bolder because he was dealing with sympathetic Whites of Philadelphia's educational elite. Indeed, Locke had little if any experience with racist Whites, a weakness uncovered later in his career when he rudely discovered that not all Whites would be charmed by his gentlemanly behavior. But at School of Pedagogy, Locke can manipulate the teachers and students because he has already moved beyond them and sees their sexual timidity and racial hypocrisy as part of the same cloth. And yet having moved beyond them, he nevertheless is still caught in their problematic—he too will perform the closet in professional situations by labeling always his interests in art rather than in other men's bodies. Calling Philadelphians "paralyzingly discreet," Locke was also describing how he himself was still caught in strategies of survival.

Becoming an aesthete, therefore, would never be enough for Locke. While he loved art for its own sake, something about the rejection of School of Pedagogy taught him that he could never be the completely irresponsible gadfly of art that his performance among his classmates and in front of his professors suggested he would become. At some point, he would feel the tug of that nexus of responsibilities his mother felt and saw on the face of those elite arranged at the Ethical Culture Society one afternoon, but directed to some new, more Black, purpose. At some time, he would drop the pose and use the style, taste, and aesthetic posturing to advance a new interpretation of American culture with his predicament and that more broadly of the Black subject, as its center. Associations with his young White aesthetic classmates would then be another social experience that provided the advanced tools to refashion American culture to make room for him.

Locke began to translate his performance of sophistication and deportment into a new rhetorical strategy in an essay written just before he left the School of Pedagogy.

> The appearance of a few faint rays upon the horizon of dramatic art has revived the interest in this most important problem of the American drama and has, at last, aroused even the controllers of our dramatic syndicates. Art lovers have long deplored the shortcomings of the American stage and have tried to awaken public interest by speaking of the "universality of Shakespeare" and the "glowing imagery of Ibsen." Here and there some party of enthusiasts would present one of their beloved works; but the theatre-going public would overlook their modest announcement to be absorbed in the huge chest bedaubed with primary colors, which blazed a path for Mrs. Leslie Carter in Zaza, or something equally ridiculous.... The real problem that was producing such outrages was the theatrical syndicates, which had control of all the great theatrical centers. No amount of literary criticism could break its power, a commercial rival alone could check its power. Such it has found in the recently established Academy of Dramatic Art.[28]

The optimistic, almost hopeful ending to this Daily Theme in Mearns's class voices a new generation of American aestheticism. Unlike Henry James, Henry Adams, and George Santayana, Locke's generation of aesthetes was not hopelessly pessimistic about American culture. Young men like Locke and Van Wyck

Brooks believed a return to emphasis on form would perhaps break the grip of Victorianism and moralizing high culture on the one hand, and the stranglehold of banal popular entertainment on the other. The postwar rebellion against Victorian American culture began in the 1890s in the adolescence of boys like Locke who attended elite institutions of higher education, who found art to be a way out of the stultifying moralism of a patriarchal culture, and who would later use the love of form, of line, and of color to challenge traditional Victorian morality notions of the role of art in American culture.

In 1904, Harvard College admitted Locke as a freshman, refusing to give him the advanced placement he requested for the years at the School of Pedagogy. It did not matter. Locke was glad to escape Philadelphia and its peculiar professional predicament. Afterward, Philip Boyer wrote to tell Locke that all the other members of his class had found positions in Philadelphia's school system. Locke wrote back that he felt quite "corrupt and contented" at Harvard.[29] Of course he did. As a Victorian, he would barely reveal the hurt and anger his ostracism from their Philadelphia that racism caused. To his mother he would reveal upon arriving in Cambridge, "If I can get situated up here, Philadelphia will never see me again."[30] More privately, to Boyer, he would express in the 1930s a barely audible sense of hurt at having been forced out of the Philadelphia nest. "Life here [at Howard University in Washington] hectic as usual. I rather envy you your somewhat more tranquil base of operations."[31]

4

An Errand of Culture at Harvard College, 1904–1905

Locke arrived at Harvard shortly after his nineteenth birthday with letters of introduction from his Central High teachers, much as his grandfather Ishmael Locke had arrived in Philadelphia with his own letters sixty years earlier. For Locke too, the letters served to introduce him to the important educators of his new community and to ensure that he would not be regarded as just another Black man. Unfortunately, when Locke arrived the second week of September in 1904, the luminaries of Harvard's faculty had not yet arrived. Only younger professors were around to monitor the freshmen entrance exams he was required to take. In his first letter to his mother, he noted: "strange to say they are not pleasant fellows—sour as crab apples. I had fun asking them where the 'big boys I have letters to' were and I wish you could have seen the expressions on their faces. I did it just for effect."[1]

Locke had fashioned a pose of the young upstart genius to reassure himself that he could handle himself in the big leagues. The remark and the letters signaled to those who might think otherwise that he was somebody to be taken seriously. First impressions mattered most. His strategy was a protective armor, for beneath the attitude of total self-confidence, arrogance, and self-possession hid considerable doubts: Would he be accepted? Would this 4′11″, ninety-five-pound man be taken seriously? Would he be segregated from and marginalized by a Boston elite that shunned close and intimate association with Blacks? Beneath Locke's tough veneer was a tender-minded boy who would confide to his mother at the end of this first letter: "I'm awfully glad to have these letters of introduction—its such a cold formal place that it would seem forbidding if I did not have them."[2]

But Locke already had fallen in love with Harvard. He continued to his mother:

> I was called up early this morning from the office.... Got breakfast and went over to Harvard. It's a <u>beautiful</u> place, quite different from the

University [of Pennsylvania]. Everything is old and staid. None of the buildings look as if they had been built within 25 years. The largest finest trees I have ever seen and the campus full of pigeons and squirrels. Neither seem to mind passers by.[3]

Later, he would gush, "You can't imagine the historical associations of this place. I have to cross the field where the men assembled for the battle of Bunker Hill every day. The Washington Elm is within a half square of the college yard and you pass Longfellow house every time you go to the Stadium."[4] The memory of the New England Renaissance of American literature was still alive at university teas, where according to Locke's fellow student Rollo Brown, one could hear "unaffected talk of what 'Mr. Longfellow' was like as a teacher—he obtrusively caused students to shift their point of view—what 'Mr. Emerson' had one day said when he was in Cambridge."[5] It was important for him to set down roots in New England's flowering ground. After visiting the Mt. Auburn Cemetery at Fresh Pond, Locke would write his mother, "Longfellow, Lowell, Phillips Brooks, everybody that was anything in New England are all buried there."[6] During the next three years, Locke would visit almost every fine arts institution in Boston and soak up its culture.

Locke was fortunate to attend Harvard before the end of its "Golden Age," which began in 1869 when Charles William Eliot became its president and revitalized both undergraduate and graduate education at Harvard. Although in Locke's time the legendary professor Charles Eliot Norton no longer taught his famous courses on English literature, others including Barrett Wendell, George Lyman Kittredge, and Charles "Copey" Copeland carried on the Harvard tradition of senior professors teaching English composition and literary history to undergraduates. Aging William James, the father of American pragmatism, still taught courses at Harvard, although Locke chose instead to study with such other stars of American philosophy as Josiah Royce, George Herbert Palmer, and George Santayana. Locke acknowledged his debt to Harvard's surrogate fathers in a 1942 reminiscence: "There I was exposed to the Golden Age of liberalism and deeply influenced by Barrett Wendell, Copeland, Briggs, and Baker, shed the Tory restraints for urbanity and humanism, and under the spell of Royce, James, Palmer, and Santayana, gave up Puritan provincialism for critical-mindedness and cosmopolitanism."[7]

Harvard not granting him the one-year of advanced standing he requested was only the first obstacle to his plan to graduate from Harvard College in three years. His entrance examinations had revealed deficiencies in algebra, history, and physics. Undaunted, Locke committed himself to taking the courses to make up the deficiencies. But his biggest obstacle was financial. Locke's correspondence with his mother for these years is a record of their difficult efforts to stretch Mary's now $560 per year salary as a teacher at Camden's Mount Vernon school to cover the Harvard tuition. Constant borrowing, late payments on rent, cashing in insurance policies, and dodging creditors composed a floating system of debts and payments that frequently bewildered and upset his mother. Locke, on the other hand, looked at the situation as a financial game. To him, any inability to pay was not a personal dishonor, but a temporary glitch in an otherwise quite acceptable process of inconveniencing others to realize his goals. Throughout, Locke managed the family's accounts, instructing his mother whom to pay and when, from whom to borrow and how much, and how to bargain for more money from her Camden job. In part, his decision-making role derived from his greater ability at juggling the accounts, but it also signified that by the time he left Camden, he had become her surrogate husband, the head of the household. In his letters he would chide her to eat well, to not "strict" herself by going without food or coal, and berate her about the tasks she had left undone.

Locke's almost daily correspondence with his mother buoyed his confidence at Harvard. It also buoyed her. His leaving had devastated Mary. In her third letter to him in so many days, she wrote, "I don't expect letters—just send a postal—I don't expect answers, but I must just talk to you until I get used to the absence."[8] She was left behind to work at an unfulfilling teaching job and deal with insistent creditors, while he was off on an exhilarating adventure. He was still the center of her world and knew it. "I dream nearly every night of you," she confided.[9]

Another cause of economic stress during these Harvard College years was Locke's desire to live the life of the gentleman. His first letter to his mother had delivered his opinion of student housing: "The cheaper dormitories are like barns and are not heated except by open grates for wood in each room—I wouldn't live in one rent free."[10] So Locke placed an ad in the newspaper and reassured his mother, who believed he might be denied accommodations because of race prejudice:

> I have a large list to choose from—I have received 8 or ten answers to my ad.... There is one answer in particular I think will suit.... From its location it must be in a charming neighborhood and is within 5 minutes walk of Harvard grounds. Still I am looking out for something better not in the way of price.... I am determined to get in [with] some good and intellectual family.[11]

By the end of his first week in Cambridge, he could write his mother with even more encouraging news.

> Well yesterday I visited about 14 boarding houses in the swellest parts of Cambridge and what do you think? Every single one but <u>one</u> was

pleasant and offered me accomodations [sic]. I have so many I don't know which to choose. Four of them when I spoke of references said I needed none but my appearance. Well I did look rather nice. I knew I would never break in if I didn't. The grey suit with the hat and grey glove—the overcoat and bag—all make their impression. One downright refused me, every other was pleasant. This New England coldness is all bosh—the pleasantest chummiest people you would want to find. One place when I mentioned Prof. Royce said "His son is downstairs now." So you can see what nice places they are. Every one offers the use of the reception room. About 5 or 6 that I have <u>already</u> [been] offered are on the streets where professors live. This seems to be the place for me—it's just extra enough.... The reason I want a real nice place is on account of the tutoring. By the by there is a colored woman, a Miss Baldwin, principal of the largest and most aristocratic grammar school in Cambridge. I am going to see her—ostensibly to visit the school—really to <u>get in</u> with her. If I could get a nice bunk up here, Phila would never see me again.[12]

Locke took Black Victorianism and turned it into an art of performance on the streets of Cambridge. He was the Black dandy, whose gray coat "and gloves" updated Beau Brummel's signature preference for the more severe black suit and cane. Gray, the preferred suiting color for medium-brown African American men of the early twentieth century, was a palette for Locke, meticulously coordinated down to the gloves and coat. Locke used his dress to trouble White expectations of what a Negro looked like and replace them with an image of the New Negro, who created a new surprising identity through the art of dress. As a Black dandy, Locke had even transcended his grandfather—he needed no references "but my appearance."

Indeed, the letter shows how much Locke believed race was essentially a performance. His dress defined him as cosmopolitan, even worldly, and not "niggerish." The success of this initial self-fashioning of his Harvard identity led him to believe that he could escape the boundaries of racial prejudice he had sensed in Philadelphia. "There is no prejudice here," he wrote his mother, "and from the impression I have made so far I am sure I can get along all right."[13] Locke did not come to Harvard as Negro to a White university, but as a man who belonged there, continuing the integrated social life he had enjoyed at Central. By contrast, W. E. B. Du Bois, who had attended Fisk University before Harvard, wrote that he "went to Harvard as a Negro, not simply by birth, but recognizing myself as a member of a segregated caste whose situation I accepted."[14] Du Bois attributed his racial self-consciousness to living in the Black undergraduate atmosphere at Fisk; without such an experience, Locke saw no reason to limit the sphere of his contacts. Accordingly, when he finally settled on lodgings at

50 Irving Street, he was very pleased: William James lived a half a block away at 95 Irving Street, and Josiah Royce's house stood two doors farther down. It was certainly a "nice-looking place to receive" White fellow students, whom Locke did not have trouble meeting.

> I've picked up acquaintanceships with 2 or 3 of the Freshmen. It's a funny-looking lot of dudes about 20–22 years of age, some eccentric with heels 2 in and more high, skin tight jackets and colored handker-chiefs tied around their rough rider hats, then some poor looking Jews—some with moustaches—and then the rabble. Of all [the] people half of them look as if they ought to be furtherest from Harvard College....I fell in today with a young man from Springfield, Mass who is really chummy. Others have started conversation but I am going to be choice and pick my company. From the very first word I knew this one was an O.K. fellow. [By the way] I didn't know there were so many coons here. Boston is thick with them.[15]

On one level, "coons" was simply one of many terms that Blacks habitually used in private to refer to other Blacks; but on another level, it was a racist reaction to other, less sophisticated Blacks. Locke strictly divided the Black community be-tween "coons," the uneducated "herd," and gentlemen and ladies, the "represen-tative" members of the race. He also gleaned at Harvard a truth of American race relations: when Whites confronted a large number of Blacks, they were more likely to think of Blacks en masse. Close ties with Blacks would make his assimi-lation into elite White culture at Harvard more difficult, especially since he wanted to appear to Whites as an exceptional individual. Locke feared the taint of inferiority would somehow rub off on him. That fear even extended to Philadelphia's Black newspaper: "I am glad to receive the *Tribune* news," he wrote his mother, "but not the *Tribune*—everything is seen here, and one must keep up appearances."[16]

By the first week of October other Black Harvard students began inviting him to join in their group activities, but he wished to avoid them so as not to endan-ger his prospects for White acceptance. Locke had to face that an enlightened Black student was expected to maintain cordial relations with other Black stu-dents on campus. He wrote his mother:

> The colored fellow whom Dr. Flounders, Rowland's principal, asked me to meet called on me this afternoon. He took me to see the "boys." Of course they were colored. All together about 9 in one house. He took me right up into the filthy bedroom and there were 5 niggers, all Harvard men. Well, their pluck and their conceit are wonderful. Some are ugly enough to frighten you but I guess they are bright. They received me

cordially ["] come around to the dances["] and that sort of thing. I staid [*sic*] the visit out for fun but I might as well have that one experience. Its my <u>last</u>. They are not fit for company even if they are energetic and plodding fellows. I'm not used to that class and I don't intend to get used to them.... Most of them are waiters up here.... Mama, don't fear I am going to associate with such fellows. Its well enough for them to get an education but they are not gentlemen.[17]

Locke's judgment was harsh and cruel: a number of excellent Black students attended Harvard during his tenure as an undergraduate. Audrey Bowser graduated from Harvard with an AB in English in 1907 and went on to a career as a journalist; William Clarence Matthews was the very popular star of the varsity baseball team for his four years as a Harvard undergraduate. Edwin Tyson and Hugh R. Francis, both of Washington, D.C., came from respectable families whose economic resources were superior to Locke's. While they did not make the kind of academic record at Harvard that Locke did, with the exception of Matthews, they graduated. Some Black students did earn money by serving tables at Memorial, where he took his meals, but White students served tables there too, without causing their fellow students any deep approbation. But those fellow White students were not as fearful as Locke that associating with working students would hurt their chances for acceptance among other Whites. His comments reveal a deeper truth—he was entering Harvard less as an individual and more as a member of an insecure Black middle class.

Indeed, Locke's status was tenuous in the first months of the fall semester. Without his Central High School connection, he very well might not have "broken in" to the circle of elite White students at Harvard as he confided to his mother:

The graduates at the table did not have anything to say to me until one happened to ask where I came from. He happened to be a Central High School man—one whom Mr. Mearns told to look out for me. He said I was told to look for a Mr. Locke. I said I am he. Then there followed the most surprised expression you ever saw, general handshaking—I was introduced to the whole table and made to feel at home. I could not help but think of the contrast and was mighty glad they could not have seen me a half hour previous in the colored den.[18]

In his letter, Locke also hinted at his role model at Harvard: "You ought to hear them talk of [Roscoe Conkling] Bruce—I bet he didn't notice them." Bruce was the son of Black Reconstruction senator Blanche K. Bruce and an honor student of his Harvard class of 1902. Not only had he won a scholarship but he had also been class orator. As his class's best debater, he had led Harvard to two victories over its rivals Princeton and Yale.[19] Bruce had won the respect of prominent professors like the philosopher George Herbert Palmer and had been popular among his White classmates. Now assistant superintendent of Colored schools in Washington, D.C., after a stint as a teacher at Tuskegee Normal and Industrial Institute, Bruce was a success story and a "representative" Negro from Harvard. Locke consciously modeled himself after Bruce, who had also been something of a snob: he could be counted on not to "notice" the less gifted Black students during his time at Harvard.

Locke seemed to have more difficulty than Bruce balancing the conflicting demands of groups at Harvard. There were the professors, and along with them social functions sponsored by the university; then White students, or "friends," with whom he sought to establish intimate relationships; and then the Black circle, from whom he remained icily distant. The first two groups might lead to advancement. "The fellows are very friendly and I'm scheming as usual to get in with the best."[20]

Interestingly, the Black students understood his game. He wrote his mother, "The colored fellows don't speak when I'm with the others. What do you think of that? To come up here in a broad-minded place like this and stick together like they were in the heart of Africa."[21] Mary supported his desire to remain exclusive, but by November, she began to sense that he might become a victim of group ostracism. She then jokingly urged him to "speak to the other fellows when they pass you, just for fun." She also chastised him about his hypercritical attitude: "You seem never to duly appreciate your colored brethren. Are the Harvard representatives particularly loud? You would think that Harvard would get the best element of the race."[22] It had. She could not understand that his behavior had roots in her early childhood admonitions to avoid "low class persons" and only associate with "refined" playmates. But for Mary Locke, who lived in a predominantly Black world, this dictum had meant associating with only the best of the Black population; for Locke, it had become a demand that he associate mainly with upper-class Whites. His letters also cautioned her against becoming too intimate with her Black women friends in his absence. "Remember me to Janie and steer clear of that club. What you want to do if you want a diversion is to go to lectures, etc." He wanted to ensure that his absence did not lead her to become more involved with the Black community and less focused on him. "I am glad you can find some diversion on Sunday," he wrote on October 13, "but do not get too thick with either Lizzie or Mary. Time I get established you will be so affiliated with the race that you won't want to leave them. Keep retired and distant with most of them."[23]

Nonetheless, despite his disparagement of Black undergraduates, Locke continued to visit with them at Harvard. He wrote his mother in November:

> Yesterday afternoon I went down to the stadium to see the last practice
> of the football team. I guess over 1500 students must have been in line

with the University band leading. I went down with a colored brother Bowser. Well he acted like a fool—talked all sorts of nonsense—the "boys" wanted [to] let me know that their annual dance and card-party— subscription $1.00 mind you [—] was to come off. They generally let the new men know ahead of time so they could introduce them to some "lady" to bring. The "lady's" name must be handed in by Thursday of next week.[24]

Over Thanksgiving the pressure to participate in the annual dance intensified.

About 10:30, my colored friend whom I have been trying to get shut of came in and said the "boys" were over in Hilton's room and would like me to come over. Of course there was nothing to do but go and I thought I would meet some whom I might like.... Then I learned what they wanted me for—to ask me to this old dance of theirs. Subscription $1 mind you. I said I have never gone and do not care to and besides I have no one to take. Oh, we'll fix that up for you and without asking me a bit they began to fix up among themselves whom I should take. You can imagine how furious I was. ["]Gentlemen I am here to study—I go to meetings of our club, I visit my schoolmates, and go to places when I have been formally introduced by friends at home but I do not go to dances and don't approve of them.["] One of them said, "Well we've counted on you and thought you were surely going." I saw the hurt and happening to have $1 in my pocket I said, ["]That's easily settled gentlemen as you have counted on me here's my subscription but I cannot go."[25]

Locke's race and class-consciousness masked a deeper concern. As a closeted queer student in an aggressively heterosexual Black student community, he wanted to avoid any setting in which he would have to perform as if he were available heterosexually. That conflict came to a head two days later:

Last night Saturday these two fellows called and said they were passing on their way to Browns and stopped in to see if I would go. Browns they explained was a sort of "house for the fellows" and Brown was a gradu- ate of Harvard, etc., etc. I had already said I had no engagement so they had me. I put on my coat and went thinking it was a few squares away. They said down Massachusetts Ave. Well they hailed a Roxbury car and I learned with a jolt that it was Mass Ave. Roxbury. One of them paid the fares and I began to think I had been sold. Well they landed at a rather nice looking house but the Brown whom I thought I was going to meet is the son who is now teaching at Tuskegee. It was the

Brown girls I found out when they asked the mother at the door if the girls were home. In the parlor playing whist was this same Matthews, Mr. Brown[,] some other fellow and four girls. Well I just grit my teeth and endured it.

Rather than the socializing in Roxbury, it was the heterosexual flirtation of the scene that made him "grit" his teeth.

After we left they told me they thought I understood and that it was the "girls at home" night for the fellows. I never fell so completely into a trap in my life—I suppose it isn't their fault for they thought I understood without explanations but you can imagine all I said. I was hot and let them know it.[26]

Mary did not think the incident was so bad and wondered why he reacted the way he did. She seemed not to realize that his hyper-Victorian policing of this incident was actually sexual panic over being forced into a social-sexual encounter with a "lady." Perhaps Locke had not told his mother about his first sexual experience with a boy, as he claimed he had done, or maybe she did not conclude that that experience ruled out future heterosexual relationships. For Locke, it did; he was sure he was not interested in "girls at home." And that brought him considerable anxiety. His vicious gendered labeling of Black women as "nigger wenches" barely deflected attention from his fear that a woman's advances might produce a socially explosive revelation.

Remarkably, Locke did attend the dreaded dance and, in spite of his promise not to stay, enjoyed himself.

They did have the hall decorated very nicely in Harvard colors and they were all dancing something like a cake walk when I came in. It was so funny that I would willingly have watched them longer if it had not been that I was on my dignity. One fellow had a dress suit, one a tuxedo, the majority black suits with <u>red</u> ties, several mixed <u>outing suits</u>. The women were simply dressed outlandishly and strange to say there wasn't a costly dress there.[27]

The dance reveals one of the deepest conflicts of Locke's entire life—his pull toward the coziness of Black fellowship and social occasions that, in fact, valued and nurtured him in ways White situations did not, and yet his hostility and standoffishness toward working-class Black circumstances, combined with persistent sexual anxiety that he would be outed and rejected if he became too visible to the Black community. Locke's sexuality prevented him having a closer relationship with the Black students. And yet he seemed to value their acceptance of him. "I find myself very cordially received by the considerable no of colored fellows here and feel very proud of the good work both scholastic & athletic some of them are doing here. Perhaps it is not within my province as a newcomer to criticize a slight tendency towards segregation when there is as little cause for it as there is here at Harvard, especially as it was at one of such gatherings that I got material to answer your questions about the football situation."[28]

Locke did not have the problem of heterosexual expectations with his White friends. None of those friends would ever have invited him to a party where there was the potential of a romantic encounter with a White "lady." Rather, his Central High friends seemed to want to avoid such situations themselves, being aesthetes for whom visiting "Cultured" sites, taking homo-social if not homo-sexual excursions into the countryside, and having beautiful experiences around Boston were the things to do. Locke took in them all with his newfound friends in tow.

> I visited the Harvard Art Museum and the big University museum... the celebrated Academy of Fine Arts in Boston and the famous Boston Library. The paintings in the library reading room are simply so magnificent as to be overpowering. I enjoyed the afternoon immensely. [David ("Dap")] Pfromm from the Central High School was with me.[29]

Locke and Pfromm, the son of a German-Jewish pharmacist in Philadelphia, met during his first week of classes. They had quickly become friends. Pfromm was a freshman like Locke, but less of an aesthete and rebel. Pfromm, who often accompanied Locke to church, did not appreciate Locke's disdain for the religious exercises, yet both enjoyed the fine stained-glass windows in Appleton Chapel. Pfromm and Locke were also friends with Charles Dickerman, another graduate of Central High and a sophomore when Locke met him in October at his table in Memorial. "Dickus," as his friends fondly called him, was already an experienced aesthete, well familiar with English literature, classical music, and modern art. By the spring of 1905, Locke had also added to his circle of close friends C. Rosenblum, another freshman who would major in English, and Bruno Beckhard, a wealthy graduate of Columbia Grammar School in New York who seemed to be at college mainly to have a good time. Locke was also friendly with John Hall Wheelock, the poet Charles Seeger, and Van Wyck Brooks.

But it was with Pfromm, Dickerman, and Beckhard that Locke spent much of his social time.

> I met Dickerman and our millionaire friend Beckhardt [sic] (the one who surprised me with his special car) and we went out to [Nonantum?] Novembeja—a beautiful lake a few miles out, toward Newton.... Well,

we went out and spent the afternoon canoeing and taking pictures. We got in late for supper—took it together and then went to Beckhardt's room. Let me tell you of the room all his furniture is in quartered oak with buff yellow trimmings, the most unique things I have yet seen—the room is simply loaded with curios—saddle, spurs, riding whips, chafery samovars for tea, old pipes, a guitar, mandolin, violin, etc.—simply great—we settled ourselves down for the evening— Dickerman made a couch for himself of pillows on the floor and started smoking a Turkish water pipe—Beckhardt started his music and went from the guitar to the mandolin to the violin, and wound up on the mouth organ. Dickerman said he played best on that—It was not much in the way of music but it did patch out the conversation which ran from baseball games to Dick's account of a spiritualistic sceance [sic] he once attended.[30]

After Beckhard's, Locke went over to Dick's room in Weld Hall to listen to him "read some new poetry that took us till one, or after, then he started to walk home with me and Cambridge was so beautiful we sat on the yard fence and talked till the clock struck two."[31] Over time, Locke's friendship with Dickerman became quite intimate. They were likely lovers by the end of Locke's Harvard years.

Perhaps aware of the contrast between his closeness with his White friends and the arms-length distance he maintained with his Black classmates, Locke explained to his mother the difference between the two as one of class aspiration. Being with his White classmates was an association that led "somewhere." Friendship, he argued, was not solely based on taste, but on the reality of whether friends could help him. This was certainly true of Dickerman, who was instrumental to Locke's introduction into broader Cambridge and Boston society. Shortly after they met, Dickerman took Locke to Civic Service House in Boston where he taught a class of "Jewish boys," and Locke was invited to perform what passed as "philanthropic work up here." Locke was looking for a way "in" to the Boston teaching scene and volunteered to come once a week to teach, even though it was unpaid. He believed it would lead to membership in the "famous Century Club of Boston, a philanthropic club to which Bruce and Booker Washington belong," as he wrote to his mother. "Bruce was a classmate of the superintendents and did the same kind of work they ask me to do." In the spring of 1905, Dickerman again eased Locke's access to Cambridge society.

I was invited Thursday Evening to a meeting of some organization— at the time I did not know what it was and on arriving found that Dickerman, a CHS fellow—now Sophomore—had proposed me for membership in the Ethical Culture club. I was elected and of course was more than willing to join. It is a club organized on the plan of the Ethical

Culture Society....I am not over interested, but as it was very kind of Dickerman and being a small club offers opportunity for meeting the proper sort of fellows, I was glad to agree to attend.[32]

"Cultured" activities were valuable intrinsically and as a means of access to "refined" fellows. And that Dickerman helped Locke socially was also part of a larger scenario: Locke was Dickerman's Black friend, whom Dickerman had decided to take on as a project. Himself a social climber, Dickerman already had made the inroads that he offered to the younger Locke as a benefit of their relationship. In Locke's letter to his mother, he elaborated on his feelings for Dickerman.

> I like him best of all the High School fellows up here—probably because I see more of him. We go down to the Civic Service House together and sit together at table. We spent part of the night talking Celtic Literature!!! He is a poet and an enthusiast—so I have to pretend to be interested. It is interesting with him—anyone else would bore you to death—but its not affectation with him. He's always that way, and he has called my attention to several mighty good books. When he sees me in the Union Library he will go get something he is enthusiastic over and insist on my reading it. Friday night he was off on Yeats, the Irish poet and after lighting his Japanese incense, sat down to read me a poetical play of Yeats and a poem "he" had written after reading it. I was a little bored but it was warm, comfortable, and I didn't mind the smoke of his old incense, so I found myself getting up to go at 12:30.[33]

Such late-night sessions had a subtle but profound impact on Locke—Dickerman moved him toward modernism. Dickerman cut the figure of a Bohemian with his Japanese incense and readings in Celtic literature, but blended cosmopolitanism and cultural nationalism together in a way that would outline Locke's future elaboration of a Black culture. But in 1904, Locke only feigned interest in Celtic literature because he wanted to be intimate with Dickerman. Homosexual desire was beginning a slow process of intellectual growth—exposing him to ideas and trends he would not have been open to otherwise. In Dickerman's room, while Locke angled for a romantic relationship, he was growing as an intellectual.

Life as an undergraduate was not just escapist romps with friends. He had a "corking good set of instructors," he wrote his mother, and he put in long hours of study, even though he didn't want to be known as a "grind." In addition to Dean Hurlbut's course in freshman composition and Professor Haskins's course in medieval history—the latter a requisite along with German because of his deficiencies on the entrance examinations—Locke took English literature with LeBaron Briggs, dean of the School of Arts and Sciences, freshman Greek literature with Gulick, Harris, and John H. White, and an introductory philosophy course jointly taught by George Herbert Palmer and Ralph Barton Perry. Locke used Harvard's liberal elective system to design a freshman curriculum—indeed his entire undergraduate education—along the lines of a classical humanities curriculum. His 1904–1905 course in Greek literature included Plato's *Apology* along with Crito, Lysias, Xenophon, Euripides, and readings from the elegiac, iambic, and lyric poets. He continued the study of Greek literature throughout his time at Harvard. He took two semesters of Greek literature from the period of the Athenian supremacy in 1905–1906, White's "History of Greek Drama" in the first semester of his senior year, and an advanced course of Aeschylus, Sophocles, Euripides, and Aristophanes in the second. He divided the rest of his undergraduate curriculum almost evenly between advanced courses in English and philosophy. In his freshman year, he had As in philosophy and history, a B+ in Briggs's course, Bs in freshman composition and Greek literature, and only a C in German (a language he began at Harvard) to spoil things. His average was good enough to win the Price Greenleaf Scholarship that he had applied for but not received upon his admission. And he had also impressed two of Harvard's most influential professors during his first semester there.

It was not until the end of October 1904 that Locke obtained a personal interview with Josiah Royce, one of the real "big boys he had letters to" at Harvard. Armed with Francis Brandt's letter, Locke marched over to 103 Irving Street and introduced himself to a somewhat skeptical Mrs. Royce. Initially, she told her young suitor that the good doctor was retired; but then noticing the letters in his hand, asked him inside, after which she took his coat and hat, and asked him to wait in the parlor. Upon reading the letters, Dr. Royce asked Locke into the philosopher's study, where they talked for about an hour.

> Well, such a room! It was small—lined up to the very high ceiling with books—dozens lying in a heap on a table at one end, a revolving bookcase in the center of the room and a large leather reclining chair in which "his nibs" was. He was hardly sitting—the chair was so big and tilted back so far that he seemed to be lying down. His body is smaller than mine but his head is larger than Thompsons. He's a genius. You know he has the reputation of being the greatest philosopher now living—and because of that and his ugliness is called "the modern Socrates." Do you know he never budged the whole 3/4 of an hour I was there. He just held out his hand, said he was glad to meet me and had me bring a chair up near this bed of his. I suppose I got a remarkable reception for the queer fish that he is. He stared at me for a minute or two and then said, "Tell me all about yourself." He made me tell how old I was, what schools I had attended[,] how I came to know Brandt, if I was of West Indian descent, if I had educated parents, if I liked

philosophy etc etc etc. What do you think of that for a cross examination? It's good I have gotten used to great men—I didn't feel strange and my nerve carried me through. It was a good chance to let him know what the family stood for. He asked, What was your father? and he got a good dose. I guess he was trying me out. At any rate he was pleased and then began to ask about my plans and to give advice. He said that it was a mighty auspicious beginning and that he would like to personally advise me on any point in my work—that he hoped to see me in his higher philosophy classes—he then even went on to ask if I had plenty of acquaintances so as not to be lonely. Told me how hard his boy had found certain courses—and so on. He was delightful in his dry way afterwards—but first he wanted to know everything, I suppose, before he let himself out. I put the finishing touches on by thanking him for the service one of his books had been to me (I had read it a few hours previous to going to his house just so I could talk about it.) and said good night and left.[34]

Locke was already a master of the academic game, in which letters of introduction, flattery, and genteel self-presentation were essential to being taken seriously by the "great men" at Harvard. Royce's patriarchal questions about Locke's family show how much class was part of the judgment of whether Locke was the "right sort"—a Black Victorian who happened to be Black (and therefore probably a "genius"). Locke, on his side, discusses Royce in terms of his physical appearance and social reputation, as a commodity to appropriate for his own success at Harvard. In that sense, Locke was a hustler at Harvard, who collected associations and connections and saw success at Harvard as depending as much on social as intellectual performance.

Yet being a hustler perfectly matched the social and academic code of his environment. Harvard's ascendancy in the latter quarter of the nineteenth century was due to its aggressiveness in innovating and refining the academic game of university self-promotion. Harvard's president, Charles W. Eliot, recognized early the necessity of first-rate graduate schools to build a reputation for undergraduate instruction, placed greater emphasis on publication than teaching in departments, saw that assembling departments of academic "stars" was crucial to the prestige of a university, and raided other universities to lure away such potential stars. The "Golden Age" of philosophy at Harvard was itself a packaged advertisement for Harvard's claim to being the best university in the world. Royce had been lured away from the University of California upon James's personal evaluation of Royce's "genius"; George Herbert Palmer had risen to the Alford Professorship less because of his philosophical ability than because of his role as a consummate judge of talent and promoter of the department's (and university's) interest and reputation; the appointment of German psychologist

Hugo Muensterberg recognized the importance of German universities and of academic scholarship, and it also brought to the department a master academic game player, who used offers from other schools to raise his salary and academic position. As historian Bruce Kuklick puts it, Eliot's faculty, while certainly gentlemen, were also "men on the make."[35] Locke correctly judged that if he wanted to be well regarded as a student, he too better be "on the make." And he succeeded. Not until his third year would Locke take a course with Royce, and Royce's recommendation for the Price Greenleaf Fellowship had certainly helped.

Locke's most dramatic reception came from Dean Le Baron Briggs in his freshman English literature course. Early in the fall semester, Locke walked up to the desk at the front of the class to turn in a daily theme. He was greeted effusively by Briggs, who

> shook hands[,] made quite a time and had me stand there talking until class was over. You can imagine how the fellows stared—there were about 150 in the class as it was our large section meeting. The colored fellow who invited me to the dance was handing in his theme just as Briggs was apologizing for being in bed when I called [at his home]. He got his ears full that time didn't he?[36]

Briggs seemed infatuated with Locke and took it upon himself a month later to introduce him first to Mrs. Eliot and then to her husband, the president at the fall University Tea. Later that same semester, Locke was again shown off by an English professor, probably Briggs, who read Locke's "examination book to the class"; and since he had cut the class, "all the fellows who have told me about it thought I staid [sic] away on purpose. I didn't know anything about it and didn't count on getting a little 'rep' for modesty."[37] Modesty was not one of Locke's strong points, but he was glad that Briggs had responded so well. Although Briggs did not give him an A for the year's work, he did write a letter of recommendation for Locke's application for the Price Greenleaf. Locke's professors were partly reacting out of their racial surprise that a Black student could do better than the average White student and also to his manner of approach to professors.

Yet Locke was also a student of exceptional ability, especially in philosophy, as one of his professors recognized. Early in February 1905, he learned that his fall semester work in ancient and modern philosophy (Philosophy 1B) was so good that Ralph Barton Perry requested a personal interview with him.

> Thursday afternoon my philosophy instructor sent for me to call on him—He gave me my mark and talked over my work—was very glad to get in such close touch with him—he was very anxious to know what I intended to do—Would I study philosophy? I said—of course. I did

intend to take some philosophy courses anyhow—so we talked those over—he complimented me on my work and asked me to come see him personally again. He is one of the younger men but quite well up—at any rate it will be pleasant to go—His room is simply ideal—books and pictures—not much else—but great—he has reproductions of frescoes and church decorations of 14th and 15th century Italian painters all around the room—I never saw such pictures in a private house in my life.[38]

Perry was the first member of the Philosophy Department to recognize Locke's potential talent as a philosopher. Although Locke moaned to his mother later that he was tired of "writing things which I don't understand" in his philosophy class, he was very able when it came to abstract reasoning and argumentation. Locke's remarks are telling in another way: in 1905, he was more interested in the pictures of medieval frescoes than in becoming a philosopher.

Locke approximated the taste of his philosophy professor during his second year when he obtained a room in Grays Hall, or as he described it a "suite rather, bedroom and study facing right on the college yard."[39] His single unfurnished dormitory room gave him the opportunity to spend weekends buying furniture, rugs, pictures, and fabric, something he thoroughly enjoyed, although he complained incessantly to his mother about the hassle of tracking down good buys. He bought reproductions of paintings at second-hand shops and had them nicely framed, thereby approximating the kind of artwork he had seen in Professor Perry's room at a fraction of the cost; he bought pillow stops, an old bolster, and made his own pillows for what became his favorite reading spot, the cushioned window seat that overlooked the yard. By the end of October, he had all of his bedroom furniture, a washstand, an oak chiffonier, and a bookcase, with only a desk and a rug to purchase to make it cozy for full-time studying.

Locke more fully enjoyed campus life his second year. His rooms allowed him to host activities for his circle of friends—Pfromm, Beckhard, Rosenblum, and Dickerman—in his quarters. He regularly studied in the Harvard Union until midnight, went by Beckhard's and Pfromm's for a brief chat, and then ended up at Dickerman's, from which he generally emerged around 1 or 2 A.M. Locke also joined a debating club, tried out for crew as a coxswain (he was asked), and attended the Ethical Culture Society meetings where he heard a closed lecture by President Charles W. Eliot. The social event of the second year came in January 1906 when Locke, along with Pfromm and Dickerman, hosted a beer night at which he not only drank beer but also played cards, though without the reprobation he had expressed about similar activities of his Black classmates a year before. In a letter to his mother, he noted that after drinking four beers, he was reminded of his father, who had loved beer, and who seemed to have been criticized by Mary for indulging it a bit too much.[40] The beer night was another sign of his transformation at Harvard: he was beginning to loosen up, to adopt less moralistic notions of appropriate behavior, and to dress more casually. As he wrote his mother in December 1905, "I beg to disagree with the universal sanction that seems to be given Mrs. Robinson's ideas of how a gentleman should dress. The benefit of Harvard is that you learn what is proper with perfect permission to be a non-conformist and be and dress and act as independently as you please."[41] Harvard provided Locke with an alternative set of values—largely those of bohemianism—which began to crack the shell of moralism with which Mrs. Locke had armored her son.

Living on campus also seemed to improve his grades. His second year was his best: his average was 3.5. Even more impressive, the grades were achieved in more rigorous courses than he had taken the previous year. He elected Dr. Maynadier's "English Literature from the death of Scott to the death of Tennyson" and Barrett Wendell's famous English 46, "The Comparative History of World Literature." And he took George Herbert Palmer's Philosophy 4, "Ethics, The Theory of Morals," while continuing his study of Greek by taking Professor Harris's course in Greek literature during the Athenian supremacy. He obtained As in all of the above, with only a C and B-, respectively, in courses in German and Economics. He was rewarded with a lucrative Bowditch Scholarship for his junior year. He was highly motivated, as he confessed to his mother: "I am watching my marks closely with regard to next year—I seem to see dollars and cents on the examination page and its quite an incentive. It is just the sort of stimulant a person needs."[42]

If there was any problem, it was that he had not yet settled on a major. Mr. Mearns, his English literature instructor at the School of Pedagogy, arranged to speak with Locke during a visit back in Philadelphia on how to go about getting honors in philosophy. Locke had already considered trying for honors in philosophy, but he was set on honors in English as well. Tension existed between his love for literature and art on the one hand, and his talent for philosophical reasoning on the other. Rather than resolve that tension into a single major, Locke believed he could take courses in both areas and succeed. He was right.

Perhaps the most important philosophy course of his second year was Palmer's course in ethics. Taking that course gave Locke an opportunity to spend time with another important patron in the Philosophy Department. Without the metaphysical interest or theoretical skill of Royce, Palmer was nonetheless the backbone of the department's idealist wing, and Locke's choice of Philosophy 4 reflected both his intellectual orientation and his appreciation of Palmer's potential importance to his later career. It also reflected Locke's undergraduate preference for the genteel tradition in philosophy over the radical empiricism and pragmatism of William James. Locke's choice of courses with Palmer suggests that he may have been attracted to philosophy because of its vision of a universal discourse that all men, regardless of race, could participate in.

Professors like Palmer and Royce also emphasized the responsibility and loyalty of the individual to the larger community and thereby reinforced the Victorian side of Locke's personality.

Palmer's Philosophy 4 had been innovative when it was introduced in the 1880s, because Palmer taught the course as a systematic exploration of philosophical problems, rather than a history of thought. Palmer wanted to teach students to philosophize, instead of merely rote-learning the positions of other philosophers. Locke's excellence in Palmer's course attested to his growing ability to handle complex philosophical problems and to think originally. He was rewarded by genuine concern and interest from Palmer. During the spring of 1906, Locke visited Palmer's home and the senior philosopher quizzed Locke on his future plans.

Then, the conversation turned toward the race question, since Palmer had known both Bruce and W. E. B. Du Bois as students.

> [He] spoke very highly of Dr. Du Bois as a man of undisputable genius, but who was a failure—he should have done much more, says Palmer, with his opportunities—Atlanta is no place for him—this is very kind criticism for Professor Palmer's wife Alice Freeman Palmer was responsible for financial help at Atlanta for years.... Palmer as usual spoke about Bruce—said he advised him to leave Tuskegee as Bruce wrote to him asking his advice. It was on Palmer's recommendation that he got the Washington position and Palmer said if I wanted to teach in Washington, he would write for me at any-time. I of course told him that I too contemplated educational work, and that both father and grandfather had done it before me. Of course he thinks it the only right sort of thing for a colored man. It is strange but they are all daft on the Negro problem and seem to think that all we think about is its solution. Well perhaps we should, but if I am to work in it, its got to afford me a pretty decent and congenial way of living, or it can go to grass. I saw he was too set in his ways to stand much in the way of opposition, but I hinted that we also had our personal problems, and should, in cases, be allowed to follow a life of self-culture as most all scholars do.[43]

In one sense, Palmer's advice was consistent with his overall philosophy of self-realization: only through self-sacrifice, Palmer argued in his treatises on ethics, could the separate self overcome alienation and achieve the highest moral aims. But Locke chafed under such advice. For him, service, the noblesse oblige of Victorian elitism, when applied racially, smacked of a double standard: the Black Talented Tenth should not aspire to equality, to "self-culture," but should educate itself only to become missionaries of culture to the masses of Blacks, generally in segregated southern schools. That was definitely not Locke's plan. Locke had come to Harvard on a pursuit of culture and imagined a role for himself as a custodian of American culture on par with those elderly men from whom he had letters of introduction. Of course none of these Harvard "fathers" could really comprehend what Locke intended to do with his education, but at least Palmer was willing to support the possibility of a year abroad and a return to graduate school in philosophy if Locke so desired.

Locke's understanding of the thorny problems of self-culture, race service, and elite White paternalism was probably advanced by his association with James Harley, the only Black student he became friendly with as a Harvard undergraduate. Locke met Harley in the spring of 1905, and he wrote his mother:

> There is a colored West Indian by the name of Harley here, and of course, he is different from the rest. He is a graduate of Howard, spent two years at Yale, is here for the year, and expects to go to England to study for the ministry and incidentally to study at Oxford—the two schools are connected. He is a very nice fellow and has become quite friendly. He criticized the colored fellows here, said they were conscious of their inferiority and justly so, that the house in which they were huddled was a "nigger Hell" he knew for he had been there, that he had noticed I was criticized as he was, and would like to know me. Where I met him was at the Ethical Society—and I think he became so very pleasant as he saw that I was "in the ring" there—I don't think it patronizing however, for he is very prominent here, a good debater—and has a scholarship. He is very well thought of, of considerable ability— believes in social equality, is the typical West Indian with their fault of being conceited also—But you know what I think of conceit—when a man has something to be conceited over I call it self respect.[44]

Locke and Harley became friends initially because of their shared disdain for the other Black students, whom they labeled as "inferior," and because both were committed to the "game" of competing with Whites for prizes and prestige at Harvard. In the spring term of 1906, Harley took a First in the prestigious Boylston Prize for Elocution. Afterward, he held a smoker in his room to which Locke was the only "colored person" invited. Like Locke, Harley socialized only with elite Whites and with each other after they met. Together they buttressed their isolation with their sense of being collaborators in the crime of aggressive upward mobility. Both faced an uncertain future as educated Black men upon graduation. No professional careers commensurate with their elite educations awaited them in the United States or the West Indies. That reality had already disposed Harley to perpetuate his education indefinitely. Born in Antigua of the British West Indies in 1873, Harley was thirty-two years old when Locke met him. Already a graduate of Howard University's Law School and a transfer from

Yale College, where he had spent a year as an undergraduate, Harley had realized he did not want to practice law, probably because there were few jobs for Black lawyers in the United States and none paid well. By the time Harley arrived at Harvard in 1903, he planned to go into the ministry; his declaration that he wished to become a minister in the Protestant Episcopal Church enabled him to obtain a Matthews Scholarship at Harvard. He majored in Semitic languages and history (the typical undergraduate major for future ministers) but excelled in elocution and planned to start his own church. Before doing so, he intended to go to Oxford, an aspiration that seemed presumptuous to the dean of Harvard College, Byron Hurlbut, who when he found out later that Harley had actually made it to Oxford, only remarked to ask when Harley was going back to help his race in the West Indies. Secretly, Harley rejected the ideology that all educated Blacks should return to serve their home communities and settled in England.

Harley provided Locke with a Black peer and a hard-nosed complement to his more aesthetic friend, Charles Dickerman. Harley's outspoken, hot-tempered, fearlessness in telling anyone, White or Black, what he thought of him or her endeared him to Locke, whose father had possessed the same temperament. That also allowed Locke to feel superior. Mary Locke made the mistake of calling Harley cultured. "What made you think Harley was particularly cultured—he is refined as any man with his training should be, but cultured!! Well [it] doesn't sit well on the fighting West Indian temperament. He is outspoken like all of them and doesn't hesitate to sling mud and sarcasm when he gets good and ready," Locke wrote back.[45]

Harley's refusal to accommodate White norms for Black behavior got him into trouble with the Harvard College administrators. After winning the Matthews Scholarship, he angered the College's tight-fisted Dean Hurlbut when he asked for more of his scholarship money to pay his living expenses and dues in the Debating Club. Hurlbut kept tight rein on scholarship money and refused to dispense funds except when he thought it appropriate. After Harley reacted angrily to Hurlbut's rebuff of his request, Hurlbut wrote to a Father Field of the Episcopal Church to inquire about Harley's "character" and financial resources. Hurlbut expressed his opinion that at thirty-two years of age, Harley ought to get a job. Father Field confirmed Hurlbut's worst suspicions. Harley had performed Sunday school work at Field's New York church with "continual grumbling," and though "very able," was unfortunately "bitter against white people" and therefore "dangerous among his own people for this reason." Hurlbut lost no time in communicating this disturbing news to Dean Hodges, for whom Harley worked in "colored mission work" in Cambridge, and to any others who would listen. That summer Harley again startled college authorities by bringing a young White woman into his college dormitory room. For that he was expelled from the dorms. Locke confided to his mother, "Don't breathe a word of this to anyone, but Harley is engaged to a white woman at Wellesley, and has taken us into his confidence. He is like all of the West Indians—they leave a trail of enemies everywhere. They are always doing exciting and preposterous things."[46]

Once Hurlbut learned of Harley's attitude toward Whites and his breach of campus (and racial) propriety, he seemed obsessed with hurting Harley, who, in turn, handed the dean a perfect weapon: a woman who had provided Harley with room and board while he was a student at Yale wrote to Harvard in the summer of 1905 to ask that Harley's degree be held up until he paid the debt. When contacted, Harley argued that because the debt had been contracted at Yale and he intended to pay it, it was "none of Harvard's business." He was wrong. Harvard had long followed the tradition that all holders of the Harvard degree must be "gentlemen" and would not graduate anyone who had debts presented against them to the college. Hurlbut lost no time in bringing this challenge before the administrative board of the college, which ruled that though Harley had completed his coursework by the spring of 1906, he could not receive his degree until he paid the debt. Finally, in March 1907, Harley paid the debt and received his AB degree in June of that year. To keep Harley's transgression visible on his record, Hurlbut stipulated that Harley's degree be granted "A.B. 1906, as of 1907." He sent letters that accompanied any requests for Harley's file to explain that the delay was the action of the board in regard to Harley's refusal to pay his debts. When Hurlbut insisted on writing a minister about the matter in spite of Harley's request that he not do so, Hurlbut recalled that Harley "told me that I had no right to do this, that I was not his spiritual adviser. I told him that I was not, it was true, a member of the church, but that I did attend it, and that I proposed to write to the Bishop." The problem for Harley as a Black Victorian was that, like Locke's father, he let White people know that they were not his superior. Perhaps this affinity to his father's fiery temperament was one reason Locke was attracted to him.

Locke adopted a more indirect approach to hostile Whites when his own financial difficulties brought conflict with the dean and the bursar of the college. In February 1906, Hurlbut informed Locke that only a portion of his scholarship money could be applied to that semester's tuition bill and that Locke needed to make up the difference. Although Locke wrote his mother about the matter, he did not press her to borrow immediately and remained sanguine about paying: "I am quite sure that I can make new plans to carry things through. The only thing that worries me is that you should worry over matters instead of looking at it as a game, which we have to play the best we can losing here and winning there."[47] But in April, Locke was called by the bursar and then by the dean and threatened with suspension if he did not pay up. Finally, he was saved by Mary Locke, who was able to obtain a bond on May 2, with Mr. Bush's co-signature, for the balance of Locke's tuition. "The bill is paid," he wrote his mother May 3, but Locke was angry.

The Bursar is satisfied.... MacDinnes, the assistant Bursar who is the exact opposite of the Bursar himself—very pleasant and accommodating, says, "Mr. Locke if you will come and see me personally whenever you get into financial difficulties and want your bill extended, why I guess we can arrange matters." I frankly told the Dean [that the bursar] had not acted gentlemanly and that I would not go to see him no matter what happened. So now it is all over, no more money to go out to the University till the 2nd term bill of July 25 which will go over to September, I am surer now than before because of Mr. McInnes friendly attitude. The Dean and the Bursar can go to Hell—the Dean (that is Hurlbut) not Dear Briggs who is Dean of the Faculty and not the College and to whom Brandt sent me is a lovable man, but Hurlbut is a perfect ass, he would do me in a minute if he dared—but he knows I have influence, and I always take care to remind him of the fact and he keeps his hands off—though you can see them itching. He said "If that bill isn't paid by May 2, you will have to leave college." I said, "In the first place, we can pay by then; in the second place I won't have to leave college for I have personal letters to President Eliot, that I can present in any emergency. Of course, I really haven't them, but I could get them if the occasion came.[48]

By labeling the bursar's actions as ungentlemanly, rather than "racist," Locke neutralized the attack on his character and asserted, in terms of the Victorian code of behavior, that he was more the gentleman than the bursar. With Dean Hurlbut, Locke could bluff his possession of "letters," another Victorian tool of respectability, to back down a man whose actions were condescending and bruising. By casting these conflicts in Victorian terms, Locke limited the labels that could be placed on his actions and avoided alienating potential White supporters by asserting racism. By contrast, Harley's vituperative put-downs of Harvard authorities confirmed the label that he was "bitter against white people" and thus a dangerous man. By avoiding a purely personal clash and asserting his connections with other significant White patrons, Locke limited the damage the dean and the bursar could do to his reputation.

Locke differed from Harley in being fundamentally an optimist about race relations. He had enough positive experiences with Whites while growing up that he did not believe that all Whites were racist. Many of them had been enablers of his success: his experience had taught him that if one behaved as if Whites were not prejudiced, if one treated them as gentlemen and acted gentlemanly oneself, more often than not Whites would treat one well. But if one approached Whites with resentment, bitterness, and blame, they would respond in kind. That was the basis of his criticism of other Blacks at Harvard. In recounting one incident to his mother, he noted:

> Tyson and the set raised quite a little stir at Memorial over the color
> question. 3 of them were at the same table, and thinking they were jim
> crowed kicked instead of acting like gentlemen and not noticing it or of
> quietly asking to be changed without giving any reasons—Tyson went
> to the Auditor and had the usual fuss....I am so glad not to be in it.
> Tyson stopped me the other evening in the yard and told his tale—
> I listened—spoke very plainly about not looking for discrimination and
> dropped the subject.[49]

His response to Tyson showed that even though Locke had not taken a course
from William James, he was performing a version of James's pragmatic theory
that truth was an outcome of our actions, not something standing outside of us.
To Locke, there was no absolute truth of racism at Harvard, but rather, racism—
and especially its impact on Black lives—was shaped by how people reacted to
incidents such as Tyson recounted. Locke's message to Tyson was performative:
"Refuse to play the victim. Behave as if you belong here and maybe spectators
will believe that you do!" Of course, Locke had had no real experience of virulent
racism, the kind that could not be tricked out of its desire to destroy. But Locke
was nonetheless expressing an early, naive version of the New Negro: the art of
Black presentation in social space could be used to preserve one's agency. Locke's
performative pragmatism mapped a path to self-empowerment, and he was not
getting off that path to indulge someone else's that was clearly not working.

Locke's approach to racism was one reason he remained highly productive
despite conflicts with the bursar and the dean over his finances that intense
spring of 1906. Not only did he achieve his highest average in his coursework
that spring but he also negotiated through the thicket of race and hierarchy
at Harvard to find his mentor—Barrett Wendell, the professor of comparative
literature he encountered in English 46 his second year. Wendell had become
something of a fop by 1906. As an heir to the Boston Brahmin tradition of elite
custodianship of American letters, Wendell had returned to teaching at Harvard
from a year as an exchange professor at the Sorbonne wearing a monocle, sport-
ing a cane, and acting like a Francophile dandy. Unlike others who experienced
the transformation of cosmopolitan living, Wendell had a theory that explained
it—that the Western literary tradition was not a universal, but a series of national, indeed, racial traditions that had evolved distinctive literary knowledges
over the centuries that crystalized into traditions that contemporary artists
could mine—and in his case perform. But Wendell was more than a dandy; he
was an institution builder, who, with his ally the wealthy Mrs. Isabella Stewart
Gardner, helped create and sustain the anchors of Boston's culture. As he wrote
Mrs. Gardner four years before he met Locke: "More and more, it seems to me
that the future of our New England must depend on the standards of culture
which we maintain and preserve here. The College, the Institute, the Library,

the Orchestra,—and so on—are the real bases of our strength and our dignity in the years to come." Locke would emulate this kind of language twenty-five years later with his own patron, Wendell's notion that Culture was a patriotic duty. When Locke met Wendell, he met a model of the kind of aesthetic activist he would become.[50]

Wendell also found something that drew him to Locke. As Locke wrote to his mother after meeting the infamous Boston aesthete:

> This afternoon I had my English conference, and a more delightful conference I have never had. Our professor is Barrett Wendell.... He is decidedly French—wears garters, smokes cigarettes and twirled his cane all during the conference but talked most entertainingly. The others left and I found myself with his highness and a Jewish rabbi. What a combination! and we talked for an hour or so on literary topics, which chiefly consisted in Barrett Wendell's reminiscences and jokes.[51]

Wendell performed for Locke because he found something interesting in the young Black aesthete from Philadelphia—a carbon copy of himself, with, of course, the exception that Locke was Black. But since Wendell's theory of literature contained a racial element, Locke was a fascinating example of something Wendell had not thought of—that a Black tradition in America had produced an aesthete who shared with him a love of the European traditions of literature. Wendell's interest helped shape Locke's emerging conception of how to make the argument for the existence and importance of a Black literary culture. In Wendell's lectures on modern literature, Locke heard a counterargument to what he had imbibed at Central High, the School of Pedagogy, even in lectures by Irving Babbitt on Harvard's campus, that Culture was universal. Wendell advocated the then-radical idea that all modern literature was fed by national traditions and all the best modern writers were those who mined those traditions. Wendell argued that since the end of the Renaissance, world literature had been essentially English, French, and German literature (and, Wendell hoped out loud, American literature), in part because literature reflected the modern period's intense nationalism. For Wendell, literature changed with the mind and character of history, and thus, by looking at literature, the critic could gauge the pulse of the people and the times. In urging the cultivation of race among artists, Locke affirmed what he had acknowledged in his English 46 notes. "I see that I am a spiritual son of Barrett Wendell's. I shall carry on his work."[52]

That last remark clarified the double errand Locke was on when he came to Harvard. In one sense, it was an errand for himself, of self-culture, to soak up as much of Boston and Harvard's aesthetic knowledge as he could gain while making himself into a Boston aesthete, a lover of art of all forms, a person who not only learned to consider in detail "legitimate works of art, but [also] everything in the world, as art."[53] But in seeing himself as carrying on Wendell's work, he was also aspiring to a larger ambition that Wendell himself had only half approximated—to be a cultural leader, to find in aesthetics, a way to refashion the Black community, no less than identity, as a work of art. What was not yet clear, even to this self-adopted son, was how to do it without the well-established cultural institutions standing behind him as Wendell had inherited?

It was not clear. But Locke's lone Black friend at Harvard provided a clue. In his Third Report of the Class of 1906, Harley recalled what happened when it was announced at the ceremonies that he had won a prize.

> Giant Grim met me at the Episcopal Theological School in Cambridge, Mass.... It was that snowy morning when Dean Hodges...announced in chapel that [Harley's submission] "Ivanhoe" had won the coveted seminary prize for the best essay on Japanese Shintoism. That $100 was too costly a matter. I got the money and was branded. I can hear their tender voices singing amid the cat-calls: "Who say dem niggers wont steal? Way down yonder in de corn feal."[54]

Like Harley, Locke was a thief who refused to be satisfied with a segregated life within Harvard Yard or a deferential posture toward other White students as their superiors. Locke was not there to worship Harvard so much as to use it to succeed in the world of culture afterward. But Locke's theft also concealed a hidden ambition—to steal knowledge of how to use aesthetics to transform a folk into a people who might free others like him who never set foot inside Harvard Yard.

5

Locke's Intellectual
Awakening, 1905–1907

Early in 1905, Locke submitted two essays for that year's Bowdoin Prize competition, "The Romantic Movement as Expressed by John Keats" and "The Prometheus Myth: A Study in Literary Tradition." The Bowdoin was Harvard's most prestigious prize for literary criticism, with an outside committee of distinguished critics who read the essays and generally awarded only one first prize to an undergraduate each year. Winning such a prize would not only enhance Locke's reputation as a literary figure on Harvard's campus but also ease his financial situation. The prize brought a cash award of $250, which he needed to pay his expenses that first year at Harvard when, without a scholarship, he barely scraped by. To improve his chances of success, Locke submitted two essays, perhaps hoping that if he did not win, he would at least catch the attention of the committee. But his written note to himself on the first one, "The Romantic Movement as Expressed by John Keats," dated January 1905, suggests who he was becoming as a person.

> I know and say now before I know definitely the Committee's decision that I am confident no more thoughtful or literary essay has been entered in this contest. It is my best work and should rank with other best work, without apologizing for the comparison. Believe in yourself—in greek "That above all to thine own self be <u>true</u>" I have resolved not to worry or be discouraged over the outcome of this; and to go on proud and determined as ever. Correct and turn this in again next year. Good Luck: Alain Le Roy Locke. Student of Romanticism.[1]

Locke was becoming an intellectual, with a precocious but confident sense that he had something to say worth saying and that he was already an intellectual voice to be reckoned with. "The Romantic Movement as Expressed by John Keats," an essay he had first written for Mr. Mearns, shows clearly that Locke already is thinking of himself as a cultural leader who someday would foment an American Renaissance.

Even at this very early period in his intellectual development, Locke's key metaphor was that of renaissance. Romanticism, he argued, was a spiritual renaissance, and to fulfill its destiny, it had to react against the classical constraints of the eighteenth century and find its inspiration in an ancient golden age. For Locke that golden age is represented by classical Greek art as distilled through Keats's poetry. "Keats was also consistently Grecian in his aesthetic doctrines. Beauty he regarded as the all-pervading spirit of the universe, and it was the true function of art, by substituting sympathy for analysis, to reveal the presence of this ideal of Beauty." Keats represented the kind of poet Locke would later long for in the Harlem Renaissance, one who was "an example of a spiritual Renaissance taking place before our very eyes!"[2] Locke's essay on Keats suggests that his vision of the Harlem Renaissance of the 1920s found inspiration in his early reading of nineteenth-century Romanticism, whose golden age, he noted, was in fifth-century-B.C. Greece. Writing later about the Harlem Renaissance, he recalled the golden age of ninth-century West Africa.

But even as a mature critic, Locke's model for a golden age in Africa was fundamentally "Grecian." Having studied Greek literature and drama throughout his undergraduate years at Harvard, he clung to ancient Greece as a model of the perfect society, as a site of freedom, rather than the discipline that Irving Babbitt and other classicists located in Greece. He was also attracted to things Greek, because Greek *love* was a period metaphor for male homosexuality. In Locke's vision of classical Greece men were enthralled with the pursuit of art and culture and with the pursuit of the love and affection of other men. He hinted at the double meaning of being "consistently Grecian" in his life when, in the following year, he wrote in his English 46 class notes that "Wendell says the lyric form of poetry is bound to vanish in translation. Wendell is a fool—(When I came to things Greek I met them as friends)."[3] Not only were Greek poems his friends but also his friends were "Greek," that is, men who shared in the pursuit of Greek love. Keats's holistic approach to sentiment and passion reflected the entire range of human emotions, and Locke may have found his voice congenial. Locke's affection for Keats and for the Romantic movement signaled that he wanted an African American renaissance that would be sufficiently creative and androgynous for both his aesthetic sense and his sexual orientation to be nurtured within it.

His second essay for the 1905 Bowdoin Prize competition revealed even more of the social role he was destined to perform. He had written "The Prometheus Myth: A Study in Literary Tradition" that spring (based on a one-page statement from his senior year at the School of Pedagogy), and it was an impressive study of why the myth had persisted throughout European history, because poets found Prometheus to be a powerful metaphor of cultural renewal. Prometheus, or the forethinker, was the supreme trickster of Greek mythology, who stole fire from the gods and delivered it (along with the knowledge and the art of how to use it) to mankind against Zeus's will. In some versions of the myth, Prometheus is also the creator of mankind who tricks Zeus into giving humans the larger portion of meat sacrifices. Zeus punished Prometheus by chaining him to a rock and sent an eagle to eat his liver, which grew back each evening. Prometheus remained chained and tormented for ages until Heracles released him. Aeschylus's play *Prometheus Bound* made Prometheus a symbol of defiant humanity, especially meaningful for Romantics such as Percy Shelley, who wrote *Prometheus Unbound* in 1818, and Goethe, who began but never finished his play, *Prometheus*. Locke argued that the recurring popularity of this myth was because of the allegorical power of its narrative.

> It was a story which in the course of time became explanatory for generations that had forgotten the actual origin of fire. [And] when it takes its place in the literature that is born of civilization, when under that universalized conception fire becomes a utility, a means to a higher end of organic life, what was an explanatory narrative becomes interpretive of a universal truth, becomes, in a word, symbolic. Out of a folk-tale, a myth is born, the Prometheus that was the cunning, successful thief or the chance discoverer is now a demi-god. Not as the product of centuries of idealizing hero-worship, however, but rather [he is] deified by his own symbolic significance when once his race has reached that state and ideal of civilization which makes literature possible.[4]

Locke is drawn to this myth because it symbolized a powerful interpretation of his emerging role—to be the thief who stole the tools of European culture to liberate a darker humanity. He noted that Aeschylus had assigned "civilization making" to Prometheus and thus the "chaining of Prometheus, is the crucifixion of civilization." Perhaps Locke could be the modern Black Prometheus who brought "civilization" to the Black population. The play "Prometheus Bound...[was]...the dramatic self-conscious moment of Greek civilization." His emergence as the modern Black Prometheus might be the "dramatic self-conscious moment" of African American civilization of the early twentieth century. But the punishment meted out to Prometheus also symbolized the sacrifice such a culture hero would have to make. In 1905, he was not ready to make it, to be "bound" to Black civilization and sacrifice his individual freedom, even though his essay showed he was toying with the possibility.

If Locke became a modern-day Promethean, one of the first things he would do would be to liberate Black thought from the twin myths of accommodationist economics or protest politics with a focus on the transformative effects of aesthetic knowledge. Like Shelley, Locke saw art as a subtle and more powerful source of reform that could begin a revolution by changing the hearts of the enlightened few. Shelley, Locke acknowledged in his essay, had brought the "political ideal of freedom into the play," for Shelley had conceived of the story of Prometheus as a modern story of resistance to oppression and had made Prometheus's rebellion the beginning of a chain of events that resulted in freedom and the fall of tyranny. By making the case for the role of myth in a people's renewal, Locke wished to substitute literature, narrative, and myth for the sociological bias and the propensity to protest that dominated Black rhetoric of the early twentieth century. In the Prometheus myth, Locke seized upon a symbol of revolutionary freedom with a double message—one had to rebel against the gods, in this case perhaps White hegemony, but also bring a deeper knowledge to the oppressed, a knowledge based on spiritual transcendence that only art could reveal.

The Prometheus myth also attracted Locke because it symbolized his dilemma. On one hand, Prometheus was just what Locke was not—not the Christlike giver of knowledge to other men, who was bereft of all personal ambition and motivated by the noblest of motives. But on the other hand, Locke was drawn to the vocation of leadership and also sophisticated enough to realize he needed devotion to a larger cause to give his life spiritual meaning. How would he balance these conflicting moral duties—the duty to one's people and the duty to oneself? The myth of Prometheus, and narratives of contemporary race service, provided such an idealized narrative of self-sacrifice and selflessness that Locke could live up to it. Yet Locke could not dismiss completely the argument of W. E. B. Du Bois that the raison d'être of the modern Black intellectual was to be an enlightening Talented Tenth, who used university knowledge to uplift the other nine-tenths. Could he accept such a role while preserving his individuality? Art advocacy might allow him to do that. But would he be accepted as a Black leader given his gay identity? What would his life mean if he completely abandoned such a responsibility? He did not know.

Locke may have been attracted to the Prometheus myth, finally, because Shelley's version held out the possibility of a resolution of his dilemma. Shelley's *Prometheus Unbound* held out the possibility of forgiveness of one's oppressors, for it was Prometheus's forgiveness of Zeus that ultimately freed him. Perhaps Locke could forgive all those who seemed to impose their expectations of the Talented Tenth on him and others. Forgiveness might also have a larger work to do, for by advocating literature over politics as a race strategy, Locke continued in Shelley's footsteps of suggesting that if one put aside one's hate for one's enemy and began to love oneself through aesthetic appreciation, that new consciousness could change the situation of Black people in America. But as Shelley's preface to *Prometheus Unbound* states clearly, such forgiveness must involve no accommodation to absolute power. Here was Locke's task—to create a basis for rapprochement between the races that avoided the accommodationism but allowed for forgiveness with dignity. Locke would have to learn to accept the rebelliousness of the Black community toward White hegemony while at the same time outlining a largely Christian—or later Baha'i—path of reconciliation. The Prometheus myth empowered Locke to believe that he could be the modern-day Prometheus if he could use aestheticism to create a new synthesis out of Black and White conflict in America.

Unfortunately for Locke, neither essay submitted in 1905 won the Bowdoin Prize. "The Romantic Movement as Expressed by John Keats" remained, in spite of Locke's confident inscription, a rather youthful piece of literary criticism. His stilted language more often obfuscated than revealed his insights. "Prometheus" was much more sophisticated, but its abstract and complex argument about the function of myth in widely divergent societies was not well integrated with Locke's rather cursory examination of the texts themselves. Of course, Locke was undaunted. He continued to submit essays for the Bowdoin competition, even revising "The Romantic Movement" and submitting it along with another essay in 1907. While the ostensible reason for such submissions was to win a prize, a more subtle kind of work was underway—to work out in his writings about European culture his relationship to the burning issues of his society.

The appeal of the myth of Prometheus led Locke to return to it in another essay, "Art as a Catharsis," probably written in 1905 for Dr. Maynadier's course on English Literature. Here, Locke defined the function of art in purely aesthetic terms and alluded to the personal considerations that underlay his reluctance to engage directly in the world of experience:

> It is a very strange thing, I think, that the Aristotelian doctrine of Art as a catharsis of passion has not come into general acceptance until of late. It is passing strange that such a doctrine should have been forced upon us by the much-despised "decadents." With what tragic and convincing irony do we hear it from those very men whose mistake it was to use their lives as a palette for mixing and experimenting with the color-combinations of literature and art. It is Oscar Wilde of all persons who seems fated to tell us "Don't let us go to life for our fulfillment, for our experience. It is a thing narrowed by circumstances, incoherent in its utterance, and without that fine correspondence of form and spirit which is the only thing that can satisfy the artistic and critical temperament." It [Life] makes us pay too high a price for its wares, and we purchase the meanest of its secrets at a cost that is monstrous and infinite.[5]

That had certainly been true for Wilde, who was convicted of indecency and sodomy in 1895 and spent two years doing hard labor in prison. Yet even before this Wilde had preferred art to life, because of its "fine correspondence of form and spirit." Locke interpreted Wilde's legal and public censure as further confirmation of his mentor's basic philosophy:

> We must go to Art for everything because Art does not hurt us. The sorrow with which Art fills us both purifies and initiates, if I may quote once more from the great art-critic of the Greeks. It is through Art and through Art only, that we can realize our perfection; through Art, and through Art only that we can shield ourselves from the sordid perils of actual existence.[6]

Only in the protected realm of art could the gay man be safe.

Yet as Wilde's case suggested, even in art one must be careful. Here, Locke invoked the magic of art to communicate by transforming emotion—not its outpouring, but its "catharsis," for such a cure "has been the immemorial custom of all artists, from the love-sick youth who cures himself with a sonnet-sequence to the genius who, possessed with the frenzy of inspiration, conquers the passion by imposing upon it the conventional forms of art-expression, and possesses that by which he was, a little while ago, possessed."[7] Since the romantic could not fulfill himself or herself in contemporary life, the cure was art that purified the soul. Goethe did it best, according to Locke, by healing himself so effectively that he never tired of calling art the sphere of man's divinity. "In art man usurps the divine prerogative of creation, and Prometheus sits in his workshop, fashioning men and bidding defiance to life and its god."[8]

Something of the loneliness and poignancy of Locke's life comes through in that last line. At Harvard, he had models in Charles Eliot Norton, Barrett Wendell, and George Herbert Palmer of sympathetic fashioners of creative men. But the gay man of the early twentieth century had few safe alternatives to a career in art: the church had been one of the oldest institutions where gay men could feel a degree of safety and community, and Locke emphasized one of the most positive results of its enforcement of sexual sublimation in the Middle Ages when he noted that "the celibacy of the Catholic clergy and the monastic regime were largely responsible for medieval mysticism, with the incorruptible yet sensuous constructions of Paradise, and the sterile love for the Bride of Christ."[9] Here Locke hinted at a gay theory of art's relationship to the emotions. Wilde, though himself married and the father of two children, had ventured something similar when he stated that the best works of art had been created by unmarried men. Prevented from finding true sexual fulfillment with the opposite sex (the theory went) homosexuals were more creative, the better artists for the sexual sacrifice abstinence imposed. The "catharsis of passion" had a specific meaning, therefore, for the cloistered gay artist: he became the artistic superior of the heterosexual because of the required suppression of sexuality. Art from such a perspective was a form of almost genetic compensation.

Locke outlined a gay tradition of "cathartic" expression whose long history stretched from the time of Aristotle through the Middle Ages to the modern Oscar Wilde. By commenting on Wilde's "mistake," Locke also acknowledged that such "catharsis" was sometimes a difficult act to pull off. Obviously, Wilde had not been satisfied with artistic sublimation, but had practically lived openly as a gay man. Here then was a warning for Locke: stay in the cathartic tradition or hazard the consequences of "mixing and experimenting with the color-combinations of literature and art." Art was a way to cloak his homosexuality and to absorb his sexual feelings, or else there was the real possibility of censure, arrest, and persecution.

Being gay, therefore, meant that Locke not only possessed a "second sight" on the hypocrisies of a heterosexual bourgeois society but also that his outsider position left him vulnerable. There were limits to how much he felt he could rebel against such a society without being exposed. Wilde had been targeted as much for his scathing criticisms of bourgeois British society as for his sexual orientation. While art was one of the realms in advanced industrial societies where criticism of the society was tolerated, even encouraged, one could go too far. Such British aesthetes as Ruskin and Pater had gotten away with criticizing English industrialism for its increasing division of labor and oppression of workers, but Wilde's sweeping criticisms of the essential bankruptcy of English bourgeois life had cost him his freedom. The closeted dandy critic was much more vulnerable than the aesthete. Why not then, Locke seemed to argue, keep things on the level of art—and disguise one's homosexuality and critique with a cloak of art, and live to write another day.

Spiritual values—Locke's "ideal of spiritual beauty"—was much safer as a pivot of critique of advanced industrial societies than its moral hypocrisies. After all, even the English bourgeoisie bemoaned the way industrialization had pushed spirituality out of everyday life. Yet Locke remained tempted to go beyond such timid indictments to wrestle with the larger threats to modern humanity. At the School of Pedagogy, Locke had already begun to write criticism of the millionaires who dominated the Gilded Age and to suggest, as he did in one essay, that philanthropy was little more than raking out the money rapacious capitalists had raked in. But Locke knew that being Black and gay, plus a public critic, would be too much: his downfall would be almost certain in early twentieth-century America if he cast himself as the Black Oscar Wilde. Better to be timid in public criticism than to skewer American hypocrisies and be locked up for it.

To avoid outing himself as a critic, Locke tended to wrap himself in the protective blanket of tradition whenever possible. Art was his way to transform the particularities of his Black or gay experience into a form that would have universal appeal. He liked that strategy too because it contained a creative challenge—to bond the individual with the tradition in such a way that new forms and new configurations emerged. That was what an artist did, as the Prometheus essay had shown, for the tradition ultimately judged the rebel in terms of whether the tradition advanced or retrogressed due to the quality of the contribution an artist made. Even rebellion signaled that the artist, no less than the revolutionary, was devoted to something outside of the self, to a tradition of expression or activism that was enhanced by the rebellion. The archive of these many separate acts of rebellion and genius was the tradition—Culture, as Matthew Arnold had put it, "the best that has been thought and known." Although Locke may have learned this specific definition of culture from Arnold's *Culture and Anarchy*, he had actually imbibed the essence of Arnold's notion from a Philadelphia upbringing that taught educated bourgeois Negroes that Culture was universal, the antidote to nationalism and, by extension, racism.[10]

In the fall of 1906, Locke would be challenged to think differently about this universal notion of culture and its relevance to subjectivity in Barrett Wendell's course "Literary Origins of English Literature." Before Wendell, Locke had adhered to a notion of culture that was close to that expressed later by T. S. Eliot, his Harvard classmate, in "Tradition and the Individual Talent": cultural tradition was that "ideal order of monuments," against which, and among which, any new work of art must be judged. Although that tradition was largely the canon of Western culture, Eliot claimed it was a universal tradition and Locke agreed. But in his second year at Harvard, at age twenty, he was challenged to place his universal notion in a historical context by Wendell. Wendell argued that all culture was national, that universalism was a myth, and that cultures were most vital when they remained on their native grounds, and works of art, written by native authors, remained in their native language and were read by their own people. This nationalism both challenged and disturbed Locke, and he struggled with it throughout this year-long course. But at the end of the course under Wendell's influence, Locke began to synthesize his universal notions and Wendell's more nationalistic conceptions of cultural production and see the potential of artists being both representatives of a transnational movement, such as Romanticism, and a national *Zeitgeist* such as Negro American culture.

The intellectual process would not be easy. Fortunately for Locke, his close friend Dickerman took the course with him, and they debated Wendell's lectures and theories in the hallways, at dinner in Memorial Hall, and on their long Sunday walks in the countryside. Dickerman, already enthusiastic about Celtic literature, the Irish Renaissance, and literary nationalism, sympathized more with Wendell's ideas than Locke. Plus, Wendell's mystical view of literature was congenial to Dickerman's, infatuated as he was with gypsies and transcendental meditation. Locke, on the other hand, seems to have had difficulty completely embracing Wendell's nationalism. While writing his thesis for Wendell in the spring of 1906, Locke had to get his deadline for submitting his paper extended twice. He also got help from Dickerman while writing it. But Locke's struggle with the paper and the two notions of tradition were not in vain: when he finally turned in the essay in May 1906, he had produced a lucidly written essay on the representative poet in dialogue with tradition, titled "Tennyson and His Literary

Heritage." His achievement was recognized. Locke received an A for the paper and an A in the course, scoring higher than Dickerman. Wendell even acknowledged Locke's paper before the class. One year later the revised, forty-two-page version of this critical essay won him the Bowdoin Prize. When examined by an outside committee of Edwin H. Abbot, Albert Matthews, and Paul E. More, the editor of the *Nation*, it was judged the outstanding essay out of the nine submitted. "We all agree in awarding the full First Prize to 'Tennyson and his Literary Heritage,' signed 'Arthur King.'" The committee went on to declare that "we are surprised by the maturity of mind shown in the three critical [winning] papers," but found "that each of the Committee, before consultation, had marked the piece on Tennyson for the First Prize."[11]

"Tennyson and His Literary Heritage" was the intellectual tour de force of Locke's undergraduate years at Harvard. Unlike his earlier submissions, this essay combined a sustained and comprehensive mastery of several of the poet's major works with an eloquent argument for the importance of tradition to any understanding of Tennyson's significance. Locke mounted a masterful defense of Tennyson by arguing that he had to be seen as an eclectic poet of the tradition, who excavated the entire European tradition of metaphors, allusions, and tropes to create poetry representative of the eclectic late Victorian age. "Of all the English poets, [Tennyson] was most conscious of his literary heritage as a craft tradition" and the most "complete exponent in recent English poetry of the conscious use of literary tradition."[12] This was important, because "Renaissance and decadence in literature are essentially the results of the revival and decay of literary tradition." Locke followed up this introduction with a detailed examination of all of the traditions, from the Greek to the English Romantic, which Tennyson had mined to create his most memorable poems. In doing so, Locke showed that Tennyson operated as the poetic mouthpiece not only of the British heritage but also the Western tradition, a synthesis of both his and Wendell's views.

For a Victorian like Tennyson, Locke realized, no conflict existed between the Wendellian notion of tradition as national loyalty and Arnold's more universal conception of tradition as the "best that has been thought and known." In the nineteenth century, from the English point of view, the best that had been produced was English, and the racial and nationalist character of that literary sensibility was evident in Tennyson. For Tennyson, "literary tradition...was an expression of a race-experience, of permanent value in itself as a contribution to art." But that loyalty to a "race-experience" did not prevent Tennyson from appropriating European poetry that had been created by other national groups:

> The Emersonian doctrine of history was literally true for him; for he too was "owner of the sphere, of the seven stars, and the polar year." Not only would he have subscribed to Emerson[']s dictum that "he who is

admitted to the right of reason, is a freeman of the whole estate" of the tradition of civilization, but would no doubt have claimed that he who is of the apostolic succession of the poets is lord and master, custodian of it all. Tennyson, then, was a true eclectic: truth, for him, was not relative and progressive as it was with Browning, but absolute and accumulative.[13]

Like many Victorians, Tennyson saw English culture as the culmination of all European history and himself as the "custodian of it all." That sense of entitlement was buttressed by Tennyson's belief in Darwinism: he saw his poetry as the result of thousands of years of cultural evolution that culminated in contemporary British poetry. That evolutionary view was so widespread in nineteenth-century British culture that even Oscar Wilde echoed it in his essay "The Critic as Artist." "It seems to me," Locke quoted Wilde as stating, "that with the development of the critical spirit, we shall be able to realize not merely our own lives, but the collective life of the race, and so make ourselves absolutely modern in the true meaning of the word modernity. To realize the 19th Century, one must realize every century that has preceded it, and that has contributed to its making." Locke observed that "this is Darwinism in literature: and Tennyson and Browning are its prophets." Even such modernists as Eliot reflected this English approach to universalism when he described the "ideal order" of artistic "monuments" as "the form of European, of English literature."[14] Even more for Victorians like Tennyson, who wrote in the heyday of British imperialism, English values were the best and most universal of values. That tradition, needless to say, rated non-English traditions inferior; but Locke did not seem concerned with that in this essay.

For Locke's essay was completely free of any criticism of Tennyson, his poetry, or his Darwinian conception of literary tradition. Perhaps that is because Locke was less interested in Tennyson as a poet than in Tennyson as a translator of tradition for a modern audience. Perhaps Locke felt that once that was established as a right of the poet, other traditions could find poets that would follow suit. For what Locke finds interesting in Tennyson is a model for what follows later in the Harlem Renaissance—that by being racial or national, a poet does not necessarily forfeit the right to be universal. Locke seems already to be laying the intellectual groundwork for a Black approach to tradition that would be as catholic and as universal as Tennyson's, yet represent alternatives to the European tradition. Indeed, Locke may have liked that the English could assert their national culture as a universal tradition, something he would urge Black poets to do in the 1920s, even as it served as a mouthpiece for the Negro American. The essay on Tennyson tended to resolve what was a psychological dilemma for Locke—how to be both a Negro and a Euro-American into a racially loyal cosmopolitan. One did it by being both loyal to one's own tradition, Tennyson seemed to be saying, and yet also seeing oneself as "the freeman of the entire estate."

Of course, from another point of view, Tennyson's eclecticism could be seen as a form of cultural colonialism, selectively raiding non-English traditions for the emotional sources it needed to create modern poetry. In a section of his essay obviously indebted to Dickerman, Locke argued that Tennyson's inspiration for his *Idylls of the King* came from the romantic Celtic tradition. Locke, however, welcomed such developments, because although Tennyson used the material solely for its poetic possibilities, he also legitimated the Celtic heritage as worthy of serious poetic treatment, thus lending credence to the Irish Renaissance movement of W. B. Yeats and others, who wished to create a modernist poetry out of Celtic origins.

Suddenly, the whole praxis of late nineteenth-century English literary culture opened up for Locke and revealed it could be turned on its head. In his notebook for Wendell's class, Locke wrote that "Europe and Asia [have interacted] 3 great times in Greece & Persia & Christianity versus Islamism. (Modify our civilization again (Yes-let it come) Japanese have undone Marathon." And then later, "Buddhistic conception of literature and religion (Dick and I)." Japanese and Irish traditions had been raided by the English, but also they had subtly influenced English and universal culture as a consequence. Eclecticism, really theft, contained the possibility of transforming the Grand Tradition. Eliot would also seek to expand the European sensibility through the modernistic inclusion of Eastern influences. But whereas Eliot's (and Pound's) notion of modernism remained European, with only a spattering of Eastern elements that fit the ascetic modernist temperament, Locke had something else in mind—the transformation of the Grand Narrative by the raided traditions. Indeed, Locke's modernist reading of Tennyson suggested the attraction of alternative cultural imaginations for the West: European poets had turned to peoples bypassed or ignored by European modernization—the Irish, Japanese, and later the African American— as sources of inspiration because rapacious imperialism and materialism had left the West spiritually bankrupt.

If the Black tradition could generate a Tennyson who could make visible the universal nature of the Black tradition, something like the Irish Renaissance that Dickerman talked of incessantly might come to Black America. It is not surprising, therefore, that at the same time that Locke was working out his ideas about tradition in his Tennyson essay, he completed another essay on Paul Laurence Dunbar, dashed off initially just after his death on February 9, 1906, that explored these issues in terms of a Black American poet. After learning of Dunbar's death, Locke wrote and asked his mother to clip all of the obituaries of Dunbar she could find, dashed off his essay on Dunbar, and then quickly sent it off to a national literary magazine. Unfortunately, it was not accepted for publication. Nevertheless, Locke delivered a revised version of the Dunbar essay as a lecture on February 9, 1907, on the first anniversary of the poet's death, to the African American audience of the Cambridge Lyceum, organized at the Rush Memorial African Methodist Episcopal Zion Church in Cambridgeport. The 1907 version of the essay has survived and shows that Locke adapted the essay to his audience: it is definitely a "preacherly text," as literary historian Marcellus Blount would put it, with all of the rhetorical conventions—such as repetition of key phrases, pauses for emphasis—of the canonical African American sermon.[15] Locke knew that an African American sermon form was the most appropriate for addressing the African American masses who assembled at the church. It is worth hearing briefly what Locke wrote to his mother about how it came to pass that he spoke to a Black church given his social distance from Blacks on campus.

> I told you Xmas I think that Barber Rhoan had been anxious for me to come down and give them a little talk—I said yes expecting not to be bothered with it—but the other day the waiter at the table asked me if I was the Mr. Locke who was announced to speak next Wednesday. I went down to see the President of the concern—a pompous, ignorant black shyster lawyer and real estate man here in Cambridge. He walked up here he tells me from South Carolina you know the breed— I daresay—without further description. Well he would like to suggest my topic—I listened patiently while he got it out—I was to speak on Adversity or What makes a Race successful. Not if I can help it, thinks I to myself—you don't make a fool of me. Of course he only suggested it but I could see he had made up his mind. I flattered and praised it, said I would take it, a wonderful subject and all that—but said perhaps it required some one of more commercial experience than I. Then I hit on the capital stroke of hinting that <u>he</u> was the only proper person to treat that subject adequately, and while the Nigger was unsuspiciously distending himself I suggested my subject and got it accepted—Well, what do you think my subject is? Its a shamefaced trick of making most out of what's already at hand—the ministers' trick of reading old ser- mons—I made up my mind to use poor Dunbar again. I almost said [it] to abuse him again. I shall have to doctor it up a bit. I took the subject purposely for if you take any controversial subject, the deacons and the parsons, and the ex deacons and sub deacons too get up, I hear, and challenge you to a debate, and haul you over the coals of their overheated imaginations. [James] Harley got into hot water—but I don't think they'll get me into any: for I don't want to precipitate a riot at my first public appearance.[16]

This letter shows Locke's movement in curves in the face of powerful people he dislikes but cannot chance to dismiss. Locke had met Mr. Rhoan, a Cambridge barber, shortly after arriving in Cambridge. Only later did he learn that Rhoan was one of the organizers of a lyceum, which like the Boston lyceums begun by Ralph Waldo Emerson and other Transcendentalists, had the mission of being a forum for moral and intellectual uplift of the community. It also provided an arena for political debates on how to solve the "race problem," a contentious issue in these days in Boston, as William Monroe Trotter, also a Harvard graduate, was challenging Booker T. Washington's accommodationist approach to race relations in Trotter's newspaper, *The Guardian*. Trotter and "his gang," as the more conservative Locke called them, had already disrupted a 1903 public lecture by Booker T. Washington in Boston, and Locke's audience at the Lyceum probably contained both Trotterites and Bookerites who would respond vigorously and publicly to any expressed preference for either leader's philosophy of social change.

> I think I'll have an audience for the barber has been talking it for a week and the waiter says, "Oh, we'll be dere." I guess they will—and if I don't succumb to the heat and the odor I guess I will be able to get through all right. . . . If I'm criticized I don't care—and I think my barber will take it as a personal insult if anyone does criticize me, and as he is known as one who speaks his mind, I'll leave it to him to defend my reputation. I'm not over afraid of my reputation anyhow, but I refuse to sell it outright by speaking of the "Uses of Adversity," "Sweet are the uses of adversity" is the only sensible thing ever said on the subject and that's quite poetical and indefinite enough to be non committal.[17]

Although Locke's speech was adapted to his 1907 audience, the surviving core of the essay reflects his concern over the artist's relation to tradition grappled with in his Tennyson essay written in the spring of 1906. In Locke's opinion Dunbar, like Tennyson, was mainly valued because of his ability to make his tradition speak. Dunbar was a cultural hero because he refused to "sell his birthright" in order to be a successful man of literature. Unlike such other writers of African descent such as Alexandre Dumas, Alexander Pushkin, Jose Maria de Heredia, and reputedly Robert Browning, Dunbar had revealed his Negro identity in his verse and expressed the Negro mind in both dialect and standard verse. Dunbar had mined the rich "folk" lore of the masses and preserved a tradition in danger of being lost because the younger generation had all but abandoned it in its effort to distance itself from slavery. By contrast, Dunbar had embraced his race tradition and contributed something in the distinctive Negro tongue to the English language. For Locke, Dunbar was the first true "representative of the Afro-American" experience in literature.[18]

Here was the first public expression of an argument that Locke would reiterate dozens of times later—that the function of the Black artist was to mine the Black folk tradition and express it in literary form. The argument appears in something of a culturally accommodationist form—Blacks should develop the distinctive folk resources of their literature to pay back the civilization from which they have borrowed, proof that Locke was a conservative in thinking about the relations of minority to dominant discourses. But he was also already transposing the race question into one of cultural exchange: Blacks could pay back, because they had something of unquestioned value. Although he was refreshing an argument W. E. B. Du Bois had made in 1903 about the spirituals in *Souls of Black Folk*, Locke was expanding it into new territory by saying Black folk had a literacy that was a "permanent endowment of literature." Locke was also adding another element: identity. It was important for the Negro writer to identify himself or herself as a "representative of the Afro-American experience," because "the Negro must reveal himself if the true instincts and characteristics of the race are ever to find a place in literature." To strengthen his case, Locke reached for the Irish analogy:

> In Ireland now some of the greatest literary men of our time are hard at work, visiting the humble cabins of the Irish peasants collecting their folk tales, their stories, and writing them into literature. They realize nowadays that all literature, especially lyric and ballad poetry[,] is a nation or race product. And in the primitive emotions and traditions of the humble people men are today finding new material and new inspiration for literature.[19]

One can imagine more than a few eyebrows being raised in Locke's audience in that Black church in Cambridge, Massachusetts, at his comparison of the Negro literary situation to that of the Irish, the bane of the Black community's existence in urban America, since the early nineteenth century in the many pogrom-like attacks on Black communities by Irish gangs and youths. But Locke was introducing something unique in "Afro-American" Studies, if you will, of the early twentieth century, a transnational perspective on the Negro in relation to the Irish in Ireland, and most important, suggesting that the Negro's relation to American literary hegemony was analogous to the colonial relationship of the Irish to their oppressor, the English in England. Locke was suggesting that what would later be called the colonial relationship of Irish literacy—its indigenous language, its songs, and its stories—to the dominant English tradition of literature was akin to that of the Negro's relationship to that same tradition. The Irish, he implied, were also looked down upon and dismissed by the English in England, but the Irish had used their native literacy to make an intervention in that discourse and make some of the finest literature in the English language. By doing so, they had vindicated themselves through literature, outside of the realm of political agitation, and made a glorious name for themselves. The Irish had been fighting for their freedom from English control for years, but of late had made a literary turn to vindicate themselves in literature. It had worked.

And it would work for the Negro, Locke declared to his audience, and Dunbar was the first proof that it was working.

Perhaps the most striking notion in the lecture was his conception of race. By listing Browning, Pushkin, and Dumas as poets of African descent, Locke initially came dangerously close to the "one drop rule" of racial identity—that Europeans with minuscule amounts of African blood should be considered Negroes. But Locke's speech ended on a much more advanced notion of Black identity—that Blackness or being "Afro-American" hinged more on identification with the people, by embodying their language in formal poetry, than on bloodlines or genealogical tracings. Blackness was, again, an act, a performative pragmatism— one was "Afro-American" by behaving, acknowledging oneself, as one.

> If we are a race we must have a race tradition, and if we are to have a race tradition we must keep and cherish it as a priceless—yes as a holy thing—and above all not be ashamed to wear the badge of our tribe. And I do not refer so much to any outward manifestation or aggressiveness. I do not think we are Negroes because we are of varying degrees of black, brown and yellow, nor do I think it is because we do or should all act alike. We are a race because we have a common race tradition, and each man of us becomes such just in proportion as he recognizes, knows[,] and reverences that tradition.[20]

Despite the fact that Locke had not taken courses directly from William James, Locke displayed in his lecture on Dunbar a pragmatist conception of race, such that being a Negro was not based on color but on "reverencing," "knowing," and "recognizing" that he or she belongs to a tradition. In that sense, Locke had layered Royce's notion of "loyalty" onto James's pragmatism, such that to be Negro meant to not desert one's "birthright," a kind of cultural inheritance or history. Here was the first public statement of Locke's mature conception of race, worked out in detail some eight years later before another audience of predominantly Black people at Howard, that race was in essence a historical phenomenon, not a biological or color-based one.

Just as striking was Locke's conception of the Negro artist. In the first statement of a position he would maintain throughout his life, Locke argued here that what made Dunbar a Negro artist was not that he was of a certain skin tone, but that he embodied the Negro worldview in his art. The Negro artist, Locke argued, must "reveal himself" in literature and identify with the "Afro-American" tradition. As would become more important later, a tension or perhaps an irony existed in Locke declaring this, not only because his social praxis at Harvard involved so much running away from contact with other Black students but also because in his essay "Art as Catharsis," he had seemed to argue that dissemination of one's emotional connections in art was what made art great. Art was also a form of hiding, a translaton of something powerful, like love, into something subtle, like poetry. And from his reflections on Oscar Wilde, Locke seemed to imply that the survival of the gay artist required concealment through catharsis in art. But the Dunbar essay was a counter-statement delivered by one who was very much conflicted about practicing that in his own life racially and sexually. Locke praised Dunbar for his courage to do what other Black poets had not been able to do—"come out" as a Negro in the English language and express the mind of the Negro in the language of the Black masses.

In making the case for an "Afro-American" (a term he used in his essay) tradition in literature, Locke was actually articulating a new theory of literature. Locke argued that Dunbar had broken with the canonical Western tradition of the artist as individual genius to enable the experience, literacy, and mentalite of the Negro masses to "speak" in literature.

> Now when Dunbar takes the crude thoughts of a negro farm and, and refines and expresses them so that they may in certain instances take their place in English literature, and take that place not only as a contribution but as a representation of the Negro, he has been of some service. . . . Dunbar is our first contribution, and however small in intrinsic worth he may be, however far down in the scale of literary values he may stand (and you must remember that that scale is set by such standards as Shakespeare and Milton) he is significant—very significant to us—for surely it is more blessed to give than to receive.[21]

That Locke could appreciate Dunbar as a "representative Negro poet" derived from the influence of his friend Dickerman, who had introduced Locke to the Irish literary revival and no doubt to W. B. Yeats, its transcendent poet and theorist. Yeats and other Irish intellectuals of the Irish League were planting libraries in reading communities across Ireland with books by Irish writers who expressed their love for the Irish people, the Irish landscape, the Irish way of life, in imaginative literature. Quite analogous to what Locke suggested at the Cambridge Lyceum, Yeats argued the people needed "imaginative" literature, not sociological or political treatises, to incite them to dream a new future for themselves based on their glorious past. Locke was speaking as the "Afro-American" Yeats when he suggested that the Negro artist who mattered embodied the Negro soul in his or her work, and Dunbar was the first to do that. It was better to give than receive, because in giving, contributing, innovating, the Negro changed the larger culture for everyone.[22]

In saying that Dunbar's life's work had meaning because he identified with the Black experience in his writing, Locke was also saying something in his first public lecture about his own future significance. Like Locke, Dunbar had been something of a conservative who had been labeled by some radicals as an accommodationist, partly because he recommended that Negroes remain in the South and partly because his dialect poems appeared to perpetuate the stereotypical "plantation" image of the American Negro. But Dunbar had also written poems that showed that he wore a racial mask and presented to White people only what he wanted Whites to see of the Negro. Those poems must have resonated with Locke, who must have known that Dunbar was a bitter man. In spite of the praise he had received for his dialect poetry from Boston Brahmin William Dean Howells, Dunbar harbored resentment that the only poetry of his that received extensive praise was his dialect poetry. Locke faced a similar predicament, despite his efforts to escape it: he would be valued in the future because of his identification of his intelligence with the Black culture cause. Like Dunbar, Locke was a reluctant representative of his people; but by identifying with the "Afro-American" experience, both were able to shape American culture in profound ways. But like Dunbar, Locke would have to will himself to be a Negro to secure his place in history, in spite of his persistent abhorrence and ambivalence about that road to power.

Unfortunately, at the first delivery of his Dunbar lecture, Locke had no real opportunity to judge its impact or reception. After walking from his room in Holyoke House to the Rush Memorial AME Zion Church in Cambridgeport in a blinding snowstorm that February evening, he was told by a sheepish lyceum chairman that few would be present at his lecture: a lantern slide lecture on the "Colored Man in Cambridge" had been scheduled at the church at the same time. To Locke's chagrin, he was now robbed of an audience for his maiden voyage as a lecturer. He wrote his mother:

> Humph thought I—I see where I come out at the small end of the hour. I can't compete against moving pictures—Finally a baker's dozen did arrive, and I read my paper, was thanked, and then tactfully suggested to avoid a debate which I suspicioned would follow that we all adjourn upstairs for the lecture. I had talked with the lecturer—a certain Virginia silver tongue, and knew what I must do to get rid of him. Says I, I will go right down and get mine over quickly so that people can come up to hear you. I was just slipping out the door folding up my manuscript and buttoning my coat when Heah yo brother—you surely aren't going to leave us—Come up—so I came up. What else could I do[?] Well I sat it out—a horrible succession of negro pictures—you can imagine what they looked like—poor pictures made into poorer lantern slides—the lecturer asked me for my photo—of course I got out of it [—] be damned if Ill stand for that insult to my countenance—he intends to travel from church to church of course, etc.—you know the whole thing.[23]

After the lantern lecture, the director made Locke promise to return again in April when there would be no lack of audience for his lecture. Although Locke agreed to return, his mother advised otherwise: "I should not bother any more with those negroes," she wrote back: "it is casting your pearls etc—you had better be in bed—than wasting your time with them."[24]

But Locke honored his promise and on April 10, 1907, delivered the lecture again, this time to an overflowing audience.

> By the way—I clean forgot to tell you about my speaking in meeting— I nearly forgot the appointment—but got out Dunbar Manuscript No. II and put it in my big coat pocket and went to dinner. Dap Pfromm asked where I was going, and when I told him he said he wanted to go along if he might—said he was going to be my biographer anyway— and he might as well be my manager too—So I took him along—and together we slopsed [sic] down to Cambridgeport—(the weather was terrible—slush, rain and snow combined) With difficulty we found the church—no lights lit and not a soul about. Just as we had made up our minds to beat it back home, de chairman came—Oh says he its only twenty minutes past eight—come right on up—We went up—he lit up the church and we sat down—"de audience be here all right—you just wait." He had forgotten his gavel so made his apologies and went home for it—giving Dap and I a chance to let off steam in a good laugh and chat while he was gone. Well would you believe it—by 5 minutes to nine I had all the audience I wanted—75 or 80 people I guess—de meeting opened with hymns—during which Dap and I sang to keep from laughing, sang with might and main—then there was a "soprano solo"— killing—perfectly killing—and then the speaker of the evening was introduced—I read from the pulpit—and Dap swears I read very well— anyhow I galloped through in about 25 minutes—for Dap and I planned to get back to Cambridge in time for 10 o'clock tea. . . . After I had finished, the discussion followed—which was a combined eulogy of Dunbar and the speaker of the evening—First the chairman, then the minister, then a Cambridge school teacher Miss Lane—then Mr. Roan, my old barber, then the audience indiscriminately—it kept me getting up bowing and thanking them—adding a remark or two between the speeches till 11 o'clock when the meeting adjourned . . . they just uncorked the champayne [sic] of oratory, and I was soaked with all sorts of mixed metaphors, just anointed with the oil of flattery till the grease ran into my eyes.[25]

Of course, by April 1907, Locke had won the Rhodes Scholarship and become a celebrity. But he attributed the outpouring of sentiment to what he said: "The whole thing was I set them thinking and am very glad I said what I meant frankly—for instead of thinking it heretical they hailed it as a new revelation." They were also intrigued by his White companion.

Dap was a great card for me—they were tickled to pieces to have me bring him and he was very cordial to them—but was as you might expect dazed and bewildered. Of course I took pains to tell him what type they represented. I am particularly glad to find that I could meet that class of people and handle them as a public audience without having to tody [*sic*] to them: and if this is typical of what I shall be able to do in the future I think I could handle the masses quite as effectively as Father—I was very surprised to hear them say to my face that they were proud I had condescended to come speak to them: it simply meant this—that you can come to them if you are tactful enough and yet not have to come as one of them. Educated colored men queer themselves with the masses by being condescending so that they resent the difference, or too familiar so that they forget it. I think I have discovered one great help in the matter of public speaking—I shall always have a white friend to accompany me—or if I ever lecture extensively I would have a white manager—it[']s a capital stunt.[26]

Locke had brought Pfromm to the lecture, but it was Dickerman, likely Locke's lover, by now, who was the unseen inspiration for Locke's maiden public speech. Dickerman, along with Wendell, had supplied Locke with the conceptual frame to see Dunbar in a new way, especially Dickerman, for in introducing Locke to the Irish literary awakening, he enabled Locke to break with the Black Victorian dismissal of the crude lyrics of the people and Dunbar's dialect poems, and see their larger significance. Locke's literary awakening at Harvard had been fueled by twin forces that would continue to shape his intellectual growth in the future—transnationalism, the need to go away from his homeland in order to come back and appreciate it more deeply, and romantic attachment, often with superlative individuals, whose love and insight helped move him to higher states of understanding of himself.

Locke could become the Promethean Black leader who could "handle the masses quite as effectively as Father"—if he wanted to. Having spent his Harvard years immersed in the tradition of his mother, of art, literature, and the pursuit of cultivation, he seemed surprised in his last year at Harvard that he could be received cordially by the Black masses. Of course, so brief a foray into "the community" did not resolve his racial ambivalence. He still privately distanced himself from other Blacks while publicly embracing them on this occasion. But what was significant is that he had embraced them socially and intellectually by presenting a lecture that made demands on Black identity but also expressed a barely articulated love for them. They had loved in return, because, despite becoming a Rhodes Scholar, he had not forgotten where he came from.

6

Going for the Rhodes

It is not clear when he began to think of applying for the Rhodes Scholarship, but in the spring of 1906, just after finishing his essay on Tennyson, Locke wrote his mother to ask her to seek out information on how one applied for the scholarships. The Rhodes was a way for a poor Black Philadelphian to acquire an education generally reserved for the elite, since the Rhodes Trust had made study abroad available to numerous American boys since beginning to select scholars from America in 1903. Set up by the last will and testament of Cecil Rhodes, the British mining capitalist who made his millions in Africa, the Rhodes Trust provided $1,500 for a young scholar from each state to spend three years of study at Oxford University. Although Cecil Rhodes had conceived of the scholarships as a way to promote Anglo-Saxon unity in the world, he had not excluded persons of color from the competition: by drawing students from the colonies and the United States to Oxford, Rhodes hoped an education at Oxford would inspire them to extend Anglo-Saxon influence in their native lands. Selection was based solely on a candidate's "literary and scholastic attainments; his fondness of and success in manly outdoor sports . . . his qualities of manhood, truth, courage, devotion to duty, sympathy for the protection of the weak, kindliness, unselfishness and fellowship; and his exhibition during school-days of moral force of character and instincts to lead and to take an interest in his schoolmates."[1]

By 1907, no Negro American had won the scholarship, but Rhodes officials had privately discussed the possibility. Some Rhodes officials even wondered whether the Trust should encourage such an appointment, but decided to refrain from any policy statement; they did not want to "venture into such a wasp's nest," as one official put it.[2] As it was, selection of candidates rested with American committees formed in each state. Probably the matter would take care of itself. With the rise of segregation in the South and the intensification of racial animosity toward Blacks throughout the nation, it seemed unlikely that any committee would select a Negro Rhodes Scholar in 1907.

At first glance, Locke was an inappropriate choice to be a Rhodes Scholar. They were typically rather athletic Americans. Not only was Locke not an athlete but also he was thoroughly indifferent to sports. As one of the tiniest students on campus, Locke had few options to satisfy the scholarship's athletic require-ment; in his senior year, he joined freshmen crew as a coxswain. Just as impor-tant, the scholarship emphasized manliness and high moral character; if Locke's homosexuality had been known at the time, it probably would have disqualified him. Indeed, his financial difficulties at Harvard might even have disqualified him, since an English gentleman was supposed to avoid even the whiff of finan-cial impropriety. But a second look suggested Locke was highly appropriate. He epitomized the bearing and attitude of the upright—and some probably would have said "uptight"—Victorian on campus, and his essay on Tennyson seemed to enthuse over Anglo-Saxon civilization and its benefits for everyone. By applying for the scholarship, Locke showed he possessed the kind of aggressive self-confidence that had made Rhodes a successful imperialist.[3]

But most important to Locke when he wrote his mother in May 1906 was that his plans for the scholarship be kept a secret. He knew that many Americans might object to a Black man winning the Rhodes Scholarship. Hence, Locke ad-opted an indirect approach to acquiring information about it: he asked that his mother place a notice in the Philadelphia *Press* correspondence columns about where information on the scholarship could be obtained. "The reason I do not want to ask up here," he wrote her, "is that Harley suffered because he let his Oxford plans get out in public, and as I want to apply for a fellowship here in June 1906, and of course it is important that they should not know of the other applica-tion." Harley did not apply for the Rhodes, which left the field clear for Locke to be the only Black Harvardian in the running. Actually, Harley's Oxford prospects seemed rather slim in the spring of 1906 given his money problems and his en-gagement. But Harley's public airing of interest in Oxford revealed an important lesson he wrote about later in his Third Harvard Report—that some Whites re-acted angrily to a Black student being so uppity as to take prizes they thought should be reserved for Whites. As Locke informed his mother, "There are Oxford men here from whom I can and have gotten ample information about the place but I have never mentioned the Rhodes scholarship question, as it is a matter of *influence* pure and simple, and it is well to keep things dark to the very last."[4]

Mary placed the notice, received a response, and conveyed the contact infor-mation to her son. Once he wrote the Rhodes committee, he learned that there were two parts to the selection process. First, he would have to pass Responsions, Oxford's entrance exams (taken by all undergraduate Oxford applicants), an in-tensive set of questions in Greek, Latin, mathematics, and history. If he passed this exam, he would then have a personal interview with a committee either from the state of his residence or the state where he attended college. Each state chose one Rhodes Scholar to go to Oxford. First, of course, he had to pass the written exam, which would not be offered until the following January. Until then he would attend closely to his mounting coursework to keep his average high and deserve the letters of recommendation he would need from his Harvard professors.

Locke had several prominent professors to choose among. He had selected three literature courses for his senior year: Irving Babbitt's rigorous "Literary Criticism in Comparative Literature," which lasted for the year, Dean Briggs's fall course on Browning, and if he gained admission, Charles T. Copeland's English 12, the senior elective course in composition. He took Professor John W. White's survey "History of Greek Drama" in the fall and followed it with an advanced course in Greek literature in the spring. But the main focus of his senior-year studies was his three philosophy courses: Palmer's course in Kantian philosophy that fall, and Royce's and George Santayana's yearlong courses in metaphysics and Greek philosophy, respectively. Locke had just met Santayana at the end of September when he had had to spend an afternoon discussing his plans for honors in philosophy with the department's current teaching faculty, Royce, Palmer, Santayana, and Hugo Münsterberg. "All professors were very pleasant," he wrote his mother.

> Royce chatted for nearly a half hour about the Negro question—asked me if I had read his paper—and when I said I was going to teach said I hope not in Atlanta. Prof. Palmer was delightful—He said [Roscoe Conkling] Bruce visited him this summer, and that he and his friends at Harvard recommended him for his position in Washington. If I want anything in Washington Palmer says he will write a recommendation— It will only be a short step to get a blanket recommendation for whatever may turn up and to "whomever it may concern."[5]

Locke had already begun to evaluate which professors might possibly write him letters of recommendation for the Rhodes.

His course with Santayana became Locke's most important that fall for two reasons. First, George Santayana was the philosophy professor who modeled most closely the kind of mature philosopher Locke would become—the aesthetically minded philosopher who lived the life of reason. Though Spanish-born, Santayana had become a Boston aesthete during the 1890s, a time of "rebellious, conceited, pessimistic aestheticism."[6] Santayana synthesized his philosophical orientation with his aesthetic sensibility to produce *The Sense of Beauty* (1898), the bible of philosophically inclined aesthetes of his "generation." His philosophy complemented the literary outlook of Henry James, who also possessed a Santayana-like detachment from his surroundings. Santayana eventually abandoned America and teaching to live in Europe, where he remained prolific, and wrote *The Life of Reason*. In Santayana's Greek philosophy course, he and Locke did not hit it off: Santayana gave Locke the only B he received in his philosophy courses that fall, while the other two, Royce and Palmer, gave him As.

A second and more important consequence of taking Santayana's course was that Locke met Horace Meyer Kallen, a Jewish graduate student in philosophy, who himself was wrestling with his identity at Harvard. Born in 1883, this son of a Jewish rabbi had been an outstanding Harvard philosophy undergraduate graduating magna cum laude in 1903. After two years of graduate study in English at Princeton, Kallen was dismissed for being an "unbeliever," a subterfuge for it having been discovered that he was Jewish. After unsuccessfully applying for a lectureship at Harvard in 1905, he became a graduate assistant in Santayana's course that fall of 1906. Locke may have met Kallen prior to Santayana's class, as he had been a social worker at the Civic Service House where Locke and Dickerman tutored. Kallen may have also been the "Jewish rabbi" that Locke referred to as being present at one of his meetings with Wendell in the fall of 1905. According to a 1971 interview with Kallen, however, their friendship dated from Santayana's class and Kallen's engagement of Locke in an intellectual debate over the significance of racial difference. Kallen remembered meeting Locke, "a very remarkable young man—very sensitive, very easily hurt—who insisted that he was a human being and that his color ought not to make any difference. And, of course, it was a mistaken insistence. It had to make a difference and it had to be accepted and respected and enjoyed for what it was."[7] Kallen credited Locke and their discussions for coming up with the phrase "cultural pluralism," or "the right to be different."[8] One wonders whether at this early stage of his relationship with Locke Kallen understood the depth of Locke's "difference" or whether Locke, as a closeted but unapologetic gay man, would have to be convinced of his "right to be different."

Kallen was a student of William James, who had argued in *Pragmatism: A New Name for Some Old Ways of Thinking* that many metaphysical arguments revolved around inconsequential distinctions of language and that serious philosophical inquiry should focus only on those "differences that made a difference." Kallen believed that racial differences were just those kinds of significant differences, real divisions of mankind in terms of traditions, beliefs, and group ideals that made a huge difference in people's lives. Kallen's concept of ethnic pluralism was equally indebted to Barrett Wendell, for it was in Wendell's class that Kallen reconnected to his Jewish identity. In a lecture, Wendell argued that the Hebraic philosophy of individualism had influenced the Puritans and later the Founding Fathers. After Kallen challenged Wendell's views as inconsistent with what the younger man knew of Jewish religion, he learned that his teacher meant the Hebraic philosophical tradition, not the religious one. Kallen underwent a conversion experience in which he adopted Wendell's interpretation and defined Hebraism as "individualism...the right to be oneself, the right to be different."

Wendell, Kallen admitted, "re-Judaized me."

While Kallen characterized himself as the mature philosopher who brought Locke to a greater racial self-consciousness as a Black intellectual, theirs was more than a disagreement over identity politics; it was a serious debate over the nature of race. While Kallen considered Locke's position naive, it did avoid an essentialism that might make race a nearly biological barrier. When Locke "insisted that he was a human being and that his color ought not to make any difference," he asserted race was not real. Race was tradition, as Locke asserted later in his Dunbar lecture, something to be chosen, not imposed by society's notion of what really mattered. Race was something he performed, with all the flexibility implicit in the term "performance," in his daily approach to race on Harvard's campus—sometimes asserting his racial identity by going to dances with other Black students, other times denying race's power in his struggles with administrators. Locke was more the practicing pragmatist than Kallen, for Locke approached race as an improvisation made and remade through our actions. While naive in one sense, Locke's conception of race was sophisticated in creating an unfinished racial landscape that preserved his agency. Nonetheless, debating these points with Kallen likely gave Locke confidence in advancing the strong voice of race pride in his Dunbar lecture.

A sign that Locke still held onto the notion that there was a universal tradition higher than any particular national identity can be seen in his decision to take a course from T. S. Eliot's mentor, Irving Babbitt, that final year. As a critic of the elective system and specialization in higher education, Babbitt was a throwback to an earlier tradition that college education should produce well-rounded "gentlemen," whose training in the classics made them into "humanists," not the cultural nationalists that Wendell was turning out. Ironically, Locke used the elective system to fulfill exactly what Babbitt felt was the point of college education. By taking a variety of courses in English, Greek, and philosophy, Locke created for himself an integrated education in the humanities. And at Oxford, Locke would enroll in the program of *Literae Humaniores*, which provided intensive training in Greek, Latin, and classical culture—the so-called universal tradition of the West.

While the year's courses challenged Locke, his mind returned to the Rhodes throughout the fall, and when he returned to Harvard after Christmas, he ignored his coursework and threw himself into studying for the Responsions. He planned to take the exams in Boston on January 17 and 18 and crammed all of the information he could into his head during those first three weeks of January 1907 to prepare. "I have been reading up my Greek and my Latin at the rate of 20 or 30 pages an hour—and am in no way near through—have not touched the mathematics as yet," he wrote his mother, just three days before the exam. Though rushed, Locke was having the time of his life. "You cannot imagine how pleasant the work is—it is for such big stakes and though I have hopes at the same time I do not expect to get it for to aim at such is even an opportunity." Bolstering himself and his mother against what was likely failure, he continued: "I suppose I should consult the oracle—what do you think? I am bound to go with the contest and even may decide to repeat it next year though if it comes then the opportunity would almost be too late."[9]

Locke took the Rhodes exams, and while waiting for the results, crammed for his upcoming college exams in the first week of February. He also took advantage of the break to bring a copy of his Dunbar essay to Professor Charles T. Copeland's office as a writing sample for his senior composition course, English 12.

As he wrote his mother, "I didn't have time to write anything new for it, and anything else would have been less well written even if it might have been better in terms of its style." It was good enough, because Locke was admitted to the course. From Copeland, known by his students as "Copey," Locke received the close attention his prose needed. Copey used his red pencil to urge Locke toward greater concreteness and detail in his writing. A comment by Copey on one of Locke's essays, "Impressions of Dante," conveys the spirit of the older man's criticism.

> A skillful combination of exposition and individualized criticism. Although you write well, your work sounds too much as if you knew you were writing. This is partly a symptom and effect of clever youth, and as such to be welcomed; but—the impression comes also in no small degree from excessive Latinity, and a kind of rhetorical rotundity of phrase[.] Your sonorous summarizings also smell of the platform. Now what I propose is that we should continue to be clever ambitious and young but that we should abate our rhetorical transports. If this be criticism, make the most of it.[10]

In response to one of Locke's impressionistic short stories, Copey continued his sound commentary.

> Such pervading obscurity of expression, such vagueness of human presentation, is excusable only when the atmosphere (to use a word that is now almost slang) is charged with imagination, when there is a poetic glamour and allurement over the whole work. Both Masterlinck and Yeats succeed from time to time in a sort of imaginative triumph of the vague. This story of yours, I regret to say, seems to me never to get far above the level of prose, and therefore I can't help regarding it as a failure; you are capable of much better things.[11]

Copeland's comments on Locke's book review of Wells's *Future in America* caught one of the weaknesses of Locke's self-conscious, self-referential style of criticism.

> [This is] a highly generalized comment on Wells's book. As it is interesting to me who have read that book, so it would be bewildering or meaningless to those who have not read it. The ideal book review I suppose constructs a working image of the book, and then either breaks or exalts that image or else walks round and about it taking cool, peering views from every point. As I have read the book I am much more interested in your critique than I should be if it were an ideal review. Nevertheless you better put what I have said in your pipe, and smoke it.[12]

But Locke persisted in the style that Copey criticized, believing, after Pater in *Studies of the History of the Renaissance*, that criticism should begin and end with one's own attitude toward the work of art.

Copeland's influence may have been more than advising to tighten his prose. Copeland modeled for Locke how to be a sympathetic literary critic that encouraged students to become creative writers. As Van Wyck Brooks recalled, Copeland as well as Dean Briggs assumed their students would become writers and offered advice on charting a literary career. Copeland recommended to Locke that he continue to write those "better things" and devote himself full-time to a career as a writer. He went so far as to give Locke names of New York editors he should contact to try placing his short stories. Later he even suggested that Locke attempt to serve as a foreign correspondent for one of the major literary magazines. Locke owed Copeland a debt for providing unconflicted support. In the spring of 1907, Copeland wrote a strong letter of recommendation for Locke's Rhodes Scholarship application.

That shortly came in handy because on February 10, he "got the very pleasant news that I had passed the Rhodes examinations." An important decision loomed. Finalists had the option of appearing for their interview before the committee of the state in which they resided or before the committee of the state in which their college was located. Because he had listed his aunt and uncle's residence at 715 Sixth Street in Philadelphia as his home address on his Harvard College application, Locke had the option of being considered from Pennsylvania, New Jersey (where his mother resided), or Massachusetts. Given the strength of candidates he would likely face in New Jersey (from Princeton), the choice came down to Pennsylvania or Massachusetts. He wrote his mother, "I must hastily get all the information I possibly can get and then do what I think best. Their [*sic*] are advantages on each side and as yet I don't know where the most lie. At present I for several reasons favor Pennsylvania—the competition is not near so strong as it will be here—But I must see and talk the matter over with the Deans and several other professors here before I decide." If he went before the Massachusetts board, he would be one of six Harvard candidates, one of whom would be selected by the "Committee on Scholarships of Harvard College...as best fitted to go before the Committee of Selection for the final choice." The advantage of the Massachusetts appearance was:

> [If I can] get the Harvard selection, I am almost sure of the appointment and the whole thing hinges on that. By registering before the Pennsylvania committee Harvard is compelled to advance me as her candidate in Pennsylvania since I am the only Harvard man competing from that state. I must decide quickly and you see it is quite a puzzle—But as the certificate holds good [as having passed the entrance exams] in even of my failing this year I can apply again next year either in Massachusetts or in Pennsylvania or in New Jersey—wherever the best chances lie.[13]

Choosing the sure thing of being Harvard's candidate, he decided to appear before the Pennsylvania committee. The only drawback was that it involved the expense of an additional trip at a time when finances were already tight. On February 28, he wrote his mother that he needed her to send him $44.45, which was all of the money left over from her living expenses for the month, to pay his term bill, due on March 2. He would borrow the money for his trip home from his friend Bruno Beckhardt and "come the regular Fall River [Line]—which is safe, if any are, and then come from Jersey City by trolley as I shall have time to do so—I think by hard work I can land the Rhodes in Philadelphia. At any rate I am going to make a vicious try for it—and will tend to other business while I am on [home turf]—Philadelphia school etc.—"[14]

Locke was not so confident of winning the scholarship that he did not want to investigate teaching opportunities in Philadelphia as well as elsewhere. His friend Beckhardt had also promised to write him a letter of introduction to Dr. Felix Adler of the Ethical Culture Society in New York if Locke decided to seek a teaching position in that city. Locke even attended a lecture at Harvard's Ethical Culture Society at which a Mr. Hapgood of the Hapgood Employment Agencies discussed business opportunities for Harvard graduates. "I have always wanted to dabble in business on the side, perhaps that's the Hawkins blood clamoring for an outlet," he wrote his mother. But clearly, the Rhodes Scholarship consumed his interest and energy as the early March trip to Philadelphia approached. "I shall try and try hard, and the Pennsylvania Committee will see that one negro has the nerve and the backing to thrust himself on their serious consideration if but for a few hours." He believed that he could eventually "go to Oxford Rhodes or no Rhodes in a few years," but would fight hard this time, because "its too good a chance to miss." Before traveling to Philadelphia, he gathered information on the competition. He was one of six candidates who would be interviewed by a committee of five college presidents, including President Harrison of the University of Pennsylvania, who chaired the committee. He thanked his mother for "the information about George Wanger [it] came in very handy—he is the only serious rival—and a very serious one. He is [the] son of Congressman Wanger, has just made Phi Beta Kappa, and is quite prominent in his class—I think myself he will get it—but I am going to give him a tussle for I shall bring down a startling bunch of references."[15] Actually, William Harrison informed Locke shortly thereafter that at this level of competition, letters should be mailed. Here was a symbol of the distance Locke had come in the academic world since he had first arrived on Harvard's campus in 1904 with his letters in hand. Locke hurried around campus that last week of February collecting letters from his most respected professors.

But something clued Locke not to ask Barrett Wendell for a letter or even to discuss his plans with him, even though it was Wendell whose theories had been most important to his intellectual growth at Harvard. It was a wise decision. Years later, Wendell wrote to Horace Kallen, a Jewish friend of Locke's, and stated: "As an American, I cannot but feel that Locke, in applying for a Rhodes Scholarship which involves some suggestion of national representation, committed an error of judgment.... The terms of the Rhodes foundation, if I am not in error, are carefully phrased to the effect that <u>mere</u> scholarship is not all that is required. The purpose of it was to ensure, so far as possible, the kind of man who might be expected in maturity to be widely, comprehensively representative of what is best in the state which sent him. At least for many years to come, no negro can make just this claim anywhere in America. Before he can, the kind of American which unmixed native blood has made me must be only a memory. It is sad—I admit—not least so to me for the reason that I am passing—perhaps [I am] of the past altogether [sic]."[16] What saved Locke from possibly having a disastrous letter written by Wendell was a "sixth sense" of whom Locke could not trust with his outsized ambition to be a "representative" American.

Apparently, Wendell was not the only one who believed it was ill-advised for Locke to apply for the Rhodes Scholarship. When he arrived back home on the morning of March 7, Locke learned that his old nemesis, Dean Hurlbut, had failed to send the college's official letter of recommendation to the committee. Locke urgently telegraphed the dean. Hurlbut did send his letter to the committee with only a perfunctory acknowledgment of Locke's accomplishments: "his connection with Harvard College has been creditable," it concluded. But more important, Hurlbut omitted any reference to Locke's financial difficulties and mailed it promptly. Here, not angering Hurlbut in their earlier conflict had paid off.

More surprising was the reaction of his mother. In what may be an apocryphal story, Locke recalled to a friend that when he arrived home, Mary Locke, now elderly, was bending over, performing the ritual for proper Philadelphians—even though they lived in Camden—of washing down the front steps of her home. Locke bounded around the corner, his tiny, 4′11″, ninety-five-pound frame brimming with enthusiasm. He recalled rushing up to her, exclaiming, "Mother, I'm home to interview for the Rhodes scholarship. Isn't that wonderful?"

"Yes," Locke recalled his mother saying, and then to his surprise, she returned to washing down the steps. Flabbergasted by her lackadaisical attitude, he queried: "Why mother, aren't you glad?" Still washing the steps and without turning her head, she announced: "I don't know why you are bothering to apply for that Rhodes thing. You know they will never give it to a Negro." Locke recalled being shocked. Standing up as straight and tall as his small frame would allow, he reputedly said: "I am going to win that Rhodes Scholarship. It is the least that Rhodes can do considering all the wealth he took out of Africa."

Although she had not wished to discourage him at a distance, she could not help voicing her opinion that it was unwise for him to apply for the Rhodes. Locke rejected her attitude that race prejudice was an insurmountable obstacle. As he remarked about one of her friends who experienced difficulty with the Camden school system: "soon she too will take up the cry of prejudice—well—I don't lay any stock in the prejudice argument though it seems to be the fashionable excuse—Lord save me from ever offering it as an excuse no matter what happened." But Mary Locke may have had another reason for not encouraging him. She may have believed his overweening confidence that he would succeed would, eventually, meet a racial barrier he could not overcome. He was hardwired for propulsive forward motion, filled with the confidence that came from never having experienced real racism.[17]

Locke's confidence was confirmed in the case of the Rhodes Scholarship. A Rhodes Scholarship committee of distinguished college administrators, including Provost Harrison of the University of Pennsylvania, and Presidents Swain of Swarthmore College, Moffatt of Washington and Jefferson College, Russell of Westminster College, and Haas of Muhlenberg College, selected him over six other candidates, all from colleges whose presidents were on the committee. Although reports circulated afterward that the committee had not interviewed Locke (and hence it did not know he was Black), he did appear before the committee at 2 P.M. on Saturday, March 9. The minutes of John Haas, the committee secretary, confirm that "after a careful examination of all letters of recommendation, and a personal conference with each candidate, the Committee unanimously resolved that while all applicants had reached a very high standard, Mr. Alain Leroy Locke be awarded the scholarship for his specially mature mentality and high, definite purpose."[18] While his record, demeanor, and personal bearing certainly contributed to his success, he may also have impressed the committee by the way in which he handled the "racial question." Locke later recalled that the committee had asked him: "Why do you want the scholarship?" While such a question was relevant to all the candidates, Locke sensed its racial import in his case and replied, "Besides the further education ... I want to see the race problem from the outside. I don't want to run away from it, but I do want to see it in perspective"—from the vantage point, apparently, that residence in Europe would offer.[19] The committee was understandably charmed by such a mature answer from a young man. As Franklin Spencer Edmonds, a lawyer, later relayed to Locke, he had made an "excellent impression" on the committee, according to President Swain of Swarthmore.

Yet in the wake of the decision, at least one member of the committee would have difficulty defending the committee's action. Provost Harrison was later asked by George Parkin, the organizing secretary of the Rhodes Trust, how it occurred that the committee had selected a Negro. Perhaps feeling he had to defend the committee's judgment, Harrison reputedly asserted that it had been a colorblind decision. Harrison lied to Parkin that the committee had received such outstanding letters of recommendation from Harvard without any mention of Locke's race that the committee members had decided unanimously in favor of Locke before the interview. They then thought it unfair to change their opinions once they learned he was Black. While it was true that Locke had received outstanding letters from his Harvard professors, one letter addressed to Provost Harrison from Dean Briggs and dated March 6 stated clearly, "Mr. A. R. Locke, a young colored student from Philadelphia, tells me that he is an applicant for a Rhodes scholarship."[20] The committee knew Locke was Black and had decided to make a statement for racial justice. But afterward Harrison found it difficult to explain how an American committee could select a Negro for the award in spite of his race. Parkin's question not only signaled the Trust's consternation if not displeasure with the appointment, but also the problem for Locke and others connected with the decision: although individual ability had won the award for Locke, it would be almost impossible to separate his winning the scholarship from the larger issues of race and Negro status in the United States.

The appointment catapulted Locke into national attention. On March 13, 1907, the New York Times announced, "Negro Wins Scholarship, Locke Gets the Rhodes Award in Competition with Fifty," and went on to state that "those who selected Locke said that merit alone won for him." As Parkin noted in the special report he prepared on the selection, "the comments of the American press have not been unfavorable."[21] Yet there were exceptions to the tolerant respect for achievement that characterized most newspaper accounts throughout the country. F. J. Wylie, assistant secretary of the Rhodes Trust, had a brother-in-law at Harvard, who felt that electing a Negro to the Rhodes Scholarships would hurt its reputation. This young northerner wrote, "Have you heard that a negro has been chosen by Pennsylvania to go to Oxford as a Rhodes Scholar? This negro, Locke, is at Harvard and from all accounts, though clever, he is decidedly objectionable. I do not know him personally, but he is not at all pleasant to look at. I do not see why Oxford should not refuse to admit him."[22]

Mention of Locke's award was conspicuously absent from such major southern newspapers as the Atlanta Constitution, the Richmond Times Dispatch, and the New Orleans Daily Picayune. The opinion of much of the South, however, was articulated by Mr. Gustaf R. West Fledt, a New Orleans businessman and a member of the board of administrators at Tulane University. He wrote the British ambassador to protest Locke's election to the Rhodes Scholarship. He claimed, "The appointment of negroes will make the Rhodes scholarships unpopular in the South." Southern Rhodes Scholars at Oxford echoed this opinion. They were shocked that a "negro" would soon enter what they had been told by Rhodes officials was a "Brotherhood" of the elect. They protested by sending a representative to London, who challenged Locke's appointment before the trustees of the scholarship. Like the Tulane University administrator, their chief argument was that the election would damage the image of the Rhodes Trust in the South. Southerners would not apply for scholarships that involved association with Blacks. Some threatened to resign their scholarships if Locke's name was not withdrawn.

From the standpoint of the Trust, canceling Locke's appointment was out of the question, "a vain hope," as Sir Francis Wylie, the Rhodes Scholarship administrator at Oxford, put it. To overrule the action of the Pennsylvania committee would have been unprecedented and damaging to the program of selection. To cancel his appointment would, as Parkin put it, "bring up the colour problem in an acute form throughout our own Empire." Nevertheless, the trustees of the Rhodes Scholarship considered the southern challenge serious enough to review the appointment at a meeting on April 16, 1907. They "confirmed the election of a black American, Mr. Alain Leroy Locke, of Pennsylvania to the scholarship for which he had been selected," basing their decision on "clause 24 of the Will," which stated that "no student shall be qualified or disqualified for election to a Scholarship on account of his race or religious opinions."[23] One wonders why they even bothered to meet, but perhaps the trustees hoped such a ruling would put the issue to rest.

It did not. Although no Rhodes Scholar resigned his appointment and none apparently refused a scholarship in the future because of the appointment, the southern Rhodes Scholars did not quietly acquiesce, but made plans to exclude him from social functions and, when that failed, absent themselves from integrated functions. The conflict also affected Francis Wylie, a former college tutor, who had begun his tenure as Rhodes secretary with the first class of scholars in 1903, and who, with his being American-born, regarded the community of Rhodes Scholars as his extended family. Now that harmonious community life was threatened by a race problem that could potentially divide the community permanently. Parkin predicted that Locke's appointment would cause southern scholars to request to be moved to other colleges from the one to which Locke would be assigned. Wylie anticipated this response and attempted to avoid a scene early in the year by trying to place scholars who might object to Locke at colleges away from the "*coloured man*." In a notebook that Wylie kept on all of the Rhodes Scholars, Locke's entry contains the note, " 'not with Mississippi or Alabama (n'd letters) not to <u>Univ</u> or <u>Lincoln</u>."[24]

Actually, Wylie had difficulty placing Locke at any college. While winning the Rhodes brought automatic appointment to the university, each scholar had to be accepted by one of the residential colleges. Every year, Wylie had some difficulty placing Rhodes Scholars, since they were not as highly prized as English undergraduates. Skill in a particular sport or excellence in a particular field of study valued at the college were factors that might overcome the fact that Rhodes Scholars came to Oxford with little social standing. No scholar, however, would be as difficult for Wylie to place in 1907 as Locke. On April 22, Wylie received from Locke a list of colleges he wished to seek admission to, beginning with his favorite, Magdalen (the college Oscar Wilde had attended), followed by Balliol, Merton, Brasenose, and Christ Church. On May 4, however, Wylie had to write him to request a new list of colleges, since all of these had refused him. Before Locke could answer, Wylie submitted his name to Worcester and then to Hertford, which on May 18 accepted Locke. Wylie wrote Locke that same day to accept Hertford. Although it is impossible to determine whether race or press attention to Locke's appointment played a part in the these colleges' decisions, he was rejected by six colleges in a year when the next most difficult case was that of Benjamin Lacy from North Carolina who was rejected by three.

Locke was displeased with his selection and expressed it in a letter that asked Wylie to resubmit his application to the colleges on the original list. "Because of the historic nature of my appointment, and the attention on my activities while at Oxford that will undoubtedly follow, it is imperative that I be situated at one of the better and more visible colleges at Oxford."[25] Hertford was one of the newest and poorest of colleges, and Locke desired a more prestigious launching pad for his career at Oxford. But Wylie wrote back that given that all of the other colleges had their fill of Rhodes Scholars, it would be unwise for him to reject the one college that had accepted him. That was certainly true, but Wylie had other motives for wanting Locke to accept Hertford. Once he had learned that Hertford had taken Locke, Wylie had written to Lacy, who had been accepted by Hertford after Locke, to ask whether Lacy would "accept as negro been acc. at Hertford." Lacy chose to be "recovered from Hertford" and eventually was accepted by Worcester. Wylie was so concerned about potential objections to Locke that he even informed a non-southerner, Mr. Shirley Townshend Wing of Ohio, that the "negro" scholar would be at Hertford. He too chose to be recovered from Hertford, eventually landing at Wadham. Clearly, Wylie took it upon himself to ensure that the racial sensibilities of White Americans would not be offended by having to reside in the same college with Locke. But in seeking to reduce the potential conflict, Wylie confirmed those feelings as legitimate. Even more tellingly, he granted other scholars the freedom to switch colleges, yet denied the same right to Locke. Wylie did not recover Locke from Hertford, nor resubmit his application to the other colleges. Although Locke had no way of knowing the elaborate maneuvers taken in his case, he sensed something was amiss and refused to accept Hertford until he arrived at Oxford in the fall. No doubt his decision gave Wylie a nervous summer. It also affected Locke: there could be little doubt now that going to Oxford as the Black Rhodes Scholar was going to be much more complicated than going to Harvard had been.

Locke's appointment also received a great deal of notice from the African American press, which interpreted his winning of the scholarship as a "distinguished honor" that he brought to "his race." In an era when Black Americans were habitually depicted as ignorant buffoons or subhuman criminals in White newspapers, the Black press seized on Locke's selection as ammunition against White racist claims that all Blacks were intellectually inferior. Had not a Negro boy in fair and open competition bested White boys? Was that not evidence that Negroes had the capacity for the highest civilization? Such newspapers also drew attention to Locke's dark complexion as a refutation of claims by White commentators that only African Americans of considerable White ancestry excelled intellectually. A newspaper reporter who witnessed Du Bois's superb valedictory speech at Harvard in 1898 had specifically mentioned his "white blood." Locke, on the other hand, was portrayed by the Black press as one of the "living refutations that superior mental possessions belong only to people of fair complexions, and those who are absorbing the highest influences are significantly uplifting the standards of their race." The newspaper concluded, "Alain Le Roy Locke...is one more example to be quoted in evidence of the brain-power that resides in the pure Negro race."[26]

He was suddenly a "representative man" to be used against prejudice and a source of inspiration for the race. Such organizations as *The American Missionary* interpreted his appointment as confirming the truthfulness of the ideology of uplift that imbued Locke's middle-class upbringing in Philadelphia. Despite all the odds, a Black man could compete with the best White students and win. Rather than complain about the inequities of opportunity, Blacks should plunge into competition with hard work and dedication. Indeed, part of the reason that both Black newspapers and northern White newspapers praised Locke and the appointment was that it confirmed an essentially laissez-faire approach to American race relations. Perhaps it was because barely a majority of Black Americans could read and write in America in 1907 that the accomplishment of a single Black man in winning the Rhodes took on such symbolic meaning.

Although this ideology of individual initiative was actually Locke's own personal racial philosophy, he chafed under the deluge of letters from well-meaning friends and unknown people who seized upon his accomplishment as a symbol of racial progress. Some were from close friends, but the majority were from acquaintances, some he barely knew and some who ruffled his sensitive feathers. Locke wrote his mother:

> I don't like Duty's letter and will write him something to that effect—as usual he meddles into personalities—he isn't very tactful—"tell him to be self possessed, self composed" grates on me—why because all these Negroes are surprised because they didn't know my plans—do they think I was taken as unawares as they—I will tell him that I expected to go abroad as a Harvard Fellow anyway and that I did not care for this muddying of a purely personal issue of my life with the race problem—I am not a race problem—I am Alain LeRoy Locke and if these people don't stop I'll tell them something that will make them—There now—I have written Duty—my good saints—but it piles up.[27]

Even those who were close family friends received letters from him that must have raised some eyebrows.

Mother's letter today brings your kind note of congratulation—and it was one of the few of its kind that I feel I can genuinely accept as implying any past or future obligations on my part. By a kind of fate it seems that I have been indebted to very few persons in order that I might the more heavily be indebted to my Mother—Yet to some I am indebted, but in a most agreeable fashion—for some _few_ have believed in me, and since whatever credit I take to myself I take because after a certain fashion I have always believed in myself—I consider as true friends _only_ _those_ who have believed and hoped with me—For this accept my most hearty thanks.[28]

Clearly, Locke wanted his achievement to be his and his close friends' only. But at a time when the American Negro was soundly criticized for the so-called failure of Reconstruction and reputed lack of substantial moral and intellectual progress since slavery, his appointment was a success that many less privileged Black people wanted to be a part of. Understandably, there were some excesses of enthusiasm. Perhaps the worst cases were letters from those who hardly knew him but sought to capitalize on his success for their own purposes. The "Brotherhood of Andrew and Philip," a Philadelphia benevolent society, elected him to honorary membership after receiving a reluctant reply to their letter of fulsome acknowledgment, and then had the audacity to write requesting a photograph of Locke that they could sell to bring in needed funds for the "Brotherhood."[29] Many African Americans seemed to want to be related in some tangential way to the Rhodes Scholar.

Mary was inundated with expressions of congratulation from distant relatives. "First Mrs. Adelaide Locke—who hurried in to congratulate and _talk_ and _talk_. I was glad to see—her—she—sent much love and told me to say _she_ was the _only_ person not surprised, because she always predicted great things of you." Mary Locke had "20 letters on hand. You see _I_ am _somebody_ too—I can't send you all—but will send you those answered, or those you have not seen. . . . The people that have been at the door and stopped me—on the St. are legions—I am going to have a sign stating that I am the mother of the prodigy." One of those letters informed him that "we have discovered some cousins or resurrected some—I haven't heard of them since [18]73—They have money and live at Wash[ington] but I never bothered—the fun of it is, that they are related on both mother's—and the Hawkins' side. So you see you are opening doors for 'ma' as well as the _race_."[30]

That was certainly the case, as Mary received congratulations from such Black society families as the Mintons and Black community leaders such as J. W. Cromwell, her husband's law school friend. Suddenly, she was invited to so many people's houses she barely had to cook dinner for several weeks. Particularly poignant was her visit to Uncle Harry and Aunt Lizzie, whose Philadelphia residence was Locke's official home address.

I could not help being amused at Harry's—They are both as proud and as pleased as Punch. Harry was alone when I went in Thurs. and disconcerted me, by breaking out and crying—said he was crying for joy—and he sobbed away, while I sat there like the dog-eyed fool.... Harry said the house had been besieged by people—black & white—The people who live around there & those people at the church I expect—to see the new "Moses" that is to lift the race. It's all one big joke to me—The race is Sensational—when your father <u>opened</u> the doors of the P.O. to his <u>race</u> it was almost the same—when he needed money and friends— they were sadly wanting. So keep your head—my boy.[31]

As her roomer Bush told her, "The people col'd. are talking about nothing else."

Talk throughout Camden centered on how a Camden boy had won the Rhodes, and therein lay a problem: one of the Camden newspapers, the *Post Telegram*, ran a story under the headline, "Camden Colored Man Wins Scholarship." When Locke heard of this from his mother, he sensed the danger immediately: if it were discovered that he actually resided in Camden with his mother, he might be disqualified from the scholarship. His March 23 letter to his mother summarized his response:

> I have seen a lawyer.... I understand that as of age I can claim separate legal residence from you. I have written to the Post Telegram as follows:
> Editor, Post Telegram
> My dear Sir
> My attention has just been called to an article in your paper for March 14 under the caption "Camden Colored Man Wins Scholarship." Many incorrect statements that have appeared in the public press have been matters of insignificant detail, and I have not troubled to correct them. But that a reliable newspaper should claim Camden residence for me is of sufficient import to warrant correction on my part. I would think it quite sufficient merely to inform you that such a statement is incorrect, rather than to ask for the usual acknowledgment in order that there be no further consequences or responsibility for what is, as yet, only a reportorial mistake, were I not legally advised to enclose a signed statement that a young man of age may have separate residence from his parents, and a directory address is not necessarily a legal residence.[32]

He then chastised her for talking to people.

> This settles the affair I hope—though I want you to watch the Telegram <u>very</u> closely for a week or so... but for the sake of the heavenly twins do keep quiet—and as to Cornish [her principal at Mt. Vernon where she

taught]—trust him <u>not</u>—I think he was responsible for it anyway—
you know he is a friend of the Post Telegram—so say nothing to him
unless he says something to you and then say I cannot say anything—
Roy has retained a lawyer...I have been ordered to say nothing. I know
Cornish put <u>That</u> in—and it all comes from you confiding in him—I have
always told you not to—Otherwise how came it that the Courier said
nothing and the Post Telegram did.[33]

But it was not her fault, of course. He had decided to claim Pennsylvania rather
than New Jersey as his home state, and it had made a difference. If he had gone for
the Rhodes in New Jersey, he would probably not have won. The New Jersey
Rhodes winner was Donald Grant Herring, a Princeton football star, inter-
collegiate wrestling champion, and excellent student. As the press noted, "The
Committee on Selection consisted of President Woodrow Wilson, Dean H. B. Fine,
of Princeton, and President Damerest, of Rutgers College."[34] The committee was
stacked with Princeton people, not the least of whom was Woodrow Wilson, who
as president of Princeton condoned the policy of exclusion of Negroes and as president of the United States was responsible for the segregation of the Post Office,
among other federal agencies. Locke had made the right choice to be considered
from Pennsylvania, but his deception threatened to come back to haunt him.

Fortunately, there was no further publicity in the *Post Telegram*. Locke had
wisely refrained from asking for a printed retraction. But such close public scrutiny of his life was beginning to cause problems. Newspaper interest and attention continued. More than a week after the announcement, he returned to his
room to discover a card slipped under his door from a reporter for one of the
Hearst newspapers who wanted an interview. The next day that reporter caught
up with him in the Harvard Union and told Locke that if he did not give him
an interview, the reporter would make up the answers and print it anyway.
Stumbling over his words, Locke answered the questions, but surprisingly, no
story ever appeared. Locke began to long for his former anonymity. "I just wished
they would stop and leave me alone," he moaned to his mother.[35]

Locke did enjoy some of the attention brought by the appointment. Suddenly
he was no longer just a bright, interesting Negro boy, but the Rhodes Scholar,
a Black genius; and that changed White opinion of him as much as Black. "Oh did
I tell you," he continued, "I got a letter from the editor of the Independent asking
me to write them an article of 2000 to 3000 words on my impressions of Oxford
after I have been there long enough to form an impression." "Did I tell you about
the dinner invitations—Well Sunday afternoon I am to go to the Downses,
Sunday evening to the Scammells—the Scammells are English people—the
father an Oxford man the son a classmate of mine, who are of course 'very interested' which means very curious—I shall go indulge their curiosity for their

uncle is an editor of the Westminster Review and it means an introduction to him." Taking a moment out from the euphoria, he mused: "Strange though, how quickly people—even cultivated men, show an increasing interest and friendliness in success—its instructive I suppose."[36]

One payoff of this new interest came that April: he was appointed to be a delegate to the three-day Episcopalian Church Conference of New England Schools and Colleges that was held in Cambridge. As a delegate, he was responsible for entertaining a visitor to the conference, dining with the group, and attending a variety of lectures.

> I met several of the boys from Groton school and they were of course very much interested in me Principal Peabody having spoken of me up there at school—they were politely curious as only fellows of that sort of training can be—so I was asked to go to Apthorp house where they were staying where a party of us chatted and talked till midnight[.] Several of them come to Harvard next September, and on second thought I was particularly pleasant to them when I thought someone of them might have to be tutored for the September exams.... However, I was very glad to have met them.[37]

He was also able to make the acquaintance of a Mr. Carleton—"a graduate of Brasemore College at Oxford—of course he talked and talked and talked—told me very valuable things, gave me several introductions to friends of his who are now Dons. 'Dons' you may as well know for now on are the younger instructors of fellowship holders to Oxford." Locke himself acknowledged that "if I had not been Rhodes Scholar I not only would not have been invited as a delegate to the conference—but if I had gone would have been a nonentity instead of the star side show—everyone was brought and I was introduced as Rhodes scholar elect until I was sick and tired of it."[38] Celebrity status was intoxicating, and Locke would have to marshal all of his self-discipline to "keep" his "head," as Mary suggested.

Newfound status also brought renewed challenges, as when he socialized with the Black bourgeoisie of Boston. On one occasion a Mrs. Etta Williamson, on whom Locke called, seemed to try to "fix him up" with her daughter.

> She is very foolish—and of course very uneducated.... What do you think they did—went out and left the Williamson girl and me <u>alone</u>— that shows how much they know about things(!)—fortunately 2 other Negro summer girls came in and I got involved in a conversation, almost a controversy over separate schools etc. They evidently tried to rag the Rhodes Scholar but got paid back with interest—I led them into the deep waters and left them there to drown.[39]

Despite such attention, Locke needed to focus his energy back on his work, which was considerable in those months after the Rhodes announcement. He had to submit his Bowdoin Prize essays in March, catch up on his coursework in April, much of which he had had to neglect during March, and translate a poem for the Sargent Prize. He needed to prepare for two exams in the condition subjects from his entrance exams—algebra and physics—that he had to pass before he could graduate. Finally, he had to take special exams in philosophy early in May, plus answer a senior thesis question, in order to receive honors.

> Tuesday afternoon from 2–5:30 I took an examination on the Outlines of Modern Philosophy—Wednesday two exams, one on Plato and one on Kant...the Department is trying to size me up—pretty thoroughly it seems—This morning [May 10] I got my special thesis subject— Professor Royce wrote out the paper—What relation has the study of metaphysics to the practical problems of life? Specify some of the uses of metaphysical study, if you see any such uses, in relation to the problems of life. If the study seems in any respect impractical or useless or dangerous define the respects in which this seems true. What particular problems of metaphysic seem to you to have the most practical import. That's a personal question if ever there was one—Prof. Royce from personal conversation with me knows I am unpractical and of course its the severest sort of a test to propose—The thesis is supposed to show philosophic power and is due in 48 hours—Well before I set to work solving the problems of life—before I monkey with the Absolute, thought I might as well be practical and write a letter to Mamma.[40]

Mary Locke remained his psychological anchor in this sea of intellectual and emotional stresses. He drew back the curtain and revealed his inner feelings only with her. "Yes, I must play the genius, but I hope you are never taken in. I need you more than anything to keep me straight." When that anchor was missing, Locke became extremely agitated, as he did the last week of May after receiving no letter from her for over a week. He dashed off a telegram to her, "Are you ill? Can wire cash. Love, Roy." His mother, needless to say, was frightened by the telegram and sent an answer back with the messenger. She had imagined something had happened to him. Afterward, he tried to explain. "Well, I was a bit worried—you know you said you would write Thursday night—and then there was no note with the money order—I thought you were sick." He continued, "You mustn't be so old fogey—nor must you ever worry me up—or sometime you'll have me coming across the Atlantic on an express steamship for nothing."[41]

Locke was feeling apprehensive in the face of their coming separation. That separation would also mean a dramatic change for her. She would move out of the house into a room in Claphans's house on the same street, since there would be no need for her to pay the expense of maintaining a full residence in his absence. More than ever, she would be in other people's care. As his Harvard commencement in June approached, he began to view it as a special occasion on which to reward her for all the sacrifices she had made for him. He wished to place her on the pedestal and show the world that here was the person who really deserved credit for his successes. He also hoped that he would have definite prospects for summer tutoring, and that he could then pay her back a bit by having her spend the summer with him in New England. Then, one of his ships came in.

> I was a bit worried over financial affairs—laying plans and worrying how we were going to come out—So I went to be on it and this morning was awakened by a letter falling with a click through the letter slot— Strange—it didn't contain money—but it contained the next best thing— good news and the promise of money—Don't cackle overmuch—but I just got notice that I had won the first Bowdoin prize with my essay on Tennyson and His Literary Heritage—That means $250, a bronze medal, a public reading and some more popularity or notoriety as it seems to be in my case—damn the luck—Well that is quite a thing here at Harvard and quite a personal vindication as I tried twice before and failed—Of course it is the largest and chiefest literary prize here—also the oldest Emerson, Holmes, Phillips Brooks and lots of other notables have won it.... Just yesterday I counted up on my Phil 9 notebook margin that I needed $500 for my plans this summer. Well here's 250 of it now.[42]

Now that finances were a bit better, Locke threw himself with gusto into preparations for his mother's trip to Cambridge for the commencement. He would find her a cheap room for the bulk of her stay, but would spend the extra money for her to be able to receive visitors in one of the better hotels for one day. In a "Letter of Instructions," he gave her detailed instructions on the types of hats, bags, and accessories she must purchase to be properly attired. Of greatest importance was the dress that she would have to have made.

> Tell Smith [her favorite dressmaker] you want a corking good dress of crepe de chine, grey or black, preferably black with some grey about the trimmings—that will do <u>for formal afternoon and evening wear</u>—Now this one dress must look right—give her free rein—only see she doesn't go to the extreme of fashion—go over patterns with her—send one she selects and I will approve and return immediately.

There was more: "begin to get your face and hands in shape. Go to your drugstore Brooks for Jolivons etc.—you will need a few little hotel articles." He concluded "a fancy parasol [is] absolutely necessary."[43]

Mary Locke began to crack under the strain to live up to his requirements with very little money on hand. "This trip is making me <u>sick</u>," she wrote on June 7, after providing lists of the hats, bags, and accessories she had priced in local stores. In addition, she had been forced into downtown stores for fittings that challenged her Victorian notions of propriety. "I had to be fitted at Gimbels for corsets today. She [Smith] <u>ordered</u> me to get corsets <u>made</u>—said I looked like I was going to 'increase the family.'" When Mary went in, she discovered to her horror that instead of paying the $3.00 she had been promised, "I was so *hard* to fit—I had to pay $3.85—3.50 for Corset & .35 for bust.... It *fits* and I am *minus* a *stomach*. I had to take off everything but my shirt and stockings. Can you imagine me? Do tear this up—but I had to tell you—I felt like an old fool—I had no idea that was the way."[44] Incredibly, she included a swatch of the black voile in her letter for his approval.

Although Mary did not make it to Cambridge until after his public reading of "Tennyson and His Literary Heritage," the commencement appears to have come off well for both of them. Not only did he graduate magna cum laude for his overall performance in his courses but he also got his honors in philosophy. Altogether, he was the star attraction of that year's commencement. Unfortunately, she was not able to stay in New England with him. Try as hard as he might, he could not secure tutoring, even with Copeland's intervention with the dean. After Mary Locke returned to Camden at the end of June, Locke continued to hustle after each fleeting rumor of work, in competition with dozens of other Harvard graduates, for another month. Indeed, his fellow Black graduates were in much worse straits: "Bowser, the 'author of Shelleyian verse' is on the Pullmans, Tyson is working on the steamboats—and from New York, Harris is yard laborer— so it goes—"[45] Matthews, the star of the baseball team, had been forced to leave college. Publicity in the Boston newspaper the *Guardian* made Locke sympathize with Matthews's plight. But the reality was clear: there were few, if any, positions of worth available to his fellow Black Harvardians, and without the Rhodes, he too would have had no prospects.

July's relative calm was broken by another newspaper incident: the *Boston Globe* picked up a story, reputedly attributed to "Pennsylvania men," that they objected "to [the] choice of the Harvard man" for the Rhodes. No names accompanied the report, which stated "the feeling among certain classes of students is against Locke's representing Pennsylvania at Oxford on the ground that he did not qualify in social standing and athletic ability. It is also rumored that the undergraduates at Harvard resented Locke's being chosen." Ironically, the newspaper article went on to contradict the report by asserting that Locke was popular among his classmates at Harvard and "was chummy with some of the best scholars." Although he "has never gone in 'strong' for athletics, principally because of his small stature," Locke was "one of the best students in college," who had been "one of the seven men of his class upon whom the college bestowed one of the much-coveted Detus," and "one of the 3 men to receive the grade A in English 12, the advanced course in English composition."[46] Locke was concerned that a Black paper would get ahold of the story and "stir things up and first thing you know my residence will be disputed." He successfully squashed the story in the *Boston Herald* by personally going to the city editor and getting it "held up in time before it spread—It only came out in their first edition which they send up in the country [for] Massachusetts and Maine etc., in the second edition for Boston it was cut out. Notice of it was left in the summary of the day's news, and the Negroes of Boston have been hunting for the article ever since I hear."[47] Maude Trotter Stewart of the *Guardian* had contacted Locke to get more information on the purported incident, but he did not answer her. In fact, this "story" was nothing more than a newspaper-created rumor, as Locke noted to his mother.

It showed, however, that it was time to leave the United States before any more "news" broke about his controversial appointment. Fortunately, he would not be going alone. His friend Carl Downes, son of the editor of the *Boston Transcript* and an excellent graduate student in English, had written to Oxford asking permission to spend a year in residence. In contrast to his reluctant endorsement of Locke, Hurlbut wrote an enthusiastic letter of recommendation to Oxford for Downes, whose grade point average and overall achievement did not equal Locke's. Downes was accepted and able to accompany Locke on his voyage. Dickerman would be coming over to visit in the summer of 1908, and Kallen would be in residence working under F. C. S. Schiller, James's pragmatist counterpart at Oxford. All in all, Locke would have a good collection of friends to ease the transition.

The day before he left it rained hard all day, which matched Mary Locke's dreary mood. She had wanted to accompany him to New York, but he convinced her it was not worth the effort; and so, she sat around all day, saddened that this was finally goodbye. The next day, September 24, Locke took an early train to New York, but apparently had some difficulty meeting up with Downes and his uncle. They were late for their ship's departure, and only by speeding through New York in a cab with Locke's trunk on top were Downes and Locke able to reach Hoboken before the *Wilhelm* departed. When finally settled safely on board, Locke wrote a farewell letter to his abandoned mother:

> Am on board all right sailing out into the ocean now—just out of sight of Liberty statue.... The boat is rocking considerable but I am not sick yet. I feel very hopeful just as if one had a new world to conquer—I have in a sense—Well here[']s good luck for both of us—I shall be thinking of you lots—and as soon as I can arrange to have you over you know I will—Well I must hurry—Mother dear do be hopeful and thankful and cheer up. Goodbye, your loving boy, Roy.

Alain Locke, England, 1908. Courtesy of the Moorland-Spingarn Research Center, Howard University.

7

Oxford Contrasts

"I find myself an excellent sailor," Locke noted in his second letter to his mother from on board the *Kaiser Wilhelm*. He was thrilled to be leaving behind America and sailing into an unknown future abroad. He had "eaten 5 meals a day—not having missed one[.] I feel the trip is doing me lots of good."[1] Locke looked forward to escaping the American race problem and immersing himself like other American aesthetes in the art and culture of Europe. While an Anglophile, Locke was also interested in Paris, Berlin, and Rome, cities associated with a new artistic modernism and avant-garde of pre–World War Europe. Europe was alive with a creative ferment his professors and fellow students had spoken of incessantly at Harvard. Now he was going to experience that Europe firsthand.

Locke also contemplated the possibility of not coming back. Before he left for England, Oswald Garrison Villard had advised him that it might be best to remain in Europe if he could make a good living there given the racial situation in America. Locke's letters from the *Kaiser Wilhelm* suggest that he was already thinking that a literary career in Europe might allow him permanent residence abroad. Life in Europe also promised a more tolerant sexual life, since homosexuality appeared to be more tolerated in European nations than in the United States. Even England, which had been rocked in 1895 by the Oscar Wilde trial, was less legally and morally repressive than the United States. And Oxford—Wilde's university—was well known as a haven for male homosexuals. Perhaps at Oxford he would find social and sexual acceptance that went beyond Harvard's. Perhaps such freedom would fire his muse and enable him to move beyond literary criticism to creative writing. Locke welcomed his trip to Oxford as a wonderful possibility of a cosmopolitan life abroad.

Locke's trip began with many of the familiar attributes of the honeymoon in Europe for Black Americans. There was "no prejudice on board," he wrote to his mother from the *Kaiser Wilhelm*, as "we have a seat at the first officer's table—that is next to the captain's table, and have very pleasant chatty table mates." He was readily accepted as a member of the ship's community and spent his time reading, playing shuffleboard, and participating in games with children. There were some interesting people on board, "the Van Remsaleavs, the Henry's (relations to [Henry] Jacobs), several Leipsig conservatory students, [and] a Mrs. Wistar Brown who has invited me to visit her in Frankfort on the Main Germany." In fact, Locke was "a mild sort of curiosity" on board, "which I rather enjoy than resent—They all come up rather shyly from behind—clear their throats as a warning signal and say So you are going to Oxford—"[2] Rather than leaving race behind in America, Locke had brought it on board where, combined with the status of being a Rhodes Scholar, it made him a celebrity.

Carl Downes's presence made this trip particularly pleasant. According to Locke, he was an "excellent travelling companion." For one thing, they were compatible enough to share expenses: Downes had changed all of his money into English currency before boarding, and then learned that the *Kaiser Wilhelm* only accepted American (or German) money. So Locke paid the expenses on board, while Downes promised to pay their London expenses, which were eventually the larger share. But Downes was an easygoing fellow and not a stickler about money matters (which Locke was) in part because he was relatively well-to-do: his father was footing the bill for his year at Oxford. Even more important, this was Downes's second trip to Europe, which made him a tour guide for Locke. This was becoming a pattern for Locke: when he entered unknown or unfamiliar situations, he habitually brought someone, usually one of his close White, male friends, as a kind of protector. He had done so when he had made his maiden speech to the Cambridge church. He now had another protector/guide as he went abroad. Locke also seems to have had a romantic interest in Downes. Although Locke had known Downes at Harvard, he had not been as close to him as some of the other fellows. Now, sequestered together for a five-day trip to England, he could determine whether Downes was also interested in him.

Apparently, the trip went well, for when he landed at Plymouth on September 30, he was in an excellent mood. "It was a beautiful landing...and we steamed up through the swellest fleet of French and English sailing vessels I have ever seen. The cliffs were beautiful—covered with dwarfish English trees, all sorts of wonderful shades of green—you really have no idea of what beautiful soft green is until you see England and I hope you will." They passed through customs without difficulty.

> Downes and I tumbled into the compartment (you know the English
> and continental trains have compartments with doors opening on
> the sides) with a Mr. Broad of New York—a fellow passenger on the
> ship who is chief musician of the Perforated Music Company in
> London—he directed us to Wards hotel—and after a beautiful 4 hours
> ride on the Great Western to London, we got in a typical London

fog—It was only 4 o'clock, but dark as 7 or 8 at home, and a pretty time we would have had finding accommodations by ourselves. We simply got into a cab and drove to Wards where they gave us a very large double room and excellent board for 30 shillings, $7.50 a week... things are much cheaper in England—this was a very nice house in the Russell Square residential district, with 2 flunkey's in full dress from early morning till night—who said yes sir and thank you if you looked at them.[3]

After a quick trip up to Oxford on October 2 to register for the term, Locke and Downes returned to London to spend the next ten days sightseeing. Unlike Locke's first days alone at Harvard where he got down quickly to work, at Oxford with Downes he took a more relaxed approach. He wanted to ease into his studies at Oxford and was glad to have Downes as a companion and guide. "Really, we did London, saw it through and through," he informed his mother. First, they explored Southampton Row and Oxford Streets, getting lost despite Downes's familiarity: "I never saw such a city—enormous—and the crowds of people and vehicles far outdoes New York—it really isn't safe to walk—or doesn't look so— and wouldn't be except that the London policemen control everything and everybody with a crook of the finger." Not only were London policemen impressive, but so was the lifestyle of the elite. "The better classes use cabs and hansoms all together—there are regular cab stands, and every house of the better sort has a cab whistle[:] you step out on your doorstep and blow your cab whistle and in less than a minute your cab's there[.]" The only drawback was that "you have to tip everybody—you ask someone a direction on the street and its a tip— every cabby expects a tip[,] but fortunately they are not large—you just have to carry around a pocket ful [l] of small coin[.]" Locke found even that troublesome because "their penny is as large and as heavy as a half dollar[!]"[4]

Once accustomed to their surroundings, Locke and Downes swept through the major cultural sites. First, they visited the National Art Gallery, which astounded him: "I never saw such a collection of pictures...the Reynolds and Gainsboroughs and Reyburns—There is an enormous collection of Turners pictures in one large gallery—some very wonderful and others quite bad to my thinking—I never saw such a collection of Italian paintings though—some of them are marvelous." He promised to send her the catalog and mark the paintings he liked the best. They also went twice to the "Royal Opera at Covent Garden—for 5 shillings 1.25 we got seats in the dress circle stalls and rubbed elbows with the upper middle class—just think of it—the upper middle class— why I suppose we belong to the lower – higher class don't we Mother—at any rate we're going up—Well we saw Carmen—a most remarkable performance and Faust not so good."[5]

Downes encouraged Locke to take in more eccentric sightseeing along with the traditional high-culture spots. "We went next night to the commonest theatre in Shoreditch and saw a bloody melodrama sitting besides innumerable Currys and Curretts (?)—old English couples who brought bread in their pockets, cut it with the old man's jack knife and munched and munched and munched like the sailor's wife in MacBeth." Back on the traditional tourist trail, they visited Westminster Abbey, which Locke deemed "the great sight of our trip. Twas very impressive." They also had time to see the Henry VII Chapel: "it contains the tombs of Elisabeth and Mary Queen of Scots—and is a beautiful example of flowery Gothic."[6] Here was the beginning of a fascination with Gothic chapels and cathedrals in Europe that would continue for years.

Locke was also able to begin making important contacts. "I must tell you that Mr. Isaka Seme—a wealthy East Indian met us—took us to the Middle Temple—the law courts—the Temple is the ancient association of English judges and barristers—they have beautiful old Gothic buildings just opposite Temple Bar Library—"[7] Seme, actually a Zulu from South Africa, had received a BA from Columbia University and was studying law at Jesus College while residing in London where he worked as a legal assistant at Middle Temple. Already an able and ambitious attorney, Seme had dreams of starting a Pan-African organization in England comprising Africans from around the world. His March letter welcoming Locke to Oxford while he was still at Harvard may have been part of his plan to enlist the Black Rhodes Scholar in his Pan-African vision. Apparently, after arriving in London, Locke contacted Seme and, in turn, the South African arranged for Locke to meet one of the most important thinkers of African descent in England, Dr. Theophilis Scholes, whom Locke described as "a negro author of some repute here[.]" Locke met Seme and Scholes on October 6, attended service at St. Paul's Cathedral with them, and then "dined with Dr. Scholes at his house."[8] Locke enjoyed being the star attraction.

Locke may have dawdled in London that first week because he had not yet resolved where he would reside at Oxford. His last letter to Francis Wylie had threatened to refuse residence in Hertford and resubmit his application to Magdalen (or one of the other renowned colleges on his original list). That would have been disastrous for Wylie, as mass confusion might have resulted if Locke had gained admission to another college, and other Rhodes Scholars had demanded to be moved out of that college. It was imperative for Wylie, therefore, to persuade Locke to accept Hertford. Shortly after Locke's October 2 visit to Oxford, Wylie invited Locke to lunch at the Rhodes Trust office in London with Dr. George Parkin. The three men discussed things "very frankly," Locke recalled later to his mother, and they persuaded him to accept the place offered at Hertford. He admitted that it was a smaller college...but a very good one[.] Magdalen[,] the college I wanted to get into[,] is very expensive and if you are not of the English nobility you get very poor accommodations—besides it is down by the river and is very damp and unhealthy—Still it is a most beautiful place—a perfect dream and I should ever so much like to be there—It was proposed that in 2 or 3 years I try the fellowship examinations and perhaps I then shall be able to go to my beloved Magdalen[.][9]

Of course, such untitled students had obtained perfectly acceptable rooms in Magdalen. But the college had selected students mainly from elite private schools such as Eton and Wykeham and had accepted very few Rhodes Scholars in the four years the Trust had operated. Wylie's advice, though self-serving, was sound: there was little chance an upstart Rhodes Scholar could muscle his way in at such a late date. And Locke did not put up much of a fight; having just arrived in England, he was enjoying himself immensely and did not want to antagonize his hosts. Indeed he impressed them with his common sense and reasonableness. Parkin, a man who had initially been skeptical about Locke's prospects, was mildly enthusiastic about Locke after their meeting: "Have just met the negro Rhodes scholar Locke of Pennsylvania the other day; He is not at all a bad little fellow himself: and I hope things will go all right. He is quite prepared for having difficulties, which he says he is already accustomed to, but he seems to be going to face them cheerfully." Parkin could not help noticing, "he has the grace and politeness of manner of a Frenchman or Italian."[10] Locke was already the Wendell-like dandy, a man who had cultivated a persona that perfectly matched the Italianate manner dominant at Oxford.

Once settled in, Locke was "tremendously pleased with Hertford." The small but intimate Hertford College stood opposite the famous Bodleian Library and Sheldonian Theatre on Cate Street. It was certainly more centrally located than Magdalen. Originally founded in 1740, Hertford College had closed for lack of funds in 1818, but reopened in 1874 through the benefaction of T. C. Baring, a noted banker. Although not one of the oldest of Oxford colleges, its recent completion of the North Quad, or New Buildings as Locke called them, gave Hertford the most modern accommodations in Oxford. As he wrote his mother, "I have elegant rooms in the New Buildings," including

a large sitter with lounge chair, morris chair, long sofa upon which 3 or 4 fellows stretch out every evening [—] it must be six or seven feet long on open grate—writing desk, sideboard, 2 window seats—hanging electric light chandelier—desk light—and for two pound $10 a term I have hired a stylish English weathered oak piano with weathered oak bench—The sideboard is for food and wines—let me tell you how we live—I have a man servant—a scout who is hired by the college—(we have to tip him though) who takes complete charge of five or six men—He comes in every morning at 7:30 makes the fire—runs the water in the bath and then wakes you up with Good morning sir what will you have for breakfast—you get up order breakfast—take a dip—dress—(and what dressing) in the morning you put on grey flannel trousers and I have a brown norfolk jacket with brown leather buttons flannel shirt (all of which had to be made to order) dress I say—put on cap and gown and go to chapel—or if you don't want to go to chapel—go to the lodge and report to the Dean—just think of it,—dressed by 8 o'clock in the morning—each college has its own chapel.[11]

What bothered him most during those first two weeks in England was that he did not receive any letters from his mother. Despite his precise instructions to address them care of the Lloyds Company in London, her letters had gone astray. Anxious to hear from her, he had walked every day since landing from his hotel in Bloomsbury to the Lloyd Company's offices on Cockspur Street to ask for letters; every time he had been disappointed. Even after he had moved up to Oxford, he heard nothing. "Saturday, the 12, I went down to London especially—went to the Cockspur street office—not a single piece of mail had been received. I then went to Wards Private Hotel[—]they had had no mail[.] I gave both of them forwarding orders when I left London." Giving in to his mounting panic, he cabled her—"Worried anything wrong. Can cable money, Roy Locke," with a request for an immediate answer, which she supplied. Reassured, he wrote on October 23, "You were surprised I guess at the cablegram, but I could do nothing else—I was never so worried up in my life. I told you, you know, to write right off—there must have been some hitch somewhere." Then, he confessed, "If I had waited till now and not heard anything, I should have sailed right off." It was worth the money, he declared, because "when we are so far away from each other I daresay it will have to be used. It cost me $7 or thereabouts, but you see I got an answer from you in a few hours." After encouraging her to cable if she needed to reach him instantly, he set up a code to use in cabling—her code name was "Stevenlock Camden," his "Hertlock Oxford"—to save money on the address in future cables. Perhaps to shift attention away from his needs, he inquired about her financial situation, because "I have been anxiously waiting your letters, for I do not know just how money matters stand."[12] But realistically, the two weeks between letters precluded him from providing the close supervision of her finances he had exercised from Harvard. More likely, Locke's panic stemmed from a deeper source: his stay at Oxford was the first time in his life that he was really separated from his mother and the stabilizing influence she had exerted in his emotional life. Locke had needed to hear from her and to feel her soothing presence, but she had not been there.

More than separation anxiety caused his burning need to hear from her: Locke had begun to experience some of the "difficulties" that Parkin had predicted for him. The best contemporary record of the racial problems Locke experienced upon his arrival at Oxford comes from a diary kept by Horace Kallen. An October 18 entry in Kallen's diary suggests that even before Locke had matriculated into the university there were discussions among the Americans about the southern Rhodes Scholars and Locke. "Tuesday night Louis Dyer [a former Harvard professor then a fellow of Balliol College at Oxford] called....Our conversation was about Harvard—Bliss Perry & Schofield & their jobs, the trubble [sic] about Locke & Meriman's damned impertinent interference; the objections of the southern Rhodes Scholars to him[.]"[13] The southern Rhodes Scholars who had tried initially to get Locke disqualified stepped up their objections to him in person. For the first time in his life, he was experiencing naked racism, directed at and focused on him.

So intense was the controversy that Kallen, in an October 22 letter, asked Barrett Wendell to lend some assistance in the struggle.

> Now I want to ask a favor of you. You will perhaps remember little Locke. The yellow boy who took Comp. Lit. I when you first gave it as English 42. He is here as a Rhodes Scholar; and some people have been in [sic] America officious and mean-spirited enough to draw "the color-line" for the benefit of Englishmen. The boy earned his scholarship in an open competition. He has said nothing to me himself. Others have deprecated his being there. But he is here, one of America's scholars, and a Harvard man. He finds himself suddenly shut out of things,— unhappy, and lonely and [he] doesn't know why.[14]

Interestingly, Kallen knew Locke was being shut out of things without discussing it with him. Kallen apparently heard the comments and noticed that Locke was absent from many of the gatherings for the Rhodes Scholars. In staking out his racial position in his letter to Wendell, who was not only anti-Black but also anti-Jewish, Kallen found it necessary to articulate the reservations of even a liberal to social contact with ordinary Negroes. "As you know, I have neither respect nor liking for his race—but individually they have to be taken, each on his own merits and value, and if ever a negro was worthy, this boy is." Kallen acknowledged that "I have remembered your warning [presumably, a warning not to get involved] and have been silent on the matter, but I listened with great anger and I have said all that I could concerning what was commendable in him, and now I want to get you to write a word to Dyer and others, if you can, to help right this wrong."

Unfortunately, there is no record of Locke's view of these early hostilities at Oxford. His letters to his mother in October do not mention any trouble. Even when he wrote her later about this period, he did not mention these problems, focusing instead on how popular he was at Oxford. According to Locke, he was showered with invitations to tea, to dinner, and to the theater from English undergraduates, colonial students, and prominent Oxford professors. Indeed, he had been invited out so much that he had had to spend almost all of his allowance for the Michaelmas term on clothes, in part because he had to have them specially made for his frame. Some days he was so swamped with invitations, he wrote his mother, that he had to change clothes four or five times a day, as he went from morning chapel to lectures to luncheon invitations to Greek lessons with his tutor, to boating exercises as coxswain, to tea with fellow Americans, and then formal dinners with Englishmen. He complained that the fellows seldom left him alone, dropping by at all hours to ask him out or to lie around on his sofa, so that he hardly had any time for reading or writing. In short, his letters to his mother seem to indicate that Oxford had so completely opened its bosom to him that he felt totally accepted socially.

Locke was fabulously entertained, but his popularity was engineered by those around him who rallied to his side in the face of the conflict. Locke may or may not have known of Kallen's correspondence, but if he did, he certainly did not relay it to his mother. As Sir Edgar Williams, the Oxford Rhodes Secretary after Wylie, recalled, Oxonians probably responded to Locke in part out of embarrassment over the "impertinence" and bad manners of the southern scholars. Wylie and his wife tried to help by contacting those they thought might befriend Locke. By the end of October, their solicitations bore fruit. "I believe you had a message through Mr. Wylie," Elinor Dicey wrote Locke, "that my husband Professor Dicey would be glad to make your acquaintance & that we are as a rule at home on Sunday afternoons from 4–5:30. Possibly Mr. Wylie only mentioned last Sunday—so write to say we shall hope to see you on the 27th." Locke went, of course. Dicey, who had taught at Harvard, was a friend of William James and a prominent constitutional law professor at All Souls College known for both his liberalism and his championship of Oxford's leadership role in the Empire. Locke wrote on his invitation: "Called the twenty seventh with Clarke— met Dicey[;] kept me talking of race problems in America. Very interesting old fellow."[15] Apparently, Locke became a regular at the Diceys' Sunday "at homes." Similarly, Louis Dyer invited Locke to Balliol College. Race was a factor in his initial reception in an unusual sense: Locke's social success was probably helped by the controversy that surrounded his presence at Oxford. Indeed, so popular did Locke become that Lady Wylie stated that Locke got "rather spoilt" while he was at Oxford. There seems to be some truth to that. As he continued in his December 1 letter:

> So many fellows have come to know me that I have to have a guest to lunch or lunch out almost every other day—I send you a lunch menu—I generally have cold game bread and butter and cheese and wine—these Englishmen drink every meal but breakfast—I have been as economical as I can but have used about $10 worth of wine already—I was wise and got some cheap but very good Italian wine Nebeollo Spumante and they think it is rare because they never tasted it before—Well we generally eat lunch undressed—don't be surprised at anything—everyone lunches in athletic togs—I am boating and lunch in white slippers—golfing stockings to my knees, short white flannel knee trousers and white sweater—my little brown knees <u>bare</u>—right after lunch I have to hurry down to the river where each college has a boat house or "barge" as they call it—Every afternoon except Sunday rain or shine I am out with my crew—trying to steer them in and out of the narrowest[,] twistiest [*sic*] little snake of a river you ever saw—I had my times at first—the coaches run or ride along the bank, the varsity coaches on horseback and coach the crew—but the coxswain in England is an auxillary coach[.] So first they taught me how to swim and then how to row[,] mind you[,] so that I could help teach the others—I am so light that I have a very good chance and someday your little duckling may be a star in English sporting world as Varsity coxswain...the other day we had our "Torpid fours" that means the fall races in four oared boats—and I had great luck—my boat won a very close race in the first heat—and through my enthusiastic yelling and steering won out in the second heat—so I just got my first athletic cup—a large silver pot—pint size with Hertford College Torpid fours, the college arms and the names of the crew engraved on it (including my own name) this gives me a good chance to coxswain the college eight oar next term—I was ever so glad as it gives me social position from the jump and gives the black eye to those people who said I did not qualify athletically for the Rhodes scholarship.[16]

According to Kallen's November 12 letter to Wendell, Locke's plan to win social position through athletics was working.

While Lady Wylie was certainly accurate, her characterization of Locke as "spoilt" was not quite fair, as it silenced the racial conflict that was his backdrop. The "attention" of others was actually a bulwark against prejudice and the isolation that would be his fate if he were not aggressively social. In one sense, he was merely continuing the plan he had begun at Harvard, whereby he sought social success as much as academic success. But it took on added urgency at Oxford, where socializing was more important and more pervasive than at Harvard, and where for Locke it was the key to survival in a hostile environment.

Locke was so preoccupied with social maneuverings that he had little time or energy for his academic work that first term at Oxford. Of course, he had come to Oxford with grand hopes.

> I shall be a gorgeous peacock when I get my last degree here [.Y]ou see I hope to be a Bachelor of Arts and a Bachelor of Letters BA and B. Litt. In three years[.] Then after 2 years (without any more study or residence) but not without certain money fees[,] the MA will be conferred on me—and then 2 years after that seven years from now in all the Doctors of Literature[—]one of the famous degrees[—]will be conferred if I have done scholarly and literary work in the interim[.] The D. Phil. robe] is a gown of crimson flannel (red flannel[,] just think of it[:] many a Georgia darky has it hasn't he[?]) with grey silk sleeves and trimmings and a red and grey silk hood. Oh what a gorgeous wrapper.[17]

The educational plan Locke revealed to his mother was actually a compromise: he had wanted to begin graduate work in *Literae Humaniores* immediately, but apparently was dissuaded by Wylie at their October 21 conference on his academic program.[18] Wylie was familiar with the desire of Rhodes Scholars from America to read for a graduate degree because almost all of the Americans had already received BAs from their American colleges, but by the middle of the term, Locke began to realize that even the work for a BA in *Literae Humaniores*, or "Greats" as it was commonly called, was going to be difficult. Their undergraduate educations in the United States had not prepared most American Rhodes Scholars for the kind of intensive study in the original Greek and Latin that was required to pass the honor exams in Greats. Although he had taken Greek and Latin as a student, Locke was not nearly as proficient in ancient languages as the average Oxford undergraduate; so, Locke had a tutor that first year. "One goes to lectures till twelve generally," he informed his mother, but "I have fewer lectures than most people because I have to go three mornings a week to a coach—a...clergyman with a wig who reads my latin and Greek with me—you see I must learn within a year to read Latin and Greek almost as English—and it keeps me stepping I tell you[.]"[19] It was particularly difficult to focus on his work with all of the socializing.

By the middle of November, Locke's letters had stopped coming. Having not heard from Locke for almost a month, his mother grew concerned. Her suspicions had been aroused by friends who told her of articles in the New York newspapers about his being the center of racial hostility from the southern Rhodes Scholars at Oxford. She cautioned him not to go out alone, because "friends here believe that the southerners may try something underhanded." In reality, the situation was worse than she knew. Early in November, these same southern Rhodes Scholars had succeeded in convincing the American Club not to invite Locke to the annual Thanksgiving Dinner.

Kallen rather matter-of-factly noted his invitation to the dinner in his November 12 letter to Wendell, "There is an American Club. It came to my notice in the shape of an announcement of a Thanksgiving Dinner to be held on November 28, to the tune of two dollars, odd, per head." The club's significance would grow in Kallen's eyes as news of Locke's exclusion got out, and the American community divided over the issue. An informal organization meant to provide Americans with a sense of community away from home, the American Club had its own rooms where Americans dropped in, but it was better known for its annual Thanksgiving meal. Although the dinner was not officially a Rhodes Scholar function, all of the other Americans were invited, most of whom were Rhodes Scholars. Apparently, the southerners threatened to boycott the dinner if Locke was invited, and in a flawed attempt to maintain American unity, the club had not invited him. But the decision to exclude Locke remained controversial and in the weeks before dinner, several meetings were held to debate the appropriateness of the club's decision. Locke's exclusion particularly angered Kallen, and even when he recalled the incident forty-eight years later it still burned in his memory.

> There were among the Rhodes scholars at Oxford gentlemen from Dixie who could not possibly associate with Negroes. They could not possibly attend the Thanksgiving dinner celebrated by Americans if a Negro was to be there. So although students from elsewhere in the United States outnumbered the gentlemen from Dixie, Locke was not invited, and one or two persons, authentically Americans, refused in consequence to attend. You might say it was a dinner of inauthentic Americans.[20]

In addition to Kallen, Professors Dyer and Dicey refused to attend the official dinner. Instead, Dicey invited Locke to the Thanksgiving Reception held in Balliol that Wednesday, November 27, while Dyer invited the young man to dine with his family on Thanksgiving. "It will give me & my two sons,—a bachelor trio for the moment as you know, great pleasure if you will dine here with us on Thanksgiving Day, Nov. 28th at 7:30 P.M. We must rejoice together for several things, among others for such brilliant November weather! May we expect you?" Of course, Locke accepted. The day's activities began with a sermon preached in Christ Church's chapel by Bishop Worthington of Nebraska, to which Locke was invited. When Thanksgiving Thursday arrived, Locke quietly attended the noonday sermon with Kallen and then accompanied his Jewish ally to a synagogue. Later that evening, Locke went to Dyer's house in Banbury Road. Yet the American Club incident was significant enough that the next day Bishop Worthington made a special visit to Locke's rooms to speak with the young man. "The Vicar of St. Phillips and St. James," Locke wrote his mother on December 1, "called on me the other afternoon much to the surprise and disgust of some I daresay with Bishop Worthington of Nebraska—who preached the Thanksgiving service for Americans in Christ Church Cathedral[.] Worthington is very much of a fool—but very pleasant."[21]

That last line gives us a feeling for the tone Locke adopted in presenting the incident to his mother and perhaps even to himself. After all, he was a seasoned Black Victorian who had successfully used his culture and civilization to circumvent problems in the past. In the same letter, he gives the impression that he was merely inconvenienced and that he had turned his exclusion from the official dinner to his social advantage.

> Mr. Dyer a retired Harvard professor has been very cordial—he is honorary fellow of Balliol[,] has married very rich[,] lives on fashionable Banbury Road—he is the acknowledged grandaddy of all Americans here—he has introduced me to some of the best of the professors, and when the American club didn't invite me to their Thanksgiving banquet—he and Professor Dicey, both honorary members of the club refused to attend and Dyer, his cousin from Balliol[,] and I ate Thanksgiving dinner together at Dyer's home. I am anxious to hear how you got over Thanksgiving.[22]

Of course, her holiday had been difficult too, because he had not been there on a day they almost always spent together. Yet it seems he wanted to deflect attention away from his Thanksgiving and racial problems at Oxford. Locke downplayed the incident in his letters to avoid alarming his mother.

Indeed, it was difficult for Locke to admit that he was wounded by racism for the first time in his life.

> I never was better or happier—never had better chances....Do let me hear about the American papers—there is nothing over here—several of the Rhodes men have asked to be introduced to me—the Southerners are silent—and my patrons Dyer and Dicey are two of the biggest men in Oxford. I visit 5 houses in Banbury Road which is like Rittenhouse Square. Send me the clippings but its all American newspaper talk—I have forgotten almost I was colored.[23]

Certainly, his not encountering Blacks on campus as at Harvard meant Locke was freed from having to define himself in terms of the Black group. Yet it is hard to believe that the incident did not hurt. Locke had never really experienced any blatant racial prejudice and certainly not the overt racial exclusion of the Thanksgiving incident. Never before in his twelve years at predominantly White Philadelphia schools or at Harvard had he been excluded from an official school event because of race. He had come to Oxford believing that he had finally escaped the racial problem, and that if he did encounter any little obstacle, his manners, sophistication, and culture would overcome it. The victory of the southerners opened the door to the possibility of other such violations of his dignity and humanity at Oxford. The Thanksgiving incident was just the first of many skirmishes and power struggles between him and them for the rest of his stay.

It is interesting that Locke chose Kallen—or perhaps Kallen invited himself—to accompany him on this holiday. Perhaps he chose Kallen because he was Jewish, or because he was older and a friendly acquaintance from his class with Santayana. But Locke may have chosen the tall, sandy-haired, militant Zionist as a masculine ally. On a day when he would certainly be observed, Locke chose the political and heterosexual Kallen over sexually ambiguous aesthetic Downes as his escort. Kallen's personality was certainly a factor as well. Kallen was already known as someone who was a fighter, who, like the big brother he never had, would take the pressure off of him. Locke repeated the strategy he had used as a young child when bullies accosted him on the way to school, and a "big boy" defended him.[24] Thousands of miles from home, no matter how good an act he put on for his mother, Locke must have again felt vulnerable, and Kallen came to his aid.

Of course, Kallen was not a completely neutral participant. He was conflicted about Locke and Blacks in general. Not only his statements about Blacks in his letters to Wendell but also Kallen's private diary confirmed he was ambivalent about Blacks. In one instance, Kallen observed that Harley, Locke's West Indian friend also at Oxford, had "more of the objectionable Negro ways than Locke." This is ironic given that Harvard professors like Wendell routinely commented and evaluated Jews with similar sensitivity to Jewish "ways." Locke, for his part, characterized Kallen's upward mobility in stereotypical terms when he identified Kallen to his mother as a "Ghetto Jew I met at Harvard who is making a social sensation." Yet at Oxford, Locke held onto Kallen's coat-tails and Kallen, for his part, felt sympathetic toward Locke's predicament. Coming to Locke's aid may have also reflected Kallen's own struggle with identity while in England. Jews in England were able to pass very easily, but Kallen saw that as a problem of Jewish identity and solidarity. In one diary entry, he confirmed that he had the darndest time telling who was Jewish, and a veritable little dance of curiosity and gesture would go on between him and someone he suspected was Jewish until one would ask delicately if the other was Jewish. But no matter how socially sophisticated Locke was, he could not pass—and thus he became a perfect case study for Kallen to reflect on the primacy of racial self-definition in the biography of Jewish—and with Locke in mind, minority—intellectuals.

Kallen recalled that when the two of them discussed the meaning of the Thanksgiving incident afterward, Locke was angry and confused and asserted that he was a human being like other human beings. Kallen concluded:

> Now the impact of that kind of experience left scars, the more so in a philosophic spirit. For the dominant trend among philosophers is always to prove unity and to work at unifications—to assert *one* humanity, *one* universe, *one* system of values and ideals which somehow is coercive of the many and somehow argues away the actualities of penalization for one's being oneself into unimportant appearances, without in any way relieving the feelings of dehumanization, the pain and the suffering; and without lessening the desire never again to expose oneself to them.[25]

Kallen credited these discussions with clarifying the true meaning of cultural pluralism. "We had to argue out the question of how the differences made differences, and in arguing out those questions, the formulae, then phrases, developed—'cultural pluralism,' 'the right to be different.'"[26]

A life crisis had erupted for Locke: his social expectations, personal negotiations, and philosophical speculations on the terrain of race were suddenly and simultaneously under assault. He had crossed over educationally, intellectually, and socially into an elite English world, but remained categorized as Black by the Americans. The reaction of Americans crystallized Locke's feelings of alienation from his homeland. As Kallen recalled:

> There were times that year when Locke thought never to return to the United States. In fact, he deeply wanted not to. He was at ease in Europe. The penalties for "color," especially in France and on the Continent, were not apparent. They were not as apparent in England as they are today. But however or wherever the penalties were laid, Locke felt he could not expose himself to their indignities. As a human being with an individuality of his own, he knew that no commitment or obligation could be laid on him heavier than anybody else's, and that the necessities of vindicating his integrity and realizing his own potentialities in his own way had the first claim and the last.[27]

Of course, on a day-to-day basis, race was not a paramount issue, because the majority of the English, especially the young undergraduates, lacked the race feeling the southerners exhibited. Yet his claim that he had "forgotten" he "was colored" is unbelievable. Locke was, after all, the focal point of several meetings and discussions among the Americans that centered on his Blackness, and the decision to exclude him from the dinner had divided the American community and forced people to take sides. Certainly, his presence had raised the issue of race in a way that neither he nor the Oxford community had had to face before.

Even after this incident, numerous other uncomfortable encounters with the southerners must have taken place on his daily travels through the narrow walkways around Oxford. He did seem to take his mother's advice and generally traveled in the company of one of his friends, if not Downes then Kallen. On one of those trips, Kallen recalled in his diary that the hostility toward Locke did not come solely from Americans. After Locke visited Kallen's rooms, Kallen recalled, "I went back with him in a great rain. A big fat person opened his gate & looked him up and down with infinite scorn."[28] Given that Kallen generally noted Americans when they entered the scene in his diary, the "big fat person" was probably English. Even Kallen's racial consciousness was exacerbated in the Oxford environment. In his diary, he recorded that "Thursday night Locke & Harley called... Locke is at Hertford College. He seems darker than at home."[29] In the overwhelmingly White and Anglo-Saxon environment of Edwardian England, even this "nut-brown man," as the historian Nathan Huggins once described Locke, stood out for Kallen in stark contrast to the overall population. If Locke had forgotten he was Colored, he was the only person in Oxford who had.

Locke's homosexuality, however, may have cushioned the racial conflicts. Being gay gave him access on a private level to the world of some English and White American undergraduates who he may very well have viewed as compensating for the public exclusion he endured. That may explain why he remained optimistic about "his chances" at Oxford. He had a trump card in the game of sociability at Oxford that the southerners could not easily match. In a letter to an anonymous friend, Locke wrote from Oxford: "Let me tell you about the men. I have met some of the best specimens among the English that I have met since School of Practice [Central High] days." Even more than Harvard, Oxford possessed a rich, diverse, and thriving homosexual community that controlled Oxford social life. In such circumstances, Locke's sexual opportunities were greater as a gay Black man than they would have been as a straight Black man. That fact leavened and assuaged the racial stress of the Oxford experience. It may have also keyed his extreme popularity at Oxford. "I sometimes have three or four invitations a day to answer or send out[.]"[30]

Some of the more attractive men were not even English. At Oxford, Locke noted to his mother, he was meeting wealthy and attractive East Indian men, who were the epitome of sophistication in their manners and tastes. He met most of them through the Oxford Cosmopolitan Club, which invited him to its fall dinner. At that dinner, which he attended with Downes, Locke met Lionel de Fonseka, the Ceylonese literary intellectual, who was studying at Merton and would become one of his best friends. He also met Satya Mukerjea, a wealthy Brahmin from the Bengali region in India. The Oxford Cosmopolitan Club, begun in early 1907, had been formed to "promote mutual knowledge and sympathy between members of the different nationalities at Oxford," a kind of international club for members to read papers and argue how best to promote cosmopolitanism. But for Locke, the group seemed to serve a dual purpose of bringing him into closer collegial connection with men who, like him, shared an interest if not indulgence in homosexuality; further, it brought him into contact with other intellectuals of color who were working out the conflicts between personal assimilation and loyalty to their ethnic or national identities. At Oxford, the club would become the most important center for Locke's working out of his future destiny in regard to his people and his country. For now it provided him with a welcome escape from the social world of priggish Americans and scornful Englishmen.

Even Locke was beginning to acknowledge why he was such a popular invitation that first term. He admitted to his mother that there was "a good deal of curiosity about your ugly duckling...teas have been given as excuses for meeting the 'chinese ? puzzle.'" That seemed to be the case when Satya Mukerjea invited him for tea. "Remember you are to come like an obedient child to my rooms for tea. Otherwise the ladies will be disappointed." Locke did not disappoint them, but afterward noted to his mother that they "are very nice but rather masculine women—in fact they are public women interested in the Woman Suffragist movement."[31] That meeting was symptomatic: although he had invitations to meet people as the "chinese puzzle," many of them came from people who were themselves on the fringes of English society. The majority of the other invitations came from Americans or from Englishmen with American wives, or from the Scots, as in the case of the Cairds, the former master of Balliol and his wife, who frequently asked him to their home. During his second term, he would begin to reveal to his mother it was with the Americans and the Scottish with whom he was most congenial, rather than those from Oxford's elite English stock. Such social activities were crucial to his sense of acceptance, but they did not add up to him feeling very good, overall, about his Oxford educational experience or powerful enough to apply himself in earnest to his studies at Oxford by the end of the Michaelmas term, 1907.

Ever since those days at the Charles Close Elementary in Philadelphia, he had struggled with being productive away from his mother. Separation anxiety often descended on him whenever he was too far away from his mother to easily refer to her unconditional love. All of his greatest achievements had been like some adult child practicing phase in which he had ventured out on his own into uncharted space, yet not too far that he could not refer to her emotionally for reinforcement. Certainly, that had been true at Harvard where almost daily letters were supplemented by quick visits back home. There was an ideal space, distance really, from her, between him and her that allowed his naturally propulsive self to roam aggressively, yet not too far to remind him that he was alone.

Now, as 1907 came to a catastrophic close for him, he felt very lonely. No one but Locke knew how lonely he felt. Despite his protestations to his mother that he was thoroughly enjoying himself at Oxford, he informed her in his December letter that he would be spending his vacation away from Oxford traveling with Downes. They would spend the first of the six weeks' vacation on the Scilly Islands on the Atlantic coast of England before going on to France. "We are going there because living is very cheap there in winter and both of us have a lot of studying and writing to do—I have had no time to think of a short story much less write one. Here['] s my chance—we shall stay there 3 weeks then sail by way of the Island of Jersey for the French coast landing at Dieppe and going to Paris via Rouen[,] a Norman town with beautiful cathedrals we want to see and write about[.]"[32] He was anxious to flee Oxford for the kind of love affair he had had in London. Traveling in Europe would be a yelling escape from those dastardly southern Rhodes Scholars who made every walk alone through Oxford's narrow streets an anxiety-filled journey.

But leaving with Downes was also the point. Here was the great experiment of his adult life. Ever since his first sexual experience, the remarkable thing was that he could be that close to someone other than his mother. Now, the second part of that story began—could being close to another male assuage the loneliness, that existential bereft feeling, he now felt more than five thousand miles away from Momma, facing the most vicious racism he had encountered in his life? Could Downes and the pursuit of beauty on the Continent heal his soul enough that he could return to Oxford and get down to work? Something led him instinctively to believe that this was his best chance to save his life.

But before he left Oxford, he was able to write "with much trouble and countless interruptions" his "impressions of Oxford." In December he sent it off to the *Independent*, which had asked him to write something for them. The resultant article, "Oxford Contrasts," appeared in print much later, in July 1909, but is a revealing interpretation of his first term's experience at Oxford. He was quick to praise Oxford for the modernity of its social life and by implication its lack of racial discrimination. But he criticized Oxford for its "medieval educational" system and its disrespect for Rhodes Scholars. Indeed, "Oxford Contrasts" remains one of the best defenses of the Rhodes Scholars against the Oxford critique that they were not up to the quality of English students academically or socially.

Locke's article is all the more remarkable given that the Americans were the bane of his existence at Oxford. In an ironic but important way, Locke responded to being discriminated against by other Americans by claiming his right to speak for them. The experience of living in England for the first time in his life heightened his American identity. He may have felt—and he may have been right—that he was excluded as much because he was an American as because he was Black. The editor of the *Independent* wished him to deal with the race question, but he had refused, except at the end. There, in an addendum comparing American and English approaches to race, he noted that the English were much more subtle than the Americans; and yet, he preferred the directness of the American to the circumspection and "indifference" of the English.

What did that mean? "Oxford Contrasts" was the beginning of the comparative study of racial attitudes Locke continued throughout his adult life. Americans believed in rigid social exclusion and separation of Black people, but the English perfected imperial racism by which the best and the brightest of the colonial subjects were plucked from their native lands, brought to England, indoctrinated with the imperial ideal, and sent back to their countries to carry out British colonial policies. Since A. V. Dicey was a prominent supporter of the notion that Oxford should be an integral agent in supplying the administrators of the British Empire, he had welcomed Locke as the type of "colonial" that he (and Parkin, another architect of the imperial role of Oxford) felt the empire needed to carry out its imperial mission. Through his growing association with colonial students in the Oxford Cosmopolitan Club, Locke was beginning to understand how imperialism produced an even more insidious form of racial practice than the brutality of the Americans. He was beginning the second phase of his race education and learning imperialism was as much the practice of race as segregation.

That Locke really preferred the naked hostility of the southern Rhodes Scholars to the more sophisticated indulgence of the English students at Oxford seems unlikely. But writing that he preferred the American version of racism was an act of cultural resistance—claiming the right to represent America regardless of those, from Wendell to the southern Rhodes Scholars, who denied him that right. Racist Americans would not deny him the right to affirm America abroad. As Locke wrote his mother, he did not want "anything Negroid to spoil his first appearance in print."[33] Southern racists would not paint him into a corner where he could appear in print only as a Negro and not as an American. At Oxford, dealing with the Americans made him Black, but dealing with the English made him American.

While "Oxford Contrasts" represented a breakthrough, his not wanting "anything Negroid to spoil his first appearance in print" shows Locke had not yet resolved the conflict the Thanksgiving incident had uncovered. He wanted to keep hidden the truth of what he had experienced that fall of 1907, that his sojourn to Oxford already had been "spoiled." He was not simply an American not taken seriously by the English, but an American denied his right to give thanks for America by other Americans. In the end, "Oxford Contrasts" masked the most important contrast of all. At Harvard, Locke had been a favorite son. At Oxford, he was a pariah.

Oxford Cosmopolitan dinner, ca. 1909. Courtesy of the Moorland-Spingarn Research Center, Howard University.

8

Black Cosmopolitan

It probably came as a surprise to Mary Locke that her son was taking such an extensive trip at the end of his first term. The previous month she had written and asked for money and he had written back that he was broke. Mary had been strapped for funds since his leaving, since fewer students were coming to the after-school tutoring and music lessons she relied on for extra money. With some justice, she might have felt that given his full scholarship, he could help her out financially and reimburse her for the money she had sent him the previous summer when he could not find work in Cambridge. But Locke's mind was made up about his vacation: he had sent his mother £18 in October and was not about to sacrifice his vacation with Downes to send her more. And he justified the vacation trip by arguing it was cheaper to live outside of Oxford. In fact, it was: he and Downes were able to board for a pound a week each while living at the Bay View Inn on Jersey. But economizing was not the major motivation. Away from Oxford, he would avoid the southerners and would be able to spend time alone with Downes, his closest friend at Oxford and probably his lover by this time. Perhaps if the affair blossomed on the trip, his creative abilities might flourish, and, in the shadow of "the beautiful cathedrals that we want to see," he might become a short-story writer and escape an academic career altogether.

True to Locke's word, he left for London on December 7, where he and Downes stayed again at the Ward Hotel, seeing the sights for five days, until they "crossed the English channel—and such a crossing—a terrible gale—decks awash all the way over—I was not seasick only sick of the sea." After landing safely, they spent the next three weeks on Jersey, "a beautiful island—cliffs and sun and sea...flowers are blooming here—imagine it," as he wrote to his mother along with best wishes for a happy Christmas.[1] Locke did not write his mother again until January 3, perhaps a result of Downes's impatience with Locke's letter writing. That impatience may signal that Downes saw loosening the umbilical cord with Mary as a condition of their greater intimacy. Locke also may have refrained from writing because there were few interesting sightseeing details to relay to his mother while he was sequestered with Downes on Jersey.

Yet even at this distance Locke remained unconsciously connected with his mother as an incident he relayed to her on January 3, 1908, attests. "I thought of you on New Years Eve—and strange I woke up at 5 a.m., the exact midnight with you [Camden time]—and thought of you—rolled over in a mechanical way and said our New Year's prayers—stopped my watch—for it was too dark to see the time—and when I awoke next morning found the watch stopped at exactly 5." After waking up early that morning, he and Downes had gone "for a 12 mile tramp over the Northwestern corner of the island." They located the romantic Castle Grosnez, but Locke found it "decidedly disappointing." It was the walk he enjoyed, "one of the best I ever took—we went right cross country—past the beautiful old Medieval manor house of St. Owens," set against the backdrop of the spectacular surf in the bay. They returned to their hotel in time to gobble down a sumptuous New Year's dinner "which started the gastronomic orgy" that eventually gave him indigestion. New Year's evening they packed and, after "a gorgeous lunch" at a French restaurant in the capital city of St. Helier, sailed to the coast of France. The heavy lunch combined with another rough crossing aggravated his stomach distress. Although it was not enough to make him sea-sick (which Locke boasted he never was), he and Downes remained on the deck during the crossing. They were rewarded with a spectacular sky that "was beauti-fully blue and spotted with large white sailing clouds—and the sea! It was beau-tiful—the Breton sea is noted for its emerald green-color and with the gulls and the sunlit green and the white crests of choppy waves to set off the contrast—it was as beautiful a marine picture as I have ever seen."[2]

His first trip to the Continent brought out the romantic in Locke and culti-vated a different side of his personality. Traveling with his friend Downes opened up his senses to the landscape, castles, flora, and foreign peoples before him. Freed from the constraints of Oxford and race conflict, Locke became intoxi-cated with the rhythm of traveling and sightseeing, and an uninterrupted love affair with Downes. For the first time in his life, he could be really free in expressing his sexuality, away from the probing glances of acquaintances. That experience ushered in a new consciousness of sexual and artistic freedom that became the touchstone of his lifelong love affair with Europe. Finally, he was enjoying a measure of openness that put him at ease. And face-to-face with the art and culture of Europe, he was at home. He would continually return to Europe to renew that connection and openness to nature and others that occurred on his first trip abroad.

Locke's mood seemed to sink once they were on the move again. After a rough crossing of the channel, he was angered by the treatment he received from French customs officials. "The French inspector asked me questions as if he thought I was a smuggler and I surly answered non, non and wished I was able to curse him in French—he poked around my trunk and disarranged my things and then passed me."[3] Was this racial? He could not tell and grumbled all the way to their stopping place, the Hotel de l'Universiti in St. Malo. Just off the coast of France in its famous fortress-island city, Locke also had trouble settling his stomach. A "heavy French supper" sent Locke out into the streets looking for pepsin tablets, which he found, "big as a nickel." After swallowing "one with great difficulty," he went to bed and was much improved the next day. His mood improved too when Downes and he toured the town of St. Malo:

> [It is] a very quaint typically French garrison town and we spent most of the afternoon walking around the ramparts—the town is surrounded by a sturdy medieval wall about twelve or fifteen feet thick overlooking the bay. We did go to the Cathedral church of Saint Vincent—but it is a miserable specimen—the nave is rather old, but they have spoiled it with barbarous additions—among them a spire that must pierce the heavens like a barbed lancet. We walked over to Saint Serran [to the southwest], where there is a Roman basilica style of church[—] much better—we struck it about sunset with the sun streaming like molten gold through some very fine stained glass windows—and some quaint old Breton women (fisherman's wives I daresay) were praying at the fisherman's altar. It was a very pretty night.[4]

Here was a nearly perfect aesthetic scene for a young man on his Grand Tour of France—a medieval church, a Roman town, and picturesque peasant women kneeling in prayer.

Locke and Downes left St. Malo on January 4 for Dol, another "quaint medieval town with a good Gothic cathedral," and then hurried on to Dinan, the prettiest of Brittany's medieval towns. There they hunted down its cathedral and "fine chateau," worked their way east, visited Mont St. Michel and Coutances, and another "fine Gothic cathedral," and then prepared to go on to Cherbourg before returning to England.[5] Although Paris was their stated destination, no mention of it appears in his few surviving letters. Interestingly, as they began their return to England, the volume of his letters to Mary Locke increased. He wrote just before crossing the channel that he hoped to get "a bigger boat and better weather" for their return trip, for he had decided that traveling on the small boat had caused him "too much nervous tension and strain."[6] On the return, however, he experienced considerable rocking and became seriously seasick. One wonders if it was the crossing or the prospect of returning to Oxford that really sickened him.

The month-long trip had been a success, not only because of what it did to achieve with Downes a level of intimacy that may have rivaled what he shared with his mother. Mary Locke seemed to sense that Downes was becoming a competitor for her son's attentions when she wrote to Locke after his return, "Oxford must be the most formal of places and I am glad you could escape and live your own life for a time—I am greatly indebted to Downes—but I may have cause to regret his kindness, should he develop you into a first class artist—and—I have to undergo the penalty of seeing my handsome (3) walls decorated with your sketches."[7] She could see that Downes was influencing her son toward aestheticism and the life of drift and artistry that came with it. As any mature woman of her time knew, that was a dangerous direction for a young man. Not only was it irresponsible and potentially immoral but also it was not very practical as a career for a Black intellectual. Mary Locke could be enthusiastic about the Rhodes Scholarship because of the honor that came with this "holiday" from responsible work; but she was also concerned that her son would become so intoxicated with European aestheticism that he would lose all professional aspiration. Her worries were not groundless. As Locke later remarked about his Rhodes Scholarship years in his second Harvard Class report, "instead of transferring my allegiance from scholarships to scholarship itself, as would have been best, I temporarily abandoned formal education for the pursuit of culture—yet fortunately, without money enough to collect blue china."[8]

But just as significant, the trip had not turned him into a creative writer. Undertaken ostensibly to get some short stories written, none survived the trip and no mention of any completed works appeared in his correspondence. A paradox had emerged that would continue in his mature years: he had difficulty translating the sexual and intellectual freedom he experienced in Europe into creative works of art. Europe opened his mind, but seldom his muse. While Europe seemed to be an essential stimulus, it made Locke content and less interested in work. Whether he knew it or not, Locke needed conflict to be productive; freed in Europe from the kind of race and academic obligations he resented, he simply enjoyed life. Just as important, intimacy with Downes had not translated into the completed short story or novel he had hoped to write while abroad.

Locke returned to Oxford around January 9 and wrote his mother that he planned to remain there before term began and catch up on his reading. He planned to stay at Merton with Downes, but Locke seemed too restless to remain the entire time in Oxford. A letter from Kallen brought an opportunity to escape again: "Dear Locke and Downes, or Downes and Locke etc," Kallen wrote from London. "Have just returned from Croydon and go to London to live in Toynbee Hall, 28 Commonweal St. until the end of vacation."[9] By January 17 Locke was writing his mother on Toynbee Hall stationery that he was back in London, having just spent the night there with Kallen. A letter fragment, also on Toynbee Hall stationery, supplies a clue why he had returned: "Dear Mr. Whitehouse: A sudden panic—about going up to Oxford." Mr. Whitehouse has disappeared into history, but the letter's mention of Locke's "panic" about returning to Oxford signifies he had not completely gotten over the Thanksgiving dinner incident and related conflicts of Oxford the previous term. Plus, he felt more comfortable in London and its more diverse and interesting mix of English culture than in Oxford. A modernist movement in the arts was emerging in

London, and Locke met one of its contributors, Jewish modern artist Louis Kronberg, and visited his studio with Downes during this brief stay in London.

On January 18, when Locke returned to Oxford, he was rewarded this time with a letter from his friend Dap Pfromm that announced that Locke had been elected to Phi Beta Kappa. He wrote his mother exuberantly about his pleasure in receiving the award: "it puts the stamp on me that even Oxford cannot ignore." Locke confided to his mother that "the one disappointment of Dr. Brandt's career was that he had not gotten the Phi Beta Kappa key."[10] Now, Locke had it or would have it as soon as he could raise the money to purchase it. Since he had not yet found his academic niche at Oxford, it was pleasing to have yet another confirmation from Harvard that he was special. It certainly reinforced his status among the other Harvard men with whom he continued to socialize at Oxford. Dap also told him that people at Harvard were still eager for news about him from Oxford. But Locke was not eager to create any. "They needn't expect anything startling from over here for quite a while. I do feel and have felt ever since I've been here that I need a little restful retirement—I would give anything to stay out of the public eye for a year or so for I want to yawn badly. Oxford is a jolly asylum—things that go on in the world are like the far-off rumblings of a volcano or the unrestrained wind—colic of the vulgar."[11]

Locke vacillated between his sense of Oxford as a comfortable "asylum" and a cold and insensitive place. When thrown together with other Americans, most of whom he knew from Harvard, his conversation often centered on the comparative advantages of the American and Oxford systems. Invited to tea with Haring on February 13 (along with Downes), Locke recalled afterward, "I asked of Harvard and Oxford contrasts—and as usual Oxford made a very effective background." Six days later he accepted an invitation to visit the Cairds of Balliol College and jotted on the back of that invitation, "Yesterday I went to lunch with the Cairds[;] they have been very nice . . . they are Scotch and have all the Scotch heartiness and very little of the Oxford superficiality and insincerity[.]"[12] By the middle of his second term, Locke was becoming a bit cynical about Oxford, perhaps because he was beginning to realize that much of the attention of the first term had been "superficial" interest in him. Prominent people continued to send him invitations; one of the most important that term came from the niece of Alfred Lord Tennyson, who, upon the suggestion of Mrs. Caird, invited Locke to come to tea at her home on Iffley Road. Locke visited her on January 26 and enjoyed himself, as would be expected of one who had devoted so much time and energy to a study of Tennyson in his Bowdoin Prize essay. Yet what could be the long-range benefits of such isolated contacts? In fact, he had gotten the invitation only because Tennyson's niece was a close friend of Mrs. Caird, already part of his luncheon circle. Locke's circle of contacts among the British was not expanding. In fact, by the end of the first year, Dicey, Dyer, and Caird would all be dead, and Locke would not be able to replace them with men of equal importance and sensitivity.

Freshmen commoners at Oxford were generally limited in their social opportunities, because they were on the bottom of Oxford's social hierarchy. They generally socialized with other members of their class in their college. Locke had greater access to clubs at Oxford because his BA from Harvard placed him in a higher class than the typical fresher. Nevertheless, most first-year students centered their social lives in their colleges, and Locke remained something of an outsider in his, because he was older and a Rhodes Scholar. His best opportunity to establish himself in the college came when he was selected to "cox the Togger eight" of his college. The college crew wanted him "because I am so light," as he notified his mother. But Locke could not swim, and furthermore, he wrote:

> [I] could not get ready, with the short notice they gave me, to pass the swimming test. I worked frightfully hard—every morning I went down to the Merton baths and was dangled on the end of a pole and belt, like a scared fish—the swimming master is awfully good. I undressed in the Turkish bath rooms and he took great care I should not get a chill—but I did several times. I really hate the water and am afraid of it—though I can swim a few strokes now and am still taking lessons.[13]

But he had to withdraw after three weeks: not only could he not swim but also he was exhausted by the physical exertion required to prepare for crew, even as a coxswain. "I was breaking under the strain—swimming in the morning—coxing in the afternoon—why I was living either in or on the water or worse had water on the brain so to speak all day long." An Oxford doctor's examination confirmed the state of his health: "poorly developed heart and valves, from long-standing heart problems," concluded Dr. Collier. "How this man got selected a Rhodes Scholar surpasses me."[14]

That he wanted to participate in crew is certain, because, as he noted to his mother, he would have been "entitled to wear my boating uniform and the college arms (white flannels with red braid binding and the college arms embroidered on the breast pocket)." Although Locke tried out again for coxing the following term, his health prevented serious participation. The avenue of athletics, through which many Rhodes Scholars found acceptance in their colleges, was closed to him. Such failures may explain, in part, why Locke remained so critical of college athletics throughout his life. At Oxford his failure at his college athletics confirmed that he was an outsider. Not surprisingly, at the end of his third term, Locke applied for and was granted permission to seek lodgings in town. If he didn't fit in, it was best to get away from his college and create a place of his own for himself and his friends.

Locke had an energetic circle of English, American, and colonial friends and he generally was content to let common interests dictate those whom he selected as friends. An accomplished classical pianist from his years at Central High, Locke rented a white baby grand piano that brought him into contact with a most lovable Englishman (a sort of contradiction in terms) but really a thoroughly cultivated classmate named Garratt, whom I hope you'll meet some day, [who] comes in now and then and plays with me. He plays the clarinet—rather well. Its an instrument I can't tolerate unless played well, but sometimes he pipes like Pan himself and I am learning to play in tune by playing accompaniments.[15]

He was even making a few friends among the Rhodes Scholars. Samuel Ely Eliot, the son of a Swedenborgian clergyman and a third-year scholar from Oregon, was also a resident of Hertford and went out of his way to befriend Locke. Eliot regularly invited Locke to lunch and by the second term was a regular member of the Downes-Kallen-Locke contingent. But Eliot was the exception: by and large, the Rhodes Scholar community was not Locke's. He felt comfortable only with a select few—handsome, aesthetic, and homosexual young men. While his homosexuality gave him more access to English males than he would have had otherwise, it did not translate into access to the Eton or Harrow underground of homosexuals at Oxford during his second term.

As the invitations fell off in his second term, the challenge was for him to find friends who could sustain him socially and intellectually through the next two and a half years at Oxford. Of course, his American friends, especially Kallen, continued to provide him access to a broader intellectual circle. During Lent term, Kallen, for example, took Locke to meet Bertrand Russell, whom Kallen had met through William James. Kallen consulted with Russell about epistemology and pragmatism, subjects Kallen was writing about in his dissertation, and he found the Cambridge philosopher an engaging and interesting critic of James's pragmatism. Kallen also seems to have introduced Locke to F. C. S. Schiller, Oxford's resident pragmatist. Among the Americans, Locke found support for his criticisms of Oxford and for his sense of himself as an American. He also began to look for ways in which a new conception of American culture might bring greater recognition of the African American contribution. Locke wrote his mother that he had become interested in the music of MacDowell (who had just died, his mother informed him) because Kallen had introduced him to it. In addition to MacDowell, the "Wa Wau people—the society of young American composers" were beginning to interest Locke as they were "trying to found an American school of music on Indian and Negro melodies. I am going to get in close touch with their work," he wrote his mother. "You know MacDowell and Dvorak were pioneers in the movement."[16] Either in their company or at their suggestion, Locke's American friends encouraged him to find examples of cultural pluralism. And Americans were his most constant companions on a daily basis: every Sunday, for example, Downes and Locke attended the Balliol College Musical Society program and often visited Kallen's rooms before or afterward. On February 9, for example, Kallen had Locke and Downes over for coffee, along with two of his out-of-town guests, one a minister from the United States.

Crucial for Locke during this second Hilary term was to make inroads into another community to sustain him. This he began to find at the Oxford Cosmopolitan Club. The papers often given there were either idealistic proposals for a "World Literature," as delivered by Queen's professor H. G. Fiedler in Locke's second term or self-interested celebrations of emerging national literatures, as delivered by the Norwegian D. B. Burchardt and the Indian Satya Mukerjea that summer term. Burchardt, for example, heralded the "new movement" in Norwegian literature of younger writers who rejected the "problem literature" of Ibsen and instead portrayed the lives and culture of Norwegian people in naturalistic novels and poetry. Mukerjea's paper claimed that Bankim was a representative artist of a Bengali cultural renaissance with far-reaching effects on Indian and "world literature." These papers confirmed Locke's belief that art was a source of national pride and racial renewal, and also, perhaps, that he could blend racial feeling with a personal commitment to a "cosmopolitan" lifestyle through aesthetics. The club seemed to take to him as well. At its March 10, 1908, meeting he was pleasantly surprised to be elected to its executive board.

The most significant friend Locke met through the Cosmopolitan Club that Hilary term was Percy J. Philip, then club secretary. In a March letter to his mother, Locke confided:

> I see I have begun a letter on this sheet to Philip—the Scotchman. Have I told you of him? I will—I met him through the Cosmopolitan Club. He is one of the best finds yet. He is a graduate of Edinburgh University who is helping Dr. Murray edit the New Oxford dictionary. I told you about going to see the workshop didn't I? Well, Philip is a charming fellow—with lots of experience. He has tramped about, lived a regular Bohemian life for several years though he is the youngest son of a Covenanter Scotch family, the very best type of democratic aristocrat. He is just a bit younger than me though I mistook him for much older. Downes, he, and I go out walking almost every Sunday—he is a capital fellow for tramping—a disciple of Thoreau.[17]

Some of that "bohemianism" surfaced in a paper Philip read before the club that praised Thoreau for "advocating absolute independence from tradition and from convention in the choice of his career by every individual." Philip had put Thoreau's experiment into practice, according to Locke, for "he has spent days and nights in the open air—I think I shall go camping with him sometime— I should feel safe with him—a strange pair we should make though—he is a giant of a sandy-haired Scotchman." Philip and Locke would become even closer in the next term when Philip would enlist Locke to take over the editing of the first issue of the club's new magazine.

Locke's friendship with Isaka Seme, another member of the Oxford Cosmopolitan Club, also intensified during the spring of 1908. Indeed, by March the Zulu from Swaziland had replaced Harley as Locke's favorite Black friend at Oxford. As Locke confided to his mother, unlike Harley, Seme was refined and cultured, a thoroughly Anglicized South African. As photographs of Seme from this period show, he was as fond of formal dress as Locke; but he had something Locke lacked—a royal attitude that commanded respect and almost homage, even from Whites. Kallen conveyed something of this playfully in a letter when he asked Locke how "His Majesty Seme" was doing. Although Seme played the role for all it was worth, it was not entirely an act: Seme could convince others that he was royalty, because he had already convinced himself.

Already a graduate of Columbia University, where he had received an AB in 1906, Seme was older than most other students at Oxford and well respected by the members of the Cosmopolitan Club, who elected him treasurer. But Seme had his eye on a higher goal: he planned to start his own African fellowship society, which would present papers to its members, like the Cosmopolitan Club, but whose real purpose would be to bring together persons of African descent in England to work for the redemption of the African continent. A card in Locke's scrapbooks noted that Locke and Seme "breakfasted" on March 3 and "talked of Tuskegee (Board of Trustees idea)." Seme was already corresponding with Booker T. Washington and had visited Tuskegee, which his cousin attended. Like many other Black South African intellectuals, Seme admired Washington for what he had accomplished at Tuskegee and may have seen it as a model for what he wished to achieve in South Africa. Seme may have hoped that Locke could assist him in gaining Washington's support for the African Society; at the very least, Locke's participation in the venture would show that the organization embraced distinguished African Americans. As Seme wrote to Washington on April 15, the African society was to be formed in England because "here are to be found the future leaders of African nations temporarily thrown together and yet coming from widely different sections of that great and unhappy continent[;] and...these men will, in due season, return each to a community that eagerly awaits him and perhaps influence its public opinion."[18] Seme wanted Washington to endorse the African Union Society, but Washington demurred and wrote back urging that any such organization avoid militancy or violence. Perhaps Washington detected something of the young man's fiery temperament even at this early stage or that the organization was potentially an African version of the Niagara Movement, the militant Black protest organization founded in 1905 by W. E. B. Du Bois and Monroe Trotter. Seme would continue to try to win Washington's support until a meeting in person finally convinced him that it was pointless. Actually, Seme's movement was closer to the ideology of the Niagara Movement, which also sought to bring together the "future leaders" of the race in a society.

Though Locke disliked militancy and race organizations, he was drawn to Seme and may have been sexually attracted to him, which may have made it easier for Locke to become involved in Seme's organizational planning. As a cultured Black Edwardian, Seme confirmed Locke's belief that one did not have to sacrifice personal standards to embark on a career as a Black leader; Seme saw himself as an eventual leader of his people. In addition, through Seme, Locke became aware of the imperialist underpinnings of his sojourn in England and gained a clearer understanding of why he seemed not to fit in in England. Perhaps with Seme, more than anyone else, Locke began to connect the two sides of the Black Victorian legacy in his own experience—a sumptuous comfort and decorous lifestyle on the one hand, and the exploitation of peoples of color around the world on the other. While both were seduced by Edwardian dress, decorum, and decadence, their association reminded each of how personally connected they were to the imperialism they abhorred. More than anyone except Kallen, Seme reminded Locke that he could become a leader of his people and a power to reckon with once he returned home.

During the second week of March, however, Locke was more focused on his vacation plans to return to France with Downes. This time, before departing, Locke held a typical end-of-term dinner with his friends at Buolo, a favorite restaurant of English undergraduates at Oxford. It became an American celebration when Lionel de Fonseka, whom Locke met through the Cosmopolitan Club, was unable to attend because he had already left Oxford. Indeed, the Ceylonese student might have felt out of place among the rakish Americans on March 14.

> Saturday night Kallen[,] the Jew Harvard instructor in philosophy who is making such an impression here—Eliot[,] the Rhodes man whom I have told you of—Downes and myself had a splurge dinner at Buolo—we were late getting off—I had been over to Harley's to tea, and it takes me so long to dress—besides I had to hurry over to Merton to try and put Downes in good humor—he always gets miff[ed] when he has to put on a dress suit—I met him on his way over—with his back collar button undone as usual—well we got off[,] had a good dinner—were considerably boozed and startled ourselves and our neighbors by boarding a tram car, going up top and singing American college songs all the way down the High and over to East Oxford when we went to the East Oxford theatre and amused ourselves by throwing break lump sugar and cheese done up in empty match boxes at the stage...we had a great time—and danced our way back to sober Oxford and serenaded the balcony windows of All Souls and Hertford.[19]

Locke could feel good about the term for a number of reasons, especially about his progress in easing the situation with the other Rhodes Scholars.

> Needless to say I was late getting up Sunday morning—Downes came over and we went out to tea to Kallen—met some more Rhodes men—they are very nice and cordial, those whom I have met—I have made up my mind to make them come to me—several have asked to meet me—two came round to call a week or so before term end—fortunately I was having Downes and De Fonseka and Garratt to coffee—and I sat them down to coffee and biscuits, port wine and fruit cake as if it were a nightly affair.[20]

Yet as he made plans to leave on vacation, he could not help acknowledging that the term had not been very productive intellectually. He had a hard time explaining, to his mother and perhaps to himself, just why this was so. "I have been very lazy mentally—the slack of Oxford is very hard to shake off—the effect is purely physical—but it cripples you mentally—the Summer term will be much better—but the weather of the winter term is shocking—fog rain and mist all the week long—not a flake of snow—but not a speck of sunshine. I could not have stood 2 weeks more of it." Instead, he escaped to London with Downes the day after writing his mother. Kallen, by contrast, stayed behind to finish his doctoral thesis, and de Fonseka planned to rendezvous with them later in Paris.

Before leaving for the Continent, Downes and Locke renewed old acquaintances in London, especially with their painter friend Kronberg. He invited them over for tea one afternoon and promised to meet them in Paris, where he would "show us the life of the Latin Quarter." After time with Kronberg, Locke and Downes continued their investigation of London sights and culture.

> We went to the Empire—a rather trashy Variety Theatre in London—a great resort of the demi-monde on the sea...we were terribly bored with the performance—we went up into the Promenade—all those theatres have promenades where the men and the women parade up and down during the performance. We were enjoying ourselves immensely, laughing at the women, their gay flashy clothes and crude wiles—when we saw a young girl so obviously different from the rest that we immediately decided she must be respectable—yet couldn't account for her being there. We went up to her—asked her what she was doing there and asked her to come out to supper—and stumbled on this very interesting story. It was quite worth while—either one of us or both of us will put her into a novel yet and told her so. It seems she is the daughter of a Danish nobleman who ran away from home with her tutor at 17—she is not only 18—has of course been deserted and was on the edge—the very edge of the London whirlpool when we chanced along—She is obviously true because we persuaded her to write back home to her parents—wrote a note ourselves and posted the letter ourselves. What do you think of that for an adventure—it fell

right into our hands—fake or no fake ... it was an interesting story and that's what we are looking for—strange stories—strange people[—] strange impressions....We haven't heard anymore about her and are just as glad of it—to get an inside look at everything without doing ourselves or anyone else any harm that is our problem and our object—a rather cynical attitude is an invariable consequent—but you cannot write without experience and cynicism—self esteem and even a self-centered interest in life are a cheap price to pay for experience.[21]

Like many other young writers of their generation, Locke and Downes shared the idea that experience, especially of the sordid, was essential to modern writing, but one wonders what Mary Locke thought of his "adventure." Did she approve of her son's slumming? Was he in England to pick up destitute young women in trashy theaters? Again, it must have raised her concern about Downes's influence on her son. The episode reveals that another side of Locke's personality was given free rein in Europe: his attraction to the seamy side of life that stood in sharp contrast to the Victorian pose of the Black Philadelphian. Perhaps such escapades were a needed counterweight to his more rigid, principled, and overly mature side, but it must have seemed to Mary that Locke was concerned with everything but his studies. That was true.

Locke stumbled into a more political adventure when Downes and he visited Toynbee Hall the next evening.

We heard a most excellent debate on socialism and nearly got ourselves into another rich experience. The man Watts, who was to open the debate, hadn't turned up when we arrived and Harvey, the warden, was quite at a loss what to do—400 working men and boys were already assembled in the Hall. I went into the lavatory to hang up my hat and coat when the door suddenly opened. Harvey had an inspiration: "Locke, won't you help us out—the speaker hasn't come—talk to them—about anything in the social line—the race question if you like—they would be interested." I was in the throes of indecision rather inclining toward not doing it for I [had earlier] heard them rag Kallen who is really a capable speaker—I was in the throes when Mr. Whats his name arrived—I did promise to come down and talk to them sometime later but with that short notice, Good Lord deliver me! We staid [sic] for tea (pm o'clock tea) bid Harvey and our good friends goodbye and hurried home to pack for Paris.[22]

One wonders what Locke would have said. As in his Harvard days, Locke seemed too timid to grasp the political spotlight when it was offered him. But the fact that he was at Toynbee Hall, this time without Kallen, suggests that he did feel some connection to the radical intellectual community associated with the settlement house.

Locke and Downes arrived in Paris during the first week of April, settled into a hotel on the Boulevard de Courcelles, and began sightseeing. Kronberg also knew Henry Ossawa Tanner, the renowned African American expatriate artist from Philadelphia who lived in Paris. It is quite possible that Kronberg wrote Tanner after Locke's visit and introduced the Black Rhodes Scholar to Tanner, for shortly after Locke arrived in Paris, he received an invitation from Tanner to come to tea. Locke received the news with aplomb. "I shall go," he wrote his mother, "and after will have him out to dinner with Kronberg and Downes."[23] Locke did spend the afternoon of April 9 with Tanner. A rumor survives that Locke asked Tanner to return to the United States and lead a Black artistic movement. Tanner refused, the story goes, but this seems more likely to have occurred, if at all, later. At this point Locke seemed on the verge of a Tanner-like expatriation. Even in the literary arena, he was more interested in gathering stories of the urban life of London and Paris than of any other Black American community.

Locke was also visually stimulated by this trip to Paris, more so by its artistic avant-garde than by Tanner's work in 1908.

> We are in Paris at just the right time—the famous Art Salon will open in a few days—the exhibition of Independent artists[,] the crazy freaks and rebelling geniuses[,] who cannot get into the Salon past the academic criticism of the Hanging Committee[,] have a vast exhibition— the strangest freakiest mixture of good and bad painting one has ever seen—we have been twice to it.... You can imagine what a collection... they hang everything—many of the things they should hang the artist himself as a more fitting tribute to art—but it's excruciatingly funny.[24]

By contrast, there was no mention in his letters to his mother of trips to the more conventional art repositories such as the Louvre or any discussion of paintings hanging in Tanner's studio.

A week later Locke was on his way back to Oxford after another rough crossing of the channel. Such a passage made him at least thankful to reach Oxford this time, where he could admit to his mother that "I have had a vacation year of it— the change—the delightful leisure," which he deserved, he believed, "after last year's hard work that told on me more than I suspected." He planned to get down to work during the summer term when the weather was warm and sunny and finally invigorating. Here Locke was not simply making excuses; many other Americans found the Oxford weather debilitating, though he seemed, for someone of his frail health, to have enormous resources of energy while vacationing. "After I am thoroughly tired out I go on a long bit on my nerves—I found that out in Paris—Downes would be absolutely done out—I would be as fresh as ever—till I got home: then I would keel over and sometimes he would have to help me off with my undershirt— (you remember I could never get them off anyway)."[25] Once again Locke seemed to be admitting that Downes was performing what had commonly been Mary's role in his life. But what Downes could not supply was the stabilizing sense of direction to get down to work that Mary had given him. Evidently, when Locke indulged the pleasure-seeking side of his personality without restraint, he ran ragged until he could not take adequate care of himself.

Not only did Locke still need his mother's stabilizing influence, she needed him as well. During the preparation for his vacation, Mary Locke had peppered him with letters asking his approval to move their home at 417 Stevens Street in Camden, New Jersey, to Clapham's at 517 on the same street. The former, Yeocum's house, had been their home for almost ten years, but it had a leaking roof, among other chronic problems in need of repair. Now that her son was not living with her, there was really no need for her to rent a house. Her bills were piling up, and she had had to buy and cook her own food. At Clapham's she could get prepared meals for $16 a week. She could also sell her furniture, since Clapham's second-floor rooms were furnished; she could even sublet one of them to Mr. Bush until her son returned from England—if he ever did. He, of course, had agreed with her decision and confessed that he felt a bit guilty that she had had to move their household by herself, while he had been "roaming Parisian picture galleries and going to Paris Operas."[26] Locke knew that his mother needed to be around other people, and she would have that at Clapham's. Moreover, her salary barely paid her expenses, and with his vacationing, entertaining, and socializing lifestyle, he barely had enough left over to send her. So, she had "gathered up the deserted household goods," as he put it, and moved down the street, an ordeal he admitted he could "hardly understand how she" managed. While he was at Harvard, he had micromanaged her every decision about the household, down to which chairs should be reupholstered and with what color fabric. He was much less concerned about such issues at this distance. He advised her to "keep cheery and do the best under the circumstances."[27]

Locke's Paris vacation also made him miss an important meeting held by his friend Isaka Seme. Apparently, Seme had tired of waiting for Locke to return from Paris and hosted a meeting on April 10 at the York House in London for all those interested in his plan to establish an African society. The meeting had apparently been well attended, and those present had voiced their support for the venture. Seme planned to hold another meeting at which the organization would be formally launched and asked Locke if he would be willing to serve as honorary secretary and assist Seme in arranging the next meeting. Seme wanted to do an extensive mailing to ensure all interested Africans in England would attend.

Locke jumped at the opportunity and may have co-drafted the invitation that Seme sent out. "We and all the friends of Africa must be filled with joy at the successful initial result of our movement. It seems to me that we have now sufficiently digested the matter, and that therefore we must meet and apply our seal to the organization" the letter claimed. The date set was Friday, May 15, at 8 P.M. What was not yet clear was where the meeting was going to be held, and Locke may have been asked by Seme to locate a suitable meeting place. Apparently, a delegation of Africans, perhaps from South Africa, was due to arrive in England, perhaps as early as June of that year, and Seme wanted them to "find us already organized and prepared to greet them." The "Vice-Chancellor of Oxford" had apparently chosen a "well-known native African Bishop to deliver a University sermon in his place" on the occasion of the delegation's visit to campus, and Seme wanted to be able to meet the delegation as the head of the African Union Society.[28] The assembled would not only decide the name of the organization and approve its constitution but also elect officers of the organization and hear Seme deliver a paper titled "The Fatherland."

While the text of that address has not been located, its title suggests that Seme had already moved beyond his earlier goal of uniting the Zulus in South Africa to a broader notion of Pan Africanism analogous to Kallen's Zionism— a call on all of African descent, regardless of their origins within the Diaspora, to look upon Africa as their homeland. Although clearly the organization was Seme's idea, that Locke signed the printed letter of invitation with his name first and then Seme's suggests Locke was committed to the effort.

When the constitution of the organization was printed, Locke's name appeared as honorary secretary of the organization and presumably the document's author. Clearly the launching of the African Union Society was a defining moment in Locke's career. For the first time in his life, he had publicly committed himself to working in a politically oriented Black organization. By identifying with the cause of African liberation, he seemed to have made the ideological step that Kallen had been urging him to take, to identify with his race as a source of political and intellectual strength. Yet it was Seme who had been able to move Locke beyond dialogue to activism and toward viewing Africa as his "Fatherland."

This step suggests something of the "double consciousness" of Locke's first year at Oxford. He was both a Europeanizing cosmopolitan and a burgeoning Black internationalist. Having spent the vacation enjoying the bohemianism and cosmopolitanism of European modernism, Locke had returned to Oxford in mid-April to begin formalizing an African identity for himself by launching an African Diaspora organization. "His Highness Seme" was the catalyst, because, unlike Downes, Seme showed that Locke's desire to live a cultivated lifestyle, to be a homosexual, to be an aesthete did not have to exclude a commitment to the redemption of Africa on a global scale. In a sense, Locke was still struggling to combine the aestheticism he enjoyed with his friend Downes with the political commitment he had begun to acknowledge with Seme and Kallen. The problem for these ethnic intellectuals abroad was that they had to find a way to make their immersion in high art and even higher living relevant to the worlds of those in their homelands whose life experience was meager if not mean by comparison. The African Union Society was a step in that direction, but still an association of elite Africans—educated Africans living in England or able to travel there easily, Afro-Cosmopolitans open to the idea of finding in their study of the Europeans the logic of African liberation.

Such a step reflected the racial fissure within the Cosmopolitan Club itself—and hence the need for an independent African club. As the Cosmopolitan Club papers generally suggested, the Europeans, and especially the English, were not truly cosmopolitan, but fiercely nationalistic and jingoistic in elevating England's interest above all others. The English were always cosmopolitan when it came to other people's countries, but not their own. What Seme proposed was for Africans to begin doing the same thing, to begin to rescue the "unhappy Fatherland," as he put it, from the kind of underdevelopment that European cosmopolitanism had brought to it. Apparently, Seme was not alone in this opinion: on May 18, H. El Alaily, an Egyptian student at Wadham, and Mukerjea, Locke's Indian friend, held a meeting to discuss forming an Oriental Club at Oxford to address the same issues in relation to the Indian and Muslim world. What made Locke's predicament perhaps more difficult was that the road he sought to carve out was as yet relatively uncharted—that of using art to activate an anti-imperialist African Diaspora renaissance centered in America. Of his friends at Oxford that summer term, perhaps only Mukerjea could provide Locke with a model of what that might look like.

Locke also began to face the problem of his academic drift at Oxford that Trinity term. He was not making sufficient progress in his Greek tutoring to be able to pursue the intensive reading of ancient texts required for his Greats BA, let alone a BLitt in the subject. His real problem was he had difficulty learning the language; but several other factors conspired to increase his difficulties. As one of his comments in "Oxford Contrasts" suggested, Locke did not think much of his tutor's pedagogical ability: "The ability to parse Greek sentences is thought to imply the ability to teach the parsing of Greek sentences."[29] Race could have added an additional complication; Mary Church Terrell recalled that when Matthew Arnold visited her class at Oberlin, he was surprised to hear her pronounce Greek because, as he remarked, he thought that Blacks were physically incapable of Greek pronunciation. The fact that an intellectual liberal like Arnold believed this suggests that it may have been widely accepted by Oxford dons during Locke's tenure. Why should his tutor expend any extraordinary effort in teaching Locke something that was believed to be impossible anyway? Such factors do not explain why Locke had difficulty, but do suggest why his environment likely would not provide him more resources to overcome it.

This was also Locke's first experience of academic difficulty. Learning always had come easily to him; but now, it was difficult, and he had no other comparable experience of overcoming great difficulty in his educational past. His lack of success raised the issue of his competence in a particularly embarrassing context: the southerners had already raised the issue of whether he deserved to be at Oxford, albeit without any reference to his academic ability. His difficulty with Greek could add fuel to the still-smoldering controversy over whether he "belonged" at Oxford at all. Moreover, the longer Locke remained at Oxford, the less he was interested in Greek and ancient history. Given his personal situation as a Black intellectual, what good was successful parsing of Greek sentences? He had already reached the pinnacle of education for a Black man; success at Greek was not going to win him a post as a classicist at one of the better American universities; and it also was unlikely to win even a temporary appointment at Oxford, even if he earned a Greats BA. Why should he marshal the Herculean effort to master something that would make him only more of an anomaly? His intellectual interests lay in literary and artistic modernism of the type that he had seen in London and in Paris, and in the counter-nationalism of the Cosmopolitan Club and African Union Society, where his Egyptian, Indian, and South African friends were his real intellectual tutors.

Locke's personal copy of the *Oxford University Gazette* for Trinity term 1908 suggests the shift in his educational attention and priorities away from Greek literature and history, and toward the modern study of philosophy, aesthetics, religion, and anthropology. From the faculty of *Literae Humaniores,* Locke planned to attend such lectures as Introduction to Philosophy by Dr. F. C. S. Schiller; Philosophy of Religion by the liberal Platonist, J. A. Smith; and Anthropology: Early Stages of Art and Knowledge by Edward B. Tylor, one of the founders of modern anthropology. From the faculty of English and Modern Literature and Languages, he had checked The Philosophy of Poetry and Criticism from Oxford's only philosopher of aesthetics, E. F. Carritt, and a course in Schiller's *Naive und Sentimentalische Dichtung* from the Taylorian professor of German, H. G. Fieldler. Unmistakably, Locke was leaving Greek literature and culture behind.

Of the choices Locke listed, the most intriguing is Tylor's anthropology course. Although we have no way of knowing if he attended Tylor's lectures, his selection in the catalog suggests that Locke was beginning to think seriously about anthropology for the first time. Moreover, if Locke's first formal exposure to anthropology came at Tylor's feet in the lecture hall of the Ashmolean, that would explain in part the quasi-evolutionary character of Locke's mature conception of culture. Tylor believed that European civilization was the highest expression of culture, and that "primitive" cultures—whether created by savage or barbarous peoples—were always earlier forms of civilization. Listening to Tylor would have helped Locke break free of the humanist notion that culture was merely the best art and literature that had been produced toward the anthropological notion that culture was "that complex whole which includes knowledge, belief, art, morals, law, custom, and any other capabilities and habits acquired by man as a member of society," as Tylor had defined it in his 1871 magnum opus, *Primitive Culture*. But Tylor's lectures would have also sanctioned an evolutionary view of humanity, the Tylorian view of culture as "progressive human development" from savagery through barbarism to modern civilization.[30] Tylor's belief in a hierarchy of culture reinforced an unfortunate tendency already evident in Black Victorian culture—that assimilating European cultural values proved Black people could be civilized. Such a philosophy of cultivation informed Seme's project as well as that of the Indian students Locke met at the Cosmopolitan Club. To assimilate was to show that one's people would progress if granted opportunity, a belief that sanctioned the sartorial indulgence and almost comically civilized manner of colonials at Oxford. No better example can be found than a photograph of a Cosmopolitan Club dinner probably held in 1908: the often lauded variety of faces and skin color of those arrayed around the table is unified by formal dress of almost smirking Edwardian self-indulgence. They all assumed in their dress, deportment, and manners a hierarchy of values and were certain that they, as the elite of their races, personified the best of humankind.

But these overly sophisticated British colonials also educated Locke about the contradictions of the Victorian rule, that no matter how dressed up they were, they were still emissaries of inferior cultures according to the British. As Lord Macaulay famously put it, he had never found an expert on Oriental literatures "who could deny that a single shelf of a good European library was worth the whole native literature of India and Arabia."[31] But because of their successful assimilation of European culture, colonial members of the Oxford Cosmopolitan Club disagreed and used the club to advance a counterargument for a cultural renaissance emerging from Indian and Arabian traditions. At the first meeting of the Oxford Cosmopolitan Club for this term, held on May 5, Mukerjea read his paper on "The Bengali Novel: Bankim" that signaled the beginnings of an independent cultural renaissance in India. The old hierarchy in which European and English values and cultural products automatically stood at the top to be worshipped by all, including the colonials, was being called into question by that collection of intellectuals assembled around the table at Buolo's in Oxford. Of course, one would not know it from simply observing the social life of the group. To the end, Locke and Seme still indulged in the symbols of European cultivation, for by identifying with them, they conferred status and equality on their efforts. In criticism, it could be argued that Locke, Seme, and Mukerjea merely wanted a colonial culture that met European standards, and in their expectations lay a profound alienation from the actual indigenous culture of their peoples. But they believed that by meeting the standards of English society and culture, they removed the stigma of inferiority from themselves and their peoples, and subtly undermined the whole project of European cultural superiority.

Beneath the swirling sea of socializing and partying lay an awakening that the old value system was crumbling and the traditional Eurocentric hierarchy was a lie. Culture, despite Tylor, could decline and turn back toward less sophisticated impulses, and that was precisely what these young colonial intellectuals believed was occurring in English culture in the period of imperialism. Locke, therefore, was too skeptical to embrace Tylor's social Darwinism, but he may have seen that in Tylor's notion that culture passes through stages an opportunity to view African American culture as an authentic "complex whole" that would evolve and progress, especially under the tutelage and stewardship of men like Locke.

Locke's immediate problem was that study for *Literae Humaniores* was no longer a reasonable option for him by the end of Trinity term 1908 and studying formally anthropology was not an option at Oxford either. Locke probably would have been reluctant to do the latter, as he continued to favor literature and philosophy with increasing emphasis on philosophy. In Locke's day, however, the only way to study philosophy on the undergraduate level was in Greats. The possibility did exist that Locke could study philosophy as a graduate student if he could present a thesis subject and get it approved for an advanced bachelor of science degree in philosophy. Locke would have to transfer out of his undergraduate concentration and obtain university authorization to read for the graduate degree. Given that he already possessed a BA from Harvard, his admission to the graduate program depended merely on his finding tutors who would agree to direct his research. Here again, his friend Horace Kallen came to his aid.

In April, Locke appears to have discussed the issue with Kallen, who wrote him afterward that he'd "told Schiller of y'r proposed change. Now you'd better write him a note and ask for an appointment to talk things over." Schiller had been educated at Balliol College and had taught philosophy at Cornell University where he met and befriended William James. When Schiller became a tutor at Corpus Christi College in 1897, he was already a pragmatist who believed that the truth of an idea came down to its usefulness in human affairs. Schiller's pragmatism made him an outsider at an Oxford dominated by idealism. While loyal to James, in 1903 Schiller adopted the name of humanism for his brand of pragmatism to emphasize his main concern that philosophy should be relevant to the human condition as lived by ordinary persons. He was an excellent person for Locke to work with, for much of the Rhodes Scholar's academic alienation at Oxford came from the irrelevance of his course of study to his experience as an American.

Locke wrote to Schiller shortly after Kallen's note and received an appointment to tea with Schiller at Corpus Christi on May 18. The meeting was very significant for Locke, as his notes on the back of Schiller's invitation suggest: "the 18th—Found Dr. Schiller alone—very cordial—very American—welcomed my plans—spoke very frankly about Oxford inattention etc.—selected subject The Concept of Value in philosophy—Stewart Williams & Schiller—Thanked him most heartily and walked over with S to James lectures. This is a great day— when I met Schiller—the whole prospect of my work and life seemed different." Schiller met a number of Locke's needs: he was a role model, for though he "spoke frankly of Oxford's inattention"—he was also successful at Oxford, and that success suggested Locke could succeed in its inhospitable environment. What Locke desperately needed was someone who would take him on seriously as a budding intellectual, to demand hard work from him, but also to do so with sympathetic understanding of the psychic pressures he was under. In May 1908, Schiller seemed to be that man.

Locke's choice of subject is revealing. By focusing on the "Concept of Value," Locke avoided a direct engagement of the traditional disputes between the Idealists and the Pragmatists over the meaning of truth or the absolute, and instead charted new waters in the emerging discipline of value theory coming out of Germany. While the works of Meinong and Ehrenfels, the two principal Austrian philosophers of value, were being read at Oxford, they were not the subject of heated debate. Moreover, values as a subject also reflected Locke's emerging sense of being at the vortex of social change.

As Locke's "note" revealed, he left Schiller's to walk over and attend the third lecture of William James's Hibbert Lectures in Oxford, which may have had some long-lasting influence on his emerging philosophical orientation. After talking throughout the year with Kallen about the conflicting appeals of Absolute Idealism and Pragmatic Pluralism, it must have been a treat to hear James's third lecture, "Hegel and His Method." Locke was attracted to Absolute Idealism, which he had learned from Josiah Royce at Harvard, because it was part of a system of certainty, which Locke instinctively and temperamentally preferred. The Absolute was the Great Mother in whom all contradictions were taken up, all conflict resolved, all emotions soothed, and all peoples regarded as one. For nineteenth-century thinkers, the Absolute gave a sense of ultimate integration that certainly was not lost on Locke's Black self. Of course, Absolute Idealism could be exclusive and dominating, demanding a kind of subservience to a higher power that smacked of the force of God in organized religion. But Absolute Idealism also contained that revolutionary element of a grand dialectical system that could accommodate the contradictions that constituted Black life and serve, as it did when adapted by Marx to dialectical materialism, as an intellectual weapon of analysis against naive believers in one thesis or another.

Sitting in the front seats of the auditorium with Kallen, literally at the feet of the master of the pragmatic method, a method that tested ideas by examining their meaning in daily practice, Locke was pried a bit further from the bosom of Absolute Idealism by hearing James argue it was not so much the dialectical method as the Absolute that made Hegel and Hegelianism untenable. Indeed, by suggesting the convergence of the Hegelian dialectic with the changing world of pure experience, James confirmed Locke could still hold onto the dialectical method of reasoning while jettisoning the Absolute and its metaphysical baggage. From James, Locke learned the dialectic was not locked up in conceptual categories, as Hegel had claimed, but was immanent in our experience. That recognition began Locke's process of shifting from the transcendent categories of the good, the true, and the beautiful into the world of his own experience, which he could access through introspection. James's example in *Principles of Psychology* modeled for the introspective methodology Locke would use in his thesis.

Most important, James, along with Schiller, showed Locke that philosophy was relevant to his life. Like James, who had undergone a spiritual crisis in his early adulthood, Locke found that he needed a philosophical answer to the crisis he experienced at Oxford. Finding a sense of professional grounding in pragmatic philosophy and in studying value theory with Schiller did not solve all of Locke's problems, certainly: he was still a Black man in a racist world. But hearing James reminded Locke that he was part of a Harvard tradition that could support him as he developed a more radical philosophy of racial modernity than Absolute Idealism would ever allow.

Two events occurred just after James's May 18 lecture that reinforced the importance of that day's events for Locke. First, Locke learned that Kallen, who had completed his thesis, was returning home to Boston to be examined by his doctoral committee at Harvard. As a parting request, Kallen asked Locke to gather up as many of the Americans as he could locate for the degree-granting ceremony for James the following week. With Kallen gone, Locke would be on his own managing his social relationships with Americans still at Oxford. Kallen's departure also meant that Locke would be even more dependent on his new relationship with Schiller to sustain his development into a pragmatic philosopher of pluralism. Second, upon returning home that Monday evening, Locke found an invitation from Farid Nameh, Satya Mukerjea, and H. El Alaily to come to tea to discuss their plan of forming an Oriental Club at Oxford. This club would be a statement of Orientalism from the perspective of the colonized, not the colonizer, and also boldly assert the superiority of Oriental forms of art over those of the European. For Locke, this club symbolized the maturation of a pluralistic philosophy wedded to anti-imperialism and counter-renaissance—a different notion of the meaning of "radical empiricism" than James had had in mind during his lectures. It would be radical in that it would narrate the experience of the West from the perspective of the non-Western. It was easier for Locke to become militant about imperialism than about American racism, and similarly, it was through the eyes of the colonized that Locke could begin to see his way toward acceptance of the criticality inherent in the African American tradition. Imperialism gave him just enough of a vantage point on racism and cosmopolitanism to allow him to begin to formulate a "critical Black pluralism" to sustain him philosophically for the rest of his life.

Locke delivered his maiden critique of the imperialist conceit when he contributed an "Epilogue" to the first issue of *The Oxford Cosmopolitan*, published in June 1908. Apparently, the "Epilogue" was an excerpt from a paper "Cosmopolitanism," which he had delivered at the club's May 29 meeting. Locke did not plan to publish his paper in the first issue, perhaps because as editor, he did not wish to appear to be promoting his own work, and perhaps because, in his own judgment, the paper, while "clever and suggestive," was also "hard to follow." Yet, once edited down into a conclusion to the rather eclectic volume, "Epilogue" was an important pluralistic statement of cosmopolitanism that resembled James's popular essay, "On a Certain Blindness in Human Beings." Locke criticized the common-sense notion of cosmopolitanism, calling it the illusion that travel and exposure enables one to understand other people. As a doctrine, it was little more than a disciplinary exercise for idealistic youth. He wrote:

> There are certain honest people who think otherwise, but they seem to be misled by a false analogy much after the fashion of the man who travels to "enlarge his horizons." It is all a shifting of the attention and interest, a juggling with the centre of a pre-determined but movable circle, and most of us are convinced and some of us perplexed on find-ing that we carry our horizons with us and are unable to see through any other eyes than our own. It is the pathetic fallacy of the sympathetic temperament to think otherwise.[32]

As James had asserted, all human beings were afflicted with a "blindness" that prevented them from seeing the world from the other person's perspective.

On a philosophical level, Locke was arguing for humans' inability to transcend their own subjective perspectives and thus to attain a cosmopolitan or "abso-lute" perspective. What was needed, Locke argued, was not the illusion of perspicacity, but the acknowledgment and acceptance of one's own cultural tradition and its limitations. Only through such self-knowledge could the truly honest social observer begin to understand what separated him or her from other peoples and cultures.

> Cosmopolitan culture, then, if it is to be truly cultivating, is a sense of value contrasts and a heightened and rationalized self-centralization... [because] few Cosmopolitans have been able to escape the exchange-formula of the simple proposition: as x is to you, so is y to me. The beautiful law of this cosmopolitan equation is that each unknown is or ought to be well known on its side of the equation. The only possible solution is an enforced respect and interest for one's own tradition, and a more or less accurate appreciation of its contrast values with other traditions.[33]

After three terms at Oxford, Locke had become more skeptical of the ideal of cosmopolitanism. While "Oxford Contrasts" had positively portrayed the Rhodes Scholarship as fostering a "patriotic cosmopolitan," "Epilogue" can be read as a critique of cosmopolitanism as essentially a disguised imperialism. On one level, the British were cosmopolitan because they traveled and ruled the world. But such cosmopolitanism was little more than "carrying their horizons with them," a perspective he tellingly called "a moveable circle." The British retained their essential self-centeredness even if it was enlarged by worldliness. Their ethnocentrism and belief in the superiority of British traditions actually justified their ability to invade, take over, and assimilate another country's land and folkways. The operational definition of the cosmopolitan was the imperialist.

The colonized who wanted to become a real cosmopolitan was tempted to become as ethnocentric about the superiority of his or her own roots as the English. But that was not necessarily easy to do. Cosmopolitanism gave the colonized, like him, "the very rare opportunity to choose deliberately what I was born, but what the tyranny of circumstances prevents many of my folk from ever viewing as the privilege and opportunity of being an Afro-American."[34] The richest phrase here is the "tyranny of circumstances," the reality that the "Afro-American" was himself or herself caught in a web of economic, political, and discursive "circumstances" that taught him or her over and over again that he or she was inferior, taught him or her to run as fast as possible away from "what I was born." Locke had been doing just that his first year at Oxford chasing European gaze and avoiding his own. But his "Epilogue" suggested Locke now realized it was a hopeless chase. The cosmopolitanism where one lost oneself in a smorgasbord of other people's cultures led to a dead end. Without the self-confidence of being English, without the arrogant traditions of domination and exploitation to anchor one's subjectivity, Locke and the colonials could never really reproduce the European approach to cosmopolitanism, which was to survey civilization and call it their own. The material conditions of cosmopolitanism were utterly different for the colonized.

Interestingly, it was in the journal of the Cosmopolitan Club that Locke publicly testified to the tragedy of that first year for him as a Black subject abroad. Not in the *Independent* but only in a paper delivered to other, similarly sophisticated Brown Edwardians could he state how out of place they were, despite being Oxford dandies and aesthetes. Encountering what constituted English cosmopolitanism forced one back on "one's own tradition, and a more or less accurate appreciation of its contrast values with other traditions." What was that contrast? That he, as an "Afro-American," lacked the kind of arrogant, global, self-validating traditions the English took for granted. For that matter, Americans lacked them too in 1908, if his article for the *Independent* was to be believed.[35]

Coming to Oxford was not a waste, however, but an opportunity to forge something transformative out of their newly discovered pluralism. The transnationalism of his experience was returning him to the value of the local, to the indigenous, to a sense of community that was his new emotional home. A later metaphor Locke used to describe Harlem was appropriate here. Oxford had become a "crucible" of Black and Brown Cosmopolitans, because imperialism—including Rhodes's—had brought them together in that one place.[36] The Cosmopolitan Club was the manifestation of this new community, which emerged out of their transnationalism, their ability through education to leave home and find a new one in their shared predicament. Their and his dilemma would define the outlook of the organization going forward. Could Locke and his new friends be Brown and cosmopolitan and yet avoid being a fig leaf for imperialism and global arrogance? Could the Cosmopolitan Club outline a path to a new humanism based on the "value contrasts" made visible by imperialism? Perhaps. And perhaps Locke's work on value with Schiller could be the philosophical foundation of such a new humanism. If so, it would emerge in dialogue with the more radical and critical essays on British colonialism he would hear in the club. But to do that work, Locke would have to sit still.

That would be difficult. Kallen, his one trusted White interlocutor, was leaving Oxford. Another bosom friend was also leaving that summer. "Downes leaves for Italy in a week," Locke informed his mother in a letter written June 18, "to spend a few weeks with his uncle who is painting there—but returns to America by the middle of July—I shall miss him very greatly—he and I have been inseparable all this year[.]"[37] Downes was headed to California to spend a year teaching and taking care of his invalid sister before returning to Harvard in the fall of 1909.

Downes's impending departure was more significant than Kallen's. The love affair with Downes had been a bulwark against the emotional cruelties of Oxford. His impending departure exposed the crux of Locke's adult emotional life. He longed for someone who would love him unconditionally as his mother did. Downes was not that person, and even more, he was a sign of the intense loneliness of adult love for Locke—it was never unconditional and never absolute, for if it were, they would never leave him.

But Downes *was* leaving and as his departure approached, Locke began demanding his mother come over and spend the summer with him in Europe. In a May 27 letter, he reacted with horror when he learned that she had pneumonia: "Do write immediately how you are—I am so fearful of sickness—why on earth do you not take good care of yourself...if you knew how important it was for you to keep hearty and well and happy—you would—take all precautions." Panic erupted in him: he needed her more than ever now that his closest friends were leaving. Nothing, not even her illness, could be allowed to prevent her from spending the summer with him. After reading her many objections to coming— her lack of funds, her lack of proper clothes, her poor health—Locke countered, "the 20 days at sea—10 days coming and going will take your whole vacation and make a good trip for you.... You would need only one good dress—the crepe de chine for dinners and that sort of thing—You need more underwear than anything else."[38] Mary, however, was afraid to come: she had little money and did not believe that it was worth the expense. But he was unyielding: "I am talking facts[;] if you can get your round trip ticket American Line leaving Philadelphia for Liverpool 2nd class $80 or less and enough clothes to be comfortable I can with what money I actually have (for I have gotten my vacation allowance) can manage comfortable six or eight weeks in Europe for you."[39]

Locke's need for his mother to replace his departing lover reminds us of the comment by his friend Douglas Stafford that Locke regarded it remarkable, after his first sexual experience, that he was able to be so close to another human being other than his mother. Downes, it appears, had become that person, had taken the place of his mother, which suggests a sexual subtext in this mother-son relationship. Now that Downes was going, Locke was emotionally exposed and desperate for "Momma."

Finally, Mary relented, and on July 4 departed New York as a second cabin passenger on the RMS *Etruria*, in spite of her health and the counsel of friends. Such friends did not realize perhaps the strength of Mrs. Locke's desire to see her "one and only." For his part, Locke garnered enough money, principally from his Rhodes summer allowance, to take care of him and his mother for the summer. When she arrived in Liverpool on July 11, Locke whisked her away to an organ recital in St. George's Hall and then to the Bradford Hotel in Liverpool for the night. He would take her to the Royal Leamington Spa to enjoy its restorative waters and then to the local summer concerts. During her eight-week stay, the two of them took in several musical concerts, visited several spas, and enjoyed evenings in Oxford with Locke's friends, Harley, Seme, Mukerjea, and Philip, who frequently invited them for dinner. By the end of July, Locke had moved out of Hertford and into Dines's Board and Lodging House, where he and his mother rested up until the second week of August.

By then Mary Locke had recovered from her illness and was ready for the second phase of her European trip—a trip to the Continent. After a brief stop in London, where the two of them took in the galleries, Locke and his mother went on to Southampton, and then across the channel to France. The high point of the trip came on September 1, when the two of them sat in the Grand Concert Hall on the Boulevard de Strasbourg in Paris, listening to Beethoven's Third Symphony and sipping champagne. Certainly, the little boy and his Philadelphia mother had come a long way.

Shortly, however, the reality of his mother's impending departure set in. Still in Paris on September 3 with her ship, the *Lusitania*, scheduled to leave Liverpool at 6 P.M. on September 5, Locke and his mother dashed madly across France and then a choppy, tempestuous English Channel to get her to Liverpool in time. In fact, when Locke returned to Oxford, he was not sure she had made the sailing. He was relieved, of course, to get her telegram telling him she had made it, but the rush, the rough channel crossing, and the overall vacation, during which he had "overdone it a bit towards the end," left him "nervous in the extreme."[40] During her summer visit, he had nurtured his mother back to health and she had fed him emotionally. Her departure suddenly reminded him, like a child who had gotten too far away from his mother, that he was frightfully alone. The question he had to answer now was this: was the emotional refueling of the summer enough to enable him to get down to work?

Percy J. Philip and Locke on horses. Oxford, ca. 1909. Courtesy of the Moorland-Spingarn Research Center, Howard University.

9

Paying Second-Year Dues at Oxford, 1908–1909

The summer had done its trick. Locke began his second year at Oxford in good spirits. Mrs. Dine, the landlady of the boarding and lodging house at 40 Beaumont Street, stepped into the vacuum created by the departure of his mother and nursed him back to health with plenty of rest, hot lemonade, and gin. She was the first of many surrogate mothers he would rely on throughout his life. A week after Mary's departure on September 9, Locke was his old energetic self again, eager to start the new term. "I seem to be waking up from last year's hibernation," he announced to his mother, "shaking off the Oxford slough, and getting ready to work."[1]

For one thing, he had new rooms. After a month at Dine's, in futile pursuit of overly expensive accommodations on fashionable Banbury Road, Locke finally compromised on less-expensive furnished rooms down the street from Dine's at 14 Beaumont Street. He described it as "the large house at the corner diagonal from Dine's. They are finer rooms than her's," he boasted to his mother, "very old antique furniture and a large oil painting by D'Eychaert, a fine specimen of the genre Dutch.... The people, Mrs. Foster, of the house have been very well to do, fine Wedgewood china and that sort of thing."[2] Mary Locke did not remember the house, yet approved: "the street is such a pleasant one and so conveniently located. I know your penchant for antiques, so suppose the furniture will just suit you."[3] She was right about the street: the house stood next door to the Ashmolean Museum; across the street stood the regal Randolph Hotel, where the Rhodes Trust held its annual spring luncheon. Locke relished lavish accommodations, because "good locations have a lot to do with an entrée into social life, and then I think it more or less a duty for me to live representatively while here—few Rhodes men had such rooms."[4]

Locke wanted such lavish accommodations, because as secretary of the Cosmopolitan Club he was expected to host some club meetings in his rooms; thirty or forty people generally attended. Not long after he moved in, he began to plan the club activities with an eye on their rewards. "Seme and Phillip were into dinner night before last. We are arranging a delightful series of papers for the Cosmopolitan Club this term—I shall work hard for it—I am a candidate for the presidency of it term after next." The first meeting of the club did take place in his rooms on October 20, but was a burden to pull off. Locke had to schedule the speaker, Hamid El Alaily, send out the invitations, and secure a caterer—at his own expense. "If ever I undertake to slave for a dishful of international hash like this [again]," he complained to his mother, "may I have all the trouble I have had." But Locke clearly delighted in such entertaining. His rooms were a museum-like exhibition of the new ideas of the Cosmopolitan Club in high style. "The meeting in the room came off charmingly well. I had Buols to cater with coffee, biscuits, fruit, cigarets, and the like. They brought in a silver urn and all I had to do was draw off and hand a cup to each one as he came in. . . . There were nearly 40 present, and we weren't overcrowded—you can judge the size of my rooms."[5]

The formality of the occasion contrasted sharply with the radical political content of the paper El Alaily presented. Just back from France, this young Europhile and president of the Egyptian Society of England was in an angry mood. In his paper, "Modern Egypt," Alaily attacked British colonial rule in Egypt, especially the administration of Lord Cromer, Britain's Consul-General in Egypt from 1883 to 1907, and demanded that England grant Egypt its independence. He rebutted British justifications for denying Egyptian self-rule, especially the charge that Egypt's independence movement lacked the spirit of true nationalism, being led by religious fanatics. Egypt's nationalist movement was both secular and religious, Alaily argued, a virtual "renaissance of the whole Mohammedan world [which seemed] to be entering a new lease of progressive life. It is an Islamic renaissance, based on science and freedom of thought, that has elevated the most long suffering people in the world."[6] The new cosmopolitanism was beginning with criticality toward the discourse of English colonialism.

Locke may have been less interested in El Alaily's militant nationalism than with the way he used the concept of a "renaissance" to imagine liberation in his country. By October 1908, Locke had heard the anti-imperialist critique of colonialism from club members. But more interesting for him was how some like El Alaily located such values as free thought, secularization, and "renaissance" in the modern Egyptian tradition, obliterating the assumption that Europeans had a monopoly on such ways of thinking. Alaily echoed that of Moustafa Kamel Pasha, cited in Alaily's paper, who had asked a year earlier in Alexandria: "what greater honor can a man yearn for than to work for the renaissance of a nation which knew the sciences, civilization and literature before all other nations? What greater source of pride can there be for a man of noble instincts than the honor of contributing to the redemption of a nation which has been the master of the human race and the educator of the world? What greater glory can souls desire . . . than that of bringing forth the Egyptian people from darkness into light, and giving it the first place among those other countries which were sunk in black obscurity when our country was the fountain of all knowledge?"[7] By invoking ancient Egyptian civilization and appropriating nineteenth-century language to announce their people's exit from the "Dark Ages," Egyptian intellectuals labeled as their own those very values the English used to deny freedom and self-determination to the colonized around the world. In a maneuver not unlike that made famous sixty years later by Malcolm X, Egyptian intellectuals fired the pride of their people by asserting that Egyptians had built astounding civilizations during a time when, as Malcolm put it, the people of Europe "lived a cave-like existence."[8]

The drawback of El Alaily's intellectual strategy was that it reproduced some of the bias toward sub-Saharan Africans who did not have Egypt's imperial past. Alaily declared, for example, that Egypt "cannot be governed like a country buried in the depths of Africa and out of contact with Europe." Did El Alaily mean to imply that the right to self-determination depended on the degree to which a nation exemplified European cultural values? It seemed so. Intellectuals of color in the Oxford Cosmopolitan Club tended to value their indigenous cultures to the extent that they had anticipated or assimilated European signs of culture.

Locke, of course, also denigrated African Americans who had not achieved the level of civilization that Europeans (and Africans like El Alaily) thought was required for the right to self-determination. As Locke wrote his mother:

> Seme and I and a Gold Coast Negro by the name of Gibson who returned to Oxford to take both his M.A. and B.C.L. (think of that you Afro-Americans!) went to a wonderful performance of Coleridge Taylor's Hiawatha. I had never heard it before. It stunned me. I have heard a great deal of music, but the emotional appeal and the native idiom of Hiawatha I have never felt nor expected to feel. I shall not stop long in London next time, but I must look him up. Strange too he is African extraction. The African mind and temperament is not self-divided, nor self-despising. Thank God for it. I don't hear the call of the Liberian herd, but I'll visit every part of Africa the climate will allow me, and what's more I do believe it a greater field than America.[9]

Locke was infatuated with elite Africans as somehow more able than their brothers in America. His heart was touched by Samuel Coleridge-Taylor's ability to allow indigenous peoples to sing in European music. Locke was looking for sublime music, not the entirely original modern music of ragtime that African Americans had created around the turn of the century. Ragtime jarred Locke's nerves and destroyed his sensibility of what art music should be. Like El Alaily, Locke's definition of success in art was constructed in opposition to Blackness, which both wrote of as the absence of civilization. But it was going to be harder for Locke than for El Alaily to build imperial cultural power out of "Afro-American" creativity, because Locke had no ancient imperialist tradition like that of the Egyptians to contest European culture. Afro-American folk forms were revising European forms, as the spirituals revised and transformed Anglican hymns. Locke wanted a home culture more nationalist, but also more sublime than what the Europeans had.

Not everyone in the Cosmopolitan Club agreed nationalism was the path forward. Har Dayal, an Indian revolutionary and a former Oxford scholar with an impeccable academic record, challenged the Cosmopolitan Club in a paper he read in November, most likely in Locke's rooms. In "Obstacles to Cosmopolitanism," Har Dayal argued that "tribalism," Har Dayal's term for nationalism, and intellectual bigotry—the demand that others conform to our ideas of group politics or be rejected—kept humanity from embracing the central idea of cosmopolitanism that we should love one another regardless of our beliefs or affiliations. What made Har Dayal's critique powerful is that it came not from an aesthete British member of the club, but from a revolutionary. The love of nation could not be completely eradicated, though its influence could be limited, Har Dayal argued, by de-emphasizing national or racial identity and replacing nationalistic history with a world history. To oppose intellectual bigotry, Har Dayal called on his fellows to form a band of men "who should undertake the duty of preaching and living Cosmopolitanism" and travel around Europe to spread the message.[10]

It must have struck Locke as deeply ironic that Har Dayal, one of the most incendiary leaders of the Indian nationalist movement, was now back at Oxford extolling the virtues of universal tolerance. Fourteen months earlier, this brilliant Sanskrit scholar had resigned his Oxford scholarship and returned to India to organize active resistance to the British government, values, and civilization. Born in 1884 in Delhi, the son of a reader in the British court and a member of the *Kayastha*, or writer caste, Har Dayal had excelled in public schools, passed numerous examinations with no mistakes, and had become the darling of the Christian missionaries at Saint Stephen's College in India before he went to Oxford in 1905 on a full scholarship. Despite being very European in his dress, manner, and taste, he became an enthusiastic advocate of Indian nationalism— another example of the radicalizing effect Oxford had on intellectuals of color. After a brief stay in India, Har Dayal was forced by a British crackdown to flee India in the summer of 1908 and return to Oxford, where he showed up at the fall meetings of the Cosmopolitan Club. Not long after his speech before the club, he left for Paris, where he joined a group of Indian radicals; he eventually broke with them because they would not join him in advocating violent resistance to British colonial rule. Har Dayal's "Obstacles to Cosmopolitanism" was a dress rehearsal of ideas that would emerge even more strongly later. In 1910, Har Dayal, in the United States, would caution Indian radicals to loosen their grip on their own native culture and allow themselves to "breathe the fresh air of Western intellectual, as well as political, freedom."[11]

At the root of Har Dayal's many ideological shifts was the idea that the Indian, read colonized, had something to learn from the West just as the West had something to learn from the colonized. He borrowed the term "renaissance" to symbolize the intellectual awakening he wanted to come from his people, where they would gain a sense of their history, culture, and destiny, and yet remain open to the positive influences of European civilization. Here was a much more sophisticated notion of revolution as well as self-culture—and a thoroughly pluralist one—than Kallen had advocated. In this quest for "self-culture," Har Dayal's Christian heritage was often more powerful than any Indian tradition. Har Dayal hoped he would find a way to meld the best of both the ascetic Indian and the rationalist Christian traditions, but unfortunately, balancing the two to his satisfaction was elusive. Consequently, he lurched back and forth between responding with ascetic transcendence to the West and responding with a violent, murderous rage.

Although Locke respected Har Dayal from a distance, they were not intimate friends; but Har Dayal may have introduced Locke to the Marxist colonial critique of imperialism and something more—the view that a truly revolutionary view of the future had to go beyond the political attack on European domination. Cosmopolitan criticality had to warn adherents that in responding in kind to rabid European nationalism, the colonized must not lose their soul to gain self-determination. Har Dayal was trying to develop a politics that reflected the sublime, transcendent spiritual existence of non-Western peoples. Indians, Egyptians, and African Americans had lessons to give to humanity beyond their rage against exploitation. A Cosmopolitan Club worth its name had to keep open the very possibility, seemingly foreclosed in Locke's "Epilogue," to transcend one's traditions and become something larger. Har Dayal's paper resonated with Locke's earlier dream to continue Josiah Royce's notion of a beloved community with African American culture, especially products like the spirituals, as a catharsis of passion and a rapprochement between the races. But such freedom dreams had no academic mooring for Locke at Oxford as they had with Royce at Harvard.

A couple of days after the first club meeting in his rooms, however, Locke did receive the good news that the Standing Committee of *Literae Humaniores* had met on October 28 and approved his request to read for a graduate degree in philosophy. That meant that he could exit the BA program in *Literae Humaniores* at Hertford College, end his futile effort to master Greek, and immerse himself in a program of independent study of philosophy that would culminate in a dissertation and a BSc. The board even accepted his dissertation subject, "The Concept of Value and Its Relation to Logic, Ethics, and Aesthetics," which surprised him. "I hadn't expected they would," he confessed to his mother, "for it was frightfully unorthodox and really too good a subject for them to allow me to corner it, I thought. I have a year to do the thesis in, with Dr. Schiller and Prof. Cook Wilson as supervisors. Generally, even if they admit a subject, they don't give one decent supervisor. So I am very lucky, especially as my old Hertford tutor opposed it: it cuts him out all together."[12]

Locke was happy that his work would be supervised by two Oxford professors outside of Hertford, for his Hertford tutor, Rev. Williams, evidently wanted Locke to satisfy the requirements for the BA before being allowed to read for a graduate degree. Williams may have been skeptical about how hard Locke was applying himself in his first-year work. He was right. But Locke already was adept at academic intrigue and took advantage of Oxford's idiosyncratic graduate regulations and greater latitude for Rhodes Scholars to outmaneuver his college tutor. A day of reckoning awaited Locke, however, if he should fail to get along well with his new supervisors. Oxford was letting him direct his education as he saw fit; but it was also giving him enough rope to hang himself, if he failed to make adequate progress on the dissertation by the year's end.

The university's support of his new academic plans invigorated Locke, and by November he was getting down to work, although his earlier problems of concentration persisted. In November, he informed his mother:

> I have just really begun serious work...and dull philosophy written in bad and involved German by Austrian Jew Professors is not easy hammock reading. If only I could be in a decent climate that didn't take the starch out of me as the Oxford weather does. I could sleep the term out here and have seriously thought of galvanizing myself into activity with acid phosphate and that sort of thing but I feel it would react on my nerves which are already too jumpy.[13]

In the end, he concluded, "really what I've got against Oxford [is] terrible disinclination to write. I don't mind thinking even in this fog—but writing! Oh the ideas that get lost for a bit of paper and ink." Locke's struggle with the weather seemed real, but just as important was his "disinclination to write" and an abhorrence of the kind of ennui that often accompanied his time alone at Oxford. Accordingly, he still found socializing his best escape from his inability to write. "You do what your neighbors wish you to do in Oxford—whether you like it or no. I have tried I don't know how many times to set to work on several short stories...but get as far as the title or the first sentence of 1st paragraph, when I am interrupted."[14]

Cosmopolitan Club friends were his most frequent interrupters. Seme was the constant companion who most influenced how Locke spent his time. Among other things, Seme convinced Locke that to be a true gentleman he must learn to ride. With Seme, Locke took riding lessons and French lessons, the latter with the daughter of a Sorbonne professor who treated both of her charges with a brusqueness that bordered on cruelty. By the end of the term, Locke had mastered riding, if not French, and went riding regularly with Percy J. Philip, who seemed by December to have supplanted Seme as Locke's main social companion. "I have become a splendid horseman," he announced to his mother on the eve of his Christmas vacation. "Last Saturday Philip and I rode 20 miles—I was fairly exhausted," but "I am going out with him again this afternoon—he is a splendid figure on a horse—I look like a jockey—but for my clothes which I got particularly proper to avoid amputations that I wasn't a gentleman after-all.... Philip has been an almost constant companion recently" and had replaced Downes as the man uppermost in Locke's romantic affections.[15]

Philip also seemed responsible for introducing Locke to another new diversion of his second year, the company of two teenage boys who lived in Oxford. Philip was friendly with Mrs. Addis, a single mother of two boys, Phillip, fourteen, and Dansey, fifteen, and infatuated with another member of the family, a young girl named Margaret of undetermined age. It is not clear from the surviving letters whether Mrs. Addis was divorced or a widow, but what is certain is that the family lacked a father and that Mrs. Addis was having difficulty rearing the headstrong boys.

While Philip's interest in Margaret was paramount, Locke's interest, not surprisingly, centered on the boys, although to be fair it should be admitted that Philip, Locke, and Sydney Franklin, a London lawyer and Cosmopolitan Club member, all seemed to feel some responsibility "to do something" for the boys, most likely to help them gain some maturity. Locke, more than others, however, appeared to sign on to what amounted to a mentoring relationship with the two teenage boys. But a curious duality existed in his relationship with these two "youngsters": as a father figure, he had their mother's permission to civilize them, but as an adult child himself, he was also attracted to the opportunity to frolic in their world of innocence and playfulness. That is the sentiment that surfaces from the first letter in which Locke informs his mother of this new relationship in his life.

> Seme is here often, almost every day... we go out driving fine afternoons—the Dines have got a stylish new trap—and let it to us very cheap. Its jolly good fun—particularly when I take the children out— the children, I must explain, for I am shamefully behind in my news, are two North Oxford boys the Addis's—Philip Aetates, 14 [years old] and Dansey Aetates, 15. They are allowed to come to tea with me twice a week and if it is pleasant I take them driving.[16]

Later, Locke informed her he had discovered a nice lake nearby where he took the boys out in small boat and let them paddle him for a good part of the afternoon. Rather than taming wild beasts, Locke approached the "children's hour" with the "youngsters" as a world of adolescent fantasy and escape much like Lewis Carroll found with Alice out in a rowboat on a lake during his time at Oxford.

Toward the end of the Michaelmas term 1908, however, Locke, along with his friend, Sydney Franklin, seemed to develop a more adult and more romantic interest in the boys, especially in Dansey. Franklin's letters provide the clues to a relationship that remains unclear today. Locke began to behave toward Dansey in ways that would later be his signature style of romantic involvement with young men. Indeed, it appears that Locke and Franklin became rivals for Dansey's affection. A letter dated June 2, 1909, from Franklin to Locke indicates that at least two crises occurred that defined Locke's attachment to Dansey. The first probably occurred at the end of Michaelmas term or just at the beginning of the Hilary term 1909: Locke decided to break off his visits with Dansey by himself in his rooms on Beaumont Street. The cause of this first break is unclear, but it seems to have occurred because Dansey failed to respond to Locke's subtle expression of interest in the younger man. Philip already had remarked in one of his letters that Dansey had failed on one occasion to understand one of Locke's letters; clearly, Locke's entreaties to Dansey, particularly given the delicacy of the relationship, were too murky to be readily understood by a teenager. At that time, Franklin interceded and advised Locke that if he would just "sit still and do nothing," Dansey would move toward Locke and respond favorably. This judgment seems to have been correct, for Locke did not end the relationship at that time. Such helpful advice was interesting given that Franklin was also interested in Dansey. "For some unaccountable reason [I have] grown extremely fond of Dansey (although I do not get the affection from him I might have hoped for)," Franklin confessed. He interceded again in the relationship early in June 1909. This time Locke did break off seeing Dansey after the latter missed an appointment, and this time Franklin urged Locke to do anything but sit still. Franklin's letter offers insights into the complexity of Locke's relationship with Dansey:

> You do not need me to say what you should do, but anything is preferable to that course [to sit still and wait]. Even getting angry with him might serve some good, as he would then realize that he would have to mend his ways, but a cold impassive waiting attitude merely kills confidence.... Besides breaking your faith with his mother, you are abandoning for one hitch the task you voluntarily undertook. You undertook to attempt to cure him of his faults, and refuse to exercise your influence because of his faults. Is it not rather a severe punishment on him to sacrifice his future because he forgot an appointment? Have you never cut an appointment yourself; if you did, did you not make excuses

and apologies which were accepted? You know quite well that what Dansey needs is the influence of one strong will, and he cannot get that influence at home. You have it in your power to give him that influence yourself by exerting your authority, and you refuse to do so for merely selfish reasons.[17]

Punctuality, according to several of Locke's lovers, was a firm requisite of being romantically involved with him. A missed appointment was an early warning signal to Locke that a person could not be trusted with his heart. Careful attention to appointments was only part of an elaborate system of rules Locke imposed on lovers, for complete control of another person was a prerequisite for Locke to be intimate. The need for complete control inevitably led to the downfall of many of Locke's relationships, since eventually everyone broke one of his "rules" and was demoted. Fortunately for Locke, Franklin intervened this time and, by calling on Locke to act in accord with his responsibility to help the boy achieve a degree of maturity, he was able to get Locke to act more reasonably. What reinforced Franklin's position with Locke was that Franklin himself gave Locke permission to act in the boy's interest alone, even if that meant forbidding Franklin's own involvement. "If you think I make your influence harder, tell me so, and I will not see him again. As for his other friendships, find out what they are and forbid them too," he continued. Emotionally, Locke had considerable control over Dansey, as was revealed in Franklin's next comment: "You once said you could get anything out of him that was in him. I thought it, at the time, a very brutal thing to say, but now is the time to use this power. It is merely false modesty for you to deny that your friendship with him is of greater benefit to him than any other. 16 is the critical age with all children, and with a boy like Dansey, the fact is emphasized enormously."[18]

Apparently, Locke relented and reestablished contact with Dansey, but he also turned the situation to his advantage and forbade Franklin from having any further contact with the boy. Locke replied to Franklin, "I shall, if allowed by Miss Addis and conceded by Dansey, assume entire and responsible control of Dansey's time and thoughts from now until my mother arrives (June 23rd or thereabouts)."[19] Hence, for the next three weeks he would attempt to get Dansey "into shape." Locke exercised a father-like authority to teach Dansey how to act, how to behave as a gentleman, and how to comport himself with others in person and in writing. Was Locke's mandate broader? Was Locke charged with the responsibility to make Dansey less irresponsible or less effeminate, less outwardly or outrageously gay? Locke was an authority on how to appear as if he were an Italian or Frenchman, rather than a gay Black American. Locke may have advised Dansey how to comport himself to survive in a heterosexual world, a kind of mentoring Locke would do with other gay men throughout his life. Nurturing Dansey as a surrogate father to a young, White Oxford boy may have reprised the role Locke's father had performed—or tried to perform—with him, that of trying to drill the apparent gayness out of him.

Even more intriguing is the question of why Locke, a man with considerable access to men at Oxford and particularly in the Cosmopolitan Club, would become so involved with a much younger man. This relationship seemed to satisfy some need in his psyche not satisfied elsewhere, a need to be the father figure, a male nurturer. Or was it an attempt of the dramatically undersized Locke to become a child again?

The ambiguity arises because Locke seemed to be under Dansey's sway as much as Dansey was under his. The master-slave relationship always contained, as Hegel observed, the likelihood that the slave would one day become the master. In this as in other intimate relationships, who was in charge was contested and changeable, as each jockeyed for psychological position with the other. At just below 5 feet tall, Locke must have felt a greater parity in size with the diminutive, but still growing teenager, Dansey, than he could ever have felt with men his own age, like the almost giant Philip. Locke found himself rather helpless in being so powerfully attracted to someone so obviously unsuitable. His subsequent overreaction to the young man's one missed appointment suggests how powerful that obsession had become and how important it was for him to protect himself in a relationship that potentially might end up controlling him.

Locke's compulsion also helped him to avoid facing the moral implications of what he was doing. He was clearly acting unethically when he exploited the mother's mandate to groom the young man by pursuing a clandestine, romantic relationship with Dansey. Locke knew that Mrs. Addis had not intended him to romanticize her son; and yet, the same Victorian society that condemned such romantic attachments in public also created the space for them to occur in private. Mrs. Addis seems not to have seen that Locke's relationship—really the relationships that several men had—with her children was sexual, or at the least sexualized, and accordingly, Locke exploited that blindness. Was it his race, his diminutive size, his Oxford standing, or his winning smile that convinced her he was safe?

Despite such private escapades, Locke eschewed any public discussion of homosexuality, even in the protected atmosphere of the Cosmopolitan Club. At the end of the Michaelmas term, a mild controversy emerged when Marsh Roberts, a graduate of St. John's College, proposed to read a paper titled, "Oscar Wilde's Place in Literature." Locke asked Sydney Franklin to speak with Roberts about his paper. Franklin replied on January 31, 1909, "I took your advice and went round and worried M-R again. Results 1: He has promised to make it the dullest and most insipid thing imaginable. 2: I am to have a censorship over the paper, and he hopes I will be sure and cut out any passage which could possibly hurt the feelings of a maiden Aunt. Will this satisfy you? He says he knows we all want to withdraw his paper and he would gladly have done so if they asked him straight out."[20] Like other Oxford homosexuals less than ten years after the Oscar Wilde trial, Locke worried public discussion of Wilde would bring scrutiny and repression down upon him and the club. That Roberts knew "we all" wanted the paper withdrawn suggests Locke was not alone in this worry. Unlike criticism of imperialism and non-Western nationalism, which was inflammatory but still permissible in the club, even literary discussion of sexuality was verboten. Yet this was precisely the issue that drew many of the club members together.

Tension over sexual issues was not the only conflict in the Cosmopolitan Club. At the end of the Michaelmas term 1908 a power struggle erupted between Locke and Roman Biske, a strong-willed German who was a member of the club and editor of the magazine. Biske was a major radical voice in the organization, and though it is unclear what started the dispute, it seemed to center around a disagreement among members over a question left unresolved by many of the papers, including El Alaily's: how were the members of the colonial world to effect change, to break the yoke of imperialism, and to lead their people from under European domination? On one side of the question stood Roman Biske, a revolutionary thinker and student of Marx, who argued vociferously that only a colonial revolution would bring about the new world order of cosmopolitanism. Har Dayal, it can be presumed, agreed. On the other side stood Locke, Mukerjea, Philip, Seme, and de Fonseka who believed that a revolutionary challenge to Western imperialism was suicidal and believed a cultural struggle was the best approach. Colonized people ought to resist by preserving their own indigenous art, culture, and sense of self-respect, an agenda Mukerjea had endorsed in his paper on Bengali literature, and Locke had implied something analogous in his early paper on Dunbar. But that position was being challenged by a group of radicals who advocated cultural assimilation and political rebellion for underdeveloped peoples. The conflict between the two camps came to a head at the end of the term, as Locke had reported to his mother on December 15: Biske "is a hair brained intriguer—we had quite a horrible clash in the last meeting of the Cosmopolitan Club and to spare the indignity of a personal issue I withdrew from next term's election list."[21]

Biske won the presidency of the club for the Hilary term, but Locke counterattacked the following term. He encouraged Mukerjea to make a special trip up from London to join Philip, Locke, and Seme in passing a vote of no confidence on Biske and his slate of Cosmopolitan Club officers. The vote was a ringing defeat of what Locke termed "intellectual radicalism of the worst kind." Such a maneuver exhibited what later would become Locke's trademark in conflicts: he would withdraw in the face of conflict, especially when challenged by superior force, only to return to counter-attack later with deadly force.

Academically, Locke seemed to do much better his second year at Oxford. Toward the end of Michaelmas term, his reading picked up and he reported to his mother that he had had a good term. He impressed his tutors during his "collections," a term-end oral examination on his progress in his thesis reading, although he still had to tolerate criticism from his college dean. His work the following term was even better, in part because he did not do as much traveling as the preceding Christmas vacation. Instead of going to Paris with Seme and then to the south of France and Rome to meet Franklin, Locke took a short tip to London and returned early to Oxford to continue his studies. After a fall term of attempting to live up to the standard of his friends, lack of funds was as much a factor as interest in his studies for his not traveling to the Continent. Yet Locke was not greatly upset, as he seemed pleased to stay in London. He roomed mainly with de Fonseka in Soho and particularly enjoyed their afternoon strolls in Piccadilly.

Locke also welcomed the opportunity to explore the London cultural scene, especially after he was elected to honorary membership in two prominent London clubs—the United Arts Club on St. James's Street and the Union Liberal Club. Although such memberships were automatically conferred on Rhodes Scholars, Locke appreciated gaining access to the United Arts Club, an arts organization that maintained a permanent exhibition of paintings, sculpture, furniture, and decorative art in its galleries. Hobnobbing around London with the cultural elite was just what Locke wanted, especially if he could do so in the company of de Fonseka, fast becoming one of his favorite Oxford friends.

Back at Oxford for the Hilary term, Locke threw himself into reading and writing. It was not easy. He complained to his mother that his subject was a very difficult one. His mother responded that he had always chosen the most difficult subjects to research. That predilection was an intellectual strength, but it imposed a special burden on him now. Value theory and classification was not only a difficult topic, but also not well developed or understood at Oxford. Most of the work in this abstract field had been done in Germany, and the work was available only by translating German texts, which slowed the process for Locke: by 1909, he was still a novice reading in German. With such an esoteric topic, Locke was limited in the number of tutors who could help him. In the case of Schiller, problems developed early in Locke's second year in the form of compensation that Schiller received for his work with Locke. Schiller was a tutor at Corpus Christi College, and because Locke was a student of Hertford, he had to pay Schiller supervisory fees during Michaelmas term, at the same time that he paid his college tuition. In December 1908, Locke petitioned Hertford to be excused from paying tuition, because he was working for a BSc outside of the college, but Hertford ruled instead that it would pay Schiller's supervisory fees.[22] The upshot was that by the end of his second year at Oxford, Locke would be working mainly with Wilson instead of with Schiller.

In Cook Wilson, Locke encountered a logician who was not sympathetic to pragmatism and not particularly sympathetic to the kind of aesthetic philosophical interest that lay behind Locke's formal study of value theory. Wilson was a rigorous tutor, however, and at the end of the Michaelmas term, he asked Locke to prepare some notes on his reading of Ehrenfels. That evidently was the "work" that he had to get back to Oxford to do. When he turned it in, Wilson was less than completely satisfied. He noted that Locke had a tendency to mix in his own critical reflections with quotations taken directly from Ehrenfels that were not set off in quotation marks. Locke needed to be more careful with his citations, Wilson commented. While the seamless quality of Locke's exposition of Ehrenfels shows that he was finally getting into the value of theory work, it also suggested that Locke was veering hazardously close to plagiarism. Wilson did praise Locke for beginning to move beyond simple descriptive exposition of Ehrenfel's theories to some critical evaluation of their limitations. But Wilson's comments also suggested that Locke was not yet doing first-rate philosophical work.

Locke began to think seriously about the possibility of taking a year off from Oxford and spending it at the Sorbonne, where he might study with the eminent French philosopher Henri Bergson. "I am tiring of Oxford," he informed his mother in a February 10, 1909, letter. "It is too relaxing mentally and physically. To return to it for a year after having been away on the continent a year (would) be an enormous advantage in every way. There is in Paris too Henri Bergson— the truest master in philosophy Europe can boast of, that is to say a truly original thinker who has not yet had time to fossilize or grow academic."[23] That plan, however, never materialized, and instead he stuck it out with Wilson and Schiller. Yet even in this environment, he could report at the end of the Hilary term that his oral examinations before these tutors had gone well. He seemed on the right track, if not tremendously inspired.

But just as Locke was gaining academic stability at Oxford, America reminded him he did not belong. Along with the rest of the Rhodes Scholars, Locke was invited to a lunch with the American ambassador, Whitelaw Reid, and his wife at their London residence, Dorchester House, on March 15. Locke accepted, but then Reid learned to his surprise that one of the scholars was a Negro. Almost certainly the southern Rhodes Scholars informed Reid of Locke's race as part of continuing their efforts to segregate him. Reid reacted hysterically and dashed off a letter to George Parkin decrying the impropriety of asking southerners to lunch with a Negro. "The question of social relationships, particularly at the table, with such people in the houses of American officials has been a burning one," perhaps referring to the tidal wave of southern outrage after President Theodore Roosevelt dined with Booker T. Washington at the White House in 1901. Reid continued: "to a certain extent the same thing is true in this country, and I have had occasion to see quite strong manifestations of feeling on the subject here as one ordinarily sees either in New York or Washington." Reid wished that Locke had not been invited, but concluded that under the circumstances, there was nothing that could be done except to "go through with it, receiving the gentleman himself with all proper courtesy and trying to avoid the possibility of either any incident unpleasant to him or to others, or any unpleasant publicity." He asked Parkin to give him the names of Rhodes Scholars who were friendly with Locke so that he could be seated next to them; the southerners would then be placed on the other side of the room.

The Rhodes Trust had another plan. Wylie visited Locke's rooms Saturday before the luncheon and asked Locke to withdraw his acceptance of the invitation. Locke refused. Wylie returned again that Sunday and asked Locke to provide names of scholars with whom he was friendly so that Wylie could seat Locke next to them. Again, Locke refused. The next morning, Locke rose early, took the train to London, changed into his formal dress clothes in the train station, and took a cab to the luncheon. Locke had his own strategy for dealing with the situation. "It was an elaborate function," he wrote to his mother, "tea courses, absolutely high watermark of all my gastronomic experiences [and] a perfect palace, Dorchester House. The southerners were sore but attended. They even asked the Rhodes authorities to urge me to recall my acceptance. I gave them to understand I attended in merely a representative capacity—was seated as it chanced by a friend." Most likely, the Rhodes officials had researched his acquaintances, and he was seated next to Chester Haring, the Massachusetts scholar and a friend of Locke's. "I conversed formally only with the hosts and a few Rhodes scholars whom I know and was the first to take leave of the hostess. I did the last quite premeditatedly, and I think it had quite an effect. They were sore I came, but sorer still that I should be the first to leave."[24]

At the time, Locke only hinted at how he felt. "After the Rhodes luncheon I simply went to see Seme—had dinner with him and left the very next day for Paris." After a racial confrontation that required all of his self-discipline, Locke needed to commiserate with someone who understood instinctively what the incident had meant.

Just at that point in his academic career when he was beginning to settle in, feel comfortable, and gain traction in his studies, Locke was told again—by the cowardly Wylie, no less—that he should absent himself from the American community in England. In one sense, it was a simple little luncheon that any strong-minded African American could move on from. But Locke had more difficulty moving on than he could admit. These social occasions meant a lot to him. And this time, unlike the Thanksgiving incident, the Rhodes Trust officials had openly supported the claim of the southern Rhodes Scholars that he should not break bread with other Americans.

Much later, perhaps when Locke contemplated writing an autobiographical essay on the incident titled "April 1909, Southern Rhodes Scholars vs. English Tory Allies," he made a brief note to himself that revealed what it had meant to him. "By this experience, and its [undecipherable] prejudice, I was converted from an individualistic aesthete into an ardent but I hope not bigoted racialist."[25]

No concrete way existed for Locke to express his anger or to heal. He had his friends at the Cosmopolitan Club, but it was questionable whether most would really understand how the incident affected him as an American. Kallen described Locke as "sensitive," and he was, in part because at some level he believed in America as something more than the land of his birth. To be an American to a philosopher like Locke meant allegiance to an idea, codified in the Declaration of Independence, that "all men are created equal." The English never claimed anything so widely democratic as the basis for Englishness. But to be an American was supposed to mean one was part of a community, because one "held these truths to be self-evident." The Reid luncheon reminded Locke of the deep hypocrisy of the American identity he could never claim as fully his.

Connecting with Seme suggested one way out—to bond with an African Diasporic sense of transnationalism. But that did not solve Locke's emotional problem. He was an isolated African American in another country, and more than ever before, he knew it. And so, with Seme's heartfelt understanding, Locke left London in the spring of 1909 and threw himself headlong into what he knew best, his personal pursuit of beauty on the Continent. With Downes gone and his mother thousands of miles away, the love of beauty remained his one remaining bulwark against the growing list of cruelties at Oxford, a slender reason to go on when precious few remained.

10

Italy and America, 1909–1910

Shortly after landing in Paris at 6:45 in the evening after the ambassador's fateful luncheon, Locke was taking in an opera, Maeterlinck's *Momma Verna*. Locke loved to hit the ground running whenever he began a trip, an approach to self-care that was becoming his preferred pattern of travel—plan ahead, attend as many of one's favorite cultural activities as possible, and chase away any feelings of loneliness. Indeed, this trip revived pleasant memories of the previous summer's trip with his mother. He stayed at the same hotel, where they had roomed, and visited old haunts they had enjoyed together. "I smiled as I passed places we had seen together—you do not know the pleasure of such memories," he wrote his mother, encouraging her to begin planning her return to Europe, and especially to Paris, the coming summer.[1] A life of beauty had its rewards.

After lounging in his favorite cafe, the Mi Carena, where he and Downes had had such a rollicking good time the year before, Locke settled down to plan his trip south in his "Grand Tour" through France, Switzerland, and the great cities of Italy. He had maps, guidebooks, and a letter of introduction to a Mrs. Alexander of Florence from Sydney Franklin, who had promised to accompany Locke to Italy over the Christmas vacation, but who now was stuck in London with his law practice. The trip threatened to be lonely until Lionel de Fonseka showed up on March 18, just as Locke had all but "given him up" as unable to make the trip. Saddled comfortably with a traveling companion, Locke took the night train for Bale, Switzerland.

With little more than a museum and a few old churches to detain them at Bale, Locke and de Fonseka left the next day for Lucerne. Their approach from the west initially obscured their view of the mountains; but, as they rounded a bend halfway through the climb up the Swiss side of the Alps, Locke and de Fonseka got their first thrill of the trip—a "magnificent view" of some of the most beautiful mountains Locke had ever seen. Once at Lucerne they spent the next three days soaking up the views. One day, after being frustrated that he could not go climbing, Locke took the cable railway, the Rigi, up the side of the mountain and was rewarded with a view of the mountains that was nothing less than "shudderingly beautiful—quite awesome." He had always known that he would love the Alps, he confided to his mother, and was pleasantly surprised that the altitude did not affect his heart negatively—given that some reported the climb produced palpitations. Locke was enlivened by the mountain air and lamented only that his mother was not there to share it. To compensate, he detailed his movements through the trip and the scenery with as much literary flare as he could muster. "A bright Sunday morning we took the boat down the Lake of Lucerne or the Lake of the Four Cantons to Flüelen—23 miles on a calm blue lake simply hemmed in by mountain peaks—some of them towards the tail end extremely high—we could see peaks twenty and thirty miles away in the clear air, and the dazzling snow-fields with blue-grey cloud shadows and a few of the higher peaks with two cloud belts and the peak still visible above them was an inspiring sight."[2]

While Locke had planned his trip around art museums and cathedrals, the landscape most enthralled him. His aesthetic sense had been crafted by the preferred recreation of Black Victorians who grew up on promenades through Philadelphia parks. He now reveled in the grander park of the Swiss Alps. To keep up the rationale of Grand Tour education, they chose routes that were most historically significant. Once their boat trip down Lake Lucerne dead-ended at Flüelen, they elected a train route to Goeschen that took them over the St. Gotthard pass, the route that Hannibal took when he invaded Rome, and that "Goethe took his Werther and his whole army of sentiments over it with the famous song on his life, Kennst du das Land—it is the only way to Italy for a students wander-jahr," Locke informed his mother.[3]

After stopping briefly at Goeschen for lunch at 3,700 feet above sea level, Locke and de Fonseka went down the other side of the Alps on a train whose brakes screeched and clawed at the mountain to manage a sensible rate of descent. Locke was awestruck by the sight of the snow-capped mountains, which "looked like peppermint candy or mounds of sugar and contrasted with the jagged rock-salt of the Swiss side. I can't tell you how I felt—I was drawn through my eyes like thread through a needle." Eager to reach Italy, they hurried through the Italian Lake District and took the overnight to Milan. Milan did not have enough historical sites to detain them very long, although Locke remarked to his mother that they saw the "wonderful cathedral" there.[4] That remark says something about his taste: unlike Oscar Wilde, who declared the ornate and elaborate Duomo Cathedral an abysmal "failure," Locke's response echoed that of the romantic poet Elizabeth Browning, who had found the spires and pinnacles of this Gothic cathedral almost as glorious as the Alps.

The next day, they pushed on, taking the train through Verona and Padua to Venice, Locke's city of dreams, where they would take rooms along the Riva degli Schiavoni, on the southern tip of the Piazza San Marco, overlooking the Grand Canal. They stayed in Venice four or five days, soaking up art, but mostly the views. At first, Venice was something of a letdown, Locke confessed: his first gondola ride was rather routine, and the famous buildings, galleries, and even its Basilica di San Marco seemed dirty and depressing in daylight. However, by the second day, he "began to know the fine points of view and the proper time of day to go to see them," mainly in the early evening, when the spectacular sunsets produced deeply hued skies—"the sky and the mist and the sun make Venice, and say what you will moonlight remakes it." Venice became a work of art for Locke in those evenings, "a dream city on a lovely night and my very best impression came sitting at Florio's a fashionable cafe in the Piazza San Marco and watching the rectangular patch of sky go through all the tones from pale mauve to purple black after the sunset." Such views brought to his mind Turner's paintings, which, as a true aesthete, Locke thought superior in some cases to the original. "The actual sunset from St. Georgio campanile over Maria del Saluti is striking enough—but Turner has made it too accessible. I had rather see his paintings of it; the sky at San Marco piazza no one can paint—it is not a scene, [but] simply a chromatic scale of colour with the same group of buildings to frame it—it is lovely."[5]

The piazzas, the cafes, and the water that seemed to buoy the entire city stimulated the romantic in Locke. That may account for why Locke wrote Sydney Franklin that he preferred Venice to Florence: Venice was more romantic, not only because of its views but also because of its men. After chiding Locke for his preference, Franklin teased Locke for "throwing your money at the first passersby." As John Addington Symonds wrote in his memoirs, Venice was a city preferred by traveling homosexual men, because of its wealth of lithe, strong, sinewy gondola men. Given that Locke's preference ran to tall, slender men, it seems unlikely that Locke would not have taken advantage of public sources of affection while visiting the city.

Locke's interest in the men of Venice may be related to the coolness of his traveling companion, Lionel de Fonseka. As Locke informed his mother, his trip with de Fonseka was not as intimate as it had been the year before with Downes in another romantic city, Paris. Downes and Locke had gone everywhere together, but de Fonseka and Locke went their separate ways during mornings, only to encounter and pass each other in squares in the afternoons. Locke and de Fonseka do not seem to have been lovers, at least on this trip, which came relatively early in their relationship. Like Locke, de Fonseka was an aesthete and a gifted wit and ironist, who could match Locke for pointed remarks and repartee. Born in Ceylon, de Fonseka was one of the funniest ironists of the Cosmopolitan Club, whose hysterical critiques of Western aesthetic hypocrisy made his companion, Locke, laugh giddily. But as a Catholic, de Fonseka found in the Roman Church what some Oxford aesthetes before him found there—a religious outlet for some of the sexual energy that accompanied aestheticism. Indeed, one of de Fonseka's reasons for making the trip was that he was interested in meeting up with his religious mentors in Rome.

Locke and de Fonseka reached Florence in early April. As before, they went their separate ways during the day and dined together in the evenings, a plan that Locke explained to his mother suited him fine—"one needs to be alone in Italy. I never spent such a profitable ten days anywhere as at Florence. I really studied." His attention shifted from the landscape to the art in Florence, as he attacked the museums, galleries, and especially the churches soaking up all that Donatello, Michelangelo, and Ghirlandaio could teach him. Florence was the "real" Renaissance, as he might have reminded Mukerjea and El Alaily, a special period in world history according to its historians when the superlative secular individual could realize all aspects of his or her intellect, from literature to art to science, and through such personal fulfillment, transform his or her culture. Locke was preparing himself to be a Black Lorenzo, whose love of curiosity, experimentalism, and art for art's sake would carry on the work of the Florentine patron. Ironically what seemed to hold Locke's attention the most in Florence were the "old church frescoes, particularly the Ghirlandaio frescoes in Santa Maria Novella." He returned to view the marvelous interior of Santa Maria Novella several times and seemed to be captivated by the lifelike spiritual dramas that unfolded on the ceilings. For Locke could not help noticing the African faces and rotund bodies in the frescoes in Santa Maria Novella, evidence that Ghirlandaio's figures reflected African and Muslim influences. Seeing the Negro inserted in the pictures of his celebrated Renaissance connected these religious frescoes to him emotionally and reconnected him to the Christian mysticism of his mother. Locke felt much more comfortable in Italy than he felt in England, because he could feel himself part of Italy and see a Renaissance that had included his own, even if only at its margins.

Locke also enjoyed taking extensive daytrips, particularly after de Fonseka went on ahead of him to Rome. Locke would often enter a church or gallery, wander about, and let the historical associations wash over him, returning to his hotel and cafe at evening. He realized that the typical traveler's program of going "to the spot where Savonarola was buried or to try to pick out the spot on the Ponte Veechio where Dante stood or Michelangelo leaned is futile and soul wearing—but to cross it haphazard and the associations flit across your mind—to lean on the bridge to look at the sunset in the Arno Valley and suddenly to think Dante & Angelo and the rest of them did the same—that's really worthwhile—it enlarges the mood without prescribing it." While using his guidebook to find a particular church or museum, or to find his way home, he preferred to wander aimlessly, stumbling into interesting situations. For "fashionable crowds I have a scent for them," he confessed to his mother, and for tramping up back streets of Florence "startling the peasants—I love to puzzle them—they don't see many of our kind."[6]

Locke took the slow road to Rome, stopping along the way at the hill towns of Perugia and Assisi. His two days in Assisi were some of the best of his trip. He had heard about Assisi as a youngster from a lecture by Griggs on St. Francis of Assisi, probably delivered at Philadelphia's Ethical Culture Society. One beautiful day he departed from the train and trudged "like [a] pilgrim[,] a tiresome climb up the hill to the town... half way up I hired an Italian laborer to carry my bag—this barefooted urchin tugged alongside with my overcoat and just at dusk with a marvelous sunset behind us, we trudged up the hill, saluting Mary at the crossroads... until just as we were getting into St. Peters gate the purple night was down upon the valley. It was an experience I shall never forget."[7] It was difficult to tear himself away from Assisi.

But with excellent timing, Locke arrived in Rome at the beginning of Easter Week and reconnected with de Fonseka, who was the guest of the Zaluetas, cousins of Cardinal Merry del Val. Through de Fonseka, Locke was able to get special permits for all of the Easter services. De Fonseka attended the opening of the Vatican gallery and had a private audience with the pope, while Locke attended church services in St. Peter's on Palm Sunday. On Good Friday he went to Mass at St. John Lateran and then over to the Scala Santa, "the stairs that are reputed to have been those of Plater palace down which Christ went after the condemnation. The stairway was jammed with loyal Catholics going up on their knees, there being no other way to get up. I went up in a spirit of emotional sincerity if not of devotional belief and found the Crucifix exposed at the head of the steps. Afterwards I took a long ramble in the Campayne with a very engaging Italian youth Umberto Zanucchi with whom I scraped acquaintance on the Pucio. We became very friendly and used to ramble out into the Campayne almost every afternoon after that."[8]

Locke also found companions among de Fonseka's friends in Rome. Rising early to view the art in museums and galleries with the best morning light, Locke would catch up with de Fonseka and schmooze with fashionable society in the afternoon at the cafes. Locke informed his mother that one evening his table contained two counts, a duke, and several Harvard classmates. Clearly, access to the elite in Rome came easily for Locke. "Rudyard Kipling was at a nearby table the other evening... Richard Strauss the great musician was involved in conversation with Arthur Lee, a Norwegian art student who is one of our party at nights and was introduced all round. These with de Fonseka's friends make a set the like of which Mothers darling hasn't heretofore entered." Of course, there were the unavoidable encounters with White Americans who resented seeing an African American abroad—"some of them look sick," he confided to his mother; but he seemed to enjoy frustrating their sense of who and what was an American. Such social conquests did not force him to entirely neglect his cultural education. "The Vatican and of course the Sistine Chapel have claimed the most of my attention." But Locke was tiring from weeks of sight-seeing and had much less energy to track down all of the famous sights; moreover, after Florence, he found Rome to be more confusing to study. Christian churches were piled on top of pagan temples, and Christian traditions were rich with pagan heritages. More tantalizing was sitting at the cafes, wiling away the afternoons, sketching out story lines and titles, with the dream of a novel taking shape in his head. His first trip to Italy had provided numerous inspirations, and rather confidently, he predicted that his first novel would be "brought forth there."[9]

Italy had stimulated Locke's sensitivity to visual beauty. As he traveled home by train through France, he continued to be moved by the landscape, especially of the Loire Valley with its "brilliant flowers sunlit against a bewildering background of greens ranging from the dark glassy green of orange leaves and rubber plants to the high pitched yellow green of flog grass—the most striking color [and] a dream country for whoever likes profusion and sharp contrast and I love both."[10] Locke was beginning to find a language to express the kind of impressionism nature and art elicited from him. Not surprisingly, the trip had restored his positive outlook and interest in his work. After a brief stop in Paris, where he watched a beautiful sunset over the Seine, and in London, where he picked up Seme, Locke returned to Oxford by the last week of April in excellent spirits.

Such a wonderful trip posed a series of challenges for Locke as Trinity term 1909 began. First, he had to resist the temptation to continue vacationing and its reverie for living. This was especially so, given that Oxford was sunny and bright that spring. His first letter to his mother from Oxford signaled the tension. Yes, he had an "enormous amount of work to do," but "I shall play tennis and boat a good deal—the youngsters—the Addis boys play tennis well and boat—they can pull and paddle me to their hearts content."[11] By the second week after his return, invigorating weather seemed to inspire him finally to tackle his thesis. But a second, higher hurdle lay in his path. His philosophical interests in aesthetics, both in the subject matter for his reflections, and also the style of writing it brought out in him, diverged sharply from what Oxford expected. From Italy, he had been able to voice to his mother his growing alienation from the academic approach to his subject. "I told you my thesis subject was 'The Concept of Value,' a study in the correlation of Logical, Ethical and Aesthetic values. If it doesn't suggest any definite idea to you, it's just what it doesn't to me. That's partly what makes it such a big subject—people have been writing all around it lately. A French doctorate thesis has come out in the last few months and missed fire. Prof. [Wilbur] Urban has a new book at which I am chiefly angry because I must buy it to say I have read it—I am sure it is bosh."[12] Instead of writing another boring academic treatise on the classification of values, Locke wanted to make an introspective psychological study of how we learn to value. His Italian trip had sharpened that sense in him, for as he had soaked up impressions from the art and landscapes, he had begun to believe that the ability to take such an aesthetic attitude on one's experience was at the root of valuation. What Locke wanted to create in value theory was analogous to what the Impressionists were creating for art theory—an investigation that ignored what we already know about objects and made visible what we feel when we sense something is of a higher value than something else. Locke's intention actually had the closest affinity to what William James had achieved in *The Principles of Psychology* and was light years away from the kind of work that Cook Wilson, a logician, or F. C. S. Schiller, a blinkered pragmatist, could sympathize with. Accordingly, Locke began to dream again of going to Paris to work with the rebel philosopher, Henri Bergson, but such an option was impossible without financial support for a year at the Sorbonne. Locke's class position limited his ability to realize these philosophical aspirations.

Locke began to despair of his capacity for scholarly work. "I have realized definitely and finally at Oxford," he wrote his mother early in May, "that I am cast for a practical career, and my scholastic pretensions have dwindled to mere ideals of personal culture." For the first time, he longed "to get back to America, and into my position—it will be a stormier and shorter reign than Booker's, but so much the better. I want a long arm and the will to use it." Locke still had the possibility of race service to fall back onto. Yet as the reference to Booker T. Washington suggested, and the subsequent discussion confirmed, Locke imagined a grandiose role for himself in African American affairs. "The danger is where as with you and papa and all the rest of us before you—you have allowed yourselves to get into too small, too petty an environment and strength, will and aristocracy are tragically useless and at the same time grotesquely comic when exercised in the cramped environment. I am as I have always told you going to hold out uncompromising until my situation comes to me—for in the meantime, I shall have as much as I can do ruling myself—a turbulent battlefield of contrasted heredities."[13]

It is doubtful Momma was pleased to have her life work as a teacher characterized as "tragically useless" and "grotesquely comic." But Locke was expressing a truth about the Reconstruction generation shared by others of his generation. His mother's generation after the Civil War had compromised with advancing segregation in the late nineteenth century to survive. Of course, Locke and many of his generation ignored that their parents had had little choice in the matter. But it was crucial for Locke to believe that he could avoid falling into the kind of career quagmire that had destroyed his father. Locke found himself thinking a great deal about his father in the days following his Italian trip, in part because, though he could not admit it to his mother, he was himself in a quagmire. He was failing at the one task over which only he had control—"ruling myself—a turbulent battlefield of contrasted heredities." "Heredities" cloaked the real contrasts—the demand to be a race leader and suppress his sexual orientation versus continuing the life of a homosexual dilettante in Europe; the near self-destructive desire to frolic with delinquent English teenagers versus putting in the hard work necessary for scholarly production; the desire for power in human affairs versus an inclination for disappearing into cloistered study, etc.—that only a strong "will" could resolve. A strong will was precisely what Booker T. Washington had and exercised to create space for himself and his race. Locke's usual strength of will and purpose seemed to have deserted him at Oxford. What would he do? That remained unclear, and ironically, Locke's purpose in these remarks was in part to fend off any expectation on his mother's part that he would be returning home soon.

Oxford might offer a path to that "practical" career rather than a scholarly one. "Chesterton is right about Oxford—it is a training-school for the governing classes—and has taught your son its lesson.... Every blasted one of the young race-leaders here at Oxford would like to see me secured for his work, his field—to such an extent that I have made up my mind to serve a great apprenticeship— to travel round the world, stopping with them in their Asiatic and African homes, before returning to America."[14] Seme and El Alaily seemed to have been the "young race leaders" most eager for him to join their liberation movements, and Seme, in particular, seemed responsible for Locke's latest conviction that he was set for a practical career: presumably after this world tour, Locke could take the bachelors degree in civil law, the degree that Seme was reading for at Oxford. Not only would law help him in the United States but also might allow him to "dabble a bit in international law—formulating plans for the admission of Asiatic and African peoples into the jurisdiction of international law. It is a subject where the legal scholars make history—Seme is making a specialty of it, as indeed he needs to for his home situation."[15] Oxford symbolized the mythic possibility that Locke could gain power as a Black man—indeed, because of the situation of Black Diasporic peoples around the globe—and live the life of the queer international tethered ever so loosely to his "home situation."

Like Seme, Locke saw Booker T. Washington as a role model and peppered his mother with questions about Washington and his plans in his May and June letters. Locke particularly wanted to know whether Washington would be coming to Europe soon, for he wanted to meet him in Europe, "on neutral ground," as he put it. Locke did not want his own aspirations for a position through Washington to be mixed up with those "Nigger pretenders," like Roscoe Conkling Bruce or Emmett J. Scott, who were scheming, in Locke's opinion, to replace Washington once he died. "The bigger shoes he leaves the harder they will be to fill—They will play dice for his toga when he dies and then find that no one of them can wear it. He is really a big man."[16] That Locke saw Booker T. Washington as a "big man" contrasted sharply with W. E. B. Du Bois's and even T. Thomas Fortune's views of him in 1909 and suggests something of the persistently conservative nature of Locke's racial vision. In 1906, Washington had surely seemed a "big man," perhaps the only Black man in America who could have gone to Atlanta and spoken to both Black and White camps in the aftermath of the race riot. But after President Theodore Roosevelt's dismissal of Black troops in the Brownsville incident, Washington's standing among African Americans had slipped, as his so-called power with Roosevelt seemed confined to the minutiae of handing out minor patronage jobs to those loyal to the Tuskegee machine. The 1909 Springfield race riot had led young Black and White progressives to come together and form the National Association for the Advancement of Colored People, an organization Washington immediately and consistently opposed. In siding with Washington, and against W. E. B. Du Bois, one of the founders of the NAACP, Locke was showing that he was a bit out of touch with progressive race forces in America and more concerned with the opportunity to use Washington and his philanthropic friends to advance the cause of Alain Locke than becoming a leader of the race back home.

Locke's academic dilettantism was not going unnoticed by the Oxford authorities. The word was getting around in that May that he was not a serious student. Hertford College was not satisfied with him as a student and George Parkin could not wait to communicate that information to President Harrison of the Pennsylvania committee that had selected Locke as a Rhodes Scholar. The meddlesome Parkin wanted to drive home with Harrison what a "mistake" it had been to select Locke and ensure something like it would not happen again. Apparently, Locke's Hertford tutor, Rev. Williams, had not forgiven Locke for abandoning the BA program and was probably behind the rumor that Locke was a slacker. Locke may have inadvertently reinforced that opinion when he petitioned Hertford that term to be exempted from paying college tuition, because he was neither studying under a college tutor nor attending inter-collegiate lectures. But the reality was that he was also not studying closely under his non-college tutors either. Rather than hugging closely to them to get clear instructions on how to approach his topic, he was avoiding them because of the difficulties he had. Not surprisingly, Locke had little more than a rough draft of the introduction to show for his efforts by the end of Trinity term. Rather than spend the summer working on the thesis, as he had promised his mother in an earlier letter, he began in June to harangue her repeatedly about making the trip over for the summer. This time she had her own reasons for wanting to spend the summer in Europe. The Claphans, the owners of the rooming house she resided in in Camden, were going to be away that summer, so they would be closing up their house. If she remained in Camden, she would have to spend the summer at her cousin Varick's, an option she "detested." So, she made the trip over, but this time accompanied by one of her closest friends, Helen Irvin, a fellow teacher at Mt. Vernon School. Mary Locke knew how possessive Locke could be and had broached the subject gingerly with him, but surprisingly, Locke was very gracious. He liked the light-skinned, refined, and respectable Mrs. Irvin, and he welcomed her, as long as she understood that "you and I will expect to have our usual honeymoon privacy in any event."[17] In the end, encouraged by Mary, Helen accompanied her friend to England, where they arrived around July 20 to begin a glorious summer vacation.

The day after they arrived, Locke whisked them away on a Thomas Cook tour through more than a dozen cities in Holland, Belgium, Germany, and Switzerland, before returning to Paris and London. Mary Locke kept a detailed journal that shows this was her "Grand Tour." Leaving England for the Hook of Holland, they traveled through Leiden to Amsterdam where they visited the Rijks Museum and reveled in all of the Rembrandts and Van Dykes. They left Amsterdam by boat and toured the island of Marken, took Mass at a local Catholic church, and went on wonderful walks to Edam, "maker of cheese." In almost every city, they followed Locke's ritual of visiting the churches, especially if an interesting cathedral was located there, and visiting the museums and the galleries. But Mary was just as interested in the quaint customs and interesting peasants they saw, and the shops and diamond cutters in the Jewish ghettos of cities like Amsterdam. Leaving Holland, they headed south to Belgium and Brussels, a city that "compared well with Paris" in her estimation. It was interesting and alive, and she particularly liked Leopold's Palace and the Negro Slave Bronzes. But it was Germany that captured her strongest attention. Arriving in Cologne on the evening of August 3, they all got their first glimpse of the famous cathedral that evening and of the Rhine the next day. "Crossed iron bridge and bridge of boats—came back to Cathedral [and] stood 4 or 5 hours to see 'Vannutelli' and cardinals. City bright with Ecclesiastics, visited Wallraf's Rickartz Museum, [saw] paintings of Leo & Bismarck. [Witnessed] the choons by priests on the steps of the cathedral, [went] back to Hotel for Air Ship [show], invited on the roof by proprietor, who opened champagne for party." Mary Locke had developed a taste for champagne on the previous year's visit to Paris. The "roofs, chimneys, towers, [were] crowded. [There were] cheers, wildest excitement, [at the] magnificent sight— [of the Zeppelin] containing 24 German officers. [Demonstration was] successful from every point [of view]."[18]

They followed the Rhine southward, stopping at Wiesbaden, where they dipped in the hot thermal springs and strolled in the Kochbrunnen, "the largest Kursall—beautiful gardens & shady parks." They left Wiesbaden the next day by train, stopping briefly in Mayence and at Frankfurt am Main, before spending two days in Heidelberg, where they fantasized about Locke attending the university. Mary particularly enjoyed Baden Baden's "lovely valley" and "hot mineral spring park." She and Alain went on lovely "river shady promenades" and said goodbye to Helen, who went on to Paris, while they headed south by train to the Swiss Alps. The Lockes revisited Zurich, Zug, Lucerne, Interlaken, Bern, Lausanne, and Geneva before turning northward for Paris. On such a glorious "honeymoon," Mary Locke must have felt blessed that she had a son so interested in sharing the high points of his cultural life with her. Her diary suggests that she approached the beautiful views and dramatic sites, with their literary and historical associations, with an enthusiasm that matched his. "Aug. 23 [Took the] train to Zug, capital of the Canton on Lake of Zug. Fine view of Rigi Pilatus and the Bernese Alps—old houses, remains of fortifications. For Catholic festival, town beautifully decorated. Lake of Lucerne or Lake of 4 Forest Cantors most beautiful scenery, described by Schiller in Wm. Tell. Got out at Tell's Platte walked to Tell's Chapel a ledge of rocks at the base of the Axenberg shaded by trees.... The morning went to Thurn, saw the Lake of Thurn by moonlight.... From Bern to Lausanne staid over night went by train. Cathedral, handsome view of Alps and Town. University and library finest I have seen.... Saw the Castle of Chillon on the way to Geneva by boat, stands on an isolated rock from the bank connected by bridge—'Bonivard' confined 6 yrs in dungen by Duke of Savoy, sometimes confused with Byrons 'prisoner of Chillon.' Went on boat to Geneva, a long, chilly sail. Mountains only partially visible, walked to R.R. stations up high steps. The Rhone divides the town into 2 parts.... Took 9 p.m. train to Paris, met Helen."[19] These sightseeing trips through German and Swiss cities would create memories for Mary Locke for the rest of her life.

The trip was good for Locke too. He had been able to study the Dutch painters up close in Holland, and on his first trip to Germany, he had fallen in love with Deutschland. The Zeppelin show had impressed him particularly with the technical proficiency of the Germans; the quaint cities along the Rhine had impressed him with their order, cleanliness, and friendliness. The Black Forest had moved him as powerfully as the Rhine: both were beauties of the natural landscape that rivaled the more monumental sights he revisited in Switzerland with "Ma." But as was always the case, these honeymoons came to an end, and after seeing his mother and Helen off to America, he returned to Oxford and Mrs. Dine's rooming house the first week of September.

Locke would soon move into more fashionable living quarters at 10 Turl Street. It was now the third and final year of his Rhodes Scholarship, and he had not progressed further than an introduction to his thesis. Earlier in February, he had told his mother that he planned to write the thesis over the summer and stand for the degree in October, with the possibility of a year at the Sorbonne; but that had been jettisoned for summer travels with her. It was becoming frighteningly clear to him that he was blocked. He read books, began writing pages, balled up the results, and threw them in the wastepaper basket, only to go out to play tennis, go riding, or escape into his fantasy world with one or more of the "children." His relations with his supervisors deteriorated as he cut appointments, came unprepared but talked brilliantly, and generally confirmed the opinion growing steadily in the minds of Schiller and Wilson that he lacked the necessary intellectual power to pull off the thesis.

As was often the case for Locke, when he despaired most about Oxford and his thesis, his thoughts turned to America. Those thoughts coalesced this time into writing what became his first major article on the American character,

"The American Temperament." First delivered before the Rationalists Club in November 1909 and later to the Cosmopolitan Club in January, Locke had been searching for a way to announce himself as a new voice on the American cultural scene and found it in "The American Temperament," eventually published in August 1911 by the prestigious and conservative *North American Review*. In 1909, when he could not find his philosophical footing, he found his voice as a cultural critic. Locke adopted the detached but sympathetic tone of Alexis de Tocqueville (whom he quoted in the essay) to argue that not only was the American character distinctive but it was also America's most recognizable product. Although long-lived, that character was not genetic, but a construction that at best was pliable enough to be quickly adopted by visitors and that at its worse became an unconscious performance by Americans to conform to European prejudices about Americans. "It is a curious but inevitable irony that the American temperament, so notorious for its overweening confidence and self-esteem, should be of all temperaments least reflective, and for all its self-consciousness, should know itself so ill. When criticised, it is either perplexed or amused; when challenged, apologetically boastful, and seemingly delights in misconception and misrepresentation. A striking instance of this singular trait is the way Americans abroad exaggerate their native mannerism and become veritable caricatures of themselves in good-natured mimicry of the national type."

Here, Locke put to good use his observations of those Americans he had encountered in Rome and probably as recently as the preceding summer's travels with his mother. It may have been on that trip that Locke, while observing American behavior, and particularly White American behavior toward him and his mother, conceived this piece. Self-caricature by Americans abroad must have been particularly irksome to a thoroughly Europeanized American like Locke, and he took advantage of the opportunity provided by this essay to deliver a telling judgment on such behavior. "In its extreme form the tendency might be characterized as living up to a libel to save the trouble and expense of legal proceedings." Such sentences also revealed Locke's ironic temperament and his emerging style, one that combined subtle humor with a stinging wit. There was, of course, a serious philosophical consequence of such superficiality, for "if only by the reactions of others do we achieve any definite notion of what we ourselves are, it is small wonder that we have cultivated the actor's manner and practice his art, only it is a strange art for an otherwise inartistic nation, a curious dependence for a free people."[20]

America had not declared its intellectual independence more than a century after it had separated politically and economically from Europe, but instead of developing a solid high culture had allowed the American national type or self-image to be defined by the purveyors of mass culture—the journalists, cartoonists, and stump politicians who painted a portrait of the American at odds with that of the elite, the artist, or the intellectual. In one sense, this was lamentable;

but in a maneuver that characterized the entire essay, Locke also found a way to laud the American temperament.

> [Americans were wise] after all, in preferring to remain artless and un-
> enlightened rather than accept contemporary art as a serious expres-
> sion of itself. Drawn by detached and almost expatriated aesthetes
> at the commands of the most disinterested class of art patrons ever in
> existence, it has no real claims except upon the curiosity of the people.
> To force an art first to digest its civilization in all its crude lumpiness is,
> after all, a good and sound procedure, and it is safe to prophesy that
> in America either the result will be representative and unique or that
> there will emerge no national art at all.[21]

Locke knew that Americans abhorred criticism and would scarcely accept blanket condemnation from a Negro Rhodes Scholar. But something more was at
work here than preparing a text the culturally conservative *North American Review*
would publish. Locke was separating himself from the long line of Boston
aesthetes who had made expatriate careers out of looking down their noses
at America, people like Henry James, Henry Adams, and Bernard Berenson.
Despite all of his internal battles, Locke was an optimist and believed Americans
could foster the conditions for the development of serious art, if they based it on
its indigenous Negro aesthetics. "American Temperament" was the place where
he put into theoretical practice what he had declared in "Oxford Contrasts," that
England had made him an American despite its superficiality and racism.
Whether standing before the Rationalist and Cosmopolitan Clubs or editing the
piece for publication in the *North American Review*, Locke was revealing the self-
knowledge he had gained at Oxford and clearing the ground for an intellectual
return to America.

But he was not ready to return yet. Locke was convinced that he might be able
to support himself indefinitely in Europe on magazine commissions. He needed
a unique angle, however, and thought he had it in his scheme to travel throughout Europe, the Middle East, and Africa, record his impressions of the race attitudes and living conditions of various nationalities, and write a series of articles
on the global nature of race. By comparing how race functioned in different
cultures, Locke believed his findings would be both a serious sociological contribution and a popular press item that would fund his continued European expatriation. Not only did he need a new project, he desperately needed a new source
of income. As he entered Hilary term, he was running out of money, Rhodes
support was nearly at the end, and his debts in Oxford were mounting. On
November 18, 1909, he had been required to appear before the Vice Chancellor's
Court because of an unpaid debt owed to an unknown W. H. Walker. Locke
signed a note to make payment of the £3, 12 s owed, plus 9 s in court costs, by

January 20, 1910. Clearly, things were getting tight for the Rhodes Scholar, who lived and traveled first class: he needed a new benefactor, a new patron for his ruminations. So, early in February 1910, he made plans to return to the United States to hunt up magazine work and to try to obtain support for his plan from the most powerful Black man in America, Booker T. Washington.

Passing up a chance to return to Italy over Christmas vacation in 1909 with Sydney Franklin, Locke saved his money and planned to sail to America on March 12. In the interim, he revised his synopsis and drafted the first five chapters of his thesis for Schiller and Cook Wilson. He had conferences with his supervisors, reported on his progress, and began translating a Latin poem for the Newdigate Prize. His main goal before leaving was "to get my thesis so under way that I can work on it at home and so the trip will not prejudice my chances for a degree. Of course, if I fail I can represent the thesis when I wish, but I should like to get the degree first shot—especially as every year delays my getting the doctorate: one cannot take the Oxford doctorate till five years after admission to the Bachelors."[22] Locke was not clear on the requirements: he could not submit the degree whenever he wished, for his college or the university could, for a variety of reasons, send him down without a degree if it so desired. Locke's error was understandable, given that the rules of the graduate program were notoriously hazy and many students were relatively unfamiliar with them. Locke's confidence was misplaced: he had not finished the thesis yet, and he was already planning on the doctorate and the opportunity to wear Oxford's "scarlet and grey gown."

On the eve of Locke's first trip home in nearly three years, his thesis was not uppermost in his mind. He began the reorganization, rushed through the drafts, but spent less and less time on it as his trip loomed. He got photographs made, "as the demand will be rather great," reworked his Cosmopolitanism essay for the "Fortnightly and Harvard club," sketched a couple speeches for Black associations in Washington and Philadelphia, and said goodbye to friends. Seme spent a whole day with Locke, in part to enlist Locke's help in his attempt to float a loan, since Seme did not yet have the money to return home. Locke even asked Sydney Franklin how might Seme borrow on his land in South Africa. Just as important, Seme wanted to get Locke to commit to coming to South Africa after he returned from America. Locke was interested, but for his own reasons: his main goal in going to America was to try and obtain writing commissions from New York newspapers, and a trip to South Africa for a brief travelogue would suit Locke just fine. He was already beginning to put together a list of places he could travel to, sketch their life and culture, and translate it all into paying newspaper articles.

On March 12, he set sail from Liverpool. Waiting until the last possible dramatic moment, he cabled Booker T. Washington from the ship.

> My dear Sir, I should be forwarding your letter of introduction from Dr Parkin of the Rhodes Trust and from my friend and fellow-student

Mr. Isaka Seme, did I not prefer to go upon the assumption that you will require none of any young man, seriously contemplating race work who asks your counsel. I am returning to America after two and a half years absence to get into practical touch with race affairs, and with the express purpose of meeting certain of our representative men. I am hoping you will be disposed and able to grant me a personal interview, and will undertake to present myself at your convenience and appointment, should you happen to be in New York, Philadelphia or Washington anytime between now and April 16th.[23]

Less interested in meeting "our representative men," Locke was more interested in meeting Washington alone and discussing with him his elaborate plan. But that would have to wait until later in the trip. Upon landing in New York, Locke threw himself into his first order of business—the hunt for editors of America's elite magazines who would be interested in publishing his articles. It seems likely he visited the *Century*, *Harper's*, and certainly the *North American Review*. Then, he left New York for a visit with his mother, and possibly a lecture before the Phillis Wheatley Society in Philadelphia.

More intriguing than where Locke went on the trip is how it made him feel to be back in the United States. It must have seemed noisy to Locke after his sensitive sensibilities had been honed by the beautiful, pre-industrial cities of Europe. Then too, there was the confrontation with racism, the recognition that everything was suddenly different, that he was now an inferior in the eyes of even the commonest White man on the streets of Philadelphia no less than New York. Being back in America in 1910 was a sharp contrast to the liberal cosmopolitanism he enjoyed in Europe. He didn't fit in, but then again, this was a business trip for Locke.

On April 18, Washington telegrammed Locke at Thomas Cook & Sons that he would meet him that evening at the Hotel Manhattan.[24] The talk went well, for afterward Mary wrote that she was surprised that "he bit so fast."[25] Evidently Washington, beleaguered on the educational front in 1910 by the emergence of not only the NAACP but also the *Crisis*, started that year by Du Bois, and increasing criticism from such Black intellectuals as Ida B. Wells, was eager to get a scholar of Locke's renown for his team, for Tuskegee perhaps. But Locke did not yet want a job. What he wanted was Booker T. Washington's endorsement of his scheme and perhaps even funding for a revolutionary comparative study of racial attitudes and race relations in different European countries. Washington, with his access to Andrew Carnegie, seemed a likely touch for funds, and Washington, perhaps thinking of the possibility of Locke on his team, endorsed, at least rhetorically, Locke's plan. The Wizard and the Fox, as his adversaries would later call Washington and Locke, had met and each had found a potential compatriot.

Locke, however, was not yet ready to return home; but he had learned an important lesson—in order to survive in Europe, he needed to keep stoking the fires of America. In "Oxford Contrasts," he had articulated a principle that was even truer now that the Rhodes was coming to an end. His value was greater in America than it was in Europe, and his continued survival as a transnational African American depended on his ability to find new sources of acclaim and support from the American side. The question left unanswered was, would Washington really bite and fund the ambitious plans of the Black Rhodes Scholar?

11

Berlin Stories

Alain Locke's return trip to England at the end of April 1910 contained a welcome surprise: the Pan-Africanist bishop Alexander Walters was also on board the *Lusitania*. The renowned bishop of the African Methodist Episcopal Zion Church, co-organizer of the Afro-American Council and, more recently, sympathizer with Du Bois's Niagara Movement was on the first leg of a maiden voyage to Africa to organize AME Zion conferences in Liberia and across West Africa. Locke and Walters conversed extensively as Locke judged him one of the most cosmopolitan "representative men of our race," committed to forging alliances between Africans and African Americans. It is likely Walters confirmed for Locke what Seme championed—that Africa was the crucial field of development for enlightened African Americans. Once Walters reached Liberia, he claimed, "a thrill of joy possessed me as I stepped from the boat on to the shores of my fatherland." Not only did this transatlantic meeting further encourage Locke to visit Africa but it also launched a lifelong friendship between the two men.

Back in London, Locke visited the *Daily News* and the *Manchester Guardian* trying to obtain additional commissions for his travel scheme before heading to Oxford. He probably would have been better off staying in London. Not long after reaching Oxford, Locke was notified he would have to appear again before the Vice Chancellor's Court because of more unpaid debts. This time his creditor was the Oxford Wine Company, whose bill he had run up hosting so many gatherings in his rooms for the Cosmopolitan Club, the Rationalist Society, and his friends. This time he owed £3, 9 s, and 1 d, and when he appeared before Judge Holland on May 27, he again could not pay his debt, even though he had asked his mother to borrow money on her salary to send to him. On June 3, he would have to appear in court yet again for an overdue debt to Admanson and O. of Oxford. The Chancellor Court Record reads: "defendant appeared. Adjourned for a week. Defendant to have the costs of today. Consent signed in meantime for payment of Debt and L1..18..0 costs as follows: L3 on 9 July and the balance on or before 1st Oct. 1910."[1]

Locke was close to destitute, unable to pay these and other debts as well. His trip to America had exhausted the family's resources, and Mary was worried. When he suggested her coming over to Europe that summer, she dismissed it as absurd. She was right. If she had come, neither of them would have any money for the fall, when he might have to return to Philadelphia. A note of criticism appeared in her letters as she learned how committed he was to remaining in Europe. Magazine and newspaper work was unreliable, she reminded her son. What he needed to do, she chided, was to "finish that darn thesis" and think of getting a job. Locke, however, remained as resolute as ever about avoiding both and staying in Europe.

Hertford College was also resolute. On May 31, the board of his college met and "decided that Mr. Locke must send in his thesis by October 10th 1910, otherwise his name will be taken off the books. As he has been adjudged to be in debt to various creditors, whilst he appears to have no means of satisfying these claims, the College decided that he should go down from Oxford on or before Saturday, June 4th; and that the above decision be communicated by the Dean to the Registrar of the Vice Chancellor's Court."[2] His high-living ways now threatened his ability to come away from Oxford with a degree. Evidently, Locke still had political if not financial resources in Oxford, since he was not sent down on June 10, 1910.

Locke's June 15 letter to Booker T. Washington exuded confidence in his journalistic plan. Things did look good. Washington had provided Locke with a letter of recommendation to Lawrence Abbott, editor of the *Outlook*, whom Locke had met in England and who was encouraging. Moreover, Locke had "been successful in obtaining further commissions in London from the Daily News and the Manchester Guardian, and am hopeful of ultimate success in the undertaking. The scheme seems to have assume[d] quite some proportions, and I have high hopes not only of making it a success as a personal and journalistic venture, but as furnishing some material of permanent value towards the comparative study of the race problems."[3] Locke knew that such a "comparative study of the race problem" was of prime interest to Washington, who himself was planning a European trip to compare the plight of the American Negro with those of the lower classes abroad. Washington was even more concerned about criticism of his policies in the press and during his long battle with his critics had gained financial control of several Black newspapers. Locke attempted to assure Washington that he could be counted as an ally in this struggle. His plan "includes as you will notice, the rights of free reprint for a number of Negro journals," he wrote Washington, but had "not made the offer as yet to any of the editors because the trip is not yet definitely assured, and because I have been contemplating asking your advice in the selection of an effective and representative list."[4]

After assuring Washington of his loyalty, Locke made his pitch.

> I am hoping further for your advice, and, should you be so inclined your endorsement, in financing the venture... as the initial expenses in the matter of photographic and personal outfit will be large as well as the expense of collecting materials, and they cannot be repaid perhaps until the entire trip has been completed; while nothing [echoing his mother] would be more hazardous than to chance it on remissions from articles as they are published. I am endeavoring to get the whole scheme assured by private guarantees to the extent of some five thousand dollars, with an initial advance of two thousand, the whole to be pro-tected by personal life insurance.... If I could, through you, be brought into touch with some likely sources, a second visit to America would be obviated, and I should be profoundly grateful.... Is Mr. Carnegie a possibility? I could, of course, see him this side.[5]

Unfortunately, Washington did not consider this speculative venture important enough to commit his or Carnegie's financial resources to it. Washington ac-knowledged Locke's aplomb in promoting his idea when writing back, "I am wholly unable to offer any direct suggestion as to how the trip may be financed, but you seem to be going about the matter in an altogether satisfying way."[6] Locke did have some prospects. Sydney Franklin alerted him that Dr. Nicholas Butler, the president of Columbia and director of the Albert Kahn Travelling Fellowship, was stopping in London at the Berkeley Hotel. Locke quickly fired off a letter asking for an interview and presenting his plan to the director. It was "just the thing you want," Franklin advised. Whether or not Locke met with Butler, he applied for the Kahn Fellowship during the next cycle.

Locke's problem in June 1910 was that no one would give him any upfront money for the venture. As his Rhodes scholarship was ending, he had no visible means of support for the coming year. There was other bad news. The Eagle Insurance Company of London informed him it would not offer him a life insur-ance policy. That policy had been a key part of Locke's plan to guarantee the in-vestment in his travel scheme by Booker T. Washington's financial backers. Locke's health was too fragile for the company to take the risk.

Suddenly, Locke seemed stuck, while others were moving on. Seme was leav-ing England to return to South Africa and begin his career as a lawyer and leader of his people. Seme wanted Locke to come to South Africa with him, but he was in no position to finance Locke's travel expenses to South Africa. Locke's rela-tionship with Dansey also came abruptly to an end. The details are unknown, but its effect was to further isolate Locke. Fortunately for Locke, Sydney Franklin came to the rescue: "I am thinking of going for an Orient cruise to Norway, leav-ing June 24 and back July 9. It goes as far north as Trondheim, and includes some of the most delightful parts of the country. You simply <u>must</u> come too, it is just the kind of holiday that will suit you, and a kind friend will provide the funds, so that need not trouble you."[7] Locke jumped at the chance to get away from Oxford, do some thinking, and spend a romantic holiday with Franklin, one of his closest friends.

By the first week of July, Locke had returned to Oxford and had begun to regard this summer as no different from any other. Although he needed to save as much of his last Rhodes Scholarship installment as possible, Locke demanded obsessively that his mother spend another summer traveling with him. As in every crisis, his need for his mother increased the worse it became. But Mary Locke insisted it was impossible for her to come over. As a substitute, she recommended that Mr. Bush, her roomer and itinerate substitute teacher, come over. Bush was a long-time family friend who was also something of a surrogate father figure for Locke. Although Bush still lacked a permanent teaching position, he had saved his money from the school year and, with a temporary position assured for the fall, was eager to see Europe. He sailed from New York on July 2 and arrived at Southampton just after Locke returned from Norway. Mary Locke thought that Bush would satisfy Locke's need for her companionship. "Remember I have had two fine summers and am happy in the memory of them. I think everything depends on your staying there and awaiting your chance with Booker."[8] She was wrong. Apparently, as Locke got closer to having to leave Oxford for good, his need for his mother skyrocketed. On July 11, Locke cabled his mother a ticket for second-class cabin passage on the *Kaiser Wilhelm der Grosse* scheduled to sail on July 12, 1910, from Hoboken, New Jersey. She was shocked by his move. "I am so worried and sick at heart," she responded. Having returned home on the evening of July 11 to find the telegram at her door, she was "two hours from sailing of vessel. This was the first I knew of any such plan. I scarcely believe I could have made it. . . . I did not dream you would try to have me come at this <u>late</u> date. My child, try and look at things in a more philosophical mood. I was surely not to come. Every plan has gone astray. Yet my boy— compel yourself to think for a little while of yourself and your career. Give your work your time and thoughts. You will best please your mother, the time soon pass, and we will be re-united again."[9]

Once Locke knew that his mother was not coming over, he desperately needed a place where he could focus all of his attention on completing the writing of his thesis—without the distractions of his friends, his debts, and his unhappy relationship with Oxford. He decided that that place was Berlin. He had liked the city when he visited there with his mother the year before; he could live more inexpensively there; and it was far enough away from Oxford that neither creditors nor inquiring Americans could find him. Then, too, his thesis on the Austrian theory of value relied heavily on the work of German scholars who lived in and around Berlin. Perhaps settling near these thinkers in Berlin would help him to finish it. Then, he could perhaps enroll in one of Germany's several fine universities and make some progress toward getting the doctorate. Like most American students of his generation, Locke viewed the German universities as superior not only to the American but also the British. A German doctorate would put a stamp on him that would transcend the Oxford degree for prestige in American academic circles. Then, he would possess the intellectual and scholarly validation he craved so desperately as he approached his twenty-fifth birthday.

Locke may have hoped that if his mother came over, she could accompany him to Berlin, calm his nerves, and help him get down to work before she returned to America. Instead, he had to settle for Mr. Bush, with whom he would travel around Europe. At the last moment, Philip, who sensed Locke's desperate need for reassuring companionship, decided to accompany him and help him get settled in Berlin. Locke left London for Paris during the last full week of July and did what he loved to do—show a newcomer, Bush, Paris. By now, Locke was not only an expert on the environs of Paris but also had a coterie of Parisian friends with whom he, Bush, and Philip were able to stay. Bush had a great time on this trip; yet on August 4, Mary Locke wrote that she was relieved to learn that he had gone off on his own. "I am glad you have Bush off your hands and I do hope you have not incurred any expense by his coming."[10] Although the details of their itinerary are fuzzy, it seems that Bush was still traveling with Locke and Philip in early August. From Paris, they traveled east into Germany, stopping at Koln and Bonn. Then, on his own, Bush took side trips to Wiesbaden and Frankfurt am Main, before all three rendezvoused temporarily in Hamburg. Locke was almost out of money, and with little time to spare, he hurried on to Berlin, while Bush remained in Hamburg, awaiting the departure of his ship for home. On the day of his departure, Bush wrote to Locke, who had arrived in Berlin and was desperate for money. "I am so sorry that I cannot comply with your request. I have had to begin on my $20 reserve before coming abroad and also had to pay $5 for the extra passage from Hamburg," when he departed for the United States. "I will see that something," he promised Locke, "is sent you as soon as I reach home. I hope you will get on all right. . . . I have had a good time, and no trouble whatever, except to try to hold on to my money that I did not spen[d] it. That I found the hardest thing to do. Try to hold out till I can get something to you from home. I send you these 20 Marks. It is the best that I can do. Keep in close touch with Cook's Office."[11]

Locke and Philip found cheap lodgings through the intercession of their friend, F. H. P. von Voss, who was in Gotha that summer. Von Voss was a tall, blond-haired German whom Locke had met at Oxford, possibly in connection with the Cosmopolitan Club, and he shared Locke's interest in young adolescents. Apparently, Voss had an appointment perhaps through the German diplomatic corps or the military that allowed him to do extensive travel and to sample the homosexual trade in a variety of cities. "Every day," Voss had written from Capri, Napoli, "I go bathing with my friends, some Germans, Italians, and

English. One day there are two English aristocrats. He [*sic*] introduce himself and ask me to come to dinner to his Hotel. I never met a homosexual man like he before. He called me sweetheart for some waiters. I told [him to] go away. He really envy about my friends. We all cannot stand him because he says that he saw us masturbating together (that is not true) & always when we tell him to go away, he says he is going to tell that we are homosexual. It is horrible. Do burn this letter!"[12] From time to time, Voss would turn up in Oxford, and more than once Locke had put him up for several days. Locke had even acted as Voss's art agent for a while, trying to sell several pictures, including a Holbein, that Voss left in Oxford. He wrote Voss when he and Philip reached Hamburg.

Locke's decision to migrate to Berlin may have been shaped by the expectation that he and Philip might be able to stay with Voss for a while, either in his native Potsdam, just outside of Berlin, or in Gotha in central Germany. That didn't happen, however. "I am very sorry," Voss wrote Locke on August 19, "that I cannot ask you and Philip to visit me for some time; but my mother just came back from Switzerland and is very ill and I got plenty of troubles with her and her doctors. When are you leaving West-Deutschland for Berlin? You can go very well via Gotha and stop here some hours or go in a Hotel. I will everything arrange it about hotels here and in Berlin if you like. I really cannot tell you how sorry I am that I can't ask you to come and visit me, as you were so kind to me and had so many trouble with me."[13] Possibly something more fundamental than his mother's illness, such as Locke's race, made it impossible and embarrassing for Voss to invite Locke to his house. But Voss atoned by meeting Locke at the train station in Gotha, repaying an overdue debt, and directing Locke and Philip to a suitable hotel in Berlin. Within another week, Locke had located a rooming house run by Frau Haupt at Grossbeerenstrasse 5. He could confide to his mother by the end of August that he was pleasantly situated in Berlin and settling down to work on his thesis.

Locke felt at home in Berlin, the German capital, in a way he never had in London or Paris. He loved the city's wide boulevards, tall modern buildings, and sumptuous gardens. Berlin exuded an openness and expansiveness that lifted Locke's mood and his confidence. Here was a city with the kind of industrial might and cultural modernity that all twentieth-century cities should offer. The cleanliness, orderliness, punctuality, and obsessiveness of the Germans matched perfectly Locke's own fastidious temperament. Berlin also possessed a bustling street culture, nightlife, and cultural ferment that made it an interesting city for an aesthete and homosexual. In Berlin, at last, Locke had found his spiritual home.

Berlin's reputation as a mecca for male homosexuals was another strong attraction. Locke's friend von Voss seemed to epitomize the freedom to develop an all-but-out gay personality in Berlin. Although Germany had passed its infamous paragraph 175 that made homosexual activity a capital crime, the law was inadequately enforced, even though some scandals occurred. A famous case was that of an army officer who was exposed as being gay, and in the aftermath of his trial, a kind of hysteria had reigned in Germany that was not unlike that of the Oscar Wilde affair in England. But just as was the case in England, when the hoopla died down, gays who were discreet—those who did not get caught or have some jealous "aristocrat" accuse them publicly of homosexuality—were left alone. The promise of such social and sexual freedom, as well as the anonymity of being a foreigner, may have made Berlin seem perfect to Locke.

But Voss's letters to Locke during this period also suggest that the love life available to him in London was superior to that of Berlin. In London, after attending some lectures at the university there, Voss wrote Locke on October 28 that "I have had the most splendid time I ever had in my life! Every evening and not for money, only for love! The youth here are beautiful. I love them." Teasingly, he questioned Locke—"are all those youths in Berlin professional or do they do it for love like here?"[14] Voss knew very well that the principal source of gay sex came from young boys from the provinces who walked the promenade along Friedrichstrasse and Unter den Linden, and made a living as male prostitutes. Locke knew this too and probably frequented the area. By the spring of 1911, Locke appears to have decided that the city and its "trade" had been overrated. "I quite agree with you," Voss wrote to Locke, "that in Berlin are not so many nice looking youngsters as in Italy, London, Paris, Cairo, and so." Planning his own visit to Berlin, Voss queried Locke: "Could you give me any idea what the fee of a nice looking boy in Berlin is in the age of 16 or 17?"[15] This Voss rather incredibly inscribed on a postcard; when Locke did not write him back immediately, Voss queried again, "Are you mad that I wrote about those boys on the postcard?" More than likely Locke was mad: he was too discreet for such bold admissions. But Voss expressed the deeper truth when he wrote, "You are only a sir if you got money? Everybody want money, money! I know it myself, but never mind. Cheer up! Don't be downhearted!"[16] Clearly, Locke, who was down to his own last pennies, was hardly in a position to pay for sex on a regular basis. Without a scholarship or a lucrative endowment, Berlin was hardly a homosexual paradise for him. That was probably good, since without distractions, Locke had little else to do but concentrate on his thesis. In Berlin, he was able to finish it.

Locke produced a brilliant analysis of value theory in his Oxford thesis, "The Concept of Value," by constructing a wholly psychological account of how values arise in human beings. Unlike writings by such major value theorists as Brentano, Meinong, Ehrenfels, Urban, and Munsterberg, Locke's philosophical discussion of values is a readable, almost lyrical account of the process by which human beings learn to value. Thus, in terms of its philosophical orientation and its literary form, "The Concept of Value" was an extension of William James's two-volume opus, *The Principles of Psychology*, into a philosophy of values. As a thesis for Oxford in 1910, however, and especially for Locke's principal supervisor and examiner, J. Cook Wilson, this was not a particularly strategic approach. In fact, by choosing to write a psychological rather than a logical account of valuation, Locke's thesis was a frontal attack on the logical tradition of value theory that Cook Wilson himself represented. Nevertheless, it was a major step in Locke's progress toward becoming a philosopher, proof that he could sustain a sophisticated philosophical analysis over four hundred handwritten pages.

Locke asked: How do our values come into being? Are values derived from feelings, desires, or cognitive judgments? The prevailing view in Locke's time was that values arose because of our desires and through the exercise of the logical, judgment faculty of our minds. By contrast, Locke argued that, while logic and reason played a role in the discrimination of values once they had arisen, we could only understand how values arose in the first place through a psychological reconstruction of the valuation process from the "experient's own point of view located and explained in terms of its own activity and its psychological implications." Using several real-life examples of valuing, Locke showed that values were "selected" on the basis of feelings, which arose in our experience, and led us to place a value upon one part of that experience. Reflecting James's insights, Locke argued valuation emerged as part of the selecting agency of consciousness. Confronting what James called the "stream of experience," our minds, Locke argued, elevated that which moved us emotionally. That became what we valued ethically, practically, or aesthetically as the good, the useful, and the beautiful. Locke's theory of value, therefore, applied James's method of introspective psychological inquiry to valuation and came up with a no-nonsense portrait of how people actually valued. Indeed, by using "real-life" examples of valuing, Locke made his work accessible in a way that also recalled William James.

What remains most interesting about "The Concept of Value" are the philosophical choices Locke made in this, his initial philosophical treatise. For one thing, he labels himself rhetorically as a psychologist in the text. This is a remarkable choice for a man who often seemed not to have a clue about his own complicated motivations and about how others reacted to him. Even more profound is his choice of feeling as the most important factor in valuation. If we assume that this essay is not only about values but also about Locke himself, a man who personally came across to some as cold, logical, and rational to a fault, he "comes out" in this thesis and throws his entire philosophical weight behind feeling. In his thesis, Locke revealed the romantic that stood behind the stoic Rhodes Scholar exterior: here was a man whose feelings drove his engagement with the world.

The autobiographical character of Locke's thesis is also illustrated by the examples he chose of value formation from his own experiences listening to music. "Let us suppose," he writes, "as usually happens, that some disproportionate variation in one of the sensation elements [of a musical composition] attracts attention, say an unusual stress, and on the basis of it we catch a rhythm movement, go along with it a little while, lose it, catch it up again until finally we have some distinct feeling of form succession in which all the other sensation accompaniments center. And then suddenly some of the sensation hooks on to the rhythm, subordinates it, and gives us a sense of time, heightens perhaps the successive feeling into a pleasurable feeling tone. This persists for a while, and then quite as suddenly again perhaps the feeling-tone spreads over the whole content. At last we have something which from the aesthetic point of view we can call a musical appreciation."[17]

Locke rewrote value theory because most value theories could not account for his experience of aesthetics. Neither logical inference nor self-interest could account for how the beautiful and the ugly were differentiated. Nor could such theories solve the mystery of "value-transfer," when one value attribute (useful, noble) became associated with another value category (logical, ethical). Such transfers proved to Locke that values were not fixed objects, but attributes transferable from one area to another. "The prevalent interchange of value predicates, as for example, a 'pretty demonstration,' a 'wrong inference,' are not to be wholly accounted for as mere verbal tropes or figurative transfers. Some real psychological linkage seems involved in certain value metaphors. For example, ethical distinctions for certain temperaments present themselves in aesthetic contrasts, and actual motives of ethical action may often be purely aesthetic or mixed aesthetic as conveyed by terms [such] as 'noble' or 'ignoble' action."[18] Only feeling was comprehensive enough to account for the ambiguity of valuation and the ways that value predicates moved from one category to another. Clearly, our feelings change about our value objects, and with those changes came shifts in the values and the categories we commonly used to order them.

Locke's focus on value shift suggests that he believed values had no permanent character: the expert and the novice might listen to the same music, but hear it differently and certainly value it differently, depending on their levels of appreciation. Since the values were attributes determined by the subject who listened and reflected the complexity of feeling that the listener brought to the experience, the expert and the novice did not share the same musical experience. Values were not even permanent for the same individual. They changed with changes in consciousness.

Such a skeptical view of values extended to Locke's view of race as malleable and changeable. At a time when Du Bois's "The Conservation of the Races" (1896) argued races were fixed entities with discrete spiritual contributions to make to world civilization, Locke took a more revolutionary position that racial character and identity changed over time, and in response to changing social and cultural conditions—and the attitude (consciousness) of the racial subject himself or herself. That view of race had its philosophical grounding in "The Concept of Value." In one context, he was certainly an American Negro; but he also was rapidly becoming a European, a man whose identity had taken on many of the characteristics of his European education. His subjectivity had evolved and so had his valuations. Locke's value theory provided a way of conceptualizing what he would eventually call the New Negro as racial identity that would shift with the changing context and valuation of our experiences.

But in 1910, the connections between his value theory and modernism in literature and art were stronger than any racial analogies. When Locke depicted aesthetic valuation, he went behind the process and described the kind of "open" and indeterminate state of consciousness that many writers and artists cultivated as a source of inspiration for their work. "Such states as objectless sadness, moods of poetic melancholy, and the like have very little or no sensational content, and involve practically no mental reactions, cognitive or conative. They are therefore, very difficult of explanation for the judgment in the desire theory of value. That they have value is beyond dispute. A little introspective analysis will reveal why. They are diffused emotional states covering, as it were, the whole field of consciousness, and leaving us room . . . to take an attitude and discriminate a relationship. And we do so through the medium of feeling. The feeling deepens somehow and we get a sense of the context as a subjective 'mood,' a phase of consciousness and its very diffusion becomes a sense of immediacy, of close identification." As Locke went on to argue, modern art was given to cultivating such moods in order to create new forms of art. "Impressionism has experimented in the creation of aesthetic values out of just such vague emotional states and to the extent it has succeeded has proved that they were values before, only much neglected and dissociated. As aesthetic values, they have been formalized and might be accounted for as a 'cultivated taste,' which would only mean the formation of a feeling disposition, but as they occur in the ordinary experience, a propos of nothing in particular, they are better illustrations of how feeling tones and feeling references condition value acquirement."[19]

Locke's reference to "diffused" emotional states as the origin of valuation suggests that he may have also had his experience as a homosexual in mind while he was writing his essay on values. "Diffused emotion" was a metaphor Locke later used in his correspondence to describe some of his feelings as a homosexual. "Diffused feelings" was Locke's longing for male companionship without any specific person or "value object" in mind. It often produced in him a state of "objectless sadness"—longing for a specific person who is absent. "Objectless" emotions, according to Locke, ultimately resolved themselves into more specific desires for some specific person, or as in the case of valuation, resolved themselves into a more definite "value-feeling-unified emotional state fused or identical with its feeling content."[20] Locke used his "diffused feelings" for bonding with any man as a source for understanding that stage in which an individual senses a value preference before conceiving of a particular object of value. In that way, some of Locke's feelings and experiences as a homosexual provided him with insight for his theory of values.

Of course, aesthetic value remained the most important model for Locke's theory of valuation. Locke believed that having values was evidence of our capacity for an aesthetic disposition toward our environment, just as desires and satisfactions were evidence of our biological nature. What Locke was developing was reminiscent of James—an account of the rise of culture in human beings that rejected biological instinct or behaviorism's "conditioned-reflex" as the origin of values. Like James, Locke was trying to avoid biological determinism in understanding human life.

The major weakness of "The Concept of Value" was that it relied too much on aesthetic valuation to model all valuation. Locke failed to demonstrate the applicability of his analysis to all other areas of valuation. He also failed to distinguish between a concept and a value, between the concept of a chair and its utilitarian value. Are these the same thing? Is learning the meaning of the chair the same as appreciating its usefulness? If this is so, Locke's portrait of learning processes needed added complexity to differentiate between learning through habit, conditioned reflex, trial-and-error, and insight learning. The absence of this refinement can be explained in terms of the rudimentary psychological theories of learning behavior Locke had available to him, but it also was due to the narrow focus he had taken. He relied too much on introspection as a methodological tool and paid too little attention to the social context in learning.

Nevertheless, "The Concept of Value" was an impressive work—more than four hundred pages of detailed argument for (1) the ability of psychology to account for valuation without recourse to logic, (2) the primacy of feeling in the origin and discrimination of values, and (3) the demonstration of how a new classification of values could be created based on (1) and (2). Locke completed part 1, chapters 1 through 9, of "The Concept of Value" on September 13, 1910, his twenty-fifth birthday; he completed part 2 on October 7, 1910. After copying them over in a measured, elegant longhand with footnotes at the bottom of each page, Locke sent the manuscript off to Oxford in time to meet the October 10, 1910, deadline imposed by Hertford College for the submission of his thesis.

"The Concept of Value" was a psychological breakthrough in Locke's life. He had written a massive, original, generative work of philosophy without having his mother with him or at a convenient distance, as had been the case at Harvard. Abandoned, alone, without even money to pay for sex, Locke had holed up in his Berlin apartment, and written his ass off. A rebirth had occurred in Berlin that prefigured what would happen fourteen years later when he was permanently separated from his mother and returned to Berlin to invent himself. His catharsis then as now came through dialogue with a city, its built and human environment that created the psychological space for a momma's boy to become a mature philosopher.

While waiting for Oxford's response, Locke attended lectures at the University of Berlin. He enrolled in five lecture courses given that fall by members of the philosophical faculty at the university. Locke took logic from Benno Erdmann, a Kantian professor; logic and theories of perception from Adolf Lasson, another Kantian scholar; nineteenth-century philosophy from Georg Simmel, the Jewish philosopher who founded modern German sociology; introductory aesthetics from Max Dessoir, a well-known professor of aesthetics; and philosophical idealism from Hugo Munsterberg, a visiting Harvard University professor. Munsterberg was the philosopher most familiar to Locke that first semester. Locke knew Munsterberg from Harvard, where he had been one of the faculty on the committee that awarded Locke his magna cum laude. Munsterberg was a Fichtean who believed that humanity possessed a metaphysical will accessible by intuition and a scientific will accessible by observation and experiment. It was Munsterberg the metaphysician who had crept into his major philosophical book, *The Eternal Values*, which Locke had soundly if sympathetically criticized in "The Concept of Value" for its idealistic notions of values. Still, Munsterberg was someone who remembered Locke's undergraduate work and probably encouraged Locke to study at the University of Berlin. Munsterberg was also director of the Amerika-Institut and as such was responsible for the growing number of Americans studying at the university. In January 1911, he wrote to Locke formally in this capacity. "In the interest of the American students, the Amerika-Institut is carrying on an investigation concerning the studies of the Americans in the German universities. We beg you kindly to aid us by answering as soon as possible and as carefully as possible the questions of the enclosed sheet in the blank spaces after each question."[21] Locke's answers are lost, but the surviving letter shows that Locke was not an anonymous entity at the University of Berlin by January 1911. If he played his cards right, he might be able to parlay his stay in Berlin into a German doctorate and then return to the United States as a complete educational success.

As always, Locke had other irons in the fire. He was writing more short stories and articles, which he was trying to get placed in American magazines. He was also still trying to obtain financial support for his race relations travel scheme, and toward that end, planned to meet Washington "this side" of the Atlantic. But after months of having his mother check the newspapers for Washington's travel plans, somehow Locke let Washington slip into and out of Berlin in January 1911 without meeting him. Washington had come to Berlin to deliver a lecture, but did not contact Locke while in town. When Locke's mother learned of the miscue, she was astounded. How could Locke have missed this opportunity? Locke himself seemed to have no explanation. Washington apologized with the excuse that he was very rushed. He encouraged Locke to obtain the articles that Washington published from the trip in the *Outlook*. In a sense, Washington told the truth: he was tremendously rushed. Washington did not have time to dally in Berlin interviewing a powerless aesthete like Locke. He had hurried back to New York to try and woo such powerful representatives of educated Black opinion as Mary Church Terrell and William Pickens, who had established constituencies and access to information on the NAACP. Locke had neither. The costs of staying away from the American scene were beginning to add up. Plus, Washington already had an amanuensis, the only job that Locke would have been interested in taking in 1911. Robert Park, a Jewish American sociologist, was ghostwriting Washington's articles on race and class relations. Indeed, what could Locke offer Washington? As he confided in a January 1911 letter to Washington after missing him in Berlin, Locke planned to remain in Berlin until he heard about his thesis results, continue to take courses at the University of Berlin, and travel to Egypt in the near future to study their race relations. Locke could not assist Washington in any useful way.

Locke did not have long to wait on his thesis results. On February 8, 1911, the board of the *Literae Humaniores* met and discussed his thesis. Present that day were Mr. How, master of Balliol, who was the chair of the committee, Professors Cook Wilson, Ellis, Gardner, Murray, Myres, and Stewart, and Messrs. Blunt, Clark, Cookson, Joseph, Matheson, Richards, and Webb. This group rendered a decision, "on the report of the examiners it was resolved not to issue a certificate to Mr. A. L. Locke."[22] Neither his examiners' report, nor the notes of the discussion that day have survived. The views of Cook Wilson, who had been both Locke's supervisor and one of his thesis examiners, must have carried considerable weight in shaping the board's decision. The other examiner of the thesis, Mr. Carritt, who was the only philosopher at Oxford who knew anything about aesthetics, was not present. Even more devastating was the board's second decision to deny him an opportunity to revise and resubmit it: "Mr. Locke having applied for readmission as a B.Sc. student on the same subject of special study it was resolved that his application be not granted."[23] With that decision, the board and particularly Wilson declared that there was nothing worthwhile or redeemable in Locke's four hundred–page thesis. For Locke, it meant that his entire struggle to complete the work had been in vain. He now had a thesis that itself had no value to Oxford.

Perhaps Locke had anticipated this outcome. Two days before the board of *Literae Humaniores* rendered its decision, Hertford College responded to Locke's request from him to be allowed to reapply to that board for candidacy for the BLitt degree, his original course of study when he had entered Oxford. Locke believed that if he failed in his attempt to have the thesis approved and to receive the BSc in philosophy, he could still hold the door open for a BLitt degree. While Hertford College gave him permission to reapply for candidacy for the BLitt, it simultaneously informed him "his name would be removed from the books at the end of the present term, unless he satisfied the College that he had discharged his debts in Oxford."[24] That was almost as impossible as his getting the BSc degree: he had no income, beyond the $30 his mother scraped together to send to him each month, and thus he had no way to pay his debts.

Like Harley at Harvard, Locke's personal financial problems had derailed his academic career. But unlike Rex, who got his Harvard AB after he paid his debt, Locke was no longer eligible for a degree after he was "sent down." That occurred on March 10, 1911.

Of course, more had poisoned Locke's relationship with his college than his debts. Locke had rebelled against the authority of his Hertford tutor, Rev. Williams, and succeeded in eluding Williams's grasp by gaining admission to the graduate program in philosophy under Wilson. That had angered Williams and set him against Locke. Locke had then moved out of his college, traveled throughout Europe on expensive vacations, and had had the cheek to have the college forward his mother's letters all over Europe, proving to his college that he was not engaged in serious study. Then, when the board of *Literae Humaniores* rejected his thesis in February, he was thrown back upon his unsympathetic college as the only possible place through which he could salvage his Oxford career. But they were thoroughly tired of the Black Rhodes Scholar from America who had embarrassed the college by running up huge debts in town and refused to be deferential about it on top of it.

Having subverted the power of his Hertford tutor, Locke seemed not to realize how dependent his getting the degree was on J. Cook Wilson, the fierce white-bearded logician at Oxford who had turned philosophy away from idealism. As a classicist, Wilson also may have heard that Locke had come to him because he could not make the grade in Greek and thus approached him skeptically. Rather than produce a thesis that followed Wilson's somewhat dated theory of knowledge and apply it to valuation, Locke wrote an entirely psychological account that rejected the logical approach to valuation! That was too much for Wilson. There was much to dislike about Wilson: he was pompous and combative, and, according to one wit, Wilson's total published work in philosophy was a footnote before his death in 1915. Wilson's ideas had been passed over by the new logic coming out of Cambridge University, pioneered first by Bertrand Russell and then by Ludwig Wittgenstein. Wilson hated the new logic, and he certainly could not stomach the new psychology of William James. Though Wilson had agreed to work with James's Oxford disciple, F. C. S. Schiller, in supervising Locke's thesis, Schiller had apparently abandoned the project, leaving Locke at Wilson's mercy. Still, had Locke been a deferential student, he might have at least been able to revise the thesis in accord with Wilson's criticisms. But Locke had not been deferential and he paid the price for that.

Oxford, the place, had defeated him. When Oxford sent him down, it did so as much because of his behavior as the quality of his work. They were done with him as a person, as a character, regardless of what he achieved as a student. The same Victorian nexus of good behavior, proper breeding, and exemplary background that had worked so many times for Locke—that buoyed his career because he was more "gentlemanly" than other Blacks—had finally turned against him. Just as his ability to play the game of deferential politics had helped him flourish at Harvard, his inability to play it effectively at Oxford had sunk him.

What had been different? The racism had destabilized him, cut him to the core in ways he had never experienced before, made him nervous and even scared for his safety. This was the first time that he had really been hated, hounded really, even when the Rhodes Scholars were not around. But he would never admit that race was the determining factor, because the whole apparatus of Black Victorian behavior was designed to manage racism as a constant enemy of Black success. Was race enough of an excuse? Some might have blamed it on his being an American and insufficiently prepared for the rigor of an Oxford education. Indeed, a series of articles had appeared in the American press that February 1911 lambasting American students at Oxford for not being very good. He learned of them because his dutiful mother copied them into her letters to him as he was absorbing the shock of his thesis rejection and imminent expulsion from his college. She did not know yet what had happened, for Locke did not inform her immediately after learning the results. He too was searching for an explanation as to why after so many successes, he had failed this time to come away from Oxford with the one thing he needed—a degree.

Early in March 1911, Locke wrote his mother that he had suddenly changed plans. He was not going to stay in Germany and try for the doctorate, after all. The only place for him was Cambridge, Massachusetts. He would come home, enroll in Harvard's graduate school, and take his degree. That sudden switch alerted her something was wrong. But not until April 2, almost two months after he had heard the news, did she learn his thesis had been rejected. "My heart goes out to you," she wrote him, "in your disappointment regarding the Thesis—yet I had expected it."[25] Her superb Victorian intelligence had taught her failure could be expected, when one did not—ironically enough, since his thesis was on values—uphold the values of the institutions one depended on. She wrote him that there was nothing to do but to stay until he earned the Oxford or a Berlin degree. He had not told her the board's second decision. It was probably too much for him to reveal to her all at once the depth and completeness of his failure.

Perhaps Locke would have been better off telling her, for she went on to admonish him that despite the setback, he could not let go of the Oxford thesis. "I know how hard it will be to take it up again, the thesis, but it must be done. You cannot afford to fail as the first and only one of your race—and more than all—for my sake—because I have my heart and soul fixed on it."[26] The last line had the ring of desperation, as if she had suddenly realized that something like this needed to have been said long ago. Indeed, before she actually learned of the rejection of his thesis, she had peppered him with admonishments and self-recriminations. She should have pressed him to work harder, she wrote to him now—three years too late. The Rhodes Scholarship had seemed so long, and she had gained so much from it herself, for she had been able to see places and things she never dreamed she would see in her lifetime.

A growing sense of shared responsibility and now embarrassment made her angry at him for letting down the race. He had let her down too. And other people would know. People at the post office were already asking her what he was doing in Germany. More well-known folk like Jessie Fauset, the prominent Philadelphia young woman, had met Mary Locke one Sunday in Philadelphia early in 1911 and asked about him too. On April 9, Mary Locke wrote him that Pfromm, his Harvard friend, had stopped by the house and asked if the thesis had gone through all right and whether he had his degree. She, of course, told Pfromm she did not know. But that story would soon be old. The pressure was building on the Lockes, both of whom had lived off the prestige of these last three years. Soon they would look much smaller in light of his monumental failure.

Mary had been a central part of his success; now she was part of his failure. Like a mythological hero, he had had to go off on a quest to become the hero he was destined to be. But going so far away from her had weakened him. It was not just the money he had lost in bringing her over two years in a row, the debts that mounted; it was that he had been unable to manage the multiple pressures on him—the racism, the partying, the sexual distractions, the painful recognition of his intellectual limits—without her stabilizing presence. At Harvard, he had had her in striking distance for easy renewal and steadying in the face of challenges. At Oxford, he had been less emotionally mature even though he was older. And the challenges had been far greater. So far away at Oxford, he had lost his balance. In Berlin, he had achieved something absolutely necessary by finishing his thesis without her presence. He had grown into manhood. But in April 1911, that did not much matter. Now, what reverberated was that line in her letter—"You cannot afford to fail as the first and only one of your race—and more than all—for my sake—because I have my heart and soul fixed on it."[27] Having failed to get the degree, he was an embarrassment to his race—and to her. How could he come home now?

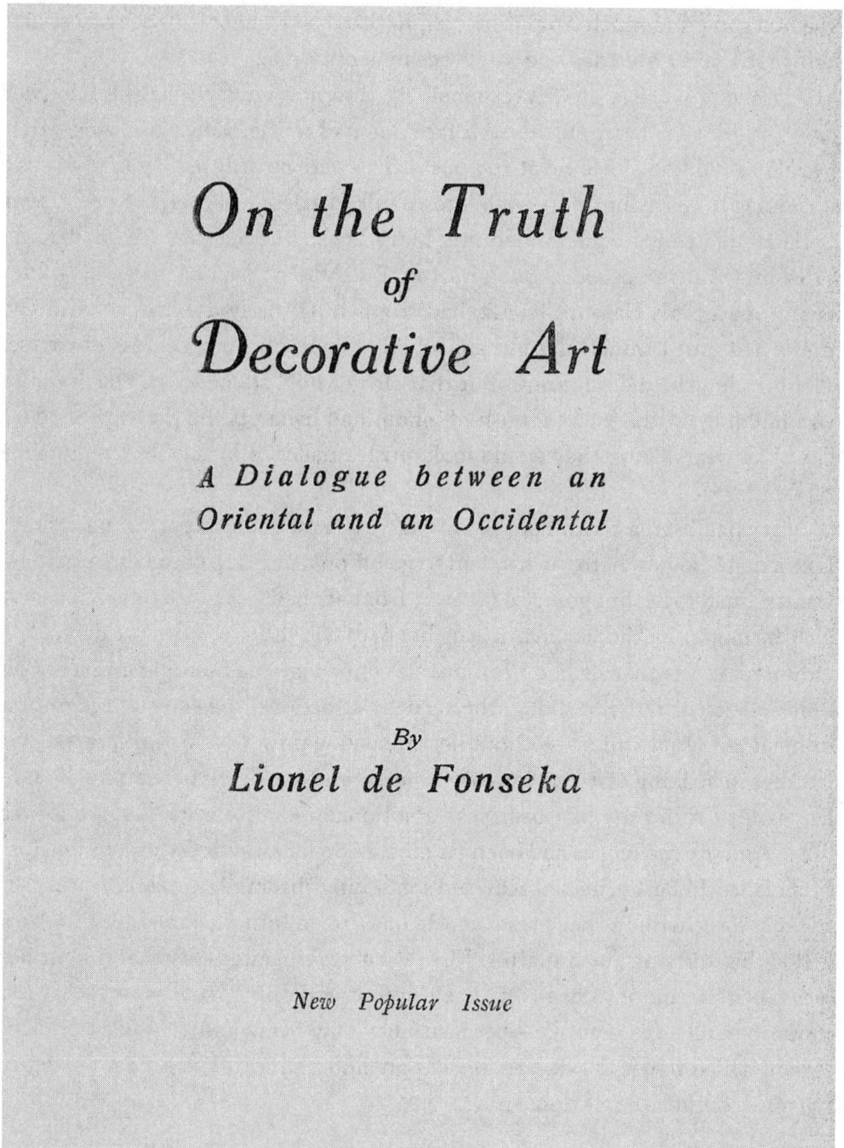

On the Truth

of

Decorative Art

A Dialogue between an
Oriental and an Occidental

By

Lionel de Fonseka

New Popular Issue

New York:
Henry Holt & Co.
1913

Title page of Lionel de Fonseka, *On the Truth of Decorative Art*, 1913.

12

Exile's Returns

Locke's exile in Berlin was interrupted late in February 1911 by the arrival of Frederich von Voss, who wanted to spend a month with him in Berlin. Voss confided that his parents objected to his going to Berlin, so he wanted to come in secret. Voss hoped he could share a room with Locke for the month, which would have helped Locke save some of his rent money. But it was not to be. When Locke met Voss at the Anhalter Station on February 27, Locke was not able to offer him a place in his apartment, most likely because Locke's very protective landlady refused. She had even shut the door in Voss's face without checking to see if Locke was home. Nonetheless, Voss's appearance in Berlin cheered Locke. Together, they walked the promenade on Friedrichstrasse, enticing the young homosexual trade. Voss introduced Locke to several of the cafes and restaurants that he knew from his earlier days in Berlin, and Voss's companionship soothed Locke's jangled nerves. Voss also introduced Locke to Charlottenburg, the lovely, tree-lined suburb at the outskirts of Berlin. Not long after that first visit, Locke moved into an apartment in Charlottenburg, perhaps taking over the one occupied by Voss during his Berlin stay. By March 9, however, Voss had returned to Potsdam and his family, and Locke was once again alone with his secret.

Locke had informed his mother and his closest Oxford friends that his thesis was rejected, but they did not seem to comprehend that he was prevented from obtaining an Oxford degree. An April 7 letter from his friend Lionel de Fonseka reflected how confused even Oxford undergraduates were about Oxford rules and regulations. "What does it mean—your name being taken off the books of the college. I hope it does not mean that you can't get a degree at all."[1] Of course, it did. In one sense, it made little immediate difference whether he got the degree or not. Unemployed and near destitute in Berlin, he would have remained so regardless of Oxford's decision. What failure to get the degree really meant was that he could not face the embarrassment such failure would cause him at home. So he kept it a secret and remained in Berlin.

It might have been better if Locke had returned home before he knew the results of his thesis. In the fall of 1910, he had been offered a job unofficially through his mother to be principal of a Black school. If Locke was back employed in the United States, he easily could have put off inquirers that he was still awaiting a decision. But he had turned the offer down. Though desperate for money, he was too proud to take a job in elementary education and too hopeful that after receiving the bachelor of science degree, he could return to Oxford for the doctorate. Having never before experienced academic failure, he had no experience of coping with it. As he sat in his Berlin hovel, penniless and alone, even he must have wondered what this failure said about him. Some doubt had crept into his consciousness ever since he had difficulty with Greek during his first year. At the time, he had been able to blame it on his tutor and subsequently on the educational system at Oxford; but a bit of self-doubt had returned during the long haul of working on his thesis, year after year, without being able to make any real progress on it. Locke, a man of supreme confidence, had begun to wonder privately to himself if he would ever finish. In a sense, it would never be finished; he would never really be over Oxford, for the rest of his life. As a good Victorian, who believed that each man was master of his fate, he could not escape the conclusion that he had been the master of his.

But academic failure rejuvenated Locke's journalistic writing. Freed from his thesis, Locke found that he could write easily and quickly again. On April 10, Locke completed an essay, "Some Aspects of Modernism," less than two weeks after seeing a similar article published in the March 29 issue of the *Saturday Evening Post* by a "special correspondent" living in Paris. That article convinced Locke that enough interest existed in the United States to get his essay published, and that there might be an income for him writing similar articles as a "special correspondent" in Berlin. But "Some Aspects of Modernism" is unique in Locke's oeuvre, because it presents an ideological argument for Modernism in the Roman Catholic Church. Another consequence of the Oxford debacle may have been that Locke contemplated converting to Catholicism, perhaps even going into the church, influenced perhaps by de Fonseka's fervent Catholicism. If so, then Locke's article was his way of defining what kind of Catholic he could become.

Locke argued vigorously that Modernism within the Catholic tradition was an authentic challenge to papal authority and not a movement toward Protestantism as the earlier article suggested. Spawned by the rise of Higher Criticism that revised biblical interpretation through the use of historical knowledge, Modernism, according to Locke, was really an evolutionary movement toward the acceptance of relativism in the Roman Catholic Church. Modernism emerged as an answer to the pragmatic problem facing the Roman Church that over half of modern church membership did not believe in such rigid church doctrines as papal infallibility. Yet such members wanted to remain in the church. German Protestantism was a response that rejected the pope, yet enshrined a new absolute truth imposed just as ruthlessly as papal edict. What Locke liked about Modernism was its tendency to see truth as progressive, as reflective of a world in the making and not already made, a precursor, perhaps, to what he would argue about the New Negro fourteen years later. "Modernist scholarship, more modestly perhaps, more wisely perhaps, expresses the prevailing relativism of contemporary thought and theory. It gains thereby in interpretative power, in literary charm, and in its relevance to the private thought and problems of the time. For the Catholic tradition, for any tradition, this is ... appropriate."[2] Locke's essay was thus a continuation of his interest in values and the necessity to accept relativism in values. Indeed, Locke saw Modernism as a blueprint for successful change in the modern world:

> The success of Modernism will mean something more than the success of a new cause; it will mean the triumph of a new method of mental and moral warfare. Springing up on the old controversial ground of religion and within the jurisdiction of Catholicism, Modernism might easily have reinstated another era of controversy and have had reactionary effects of the greatest consequence. [But] with rare caution and unusual success, Modernism has refused to compromise itself by joining issue with the opposition, and has achieved thereby its unique character and advantages. Reform movements of consequence, in the religious as in the political world, have hitherto been of necessity partisan and revolutionary in character; and although they may have taken origin out of the most abstruse issues, have scarcely ever been prosecuted or carried on the intellectual plane.[3]

Locke was suspicious of revolutions because, in their total repudiation of a tradition, they tended to resurrect a dogmatism often as bad as or worse than that which they sought to replace. Locke disliked Protestantism because in its rebellion it had become totalitarian; he liked Modernism because it preserved the Catholic tradition at the very moment that it reinvented it. "The steadier undercurrent of events, even in Germany, gives clear indications that Modernism has more in common with a Renaissance movement than with either a Revolution or a Reformation."[4] Locke approached the Catholic tradition as an intellectual tradition of rigorous engagement with and debate of spiritual issues. Locke sided squarely with the reformers in historical Catholicism.

Locke's sexual orientation may have conditioned his insistence that the church recognize the relativism of moral values, even though he did not mention sexual issues in his essay. He was well aware that the Roman Catholic Church was a harbinger of many homosexuals and that it must liberalize its doctrine or sink into complete hypocrisy. Clearly this was a problem that did not face the Catholic Church alone, as a letter that Locke received two weeks after finishing his essay attests. His Chelsea London friend Jayston Edwards confided to Locke:

I have been the guest of a man at the Isle of Wight—he is a parson too. He is a very nice man but I had suspicions at first that I was accepting his hospitality under false pretenses. Sunday, expectations of his were not realised. Physically he did not attract me at all. However we remained friends and he took me into his confidence entirely. He had been 5 years chaplain to a bishop in India and knew them of all colors. He had a young friend of 22 a pupil at a farm who was also so disposed and whose whole life and being were absorbed in the pursuit of boys, etc. I went to hear my host, the parson, preach and wondered how he had the brass to talk about priority, hypocrisy, etc.[5]

The Modernists argued against the hypocrisy typical of "parsons" in the church who habitually railed against homosexuality but practiced it themselves. Locke's essay outlined what he required of any religion he embraced: it must preach what it practiced and frankly acknowledge the relativity of all normative dictates. It must embody a methodology of social reform and be responsive to it. Ultimately, the Modernist movement Locke depicted in 1911 failed to conquer its opposition, which may be one of the reasons that Locke never converted to Catholicism.

But an unanswered question remains: why would Locke turn to writing an extensive essay on reform Catholicism after failing in his quest for an Oxford degree? Perhaps he sought a form or forum of absolution for his Oxford failure. Catholicism, Locke believed, had had the good sense to formalize the process by which if one confessed one's sins, one was forgiven, and allowed to go forth a new man. The process of how to become a new man was a central thread in Locke's philosophical life. Here, Locke acknowledged he himself needed absolution from his sins as long as he did not have to view his homosexuality as a sin. That he continued to write—and such a powerful essay as this—suggests that his ego had not been destroyed by that failure. Writing "Some Aspects of Modernism" may have started the process of absolution he desired without his having to take the step of joining the Catholic Church. For writing that essay may have concretized that his refusal to bend to Oxford's strictures, to accept what he clearly felt was the hypocrisy and despotism of Oxford's system, had, perhaps, saved him as an independent thinker.

While Locke enjoyed writing "Modernism," the essay, sadly, was not published. It is not clear why. Perhaps the problem for Locke's journalistic aspirations was that his subjects were too esoteric to command a wide American readership. If he really wanted to become a journalist, he would have to return to the United States and work in a newsroom or on the staff of a magazine. Locke, however, wanted to start at the top, as a foreign correspondent, but he was not famous or even well known enough to be published regularly doing that. In Germany, Locke was beginning, slowly, to realize that he needed a regular income, from teaching or something else, to sustain him until he could establish a reputation as a writer. That line of thinking brought him back to the Oxford problem.

Sometime in the spring of 1911, Locke decided it was time to become serious about getting the German doctorate. In May 1911, he matriculated into the university for study under the philosophical faculty and took a full complement of courses: two courses, a lecture course in the history of philosophy, Kant and Idealism, and a seminar on Kant's Antinomies, from Professor Riehl; another lecture course on fundamental problems of philosophy from Professor Lasson, plus a course on the philosophy of Will and Action from Professor Munsterberg. But the most important courses he took that spring bridged the divide between philosophy and modern sociology: Analysis of the Fundamentals of Science, and Problems of Modern Culture taught by Germany's premier sociological theorist, Georg Simmel.

Simmel was an interesting mentor for Locke, as he, like Locke, was a perennial outsider. Although a brilliant Kantian scholar, prolific writer who wrote on such esoteric subjects as *The Philosophy of Money*, and founder of modern German sociology, Simmel never received an appointment as a full professor at the University of Berlin because he was Jewish. Simmel also was disparaged because he was a thoroughgoing Modernist, who did not suffer the romantic nationalism of Volkish philosophy sweeping academic circles in the late nineteenth century. He argued that gradual, painstaking, and democratic reform was the best solution to modern problems in a world without a priori certainties.

Simmel's classrooms confirmed Locke had been on the right track in "The Concept of Values." According to Simmel no certainties, no fixed unities, existed from which ideas of law, morality, religion, and society could be developed in modern societies. Modern values were essentially pragmatic "social unities" in a fluid state of interaction, and they bound dissimilar elements and peoples together despite the social distance of modern, urban living. A creative tension existed in modern societies that responded to changes in population and attitudes that reestablished a society's equilibrium after incorporating new elements. Unlike such German sociologists as Ferdinand Tonnies and Ernst Troeltsch, who romanticized traditional German society as possessing greater unity, stronger values, and more Gemeinschaft, Simmel argued modern society was actually superior to past rural societies because it demanded more of its individuals. Only in the city, he argued, and especially in Berlin, could the citizen become a true individual, for in rural communities, the need for social control imposed a rigid conformity on community members.

What Simmel meant for Locke can best be seen by comparing it to Du Bois's intellectual debt to Gustav Schmoller, whom the older Black scholar studied with at the University of Berlin fourteen years earlier. Whereas Du Bois learned sociology as a highly detailed, empirical science of observation of social phenomena,

Locke learned sociology as a theoretical inquiry into how modern society functioned as a system. Schmoller's thinking might have been responsible, in some
respects, for Du Bois's attachment to the notion that societies, no less than race
groups, should be understood in terms of fixed, transcendent ideals.[6] By contrast, Simmel suggested all modern social entities like races were fluid constructions produced by the overall system of a society. Actually, Locke had the benefit
of familiarity with both Simmel and Schmoller, as Locke found his way into
some of Schmoller's lectures, where he imbibed this conservative professor's
Marxist-inspired analysis of class and class groups. What Locke wanted to do,
however, was to combine the economic approach to race conflict that came from
Schmoller with Simmel's more social psychological engagement of society as
a social organism. In that synthesis, Locke believed, lay the best of what modern
society could offer.

There was an aesthetic benefit for Locke in taking Simmel's classes in 1911:
by then, Simmel had become an aesthete, who responded to early twentieth-
century German modernism in art by evolving a "sociological aestheticism."[7]
Though Simmel extolled the virtues of modern life, he nevertheless developed in
the early 1900s a utopian vision of what society could become if it became more
responsive to the spiritual enlightenment of its best artists. Simmel developed
an elitist utopianism that held some artists and scholars in great esteem as "persons of distinction" whose vision could give meaning to an increasingly chaotic
world. In the first decade of the twentieth-century, Simmel surrounded himself
with such writers and artists as Ranier Rilke, Lou Salome, and Stefan George,
and wrote extensively on how the artist was a messenger of social and spiritual
enlightenment in modern society.

The Berlin of Simmel's day witnessed a Secession movement that, like its
stronger cousin in Munich, expressed younger artists' rejection of the taste of
Imperial Germany. Refusing to show their work in official, state-sponsored exhibitions, artists like Max Lieberman held their own independent exhibitions at
which Symbolist, Impressionist, Cubist, and *Jugendstil* art was jumbled together.
Caught up in the enthusiasm of revolutionary art change, Simmel tried to organize a salon in his Berlin home of like-minded artists, critics, and scholars
whose fellowship he believed would foster a renaissance in Berlin. Although
such Modernist intellects as Simmel, Rilke, Kandinsky, and others would lose
the battle against anti-Modernist forces in prewar Germany, Locke's exposure to
this milieu provided him with a model of the kind of aesthetic community he
wanted to live in. Simmel even modeled the type of philosopher that Locke
wanted to become—an engaged scholar who moved outside of the academy to
transform his culture.

Despite the intellectual stimulation of studying under Simmel and visiting
Secessionist exhibitions, Locke's financial problems forced him to leave Berlin.
By June 28, Locke had become desperate, as de Fonseka's reply to a previous

letter from Locke suggests. "I don't know how hard-up you are," de Fonseka wrote his friend. "I gather from your defiance that you are pretty hard up. I think you had much better come to England and stay with me,—at least for a time. I am sending you either three or four pounds tomorrow through Cook's,—so mind you call for it when you get this letter. I think it will pay your fare over. If you have an outstanding landlady's bill, let me know by return and how much the bill is. You could live here on nothing."[8] Just as important to Locke as de Fonseka's kind offer of free room and board was his assurance that his landlady would shield Locke from his creditors.

> You need not be afraid of Oxford creditors—they haven't got me and I owe some £90. Two or three gentlemen have called at 45 Ashburton Mansion with summonses for me—but Mrs. Frost encloses her card and sends the summonses back to the Registrar of Oxford County Court objecting to having summonses left for me, against her wish, at her private address (II) refusing to pay the postage to forward these summonses on to me in France, (III) refusing to save the summons of the Law the trouble of discovering my address in France. You can have your letters sent to 45 Ashburton Mansion, or to Cook's office—no one need know that you are at 131 Cheyne Walk, [London].[9]

Lionel de Fonseka's offer and good humor was a godsend: Locke was finding it increasingly difficult to survive on his mother's monthly $30 contribution, and even that source of funds threatened to dry up as summer approached and her school year salary ended. For de Fonseka, eluding Oxford creditors was still a game; for Locke, being protected was serious business. The last thing he needed was to be arrested and have that information get back to the United States. The monthly contribution from de Fonseka's wealthy Sinhalese father to his son's education made it possible for him—and now Locke—to live on fashionable Cheyne Walk in Chelsea. His father thought that his son was studying for his BA in modern history, with an eye to going on to get a bachelor in civil law. But de Fonseka had passed up taking the exam for this year because, in his words, "I have done no studying."

One reason de Fonseka invited Locke to spend the summer with him was that he wanted Locke to help him flesh out a book—a dialogue between an "Occidental" and an "Oriental" over the relative merits of each civilization's conceptions of art. De Fonseka's idea was that such a dialogue would demonstrate his great insight—that decorative art, what he believed "Oriental" art excelled in, was actually the highest form of art. Western art was decadent, because its aesthetic impulse was invested in art "objects" put on display in museums, whereas in the East "daily life is beautiful." True art was alive in the "Oriental" societies: "the ancient Sinhalese, who do not paint pictures, but decorated objects of daily use" were the true artists. De Fonseka rejected English aestheticism, because "to look on art as 'an escape from Life' is corrupt: a confession that in the West art is kept in a compartment. In the East, art is a product, an adjunct, and an <u>unconscious</u> expression, [a] symbol of daily life—really a 'mirror of life.' "[10]

De Fonseka's theory turned the West's denigration of Oriental art—that it was primarily decorative and lacked morality and sophisticated emotion—back on Western art as its weakness. Decorative art enhanced space with spiritual possibility, as the West had itself once done during the Renaissance. "Western art [is] most successful when decorative, e.g. the frescoes meant to decorate the walls of Santa Maria Novella in Florence by Ghirlandago, Rafael's decoration of the roof of Sistine Chapel." These were the same decorations that had moved Locke and, interestingly enough, included non-Western figures. For de Fonseka, that high-water mark in Western art had been replaced in the contemporary period by the artlessness of the recent coronation of the new king of England, which de Fonseka judged "a failure—in Ceylon they do these things as they ought to be done."[11] Now certain that he had a demonstrable critique that could be developed into a book, de Fonseka drew Locke to London to "midwife" his book.

Locke was excited by the prospect of helping de Fonseka with his book, but he had his own reasons for accepting the offer. He had learned that Felix Adler's Universal Races Congress was due to be held in London from July 26 to July 30. Adler was the founder of the Ethical Culture Society that Locke and his mother regularly visited in Philadelphia, especially since it was an integrated forum of lectures by America's best minds. The secular society promoted nonsectarianism, interracial tolerance, and world peace, values Adler hoped to promote by bringing together international authorities and delegates at a Congress that would launch, he hoped, an international peace organization. Although the organization never materialized, the Congress was a success, as thousands of scholars, professors, diplomats, and laypeople descended on the University of London for four days to read and hear critiques of pseudoscientific racism, analyses of imperialism, and proposals for greater racial harmony. If Locke was to be *courant* on race issues, he needed to be at this conference and "back in circulation" with the community of scholars and activists working for racial reform in America. Although still a fan of Booker T. Washington, Locke realized that he needed to broaden his contacts, especially since Washington had so far not really helped Locke's plans. The NAACP would be present in force at the Congress, in part because John E. Milholland, one of its founders, was also a co-organizer of the Congress and had secured travel funding for some of its most prominent members, including Mary White Ovington, William A. Sinclair, and W. E. B. Du Bois.

Locke evaded his creditors and arrived in London around the third week of July 1911. After settling into de Fonseka's luxurious digs on Cheyne Walk, Locke hurried over to the University of London's Imperial Institute just in time to hear the papers presented the first day at the Races Congress. At the first and second sessions Locke heard three of the most important papers that he would hear at the whole conference—"Race from the Anthropological Point of View" by Professor Felix von Luschan of the University of Berlin, "Race from the Sociological Point of View" by Professor Alfred Fouillee of the University of Paris, in the first session, and "The Instability of Human Types" by Professor Franz Boas of Columbia University in the second session. Locke may have been familiar with von Luschan from Berlin, as the renowned curator who had bought Europe's most valuable collection of Benin sculpture at an auction in Britain. Respect for African art and for the people who created it lay behind von Luschan's assertions that morning that African peoples possessed highly developed cultures and lifestyles that were superior to those of Europeans. As a man who liked to shock his audience, Luschan went on to assert that the average African was cleaner than most Europeans, that beauty was relative and not confined to the White race, and that variations in color among humans were caused by environmental factors. Luschan's radical assertions were counterbalanced, however, by his conservative belief that racial barriers had a positive role to play in human affairs, that segregation of the races was unavoidable, and that nationalism and even war were necessary to human civilization. His discrediting of the cultural basis of White superiority jibed quite well with the argument that de Fonseka was struggling with at his writing table while Locke attended the Congress.

Yet it was a paper read by Alfred Fouillee after von Luschan's that probably had the most influence on Locke. Fouillee's paper confirmed what Locke had argued about values in his thesis, only applied to race. As Locke sat listening to Fouillee's lecture in the stuffy Imperial Institute, he must have thought he was hearing himself lecture. "Every idea contains within it," Fouillee said, "not merely an intellectual act, but also a certain orientation of sensibility and of will. Consequently every idea is a force that tends to realise its own object more and more fully. This is true of the idea of race, just as it is true of the idea of nation. Hence we have (I) a certain self-consciousness in a race, imparting to each of its members a kind of racial personality; (2) a tendency to affirm this personality more and more strongly, to oppose it to other racial types and secure its predominance. In other words, the race-idea includes within it a race-consciousness."[12] In an odd way, here was a pragmatic theory of race: a group tended to adopt and even try and live up to a tendency that was identified with or subscribed to a group. That insight would become one of the key ingredients of Locke's own lectures on race in 1916.

Another paper delivered during the second session by Franz Boas backed up earlier speakers' assertions that race was a mode of consciousness, not a biological reality. Based on research gathered while working for the Immigration Commission, Boas's paper "Instability of Human Types" showed that racial characteristics varied so much under environmental conditions that there were actually no stable physical characteristics that reliably distinguished humans by race. Boas's research had shown that the head size and shape of immigrants had changed over generations, and that skin color varied within groups as much as it varied among race groups. No one factor correlated always with a race group, and many factors, stereotypically associated with one group, could be found abundantly in other groups. Racial characteristics resembled what Locke had discovered about value attributes: they moved across racial lines as values moved across ethical, aesthetic, and utilitarian lines in value theory. Boas's work confirmed that racial categories were just as inaccurate as the value categories that Locke critiqued in "The Concept of Value."

Race consciousness was so powerful because it was practiced self-consciousness. Racial prejudice gave those who held such attitudes a heightened sense of purpose and legitimacy, reinforcing their idea of themselves. "If an ethnic consciousness gives a race greater solidarity and inward unity, it has, on the other hand, the disadvantage of culminating nearly always in an assumption of superiority and for that very reason, in a feeling of natural hostility," Boas explained.[13] What was the best way to deal with the intensity of racial ideas and feelings? Fouillee had answered we should oppose racist ideas with "the force of other ideas which contain a different set of feelings," and the most important of these were scientific ideas. Boas modeled the power of the social scientist with his clinical deconstruction of race as a biological concept. Locke was naturally drawn to the role of the scientist, especially after studying with Georg Simmel, for science not only promised a pose of detachment, which Locke liked, but also a sense of community with other like-minded scientists. "Men of science, be their colour white or yellow, hail one another as brothers."[14] The Universal Races Congress convinced Locke that a scientific critique of race was a real option for him to create a community around his modernist ideas. Five years later Locke explained what the Congress and the scientific vocation had meant to him:

> Ever since the possibility of a comparative study of races dawned upon me at the Races Congress, in London in 1911, I have had the courage of a very optimistic and steadfast belief that in the scientific approach to the race question, there was the possibility of a redemption for those false attitudes of mind which have, unfortunately, so complicated the idea and conception of race that there are a great many people who fancy that the best thing that can possibly be done, if possible at all, is to throw race out of the categories of human thinking.[15]

Locke had been planning a "comparative study of races" for some time as a journalistic project, but the Congress revealed the benefits of a scientific investigation of race to demolish the claims of the pseudoscientific racists and create space for a progressive race politics. The Congress, therefore, outlined a future vocation for him as well as a future role as the voice of a progressive-minded community.

That role seemed particularly open to Locke after he heard W. E. B. Du Bois's speech in the sixth session. Du Bois's paper conceded the theoretical discussion of race science to others, and instead presented a detailed narrative history of the Black experience in America from slavery to the contemporary era, packed with tables and lists of facts about Negro poverty, education, birth rates, and lynchings. He concluded with a critique of Booker T. Washington's racial program. This was understandable, given that Washington, in London on a speaking tour in 1910, had given his listeners the impression that the situation of African Americans in America was dramatically improved. Such political infighting and programmatic squabbling left the field of a theoretical investigation of race by a Black social scientist wide open, Locke believed.

Israel Zangwill's talk, "The Jewish Race," at the fifth session of the Races Congress, came closer than Du Bois's to outlining an approach Locke felt he could use as a future race leader. Zangwill gave a brief overview of Jewish history, but focused on what he believed was the "real Jewish problem," the problem of self-preservation of the Jewish identity, a problem that he believed had to be solved by Jews themselves. While pogroms and other forms of Jewish oppression were real, a different kind of problem emerged where nations welcomed Jews: "a minor form of Crypto-Judaism was begotten, which prevails to-day in most lands of Jewish emancipation, among its symptoms being change of names, accentuated local patriotism, accentuated abstention from Jewish affairs, and even anti-Semitism mimetically absorbed from the environment."[16] As a result some Jews embraced wholeheartedly their expatriate cultures, forgot their own, and became the best exponents of their adopted national cultures. Such a "chameleon quality" of diasporic Jews made them excellent actors, artists, and critics, for "if a Russian Jew, Berenson, is the chief authority on Italian art, and George Brandes, the Dane, is Europe's greatest critic...all these phenomena find their explanation in the cosmopolitanism of the wandering Jew."[17] Instead of becoming a rabid nationalist, Jewish intellectuals often became ardent internationalists.[18]

This lecture must have also pricked Locke's conscience a bit. Was he not the perfect example of the kind of cosmopolitanism that Zangwill described in his lecture, a man who had spent most of his last three years further assimilating European art, literature, and culture, even though he himself had lectured the limits of cosmopolitanism in 1908? Just writing about it had not solved the problem. An act of will was needed by Jews (and by inference, Blacks) to will themselves a self-consciousness as a displaced nation. Zangwill shifted away from Du Bois's focus on the external forces that acted on the group to an analysis on what a minority needed to do to save identity. What Locke heard was a clear clarion call for Jews to accept responsibility for the preservation of Jewish culture, and by analogy, for Black intellectuals to do the same with Black culture. Rather than abandon the masses of the group, an option always open to the more educated members of the assimilating race, the minority intellectual had to find a way to build up the group itself.

Zangwill's lecture counterbalanced the cosmopolitan scientist role that Fouillee had outlined earlier in the Congress. Locke knew science alone would not solve the African American problem. Locke knew that he needed to find a way to galvanize the Black community as much as to neutralize the White community's scientific racism. But how? Fouillee provided a clue in his lecture when he had stated that "an ethnic consciousness gives a race greater solidarity and inward unity," because such a "self-consciousness in a race" imparts "to each of its members a kind of racial personality" that they affirmed "more and more strongly" over time.

Locke's originality as a thinker came in how he put together what he heard from Fouillee, von Luschan, Boas, and especially Zangwill, at this Congress. Locke heard that racial self-consciousness produced a sense of solidarity and inward unity that empowered the White community in competition with others. While Fouillee had spent the rest of his lecture detailing how such self-consciousness ought to be suppressed, Locke determined he needed to find a way to promote such a self-consciousness in the Black group. Certainly, Locke wanted to foster a Black community in which he could live, in which highly assimilated men of the world could be comfortable. And Locke worried that racial self-consciousness in Blacks might transpose into the kind of hostility toward others that characterized European nationalism. Zangwill had also given Locke a hint of what could be the device for fostering such nationalism—a focus on making a contribution to one's own culture, to inventing one's own tradition, as a way of holding onto and building esteem in one's own group. Other papers at the Congress that caught Locke's attention were John A. Hobson's "The Opening of New Markets," which outlined the economic motive behind imperialism, and D. B. Jayathaka's that delivered a scathing critique of Christianity and its missionary effort in Ceylon. "Christian methods of conversion must change," the London *Times* reported him as saying.[19] Du Bois later remembered this speech as a "dramatic incident" at the Congress. The organizers seemed to recall it as well, as an example of the kind of inflammatory statement that they did not wish to see at the conference. As the conference wore on, such speeches were curtailed.

While Locke enjoyed the Congress and the access to information he needed, he was also glad when the last session of the Congress ended on July 29. He relished spending more time with his host, the aesthete de Fonseka, who was consumed with writing his book, and increasingly in need of Locke's help. As much as Locke liked the Congress, he still preferred the company of aesthetes and the opportunity to give ideology an aesthetic form, as de Fonseka's book did. De Fonseka's text of cultural resistance took the insight that the Ceylon delegate to the Races Congress had outlined—that Western cultural influence tends to denigrate traditional Asian culture in the eyes of Asian peoples—and turned it into a scathing, irreverent attack on Western aesthetics and an impassioned recommendation to Sinhalese people to value their own art traditions. His book outlined how to answer the Western racial practice of discursive validation by deconstructing the Western tradition and substituting a non-Western tradition to build pride and independence among the colonized. Locke was imbibing an anti-colonial model of aesthetic education as a tool of Black self-emancipation back home. As de Fonseka put it: "This dialogue is written primarily for the people of Ceylon. Sinhalese art has hitherto been strictly decorative, and as a Sinhalese I view with regret the modern tendency in Ceylon, under Western influences, to abandon our tradition in art and life.... It is regrettable that the rise of Western commerce should involve the decline of Eastern art; but though regrettable, it is not inevitable.[20] That last statement provides a sense of what de Fonseka and Locke were up against—economic domination of their peoples—and their faith that aesthetics could interrupt those forces of alienation and stimulate the cultural regeneration of their peoples.

Of course, de Fonseka's argument was problematical in several senses, as it accepted as true a kind of fixed construction of "Oriental" and "Occidental" cultural identities produced and disseminated by European imperialism. Was there nothing more diversified and varied than an "Oriental" or "Eastern" aesthetic? As was characteristic of much of the cultural apologetics of this generation of colonial intellectuals, cultural resistance was seen in terms far more related to English cultural imperialism than to the reality of cultural life in the "Orient." Yet the book did succeed, perhaps better than the Races Congress, in bringing into the open the conflict between colonial cultural nationalists who wished to preserve aspects of their culture during modernization, and imperial intellectuals who wanted to preserve the hegemony of British culture even as they advocated liberal anti-racist politics.

It is unclear what role Locke played in the writing of *On the Truth of Decorative Art*. Years later Locke referred to this collaboration as his first experience of "midwifing" a book. The book was certainly de Fonseka's, who brought to the project both the idea and most likely the dialogue form, borrowed from Oscar Wilde's "The Decay of Lying." Locke may have written some of the text that went into the dialogue, especially the voice of the "occidental," who at times had to make the argument for the social realist school of art, as when he queried, "Do you think then that it detracts from the dignity of an art to be used as an instrument of social reform?" Working with de Fonseka helped Locke imagine the kind of argument that he would level at the social reformers of the Negro establishment, who themselves would argue for the propaganda value of Black art over its aesthetic, imaginative, or decorative aspect. But the midwifery role carried within itself its own frustration. Once again, as with his conversations with Kallen, Seme, El Alaily, and other intellectuals in England, Locke was working on their problems, their texts, and their resolutions. Working on the dialogue, however, did help. It got him collaborating with another minority intellectual in a counter-hegemonic project that legitimated Locke's resistance to English discourses of domination of darker peoples. It also suggested a model for a non-hypocritical approach to the question of minority cultural identity. The dialogue was in fact inside Locke and de Fonseka themselves: they were dialogic constructions, a conversation of opposites, highly assimilated and educated "Occidentals" trying to find a path back to the "Oriental" in themselves—the people they had been before they became Oxonian intellectuals. *On the Truth of Decorative Art* showed that dialogue itself was productive, not destabilizing as was implied by the concept of "double consciousness," and creative in giving voice to those who had mastered the European tradition, but still, as Locke had said in "Cosmopolitan" found their way back to their own traditions. Even though they did not finish the book that early August, Locke had helped get most of it done, and it was published in London in 1912.

Even with de Fonseka's hospitality and the stimulating collaborative work, Locke's personal problems were mounting in August 1911. He had very little money and was still adrift in England. He did get some good news. His mother wrote him early in the month that she had gone for the "99th time" to the shelves of the library and finally found his article, "The American Temperament," published in the August issue of the *North American Review*. She confided that she "nearly dropped—I had no idea that I should live to see it."[21] Payment for that article would be mailed to him shortly in England. Lack of funds, though, blotted the joy of publication. Locke did not even have enough money to pay his landlord in Berlin the back rent he had owed her since April. Since May he had been fleeing the debt he owed another landlady, Mrs. Addis, with whom he had lived in the spring of 1910 before leaving for Berlin. Now she had had a Reverend A. Parker Fitch writing his mother, the head of Oxford, and the head of Harvard trying to embarrass him into paying. Had Locke done so, however, he would have been penniless. Despite the embarrassment of these debts, he held onto his precious few dollars. He also held on to the notion of remaining in Europe, even though to do so might leave him marooned without funds to get back to the United States.

Locke's decision to stay in Europe without a source of income flabbergasted his mother. Mary had to borrow during the summer to send money for his board even though he was living with Fonseka rent-free. The lenders "think I am help-ing you. They must know something of the situation." She was beginning to be critical as well: "What a pity you let so much money slip thro your hands and got yourself in this fix."[22] After one of his manuscripts was returned to her in Camden, she concluded that he would "never make a living at that. Could you not qualify to teach French or German in some of the colored high schools," back home?[23] At the end of June, she advised him, "You must settle on something." Even he began to realize that was true. Locke had hoarded enough money from the $60 his mother sent him in July so that he could return to the United States if he had to. But how could he return to the United States as a failure, without his Oxford degree, and an embarrassment now to his race? In a fit of desperation, he wrote her that perhaps he might still go to Egypt. As usual, she encouraged him. But both of them knew that salvation lay in the other direction.

Despite nearly becoming a vagabond, Locke's exile in Europe after Oxford had not been a waste. Having studied under Simmel at the University of Berlin and then attended lectures by Boas, Zangwill, Fouillee, and von Luschan at the Universal Race Congress in London, Locke had given himself a post-Harvard education in the emerging fields of sociology, anthropology, and race studies that would fuel his thinking for the rest of his life. He had deepened his ability to think about the Negro situation in the United States from comparative sociological and cultural perspectives, and become a philosopher of the social sciences even while failing to get the kinds of degrees he wanted. Hunkered down with de Fonseka in Chelsea, he had helped write a dialogue that recalibrated the cultural relationship between the East and the West and articulated a new Sinhalese self-consciousness that prefigured the New Negro's. With de Fonseka, Locke also had rehearsed his mature role among African American writers—to be a midwife if not the mother of their "pen-children." Most important, Locke had learned something profound about himself and the race, that transnationalism was the catalyst of his and the Negro's advancement in the twentieth century.

Faced with complete destitution, and worse, the prospect of arrest and imprisonment in England for his unpaid debts, Locke decided to come home. Sometime before that decision, he made an equally important decision: he decided to lie and state publicly that he had received the Oxford degree. He made that decision sometime between his matriculation at the University of Berlin on May 6 and his return to America. On the inside of his registration folder appears a record of his degrees. BA was printed, but "B. Litt." appears in Locke's handwriting, as if it were added later. Locke decided to represent himself as having received the BLitt, his original degree course.

Locke probably made that decision early in August, as he prepared to return to the United States and realized that he had no other way to save face. In one sense, he needed to find some way to put the Oxford situation behind him so that he could get on with his life. With the distance, both culturally and geographically, between Oxford and the educational establishment of the United States, it would be unlikely that anyone would discover the truth. Oxford certainly had nothing to gain from embarrassing him, especially as its own racial treatment of him might get out in the papers. Always the rationalizer, he justified the lie as necessary to avoid an unnecessary racial conflict. But the lie cost him. Although he was never discovered, it haunted him, so much so that twenty-five years later, he woke up at 4 A.M. one morning, and scribbled a note of justification to himself:

> The only basis upon which I could reasonably or in full justice to myself be expected to publicly admit my failure at Oxford University would have been a full public statement of the peculiar circumstances of the case. The whole story even now and more so then would have released a storm of public discussion and inflammatory [debate] harmful to the best public interests of all concerned, especially those of the special constituency that had been foisted upon me by sensational publicity attending my appointment as the first Negro appointee to a Rhodes Scholarship. I should have had to publicly complain of arbitrary procedure [and] discrimination which so far as it related to the degree examination itself was in my best judgment personal rather than racial, but which would immediately have been construed as racial by the public opinion, especially in view of the frequent recurrence in my Oxford career of instances of racial discrimination, two instances of which had already appeared by cable report in the public press. I thus deliberately resorted to strategic coverup at the great risk of personal honor and peace of mind and expectation of a correction of the matter by my entry for another Oxford degree and later by the subsequent election and academic success of a stronger or luckier successor. For I should have had to bear the additional blame of being largely responsible for the nonelection of Negro candidates for these scholarships during this period of 25 years.[24]

With the door to an Oxford degree closed, Locke convinced himself that to lie about having received it was an act of noblesse oblige so as not to embarrass the race. He also believed that in a public squabble race spokespersons would seize on racism to rescue his reputation by disparaging Oxford's. Perhaps the honorable aspect of his note is his unwillingness to attribute his own failure to racism. No, it was personal, despite that Oxford acted poorly from a racial standpoint. Having criticized other Blacks when he was at Harvard for using race to excuse their own failure, Locke at least was honorable enough to refrain from invoking it here.

Yet Locke's justification remains unsatisfying and unconvincing. Ethically, it was wrong to lie about the degree, and he knew this instinctively. Moreover, he benefited personally from the lie, for it made him into a success story, confirmed what those of the race wanted to believe about him, and gave him a career as a major Black intellectual that would certainly have been compromised if it had been known that he had failed at Oxford. His reminiscence is unsatisfying mostly, because it does not do justice to his anger. How dare Oxford do this to him, how dare they try to embarrass him and his race! As he sat in Berlin and then in London brooding over the predicament, he must have come to feel that race had something to do with it. Weren't the stories legion at Oxford about the English nobility who wasted away their time partying and drinking, only to emerge with a face-saving degree, a Gentleman's Third? Why not him? Because he was Black? Because he was American? Or simply because he was the "spoiled" Locke? He couldn't know for sure, but he had to feel it was unfair. Since they had treated him unfairly, he would return the favor and reject Oxford's right to judge him. He lied about the degree, partly to protect the race, but also to assert that he *had* earned his degree, whether Oxford agreed or not.

Locke's decision also suggests his cynicism toward Black people. He was going to give them what they wanted anyway. Hadn't Black people been responsible, in part, for the "sensational publicity" that had surrounded his appointment? Hadn't he just wanted to go off to Oxford on his own, be left alone, and disappear? And hadn't the Black press, the Black clergy, and the Black progressive establishment violated his privacy by making him a symbol of Black intelligence? Didn't they owe him something in return? It served them right for their intrusion into his personal affairs. Locke would encourage the applause of hundreds of unsuspecting Black bourgeoisie for his success. They needed culture heroes. He would give them one, whether he was one or not.

As Locke sailed home from England sometime in August, he brought home some additional baggage. Having used race to justify to himself his cover-up of the truth, he owed Black people in a way he had never owed them before. That was what the guilt about Oxford would do to his soul. In the final analysis, perhaps lying about the Oxford degree helped him. Had he gotten the Oxford degree, he might not have been so driven to make a real contribution to the race struggle, might never have become Alain Locke, the race leader. Failing to get the degree and lying about it imposed a heavy burden. Disembarking to New York, Locke returned home in 1911 carrying a debt it would take his entire life to work off.

13

Race Cosmopolitan Comes
Home, 1911–1912

Coming back to the United States in the fall of 1911, Locke was welcomed by Black America despite his having been away so long. Since he had been gone, the NAACP had emerged and W. E. B. Du Bois's *Crisis* had captured the imagination of educated African Americans. Booker T. Washington was still the most powerful Negro in America, but his star had dimmed after Taft won the White House in 1908 and reduced Washington's influence over federal appointments in the South. In the shadow of contested Negro leadership, a new diversity of opinion had emerged among Black political voices that made the African American intellectual climate open to Locke's unique perspective on race. Perhaps closest to Locke's views were those of older, African American thinkers who were nationalist in philosophy, but conservative in personal style and political action, men like John Bruce of New York and John Cromwell of Washington who served as custodians of culture in the Black community. They used their influence to raise the quality of debate among the African American bourgeoisie in emergent literary and historical societies that featured lectures on politics and history, poetry readings, and music and art exhibitions. When he returned to Philadelphia, Locke found that men in these societies were eager to provide him an opportunity to announce himself as a new voice in African American discourse. Not long after he settled in at 579 Stevens Street in Camden with his mother, Locke was heading out on the speaking circuit.

The American Negro Historical Society in Philadelphia invited him to speak on October 24, and William C. Bolivar, a family friend and contributor to the *Philadelphia Tribune*, had probably alerted fellow society members that Locke was back in the Philadelphia area. Bolivar may have brought Locke to the attention of Levi Coppin of the Baltimore Bethel AME Church, where he spoke on November 2. Coppin was married to Fanny Jackson Coppin, formerly the head of the Institute of Colored Youth in Philadelphia that had educated both Pliny and Mary Locke. Alain's parental network came alive. Locke coupled the trip to Baltimore with a trip to Washington, where he spoke at Howard University and was introduced to Washington society by Roscoe Conkling Bruce, superintendent of Washington's Black schools. Locke seems to have made a great impression. Locke wrote his mother:

> Having veritable ovation. Young Bruce gave smoker last night—all the younger men & Judge Terrel[l were there]. Have seen all old-timers including Mrs. Langston. Too much news to tell—had fun at Howard. Don't worry, keeping up though very tired. To speak possibly before Bethel Literary in Washington ten days or so...also speak before Negro Historical of New York if time permits. Crummel is arranging this and proposes me next meeting for election to the Negro Academy.[1]

Although Locke had done everything he could to remain in Europe, he was actually happier and more energetic in America, a train ride away from his mother, but also speaking to a Black patriarchal audience that embodied the energy and activism of his father. He was also giving talks to people who actually wanted to hear him, looked up to him, and celebrated him as one of their own. Only Black people in America would praise him for having "brought such distinction to the race," as Rev. Levin Coppin put it, and such praise buoyed Locke's spirits and reaffirmed that he was somebody special. Throughout his life, Locke acted as if he did not need such confirmation, but he did, especially now.

Locke was especially pleased by how the elders of the race embraced him and his standard speech for 1911, "The Negro and a Race Tradition," where he argued Black intellectuals must see themselves in terms of race. This message played well in these historical societies, and Locke made sure he linked it to praise of the elders, such men as the late president of the Philadelphia Historical Society, Mr. Adjer, who had, as Locke put it, stood for tradition "persistently, effectively, quietly, unassumingly—almost silently." Ironically, the man most alienated from his father was quite comfortable praising the tradition of Black patriarchy to introduce himself to the Black community. But that rhetorical maneuver was the set-up for the Oedipal Locke to emerge and reveal his real message—his critique of the "antiquarian" tradition that Adjer and others had institutionalized in these societies, the "tradition of personalities, incidents, a tradition of records, but records that were at the same time souvenirs." In 1911, the Negro needed a different kind of tradition, of "racial-consciousness rather than race-memory, of race culture as distinguished from but not opposed to race history." As a kind of Promethean coming to them from Oxford, Berlin, and the Universal Races Congress in London, Locke brought the new knowledge of a scientific rather than the hagiographic story of individual Black successes. Negro historical societies needed to break with their provincial past and begin to think about the predicament of the Negro in comparative terms. "Our problems in the matter of history," Locke noted, "have their analogies for the average American, for the

American's broken past we have a forgotten past, in place of his voluntary revolution we have involuntary transplantation."[2] Most Negro historical societies avoided the discussion of slavery—the great "transplantation"—because it embarrassed them. But Locke argued Negro Americans could not hide from the pain of slavery and worsening contemporary race relations by perpetuating a sanitized history.

Locke even skewered Du Bois to drive home his point that the Negro intellectual had to be relentless in thinking in terms of a Negro intellectual tradition. In a revised version of the lecture Locke delivered to the Yonkers Negro Society for Historical Research in New York on December 12, Locke critiqued that line in Du Bois that gave the illusion that in the realm of culture the Negro intellectual was a peer.

> Few indeed are those of us who have escaped entirely the subtle seduction of this illusion, all of us at certain times or in certain moods are its victims. I think of the momentary lapse of an almost irreproachable scholar who was tempted into the rare boast that he joined hands with Shakespeare & Plato above the color line[.] Was he anything less of a Negro in Shakespeare's world or in Plato's presence? Intellectual affiliations may be a philosopher's solace for denied opportunities; and dead poets may be more friendly & sociable than living ones— they should be certainly to the scholar, but what a warped sense of personal identity it displays to associate the Negro personality with these pains & the disembodied self with the pleasures & compensations of life. Not that one need think [badly] of the situations which may make Plato & Shakespeare mental refuge from physical pangs and social disgusts, but that one track the error and review the issue inducing in the minds of the best informed and most valuable of the race the dilemma of conflicting loyalties and the pangs of a divided consciousness.[3]

Locke was feeling quite cocky up in New York to crack on Du Bois's fantasy of transcultural communion above the color line. But after his experience at Oxford, Locke could not read the lines in Du Bois's *Souls of Black Folk* and not gag.

> I sit with Shakespeare and he winces not. Across the color line I move arm in arm with Balzac and Dumas, where smiling men and welcoming women glide in gilded halls. From out the caves of evening that swing between the strong-limbed earth and the tracery of the stars, I summon Aristotle and Aurelius and what soul I will, and they come all graciously with no scorn nor condescension. So, wed with Truth, I dwell above the Veil.[4]

Certainly, the "great men" of Oxford had "winced" in Locke's presence, had not treated him "graciously" but with "scorn" and "condescension." Culture could not wash away the racism endemic to knowledge dissemination in the West and the Negro could not "glide" across centuries without race dogging one's tracks. "From the fact of being a Negro there is no escape—no, not even in education and culture," Locke went on. "No individual or group can break loose from its ethnic tradition without landing ultimately in an historical dilemma."[5] Before these historical societies, Locke was returning from his educational odyssey to tell his listeners the "Truth"—that educational elites never forgot that one was Black. The good news was the silver lining that exclusion created agency—to build one's own stately mansions, one's own tradition of excellence in reason and art in the world of culture.

After his Yonkers lecture, the members of the Historical Society hailed him, especially John Bruce and Arthur Schomburg, the founders of the society. As Bruce wrote to Cromwell, who had recommended Locke as a speaker to Bruce:

> Well, Locke came over and gave us a splendid talk. We kept him all of Saturday night and all day Sunday and part of Sunday night and parted with him with some reluctance. He is a worthy son of a worthy sire. I remember his father. Everybody here who met the son is pleased with him. My! but he is a mite of a chap, but "he had a mighty intellect and talking ways." I liked him much and felt that I had always known him. Mrs. Bruce was "carried away with him but she has returned." ... I tried to give him a decent press notice in the local papers ... and a fair resume of his paper which was a thoughtful and scholarly effort.[6]

Locke had won over his hosts because of his father, because of his excellent bearing and manners, and because he was able to present himself as the new Black voice. As he wrote his mother, "I was hailed all around, bravo, better than Du Bois, etc."[7]

The problem was that Locke had not completely accepted the lesson he shared with his listeners in "The Negro and a Race Tradition." While characterizing Du Bois as naive, Locke himself was still dreaming. At the very moment Locke was lecturing American Black intellectuals about the benefits of sticking to one's own traditions, he was busy as ever trying to break free of them, still regarding elite White Americans and Europeans as the really high-minded people of culture, and still dreaming of spending his next two years in a comparative race study travel scheme that would in effect allow him to hobnob with White people in Europe, not Black people in America. His cynicism was not confined to Du Bois, for as Locke wrote his mother about his lecture, "all you have to do is to tell Negroes how much you love them and they will sing your praises to the high heavens."[8]

Of course, Locke would hardly have impressed John E. Bruce, the Black journalist and racial nationalist if he had argued, as was possible, that as a Europeanized Black intellectual he still suffered from the kind of "double consciousness" he critiqued in Du Bois and that, in fact, Locke saw that double consciousness as a strength rather than a weakness. Bruce, who worked as a clerk in the State of New York's Treasurer's Office, epitomized the kind of race consciousness Locke described in his lecture: he was a politically savvy Black Republican who believed self-organization if not self-segregation was the only salvation for Black people in America. Bruce's racialism did have its pathological aspects—the dark-skinned Bruce was extremely color-conscious. In a letter to John Cromwell, Bruce wrote that after hearing Kelly Miller lecture forcefully in New York, "I'm glad that he isn't yaller."[9] Such prejudice did not stint Bruce's praise of the light-skinned Du Bois, however. But what endeared Bruce to "The Negro and a Race Tradition" was that a young African American could go to Oxford and Berlin and come back to America to recommend Black consciousness as the road forward. To do that required Locke to hide the complexity of the man that education had actually created in him.

Locke was not only performing race, but also masculinity. This "mite of a man" continued, in Bruce's eyes, the tradition of outspoken Black masculine leadership that the post-Reconstruction generation was known for. That Locke could appear as fierce and manly a leader as his own father, and be culturally more sophisticated boded well for men like Bruce, hoping that the next generation would carry over the virtues of his. Locke viewed Bruce as a kind of sympathetic uncle, someone who though mired in the old tradition, supported the cultural approach to race that was the subtext of Locke's "Race Tradition." Locke showed he was already adept at managing the generational struggle between himself and the older generation of Black intellectuals by presenting himself as their heir and not a threat to their leadership.

When Locke left Bruce's residence at Sunnyslope Farm in Yonkers that December, he gave the impression, ironically, that he would be returning shortly to Berlin. Interestingly, the path to a Black tradition lay through the Teutonic Empire. His listeners knew he was a thoroughly Europhile Negro, but they accepted him nevertheless, because he seemed to be on a mission for them, one that would carry him back to Europe to take another of its intellectual prizes. But Locke was so deeply in debt and his lectures netted him so little he had no choice but to remain in America. On January 1, 1912, alumni of his high school entertained Locke in Philadelphia, and on February 15, he was back in Washington, D.C., giving a lecture to local teachers. This was arranged by Cromwell, who seemed to take a personal interest in trying to get Locke established in the capital. The lecture brought him $25, considerably more than the usual $10 he received from the historical societies, and it gave Locke a chance to hobnob with the Washington elite. "I am returning tonight," Locke wrote his mother on February 17, "although invited to stay over and of all things to go to the Assembly with W.H. Lewis. Dined with Lewis last night. Lunch with him to day. Speech a success, delivered two others since. Bruce matter pending and somewhat doubtful."[10] Lewis was a graduate of Harvard, a lawyer, and a prominent lieutenant of Booker T. Washington. So was Bruce, who had led Locke to believe there might be a place for him in the District of Columbia school system, which never materialized. But Locke did not want to become a public schoolteacher, at least not yet, not until all other possibilities, especially the possibility of returning to Europe, were exhausted.

Indeed, John E. Bruce was surprised to learn from Cromwell early in February 1912 that Locke was still in the United States. Bruce was pleased, however, since "I may yet get another chance to meet him before he leaves these shores. Remember Mrs. Bruce and myself to him most kindly and say that we are looking forward to seeing him at Sunnyslope ere he says farewell to America."[11] Bruce was probably surprised as well when he learned early in March through the grapevine that Locke was to accompany Booker T. Washington on a trip through the South. Bruce did not like Washington and considered him a toady to the White people. Indeed, Locke's lecture had prompted Bruce to write Cromwell that "I could not help thinking what a Jonah Booker Washington is to the race, and what a mistake his propaganda is. Alain Le Roy Locke was born to scholarship. He'd never make either a good gardener or a good shoemaker and there are thousand[s] of our boys scattered all over this country who like him only want freedom for their wings."[12] While at Sunnyslope, Locke had not let on to Bruce that he was friendly with Washington, and most of his African American patrons did not know until he had left on this trip that such was the case. During the first week of January, Locke would meet Washington in Philadelphia and assist the Wizard in meeting his train south to Tuskegee.[13]

While Bruce and Cromwell were helpful in obtaining speaking engagements at African American historical societies, only a man of Booker T. Washington's stature could bring Locke's name to the attention of the White intellectual establishment. That was Locke's main goal at the beginning of 1912. He wanted to make another run at the Albert Kahn Travelling Fellowship, and he needed heavyweight influence. As Locke had learned, Washington was reluctant to put his influence behind someone he did not know well. Locke needed time with the Wizard to build some rapport, and that opportunity came in late February when Dr. S. G. Elbert of Wilmington, Delaware, withdrew from a trip through Florida organized by Washington. This was one of his annual trips through the South, on which Washington stopped at numerous small localities and made speeches designed to secure White finances for his education projects and build popular support among the Black southern community for his policies. Locke jumped at the opportunity to observe the Wizard at work. Washington seemed pleased as well, writing Elbert on February 26 that he was "glad to have Mr. Locke take your place[;] he will have no expense at all during the trip through Florida and only his expense to florida [sic] and return after tour is complete[;] tour begins at pensacola [Florida] march first."[14] Washington's reference to Locke's expenses was designed to allay Elbert's concern that Locke would not have enough money to make the trip. Elbert still insisted on Locke coming down to Wilmington for dinner and a conference before catching the train to Pensacola. Unfortunately, Locke missed the train that would have given him enough time to dine with the Elberts. When he arrived at the Wilmington station with only a half hour to spare, Mr. Elbert came down to the station and attempted to press a roll of "bills, I don't know how many" into Locke's hands, stating that he could borrow for the trip if he desired. Locke respectfully declined, although he promised to wire Elbert if he did run short during the trip. For Locke it was good to know that finally he was encountering some sympathetic Whites who could help him financially.

Elbert's offer was appreciated, because Locke felt considerable uncertainty about what lay ahead of him on his maiden voyage south. Since Washington would not be boarding until Montgomery, Alabama, Locke started his first trip through the South alone. The trip went well, however. He was not Jim Crowed in his riding car before reaching Alabama, although he could not eat in the Pullman car. Instead, his meals were "served on a Pullman table put up at my seat. How much trouble they go to save their old prejudice," he casually informed his mother. While writing her from the observation car as the train traversed Georgia, Locke noted, "as I write this an old confederate opposite sits & glares. I guess it makes him angry that I can write." Generally, though, Locke was able to concentrate on what he had really wanted to see, the South. "The trip is beautiful—but what a poverty stricken land white & black. I am observing closely for journalistic material."[15] The pace quickened after Washington and his party boarded. They made their first stop on March 1 in Pensacola, and the *Pensacola Journal* on March 2, 1912, documented the Wizard in action. "Dr. Washington... gained the sympathy of both races immediately in his audience by asking the negroes present to sing a few of the old-time plantation songs." Washington cooed White southerners with the sounds of slavery, reassuring them his Negroes were no threat to White supremacy. More concretely, "sensible advice was given to the negroes with reference to dependability to labor, with reference to idleness and crime, and on the other hand the white man's responsibility in the direction of negro education and progress was emphasized." By voicing Henry Grady's New South paternalism, Washington hoped to foster White support for Negro education by claiming it would make Blacks better laborers. But the people standing on stage with Washington were not day laborers, but prominent Black individuals in business, education, and the church: "J.C. Napier... Chairman of the executive Board of the National Negro Business League; M.W. Gilbert, president Selma University... Bishop G.W. Clinton, A.M.E. Zion Church... George C. Hall, physician and surgeon, Chicago, Ill. Alain Le Roy Locke, Rhodes Oxford Scholarship Student."[16]

Locke wrote his mother that, except for Washington and Emmett Scott, Washington's second-in-command at Tuskegee, he was the star attraction. Locke's claim was supported by the enthusiastic applause of the Black audience that greeted him at Pensacola. Such a welcome also supports historian Richard Potter's contention that the Black people in the audience understood that the spirituals and Washington's rhetoric were intended to camouflage an opportunity to celebrate Black achievement. Still, Washington felt that even this delicate balance had to be adjusted as the party traveled southward. After the Pensacola reception, "W[ashington] questioned the advisability of mentioning the Oxford University scholarship affair farther south in Florida, where feeling is more adverse. Mr. Napier did the stunt and is of the uncompromising sort to repeat it." Locke seemed to react as if he had been taken down a peg, for he continued, "I shall see that he does and have something to say on the question to B.T.W. at the end of the tour."[17] Locke's name actually disappeared from the record of the next stop at Ocala, but he was listed as speaking on "schools and scholarship" at Lakeland, Florida. Washington was right about the "more adverse" feeling farther south. For the day that the party reached Jacksonville, the town was hysterical over the capture that same day of five African Americans accused of murdering a local shopkeeper and assaulting his wife and two children. "Wild were the scenes enacted last night," reported the *Florida Times-Union*:

> A mob consisting of several hundred men, women and youths gathered at the corner of Forsyth and Ocean streets, and from there proceeded toward the police station. There a squad of policemen, with drawn clubs, held the crowd at bay, but after several ineffectual rushes they were finally dispersed with a stream of water directed at them by men from the central fire station.[18]

The crowd, however, was not confined to the jail. As Locke informed his concerned mother, "You will have seen by the papers that a lynching was narrowly averted here—we could hear the mob howling while Dr. Washington was speaking—the party were [sic] conducted under police escort safely home—Dr. Washington slipping out while they were singing. It was brave of him to continue his speech at all." Not surprisingly, Washington's speech was not reported in the *Florida Times-Union*, as both headlines and secondary stories detailed how effective sheriffs had been in capturing the alleged perpetrators and preventing a lynching. Such coverage was responsible at least in that it reassured an outraged community that justice was swift and mob action unnecessary. But it also showed how irrelevant Washington's message had become. As James Weldon Johnson recalled in his autobiography, *Along This Way*, Jacksonville was no longer the city of harmonious race relations it had been during his childhood, because the White populace had changed: it had rejected the paternalistic ideology of Henry Grady and adopted the turn-of-century view that the Negro was a beast that had to be kept down, and failing that, killed. It was wise Washington skipped out.

Writing two days after the near riot, Locke put the best face on the situation. "Yesterday things quieted down and we had the day of the trip visiting the schools and business enterprises of Jacksonville." But some members of the party had seen enough by Thursday. One was J. C. Napier, who "wanted me to go to Nashville with him and I was going, but he left suddenly night before last when the mob broke out."[19] Despite his calm reassurance to his mother, Locke himself had been shaken by this display of naked White power. One of the members of the group remembered in an interview that Locke cowered in the man's arms as the party was whisked away with the crowd yelling outside. This nurturing fellow could not understand what frightened Locke so much. Of course, Locke was not above using such a situation to ferret his way into a man's arms. But Locke had stumbled into a situation that really rankled his nerves. Earlier on the way to Montgomery, he had joked in a letter to his mother that he would finish an essay he was writing on lynching when he returned to Philadelphia, "if I am not lynched myself." Suddenly, he had come face to face with the reality of southern murderous violence; and he had reacted with all the pent-up fear he had carried within himself from the moment he had "crossed the line" into the South.

That incident left a mark on Locke's mind. Regardless of the wonderful subsequent receptions for him as he completed his southern tour, something in him resolved not to take a job in the South if he could at all help it. True, he was lionized at Jacksonville the next day, once the threat of a lynching had passed, and Jacksonville's thriving Black business and academic community had properly welcomed him. Arriving at Tuskegee, he received the kind of introduction accorded a returning military hero. "The whole school paraded yesterday in my honour and I walked inspection up and down the lines with the Captain in charge. Last evening I made my second address to the school, quite a good speech—I had been invited to two faculty meetings and had addressed them— also the men's club gave me a smoker and supper and the boys of the Glee Club serenaded outside." Yet Locke could not dispense with his cynicism even at this moment of southern Black community embrace. "It pays to tell Negroes I am of you with you and for you. Three cheers for the Negro," he concluded to his mother.[20] His real reason for visiting Tuskegee was not to consider joining its faculty, but to have a personal conference with Emmett J. Scott at which the two of them would draft "Booker's letter of endorsement" for the Kahn Fellowship. Upon leaving Tuskegee on March 19, Locke proceeded to Atlanta Baptist College (later known as Atlanta University), where he enjoyed a personal conference and tour of the facilities with John Hope, its president. Locke liked what he saw of the campus and the faculty, but could not help recalling that just six years before the town had erupted in one of the worst race riots in southern history and forced Du Bois out of the South and academia and into work for the NAACP.

Perhaps the only place of significance Locke did not visit was Fisk University, but Mr. Napier's flight had precluded that. For all of its educational development, the South still represented for Locke a step back into the Dark Ages.

Perhaps the most humorous interchange of the trip occurred between Locke and Carl Diton, his former Central High classmate, who was music director at Payne College in Augusta, Georgia. Locke wrote to Diton from Jacksonville to find out if he could get any paid speaking engagements at Diton's college. Diton was at first shocked that Locke had written him, since after his graduation, Locke had always discouraged Diton's attempts to establish a correspondence, let alone a friendship. When Diton had tried to contact Locke when he went to Germany in 1911 to study music, Locke had kept Diton from knowing his whereabouts. Now in the South and near destitute, Locke needed his "old friend" Diton, but he was not fooled. "Your letter of the 9th," he wrote, "came rather as a surprise to me for I was thinking that you had about arrived in Europe.... Knowing the calibre of your works I should deem it unwise to present you or have you presented here—that is, unless you have changed your style of expression from that which you use when talking before our historical societies. I am much afraid that these folks would be apt to miss the point." Of course, "if your 'hard luck' tale is really true, why I think that I can scare up a crowd of a hundred and fifty—or two to hear you talk at ten cents a piece. Probably you'll realize ten, fifteen or twenty dollars therefrom. But don't count upon it."[21] Later, when it was clear Locke was not coming, Diton quipped, "I think you are making a mistake in not seeing Fisk. What's your hurry? You've been going to Europe since November. Why not put it off some days later and take a faster steamer?"[22] Once again, Locke was using Europe as an excuse, but his real hurry was to get to New York for conferences with Booker T. Washington and the trustees of the Kahn Fellowship. His exchange with Diton showed, however, that Locke needed to repair bridges with former friends and Black intellectuals whom he needed if he wanted to become a Black leader of influence in the United States.

Hurrying north, Locke arrived in New York on April 11 and, using the Hotel Marshall at 127 W. 53th Street as his base of operations, began his campaign for the Kahn Travelling Fellowship he needed to fund his travel-research trip through Europe and Africa. Having won late admission to this year's competition, Locke wanted to build support among the trustees for his project. At first it was hard to get appointments, but once Washington's letter to Nicholas Murray had arrived, Locke met with several officials, including the chief commissioner of the fund. His New York stay also allowed him to connect with significant Black intellectuals and artists. He dined with Du Bois on April 14, met the emerging young Black artist, Lonsdale Brown, and returned to Bruce's Sunnyslope farm. Unfortunately, all of Locke's efforts were for naught. As he informed Washington on May 20, the Kahn committee turned him down. The project was very expensive (around $5,000) and would have involved allowing

Locke to sell articles from the research trip to various newspapers, which may have reduced its value in the eyes of the trustees. Race, of course, may have been a factor, since no other Black man had received such a fellowship. But Locke refused to consider race a reason and surmised instead to Washington that the Kahn people were favoring older men who had teaching experience. If that were true, then there was nothing left for him to do but to postpone returning to Berlin, obtain a teaching position in the United States, and apply for the fellowship again the next year. In truth, it mattered little why the Kahn people had turned him down; without the fellowship he could not return to Berlin. From May 1912 on, he began to search in earnest for a teaching post at one of the Black colleges.

But which college? Howard University was the most prestigious and the most practical, located in the nation's capital, just outside of the South and close to Camden and his mother. As the only bona fide Black university in America, Howard possessed a respected medical school, a well-regarded law school, and a federal subsidy that made it one of the most secure academic institutions in Black higher education. But in the fall of 1910, Locke had alienated officials at Howard. Apparently, someone at Howard University in a position of authority, perhaps Dean Kelly Miller, had written to Locke asking if he would be interested in the possibility of an appointment at Howard. The "offer" was exploratory and tentative, but Mary Locke believed it was serious. "They were willing to offer you a chair," she wrote her expatriated son, "but were surprised by your letter. In light of it, they could not proceed further."[23] Most likely, Locke rebuffed their offer, because despite his severe financial problems in 1910, he remained committed to staying in Europe. Locke believed he could obtain the funds to finance his research travel plan, and he did not want a teaching commitment to stand in the way of realizing that dream. Locke may have felt that teaching at any Black college, even Howard, was a step down for him, and some of that condescension may have crept into his response. From Howard's standpoint Locke's lack of interest must have been surprising, since it was the most prestigious African American institution of higher education in the nation, and his best opportunity to have a college teaching position outside of the Deep South.

Apparently, the cool feeling toward Locke lingered, for when he visited Howard in November 1911, Locke contrasted the enthusiastic reception elsewhere on his Washington trip in a letter to his mother with the cool one at Howard. A return trip to Howard in February 1912, when Locke spoke to Cromwell's teacher association in Washington, did not immediately increase his prospects. By the spring of 1912, Locke realized that he needed a go-between to resuscitate his candidacy. Again, he turned to Washington, who had been a member of Howard University's Board of Trustees since 1907. After making a formal application for a position at Howard in July 1912, Locke wrote Washington asking whether he would "use your influence on my behalf" with the "proper authorities at Howard."[24] Washington spoke with Kelly Miller, who informed Washington that nothing was available in the College Department, but offered to speak with Dean Lewis B. Moore about a possible appointment in the Teachers College. The Teachers College offered the kind of teacher preparation courses that Locke's mother and father had taken at the Institute for Colored Youth. Although this was not the academic appointment Locke hoped for, it was a job and he desperately needed one. Over the summer, Miller and Lewis worked out an arrangement whereby Locke would be offered a position in the Teachers College, with some minimal classwork in the College Department. To be considered for the position, Locke had to fill out application forms that required him to confront, once again, the issue of his Oxford University degree. Again, he put down that he had received a BLitt degree from Oxford in 1912. Actually, it probably was not necessary: having an AB from Harvard was quite enough to land a teaching job at Howard University in the early twentieth century. Moreover, his training at the Philadelphia School of Pedagogy probably played a greater part in recommending him for the kind of work he would be doing in the Teachers College. Nevertheless, by 1912, Locke had become committed to the notion of representing himself as a degreed student from Oxford. It certainly did not hurt his chances: on September 14, he received this telegram from Moore: "Elected Assistant Professor Salary One Thousand Dollars Congratulations."[25]

Ironically, on the very same day, Locke received an offer from Washington to teach at Tuskegee if Locke had not already obtained work. Locke's predicament recalls that of W. E. B. Du Bois, who received an invitation to Tuskegee days after accepting an appointment to Wilberforce University. In his autobiography, Du Bois reflected on how his life might have been different if the Tuskegee offer had arrived prior to the one from Wilberforce. Unlike Du Bois, Locke had a real choice, since both offers arrived the same day. But there was no doubt in Locke's mind that he preferred Howard to Tuskegee, and he hurried off a letter to Washington to inform him that Howard had made the offer. "I was about to write you news of this, and to thank you for your very valuable and timely help in the Howard matter, when your letter with its still greater willingness to assist me in getting placed arrives to put me still more in your debt." Locke tried to soften his rejection of Tuskegee by promising Washington to "serve your very best interests at Howard and elsewhere, until I more than repay you for your deep personal interest."[26] Both Locke and Washington may have realized that a "direct apprenticeship under" Washington might have had disastrous results for Locke—as well as for Washington. Washington knew that Locke was better placed at Howard. His abstract discussions of the comparative nature of racial attitudes and the conditions of cultural development were out of place at Tuskegee, where the practical training of the Black masses dominated instruction. Nevertheless, it would have added an interesting twist to Locke's career if Howard had not made the offer and he had been obligated to go to Tuskegee. Perhaps teaching at Tuskegee would have inspired Locke to make southern African American culture the focal point of his interest, instead of the northern urban culture of New York and Washington, D.C. And the opportunity for Locke and Washington to team up to create a program of liberation at the intersection of art and economics could have been paradigm shifting for early twentieth-century Negroes.

But Locke could not overturn his bias and perhaps real fear of the South. His trip with Washington through the South had not stimulated Locke's literary creativity. Although he talked of writing up his experiences, no literary sketches of southern Black life had resulted from the trip. While the South was the cradle of African American civilization, northern-born, it was not his civilization, so marked was his sense of social difference from the heirs of slavery. Locke regarded the Black South as best observed from a safe distance. In that sense, Locke remained indebted to Howard as well as Washington, for Howard had rescued him from a fate he must have regarded as just this side of death—the prospect of living in the Black Belt of Alabama in 1912.

Even so, Locke's Howard appointment was a bittersweet victory. Remaining in the United States meant leaving behind the lifestyle that he and his friends Seme and de Fonseka had enjoyed in Europe. Instead of just visiting America long enough to secure funding to return to Europe, he was now settling into an American lifestyle, shouldering the tasks of race leadership, and closing off opportunities and freedoms that he had enjoyed living abroad. One of the most important was sex. Since his return to the United States in the fall of 1911, Locke had been living with his mother and the Claphans at 579 Stevens Street. Except for brief trips away from home, Locke lacked the kind of privacy he needed to entertain male guests in Camden. During the year since his return, he probably had contacted his former lover, Charles Dickerman, and enjoyed a rendezvous or two. He also attended a Central High reunion in January 1912 at which he may have revived old acquaintances and intimate friends. But these interludes of romance and possible sex were far more limited, hidden, and brief than those he had been able to regularly enjoy in Europe. At least in his first year back, returning to America meant giving up his sexual freedom for a life of far less frequent and far more compromised pleasures. In January 1912, he was approached by a Mrs. J. Elwood Camagy to address the Alpha Male Choral Society, a boy's choir in New Jersey. After inquiring and learning that the singers were young teenagers, Locke took the time out of his busy campaign for the Kahn Fellowship to speak to the choir. The boys were mightily impressed with Locke; and so, apparently, was Locke impressed with them. Two days later, he wrote asking whether he might visit the boys at their next meeting. She said yes, although it is not known whether he returned. Here was one of the few compensations of his American return—he could use his iconic status to bring himself into contact with young men he could be attracted to. But such sublimated settings of hidden pleasure were a far cry from the kind of ecstatic homosexual freedom he had taken for granted in Europe. As his friend Lionel de Fonseka somewhat tactlessly recounted again and again in letters to Locke in 1912, London had exploded with vibrant new establishments that even the police knew catered to homosexual interests.

If Locke could not live the cosmopolitan lifestyle itself by returning to Europe, he could at least write about it, and in doing so, try and create a synthesis between his commitment to the race tradition, which he had eloquently outlined in "The Negro and a Race Tradition," and his still-burning commitment to being a cosmopolitan, a player in a larger, universal community of thinkers and peoples. Just ten days before he learned of the Howard University offer, Locke penned a letter to Miss Cutting, his editor at the *North American Review*, which documents his continued theorizing about cosmopolitanism in 1912. A critical essay in two parts, "Cosmopolitanism and Culture" was a major statement of Locke's philosophy of cultural pluralism and of what today would be called Cultural Studies, a demand for a criticism that "must be synthetic... must establish the linkages of facts, [as well as be] capable of administering a system of cosmopolitan culture. Had such a criticism kept pace in art and letters with our modern practice, our culture would have been more sound, more sane and more permanent. But with a steadily increasing need for it, criticism of that type has lapsed; so that for even the right conception of it, we must go back to Sainte-Beuve, to Taine and Renan, to Matthew Arnold."[27]

"Cosmopolitanism and Culture" rejected what would later be called the New Criticism that studied a work of art removed from the world in which it arose. Instead, Locke suggested cultural critics return to an older form of criticism that Arnold's generation of critics had advanced, even though their racial politics had been reactionary. Arnold had pioneered a new kind of cosmopolitan criticism, for Arnold had not been afraid to "universalize the English temperament even at the cost of denationalization in some essential respects."[28] But Arnold also had had the good sense to realize that something of the English national character must be preserved even when modern English criticism became cosmopolitan. Arnold's criticism was both English and European; what Locke wanted to do was to expand that kind of cosmopolitan criticism beyond Europe to encompass the broader world of cultures, such that he and others could be both African American and cosmopolitan, even though he did not mention that dichotomy in this essay. He wanted to be able to insist that one's national "voice" be retained in any world literature, while at the same time preserving the openness that allowed a culture to be open to others.

But Locke's essay was noteworthy for being one of the first critiques of modernism from a postcolonial perspective. Locke made the argument that cosmopolitanism in literature and art was most often a raiding of other cultures, especially non-Western or colonial ones, for the forms the West could then appropriate for its own purposes, and then congratulate itself for being "cosmopolitan." As in the earlier "Epilogue," Locke argued true cosmopolitanism needed to be more than intellectual imperialism. Unfortunately, that had defined how the West had responded to Japanese art and culture:

A few years ago a discovery of Japanese art was the incident of the artistic decade, a startling revelation of civilization strange and new to us. A proper use of its contrast values was perhaps the very thing Occidental civilization most needed at the time. The diversity and incommensurability of the two traditions, the profound psychological and racial differences were a challenge and an opportunity for any culture professing cosmopolitanism. But the incident has come and gone without even having proved or disproved our notion of cosmopolitanism. The results of the encounter should have been momentous, instead of being in point of fact almost negligible, and the defects of our cosmopolitanism have been the causes of this failure: a faculty of appreciation too fluid to be retentive, an inability to comprehend and respect marked and representative national or racial contrasts because the sense for contrast amongst us has atrophied through neglect and disuse, and a facile eclecticism which refuses to interpret alien things in their own terms and according to their native values.[29]

Cultural respect for non-Western culture was still something Western artists no less than cultural custodians had a hard time practicing when they encountered sophisticated cultures that were not Western. However much the West congratulated itself on its cosmopolitanism, "there was more real power of assimilation in the subtle nationalism of Japan than in our diffuse and careless cosmopolitanism."[30]

Rather than hobnob with Shakespeare and Plato above the color line as Du Bois had recommended, Locke wanted to build a cosmopolitanism out of the national traditions of the non-Western peoples. A sophisticated praxis of universalism was already practiced by non-Western cultures like the Japanese that put Western pretenses to cosmopolitanism to shame. Western cosmopolitanism was mainly a lifestyle for alienated intellectuals who wanted to escape the provincial confines that existed in any culture. Oscar Wilde had epitomized this attitude by calling the critic the physician of world culture. While such megalomania was ennobling of criticism, it ultimately was bad for art, for "the artist has found it impossible to use the universalized and disintegrated culture tradition as the constructive basis for creative work." The literature and art that had expressed itself in terms of cosmopolitanism and universalism "has been for the most part so superficial and uncreative that it is not amiss to call it sublimated journalism."[31] Likely, Locke had the novels of Henry James on his mind, for they depicted in all their nuance the life of the "transit class." Alienation was the concomitant of American cosmopolitanism, the elite disgusted with the lack of refined culture in America.

There was an alternative. Younger writers and artists were embedding themselves in the life of their people and discovering the life of the "province and the social underworld" through "the study of dialect, folk-lore, provincial manner-isms and community-life, and of the psychological exploration of those dark mental universes of the untutored peasant, the mentally abnormal, and the so-cially unfit."[32] Rather than trying to escape into expatriation, the true modernist artist, Locke the expatriate declared, needed to create literature out of the "in-termediary units" of nation, locale, and province, that the critics claimed limited and destroyed art. Here were the lessons he had learned from traveling with Downes in London: the new literature would be a realism that knitted together with the local and subversive into culture. Locke put that theory into practice in his fictional village story "A Miraculous Draught," also submitted to Miss Cutting. It developed a local legend about a Breton fishing village into a short story whose universal appeal came from how well it embedded the reader in locale. Art resided in the "smaller world, which criticism and cosmopolitanism have been breaking down," an argument consistent with his Oxford thesis, "The Concept of Value," that values emerged from and gained meaning in a social con-text. The particularities of the valuing literary experience—its history, its sense of place, and its social relatedness—produced aesthetic value, not paeans to drift and wayward seeking. Already evident in this essay was how far Locke had come from the Boston aestheticism of his Harvard undergraduate days. Philosophically, he was circling back to the position he articulated in that Cambridge Lyceum about Dunbar—that the true artist could not escape his or her birthright through cosmopolitanism.

Given how thoroughly he critiqued cosmopolitanism, one wonders why Locke called his essay "Cosmopolitanism and Culture." Why not just focus one's whole career and life on the "conscious revival of obsolescent bodies of culture tradi-tion like the Celtic, Provencal, and the like?" The answer was simple: he needed cosmopolitanism to see something of value in his home culture. More concerned than Kallen that an unreflective embrace of difference and nationalism would lead one into a Gulag of imprisoning provincialism, Locke kept including the cosmopolitan, even when he argued against it, to remain free. Ethnic particular-ism must be part of a Hegelian-like becoming toward something larger, a path to a sense of world community, or become a trap. Cosmopolitanism and culture were a dialogue that defined who he was as an intellectual.

On a practical level, "Cosmopolitanism and Culture" was his way of talking himself into coming home. America was the only country that would support Locke as a Black intellectual. He knew that now. America also was where his mother was. But he would always be here and elsewhere, a liminal figure, an out-sider to America spiritually and intellectually regardless of how much he symbol-ized Negro success for others. The trick was to use that alterity to create a more cosmopolitan "culture" at home. If he failed at that task, he would become little more than another Barrett Wendell, an exile at home.

Locke, his mother, second from the left, and unidentified group, ca. 1915. Courtesy of the Moorland-Spingarn Research Center, Howard University.

14

Radical Sociologist at Howard University, 1912–1916

"What a day to leave!" wrote his mother, after Locke traveled from Camden to take his new job at Howard University. "Yet I am reminded that you go away in a storm—It rained when you left for Harvard and sinfully poured when you left for Eng[land] the first time[.] Is it ominous of what will happen at Harvard [*sic*]?" Clearly, the rain had not been a consistent predictor of things to come— he had succeeded beyond her wildest dreams at Harvard and failed in ways she could not have imagined at Oxford. The rain did capture her mood of being left alone again and the curious way that his successes always took him away from her. The compensation this time was that he would be earning money and be a mere three-hour train ride away. Mary Locke may also have sensed in that rain the uncertainty of what lay ahead of him at Howard University, the "capstone of Negro education," and Washington, D.C., the uncrowned capital of Black society. Both were tough, challenging institutions of Black America, and she could not help feeling that her son, whom she still thought of as a little boy, was not ready for that world awaiting him. She expressed those feelings, as she habitually did, in words of motherly concern. "I do wish you had your rubbers— so foolish in this storm not to take them. I am very anxious about you in every way."[1]

At age twenty-seven, however, Locke was ready to construct an adult identity for himself as a Black professional. Howard was the best place for him to do that, as fatherly Bishop Levi Coppin confirmed: "There is where we want you to be, because it is really <u>our</u> principal school. You are now <u>placed</u> and this gives you a chance to make your way to special work. Your splendid ability coupled with exemplary character will do the rest."[2]

It was also the right time for him to come to Howard. Founded in 1867 to teach the freedmen, Howard had weathered late nineteenth-century attempts to make it a school for vocational training and become a good liberal arts university by the twentieth century. Howard produced most of the African American teachers, doctors, and other professionals. It also possessed the best faculty in

1912: under outgoing President Wilbur Thirkield, Howard had hired Ernest Just, Benjamin Brawley, and Thomas Montgomery Gregory, all Ivy League school graduates, who would distinguish Howard in biology, literary criticism, and drama over the next decade. Over the next twenty years, Howard University would become known as the "Black Harvard," because it attracted the increasing number of brilliant Black graduates produced by Harvard as well as other Ivy League schools who could not teach in the institutions that had educated them. In the 1910s and 1920s, Howard would add historians Charles Wesley and Carter G. Woodson, sociologist E. Franklin Frazier, political scientist Ralph Bunche, economist Abram Harris, poet Sterling Brown, and critic Arthur P. Davis to its faculty during what could be called Howard University's "Golden Age." Arguably, that "Golden Age" began when Alain Locke joined the faculty in 1912.

Locke came to Howard University believing that his responsibilities in the Teachers College would be secondary to his leading the more academically rigorous College of Arts and Sciences.[3] But during his first four years at Howard, he worked constantly in the pedagogical Teachers College, and with his relatively low salary, that was disappointing. Not only did the College of Arts and Sciences have better students and more disciplinary-based courses but also it had Kelly Miller as its dean. Miller was a broad-minded intellectual in addition to being a professor of mathematics, an academic visionary who pressured the university to offer modern language courses, to establish a Negro Academy to study Black history, and to allow him to teach the university's first course in sociology in 1902. Miller was also a public intellectual, who charted a middle course politically between Booker T. Washington and W. E. B. Du Bois, and believed, as Locke did, that objective, scientific study of the Negro was the best answer to racists. As a pragmatist, Miller believed "race advancement" was in the hands of Black people and translated that perspective into a series of demands to make the school a center for teaching and research about the African American experience. But Howard's conservative board of trustees rejected most of Miller's proposals, creating conflict between Miller (and younger race-conscious Black professors like Locke around him) and the administration at Howard.

Locke's fate was in the hands of Dean Lewis B. Moore of the Teachers College. Unlike Miller, who may have still resented Locke's 1910 snub of the college, Dean Moore was very enthusiastic about Locke, whose presence bolstered the prestige of his Teachers College. Moore also valued Locke's previous training in pedagogy in Philadelphia. For his part, Locke made jokes about Moore. He told his mother that when he discovered Moore sleeping on a train, the dean resembled a giant walrus. But Moore was a powerful dean at Howard University. He was one of the few faculty who held a PhD and was also a skillful power player, who got his way at Howard University more often than the outspoken Miller. He was also a competent teacher of philosophy, as Locke discovered when he took over Moore's course in Kantian philosophy when the dean was away from campus. Moore had been the one who decided to hire Locke; whether he liked it or not, Locke's future was in the hands of this formidable patron at Howard.

Moore's hiring telegram to Locke had not left him with much time to prepare for his new position. But after hurrying to Washington and moving temporarily into Mrs. Maggie Walker's rooming house at 1610 15th Street NW, Locke threw himself into the fall semester of teaching. As an assistant professor of the teaching of English and instructor in philosophy and education, Locke taught five courses in English and assisted in a course by Moore on the history and philosophy of education. He taught English Curriculum for Secondary School, English Speech and Usage for Teachers, and Type Forms of English Literature. He particularly liked the Type Forms course, because it allowed him to showcase his knowledge of such literary forms as the epic, the lyric, the ballad, and the novel. His two team-taught English courses—The Teaching of English Language and Literature with Montgomery Gregory and Ethel Robinson, and English Composition, again with Professor Robinson—rounded out his English offerings. Locke was hired primarily to teach English to those who would be teachers, and in some semesters, he would teach English for elementary schoolteachers, as well as additional philosophy and education courses. His rotation of courses remained roughly the same for his first three years at Howard, and a report he submitted to Dean Moore in 1915 gives a sense of how Locke approached these courses. The course in Teaching of English was quite satisfactory, although plagued by its low enrollment. "Undoubtedly registration will be larger as soon as our regulation that students take the methods course in their major subject goes into effect.... The course in Type forms will next year be given at a more favorable hour, and is so scheduled. MacMillan Co. have accepted the M.S.s. of the course and if publication should ensue in time for the Fall list, the course will have its own text next year." Of course, the low registration in his classes might suggest that Locke was not yet a popular teacher. On the other hand, his comment about Macmillan publishing a text for "Type Forms" suggests that Locke cared enough about that course to pull together a textbook for publication. What most troubled him was the poor preparation of the students. "Regarding the Course in the Literature of Elementary schools, I have found the work very handicapped through deficiencies in the rudiments of English grammar, pronunciation and reading, and I must suggest that either next year pupils be required to take the course in Oral Drill and Speaking that we contemplated and have in the Catalogue, or else the course postponed to the Sophomore year." Locke had little tolerance for, and perhaps little knowledge of, how to teach those students who were reading at a low high-school level. How could he teach the type of English needed to teach in secondary school when his students could barely read at that level themselves? He admitted work had not gone particularly well in English Composition, because he was prevented from using his "own method" of instruction in that course, presumably because of his co-teacher, Miss Robinson.[4]

Locke preferred the philosophy courses and obtained permission to teach sections of courses that Moore offered previously by his second year at Howard. "The hours that this year were kept open for [my] assistance in the Philosophy courses are available next year, and I suggest an earlier ascertainment of pupils schedules, should you still contemplate assistance in that work." Locke felt that "the course in Logic and Ethics went as usual," but, he hoped to improve it by changing the text the next year. He reserved his greatest enthusiasm for Philosophical Bases of Education, a team-taught course that was going very well until two of the four teachers fell ill, and the other one quit.[5] The picture that emerges is that Locke was a dedicated, innovative teacher, who had yet to hit his stride with the students. Locke wanted to shift entirely to philosophy and education and leave the teaching of English skills to the other professors. Accordingly, Locke's second correspondence with Moore is punctuated with requests to be promoted from an instructor to an assistant professor of philosophy and education. Perhaps Locke already dreamed of becoming Howard's future professor of philosophy, but his more immediate need was to increase the $1,000 a year salary that came with being an instructor in the Teachers College.

Locke's family friends and school acquaintances eased his first-year grind at Howard University by introducing him to Washington's Black society. The social elite in Black Washington were famous for their sophisticated social set, dominated by private clubs, sumptuous northwest Washington homes, and considerable political clout garnered by such federal appointees as Recorder of Deeds; a former Reconstruction governor, P. B. S. Pinchback; and Robert Terrell, a federal judge. To gain status in such a society, one needed a patron, and Locke's most prominent and indulgent patron was an old family friend, Major Christian Fleetwood. This tall, refined, and retired military officer was one of only sixteen African Americans to receive the Congressional Medal of Honor for heroism in the Civil War. Fleetwood, as a sergeant major of the 4th United States Colored Troops at the battle of New Market Heights and Chaffin's Farm in September 1864, had grabbed the Union flag after two color-bearers had been shot and, in the absence of any officers, had rallied a group of reserves to attack the fort during the final successful battle of the engagement. Fleetwood was a member of the Acanthus Club, a prestigious African American gentleman's club in Washington, and a prominent member of the Black elite of the city. A widower with two daughters, Fleetwood was an old friend of Mary Locke, perhaps from the Institute of Colored Youth days in Philadelphia, but at least as far back as the 1880s, when Pliny had been an appointee at the Treasury Department. When Locke first visited Washington in February, Mary Locke encouraged him to look up the old family friend. When Locke wrote to apologize for not calling on him, Christian Fleetwood replied in the rococo prose of a seasoned Black Victorian. "Knowing from experience how impossible it is to get to see all whom one wishes to see, in a limited time, I have the largest charity and consideration."[6]

Once they connected, Fleetwood took Mary Locke's only son under his ample social wings. "Major Fleetwood took me last night to Miss Lucy Motens. [I] was invited back to an exclusive coterie of intellectuals next Wednesday. Chris likes this sort of thing—he chaperones well." The Fleetwoods seemed to adopt Locke as their own, often inviting him over, and holding a special reception when his mother spent Thanksgiving in Washington. "Ask your mother," Fleetwood wrote Locke, "to kindly send me a list of the friends whom she remembers from earlier days and whom she would like to see. And as far as practicable we will try to gather them together (informally) to meet her again." Socializing with the major and his daughters was good ballast to Locke's heavy teaching responsibilities. "Going out now to Fleetwoods," he reported to his mother. "Class work and other stuff very heavy, but going nicely. Cannot get home till Saturday morning—important meeting on Emancipation down here, and Major Wright and Bishop Walters on the string."[7] The next month, Locke was again bogged down and unable to get to Philadelphia for the weekend, and again the Fleetwoods provided needed diversion. "I am having the deuce of a lot of work to do. Particularly for Dean Moore. I hope the tickets for the Boston Symphony have come, in which case meet the train due 7:40 at Broad Street Station. I took the Fleetwoods to hear [Roland] Hayes. He really has a fine voice. So much for my personal debt to them. I got out cheap as usual."[8] Even after Major Fleetwood died on September 28, 1914, his daughter, Edith, continued to invite Locke to intellectual club meetings.

Of course, Locke's father's friend and Howard Law School classmate John W. Cromwell, and Locke's own Harvard colleague, Roscoe Conkling Bruce, steered Locke through the social intricacies of Black Washington. Of the two, Locke grew closest to Bruce, although Locke found aspects of Bruce's social conduct almost ridiculous. "Bruce Evans summarily dismissed," Locke wrote his mother, "from the Armstrong school—more scandal. Bruce (Roscoe) just wallows in this sort of thing. They are the limit down here."[9] Gossip, innuendo, and scandal dominated social relations in Black bourgeois Washington, in part because the number of Black aspirants far outnumbered the number of respectable federal and local positions available. Bruce himself would become a victim of scandal in 1919 and lose his job as administrator in the District of Columbia. There also was the possibility of scandal for Locke. Eventually, someone would begin to wonder why such an eligible and socially acceptable gentleman was not married, and then the gossip and rumors would start. Locke knew he could never feel completely comfortable in Washington, because no matter how much he excelled academically or socially his sexuality made him an outsider to its patriarchal culture.

Managing his sexual orientation within the context of being a Howard University professor came to symbolize how Locke managed his alienation from bourgeois Black life generally. As a letter from his friend de Fonseka in March

1913 shows, it was difficult for alienated aesthetes like them to identify fully with their professional roles. "I wish you hadn't become a Professor," de Fonseka chided. "You will get fossilized like the rest in no time. You will no longer be the charming sceptic that you were." That was unlikely, given Locke's basic personality; but de Fonseka had picked up something about the new Locke that he had sniffed out the year before: in taking up "stump speaking," as de Fonseka called Locke's lecturing before Negro historical societies, Locke revealed that he was willing to become an ideologue in order to get power. "You will inevitably," de Fonseka continued, "have to adopt some comfortable creed and batten and fatten on it in order to fill the chair that you occupy." How far would Locke be willing to go, to sell out, de Fonseka implied, to become a success? "Alas, for the young men who start life with a perfect outlook and end by accepting a useful Professorship. Would not Wilde have wept if he had lived." His recommendation? "Chuck your job, my dear fellow, universities were once the repositories, but they are now only the cenotaphs of thought."[10]

With his debts, Locke was not about to "chuck" his Howard job. But de Fonseka's teasing captured something of the tension in Locke's life as a professor—it could never embody all of his creativity as a person. A double life was required to survive at Howard and Washington, D.C. Advocacy of art and literature away from the university would give him spiritual sustenance and allow him to express his sexuality in his artistic interests and among of his artistic friends, while remaining relatively strait-laced in his professional life at Howard. But his rigid division of work and love, of ego and id, and of America and Europe would become a punishing self-discipline, for he had to have the energy to sustain two lives—an increasingly authoritarian academic and a flagrantly subversive aesthete. It was the former that de Fonseka could not stomach; he could not become a spokesperson for the establishment, even the Sinhalese establishment. "Philip," de Fonseka continued, "has excommunicated himself by marriage, as you say—that is pardonable. But you have excommunicated yourself for the means to marriage. I have once for all chosen my path in life—that of a vagabond."

De Fonseka lied. He also stood on the brink of a similar transition into the fossilized life of the professional. After *The Decorative Theory of Art* had been published, de Fonseka's father had traveled personally to Oxford to communicate his anger about his son writing books on aesthetics instead of preparing for the law. De Fonseka Sr. demanded his son complete his studies, return home, and get married, which de Fonseka Jr. agreed to do—although de Fonseka said he would marry a European, not a Sinhalese, woman, because, as he put it, he needed some complexity in his life. De Fonseka did return home, become a lawyer, and disappear from the literary world after he reached Ceylon. Although Locke had "accepted a useful Professorship," he had not accepted masquerading as a married bourgeois to save his private reputation from rumor and scandal.

But de Fonseka had put his finger on a problem: by becoming an academic, Locke was giving up the kind of intellectual freedom he had enjoyed in Europe for the insularity of the ivory tower. By choosing an academic post, Locke protected himself from having to dialogue directly with the public to earn a living. John Bruce, Arthur Schomburg, John W. Cromwell, William Monroe Trotter, and W. E. B. Du Bois, whether university trained or not, were intellectuals whose continued existence depended on their relationship with the Black public to survive. Their social voice was crafted in response to the daily struggles of Black people and the criticality that bubbled up from the experience of race in America. Joining Howard hampered Locke in sensing his audience, as he nestled in an academic institution dominated by a White president and a conservative board of trustees. But American intellectual life was shifting away from generalists who often wrote in a variety of genres for newspapers, magazines, and social welfare journals toward specialists who taught at universities and published in scholarly journals. The days when people like John Bruce, who worked as a clerk in the Treasury Department, could be regarded by the White power structure as authorities on the Black experience, were quickly passing. What neither de Fonseka nor Locke could see, however, in 1912, was that a "useful Professorship" was not even a certain path to the kind of power Locke longed for and de Fonseka feared would warp his friend.

Indeed, Locke did not have much power in 1912. The key, of course, was to tap into the institutional power structure at Howard. Locke wasted no time in trying to find out who were the influential figures at Howard and how he might ally himself with them. Chief among his early allies was Alexander Walters, the influential bishop of the African Methodist Episcopal Zion Church and Howard trustee. Having met Walters on board the *Lusitania* in 1910, Locke renewed their relationship when he came to Howard, working closely with the bishop after Locke was elected secretary of the Teachers College faculty in February 1913. That post brought with it a spot on "Bishop Walter's Council," his organization for lobbying Congress on behalf of the university.[11] Walters's political stock had skyrocketed after the election of Woodrow Wilson to the presidency in November 1912, for Walters was one of the few Black Democrats, and he hoped to serve Wilson as Washington had served Roosevelt—as the trusted Black advisor who dispensed presidential favors and influence. Perhaps Walters's influence might help improve Locke's position at the university and gain him access to Wilson. From his part, Walters liked having a trusted lieutenant like Locke at the university. The collusion developing between Locke and Walters can be gleaned from a letter Walters wrote Locke on April 9, 1913. "Your 'special' just received, too late to even telegraph you to go to Brooklyn. I hardly think it is necessary for either one of us to be on hand. Our close connection with the administration makes our position secure." Locke and Walters shared a taste for political intrigue and a talent for organizational gamesmanship. "I do not think that we have anything to fear from that source," Walters continued. "I was urged by the chairman of the committee to be present, it looked to me to be a trap, hence I decided not to go."[12]

But Wilson's record on civil rights turned out to be so disastrous, that there was no chance to turn association with Wilson into political capital in the Black community. As early as the spring of 1913, Wilson had asked all the prominent Black federal appointees from previous administrations to resign and then refused to appoint African Americans to replace them. Simultaneously, Wilson made it known that he would not appoint any Negroes to positions in the South, because it would anger Whites in the region. Over the summer of 1913, Wilson supported subordinates in the Treasury, the Post Office, the Bureau of Census, and the Bureau of Printing and Engraving who instituted a policy of segregating Blacks and Whites in the working, eating, and restroom environments of these government departments. A storm of protest erupted from the Black community, and even such friends of Wilson as Oswald Garrison Villard, the secretary of the NAACP, who had earlier sought Wilson's endorsement of a Race Conference, released to the press an official NAACP letter condemning the administration's segregationist policies. Even worse for Alexander Walters, when Wilson was challenged on his belief that Negroes favored segregation, Wilson claimed that a number of Black leaders agreed with him; when Villard and others asked for their names, one of Wilson's subordinates let it be known that Walters was one of them. Whether true or not, this rumor led to Walters's resignation from the NAACP and tarnished his reputation among the Black intelligentsia.[13]

Here was one of the pitfalls of alliances with conservatives during a time of increasing protest from progressives, but Locke appeared not to recognize them. He continued to support Walters and Wilson, despite the worsening situation, even though Walters informed him little good could come from an association with Wilson now. "With you," Walters wrote to Locke on September 3, 1913, "I cannot but believe that Mr. Wilson intends to make good; but I fear that he has let his most favorable opportunity pass. So far as the colored people are concerned untoward sentiment has crystalized against him; and he will never be able to retrieve his lost prestige no matter what he may do in the future to aid them."[14] Locke enthused about Wilson in part because he had made a proposal to Wilson, perhaps through Walters, and hoped to benefit personally from his administration. Here was a weakness in Locke's political vision: his private schemes for gain from certain officials made it difficult for him to identify with rising Black anger against them. Locke even criticized, privately of course, friends such as Roscoe Conkling Bruce who responded to the segregation crisis by joining the NAACP. "It is disgusting," he wrote his mother, "to see the way these Negroes down here, Bruce etc. flop over at the slightest change of fortune. They are all Villardists now."[15]

Locke was correct to see Bruce as an opportunist, who had supported Booker T. Washington's policies when they were in vogue and helpful to his career. But at least Bruce was cognizant enough of the mood of the Black community to sense when it changed and that he needed to change with it. By contrast, Locke characterized the racial climate under Wilson as "the slightest change of fortune." This was absurd. Even in Washington, D.C., where Negroes had been excluded from downtown hotels, theaters, and restaurants for years, Wilson's election spread segregationist sentiment to the point that the Central Citizens Association demanded streetcars of Washington, D.C., be Jim Crowed. Although a well-organized, NAACP-led protest blocked the effort in April 1913, over the next three years, six bills would be introduced in Congress to segregate the District of Columbia streetcars, and Congress would pass an anti-intermarriage bill for the District as well.

Locke's abhorrence of protest blinded him to the realization that Black politics had shifted and he needed to shift with it or risk not being able to speak as a representative voice. His loyalty to past friends, a noble attribute, marginalized him politically in the 1910s. "Today [I have] a rather important conference with Walters," he announced to his mother in January 1914, "who is about to form an alliance with Booker T. largely at Booker's initiation strange to say. I have large prospects under such leadership. Walters swears by me."[16] It was not strange that Washington sought an alliance with Walters, given Washington's own declining support among Blacks. By contrast, NAACP membership soared, and NAACP leaders such as Villard and Du Bois became heroes to most Black people. Locke's "large prospects" were rather diminutive considering how invested in conservative Negro leaders he was in 1913.

Locke's views were somewhat more typical of the older Black bourgeoisie of Washington, D.C., who, though faced with worsening race relations in their city, also tended to respond with acquiescence, which was less a political philosophy and more a sign of their inability to stem the worsening tide. Such conservatism had made sense in the nineteenth century, when the African American elite, especially light-skinned bourgeois, had been able to thwart segregation by gaining access to otherwise all-White establishments because of that conservatism or their skin color, or both. But by the second decade of the twentieth century, such access was gone. This was particularly problematical for Locke, given that he had always dined in the best restaurants and shopped at the best stores. Now, in segregated Washington, he could only enjoy a nice dinner in the Union Station restaurant, a federally supervised facility. Once again, America forced upon him the politics of escape. When the school year closed in 1913, he hurried off to the Harvard commencement, where he could hobnob with his former classmates, Pfromm and Dickerman, and enjoy the Boston symphony, the opera, and the theater free of segregation.

Locke could not afford to go to Europe that summer, yet upon his return to Camden from Boston, he longed to avoid hot, segregated Washington and avoid remaining in his mother's cramped rooming-house apartment in Camden. His outstanding Oxford debts lingered; he had paid off only part of what he owed with his meager Howard University salary. Locke had deliberately held back from paying off all of the debts, especially those owed to Mrs. Addis and others who had angered him, in order to save something for a summer vacation. But where could he and his mother go where they would not be segregated or, worse, excluded altogether. Europe had spoiled them, and it was hard to settle back into the rituals of raced space in America. Locke also wanted to avoid the typical Black bourgeoisie watering holes like Saratoga and Cape May.

Perhaps at the suggestion of one of his friends, Locke elected to spend a good part of August with his mother in Bermuda. Scrapbooks in the Locke Papers are filled with postcards from this trip, with picturesque views of "Moonlight at Bathing Bay, Bermuda," "Leaving the Devil's Hole, Bermuda," "Kyber Pass, Warwick, Bermuda," and the "Royal Palms at Paget, Bermuda." Like many of the Black bourgeoisie, Locke felt hampered by the constraints of segregated vacationing in America; but he sought and found a tropical paradise just off the American shore that embodied all of the Victorian imagery of paradise that he and his mother had come to value in their vacations. In viewing the photographs of Locke in all-white shirts and shorts, his brown knees exposed, and of Mary bedecked in sun-protective hats and veils, one can sense what this Caribbean island meant to them—another honeymoon closer to home.

When Locke returned to Howard University that fall of 1913, he confronted again the reality that he was stuck professionally at Howard. Over the summer, his closest friend among the teachers at Howard, Montgomery Gregory, had obtained a position as an assistant professor of English in the College of Arts and Sciences under Kelly Miller. Locke remained in the Teachers College teaching reading and writing. Gregory had a Harvard pedigree as well, being a graduate and a protégé of George Pierce Baker, the great Harvard dramatist. Kelly Miller and others at the university had dreams of a university drama group, and Gregory was picked to start what became known as the Howard Players. Gregory also became Miller's main teacher of English literature and public speaking in the pre–World War I years, teaching American Literature and the Novel, the Elizabethan Drama, and Debate and Composition. These were all courses that Locke would have liked to teach. Locke complained in several letters to his mother in 1913 and 1914 that Gregory's mother was "pushing her son ahead." Although Locke got along quite well with the fair-complexioned, curly-haired Gregory—he would later assist Gregory in forming not only the Howard Players but also the Howard Stylus, a literary club—it was difficult for Locke to see a man his junior promoted ahead of him.

Locke did have some professional opportunities. Not long after he accepted the job at Howard University, Locke was contacted to help organize northern semicentennial Emancipation expositions, one at Atlantic City, the other at Philadelphia. Such expositions were designed to advertise the gains the race had made since 1863, and hence one reason Locke was recruited: he was the winner of the Rhodes Scholarship. But Locke also used the exposition to advocate for a research program that could carry out a sociological analysis of the New Jersey Negro in concert with what he had learned at the Universal Races Congress in 1911. Locke wanted to move beyond simply holding a fair that celebrated the Negro's arrival in the twentieth century and success at assimilating White American middle-class accomplishments, which was often the focal point of such expositions. But Locke lacked a research team or a community of like-minded comparative theorists to carry out a comparative world analysis of the Negro community in New Jersey. Locke could not transform the celebration program into the kind of examination of this northern urban community with the international scholarly vision he brought with him from abroad.[17]

But in truth, Locke's mind was not really focused on sociological research or the Emancipation celebration, but on advancing his career as a teacher at Howard in 1913. The only way to advance his academic standing at Howard was to get a PhD. Indeed, there was no reason to worry about his failure to get the Oxford degree: he had put down that he had it, and it still didn't matter; it was just another bachelor's degree as far as Howard was concerned. He needed a PhD, the pinnacle of academic distinction in the United States, and his trip to Harvard over the summer had rekindled his desire for graduate study at Harvard with his favorite teacher, Josiah Royce. If he could find a way to get to Harvard in the coming years and obtain a PhD, perhaps he could get promoted into the College of Letters and Science and get more salary. But study at Harvard was expensive, and he was not at all certain that he could get in: letters from the head of the Andover Theological Seminary about his welshing on the debt to Mrs. Addis had probably not helped his reputation. For that reason, his thoughts began to turn to Berlin in the spring of 1914, for he was still enrolled under the philosophical faculty at the German university.

Locke left for Berlin probably in late June 1914 taking his mother with him. Of course, this was not surprising. Since being back in the United States, he had settled down and been very productive at Howard in Washington, D.C., with his mother close by. Perhaps he decided to take his mother with him to Berlin to help him get the doctorate or perhaps simply to get him settled before she returned to her teaching job in Camden—it's not clear which. Indeed, Mary Locke may not have known exactly what his plans were. After the crossing, they stopped briefly in England, and then went on to Berlin, where Locke set about trying to register for fall classes at the University of Berlin. Mary accompanied him even though she believed going to Germany unwise. "I was impressed not to come," as she wrote her cousin Varick from Berlin on August 4. "But Roy is so determined, he wanted to increase his salary or get a better position at Howard by continuing his studies here."[18] Locke ignored negative advice from other people, so it is not surprising warnings from her friends did not deter him. But when a Serbian nationalist assassinated the archduke Franz Ferdinand of Austria-Hungary at Sarajevo on June 28, a chain reaction led to war by the end of July. It certainly caught the Lockes by surprise. "War declared in Germany, July 31, 1914," Mary Locke wrote in her diary. Alain and Mary Locke heard the "declaration of war read by [the] Kaiser from [a] balcony window of Place amid crowds of people, who with cheering and shouts expressed their joy and approval. The vast multitudes united in singing 'Praise God from whom all blessings flow.' The bells of the Cathedral opposite began to play German hymns and national airs. The Kaiser accompanied by his whole family went on foot to Cathedral to service of prayer and praise."[19]

They were now trapped in Berlin. Since Germany was at war with almost all of its neighbors, the kaiser closed its borders, making it impossible to leave. Twenty-five thousand Americans were detained in Germany on the excuse that all trains must be commandeered to move troops and military equipment to the front. German officials were also very concerned about spies and wanted to ensure that no one with classified materials or photographs of military preparations slipped out of the country. Although Germany assured American officials that Americans would soon be released after mobilization had been completed, the situation worsened when Britain declared war on Germany on August 7. In Berlin, Germans rioted and stoned the British embassy and became suspicious of anyone speaking English. Germany also cut off all communications and financial transactions with London, stopping mail service between England and Germany. This action cut off the Lockes from a hundred dollars awaiting them at Cooks in London. Even "the University of Berlin closed... students in great numbers, with uncovered heads, marching through the streets, singing the 'Watch on the Rhine'—in which they are joined by crowds in the street." It did not take Mary Locke long to conclude that "we are in a terrible situation, the whole country seems to be at war—the city of Berlin is under martial law. Roy has his American passport and has registered at the American Embassy. [Our] only hope in getting out of this is that the U.S. will send warships to take the Americans home and that we may be included. The Embassy is crowded with Americans." Unsure that they would ever make it back alive, Mary Locke sent her cousin instructions to "go to Claphans—get the cedar chest open, it has all papers belonging to us. Roy is insured in three companies, Metropolitan of New York, National Benefit of Washington and an accident policy. I have about $500 due on Metropolitan... sell everything you can, let the other debts go and whatever there is, use for Money. Do this as quickly as you can."[20]

Perhaps Mary Locke hoped Varick could wire money to Berlin, but that was hopeless: all diplomatic and financial communications between the United States and Germany had been cut off. By August 7, their Berlin landlords, fearful that the Lockes, like many other Americans, were out of money, demanded that the rent be paid in cash every morning. Fortunately, Alain and Mary Locke had budgeted carefully for the trip and still had money, unlike the hundreds of Americans who crowded the American embassy trying to get advances on suddenly worthless checks. Actually, the Americans were the lucky foreigners in Berlin, for all others were suspected of being spies. "A Russian was dragged out of the house in which we are staying," Mary Locke continued to Varick, "his wife left penniless, and he sent to prison. They have shot a number of Russians, whom they suspected of being spies—as you walk along the streets, you see men arrested on every side as suspects. Last night the English Ambassador [Sir Edward Goschen] tried to leave, his auto was stoned, and he was forced to take refuge in a hotel." Being African American helped in this situation. "The police opened Roy's door early in the morning a day or so ago, saw his black face in the bed, and went on. They were searching the house for Russians and Frenchmen."[21]

In fact, the Lockes escaped any harassment from the Germans and were able to move about freely in the capital of the Axis powers. Locke seemed to enjoy being in Berlin at such a propitious moment in modern history. As a German sympathizer, he believed that Germany would win the war and teach the British a lesson, and he seemed to be enthralled by the war preparations. He was thrilled by the show of patriotism on the part of the German people, at the organized way Germans prepared themselves for the war, and at the spirit of elation with which even Berlin's art, theater, and music people took trains to the front. Here was the spirit of nationalism that he appreciated in the Germans and wished for among the African Americans back home. There was always something of a martial spirit in Alain Locke, a man who thought of himself as a literary general. On a more practical level, Locke also approached being a trapped American with the kind of organization that he esteemed in his German friends. He attended all of the mass meetings at the American Embassy, had his passport updated, with his mother listed as his wife (a diplomatic move to simplify his exit), and had a personal meeting with Ambassador James Gerard to ask that he and his mother be given special and early passage out of Berlin. Since both Locke and his mother were schoolteachers, whom the American press had identified as persons particularly in need of quick exit from Berlin, Locke had every expectation that he would receive special treatment. As a former Rhodes Scholar, Locke may have felt that he possessed the cachet to prevail on Ambassador Gerard for a quick exit from Berlin. For now that there was no hope of continuing at the University of Berlin, he needed to get back to the United States and into his position at Howard University as quickly as possible. A quick exit would also allay his mother's mounting anxiety.

Locke's early departure was not to be, however. On August 12, Ambassador Gerard led a train of four hundred Americans out of Berlin that stopped in Amsterdam and then in Rotterdam, Holland, where "a steamer on the Holland-American line" brought the distraught Americans to the United States.[22] Locke and his mother were not among those "rescued" by that first train out of Berlin.

The reason appears to have been racial. In October, after he did make it out of Berlin, Locke informed Gilchrist Stewart, a deputy clerk in the New York State Assembly, that Gerard had informed him that Locke and his mother could not leave on that first train, because of the "color question." Apparently, Gilchrist Stewart had heard of Locke's experience from someone else, possibly John Bruce, and telegraphed Locke asking for confirmation. "Wire me at my expense 203 Broadway if report is true that Ambassador Gerard told you to wait until he [had] taken care of the whites marooned before taking care of any colored."[23] Locke's reply, scribbled in his hand on the telegram, confirmed that that was true, along with his usual attempt to play down the role of racism in his life. "It is true that Ambassador Gerard in private conversation admitted reluctantly that color question prevented granting special accomodation [sic] claimed and promised re personal transportation, even condoning situation. Case special |personal| however without reference [to] others. Would [deprecate?] newspaper or sensational use of facts because of extreme courtesy and consideration [by] other officials and members of staff [and] also because vigorous protest was lodged there and later in influential official quarters. Had considered and have no objection however [to] sensible use of generalized charge in New York campaign."[24] The "charge" was important because Gerard was the Democratic candidate for senator from New York in the fall, and such Black newspapers as the New York Age had come out for the Republican candidate. The charge seems not to have made it into the newspapers, however, or to have been part of the campaign in any way. Still, if true, the incident shows how pervasive American racism was even in Germany at such a cataclysmic moment.

The Lockes were not the only African Americans in Berlin. Hazel Harrison, the pianist, had come to Berlin to study with Borsini, while Kemper Harreld, the violinist, accompanied by his wife, was spending the summer there taking lessons from master violinist Siegfried Eberhardt. Kemper Harreld kept a diary of his experiences in Berlin that detailed the formal declaration of war, the patriotism of the German people, and the kind treatment the Harrelds received from the Germans. Like Locke, Harreld seemed to be relatively unperturbed by the war preparations and continued his lessons with Eberhardt at the latter's residence through the second and third weeks of August. Interestingly enough, the Harrelds and Miss Harrison also remained in Berlin after the departure of the August 12 train, but Harreld made no mention of race or discrimination in his diary. "First train leaves tomorrow for Holland since the mobilization began. Many Americans who have surcured [sic] passage on Holland ships to America will embrace this opportunity to travel to their ships."[25] Given that the Harrelds' ship reservations to depart London for the United States were not until August 29, they had not attempted to leave on the August 12 train. The Harrelds probably only learned of Locke's experience on the seventeenth, when the Harrelds had "Miss Harrison, Mr. Locke and his mother come for coffee." Even then the

Harrelds might not have learned of Locke's experience, since Locke might not have felt that it was politic to mention his attempt to obtain special treatment.

In any event, a second train arranged by Ambassador Gerard left Berlin on August 25 with four hundred Americans on board, including Miss Harrison, the Harrelds, and the Lockes. It moved very slowly through the German countryside "for fear of accident" and arrived the next day at "the border town of Bentheim." After having their passports and tickets checked, the passengers continued on the same train to the Hague, where they disembarked. Unfortunately, the "Hotels in the Hague and Rotterdam [were] unable to accommodate Americans who must wait for ship transportation." We don't know how Locke and his mother fared, but they seemed to tough it out with the Harrelds and Miss Harrison until the next day, when all left the Hague for Flushing. They went aboard "ship at night," so as not to attract attention, and crossed the English Channel to Folkestone, where they took a train and arrived in London late in the evening on August 28. Harreld was pleasantly surprised to learn that "our return reservations purchased in America is good." Locke and his mother were not so lucky: Mary Locke had booked her return passage to the United States from Bremen, Germany, and Locke himself had not even had a reservation to return since he had believed he would be staying in Berlin indefinitely. So, in the midst of "great excitement in England over German victories in Belgium and France," Locke and his mother had to scrounge for whatever accommodations they could get. Josephine Harreld Love recalls her parents telling her that the Lockes returned on the same boat, but had to book passage on steerage—a real indignity to Mrs. Locke. Earlier, in 1911, when Locke had proposed coming home with little money, his mother had stated, "whatever you do, do not come over on steerage—the disease, the filth, I would be crazy with worry."[26] But in this desperate situation, both Locke and his mother had to put their class fears aside. Indeed, they were not alone: millionaires, according to press reports of the time, were electing steerage over remaining in a sinking Europe. As with war generally, the Great War was breaking down class barriers, if only on the trip home.

Once Alain and Mary Locke landed in New York, they hurried home, Mary Locke disembarking at Philadelphia to report late to her school in Camden. The Camden Black community already knew that she had been detained in Berlin, and she was inundated with visits from nosy neighbors and school colleagues. A note from the ambassador about why she was delayed smoothed over whatever problems her lateness caused with school officials. The situation that faced Locke is more unclear: Had he informed the Howard administration he would not be coming back for the fall? Or had he simply not told them he might not be back? It is unclear, but Locke appears to have gotten his old job back without a hitch.

Locke also gained a more radical voice. Being in Europe at the beginning of the war inspired him to revisit his criticality about imperialism that he had explored in his talks before the Oxford Cosmopolitan Club and that he had planned to develop in his aborted comparative race studies lecture series in Europe. The Great War confirmed what he had been working himself toward intellectually for sometime—that imperialist rivalry would one day lead to Europeans attacking one another and revealing that their so-called civilization was little more than naked violence and power. The war unveiled the dirty little secret of European domination, that imperialism was a racial virus that now infected those who had spread it. With this theme amplified by his German internment, Locke approached John Bruce of the Yonkers Historical Society about delivering a new address. On September 26, he returned to Yonkers to deliver "The Great Disillusionment," a powerful paper that argued that World War I was a race war, which had broken out between the two arms of Anglo-Saxon civilization, England and Germany, over the spoils of empire. Locke argued that it was not the outcome of the struggle, but its outbreak that was most significant. The first consequence of the war was the breakup of the Anglo-Saxon partnership in the spoils of imperialism. "Up to a few days ago England[,] America[,] and Germany were custodians of Anglo-Saxon civilization[.] Now before the youngest as a neutral spectator, the elder partners struggle in [a] death-grip" for control of that civilization. Britain had created the imperial model in its naked grab for trade and raw materials in Asia and Africa, but "as modern imperialism came more and more to be a racial matter, the philosopher and statesmen were forced, even in view of their bitter rivalries, to assert the co-partnership of European nations[.]"[27]

Apologists for empire had rationalized imperial domination in social Darwinist terms as the White man's burden of bringing progress and civilization to barbaric Asian and African peoples. But the war showed that European civilization was itself "barbaric" and unable to resolve its disputes in a rational manner. The war exposed that "civilizing" the Colored races had been only a pretension, that the lust for empire and world domination had been the main motivation of imperialism. Once the spoils had been divided up and there were no more easy pickings for the latecomers like Germany and Russia to the rape of Africa and Asia, the imperialist nations had gone after one another's holdings. The second consequence was that the war delivered a fatal blow to the notion that Europe had an inalienable right to rule. "Indeed, one of the predictable results of the war will be its inevitable lesson to other races and alien civilizations that I trust will forever make impossible the Frankenstein of the nineteenth-century—the pretensions of European civilization to world-dominance and eternal superiority." While the war did not mean the "end of the enterprise . . . it does mean the lapse of the old charter, the divine right of certain nations to govern others. For whichever nation wins[,] empire can no longer mean the God-given privilege to rule the world."[28]

Interestingly, Locke found confirmation of this view in an editorial on the war in the September 1914 issue of the *North American Review* that he read to his Yonkers audience:

Consider the possible reactions of this European conflagration upon the world at large. Up to a month ago the white race was master of this planet. Africa was absolutely beneath European sway, while in Asia only the island Empire of Japan had made good its position.... But in these last ten years a strange breath has passed over the Asiatic world. The victories of Japan have awakened the dormant spirit of the East, and the countless millions of the Orient, once so passive, to chafe sullenly at the European yoke. India is seething with unrest at the British "Raj"; "unchanging" China is changing at last, and their teeming populations are beating fiercely against the white man's own frontier and answering his exclusion laws with threats and menaces which portend still mightier race struggles in the years to come—struggles beside which even the present battle of the nations might seem tame indeed.[29]

Locke acknowledged, "Many will dispute the fact that the imperial rivalry is the ground cause of the present conflict." Even most of the African Americans in his 1914 audience probably believed that militarism, navalism, or petty conflicts between European emperors were more likely causes. But Locke argued forcefully, "An examination can as easily substantiate this claim as well now as history must later. To my mind the most certain proof that this is [the] main issue between Germany and Great Britain is the hysterical assertion of each that they are fighting for the same thing," for "a leadership that only one can exercise. This is the essence of the imperial idea: it is not as nations but as empires that Germany and Britain rival each other.... What lies back of the most commonly asserted cause, militarism, with its complement of navalism, are in their modern forms a product of empire." Imperialism, in Locke's analysis, was not solely the racial domination of India by England—it was also a policy by which the elder imperial nations tried to draw into their orbit other European nations as junior partners; what was "Germany['s] sponsorship for Austria, but the tutelage of a younger and more unsuccessful accomplice at the imperial game. What is Russia's shibboleth, the Pan-Slavic idea—another imperial scheme." Rather than a war of cliques and emperors, it was "nearer the truth to say that it was a war of peoples—a race war—but truest of all, and worst of all, it is a war of ideas, for the utopia of empire and the dream of an unlimited and permanent overlordship."[30]

The Great War destroyed the pretension that Europeans pursued imperialism and colonialism to "civilize" the non-Western peoples, since now Europeans were acting in the most barbaric way possible—eschewing diplomacy and negotiation to kill millions of their own peoples. Locke was invoking here a version of Plato's discourse on justice, in which Socrates argues that justice is never simply the "right of the stronger." By that logic, the Great War is not a just war, since justice involves rulers acting in the best interest of those whose welfare has been entrusted to them. By the same logic, imperialism was exposed by the war as unjust, for instead of being pursued in the interest of the ruled, it was in fact pursued for the naked self-interest of European nations. Once that self-interest could not be satisfied by more bounty from the colonies, they turned on one another and exposed that greed was their only real motivation all along. While such an exposé hardly seems earth shattering today, it was an important critique to his African American audience that was wrestling with its own ambiguous relationship to Africa and subjected to the ideology of the civilizing mission of Europe as imperialism's justification in Africa.

But what made Locke's analysis most radical was that he described the Great War as a race war that now divided the Europeans themselves. The war had broken out at the center of the "great European civilization, rather than at its extremities" in Africa or in Asia, because European nations or empires now competed with one another to determine whose empire would dominate not only Africa and Asia but also the rest of Europe. Europeans were speaking of other Europeans in racial terms—as inferiors, as barbaric, and as backward—terms that had generally been reserved for the peoples of Africa and Asia. The hatred that burst out in Europe in 1914 was not just a conflict between ruling elites, but a racial feud whereby "in each country the common folk feel their existence is in jeopardy. Possessing often a common culture and tradition, they are nevertheless forced to regard themselves as bitterly estranged. The epithet of barbarian and enemy of civilization is hurled at blood brothers[;] the idea of Empire, the nemesis of alien races, has turned upon its authors." In places like the Alsace-Lorraine, people who had lived side by side for centuries now regarded themselves as different as races. "The Great Disillusionment" expanded the notion of race to show the way in which the average European was a victim of the kind of racial polarization that imperialism had spawned.

The Great War was clearly a case of chickens coming home to roost, as "the idea of Empire, the nemesis of alien races, has turned upon its authors."[31] The war was a morality lesson "that like a handwriting on the wall, suddenly looms up out of our darkness before us" to teach us what are the consequences to those who dominate the political and economic lives of others. Since the Great War was not a just war, African Americans should distance themselves from the conflict.

> In my first communication to this society in 1911[,] I distinctly claimed that we should be prouder as a people of having acquired this [European] civilization and culture than of having it as an inheritance. I said this first in the interests of sincerity[.] I thought our culture would be sounder if we made no false claims to it, and had a sense of our own racial and ethnical past as a foundation upon which to rear it[.] But now not merely for our own pride's sake[,] but to avoid their shame, let us realize and confess that the civilization which is at war with itself is

not ours in the intimate sense that we owe it a blood debt or even an irrevocable allegiance.[32]

Locke's declaration that African Americans did not owe a "blood debt or even an irrevocable allegiance" to the "Anglo-Saxon partnership" came close to advocating the Black nonparticipation in the war, should "the youngest as a neutral spectator," America, be drawn into this war over the future of the Anglo-Saxon partnership. Followed to its logical conclusion, Locke's cultural nationalism led to a conscientious objection for racial reasons. That certainly went beyond the kind of neutrality that Woodrow Wilson could have endorsed.

It also went beyond the analysis of Locke's intellectual rival, W. E. B. Du Bois, who, in a November 1914 editorial in the *Crisis*, also argued that imperialism was the underlying cause of the war. Coming so soon after "The Great Disillusionment," Du Bois's editorial may have been inspired by news of Locke's well-received lecture. But Du Bois's editorial focused more narrowly on Africa, whereas Locke went further and argued that imperialism not only explained the origins of the war, but that Europe itself was a racialized continent. Where Du Bois believed that Black interests lay in defending the British, who as colonizers were not as bad as the Germans, Locke concluded that England and Germany pursued the same policies: "it is simply a question [of] which is the most efficient agent, the weapon of conquest or the weapon of maintenance, physical force or material resources."[33] Clearly, Locke found in "The Great Disillusionment" an independent voice and a more thoroughly transnationalist viewpoint on the war than that of Du Bois. Ironically, it was Locke's closer connection with the European experience, and his own love of Germany, that gave him the more revealing critique of imperialism as something that embodied but transcended color.

Locke had found a way to win the acclaim of the society's members, as his speech was greeted, at least according to his letters back to his mother, by thunderous applause, general approval, and cries of "better than Du Bois." This latter must have been particularly satisfying, for in truth, he had been working in Du Bois's intellectual shadow since returning to America in 1912. "The Negro and a Race Tradition," as well as Locke's subsequent lectures on the education of the Negro, worked within lines that had first been drawn by Du Bois. Now, Locke had an issue that was his, or so it seemed, until the November editorial, and Du Bois's more formal article on the subject, "The African Roots of the War," appeared in May 1915 in the *Atlantic Monthly*. After the latter article appeared, Du Bois would be known as the African American intellectual who provided an imperialist analysis of World War I. That occurred, in part, because Locke's speech was never published.

Once again, Locke struggled with his continuing problem of invisibility. Du Bois's piece, of course, deserved its reputation. Reading "The Great Disillusionment" and "The African Roots of the War" confirms how much more scholarly and detailed was Du Bois's essay, especially when compared to Locke's sketchy, but more challenging racial deconstruction of the idea of imperialism. But, Locke's analysis deserved a broader hearing, for it took the discussion of imperialism out of the narrow confines of the impact of African colonialism on Europe and suggested before Du Bois that imperialism was the international practice of race in a way that anticipated the kind of critique that Lenin would advance in his "Imperialism: The Highest Stage of Capitalism." Where Lenin analyzed imperialism as an example of "late capitalism," Locke analyzed imperialism as a metastasized stage of racism. Indeed, "The Great Disillusionment" owed a debt to Marx as well as Lenin, showing that Locke in Berlin and in the Oxford Cosmopolitan Club had learned enough Marxism to transform it into a critique of imperialism from a colonial perspective. Locke's cosmopolitan sojourn to Oxford and Berlin was beginning to pay off in a radical sociological analysis of race in ways that Marx had analyzed class—as the pivot of contemporary global economic and political domination. And just as Lenin later saw the war as a turning point in the world history of the class conflict, Locke saw the war as the turning point in the history of a race conflict, for it exposed the fundamentally ideological nature of imperialism. And its signature insight that race defined the relations between European nations would not be flushed out in more detail until 1983 and the publication of Cedric Robinson's *Black Marxism: The Making of the Black Radical Tradition*.

Locke's speech before the Yonkers Historical Society also allowed him to renew his relationship with John E. Bruce. Bruce had argued in private correspondence with John W. Cromwell that Alexander Walters would fail in his attempt to turn his status as a loyal Black Democrat into political capital for the Negro once Wilson was elected. By the fall of 1914, it was clear that Bruce had been right, and he probably used his time with Locke, whom Bruce saw as a protégé, to emphasize that point. Bruce probably tried to wean Locke from too close an association with Walters and the Democratic Party, which Bruce believed was fundamentally inimical to the interests of the Negro. It was probably at the dinner and festivities that followed Locke's address that Bruce learned of Locke's experience with discrimination at the hands of Ambassador Gerard in Berlin. Later, Bruce probably passed that information on to Gilchrist Stewart, because Bruce viewed Gerard's defeat as a blow against the Wilson administration that had put the reluctant ambassador up for the New York Senate. Locke's reply to Stewart showed that, although he often eschewed politics, he was willing to contribute to the struggle against Gerard and the Democratic Party in New York. Locke's visit to Bruce's Sunnyslope farm, therefore, drew Locke into the Republican fold. Shortly after Gerard's defeat in the November election, Locke wrote his mother, "Things are looking up for our friends, the Republicans and the Germans."[34]

That fall, war was Locke's consuming concern, such that he was almost "bankrupting myself" buying papers to follow each punch and counterpunch of the

European conflict. Locke enthused over every German victory and even the rebellion of the South African Boers—anyone who threatened the hated hegemony of the British. Part of that enthusiasm derived from Locke's belief that armed struggle connoted to a people a degree of self-respect. "Our friends the Germans are looking up these days—it is wonderful isn't it? I am sorry no colored race has had the courage of the Boers, but I think like the rest of us they'll imitate now that someone else has started."[35]

Such harsh judgments came easily for Locke. He used a similar one to casti-gate an old acquaintance, Jessie Fauset, a fellow Philadelphian, who was coming up to Howard University every week. Fauset graciously invited him, along with her chaperone, Helen Irvin, over for dinner in November 1914. "I called on Jessie Fauset last night—(at her written invitation) she comes up each week to the University and is more civilized and sensible than she was I think. Like most strong medicine the war seems to have driven some insane people sane as well as made many mad who were not."[36] Such a harsh response to such a friendly gesture as an invitation to dinner suggests that something else was going on. Was Fauset's more "sensible" behavior Locke's way of stating that she was no longer as forward as she might have been when they first met during his under-graduate days at Harvard? Had Fauset been attracted to Locke in those early years until she heard through "the grapevine" that Locke was gay? Locke may also have been attracted to Fauset, but knew that he could only go so far with such an interest. It may have then been far easier, therefore, for Locke to deal with her once she was less aggressive. Or Fauset may simply have been inter-ested in a position at the university and believed that Locke might help her obtain it. Certainly, she would be on her best behavior in such circumstances. Given that she never got hired, Fauset may have also gained a negative message from her attempt at rapprochement with Locke. Perhaps no matter what she did, Fauset could expect little if any support from him. As Locke became more popular on the Washington social scene, he had to use his sarcasm and deprecating wit to keep his involvement with women at a safe distance.

Things were also looking up for Locke on the academic front that fall of 1914. The time seemed to be right to begin building a base for himself as a cutting-edge sociological thinker at Howard University. In December 1914, a White trustee, Dr. Jesse Moorland, donated his enormous collection of books, manuscripts, and statuary on the Negro to Howard University. Kelly Miller had encouraged Moorland to donate his collection, as part of Miller's plan to make Howard a center of research on African American life and culture. Miller gambled that the university would be unwilling to reject the contribution of a White trustee as well respected as Moorland. The university graciously accepted what became known as the Moorland Collection and with it Moorland's recommendation that a special room in the library be set aside to house it. Suddenly, a place existed on campus devoted to the study of the Negro, and Locke joined Miller in recommending that a Negro history museum be established at Howard University for the collection and study of African American artifacts and memorabilia. Locke also proposed that the university hire a full-time researcher to produce a bibliography of the collection and other works of *Negro Americana* that would be collected in the library. Ultimately, this library would become a center, in Locke's view, for what would become Black Studies. As with most of Locke's schemes, his personal advancement was part of the idea: Locke intended that he would be appointed the bibliographer. He even lobbied Booker T. Washington with examples of the kinds of materials that he and Miller wanted to see collected in the bibliography of Negro-Americana.[37] Although the board thought the idea important enough to refer it to a committee for further study, it ultimately turned down his request. Did the board react to Locke's proposal out of its racial conservatism or against the obvious self-interest of Locke in the project? While this is unclear, the decision blocked what was a legitimate attempt to establish the first African American Studies program at a Negro university.

Undaunted, Locke redoubled his efforts to win approval of another of his proposals, a course he wished to teach on race theory and practices. Actually, he had submitted the same proposal early in 1914, when Howard's board of trustees had rejected it. Locke then repackaged his course into a series of five lectures he proposed to give outside the curriculum, under the auspices of the campus NAACP, but that too was blocked effectively in April when the board of deans decided he could say all he had to in one lecture evening. Not to be outdone by his opposition, Locke decided to submit his race course proposal during the summer for inclusion in the fall 1914 curriculum. Again, it was rejected. In January 1915, in the afterglow of the school's acceptance of the Moorland Collection, the climate at Howard was right for another attempt by Locke to teach "a new course I wish to give if I am to be here next year."[38] Although this proposal was also rejected, it paved the way for permission to give the course in the five public lectures, on campus, with the support of both the NAACP chapter and the Social Science Club at Howard. Locke delivered those lectures in 1915 and was able to synthesize all he had learned in the Oxford Cosmopolitan Club, at the University of Berlin, the Universal Races Congress, and his own experience of the European war mobilization to express a new way of thinking about race in America and in the world.

But it would be another year before Locke got to deliver the lectures to the influential audience he wanted to reach and deliver them on campus at Howard University. On the afternoon of March 27, 1916, a terrific rainstorm raged in Washington, D.C., and worried Locke as he hurried to the lecture hall of the Carnegie Library on Howard's campus, umbrella in hand, to the first of his five lectures he would deliver that afternoon. Last year's audience for the lectures had been small and bereft of the more famous people at the university. He was delivering them a second time because he needed to reach a larger audience this time, especially Howard's influential circle of deans and administrators. He was giving the lectures to gain an appointment in the College of Arts and Sciences and to establish an institute of race relations at Howard. As William Sinclair, a trustee of Howard University, put it in a letter to President Newman, Locke planned to establish at a Black university the kind of Sociology Department that Columbia University was beginning to found.[39] At the very least, Locke hoped that if his lectures were a success, they would make the case that he belonged in the College of Arts and Sciences with Miller. Spectacular success might mean he would be recognized as a new sociological authority and given an opportunity to lead a race studies center at Howard.

As Locke paced the stage for several minutes before beginning, the hall filled as people slowly came in from the heavy rain, hung up their raincoats, and settled into the hardwood seats in Carnegie Library. The stenographer, a White George Washington law student Locke had hired to record the lectures, sharpened his pencils and readied his pads while the compulsive Locke looked nervously at his pocket watch. By the time Locke delivered his opening remarks shortly after 4 P.M., the most important Howard people had arrived, including College of Arts and Sciences dean Kelly Miller and Locke's own dean Lewis Moore.

Begun on the last Monday of March and continued each afternoon of the following four Mondays in April, Locke's lectures laid out a new sociological theory that race was not a biological but a historical phenomenon. In his first lecture, "The Theoretical and Scientific Conceptions of Race," delivered that first rainy night, Locke used the work of Franz Boas, specifically his Race Congress lectures, "The Instability of Race Types," to show that racial characteristics were not innate or permanent. Recent anthropology had found that physical traits—skin color, head size, hair type, and so forth—varied dramatically within groups, such that one could find dark-skinned and very light-skinned Negro Americans; and one could find similar traits (hair texture, for example) in a variety of different race groups. Even within a group, Boas's research had shown that certain physical traits, specifically head shape and size, changed over time with changes in the social and cultural environment of immigrant groups. Locke concluded that there were no static factors of race and therefore no permanent physical characteristics that were possessed by any race.

In 1916, Boas's work was known to only a handful of Americans and would have to wait until his graduate students Ruth Benedict, Melville Herskovits, and Margaret Mead popularized his views in the 1930s and 1940s. In 1916, Locke was the intellectual who most fully realized that Boas's insights revolutionized racial science by shifting the burden of proof onto the racists and took from them the sanction of anthropology. Locke's first lecture demonstrated there were no static factors of race, that even physical characteristics changed with alterations in the social and cultural environment, and went even further than Boas to assert that biology had no influence on race types. Race was simply another word for national or social groups that shared a common history. It was culture—social, political, and economic processes—that produced racial character, not the other way around.

What then, the listener in the Faculty Club might have asked, was the significance of race? Locke answered such a question in lecture 2, "The Political and Practical Conception of Race," by arguing that race mainly defined one's relationship to power. Here was the lesson he had delivered in "The Great Disillusionment," that one's race was really just one's reputation, that being the inferior race was just the record of having lost out in conflicts like the Great War raging in Europe. Races had begun as extended kinship groups with a sense of us-versus-them developing as a kind of blood relationship; but that was all fictive now after generations of mixing of different groups, such that now, races were imagined national or social groups that competed for scarce resources and used racial discourses to justify their seizure of more of those resources for their own group. Imperialism was thus little more than the practice of race, the use of power to take what one wanted, and justify it with a rhetoric, a mythos, of inherent difference.

What was perhaps most interesting about these lectures is what Locke did on the third Monday in the lecture "Phenomena and Laws of Race Contacts." For there Locke donned the hat of the sociologist and analyzed race as the vortex of modern social relations. A history of race contacts might be interesting, Locke opined, but what was really needed was a sociology of race contacts, an analysis of how groups of people interacted through race, and how race perceptions shaped group interactions. Like Marx, Locke asked his listeners to look behind the apparent nature of conflict—class conflict for Marx, race conflicts for Locke—and see those racial conflicts as originating, "after all, not in the mind, but in the practical problems of human living." Racial categories were usually class categories that had become hereditary, such that certain jobs were performed by certain groups of people, such that the slave or the servant came to define what many people thought of when they said Black. Competition for scarce resources—money, status, reputation—was the underlying cause of most racial conflict and perhaps the key to understanding why racial conflict increased or subsided in relation to poor or improving economic conditions. Indeed, one of the reasons for the ebb and flow of racial feelings was that elites manipulated race feelings to divide and conquer the working classes. That insight revealed an even more fundamental one: race feelings changed over time in response to changing historical conditions and racism passed through distinct phases in response to varying economic conditions.

But Locke was unwilling to reduce race to simply a reflection of class conflicts or interests like traditional Marxists. Race was a social psychological calculus by which a group or people measured its success in relation to others. Racial feelings had some as yet undetermined relation to population such that racial feelings often changed with removal of formal barriers or dramatic changes in population. Racial feelings often changed in relation to perceived changes in the social status of a group and were particularly prevalent in democratic societies where in the absence of aristocratic barriers to upward or downward mobility, competition for status and power was open to all. Race was thus a tool used in competition for scarce resources but also a feeling about the fate of one's group that reached down into the emotional psyche of a people. That was one of the reasons racial feelings could be so virulent and passionate, often more violent than class feelings. Race, in other words, deserved its own sophisticated sociology to understand how modern societies functioned but also suffered because of race perceptions and relations.

Even though there were no fixed biological indicators of race, thinking of oneself as part of a race persisted, because once constructed by a society, race consciousness shaped how people reacted to one another, particularly in competitive social situations. Locke's intellectual innovation was important for his time for it solved the problem faced by other Black intellectuals of how to reject scientific theories of biological racism without also having to jettison any possibility that Blacks could regard themselves positively as a racial group. Such Black intellectuals as Alexander Crummel, John Bruce, and W. E. B. Du Bois believed that African Americans needed a positive conception of race to restore Black self-esteem in the aftermath of slavery and Reconstruction. But most of these intellectuals found themselves unconsciously buying into nineteenth-century notions of race when they spoke about the Black group as a race. For example, race seemed to be a fixed and permanent entity in Du Bois's essay "The Conservation of the Races" (1897), when he wrote that "in our calmer moments we must acknowledge that human beings are divided into races; that in this country the two most extreme types of the world's races have met."[40]

Locke's more flexible sociological approach to races occurred also because he was constantly injecting the comparative perspective into his lectures. Locke's discussions with other colonial intellectuals at Oxford and his European traveling experiences convinced him that other groups experienced racial or group prejudice that was on a par with that suffered by Blacks in America. Particularly in lecture 4, "Modern Race Creeds and Their Fallacies," Locke compared American racism with European anti-Semitism and found the latter as intense in places like France as anything he had witnessed in America. Europe had its own internal race conflicts, between northern and southern, western and eastern Europeans, such that Lithuanians who revealed their national identity by their accent found themselves discriminated against in Austrian restaurants. Race and racial divisions, categories, and conflicts were always constructed out of the particular histories of societies in which they occurred, such that in Austria, the Lithuanians, or in France, the Jews, were the "niggers" of those societies. Locke stressed the comparative approach because he wanted to free his listeners from the belief

that their experience of oppression was unique in world history and so unprecedented that no way existed for them to grapple successfully with it in the
American racial situation.

What Locke most wanted to give his listeners in the lecture hall of Carnegie
Library was a sense of their agency in America. Since race attitudes changed over
time, hope existed even in the America of 1916 for Black Americans to shape
their future. If Locke's analysis was correct, then the American racial situation
would change, inevitably, and with it Black prospects for empowerment in
America. Therefore, the question was, how could African Americans respond to
their historical situation in such a way that they could improve the prospects for
the race as a whole? Locke's answer, articulated in lecture 5, "Race Progress and
Race Adjustment," echoed and updated what he had argued in "The Negro and
a Race Tradition" and "Cosmopolitanism and Culture." Although race was a
biological myth, it was a powerful historical myth that unified those peoples
who believed in it. In practical terms, a sense of racial solidarity was essential to
the success of modern nations or groups. Locke believed that African Americans
needed a sense of racial consciousness to compete with other groups in a modern
capitalist order.

The problem, of course, was how to mobilize Black people to succeed in a
system that was stacked against them in terms of the message that racialized
American society delivered relentlessly to African Americans. Black people
needed to develop a stronger sense of race consciousness, of pride and group
self-respect, the positive characteristics of race, while avoiding its more perni-
cious manifestations in prejudice, racism, and xenophobia. Locke recommended
focusing on the artistic and cultural celebration of race or national consciousness, instead of its political forms. European examples again supplied Locke
with his most compelling models, especially "[t]he Celtic and the Pan-Slavic
movements in arts and letters—movements by which the submerged classes are
coming to their expression in art—seem to be the forerunners of that kind of
recognition which they are ultimately striving for, namely, recognition [of an]
economic, [a] civic, and [a] social sort; and these [movements] are the gateways
through which culture-citizenship can be finally reached."[41]

Locke wanted to alter American racism by strengthening African Americans'
ability to compete more successfully with other groups by amplifying their group
sense, their group self-esteem and self-respect, and through amplifying their
positive sense of race consciousness, increase their power. The way he advocated
doing that was through literature, art, and music—the literacies of Black culture. That process had already begun under slavery when Blacks and Whites,
slaves and masters, lived in such close proximity that the powerful African-
based forms of Black American culture had powerfully shaped the folkways,
music, and formal culture of southern America. Even in the late nineteenth and
early twentieth centuries, cultural exchange was occurring between Black and

White cultures under segregation because exclusion and separation actually heightened assimilation, in Locke's analysis, because the oppressed and oppressors became more curious and desirous of precisely those things, those forms, that were verboten by official racial policy. America was already a composite culture, despite all the efforts of racial segregationists. What Locke recommended is that Black Americans capitalize on their cultural agency and turn the "reign" of their culture, eventually, into a source of political and economic freedom. Here was Locke's theory of the social use of art to attain culture-citizenship.

Locke's Race Contacts lectures were a bold attempt to provide a clear sociological argument for the emergence of the New Negro. The Race Contacts lectures showed that Locke had made himself into a keen theoretical sociologist of race in Washington, D.C., by 1916 just as "The Concept of Value" had showed Locke had made himself into a philosopher in Berlin by 1910. His sociological modernism consisted of his ability to reveal that race relations were changeable, liminal, and unfinished—something that Black people could contribute to redefining through their consciousness and actions. These lectures were also his most militant statement of his views, fueled perhaps in part by his anger over the war and the militant turn that Black political discourse had taken in America by the mid-1910s, of the possibility of a cultural revolution in America. They were radical in their sociological mapping of how race worked in modern capitalism to ensure the continued success of certain ethnic groups in stealing a disproportionate amount of the world's precious resources. But Locke studiously avoided any recommendation of organized protest by Black Americans in his lecture on "race progress." In recommending art and culture as the path of Black liberation, Locke built on his subtle observation in the lectures that a sociology of race relations revealed that the most powerful races could not control the interactions between themselves and other less powerful groups no matter how hard they tried. The less powerful groups or races had in fact profoundly shaped culturally and socially the so-called dominant groups, and within that scenario there was hope for the Negro. Could art and cultural influence seduce the powerful into a more humane approach to race contacts? If race was in essence consciousness, might art and literature that emerged from and shaped consciousness be a tool for change?

Once concluded, Locke felt that his 1916 lecture series was a success. Locke was especially pleased that he obtained a near complete transcript of his remarks that were delivered each Monday from scattered notecards. His White stenographer not only took down the notes but typed up the transcripts and gave them to Locke to edit. The previous year's stenographer had failed to attend all of the lectures and had not produced a coherent record. Locke read the difference as racial. "Yesterday I spent nearly three hours trying to get or persuade various <u>colored</u> stenographers to no avail. I phoned a white stenographers bureau, and in a half hour a law student at George Washington University appeared...exactly on time. Says he will make cut rates as he is 'glad to get the practice'...the difference!"[42]

Locke also had created his own permanent record: he had spent much of February and early March writing and privately publishing a pamphlet-sized syllabus that summarized the lecture contents and gave suggested additional readings. The syllabus suggested the tremendous range of Locke's reading, from Edward Blyden's *Christianity, Islam and the Negro Race* and *Glimpses of the Ages* to such obscure foreign-language texts as Hertz's *Moderne Rassenprobleme* and Beaulieu Leroy's *De la colonisation chez les peuples modernes*. Particularly strong was the large number of histories and studies of imperialism and early twentieth-century race thinking. Locke was pleased with the clean printed copies of the syllabus, even if they were not ready until the end of his lectures.

Unfortunately, while Locke's lectures in 1916 succeeded in attracting key figures of the administration, they had little immediate impact on the Black political discourse of the day. "I gave the second lecture," he wrote his mother on April 3, "last night to a small and rather indifferent audience." That lecture, "The Practical and Political Conceptions of Race," was his boldest lecture on race and British imperialism and missonarism. But when he concluded his final lecture on April 24, there was little response from the Howard community, which was distracted by other issues. During the second week of Locke's lectures, a student strike had erupted on campus and had consumed the attention of the faculty, the deans, and the board of trustees for nearly two weeks. This strike also reduced attendance at his lectures, which must have seemed irrelevant to most of the students involved in the uprising. Actually, the lectures were not, for Locke could have predicted with his theory that such a generational rebellion was due, for race attitudes, even within the oppressed minorities, were also subject to change. On April 9, he notified his mother:

> We have been having the devil of a time. Since Tuesday the whole student body has been on strike against the arbitrary discipline of the President and the Deans—Dean Cook precipitated the trouble, but it has been brewing a long while. I, of course, sympathize with the students but have not let it get known. Gregory on the other hand largely because of the debates which have had to be postponed has been very partisan—openly—and has I fear gotten in bad with the authorities. Sinclair is here—and I am having him take up the matter of my leave of absence while here.[43]

With Booker T. Washington dead, the New Negro was in a protest mood and ready to attack inherited authority that kept the African American intellectual community in check. Unfortunately, because of his dismissive attitude toward protest, Locke lost the support he might have gotten from students at his lectures. Locke's posture of scientific objectivity, on the one hand, and cultural expressiveness, on the other, was not the political fashion.

Of all those who attended, Kelly Miller may have been the person who most appreciated Locke's contribution, although even he had been there only sporadically. Miller had written a scathing critique of President Wilson's policy of segregation and had lectured before the Washington, D.C., Mu-So-Lit Club in 1915 on the impact of the world war on race relations. Miller sympathized with Locke's advocacy of increased race consciousness and respected the scholarship Locke had reviewed in compiling the lectures. After the lectures, Miller approached Locke about lecturing in Miller's course on sociology in the College of Arts and Sciences that was planned for the fall. That course would feature lectures by Robert Park, the Chicago sociologist and Booker T. Washington amanuensis, whose work Locke had reviewed in his lectures.[44] But Locke declined the invitation.

Locke's reference to "the matter of my leave of absence" in his letter acknowledged that he had applied for and been admitted to Harvard's graduate school in philosophy with an Austin Teaching Fellowship to help with expenses. Once his leave of absence was approved, Locke's mind pleasantly turned to Harvard, especially after he learned that he would be exempted from the preliminary graduate school examinations. It would not be long before he would begin graduate coursework in philosophy at Harvard, under the special direction of Josiah Royce, he hoped, and begin consolidating his academic position in Howard University in the only way that he could—by obtaining a PhD.

Rainy days had bookended the four years Locke had spent at Howard University in one of the most productive periods of original thinking in his career. At thirty years of age, he had found a working formula—a job teaching in the major Black university in America, a fawned-over lecturer on the Black historical society circuit, and an indulgent mother three hours away by train from his home in Washington, D.C. While he had chafed at having an entry-level job in the Teachers College at Howard, he was nevertheless functioning as one of the most propulsive thinkers on campus.

Yet this dynamic period of original thinking and working as a public intellectual was coming to a close. Harvard beckoned and a new set of challenges loomed.

Francis Gregory, Locke, and William Stanley Braithwaite (seated), ca. 1916. Courtesy of the Moorland-Spingarn Research Center, Howard University.

15

Rapprochement and Silence

Harvard, 1916–1917

Locke always loved Harvard, loved its architecture, its Yard, even the smell of the grass at Cambridge's Mt. Auburn Cemetery, where he could wander on his light days of classes and visit the graves of the leaders of the New England Renaissance, the only renaissance America had known. He remained a Boston aesthete despite the many turns in the road his intellect would take afterward and was just a bit giddy as he contemplated that spring of 1916 the possibility of returning to Harvard. With his Race Contacts lectures over, he began to imagine what it would be like to get the doctorate from the place of his most spectacular triumph academically and socially. But a fear lurked in him as he planned for that return. Since his undergraduate years, he had tasted failure. He needed the PhD not only to get a promotion at Howard but also to keep pace with Du Bois and join the coming generation of Black scholars, all of whom would have PhDs. Without a PhD, he would remain a mere prodigy, a bright little boy; with it, he would be a man among the leading scholars of the race, likely a full professor in the College of Arts and Sciences at Howard in a couple of years. A bit of nervousness crept in as he went about preparations to leave for Cambridge— not doubt about his ability, but about the unknown that had derailed in Oxford and Berlin.

For once at Harvard, where he would be able to enjoy his romantic friendships without Howard's restraining eyes, a danger would emerge. Unlimited freedom of romantic association had been partially responsible for his debacle at Oxford. Harvard in 1916 was likely his only chance to get the PhD, and he could not afford to risk disaster again, especially since attending any failure in the United States would become public knowledge. Instinctively sensing the danger, Locke began to think of taking his mother with him to Harvard. Shortly after learning that he had been awarded the Austin Teaching Fellowship at Harvard, he wrote his mother that "barring slips, here's to our year in Cambridge."[1] The almost romantic quality of his comment covered up a more practical consideration—in this final struggle to get his terminal degree, Locke needed his mother close at hand to maintain his psychic stability and restrain his self-destructive impulses for sexual excess, high living and overspending.

Mary Locke began to play this role as early as the summer of 1916. As soon as Locke obtained a leave of absence and "$350 or $400 of my salary" from Howard, he traveled to Boston to scout out living arrangements. Initially, Locke stayed with William Stanley Braithwaite, who suggested some lavish and expensive rooms for Locke and his mother. Put off by the price, Locke lost the rooms, and then lamented that he had not taken them. He also discovered that he would face more serious obstacles in renting a room than he had imagined. Racial prejudice had increased dramatically in Boston since his undergraduate days. "I am up against a difficult proposition—considerable prejudice—and colored places scarce—and undesirable," he informed his mother.[2] It was no longer his undergraduate days when he could just present himself to landlords in his fine coat and hat, and obtain a room. Here was a concrete example of his observation in the Race Contacts lectures—that race feelings changed over time, hardening in the era of the European war and Wilson's segregationist policies. Unwilling to take a place in a Black rooming house, Locke began to consider seriously the suggestion of William Lewis, a Black lawyer and one of Booker T. Washington's former operatives, to get an apartment in a White building by mailing in his lease and deposit, and then letting the neighbors howl when they discovered that the Lockes were Black. Mary Locke's response to both Braithwaite's and Lewis's suggestions set the right tone and the priorities for coming year: "I am sorry you are having a time to locate rooms," she wrote him on June 28. "The apartments Mr. B[raithwaite] selected were too expensive. I have been wishing you would just engage board for both of us. Surely you could find some suitable place—it would save so much expense and worry for just 10 months— stow the furniture (storage) we have, and start fresh at light housekeeping (flat) in Washington in the fall of 1917. I cannot see how we are going to manage to move things up to Cambridge—then back to Washington. Or get furnished rooms—with some one.... Do not have the risk and trouble of being put out of white apartment house—or even having trouble with them. You need a quiet mind—and peace."[3]

Mary's letter reveals that they also planned to live together once he returned to Washington, D.C., and for the rest of her life. Paying to live separately in Camden and Washington had seemed a waste of money by 1916, especially since he had not been able to increase his salary while at Howard. His mother retiring from her job in Camden seemed appropriate now, especially as she would be able to bring her retirement money to Cambridge and then Washington, allowing them to live more comfortably together than separate. But the decision also meant a change for the foreseeable future. For the last twelve years, he had lived on his own, beginning at Harvard and ending at Howard. In both of those instances, being connected to her but also on his own had resulted in his most spectacular successes. What would his productivity let alone his personal life be like once he shared domestic space with her every day?

Answers to those kinds of questions were less pressing than the challenge of finding rooms before the fall term began. But as usual Locke delayed even that challenge in order to enjoy the intellectual freedom of Cambridge immediately. Staying that summer with Braithwaite, the Boston poet, critic, and anthologist who was the son of a very light-skinned British Guianan of French, English, and Creole ancestry, was a pleasurable interlude before he figured out the matter of housing. The son of a West Indian patriarch who taught his children the French language and Victorian manners at home, as well as to avoid social contact with American Blacks, Braithwaite left school for work after his father's early death. He was rescued from a laborer's life while working in a printer's office when he discovered his love for poetry while setting to type John Keats's "Ode on a Grecian Urn." Braithwaite's first book of poetry, *Lyrics of Life and Love* (1904), showed the influence of Keats and Shelley, but his second, *The House of Falling Leaves* (1908), announced a mystical and modern voice. That modern voice gained maturity and authority in his critical articles in *Century*, *Scribner's*, the *Atlantic*, and the *Boston Evening Transcript* and reached its greatest influence in Braithwaite's annual anthologies of magazine verse that introduced such younger poets as Carl Sandburg, Edgar Lee Masters, Conrad Aiken, and Amy Lowell to a broader audience. Braithwaite was not a race poet or race critic, but someone who encouraged Black writers to focus on the craft, the form of their art, even to the point of avoiding race themes altogether. And his success in insinuating himself as a critical voice in the poetic modernism of the early twentieth century suggested that one need not be confined to race if one had the chops to perform mainstream modernism in one's poetry.

Locke's Howard colleague, Montgomery Gregory, probably introduced Locke and Braithwaite, whom Gregory may have known from his undergraduate days at Harvard. Braithwaite had already taken a liking to Gregory in 1915 and had collaborated with Gregory to edit and publish the *Citizen*, a magazine of African American literary and cultural discussion. Braithwaite's first letter to Locke was a request for an article for the *Citizen* on the literary significance of Booker T. Washington, who had just died. Braithwaite wrote Locke again in April 1916, when Braithwaite was planning a poetry reading and lecture trip to Howard University. Invited initially by Roscoe Conkling Bruce to lecture to the Washington teachers association, Braithwaite had added Howard at Kelly Miller's suggestion, but relied on Locke to chaperone him around campus. Locke was flattered by the attention and inspired by Braithwaite's presence, which included a lecture, "Current American Poetry," that resonated with Locke's analysis that the European war was a turning point in culture. For Braithwaite, however, as he stated in his introduction to the 1916 *Anthology of Magazine Verse*, the European war was catalyzing a renaissance of American poetry that had begun in the poetry of Edgar

Arlington Robinson, Robert Frost, Edgar Lee Masters, Anna Branch, Amy Lowell, and James Oppenheim. While most had begun writing before the war, after the conflict broke out their "body of work has ascended with convincing proof of power on the wave of the great European war."[4] Braithwaite was an important literary influence on Locke because he rejected Ezra Pound's advice to modern American poets to divorce their poetry from the American social environment, and advocated, instead, that poetry respond to social forces without becoming social propaganda.

When Locke arrived at Braithwaite's residence at 27 Ellsworth Street in Cambridge around June 21, an additional pleasure was that Gregory was also spending part of his summer there. Perhaps Gregory was also experiencing the longing to return to the place of his triumph as a Harvard undergraduate and the prize Black student of George Pierce Baker. Locke, Gregory, and Braithwaite talked of poetry, of the drama, and no doubt of the central conflict Locke and Gregory had been involved in that year in Washington—their recent disagreement in the Drama Committee of the Washington, D.C., branch of the NAACP over the kind of theater the committee should produce. While the committee members—Laura Glenn, Clara B. Bruce, E. C. Williams, Anna J. Cooper, Carrie W. Clifford, Georgia Fraiser, E. E. Just, Montgomery Gregory, and Locke—agreed on what they were against (the savage caricatures of Black life that dominated the American popular theater) they disagreed on what kind of drama should be presented to the Washington Black community. Some on the committee, including activist Anna J. Cooper, believed that Black drama should be political and critique American racism. That wing succeeded in convincing the rest of the committee to support the production of Angelina Grimke's three-act play "Rachel," which opened at the Miner Normal School auditorium on March 3, 1916. Apparently, Locke and Montgomery had supported the production of "Rachel" with the understanding that afterward the repertoire would expand to include "folk-drama" and plays about Negro life written by White authors. But shortly after "Rachel" opened, Locke learned that only more political plays would be put on, and he promptly resigned from the Drama Committee, explaining in a letter to Archibald Grimke, head of the Washington, D.C., branch, that "an utter incompatibility of point of view—something more than a mere difference of opinion—indeed, an abysmal lack of common meeting ground between myself and the majority of the members forces my retirement. It was my impression that . . . other types of race or folk play should be considered along with the problem-play on their respective merits, and probably one each of several kinds experimented with, but most of all I had anticipated and regard as fundamental, the careful consideration of the work that has already been done in the field of drama with ourselves or our problem as the subject if only as a point of departure and an attempt to enlist the influence and interest of men who are already fast becoming authorities on the matter of modern playwriting and presentation."[5]

Locke and Gregory were critical of "Rachel," because, as Gregory recalled eleven years later, its chief limitation was "shown by the announcement on the program: 'This is the first attempt to use the stage for race propaganda in order to enlighten the American people relative to the lamentable condition of ten millions of Colored citizens in this free republic.'" That view of art was precisely what Locke and Gregory objected to, as Gregory also recalled: "a minority section of this committee dissented from this propagandistic platform and were instrumental later in founding the Howard Players organization, promoting the purely artistic approach and the folk-drama idea."[6] It is possible that these conversations with Braithwaite in Cambridge laid the foundation for Locke and Gregory to establish the Howard Players later in 1919.

Beneath the art versus politics debate were others over race and class. To fight racism, the committee wanted plays that featured only middle-class Blacks as characters, whereas in George Pierce Baker's classes at Harvard, Gregory had imbibed his drama teacher's dictum that modern dramatists should draw material from and develop a realist portraiture of the lower-class folk. Locke believed that Black drama needed to reflect the revolution in storytelling, stage direction, set design, and costume seen in White modernist theater. But the politically minded members of the NAACP Drama Committee wanted nothing to do with such plays as "The Nigger," by White playwright Edward Sheldon, which opened in New York on December 4, 1909.

At stake here was more than meets the eye, more than simply whether plays by White dramatists or about lower-class Black sexuality were offered to bourgeois Black audiences in Washington. Locke and Gregory had mounted a resistance to the very notion that protest to racism was the essence of Black identity. Was Black aesthetics going to explore the subtle, sublime, and quiet dimensions of Black humanity as well as the robust?[7] African American life contained many other episodes of dramatic significance than the encounter with and struggle against White racism. Everyday life, the wrestling with one's inner self-destructive tendencies, the pains of adolescent life, the tribulations of families arriving in the city and leaving back home memories and departed ancestors—all of these and more were subjects Locke and Gregory wanted the theater to encourage young writers to explore in connection in the Black theater to open up the psychological dimension of modern Negro life. But that would never happen in a drama narrowed to the proposition W. E. B. Du Bois would express in print ten years later—"all Art is propaganda and ever must be, despite the wailing of the purists. I stand in utter shamelessness and say that whatever art I have for writing has been used always for propaganda for gaining the right of black folk to love and enjoy. I do not care a damn for any art that is not used for propaganda."[8]

Locke and Gregory, of course, wanted a drama that showed Black folk could already love and enjoy despite the terror of racism. Indeed, their view went to the core question of twentieth-century Black aesthetics: could art show that

Black people have an existence, a being, a worth, beyond the debate about their worth generated by White racists? Black aesthetics was thus an absolutely essential way to reveal Black humanity in all of its complexity. But Locke had resigned from the NAACP Drama Committee because he knew that the political establishment that drove Black bourgeois aesthetics in 1916 would not allow that kind of dramatic exploration. Talking with Braithwaite over the next year would strengthen Locke's resolve to refuse to participate in an aesthetic politics that denied the deeper dimensions of Black humanity.

Mary Locke soon joined her son at the end of June, after vacating her home and moving up to Cambridge. Both stayed at the Braithwaites' into the month of August, until Locke, ignoring his mother's advice, obtained lodgings at 552 Newbury Street in the heart of an all-White, middle-class Boston neighborhood. Although most of the inhabitants of the three- and four-story brick row houses on Newbury Street were renters rather than owners, Locke and his mother were certainly the only Black residents. Locke had followed, probably, William Lewis's advice and secured the lease through the mail, and then weathered the storm of indignation when they moved in. The neighborhood apparently did not protest too much. The location was convenient: Locke could walk the four blocks from his home to Massachusetts Avenue, where he could catch a bus or trolley to take him across the Charles River to Cambridge. Most important, 552 Newbury Street was probably the least expensive housing in an all-White neighborhood that he could afford. And being in an all-White neighborhood was essential to Locke. He knew his White friends, especially his Central High School friends, would be uncomfortable visiting him in a Black rooming house.

When Locke enrolled in Harvard that September, he received a shock: Josiah Royce died suddenly. Locke had returned to Harvard in part to study with Royce: the California-born idealist had been the first Harvard philosopher to befriend him in 1904, had been his major professor during his undergraduate career, and had written a strong letter of recommendation for the Rhodes Scholarship. Not only had Royce extended himself personally with Locke but also modeled the kind of philosopher Locke was becoming, a social philosopher akin to the old New England minister. Men like Royce and James cultivated a public audience for their writings, and Locke wanted to follow in their footsteps. Royce's death, however, removed the one man in the Harvard Department of Philosophy whose vision of the philosopher's vocation might have helped Locke find a way to integrate his public and social concerns with a career as an academic philosopher.

Who would Locke work with now? James had died in 1910, and George Herbert Palmer, who, next to Royce, had been Locke's friend in the department, had retired in 1913. Hugo Munsterberg, who had interested himself in Locke at the University of Berlin, died in 1916 as well. Locke's Oxford friend and intellectual ally, Horace Kallen, also was gone. At a time when the Philosophy Department was attempting to rebuild, Harvard president Lowell blocked the appointment of Arthur Lovejoy, Bertrand Russell, and John Dewey because he disapproved of their character. As a result, Locke entered a much weaker Philosophy Department in 1916 than he had graduated from in 1907. William James, Josiah Royce, and George Santayana were probably irreplaceable, but the remaining faculty was not even the best in the country.

Further study with Royce would, however, have been a step backward for Locke. He had already moved beyond Royce's idealism in his Oxford thesis. Harvard's younger generation of philosophers better served Locke's main purpose—to get his PhD without a great deal of difficulty. There was the German-born Oxford graduate R. F. Alfred Hoernlé, who had received an assistant professorship after visiting at Harvard and who was widely liked because of his geniality. Hoernle taught Metaphysics, Royce's old course, and Logical Theory to Locke, and they seemed to get on very well. Locke also seemed to enjoy very cordial relations with Henry M. Sheffer, the Jewish lecturer in the Philosophy Department during Locke's graduate year, who was a brilliant logician. Sheffer taught Locke logic and corresponded with him years after both had left Harvard. But the most important philosophy professor for Locke would be Ralph Barton Perry, who had introduced him to modern philosophy in his freshman year, had administered Locke's honors exam in 1907, and who had tried to get Locke a scholarship to return to graduate school in 1911. Perry was a tall, wiry, clean-cut man who epitomized what Lowell looked for in his faculty: he was a White, Anglo-Saxon Protestant, mildly anti-Semitic and pro-war. Perry not only wrote several books and essays linking the German war effort with German philosophy, but traveled as a recruit to the military training program at Plattsburg, New York, in the summer of 1916 to become a "citizen soldier." He seemed to like Locke a great deal and to be genuinely supportive of his attempt to become the first Black American to secure a PhD in philosophy from Harvard University.

Locke excelled in Hoernlé's Logical Theory course that fall of 1916, in part because the course played to Locke's strength. It focused on the "comparative study of Logical and Epistemological Theories with special attention to Bradley and Bosanquet, Russell, Husserl, and Meinong"—philosophers with whom he was familiar from his Oxford thesis research. It was a rigorous course, but Locke liked Hoernle and applied himself diligently to his studies, passing a particularly difficult set of examinations in November. Then, Locke wrote for the class one his best papers of the fall semester, "A Criticism of the Bosanquetian Doctrine of Judgment Forms." It was a brilliant critical analysis of Bernard Bosanquet's tendency to oscillate between a genetic, psychological approach to value judgments and a Hegelian dialectical approach. Locke showed that despite Bosanquet's pose of keeping the question open as to which methodology was the best for analyzing judgment forms, Bosanquet had subtly decided on the Hegelian over the psychological approach. By critiquing this tendency in Bosanquet, Locke declared his allegiance to the psychological account of how values emerge in human consciousness. Locke's paper also reveals his reason for backing the genetic account, for when he quotes Professor Baldwin on the subject, he indirectly states his own belief: "this natural genesis forbids our taking these principles out of their context and treating them as having miraculous and mysterious ontological virtues."[9] For Locke, the psychological approach to valuation preserved the relationship of values to their social context, and, in particular, preserved the sense that feeling was as much a part of the valuing process as reason. What is also remarkable here is how easily Locke writes with command and assurance about exceedingly technical issues in logical theory and the theory of values, despite having spent little time on such issues in the six years that intervened between his Oxford thesis and his first semester of graduate school in 1916. Hoernlé rewarded Locke's effort with this comment on his paper: "An exceedingly interesting piece of work, which I have read with pleasure and profit."[10] The Bosanquet paper proved that Locke belonged in Harvard's graduate program in philosophy.

Locke would have chosen Perry's year-long seminar on Ethics and the Theory of Value, Philosophy 20, regardless of Royce's death; but this seminar took on heightened importance in Locke's plans once his former mentor was not available to direct his dissertation. Perry represented the shift of Harvard philosophy toward professionalism, increased specialization, and the invocation of science as the model for philosophical inquiry. He was also the department's foremost authority on value theory and the only man who could direct Locke's PhD dissertation on value. Perry had taken William James's argument in *The Principles of Psychology* that interest was the key to consciousness and transformed it into a definition of value: interest was the key to why humanity valued the good over the evil, the truth over falsity, and the beautiful over the ugly. According to Perry, a value was nothing more than "the fulfillment of [a] bias of interest. An object would be said to possess value in so far as it fulfilled interest."[11] By contrast, Locke identified value with the ability to rise above naked interest and passion. He did not believe that simple interest could explain all of valuation. But he had also learned something from his disastrous attempt to force his psychological interpretation of value theory on Wilson and the other logically inclined philosophers at Oxford. Perry was Locke's best hope for success at Harvard, and it did not make sense to make a frontal assault on Perry's definition of value as the core of Locke's dissertation. So, Locke devised a more academic, more circumspect thesis than the one he had submitted to Oxford. Locke shifted the emphasis to a less contentious ground—the problem of classifying values into categories in the theory of value. When Locke read the outline of his dissertation in Perry's seminar on January 18, he had revised the argument of his Oxford thesis: the nature of valuation could best be discovered by observing how well explanations of valuing sorted our values into usable categories. For this problem of classification, Locke argued, the only reasonable approach was a "functional analysis and the genetic method as proper to the inquiry."[12] Locke also sharpened his critique of idealist theories of values by arguing that they failed to adequately explain how humans sorted values into their categories. Value categories emerged not from the idea of value, but from the practical, everyday experience of valuing. His argument came down to this: if we followed out how valuing worked in everyday experience, we would discover that Locke's definition of value, as educated feeling, was the most adequate to classifying values in their appropriate categories.

Perry responded positively to Locke's outline at the end of the first semester, a sign that Locke had successfully cleared a major hurdle of his graduate year at Harvard. Then, during the second semester of the weekly seminar, Locke, along with the rest of the students, developed his outline into a rough draft, titled "The Types of Classification in the Theory of Value." In addition to attending classes, Locke devoted considerable recreational time to those extracurricular activities that he deemed "cultured." He was a member of the Harvard Philosophical Club, attended most of its meetings, and used them to deepen his relationships with his professors. Locke's scribble on the back of an invitation to the February 23 meeting at which Professor Hoernle spoke reveals something of Locke's easygoing manner in interacting with his superiors. "Went. Met Dr. Langfeld on the way—talked of Harris. Entered room late. Dewey Philosophy [apparently Hoernle's subject] Downstairs Hoernle's apology—fine talk with Sheffer [about] Freud, etc.—then Hoernle & Mrs. H. Left."[13] He also felt most comfortable socializing with his peers in the Central High School Club at Harvard, which elected him to membership shortly after he arrived in Cambridge. Presided over by his friend, David A. Pfromm, now a lawyer in Boston, the CHS club met at the homes of prominent members and at Boston cultural shrines such as the Copley Theatre, where on February 8 they witnessed the Henry Jewett players "present 'MILESTONES' by Arnold Bennett and Edward Knobloch." Dickerman was often present at such club meetings, allowing Locke to re-create the triumvirate of Pfromm, Dick, and Locke from his undergraduate days. As before, Dick and Locke planned writing projects together and may have renewed their former romantic interests, although in 1917, "Dickus" seemed increasingly preoccupied by the war, which he was convinced would likely stimulate literary activity in the United States. Sometimes, such extracurricular activities synchronized with Locke's graduate work to make for exceedingly pleasurable and syncretic days. "Read Outline to Perry's seminar," Locke scribbled on the back of an invitation to the January 18 meeting of the CHS club. "Braithwaites Next. D A P[fromm at the Harvard] Union had dinner there—splendid discussion of Dick & the War. Then to Fairfax Squires (Gross for the first time). Afterwards with Jamie Miller to the Square. Fun Day."[14]

Locke felt at home at Harvard, because there he was able to balance his academic and non-academic responsibilities such that they did not divide him, as they had at Oxford. In Cambridge, he could have friends, meet up with them without concern of who was checking on him, and then go to classes, have intellectual discussions with the likes of Hoernlé, Perry, and Braithwaite, and not feel torn by the contrasts. For the first time, Locke found it easy to connect the philosophical and the literary sides of his intellect in Cambridge through what emerged as a rather consistent preoccupation with the psychological dimensions of human experience. His formal studies of the psychological dimension of valuation with Perry resonated with his informal discussions with Braithwaite that a Negro literary aesthetics of the future must be open to the psychological as well as the political dimensions of the Black experience.

Spending a year at Harvard also allowed Locke to reconnect with the generation of young Harvard graduates that was shaping the American literary rebellion of the 1910s, the cadre of Van Wyck Brooks, Lee Simonson, Harold Stearns, and Walter Lippmann who would combine aesthetic and political revolt. Some of them had been his classmates, such as Lee Simonson, the modernist set designer and authority on the new American theater, who wrote for *Seven Arts*. Simonson, whom Locke probably reconnected with at several dinners, may have introduced Locke to the magazine. Locke, in turn, introduced it to his Oxford friend, de Fonseka. Locke's recommendation of the *Seven Arts* to de Fonseka signaled that Locke's taste was shifting away from older, conservative magazines like the *North American Review*. Moreover, by recommending the *Seven Arts* rather than the *Masses* to his Sinhalese friend, Locke also showed that he sympathized less with the *New Masses'* Marxian-inspired debates in that magazine and more with the Freudian-inspired cultural revolution that contributors to *Seven Arts* seemed to believe lay ahead. Romain Rolland's essay on America in the November issue of *Seven Arts* was typical of this optimism, for the author seemed to believe that in America would begin a worldwide cultural liberationist movement. Unfortunately, Locke did not contribute anything to the magazine.

Life in Boston offered a near idyllic social life and world for the Lockes. There were frequent visits and dinners with the Braithwaites, of course, but also a chance to visit frequently with the Philadelphia-born artist and intellectual Meta Warrick Fuller, who had studied sculpture with Rodin and been a sensation in Paris art circles before settling down in Framingham, Massachusetts, with her husband, the psychiatrist Dr. Solomon Fuller. They entertained the Lockes repeatedly during his Harvard year. Being at Harvard also meant the opportunity to reconnect with Dickerman, who by the fall of 1917 was nicely ensconced as an instructor of English at Mt. Holyoke Collection. That year also brought new friends into his life. He met and befriended Plenyano Gbe Wolo, the outstanding son of the chief of the Kru tribe in Liberia, who had entered Harvard in 1913. Known on campus as "the African prince," Wolo was a member and vice president of the Harvard Cosmopolitan Club and, like Locke, interested in finding a way to utilize an American education (he went on to obtain a BA from Harvard, an MA from Columbia, and a BDiv from Union Theological Seminary) to leverage the independent economic and social development of African people.[15] Blending a social life with new and old friends, in the nearly constant company of his mother provided Locke with a social life that seemed to buoy his creative spirit.

Locke contributed an important article to the *Poetry Review*, William Stanley Braithwaite's fledgling journal, on the Belgian poet Emile Verhaeren, one of the Symbolists and a favorite of Amy Lowell, another contributor to *Seven Arts*. Locke's essay was a commemoration of the recently deceased Verhaeren and showed Locke's familiarity with both the poetry and prevailing critical opinion of Verhaeren. But the essay's real significance was Locke's discussion of modernism in literature away from the issues of Black writing and racial politics. Verhaeren had been one of the founders of the Belgian Renaissance, a national movement of literature that had emerged in the 1880s as Belgium reacted against the political and cultural domination of France and Germany and struggled for national self-determination. The movement began with the study of Belgian history, caught flame with the establishment of *Art Moderne* and other literary reviews in Brussels, and blazed in the work of Camille Lemmonier in fiction and Verhaeren's painter-like portraits of Flemish peasant life in poetry. Eschewing sentimental idealism, Verhaeren depicted Belgian life, in such early books as *Les Falmandes* (1883), with the "crude defiant realism" of the modernist, according to Locke.[16] Verhaeren wrote about peasants with an eye on their vices, brutality, and criminality, and avoided fin-de-siècle decadent aestheticism and the hyperrealism of Émile Zola. Verhaeren was

> the greatest exponent of modernism in poetry. In so styling him, we rate as the really vital modernism in the art, not the cult of sheer modernity of form and mood,—the ultra-modernism in which the poetic youth exults, but that more difficult modernity of substance which has as its aim to make poetry incorporate a world-view and reflect the spirit of its time. The task,—ancient and perennial in some respects, of getting the real world into the microcosm of art without shattering either one or the other, was unusual in Verhaeren's day. No life has been harder to transmute into art than modern life, and in no art so difficult as in that of poetry. Yet this was the master-passion of Verhaeren's temperament and the consummate achievement of his work.[17]

In his later work, Verhaeren had extended poetic modernism by exploring the symbol of modern life, the city in such works as *Les Campagnes Hallucinees* (1893), *Les Villes Tentaculaires* (1896), and *La Multiple Splendeur* (1906). Just as the city had been the sign of the modernity of Simmel, the Berlin sociologist, the city symbolized for Verhaeren the real, the throbbingly actual. "It is obviously not the city as such—indeed Verhaeren never quite escaped his old preoccupation with peasant folk and country life in all their Flemish provinciality—but the city as a symbol, a point of view, behind Verhaeren's real gods, Humanity and Force."[18]

Such views help situate Locke's modernism within the context of his times. Locke embraced the modernism of the *Seven Arts* magazine, rejected moralistic progressivism, and advocated a revolution in literary taste to accept the franker, more Freudian discussions of sexuality, the moral uncertainty of modern life, and the sordid lives of the poor in the cities. That was the challenge of modern poetry that Verhaeren had met and Negro literature would need to meet—adopt a radically new content and derive new forms of expression, as Whitman, another Locke favorite, had done in *Leaves of Grass*. But Locke was not sympathetic to what he called "ultramodernism," whose main goal was a complete rebellion against tradition in form and the artist's responsibility to reflect the life of the people in content. Locke liked Verhaeren, because for him, the "real did exist," and he revolutionized form because he knew that the classical tradition's insistence on grace, balance, and symmetry could not accommodate the contrast, contrapunctuality, and dissonance of the modern urban reality. Verhaeren exhibited something akin to the blues aesthetic that later poets like Langston Hughes would try to capture in poetry of Black urban life. The challenge for modernism, Locke believed, was to extend the reach of poetic beauty to accommodate the raucous diversity of modern life.

The Verhaeren reflections elucidate what Locke was trying to achieve in his formal philosophical discussions of value and beauty that spring of 1917. Locke sought to answer the late nineteenth-century attack on values led by Nietzsche, who, once he declared God dead, asserted that the system of universal social values, derived from God or an Absolute, was dead too. No longer could we depend on the existence of transcendent ideals or argue that standards of the good, the true, and the beautiful existed for all peoples. Locke agreed that people perceive values differently, and that no God or universal intelligence can be posited that creates ideal value types. But Locke rejected the extreme of the position that insisted, as Nietzsche did in *Thus Spake Zarathustra*, that now the individual, the super-individual, was the only source of values. Instead, Locke wanted to reestablish socially shared values on a psychological basis and argued that certain values are products of the way people habitually perceive their experience. He found a metaphor of what he wanted to say in formal value theory in the psychological research of A. Mussell, who wrote on color and sound perception. In a series of psychological experiments, Mussell determined that large numbers of people habitually perceived certain colors and sounds as complementary or harmonious, and that these colors and sounds were habitually grouped together when experiments were repeated with the same or different subjects. Mussell had developed a qualitative scale of color and sound apperception, and Locke took that as more than an analogy of what happened when people perceived certain values as harmonious or complementary to one another.

According to Locke, complementary "color and sound sensations are <u>felt dif-ferently</u> from the type of sensation lacking that <u>aspect</u>, and such aspects of sen-sory experience are called 'values'—not merely by analogy, I think, but because they really are a type of value, in an elementary way as a conditioning of experi-ence principally in terms of its affective factors."[19] Since Mussell's work was based on direct perception rather than reflective comparison, Locke argued by analogy that valuation contained gradations of qualitative discrimination such as harmonious, inharmonious, and unharmonious. In short, Mussell suggests that people's qualitative sense is shared and can be measured scientifically, such that one can claim, without reference to some ideal notion of values, that socially shared values exist. Despite the dramatic diversity of experience and sophistica-tion, there is something fundamentally similar about the experience of an art critic viewing a Rembrandt in a museum, of a peasant viewing a Belgian countryside, and of an African artist carving a tribal fetish—all would sense their experience as somehow harmonious. Something aesthetic connected the experience of all of them. Locke's modernist approach to art, literature, and philosophy was de-signed to rescue that which was "ancient and perennial" in values from the dustheap of nineteenth-century idealism and re-establish them on the more scientific foundation of twentieth-century psychology.

By the end of the spring semester, Locke had gained a reputation for his psy-chological theory of value and developed his outline into a rough draft essay of his dissertation, "The Problem of Classification in the Theory of Value." He had convinced Perry of his capacity for first-class philosophical work and gained the professor's support for his dissertation subject. Locke had also gained the esteem of his other professors that year: Locke completed his graduate year at Harvard with straight As except for his only B in Sheffer's class in logic. Whether because of his mother's reassuring presence or his own greater maturity, Locke excelled that year in his studies and regained the earlier academic form of his undergraduate years at Harvard.

Locke's success may also have been related to his reluctance to involve him-self in African American projects, a posture that may have been strengthened by his Harvard experience. Locke completed a bibliography of slave narratives during the fall of 1916 and sent a copy of it to Arthur Schomburg. Locke wrote that he was thinking of submitting it to Carter G. Woodson's *Journal of Negro History*, but he never did. Locke was too busy with his studies. "I have great facilities here for research," he informed Schomburg, "but little time to exploit them."[20] During his second semester, Locke did manage to pen a tribute to his old mentor Bishop Walters, who died in January 1917, but only reluctantly. Invited by Walters's wife to come to Philadelphia to attend the bishop's funeral, Locke had declined: not only did he hate funerals but also he could not leave Cambridge because of his work. But when Lelia Walters offered to pay him for a written tribute that could be published, Locke agreed to write one, and it provides an interesting insight into this Harvard aesthete's critique of political leadership. Locke used Walters's death to deliver a sharp critique of how Black people treated their leaders:

> I know the good spirit of Alexander Walters will pardon that I take him for the text. It is no secret that beneath all of his success, over all his other satisfied ambitions, above and beyond all the honor that came to him, there was a tragedy in his life. Did I share it only to betray it? No, I consecrated it to this moment of its proper and highest use.... With what brave optimism Bishop Walters strove to the end to be saved from despairing of Christian leadership among us? He had the instinct for leadership as all really great men have. He had a position which was a constant reminder of the highest and most responsible type of leadership. He had a charge and a flock to keep. It is sad to think that the best definition and example of human leadership is built upon an analogy... of the shepherd and the flock. I am not propounding dark or idle riddles when I ask again "What sheep is it that knoweth not his own shepherd?" I wish I could say that we were a shepherded and shepherdable people with the same certainty that I can say "This man was a shepherd of his people." Too often we take the wolf for shepherd, or scatter because of bells tinkling from many directions[s]. Trust in men is afterall the basis of trust in principles. And I see on every hand a growing distrust among us which is sapping at the source the vital force of race life, the belief in and respect for the man of disinterested motive and unpurchasable loyalty.[21]

Walters had been a kind of hero for Locke, a replacement for his own father, as a political figure who, though powerful, was also humane. Walters was nurturing, selfless, and devoted to the cause, and still had been unable to mobilize the race. "The motives of his leadership were clear and unquestionable: of how many can this be said? Loyalty,—the sterling basic metal of manhood and leadership among men was never better exemplified among us than by this life and character."[22] Locke read Bishop Walters's death, which most African Americans hardly noticed, as an ominous sign: one could give one's all to Black people and still not be loved. In one sense, Locke was simply being naive: such leadership was always a sacrifice, because the leader was always betrayed by the masses. That did not keep true leaders from taking on the shackles of leadership, but it did give pause to Locke. He needed more of a payoff for race leadership if he was to disturb the quiet equipoise of his life to descend into the battle of Black leadership. By criticizing Black people's loyalty, he really defined the limits of his own: without enormous support from the people, Locke could not guarantee that he could be "the man of disinterested motive and unpurchasable loyalty" that he argued

Walters had been.[23] Locke had been wounded by the rough and tumble of academic and political conflicts in Washington and wondered in this article if it was worth it.

Something of Locke's detachment, his willingness to sit on the sidelines and simply observe the courage of others, seemed to peak during and after his return to Harvard for graduate school. Even when Woodrow Wilson led the United States into World War I and African Americans responded throughout the country with unbridled enthusiasm for the war effort, Locke remained unmoved. He did like to go down to the Harvard stadium and watch the Harvard men go through their military drill, but that was more of an aesthetic experience for Locke than anything patriotic. Apparently, he responded favorably to Montgomery Gregory's urgent request in May 1917 to contact New England ROTC representatives about the possibility of Negro officer training facilities. As head of the Committee of Negro Men at Howard University, Gregory was leading the effort at the "Capstone of Negro Education" to force the War Department to set up a separate camp to train Black officers, largely because the Department's current facility at Plattsburg was for "Whites only." Locke appears to have responded to Gregory's request, but that was about all. After the spring semester came to an end, Locke remained in Boston over the summer, working on his dissertation and assisting Braithwaite with his editorial projects. By contrast, Locke's dissertation director, Ralph Barton Perry, left Cambridge for Washington to become Secretary for Military Training of College Men. Montgomery Gregory enlisted in the army for officer training once Secretary of War Newton Baker declared that facilities would be established at Des Moines, Iowa, for the training of Black officers. Locke was wise to stay put. After all that he had suffered for failure to get his Oxford degree, he needed to commit all of his energies to his dissertation. But as the year at Harvard, and the summer too, came to an end, it was clear that Locke had chosen the path of inner quiet rather than engaged Black cultural leadership. He had developed at Harvard a new, philosophically and literarily rich conception of the kind of work our psychology does in creating and sustaining experiences of value. But he had also come to believe that that view and its complexity was not welcome in the Black world he was returning to.

An unconscious rhythm of maternal intimacy was also now visible in Locke's creative life. Spatial distance between him and his mother affected his ability to produce. When he had left Camden for Cambridge and Harvard in 1904, Locke had sought and found an ideal psychic distance from his mother—hundreds of miles away yet close enough for constant, almost daily referral and renewal, yet with enough freedom to roam intellectually and personally; in consequence, he had grown in his studies and in his personal intellectual adventurousness. But when he had left her for England and Oxford and too great a distance, his psychic connection with her was broken, leading to panicky episodes and the absence of internal calm, precisely when circumstances meant he needed her most.

His failure to get the Oxford degree taught him a lesson. Recognizing that he needed her stabilizing presence to get the German doctorate, he insisted on her coming despite the horrific timing of the decision. Once the war's outbreak ended abruptly their honeymoon in Berlin, they were separate again, but he was seemingly renewed again by the heightened drama of their forced intimacy on his return to live separately in Washington. Being merely a two-hour train ride from Philadelphia, Locke had embarked on some of his boldest and most original thinking, writing, and public speaking—reminiscent of Harvard.

Locke had taken Mary to Harvard to ensure he would succeed at a graduate career that had stumbled without her. In his rapprochement with her and Harvard, he had healed his wounded student self. Now, after a successful year at Harvard, Locke was headed back to Washington with her. With Mary by his side, he had nestled back into the Black Victorian voice of the settled bourgeois, his psychic needs met, his public criticality quiet.

16

Fitting in Washington, D.C., 1917–1922

Locke began looking for an apartment in Washington long before he left Boston. It was good that he did, for after Wilson's declaration of war on April 6, 1917, housing was scarce in Washington, as his real estate agent, R. R. Thompson, informed him. Family friend Helen Irvin, now living and teaching in Washington with her husband, put Locke in touch with Thompson. Thompson's son, a student in her class, informed the elder Thompson that Professor Locke of Howard University was looking for an apartment. Thompson informed Locke that a second-floor apartment in a three-story Victorian building at 1326 R Street had been recently vacated. That would be of negligible historical significance except for what Thompson revealed of the racial protocol of Black housing in the District of Columbia. "This is a three family apartment building each containing five rooms, bath, rear porches, hot water heat, janitor service and which have been renting to whites at $32.50 but [which are now] for rent to colored at $30.50 for the first two and $29 for the top one."[1] Black tenants paid less than Whites, apparently a reversal of the practice in New York. Even more interesting was Thompson's explanation for why the second-floor apartment was still empty, a month after the owner had moved out and the real estate agent had received several applications to rent it. A "white tenant is still in the first [floor] flat and will be there till about the 1st of Aug., and therefore my other tenants cannot go in, to avoid friction, until Aug. 1."[2] While the block was integrated, individual buildings had to remain all White or all "Colored," and Thompson was not about to buck protocol in a southern city.

As soon as the first-floor tenant vacated, Thompson would be able to turn the apartment building over to the Lockes if they moved fast. As Thompson informed Locke, "Owing to the war a large number of people are now beginning to come into Washington, the work of the departments having doubled in some instances. This, I understand is expected to make the houses and apartments scarce. Even though most of these are Whites the average abandonment of houses and apartments by them to colored will cease which cause quarters for colored to be equally as scarce."[3] Unlike such industrial cites as Chicago and Pittsburgh, whose wartime population increases were due to the avalanche of southern Black migrants, Washington's population expanded because of the in-migration of White professionals to staff the bureaucratic war machine. Thompson's strategy worked: Locke took the apartment, even though he had to rent it from August 15, rather than his preferred date of September 1, to ensure he would have a comfortable place for him and his mother near Howard University.

Bringing his mother with him meant a loss of freedom in Locke's life in Washington but also a number of gains. He would not have to worry about how she was being cared for; he would take complete control of her affairs; and by husbanding her find a degree of fulfillment as the man of the house. At the same time, she would give him the structure to finish his dissertation and obtain his PhD. Living together with all of their things in one city and in one house, Mary Locke was able to sustain the kind of stable, nurturing environment that she had created for him in Boston. Setting up household with his mother in northwest Washington also improved his sociability. Locke not only had someone to come home to from teaching at Howard University but also someone who accompanied him to teas, dinners, and walks with his close friends. Cohabitation with her seemed to improve his mood as well, in large part, because of her personality. She represented the best qualities of Locke's nature, and being around her amplified his friendliness, openness, and gentlemanly bearing. He seemed at peace devoting himself to caring for the one person who had devoted her life to caring for him.

Mary Locke's presence in Washington also allowed Locke to introduce her to his developing religious interest in the Baha'i faith. While the exact details remain sketchy, Locke apparently became interested in the Baha'i after being recruited by Louis Gregory. The Baha'is were attractive to Locke as to other middle-class Black communities in Chicago, New York, and Philadelphia for their quiet nondenominational religion, their notion of the oneness of humanity, and the call for believers to be tolerant of other religions and devote themselves to service for the betterment of humanity. The Baha'is also possessed a progressive social agenda that fit well with Locke's mildly progressive goals of world peace and humanitarian tolerance for all peoples, especially their advocacy of the equality of the sexes and tolerance of homosexuality. Not long after they arrived in Washington, the Lockes became regulars at the services of this Persian faith.

Having his mother with him in Washington also increased Locke's social acceptability. Those prying people who needed an explanation for why this attractive thirty-two-year-old man had never married now had a ready answer: he was devoted to his mother. The social invitations Locke received increased between 1917 and 1922, as Black Victorian Washington invited Locke and his mother over for tea, for dinner, or even for those "at home" drop-in hours that were so favored by upper-crust Washingtonians. Of course, Locke had received his fair share of invitations when he lived in Washington alone, but these increased dramatically, a sign perhaps that Locke was perceived as safer with his mother around. Even official celebrations, such as class reunions, invited them both. At dinners, Mary Locke supplied the easygoing ballast to her son's often prickly personality, while Locke added fame and sparkling, witty conversation to an evening. Locke liked such gatherings more than he admitted.

One escape from his almost all-consuming mother relationship was Locke's involvement in the war mobilization effort. Students and faculty at Howard had reacted enthusiastically to NAACP chairperson Joel Spingarn's March 1917 speech on campus that called on the War Department to establish a separate camp to train Black officers. Historically, White officers had always commanded African American troops, as the army saw African Americans as followers, not "officer material." Spingarn's proposal met resistance not only from the army but also from some elements in the Black community, specifically some newspapermen, who believed the separate camp was acquiescence to segregation. Encouraged by Montgomery Gregory and other faculty members, Howard's students drafted petitions, interviewed congressmen, and created a groundswell of support for the camp. With the national support of W. E. B. Du Bois in the *Crisis*, the lobbying effort forced Secretary of War Newton Baker, who worried that the denial of officer training might hurt the morale of Black servicemen, established a camp for Black officer training in Des Moines, Iowa, in May 1917. Although Howard missed out on the opportunity to have the camp there, the university was selected by the Federal Board of Vocational Education that September to help train radio operators for the Army Signal Corps. In response, Howard's School of Manual Arts and Applied Sciences set up a technical training course that began on November 19. By May 16, 1918, it was training three hundred Black "draftees from the District of Columbia." Indeed, Howard was virtually "taken over by the government" in the spring of 1918 to train soldiers in radio and technical Signal Corps work. Locke knew that if he wanted to fit in with wartime Howard, he must define a role for himself in the mobilization movement on its campus.

Locke's disadvantage was his late arrival in the war mobilization at Howard. By September 1917, two hundred students and professors, including Gregory, had already left for the Des Moines, Iowa, camp. As early as August, Gregory had written to Locke, "I'm going to carry out our ideas in active service in the field— you must handle situation at home—at Howard!! Howard is in critical and precarious condition, needs strong & tactful strategist to guide her course.... Will turn material over to you...you can manage it."[4] Gregory needed a man on the inside at Howard to create leverage on the War Department, and Locke was perfect for such behind-the-scenes maneuvering. Gregory's reference to "our ideas" suggests that Locke shared Gregory's view that war was an opportunity to demonstrate Black leadership ability. Black Progressives such as Locke, Gregory, and Kelly Miller held the view that tolerance for African Americans improved during wartime, because the threat from an external enemy raised the value of Black manpower in White eyes. Despite such aberrations as the East St. Louis riot in which Whites attacked and burned the Black community in response to wartime migration and increase of the Black population, Black Progressives believed that Black support of the American involvement in the war ultimately would translate into greater recognition for Blacks after the war. That belief was particularly serviceable for Locke, as it allowed him to silence his 1914 condemnation of the war as a White man's war and embrace the mood of patriotic loyalty that had swept the country.

As always, Locke wanted to capitalize on opportunities to advance his career and increase his salary, especially now that he was caring for two in expensive Washington, D.C. Others were profiting more from the war. Shortly after Locke arrived in Washington, another African American received the most important job for a Negro in the War Department. That man was Tuskegee Institute secretary Emmett J. Scott, who became Special Assistant on Negro Affairs to Secretary of War Baker. While Locke would certainly have preferred that job for himself, he also viewed Scott's appointment as a blessing: he and Scott had had cordial relations when Locke had visited Tuskegee, and Locke hoped to turn his unofficial role as a liaison at Howard into an official position on Scott's staff. Immediately after the announcement of Scott's appointment, Locke wired Scott to offer to meet and talk things over. Scott's reply—that he was still "waiting certain definite instructions from War Department before I can wire hour of arrival"—set the tone of their relationship: Scott kept Locke at a distance. He was suspicious of Locke—and other Blacks—whom he believed might be trying to usurp his power or limit his maneuverability. While Locke and Scott would meet from time to time during the next two years of war work, nothing like the official appointment Locke longed for materialized.

But Gregory kept the pressure on Locke to serve as a liaison and continued to provide him with information about the conditions and mindset of Howard recruits at the Des Moines Camp. Early in October he reported that African American recruits in Des Moines were "blue" over the "Houston affair," the case of Black soldiers who attacked White southerners who had taunted them on the night of August 23, 1917, in Houston. In the riot that resulted twenty persons died—four soldiers and sixteen civilians. The soldiers were to be court-martialed and condemned, without a serious investigation of the causes of the disturbance. So eager was the army for a quick conviction that the army had conscripted several of the Black officers at Des Moines to secure a "confession" from the Houston men. Gregory, like many African Americans, felt that the affair was another sign of the unfair treatment of Black soldiers by the army. "Be sure to keep in touch with Scott and situation generally," Gregory pleaded. "[We] look chiefly to you as our representative there."[5] Ultimately, Locke had no influence and thirteen of the Black soldiers were hanged on December 11 without any opportunity to appeal their convictions.

Locke's only significant role may have come in April 1918, when Gregory asked him to block the army's attempt to break up the artillery unit for training African American officers at Camp Dix, where Gregory was stationed. Most African American officers had been assigned to infantry training, at best, and to labor battalions, at worst, so the loss of this artillery unit symbolized the betrayal of the army's commitment to treat African American officers equally. "Hell is loose!" he informed Locke:

> They are breaking up our artillery as fast as they can. 450 of our men are packed ready to be transferred on order from Washington. Then this morning the 3 most important field officers here, the men who have conducted the instruction, etc.—are removed to other places....We have nothing but skeletons of 2 regiments left. Col. _____ tells me that these moves spell the doom of our artillery arm of the division. For God's sake get those men down there to do something at once! They should go to Baker at once and demand that the War Dept. act frankly— either [drop] the whole business or treat it fairly.[6]

Locke may have had some impact, for on April 23, Gregory thanked him for interceding with Scott, who had "gotten order, transferring the enlisted men, cancelled. I couldn't reach him in Phila[delphia] but talked with him over phone. Hope you saw Baker. He should know that the leading men of the race are awake to conditions and that the colored division must get fair considerations at all times & in all matters. This one order is merely one isolated incident."[7] Certainly, that was true. Black soldiers trained at southern bases were bombarded with racist insults from the surrounding communities and treated with contempt by White officers. Even in the northern camps, African American intellectuals like Gregory recognized the lack of seriousness in their training and preparation. "So far we haven't done a damn thing but sleep," he reported from Camp Dix. It's time for the younger generation to assert itself....I believe in true loyalty and patriotism, but a positive patriotism, not a slavish one."[8] Gregory was beginning to see through the veil of African American officer participation that second-class treatment remained for Blacks in the armed services despite the token of the officer training camp. Gregory's experience warned that little substantial changes in domestic race relations were likely to result from Black mobilization during the war.

Locke's involvement in the war effort did solidify his relationship with Professor Perry, for it provided Locke with a convenient excuse for his lack of progress on his dissertation. Although "The Problem of Classification in the Theory of Value" was dated September 1, 1917, the entire dissertation was not completed until the end of the fall semester, considerably after its promised date of completion. Sometime during the fall Locke wrote to Perry to explain "my apparent dissertation from my philosophy work; and I feel especially so now that I am the unwilling means of crowding your last days at Cambridge, this semester with thesis reading and possibly a topical exam. Since mid-August, I have been terribly caught up in political affairs: a trip of investigation to East St. Louis for the NAACP, a visit to the Des Moines Camp, and since October quite a deal of work as an assistant to Mr. Scott, advisory aide to the War Department on the colored personnel of the army."[9] Locke was not above appealing directly to Perry's interest in military preparedness: "In fact the possibility of some more definite connection with our guard Division when it is organized is one of my motives for wanting to get the degree matter over if possible.... Though rewritten in large part the thesis is I fear more patched than retailored. However I shall stand by it and all my other shortcomings."[10] Locke stretched the truth considerably. He was not an official assistant to Scott. No evidence exists that the NAACP sent him to East St. Louis or that the naturally timid Locke would have gone if he had been asked. His reference to a place in Felix Frankfurter's office was perhaps closer to reality: he may have occupied a desk in Frankfurter's office, for it is unlikely that Locke would have dared lie outright to Perry about that. But Locke was adept at maximizing the sense of commonality with the military-minded Perry and suggesting that Locke, like Perry, was an academic in arms. This martial bonding, combined with the hard work he put in that fall semester on the dissertation, paid off for Locke. Perry, along with his other readers Hoernle and Sheffer, was pleased with Locke's dissertation. When the doctorates were awarded in June 1918, Alain Le Roy Locke became Dr. Locke, the first African American to secure a PhD in philosophy from Harvard University.

Completing his PhD did not end Locke's relationship with Perry. That summer, Perry contacted Locke with a surprising request. He was about to receive page proofs of his forthcoming book, *The Present Conflict of Ideals during World War I*, and Perry had no time to check the voluminous references. He needed someone with access to the Library of Congress to check them for him and wondered if Locke knew any responsible person who would do it for pay. Immediately, Locke volunteered his services and did the work promptly, not only checking the sources, but also writing other professors, such as Sheffer and Hoernle, for leads on books he could not locate in Washington. That Perry selected Locke shows something of his confidence in his student. At the same time, checking references was the kind of work graduate students were asked to do by their professors, often without attribution or acknowledgment. Something of Perry's character is revealed by the fact that on the first page of his book, he thanked "Alain Le Roy Locke for his assistance."[11]

Locke undertook this work not only because he viewed it as an opportunity to repay Perry for his PhD support but also as a way to gain Perry's support for his plan to establish a Student Army Training Camp at Howard University. As Secretary of Military Training for the War Department, Perry was responsible for ensuring that institutions of higher education supplied their percentage of officers to the war effort. It seems likely that Perry was a sympathetic voice in the War Department's Committee on Education and Special Training for Locke's plan to establish at Howard University the first ROTC (or its wartime name, SATC or Student Army Training Corps) training camp at a Black university. Beginning in the 1918–1919 school year, the War Department planned to establish SATC units at colleges with one hundred or more male students and to train specialist instructors for those individual college units at three regional training camps during the summer of 1918. Black college students would not be welcome at these camps, and considerable criticism erupted in the Black press about the lack of any provision for Black college students. Some Blacks even went so far as to suggest that the military training at Fort Des Moines was exactly the kind of inculcation of discipline that the Negro needed. Herein lay Locke's opportunity. Though the particulars remain unclear, Locke secured on July 17 the War Department's approval to hold a summer training camp for Negroes at Howard University from August 1 to September 16. Even though the army did not plan to commission any more Black officers, Locke (and others) wanted to keep the pressure on the War Department by showing that qualified officer material existed in the Black college community. By setting up the training camp at Howard, Locke drew attention to its premier role in the Black officer training effort and secured esteem for himself as the chairman of the Negro Student Army Association.

In that role, Locke traveled to Camp Mead to observe how a regular army camp was run and helped select the trainees from the hundreds of college students who applied from Fisk, Wilberforce, Atlanta, Lincoln, Hampton, and Tuskegee. Locke also recruited Lieutenant Russell Smith to be commanding officer, and several other officers, including Montgomery Gregory, from the 349th and 350th Field Artillery at Camp Dix to serve as Smith's assistants at the Howard camp. Apparently, these efforts met with success. More than 457 Black college students enlisted in the army for sixty days, attended the camp, and were discharged with most receiving certificates as graduates entitled to serve as instructors at the colleges to which they returned. Locke also spoke at a September 14 ceremony that honored the graduates. Standing before Major Ralph Barton Perry, Emmett J. Scott, and J. Stanley Durkee, Howard University's new president, Locke claimed:

> [The camp's graduates were] in Mr. Braithwaite's fine phrase, part of "the reserves of Peace." They commemorate, therefore, not themselves, but the spirit which actuated them and the nation at the same time. This spirit is still the hope of this nation … and no less, the hope of our race. All our institutions must conform themselves to it, but most especially our universities. For theirs must be the policies of the future, not

the policies of the present: and their proper wisdom is not the expedi-
encies of middle-age, but the hopeful ideals of youth [and] the vision of
a new social order.[12]

In "The Role of the Talented Tenth," published after the war, Locke reiterated his
call for a "new social order" and his belief that new leadership opportunities
awaited talented African Americans in the postwar world. Locke forecasted that
future leaders would be selected more democratically, on the basis of merit
rather than privilege or race, and this camp, however limited in scope, was part
of the effort to prove Negro worth and merit.

The camp had been a significant racial experience as Locke noted in an article
on the camp in the *Howard University Record*. "In addition to the military training, there was the beneficial association for the first time of so large and representative a body of Negro schoolmen; and this affiliation of the colored schools,
acknowledged by the formation of the Negro Student Army Association by the
members of the camp,—has revealed to Howard a new mission in educational
leadership."[13] The military program had furthered what Locke had called for in
"The Negro and a Race Tradition"—a heightened sense of collective race consciousness among Black youth. The success of the camp might also convince
Howard to awaken to its "new mission in educational leadership" of serving as a
race center, something Locke had advocated at Howard for years.

Locke's enthusiasm for war preparation stopped short of actually joining the
army. When his Camden, New Jersey, draft board contacted him in October
1918 to inform him of its plan to reclassify him as eligible for the draft, Locke
quickly sent his board a report about his medical condition—it was poor—and
instructed Major Smith, the SATC commanding officer, to write the Camden
board that Locke was "a graduate of the Students' Army Training Corps" and an
"Assistant Personnel clerk of this Unit." Of course, Locke may have been an "assistant personnel clerk" of the defunct camp, but more likely he merely utilized
this title to strengthen his claim for "deferred classification." The camp had been
a way for a non-soldier to participate in the war effort without actually serving.

That Ralph Barton Perry would be supportive of Locke's separate camp idea,
even to the point of speaking at the September 14 ceremony commemorating
the camp, deserves comment. In a strange way, Perry and Locke were drawn together by this military proposal into an intimacy that they would never share
afterward as fellow philosophers. After the armistice was declared and Perry returned to Cambridge, they had little further contact. Perry never took on Locke
as a philosophical protégé. In part, this was due to the overwhelmingly segregated character of higher education in America, particularly where the teaching
of philosophy was concerned. It would have been impossible for Perry to call
Locke back to Harvard as James had called back Perry years before, and both
Locke and Perry knew that. Indeed, the only real relationship that Locke would

have to his former graduate department in the coming years would structurally resemble that of the segregated war effort: Howard emerged in the 1920s and 1930s as the feeder school for young Black Harvard philosophy graduates who would be recommended to Locke. Albert Dunham was perhaps the most important Harvard philosophy protégé who would come to Howard to teach under Locke's tutelage. In that sense, the wartime collaboration between Perry and Locke symbolized the limits of their progressivism: even those who were liberal in their racial sentiments ultimately perpetuated the system of segregation by accommodating it.

Racism, of course, was not the whole reason that Locke's PhD in philosophy from Harvard led him to a disciplinary dead end. Locke had the misfortune to write his dissertation when the kind of speculative, broadly appealing philosophy that had flourished during Harvard's Golden Age no longer prevailed. Like Perry, philosophy in America in the 1920s and 1930s became "scientific," logical, and professional and lost its popular audience of the 1890s and 1900s. Had Dewey been at Harvard, and Locke been able to work with him, Locke might have been mentored to develop a broader philosophy of experience out of his study of aesthetic valuation. Both Locke and Dewey saw the root of aesthetic consciousness in the emotions rather than logical, reflective knowledge, and called for empathetic openness to our experience to realize the aesthetic dimension in our lives. More than any specific philosophy influence, Dewey would have offered Locke the opportunity to work with a social philosopher of the first rank and share in Dewey's success as a public social philosopher. By contrast, Perry could not guide Locke into a successful social role as a powerful social philosopher because Perry was not one himself.

Dewey would not, however, have saved Locke from the pitfall of naively believing that the war would bring meaningful democratic change to America. Even W. E. B. Du Bois had advocated that Blacks "close ranks" during the war, because he too believed the world would be better for African peoples after the Allies won. Du Bois also attended the Versailles Peace Conference and the Pan African Congress in 1919 with the belief that the Allies would liberate Germany's African colonies as the logical consequence of a war to make the world safe for democracy. But after the armistice, the Allies quickly parceled Germany's remaining colonies among themselves and ignored pleas from Africans and African Americans to grant such colonies sovereignty or even outline anything more than a token nod to future self-determination in the African Mandates established by Article 22 of the League of Nations Covenant.

At home, urban White Americans sent an even clearer signal that the war would not result in better treatment for African Americans. In several northern cities, gangs of young Whites attacked Black neighborhoods during the summer of 1919. In Chicago, the attacks seemed to be a response to Black encroachment on working-class White neighborhoods as a result of the wartime migration of southern Blacks. The *Washington Post* essentially started a riot by running an announcement on the morning of July 21 that servicemen would assemble that evening to respond to a recent trend of attacks on White women in the city. That evening a roving band of youths and servicemen attacked isolated African Americans, pulled them off of street trolleys, and invaded the southwest and northwest sections of the Washington Black community. The police stood by and refused to restrain the Whites, but unlike in East St. Louis, Blacks fought back with unexpected ferocity and killed several Whites. Eugene Holmes, later Locke's colleague in the Philosophy Department, claimed that Locke served as a go-between for Black and White neighborhoods during the riot. But this seems as unlikely as Locke's reputed trip to East St. Louis shortly after its 1917 riot. The Washington riot did not create armed camps, as was the case in the two-week-long Chicago riot, but took the form of sudden violent attacks on innocent bystanders, regardless of their social standing. Another Howard University professor, Carter G. Woodson, recalled that he narrowly avoided a marauding band of White servicemen by ducking quickly into an alleyway between houses. Woodson, who had recently been appointed dean of Liberal Studies at Howard, would later become a member of the Central Advisory Council organized by Emmett J. Scott to research the causes of the riot. Locke's name was absent from the list of members. More likely, Locke's first concern was to protect and calm his elderly mother, who must have been greatly frightened by the rioting, some of the worst of which occurred not less than five blocks from their home.

Yet the story of Locke's mediation, evidently told to Holmes by Locke, is significant in this respect: it tells us something about Locke's vision of himself and the society around him. Locke saw himself as a harmonizer between Black and White civilizations, and at a moment when both groups seemed their least civilized, Locke dreamed of a larger, harmonizing role for himself. But little mediation was possible in Wilson's Washington. After the rioting, feelings on both sides hardened. No citywide interracial fellowship organization emerged, and no sustained interaction emerged between the "talented tenths" of either group. In the early 1920s, segregation spread in Washington, culminating in the 1922 insult of the segregated bleachers for those wishing to view ceremonies at the installation of the Lincoln Memorial. Such patent segregation must have been particularly difficult for Locke, who thrived in cities where access to all cultural and social institutions could be taken for granted. It must have also been difficult for Mary Locke, who was used to going to such prestigious downtown department stores as Wanamakers in Philadelphia without fear of discrimination. In Washington, D.C., she'd be barred from entering Garfinkels. For Locke and his mother, therefore, the riot defined the cramped racial space they lived and moved in in Washington. And for a philosopher of race relations, the riot showed war had not opened new opportunities for Negro leadership.

Beneath Locke's optimistic postwar predictions lay a deep and abiding skepticism about the prospects for Negro progress. In that sense, Locke was not too surprised by the riot, almost predicted by the author of *Race Contacts* when he observed, "Adjustment in society, coming about, as it has so very often, by legal enactment, in itself generates violent changes. And a violent change in one direction is apt to be followed by a reaction, so that a sort of series of waves, on the one hand, of moral reform, and on the other hand, of social reaction, seem inevitable under most conditions."[14] Although the progressive adjustment he had predicted was not the result of "legal enactment," the Great Migration, the distinguished service of Negroes in the war, and the renewed clamor for democratic rights by such groups as the NAACP constituted a progressive step forward that inevitably met a counter "social reaction." Locke knew the Black Victorian ideology that Black merit would be rewarded was deeply flawed. Oxford had taught him that. Hence, when Locke stood before those SATC graduates on September 14 and pronounced the way open for Negro advancement after the war, he only half believed his own words. He knew that being responsible, serving one's country, and joining in the idealistic struggle for democracy did not guarantee justice for Black folk. Like so many others of his generation, however, Locke had no alternative to professing the standard faith in Black Progressivism and Black Victorianism on such public vocations.

Locke's skepticism ran even deeper. He believed, privately of course, that Black people fell short of having earned the respect of Whites. Was it true, as the Black newspaper the *Washington Bee* asserted during the riots, that Black people in Washington had proven by their public behavior that they deserved to be treated as equals by the White population? Although never expressed publicly, Locke was a racial conservative about such issues and skeptical about whether the Black masses behaved in a consistently civilized manner and appreciated the finer things in life that he valued. Such ambivalences about Black people and the prospects of Black progress made it difficult for him to assume the leadership role he imagined for himself when he claimed that he had helped resolve the riot.

Like many of his peers in the aftermath of the riot, Locke retreated into the pursuit of culture—at Howard, at the Bethel Literary and Historical Society, and at the "at home" get-togethers of middle-class Black Washingtonians who lived in the northwest quadrant of this segregated city. The Lockes resided in its Black intellectual and cultural center: just across the street was the District Branch of the NAACP, the home of Shelby and Mrs. Davidson, who were close friends of W. E. B. Du Bois, and a host of other dignitaries in the NAACP. Nearby lived Roscoe Conkling and Mrs. Bruce, Georgia Douglas and Lincoln Johnson, Edmonia Taylor and Harriett Butcher, and a host of other influential Black Washingtonians. Within this world of fine homes, the Lockes carved out an insular social life. Unfortunately for Alain Locke, it was more his mother's world than his. He came to feel that the cultivated Black world of such places as Washington—and

Philadelphia—was suffocating after London, Paris, Berlin, and even Boston and New York.

It was a life William Stanley Braithwaite seemed to value from a distance even more than Locke. "How is Mrs. [Georgia Douglas] Johnson?" Braithwaite wrote to Locke on the last day of the riots. "Her last letter I've not had a chance to answer. And Harriett—how is she? I saw some star dust scattered at the N.A.A.C.P. meeting here in April—and twas she [in] fact—star dust!"[15] Here Braithwaite expresses a joy in the women of Washington that Locke could never muster, perhaps because of his sexual orientation and his feeling that he never fit into that society. Braithwaite seems to have understood, though, that Locke needed to get away from that world. "Emma and I have discussed the possibility of you and your mother coming up here in August to visit us. We've got a pleasant and roomy... for both [of you] to come and enjoy. There's a deal of things I want to talk over with you too: you must get into writing."[16]

Braithwaite sensed Locke was drifting intellectually. Thirty months had elapsed since his last serious literary effort was published: the *Poetry Review* article on Verhaeren. Braithwaite also sensed that such unproductiveness derived from his filial loyalty. "Come up with your mother and we'll talk about the many things I haven't time to write about just now." Then, Braithwaite teasingly mentioned "the anthology of prose and verse from colored authors [James Weldon] Johnson's been after me for over a year to join him in making. I half way promised. But there are infinitely better things to do. Come and I'll tell you."[17] Finally, "Locke bring your mother up here!" It is not clear what was really stifling Locke—his mother, the riots, the Washington social world, the lack of a sexual outlet or lover, or his own reticence about becoming a public intellectual. But what is clear is that others, Braithwaite and James Weldon Johnson, were beginning to chronicle Locke's natural subject—the new developments in African American poetry.

Unlike Braithwaite and Johnson, of course, Locke had recently completed a PhD dissertation, set up the SATC camp, and returned to full-time teaching. He would not have been remiss in wanting to give public criticism a rest. Moreover, in 1919, with his PhD in hand and the war over, it was time for him to consolidate his position in the university. That process began that fall of 1919 at a time of great optimism at Howard. A new president, J. Stanley Durkee, had started what promised to be a progressive reorganization of the university system. He did away with the old College of Arts and Sciences, substituted a more humanities-based School of Liberal Studies, and replaced Dean Kelly Miller with the Harvard-trained PhD historian Carter G. Woodson, who had already pioneered his Association for the Study of Negro Life and History and his *Journal of Negro History*. Locke's new degree, therefore, put him in step with the increased emphasis on professionalism at the school. Accordingly, that fall, he became an assistant professor of philosophy in the new School of Liberal Arts and was freed of teaching such courses as English Speech and Usage in the Teachers College. He could offer a comprehensive program of courses in philosophy: Ancient and Medieval Philosophy, Modern Philosophy, Logic, Present Philosophical Tendencies (with special focus on the work of his mentors, William James, Josiah Royce, and Henri Bergson), two courses in Aesthetics, and most important, Social Philosophy. The last was an "advanced course in theories of society and social culture, with special consideration of the racial interpretation of history, and the role of races and nations as types of social culture"—essentially the sociological "survey of race contacts and interracial relations" that he had wanted to teach at Howard University since 1914. Though Locke must have felt some regret that his ally, Kelly Miller, had been demoted to the deanship of the less significant Junior College, he must have read the reorganization and the approval of his sociological course on race as signs that the administration was willing to adopt Locke's recommendation that Howard become the center for African American research and scholarship in America. More significant, Locke's undergraduate program in philosophy was the only one in the nation to make sociological theory an integral part of its curriculum.

Although Locke was glad to have solidified things at Howard, his heart was not in it. In a letter written in 1923 to Langston Hughes, Locke characterized Howard as "a cultural backwater, even though at the nation's capital." Locke longed to be the center of a "literary and art coterie," but believed that "it cannot be here. And yet—I have always been attracted to Howard and in spite of much disillusionment am still intrigued with its possibilities."[18] Something of Locke's paralyzing equivocation, the back and forth of being alienated from and yet "intrigued with" Howard's "possibilities," is revealed here. Despite his involvement in broader faculty issues—he resumed his role as secretary of the faculty in 1919—Locke did not form relationships with any of the new professors appointed to Howard. He was only distantly connected with Woodson, despite Locke's respect for Woodson's *Journal of Negro History* and his program of African American historical research. He was not especially close to Benjamin Brawley, who arrived as a rising star in English literature. The relationships Locke sustained at Howard—with Ernest Just in biology, with Kelly Miller in sociology, and with Montgomery Gregory in drama—all derived from before he had returned to Harvard. Despite all the good things that were occurring at Howard, Locke remained an aloof and distant figure.

The one important exception was Locke's relationship with Montgomery Gregory and the Howard Players that they helped to launch in the early 1920s. Both Locke and Gregory had been faculty supporters of what was called the "Howard University Dramatic Club" until 1921. But under the direction of department chairman Professor G. David Houston, the "Dramatic Club" had produced mainly light popular drama and comedy, written by White playwrights, and put on for an entertainment-minded Black public at the Howard Theatre, located just below the campus at 7th and T Streets. This type of dramatic entertainment fulfilled Howard's obligation to generate bourgeois diversion for Black people. Montgomery Gregory rose to become chairman of the Drama Department and gave it a more modern and racially self-conscious raison d'être. Gregory remodeled the department along the lines of George Pierce Baker's Harvard Dramatic Workshop to be a laboratory to train a generation of actors, playwrights, and set designers who would pioneer a realist drama of the American people. Gregory was a cultural pluralist, who believed Black talent and the Black experience had something distinctive to contribute to the American Drama; and he believed that that contribution was best nurtured in a Negro theater that drew upon plays by Black and White playwrights to portray the Black experience. The key was to produce plays that focused on the life of Black people, or developed the artistic possibilities of the Black theme, without succumbing to a purely propagandist attack on White racism. Hence, after assembling a talented staff of local director Marie Moore Forrest, Provincetown Players set designer Cleon Throckmorton, Howard University student artist and costume designer Alma Thomas, and Alain Locke, as head of dramatic composition, Gregory created the Howard Players to disseminate this Negro drama to a wider audience.

Locke's official role in this movement was conceivably the most important—the training of a generation of Black playwrights. He tried to foster that first by teaching Dramatic Composition in the English Department, a course he continued to teach even after he became chair of the Philosophy Department. But Locke and Gregory also explored new ways to generate enthusiasm for playwriting. In the spring of 1920, they announced "a contest for the writing of original One-Act Plays" by students "in the Junior and Senior Colleges." Suggestions could be "had from Professors Locke, Johnson, and Gregory" for suitable topics for the plays, and the winning play would bring $25 to its author. Locke may very well have been the originator of the writing contest idea and may have suggested it to Charles S. Johnson, who later used it to stimulate the writing of poetry and short fiction at *Opportunity* magazine. Eventually, such efforts would yield results. On January 17, 1922, the Howard Players put on "As Strong as the Hills," a collaboration between a Dunbar High School student, who wrote the story, and a Howard student, who did the dramatization; and in 1923, the first play written by a Howard University student was performed by the Howard Players. In the coming years, the Players would perform "Genifrede" by Helen I. Webb, of the Class of 1923, and "The Yellow Tree," by DeReath Irene Busey, of the Class of 1918. But Howard students did not write most of the plays performed by the Howard Players in the 1920s. White playwrights, especially Ridgely Torrence and Eugene O'Neill, or Black professional playwrights, such as Willis Richardson, wrote them. In one sense, the fault may have been partially Locke's. Although he knew a good deal about poetry and fiction, he was not the best person to teach dramatic composition. On the other hand, Howard did not attract the kind of talent needed to produce a new generation of Black play-wrights, and this lack of talent would be a continuing problem for the Negro Theater throughout the 1920s.

The production that garnered the greatest attention for the Howard Players was its 1921 production of Eugene O'Neill's *Emperor Jones*, a play written by a White playwright, but distinguished by the performance of a Black actor, Charles Gilpin. Indeed, Black talent seemed to be more plentiful on the acting side and the success of *Emperor Jones* testified to it. Gilpin's origination of the title role of the demonic, frightening, yet tormented Pullman porter Brutus did as much to launch the fame of O'Neill in New York as O'Neill's script launched the new Negro drama when the Provincetown Players production opened in November 1920. The *New York Times* noted that the play "weaves a most potent spell, thanks partly to the force and cunning of its author, thanks partly to the admi-rable playing of Charles S. Gilpin in a title role so predominant that the play is little more than a dramatic monologue. His is an uncommonly powerful and imaginative performance, in several respects unsurpassed this season in New York. Mr. Gilpin is a negro."[19] While generally praising Gilpin, some Black re-viewers of the play criticized O'Neill's play for choosing as its central character an African American criminal who was "the lowest and most degraded character one would wish to meet." In fact, the play was more of an American fantasy than a portrait of African American reality, a play that fused in one character all of the complex fears and infatuations with Black power that many in White America believed lurked just beneath the veneer of civilization in most Black men. Gilpin, by playing the role hugely and histrionically, but also with a brooding introspec-tion, transformed what could have been a caricature into an existential medita-tion on the problem of evil in the West. When Gregory and Locke heard about the play, they secured free tickets to the Provincetown production through Cleon Throckmorton. Awed and astounded by Gilpin's performance, they approached Gilpin after the show and gained his approval to perform the title role with a cast of the Howard Players in Washington. Gilpin was enthusiastic about the pros-pect, because of the chance to perform the play with an all-Negro company and the opportunity to add to his meager Provincetown Players salary. Once Gregory secured permission from O'Neill to perform the play after it closed in New York, Gregory enlisted Throckmorton to reproduce the splendor of the Harlem stage in Washington's downtown Belasco Theater. When Gilpin finally performed the role on March 28, the Howard Players had their first hit.

Not only were press reviews favorable, but one of African America's toughest critics enjoyed the Washington performance as well. On April 4, W. E. B. Du Bois wrote to Locke and Gregory his opinion that "the work was exceedingly well done and most promising for the future."[20] The magisterial editor of the *Crisis*, who would sharply critique White interest in the Negro theme later in the 1920s, evidently approved of O'Neill's play and the Howard Players' performance. Such acknowledgment confirmed the significant progress that the Dramatic Department had made in the year or so that Gregory had been in charge. But Du Bois also acknowledged something else. "I have asked Mr. Locke," he continued, "to kindly prepare an article for THE CRISIS, which I trust he will."[21]

Du Bois's request provided an opportunity to give national attention to the Howard Players and the drama program at Howard University. In asking Locke to do it, and not Gregory, Du Bois suggested that Locke was the more important person to chronicle the new effort. Locke had something that Gregory lacked: he had fame, because of his Rhodes Scholarship, an achievement that had made him a household name to African American intellectuals. Du Bois, as an elitist, tended to recognize only those like him who had distinguished themselves at the highest levels of achievement. Locke had a PhD, while Gregory only had a BA, though from Harvard. This request may have stimulated Gregory to write his own article, since seven months later, Gregory published "For a Negro Theatre," in the *New Republic*, an even bigger national magazine than the *Crisis*. By contrast, Locke's article would not appear until December 1922.

The slight to Gregory did not seem to affect their relationship. He and Locke collaborated again later that year to produce Ridgley Torrence's play, "Simon, the Cyrenian," which opened at Rankin Chapel on campus on December 12, 1921. This play, another by a White playwright, was the story of the African who, according to the Bible, took up "the cross that he might bear it after Jesus." Throckmorton transformed the staid Rankin Chapel into a Middle Eastern bazaar, and Howard University students acted all of the parts. Coordinated to open at the same time as the Arms Limitation Conference being held in Washington, the Rankin Chapel not only introduced the delegates to Howard University but also to Black culture through a musical program that included spirituals sung by the Howard Glee Club. This followed the tradition of literary and historical society meetings; but by focusing on the spirituals, the program was intended to convey a fuller interpretation of the "musical development of the Negro." In language that seems rather Lockean, the program notes informed the uninitiated that "Roll, Jordan Roll, Swing Low and Steal Away are spirituals of the pure folk-song type. Go Down Moses and Deep River are arrangements by the distinguished contemporary composer of the race, Harry T. Burleigh. The Juba Dance is a composition on a Negro folk-dance motive, by Nathaniel Dett, the Musical Director at Hampton Institute and a leading representative of the younger musical school." Locke may also have been responsible for including a selection from his favorite, the "Anglo-African composer, Samuel Coleridge-Taylor, the most representative of our composers, [who] is reprented [sic] by his Scenes from an Imaginary Ballet."[22]

The year 1921 ended with as much of a dramatic success for the Howard Players as it had begun, largely due to the collaboration of Locke and Gregory. Gregory was the man out front, managing the department and the Players, securing Howard University administrative support, and creating an advisory board of Eugene O'Neill, Percy Mackaye, Heywood Broun, and other authorities in the American drama for the Players. Locke was the behind-the-scenes coordinator, who performed the less glamorous duties of working with actors, designers, and costumers to make such productions a success. Locke's name was often mentioned in the correspondence that Gregory received during this period, as visitors to performances praised the Howard Players. But Locke's involvement also suggests what was the distinctive characteristic of Locke's role in Black cultural affairs in the early 1920s—he seemed most comfortable when he functioned backstage to more powerful personalities.

Locke may have felt on the margins of the Howard Players' success, because its playwriting campaign, his primary responsibility, was not very successful. The lack of plays by Black playwrights would become increasingly problematic for the Howard Players. For example, when Gregory sought to perform Ridgeley Torrence's "Simon, the Cyrenian," he was told that the Howard Players ought to perform plays by Black playwrights instead. Even Ridgley Torrence declined Gregory's offer to put on the play. He would not commit to paper the reason for his reluctance, only stating that he would confide in Gregory when they met. But the implication was clear that Torrence may not have wanted to produce the play again, perhaps because of the possibility of Black criticism. The time was rapidly approaching when the claim of the Negro Theater movement to self-conscious recognition in the American Drama movement would depend on generating a corps of accomplished Black playwrights, and they were not to be found at Howard.

The best Negro writing talent of the early 1920s was in poetry, not drama. In New York, the Jamaican-born Claude McKay was holding forth at the *Liberator* where, as literary editor, he was well positioned to publish young Black poets. With two volumes of dialect poetry published in his native Jamaica, with several poems in Locke's favorite Lost Generation magazine, *Seven Arts*, and with a book of poetry, *Spring in New Hampshire*, McKay was, in the opinion of William Stanley Braithwaite, African America's most accomplished living poet. Yet, it was a Washington, D.C., poet who was the most important to Locke in this period: his family friend, the tall, sinewy, "New Woman" poet, Georgia Douglas Johnson. An intense, light-skinned, bohemian wife of Washington's elderly recorder of deeds, Lincoln Johnson, Johnson was well known to the readers of the *Crisis*, which had published several of her poems in the late 1910s. Her first book of poems, *The Heart of a Woman* (1918), explored the woman as mother and culture bearer and suggested that through such roles, women achieved a spiritual power that transcended that of men. Johnson then struck out in a new direction to focus more specifically and intensely on racial themes in her work. Interestingly, that is when she turned to Locke and asked him if he would "go over some manuscript with me in a critical way."[23] That she turned to Locke at this juncture in her career is significant. While Braithwaite was unquestionably the premier

African American critic of poetry writing in the early 1920s, Locke was younger and more encouraging of Black writers to develop the racial theme in their work. Along with Gregory, again, Locke had started the *Stylus*, a literary magazine at Howard, to publish the writings of students and encourage them to explore race aesthetically as a doorway to a unique universalism in modern spiritual life. Such a dialectical view of art was consistent with the position Locke had maintained on Emile Verhaeren and contributions to the symbolist movement. Also, like Verhaeren, Johnson's poetry was not "ultramodernist," and that also endeared it to Locke. Rather, hers was a deeply mystical search for spiritual fulfillment for the alienated, modern woman.

Shortly after asking Locke for his critical help, Johnson dropped off some of her newest poems to Locke at his home, a practice she continued over the next two years. A dutiful editor, Locke spent several hours making deletions and suggestions, emendations and additions, as he provided sympathetic criticism. These poems would eventually become Georgia Douglas Johnson's second book, *Bronze*, which appeared in 1922. Originally, Johnson asked Locke to write the foreword; but then, perhaps in a move designed to give her work greater credibility, she enlisted W. E. B. Du Bois to write it. That she and Du Bois were romantically involved may have also shaped her decision. She may have regretted the change: in his generally appreciative foreword, Du Bois could not refrain from stating that some of Johnson's words "were simple, some trite." For Locke, the switch was another reminder of his second-class status whenever Du Bois was available. But Johnson's debt to Locke was considerable, and she acknowledged it by thanking "Professor Alain Leroy Locke, of Howard University" on the first page of the book, "for helpful criticism."[24]

Earlier, on August 20, 1920, Locke had received a different kind of invitation: Georgia Douglas Johnson was having some friends over to her bayfront brick Victorian home at 1461 S Street in northwest Washington that next Saturday, and she wanted Locke to join them. "Please bring your mother. Say to her that [I] hope that she will be with us." The extra special encouragement was needed, Georgia probably surmised, because this Saturday evening would not be the typical Black bourgeoisie "at home" to which Locke and his mother were regularly invited. This was to be a literary evening, perhaps the first meeting of what would become the regular "Saturday nighter"—get-togethers of Johnson's Washington Salon for writers, artists, and Black intellectuals who were in town. The star attraction of this Saturday evening was to be none other than Jean Toomer, who was just back from New York where he had been exposed to the readings, artwork, and bohemian pursuits of literary New York. "Mr. Toomer," Johnson continued in her invitation to Locke, "wishes to show us his books also. He says that he has some very good finds."[25]

Of course, Toomer himself was as much on exhibit as his books. Born Nathan Pinchback Toomer in 1894, Black Washington's thin, frail, sallow-colored poet was a precocious, intense, and mesmerizing young intellectual who was tortured by his ambiguous racial heritage. Toomer was the maternal grandson of P. B. S. Pinchback, the only African American governor during Reconstruction and a man who chose to live as an African American (he was the son of a slaveholder and a mulatto slave) though he was phenotypically White. Toomer would find that choice more difficult to make. Passing for White gained him acceptance to several midwestern colleges, but Toomer never completed a course of study and drifted until 1918, when he began a period of intensive reading and writing that culminated in his first short story, "Bruno and Paul" (an interracial romance), and a nervous breakdown. When Toomer recovered, he changed his name to Jean, rejecting both his father's and his grandfather's names for one he chose for himself, a sign not only of his independence, but also his new resolve to become a writer. When Toomer returned to Washington, D.C., in 1919, he began to explore his African American heritage and that apparently led him to Alain Locke. In November, Toomer wrote Locke asking, "Will it be convenient for me to come around this Thursday, Nov. 13?"[26] Several other letters followed, all arranging for meetings during which Toomer could discuss his emerging ideas with Locke. Toomer seemed to find in Locke an alternative to the conservative, Black Victorian father figures that dominated social and intellectual life in Black Washington, perhaps because Locke was already beginning to be known as a sympathetic uncle to a younger generation of writers and artists.

Unlike McKay, whose poem "If We Must Die" had captured the feeling of militant protest of the 1910s, Toomer's poems and short stories launched a romantic search for the self through a meditative engagement with the African American experience. Toomer wrote in a dreamy, impressionistic style that seemed to capture what it felt like to experience life aesthetically. Unlike some in the Black literary establishment who disparaged his work—McKay refused Toomer's poems for the *Liberator* criticizing them for lacking of focus—Locke was one of the first to take Toomer's work seriously, in part, because Locke's own literary work, especially his short stories written at Harvard and Oxford, manifested a similar impressionism that exuded from Toomer's work. In the early 1920s, Toomer also was developing an aesthetic view of the African American folk experience in his writing that Locke was sympathetic to as well.

Johnson's letter of invitation to Locke noted that Toomer "has met some very delightful writers of New York and has improved immensely." Whether it was his writing or his personality that Johnson is referring to remains unclear, but Toomer seems to have become more sophisticated socially as he became more convinced internally that his true identity was that of a writer. His quirks, such as his extreme excitement over obscure philosophical ideas, would likely be overlooked in the group that Johnson had assembled at her home. Mary Burrill was slated to be there, the lesbian lover of Lucy Slove, the new dean of women at Howard University. Burrill's presence suggested the sexual and social liberalism of Johnson's gatherings: here was a community that accepted the diversity in Black bourgeois Washington. During the coming years, Johnson would sustain this oasis of tolerance for the outlaw spirits of the Negro Renaissance. And Locke, despite his Howard University credentials, was one of them. In a very real sense, he could feel comfortable for the first time in Washington when he was at her S Street Salon. He knew that at least there he was not the only one who was queer. In that sense, Johnson's home became one of the few sites of community for Locke in Washington, D.C. It was not his mother's Washington, but his own.

PART II

ENTER THE NEW NEGRO

17

Rebirth

We do not know when Mary Locke began to decline. We do not even know what illnesses plagued her in her later years. But it is clear that as the 1920s dawned, Mary Locke was considerably less robust than she had been in the 1910s. We know that because of a remarkable photograph of Mrs. Locke, taken presumably sometime in the early 1920s, of her sitting peacefully in the second-floor apartment on R Street. Mary Locke is seated leaning on a Victorian parlor table with a slender vase next to her, looking into the camera with her soft eyes (see page 4). She is dressed in a beautiful embroidered shirt, her hair nicely uplifted back from her face, and she greets the camera with a controlled, but almost sad smile. She looks the part of the refined, contented, and dignified mother. She also looks considerably thinner and less vigorous than in the photographs of her during the 1913 trip to Bermuda. Now, she appears a bit frail, almost tired. Mary Locke had entered the last season of her life.

Locke responded to his mother's decline in health in a variety of ways. For one, Locke stopped going to Europe in the early 1920s. He surmised that she could no longer stand the strain of a transatlantic crossing and the heavy walking required of European sightseeing. Instead, he found stateside resorts where they could vacation during the summers. He told one correspondent, "Mother and I have been in for repairs at Saratoga, at the summer resorts."[1] Although Locke did have a weak heart from his childhood bout with rheumatic fever, and suffered from gout and other common ailments from time to time, he was nonetheless a healthy individual. By exaggerating, if only so slightly, his own medical needs as his mother's health declined, Locke preserved a bond with his mother that her advancing age threatened to sever. Locke had always identified with her—"took after her," in the words of Metz T. P. Lochard, a Chicago *Defender* editor and close family friend—and that identification extended into her infirmity. In the early 1920s, illness bound them together just as wanderlust and sightseeing had linked them in the years he was abroad.

As Mary's health declined in 1921, they were more cautious in the invitations they accepted with the upswing in their popularity as a couple at homes in Black Washington and with increasing demand for Locke's assistance to Washington's

writers as a private critic. Mary needed more time to get dressed and greater recovery time from even the least stressful outing. In those downtimes when
Locke was not teaching or providing her care, he ventured out to see his literary
friends. After Georgia Douglas Johnson, Jean Toomer was becoming a closer
friend. Entering an almost manic phase of writing in the early 1920s, Toomer
wrote Locke frequently about his literary pursuits and often dropped by Locke's
apartment. Toomer was struggling to carve out a literary career for himself at a
time when he was under considerable pressure from his father to choose a professional career such as teaching, medicine, or law. He seemed drawn to Locke as
a sympathetic ally in the struggle to make a career as a writer and avoid the psychological death of sinking into a comfortably bourgeois professional career.
Something in Locke's council encouraged this rebellion, just as he himself had
resisted as long as possible becoming a "professor." Toomer dreamed of becoming the center of a literary salon and tried to enlist Locke in that effort. At his
home at 1341 U Street, "I have managed to hold," Toomer wrote Locke on
January 26, 1921, "two meetings of a group (Mary Burrill, Georgia Douglas
Johnson, Miss Scott (of Howard), Mary Craft, E.C. Williams, Henry Kennedy,
and myself) whose central purpose is an historical study of slavery and the
Negro, emphasizing the great economic and cultural forces which have largely
determined them."[2] The knitting together of the study of the material conditions
of Black life with the "cultural forces" that "determined them" might be reminiscent of Locke's consuming interest in his Race Contacts lectures, transcripts of
which lay dormant in Locke's drawer at 1326 R Street.

But Toomer's reading group actually reflected his consuming search to define
his racial identity and explore "the actual place and condition of the mixed blood
group in this country." He admitted, "The subjects may be a trifle elementary for
you, but now that we seem to be underway, I certainly would like to have you join
us . . . whenever the time will permit. And if she would enjoy it, bring Mrs. L by all
means."[3] When Toomer later referred to this aborted literary salon in his thinly
veiled autobiographical play, "Natalie Mann," the play's hero and Toomer's alter
ego, Nathan Merilh, claimed his salon failed because its society matrons would
not allow expressions of real emotion and creativity at the meetings. In real life,
Georgia Douglas Johnson and Mary Burrill, the actual salon's female participants, were anything but society matrons. Toomer's salon actually failed because he left Washington for a teaching job in Georgia and discovered that in the
South, "there is poetry here—and drama, but the atmosphere for one in my position is almost prohibiting." It also catalyzed his voice as a Black writer and led
him to produce in his novel *Cane* "something . . . that will surprise most people, if
not yourself," as he wrote Locke.[4]

Even had Toomer stayed put, Locke probably would not have joined a group
grounded in Toomer's obsession with his racial origins and not one Locke would
have subjected Mary Locke to. But Locke was probably flattered by Toomer's in-

vitation, which symbolized his growing stature in the Black literary world of Washington and in Toomer's life. From 1921 to 1922, Toomer let Locke read and criticize much of the poetry that he published in the *Little Review*, the *Double-Dealer*, and the *Broom*, which was some of the best African American poetry written at the time. It was good that such an emerging poetic talent valued his counsel. Locke was at the center of what could soon be called a literary movement, though not its publicly recognized leader.

As early as February 1922, Mary Locke's close friend, Helen Irvin, warned Locke that his mother did not seem well. "I have been exceedingly anxious about her, recently. You know how brave she always is and how nonchalant in speaking of her own condition, but I haven't at all liked recent little things that I could read between the lines of her letters."[5] Because these letters have not survived, we do not know whether Locke agreed with Irvin's observations or had already surmised that his mother was dying. On April 23, just two months later, Mary Locke passed.

Locke reacted well, at least initially. As his lover and friend William Crusor George wrote later, such self-control was a basic tenet of Locke's personal philosophy: one should take "otherwise 'bad news' in an unusual manner... [and] instead of being blue or sulky... [be] happy and lively."[6] Yet even Locke had to acknowledge that in his effort to deal with the shock of her loss, he had to indulge a few "idiosyncrasies," as he put it to Helen Irvin. His most public idiosyncrasy was inviting twelve of their closest friends to a wake in his house. Locke later claimed that he and his mother had discussed her death in detail and had agreed that a funeral and cemetery burial were unnecessary and that something simple and genuinely spiritual was more appropriate. That image was communicated to a friend of Helen Irvin, who had attended. "I had a really beautiful letter from Miss Hunt.... She spoke of the very sweet natural picture that your mother made lying there on the couch in her pretty grey dress with just a few blossoms here and there and none of the heavy scent that one usually associates with such occasions." Further, "I have always felt that Dr. Locke's influence over his students must be strengthened by his devotion to his mother and his tender care of her—and I am sure that this last scene will remain with them all their lives, to help them see life whole with death, a beautiful part of it."[7]

The wake appeared to some as an appropriate way to honor a great mother love. Another interpretation surfaced among some of his mother's peers. A fascination with the details of the setting persisted long after the event, which entered Black Victorian Washington's folklore through numerous retellings of the story, especially the rumor that Locke seemed to continue to speak to Mary Locke as if she were alive. It was as if they were just socializing "at home." What those who snickered or howled realized and then expressed, rather untactfully, was that there was something pathological in his love for his mother.

Almost as controversial as the wake was his decision to have Mary Locke cremated. Isabella Claphan, of the rooming house that was Mary Locke's last
Camden home, expressed the typical sentiment of the time: "was sorry that you
had your mother's body cremated."[8] Most Christians opposed cremation because such destruction was believed to eliminate the possibility of a resurrection
of the body. Some argued that the insistence on burial reflected the self-interest
of the clergy, who historically owned the burial grounds. It seems surprising
that a good Christian like Mary Locke would agree to this departure. Locke's
needs may have played a great part in this decision. Not only was cremation
cheaper but served Locke's emotional need to keep his mother close at hand.
Locke kept the urn that contained her ashes on the mantel of the fireplace.
It was powerful enough years later that Countee Cullen, a Black poet who stayed
over at their apartment one night while Locke was away, spent the night walking
the streets of Washington, rather than sleep in the apartment alone with
Mrs. Locke. In some ways, she had not left.

In other ways, it was brutally clear to Locke that she was gone. For most
people, of course, the death of one's mother is one of the most traumatic experiences of life. But for Locke the impact was heightened by the lack of a spouse or
a family to lean on in such a crisis. His mother's death highlighted how alone he
was as a single, gay, Black male in Washington, D.C. Locke did have a small circle
of friends, and it was one of these, Georgia Douglas Johnson, who came forward
and tried to fill the enormous psychological vacuum of his mother's death.

It would be several years before he would complete his grieving, and, in another sense, the gaping hole in his life would not be filled until he found another
mother figure. Meanwhile, he had to live with the recognition that he had lost
the one person who provided him with unqualified love and adoration. With her
departure, moreover, Locke sought an immediate substitute for some of the
affection he had lost. Suddenly, he was a little more desperate in his search for
friends and freed to pursue them more aggressively than ever before. No longer
would he have to rush back from events to make sure that she was all right.
No longer would he have to share the apartment with her and be limited in the
kinds of activities he could pursue with friends and lovers. Yet his newfound
freedom came at a considerable cost. Without his mother to help him maintain
his balance, his emotional life would become a series of highs and lows dominated by his interactions with friends and lovers. Having lost his symbiotic partner in life, the newly vulnerable Locke lacked the emotional pillar that had
enabled him to be aloof and uninvolved with even those he cared about. From
now on, Locke would need much more from those he called *Mon cher*, and when
they failed to deliver it, his rage at their disappointments could reach self-
destructive proportions.

A case in point was his relationship with William George, a young man of sixteen when Locke met him in 1920. Locke had asked William's older brother,

John George, whether he would work for Locke as a secretary during the summer, and when John was busy, William offered his services. Having already "completed three years in the business department at Dunbar High School," as his first letter to Locke announced, William believed he was well qualified for the job.[9] Locke took William up on his offer. But while satisfying the need for someone to type his letters, which Locke later described as the "pretext of serious work," Locke developed romantic feelings for William, which Locke apparently struggled to control even before Mary Locke's death. An undated letter written by George to Locke suggests that George seemed to appreciate the relationship as well. "Before I begin work," William wrote, "I must tell you how much I enjoyed my stay last night." William's visits to the apartment had already shifted from solely work sessions to "engagements," during which Locke introduced William to classical music, discussed the boy's future plans, and gave advice. As was the case in Locke's attachment to "the children" during his second year at Oxford, Locke's adult romantic attachments almost always exhibited a parental dimension. Emotions of a different character are revealed by Locke's handwritten note at the bottom of another of William's letters. "Tuesday—9,15—Two letter scene—took the love letter—Even came—ice cream walked out Mass Avenue with... [He] ran off for rehearsal. Wednesday—9,15 Walk—R St New Hampshire—sat in Sheridan arch—walked out Mass ave returned R St. Mother Courtship days—I am afraid those will never come. William Alain Home—first welcome kiss."[10] Locke's note suggests that he may have discussed this growing infatuation with his mother, and then lamented that the "courtship days" she enjoyed with his father Pliny would "never come" to him. Given that Locke was primarily attracted to late-teenage boys, it was certainly true that he would probably never have the kind of peer relationship of courtship that his parents had enjoyed. Mary Locke may have helped him keep some perspective on such attachments and advised him to manage such relationships so that they did not threaten his position as a Black professional in Washington.

On April 2, three weeks before Mary Locke's death, Locke and George ended their professional and friendly relationship—at least for a while. Some light is thrown on George's feelings by an undated letter he wrote after the breakup.

> Now that this matter is past and had been forgotten, I hate to refer to it. I felt that many nasty little remarks made by fellows whom I knew you had befriended and by fellows who knew nothing at all about you. I felt these remarks deeply because I knew they weren't true and the more I'd either refute or argue these statements the more the fellows would kid. I did not seem to mind so much as far as I was concerned for I didn't give a damn, but in the presence of a group of folks it was of course embarrassing. It hurt me to know how fellows you had helped and who seemed to be your friends could say such things knowing they

weren't true. I am sure this had some kind of psychological effect on me for I found coming to work a more and more difficult task even though I knew that the remarks were lies. You probably understand. I guess the climax came when we broke off.[11]

For his part, Locke may have come to feel that the relationship had reached a dead end: William's naiveté suggests that Locke had kept their relationship platonic and may have felt that it was no longer worth the effort.

Two weeks after Mary Locke's death, Locke resumed his relationship with George. He asked the eighteen-year-old to write a letter outlining his future plans and to include a copy of his academic record. William complied but confessed, "I am ashamed to show [the record] to you because I am afraid you will be disappointed." Locke also recommended they resume their prior connection, which William quickly accepted. "You[r] proposition appeals to me not only because I know that association with you means advancement mentally and in maturness [sic] but because I feel you are a true friend and seem interested in my advancement," although William also confessed that he could not see why Locke was so interested in him, given his modest intellectual and cultural attainments.[12] Their resolution to be friends again, however, collapsed on George's inability to keep their appointments. On May 17, George wrote and apologized for not showing up and gave as his excuse that on his way over he met up with "the 'gang' and they persuaded me to go to the Dunbar Theatre. I am not usually persuaded as I have a vary stubborn will." Perhaps he was subjected to peer pressure not to spend the evening with Dr. Locke. A week later, George, adopting a more defiant tone, asserted, "between being fagged out by this war weather and doing extra work for Mr. Lucas—I find little time—if any—[to] get around. I do not think I can possibly get around again until after the first when I shall be glad to offer my rotten services."[13]

Apparently that was not good enough. On or around May 28, Locke wrote the following letter to William's mother. "I regret to inform you that I have been compelled to address the following letter to your son William.

Dear Mr. George,

Very shortly after the discontinuance of our business and personal relations on April second, one might have expected of any gentleman the return of my apartment keys. I requested them ten days ago, and again yesterday: it is not a matter that you could likely have forgotten.

I am sorry to have to drop consideration and gentility in the few remaining dealings it is necessary for us to have. I consider it now to be my duty to inform your parents of my reasons for discontinuing employment and friendship. I shall expect you to sign a personal note for your indebtedness from April 2nd, advance payment in the sum of thirty-five dollars, to be paid on or before August 31st, and I shall adjust any further outstanding matters only through your parents as your representatives.

With best wishes for your future, in spite of the attitude your behaviour has made necessary, I remain, very truly yours.

I am myself partly to blame I suppose, in the over-sympathetic manner I have treated William, but I have regrettably found it impossible to continue without loss of self-respect on my part, and character damage on his. His chief fault has been utter irresponsibility. I have no desire to cause him chagrin or chastisement, but feel it my duty to hold myself to any account you may wish to have me make of the situation as it has arisen and exists between us. If you require none, then I shall merely request that you see that he discharges the obligations mentioned in my letter to him.[14]

This suddenly hostile change in attitude toward friends and lovers would become a Locke trademark in the 1920s—a vindictive rage that had been better managed while his mother was living. Now, there was no one with sufficient credibility in his life to make him hold back once someone violated one of his cardinal rules. Suddenly, as later friends would acknowledge, Locke, the ultimate friend of budding young talents, could turn into a monster. William's reply shows how devastated he was by Locke's blow. "Dear Dr. Locke, I am heart-broken—I've never felt so bad in all my life. It would not have been so bad if mother had not seen the letter but she did see it and is worried to such an extent that I'm sick. She, of course, thinks everything—that I have gotten in trouble or something like that. I've explained to her as best I could & hope this evening everything will be straightened out. I am sorry, so sorry, that I did keep the keys for such a length of time and could give you no excuse other than what I told you. I know how highly you value promptness & should have returned the keys." By retaining the keys, William compromised Locke's privacy and heightened his sense of vulnerability that William or his friends could walk right into his flat whenever he pleased. Such a degree of access was excruciating to Locke, but what Locke was really mad about was that William was not using the keys to come by and spend time with him, that he had made and broken several engagements, and that he had, in the final analysis, deserted him. William disappointed him at a time in his life when he desperately needed companionship. In that sense, Locke's letter was not completely honest about his reasons for being angry at William, and William was smart enough to point it out. "You[r] letter stated that 'working & friendly relations ceased to exist.' I did not know that friendly relations had ceased to exist for you gave me the distinct impression that we would at least be friends." They had continued to be friends, actually closer friends than Locke would have liked Mrs. George to know. But once George had shown himself to be unreliable—again—Locke turned on William. William acknowledged:

> I had noted your manner toward me and at once felt a great change & often wondered why you seemed so hostile. I did not know that by not giving the keys back what an ungentlemanly or ill-mannered thing I was doing.... I should have agreed the day I quit to settle the balance with you when I got work this summer. I can[']t go on,
>   Sincerely
>   Wm. C. George

> I often thought of calling to see you but your manner was so hostile & changed that I was perplexed. WCG[15]

What often surprised Locke's friends about the sudden eruption of hostility toward them was that it seemed so out of proportion to the transgressions that produced it. In truth, when his friends or lovers failed him in some minor obligation, it triggered a realization in Locke that they could never deliver the kind of unqualified regard he had received from his mother. William's error was that he had failed to dedicate himself to pleasing the older man who took such an unusual interest in him. On one level, it was simply a matter of sex: Locke wanted William, and yet had to be careful not to make his desires too explicit. Locke was angry that William did not understand and reacted similarly to those who were later physically intimate with him. Beyond sex, Locke wanted William to put the rest of his life on hold while he devoted himself to fulfilling Locke's needs. Though Locke knew on a common-sense level that such devotion was unlikely, if not impossible, for another adult—especially a young adult like William—he still stubbornly demanded it and became enraged when he realized he would not be getting it any time soon. Less naive young men also found Locke's hostility difficult to understand because the violations of Victorian propriety (the returning of keys, paying of minor debts, unwillingness to keep appointments) that triggered Locke's rage were minor compared to Locke's infinitely more serious transgressions of Victorian morality—the frankly sexual agenda he carried into many of these relationships with men. But for Locke, homosexuality carried with it no moral baggage whatsoever: for him, his main concern about sexuality was whether it contributed to or detracted from one's creativity. Sex was morally neutral to him. But he did recognize the power of conventions in sexual areas, and in subsequent letters to William that summer in which Locke apologized indirectly for his vindictive attack, he not only admitted that "I love you," but that his "greatest problem and concern is to keep it within the bounds of convention, and to make it function helpfully in your life."[16] Locke could not control the intensity of his feelings and find an acceptable outlet for them within the bounds of a conventional relationship.

Finally, Locke realized that their relationship had no real chance of success as a romantic, loving relationship, and, accepting that, he let William go. "My dear George, Please feel that I appreciate your motives and intuitions—but I quite understand the tragic impossibility as well. I have experienced this sort of thing before. Please let me help you with your school plans just to repay you for what you have already done for me—for even the hope of a few weeks has been a beautiful experience and will be a beautiful memory."[17] William did continue to drop by from time to time, and as Locke prepared for his summer trip to Europe, he and William agreed that the latter would continue to serve as an intermittent secretary, especially while Locke was abroad. That kind of relationship was still within the "bounds of convention," and he would have to be satisfied with it. He needed to get away for several reasons—not only to ameliorate the pain of his mother's death but also to distance himself from the pain of the impossible love that he could not enjoy in Washington, D.C.

Even before this explosion in his relationship with William, Locke had invited Dickerman to accompany him to Europe. Such companionship was now even more desirable, and it was one that was socially acceptable. Even Helen Irvin approved. Unfortunately, by the end of June, Dickerman informed him that he could not make the trip; Locke went ahead, obtained second-class tickets on the SS *Aquitania*, and sailed from New York Harbor on Independence Day.

Leaving America behind invigorated Locke's muse. From on board he mailed two poems to William George, "Mon Cher, You will find enclosed two manuscript poems. They both grew out of the one I spoke of. Please copy them very carefully. Double space on separate sheets and type at the bottom 'Submitted for publication in The Dial.' Mail to 'Editorial Rooms. The Dial, 152 West 13th St. New York City'—putting my return address, 1326 R Str both on the Manuscript and the envelope." Technically, the poems had been inspired by this new relationship, but it was only upon leaving America that Locke had been able to write them. "You may keep the manuscript copy as souvenirs of June 29th and 30th—if you wish. . . . Do you like them?"[18] Rather quickly after his mother's death, Locke's relationship with George had escalated, now encompassing secretary, romantic interest, confidant, and erstwhile muse. But it was the trip that was really helping Locke. "We have splendid weather—I am writing almost constantly—proof that it is Washington and not softening of the brain (as I had begun to fear.) . . ."

> To get back to the ship—most of us are just eating, drinking, dozing[.] There are several splendid musicians aboard—I used to write a great many letters from the café's abroad—where there is always good music—it made a difference in the letters—they weren't so prosy. You

may get one or two prose-poems of the sort—don't take them too seriously—if you don't understand or like them, put them aside—and I'll put them in my diary when I get back.... Sincerely your friend, Alain Locke.[19]

Sailing across the Atlantic released Locke from the double consciousness of being Black and being gay that constrained his creative life in Washington. While he flirted with William George in private, in public Locke had to fit his identity within the heterosexually defined reality of Black Washington. He had to be on guard constantly to cloak his sexual interests to avoid the social stigma of being a public homosexual. Of course, among certain persons, such as the boys with whom William hung around, Locke's sexual orientation was known. But in Black bourgeois Washington, it was ambiguous. To keep it that way, Locke had to sustain an identity that was consistent with a heterosexually defined and socially validated definition of male when participating in conventional social situations, either up at Howard or at others' homes.

Locke was living out a gay version of Du Bois's conception, popularized in *The Souls of Black Folk*, of "double-consciousness, this sense of always looking at one's self through the eyes of others, of measuring one's soul by the tape of a world that looks on in amused contempt and pity. One ever feels his two-ness... two souls, two thoughts, two unreconciled strivings; two warring ideals in one dark body, whose dogged strength alone keeps it from being torn asunder."[20] No wonder it was difficult for Locke to be creative in Washington, where his survival as a member of the Black bourgeoisie demanded he suppress his real feelings and wear the mask. Abroad no one cared whether he was gay or not, so he could drop the mask. Locke's life struggle would be to merge his "double self," as Du Bois put it, "into a better and truer self."[21] On this trip to Europe, Locke was able to achieve a little bit of that by giving poetic—still metaphoric, but nevertheless public—expression to his new love. Locke's elation was also related to questions of class. On board the *Aquitania*, Locke could live the life of the leisure class— eating gourmet food, drinking fine wine, enjoying the company of orchestra musicians—with an intimacy impossible in segregated Washington and he could believe himself to be just another member of the middle or upper class steaming his way to Europe on vacation.

Even so, Locke's mood was tempered by his loss of his mother, which he sensed peculiarly at sea. Thoughts of his own mortality and what would happen if he suddenly died crowded his mind. His feelings led him to pen his first will. "I Alain Locke, being of sound [mind] and mentally and legally competent to decide...name Helen Irvin Grossley...as my sole executor or in event of her death or incapacity Arthur W. Claphan of 579 Stevens St., Camden." The choice of Helen Irvin was not surprising: not only had she been his mother's closest friend, but in the month after the funeral, she had tried to comfort him in his

loss and suggest ways that he give up his apartment and store his effects—
including the urn of his mother's ashes—while he was away. While he did not give
up the apartment, he did store his most valuable items in a safety deposit box.
She had also wondered whether he would be willing to send her the letters he
had written his mother from Harvard and Oxford, so that she might edit them
for publication. Again, he had demurred, but something of her interest was
reflected in his decision, in the rest of the will, to give his "manuscripts, books,
and papers . . . and ornamental ware, pictures etc to Mrs. Helen B. Grossley."
He willed his "clothing and personal articles or such of them as he may desire
to [his] cousin, Ross Baker Hawkins," whom Locke shunned for the most part.
Finally, he gave $200 to a memorial to St. Mary's Chapel in the name of his
mother, "$500 for the publication of any manuscript or memorial volume and
the balance of the estate to be given to Howard University toward some worthy
object such as student aid, English or Drama prizes, or the scholarship fund as in
view of the amount available my executor may deem best." If some foundation
or scholarship were to be established, he wished it to "bear the memorial name
of my parents, Pliny Ishmael Locke and Mary Hawkins Locke rather than my
own, in honour of their great sacrifices for me. It is my idea that whatever memorial of mine beyond my life work in the institution there should be the donation of my pupils, whom I urge to give freely to their alma mater." Without a
family or children of his own to whom he could give his legacy, Howard University,
despite all of his criticism of it, and its students, surfaced at this moment as the
surrogate family to receive his patrimony.

For the moment, Locke was leaving all that behind as he slipped into
Southampton, spent a few days in London, and went to Paris, where he arrived
on Bastille Day. A lot had changed since he was last in Europe. He now had
money—after years of working at a fairly good job and saving as much as he
could. And with his mother dead and prying eyes of America far behind him,
Locke could now indulge without any obvious restraints. In a sense, he was
attempting to subsume his mother's loss in affection from other men. And he
could now pay for those sexual favors, unlike during his student days in Berlin.
Before leaving Washington, he had pestered Georgia Douglas Johnson for
Claude McKay's address in New York, because Locke knew, from some previous
meeting, that the Jamaican-born poet, who was bisexual, knew of a particularly
good gay brothel in Paris. Unfortunately for Locke, by the time that Johnson
obtained McKay's address, Locke had already sailed.

After stopping at his favorite hotel to bathe and change clothes, Locke bought
a ticket to the opera, ate a quick dinner at his favorite restaurant, *Duval*, and
made his way directly to the Champs-Élysées, the boulevard of promenading
gays in Paris. For the next five days, Locke would spend almost every evening at
the opera, dining at his excellent but inexpensive restaurant, and then cruising
the Champs-Élysées. The culmination of his sexual escapades in Paris would

come Saturday night, when he returned from the boulevards, changed the ribbon in his hat, and went to a "Homo Ball" at "Madeline till 12:15."[22] For the first time in a long time, Locke could relax in an environment where he was comfortable.

That sense of freedom and acceptance catalyzed his ability to produce his first essay of the Negro Renaissance. Following a brief visit to the World War battlefields just outside Paris, Locke returned to London for a week and worked on his essay on the theater for the *Crisis* that Du Bois had invited him to write in March 1921. Perhaps to gain inspiration, he took a day trip to Stratford-on-Avon to view Shakespeare's old Globe Theatre. In the shadow of that monument to English drama, Locke seemed to imagine that the Negro theater movement possessed a similar potential to be to African American life and culture what Shakespeare's drama had done for the English. European art and culture always had functioned in this double way for Locke—as a vantage point outside of American conditions from which to view African American creativity and as a model for what that creativity could become. Thinking of Black theater in the context of Shakespeare not only held up a superlative standard for Black playwrights to emulate, but symbolized that larger significance of the Negro drama for world history. As such, Shakespeare had made a universal contribution by expanding the pathos and comedy of Elizabethan life into a drama for all of humanity, which the Negro dramatist must always aspire to, even if he or she failed in the attempt. In embracing Shakespeare's model, Locke was drawing attention to Shakespeare's achievement—that of making English drama the standard for world drama and the English Renaissance the model for the coming Negro Renaissance.

"Steps Toward the Negro Theatre" was his most inspired piece of writing yet, one in which he found his critical voice and established his critical posture on Black literature for the 1920s. In this article, Locke fused together the two sides of his professional identity—that of the aesthete of his Emile Verhaeren essay and the race spokesperson of "Race Contacts." Locke went beyond Montgomery Gregory's frankly promotional piece for the *New Republic* by issuing a challenge to the actors, playwrights, and patrons of Negro drama and thereby establishing himself as the conscience of the Black aesthetic movement:

> Culturally we are abloom in a new field, but it is yet decidedly a question as to what we shall reap—a few flowers or a harvest. That depends upon how we cultivate this art of the drama in the next few years. We can have a Gilpin, as we have had an [Ira] Aldridge—and this time a few more—a spectacular bouquet of talent, fading eventually as all isolated talent must; or we can have a granary of art, stocked and stored for season after season. It is a question of interests, of preferences—are we reaping the present merely or sowing the future? For the one, the Negro actor will suffice; the other requires the Negro drama and the Negro theatre.[23]

Here was a demand that the race build something permanent in the history of the art.

Key to Locke's argument was the notion that just living off of the momentary success of Black actors in roles created by White playwrights and performed before predominantly White audiences was not enough. Black actors were handicapped by the commercial theater, which forced them to appear in blackface and in vaudevillian comedies if they wanted to make a living as an actor. "Our art in this field must not only be rescued from the chance opportunity and the haphazard growth of native talent, the stock must be cultivated beyond the demands and standards of the market-place, or must be safe somewhere from the exploitation and ruthlessness of the commercial theatre and in the protected housing of the art-theatre flower to the utmost perfection of the species."[24] Only a Negro theater endowed by such a major Black university as Howard University could provide the kind of hothouse an authentic Black drama needed to survive.

Why Locke relied so much on the flower metaphor in this essay on the theater remains a mystery. His choice may have been inspired by something as mundane as the fields of lilies he had seen growing out of the grave-filled battlefields he had visited. Or it may have been inspired by *The Flowering of New England*, a book on the American Renaissance of the 1800s written by his classmate, Van Wyck Brooks, and published that year. The flower metaphor worked better than the renaissance for Locke now because, in truth, what he imagined was more of a flowering than a rebirth. Flowers also highlighted the delicacy of what Locke proposed. Locke wanted a drama that was devoted to Beauty in a way not predominant in American theater. This new race drama had its strongest analogies in the university drama centers of White America and not in the thriving Black commercial theater circuit, which was still dominated by "stereotyped caricature and superficially representative but spiritually misrepresentative force . . . of the 'bootstrap-lifting kind,' from the pioneer advances of Williams, Cole, Cook, and Walker, to the latest achievements of 'Shuffle Along.'" In that world, "the dramatic side has usually sagged . . . below the art level"; what the Howard Players sought when they began collecting for a Negro theater was an alternative to the commercial Howard Theatre on its doorstep. There was the rub—the Black community was being asked to patronize and support an intellectual drama of little commercial appeal. Locke knew that such a demand was probably premature in 1922, but he wanted to raise the self-consciousness of his community as to why this was important to do.

Even more remarkable was Locke's willingness to expose how contested the movement was in establishing a non-propagandistic drama in the Black community. He recounted, for example, the struggle within the Washington branch of the NAACP, which broke apart over the issue of propaganda plays. "If ever the history of the Negro drama is written without the scene of a committee wrangle, with its rhetorical climaxes after midnight—the conservatives with their wraps on protesting the hour; the radicals, more hoarse with emotion than effort, alternately wheedling and threatening—it will not be well-written." As he went on to admit, "the movement has, of course, had its critics and detractors," most of whom merely suffered from shortsightedness. Ironically it was more difficult to get plays written and performed that focused on the Black theme than those that focused on so-called universal themes. And those plays that merely dramatized the race problem had more immediate support than those that explored the culture and community of Black people as it was lived. Locke left the distinct impression that the tradition of caricatured misrepresentation in the larger American commercial theater had left the Black intellectual community afraid lest any exploratory theater produce more grist for the mill of American racism.

In "Steps Towards a Negro Theatre," Locke seemed to have found the courage to voice the criticisms and concerns that had animated him and Gregory in 1916 when they left the NAACP Drama Committee. For example, even as important as were the achievements of the Howard University Dramatic Club since that time, Locke boldly suggested that Negroes could not achieve this transformative cultural flowering alone. Success would require more than simply the best effort of Blacks; Whites would also be involved, necessarily, in fostering the conditions for a viable Negro theater. "A movement of this kind and magnitude is, can be, the monopoly of no one group, no one institution, no paltry decade." Locke's essay was to sell the Black bourgeois community on the importance of a Negro theater as not a segregated theater, but a way into changing the whole basis and tenure of culture in America. By linking his argument to Shakespeare, Locke was trying to get the attention of the Black bourgeoisie who read the *Crisis* and who, as he suggested, were more comfortable attending plays by Shakespeare than patronizing plays on the Black experience in America. What he intended in the reference to Shakespeare was that the English people had become a great people because they nurtured, supported, and celebrated the work of their playwrights, and if Black people wanted to become great, they would have to do the same. Like the educational courses accompanying the summer Shakespeare festival, he called for the African American bourgeoisie to support the educational programming of the Howard University theater movement. Just as the Italian Renaissance needed a classical, Grecian model to inspire its creative modernity, so too a Black American Renaissance, taking place in the center of what was still a largely English culture, could not err in getting its inspiration from the greatest English playwright who had ever lived. Shakespeare and the English Renaissance represented the refined aesthete in Locke, the man of old-world values and conservative nationalism.

Why had it taken Locke so long to articulate his critique of Negro culture as well as its possibilities? Was it his desire to fit in to Washington as he came back from Howard? Or was he waiting for the demonstration of the success of the psychological drama in the Howard Players program that he and Gregory put together to assert that a non-didactic Negro drama could say something important without being embarrassing? Or was it that he had become too comfortable nestled with mother in northwest Washington to be fundamentally intellectually rebellious? One factor may have been that staying in the United States caring for his mother and building his brand at Howard University had cut him off from the cosmopolitan sampling of elite culture that was like food for Locke's muse. He saw Othello performed at the Shakespeare festival on August 5, and it symbolized for him what the Negro theater could accomplish. For Desdemona had seen through Othello's "visage" to the beauty of his mind and Shakespeare had done the same—seen through the prejudices of Elizabethan England to the mental genius of the Moor. Shakespeare's transcendence served as a metaphor for what Locke hoped the Negro theater would accomplish in America—express the Negro mind. Sure, Blacks had music; but Locke believed, somewhat unfairly, that Black music did not communicate the ideas that an intellectually rigorous Black culture needed under modernism. Locke had a point. Within the American context, musical genius was qualified, compartmentalized, and ultimately marginalized as a sign of Negro genius but also a devalued symbol of entertainment, frivolity, and nonsense since the days of Thomas Jefferson.

One other factor was pivotal—for six years Locke had suppressed the subversive side of his personality, the rake who loved checking out the new clubs in London that de Fonseka had spoken of years ago, visiting brothels in Paris, cruising Champs-Élysées, and diving into queer culture of Berlin. Finally, he was able to indulge that side of his personality and it catalyzed something in him. After two weeks in England punching out his obligatory article to the *Crisis*, Black America's quintessential Victorian monthly, Locke was ready to enjoy the pursuit of sex and raucous entertainment in the city he called "home." Arriving August 14 at Berlin's Banhof Station, Locke took the elevated to Unter den Linden, where he stopped in Thomas Cook and Sons to see if he had received any forwarded mail from such people as Helen Irvin, Georgia Douglas Johnson, and even William George. Berlin was far enough away from America that he could be truly anonymous, since almost nothing that he did there would get back to the United States. Berlin allowed him the opportunity to don his personality as the gentleman rake, who searched the Passage at the intersection of Unter den Linden and Freidrichstrasse for young men on the make. On his last visit Locke had had his mother along and though she "understood," he had not been as free to sample the Passage's offerings as he had been in his student days. With Germany's disastrous run of postwar inflation thousands were plunged into poverty, which stimulated prostitution. Americans like Locke had their pick of the trade.

Berlin during the 1920s was a street theater, where bars, cabarets, nudie nightclubs, and traditional theaters developed revues and vaudevillian entertainment to attract the paying tourist. Berlin became a showplace for the well-heeled visitor, whether European or American, as street barkers, pimps, male and female prostitutes, and every sort of entrepreneur vied with one another for the visitors' non-German money. Berlin possessed an urban energy and excitement that exceeded all other capitals. Increasingly in the rest of Germany, resentment grew against Weimar sexual permissiveness and cosmopolitan openness to foreigners and ultimately crystallized into rank-and-file German support for the increasingly violent right-wing nationalism that labeled the freewheeling lifestyle of Berlin, and especially its Jewish intellectuals, as threats to the "real" Germany. Just two months before Locke arrived, Germany's popular Jewish foreign minister, the millionaire industrialist Walter Ratheau, had been killed in his chauffeured automobile in broad daylight. Perhaps another part of postwar Berlin's attraction to Locke was this tension between its sexual and intellectual freedoms and its foreboding quality of violence and horror that eventually would sweep away such liberalisms.

Berlin also attracted Locke because of its modernist theater, which had blossomed after the war into a political critique of the generals and the bourgeoisie who had led Germany into that disastrous war. The abdication of the kaiser in November 1918 had precipitated a revolutionary period in Germany, during which Bavaria became communist and writer Ernst Toller became the head of the "Red Army," before social democratic forces overwhelmed Munich in 1919 and consigned Toller to prison. Afterward, many writers and artists continued to sympathize with the workers and soldiers who had dared to attempt to create a revolutionary Germany. The armed struggle revitalized the prewar Expressionist movement in art and the theater, within its postwar mission of opposing the nationalist forces that Toller and other artists believed were leading Germany into another catastrophe. Such playwrights wrote, and traditional and working-class theaters produced, a stream of plays that hammered away at the national leadership and German bourgeoisie for their complicity in the war and the counter-revolution, and yet articulated faith in the spiritual transformation they believed was still possible for the German people.

Locke saw some of these plays on his second night in Berlin. He visited Max Reinhardt's Grosses Schauspielhaus, Berlin's huge auditorium that sat more than five thousand people, and saw four plays by Expressionist and Dadaist playwrights. C. F. W. Behl's "*Sakrament der Erde*" (The Sacrament of the Earth) began with a soliloquy from Ernst Toller's "Requiem"—"They have killed him, The Man of Merciful Eyes, The Man of true heart"—and concluded with a long lament to those imprisoned and murdered. That evening Locke also saw a scene from Toller's unpublished drama, "Hinkemann," written during his imprisonment at the fortress of Niederschonenfeld. The scene presented at the Grosses Schauspielhaus in 1922 was a dialogue from the play in which Eugene Hinkemann, the invalid, who was castrated during the war, asks a member of the petite bourgeoisie what he should do now that the war is over and his faith in the "imperialist" conflict has been shaken. The man tries to reassure Hinkemann with realism: "Only peaceniks believe the ideas. Have no misgivings about the affair. People want blood! Blood!!"[25] Unfortunately, Hinkemann cannot make himself understand or truly believe that such war is really in the people's interest or what the people desire. When the complete play was performed in Dresden in 1923, it resulted in a political upheaval and a vociferous debate about the theater. Locke, therefore, got a preview of one of the Weimar period's most controversial plays, which showed the Berlin theater at its most self-critical. As Ludwig Marcuse's *"Der Kampf ums Theater,"* the last play performed that evening, attested, there was a war going on in the Berlin theater.

Perhaps the most disturbing offering of the evening was the third play, Walter Mehring's *"Die Schuld der Juden am Weltkrieg, der Revolution und den nivellieren-den Witterungsverhaltnissen"* (The Guilt of the Jews in the World War, the Revolution, and the Socialist Atmosphere). Mehring was a famous Dadaist, who published numerous magazines, staged "happenings," and produced plays designed to shock bourgeois audiences out of their complacent addiction to art as somehow above social conflict. Dadaists called for a frontal attack on the art establishment and the bourgeois sense of value that underlay it. They used collages, simultaneous recitations of poems, verbal fragments, and sound pictures to create art forms that fused the fragmented nature of the metropolis and the political movements of the day. Mehring's play symbolizes that such criticism of the bourgeoisie from the left could also coincide with the anti-Semitism of the right. Even Reinhardt, himself a Jew, could present a play in which the chimerical argument that Jews were responsible for Germany's loss in the World War could be articulated. This too was Berlin in the 1920s—a city whose modernism was laced with the racist belief, on the left and the right, that the Jews were to blame for Germany's postwar disintegration.

Locke's reaction to the temper of racism that echoed during his visit to Berlin was not recorded and can only be guessed at from later comments and his racial temperament. In the United States he tended to dismiss racial incidents as of little importance, exaggerated by the purported victims; thus, he may not have taken particular notice of foreign racism, especially since the targeted race was not his. Even though Locke had close Jewish friends and had compared anti-Semitism and American color prejudice, he may have ignored the racial undercurrents of postwar Berlin because of the personal freedom he enjoyed in that milieu. And in 1922, it was not yet clear how dominant right-wing anti-Semitism would become by the early 1930s. Locke's interest was not in the content of these plays—he hated didactic, overly politicized drama—but in their new and bold forms. Here was drama that was being fashioned out of the stuff of social conflict, and in its use of dialogue, background, and graphic sets, it set a standard for the agitprop political theater of the 1930s in America. Locke probably noted the racial discourse of the plays that he saw and then moved on.

There was much to move on to, and Locke seemed to take in a different theater every night. He probably attended Leopold Tessner's Staatliches Schauspielhaus, which presented classical plays from Sophocles to Shakespeare, but interpreted them in a modern idiom that made them speak to the urban milieu and consciousness of the 1920s. Tessner pared down the stage, the set, and the lighting and presented classical characters with a modern sleekness and severity that made them startling to watch. This theatrical style that privileged the projection of character over physical expression engaged Locke's taste. Locke wanted an African American modernist aesthetic that would engage on the deepest levels of interiority, the ability of the African American actor and performer to dig deeply into the soul of the race's experience and reveal something that was transcendent. What Locke found in the theater world of Berlin was a kinetic dramatic energy that raised the level of liveliness and seriousness about life. Yes, Berlin was full of contradiction; but those conflicts were heightened and wrestled with in public, not behind closed, closeted doors as in Washington, D.C. In Berlin he could feel himself come alive.

That sense of liveliness for Locke in Berlin surely came from the friends that he had there. From the moment he arrived, he met and interacted with such people as "Werner Land + seine Freund," "George Lange + Freundlag," and a host of others whose identities survive in such initials as "F.R.M." More than likely, one of them took him to the Grosses Schauspielhaus and introduced him to the latest in Berlin theater. It is very likely that such friends also took him to the latest cafes, such as the Romanische Cafe, where painters, writers, publishers, journalists, actors, and bohemian intellectuals gathered to smoke, drink coffee, and indulge in the most important pastime of postwar Berlin—talk. While it is doubtful that Locke gained access to the inner circle of such artists as George Grosz, Emil Orlik, and Max Slegot, or that of the writers Bertolt Brecht, Heinrich Mann, and Joseph Roth, who congregated regularly at the Romanische, it is likely that he was enough of a regular by the end of August that he could sit comfortably and engage in dialogue in such cafes. In such company Locke would have heard discussions about the visit that year of Sigmund Freud to attend a psychoanalytic congress in Berlin, and even franker discussions of sex in relation to Magnus Hirschfeld's recently established Institute for Sexual Science, which would become a center for research on homosexuality in Germany.

Locke gained from association with his Berliner friends the ideology of youth in Germany that was really a Weimar lifestyle. Stephen Spender has captured something of the spirit of such associations in his autobiography, which records his experiences first in Hamburg and then in Berlin during the 1920s.

> My host introduced me to his friends, who invited me to parties in their
> bed-sitting rooms and studios. We went swimming in the lake and for
> excursions in canoes. To these young Germans who had little money

and who spent what they had immediately, the life of the senses was a sunlit garden from which sin was excluded...their aims were simply to live from day to day, and to enjoy to the utmost everything that was free: sun, water, friendship, their bodies....Thousands of people went to the open-air swimming baths or lay down on the shores of the rivers and lakes, almost nude, and sometimes quite nude, and the boys who had turned the deepest mahogany walked amongst those people with paler skins, like kings among their courtiers. The sun healed their bodies of the years of war, and made them conscious of the quivering, fluttering life of blood and muscles covering their exhausted spirits like the pelt of an animal....I went to the bathing places, and I went to parties which ended at dawn with the young people lying in one another's arms. This life appeared to me innocuous, being led by people who seemed naked in body and soul.[26]

Locke, who as a young child had been chastised by his mother to stay out of the sun—"you're black enough already!"—"found a sense of physical release in this fraternity of German youth: he was, after all, already 'mahogany.'" Connected with this sunbathing, canoeing, and enjoyment of the outdoors was a belief in the restorative powers not only of nature, but of youth, of being "advanced" in one's thinking about gender and sexual orientation. There was an acceptance of one another as quintessentially "modern" and open to the reformation of relationships based on that modernity. Thus, while race was certainly present in the background, color was not an obstacle for Locke. This youth culture fostered a spirit, a verve, and an attitude toward progressive relationships that invigorated Locke and gave him hope.

Locke recorded the restorative effect of friendship in a poem that he wrote on September 1, 1922, while he was still in Germany.

Friend
Life gives dark hours,
takes away hope, joy, and desire to act (Lust),
[we] can give balm to the heart
to the wounded heart in the breast.
Pale and dim/sad looks the eye
[unintelligible] mouth
all hope lies in the dust
with love in the night and bottom
Only then does the anxious heart know
what the true friend was to him
what, when we enjoyed wine, pleasure and song,
he [got] what he always asked for.

Though incomplete and poorly expressed, Locke's poem suggests that his mother's passing robbed him of his "desire to act," which he seemed to regain in Germany in the company of his friends.

He also regained his sense of direction. Bonding with a youth culture was not simply an isolated, decadent social practice for Locke, but an embrace of the spirit of catharsis that undergirded the artistic revolution in Berlin. What Locke found there was an art movement inspired by the youth culture and its vision of modernity. "It was a renaissance," recalled Sol Hurok, a Jewish émigré from 1920s Berlin, as he looked back fondly on the period when Locke was in Berlin. "It was a renaissance...the greatest renaissance in this century? Now how would you translate that into words?"[27] Locke agreed. Although publicly more identified with the Harlem Renaissance, Locke was inspired by the German one that satisfied his intellectual sense of what a modern art movement should be, and his personal sense of what a youth movement should do to one's soul. In Berlin, he found dramatists who translated the classics into modern forms, and architects and designers, as in Bauhaus, who transformed interiors and exteriors with the crisp lines of the industrial age. The youth-driven attitudes of modern human relationships coalesced in Germany with a more critical, aesthetically demanding art and culture. The interpenetration of art and life in modern Germany bonded him to that country. It inspired in him the kind of intellectual and personal renaissance he needed to revive and reinvent himself. Now, he could return to America with a vision of what he wanted African American culture to become.

Before leaving Germany, however, Locke took the train first to Munich and then to the little village of Oberammergau to witness an ancient, vital tradition. There he attended an outdoor performance of the Passion Play held every ten years by village residents who had performed the play ever since the Middle Ages. At that time, the village had been decimated by the plague. As their numbers dwindled, the Oberammergau villagers had sought divine intervention by enacting the Passion Play of the death of Jesus. The plague subsided and, believing its cessation was an act of God, the villagers continued to perform the play every decade. Locke must have learned in Berlin that this play was due to be performed in 1922 and took the trip south to see it. It certainly completed his study of the theater that summer. The Oberammergau Players did not merely perform the play, but lived their assigned roles in the years between performances, often seeming to become the characters they played. This was the ultimate commitment for an actor. Locke could not miss it. Here again, Locke would have bracketed and screened out the racism of these performances that voiced ancient Christian hatred for the Jews as killers of Christ. For Locke, though, this performance symbolized the spiritual renewal that came from immersion in tradition, in this case the Christian tradition of his mother. In a sense, tradition had become, by now, a kind of mother to Locke. By honoring tradition, as he had his mother, he could reassure himself that he would never abandon his soul in the process of becoming a modern Alain Locke.

Locke's sojourn abroad also may have involved a detour. Shortly after the death of his mother, Locke heard from his distant friend Plenyono Gbe Wolo, whom he had met while at Harvard as a graduate student. Wolo was returning to Liberia with the financial support of an array of powerful White backers such as Harvard president Abbott Lowell and Thomas Jesse Jones of the Phelps Stokes Fund.[28] Wolo started a school in his village, ostensibly to train a new generation of Liberian youth to follow in his footsteps of Christian faith and Anglo-American education, but really to utilize his education and critical assessment of Western colonialism to bring about an independent development for native Africans in Africa. Apparently, Wolo wanted Locke to join him in Liberia in this work of educating his people but also turning the Firestone rubber interest in Liberian raw materials for the production of tires into something economically sustainable for native Liberians. Here was a different kind of transnationalism for Locke from that of Berlin, the possibility of an economic partnership through a triangle of Howard University, Berlin, and Grand Cess, Liberia, to foster an independent African economic power base. Wolo was also a young man who combined aggressive national self-promotion with personal sensitivity.

Perhaps bonding with Africa and perhaps visiting with Wolo was also part of Locke's healing process. Locke's passport contains an entry for Liberia— perhaps a suggestion he may have traveled to Africa during his mourning in Europe. Even the idea of Africa brought a recurring tease—an empire of his own through which he might, with African intellectuals like Wolo, who later worked for the Firestone Company, find an economic basis for the Black renaissance. A triangle of Howard education, African brotherhood, and Europe modernism was in his thoughts as he returned home early in 1923.

Locke's time abroad in the aftermath of his mother's death gave him a more complex notion of a renaissance of African American aesthetics than other Black thinkers in the United States. In the Germany of the 1920s, *volk* culture was the backdrop of a modernism just as a rich tribal tradition was the backdrop of Wolo's attempt to forge a new, progressive African educational system in Liberia. Homosexuality and the possibility of an adult, leadership role in the future of his people seemed to fuse in Locke after this trip. They no longer led in opposite directions as they often did while his mother was alive. Something had broken— not just his attachment to his mother, but also his attachment to a double consciousness that was self-defeating. He would forever afterward stare down those who wished to block his path to Black leadership because of his sexuality. He would let his vision do the talking for him. For now he had one.

18

Mother of a Movement,
Mothered in Return, 1922–1923

An August letter from Jean Toomer was waiting for Locke when he reached Washington that fall of 1922 and forecast his future role in African American affairs. "I liked your criticism," Toomer wrote. "The cocoon is both light and intense. Dickerman has not returned the Ms. but there is no hurry. Little Review has the original."[1] In addition to serious, sympathetic criticism of his poetry, Locke had provided Toomer a sense that he was important as an intellectual and a human being. That Toomer valued Locke's appreciativeness runs through almost all of his correspondence with Locke, but is expressed in a letter to Georgia Douglas Johnson in contrast to his treatment at the hands of Du Bois:

> Yesterday I called up Dr. Dubois. At first he didn't remember me, even after mentioning the fact that you and he had talked of me. In fact it wasn't until I chanced to mention my hike up here, that the light burst— or rather filtered through—it wasn't a very strong light—He ended up by saying that if I would send some of my stuff to the office he would be glad to look it over. Now I really had expected something more. Any editor would have said as much as that. Anyone with two ounces of curiosity (literary or otherwise) in his make up would rather like to look over new material. I had thought he wanted to get in touch with me, even possibly to know me. Does he expect to do so by looking at my writings? If I were mature he could expect to see the man in the writer. But of an immature youngster? Why no more than a chick can truly express himself within his skill. No, it will be some years before Jean Toomer the thinker, the feeler, the man in love with life in toto, passions, vices, sorrows, despairs—all of life, will be able to put half what is in him on the cool surface of a white sheet of paper. That is art. And as yet I am far from the finished artist.[2]

Toomer's letter reveals something important about the Negro Renaissance—it produced New Negroes, unique personalities, not just unique art. And it reveals something important about Locke: he was willing to nurture these precocious personalities, because he believed young talents needed their creative potential and spiritual qualities recognized in order to blossom. Toomer's letter reflected what some other young African American writers also felt, that Du Bois's infamous aloofness was particularly hurtful when directed at young writers who approached him.

W. E. B. Du Bois did have the pride of place as father of the new movement. Since he began publishing the *Crisis* in 1910, Du Bois had included poems, fiction, and artwork in each issue, a subtle statement of Black people's humanity and an effective outlet for Black creative writers and artists. Du Bois had even prophesized in 1920, "I think we have enough talent to start a renaissance." But instead of actively cultivating that movement, he turned that over to Jessie Fauset, now literary editor at the *Crisis* and his eventual lover, in order to spend his time chasing his ill-fated dream of the Pan African Congress. Du Bois's dismissiveness may have been Oedipal, since he may have viewed these rising young, male Black writers as eventual competitors.

Locke, on the other hand, was not even a minor published poet or novelist like Du Bois. Whatever the personal significance of his poems written during his sailing to Europe, the *Dial* informed him soon after he returned from Europe that it would not publish them. Unlike T. S. Eliot or Ezra Pound, Locke could not use his own creative output to steer modern Black literature in the direction he wished it to go. But Du Bois's coldness created an opening for Locke. By warm concern, willingness to talk, and ability to introduce writers to other writers—note that Locke had introduced Toomer to Dickerman, Locke's literary companion from Harvard—Locke became a literary mother, who opened his home and his intellect to young writers. Of course, Georgia Douglas Johnson had been doing this kind of thing for years. But after his mother's death, Locke was able to take on her role with them, because he believed that their personalities needed nurture as much as their writing needed criticism. The death of his mother encouraged him to become the mother of a generation.

As a philosopher, Locke was willing to tussle one-on-one over ideas, especially educational and philosophical questions Toomer was struggling with at the time. Toomer found that attractive. The following letter gives an inkling of the kind of dialogue between them.

> A propos of our talk last evening, M. H. Hedges in this weeks "Nation" in an article, "The Teachers Real Dilemma" takes our point in question, extends it to include the college student generally, and makes his statement, succinctly, "The undergraduate of American colleges has been pictured an enthusiast; the fact is, he's a stone." He supports this assertion by indicating the students absorption in the petty rituals of college

life while the grand gestures and convulsions of the social world are
passed by, unheeded.[3]

Toomer concludes the letter by observing that Hedges never answered the question they were concerned most with—why is the undergraduate a stone? Locke
and Toomer had been discussing why education in American colleges and universities was a failure—a subject dear to Toomer's heart after dropping out of
several colleges and close to Locke's concerns as he was becoming increasingly
frustrated with the students he was teaching at Howard. But while Locke framed
his frustrations in terms of teaching at a Black university, Toomer argued the
real cause was the triumph of economic and materialistic motives among the
modern bourgeoisie. For Toomer, the problem of Black middle-class students at
Howard was no different than that of White students at Columbia: all were being
dragged down by puritanism, on the one hand, and materialism, on the other.
When Toomer scandalized the Black bourgeoisie of Washington in his play
"Natalie Mann," written that fall, his target was not so much the race as the
sexual repression and superficiality of the Black middle class. They were destroying the soul of the Black community, and the roots of those destructive forces
were, for Toomer, deeper than race.

That fall, Locke delivered a critique of bourgeois notions of education and
culture in his Freshman Class address that may have been indebted to his conversations with Toomer. In the speech, later published as "The Ethics of Culture,"
Locke advanced the proposition that the purpose of education was not to secure
a job or wealth, but to cultivate a unique personality. Locke was updating
Matthew Arnold's argument in *Culture and Anarchy* in critiquing the middle
classes also for what Toomer found objectionable about that class—its materialism and self-indulgence. Modern Black students were no different than the
English middle classes—no longer expanding their souls in college, but graduating more dead than when they entered; an echo of Toomer's narrative. To be
educated, a student needed to reclaim the right to cultivation as an end in itself,
as the thing for which other things should be done. In refreshing the Aristotelian
notion that Beauty, Knowledge, and Justice should be pursued for their own
sake not as a means to some other end, Locke sought to return education to its
classical foundations.

But Locke also spiced up the lecture with the Toomer-like notion that such
educational enrichment required breaking with the puritanism and the rank materialism that dominated mainstream American higher education. Locke sought
to encourage Howard's students to break with the society that lived only in the
material present, and instead live boldly for their spiritual selves by cultivating
a self, borrowing from the self-indulgence of Walter Pater, that viewed Beauty,
Justice, and Truth as its highest personal goals. Education taught one those
things for which everything else was lived, and if it stopped short of that, it

shortchanged its students. Locke was emboldened by his conversations with Toomer to make a stronger critique of bourgeois notions of culture than he would have otherwise. While Locke would later view this period as one where he was "less of a professional philosopher, and more of philosophical midwife to a younger generation of Negro writers," his freshman lecture suggests that those like Toomer "midwifed" him as well to blend his classical notions of Culture with a searching criticality of contemporary education.

The midwife metaphor hailed from Locke's days in England living with de Fonseka, helping to bring into birth de Fonseka's book *On the Truth of Decorative Art*. Locke helped de Fonseka write the book by serving as a sounding board and interlocutor. But Locke had done relatively little mothering of de Fonseka himself: he was not a wounded soul like Toomer or others of the Black renaissance Locke would become especially close to. The truth of Locke's relationship with the writers of the early 1920s in the renaissance was something less and more than midwifing of the de Fonseka variety: he was not directly as influential in the writing of their books as the metaphor might suggest. Toomer, for example, produced his best writing when he abandoned the world Locke was comfortable in and tramped the sidewalks of Seventh and T Streets in Washington, D.C., where lower-class migrants from the South congregated; or when Toomer walked the dusty roads of rural Georgia among people Locke could never have associated with. While Locke could tinker at the edges of texts Toomer wrote, the new literacy of modernism and primitivism exuding from Toomer's *Cane*, for example, was not something Locke could "midwife," although he could appreciate its great Beauty. What Locke, and to a certain extent George Douglas Johnson, *had done* was perhaps more important for Toomer than textural criticism—they had supported him psychologically as he careened intellectually in Washington and sought to find his bearing as well as his literary voice. They gave him unqualified acceptance. That had allowed him to go South on his practicing phase of exploration, out of sight of these Black mothers, and like Odysseus bring its literacy back to bourgeois America in *Cane*, published in 1923. Locke could take credit for nurturing the complex subjectivity that created that art more than the art itself.

But Locke's mothering was also a failure. Soon after publishing *Cane* and leaving Washington in 1923, Toomer would surrender some of the complexity of his vision to the religious doctrines of George Ivanovich Gurdjieff and spend the next several years trying to convince Harlemites and others that Gurdjieff's philosophy was the way out of the dilemmas and contradictions of American racism. Toomer also made a public campaign of denying he was a Negro. This embarrassed Locke as well as others and signified Toomer was a lost soul whose wounds Black mothering could not heal. Thereafter, he abandoned the type of Black modernist voice he had found in *Cane*. What were the reasons? Might one have been too intimate a form of mothering from Locke? While no proof exists, an autobiographical fragment in Locke's Papers suggests that Toomer may have been one of the young men that the Socratic Locke admitted he could be accused of "spoiling." Was that spoiling sexual? It seems possible.

Another promising African American writer entered Locke's life precisely as Toomer was coming under other influences. A letter from Countee Cullen, the brilliant high-school student, poet, and vice president of his class, also greeted Locke upon his return from Europe. "Through a Mr. Cobb, a student at Amherst," Cullen announced in his first letter to Locke, "I have learned that you are our race's sole representative as a Rhodes scholar. As I am desirous of bending my efforts toward such an award, I am writing you in hopes that, aided by the advice of one who has gone that way, before, I may marshal my efforts in the most logical and effective manner. I am not known to you personally, but you may have heard of me in some small way through the press."[4] More than likely, Locke already knew the nineteen-year-old through Georgia Douglas Johnson, Jean Toomer, or Claude McKay. As the adopted son of Rev. Frederick A. Cullen, pastor of Salem Methodist Episcopal Church in Harlem, and a graduate of prestigious DeWitt Clinton High School in New York, Cullen had gained public attention when his poem "I Have a Rendezvous with Life" won a prize from the Federation of Women's Clubs in 1921.

Countee Cullen was an outstanding student, who in fall of 1922 had enrolled in New York University. That he was already contemplating applying for the Rhodes Scholarship shows something of his precocious self-confidence; indeed, that Cullen entertained applying for the scholarship confirmed Locke's belief that in winning the Rhodes, he had opened up this option for young Black men. But something more was operative as well in Cullen's desire to become acquainted with Locke. "I trust that I may be allowed to know more of you, for next to the attainment of a goal, is the pleasure of knowing those favored ones who have been fortunate enough to reach that goal."[5] Did Cullen already know of Locke's reputation as a closeted homosexual? But Locke's scribble on the back of this letter shows he read Cullen's letter as opening to a potential romantic relationship: "I saw thee in a multitude of things," Locke wrote, "and in my fowling net snared your soul." Evidently, something in Cullen's letter—its self-indulgent elegance, rotundity of phrase, or fawning coquettishness—signaled to Locke that Cullen might be gay and available.

That Locke reacted so aggressively to Cullen's introductory letter suggests a danger in Locke's approach to midwifery. The "fowling net" metaphor signified that Locke saw himself as a fisherman ready to snare unsuspecting prey. That posture would alienate some young writers, but Countee Cullen seemed to appreciate Locke's interest in him. When Locke invited him to spend an evening at his apartment, Cullen accepted and afterward wrote, "You cannot, I am sure, appreciate the value I place upon that visit. I hope it was, enjoyable as it was in itself, merely a prelude to a greater intimacy between you and me."[6] On one level, of course, Cullen simply wanted the support of a powerful literary ally. Cullen appreciated Locke's offer to send some of Cullen's verse around to other Black literary scions, such as William Stanley Braithwaite, though Cullen drew the line at "J. Weldon Johnson. I do not care to curry favors." Cullen also welcomed the opportunity to join a literary group Locke said he was forming. Cullen also wanted to know "Have you any influence with publishers?" Without the kind of support from White literati that Toomer enjoyed, Cullen needed Locke to help transform his dreams of literary success into a reality.

Cullen wanted something more. As a young gay African American struggling with his sexual orientation, Cullen also needed the kind of emotional and personal guidance that only Locke could provide. "Your letter was an excellent and effective stimulant for a rather depressed young man; please continue to imbue me with the delightful nonchalance of your philosophy of life," Cullen wrote on January 29.[7] "You can realize how delighted I was to hear from you by the promptness of my response. Your letters are such a source of pleasure and inspiration that I find myself wondering how great a delight it would be to have you here in the city to talk to me often," he continued on February 20. Cullen wanted someone to whom he could bare his soul about the frustration he was experiencing in his personal life. "Of course, a creator always has questions to bother him, questions of moral and social conduct—but half the time he keeps these questions locked in his breast. One never knows when a question will cause his dearest friend to eye him askance."[8] Could he be completely honest with Locke? Locke answered affirmatively, because such a deeply personal relationship with a younger artist was precisely what Locke wanted. In his reply, Locke admitted, "one's intimate confidences often seem foolish even to the best intentioned confidantes. I think I may assure you of but one standard of judgment,—and that is the law of a man's own temperament and personality. But one cannot often discover this, especially if there are convention-complexes except through <u>confessional self-analysis</u>." Locke encouraged Cullen to confide in him as part of a healing process that was essential to creativity. "If I were inventing a religion I would try to work out some beautifully ritualistic mode of reciprocal confession and make all the conception of punishment and reward psychological and self-inflicted."[9]

Locke wanted to reproduce the reciprocal confessional relationship he had with his mother with Cullen. Its goal was not religious in the traditional sense, but spiritual nonetheless, in unlocking the emotional resources for creative expression. Locke was not above using such advice and confidences to draw young writers into deeper emotional relationships than they anticipated. But with Cullen that was not a problem. Locke was getting something out of it too. By practicing a kind of confessional self-analysis with Cullen, Locke was getting back some of the benefits of the reciprocal relationship with his mother. And in promoting such confessions from Cullen, Locke believed the meditative self-revelations would also have a therapeutic role in Cullen's life.

Perhaps the first item on Locke's agenda with Cullen was to bring resolution
to the younger man's fitful dilemma about his sexuality. When Locke met with
Cullen in New York on February 24, he recommended that he read Edward
Carpenter's *Iolaus: An Anthology of Friendship*, an informal history of the idea of
male friendship in African, Greek, and modern societies. This awakened Cullen
to the knowledge of a tradition of male bonding that stretched across the centuries. Cullen "read it throughout one sitting" and was elated that so many had felt
the way that he did; but then he despaired when the realization settled in of how
difficult such relationships were going to be for him.

> Tuesday young [Ralph] Loeb was to have come to see me. He did not
> come. I was keenly disappointed. He wrote no letter. Thursday morning
> I wrote to him, asking him to attend a concert with me to-morrow
> (Sunday) afternoon. It is now Saturday night—and although there
> has been time a—plenty, I have not heard from him. So what I had
> envisioned as a delightful and stimulating comradie [*sic*] is not to be.[10]

Searching for the reason that he had been so unceremoniously ignored, Cullen
came up with this, something that Locke was already quite familiar with:
"I suppose some of us erotic lads...were placed here just to eat our hearts out
with longing for unattainable things, especially for that friendship beyond
understanding."[11]

Thus ended the first phase of Locke's involvement with Cullen's sexuality and
began the second, for Cullen closed his letter by asking Locke write to Ralph
Loeb directly. He particularly needed Locke's sophistication as a letter writer
to make Loeb realize that Cullen was romantically interested in him. Although
Cullen claimed that he and Loeb understood one another, he was unwilling
to act on that knowledge, for fear that to "bend the twig" that way might, to
continue Cullen's metaphor, break it—and send Loeb into a permanent retreat.
Locke's greater sophistication in the art of raising an issue such that only another gay man would react to it came in handy on such occasions. We do not
know whether Locke wrote to Loeb, but he probably did. Part of Locke's role as a
literary mother, therefore, involved satisfying Cullen's emotional needs as well.
That intimacy was signified by a change of voice—in his April letters, Cullen
began addressing Locke by his boyhood name, Roy. It was as if from that point
they were less mother and son, and more, brothers in arms.[12]

Cullen went off chasing another man in April 1923, a German named
Friedrich, whom he may have met through Locke. Cullen had no problem with
propriety with Friedrich, since he seemed to already share Cullen's sexual orientation. But for some reason, Friedrich did not offer a satisfying "adjustment"
to Cullen's need for companionship. Perhaps Cullen's lack of satisfaction came
because Friedrich was German. Such a relationship did not offer either the

permanency of an American affair or the invisibility of a Black one. Although Cullen and Locke frequently became infatuated with White men and foreigners, they preferred Black lovers, in part, because, as Locke put it, he wanted to "preserve a racial heart." Cullen was less racial in his preference, but nevertheless mindful of the pitfalls of interracial dating across the sex line. Cullen's poem, "Tableau," written during this period and dedicated to Donald Duff, a White American with whom he became infatuated after Friedrich, addressed this issue.

> Locked arm in arm they cross the way,
> The Black boy and the white,
> The Golden splendor of the day,
> The sable pride of night.

Cullen continued on to address the stares that such walks elicited from those behind blinds. While such promenades, as they had been for Locke at Harvard, were viewed as innocent boyhood bonding in elite environments, those in the Black community familiar with the tradition of White men coming into Black neighborhoods to find Black young men might suspect. But by wrapping the poem's voice in the righteous indignation of racial liberalism, Cullen kept the focus on breaking the color line, cloaking the sexual taboo also broken. The poem thus makes the point subtly that color and sexual prejudice come from the same limited minds among the "dark folk" and the "fair folk." But "Tableau" also exemplified Cullen's problem as a writer—his language cloaks rather than exposes his feelings. Cullen could not find the voice to say what he felt, as a writer and a lover, largely because he feared rejection. Despite glorious lines about how the lovers were "oblivious to look and word," Cullen found it difficult to lock "arm in arm" with them in print and in person.

Cullen's predicament created a need for the more aggressive voice of Alain Locke, both as a sexual interlocutor and as a mother-like figure. Locke believed that the key to Cullen's productivity was accepting that he was gay. On one occasion, Cullen ended an attempt at a relationship with a man because he thought it kept him from finishing a poem. At other times, Cullen seemed to need the energy of such relationships in order to be creative. This certainly seemed to be the case in his infatuation with Llewellyn Ransom. Once again, Cullen asked Locke to intervene, this time to discover whether Ransom was "sincere." Cullen needed to know whether what Ransom offered was simply "kindness or what [Cullen] most desired it to be." Locke eventually succeeded and Cullen was elated. "L.R. was here last night, and we quite conclusively understand one another...I shall write now, I am sure....There is so invigorating a relief in being happy!"[13] Such an admission must have heartened Locke. By involving himself in Cullen's love affairs, Locke hoped he was clearing the emotional ground for Cullen to become a great writer and use his turmoil to fuel his poetry. Locke liked the cloaked poetry that Cullen produced, for it was the kind of confessional self-analysis that Locke himself indulged in, articulating the universal love of mankind, rather than the exhibitive decadence of the flesh. Thus in 1923, Cullen seemed headed toward becoming the kind of artist that Locke wanted to lead the Negro Renaissance.

Unfortunately, the emotional stability brought on by the relationship with Ransom was short-lived. Cullen's problem, like Locke's problem, was deeper than simply finding a suitable lover or accepting that he was gay. It was that being gay conflicted so strongly with the role that he was increasingly expected to play by the Black community. Cullen was the darling of the Black bourgeoisie, with his refined, Victorian manner, diction, and dress, whom all the elders of the race looked to as representative of what the younger generation should be. Cullen was caught between wanting to be a representative African American, which entailed being a credit to one's race, an exemplary American, and a man of the highest moral values, and wanting to be himself, a gay man who was remarkably sensitive and open to other people. The latter contradicted, in the minds of Whites and Blacks, what it meant to be a representative Black intellectual. And Cullen did not want to give that up either. Not two months after his revelation in reading *Iolaus* and a month after his successful courtship of Llewellyn Ransom, Cullen could write to Locke and say, "I believe I had found a possible resolution to my problem."[14] That resolution was a young lady, Yolanda Du Bois, W. E. B. Du Bois's daughter, whom Cullen hoped to seduce into marriage. Such a successful adjustment might allow Cullen to maintain his status within the Black bourgeoisie as a closeted homosexual who was married.

Locke advised Cullen to avoid marriage—and its hypocrisy, at least in romantic terms. But in the very same month that Cullen was considering marriage, Locke almost considered it himself. His old Oxford buddy, Isaka Seme, came back into his life in December 1922. Seme wrote Locke from London stating that he was now the South African Zulu chief's right-hand man and wanted to invite Locke to South Africa to head up a mammoth educational program. Locke seemed interested. As Helen Irvin wrote to Locke, "Africa! Heaven's sakes, my boy! That is a leap! But I think it would also be a great opportunity for you."[15] As always, there was something about explorations of the African self that intrigued Locke, as something elemental (if not essential) that could not only lift him up, but free him from the loneliness of being Other, gay, and human in America. But there was just one little snag. Seme asked whether Locke had gotten married. Seme had gotten married, and the implication was that it was a political necessity. Locke wrote back that he too was interested in marriage. Seme believed he might be able to fix Locke up with someone of rank in the tribe. Locke shuddered and wrote back asking whether he would at least get to see the woman before marrying her. Although Seme assured Locke that he would have such a chance, his enthusiasm waned for the prospect and, when the deal fell through, he was rather relieved. He may have warmed to the prospect of another woman who would serve a maternal role like his mother had for most of his life, but to marry a woman, especially one he knew little about, would be simply too much. Cullen had not reached that stage of self-knowledge yet. Locke might fantasize about the benefits of marriage, especially as a gateway to Africa; but he never went through with it. Cullen did, and his relationship with Locke declined afterward.

One area where Cullen could potentially help Locke was in nurturing the older man's still simmering desire to be a poet. In a February 1923 letter to Cullen, Locke promised to enclose "a manuscript poem on which I invite your most professional reaction. Primarily, of course, it's just an exchange courtesy, which I have been following with friends now for a number of years. I write verse for private circulation and consumption only."[16] Of course, this was not strictly true: Locke had submitted poems to publications and been rejected. But he had been showing his poems to such friends as Georgia Douglas Johnson for years; that he was willing to show Cullen some of his work established the basis for a reciprocal relationship between them. But Locke failed to include the poem. Cullen persisted. He then forced this from Locke's hand. "I have been most pro- saically busy and have little time for poeticizing except a few minutes of medita- tion I get before going to sleep, or before deciding to wake up fully, or in the bath-tub."[17] Locke was probably too timid to submit his poetry to the younger published poet to review. Nevertheless, something of Cullen's generosity and sense of reciprocity comes through in his offer.

Another area where Cullen did help Locke was in advising the older man about *his* personal relationships. Although Locke was the more experienced homosexual, Locke's own life by 1923 was in such emotional turmoil that he needed help. Locke was trying to reestablish a romantic relationship with William George in the spring of 1923. The basic conflict—that Locke wanted George as a lover and George did not want to be that person—resurfaced and grew until it exploded. Locke was still stuck trying to cultivate romantic rela- tionships with inappropriate, that is, young, inexperienced men. In part, this was due to Locke's physical requirements in a lover. Locke liked slim, attractive, and lean young men, and the man who continued to fill that bill was William, who, by February, still resisted Locke's advances, but remained enticingly intimate nevertheless. Cullen counseled Locke not to take William seriously, although this advice did not seem to avoid a flare-up sometime in April. Almost to direct Locke's attention away from that disastrous relationship, Cullen began to introduce Locke to other men. One of the most important of these would be Langston Hughes.

Arriving in New York in 1921, Hughes was far more enthralled with Harlem than with his studies at Columbia, and after only a year of credible study of lit- erature and foreign languages, he dropped out in the summer of 1922. Before leaving Columbia, however, Hughes was introduced to the staff of the *Crisis* by Jessie Fauset, who, as the magazine's literary editor since 1919, had been publishing Hughes's poems. Though shy and elusive, Hughes made friends easily with the *Crisis* staff, winning over not only Du Bois but also Augustus Granville Dill, the gay business manager of the magazine. Like Toomer, Hughes was a handsome, gifted descendant of the Black bourgeoisie who rejected its values and pretensions. Hughes was much more interested in the Black masses than in the overly assimilated Black elite, but unlike Toomer, Hughes was already a race man in 1922. His closest friend among the young core of African American writers was Countee Cullen, whose home became a kind of rendezvous spot for Hughes, and whose knowledge of New York's goings-on helped introduce Hughes to the world of the literary intellectual. Together they attended numerous plays and concerts and became close friends. Cullen, already smitten by the young Hughes, was unwilling to declare his affections openly. Thus, on January 12, 1923, believing that Locke needed a lift, Cullen sent Hughes's address to Locke with the recommendation: "Write to him, and arrange to meet him. You will like him; I love him; his is such a charming childishness that I feel years older in his presence, although he is my senior by the margin of a year—I think."[18]

Hughes's "childishness" was a pose. Hughes wanted to be free to pursue the life of the vagabond, which he saw as integrally connected with the vocation of the poet; and innocence and lack of acknowledgment became key weapons, along with his elusiveness in protecting himself from entrapping relationships with men or women. Such a pose would come in handy in his dealings with Locke, who from the first letter he wrote to Hughes, seemed to view Hughes as a potential lover. While Locke was generally on the lookout for such relationships, his need for such an involvement was even greater than usual in the first months of 1923. Faced with the prospect of losing William, Locke was even more desperate to find a new love; and something that he had learned about Hughes, either from Cullen or from others, led him to believe that Hughes might also be interested in such a romantic relationship. Several people, Locke confided in his January 17 letter to Hughes, insisted "on my knowing you. Some instinct, roused not so much by the reading of your verse as from a mental picture of your state of mind, reinforces their insistence."[19] Locke created a fantasy about Hughes being an ideal match—a young man who was lean, handsome, and tan, but also intelligent and talented. Perhaps with this young descendant of his father's dean at Howard University, Locke could find fusion between his romantic and his literary interests.

Hughes, for his part, was flattered by Locke's introductory letter and wrote back an excellent reply that seemed to confirm his interest. But Hughes was perched out of reach at Jones Point, New York, where he was serving as a mess man on a ship. This suited Hughes, as he preferred to manage intimacies at arm's length, with no overt pressure to declare one's intentions, romantic or otherwise.

That approach did not satisfy Locke, and he was not about to let something as fixed as geography keep him from finding out whether Hughes was a prospect. Accordingly, Locke wrote Hughes on February 10 that he was planning to come to New York around Washington's birthday and would love to visit Jones Point to meet Hughes. "First impressions count with me, and I rather suspect with you also and I am quite nervous, either through anticipation or some deeper instinctive feeling about our first encounter."

Hughes, however, was unnerved by the prospect of Locke meeting him at Jones Point. "It would be inconvenient for you to come up to Jones Point and I can't come down to the city," Hughes explained. "This is the most out of the way place and our ship is...a good half mile of slippery gang-planks and icy decks from the shore landing," and therefore a danger to Professor Locke's safety. Perhaps more truthfully, Hughes confided his fear that "at the end of your journey, you would find a very stupid person....I am always dumb in the presence of those whom I want to be friends with."[20] There was some truth to that: at the *Crisis* meeting, he had felt dumb and stupid in the "presence" of Du Bois, Fauset, and the other staff members. But there may have been something more: as his biographer, Arnold Rampersad, suggests, Hughes may have picked up that Locke was interested in more than a professional, literary relationship. By stopping the visit, Hughes took control of their relationship and set the terms on which they would meet. Locke discovered his aggressive approach to relationships had not worked in this instance.

Of course, Locke vented his disappointment on Cullen. Hughes "doesn't need any more humoring than he has already had," Locke informed Cullen. To Locke's mind, all the attention New York had showered on Hughes had spoiled him, and Locke appeared finished with the young man until Hughes, realizing such an ending to their relationship was not in his best interest, resumed the correspondence after a month of silence had passed. During that elapsed period, Hughes inquired of Cullen, after learning that he had visited Locke again in Washington, whether Locke "was married?" Learning that Locke was indeed still a bachelor at thirty-eight probably resolved whatever ambiguity Hughes had about Locke's intentions. Accordingly, Hughes resumed the correspondence on April 6. "I am sorry I have been so long in writing you....I did enjoy your last letter a great deal and I believe that you are a <u>sympathetic</u> friend. So many aren't. They are only well-meaning." Hughes acknowledged and developed upon Locke's earlier references to "classicism," asking: "Do you teach Greek or the classics? I have read nothing but the Odyssey and a few of the tragedies but I love them. They were the only things college gave me (other than a supreme dislike for college)." Hughes also sent Locke some of his poems, described his reading interest in Nietzsche, Joyce, and Whitman, and detailed his recent theater and opera engagements. "Down in New York I saw 'Will Shakespeare,' Jane Cowl's 'Romeo and Juliette,' Nazimova's 'Salome,' and the Moscow Art Players do 'The Lower

Depths.'" He lamented that he "didn't get to hear a single opera this winter, and I wanted to, especially those of 'The Ring.' But I did both hear and see 'Liza' and it's a perfect diamond of joy! Didn't you think so?" Then, Hughes concluded his letter by acknowledging that "you must be a charming friend for poets...I do want your help, and friendship, and criticism. And how good you are to offer them to me!"[21] Though still mad, Locke was won over. It was the first of many letters from Hughes to Locke that established their many shared interests—love of the theater and the opera, of travel, of the outdoors and beautiful foliage, and of wandering for days in the woods in what Locke would call a "wandervogel."

Still, his basic problem remained—there was no one among the young men Locke had befriended and pursued who was right to be his lover, to extend to him what he wanted most, an unconditional, unqualified love. Little more than a year after his mother's death, a crushing kind of loneliness began to descend on Locke, such that the times alone at 1326 R Street became like living in a dungeon, abandoned by even those who said they wanted to "get to know you" and so forth. The fear loomed that once they did "get to know him," they did not want to be with him and quickly abandoned him for someone younger, handsomer, and less quirky and demanding.

But Locke refused to let crushing loneliness and failed attempts at love affairs defeat him. Locke was distinguished by a powerful personality trait—the ability to compensate for private tragedies with public triumphs. Even while suffering alone without his mother or a viable lover at the beginning of 1923, Locke was able to fashion a new social identity for himself through writing, by turning himself into a Black cultural voice whose public criticality of White misrepresentations of Black culture and lobbying for expanding the role of Black creative writers would define the New Negro intellectual of the 1920s. Locke still faced the challenge of how to relate his rarified, stuffy, aesthetic temperament to a mass audience of Black readers still focused on political protest or economic self-advancement as the solution to the Negro's declining social reality in America. Nonetheless, something of the personal energy he derived from working privately with these young writers gave him the courage to try and reset the African American public agenda on what he, Hughes, and Cullen could agree on—the belief that the Negro would be liberated by great writing before anything else.

Locke's success in this crusade would depend on some developments he did not embrace. In 1923, Eubie Blake and Noble Sissle, the African American creators of the 1921 Broadway hit musical *Shuffle Along* would open *Runnin' Wild*, their second successful musical revue and introduce to America the most popular dance of the 1920s, the Charleston. Black vaudeville follies on Broadway were not Locke's idea of "culture." Closer to his sentiments was the opening of Eugene O'Neill's controversial play about miscegenation, *All God's Chillun Got Wings*, at the Fazi Theater in Washington, D.C., where it enjoyed a brief run before it traveled to New York the next year and sparked a national debate over whether the Black lead, performed by Paul Robeson, should be allowed to kiss a White woman on stage. That year also saw an African American playwright, Willis Richardson, break the color line in serious Broadway theater when his play, *Chip Woman's Fortune*, became the first African American–authored play to be performed on Broadway. Things were definitely looking up when Jean Toomer's *Cane* was published that fall. But it was Black popular culture that had created a viable market for Black cultural production in America. In music, Bessie Smith began a very popular recording career in 1923, King Oliver's Creole Jazz Band made thirty-seven recordings with the legendary Louis Armstrong on trumpet, and Duke Ellington began performing in New York City.

Perhaps most important, the National Urban League, founded in 1910 to assist Blacks who had migrated to northern cities, began publishing *Opportunity* magazine in 1923 on a monthly basis and became the important outlet for the poetry, short fiction, and essays of the younger generation of writers during the 1920s. What Locke needed more than anything else was a sympathetic publisher, who could bridge the gap between the high-minded prose of a literary stylist and the popular tastes of a mass magazine–reading audience. He found that in Charles S. Johnson, who used his position to promote Locke and the magazine's literary credentials almost from the moment that the journal began publishing.

Eight years Locke's junior, Charles Spurgeon Johnson held a PhD in sociology from the University of Chicago where he had studied under Robert E. Park and adopted his notion that race relations inevitably passed through a cycle of contact and conflict to collaboration and assimilation. While in graduate school, Johnson had worked as director of research for the Chicago Urban League through the race riot of 1919 and produced an exhaustive yet optimistic report on the riot: race relations could still improve, despite reaching their nadir. Johnson was a behind-the-scenes manipulator who possessed the personal adroitness of Booker T. Washington and a belief that skillful management of human and financial resources of the liberal establishment could bring progressive advance in race relations. More than an ordinary sociologist, Johnson was a man with a mission to change American race relations and had a novel way of doing it. Having gained a love of Western literature as a child, Johnson saw his appointment as director of research and investigation for the National Urban League in 1921 as an opportunity to forge a community of writers, publishers, and patrons that would rehabilitate the image of the Negro in American life through art. Johnson made sure that *Opportunity* published enough articles on crime, disease, and other social problems to satisfy the League's social reform agenda, but he also sought out the young literary voices of the 1920s to serve his larger purpose of building the broad literary and cultural movement he believed would transform race relations in America at large. One of the first writers

Johnson approached was Locke. With his Harvard BA, PhD, and Rhodes Scholarship, his association with the younger writers like Toomer and Cullen, and his reputation as a literary critic, Locke possessed the aesthetic credentials that Johnson sorely lacked.

Locke also possessed the ability to write pithy, provocative, intellectually rich social and aesthetic criticism. On January 4, 1923, Johnson had written Locke and asked him to review for *Opportunity* "a play centering around an alleged phase of Negro life in Washington," "Goat Alley," adding, "I have tried to convey to you in person our great satisfaction in your expression of interest and cooperation in this field."[22] Locke's quick response suggests his enthusiasm. Hurriedly reading the script of the play, Locke sent a pithy, biting review to Johnson by the thirteenth, just enough time for it to be published in the February issue. The review was a success, largely because Locke voiced the emerging African American criticism of White literary interest as inevitably fascinated by the most sordid of stories of Black people's lives. Johnson hinted at this when he introduced it to Locke as a play on "an alleged phase of Negro life in Washington." Locke put it in a more straightforward manner: *Goat Alley* was "a play of the tragic, sordid sort that is happening the world over in the life of the submerged classes," with "Negro dialect and characterization" thrown in. As a result, the play was not "inevitably and spontaneously racial" and left "a painful impression of having been written to show the Negro up."[23] As might be expected, middle-class Black intellectuals did not feel the race needed more stories about how bad life was among the Black lower classes. But Locke's review made its case wittily and suggested if the Black bourgeoisie were to have its kind of plays, they would have to write them for themselves. Shortly after its publication in the February issue, Johnson wrote: "Several persons have commented favorably on your review as being better than the play itself."[24]

Here was Locke's real gift as a writer—using irony, wit, and gift for metaphor á la Oscar Wilde to expose the hypocrisy and stupidity of poorly executed literature and theater. In his next article for *Opportunity*, Locke showed he was more than just a literary critic. Reviewing Abbott Lawrence Lowell's *Public Opinion in War and Peace*, Locke stated that he was not taking issue with the arch-conservatism of Lowell's views, a statement that was ironic given that his review was an opportunity to dress down the current Harvard University president for reversing the racial liberalism of Locke's undergraduate years. Lowell was a man of aristocratic privilege who caved in to rising demands for racial segregation and denied African Americans the right to live in freshman dorms in the Yard in the name of tradition that had not existed before him. But rather than attack him on his racism, Locke dismissed Lowell as an observer of broader social forces like public opinion, because he lacked any "consistent general hypothesis as to the causes and course of large scale social movements." Though "sage and accurate in detail, illuminating in historical perspective, penetrating in the analysis of prevailing differences of social theory, the book is nevertheless platitudinous, and almost specious in basic theory and ground conclusions." As a Boston aristocrat, Lowell still believed "God and the upper classes in consultation or pre-established harmony ordained and planned society," instead of the new sociological view that "the forms of society themselves grow out of the cleavages of opinion and the clash of group interests. Society has always expressed the people, even when government and institutions have repressed them. Society is a mass phenomenon."[25] Locke attacked Lowell on the high ground, in terms of his ignorance of contemporary social theory, his out-of-date-ness, rather than his racism. The test of the true social observer was to bend with the times, to adapt to his circumstances, and adjust to one's times, despite their dissimilarity from one's own temperament. By those standards, the current Harvard president was a decided disappointment.

Johnson was even more pleased with this review than the first, perhaps because of his own greater knowledge of the subject matter: "You have done a mighty fine piece of work in this review and the point of view of your criticism makes Dr. Lowell's method seem ultra-conservative. Have you, by the way, read Walter Lippmann's "Public Opinion?" It is I believe, more nearly in accord with a realistic conception of this social phenomenon and with your own implied idea and very [much] more penetrating than Dr. Lowell's."[26]

By the time Johnson wrote these lines of praise, Locke had turned Johnson's enthusiasm for his writing toward something much more important to Locke than simple play and book reviewing. For what was really important in Johnson's June 6 letter was what followed: "The matter which you, Mr. Jones, and I discussed has indeed been taken up here and there have been several responses to letters sent to a selected group of persons which hold considerable promise and are to be followed up by interviews."[27] That matter was Locke's request, made at a meeting with Johnson and Eugene Kinckle Jones, the executive director of the National Urban League, to raise money for a fund of at least several hundred dollars to finance his six-month trip of research through Europe and Africa. In addition, Locke asked Johnson to act as a literary agent and help place several of these articles in major White periodicals that could pay for them. Although the exact details of the proposal are unclear, it appears that Locke's understanding was that his trip would produce a series of articles on the broad theme of the Negro contributions to Western civilization, and those that did not sell to White periodicals would appear in *Opportunity*. With this proposal, Locke added on to his trip's responsibilities to study the conditions of colonial troops serving in Europe, to do research for the American Negro Academy in European libraries, and to represent Afro-America at the opening of King Tut's tomb as a foreign correspondent for *Opportunity* magazine. Indeed, he even requested and received a letter from Johnson certifying that he was such a correspondent.

The elements of Locke's new internationalist role dated back to 1911, when he tried to get Booker T. Washington and then the Albert Kahn Travelling Fellowship to fund a trip through Europe writing and publishing articles about race. Then, the primary motivation was to support himself outside of the institutional structures of Black life. But, in January 1923, when he started to put together his new plan for writing articles about race and culture abroad, he had a job at Howard University and needed the project mainly to escape the limitations living in America and especially Washington, D.C., imposed on him as a gay Black man. Just as important, though, the world of international Black affairs had radically changed by 1923. Now, there was a new race consciousness shaped inexorably by Marcus Garvey and his cry of "Africa for the Africans." Locke's plan to write about race and culture from around the world could not focus just on Europe; it had to include Africa as the other pole in what would be a world systems perspective of race.

Locke had found just what he needed on the front page of the February 17 issue of the *New York Times* where he read an article announcing the British had found and opened the tomb of the pharaoh Tutankhamen in Egypt. Seeing an opening for himself, Locke crafted an argument that he, as a Black philosopher and budding theoretical anthropologist, ought to be present when Howard Carter, the English archaeologist, reopened King Tut's tomb in 1923, to resume excavating the tomb. Should not he, Alain Locke, heir to Rhodes's rape of Africa's resources for British wealth, and an Aframerican, his term, be present to witness and write about a twentieth-century excavation that proved the glory of African civilization? Being at the excavation would yield a series of additional articles that Locke could publish in *Opportunity* or perhaps mainstream magazines upon his return.

One potential obstacle to the plan had loomed. To get the fall quarter off from teaching at Howard, Locke needed the support of Howard University president J. Stanley Durkee for a trip justified mainly by its focus on the research he would do in Africa. Locke worked assiduously to present the scheme before the president and even got a letter from a French anthropologist supporting his research project. But Locke was a neophyte when it came to research in Africa, while another scholar, William Leo Hansberry, with an extensive research and teaching program in African Studies, was being considered for a position at Howard University in 1923. Hansberry was an Afrocentric historian with a well-articulated research and teaching plan for African Studies and also a friend of Jesse Moorland, the Howard University trustee, who had donated his extensive collection of books and artifacts of Black history to the university in the 1910s. Moorland liked the idea that Hansberry's research would be connected to his collection and supported his work.

Seeing Hansberry as someone the university might believe was better qualified than him to undertake research in Egypt, Locke sought to undermine Hansberry's appointment. In the end, William Leo Hansberry gained his appointment at the university and Locke gained support from the university to take his sabbatical, but not before a nasty fight that resulted in Moorland, and even Durkee, viewing Locke as a nasty academic infighter. Locke was often so driven by his personal agendas that he engaged in attacks on others that undermined wider support for his projects. Instead of trying to make common cause with Hansberry, whose expertise Locke could have used, his competitive stance destroyed any possibility of an alliance after the trip. The memory of that fight would come back to haunt him later when he would be in the fight of his life at Howard University. Nevertheless, somewhat brutally, by May 1923, Locke had won permission to spend six months away from Howard and to get funding from Howard for his research trip.

Locke then returned his attention to raising more money for the trip. Howard University had turned down his request for financial support for his research, so he needed help from Charles Johnson and Eugene Kinckle Jones to raise money for trip. A month after Johnson's favorable letter, Jones wrote Locke shortly after he left for London the following note:

> I thought you would like to know something about the development in my efforts to secure some funds to help in the investigations and research work which you are planning to do. The Rockefeller group turned us down with the simple statement that "it would not seem advisable" to provide the fund. Mrs. Henry G. Leach, however, expressed her regret at not being able to give the total amount, yet she pledged $100.... I have not had a chance to talk with Mr. Wood in detail about this matter. I shall make every effort to secure as much of the fund as possible. At least we can count on a part, if not all, of the amount.[28]

Such a proposal showed Locke's cheekiness. But from his perspective, why shouldn't the magazine underwrite his research? He was already writing unpaid articles for *Opportunity*, and this trip would yield even more for the magazine. The funding would ensure Johnson a series of interesting articles and tie Locke more closely to *Opportunity* magazine. What Locke may not have fully realized was that the money subtly transformed the meaning of his trip. He was now on an errand not only for himself but also for Johnson and for *Opportunity* magazine to produce a popular rendition of his travel experiences, rather than the scholarly research he had promised Arthur Schomburg and the American Negro Academy. Yet such a transition was consistent with Locke's vision of himself as not just an ivory tower professor, but also a public intellectual, who would use his research and philosophical skills to raise the level of public discourse about race and culture in America.

While Locke succeeded in his efforts to create new opportunities for himself as an international Black researcher and journalist, he was still wrestling with a

young man who had suddenly become by spring of 1923 more important emotionally to him than he could have anticipated. For just as Locke made plans to
abandon the more academic world for six months of traveling abroad, he also
began to connect more intensely with Langston Hughes because he stimulated
Locke's capacity to enjoy the non-academic side of life. As Hughes wrote in his
April 6 letter from Jones Point:

> I shall perhaps be here only a month or so more, until spring comes
> over the high hills and down to the river's edge. There are fruit trees all
> along the west bank waiting for flowers. I've had a glorious winter. I've
> made strange friends for whom I care a great deal. And met many poets,
> although they never write their poems.... Of course, I'm stupid and
> only a young "kid" fascinated by his first glimpse of life, but then often
> so many years in a book-world and so much of striving to be a "bright
> boy" and an "intelligent young man," it is rather nice to come here and
> be simple and stupid and to touch a life that is at least a living thing
> with no touch of books.[29]

Hughes encouraged the romantic, adventuresome, open-hearted love of life in
Locke that he indulged when he was fancy-free and out of sight of the Black
bourgeoisie. Hughes seemed to recognize this and tried to build upon that connection in his subsequent letters that enthralled Locke. Even before he had met
Hughes, Hughes's spirit conveyed in such letters uplifted Locke during what
psychologists often call the midlife crisis phase, a time of reflection on and dissatisfaction with what he had accomplished so far, and an intense yearning for a
sense of renewal and commitment to new values. Given his drift after obtaining
his PhD and the recent death of his mother, partially the rationale for that drift,
Locke needed a new, revitalizing future. Hughes seemed to offer that to Locke.

Hughes had more practical objects in mind in renewing his correspondence
with Locke. In his letter, Hughes inquired whether Locke would "help him." "I am
sending you an envelope of poems.... I am afraid that none of them are particularly good, but if you should like any of them well enough to send them out for
me, I would be very glad. I had thought of *Poetry* and *The Little Review*, but then
I was afraid that I was not good enough for one nor eccentric enough for the
other."[30] Locke agreed. "Your estimate of your poetry is about correct," he replied; "the newer technique is too strained—the other is not quite mellow enough.
By the way hasn't Countee mellowness to a fine degree?"[31] This was all true, but
it was also designed to send the message that praise and promotion came to
those who allowed an intimate friendship to develop. Yet Locke did not close the
door on Hughes. Locke would send some of his poems around and try to cultivate a friendship within the limits that Hughes imposed. Of course, he would
prefer to be "located somewhere nearer you and be the mentor of a literary and

art coterie—we have enough talent now to begin to have a movement—and express a school of thought."[32] Hughes agreed, as he stated in his next letter, though he worried that if Negroes created a Black Greenwich Village, that it would not be one that put on airs.[33] While sex remained a subtext in their relationship, the literary aspirations were not all facade. Locke did want to be involved in a literary coterie, and while he believed that Toomer excelled over Hughes in the ability to "transmute the colloquial into the poetic," he still reassured Hughes that "each [has] his own gift, my boy, each his own gift."[34]

Buoyed, perhaps, by the notion that Hughes might have feelings for him, Locke shared his travel plans. He planned to take a leave of absence after the summer in order to visit Egypt and some parts of East and South Africa, as part of his plan to visit his friend Isaka Seme. Locke needed to "shake off the academic bookshelf dust with the dust of the road." He would begin his trip with an extended vacation in Europe. Perhaps Hughes would be in Europe too—at least that was what Jessie Fauset was saying. Hughes was dying to go to Europe and commented in a follow-up letter: "I wish I was going with you."[35]

Locke interpreted that somewhat casual remark as an indication that Hughes might be willing to go to Europe with him that summer. He began to plan in late April to arrange his travel so that Hughes could come along almost for free. Even Cullen encouraged the idea. "Oh, it would be wonderful if he could go with you this summer. I would delight in nothing more than in that, not even in going myself, although I do wish with all my heart and soul that I could afford the trip. Langston ought to be able."[36] Cullen even wrote to Hughes encouraging the idea, for he believed that "each of you will be such inspiration for the other.... Here's hoping that you and Langston see King Tutankhamen's Tomb together this summer. If you do, I shall be along in spirit."[37] This was quite an endorsement, for Cullen himself longed to go on the trip, but was not invited. Just as plans crystallized, Hughes unsurprisingly backed away from the trip and departed New York Harbor on a boat headed for Africa. Locke was furious. "As to Langston," Locke wrote to Cullen, "he is a fool—never again—I swear it. For example I had an invitation to the Bahaist center at Haifa so worded as to include him." Now Hughes would not be there. "Naturally, I am depressed—you as a bus boy and Langston as a galley slave. Are we an accursed tribe?"[38]

Actually, Locke had not offered to pay Cullen's way to Europe, something that Cullen would have jumped at if Locke had offered. While Locke explained his lack of an offer in terms of lack of resources, the truth was that Locke did not feel toward Cullen as he felt toward Hughes. But Hughes was not biting.

Why was Hughes so elusive? Was it that he knew Locke was a homosexual and felt that Locke was coming on to him too aggressively? Perhaps. Hughes was hard to pin down with everyone, even those less aggressive, such as Cullen, and those more heterosexual, such as Jessie Fauset, who was also courting him. Clearly, Hughes avoided emotional intimacy, even though he craved companionship.

It was not that Hughes was opposed to homosexuality, since on that very voyage to the coast of Africa, he would have his first homosexual experience. Hughes was not sure what a summer traveling with Locke would be like and decided at the last minute not to risk destroying the relationship. But for Locke, that had already occurred.

Cullen, however, sought to steady the older man's nerves. "I'm glad you are going; if you are wise you will get a much needed rest—and also, if you are wise, you will solve your problem over there." That problem, of course, was Locke's craving for sexual companionship. And he did have plans. He planned to visit his young German friend, Rudolph Krause, who had been looking forward very expectantly to Locke's visit. But most important, Cullen counseled understanding on Locke's part toward Hughes, with whom Cullen had spent time in Brooklyn:

> I showed him your letter and of course, he wanted explanations. He was
> sympathetic but I do not believe that he fully understood the situation.
> I am convinced that he is a nature that would not fully apprehend the
> significance of such a thing. Perhaps that is also the case with William.
> He is probably unaware of what he has done, and, doubtless, blames you.[39]

Locke was not able to take responsibility for having pushed Hughes in a corner, from which Hughes, like William, had extricated himself. After another condemnatory letter from Locke, Cullen commented, "I think you are probably doing Langston an injustice. We shall talk of him when I see you. I am sure you both have not fully understood one another. Don't come to rash conclusions." Like Mary Locke, Cullen was cautioning Locke not to let his incredible temper destroy his relationships. This was especially prudent since Locke was still interested in Hughes. In connecting Locke's situation with Hughes to that with William, Cullen had hit upon a truth about Locke's reactions to nonchalance, unpredictability, and irresponsibility. Locke overreacted with almost murderous rage to those who refused to love him, rather than work through his hurt feelings to a modus vivendi with a friend.

Locke edged toward recognition of the unsuitability of a romantic relationship with Hughes as he boarded his ship for Europe. As he spent many delightful hours with Rudolph and his family in Germany, Locke forgot for a while about his twice-broken American heart. Happy once again to be away from America and loved by someone he could trust, Locke began to dream of what life would be like always to have such love. He even began to dream of what it would be like to bring Rudolph to live with him in Washington. Fortunately, he confided these thoughts to Cullen and heard the advice he needed to hear.

> Tell Rudolph I appreciated his postscript on your card. And, further,
> as regards Rudolph, I have been seriously thinking your situation over,

and I urge you to act prudently. This admonition is necessary because you have enough of the artist in you to be scornful of consequences. There are some people in Washington who would give their hope of heaven for a chance to hurt you. So, I advise you to surfeit yourself this summer and to abandon any prospects that might prove chimerical and disastrous in a cold place like Washington—this for your good and Rudolph's.[40]

Locke could not live openly with a young White man in Washington, as Cullen's "Tableau" had foreseen. In a moment of courage, Locke might believe he could cast aside the stares of the "dark folk" and the "fair folk," but it was simply not true. Cullen suggested the "dark folk" were primarily responsible. Locke was already a lightning rod of suppressed anger over his "closeted openness." To remain an influential man of color, Locke, like Cullen, had to live his love life in a closet that also constrained his literary voice. Cullen closed his August 23 letter with a poignant admission of how frustrating his life had become in America. "I have lost track of Donald, although I have written several letters to him."[41] Locke had that to look forward to when he returned—more of the same from the Donald Duffs, the William Georges, and the Langston Hugheses of Black America. Instead of a lover, he would remain a perennial mother of disobedient children back home.

No wonder Locke had taken a leave of absence for the fall. He needed to be away for as long as possible.

Europe Before Egypt

Egypt, it must be admitted, was more of a fantasy—and a rationale for funding—than an eagerly anticipated destination that summer of 1923. Locke's summer was spent mostly in Europe. Indeed, when he left America, it was not certain he would get to Egypt. As of June 28, Helen Irvin, who was looking after his apartment at 1326 R Street, wrote him, "I do hope you will find it possible and profitable to make the trip to Egypt."[1] Despite his various appeals, Locke did not have enough money to finance the trip to Egypt when he left America in June. Even as late as October, Roscoe Conkling Bruce and Arthur Schomburg still solicited funds for Locke, although by then they were having some success. The problem was, they did not know where he was! Bruce and Schomburg were "a bit surprised" not to have heard from Locke "in regard to your progress. We are raising a fund for the purposes of helping out with expenses, but since you do not write we cannot send it, til we know where you are physically and tuntankahmerizally." Of course, he was not responding because he was hold up in Europe with Rudolph rather than in Egypt with Tutankhamun. His friends' continuing efforts to finance that Egypt trip resulted in some humorous accidents. "Easeley Hatford, on the yard sent in by mistake her contribution two pounds to your beloved friend [Carter G.] Woodson, and got in the air and he is full of malicious envy. Schomburg is having a photostat copy made, to send you as soon as he can locate you. Another contrary member of the wealthiest negro in central america known as the Cocoa King has sent a substantive contribution and Schom and I have done our part as others will do there[']s." The rub was that Locke had to be more forthcoming. "Now keep us posted of your whereabouts prospects, and doings as we are sincerely interested as you must know and want your mission to be a successful one. Woodson says you 'must have a look in at the tomb, and that you may get to Egypt—that you are having a good time in Europe' malicious envy, etc."[2] It was as much an open secret that he was more interested in going to Europe than to Egypt as that he was a homosexual.

Woodson was "envious," because, having resigned his deanship at Howard University to launch the Association for the Study of Negro Life and History, he could not afford such a trip given that the Association barely made enough to keep its doors open. Locke, by contrast, had a paying university professorship and was taking money out of the purses of Black nationalists—even Central American nationalists like the Cocoa King—to travel as Woodson never could. But the caricature was unfair: Locke did want to go to Egypt, but his interest in Africa was not of a historical antiquarian kind that Woodson—and to a lesser extent, Leo Hansberry—wanted to do in Africa. For Locke, study of Africa, and especially Egypt, was not focused mainly on compiling its history, but to use that history to create a pathway for Africans and "Afro-Americans" as pivotal players in the emerging present. Egypt was part of Locke's continuing sociological study of race contacts and how non-Western culture serves as a critique of modern race creeds that asserted White supremacy. Studying Europe was as important to that critical intervention as peeking in at King Tut's tomb, though, as a mild Afrocentrist, Locke knew promoting his trip as representing the race at King Tut's tomb would get race men and women to contribute to it. And there was an emotional component to Egypt for Locke as well—it functioned as a kind of imagined racial Mother—if he could get to her.

But first, Locke had to devote himself to tasks for those who already had financed his summer trip. As soon as Locke arrived in London in July, he began to interview people, such as Sir Harry Johnston, the British authority of colonial Africa, who might help him gauge the significance of France's use of colonial troops in its occupation of Germany—this for an article Johnson wanted for *Opportunity*. He continued his interviews when he reached Paris during the second week of August for a different kind of service—a secret mission Johnson wished him to undertake to investigate the status of Du Bois's Pan African Congress. In the process, Locke met a man named M. Bethon and asked Bethon at Johnson's behest to write an article for *Opportunity* magazine on the second meeting of the Congress Du Bois was organizing to take place that October in London. The request had an impact that evidently pleased Johnson:

> Your activities on the other side are being felt here more strongly than I had suspected for so short a period. You might be interested in an incident that occurred yesterday. Very shortly after I had received your letter telling me that you had asked M. Bethon to prepare an article for us on the Pan African Congress, Dr. Du Bois called up and asked if we had received an article from him. We had not, of course, and he asked to come over and talk about it. When he came, he claimed/explained/ that M. Bethon had written Mrs. Hunton and another person . . . telling them that he was planning to discuss the Pan African Congress in OPPORTUNITY.[3]

The request inferred that Bethon would be a critic of the Congress. Du Bois, fearing that an attack appearing before the actual conference would injure its chances for convening and for its continued existence, was extremely anxious that no such article appear before he had a chance to meet with Bethon, probably in Lisbon, Spain, in October: "There is no decision, of course, that can be made definitely yet for I have not seen the article. I did give him assurance that if such an article did come to us and seemed to merit publication, he could have an opportunity to carry an answer to it as a companion article."

Johnson relished this incident, because Du Bois's *Crisis* was *Opportunity*'s main competitor, and Du Bois's visit conceded that *Opportunity* had become a significant player in the game of Black international political media. Here, Johnson was making a bid not merely to become the center of discussions of literature, visual art, and aesthetic commentary but also international politics and race leadership. Despite its success in becoming the voice of educated Black commentary, the *Crisis* had declined by 1923 in the numbers of copies sold and in legitimacy: Marcus Garvey's huge mass movement and rival publication, the *Negro World*, had called into question Du Bois's right to be called a popular African American leader. While Du Bois had succeeded in having Garvey arrested in 1923 on charges he solicited funding fraudulently through the US mails, Garvey's more global aspirations for a unification of all African peoples was far more popular than Du Bois's self-absorbed Pan African Congresses. By asking a European delegate to the Congress what he thought of the Pan African Congress, Locke was threatening to expose the whispered truth that the Pan African Congresses merely reflected Du Bois's all-consuming agenda and not the voices and perspectives of colonized Blacks around the world. Johnson liked Locke's maneuver because it forced the great Dr. Du Bois to descend from his pulpit at the *Crisis* and come over to the offices of the Urban League—a vivid sign that he would have to take *Opportunity* seriously in the coming years.

Locke resented Du Bois, because Locke felt Du Bois never accorded him the respect his educational accomplishments deserved. Even after writing "Steps Towards a Negro Theatre," a major statement on the Black theater for the *Crisis*, Locke was not approached by Du Bois to become a featured contributor to the *Crisis*. For his part, Du Bois may have had his own feelings of rivalry with a younger Black man whose education was comparable, coupled with a suspicion that Locke could not be trusted because of his earlier association with Booker T. Washington. That association also suggests the philosophical difference between Locke and Du Bois: Locke rejected Du Bois's brand of Black protest as the most effective strategy against racism. The NAACP's frontal attack on White racism to Locke had failed to turn the tide, as the segregation of the federal government under Wilson, the 1919 race riots, and the organization's failed campaign for a federal anti-lynching bill in the early 1920s showed.

Locke believed it was time to try something other than haranguing Whites ad nauseum about racism. Why not try sound intellectual criticism of racists as social anachronisms, combined with seducing the more liberal Whites to become allies of progressive race relations? Locke placed greater faith than Du Bois in the power of literature to change Whites by transforming the language and images of racial discourse. Locke wanted to flip the emphasis from political and sociological analyses, which dominated African American thought in the 1910s, to the aesthetic and anthropological approaches that stressed cultural traditions and social transformations because they promised to give agency to what Negroes could do to shape their own futures. In coming up with a new philosophy of cultural advance, Locke wanted to displace Du Bois's monopoly on enlightened Black thinking and allow others, like Johnson and him, to represent the African American mind.

By 1923, Locke was beginning to articulate his new perspective in his *Opportunity* articles and gaining intellectual recognition for it. In August, for example, one of his most significant articles, "The Problem of Race Classification," a review of Roland Dixon's book, *The Racial History of Man*, appeared in *Opportunity* and brought the following letter from Melville Herskovits, the New School of Social Research anthropologist: "That review of Dixon's book which was in last month's Opportunity was the best I have seen yet, barring none. The man who wrote it has a grasp of the subject that makes me wonder if he himself isn't a physical anthropologist instead of a philosopher. It was great! If he comes to town, I hope you will see that I get a chance to talk with him."[4] Written just before Locke left for Europe, "The Problem of Race Classification" was impressive not only because it attacked Dixon's views, but because it dismantled Dixon's analysis by exposing the contradictions in its science. "The paradox of Professor Dixon's book is that recognizing so clearly that the criteria of race-type which he chooses cannot be expected to conform with descriptive accuracy to the 'natural race groups,' he nevertheless persists in treating them in his conclusions as historical strains or actual races...and [as] responsible for characteristic effects and influences throughout human history." Just as Locke's PhD dissertation had exposed the gulf between abstract value categories and how values actually were used in human experience, here too Locke showed "there is a flagrant inconsistency involved in treating these abstract race-types as equivalent to actual sub-species or natural and cultural race groups."[5] Dixon himself admitted this distinction and then went right ahead and contradicted his own caution by using these categories to describe actual living social groups. Here was Locke's approach at its best—simply maximize the contradictions in racist thought and let it collapse on its refusal to agree with facts.

Locke concluded of Dixon's research:

> One need only call attention in this regard to the fact that on Professor
> Dixon's own criteria and comparison, the relationships of cephalic indices link peoples as different in physiognomic and cultural type as the
> Proto-Australoid [one of Dixon's own abstract race types] and the

Mediterranean—whereas the Proto-Australoid and the Proto-Negrooid, linked culturally and geographically, exhibit quite the greatest divergence in cranial indices of any of the eight primary types. One more anthropologist goes over to the idols of the tribes.[6]

"The Problem of Race Classification" brought *Opportunity* scientific attention, not only from Herskovits but also Franz Boas, the father of modern anthropology, who contacted Johnson favorably about the review. That confirmed Locke's increasing value to the magazine. Even Dixon contacted the editor to state he would answer Locke's review by letter, though no such letter survives in the Locke Papers. It is unlikely that he wrote one: in the face of such a disarming and devastating review, Dixon would have had little to write in his own defense.

The same month "Race Classification" appeared, Locke was in Paris, working on a new article on the most exciting writer to appear in French literature in recent years—Rene Maran, the bespectacled Martiniquan author whose novel, *Batouala*, had appeared in 1921 and turned the literary world of France upside down. Educated in Bordeaux, the thoroughly assimilated Maran had spent several years as a colonial official in Equatorial Africa and then authored a story of life under French colonialism that exposed the barbarity, cruelty, and sloth of French occupation. Yet remarkably, the French literary establishment awarded the novel France's highest literary award, the Goncourt Prize; afterward, a storm of protest erupted in the French press over why Frenchmen honored such an indictment of French rule. White French writers, some of whom were also former colonial officials, rushed into print a slew of "antidotes" to *Batouala* that provided a more romantic view of African life under colonialism, but also provided a more humane view of Africans because of Maran's book. Locke seized upon this development as symbolic of what he wanted to occur in the United States—a transformation in the representation of people of African descent by the literary work of a Black author. That observation led him to write his finest article in *Opportunity* to date, "The Colonial Literature of France," appearing in the November 1923 issue of the magazine.

"Colonial Literature" was a breakthrough, not only in style but also in substance, because the article not only updated his critique of imperialism and colonialism in the Race Contacts lectures but also amplified his suggestion in Lecture Five that cultural practice—colonial literature—could transform imperialism. For Locke, publication of Maran's *Batouala* (1921) was a watershed event, because it inaugurated "a new colonial literature for which no allowances and apologies need to be made."[7] Rather than caricaturing the colonialized subject as subhuman and incapable of self-determination, the new colonial literature painted the African as complex and human. Rather optimistically, Locke argued the normal hierarchy had been upended: a work of literature—Maran's novel—was now transforming the discourse of colonialism by advancing a counter-discourse that opened a new front in the cultural struggle between the colonized and the colonizer. Rather than political protest or sociological exegesis, a work of imagination had brought about a revolution in feeling. For the very popularity of Maran's novel had symbolized that the French White public was ready for a change.

> With the stylistic capacities of a Flaubert or a de Maupassant, Maran seems almost to have chose to be the Zola of colonial literature, and with cruel realism and cutting irony has sought to drive the lie and hypocrisy out of its traditional point of view. It was heroic work—and required to be done by the Negro himself—this revolutionary change from sentimentality to realism, from caricature to portraiture. And if I am not very mistaken, Maran's real thrust is more anti-romantic and anti-sentimentalist than anti-imperialist: it is the literary traducers whom he would annihilate. Let us have the unbiased truth and the same angle of vision for all; that is Maran's literary creed.[8]

That last caveat was important for Locke: describing "Maran's real thrust is more anti-romantic... than anti-imperialist" allowed White people into the discourse without forcing them to be unpatriotic. As evidence, Locke examined several other books, White-authored novels like Gaston-Joseph's *Koffi* and Jean and Jerome Tharand's *Samba Diouf's Adventure* as part of this new literature, even though they were not as good as *Batouala*. Not only were these other novels less well written, they also kept the "real dilemma of colonialism concealed behind the cloaks of optimism and rhetoric." But Locke included them to suggest they were trying to function as writers as "neither of the race partisans nor of the colonial apologists... but of those of the social surgeons."[9] By sanctioning these novels, Locke sought to show that Maran's novel was a catalyst forcing serious writers into this new wave of "colonial literature." By such an inclusive maneuver—similar to what he would do in the 1930s by including White-authored novels in his retrospective reviews of Negro literature—Locke signaled that the movement he described was a new, more inclusive domain of imaginative literature rather than a partisan literary ghetto. In effect, Locke sought to create an incentive for the French to transcend their racism through writing even if they remained colonials in their daily practice.

Such an agenda had its risks. For while Locke argued that the best of this new literature was Maran's *Batouala*, Locke devoted more space to discussing the plots of these romanticized books than to Maran's book. Was that because he found White paternalist interest in the Black experience more significant than a Black writing angrily about the rape of colonialism? "The Colonial Literature of France" was the first of Locke's articles during the 1920s to open the door to Harold Cruse's criticism in *The Crisis of the Negro Intellectual* (1967) that Harlem

Renaissance intellectuals bought into the notion that generating White paternalistic interest would further Black cultural liberation, rather than investing wholeheartedly in a separate, Black nationalist literary movement. Even more important, Locke's new position was at odds with the central insight of his unpublished lectures Race Contacts, that racist ideologies emerged from the *practice* of race and changed only in relation to changes in the daily life of race contacts. Locke anticipates Herbert Marcuse's view in *The Aesthetic Dimension* (1977) that some forms of literature—the nineteenth-century period of romantic literature, for Marcuse; the twentieth-century period of colonial literature, for Locke—could provide a utopian image of a world that does not yet exist.[10] Locke was betting that even a literature that romanticizes colonialism could open up a space for a more humane view of the colonized before the daily practice of colonialism changed. But Locke also could be guilty of romanticizing this new "colonial literature" as a benign province of collaboration. Another, more compelling view was that such literature was an arena of conflict in which the White French writers tried to displace Maran's more critical appraisal with their more romantic portrait of colonialism.

One of the authors Locke reviewed in his article directly contested the revolution in colonial attitude implicit in Maran's novel. In his preface to *Koffi*, Gaston-Joseph attacked Maran as a traitor whose book spread vicious lies about the African under French colonialism. Gaston-Joseph's novel was written to counter Maran's representation of French colonialism and was part of a counterrevolution that included some French publishers, who refused to publish Maran's subsequent novels, because they believed *Batouala* had been an abomination. Although Maran's *Batouala* had won the Goncourt Prize and was popular with the French public, the ruling elite in France hated this work, especially because of the acclaim and popularity it had received. But one would not learn any of that from Locke's article, which silenced the conflict Maran's novel had produced in the French literary establishment. Why did Locke downplay this aspect of the story in "The Colonial Literature of France"?

Did Locke deliberately hide the French antipathy to Maran? Probably not. But Locke's Enlightenment faith in the possibility of the imagination to transform racism was rooted in his own personal need to find a sense of purpose in the work he now was committing himself to. Motherless, alone, abandoned, really, by even those who were friendly with him, he needed a cause célèbre to give his life meaning. Locke's step back from the searing indictment of *Race Contacts* was calculated to enable him to move beyond the study of race to actually change race relations. To become an aesthetic activist, he had to be a pragmatist, and behave as if it were true—that a literary rapprochement between warring ideological interests was occurring, even if the principals could not yet speak to one another. Implying that they had already was just a bit of slippage he could live with. A slippery racial politics was also part of it, for Locke was walking a tightrope: he must encourage, support, and celebrate Black literary accomplishment, and yet not celebrate it as a Black thing for fear that it would produce a counter-reaction of Black racism and self-segregation that would destroy the first fruits of an opening of colonial minds. And that would be bad for Locke. In "Colonial Literature," Locke was constructing a role for himself as a critic above the fray—the "objective" and racially impartial man of the Enlightenment, even more than the passionate man of renaissance. Colonial literature, like Black literature, must seize White attention, by defining the movement as being as much about them as Black people. From now on, while his essays and articles were statements of truth, they were also constructing a new subjectivity. In a sense, the faith he had in colonial literature was the faith he had in himself—to shape a new world despite the obstacles placed by racists who refused to see reason instead of race. If the French public could confront the blasphemy of French colonial exploitation and do it forcefully, honestly, and courageously, there was hope for the Americans as well.

Locke's enthusiasm for what was happening in French colonial literature mushroomed once he arrived in Germany, sometime in early August, and began to study the issue of Black French troops in Germany. For over a year, press reports in America had carried stories of how colonial troops of mainly African soldiers had been used by France to occupy Germany after the World War and how Germans saw these Africans as an "abomination" on its citizenry. "If one would believe the German pamphlets and posters," Locke wrote in "Black Watch on the Rhine," the second of his *Opportunity* articles written abroad, "France is maintaining and abetting an army of black rapists in the heart of a civilized self-respecting people."[11] To investigate these reports, reputedly under a commission from the League of Nations, Locke left Berlin not long after arriving and traveled throughout southern and eastern Germany, visiting Coblentz, Konigstein, Wiesbaden, and Mayence, in an effort to document African troop behavior.

Locke's first surprise was that there were so many African troops in Germany. Almost every French unit he encountered had some, often the majority, and organized completely without the segregation characteristic of American troops in the World War. Not only were they dispersed throughout the French army, but they also could be found at all ranks, several as officers commanding White French soldiers—something unheard of in American or British armies. He also found that African troops had been seriously misrepresented by the newspapers and the Germans. At Coblentz, "I stood one night for nearly three hours—until nearly one . . . and watched them come in . . . and they were almost without exception, merry, smart, and sober—as a sample test it by no means bore out the rumors that have centered particularly about the colored troops at Coblentz." In Konigstein, he "met many obviously respectable women walking unescorted as far as two kilometers from the town, through the wooded lanes, as late as ten o'clock—which is late in a small village town—obviously safe in mind and body."

A German magistrate informed Locke that the people had had "more trouble with the hundred or so Frenchmen (mostly of superior ranks) than with the nine hundred or so who were African."[12] Locke concluded that the German propaganda machine had maligned African troops not because they were salacious, but it was a useful tactic to try to get all occupying troops removed from Germany.

But as the article progressed, Locke became preoccupied with the French racial attitude and transformed what was supposed to be a study of African troop behavior in Germany into something more—a comparative study of "Anglo-Saxon" versus "Latin" or French race practices. His conclusion: the French mind was remarkably free of the need, so dominant in the "Anglo-Saxon mind," for segregation and caste division of troops along racial lines. In the French forces in Germany, Locke found that the French had deployed African troops throughout the army, as officers and regular soldiers, in a "kaleidoscopic" pattern of race, color, and class. "France has made an expediency of her virtue, and not as the others, so often a virtue of expediency—having always been traditionally fair to her colored subjects, she now finds that it pays to be—and very candidly, very opportunely, she has made her colonial forces the back-bone of her military occupation."[13] The White French, in short, had thoroughly assimilated the African and transcended the European's traditional racial bias. Interestingly, the French Africans had remained self-consciously Black:

> I have heard it repeatedly said—often as if it implied something desira-
> ble, that the colored Frenchman was merely a Frenchman who happens
> to be colored. But here...there was observable something quite differ-
> ent and, in my judgment, something finer and more desirable. French
> in many respects...these men were nevertheless quite thoroughly and
> self-respectingly native to the core, without the least sign or symptom
> of deracialization.[14]

A clearer example of Locke's cultural pluralism could not be found than here. Almost incredibly, in Locke's romantic vision of Afro-French colonialism, Blacks remained nationalistic and committed to self-determination (to a return home to Tunis or Martinique, for example) despite being completely comfortable in the bosom of post war French fraternity.

Locke's own personal feelings toward the French occupation drove this almost homoerotic sense of French military culture as raceless male bonding with Africans. France and French-occupied Germany accepted him in ways unthinkable in America or England, and yet that acceptance did not smother him: he could still be himself, still feel apart, and still maintain his identity; and that combination of acceptance and separation, of union not unity with the French, shaped what he longed to celebrate about the French. "I was instantly recognized and warmly welcomed as colored...which was indeed a relief after having been for months localized even by most intelligent Europeans as from almost every corner of the earth but the right one. One correction I did have to make—in spite of my bad French, I had to disclaim in turn African birth and French citizenship. And then I was in for apologetics—these men knew about the color question in America."[15] Under such a tolerant racial atmosphere, Locke must have longed to trade his American identity for a colonial one that lacked racial segregation and the personal alienation from others of African heritage. That personal dimension was both the strength and the weakness of "Black Watch." Locke created a felt experience for the reader of the article, as if she or he was traveling through occupied German territory, visiting town after town, looking in on jovial but respectful African soldiers and conflicted Germans and enlightened Frenchmen trying to balance the racial and national complexities of the occupation. But because he was catered to as a very important foreign observer, Locke tended to exaggerate to that reader the liberalism of the French.

This became apparent when Locke's newfound friend, Rene Maran, responded to Locke's article in a letter, first published in a French magazine, and then reprinted, along with a Locke rejoinder, in *Opportunity*. Maran expressed his belief that the American professor had been tricked. "Your article recently published in *Opportunity*... is well done ... but unfortunately for us who know what is really beneath it all, what you recount, though doubtless true enough in itself, does not in any way appear to us worthy of praise." The French, Maran informed his colleague, were two-faced: the French government had smiled in Locke's face, but had laughed behind his back, for their racial policy was just the opposite of what Locke believed it to be. They *had* made a virtue of necessity: without African troops, France could not have occupied Germany for so long. Therefore, they had indulged the African troops and lavished praise on them, but the racial fraternity was calculated and disingenuous. "We are tolerated here, it is true, as one can especially realize who considers who on account of the decline of French man-power, they have increasing need of us. But that has not hindered France up to the very present from using every method to block our way to posts of prime importance."[16] Yes, Maran believed, the French people were more humane than other Europeans, but the government was just as manipulative and even more cunning than other imperialists. What Locke had failed to see was that underneath the veneer of racial tolerance was the iron fist of colonial exploitation and French superiority.

Maran's comments also derived from his personal experience: he was not "welcomed" by the French intellectual establishment after *Batouala* won the Goncourt Prize in 1921. Nor had Maran witnessed any change in French colonial attitudes after the publication of his and other books such as Locke announced in his article. Maran's critique revealed that a softness had crept into Locke's analysis of colonialism: in "Black Watch," for by emphasizing the signs of progressive change in France's imperialistic policies, Locke had failed to reveal—or perhaps even to see—that such progress might constitute a more advanced form of exploitation. As such, Maran's comments amounted to an indictment of Locke as an unconscious collaborator with French colonialism, whose misreading of the situation exonerated the French not only from their racism but also from the need to end the colonial system itself.

Locke's answer to Maran was published with Maran's critique and suggested that however inaccurate his perceptions were as a portrait of French colonialism, they were accurate as a comparison of French attitudes with American racism. The French were different from the Americans and the British when it came to how they treated people of color, especially Blacks who were not their own colonials. Indeed, as critical an observer of people as the outspoken Claude McKay wrote to Walter White in the spring of 1924 and attested that the French were different: they left him alone in the south of France and allowed him to forget for a while that he was Black. This was not an illusion, although it was also not a good index of how the French actually felt about colonial Africans. At this stage in their colonial history, the French did not need to segregate and demean Africans and people of African descent personally in order to use them and feel superior to them. They realized there would be less resistance from the oppressed if the intelligentsia of the colonies believed that they too were French. As the Algerians would later discover, the French could be as ruthless as the British or the Germans when French interests were threatened by the colonized. But what Locke stated much too generally and sweepingly still retained a grain of truth: the French did not enforce a spatial and bodily segregation toward African Diasporic peoples as the British and the White American did, and that made living around them more pleasant than living among Anglo-Imperialists.

But Maran had identified a fundamental problem of Locke's project. He was still in love with Europe and light years away from the kind of condemnation of colonialism that Aimé Césaire issued in *Discourse on Colonialism* (1955). There, Césaire would announce that because of colonialism, "Europe is unable to justify itself either before the bar of 'reason' or before the bar of 'conscience'; and that, increasingly, it takes refuge in a hypocrisy which is all the more odious because it is less and less likely to deceive. *Europe is indefensible.*"[17]

There were many reasons Europe was still defensible to Locke in 1923, but that he could not see Maran's point goes to a more fundamental epistemological problem that Locke had—and which he had, ironically, tried to expose in Du Bois by asking Frenchman Béton to write an article on the Pan African Congress. African American intellectuals wished to carry out an Afro-Diasporic project or Pan African Congress, as Du Bois put it, without allowing the voices and visions of the African colonized to be fully heard in that collaboration. Locke was actually falling into the trap he had identified in his article, "Cosmopolitanism," in the *Oxford Cosmopolitan*—that the cosmopolitans most often failed to see the world from the Other's perspective when they traveled the world. Locke was doing the same in 1923. Had Locke actually talked extensively with those African soldiers or shown his article to Maran before publishing it, he might have had a more dialogical view of what was happening in France and Germany in relation to the African. He might have learned something of the more insidious ways the French excluded the colonized from their notion of humanity even as they did not impose on them the kind of spatial segregation and dehumanizing body politics of the Anglo-American racial code. As Locke revealed in his response to Maran, he was mainly comparing the French race practice to the American. That was the problem.

All such Pan African or Afro-Diasporic projects hid a profound truth—that the racial formation that African Americans had created out of their encounter with American racism was quite different from those created by colonized Africans or native-born Black Europeans, at least the elites. That different attitude toward, for lack of a better word, Blackness was another source of Maran's anger toward Locke. The bulk of Locke's article was not about White French, but about how the French Africans contradicted the racist stereotypes advanced by the Germans. These Africans were civilized, not through complete assimilation of European culture, but through a sense of "native" pride and racial self-possession that transcended the behavior of Europeans. To Locke, they exemplified nearly a Black Victorian poise toward life that showed they were not deracinated by immersion in European life, but exhibited a kind of regal race consciousness. This was too much for Maran, whose criticality toward French society was not designed to separate from Europe but to be let in on equal terms.

Locke's article highlighted what African Americans had created out of their encounter with the harsher Anglo-American code of racism—a racial counter-nationalism or *nation* within the nation consciousness that spawned a separate Black consciousness within whichever colonizing nation the slave trade or colonialism had deposited them in. It would not be until the next generation of Aimé Césaire and Leopold Senghor that there would emerge a generation of French-speaking African intellectuals that fused in the Negritude movement Maran's hot anger against the colonial system with Locke's search for a "Black soul." In 1923, even relatively naive African Americans like Locke knew the African American had created a distinctive culture and community out of the encounter with abject Anglo-American racism. The question was, what had non-elite Africans created out of their encounter with the fist-in-the-glove racism of the French? Locke saw examples of a self-determining racial identity peeking out from the African wartime encounter with German, English, and, according to Maran, French racism. Locke was not saying that these Africans had the same consciousness as that of American Blacks, but something he found imminently finer—a composite cultural identity that took the best from the Europeans, especially the French, and bound it with an Africanness to create an African abroad who was self-confident, self-possessed, and free. As such, Locke shouldered a more complex agenda in "Black Watch" than credited by Maran. What Locke fashioned was not only a rosy view of French race relations but also an optimistic view of the prospects for a Pan-African subjectivity to emerge out of the clash of cultures the World War had produced. Ironically, Locke was finding this subjectivity most powerfully expressed in Berlin.

For in Berlin, Locke found an agreeable circle of Pan-African expatriates, of whom Claude McKay was the most important. Certainly, Locke already was familiar with McKay's work. Born in 1889 in Clarendon Parish, McKay had startled America with his sharply retributive poem, "If We Must Die," published in a radical White magazine, the *Liberator*, in 1919, for it asked Blacks to retaliate against White mob violence in the Chicago race riot. He had then coedited the *Liberator*, traveled to the Soviet Union, and published a book of poems, *Harlem Shadows*, by 1922 that was well received. But Locke probably had not met McKay or made his acquaintance before the summer of 1923, when McKay was holed up in Berlin. In August 1923, their relations got off to a great start, perhaps because McKay, who was bisexual, turned Locke on to several bisexual bars in Berlin, and because the boisterous, manipulative, deeply conflicted McKay anchored the Black expatriate community living in Berlin. McKay recalled that community after both had left. "I left Berlin in October—just in time to enter hospital in Paris [after the constant round of partying that went on]. I grew ill again with pneumonia just after getting out round Christmas time—and I really thought I was going to die then—my whole system was so debilitated. But a couple of friends rescued me and sent me here to the south of France where I am also working on my <u>novel....</u>The gang all went to pieces in Berlin. Some went to America, others to Italy, Charlie Ashleigh arrested and deported to London."[18]

Locke enjoyed his summer in Berlin in part because of "the gang." From childhood up he was pushed to achieve great things; he was taught to be disciplined, responsible, respectable, and aristocratically controlled in all that he did. Locke had developed early, been hailed as a genius, and then had lost it, even though he continued to seek fame as well as the honor and respect of his race. The combination of respectability and eagerness to please had welded him into a tightly wound man, who seldom, if ever, seemed capable of letting his hair down. Finally, abroad this summer of 1923 in Paris, in southern German towns, and now in his beloved Berlin, he could relax—or at least hang out in the cafes with friends, talk intellectual trash, shoot his biting, sarcastic wit, and be the jovial, unmasked Locke.

In part, it was because sex was not an issue. Locke had rekindled his love affair with Rudolph, spent a great deal of time being dined and entertained by Rudolph's family, and felt marvelously comfortable, especially considering the extremely favorable exchange rates as the German mark plummeted to all-time lows in 1923. Locke and Rudolph had accepted that the two of them could never live together in Washington, so they were enjoying as much of their companion-ship in Berlin, though laced through with the pain that this too would soon be gone. For a moment, Locke could relish the unqualified acceptance of his young German lover.

But the Black expatriate community in Berlin was also a reason he was elated. Unlike in 1922, there were more Black people in Berlin, who transformed Berlin's bohemian nightlife into something more multicultural. Finally, here was a com-munity whose joie de vivre and intellectual interests matched, or outdistanced his own. Almost every night he could go out to one of his favorite cafes in downtown Berlin, see and drink with diasporic Negroes as alienated from their hometowns as he was from his. Here was the precursor to the kind of New Negro community he would declare existed in Harlem two years later. Why? Because in Berlin, creative Black intellectuals could indulge all sides of their complex per-sonalities, feed all of their sexual and intellectual proclivities, and be fully outra-geous without having to look over their shoulders at the bourgeoisie, White or Black, for being artistic rebels of one kind or another. In Berlin, these race cosmopolitans were comfortable discussing European and American modernist literature, classical music, ballet, and the opera in multiple languages while still being provocatively Black. A new kind of Pan African emerged in Berlin—an Afro-Diasporic subject with a worldliness and breadth of knowledge absent from the nineteenth-century Negro intelligentsia they replaced with an openness to modernist European cultures that was absent from the Black nationalisms of the 1960s.

There were limits, however, and plenty of personal rivalries. An intense intel-lectual rivalry characterized this community that sanctioned the right, as Black modernists, to skewer one another's intellectual biases or cultural tastes as old-fashioned. No one was better at that than McKay, who recalled walking through the Tiergarten with Locke in Berlin in 1923. "And walking down the row, with the statues of the Prussian kings supported by the famous philosophers and poets and composers on either side, he remarked to me that he thought those statues the finest ideal and expression of the plastic arts in the world. The remark was amusing, for it was just a short while before I had walked through the same row with George Grosz, who had described the statues as 'the sugar-candy art of Germany.' When I showed Dr. Locke George Grosz's book of draw-ings, Ecce Homo, he recoiled from their brutal realism."[19] Grosz, the radical German artist and critic, was the quintessential artist of Weimar German art, fusing a powerful cartoonish realism with a criticality toward the shibboleths of Bismarck Germany. Clearly, some of the politics of interwar Germany outdis-tanced Locke's own.

Locke's taste in German art was old-fashioned and modernist too; but McKay's remembrance, which may have been affected by later conflicts between them, hides what Locke really liked about this particular row of sculptures in the

Tiergarten. McKay gives us a hint, though, when he describes that Locke and he were looking at "the statues of the Prussian kings supported by the famous philosophers and poets and composers on either side." It was great "plastic art" to Locke, because of the *work* this art did! Unlike a socialist dilettante like McKay, Locke brought into the Afro-Diasporic intellectual community in Germany a racial nationalism that did not exist even in McKay. Recall that Marcus Garvey's racial nationalist project flourished in the United States, not in Jamaica, where color and class within the Jamaican nation made Black nationalism an uphill battle for Garvey. Locke gravitated to Germany not only because of its aesthetic and sexual tastes—but also because he saw it as emblematic of the African American struggle. Part of his enthusiasm for Germany during the World War derived from his sense that Germany had to fight its way to nationalism, just as Italy had to during the Renaissance. A disparate and diasporic people needed an art to suture its political body together. Tiergarten "statuary" chronicled something Grosz could take for granted but that Locke could not—that Blacks were a nation or at least a people with its own aspirations and agenda. Locke wanted an art that depicted a Black national identity like the German national identity that was available for Grosz to deconstruct.

One did not have to go to Berlin to see how Europeans used such art to advance their national identities: a casual walk through Rome almost always encountered busts depicting the great minds of Greek and Roman poetry, politics, and philosophy. Nowhere, however, in America in 1923 could one walk and see anything like a visual celebration of Black accomplishment. Perhaps, for McKay, that was a good thing, but for Locke, art could become self-critical only after it was established as a secure national formation. It was easy to caricature him. But that caricature actually hid what even McKay, in his later work *Harlem: Negro Metropolis*, came to appreciate—that the signal feature of African American life in Harlem was a racial nationalism that gave Negro people agency in a White world seemingly devoted to their social death.

Perhaps Locke had a sense of the smirking attitude with which McKay regarded him, because when Locke finally left Berlin for Egypt he did not inform McKay he was leaving. Perhaps Locke realized he needed to keep this personal decision—and perhaps his ambivalences about going to Egypt—hidden, lest it become fodder for more diasporic mirth. "I didn't even know whether you had gone to Egypt or not," McKay complained afterward. He kept others in the dark as well. Helen Irvin wrote to him in November, "I'm wondering if you have decided to go on to Egypt,"[20] after receiving several manuscripts by mail after he had begun his journey south. Locke was still hesitant, after months of planning, preparation, grant making, and leave-taking, to commit publicly to exploring the continent of his ancestors. Why?

It probably was foreboding for this fastidiously prompt, obsessively neat, and compulsively clean Black Victorian to go into a hot, dirty, differently ordered country of people Locke probably regarded as a lot more civilized three thousand years ago than in 1923. For a frail, chronically ill little man, whose colds, flu, and infections rendered him dysfunctional for weeks, the fear of illness was real. Also real was the threat of robbery, theft, or murder in Egypt. Make no mistake—Locke was most comfortable in Berlin which, even in its down years during the 1920s, was one of the most meticulously ordered cities in the world. Locke was leaving that for the unknown shores of an African nation where clocks were guides, not rigid markers of time of arrival. That Locke hesitated was natural, even if it did not fit his master narrative that all African Americans should travel home one day to Mother Africa. It was a dream of a potential African American leader, but a nightmare for the diminutive, obsessively sanitary Alain Locke.

Yet he went, though not before a brief detour to Vienna. On September 24, he left Berlin for Vienna, in part to be there to hear a concert on October 1 by the first African American vocalist to challenge the color line in modern concert singing, Roland Hayes. Though there had been others before him—most notably the "Black Patti," Sisserata Jones—Hayes was the first to be taken seriously as an artist. Black singers were often acknowledged as superior in sheer range and volume to White singers—already in the early 1920s—but were considered musical athletes, people whose "natural born" talent shown through their lack of musical training. Indeed, Locke bought into elements of this argument, for when he came to write about Hayes's accomplishment, he stressed repeatedly that his success was the result of discipline, hard work, and musical training, not innate talent. Raw talent did not advance the argument Locke wanted to make—that the Negro artist was superior because of practice, hard work, discipline, and refinement of technique, rather than because of what White people commonly attributed to nineteenth-century Black singers—"Dey show got rhythm"—and in this case, the big Black voice. For Locke, that Black voice was as much a stereotypical loadstone as the big Black body, so that the refined, whisper-voiced Roland Hayes—Locke called his voice of "medium volume"—was a perfect symbol of what he wished to advocate for the Black artist. Locke wanted the Black artist to flourish through cultivation and high ambition; such characteristics would produce a voice that could be heard around the world, in all the best music halls of Europe—where such a voice was more appreciated anyway. And then Hayes returned to Boston and New York and Philadelphia and the music directors who would not have given him an interview before his European triumphs, now said, "Will you sing for us?" Then the story would be, as Locke put it: "So an Acropolis [of racial segregation that denied Hayes the right to sing in American fine art concert halls] has been captured by the shrewd strategy of a flank attack."[21] That "flank attack," again, was going to Europe.

When Locke caught up with Hayes on his own flank attack in 1923, the concert singer was already a European celebrity, having given a command performance before King George V of England at Buckingham Palace and having sung with Paris, Berlin, and Vienna orchestras. Even more, European critics had embraced him. One from the *Mittag-Zeitung* wrote: "Not as a Negro, but as a great artist, he [Hayes] captured and moved his audience."[22] Here, again, was the dichotomy. Thus, it was not surprising that on September 24, a month after getting his visa for Egypt, Locke decided to hear Roland Hayes sing before going down to Egypt land. Locke came to Vienna to witness something as important to him as the reopening of King Tut's tomb—"the music capital of Europe" shower its affection on the Negro from Georgia Europe had adopted as its own. Locke would record the importance of this concert in his article, "Roland, An Appreciation," published in *Opportunity* in December 1923, just after Hayes sang with the Boston Symphony for the first time.

Attending Hayes's October 1 concert in Vienna at the Mittlerer-Konzerthaus, Locke got what he came for.

> [It was the musical event of the season as testified by the presence of] several critics [who] missed Jeritz's annual leave-taking of the Opera to attend; that Madame Arnoldson Fischoff, the primadonna who has sung with the greatest tenors of two musical generations from Tamango to Bathstini, requested an Italian aria as an encore and declared it "perfectly sung;" that the creator of the role of Parsifal declared very generously that he would have given half his career for such mastery of the mezza-voice; that occasional Americans of the foreign colony spoke with pride of "our American artist" whom until recently they could never have heard without condescension and in some parts of our country, proscription and segregation.[23]

Europe was granting Black people the kind of recognition, indeed the kind of respect, that they sorely missed in the United States. It was an important confirmation of a little known fact, according to Locke. "We have as a group more artistic talent and fewer artists than any other; nature has in music done too much for us—so that in this musical generation we have produced but two artists whose equipment can challenge the international standard—Roland Hayes and Hazel Harrison." Other Black artists could gain acclaim if they too "challenge[d] the international standard."[24] Rather than settling for the kind of provincial acclaim that many a local talent had settled for, especially talented Blacks in a segregated and circumscribed White America, Hayes had sought out and studied with the best in America and abroad, and then tested his voice in concert halls throughout Europe against the best tenors in the world. He had avoided the "quicksands of the double standard," the particular nemesis of talented Blacks, imposed by Black and White Americans alike, who hailed the exceptional Black talent as already an artist, long before he or she was. Holding Black talent to a lower standard of evaluation because of the reality of segregation was particularly affronting to Locke—it meant to lower oneself to the "vogue of the Negro." Given his own challenges putting his talent to the international test by being a Rhodes Scholar, Locke could take a special joy in Hayes's triumph; Hayes was like a son who had succeeded where the father had failed, and in doing so had helped to erase the pain of the earlier fall.

Today we might lament the corollary of Locke's position—if Europe was the objective standard of Black excellence, then excellence was denied African American forms of music that were not Europeanized. Such bias limited his taste as a critic. But the belief in Europe as the ultimate cultural standard had unique meanings in 1923. Then, Europe was the epitome of culture, for most intellectuals, and an important leverage for Black intellectuals like Locke who saw culture as an ideological weapon: European recognition of Black artists put the lie to the White American argument that African Americans were kept out of opera houses and concert halls as performers because they were inferior. Without access to European cultural arenas, Black artists would be frozen out like Black baseball players who, because they could not compete against White players, could not prove—perhaps to themselves as well as others—that they were as good as if not better than their White counterparts. European recognition allowed Black artists and intellectuals to show not only the racism but also the cultural inferiority of the White American elite who, once Europe sanctioned Hayes, rushed to book him in the United States. American culture was as much of a slave as it imagined the Negro to be. For imbedded in the argument for a "single standard of judgment" was a Black aesthete's belief that if African Americans worked hard to earn European recognition, they could substitute European opinion for the negative one streaming from American critics continuously and internalize a higher standard of excellence despite American racism.

Without the European bias, Locke's argument boiled down to Ralph Ellison's later position in "The Little Man at Chehaw Station," an essay on how Helen Harrison, the European-trained pianist and Locke's friend, demanded of Ellison to "always play your best even if it's only in the waiting room at Chehaw Station because in this country there'll always be a little man hidden behind the stove...and he'll know the *music*, and the *tradition*, and the standards of *musicianship* required for whatever you set out to perform!"[25] Ellison used this example to argue for the critical astuteness of one's audience and its demand that the artist is loyal to his or her craft, regardless of how mean the circumstances of its performance. This sense of living up to a single standard of excellence in the arts knit together Locke, Hayes, Harrison, and a generation of African American artists, whether they succeeded against racism or not. Ellison's argument, when added to Locke's, meant this: you had to be your own toughest critic, even when one's audience would tolerate less. That sense of a single standard of excellence in the arts set the limit on Locke's cultural relativism. Locke retained a belief in universal values of excellence, even if the content of the aesthetic product varied, for it was only in the universality of form that true equality was possible. That was what Europe meant to him, regardless of whether it was Prussian statuary, Alfred Loos's modernist architecture, or a Hayes's rendering of an African American spiritual.

Locke told the Roland Hayes story for another reason: it showed those back home that a Negro could excel on the international stage and retain his cultural identity. Performing up to a European standard did not mean "deracialization," for like the colonial African soldiers in French uniforms, Hayes had remained Black by insisting on singing the spirituals in all of his concerts, and, according to Locke, with some difficulty. "That which might have been expected to make Mr. Hayes' career easier upon the basis of a novelty has really, to my knowledge, been a difficult crusade....Accompanists have often failed to interpret them properly, critics have been condescending toward them while nevertheless wholly favorable to other classical number...orchestral traditions [have had to be] broken to allow them as part of several programs."[26] But Hayes had persisted and succeeded in winning acceptance of the spirituals as "art songs," even if "not always an admission of equal value...always there has been conceded a seriousness of purpose and mission and loyalty to self."[27] In other words, Locke saw in Hayes a sign of what he would tell young Black artists that when one enters European spaces, it does not require one to become White and abandon one's cultural heritage. Rather, one brings the tradition that nurtured you— Hayes grew up in the Baptist Church and sang with the Fisk Jubilee Singers while a student at that university—and demand that others accept it in accepting you. The result of Hayes's campaign was to introduce African American music internationally and win acceptance of the form "upon an art plane." And the achievement was permanent: today, the singing of spirituals by classically trained singers such as Kathleen Battle and Jessye Norman is commonplace and unquestioned.

Locke's appreciation, however, did not tell the whole truth about his newfound friend. Hayes was also the most Europeanized of Black American singers. The Germans loved him, because he sang German lieder almost exclusively, except for an occasional aria and a spiritual or two. Hayes had won his way into the hearts of the Germans, Austrians, and Italians by paying them the highest compliment of singing their songs. Though born the son of a slave in a cabin in Georgia, Hayes had taken to the acculturation communicated through music teachers in the South and become completely enamored of the world that generated Mozart, Haydn, and Schubert. Hayes adopted Europeans and their culture (he dated his letters, for instance, in the European form of day first, then month and the year), stayed in the best European hotels he could afford, socialized with Europe's musical elite who invited him into their homes, and felt, quite naturally, more at home in Europe than stateside. Yes, he did sing those spirituals. But he sang them as European art songs, and only sang them on programs with

such European art songs, thus elevating the spirituals, Locke would have believed, from their dusty Georgia origins to concert hall material—not only by
association with European songs but also by the way that he sang them, with
a diction, a serenity, a reverence that was transcendental and airily European.
Hearing Hayes sing the spirituals reminded one much more of the Viennese concert hall Locke heard them in than the slave cabins they—or he—hailed from. In
a word, he had transformed himself into a Euro-Negro who was an ambassador
of everything Locke hoped for in the coming New Negro artist. In that sense,
Locke's article wrapped Hayes in the cover of racial contributions and provided
an interpretation of Hayes that was flattering as well as racially progressive.
Not surprisingly, when Hayes wrote Locke after the article was published, Hayes
was pleased with it. "Now for the 'article'... it is the most masterful piece of
writing and it has thrilled me beyond words. My dear boy, it is truly wonderful."[28]

Hayes had something else that Locke may have longed for, but which neither
Locke nor the Harlem literati had: Hayes had performing talent, and hence, a
paying audience that subsidized a grand lifestyle in Europe. Sure, it was nice for
Locke to have a few subsidized articles in *Opportunity*, but that was nothing
compared to the booked concerts that Hayes had.

> We are filling 10 concert dates in Czechoslovakia, one in Budapest, and
> two in Berlin. I shall be in Berlin to sing on the 10th of May. My London
> and Paris concerts have been one triumph after another. I sang again in
> Paris with the Cologne Orchestra on March 22nd. Dear Boy, my life is so
> beautiful and satisfying now that my cup of joy remains perpetually at
> a state of overflow. I never expected to have been so happy in this life as
> the success of my work (which is my meat and drink) has brought me.
> My darling Mother passed on to bring all of this to me and I recognize
> her Individuality and her great love in it all.[29]

The love that Hayes's mother had given him provided him a career as a singer,
who could travel grandly through Europe with his companion and his manager.
Apparently Locke poured his heart out to his friend in the fall of 1923, perhaps
about his long-standing need for a permanent companion of his own. "Dear
Locke, I have had all your kind communications and I have been more than
mindful of you and them, but my duties have been too great and numerous to
write you. I have felt oh! so concerned about you and have wondered if there was
anything I could do to assist you in any way. Dear boy, if I can do anything you
have only to be reminded of what I told you in Vienna that holds for all time."[30]
Precisely at the time when Locke had to give up the prospect of living with
Rudolph, Hayes had a lifestyle that imposed no restrictions on him, and in sympathy with his lesser plight, Hayes offered Locke an older brother's shoulder to
lean on. Plus, because Hayes was talented and loved, he had carte blanche to the

elite European cultural class that even the Rhodes Scholar from Philadelphia did not usually count among his friends. "I was in Vienna a few days ago for one day only," Hayes confided in the same letter, "and I spent a delightful two hours with mutual friends, his Excellency and Frau Twardowski, Frau Wassermann, and Baron Berlesps." Hayes had introduced Locke to some of the singer's friends: "They all spoke warmly of you and were most interested to hear of your profitable visit in Egypt. They all received your cards and were much elated over the fact that you thought of them. I saw Herrn Fruhmann, too, who was also anxious for news of you. You will be sorry to know that he has just lost his dear mother. She was so fond of you. Lawrence has also met these friends with me."[31] Hayes's Viennese friends should not have been surprised that Locke had remembered them enough to send them cards from Egypt: they were the type of Viennese that Locke wanted as real friends. Hayes was living the kind of life Locke longed for. Concerts in the best opera houses, completely free of segregation—racial but not class—was fine with Locke. But even more than class, what the Berlin and Vienna set offered Locke was a milieu that truly appreciated the arts, really lived for the arts, and in doing so met his aesthetic tastes. Here was a society in which the finest china, the best silver, two-hundred-year-old silver chalices, beautiful evening gowns, and spectacular chandeliers in even more spectacular homes dazzled as if alive. Locke loved all that and those whose primary loyalties were to aesthetic things, not political causes.

The Hayes meeting and article suggest something of the complexity of Locke's motives en route to Egypt. One of them comes from Locke the aesthete, who headed to Egypt as he went to Hayes's concerts to honor the art that Black people had produced and to find in the artistic renaissance of King Tut's reign in 1300 B.C. inspiration for a contemporary artistic awakening in Europe. In that sense, his trip south conformed to a narrative of Northern European homosexual aesthetes who traveled to Italy, Greece, and the Middle East to explore a world of unqualified artistic accomplishment and the more tolerant social and sexual world of the Mediterranean. Locke was part of an intellectual and cultural tradition, informed by the works of Johann Winckelmann and other closeted classicists who had created an idealized image culture in Greece. But in this instance, another motive came from Locke as a Black man. He could not really claim Greece or Italy as part of his ancestral heritage the way that Winckelmann, Walter Pater, Oscar Wilde, or John Addington Symonds could. Egypt, however, was another matter. It could be his in a way that it could not be theirs. Egypt could serve as a classical past of a broadly Pan Africanist, African American consciousness, even if Egypt was technically a bit distant.

True, Egypt was, in North Africa, geographically quite removed from direct genealogical lineage. But for a Black intellectual of Locke's generation who had been influenced by such early writings as Edward Blyden's *Islam, Christianity and the Negro Race*, the notion that Islamic Africa was as much or more a part of the heritage of African Americans was not a leap. Indeed, it became his public rationale for the trip—the notion that as a Black American, he had an interest in and a right to be a witness and interpreter of the King Tut tomb excavation. Implicit in this idea was the notion of Black Studies—that certain areas of studies, such as Egyptology, were not just human studies or part of the humanities, but the particular interest and province of Black scholars, and as such, the arena of Black scholars like himself. As a Black philosopher, he was going to Egypt as an aesthetic or cultural nationalist, whose Pan-Africanist purpose was to mine what he, after Edward Blyden and others, regarded as an archive of African knowledge in the tomb of King Tut. Locke had to go to Egypt because it was an African nation, the only one he knew that also had been a world civilization.

Locke still needed an intellectual perspective on his trip that went beyond the Afrocentrism of Edward Blyden. He found this in books he purchased and lectures he attended while in Vienna. In addition to the opera, the art museum, the anthropological museum, and two Hayes concerts in Vienna, Locke also found time to sign up for the winter semester of open academic lectures at the Vienna Internationale Hochschulkurse. Catalogs in the Alain Locke Papers at Howard show that Locke heard lectures on the history of German literature in the nineteenth century, and the development of theories of national character, and purchased recently published books by Sigmund Freud and Leo Frobenius, the German archaeologist. Such work may partially explain why Locke was going to Egypt rather than sub-Saharan Africa at this time. Frobenius did extensive research in Egypt and North Africa, some of it leading to his famous rock painting studies. Shortly after attending these lectures, Locke wrote to Helen Irvin that he had tried to get permission to translate one of Frobenius's works into English, a prospect she enthusiastically applauded, "You must be having a wonderfully interesting time of it and how splendid about the Frobenius translation! That of itself justifies the trip, no matter what may be the attitude of Howard."[32]

Frobenius was popular with African American intellectuals because he argued that African cultures were commensurate with European and Mediterranean cultures generally. Born in Berlin in 1873, Frobenius was a professor of cultural anthropology, a curator of a museum, and a prolific writer on "rock painting" and other symbolic forms of African peoples. He had also been the first German scientist to attack social Darwinism and the notion that some cultures were inevitably "primitive." Conducting excavations in Germany and North Africa, he found comparable rock paintings and concluded they were part of the same basic civilization. He bolstered his claims about the aesthetic excellence of African cultures when he discovered the beautiful Benin sculptures in Nigeria during one of his excavations. His writings influenced many intellectuals of African descent, including Leopold Senghor and Aimé Césaire who used his books, particularly his *History of African Civilization*, to provide scientific groundwork for Negritude in the 1930s. Senghor's response to Frobenius may be a clue to Locke's infatuation, for Senghor admitted that Frobenius's research that glorified African civilization helped to wean Senghor and other highly assimilated Africans from their cultural worship of European civilization. Europe *was* a key to a new African Diasporan consciousness.

Studying Frobenius at the Vienna University may have helped Locke contextualize his role as a philosopher headed for Egypt. For as an archaeologist, Frobenius argued that the true scientist of culture had to move beyond mere collection of data to its intuitive interpretation. Frobenius saw himself as a philosopher of peoples. Frobenius also validated Locke's coming trip south in another way, since his earliest work had been in North Africa, where rock pictures revealed a world of symbols and drawings that substantiated the idea that cultural and religious transfusion had been going on for centuries between Egyptian and other African cultures. Rather than simply an isolated civilization, Egypt was part of a broader cultural exchange that extended beyond Africa into the Mediterranean. As such, an Egyptian trip was not simply a nationalist sojourn of self-discovery and hence mainly a "Black" thing, but also something more—a quest to learn concretely how cultural exchange created civilization, something that he had only theorized about in his Race Contacts lectures. Frobenius was a key to a sense of the African heritage as TransAfrican.

The reference to Freud is even more provocative. In his catalog to the academic lectures in Vienna, Locke underlined Freud's *Totem und Taboo*, published in Vienna in 1913, *Group Psychology and the Analysis of the Ego* (1921), and *Das Ich in Da Es*, just published in 1923. Freud was an avid collector of antiquities, particularly Egyptian artifacts, and had a copy of Howard Carter's *The Tomb of Tut Ankhamen* in his library. Turning to Freud's *Totem and Taboo* allowed Locke to approach the study of Egypt as a psychological narrative, rather than simply a political one. Freud's *Ego and Id* may have buttressed the psychological implications Locke would derive from Egypt. In this work, Freud developed fully his theory of the death drive, which he had begun to present in *Beyond the Pleasure Principle* in 1920. Locke's interpretation of Egypt in "Impressions of Luxor" would resonate with comments about how Egyptian culture was a "peculiarly death-worshipping" culture.[33] Reading Freud's death instinct as a trope for Egyptian civilization may also have said something about Locke's personal feelings as he left Vienna for Trieste and then sailed on to Brindisi and Venice. Rather than *Death in Venice*, his trip to Egypt was a reminder of a death in Washington, D.C., the death of his mother, whose funeral had also told his friends and colleagues in Washington that he, Alain Locke, was also a man who worshipped the cult of the dead. His home, where he had preserved his mother for a week or more, had become something of a tomb, and a sign of a Black Victorian culture that not only worshipped the mother as a kind of god but also worshipped the past in a stultifying, deathlike manner, the glorious past of the nineteenth century.

Now, as a Black intellectual, Locke was trying to lead a movement into the twentieth century of new subjectivity. Leaving Europe had been almost as difficult as leaving his mother. To stay in Europe was to succumb to a death similar to that of those diasporic Negroes who had settled for an identity as a minority or a dilettante. Locke wanted an empire of his own. But to get it he had to undergo a spiritual journey, a catharsis, to open up a side of him usually silenced in his writings. Despite having avoided it for so long, Locke left Europe for Egypt and rebirth in the valley of the dead.

His Excellency Belata Heroui, Abyssinian Envoy to Egypt, ca. 1923. Courtesy of the Moorland-Spingarn Research Center, Howard University.

20

Egypt Bound

Locke began his trip into Africa by steamer, reaching Alexandria, Egypt, the second week of October. But after only a day or two of rest in Alexandria, he doubled back to the Middle East. Bonding with Africa would have to wait until he took advantage of an invitation to spend a week or so at the Baha'i shrine at Carmel in Haifa, Palestine. Locke was in no hurry to get to Haifa, either, for he took an indirect and leisurely sea route to Palestine that allowed him to visit several areas within Greece. His steamer landed on Piraeus, the Greek city near Athens, then on to the island Lesbos, before reaching Constantinople on October 14. Locke was not simply going to Africa: he was constructing a Grand Tour of the European Mediterranean and the Middle East, and he was taking his time.

Although reluctant to go directly to Africa, he was also intellectually alienated from the West. So, Locke split the difference and journeyed to Constantinople, the capital of a Byzantine tradition that was non-Black and non-Western. Of course, Constantinople had been Westernized and its dominant religion was Islam by the time of Locke's visit. But in 1923 Constantinople still preserved some of the rich religious, artistic, and literary traditions of the Eastern Christian Empire, especially in its wonderful churches that punctured this Turkish capital's skyline.

Always a fan of visiting cathedrals, Locke probably spent most of his two days in the city studying the "basilicas" or "royal halls"—the first large Christian churches, built after A.D. 311 when Emperor Constantine decided to legalize Christianity to consolidate his state power. The surviving basilicas housed a lavish Eastern Christian art that was flush with Greek and Roman imagery. The Byzantine Empire had had the capacity to absorb influences from without, but still retain its own unique cultural focus—that was the kind of Black society Locke wished to promote in the Negro Renaissance.

Locke was also fascinated by the intellectual society that had flourished in Constantinople. From the fourth through the fourteenth centuries, Byzantine emperors had placed a high regard on education of civil servants and demanded that officials have knowledge of the classics and be able to write. A courtly elite of intellectuals and scholars emerged to educate this clientele. If one did not obtain a political appointment, a bright young man could "become a scholar, hunt for manuscripts, edit an ancient author, prepare an anthology of useful sayings, sacred or profane, collect proverbs, write a commentary on a scientific text, or publish an encyclopedia." Locke had left behind that kind of world in Oxford and still longed to re-create it in some institution in America. Going to Constantinople, therefore, signaled what Locke was looking for in going to Africa, a conservative, settled, monumental civilization that had managed to embody the search for power, the love of religion, and the order of a settled so-ciety. In going east, he was hoping that he could find in the past a less Western notion of what African American intellectual life could become.

A train and another steamer brought Locke to Haifa, where he was welcomed to the shrine of the Baha'is by their new leader, Shoghi Effendi. The invitation had come to him through the efforts of Louis Gregory, an African American who had recruited Locke for the Baha'is and who became, in the 1920s, one of the most influential American Baha'is. Shoghi Effendi was shy, somewhat halting, and inexperienced without the charisma of his predecessor, Abdúl-Bahas, and that had led some believers to openly question whether Effendi was capable of leading the religion. But by 1923 the American Baha'is were firmly committed to their new leader. Gregory had been elected to the National Assembly and was well positioned to advance his long-term goal of making the American Baha'i movement the most important religious force in the fight against racism in America. Gregory wanted Locke to head a series of interracial amity conventions and succeeded in getting Locke to chair the first, held in Washington, D.C., in 1921 and another held in the spring of 1923. Gregory had probably arranged for Locke's invitation in the hopes that exposure to Effendi would persuade Locke to commit himself fully to the faith, something he had not yet done, and to becoming a public spokesperson for the faith.

But that does not explain why Locke accepted the invitation. Of course, the opportunity to visit Haifa, Palestine, and the famous Baha'i shrine at Carmel was attractive. But coming to commune with Shoghi Effendi signaled something deeper than sightseeing. Locke was also on a spiritual quest to excavate the remains of his past and try to erect a new, more authentic self. Locke hints at this complex process in his article "Impressions of Haifa," published in the 1928 issue of the *Bahá'í World*. "Whether Bahá'í or non-Bahá'í," he writes, "Haifa makes pilgrims of all who visit her. The place itself makes mystics of us all, for it shuts out the world of materiality," which Locke wearied of after three months in Europe. "I cannot describe it except to say that its influence lacks the musti-ness of asceticism and blends the joy and naturalness of a nature cult with the ethical seriousness and purpose of a spiritual religion." It was an attempt to put the halves of his personality together, for, as he noted, the shrine at Carmel "is an ideal place for the reconciliation of things that have been artificially and wrongfully put asunder."[1]

Locke's interest in Baha'ism was closely related to his mother. Although she had been raised as an Episcopalian, Mary Locke had embraced Locke's enthusiasm for Baha'ism. In a letter, right after his mother's death, he wrote, "It was her wish that I identify myself more closely with" Baha'ism; and thereafter, he did contribute more time and energy to his work with Gregory.[2] But Locke also remained somewhat aloof from the Baha'is, and rather than commit wholeheartedly to them, seemed more involved in a pursuit of catharsis through sex. By the summer of 1923, he seemed ready for a change and sought the spiritual calm his mother and the Baha'i faith had instilled in his life. Spiritual pain seemed to bring Locke to Haifa, and he came to find relief. Locke also could see in the Baha'i religion the possibility of bringing together the mystical side of his personality with his social and political commitment to advance race progress. Louis Gregory had advanced the agenda that the logical outgrowth of the Baha'i commitment to advance peace and tolerance was to foreground a program to advance racial harmony in America. Despite those incentives, Locke remained reluctant to commit more of his time to the Baha'i faith in the early 1920s.

Still, something touched Locke in Haifa. His article on the visit is written in a completely different voice from that of his European ones. When he writes of Haifa, we hear the voice of a philosophical aesthete, whose senses have been enlivened by the search for peace in a place of spiritual worship among natural beauties.

> I shall never forget my first view of it [Mount Carmel] from the terraces of the shrine. Mount Carmel, already casting shadows, was like a dark green curtain behind us and opposite was a gorgeous crescent of hills so glowing with color—gold, sapphire, amethyst as the sunset colors changed—and in between the mottled emerald of the sea, and the gray-toned house roofs of Haifa. Almost immediately opposite and picking up the sun's reflection like polished metal were the ramparts of "Akka," transformed for a few moments from its shabby decay into a citadel of light and beauty. Most shrines concentrate the view upon themselves—this one turns itself into a panorama of inspiring loveliness. It is a fine symbol for a Faith that wishes to reconcile the supernatural with the natural, beauty and joy with morality.[3]

In his own life, Locke had not been able to reconcile his desire for spiritually rewarding work, his commitment to racial struggle, his overwhelming egotism, and his consuming desire for a young male lover with what most people considered "morality." But in the hard, rocky fortress of Carmel, he was able to nourish the hope that such rapprochement was possible through transcendence and spiritual companionship. He seemed to find the latter in Shoghi Effendi, who himself was in a kind of hiding after having been maligned by American Baha'is as not being a strong enough leader. Even more seriously, traditional enemies of the Baha'is, the Islamic nationalists, had begun burning and killing Baha'is. Locke's presence seemed to buoy the distant, younger Effendi, and they became friends as he led the Black philosopher around the citadel's grounds.

The death chambers at Carmel particularly moved Locke. "The shrine chambers of the Bab and 'Abdúl-Bahá are both impressive," he wrote in "Impressions of Haifa," "but in a unique and almost modern way the ante-chambers are simply the means of taking away the melancholy and gruesomeness of death and substituting for them the thought of memory, responsibility and reverence." He went on to explore the meaning of success for a spiritual leader, and by implication, the meaning of his life, concluding "the death of the greatest teachers is the release of their spirit in the world, and the responsible legacy of their example bequeathed to posterity. Moral ideas find their immortality through the death of their founders." Very likely Locke reflected upon what moral idea his life would immortalize, what legacy would be his, and what role he was destined to play in world affairs. As yet, all of these were vague. Locke had failed to commit to any definitive cause outside of him. He had no family, no real allegiance to the Washington community, and no public identification with any political movement for social change. Locke seemed to learn here the existential lesson that only by giving oneself wholly to a cause, perhaps as a martyr for a movement, could one gain immortality. Unlike Locke, Shoghi Effendi had done so and had Carmel as "a constant source of inspiration and vision from which to draw."[4]

Locke was drawn to Haifa as a place of spiritual inspiration where he could escape the racial narrative and dwell on the tragic nature of all human existence—that we live, struggle, and die regardless of our accomplishments. That tragedy, so evident in the death chambers, was far more universal than the tragedy of Black life in America. At Haifa, he could walk with his friend and hear the higher frequencies of his life—sit awhile and reflect on the eternal question: what would be the meaning of his life? That awakened consciousness must have brought him back to his mother, and he must have longed to bring her to this hallowed place, where they could have commune in that silent way they communicated without speaking. Here, with Shoghi, Locke did not have to be the race man, the deliverer, as perhaps he had to be with Louis Gregory, who wanted him to do the work of making the American Bahai's racially relevant. Locke was tired already of what lay ahead for him—performing the role of the race man always hustling for the next accomplishment for the Negro to be put, like a notch, on his belt. Here, making a career out of the Black experience seemed a waste of his limited time on earth. So many had allowed race struggle to define them; by coming to Haifa, Locke said that he refused to let his King Tut rationale define what was really a spiritual journey to find himself in a world that treated him with mild, even rude dismissiveness. Too much focus on hustling or reacting to the crudeness of his enemies was ultimately as dehumanizing as anything the people at Oxford had done to him. His life was more than a race struggle—it was a transcendental quest for meaning and inner peace in a hard, unyielding world.

Locke was not alone in his spiritual quest. During the 1920s, other Black artists and intellectuals, including Countee Cullen and Jean Toomer, sought a mystical way out of the racial narrative, realizing that that narrative ignored the complexity of their personalities and their sense of the world. While Locke was flirting with Baha'ism in Palestine, Jean Toomer was transitioning out of writing race-inspired literature to adopting the ascetic philosophy of George Gurdjieff, who advocated that a higher spiritual consciousness would ultimately eliminate race consciousness forever.[5] But unlike Toomer, Locke could not completely abandon race consciousness to commit himself to mysticism. He was too much of a realist to believe that race prejudice in American life or world imperialism could be eradicated simply on the basis of the Baha'i or Gurdjieff appeal to universal tolerance. Locke's devotion to the spiritual brotherhood of all humanity was balanced by a desire for power for himself and his kind. Power—something both father and son respected and used frequently to defend themselves—was necessary and with it, almost inevitably, came a level of spiritual disquiet and tension.

Locke's ambivalence was a struggle with a deeper philosophical conflict. To become a full-fledged Baha'i meant to devote oneself, according to American Baha'i spokesperson Charles Mason Remey, to "the attainment of the Universal Consciousness by all human kind through the spiritual oneness of the peoples of all religions, races, nations and classes."[6] Philosophical idealism still lurked in Locke's intellectual outlook, and even as an adult, he longed for a kind of prenatal unification with the world that discourses of spiritual oneness promised. But as early as his Oxford years, he had rejected *oneness* or philosophical idealism in favor of "pluralism" and a philosophy resistant to absorption into any version of oneness.

By 1923, it was no longer simply that others perceived him as different, but that Locke had embraced difference as his personal code. No matter how welcoming the Baha'is could be or how attractive universal brotherhood was, Locke remained convinced that universalism would ultimately crush his identity. Sexuality was as much a part of this existential outlook as race. He didn't want to be absorbed in some collectivity that denied the undistilled parts of his identity, for example, of being a queer Black man who loved art and had not completely separated from his mother, among other things. He carried a near phobia that something essential about him would be filtered out in any collectivity that did not recognize the irremediable quality of "Lockus." He now faced the question that he had avoided for nearly the two years following the death of his mother. How could he reconcile the contradiction between his desires to ally himself with a universal spiritual message with his equally powerful desire for a particular, undissolvable cultural identity? He began to locate the answer in Cairo.

Early in November, Locke left Haifa for Cairo, seemingly an odd choice for a Black man in search of his African roots, given that most African Americans came from West Africa. Locke, however, did not agree. He said as much in an article, "Apropos of Africa," published in the February 1924 issue of *Opportunity*. It was ridiculous, he asserted, for "Afro-Americans" to limit their prideful identification with Africa to its "West Coast,—erroneously regarded because of the accidents of the slave-trade as our especial patrimony, if we ever had any. But the colored millions of America represent every one of the many racial stocks of Africa, are descended from the peoples of almost every quarter of the continent, and are culturally the heirs of the entire continent." The American Negro is "the physical composite of eighty-five per cent at least of the African stocks." From this perspective, "the American Negro is in a real sense the true Pan African."[7] While the argument was self-justifying, it also made prophetic sense and pushed back against the rigid ancestralism that would later take over identity politics.

Locke certainly knew that few if any Egyptians or Ethiopians had come to America through the Atlantic trade system. His argument was at base apologetics, an attempt to counter Eurocentric arguments made by some Egyptologists that Egypt was not part of "Black Africa" and hence not part of the American Negro's continental homeland. Locke attacked that argument in "Impressions of Luxor," his second article about his trip to Egypt, published in May 1924 in the *Howard Review*, where he argued that Egypt's aesthetic splendor had been "focalized here in an African setting" and "in a polyglot civilization that must have included more African, and possibly even Negro components, than will ordinarily be admitted."[8]

In effect, Locke was suggesting that African Americans were "Pan Africans" at heart, representatives of a "polyglot civilization" that had come into being through the Atlantic slave trade, a vast mixing bowl of peoples and cultures that made African Americans as much Arab as African. This was radical anthropology but less than radical political philosophy. It might have made sounder political sense to argue, as he had in *Race Contacts*, that African Americans and Egyptians were linked together by both living under a system of imperialism orchestrated by Anglo-Americans and the English. But that would not lead us into King Tut's tomb but into British Egyptian political relations that were tense in the 1920s as calls for nationalism and self-determination, really independence from England, were rife in Egypt. Despite the knowledge he gained of anti-colonialism in the Oxford Cosmopolitan Club, Locke had chosen the cultural road of linking Egyptians and African Americans through a less radical and more gendered line—all of Africa, he reasoned, was our "especial patrimony...if we ever had one." That last hint of irony—or was it sarcasm—suggests he knew that a direct African heritage for twentieth-century American Negroes was an imagined tradition. But including Egypt in the African American "patrimony" made it easier for his Afro-Anglo Saxon audience to identify with Africa. Here was the other side of the apologetics. Like his Black Brahmins back home, Locke still was not ready to identify with the non-literary, non-scholarly, and non-linear cultures of West Africa. His solution was to identify with the more Europeanized Africa. Ancient African cultures in Egypt and Ethiopia were both part of the Western tradition and precursors of it—alternatives to the modern Western European narrative that all that was civilized was White. Egypt possessed cultural traditions that could stand up to Europe, indeed, prefigure Europe's historicity, spirituality, and, most important, social and political order. With a longer history of civilized living than the Greeks, Egypt possessed a cultural splendor that made defining African Americans as "Pan Africans" palpable. Anglo-Americans might claim an undocumented lineage to the Greeks; Locke would match their hubris and claim African Americans as the heirs of Egyptian civilization and dare anyone to prove him wrong.

Egypt was attractive, because Egyptian high aestheticism pioneered the use of art to revitalize an empire. After the death in 1350 B.C. of the pharaoh Akhenaton, who had brutally converted Egyptians to sun-god worship and imposed monotheism on the masses, King Tutankhamen had reversed that religious decision, reinvigorated Egypt, and extended its influence over the Nubians, the Syrians, and the Cretans. In part, this domination was symbolic: King Tut's minions had produced thousands of beautiful thrones, chariots, walking sticks, jewelry boxes, and other accoutrements of power that celebrated the traditional gods of Thebes. Locke dreamed of returning his people to their ancient traditions by using art to rejuvenate African Americans after a period of decline under what he believed were false prophets. Under King Tut, aestheticization of the male body, especially the young male body of King Tut, reached its apogee. The remarkable treasures of King Tut's tomb testified to the tremendous love of Egyptians for their boy king. Going to King Tut's tomb might reveal how art that glorified the Brown male body could turn a divided and contentious people into a powerful nation.

Given that aesthetic history, one would expect Locke to embark for Luxor, King Tut's tomb, immediately after arriving in Egypt. But instead he dallied for several days in Cairo. Getting down to work was a slow and difficult process for Locke. "I was terribly uncomfortable in Africa at first," Locke confessed in a letter to Montgomery Gregory shortly after he finally made it to Luxor in early December.[9] Locke's discomfort was not only due to Egypt's cultural strangeness, but also its lack of the kind of immediately accessible English-speaking bourgeois world he had come to depend on in Europe. Locke thrived on an elaborate set of conventions, protocols, and connections proscribed by Victorian culture. In Egypt, he felt vulnerable, because he lacked access to that kind of social infrastructure. The British imperialists were the ruling class in Egypt in 1923, and

Locke hated the British. The indigenous elite spoke Arabic, a language he did not. And they were Islamic, the traditional enemies and persecutors of his beloved Baha'is. It was not clear with whom he could connect.

So, Locke did all the things that thousands of tourists from Europe and America did in Egypt—he visited the bazaars on narrow, crowded streets of Cairo and took time to visit the pyramids outside the town and the majestic Sphinx, using another man's non-transferable card. Locke may have had a sexual motivation for staying in Cairo. North Africa had a reputation as a place where homosexuals from abroad could find lovers. Egypt was far more tolerant than the United States of same-sex relationships, especially before marriage, although such relationships often remained ambiguous. While in Cairo, Locke appeared to find a young friend in Kamal Hamdy. Locke even wrote and sent pictures of Washington to him after he returned home. "Kamal—here is a comprehensive view [of Washington]. But after all—I love the quaintness and age of Cairo—and of course you."[10] Unfortunately for Locke, his letters and postcards were returned, undelivered.

Whether from an item in his travel guide or a tip from Arthur Schomburg, Locke visited the old Roman fortress of Babylon just outside of Cairo. Nestled in a lovely enclave of courtyards and gardens stood a small museum founded in 1908 by Marcos Simaika Pasha, a leading Copt, to preserve the history of the Christian Church in Egypt. The Copts were Egyptian Christians who had rejected Roman Catholic, Byzantine, and Greek Orthodox Church authority and developed a uniquely African branch of Christianity. Theologically, the Copts were distinguished from both the Roman Catholic and the Eastern Orthodox churches by their insistence that Jesus Christ had one and only one divine nature (monophysitism) and not the dual nature of Christ (human and divine) decreed by Byzantine theologians in A.D. 451. The Copts possessed a complicated, overlapping identity. As Christians, they were a religious minority in Islamic Egypt; but as Egyptians with a long history of resistance to Roman and Byzantine hegemony, their struggles for independence echoed Egypt's own desire for national self-determination during the centuries following the decline of the pharaohs. A unique cultural phenomenon, Coptic art and culture incorporated Greek, Roman, Byzantine, Nubian, and Islamic forms into distinctive syncretic styles in architecture, woodworking, sculpture, literature, and textiles.

In choosing to visit the Coptic Museum, Locke began his formal study of African culture at its most composite site, even though the Copts had no real connection to Black Americans. But Locke liked the Copts because they were an independent, wealthy, and fiercely proud people who were understudied in the West. "For these people," he argued later in "Apropos," "the martyrs and guardians of Christianity in Africa, and their interesting history and institutions, we should cultivate a very special and intimate interest." The "we" referred to the educated Black American community, which Locke believed needed to hear the central message of Coptic history: racial or cultural minorities could survive and maintain their integrity through group loyalty.[11] Starting with the Copts of Egypt meant rejecting an essentialist relationship to Africa for African Americans and embracing one based on a pragmatism—the American Negro, surrounded by adversaries, should behave as the Copts had.

Locke's visit to the Coptic Museum was his attempt to find in Egypt an example of the kind of group identity and struggle for cultural self-preservation he wished to foster among African Americans. That group identity was concretized in the museum, which only existed because of the collective consciousness of the Coptic people. "In ten years," Locke wrote, "six of them almost useless to the project because of the war, and with only limited private funds, but with the great intangible capital of group loyalty and cooperation, Murcos Samaika Pasha has assembled in competition with the great endowed museums of Europe and America a collection of Coptic antiquities which almost rivals the best in any line of special collection and in variety outmatches all."[12] Racial and ethnic communities survived because of the willingness of their leaders to create institutions of cultural self-preservation.

Key to Locke's enthusiasm for the Coptic Museum was that he was met and befriended by its founder and director, Marcos Simaika Pasha, a wealthy, middle-aged man, who gave Locke a tour of the museum. Simaika led Locke through a series of large rooms with marble slabs, carved tiles, stained glass windows, and wood-carved doors and ceilings from old Coptic houses and churches that had been installed in the structure of the museum. Entire pulpits, shrines, and altars were re-created in some rooms, while framed segments of wall paintings and ornate textiles of favorite biblical scenes were hung in others to facilitate meditation.[13] Instead of exhibiting the art and artifacts as archaeological curios or modernist art objects, the museum reproduced the religious context in which the artifacts were originally used. The larger intention was to convey to the visitor the spiritual feeling of worship of their churches and suggest their religion was the most important part of their ethnic identity. The museum was a shrine to the people and their history. That suggested to Locke the rationale for an African American–controlled museum in America: it was cultural self-determination, the ability to show through an exhibit what the intelligentsia of the African American minority believed were the most important elements of their culture. Locke did not yet know for certain all those elements, but one of them would be the linkage between African Americans and Africans.

As Pasha led him through the museum, he lectured Locke on how the preservation effort of his museum fit within a larger Egyptian narrative of national pride. Pasha spoke of how the Egyptians were perhaps the first to invent the alphabet, the first to manufacture paper, and the pioneers of drawing, painting, and sculpture. Then he led Locke down the steps to the lower chamber and showed him the museum's collection of precious Coptic- and Arabic-language manuscripts that lay open in glass library cases. For Pasha, the Coptic manuscripts continued the ancient tradition of Egyptian primacy in writing, learning, and religion, and refuted Europeanist claims that the West had a monopoly on civilization. Here was the literate, ordered African tradition Locke had been looking for. And here, in Pasha, Locke found proof that there were African intellectuals as nationalist-minded and race conscious as he was.[14] What Pasha and the Copts represented for Locke was something he had not mentioned in his application to go to Egypt: they were modern, complex, racial but also spiritual humanity in search of meaning.

Not surprisingly, the two men became friends, and Pasha invited Locke to his home to meet other Copts and the Abyssinian envoy to Egypt, His Excellency Belata Heroui. The slender, dark-skinned, regal-looking Heroui, with numerous pre-Christian and Christian crosses on his chest, was in Cairo on his return from Geneva where he had argued the case for the inclusion of Abyssinia, the ancient name for Ethiopia, into the League of Nations. Heroui was one of the most educated men of Abyssinia, an author, a devout Christian, and, like Pasha, a member of the African intellectual elite with whom Locke could identify. After congratulating Heroui on his success at Geneva, Locke discussed with him his dream of an intellectual alliance between African Americans and Abyssinians, the only non-colonized people in Africa. Locke also questioned Heroui about the European and White American discourse that Ethiopians did not consider themselves Negroes and shunned any association with them. Heroui disputed that, promising that Ethiopians would welcome a closer friendship. Locke then proposed an exchange program by which African American students from Howard would be allowed to travel to Ethiopia and Egypt to study their peoples and cultures, while Ethiopian and Egyptian students would be sent to Washington to study at Howard University. Apparently, Heroui was enthusiastic about the plan and encouraged Locke to contact him the following year.

In fact, both Pasha and Heroui were enthusiastic about Locke and his ideas, which buoyed his enthusiasm about Africa. Talking with them confirmed that a transnational racial connection existed between him and at least some African peoples. "Certainly it was most pleasant," he reported in "Apropos," "to be assured by their most representative men that they regard us with a brotherly and lively interest and would welcome more cordial and intimate relations. Ethnologists may argue and dispute all they like, but a felt brotherhood and kinship is pragmatically a fact." Meeting these two "representative men" in Africa suggested a basis exited for an alliance along Pan-African lines.[15] These men embodied the political gravitas of African Christianity.

Locke encountered an African patriarchy in Cairo that appeared to accept him as a brother. After all, Egypt possessed a very patriarchal society in which men were the lords of their households and communities in ways quite distinct from Locke's experience growing up in Black Victorian America, in which his mother held considerable power in the household while her husband was alive, and elite African American women influenced dramatically their religious and secular communities. The fraternity of African men he met in Cairo was inspiring. Here were African men who were free, independent, and serious; men who exercised power in their communities without the twin authorities of White men and Black women to affect what they did or said. The closest he had come to this kind of patriarchal acceptance was among people like John Bruce of the Yonkers Historical Society and Alexander Walters at Howard. But they were father figures, who treated him like a surrogate son. In Cairo, he was recognized not as a son, but as a man—a peer—by powerful African men.

Another factor that helped cement Locke's interest in the Copts and the Abyssinians was that they were among the most tolerant of his homosexuality. The Africa that Locke imagined was a cosmopolitan, intellectual, sophisticated, and sexually liberal Africa that was race conscious, intellectually serious, prosperous, and socially tolerant of diversity. Locke's vision of what was "Apropos of Africa" also contained what was *apropos* for him.

Eventually, Locke left Cairo on board one of the tourist steamers of the Anglo-American Nile and Tourist Company headed for Upper Egypt. Traveling down the Nile by tourist steamer was to see Egypt in luxury, though Locke went second-class. Initially, he was not comfortable enough with Egypt to venture off the boat, viewing the pyramids and other monuments from what his guidebook described as "a floating hotel." That began to change as he worked his way farther south. After spending the night in port at El-Balyana, Locke and a party of sightseers took a donkey excursion to Abydos, where the famous temples of Seti and Rameses, and the Christian monuments at the Coptic Monastery are located. Locke enjoyed both the beauty and the religious sentiment of these monuments to Egyptian power and religion. Next he visited the ruins of the Temple at Dendereh, one of the most impressive of Egyptian monuments, and then on Thursday, reached Luxor, where he took an excursion to its famous Karnak Temple.

Locke continued on the full twenty-one-day Nile trip through Upper Egypt and the Sudan. After reaching Karnak, the natural terminus of his steamboat voyage to Luxor and the tomb of King Tut, Locke continued south to Edfou, where he visited its fine monument that, according to his guidebook, "stands with its two enormous pylons high above the town like some huge Norman castle." Then, on his twelfth day out of Cairo, he reached Assuan, where his particular interest was to visit the island of Philae and the First Cataract or Rapids of the Nile. Locke then boarded another steamer and continued farther south to the Second Cataract. In his guidebook he checked this passage. "At Kardash (615 miles from Cairo) is a quarry and a small temple, which form one of the most beautiful bits of river scenery on the Nile."[16] Locke's racial interest in Africa did not curtail his appreciation for the picturesque and the sublime. But the peak moment in the southern excursion must have been the next day when he reached the stunning locale at Kalabsha in the Sudan, where the Nubians, a dark-skinned African people who were dominated but never completely absorbed by the Egyptians, lived. Locke left his steamer and took a train to Khartoum, where he spent a couple of days resting and surveying the vast Sudan, before doubling back.

Locke reached Karnak, just below Luxor, during the first week of December and secured hotel accommodations at the Assouan Cataract Hotel. Locke was finally becoming comfortable in Africa, in part, because it was one of the few places that an African American could be treated like a king for a couple of dollars and a song.

> How I can ever come down from these things, I don't quite know—its a worse tumble than from Oxford. For example, yesterday my share of the retinue was one donkey, one donkey-boy, one guide to tell the donkey & donkey-boy where to go, one sub-donkey-boy to carry my lunch basket, who incidentally flicked the flies away with a fly-whip while under way—all dog-trotting along in the sizzling sun—we covered 18 miles, were under way from 8 AM to 5 30 PM with stops, of course, and the whole affair cost $4 no 3.30, including ferriage across the Nile for the batch. And as to entering this hotel, here is a diagram
>
> —gateman
> —Porter
> —Boy to dust you[r] shoes
> —manager or his deputies to smile & say good evening
> —hall porter
> —corner man to see you turn in right direction (he always knows where you are going)
> —Arab servant or chair bearer who sleeps with one eye open and rises like a Sentry and then your blessed room-door-one insiders well before running the gamut.[17]

Despite his real desire for a peer relationship with Africans, his private correspondence reveals that what he also wanted was to be treated like a god. The challenge for Locke as he resumed his now almost-compulsive visitation of tombs was to find some deeper synthesis of his conflicting feelings about Africa for African Americans and for himself.

After a couple of days resting in his regal hotel and sightseeing among the local monuments, Locke took a donkey team across the river to Luxor and confronted the main reason for his six-month sabbatical: the excavation of King Tut's tomb. The second year's excavation by Howard Carter and his team had commenced in October, when Locke was en route to Haifa, and there was little to see. In the winter of 1922, after the tomb had first been uncovered, curious visitors often caught glimpses of the priceless artifacts that Carter and others carted away for labeling, photographing, and cataloging. By contrast, the second year's work of breaking into the burial chamber of the king had gone very slowly and had yielded few immediate treasures. Once Carter and company demolished the partition wall separating the antechamber and the burial chamber and cracked open the huge gilded shrine inside, they learned that more shrines stood between them and the remains of King Tut. The task of disassembling each of the four shrines was slow, tedious, and undramatic. Not until February 1924 could they lift the lid of the yellow-gold sarcophagus that held King Tut's remains, when Locke had been long gone. When he arrived in December 1923, Carter and his team were finishing work on the second shrine and beginning work on the third. Carter's rising anger at the numerous official visitors to the tomb demanded by Egyptian authorities and the rising tensions within his own research team had led him to decide not to admit almost any new visitors into the tomb. This was a monumental setback for Locke, who had hoped all along to represent the race by getting a glimpse of Tut in the tomb.

Such exclusion, especially by an Englishman, galvanized Locke into action. Unwilling to accede to Carter's blanket restriction, Locke visited the tomb on several occasions in December to try to gain access. "Tut is the most exclusive creature on earth," he confided to Gregory. "There is just a chance before leaving of stepping over the threshold at the journalist's second fortnightly view; but only a chance—and that through Egyptian channels. Carter is a bear." Evidently, Locke had taken his case to the Egyptian authorities who, like the Coptic and Ethiopian intellectuals in Cairo, responded favorably to the rationale of an African American nationalist interested in Egypt and the excavation. Indeed, from Locke's letter, he had successfully pitched the story of his visit—that he was in Egypt to represent African American scholarly interest in the excavation—to American and French archaeologists on the scene. "There have been surprising reactions—for example Mr. Winlock in charge of Metropolitan Museum staff was cordial enough over the idea of colored men investigating E[gypt] to throw in a luncheon and carte blanche to their excavations."[18]

Writing about this portion of his visit in "Impressions of Luxor," Locke echoed Winlock's interpretation that excavation of the tomb would never have succeeded without the "spirit of cooperation among the various agencies," especially from the "staff of the Metropolitan Museum of Art, led by Arthur Winlock." By crediting the Metropolitan, Locke took away some of the self-inflated credit of Carter. Although Locke's report was his revenge on Carter for keeping him out of the tomb, Locke's observation was also one of the many little truths of the King Tut tomb that seldom reached the public. Carter had seized upon the discovery as his property, not that of the Egyptians or the scientific community at large. Another hidden truth was that it had been Carter's Egyptian helper who had actually discovered the hidden step that had led them to King Tut's tomb. But that fact had been lost in the swell of press for Carter. Locke had arrived in Luxor when many people, not only the Metropolitan staff but also the Egyptian authorities, were tiring of Carter's self-inflation and his sole control over the excavation of the tomb. As Locke wrote in "Impressions": "The conflict with the Carnevon expedition has reached the flash point and the preference of the Egyptian officials is for the research to be carried out by its own archaeologists and if that is not possible by the French who are seen as less imperialistic than the British."[19] Here again was an echo of his view in "Black Watch on the Rhine" that the French were "less imperialistic."

As a practical matter, though, the Egyptians lacked the corps of scientifically trained archaeologists needed to carry out such work, and that opened the door for Locke's plan to educate such a corps of African American scholars at Howard University to do such research in Africa. In the charged nationalist atmosphere of the tomb's excavation, his plan found welcoming ears. Locke believed that if he could gain support for his plan in Egypt for Howard University participation, he could return to Washington and drum up support for a Howard University research mission in Egypt. Locke recognized that even Howard did not possess the kind of archaeologically trained experts needed, but here again he was lucky. Excluded from active participation in the British and American excavation work, Locke contacted the Institut francais d'archaeologiel orientale's mission in Luxor about the possibility of Howard University students being trained by the French Institut and then assisting with the Institute's own excavations in Luxor.

Although Locke was not able to meet George Foucart, the director of the Institute and a renowned archaeologist, before leaving he wrote Foucart a letter outlining the plan and received an enthusiastic response in January. "I attach extreme importance," Foucart wrote, "to the realization of our common enterprise. We can envision (a) scientific cooperation, (b) official administrative cooperation, (c) material realization (financial, etc.). It is important that these arrangements are done soon with proper suggestions. I am solicitous of all of your suggestions, I want your responses and all of your input in our decisions. [I envision] a premier program (between your university and my department)."[20]

It is hard to imagine a more successful accomplishment of his Luxor trip: here was a major French scholar willing to work cooperatively with him and Howard to train Black American students to do scientific research in Africa. Unlike the relationship he had broached in Cairo, his arrangement with the French Institute would not only legitimate a research mission to Egypt but also provide the scientific training Locke knew was so wanting on his home turf. Despite his misgivings, there were professional opportunities merging for him and like-minded African Americans in Africa. And if he could pull off establishing a relationship between Howard and the French Research Institute, he might be able to bring to his university a scholarly reputation in the anthropological study of Africa that would even rival the British.

There was, however, another side to Locke's experience of Egypt, which is buried in "Impressions." Along with his official, diplomatic, and scientific mission to Egypt, there was also psychological digging going on. "Impressions" began not with a trumpeting of his new scientific alliance with the French Institut, but instead with a long mediation on the Egyptian cult of the dead. "The cult of the dead, her most dominant and persistent concern, made the tomb the depository center of her civilization, and except for that fact probably nothing would have remained to solve in any concrete way the historical problem of Egyptian life and culture." Locke was fascinated by the concept of immortality and also sought a way to immortalize himself. In Egypt, he saw that building monuments and donating one's vital spiritual possessions to honor one's civilization was one way of achieving immortality. "From Napata, in the extreme south, to Gizeh, near Cairo, a distance of eleven hundred miles, scattered at intervals that are closing up with each new discovery are the graveyards of the dynasties of this characteristically death-worshipping civilization."[21] Black culture in America was also fascinated with death. Slaves retained African burial practices and ceremonies, especially as they were encouraged to seek fulfillment in an afterlife. The Black middle class held spectacular funerals and wakes of the Black American middle class, and Black Victorian culture was suffused with ornate celebrations of the dead. The trip to Upper Egypt seemed to open up feelings of mourning in Locke, the Black Victorian, surrounding the death of his mother and his own attempts to preserve the self that animated her body even after she had gone on. Egypt, therefore, touched that side of him that he was exploring privately, the feelings of loss of the kind of nurture that his mother had given him. In Egypt, he found a motherland that touched his feelings for his lost mother.

Unfortunately, while Locke's visit to Egyptian tombs rubbed open his search for meaning in a world without his mother, it did not provide any answers to that search. This is odd because King Tut was, as an adult child, the embodiment of what Locke, a child-sized adult, should have dreamed of becoming for his people. But Locke seemed to be put off by the aesthetics of ancient Egyptian civilization. Perhaps it was too much death, too much the Black Victorian splendor amplified. It failed to answer his question of how to create a renaissance of art out of his encounter with Egypt. Locke found its art—and historical moment—largely decadent. "Tut-ankh-a-men's tomb...has already revealed an extraordinary and apparent sudden flowering in the artistry of this period. [Its] objects already displayed in part at the Cairo Museum are not merely fine in one aspect of art, they are indeed the most richly composite art in the world, and only a certain wizardry of craftsmanship keeps them from being in bad taste as too ornate." Without such "wizardry of craftsmanship," the art would be in "bad taste" and "too ornate"—not a ringing endorsement. It was not as an aesthete, but as a philosopher of culture that Locke could embrace what he found in Egypt.[22] A spiritual emptiness seemed to be at the center of a culture that covered itself with incredible opulence and flash. It was all too gaudy to him, almost as if he were reviewing a Black working-class funeral back home.

But there may have been another reason Locke recoiled. Seeing the way ancient Egyptians honored and loved their boy king, probably barely shorter than Locke himself, it could not have been lost on him that there was nothing he could do that would ever elicit that kind of adoration for him. This whole trip had been about death and the underlying question, what would be his legacy? What would he be remembered for? Given how he was treated as someone barely tolerated—McKay's caricature was probably just a smidgeon of the snickering about Locke just out of earshot—Locke was not going to be wrapped up in the twentieth-century sarcophagus and be preserved for centuries as an icon of African American deliverance. Instead, he was wrapped in invisibility, the little man ignored. He could not but come away from this model of splendid hero worship feeling a bit jealous and dejected, for nothing yet suggested that saving the race like Tut had saved his civilization would result in anything but disappointment for Locke. Looking that far in the past showed how far African people had fallen to get to America. It showed as well how quixotic his own quest for a renaissance of Black people in America really was.

Back in Cairo, Locke seemed to regain his balance. Once again the purview of the Coptics and their aggressive self-reliance seized his consciousness and he felt renewed and able to act. He arranged to receive on consignment a cache of Coptic antiquities to be shipped to the United States for him to try and sell. Under the aura of Simaika Pasha, Locke became the engaged curator and potential African scholar. With the African Christians he could play the rescuing, liberating authority figure that their patriarchy had inspired him to want to be. With the Coptic art, he could represent it back in America as something he—not Carter—had discovered. Locke had also seen what a self-conscious, inspired minority in the Copts could do if they steadfastly held on to their traditions in the face of attacks from Islamic Egyptians and British imperialists. In Cairo, he found a racial mission that met his psychological needs for mastery and control and was wrapped in a rationale of selfless service to other Brown people.

Nevertheless, Locke was ambivalent as he left Egypt. The dominant odor of his trip to Egypt remained that of embalming fluid and only uncertain answers of deliverance for a modern people—or for him.

21

Renaissance Self-Fashioning in 1924

Ocean values—what Herman Melville called the consciousness freed from earthbound concerns to explore what is liminal and transcendent in human life—were Locke's values as he made his way home. Such values explained why he was so attracted to ocean travel—it was freeing. Of course, when he talked about his transatlantic travel to his friends, he spoke of needing to get away to "shake off the academic dust." But the real dust was his Black Victorianism, heightened in the United States, transported with him when he went abroad, but loosened in Europe and in Africa. It was loosest on board, where he could put intellectual pretensions aside and wallow in the purely social status that came from traveling on luxury liners. There, in 1924 between Europe and America, he could relax, gaze out over the white froth churning behind the HMS *Tyrrhenia*, and allow his mind to go. Slowly, however, as he approached New York, he began to lower the mask—the racial mask that hid his multifarious personality of professor, diplomat, and homosexual aesthete behind the persona of the race man. That transformation happened every fall when he returned from a summer abroad and occurred this January as well.

But there was something else this time. After six months abroad, presumably on a racial mission—to Africa, no less—people would want to know what his errand into European and African civilizations had yielded him, and them. He must try and relate what had happened to him during these last six months on sabbatical to a discourse on race that was only part of his motivation and part of his experience on the trip. What would he say to Charles S. Johnson, Eugene Kinckle Jones, Arthur Schomburg, his colleagues at Howard, friends like Cullen and Hughes, about Africa and what it meant to the American Negro? What did his trip to Africa mean to him? Why had he spent so much of the trip in Europe, rather than in the Motherland? He didn't really know. He had no firm answers. He must try and discover a way to turn this recent "sabbatical," another expatriated absence from the cultural and political scene in America, into some kind of personal capital or fall further behind.

So far, despite his outsized ambition, Locke was a shadowy figure in African American affairs, a person of unquestionable academic pedigree, but with little of a scholarly public production to show for it. Locke had not been a bold pioneer either in scholarly or public discourse in the years from 1918 to 1922, largely because of his husbandry of his mother. That defined a key aspect of Locke's personality: one side of him longed for the kind of intimacy, nurture, and supportive environment—a kind of nurturing medium—he had experienced with his mother. And so far, that side of him, that Locke had been transferred from the receiving end, with his mother, to the delivering end with his private encouragement—mothering of the artists he knew personally. But this was all hidden, behind the scenes, in the back room, so to speak: the burgeoning writers movement to blossom needed a larger than life leader.

Locke at thirty-eight was on the verge of middle age and a decision: what was he going to make of his life? He needed to effect a kind of self-integration in the coming months that would tap into that emotional side of his personality, that would allow the ocean values of his life, the circulation of art, literature, and culture that he had indulged as a transnational man abroad, to integrate with the more aggressive, propulsive, domineering side of his personality, if he were to become a leader in America. Locke had to write himself into the history of the present by creating a bolder, conversation-changing voice, and make others read him to understand themselves. He had to change how people talked about the Negro if he wanted to change how people talked about him.

To achieve that, he had to direct the aggressive, outward-leaning, competitive, scheming side of his personality toward a larger cause—the notion that art and culture could revolutionize not only what it meant to be a Negro, but also what it meant to be an American. Despite his ironic detachment from, indeed, profound distaste for, most African Americans, Locke would have to create a public persona for himself as the voice of Black art and culture, and further, create the intellectual argument for what that meant and why it mattered. He had to invent a Negro corporate identity and believe in it himself, and make others believe it as well—that as the proselytizer of art and culture, he could convince America, indeed the world, that through art, the Negro could be free.

The key question was whether his audience would accept him as the messenger of that grand idea. As McKay's reference to Locke in Berlin shows, there were considerable doubts about him as a leader of Black literary modernism even among those most likely to be his lieutenants. Was he their best hope for turning the Negro into an aesthetic powerhouse in the postwar world? Even his closest friends in January 1924 would have doubted that after yet another year of his escaping the American Negro. But however doubting others were, Locke came home in 1924 with a conviction—that if given a chance, he could use Black aesthetics to teach the Negro how to be relevant, interesting, and international, but most of all, modern.

That message was embodied in the ship that brought him home. The *Tyrrhenia*, the newest member of the Cunard line, having just been commissioned in

1923, was a symbol of adaptation to change. Lighter, slimmer, more efficient than the *Lusitania*, sunk by German submarines in 1915, the *Tyrrhenia* was a sign that the prewar trend toward huge, luxurious, but inefficient ocean liners had ended. The financial costs of the World War, the decline in the number of immigrants traveling to America, the postwar economic depression that gripped Britain and America, all imposed on British companies like Cunard Line the need to create leaner, more svelte vessels to keep business profitable. Not only shipping but also intellectual life was changing in the post–World War world, and Locke sensed that Negroes needed to change with it. Negro leadership must streamline and update its approach to racial politics in America. No longer would simple economic uplift galvanize White support as it had in Booker T. Washington's days. No longer would pointing out the racial injustices of America build political leverage for the Negro, as W. E. B. Du Bois had believed. Maybe a lighter, nimbler, more svelte Negro could cut through the turbulent waters of the conservative 1920s and actually be heard.

Hurrying down the gangplank upon reaching New York on January 3, 1924, Locke went directly to the offices of the National Urban League to meet with Charles S. Johnson, clearly his most important ally in effecting his renaissance as a writer and public intellectual. At their meeting, Locke reported on his trip, Johnson summarized developments in America, and together they planned the articles Locke would publish in *Opportunity* magazine. Either in the office or just after leaving it, Locke jotted down an intellectual inventory of what he must do to act upon what was most important from his journey.

I. 5 copies of Kerlin's Book & 1 personal (Woodson)
II. Write Culin (suggest Dunbar Art Exhibit)
III. Rush article on Barnes Foundation +
IV. Crisis + Johnson Anthology
   +special piece on 3 vols.
   /Andre Demaison + (Kerlin)
   /Jean Tharud
   /Paul Guillaume + (Kerlin)
   \Dr. Barnes
   \Appolonaire [*sic*] (Kerlin)
V. \Finot[1]

Robert Kerlin's book *Negro Poets and Their Poems* had just appeared, published by Woodson's Associated Publishers. Johnson brought this and other publications to Locke's attention to enlist him more closely in his plan to transform *Opportunity* from being the journal of the prosaic National Urban League into the leader of a new cultural awakening of American Negroes. Kerlin, a well-educated English literature scholar known for *Voice of the Negro*, a collection of letters by northern, working-class Black migrants during the World War, anthologized in his second book the writings of young Negro poets, including a detailed interpretation of their work as evidence of a "present renaissance." The Kerlin book got Locke's attention: events were picking up steam, others were now seeing what he was seeing, that the moment was propitious for him to assert his vision of what Negro literature could be, and do, before others stole his thunder.

But the list also recorded a synergy altogether absent to Kerlin's anthological efforts. For the list linked literature and art in a new way. Johnson informed Locke of what should be his first order of writing on his return—"Rush article on Barnes Foundation"—and helped Locke recognize that his most important intellectual influences from the trip were those July days in Paris, silenced in his other correspondence, when he had met Dr. Barnes and Paul Guillaume, and learned about Guillaume Apollinaire, the man who had introduced French modernist artists to African art. Barnes, Guillaume, and the whole Parisian fascination with African art highlighted that French and British interest in African art and culture was peaking in 1923–1924 and that American Negroes needed to find a way to exploit that new interest for their own agenda. That Locke had met Barnes and represented himself as competent enough to discuss Barnes's obsession—West African art—made him enormously valuable to Johnson. An article by Locke on Barnes's newly created museum to promote transformative arts education with African and modern art might flatter Barnes into opening his coffers for contemporary Black artistic expression—and *Opportunity*. Here was an alternative engagement with Africa from the death chambers of Egypt—it was alive, and modern. Locke and Johnson linked European modernism with the indigenous flowering of African American talent in poetry in provocative ways, such as the mention on the list of an art exhibit on Dunbar to the Brooklyn Museum under the auspices of Stewart Culin, the noted collector of indigenous peoples and African art. Here was the staging of Black culture as spectacle that Locke needed to make Negro literate traditions—and himself—visible.

The meeting epitomized that Locke's greatest accomplishment on his trip abroad was to have consolidated his relationship with Charles S. Johnson, who took the risk to publish Locke's articles on abstruse subjects, and thoroughly enjoyed what Locke had already produced. And Johnson held up his side of the bargain, putting Locke in connection with other publishers who might pay him for his articles. Johnson put Locke in touch with Paul Kellogg that February as such a possible paying outlet, since *Opportunity* was not. And it was Johnson who had promoted Locke and his European research with Eugene Kinckle Jones, the executive director of the Urban League, who had provided Locke with $100 checks to defray the costs of his recent trip. Johnson and Locke shared a desire to dominate African American opinion in the 1920s and a fierce rivalry with W. E. B. Du Bois and his preeminence among educated African Americans.

Together, they would knock Du Bois from his perch as the most listened-to-voice on Black culture in America.

Locke had scant opportunity to linger and listen more to Johnson, because Howard University's winter term had already begun. Rushing from his meeting, Locke boarded the train south and taught his class in social philosophy the next day. He probably began writing an article for Johnson not mentioned on his list—"Apropos of Africa"—which appeared the following month. Johnson wanted an article critiquing the recent flurry of activity on the question of Africa and the competition between W. E. B. Du Bois and Marcus Garvey on who represented the most progressive Negro vision of the continent. While in Paris, Locke had tried to get Isaac Beton to write an article critical of Du Bois's handling of the Third Pan African Congress, but Beton was reluctant to take on Du Bois in print. Johnson pressed for an article that would clear an intellectual space for *Opportunity*'s emergence as a voice in African affairs. Locke decided to write it himself. With Du Bois still in Europe trying to rescue the Third Pan African Congress from failure and Garvey in jail for mail fraud, Locke had the ear of his American audience of educated Black thinkers to himself early in 1924. Locke used the article to construct an image of himself as the more reliable arbiter of racial policy on Africa than either of them.

Locke used the article to say something he had wanted to say for some time, that American Negroes needed to connect with Africa if they were to become a world historical people. Here we see Locke's willingness to take on the shibboleths of his own race, specifically the reluctance of American Negroes to identify with the continent of their origin. "Except from the point of view of religious missionarism, it has been until recently almost impossible to cultivate generally in the mind of the American Negro an abiding and serious interest in Africa." Instead, the racial embarrassment was that "politically, economically, scientifically, culturally, the great concerns of this great continent have engaged the Caucasian and primarily the European mind. The sooner we recognize as a fact this painful paradox, that those who have naturally the greatest interests in Africa have of all other peoples been least interested, the sooner will it be corrected."[2] The authority with which he delivered this blow to the pride of Negro Americans was new—he seemed to have strengthened his sense that a TransAfrican identity was the only appropriate one for the American Negro and that he had the right to shame the recalcitrant among the race into adopting that view. This was, of course, deeply ironic, since Locke barely had been able to force himself to go to Africa. But that struggle gave him the authority, the strength of voice, to speak out against a problem his own reluctance to go to Africa had made visible to him—and to some others, like Woodson.

Locke was beginning to find a way to use his autobiographically grounded conflicts to make telling public statements about the psychic health of the Negro. Each of Locke's new major essays involved subject matter or argument that was drawn from his own life or his struggle with a particular issue in his life, and the essays gave him the opportunity to externalize and critique the problem as if it were not his. Since the critiques were almost always phrased in terms of "our problem" or "our predicament," as a race, which included him, he subconsciously included himself in the problem he examined. In "Apropos of Africa," he addressed his own running away from things too Black, like Africa, throughout his life. Despite his brief visit, he had come around to Africa, but he was still as detached from the land of his ancestors as he was before 1923. Even in this article, he spends a good deal of time arguing that all of Africa is the American Negroes' homeland. That argument functions here to justify that almost all of Locke's references to Africa are from non–West Africa, the part of Africa—Christian and northern—that he was most compatible with culturally. Out of a kind of racial opportunism, he embraces Africa as a discourse and chastises other Black bourgeoisie who haven't "seen the light." His attack on the Negro bourgeoisie becomes in essence a self-flagellation. Yet the article is a kind of parable of what the Negro intellectual must confront, his or her past in and out of Africa, in order to fuse the split selves of a dismembered identity together and find a being with something to say to the rest of the world.

Locke continued the critique, suggesting that the avoidance of Africa reflected the brainwashing of the Negro by slavery and post slavery apologetics. But a new generation was maturing that knew "slavery only as history," and thus it was time "to cast off this spell, and see Africa at least with the interest of the rest of the world, if not indeed with a keener, more favored, regard." A renewed interest in Africa had an analogy in the new self-awareness of European immigrants, who after being taught to disavow their homelands, now embraced their transatlantic identities. "From the thirties to the nineties, the average Irishman was half-ashamed of Erin in spite of lapses into occasional fervent sentimentalism; and even with the sturdy Jewish sense of patrimony, Zionism has had its difficulties in rekindling the concrete regard for the abandoned fatherland. Only prosperity looks backward. Adversity is afraid to look over its own shoulder. But eventually all peoples exhibit the homing instinct and turn back physically or mentally. And we American Negroes in this respect cannot, will not be an exception."[3] Locke was bringing to the surface something in his writing that had been dormant ever since his speech before the church in Cambridge about Dunbar, a biblical rhythm and style to create the sense that he was a Moses speaking to the deliverance of his people.

When it came to commenting on Du Bois and Garvey, Locke was more measured, but praised Garvey for opening the way to a transatlantic alliance with enlightened African leaders. That was modern. The popularity of Garvey's "Back to Africa" campaign showed that "the feeling of the masses [is] more ready and ripe for action than the minds of the leaders and the educated few." That was the "chief service and mission" of the Garvey movement, which "stirred the race

mind to the depths with the idea of large scale cooperation between the variously separated branches of the Negro peoples. This is without doubt the great
constructive idea in the race life during the last decade and must become the
center of constructive endeavor for this and the next generation."[4] Here was a
class analysis that the Black masses were more alive with the new subjectivity of
acting and thinking in the race's self-interest, of having an agenda, and operating out of it as a world historical people should, than the bourgeoisie from which
he came. Why did the oppressed, isolated, segregated, and undereducated Black
masses have more of a Black transnational consciousness than Du Bois's Talented
Tenth? The obvious conclusion was that the latter were still hoping to make it
in America on the White man's terms. Garvey had seen through that more than
Du Bois, Locke implied. Garvey had created a new market for race ideas. To
broaden his own market, Locke republished this and a couple of other similarly
praiseworthy articles about Garvey in the *Negro World*. While acknowledging the
failure of the "Back to Africa" business venture, Locke argued "Back to Africa"
was a metaphor of a healthy transnational identity for American Negroes that
allowed them to overcome the negative brainwashing they received about Africa
from Western culture. The challenge of what to do with that metaphor fell
squarely on the shoulders of Negroes themselves. "Wholly self-initiated and
self-supported trade intercourse with Africa would have been in itself a wonderful demonstration of the practical economic ability on the part of American
Negroes as well as of a modern and constructive interest in their African
brethren."[5]

Locke judged Du Bois as even less successful than Garvey because Du Bois
was up against a greater obstacle—the reality of European colonial control
in Africa.

> The greatest difficulty is in bringing African interests together; that
> task once achieved, it will be comparatively easy to link up with the
> American groups. This is especially the problem of the Third Pan-African
> Congress, which has just concluded its sessions. In the present situa-
> tion when national feeling, especially that of the French and Belgian
> contingents, threatens to disrupt the feeble unity of action already
> achieved, it is very necessary that the American Negro, the most disin-
> terested party, should assume very direct leadership and responsibility
> for the movement, insisting upon keeping dominant the Pan-African
> character of the scheme.[6]

African leaders' "national feeling" was a colonial loyalty they could not dispense
with or risk losing their positions as leaders of colonized nations. Strangely, the
Negro in the United States had the freer hand. Rather than blame Du Bois as he
had recommended Breton do in his article, Locke argued that, "if the movement

should lag," it would be "an indictment of the intelligence, perspicacity, and race-mindedness of the American Negro," not Du Bois per se.[7]

How was someone like Locke, without the histrionic personality of a Garvey or the backing of the NAACP like Du Bois going to be able to enhance African consciousness among Negro Americans? Locke's third way was to make the study of Africa the foundation of African American education. Locke called on the institutional structure of Negro higher education to take up this work. As he had written to Dean Kelly Miller, in 1914, Locke wanted to turn Negro American colleges and universities into world-renowned centers for the "study of African art and archeology" along with African history, politics, and culture. Now, he brought that idea out as a part of the strategy of TransAfrican awakening. "Instead of being reluctant, our Negro colleges should be eager to develop special scholarship in these directions; in the cultural field, here is their special and peculiar chance to enter the academic arena and justify themselves."[8] Unfortunately, Carter G. Woodson and Leo Hansberry had lacked adequate "financial support of the people and the active participation of the talented tenth" at institutions like Howard. Such institutions ought to seize this "very psychological moment in African studies" to launch a "well-planned and well-supported research investigation in Africa." Locke wanted to train a new generation of humanists and social scientists that would be prepared to take research and other positions of authority in the new and expanding areas of African Studies. Locke even volunteered that a White Egyptologist had approved of Locke's suggestion of having research in Africa done by African Americans. The prospect of "an African mind applying itself to ancient African manners and customs" was both attractive and perhaps productive of insights that Europeans might miss.[9]

Here was the first statement of what Locke would call the "passport of color," that is, that the subject called the Negro brought with it a set of knowledges Whites did not have, knowledges tied to the experience of growing up in and living Black life. Such a Negro American researcher would find reciprocity with the kind of Africans who were similarly sophisticated, such as cultured and race-minded Coptics and Abyssinians, such as the Abyssinian envoy to Egypt, Belata Heroui, who encouraged the idea of closer cooperation between Abyssinia and Black America among intellectuals and scholars. Locke included a picture of Heroui in the article to show that this regal, Black gentleman epitomized the learned African elite African Americans could ally with through higher education. Coptics and Abyssinians also had an economic reputation as some of the most entrepreneurial people in Africa. Here was the Booker T. Washington dimension of the TransAfrican connection Locke foregrounded along with the cultural: African Americans' economic destiny could be enhanced by less fantastical commercial ventures than those started by Garvey. Those things apropos of Africa were also apropos of the Negro, since the latter needed economic leverage to survive in America.

Where was Locke or any other African American going to find the institutional support to carry out this transnational educational partnership with Africa? Unfortunately, most Negro institutions of higher education had not advanced beyond their Reconstruction-Era beginnings: teaching basic reading and writing skills, and training professionals in law, medicine, and education remained the raison d'être of Black education. Creating a core of pioneering African-minded Negro American scholars was antithetical to the imaginations of most White administrators who ran such colleges and universities. The one possible exception was at Howard, where President J. Stanley Durkee had been very supportive of Locke's suggestion that Howard make African anthropological research a part of the university's commitment. Durkee responded favorably when George Foucart, the senior researcher of the French archaeological mission at Cairo, wrote Durkee to propose that Howard students become part of the archaeological project. The interest of Foucart enabled Locke to apply for a leave of absence during the fall of 1924 to pursue the plan to educate Howard students in archaeological work in Africa. Durkee wrote enthusiastically to Foucart, "This is work that I am very pleased for Howard to be involved in for it is something I have dreamed of for years. We will endeavor to send at least one student with Alain Locke this fall, with others to follow according as the university can raise funds for that purpose."[10] Such correspondence belies the idea that Durkee, Howard's last White president, was unalterably opposed to African American scholars' efforts in this area or that Locke turned to other institutional sources because Howard was fundamentally opposed to this kind of work.

Nonetheless, the energy for a transnational African movement emerged from another source in 1924, an art awakening occurring in Europe and America. For Locke's most important experience of modernism had taken place in Paris, where he had met Albert Barnes and listened to his lectures on how Paul Guillaume and Guillaume Apollinaire had brought European aesthetic recognition to the genius of West African art. Locke had resisted Barnes's argument initially, because Locke had been educated in that representational system that extended from the Italian Renaissance up to the great British artists of the late nineteenth century, and he loved all that. He saw himself in the mirror of a Western representational art tradition with one huge problem—he was Black, and it was White; and Western culture served the agency of Europeans and White Americans, not Negroes. To become modern, Locke had to find a way to acknowledge to his audience that his indulgence of things African and Negro in Paris had affected him more than Africa had.

That came in the most remarkable article he wrote in 1924, "Max Rheinhardt Reads the Negro's Dramatic Horoscope," where Locke portrayed in print Johnson and himself as a team whose Negro middle-class attitudes were challenged and transformed by their interview with Max Reinhardt, the German director and impresario, whose lavish production, *The Miracle*, had opened in New York in

January 1924. Locke and Johnson had sought an interview with the great director, because Locke had heard in Europe that Reinhardt had spoken highly of the
possibilities of working with Black Americans in the theater. Reinhardt even
wanted to do an all-Black production of *The Miracle*, a pageant to the life of Jesus
Christ praised in the American mainstream press. Of course, Locke and Johnson
knew that part of the praise derived from the fact that Reinhardt was a famous
European director, and if they could get him to sanction their efforts to promote
African American drama, it would legitimate their agenda.

When Locke and Johnson sat down with Reinhardt in his New York hotel
suite, Reinhardt shocked them by saying he wanted to mount a production built
around the artistry of Black vaudevillian actors.

> We didn't enthuse. What Negro who stands for culture with the hectic
> stress of a social problem weighing on the minds of an over-serious mi-
> nority would enthuse? Liza, Shuffle Along, Runnin' Wild! We had come
> to discuss the possibilities of serious Negro drama, of the art-drama,
> if you please. Surely Director Reinhardt was a victim of that distortion
> of perspective to which any one is liable in a foreign land. But then, the
> stage is not a foreign land to Max Reinhardt.... So we didn't protest,
> but raised brows already too elevated perhaps and shrugged the shoulder
> that carries the proverbial racial chip.[11]

Instead of suppressing the blindness of the Negro middle class toward modernist Negro theater conflict, Locke publicly mused on it and showed the benefits
of dialogue with a European modernist for the future of Negro art. He made it
the centerpiece of the article he wrote of the interview. By doing so, he moved
the essay away from simple race self-promotion into a surgical exposé of their
middle-class self-consciousness.

Herr Reinhardt read the gestures swiftly.

> Ah yes, I see—you view these plays for what they are, and you are right;
> I view them for what they will become, and I am more than right. I see
> their future. Why? Well, the drama must turn at every fresh period of
> creative development to an aspect which has been previously subordi-
> nated... to the most primitive and the most basic aspect of the drama
> for a new starting point—and that aspect is pantomime,—the use of
> the body to portray emotion. And your people have that art—it is their
> special genius. At present it is prostituted to farce, to trite comedy,—
> but the technique is there, and I have never seen more wonderful
> possibilities. Somebody must demonstrate its fresh artistic value.
>
> Now we understood. Baronial hotel armchairs moved as lightly and
> as instinctively as ouija boards.[12]

The question remained: "But how, Mr. Reinhardt, are we to develop these,—especially in the face of exploitation?" "Only you can do it, you yourselves. You must not even try to link up to the drama of the past, to the European drama. That is why there is no American drama as yet. And if there is to be one, it will be yours."[13]

It would be an Irish playwright who twenty-five years later would make the kind of progression that Reinhardt predicted of Black vaudeville to avant-garde in his breakthrough play about human alienation in *Waiting for Godot*. As the playbill for a Washington, D.C., production of *Waiting for Godot* noted: "The performances reflect the varied sources for this particular production: the circus, American Black vaudeville, commedia del arte, and early film. (Beckett's hat-switching routine is straight out of the Marx Brothers.) From vaudeville in particular, we find: unbuttoned flies, insistent bladders, dropped trousers, broken embraces, unexpected blows, speaking while chewing, juggling hats, body odors, farts, and objects that defy manipulation."[14] Much of American slapstick comedy, not just the Marx Brothers, was built on the antics, the physical dishevelment, clashing, incongruent gestures and patterning of Black vaudeville. But in *Waiting for Godot*, vaudeville supplies the architecture of the play's meditation on life and death in a world without God—a connection most effectively embodied by the two Black actors, Thomas W. Jones II and Donald Griffin as Didi and Gogo in the Studio Theatre's *Waiting for Godot*.[15] Performative jabber becomes existential nonsense in Godot, which is precisely what Reinhardt foresaw as the contribution of Black performance to modernism—a formal innovation that captured the feeling of modern life. "With such control of body," Reinhardt concluded, "such pantomime, I believe I could portray emotion as it has never been portrayed,—pure emotion, almost independent of words or setting. It is really marvelous. You are perhaps too near to see it."

"Max Rheinhardt Reads the Negro's Dramatic Horoscope" brilliantly suggests Locke's willingness to reveal his class blinders in print. It reminded his readers of something he himself perhaps had forgotten since his speech on Dunbar—that it was form and formal inventiveness that defined Negro genius. But even if he wanted to take up Reinhardt's challenge—"there is no American drama as yet. And if there is to be one, it will be yours"—Locke lacked the resources to create what in effect would have been an experimental American theater.[16] How could he train a generation of Black playwrights to create high art out of Black working-class performativity on a professor's salary and a National Urban League travel allowance? He could not. Thus, while Locke pressured Howard for more release time to lead this anthropological mission to Africa and continued to publish with Charles Johnson at *Opportunity*, he opened another cultural front in 1924 with Walter White, the assistant secretary of the NAACP, around Locke's idea to secure White money to create an independent institute of Black Cultural Studies in America. After launching his classes that winter term at Howard, Locke returned to New York to meet with White.

Locke's enthusiasm for the possibility of a new American culture spilled out afterward in a letter to White. "There is every indication,—here and abroad of increasing interest in the artistic possibilities of our race material and of our race temperament.... The demand as far as the artistic material already available in drama, music, painting and the decorative arts is even now outstripping the supply of competent interpreters and producers, and the recent success of Roland Hayes shows that country-wide appreciation and recognition awaits the exceptional type of talent."[17] Locke's letter fit Walter White's agenda to get Herman Lieber and George Eastman to fund a foundation to support the training of Negro artists. Lieber had made money in the music business largely by profiting from Black musicians' songs by purchasing the reproduction rights of written-down versions that were copied by Whites. Lieber expressed his desire to fund an institute to study Black music.

White used Locke's recent trip to Europe to try and land the deal. "Mr. Alain Leroy Locke, of whom I have spoken to you before," White wrote to Lieber, "told me many interesting things about the deep interest in Negro art which is now being manifested abroad."[18] White forwarded Locke's letter to Lieber, telling him that he did so without Locke's knowledge, although in reality White had asked Locke to write the letter specifically to send to Lieber. This highlights that White was a player as well. Locke, White, and Johnson shared the belief that only through behind-the-scenes manipulations could Black cultural advancement be achieved. They also believed it was fair to seek funding from White patrons, given that Black cultural productions had fattened the wallets of untalented Whites for years. As White wrote to Locke after he drafted the letter for Lieber: "I am glad that you emphasize so splendidly the interest in Negro art which is being manifested in Europe. I, myself, have been tremendously pleased during the past few days by similar indications both in Europe and in America. On[ly] yesterday, I took Miss Rebecca West (the English novelist and critic[,] and Konrad Bercovici to Abyssinian Baptist Church and afterwards we went about a bit visiting some folks in Harlem. Both of them were tremendously impressed and we made plans for other visits which I think will materialize in interesting articles on what the really worth while colored people of New York are doing and are capable of doing."[19] Then, returning to basics, White concluded: "As for the Lieber-Eastman project, I need hardly say again that I am going to keep after it as vigorously as I can without injuring their interest in the scheme."[20]

Since White was not grounded enough in Black aesthetics to flesh out a proposal for Lieber's institute, he contacted Locke a couple of days later to write one. Locke's proposal for an "American Institute of Negro Letters, Music and Art" took Lieber's original vision of a conservatory of Black music and turned it into an institute of Black culture with "five departments—Music, Drama, Literature and Folk-Lore, Design and Painting, and Sculpture and African Crafts." Such an institute would be "organized about a teaching faculty" and a "Conservatory of

Musical and Dramatic Art" that would award scholarships, prizes, and awards to talented Negroes, particularly important, Locke argued, because the American Academy of Letters and Art denied recognition to Blacks. With "a small nucleus of selected students in the several lines under its direct supervision" the institute would "be able to stimulate talent all over the country along several desirable lines of new artistic endeavor. This could be done primarily through the awarding of prizes and the holding of competitive exhibitions. Indeed I know of no other way in which productive creative effort can be more effectively or immediately stimulated."[21]

Some categories of prizes would not be awarded exclusively to Blacks, but to Whites, as works of the "race drama" could be written by anyone. Such an institute would galvanize the work of the Howard Players and the art movement in Chicago, Locke argued, by rewarding talented students who emerged from other training institutions. Locke promised a race relations payoff: "no foundation could be more stimulated at the present time in the racial effect or more conducive to the promotion on the part of the general American public of a more sympathetic and revised estimate of the capacities of the Negro race as a group than just such a plan adequately endowed and competently administered."[22] That "revised estimate" was the key outcome, for the resulting artistic productions would show the Negro as a creative agent not a passive recipient of American and world culture.

Unfortunately for Locke, the institute never materialized. Lieber was supportive and impressed with the people White lined up for such an institute, for Locke had penned the names of William Stanley Braithwaite, W. E. B. Du Bois, James Weldon Johnson, Claude McKay, Benjamin Brawley, Walter White, Carter G. Woodson, and himself as the initial board of directors. But the project was too ambitious for Lieber and Eastman, who were businessmen first and patrons of the arts as an afterthought. Both were primarily interested in Negro music, whereas the focus of Locke's proposal was drama, literature, and the visual arts, not profitable arts. Importantly, Locke's proposal avoided any reference to the blues, jazz, and other working-class music forms that were overtaking American popular music in 1924 and making money for Lieber. Locke's proposal did not fit Lieber's narrower intentions, which may have been to create an institute to "study" Black music so as to make it easier to seize its reproduction rights.

Locke had refashioned himself as the renaissance architect of Black culture. He was no longer at sea. But he still lacked what he had always lacked, an enabling patron.

22

The Dinner and the Dean

"We want you to take a certain role in the movement," wrote Charles S. Johnson to Alain Locke on March 4, 1924, and thereby changed his life and the future of Negro literature forever. "I may have spoken to you of a little group," Johnson continued, "which meets here [at the offices of *Opportunity*] with some degree of regularity, to talk informally about 'books and things.'"[1] That group included a number of young people Locke already knew well: Countee Cullen, Jamaican-born aesthete Eric Walrond, budding Symbolist poet Gwendolyn Bennett, and Cullen confidant Harold Jackman, as well as *Crisis* literary editor Jessie Fauset, her friends Eloise Bibb Thompson and New York City Librarian Regina Anderson, along with Johnson himself. On one level, such meetings were little more than a New York version of Georgia Douglas Johnson's "Saturday Nighters." But because Charles S. Johnson hosted the New York meetings, they were something more. Johnson saw the literary group as a new answer to the question, what should the Negro do? Write—without propaganda or special pleading for the Negro cause—but with confidence that creative writing by Black people would ultimately help liberate a people. One way to instill such confidence was to meet regularly.

> There have been some very interesting sessions and at the last one it was proposed that something be done to mark the growing self-consciousness of this newer school of writers and as a desirable time the date of the appearance of Jessie Fauset's book [*There Is Confusion*] was selected, that is, around the twentieth of March. The idea has grown somewhat and it is the present purpose to include as many of the newer school of writers as possible,—Walter White (who in a sense is connected with this group), Jean Toomer, and yourself.[2]

The collection of participants reflected the cleavages of the early Harlem Renaissance: the real members of the "new school" in New York were Hughes, Cullen, Walrond, and Bennett, while Toomer and Locke were Washingtonians, and thus slightly removed. Locke and Fauset were also a half generation older in age than the rest. Locke must have been flattered to learn that he was included in the "new school" of writers when he had not published a poem or novel.

"But our plans for you were a bit more complicated," Johnson continued. He wanted Locke to serve as "master of ceremonies" at "a dinner meeting, probably at the Civic Club, to which about fifty persons will be invited: Carl Van Doren, H. L. Mencken, Robert Morse Lovett, Clement Wood, Oswald Garrison Villard, Mary Johnston, Ridgely Torrence, Zona Gale, and about twenty more of this type. Practically all of these are known to some of us, and we can get them. We are also including persons like Dr. Du Bois, James Weldon Johnson, Paul Robeson, Montgomery Gregory, Georgia Douglas Johnson."[3] Interestingly, neither the group nor the meeting had been noted on the list Locke carried away from his January meeting with Johnson. Most likely, the idea to have the Civic Club meeting or Johnson's decision to use Locke at the occasion had materialized later.

Johnson asked Locke to perform the most important role at a dinner that was the first of its kind—an interracial communion between Black writers and White custodians of American culture to break bread and try to find a common language to talk about a literary awakening in America built around Negroes writing poems, short stories, and novels about the Black experience in America. Johnson needed Locke to be more than simply an emcee for a dinner. In truth these young Black writers were not yet a school or a movement of thought, but a younger generation of writers who, though less talented and untested, resembled the younger generation of White American writers, such as F. Scott Fitzgerald, Ernest Hemingway, and William Faulkner, who were defining a new American literature independent of European models. United less by ideology than by a sense that as Negro writers they had something to say if only their race and their inexperience were not held against them, their reigning metaphor was the "new," that they had something "new" to say, even if what that was remained a mystery. Johnson was asking Locke to come up with an interpretation acceptable to young writers, old race leaders, and tentative White literary allies so that they could find common language to talk about the prospects for a vital Negro literature. Locke's academic credentials allowed him to validate the potential of these young writers to contribute valuably to American civilization.

Of course, the 1920s generation of writers was far from the first collection of Black writers to command national attention, which had begun in the eighteenth century with Phillis Wheatley and Jupiter Hammon and continued through the nineteenth with William Wells Brown, Frederick Douglass, Francis Harper, and Charles Chestnutt. By the beginning of the twentieth century, some writers, such as Locke's favorite, Paul Laurence Dunbar, had brought not only distinction to the race, but also promised to supply a new American language of the soul. But for the most part, these young writers of the early 1920s rejected Dunbar's dialect poetry and were uncomfortable increasingly with the expectations of Black progressives like Du Bois that Black literature should be "representa-tive" and bring "credit" to the race. Writing with a consciousness of the race responsibility felt like a burden to these young writers, which is one reason they gravitated to Johnson rather than Du Bois. Locke was sympathetic to their desires as well. Modernist literature in the 1920s was gritty, urban, sexually and psychologically complicated, and filled with unsavory characters—especially the literature emerging from Hemingway and Fitzgerald. If Blacks in America were to make an impact in literature, they had to be in step with modernism in litera-ture, but also free to create something new out of the mix of race, culture, and experimental fiction that was coming to the fore in 1924. Although it was un-likely that Johnson was aware of all of the literary subplots in his little group, he knew that moralizing control of Black literature was weakened and almost dead. Indeed, as he revealed in his letter to V. F. Calverton at the *Modern Quarterly* praising Locke: "He believes as I do," Johnson wrote, "that the frank and unapol-ogetic discussion of subjects long tabooed will be a distinct step in the direction of creating respect for ideas which is necessary to any sort of living together."[4]

Johnson's agenda for the evening was to position *Opportunity* as the forum for this new "frankness." But his decision to hand the master of ceremonies role over to Locke signaled Johnson's sense of his own limitations and the riskiness of the role. He felt more comfortable orchestrating the evening from the wings and needed someone he could trust as its conductor. To assert this new freedom within the African American narrative could expose the writers to criticism, either from White literati, who might claim these young Black writers were not ready, or from the Du Bois intellectual camp at the *Crisis*, who would be jealous of *Opportunity*'s growing influence over the writers. Locke was sensitive to the romantic aspirations of the younger writers coming to maturity in the 1920s, but concerned as well to uphold the Christian-Enlightenment project of their elders that art had meaning as part of society's need to thwart racism. Locke was aesthetically ambiguous enough to be acceptable to the young artists and cre-dentialed enough to have the respect of the White literati invited—at least in theory. For the other intangible personality ingredient that Johnson had taken into account was Locke's temperament: he would have no problem standing in front of the White and Black intellectual elite of New York and asserting with wit and hauteur that this was the coming new wave in American literature.

Though flattered by the invitation, Locke demurred. Though his response has disappeared, Johnson's reply indicates that Locke had misgivings, especially if it was a dinner to honor Fauset and her novel. "Walrond was in this morning and I conveyed to him the gist of your letter, and he agreed that we never conceived of the dinner as a tribute to Fauset in particular or anyone else, but as a mechan-ism to honor the movement of younger writers. There seems to be a strong sen-timent to have you serve as masters of ceremonies for the evening. I regard you as a virtual dean of the movement."[5] Something in Locke's antennae had picked

up that this party was to be for Jessie Fauset and her novel of bourgeois manners, which he detested but favorably reviewed, and he wanted nothing to do
with representing her novel as exemplary of the new literature. Once Johnson
silenced that anyone in the Writers Guild might see it as a celebration of Fauset,
Locke went along willingly, because Locke was an outsider and had been asked
to be the leader in the arena he cared about deeply. After six months abroad and
years of disconnect from the American scene, here was a chance to publicly identify himself with the new literary movement in a role conferred on him by
Johnson, one of the few male leaders to ever have that kind of confidence in him.

Locke threw himself into the project now that the dinner was his "coming out
party" as well. He reviewed Johnson's invitation list and reminded him to invite
Du Bois, who had been left off the list of invitees. Johnson explained the oversight as the result of there being two invitation lists, one for the Civic Club
dinner and the other for "a dinner for Dr. Du Bois, which Miss Fauset is getting
up." Locke went on to try to get Jean Toomer to attend the dinner—without
success. Johnson also relied on Locke to select the two people to be asked to give
formal remarks at the dinner and most likely he was the one who suggested that
Gwendolyn Bennett and Countee Cullen read their poems. Locke also recommended Johnson secure a note taker to record the remarks made on the occasion. Johnson then sent an invitation to Albert Barnes, the eccentric Philadelphia
millionaire chemist and African art collector, who agreed to attend.

As March 21 approached, participants became nervous. A week before the
dinner, Bennett wrote Locke, "I am so glad that you have agreed to come. I feel
the utter necessity of your being there." Bennett was even more grateful he
would be out front when the day of the event arrived. "You are particularly
appreciated," she wrote to Locke, "because of the tremendous and unswerving
confidence that you have in us. Your faith in our utter necessity is particularly
helpful as I find that my mind is not clear on the eve of this momentous event."[6]
Even Johnson seemed nervous. After confiding in Locke that "the thing has
gone over big, nothing can be allowed to go wrong now," Johnson asked him to
come up early that day to help him finalize the evening's program. "I would like
to see you as early as possible to have the first talk about plans, and probably,
we shall have to do most of the arranging of the program then."[7] After a short
introduction by Johnson, Locke would discuss the significance of these new
writers, and then introduce Carl Van Doren who would outline his hopes for the
Negro writer. Then, Horace Liveright, the publisher of *Cane* and *There Is Confusion*,
would make a few remarks about the publishing scene for Negro books, a market-
reassuring strategy most likely recommended by Johnson. After, Gwendolyn
Bennett, Countee Cullen, and a few others would read poems and give testimonials.
Jessie Fauset would give the closing remarks.

Work on the program concluded, two of the smallest African Americans—
Johnson was only 5´2˝—proceeded to the Civic Club dinner, dressed to the

nines that Friday evening. Locke began his remarks by arguing that a new sense of hope and promise energized the young writers assembled, because they "sense within their group—meaning the Negro group—a spiritual wealth which if they properly expound will be ample for a new judgment and re-appraisal of the race."[8] Although Locke's optimism has led critics to claim that he promised Black literature would solve the race problem, his language was actually quite cautious. Negro literature would "be ample," that is, sufficient, to contradict those Whites who claimed Blacks were intellectually inferior "if they [i.e., the Black writers] properly expound [it]." Their success would allow "for a new judgment... of the race" if Whites were willing to render it.[9] But there are no guarantees.

More powerfully expressed was Locke's belief that by avoiding a literature of racial harangue, the new group of writers could make a broader contribution than those who had come before them. Locke advanced a new concept, that of generation, to suggest this was a new cohort of Black writers possessed of a devotion to literary values that set them apart from their forerunners. For example, Locke introduced Du Bois "with soft seriousness as a representative of the 'older school'" of writing. That seemed to put Du Bois slightly on the defensive and felt called upon to justify writers of the past as "of necessity pioneers and much of their style was forced upon them by the barriers against publication of literature about Negroes of any sort." Locke introduced James Weldon Johnson—a writer of poetry, music lyrics, and a novel—"as an anthologist of Negro verse"—another dig, since Johnson was a novelist, a lyricist, and a poet, in addition to editing *The Book of American Negro Poetry* and writing a powerful introductory essay. Locke did acknowledge him for having "given invaluable encouragement to the work of this younger group."[10] By defining these NAACP literary scions as elderly fathers and uncles, Locke implied their virtual sons and daughters were Oedipal rebels whose writings rejected the stodginess of their literary parents. Against the backdrop of an ornate Civic Club dinner, with its fine china, polished silverware, and formally attired White patrons, Locke issued a generational declaration of independence for the emerging literary lions of the race.

Carl Van Doren then laid out what the White literary press wanted from the younger Negroes: art not anger. Gingerly but tellingly, Van Doren ventured that the literary temperament of the African American, whether produced by African or American conditions, was distinguished by its emotional transcendence, its reputed ability to avoid haranguing White America for its obvious wrongs and turning suffering into works of unparalleled beauty. Young Black writers had to sit and listen to Van Doren declare that "long oppressed and handicapped, [Negro artists] have gathered stores of emotion and are ready to burst forth with a new eloquence once they discover adequate mediums. Being, however, as a race not given to self-destroying bitterness, they will, I think, strike a happy balance between rage and complacency—that balance in which passion and humor are somehow united in the best of all possible amalgams for the creative artist."[11] A certain amount of condescension was the cost of liberal White support.

To illustrate the newer emphasis in the younger writers, Gwendolyn Bennett then read a poem, "To Usward," she had written expressly for the evening.

> And some of us have songs to sing
> Of jungle heat and fires;
> And some of us are solemn grown
> With pitiful desires;
>
> And there are those who feel the pull
> Of seas beneath the skies;
> And some there are who want to croon
> Of Negro lullabies.
> We claim no part with racial dearth,
> We want to sing the songs of birth.

Bennett's poem reinforced Locke's theme for the "newer school," that of a new "birth" and, in particular, a generational rebellion to break "the seal" of a Black Victorian tradition that had strangled self-expression.

> And so we stand like ginger jars,
> Like ginger jars bound round
> With dust and age;
> Like jars of ginger we are sealed
> By nature's heritage.
> But let us break the seal of years.

This "seal" was "the seal of years," that is, of tradition, that privileged race—"nature's heritage"—in the writing of the "older school." Bennett ended with a collective call to arms, which is probably why Johnson selected it to be published in the May issue of *Opportunity* in an article on the dinner.

> But let us break the seal of years
> With pungent thrusts of song,
> For there is joy in long dried tears,
> For whetted passions of a throng![12]

Next followed Horace Liveright, stating even more forcefully that the younger writers must avoid the pitfalls of minority literature, especially the "inferiority complex" he had detected in the writings of oppressed peoples who tried to counter negative mainstream stereotypes with saccharin portraits of their own people. For Negro writers "to do the best writing it was necessary to give a rounded picture which included bad types as well as good ones since both of these go to make up life." Remarkably, Liveright did not mention Fauset's novel, but enthused instead over Toomer's, with its mix of middle-class intellectuals, racy southern women, and Symbolist stream of consciousness. Liveright did mention that the book had sold only five hundred copies to date. Such remarks could not have been better for Locke and Johnson than if they had scripted them, for they reinforced their message that young Black writers were going to have to avoid the racial harangue of earlier Negro creative writers if this generation wanted to get published. Although Van Doren acknowledged "Negro writers must long continue to be propagandists," their future promised something more—the prospect of a Negro art that was open, honest, vulnerable, and self-critical.[13]

Perhaps to compensate for the challenge to Du Bois and *Crisis*, but also to acknowledge her intellectual and emotional dependency, Fauset spent her speaking time thanking Du Bois for the support she had received from him. Fauset also mentioned that another publisher had rejected her novel initially on the ground that "the cultured Negro forms so small a portion of the community that the book would be of little social interest."[14] That remark sanctioned Du Bois's belief that White publishers would not publish good novels about middle-class Black people. After her remarks, the dinner concluded, but not the debate that had been broached.

The dinner was a modest success. Bringing Black and White literati together in one room, Johnson had facilitated the kinds of interactions that made publishing contracts and critical recognition more likely for the youngsters. Albert Barnes, who had also spoken briefly, later wrote to the philosopher John Dewey: "I don't care how you spent Friday night, you could not have spent it as wonderfully as I did. I met a young man, Walrond, who is really first rate, and I want him to look you up as he aspires to enter Columbia University in the fall."[15] Those kinds of recommendations advanced careers. The dinner drew attention to the magazine as unique in fostering interracial contact and exchange over literature. Johnson and Locke had helped African American literature seem more marketable than it was before the dinner and gave a sense of recognition to a group of young writers testing the publishing waters with their first products. Negro literature now appeared to be as marketable as music and other cultural commodities that could be purchased by a growing White, largely urban public. Not surprisingly, Locke and Johnson were pleased with the outcome of the dinner.

Jessie Fauset was not. Eight years later, in response to Locke's critical review of her novel, *Comedy, American Style*, Fauset reflected on that evening:

> I have always disliked your attitude toward my work dating from the time years ago when you went out of your way to tell my brother that the dinner given at the Civic Club for "There Is Confusion" wasn't for me. Incidentally I may tell you now that that idea originated with Regina Anderson and Gwendolyn Bennett both members of a little literary club with which I was then associated. How you and one or two others sought to distort the idea and veil its original graciousness I in

common with one or two others have known for years. And I still remember the consummate cleverness with which you that night as toastmaster strove to keep speech and comment away from the person for whom the occasion was meant.[16]

Clearly, Fauset was under the impression that it was to be a celebration of her accomplishment and had to sit through an ordeal of self-congratulation before any direct acknowledgment came to her at the end. Arnold Rampersad suggests that this was particularly egregious, not only because of her novel but also because of the role she had played as a midwife of the movement. She deserved more credit than Locke as a "midwife" to this younger group of writers, since, as literary editor of the *Crisis*, she had been the first to publish Langston Hughes, among others. Historian Thadious Davis also argues that the dinner was a watershed in Fauset's influence in the renaissance. Afterward, younger women writers like Nella Larsen looked to Charles Johnson for support and contacts, rather than Fauset. By minimizing her at the dinner, Johnson and Locke decentered Black women as leaders of the Harlem Renaissance movement, and Locke is generally seen as primarily responsible for it.[17]

Locke deserves to be criticized, but it's worth remembering that he accepted the role of "master of ceremonies" only after Johnson and Walrond assured him Fauset was not the reason for the dinner. If the dinner originated to mark the publication of Fauset's novel, then Johnson transformed it into a coming-out party for *Opportunity* and a new generation of Negro writers. Interestingly, one of the originators of the group, according to Fauset, was Gwendolyn Bennett, who, beyond showing enthusiasm for Locke's participation, narrated the dinner as a celebration of the "new school of writers." Indeed, she felt buoyed after the dinner by the attention given *her* on the program. Would it have made sense for Johnson, the editor of *Opportunity*, to host and pay for a dinner to celebrate Fauset, the literary editor at the *Crisis*? Obviously not. But Johnson probably knew that Fauset expected to be the center of attention, recognizing the role she and the *Crisis* had played in advancing Negro literature. Perhaps that explains why Johnson was so eager to have Locke play the role out front as "master of ceremonies." If Johnson's not-too-subtle plan to displace Fauset and the *Crisis* crowd backfired, Locke would take the blame, as has been the case. As a gay Black aesthete alienated from the Philadelphia Black bourgeoisie, Locke was perfect for the job of displacing Fauset, the not-so-secret lover of Du Bois, and the *Crisis* from their positions of leadership in the new literary movement.

But imagine how Johnson must have felt when he picked up the New York *World* on Saturday morning and read the headline: "Negress Novelist Honored at Dinner. Miss Jessie Fauset, A.B., M.A., Is Guest at Celebration of Publication of Work." Johnson had specifically recruited the *World*'s editor Louis Weitzenkorn to the dinner to get favorable publicity for the evening, but Fauset had trumped

Johnson. Weitzenkorn's article recounted, "Miss Jessie Fauset...was principal guest at a dinner given in the Civic Club...by other writers, musicians and publicists of her own race. Her publisher, Horace Liveright, head of Boni & Liveright, was nearly the second guest of honor." The *World* article made no mention of *Opportunity* magazine, Charles S. Johnson, or Locke. From the standpoint of the New York White press, the event had been for Fauset and she had been well honored. Indeed, that is the same impression that surfaces from the popular Black press that covered the event. According to the *New York Age*, "An interesting event was the dinner tendered by the Writer's Guild, a group of the younger element of Negro writers and creative artists at the Civic Club, West 12th street on Friday evening, March 21, in honor of one of its members, Miss Jessie Fauset, celebrating, in a measure, the publication of her last book, *There Is Confusion*, recently issued from the press." Again there was no mention of Locke or Johnson, but there was a registering of Locke's generational discourse:

> Among the 125 guests present, many of whom were distinguished literary lights of both races, were exemplars of both the old and the new schools of writing, and many good-natured quips and witty sallies were bandied back and forth among those who won their literary spurs in the old fashioned world of literary purity and those of the modern intelligentsia who have discarded the candlelight for electricity.[18]

Here was evidence of Locke's "consummate cleverness...that night as toastmaster" expressed in the "many good natured quips and witty sallies" that irritated Fauset, but that announced the writers assembled as a "modern intelligentsia." At the very least, the *World* and *Age* reports suggest the personal and gender conflict was relatively invisible to outsiders since the banter was recorded as "good-natured." That view was also shared by Countee Cullen, certainly an insider, who, when he wrote to Hughes about the event, recalled it as a celebration of Fauset's book. Whatever else one can say about the dinner, Jessie Fauset certainly won the contemporary media contest.

So furious was Johnson about the media coverage of the dinner that he set Eric Walrond, a contributing editor to the *World*, the task of writing another review of the dinner. But it never appeared. Indeed, the lack of an article communicating *Opportunity*'s interpretation of the dinner's significance led Johnson ultimately to write his own unsigned review of the dinner, "The Debut of the Younger School of Negro Writers," printed in the May issue of *Opportunity*. Walrond, no fan of Fauset, finally got a chance to express his opinion of her when he penned a review of *There Is Confusion* in the July issue of the *World*. Walrond wrote: "This is not a book for the old or the young. It is rather awful." That review so angered Langston Hughes that he threatened to punch Walrond in the nose. What the review, the dinner, and the blame apportioned to Locke shows is that the dinner was "momentous," as Bennett put it, the perfect emblem of the gender and ego conflicts of the renaissance.

Locke's attempt to steer the evening and the White publishers away from Jessie Fauset makes sense if we recognize that, for Locke, the Civic Club dinner was his opportunity to fashion a New Negro literary identity that was queer (in both the sexual and modernist senses of the word) and disturbing to the Black bourgeoisie. In other words, an incipient war over the taste of the literature being written by these younger writers was taking place because of the gender and class conflicts in the movement. As literary editor of the *Crisis*, Fauset was already beginning to reject some of the newer poetry and short fiction of Langston Hughes and other close friends, including even poems Du Bois thought were acceptable, because they conflicted with her Victorian taste in literature. After the March 21 dinner it was not so much that women could not be part of the movement or that every man would be promoted, but that a certain type of man and woman—a sexually ambiguous Black writer such as Nella Larsen and Zora Neale Hurston became dominant in the renaissance that followed largely because of the taste of literary men like Locke, Johnson, Van Doren, and even Liveright, who was clearly more enthused by *Cane* than *There Is Confusion*. Modernism was seizing the day, and those Black books that conveyed it were celebrated, along with their authors.

But another factor was evident as well. The March 21 dinner was also a coup d'état for the gay writers of the Black movement. Historically, the out-group, the gay and bisexual authors were now in. The dinner may have been a watershed for Fauset, but it was also a turning point for homosexual and bisexual artists and critics—Cullen, Walrond, and Zora Neale Hurston, the latter who startled the assembled guest by yelling "color struck" when she entered the room late. Outrageous, unpredictable, sexually uncategorized male and female writers and personalities had stolen the White gaze away from the staid and predictable heterosexual bourgeoisie. In a movement takeover by gay and sexually ambiguous Black men, a Victorian, like Fauset would lose out.

There may have been other reasons why Locke went along with Johnson's plan to marginalize Jessie Fauset. In an interview, Arthur Fauset, her brother and a close friend of Locke, explained that another source of tension between Alain and Jessie was color. Located in Philadelphia, the Fauset family was really two families divided somewhat along color lines—Arthur from the darker, less accomplished side of the family; Jessie from the lighter, more respectable relations. Locke knew that Jessie Fauset disparaged the darker side of her family, which incensed Locke, who abhorred color consciousness among African Americans. Jessie Fauset epitomized for Locke the obsessive class and color consciousness of the Philadelphia Negro elite that he believed crippled the possibility of great Negro writing. She further symbolized the condescending ways in which the Philadelphia bourgeoisie treated sensitive, aesthetic men. Even if

Locke was "sorely uninformed" about the early Harlem Renaissance movement, as Jessie Fauset claimed in her letter about the incident in the 1930s, he was very well informed about how the bourgeoisie of Black Philadelphia used color prejudice to undermine the sense of belonging that he believed was essential to the reconstructed or New Negro community he hoped to build.

But in the final analysis, none of these considerations excuse what Locke did to her at the dinner. Something about his identity as an outsider gave Locke the entitlement to be mean and cruel. Even if he was seriously annoyed with her book or believed that the new school of writers needed to turn its back on her moralizing attitude, he should have realized that a dinner, especially coinciding with the publication of her first book, was hardly the place for a put-down.

Sexuality obviously was a factor in this conflict—the years of subtle sexual tension between Locke and Fauset from his Harvard days until now, his distaste for her as an exemplar of all that he hated about the Philadelphia bourgeoisie, his rivalry, perhaps, with her for the affections of Langston Hughes. But in taking out on her his class and sex frustrations in a public forum, he robbed the Negro Renaissance of a chance to form the kind of beloved community his mentor at Harvard, Josiah Royce, called for. By diminishing her, he diminished himself and his capacity to get others to follow his lead as the new voice of the movement—especially the group of women writers who honored her with the dinner idea. His action exposed the possibility that the Black aesthete takeover of Negro literature in the 1920s would stumble by reproducing the same hierarchies and travesties of silencing that mainstream American literature visited on the Negro writer at large.

Locke should have recognized that Johnson had manipulated him into doing his dirty work. Locke could have pivoted his remarks so that he would not be pegged by history as the spoiler of the occasion. But Johnson had counted on Locke's enmity toward Fauset to do what Johnson wanted done. And when Locke saw that she was weak enough that evening to be displaced, he took the bait, and enjoyed doing it. A more generous approach to her at the dinner would have allowed Locke to recruit Fauset as an ally. In September 1924, she decided to take a leave of absence from her job at the *Crisis* and go to Europe to work on her second novel. The real reason for her hiatus was that her relationship with Du Bois had deteriorated, and Du Bois was ready to take over her duties now that the literary renaissance had gathered steam under *Opportunity*. A more gracious approach to her at the dinner might have allowed Locke to become more influential with the entire group of young writers than either Du Bois or Charles Johnson.

The *Opportunity* dinner symbolized the success and failure of the Negro Renaissance. Through brilliant scheming, Locke and Johnson created a context for the young writers of the 1920s that was unique in American history—an interracial dinner that convinced its participants that Black writing mattered to the rest of America. But the manipulative strategies behind the event ultimately doomed the movement to being something smaller than it could have been. Rather than putting down an ally, what the movement needed was an ethics of collaboration that buoyed one another. That did not require silencing of serious criticism of literary work, but refraining from reproducing inside a Black literary movement the old masters' trick of pitting the slaves against one another to maintain control. Diminishment of one another meant, in effect, that the "younger generation of Negro writers" had not solved the problem of how to collaborate as a group and maximize their meager resources.

Locke's competitive approach to his role at the dinner defined the limits of his capacity to lead. Despite the loftiness of his vision, he would be held back as a creator of community by his failure of empathy. It limited his ability to get people to follow him. They never knew for sure when he would turn on them, as Fauset must have felt after the dinner was over. He was often perplexed when people held grudges against him for this type of behavior. Indeed, he probably was surprised to learn in 1933 that Jessie Fauset was still hurt by how he had treated her that Friday night nearly ten years ago.

23

Battling the Barnes

Where does an elitist, mildly Afrocentric impresario of the arts go in 1924 to get backing for his Negro awakening, given his penchant for alienating Black support? The answer lay there waiting for him after he arrived from Europe. Early in 1924, a short note came to Howard University asking for the name and address of a philosopher on "your staff whom I met in Paris a couple of months ago whose name I forgot."[1] The man who sent the note was Albert Barnes. When Locke met Barnes in 1923, he was a millionaire industrialist on one of his whirlwind trips to purchase European modernist and African art and engage anyone who listened in long, convoluted conversations about both. Barnes had built a mansion in Merion, Pennsylvania, and assembled one of the largest collections of modern and African art in the world. He had formalized that collection as the Barnes Foundation in 1922 to thumb his nose at the Philadelphia art establishment, which he believed was dominated by mindless bluebloods who knew nothing about modern art and looked down on him as uncultured arriviste. Like Locke, Barnes was born poor in Philadelphia but had graduated from Central High School at the bottom of his class and attended graduate school in chemistry, in Germany, without obtaining a PhD. He also shared with Locke a capacity for duplicity. After years of study, Barnes lacked the ability to create new chemical compounds. So he teamed up with a German chemist whom he brought to the United States and encouraged to create a silver nitrate compound called Argyll, which Barnes later took credit for inventing. Barnes went on to build a company in Philadelphia to manufacture and distribute the compound, which made him millions. Barnes also had a visionary conception of what the corporation should be: he invested in the psychology of his workers and required them to attend classes on William James and John Dewey at his factory. Barnes wanted to overcome the alienation typical of the American workplace and foster the kind of creativity among his workers that would make them his equals. In practice, however, Barnes contradicted this philosophy with a dominating personality that ran the factory and everything about it with an iron will.

Gender and race shaped his notion of power. Barnes's two closest assistants—young White women—were described by one man as his "shadows," women who never articulated an idea that had not already been cleared by Barnes. Most of his workers were African Americans dependent on him for a livelihood and forced to participate in his educational programming whether they wanted to or not. Ever since his mother took him at the age of eight to a camp meeting outside of Philadelphia where he heard the itinerant preaching and religious singing of African Americans, Barnes had been convinced that Blacks had greater spiritual capacity than Whites. On the other hand, according to Arthur Fauset, who worked at the Barnes Foundation, Barnes "was sadistic: he loved to demonstrate his power, and fought to make blacks love it and him. One of his favorite sentences was 'I told them [the white Philadelphia elite] that if they didn't let me have that place for the museum, I would take my house and rent it to Negroes and see how they like that.'"[2] As the philosopher Bertrand Russell, who worked at the Barnes Foundation in the late 1930s, put it: Barnes "liked to patronise coloured people and treated them as equals, because he was quite sure that they were not.... He demanded constant flattery and had a passion for quarreling. I was warned before accepting his offer that he always tired of people before long."[3] Clearly, Barnes and Locke would be well matched in the coming contest over who would be the voice of African art in America, since gender and race were issues of power for Locke as well.

Barnes was not the only rival Locke faced in what would become a battle royale over who would introduce America to the power of African art. Both Walter White and Charles Johnson were in the struggle over who would most profit from the effort to link the cultural significance of African art to the African American literary awakening.[4] Johnson had been interested in African art since 1923 and wanted to publish his own article on the subject, along with Locke's on the Barnes Foundation, in a special issue of *Opportunity* in the spring of 1924. Johnson also saw the African art issue as a hook to land Barnes for a much larger contribution of money to *Opportunity* along the lines that Locke had proposed to Lieber. If Barnes could be encouraged to make a long-term financial commitment to the work of the magazine, Johnson might be able to move *Opportunity* out of straitjacketed social reform publishing for the Urban League. Johnson respected Locke, but was wary of him. And Locke did not want to become Johnson's boy. White aspired to become something more than an assistant secretary of race relations at the NAACP. Interestingly, the careers of two highly educated Black men seem suddenly to hinge on the successful advertising of an art form most Americans knew nothing about.

This was not the first time that Barnes had been approached to help fund and propel a complex project for social liberation. In 1919, Horace Kallen had contacted Barnes about his plan to create an international movement during the Versailles Conference to establish the State of Israel. American Jewish support for this idea was lukewarm at best, and international opinion was even more skeptical. Barnes, however, was supremely confident that if he were allowed to negotiate the issues, he could have the whole matter resolved in a matter of days. Kallen wanted Barnes in the delegation at Versailles, but Barnes decided not to go, in part because he would not head the delegation, and hence said he was therefore skeptical about its success. As would prove to be the case in his dealings with African Americans, Barnes wanted, indeed needed, to be the center of attention and have total power over any effort that included him.

Barnes was different from other potential patrons like Lieber because Barnes was an intellectual. He had developed a coherent theory of art, grounded in his early study of art with the American realist William Glackens, his reading the art criticism of Clive Bell and Roger Fry, and his personal conversations with contemporary European artists. Barnes imbibed early how to look at paintings as a play of forms, not as representations of the world. Barnes moved beyond Fry to insist these formal relationships could be studied scientifically to see what a painting had to teach. Barnes believed that this ability was a profoundly transformative experience, giving the student/viewer a sense of authority that Barnes believed traditional education denied students. Whether workers or art critics, those who "learned to see" pictures in this way could develop a new, modern subjectivity. In practice Barnes seldom allowed any but a few sycophants recognition as aesthetic visionaries; and he was always the one who decided who was one. His books, essays, and correspondence lambasted others, especially noted art critics, for not viewing art and teaching art appreciation his way.[5]

On January 24, Barnes wrote to Locke asking him to be put in touch with the best writings of the young educated Black community. Barnes felt he already knew a great deal about uneducated, working-class Black people, "with whom I have worked every day for more than twenty years."[6] But Barnes wanted a cross section of works by the "negro poets, writers, thinkers, musicians and other creators who have risen above the average" for an article he had been asked to write for *Ex Libris*, a Paris journal. The invitation was important to Barnes, even though the journal was essentially a mouthpiece for Paul Guillaume, Barnes's close friend and art agent. Barnes was pleased with the list Locke sent. He wrote back: "isn't Miss Grimke a star of the first magnitude?" Locke was glad he did not have to respond to this in person, since he did not much like Miss Grimke's work. Locke's assistance was enough for Barnes to grant Locke's request to visit the Barnes Foundation, but he wanted Locke to help him get his article republished in an American journal.[7] Johnson reasoned that Barnes might allow the essay to be published in *Opportunity*, which might further attract Barnes to the fold of White supporters of *Opportunity*'s program.

At Johnson's urging, Locke had invited Barnes to the Civic Club dinner, where he was enormously impressed with James Weldon Johnson, who spoke. But a problem emerged after the dinner. Walter White was seated next to Barnes and during the evening's conversation, discovered that Barnes was an authority on African art. Apparently, White also wanted to write on the larger significance of African art and was then working on his own article, "If White Were Black," on Black art and its broader implications, to be published in H. L. Mencken's newly launched *American*

Mercury. White made the mistake of writing an obsequious letter to Barnes asking him to critically examine a draft of the article.[8] Barnes replied immediately:

> You wish my opinion, you told me, upon what you have written upon negro plastic art. I'll give it [to] you frankly because I want negro art to come into its own, on its own merits and discharged of the load of bluff, bunk and nonsense with which it is now burdened. Hence, I think that practically everything you have written from page four to page eight inclusive should never, for the negros' [*sic*] sake, be published.

As if that rebuke was not enough, Barnes went on to detail:

> What you state in many cases as facts are demonstrably untrue. Stewart Culin is one of the most loveable, other-world souls that I know; he is also a mental cripple, a hopeless doddering old ignoramus in anything which relates to art. [Carl] Einstein is a mental giant and connoisseur compared to him—that doesn't detract anything of truth or sobriety of statement from my public assertion the other night that Einstein is a colossal bluff. De Zayas is in somewhat the same class as Einstein with dullness substituted for Einstein's Clive Bell-like counterfeit thinking in smooth, slick language. But don't take my word for anything I've just written upon those men. For the sake of the negro we both love—the negro who is a clean, simple, honest person—I suggest that you go to Paris and ask Paul Guillaume, the man who was the first to recognize what negro sculpture is as an art form.[9]

Barnes suggested to White that he "let the sole reference to negro plastic art be what Roger Fry has written. The rest of your references are the literary equivalents of prostitution."[10]

What Barnes really objected to in White's article was his references to other Whites as authorities on African art. To show who was really the authority on African art, Barnes sent White a copy of his own article, along with a letter he had written to Charles S. Johnson defining what was significant about African art and his strategy for bringing that significance to the American public. More than just promoting his own article, Barnes was enlisting Johnson and the other "fine brains I saw at work the other night" at the Civic Club dinner in his worldwide crusade to gain the long overdue recognition for West African art that had been denied it by White institutional interpreters of art. Barnes, however, did not think much of White's ability. "I saw the other night," Barnes wrote Locke of White, "that he's a light-weight but his manuscript has revealed a cheapness which I hardly suspected."[11]

White, however, seemed not to realize how much Barnes disliked his article and wrote Barnes asking if he could quote from "The Temple" and the letter to improve his own article. Barnes replied that such liberal quotation as White suggested would compromise the value of his own article. Barnes then had Johnson send copies of his articles, "The Temple" and "Negro Art in America," to H. L. Mencken at the *American Mercury* for consideration for publication. As he wrote White, "That need not conflict with your article for the same journal because what I have to say is the logical preparation for your statements."[12] Mencken replied that he did not publish articles at that time on foreign subjects and that he already had an article commissioned on Negro art by White. That infuriated Barnes. He then demanded that White return his article and the letter immediately and threatened White and Mencken with legal action should his name or his words be mentioned in White's article.

Barnes believed the *Mercury* was a better venue for his article than *Opportunity*, and once Mencken rejected him, Barnes became consumed with destroying White's reputation. He proposed to Locke and Johnson that James Weldon Johnson, the secretary of the NAACP, be made aware of White's "betrayal" of the Negro in his article. Barnes also had laid a trap for White: "In my second letter to White I suggested a conference with C.S.J. and J.W.J. in the hope that one of them would get wise. White, I think, is a personal pusher, and he may see what I meant and duck the conference." White did "duck the conference": he had the advantage over Barnes of having access to the *American Mercury* to express his interpretation. And Barnes had put White in an almost impossible position: he discredited all of White's references to authorities in his article, but then refused to let White cite the only person that Barnes approved of: himself. Despite his stated desire for collaboration in advancing the cause of African art, the cause was mainly to advance his authority on the subject. Once he realized Mencken would not publish his article, he wrote White telling him that "the negroes with whom I work read your article" and had prepared a letter to be sent to the NAACP stating that they believed it should not be published. Barnes then stated that he had succeeded in "stopping the proposed formal protest," but with the implied threat that if White failed to comply with Barnes's wishes, he would have the letter mailed. Barnes also wrote Locke that he left open the possibility of a public debate with White and that, if he could get White to take the bait, he "could be eliminated from negro public life." This conflict said something profound about Barnes: he was someone who could not tolerate anyone rejecting his self-promotion. What he did not realize was that he actually was modeling behavior for his erstwhile ally in this campaign against White: Alain Locke.

Being narcissistic himself, Locke quickly realized that it was unlikely Barnes would fund the independent arts institute Locke desired. Already astute at sizing up adversaries—and especially White ones—he sensed Barnes was the type of White man who needed Black people around to worship him, but would rebel at supporting someone else's operation. So to feed that need, Locke recommended a number of African American intellectuals and artists to spend time at the Barnes Foundation, from Arthur Fauset to Aaron Douglas, the St. Louis–born

illustrator and budding Black artist. Fauset was genuinely interested in a revolutionary, working-class pedagogy and for a while thought that Barnes's system
of John Dewey–like educational radicalism could be revolutionary. The Aaron
Douglas connection served better Locke's main agenda to gain access to Barnes's
magnificent African art collection for African American artists, for Locke believed that if Black American artists could be exposed to African art it would
reawaken in them a visual arts facility that had been atrophied since slavery.

Locke was attempting to use Barnes to gain access to a Black art form that
White people controlled in Europe and America. In 1924, African art was not
readily available for viewing in American collections. A sense of Locke's motivation in this context comes from Fauset: "Locke was insatiable when it came to
things having to do with acquisitions that were going to be important in the
black peoples lives."[13] Whereas Barnes wanted to get control of African art to
enhance his reputation as a radical arts theorist, Locke wanted control of African
art as a Black people's birthright and as a means to convince contemporary Black
artists that they were heirs to a mighty African visual arts tradition. It only
would be a matter of time before conflict between this new, overweening father
figure and the upstart virtual son came to a head.

After several postponements and delays, Barnes finally had tested Locke and
Johnson enough to allow them to visit the Barnes Foundation on April 6. Located
in a beaux arts mansion designed by Paul Cret, the Foundation welcomed the pair
through the commanding neoclassical entrance into a round main hall. There, the
six-foot-tall Barnes lectured the two diminutive Black intellectuals all day. When
Barnes was not lambasting Walter White and his transgressions, he was expound-
ing on African art and European modernism and the psychological principles he
used to arrange the art on the walls of the galleries. Johnson was not exaggerating
when he wrote Barnes afterward about "how extremely I value the opportunity
which you made possible to be in contact with your amazing collection of modern
and primitive art and with your own trenchant, kaleidoscopic intellect."[14] This visit
may very well have been the first time that Johnson had seen African art up close.
It was not, of course, the first time for Locke. He had seen a selection at Guillaume's
Paris gallery in July, and, likely before, while he was a student in Berlin.

Nevertheless, the visit awakened something new in Locke and catalyzed an
immediate and dramatic shift of emphasis in Locke's writings about things
African—from his earlier focus on North and East Africa to one firmly attentive
to West Africa. Little to no formal discussion of West African art existed in
Locke's writings before this visit, and a considerable, wide-ranging, commitment to such art erupted afterward and continued for the rest of his life. At the
Foundation that Sunday, he saw clearly how he could use African art to advance
his cultural agenda. Something emotional clicked as well, for afterward Locke
became an avid collector of West African art.

Locke also imbibed Barnes's enthusiasm for African art's significance to
modern art. Barnes displayed African art alongside modern European art and

demonstrated its influence on cubism and modernism with unmistakable visual comparisons. The arrangement of the two bodies of art together showed that people of African descent had a claim on the most powerful art revolution of the twentieth century and armed visitors with compelling evidence of the influence of African art on cubism, especially. In the 1920s, radical modernists believed that African art had directly influenced Pablo Picasso and others, some even going so far as to argue that French artists had copied the African art forms verbatim. The difference was that Barnes collected the art that proved the point. Barnes had collected African pieces that directly correlated to these modern art creations, sometimes after conversations with the European artists themselves about their inspirations for their works. Seeing those eye-popping interconnections made clear to Locke and Johnson that African art was on a par with the best of European art—ever.

The day after the visit to the Barnes Foundation, Johnson swung into action. He wrote Barnes that he planned to publish Barnes's article "Negro Art in America" in *Opportunity* in a special May issue dedicated to African art. Johnson was eager to move ahead with the special issue, especially in light of possible competition with White's article in the *American Mercury*. Johnson also planned to include his own article in an issue, but was overwhelmed with work and other responsibilities in April and had to be away from the office in the weeks leading up to publication. In Johnson's absence, Locke made most of the decisions about photographs, layout, and so forth, for the issue. This was only one of several occasions in Locke's life in which he ghost-edited issues, exhibitions, plays, or books, but this time it caused him great stress. Johnson wondered why Locke became so agitated during the mock-up. "I think it was made very clear that we were dealing with materials about which your judgment was superior even to mine, and that you would be in New York to see the proofs and make suggestions on the final form....I am glad that what could easily have been guessed as my wishes in the matter were respected....But for goodness sake don't let African art be your Nemesis."[15]

Why was Locke so disturbed? A conflict between Barnes and Locke is the most likely source. After the issue appeared, Barnes was furious because he believed that Locke had plagiarized his ideas in Locke's article "A Note on African Art." While the *Opportunity* issue also included Barnes's article "The Temple," Locke's article better communicated the ideas that Barnes had communicated orally to Locke and Johnson. John Dewey claimed Barnes suffered from an inferiority complex that inhibited him as a writer, and he often sought others to codify his ideas. But Barnes was intensely jealous of anyone he did not choose expressing his insights. Locke's stress may have been linked to his knowledge that Barnes would believe he had been overthrown by Locke's more powerful presentation of the notion that African art was the leading edge of a modernist revolution in aesthetic form. Barnes's article was stuck in the details of his own personal entry into African art and Paul Guillaume's Paris studio, which left the door open for someone, in this case Locke, to give better expression to the central idea—that African art was the most significant contemporary influence on modern art and was produced by Black people in Africa. Barnes felt cuckolded, and Locke knew he would feel that way.

Barnes was angry even though Locke fawningly acknowledged Barnes and his collection throughout "A Note on African Art," as did the rest of the issue. The editorial page had a tribute, "Dr. Barnes." The issue also included Paul Guillaume's article, "African Art at the Barnes Foundation," with numerous credited photographs of Barnes's artwork. Moreover, Barnes's own essay, "The Temple," credited Guillaume as the original person to recognize the importance of African art for modern art and lauded his studio for creating an atmosphere of free intellectual exchange where Barnes learned much from Roger Fry, Jacque Lipschitz, and Waldeman George. He concluded: "No psychologist would deny that what we like, we must share with others to obtain its full savor."[16]

It seems, though, that when Barnes savored what he had shared with Locke at the Barnes Foundation, it left a bad taste in his mouth. This kind of sharing is precisely what the mentoring role in patronage is supposed to be about. Locke was essentially the mentee—the understudy to the master and saying in his own words what Barnes wanted said. But Barnes had not yet said it well in print himself. Of course, Locke was also the only aesthete, with a world-class aesthetic rather than social science education. His exposure to modernism in his years at Harvard, Oxford, and the University of Berlin, and also with his friends like Dickerman and de Fonseka, allowed Locke to understand Barnes and use his insights nimbly to advance his own cultural agenda. Barnes had made the mistake of lecturing to the one Negro who understood him.

After the issue was published, Barnes wrote Locke to say that he did "like the African Art issue very, very much and it did, as you say, spread out the subject nicely." More privately, he also did a ten-page exegesis of Locke's article, going line by line, and writing "mine" by those sentences he felt were taken from his talk and writing "platitudes" by those lines that expressed Locke's ideas. Barnes was also displeased Locke had had the temerity to inject his own ideas and agenda into his discussion of African art. Locke had constructed himself as an authority on African art through the language and tone of the article. And Locke had not thanked Barnes enough. Lack of gratitude on the part of Negroes who received patronage was a frequent lament of White patrons of the period.

Barnes then took another jab at Locke in the letter: "This damned nigger question is getting to be quite a time-consumer for me. Twice a week I lead an attack on some of their own prejudices and every once in a while it gets so warm that I keep my eye peeled for a razor-flash."[17] The use of the word *nigger*, at a time when Du Bois and others were demanding its erasure from respectable discourse, was both Barnes's way of degrading Blacks and asserting his entitlement to use the term because he was so "in" with Blacks. But the reference to the flashing of the razor, while a demeaning stereotype of primitive Black violence, also revealed more than Barnes intended. If truly a sign of Black anger, it suggests that even the working-class Blacks in his employ were beginning to tire of his presumption he knew better than Negroes what was best for them.

Barnes's idea—that African art had taught European artists what was, in essence, modern art—was quite radical in 1924 and is still resisted by canonical modernist art history. But Barnes had the art to prove the point, and this is why Locke put up with Barnes for years: he had the art Locke needed to make his stronger point that European artists had stolen the formal inventiveness of African artists to launch modernism in art. A thirteenth-century Zouenouia statue, whose photograph from the Barnes Foundation Locke published on page 136 of his article, was followed by a photograph of the Modigliani stone on page 137 to show how strikingly similar in form, conception, and sculptural execution the modern copy was of the African original. Barnes's collection showed more than coincidence or psychological obsession with exorcism- or fetishism-inspired modernist artists like Modigliani and Picasso—it was formal lessons that African art had taught European modernists of how to create paintings and sculpture conceptually, not representationally.

But Locke diverged significantly from Barnes in the use to which he wanted to put African art—to awaken young Negro artists to see African art as inspiration for making a great African American art in the twentieth century. Locke ended on a strong charge to Negro artists to follow their African ancestors, reject Western academicism, and create a revolutionary, formally new art of their own. Why? Because up until 1924, the argument for a Negro American art movement had rested on content—that Negro visual artists like their literary cousins should be encouraged to create because they had been denied that recognition in the past because of racism. Or a Negro art was needed, à la Du Bois, to fight against visual racism by creating an archive of beautiful, dignified Negro faces and bodies. But Locke articulated a different Weltanschauung for African American art—as a demand to build on the formal aesthetic genius of their ancestors to create a revolutionary new American art on the basis of form. The resultant article was no longer simply Barnes. The discovery of the African conceptual revolution in art by a Black intellectual was taken as permission for contemporary Negro artists to equal what European modernists had achieved. That was never Barnes's intention. Once again, as with Hansberry, so with Barnes, Locke was not interested in valorizing the past, but in using that past to launch a contemporary art movement.

By making that change, Locke came out from under Barnes as his tutee, and regarded, in effect, Barnes as his research assistant, as someone who had been in the library, so to speak—or in this case the Paris galleries—had found some new research, delivered it to the professor, and now saw it stated in print. Of course, Black people were thankful for Barnes's services, especially for delivering to them the knowledge that they did not need White people to create great art. Barnes's theorizing was a breakthrough in acknowledging that African art had pioneered in effect, a conceptual art that opened a doorway to cubism and abstraction. Locke was grateful for that insight. But he refused to pay back Barnes for that knowledge by becoming his intellectual servant. Instead, as he did with Max Reinhardt's observations, Locke used Barnes's knowledge to launch his own subjectivity as the foremost African American authority on African and African-derived art.

Sometime in the writing of his article and the editing of the issue, therefore, Locke decided to accept himself as the Prometheus who stole knowledge from the man who acted like a god. He knew that Barnes would revile him as a thief. But Barnes himself stole this knowledge from others and peddled it—like his zinc formula—as his. Reinhardt had been more generous, perhaps recognizing he could never be the one to advance a Negro American artistic agenda. Barnes had no such humility: he wanted the credit for "discovering" African art and authority for determining the correct interpretation of it. Locke decided to appropriate while augmenting Barnes's interpretation so effectively that Barnes could never prove Locke was wrong.

Of course, Barnes would try and discredit him, but the truth was that Barnes did not have the institutional network to stop Locke. Indeed, Locke through Johnson, and White through E. L. Mencken, had publishing access that Barnes lacked. He needed them even more than they needed him to get an airing for his ideas. And no matter how boisterous Barnes was, or how cavalier in throwing around the N-word, ultimately, he couldn't control Locke and that made him exceedingly angry.

A corner had been turned. A New Negro was emerging, who did not have to kowtow to a White man who was "in the game." Locke had been psychologically well endowed to resist Barnes's hegemony, since after Locke's struggle against his father, he had a deep well of Oedipal resistance to draw upon. But tussling with a pathological White man involved risk, for it required Locke and those after him to manifest a kind of courage in cultural combat with powerful Whites that seldom had been successful before. What made the New Negro subjectivity new was the willingness to assert that Negroes had a right to theorize about their aesthetic traditions and benefit from them without having to grovel for every nickel they received from White supporters. This position would be tested in the coming years.

But for now, the new attitude was evident in a letter Locke wrote to the Abyssinian minister Belata Heroui about an impending visit of White philanthropists. "I am sure, that since they represent . . . the characteristic attitude of the white race, which even when philanthropic, needs constantly to be watched and safe-guarded[. I am sure] that the Wise perspicacity and skilfull [*sic*] diplomacy of yourself and associates has already sensed this and met the situation adroitly. The interests which they represent can then be wisely used, without danger to that most precious of all things—Abyssinian national feeling and sovereignty."[18] The Barnes episode had been a case study for Locke in how such interests could be wisely used, but also wisely "watched and safeguarded," lest they destroy the early shoots of "that most precious of all things"—African American "national feeling" and cultural self-determination.

Langston Hughes, 1927. Photograph by James Allen. Courtesy of the Moorland-Spingarn Research Center, Howard University.

24

Looking for Love and Finding
the New Negro

Locke emerged in May 1924 relatively unscathed from his conflicts with Barnes and Jessie Fauset. Barnes seemed afraid to attack Locke publicly: now that their names were linked in *Opportunity*, which had published his article, even he realized he would look ridiculous attacking a fellow contributor and the ghost editor of the volume. Fauset fumed in private or with her female friends, but Black respectability protected Locke once again.

By contrast, Locke was not well protected emotionally. In early June, William, his young lover, left Washington to work on a boat as a waiter. Neither Locke nor William was enthusiastic about the idea, but William took the position because it offered a chance to travel and mature somewhat. This removed the primary source of Locke's emotional turmoil, because William refused to allow Locke to control his life or his affections. After months of fruitless struggle between them, Locke's nerves were frayed and he was glad to see him go. He also soured on ever finding a romantic interest to fill the emotional void in his life. Why Locke had invested so much in that unrewarding relationship was unclear, even to Claude McKay. "You know some parts of your first letter mystify me rather. I thought I was persuading you all the time not to take that Washington disappointment so badly but I never reckoned on you entering upon experiences of 'diffused emotion.'" Locke had begun traveling almost every weekend to New York, staying at the YMCA in Harlem, and visiting emerging gay nightclubs and cabarets where he could meet young men. Nevertheless, as he confided to McKay, these random sexual encounters were neither emotionally satisfying nor creatively stimulating.[1]

Even as Locke fell apart without William, there were some benefits. With William out of the way, Locke was freer to develop his relationships with young writers in Harlem and elsewhere who sought educational and professional advancement. That Locke adhered to such a philosophy is clearly indicated by the educative or paternalistic nature of his relationships with such young writers as Eric Walrond, Countee Cullen, and Langston Hughes over the next three years.

To the extent to which he helped them to become mature, educated, and accomplished artists, he could rationalize the pursuit of his own sexual satisfaction with them as making a race contribution. If he elevated the level of accomplishment these young men reached, then, in the long run, their careers and more broadly Black achievement would spiral upward. Such male-male relationships could be reciprocal in their production of artistic excellence for the race even if they were not reciprocal in desire.

Often, in practice, this still produced more difficulties than satisfaction for Locke. Sometime in late 1923 or early 1924, Locke had developed a close, perhaps even a sexual, relationship with Eric Walrond. It exemplified Locke's educative approach. "You ask me to write you regarding my plans," Walrond wrote to Locke on June 4. "In the fall I must be at school. As regards writing, I am not going to look at that novel until I get back to the city. I am not really worried about the problem of revision—that I know is something I must do leisurely and in conjunction with my rising (I hope you'll pardon the epithet) powers." Locke had chastised Walrond for being lazy and failing to follow through to completion his many short stories, novels, and other writing projects. He also advised the young Jamaican on his best career moves. But such efforts did not result in increased intimacy between them, and the pressure to excel may have had the opposite effect. Walrond promised to spend a weekend with Locke in June, but canceled the day he was supposed to show up, citing nervous tension and depression. "I do not think," he wrote, that "it would be fair to you, nor would I be doing myself justice, to come down to Washington in this high-strung, unnatural, morbid, discontented state of mind. For it seems strange, yet it is true, that ever since I have known you I have not been really myself."[2] The pressure to meet Locke's expectations sometimes made many want to distance themselves from him.

Mercifully, Cullen did come to Washington and spend a weekend with Locke in June. But Locke and Cullen were not seriously attracted to one another. Locke received what meager sexual favors he obtained from Cullen, because he mentored Cullen psychologically. Ironically, Locke served as a go-between and model of emotional stability to Cullen, who struggled desperately with his own unrequited love. Cullen was a comrade, perhaps an occasional sexual partner, but not a lover. Additionally, the corpulent Cullen lacked the slender build that Locke desired in lovers.

Even before William's departure, Locke had renewed his correspondence with the most elusive and attractive of the Harlem writers, Langston Hughes. Remarkably, Locke and Hughes still had not met. After Hughes disappointed him, Locke swore off any further correspondence, but Cullen—returning the favor to serve as a go-between—facilitated their reconciliation. Cullen had received a letter from Hughes early in 1924 that stated he wanted to resume his education; but this time he wanted to attend a Black college, possibly Howard.

Cullen encouraged him to contact Locke, who exchanged a couple of cautious but cordial letters with Hughes. Then, suddenly, a February 2, 1924, telegram from Hughes ratcheted up the intensity of their relationship. "MAY I COME NOW PLEASE LET ME KNOW TONIGHT WIRE LANGSTON HUGHES." Locke did not immediately answer the telegram. Two days later, Hughes explained. "Forgive me for the sudden and unexpected message I sent you. I'm sorry. I should have known that you couldn't begin in the middle of the term and that I wasn't ready to come anyway. But I had been reading your letters that day and a sudden desire came over me to come to you then, right then, to stay with you and know you. I need to know you. But I am so stupid sometimes. However I am coming to Howard and I want to see you and talk to you about it."[3]

Why did Hughes, inclined to avoid Locke, suddenly change course? Probably, a number of considerations coalesce to create a sense of urgency in Hughes. He was a young man without means. Without somebody's help, he could not obtain an education. Locke had already proposed to pay his way abroad: perhaps he could live with Locke in Washington and obtain tuition and room and board. While the wily side of Hughes saw Locke as a means to an end, the artist also was attracted to the persona Locke had created in his letters of a Black aesthete able to introduce Hughes to the life of art and writing as an ideal. Hughes had never encountered anyone with such a romantic commitment to the life of art; his desire to "know" him was partly a desire to know himself as an artist and writer. Having experienced his first homosexual encounter and then having fallen madly in love with Anne Coussey, a middle-class Anglo-African, Hughes's "sudden desire" to come to Washington and "stay with you and know you" may have expressed a need to learn something more about his own complicated sexual identity by meeting Locke.

Locke weakened and decided to take a chance and propositioned Hughes. "Perhaps you will come to Howard—that emboldens my desire to have you with me...here you would have no expenses whatever if you could collaborate with me in my work and help me with my writing. May I suggest this?" Locke's needs went beyond ordinary "research assistance," as he explained. "I am humbly and desperately in need of a companion—several hoped—for things have failed utterly. My only recourse is a German friend [Rudolph] who with difficulty would fit into the local situation. Countee has put my moral problem to me beautifully and with precision—'Please keep a racial heart'—he says. I know I should—the question is, can I—may I?"[4] When Hughes failed to answer Locke's provocative letter, Locke sent Hughes a Howard catalog, advising that he too would be in Paris that summer, but avoiding any proposal to get together. He also wrote Hughes about his love for the romantic sights of Paris, but emphasized that he would be occupied with other people and business that summer.

Locke also made some connections for Hughes. He secured an invitation for Hughes to lunch with Albert Barnes and Paul Guillaume and visit the latter's

Galerie. Once in Paris, Hughes found Barnes distasteful, but loved the gallery and its collection of African art. Most important, Locke announced that he wanted to publish Hughes's best poems, especially "Danse Variation," which Cullen had shown him, in "a special issue of the *Survey Graphic* devoted to Negro life." Prominent publication in such an issue would, of course, benefit Hughes. All of these maneuvers showcased that Locke was a valuable patron to Hughes who would be rewarded by the association. It nicely deflected attention from Locke's emotional neediness. The tactic worked. Early in June, Hughes wrote that he would try to remain in Paris until Locke arrived. Locke remained cool in his letters to Hughes, even as he anticipated the opportunity to "spend a few days in Paris with you before you flit." This casual line was just a pose, since Locke knew he had a competitor.[5]

That same month, Jessie Fauset wrote Hughes asking him to remain in Paris until she arrived in October. It was no secret that Jessie Fauset always beamed radiantly whenever she had Langston Hughes in her midst. Of course, her age— she was over forty—his perpetual absence from New York, and her professional and sexual relationship with W. E. B. Du Bois complicated whatever romantic relationship she might forge with Hughes. But when her relationship with Du Bois deteriorated that spring, and her novel became a publishing success, she took a leave of absence that fall, perhaps already planning on pursuing Hughes. Romantic attention from Hughes would allow her to regain her self-esteem, play the older, wiser lover, and perhaps find her muse. "You can take me to all the dangerous places and I can take you to all the beautiful ones," she wrote in April.[6]

Even more important, Hughes, in May, looked forward to her arrival. To Harold Jackman, a close friend of Countee Cullen, Hughes confided that he regarded Jessie as "a woman of charm, my own brown goddess."[7] That news, undoubtedly communicated to Locke by Cullen, could not have made Locke happy. Despite all of his assets, he was still less desirable to Hughes than an older, late-Victorian woman. What was "an old girl," as Locke sometimes called himself, to do? Get to Paris as soon as possible! But Locke had many responsibilities to fulfill before he could leave New York.

Paul Kellogg, the editor of the *Survey Graphic*, had approached Locke and Charles S. Johnson at the *Opportunity* dinner about doing a special issue of his journal, *Survey Graphic*, on the younger writers' movement. It may have been Kellogg's idea to connect this literary awakening to Harlem, the vibrant northern neighborhood of Manhattan that had become the ideal destination of Blacks migrating out of the South and the West Indies during the 1910s. It is not clear whether Kellogg envisioned them as co-editors of what became known as the Harlem number or as having different titles and functions. But Kellogg planned meetings to include both Locke and Johnson, because Johnson was already a known quantity—a skilled editor and confidant of many of the young writers

Kellogg wanted in the issue. Moreover, Johnson was perhaps the most knowledgeable person in New York about the sociological landscape of Harlem.

But practically, Johnson was already editing a major magazine with only a tiny staff and traveled constantly to gather information and represent the Urban League. A turning point came when Kellogg planned a critical meeting for the three of them on Saturday, April 19, but Johnson had to cancel due to a business trip. Kellogg went ahead with the meeting with Locke alone. The *Survey Graphic* editor was getting anxious, because he had planned the Harlem number to appear in the fall, but as yet had no plan or outline for the issue.[8]

Locke came up by train that Friday and arrived the next morning at the *Survey Graphic*'s offices at 112 E. 19th Street. At noon, Locke and Kellogg lunched at the Civic Club, then returned to the *Survey Graphic* offices, where Kellogg asked him to prepare an outline of the issue. Locke returned home, penned the outline, mailed it, and then learned on May 10 that Kellogg and his staff liked it and, with certain modifications, would use it to begin to contact contributors, most of whom Locke had suggested.[9] From then on, Johnson had a diminished role, and Locke was clearly the guest editor of the issue.

Rumors spread that Locke had pushed Johnson aside. It would not be surprising if Locke had used his meeting with Kellogg to convince him that he was the best man to edit the *Survey Graphic* number. Less tightly scheduled than Johnson, Locke also was able to devote his full attention to the issue. Given that the *Survey Graphic* staff already possessed considerable sociological and marketing expertise, Kellogg may also have felt that his greater need was for someone who brought a completely different aesthetic talent to the project. Kellogg and Locke also hit it off personally, for they subsequently remained friends and collaborators. Most important, Locke's outline promised to make Kellogg's Harlem number one of the most original investigations of Black life yet published. Although Johnson had pioneered the use of a race magazine to market Black literature, the leitmotif to the main story of each issue was the social problems encountered by Negroes. By contrast, Locke's outline emphasized the literary and cultural history of Harlem in such articles as "The South Lingers On," "The Tropics in New York," "The Negro Digs Up His Past," "The Negro Brings His Gifts," and "Jazz at Home." Moreover, most of the authors he proposed—Rudolph Fisher, W. A. Domingo, Eric Walrond, Rebecca West, Arthur Schomburg, and J. A. Rogers—were writers or historians, not the usual Negro authorities. By putting poetry, belles-lettres, and historical anthropology ahead of sociological reports, Locke privileged the agency of African Americans and minimized Progressive-Era objectification of the Negro as the sick man of American democracy. Not only had he separated himself from other race sociologists, but he had also discovered the theme of his work for the rest of the 1920s—that in places like Harlem, a distinctive, contemporary, and urban African American culture had emerged. Nothing in the prior issues of *Opportunity* suggested anything as complex as Locke articulated in his outline.

Locke's metaphor for the special number—"The New Negro"—also was compelling, especially the way Locke planned to employ it in the issue. Of course,
New Negro was a concept that had been around in African American newspapers, books, placards, and pamphlets since the 1890s—usually referring to a
generation of Blacks born after slavery who rebelled against the stereotypes imposed on ex-slaves. Booker T. Washington had seized the term to title his 1901
book that heralded a new, more economically self-sufficient Negro, who rejected
the paternalistic arrangements started under slavery and embraced self-dependence and entrepreneurship in a laissez-faire economic world to define a new
identity for themselves. In the late 1910s, the New Negro gained a militant label
when Black migrants, who migrated to northern cities during the World War,
fought back when attacked by Whites who sought to drive them from urban
Black communities. By 1924, the New Negro was also associated with Marcus
Garvey's Universal Negro Improvement Association and its demand for Blacks
to pursue a separate, independent economic and political agenda in the United
States and plan to move "Back to Africa" to create a great African nation. By appropriating the term, Locke sought to evoke all of these prior references but to
add a new one—the idea the New Negro was a generational awakening in the
city, especially in Harlem, where the streams of the uneducated and educated of
the race came to Harlem out of a sense of *opportunity*, not flight from oppression. As Locke stated in "The New Negro," a synopsis of his introductory essay:
"The North meant freedom to the elder generation; the city means opportunity
to the younger." In one sentence, Locke changed the argument of the issue from
being about "the Negro problem" to being about the consciousness of a younger
generation of Negroes in the city.

This New Negro conceptual frame allowed Locke to keep his promise to
Hughes to put the younger generation "out front" and make youth the principal
embodiment of the "New Negro" attitude. Locke pushed "youth" in part because
of the Sonnenkinder orientation he had imbibed in Berlin, that the youth were
the deliverers of a new spiritual nationalism, whether in Germany or America.
Locke also was sexually infatuated with young writers and wanted to make young
male bodies icons of the Negro Renaissance just as they had been idols of the Italian
Renaissance. Even more politically, by focusing on youth, Locke interrupted the
dominant racial narrative in America of Negroes as an undifferentiated mass.
Youth forced White and Black ideologues to add a new concept—generation—to
the prevailing lenses of race and class used so extensively by Du Bois and such
other Black radicals as Hubert Harrison and Chandler Owen. Youth symbolized
the possible renewal of Black culture by a new generation of young, gifted, pre-
cociously expressive writers—not politicians, street corner preachers, or labor
organizers. Idealism replaced a materialist analysis of the Negro and brought
with it the possibility of transcendence of America's race problem rather than
further submersion in it.

The shift to culture was consistent with what Kellogg had defined as the orientation he wanted in the *Survey Graphic*, as opposed to the more rigorously sociological *Survey Mid-Monthly* that Kellogg also published. Since 1922, he had turned the *Survey Graphic* into a popular venue to provide educated, upper-middle-class urban readers with "graphic" portraits of ethnic peoples. Previous numbers were on gypsies and Mexicans, the latter an issue, guest edited by novelist Katherine Anne Porter, that sought to capture the spirit of the Mexican Revolution rather than provide an exhausting sociological analysis of why it had occurred.

Once Locke was in charge of the issue, though, he was more responsible than he wanted to be for securing the contributions, especially as his summer travels loomed.[10] Locke had difficulty getting fresh material for the issue. Kellogg urged Locke to "ask people to get their manuscripts in by June 10."[11] By the end of June, only one contributor from the thirty contacted, Albert Barnes, who of course had already written his contribution, had sent it in. Locke leaned on the notoriously tardy Eric Walrond to get started on his essay on West Indian culture and chided Arthur Schomburg, who had difficulty writing in English, to transcribe his largely oral insights into Afro-European history into written notes for what became "The Negro Digs Up His Past." Locke's new angle on the Negro brought with it the challenge to get creative writers and self-taught historians to produce trenchant cultural reporting on a deadline. A long, frustrating process had just begun.

Even in the area he knew best, poetry, the going was tough. Most poetry on hand was by James Weldon Johnson and other older and previously published authors. Locke leaned on Cullen, to whom several of the New Negroes regularly sent their latest material, to gather material for him. Cullen, in turn, showed these items to Locke, who then wrote and requested them from the authors. But that did not guarantee new material for the *Survey Graphic*. Locke read Hughes's "Danse Variations," and then wrote to Hughes. "Countee Cullen showed me Danse Variations and I love it so much. I would like to use it for a special issue of *Survey Graphic* I am editing."[12] But months earlier, Hughes had sent the poem to Augustus Dill, who had taken over Jessie Fauset's duties at the *Crisis*, and he planned to publish it that summer. By the end of June, Locke had precious few new poems on hand.

Another significant hurdle was to find sympathetic White observers to portray Harlem as a cultural entity with something to add to America and the world. Here, Locke's own contacts helped most. He tapped Melville Herskovits for an anthropologist's view of Harlem, but since he was a relatively unknown student of Franz Boas at this time, Locke needed a more well-known observer to validate Harlem's significance. Rebecca West's name surfaced, but she was a contact of Walter White's, and Locke hesitated since they were still on less than good terms after the Barnes conflict. Kellogg suggested Locke "take Mr. White into your confidence about the special issue we are getting up" in order to get him to enlist West in the enterprise. Locke failed to act.

Locke had a real stroke of luck when Kellogg proposed to use German-born artist Winold Reiss to illustrate the issue. Reiss had done strikingly beautiful portraits of Mexican revolutionaries and peasants for the special Mexican issue of the *Survey Graphic* in May 1924. Apparently, Kellogg contacted Reiss about whether he would be willing to do a series of portraits of "Harlem Types" that could be used by the magazine. Reiss jumped at the idea, but here again there was a catch. He needed some contacts and some sitters, and once again, that is where Locke came in. "You write," Kellogg replied to a Locke letter early in June, that "'I shall make New York again June 11th as agreed upon. Could Mr. Reiss in the interim however look up a few types? I will write him if you say so.' My impression is that Mr. Reiss was largely going to lean on you and Mr. Johnson and people you could get to cooperate to find him the types. Why don't you drop him a line and keep his interest simmering."[13]

Locke did not know many "types," a euphemism for "authentic, full-blooded Negroes," usually found among the working class. Reiss had left New York City by mid-June to spend the summer in his Woodstock home. With few written contributions on hand and no artist around, Locke left for Europe. The best that could be hoped for was that over the summer the contributors would at least start their articles, and Locke could urge them to completion once he returned from abroad. When that would be was also unclear. Initially, he had applied for a fall leave of absence to pursue the African research trip he had planned the previous year and was ready to launch in Egypt through the auspices of George Foucart and the French archaeological mission. He planned to meet with Foucart in the south of France, after visiting Hughes in Paris, and then, if conditions were favorable, to proceed to Egypt, again, for the fall excavation season in 1924. Locke also had received an invitation to meet Belata Heroui, the Ethiopian ambassador, to further pursue Locke's plan to interest Ethiopia in sending a contingent of students to Howard and allowing a mission of Howard students and faculty researchers to go to Addis Ababa. With such a full plate of possibilities awaiting him, Locke planned for a long stay. He packed thoroughly and also arranged to sublet his apartment to a group of students for the summer to help cover his expenses since the Olympics had driven up prices in Paris for the summer. Once Kellogg finally released him from further efforts to squeeze contributors, Locke sailed in early July for England.

Locke's first destination was London, where he planned to visit the Empire Exhibition. He wanted to see the African artifacts that the British had brought out of colonial Africa, particularly Nigeria, and the representation of the Africans in the exhibit. Since seeing the Barnes Collection, Locke hungered to see more African art. Once again, a visit to England confirmed his hostility to the British:

in racial and colonial terms, they continued to provide the most devastating and degrading images of Africa and African civilizations in Europe.

Upon arriving in Paris, Locke continued to delay his visit to Hughes. Perhaps he too was a bit anxious about the meeting, in case they might both be disappointed. So, keeping plans he had made before sailing, he met up with Melville Herskovits for a visit to Paul Guillaume's gallery. This constituted a minor drama in itself. Locke surprised Guillaume by arriving at his gallery on July 12. Guillaume, after learning of Locke's "lack of gratitude" toward Barnes, had promised Barnes to refuse to allow Locke to visit his gallery again. But Locke showed. Because he arrived with Herskovits, whom Locke introduced as a very important anthropologist and student of Franz Boas, Guillaume allowed them both in, but followed them around seething with anger. When he noticed them looking intently and approvingly at a particular work of art, he sighed under his breath, and mumbled to himself that it was not an important work of art. Locke, of course, wandered around blithely, showing the splendid items of African art to Herskovits as if he owned them. After the visit, Guillaume wrote to Barnes that if Locke ever returned to his gallery, he would give him a tongue-lashing about his treatment of Barnes. But he had not had the courage to do it when he had the chance in the fall of 1924, and Locke would not give him another chance.

Finally, Locke took the subway to Montmartre, the working-class Parisian district he did not like particularly and sought out Langston Hughes. After climbing the steps to an attic on the Rue des Trois Freres, Locke knocked on the door, and answered, "Alain Locke," when Hughes queried through the closed door, "*Qui-est-il?*" Hughes opened the door, quickly dressed, and took Locke down to a little bistro near the Place Clichy where Locke bought him lunch. According to Arnold Rampersad, "At lunch Locke talked effortlessly of many things, but in particular of editing a special issue, on the Negro question, of Paul Kellogg's influential magazine Survey Graphic."[14] Afterward, they made plans to get together again.

Locke and Hughes spent the next two weeks together, going sightseeing and enjoying entertainment as Locke introduced Hughes to an elite cultural side of Paris that he had not visited before. Locke took Hughes to the Louvre, to the Opera Comique, to the ballet *Taglioni chez Musette*, and to such beautiful gardens of Paris as the Parc Monceau, whose lush vegetation and secluded benches had made it a favorite of Locke's mother. Locke and Hughes also broadened their intellectual contacts while together. Hughes met Rene Maran for the first time, and Locke and Maran renewed their debate over Locke's portrayal of French colonialism. Locke had been elected a foreign member of the French Colonial Academy, and it is likely that he took Hughes to some of the receptions hosted by the Academy. Near the end of July, Hughes wrote to Cullen ecstatically: "Locke's here. We are having a glorious time. I like him a great deal. I only wish we could be together all summer. I'm enjoying my last two weeks in Paris more than any others because Mr. Locke is here."[15]

A man of learning like Locke did not want just sexual rewards, he wanted to fall in love, and that was precisely the effect of Locke's romancing of Hughes. On Hughes's last day in Paris, the two of them took a "trance-like walk up the Champs Elysees." At the Arc de Triomphe, they turned east, walked down the avenue Foch, with its sumptuous lawns and townhouses, and entered the Bois de Boulogne, Paris's largest and most beautiful park. On a hot, August afternoon, the heavily wooded Boulogne, with its two lakes and marvelous waterfall, had a magical effect on Locke. After a brief evening stop back at Hughes's rooms, Locke, rather than his protégé, had fallen in love.

The next day, August 9, Hughes left on a trip to Italy with friends he had met at Le Grand Duc, the jazz club run by the African American aviator Eugene Bullard where Hughes had worked during his stay in Paris. Hughes agreed to meet Locke later in Venice, but Locke could not wait until then to continue his courtship. He opened up his heart to Hughes in a letter written the day after he departed. "Today the atmosphere is like atomized gold, and last night you know how it was—two days the equal of which atmospherically I have never seen in a great city, days when every breath has the soothe of a kiss and every step the thrill of an embrace. I needed one such day and one such night to tell you how much I love you, in which to see soul-deep and be satisfied—for after all[,] with all my sensuality and sentimentality, I love sublimated things and today nature, the only great cleanser of life, would have distilled anything. God grant us one such day and night before America with her inhibitions closes down on us. And then perhaps through prosaic hours and days we can keep the gleam of the transcendental thing I believe our friendship was meant to be."[16] Apparently, at the end of that night, Hughes had granted Locke some undisclosed intimacy—a long hug, a kiss, or something more—and afterward, Locke was eager for a lot more.

Arnold Rampersad suggests Locke's letter stunned Hughes, who received it after a week of sun and frolic with his friends in Desenzano, the village near Lago di Garda in northern Italy. While he had developed an intimate friendship with Locke, he had not fallen in love with him. One can readily understand how Hughes felt: Locke was crowding him, pushing him into a sexual relationship that he did not want. Moreover, the request for further intimacy carried a threat. Locke might withdraw his offer to subsidize Hughes in his quest for a college education. He responded with innocence, ignoring for the moment the reality that he wanted Locke's financial help without having to put out sexually. "I like you immensely," Hughes wrote to Locke, "and certainly we are good 'pals,' aren't we? And we shall work together well and produce beautiful things."[17] Hughes proposed to continue their friendship without sexual involvement, but that was not what Locke had in mind. For him, friendship did not exclude—indeed, at its highest level required—a sexual relationship. Of course, such behavior was not unique to Locke or to the gay community. W. E. B. Du Bois expected sexual and intellectual companionship to go hand in hand when he was attracted to women, especially those, such as Jessie Fauset and Georgia Douglas Johnson, whom he helped.

But the story is more one of pathos and unrequited love than naked exploitation. Locke did not want a prostitute—he wanted a companion, a partner, who lived with and inspired him. His financial "carrot" emerged out of his insecurity that as an aging gay man he could not attract a young man of quality like Hughes without some leverage. What he longed for, of course, was for Hughes to love him. Hughes had granted Locke some minor sexual request after the latter revealed the depth of his emotional desperation. "Remember," Locke wrote afterward, "that it was only Thursday that out of the almost suicidal depths of despair and discouragement you gave me your brotherly hand of help and hope. My thanks are as profound as the need was—my hopes as high as my renewed ambitions." Such an expression of need is painful to read. It was also degrading, something Locke acknowledged. "Please insist on work—hold yourself dear and do not let my great passion cheapen you," even as he insisted on its sexual, indeed procreative nature, "and let our association breed beautiful things, like children to hallow the relationship."[18]

Here was another aspect of Locke's desire. He knew the *Survey Graphic* project would challenge him as a writer: Locke had already failed to turn in the draft of the introductory essay. With Hughes as his live-in companion, Locke believed he would have found his muse—"how I marvel at your creativeness," he had written to Hughes just weeks before. What Locke wanted was a complex relationship that would address all of his emotional and creative needs. Of course, sex would be a part of it, and there Locke knew he asked for something Hughes did not want to give. But desperate for affection, Locke lowered his sights, held out his financial proposal, and asked, almost demanded, what he knew might "cheapen" Hughes. Locke was sophisticated enough to realize, after the fact, when he had come on too strong. "All the nicest things seem to be happening after you have left," Locke wrote to Hughes after silence had followed his previous confessional letter. "Shall I catalogue them—this shall be in the epic not the lyric strain—was the last letter too lyric? (forgive me)."[19] Hughes decided to wait until Locke reached Italy.

Locke hurried to complete his professional responsibilities in France before heading off to Italy and Hughes. He had dinner with Belata Heroui and the following day had a session alone with Ras Taffari, the future Haile Selassie. Locke asked Taffari the same question he had asked Heroui in 1923: did the Abyssinians consider the American Negroes their brothers? According to Locke, Taffari responded by saying that "a man should always be able to come home." This rather ambiguous but positive answer spurred Locke on to suggest the remainder of his plan, especially the idea that Ethiopian students should come to Howard University and study.

Several years later, Locke admitted that he did not have much success with this recommendation, as most Ethiopian students who came to the United States went to White colleges and universities. Potentially more promising was his meeting with George Foucart. The details of this meeting are sketchy, but apparently Foucart delivered the news that French archaeological operations were temporarily on hold because of the upsurge in nationalism and violence in Egypt, especially over the Carter excavation. Suddenly, Locke was freed from what had been the most promising research possibilities of his trip, the return to Egypt and his engagement in real archaeological research. But he was also freed to spend more time in Italy in pursuit of Hughes. Locke left shortly after his Foucart meeting for Venice.

Locke arrived in Verona just after the first of September. Again, the nearly idyllic whirlwind of sightseeing ensued. According to Rampersad, "They visited the tomb of Juliet and sent Cullen a postcard. In the late summer mist, Venice was a spectacular vision; the Rialto, the Doge's Palace, and the Bridge of Sighs were far more vivid than he had ever imagined they would be. They rode in gondolas on the canals, and visited the house where Wagner lived when he wrote *Tristan*, and where he died. Joining the throng of summer tourists, they scattered pigeons in the Piazza San Marco; they listened to the municipal band and watched fireworks burst over the water."[20] This time something went wrong. Hughes became "restless" as he listened to Locke talk on and on "about Titian and Tinotoretto, Caravaggio and Canaletto, this *palazzo* and that *ponte*." Hughes got tired of "Locke talking, always talking," and, as he recalled some sixteen years later in his autobiography, *The Big Sea*, "began to wonder if there were no back alleys in Venice and no poor people and no slums.... So I went off by myself a couple of times and wandered around in sections not stressed in the guidebooks. And I found that there were plenty of poor people in Venice and plenty of back alleys of canals too dirty to be picturesque."[21] Afterward, Hughes had made up his mind not to live with Locke in Washington.

Locke and Hughes, as would be much clearer in 1940 than in 1924, held to two different theories of culture. Hughes felt his art would testify to the dignity, the genius, and genuineness of the poor of any culture, but especially the African American. For Hughes, culture began and ended with the masses. Locke, on the other hand, believed that although art grew out of the soil of the working-class experience, the best art and culture was that which evolved through discipline, learning, and purification to become sophisticated art. Both agreed that culture came from the bottom up. They differed on what the artist did to that folk art to make it art. Hughes believed the Black writer should listen to the life, speech, and pronunciation of the working class, and try to reproduce it, at least its thought. For Locke, culture was a theory of progress, of movement upward from the specificity of the folk experience to artistic forms of greater complexity and greater universality.

But it does not completely explain why Hughes reacted the way he did to Locke. For all his elitism, Locke had walked those back streets and dark alleys as a student at Oxford, long before Hughes did. Hughes was not so naive not to realize that there were dirty, stupid, untrustworthy, poor people in every country, and he did not need to leave Locke to realize this. What must have been occurring in Locke's conversation was a representation of who the Venetians and the ancient Italians were. Locke narrated how beautiful they were, how they had turned their suffering and struggles into fine art, and potentially how that differed from how American Negroes responded to their troubles and struggles. Indeed, there is a long tradition among Black intellectuals of lamenting that Negroes had not created the kinds of really fine art out of their struggles—with the exception of the spirituals—as the peasants of France and Italy did. What likely rubbed Hughes the wrong way is that such a view was accompanied by a denigration of the African American poor by comparison, the very people that Langston Hughes felt closest to.

This talk was not divorced from the politics of homosexuality, either. When Rampersad writes about this encounter, he situates it in the literary context of Thomas Mann's *Death in Venice*, a book that Hughes picked up afterward and read on the way back home. That story of an elder homosexual's ultimately fatal infatuation with a younger boy probably did resonate with Hughes's own feelings. But the book that epitomized what Locke was doing was *Stones of Venice*, in which John Ruskin narrated how he led his students on a tour of the art of Venice in precisely the ways Hughes recollects that Locke did that summer of 1924. It was a continuation of the seduction scenario of Paris. But in Venice something clicked for Hughes that his homosexual tradition was not that of the aesthetes but the masculinist tradition of same-sex love with sailors and other rough men. After hunting out the "common people" in Italy, Hughes would eventually explore and find his poetic inspiration among "common people" that fall away from Washington, D.C., away from Locke.

Hughes became tired of Locke in a way that would be experienced by others who were otherwise attracted to him. This was the tragedy of much of Locke's romantic life—that he was inept at expressing his love for people in a compelling way. He exposed to Hughes, as Rampersad puts it, "what it might be like to live with Locke."[22] By 1924, lecturing to other people had become a way for Locke to avoid intimacy and defend himself against emotion, in this case, his mounting fear of rejection by Hughes. Locke felt that if he expressed his love directly, he would be rejected, because Hughes did not love him. So Locke just talked, hoping that the talk would seduce him, but it drove him further away, because it was a monologue.

The poet found a way to get out of having to return to Washington with the critic for the beginning of Howard's fall semester. On a train to Genoa, Hughes's passport and all of his money were stolen while he slept alone in third class. He could not, therefore, enter France. Locke, exasperated no doubt with this stupidity, lent him a "few lire," Rampersad writes, and "hurried on to be sure to catch his own boat back to the United States. Perhaps his ardor had cooled, as well; certainly, he made no further attempt to help Hughes."

Locke left Langston Hughes in Genoa, not to catch a boat home, as he led Hughes to believe, but to take a train to his hideout for the next three weeks—San Remo, a tiny seaside town on the Italian Riviera. That Locke left Hughes stranded for the month of August 1924, in Genoa without money, while Locke lived and worked in a wonderful hotel on the beach of San Remo suggests Locke had had enough. In fact, he had gotten what he needed from Hughes. After a spring and summer of writer's block, Locke was able finally to pen the first draft of his essay, "The New Negro," that became "Enter the New Negro," in *Survey Graphic*. Locke's summer romance had achieved its desired effect of inspiration for a new statement about what it meant to be a Negro in 1920s America. Indeed, that Locke was able to separate from Hughes even though he loved him represented a step forward in Locke's maturation.

Locke also had separated successfully from another ally and friend even before meeting up with Hughes. In a letter, now lost, that surprised Charles S. Johnson, Locke severed his professional relationship with Johnson. Locke struck deep at his patron's integrity by claiming that *Opportunity* was exploiting the young writers of the movement because, as in Locke's case, most of them were not paid for their submissions. Of course, Locke's accusation was preposterous—most magazines did not pay for poetry submissions—but it hurt Johnson, who wrote back trying to repair the breach. In many cases, not the least Locke's, as Johnson explained, the editor had introduced Black writers to other magazines and book publishers who had paid them for their work. "If you had not added the point to your note by affirming and emphasizing the deliberateness of a momentary exasperation, warranted perhaps by the aspect of our common circumstance but quite unlike you—but what can I say? I agree with your sentiment regarding pay for contributions, regarding our great indebtedness to you, and regarding the justice of getting for you support in your efforts for us to the amount of the first figure mentioned by you, and even more if possible. But I am keenly pierced by the sudden tone of your letter and the unfortunate texture of your arguments."[23]

Johnson's confession, while Locke was in Paris, that *Opportunity* magazine could not pay him to write a series of articles on the Negro in Europe and Egypt probably triggered Locke's summer outburst. Without that guarantee of funds, Locke could not afford to spend the fall in Egypt and would have to return to Howard. That was not Johnson's fault, as he noted in his letter: "It may seem to you an utterly useless process but we must be able to convince our contributors that the European materials (which make remarkably good feature material for the magazine) have a direct relation to the local problems of Negroes. I wish we were a well-endowed literary magazine. I do not yet count the issue entirely hopeless."[24] Johnson had been the only person to give Locke the publishing outlet to re-create himself as a public intellectual, whose writing gained a general educated audience among African American readers because of that exposure. But Johnson had also needed Locke as a commodity whose credentials and exquisite prose gave *Opportunity* the intellectual cachet to compete with the *Crisis*. Johnson also had used Locke to deliver a stinging blow to Jessie Fauset in such a way that Locke became the fall guy. Locke also may have been angered by Johnson's decision to publish Rene Maran's letter that criticized Locke's positive assessment of French colonial attitudes in "Black Watch on the Rhine."[25] It is tempting to speculate whether Johnson decided to publish the letter as a payback for Locke's stealing from Johnson the control of the special Harlem issue of the *Survey Graphic* the preceding spring. But regardless of motivation, Locke viewed the publication of an embarrassing letter as a public indictment of his judgment. Johnson, Locke believed, did not have his interest at heart.

Locke's letter to Johnson was probably just a rude way of freeing himself from a stifling relationship. The pattern had emerged in Locke's dealings with Barnes and would repeat itself throughout his life with older, more powerful men. Locke had bonded with Johnson as a patron when he lacked a mature public identity, but it was only a matter of time before Locke would have the Oedipal tug to reject Johnson as an unreasonable, overbearing father figure. But the separations from Barnes, Hughes, and now Johnson coincided with a spurt of productivity for Locke as a writer, lasting roughly from the summer of 1924 through the spring of 1927. Separating from people he needed but who could not extend unqualified acceptance and love stimulated him to express an independent vision in his writing and editorial work. Locke rebelled against patrons, Black and White, and as well as lovers, because of that he gained psychic strength to become the New Negro himself. And he had the strength to choose a place to write that was his kind of place. Of course, there was more to San Remo than simply the memories of a kiss with Hughes or an imagined betrayal by Johnson. The coastal town of San Remo was a Mediterranean paradise beloved by tourists in August and September for its cool, ocean breezes. Locke arrived in San Remo at the height of the tourist season, suggesting that he had made reservations long in advance of his arrival. That Locke chose San Remo at its most bustling suggests that what he liked was its energy, its flamboyant beach antics by native boys and tourist crowds, as a place where this often lonely intellectual would not feel alone.

San Remo might seem an odd place for an African American intellectual to write an essay on the New Negro in America. Indeed, we might go so far as to suggest it is a frame clash—between the conceptual frame that to write persuasively about the Black community one should be embedded within it, on the one hand, and the cosmopolitanism framework that Locke was a transnational man of the world who was not just a race man, on the other.[26] That clash was audibled in Carter G. Woodson's quip the year before that Locke was enjoying himself in Europe and not hurrying to Africa. But Locke was trying to transcend the stereotypical logic by which the Negro was commonly defined as a broken minority in America and replace with one in which the Negro is the result of a dialogue between Europe and Africa. That dialogue was seen as a clash—and a ridiculous one at that—by Zora Neale Hurston, who later would quip that it was ridiculous for Countee Cullen to go to Europe to write Black poetry. But in addition to the silencing of the reality that Black homosexuals enjoyed much more freedom to think and write in Europe than in homophobic America is a more profound gesture; the dismissal relegates the Negro to a spiritual ghetto that Locke is desperately trying to escape.

Going to San Remo was precisely what he had been suggesting as valuable in the earlier essay "Cosmopolitanism and Culture"—that a dialogical relationship exists between worldliness, the life of the wanderer, the ability to see oneself from the vantage point of a new setting, on the one hand, and being embedded in one's own culture, one's own history, on the other. San Remo became a rich opportunity to skate across the contradiction into a new appreciation of what is actually valuable about Black people, of the beauty of Black people. While dozens of White American writers and artists are flocking to Europe to find their muse, Locke is hanging in San Remo to unleash his—and try to see Black people as a world people, not a broken American minority. Escape to San Remo was critical to being able to return to America with something new.

Italy, of course, had been the last nation to experience a renaissance of the impulse that Locke felt so strongly in Venice during those days he walked and talked with Hughes. That impulse was the desire to live one's life in search of aesthetic perfection. Florence presented the closest model of a city that celebrated its artists like warrior heroes and renowned their struggles with form like accounts of soldiers on the battlefield. I suspect Locke chose San Remo as his urban muse, not Florence, because he sensed he needed to distance himself from the canonical center of Western art in order to imagine a Black version of it. He was after something elusive—a new view of Negroes that would change his own negative view of them. Northern Italy, especially around San Remo, had a peasant culture whose rich heritage allowed Locke to see the poor Black southerner as a culture bearer. Italian culture narrated their poor as noble and triumphant and that offered Locke a model for seeing the Black poor as propulsive and beautiful. San Remo allows Locke to escape all that negative programming he had gained from his mother and the Black Victorian tradition that denigrated poor Black people as uncultured and worthless. Never in America would the Black "peasant," really ex-slave, be portrayed as noble and beautiful, as the Italian poor are regarded in Fellini's *Roma*. In San Remo, for the first time, Locke was able to overcome his writer's block and sketch in writing a compelling image of a New

Negro that was not fundamentally elitist, that embodied "the Negro." As he informed Paul Kellogg, "This to ease your mind somewhat about the Harlem Issue. I have been settled down here for quite a little working on my mss and the other manuscripts, and from the way things are going can assure you of bringing home a full kit."[27]

Locke's struggle for an autonomous voice helped him retell the story of the Negro as the struggle for self-determination in his earliest typed draft of "The New Negro."

> The life history of the Negro in America falls into three phases when we consider basic causes: In the first of these his fortunes were determined largely, almost solely by the attitude of white Americans towards him, with the Civil War and Reconstruction he passed into the second phase where though in a way still affected by public opinion, he was primarily at the mercy of conditions, in the clutches of the environment so to speak. With the Great War and the migration, the third phase of relative independence of conditions has commenced; the Negro today is moving under the control of his own objectives. It is not that he still does not have to pay an extortionate and heavy toll to conditions, but mass-movement is nevertheless under way. The spirit of self-determination has struck fire, so that while public opinion and social conditions may still press and modify, they cannot any longer play the primary role. It is a question now of what the Negro wants, and the price of effort, sacrifice and self-direction that he is willing to pay for it. Public opinion used to lead, and has controlled, now at best it must follow and understand. Even the so-called leaders of the Negro group are no longer controlling factors—the most significant movements of the last few years have taken most of them by surprise,—the more progressive have merely fallen into line with what they have not initiated. The Negro is not only changing habitat, he is changing his habits, it is not merely a question of continued progress but a question of a new psychology.[28]

Here was the New Negro—a "psychology" of "self-determination" to "move under the control of his own objectives" and not be controlled or directed by the objectifying frames of others. In Europe, being mobile himself, Locke broke out of the old frameworks and saw the migration of hundreds of thousands of Black southerners into the urban North as that historical moment when the Negro became a *subject*.

For Locke, geographical change was the result of a *changed mentality* in the Negro. "The wash of this tide on the beach line of the northern and mid-western industrial centers, the influx of migrants into a center like Harlem is to be explained more in terms of a strange new vision of opportunity, of social and economic freedom, of a spirit to risk more on a chance of improvement of conditions than a blind flood started by the currents of war industry, or the pressure of poor crops and the boll-weevil or increased social terrorism in certain sections of the South, however contributory any or all of these factors may have been. Something more than the old loyalties and ambitions and compensations stirs today in the average Negro mind." Remarkably, writing from San Remo, and after his romantic tussle with the working-class-minded Hughes, Locke could acknowledge that poor southern Negroes who embraced disjunction, chaos, and unpredictability by throwing themselves headlong into the completely foreign world of northern and urban Black communities were now redefining the Negro. It was not the Black intellectuals who were leading; they were followers. The Black poor were the leaders—the first Black modernists of the renaissance issuing a challenge to the rest of the race: "The question is no longer what whites think of the Negro but of what the Negro wants to do and what price he is willing to pay to do it." [29]

In one fell swoop, Locke had rewritten modern African American history. Gone was the sense one always received from reading Du Bois that the history of the Negro since the Civil War had been a long history of degradation at the hands of Whites. Locke's history was a narrative of reinvention and focused on the most elusive of attributes that emerged as a triumphant positive—the ability of Black people to transform their futures by reacting creatively to their present. In Europe that summer Locke was freed to fashion a different Negro history, in his own image, as the triumph of subjectivity over all those forces that tried to control Black people—and him. Rather than an object buffeted about by more powerful others, the Negro was, like him, able to invent a new identity out of tragedy, just as he had remade himself after his devastating experience of racism at Oxford. Europe remained important because the key to the New Negro was his or her mobility, an eager leave taking of the South that reflected a mental freedom that transcended oppression. The African American was the quintessential transnational, moving between different nations, which the South and the North virtually were, just as Locke had ranged back and forth across the Atlantic constructing a new mobile intellectual identity. Locke, ultimately, could identify with the migrating peasant because that's what he was. His personal narrative gave him a template for conceptualizing the psychological liberation for the Negro. He was unloved. So was the Negro. Both would remake themselves as crucially important to modern American history.

The Great Migration was Black subjectivity emptying through space—not just an idea or discursive trope, but a concrete manifestation of African American agency through the spatial turn. Black people changed "what time it is," by moving through space; and by chronicling it as revolutionary, Locke showed the spatial creativity of the New Negro—turning segregation into aggregation by moving away. Usually, outmigration was conceived of as a random disruption of community. But in Pittsburgh, Chicago, and New York, the Georgia Negro met the South Carolina Negro and the already settled New Yorker and Chicagoan, and formed a new, truer community. People who came from different spaces created a new space of Blackness in the North that welcomed the refugees from Jim Crow America. And Locke was a refugee himself, migrating intellectually through space by returning intellectually to Blackness by embracing his transnational mobility as itself a sign of the New Negro. He moved, and so did they—unlettered, untutored, poor, and distraught African Americans, West Indians, and Africans—and found themselves in one another. From San Remo, Locke could feel the Negro migrant as a lower-class version of himself, someone rebelling against the social death America intended for them by leaving and then, remarkably, finding a truer home away. Here, the notion of home itself was revised—not the place where one's ancestors were buried, in the rural South, in Africa, but in a new urban America. Moving was not fleeing—it was reinvention of subjectivity in Harlem, Chicago, and Pittsburgh, which were not refugee camps but new triumphant examples of traversing space and making place.

Subjectivity was the first breakthrough of San Remo, for Locke was able to see the Negro as subject transcending oppression by navigating space. Class was the other. For the first time, Locke saw the Black masses as the progressive agents of change in America. "The New Negro is essentially a mass-made advance," he opined in "The Negro Mind," another draft written in San Remo that was incorporated into "Harlem," eventually the lead article in the *Survey Graphic*.[30] This was a long way from "The Role of the Talented Tenth" that he had penned right after his PhD. Given that Locke was one of the most elitist educated men in America, the question worth asking is, was there something beyond being in San Remo with its Europeanized view of the poor that gave him greater empathy and understanding of the historical power and agency of the working-class Negro?

The summer love affair in Europe with Hughes had also helped to catalyze this breakthrough. Falling in love had awakened Locke's passion and connected him with someone else and increased his capacity for empathy, which always enabled his ability to write. But the second part of the summer's love story was just as important to his new writing. Having found love and then realized it was unrequited, he had had the self-love to move on without it, and be free. It was a metaphor of what the New Negro faced and did. Rather than lament that tragedy or be bound forever trying to earn or win this life that was withheld, the New Negro had picked up her bags and left in an act of emotional, psychological self-determination.

Locke may not have gotten love from Hughes. But he got something he needed even more. Dialogue with a thinker with affection and affinity for the Black working class helped Locke to write the clarion call of the New Negro as the psychological liberation of the race led by its least-educated members. When Hughes published his recollection of that summer in *The Big Sea*, Locke disliked its portrait of their time together in Venice not only because it was unflattering to him but also because it was one-sided. Loving Hughes made Locke listen and appreciate Hughes's love for and insight into the Black working-class humanity—an intelligence, a wisdom, about how to deal with America, how to deal with life and its many tragedies, that was distilled into folk culture. After listening to Hughes talk about the blues and jazz, forms that Locke abhorred, Locke looked at the papers and summaries from Johnson and Kellogg on his desk and saw a pattern they had not seen—that the Black working class was driving change in the early twentieth century. The New Negro refused to be a slave to anyone and chose to model for the world that the object of any oppressive situation can free himself or herself if he or she ignores the discourse of the official culture and embrace of self-love. Black working-class love for one another had freed them and the New Negro from mental slavery, and that was the grit and independent psyche of the Black masses. Langston's love of working-class Black people had freed Locke to see them as metaphysical beings whose consciousness, not their objectified bodies, had changed African American history by choosing to leave the South. Langston had embodied a beauty that had opened Locke's consciousness to the agency of the Black working class.

Locke's other essay from San Remo, variously titled "The New Setting" and "The Harlem Scene" (it became "Harlem," the lead article in the *Survey Graphic*), showcased the third breakthrough of his new thinking—that the continued formation of the New Negro identity was tied to space, to the new "environment" that allowed the Negro to escape being a mere victim of "environment" in the nineteenth century. A "renaissance" of Black culture was occurring in Harlem, because this new space was not a ghetto, but a crucible in which a diaspora of Black peoples was mixing and crystallizing the New Negro identity. "It [Harlem] has attracted the African, the West Indian, the Negro American; has brought together the Negro of the North and the Negro of the South; the man from the city and the man from the town and village; the peasant, the student, the business man, the professional man, artist, poet, musician, adventurer and worker, preacher and criminal, exploiter and social outcast. Each group has come with its own separate motives and for its own special ends, but their greatest experience has been the finding of one another. So what began in terms of segregation becomes more and more, as its elements mix and react, the laboratory of a great race-welding." Here Locke flipped the typical parallelism of American society, in which the city destabilized community. "Hitherto, it must be admitted that American Negroes have been a race more in name than in fact, or to be more exact, more in sentiment than in experience. The chief bond between them has been that of a common condition rather than a common consciousness; a problem in common rather than a life in common. In Harlem, Negro life is seizing upon its first chances for group expression and self-determination."[31] Self-determination here was an act of valuation, as Locke's value theory came through here as well.

"The question is no longer what whites think of the Negro but of what the Negro wants to do and what price he is willing to pay to do it."[32]

Locke wanted the New Negro to become cosmopolitan. "What we may be witnessing is the renaissance of a people as realistic as those more detached phenomena we associate with a liberated Ireland or a Mexico churned by racial revival."[33] The reference to the Mexican Renaissance, especially as a "racial revival," is revealing. What distinguished a renaissance was the idea that the political and social energy of the New Negro or New Mexican was translated into a distinctive style of expression that connoted a unique cultural identity. That identity was linked to a willingness to develop the art that drew upon and fed that identity of an urban particularity regardless of what the outside world thought about it. African Americans did not possess a separate country, even though after hundreds of years of separate treatment they did possess a distinctive cultural style, or "Negroness." In arguing for Harlem as a space for self-dependent, self-sustained cultural activity, Locke did not envision the Negro Renaissance as exclusively Black. Rather, like the Mexican Renaissance, which also welcomed White artists who could delineate "Mexicanness" out of their dialogue with the people, Locke welcomed White contributions to the portrayal of Negroness. In that sense, African American renaissance would not reproduce the error of American racism, but would evolve to its fullest potential if it was transracial and transnational.

Locke cited that sense of collective self-renewal and self-love in Harlem— "another statue of liberty on the landward side of New York." By situating freedom in a particular space—the Harlem section of New York—Locke linked the cultural to an urban geography as the guarantor of the New Negro's freedom. The Statue of Liberty metaphor reassured the reader that Harlem space was not a separatist space but integral to the definition of America as a beacon for and fulfillment of the desire for freedom like that of all Americans. "It [Harlem] stands for a folk movement which can be compared only with the pushing back of the western frontier in the first half of the last century, or the flow of immigration which swept in from overseas in the last half. Numerically far smaller than either... the volume of Negro migration is such that Harlem, itself but one of these northern settlements, has become none the less the greatest Negro community the world has known—without counterpart either in the South, or in Africa."[34] By referring to it as one such settlement, Locke unknowingly answered future critics who argued that the "Harlem" Renaissance, because it left out Black Chicago, Black Cleveland, and so forth, was a misnomer. Harlem was exalted over all others, because it fashioned the New Negro out of the greatest degree of international and diasporic diversity beyond that of other Black northern communities. It was the only completely cosmopolitan—Black and White, Mexican and American, southern and northern, European and African—community in the world.

Locke's enthusiasm for Harlem reflected his sense that it was the one place that welcomed Black homosexuals in America. Many of the writers he was mentoring in the New Negro movement were gay, complex personalities who foregrounded race in their identities while powerfully shaped by their sexual orientation. The choice of the term "renaissance" reflected Locke's awareness that many of the Italian Renaissance artists were gay, and that art had been their way of shaping their culture despite the marginality they felt from bourgeois social norm. Could not this be a form of salvation for his Black and queer spirits and the race as a whole—to find in creativity a language that would allow diverse personalities to speak to one another as loving human beings, less intense but akin to what he had sought with Hughes? Could love and beauty be the basis for community?

All of these hung like suspended possibilities in a concept whose strength and weakness resided in its closeted nature. Sexuality was hidden in plain view in the New Negro, who was new precisely because he or she was not fixed sexually, racially, socially, by the term. But this lack of fixity also brought instability, something Locke himself wrestled with. And yet ambivalence was refreshing in the Negro in 1924. "New Negro" had a frisson that "double consciousness," "Talented Tenth," even "Africa for the Africans" lacked. The New Negro was appealing because it was unpredictable. It was as unfinished as the essay Locke wrapped up in his folders as he left his veranda in San Remo and prepared to come home. But it had something new—a new mixture of the Negro to offer, one of equal parts identity, beauty, and justice led by queer men and women of Black America in tandem with their straight brothers and sisters. His was one way to add in queer people to a larger struggle to free the race from its White as well puritan demons.

Locke's New Negro possessed an ambivalence and a roominess largely foreign to other conceptions, because its promise was a community that would reflect his take on his racial and sexual identity. Despite all its vagueness, the New Negro Locke formulated in San Remo built upon the Olympian self-confidence he had carried within him since he was a child. Like him, the real New Negro must be uplifted and cosmopolitan rather than morose. "This new psychology is radical in tone,—even it is for the most part pitched to a negative and often depressing attitude of resentment. Only in a few has it worked out to a spirit of cheerful and optimistic self-dependence. There are two ways of being independent,—being self-reliant and confident and being disillusioned and resentfully negative. Much depends on the education of the younger Negro as to which direction this psychology will take. Personally I favor nourishing it to the fullest extent especially along historical, artistic and cultural lines into a developed sense of self-dependence and independence."[35] Of course, such a formulation hid all the pain and suffering he and the "younger Negro" endured in trying simply to exist in a heartless world of racism and homosexual rejection.

Looking for love had ended in giving birth to the New Negro. It was not an end, but a beginning—and a powerful one. As his ship wound its way again into New York's harbor, Locke was coming home with a "full kit." Beauty had done its work.

25

Harlem Issues

When Locke arrived in Washington the third week of September 1924, he found two letters. One, from Claude McKay, encouraged him to get professional help with his problems. "You know if you're neurasthenic," McKay wrote, "you ought to see a psycho-analyst—if you cannot help yourself.... Dr. A.A. Taunenbaum of New York is a fine understanding chap. He's a friend of mine—slightly neurasthenic himself[,] which makes him a better and more sympathetic analyst." McKay closed the letter with the advice that "you'd better to destroy this letter."[1] Locke did not. He did not seek psychological help. While abroad, he had shared with McKay that sometimes he became so disturbed that the only antidote was random sex, which did not really cure the problem of his neurotic tension. It was also dangerous, aggravating his paranoia about discovery as a homosexual. McKay, however, did not know about Locke's falling in love with Langston Hughes. The other note was more important. "I am sending this to Howard University in case you go directly to Washington," Paul Kellogg, the *Survey Graphic* editor wrote, "just as a bit of welcome and an expression of renewed interest in the project."[2] Kellogg had not known that Locke had been working feverishly on his introductory essays during his last days in Europe.

The two notes were connected. Having fallen in love and been rejected, Locke returned to the United States an exposed wire. Work on the New Negro had been a balm in San Remo; now, work on Harlem provided a cladding to cover his damaged but pulsating interior. Partly, it was Harlem itself—a teeming city within a city filled with Negroes from all over the world who did not judge him, as he felt judged in Washington. Harlem attracted "the African, the West Indian...the Negro of the North, the Negro of the South...the peasant, the student, the business man, artist, poet, musician, adventurer and worker, preacher and criminal, exploiter and social outcast"—the last a reference to himself—such that finding one another in its non-punitive environs, a race bonding and community emerged.[3] In Harlem, Black people escaped the normative gaze of a White society, because they immersed themselves in a Black majority. Surrounded by the successful and the criminal, Locke felt at home in Harlem, because he was a little of both.

Kellogg's note also foretold that the *work* on the Harlem issue would bring some internal harmony to Locke's neurotic tensions. For the first time, he was filled with a more powerful sense of advocacy than had suffused him when writing about Cairo or Black soldiers on the Rhine. Now, he was fighting for an American home for Black creativity and for his own kind. Writing about Harlem transformed him into *the father*—the seed layer whose prodigy was a place, unique even among Black American cities, for the poetry of the Black experience to blossom. Locke argued that Harlem, unlike Chicago or Philadelphia, was a twentieth-century mecca devoted to the production of great literature and art just as Charles Eliot Norton and Barrett Wendell had predicted for Boston in the nineteenth century. But Locke was also fathering a gay Black community in Harlem for ostracized queer creatives. They would be front and center, the leaders, the representative men—and they were usually men—rather than the Black bankers, protest leaders, and preachers. Harlem was the street on which the outliers could walk in peace. They would create a new African American literature, theater, and visual art that could, if allowed, transform American culture. Locke's response to Kellogg's letter was to build something far beyond what Kellogg originally had intended—a permanent house in the American imagination where young, tortured, and resilient Black technicians of the sacred could say "I'm home."

But the two letters at 1326 R Street, NW, also foretold conflict. For the first time in his career, Locke was in charge of a White publication, something that ensured a broader, more national platform for a Black message. Such a strategy carried risks. Though Locke was guest editor, Paul Kellogg made the final decisions. Choosing to work closely with the *Survey Graphic's* White editorial staff, Locke would have to tolerate the timid liberalism of progressives, who, despite their modernism, did not want to produce an issue that challenged directly the racial etiquette of segregation, even while they celebrated African American culture. How was Locke going to represent the bubbling racial self-assertiveness of young, Black writers in a magazine whose editorial staff did not want to be known afterward as the voice of militancy or social equality? Locke wanted a White publisher because he believed that Black liberation would proceed further if it dialogued with White attitudes. To do that forced him into a more difficult position than Harold Cruse and other critics cited—he had to create a modus vivendi between Black self-determination and White cultural hegemony if Locke's "little renaissance," as he later called it, was to become the nationally and internationally known Harlem Renaissance of the 1920s. By the end of the *Survey Graphic* project, Locke would call himself a "referee" of feuding camps. But rather than feel daunted, Locke seemed buoyed by the challenges and plunged right in.

A subtler conflict underlay the racial one. While Kellogg, the White editor, made the final decisions, Locke was the "head Negro in charge" with a unique opportunity to shape the definition of the New Negro in his own image. Locke had to mediate between his role as a caretaker and representative of younger artists' interests and his own increasingly powerful interpretation of what he thought the New Negro should be. The tension was not simply external; it was a tension in Locke. There was an aesthetic Locke who avoided conflict with Whites and wanted a notion of Blackness grounded in beauty and a radical Locke who had developed an imperialist analysis of Black-White relations that had appeared in the Race Contacts lectures. Which was going to dominate the Harlem issue? And which was going to make his reputation as a Negro spokesperson in the politically conservative 1920s? Here was a chance to perform on a national stage the through line of his life—to be a harmonizer of divergent values, personalities, and communities via art. He was not going to let that slip through his fingers.

Conflicts that fall epitomized, however, the dangers of his new calling. Locke had written his friend McKay and told him that he did not want to publish "Mulatto" in the *Survey Graphic*'s special Harlem issue, because it is was too strong for the White people at the *Survey Graphic* On October 7, McKay wrote back angry.

> Your attitude towards the "Mulatto" is that of Booker T. Washington's in Social Reform, Roscoe C. Bruce in politics and William Stanley Braithwaite in literature. It's a playing safe attitude—the ultimate regard of which are dry husks and ashes! Why mention the Liberator? It's a *white* paper and "Mulatto" is not stronger than "If We Must Die" which the Liberator first published. I guess if the Liberator had not set that example not a Negro publication would have enough of the "gut" you mention to publish it! It isn't the "Survey" that hasn't gut enough. It is you. The survey editors would not mind. There are many white people that are longing and hoping for Negroes to show they have "guts." I will show you by getting a white journal to take Mulatto. Send it back to me at once. No wonder the Negro movement is in such a bad way. No wonder Garvey remains strong despite his glaring defects. When the Negro intellectuals like you take such a weak line![4]

McKay concluded his letter by threatening to pull all of his poems from the *Survey Graphic* if Locke did not publish "Mulatto." The threat went deeper. "I do not care to be mentioned at all—don't want to—in the Special Negro number of the Survey. I am not seeking mere notoriety and publicity. Principles mean something to my life. And if you do publish any of the other poems now and leave out 'Mulatto' after this protest you may count upon me as an intellectual enemy for life!"[5]

While surprised by McKay's reaction, Locke was unfazed. "Glad to have your ultimatum," Locke wrote back, "and will publish Mulatto subject to approval by the Survey."[6] That last line is revealing. Although critics have taken at face value McKay's main contention that Locke rejected McKay's poem because of Locke's political conservatism, it seems clear that Kellogg surely would not like a poem in the Harlem issue that advocated murder of one's White father as the appropriate response of a mixed-race "bastard" parentage. The poem's expression of patricide as a means to the "utmost freedom that is life" struck a note of racial hate not present elsewhere in the issue. The poem focuses attention on White racism and suggests that murderous retaliation was the right response to such racism. Probably, Locke told McKay the truth that Kellogg and the *Survey Graphic* staff did object to the poem.

Kellogg is on record as opposing another submission to the issue that drew attention to Black life as a consequence of White racism. In the case of Kelly Miller's article, "Harvest of Race Prejudice," Kellogg wrote Miller himself asking him to shift the focus from White racism to the pathologies of the Black community. "Your essay focuses on the numerous instances of white racism with which our readership is already familiar. We are striking out in a new direction in this issue, one that focuses on the life and attitudes of the black community over those of the white. Can you not bend your article toward documenting those examples of black racism and Anti-Semitism which are the unfortunate harvest of color prejudice in places like Harlem?"[7] Kellogg was not neutral when it came to submissions that focused on White responsibility for racism. That was precisely what the poem "Mulatto" did. It's doubtful Locke would have written McKay about the poem if the special issue was being published by *Opportunity* instead of the *Survey Graphic*. While Locke objected to the poem for his own reasons, it seems likely he was reflecting the feeling of the magazine when he wrote to McKay.

But it's also doubtful Kellogg would have removed the poem without Locke's support. For a White liberal editor of a magazine devoted to Black self-expression in this number to refuse to publish McKay's poem would have carried risks. If that kind of information got out into the Black community, the legitimacy of the project could be undermined. Interestingly enough, Miller refused to change his article to meet Kellogg's demands, and Kellogg did not keep that article out of the issue. In the end, the final decision not to publish the poem probably was Locke's.

Why did Locke want to drop the poem? "Mulatto" was part of the militant counter-discourse of the New Negro that held White people accountable for past crimes, a protest Negro literature evident as early as Grimke's *Rachel* that Locke saw the New Negro poetry displacing. It's elegy to retaliation also had social relevance in that retaliation against White rioters had been a significant moment of New Negro consciousness in the Chicago race riot of 1919, as McKay had memorialized in "If We Must Die." This poem, however, implied that children of mixed-race couples should give in to murderous rage toward their White fathers. But Locke's question would be, after you murder your father what then? Locke may have resented the poem because it brought up unconsciously his own murderous declaration of independence from his father. Thus, the problem of how does the son become a man was not specifically racial, even though, in some sense, the poem's brilliance was to cast it in those terms and make a common psychoanalytic journey a racial one—that the Negro to be free must kill the White father within. Locke's argument might be that it was not the right time. But in some ways, it was: if the New Negro Renaissance was to effect a real catharsis, create a truly unique literature, was not a symbolic murder of what Cornel West called the "white normative gaze" precisely what was needed?[8] McKay had declared for a radical, Oedipal liberation that was strangely appropriate for its time.

But this was not Locke's message in the *Survey Graphic*. Locke's philosophy of art was to create a kind of cocoon of positive self-valuation within the temple of art, to turn away from self-destructive impulses connected to White patrimony of various kinds, in order to survive at something that was impossible for most White people to imagine—that Negroes could become first-order artists and intellectuals. Locke wanted to remake the Negro's past for psychic support in the present and future. Emerging in the era of the triumph of Jim Crow segregation, the Negro artists or intellectuals lacked any legitimacy in White America. There were few affective sources of support for a Black vocation of the mind. Faced with such formidable opposition, Locke felt that attacking that edifice was fruitless.[9]

Could not even the mixed-race son of a White rapist refuse to define himself in reaction to that fact and instead embrace the sun? Locke found that kind of internal freedom in Langston Hughes's poem "Dream Variation," in which the young Black person "flings" his or her "arms" and dances "till the white day is done," an exaltation of life despite challenges, where Whiteness becomes something to be waited out rather than attacked, an anachronism like the day about to become night. Locke was looking for poets to show a kind of moral superiority over racism, rather than a getting down in the muck with the enemy. But getting dirty was also part of the New Negro, and Locke had already started to clean it up.

If Locke rejected the poem purely on the basis of his aesthetic judgment, why did he not explain it as such to McKay? Locke could have written to McKay and said what every editor has said to an author at some time or other, that is, "Hey, I don't like that poem and I'm not going to publish it in the *Survey*." Locke could have rejected the poem more effectively without eliciting the White authority. Why didn't he? Something in Locke may have made it difficult for him to simply assert his authority with McKay. Perhaps because they had been friends, it was difficult for Locke to tell him he detested the poem. Locke had developed the tendency to avoid taking the responsibility for difficult decisions. He was still hiding behind a mother figure, in this case Kellogg (before it was Charles Johnson), instead of stepping out front and rebelling against the overprotective mother in him. In this, the Black Victorian in him became an easy target for McKay and other young artists who would come to suspect that Locke's literary decisions were based more on racial politics than aesthetic judgment. But in some sense, at this stage of the movement, his decisions had to take into account racial politics. Locke's role as guest editor of the *Survey Graphic* was to move Black writers into the mainstream. In the end, the price of mainstream access was compromise on message. Locke knew that, and so, in the end, did McKay, although neither seemed willing to admit it.

In November, Locke wrote to Kellogg: "McKay in his last letter is off his high horse. Says that perhaps I know best, etc. I take that as permission that we don't have to use 'Mulatto.'" When the *Survey Graphic* special number was published, "Mulatto" was not one of the poems included, and McKay did not seem that upset. He wrote the day of its publication to ask Locke to find some AME hymns, and stated, "But how can I fight you from way over here? How can I? So better let it be as it is. Tell me about yourself?"[10] In the immediate aftermath of the publication of the *Survey Graphic* number, McKay made little complaint, perhaps because he needed his relationship with Locke to continue, since Locke supplied him with money on a regular basis.

Not publishing "Mulatto" did not mean that Locke avoided all militant poems in his selection for the issue. Locke did publish McKay's other militant poem "White House," which, despite his change of its title to "White Houses" (to avoid the possibility that readers might see it as a critique of the presidential residence) remains a powerful protest against the exclusionary power of racism. What distinguished this poem from "Mulatto" in Locke's thinking was the way the poem contained its anger in the resolve to struggle against prejudice, as in its last two lines that perfectly captured the mood Locke wanted to hear from New Negro poets:

> Oh I must keep my heart inviolate
> Against the potent poison of your hate.

Locke acknowledged in his essay "Youth Speaks," which introduced the poetry section in the *Survey Graphic*, that "there is poetry of sturdy social protest, and fiction of calm, dispassionate social analysis. But reason and realism have cured us of sentimentality: instead of the wail and appeal, there is challenge and indictment." From Locke's perspective, "White Houses" was challenge and indictment, whereas "Mulatto" was "wail and appeal." Interestingly, Locke's judgment about "Mulatto" seems to have been borne out by the canon, since it is not one of McKay's poems reproduced in anthologies of Black literature. Locke preferred the McKay poem "Like a Strong Tree," with its stirring lines:

> Like a strong tree that in the virgin earth
> Sends far its roots through rock and loam and clay,

*   *   *

So would I live in rich imperial growth,
Touching the surface and the depth of things,
Instinctively responsive unto both,
Tasting the sweets of being and the stings,

                    *   *   *

Like a strong tree against a thousand storms.[11]

That was the note Locke wanted in the *Survey Graphic*, the sound of poetic strength and resiliency in spite of oppression, not wails of bitterness and ill-founded revenge.

Other poems signaled the notion of spiritual triumph over the materiality of Blackness lived by women in America. Anne Spencer's *Lady, Lady* combined racial identification with a feminist exposé of Black women's alienation.

Lady, Lady, I saw your face.
Dark as night withholding a star...
The chisel fell, or it might have been
You had borne so long the yoke of men.

Locke wanted poetry of the Black particular that showed how a universal message emerged from Black lives:

Lady, Lady, I saw your hands.
Twisted, awry, like crumpled roots,
Bleached poor white in a sudsy tub,
Wrinkled and drawn from your rub-a-dub.

Service to Whites and patriarchy had aged a woman nevertheless triumphant in the eyes of this Black woman poet.

Lady, Lady I saw your heart,
And altered there in its darksome place
Were the tongues of flame the ancients knew,
Where the good God sits to spangle through.[12]

Rather than a poem of protest, *Lady, Lady* burrowed into the pain of Black women's labor to excoriate what it meant to be Black, working class, and female in post slavery America. Here was what Locke was after—a sense of Beauty that challenged Western norms of who and what was beautiful and found it in the materiality of Black life.

While his controversy with McKay simmered, Locke traveled to New York over the October 24–26 weekend to meet with Kellogg and assess the status of the issue. At the offices of the *Survey Graphic*, he saw firsthand what manuscripts had come in, and how the *Survey Graphic* staff had reacted to them. He supervised the final draft of the letter that the *Survey Graphic* sent out announcing an art contest of work by African American artists that could be used in the magazine. His nemesis Albert Barnes had even consented to be one of the judges for the contest. Locke and Kellogg also discussed the paltry number of contributions that had come in by the end of September. Locke's first choice to do an article Locke wanted written on the psychology of the New Negro, had not yet found an author, since Benjamin Karpman, Locke's psychological confidant, had backed out over the summer. Even more disheartening, some of the submitted articles were so incomplete or poorly written that they had to be rewritten before being submitted for serious copyediting. It would be impossible to get the issue out by December, as Kellogg had originally planned. On Saturday, October 25, Locke took Kellogg to a Roland Hayes concert, to get a breather from the pressures of the looming issue.

That weekend also probably included Locke's first opportunity to look at the art Winold Reiss had produced for the issue—either at Reiss's studio at 12 Christopher Street or the *Survey Graphic* offices, where Reiss brought photographs of the artwork from time to time. After his summer in Woodstock, Reiss had started drawing portraits of African Americans from Harlem even before Locke got back from Europe. Reiss possessed a remarkably open, warm, and infectious personality, one he had used to great effect in his travels to Browning, Montana, in 1919 to draw Blackfeet Indians. Arriving in Browning in a snowstorm in November of that year, this Prussian artist quickly made friends and got prominent Native Americans to sit for portraits for him. He had done the same in 1922, when, armed only with his pastel boards and pencils, he had traveled on foot to rebel-infested Tepotzotlan and Cuernavaca, and drew bandits and Zapatista soldiers in compelling and sympathetic portraits. He began to do the same thing in Harlem, traveling uptown with his brother Hans, who spoke better English, to stop and entice African Americans, whose faces struck his fancy, to pose at his studio at 12 Christopher Street in Greenwich Village. By the time that Locke and Kellogg had started meeting, Reiss had already produced such portraits as "Mother and child," "Girl in a white blouse," "A Woman from the Virgin Islands." Reiss also had drawn a portrait of a man from the Congo, who lived downstairs from Reiss's studio and refused to cut his hair. The resulting portrait, "Congo: a familiar of the New York studios," with its globe-like Afro, became one of the most powerful statements of African identity in the issue.

Even though Locke had wanted to have an African American do the artwork, Reiss's portraits already showed he was the right artist for the job. Visual art by Negroes was slow to materialize. The art contest he had organized the previous spring had failed to produce much quality work from African American artists. But Reiss's portraits were powerful visual statements of Negro identity. What seemed like a contradiction to have a German artist illustrate a declaration of

Black cultural awakening was actually a rich opportunity, for Reiss invigorated the image of the Negro with a *Neue Sachlichkeit* visual aesthetic that was altogether absent among American artists. His portraits broke with the caricaturist representations of Blacks in American popular and fine art traditions and also with the romantic bourgeois photography Du Bois used in the *Crisis* to create a counter-discourse to racist iconography. His portraits were powerfully etched moderns, enlivened by Reiss's training in Jugendstil poster design that made their transference to print media result in no diminution in their visual power. Du Bois's illustrations had the look of old Victorians. Reiss's were modern. And unlike the visual satire of George Grosz's cartoons, Reiss's drawings placed the viewer face-to-face with the sitters who looked back with the seriousness of peers.

Locke would have more success getting Reiss to produce art that fit his agenda for the issue than he had with the writers. The portraits done so far were good but almost all of them were of working-class Negroes Reiss had met on the streets of Harlem. There were no artists and intellectuals, like Locke, represented so far in Reiss's collection of sitters. They too, like the migrants from the South, the African, and the West Indian, were part of the new community Locke argued had emerged in Harlem. The gallery of pictures had to include their portraits to visualize their influence. Locke also knew that if he published an issue that just portrayed working-class Negroes the Black middle class would cry foul and declare the issue unrepresentative. But getting the normally reticent and cautious Black middle class to sit for a German artist was a challenge. Locke flew into action. He called on Elise Johnson McDougald, the New York social worker and women's rights leader, to suggest some people who might sit for Reiss. She had emerged on his radar screen during his debate with Kellogg over whether an article on the Negro household should be included in the issue. Kellogg wanted something that would point up the problems and difficulties of Negro home life in Harlem. Locke resisted that idea, arguing that such an article was too sociological and controversial. Instead, Locke recommended a more broadly focused essay on women and the race issue. McDougald was a compromise choice, given that she was both a social worker and a women's rights advocate. The resulting article, "The Double Task: The Struggle of Negro Women for Sex and Race Emancipation," better fulfilled Locke's aspirations than Kellogg's by boldly attacking the cultural issue of the representation of Black women in the popular media of the day and painting a compelling portrait of the self-consciousness of African American women fighting against such representations in their daily lives. Her draft of her article was turned in early and convinced Locke to ask her to bring some professional Black women to sit for Reiss. "I was glad to co-operate in making the Survey Graphic—Harlem number well-rounded. I took 5 young women down and he selected 3 of them." One of the three, a portrait of Regina Andrews, became "The Librarian," and a double portrait of two others became, "Two Public School Teachers." Reiss also cajoled the strikingly beautiful

McDougald to sit for a portrait. As McDougald noted, Locke initially declined to sit for a portrait.[13]

Locke also got artists and friends to sit for Reiss. A letter from Countee Cullen attests to Locke's quick work. "Harold [Jackman] was here and had dinner with me this evening; he is quite beside himself with pleasure; he is to go to Reiss Wednesday for a sitting."[14] Jackman's portrait, which Locke titled "A college lad," was one of the most arresting of the assembled gallery, along with that of Paul Robeson, doing his Emperor Jones grin. In the end, Locke's collaboration with Reiss in fashioning the gallery of portraits in the Harlem issue of the *Survey Graphic* made profound argument—the people themselves were the most spectacular offering of the Negro Renaissance, a new identity of American, and that subjectivity was more important than the literature that they produced. The New Negro was the thing.

Sometime in December 1924, Locke began to compose the imagery of the issue by selecting portraits that exemplified the argument of "Harlem." He chose dark-skinned and light-skinned Negroes, the uneducated and "a woman lawyer," girls and boys, independent women and mothers, laborers and dandies—all placed side by side to show a community of middle- and working-class Negroes. He visually represented "the African, the West Indian, the Negro American . . . the peasant, the student . . . the artist . . . musician, adventurer and worker" in a gallery of difference that put them in conversation with one another. The *Survey Graphic* itself visualized his argument that a "fusing of sentiment and experience" and a "great race welding" was taking place in Black America.[15]

Once Locke had the art side of the Harlem number under control, he turned his attention to two other pressing concerns: the paltry number of contributions that were ready to go to the copyeditor and financial support for the issue. Kellogg was trying to get Barnes to help pay for the publication, but Barnes, as usual, was tricky and elusive. The cost of the number was mounting, and to absorb that cost, Kellogg delayed publication. This special number was more expensive—with extensive commissioned artwork, numerous contributors, poetry, short fiction, and research articles—than others Kellogg had produced in the past. But while Locke worried with Kellogg over the issue's cost, there was really nothing Locke could do to defray the costs—his relationships with Barnes and Lieber were not such as to allow him to approach them directly for funds. Without any way to advance the finances of the issue, Locke focused on revising and editing some of the weaker submissions.

Locke intervened in Arthur Schomburg's "The Negro Digs Up His Past" and J. A. Rogers's "Jazz at Home" most substantively. So poorly organized was Schomburg's submission, Locke claimed, that he had to rewrite it. The resulting article was a collaboration. For example, the lead to the article reads: "The American Negro must remake his past in order to make his future," one of Schomburg's recurring themes, though nowhere expressed as succinctly as here. Then, "Though it is orthodox to think of America as the one country where it is unnecessary to have a past, what is a luxury for the nation as a whole becomes a prime social necessity for the Negro. For him, a group tradition must supply compensation for persecution, and pride of race the antidote for prejudice."[16] Those sentences sound like Locke. He ended with the main conclusions Schomburg had reached after a lifetime of collecting—that the Negro had been a collaborator in his own liberation struggle, that Negroes of talent were typical of Colored peoples, not exceptions, and that the "record of creditable group achievement" was of national and world importance. But Locke strengthened Schomburg's claim to be modern by emphasizing that the New Negro preferred a "scientific narrative" rather than the older, exclusive, antiquarian chronicle of the Negro's woes. This helped, because Schomburg was himself an antiquarian, mainly a collector and not an academically trained historian. But Locke valued self-motivated collecting and sifting through one's history as a sign of the self-conscious intellectual agency of the New Negro and foregrounded Schomburg as a pioneer of that. Again, to visualize that practice, Locke published the photographs of book and manuscript title pages from Schomburg's collection that made this article fit nicely into the issue's overall agenda—that to be a New Negro meant to plumb one's history for a more self-conscious future.

Locke's transformation of J. A. Rogers's submission, "Jazz at Home," had a less positive result. Locke's moralizing, even condemnatory, tone toward jazz produced an article that was curiously ambivalent about an art form the issue introduced as indicative of the New Negro. "The earliest jazz-makers were the itinerant piano players.... Seated at the piano with a carefree air that a king might envy, their box-back coats flowing over the stool, their Stetsons pulled well over their eyes, and cigars at an angle of forty-five degrees, they would 'whip the ivories' to marvelous chords and hidden racy, joyous meanings, evoking the intense delight of their hearers who would smother them at the close with huzzas and whiskey." While a deft portrait perhaps of Willie "The Lion" Smith, it drips with condescension. "For the Negro himself, jazz is both more and less dangerous than for the white—less in that, he is nervously more in tune with it; more, in that at his average level of economic development his amusement life is more open to the forces of social vice. The cabaret of better type provides a certain Bohemianism for the Negro intellectual, the artist and the well-to-do. But the average thing is too much the substitute for the saloon and the wayside inn."[17]

Locke responded to jazz more as a late Victorian than a modernist, who saw jazz as a loud and wild music culture that lacked, from Locke's perspective, the kind of rigor and reflection crucial to art of value. Jazz was a trick, Locke believed, because it suggested that natural talent, rather than study and perfection, was in control over an instrument. Here, Locke's ignorance of the rigorous practice schedules of bands kept him from seeing jazz as an intellectual activity. His moralizing analysis confined jazz—indeed music—to second-class status in the Harlem number. Insinuating his own negative moral feeling into the article brought a post-publication response from Rogers. "As to mine, I am much indebted to you for your editorship of it. Nevertheless I am inclined to say in all good nature that there was injected into it a tinge of morality and 'uplift' alien to my innermost convictions. For instance after a careful weighing of the matter, I am inclined to think that of the two evils the church and the cabaret, the latter so far as progress of the Negro group is concerned is less of a mental drag. On second thought I have decided, however, that your action is for the best."[18]

November and December were slow months of work on the *Survey Graphic*, in large part because of contributors' delays in submitting their articles. By December 2, Geddes Smith, the managing editor of the *Survey Graphic* wrote to Locke that they were still awaiting final versions of six articles. Benjamin Karpman had promised to take another stab at the article on the psychology of the Negro, but soon gave up on it. Another article, by Bruno Lasker, had been received, but Locke and the editors had decided it needed substantial revisions. That still left four articles—Kelly Miller's on race prejudice, Winthrop Lane's "Ambushed in the City: The Grim Side of Harlem," George Haynes's "The Church and the Negro Spirit," and Locke's own revision of his New Negro article—not in hand. When Locke came up on December 12–14 to work on the *Survey Graphic* the conclusion they all reached was that the issue would again have to be postponed until March. Apart from outstanding articles, the business office had complained it did not have enough time to get out an issue for February. The editors also gave Locke an ultimatum: they needed his final version of the New Negro by the next weekend.

Locke finally turned that in after acceding to the editors' request to shift away from his social history of Black thought toward a critique of contemporary views of the Negro—an edgier concept buried deeper in the earlier draft. "In the last decade something beyond the watch and guard of statistics has happened in the life of the American Negro and the three norns who have traditionally presided over the Negro problem have a changeling in their laps. The Sociologist, The Philanthropist, the Race-leader are not unaware of the New Negro, but they are at a loss to account for him." So began the essay in the present, with a critique of the established "authorities on the Negro problem."[19] After struggling with it for several weeks, Locke found a way to change the article from a mostly nationalist statement of Black self-determination to a critical attack on Black and White thinking about the Negro.

The *Survey Graphic* editors were very pleased with what he had done. Geddes Smith noted to Locke when the managing editor was shaping the essay to fit within the allotted space that "if you will let me say it, I think that for sustained brilliance this essay strikes a note which we don't often achieve in The Survey, and I am reluctant to fit it to any procrustean bed of space. If you say so then we shall somehow contrive to alter our layout so as to give this article four consecutive pages."[20]

Problems nevertheless continued with other contributors. While all the poetry that Locke had selected for the issue had been revised and resubmitted well before Christmas, a blowup with Countee Cullen threatened to remove one of the most important poems in the issue. Back in October, Cullen had let Locke have his poem "Heritage," the best unpublished poem in the issue. Indeed, Cullen gushingly had told Locke that "you need never beg for any of my work that you desire to use; whatever I have is yours for the asking."[21] But a week later, Cullen was already pulling the poems "For Dunbar" and "For a Mouthy Woman" from the publication, because they had previously been sent to *Harper's*. Then, Cullen stated he would pledge "Heritage" exclusively to the *Survey Graphic* only "if they are willing to pay fifty dollars for it," because that was the first prize money for the upcoming *Opportunity* poetry contest, and Cullen was sure that he would win it if he entered it there. Locke knew that $50 was considerably above what the *Survey Graphic* paid contributors, especially for one poem. He had to find a way to argue for the poem with the *Survey Graphic* people in order to get as much money as possible for it, while at the same time not discouraging Cullen by revealing immediately that his fee was too high.

Increasing Locke's leverage was Cullen's emotional neediness. His October 31 letter confided in Locke, "L.R. was here Wednesday night—until late. I was painfully distressed, and he was very kind. But I am not certain whether it was mere kindness, or what I most desired it to be. It may be cowardly in me, but I am depending upon you to find out for me."[22] This latter confidence referred to Cullen's belief that, if he could have a secure relationship with a man he loved, his muse would be "invigorated." This related to the "Heritage" issue, because Cullen's insistence on the $50 came out of his belief that "I doubt that my muse will supply me with anything else as good for the *Opportunity* contest." In one sense, Cullen's request for assistance in ferreting out whether "L.R." was in love with Cullen was simply a request from a friend, but Locke may have also felt that he was doing this extra favor to get a break from Cullen on the matter of payment.

At the same time that Locke succeeded in fixing Cullen's love interest, the editor lobbied the *Survey Graphic* staff about the importance of "Heritage" to the issue. He arranged to have it featured on two pages in the middle of the issue, with photographs of African art from the Barnes Foundation around it. The importance of this poem to Locke was immeasurable, for it was the poem that best captured the renaissance theme he wished to encourage among the younger poets, by meditating on the meaning of the African past to Black Americans. Perhaps the ambivalence of the poem's approach to the African heritage led Locke to pass it back to Cullen for revisions. By the end of November, Cullen had had enough of Locke's suggestions. "Please relinquish me from revising <u>Heritage</u>. Either take it as it is, or give it back to me. I simply cannot do anything with it. I have toiled over it for hours—for your sake—to no end."[23] Of course, Locke took it. And he asked for and received several other poems, some of which he published in the issue.

After submitting the final form to the *Survey Graphic* on December 9, Cullen asked, "Do you think you can manage to have them pay me before Christmas?"[24] By December 20, Cullen was even more insistent: "I hate to trouble you, but unless I receive some money from the Survey people I shall be terribly embarrassed during the holidays. For me to go to Mr. Kellogg does not seem in the best taste, but I shall be forced to do that unless I hear from him by Wednesday morning. I am absolutely without money, and to call on my father would necessitate explanations which I do not care to give."[25] Locke agreed that it would be "unseemly" and wrote Cullen not to communicate with Kellogg. Apparently, Locke had gotten to Kellogg to pay the poets before Christmas, "$40 for Cullen (we are all for using Heritage), $20 for Langston Hughes, and $25 for Claude McKay," as Kellogg noted on December 19. But when Cullen got his check for $40, he was angry.

"Mr. Cullen called up a bit upset about my letter of yesterday enclosing check for $40," Kellogg wrote Locke two days before Christmas.

> He didn't think the $40 check should cover the other poems. . . . I talked with him, saying that my understanding (and I thought yours) was that this was to cover all; but that we didn't want by any chance to exploit him; that he was quite free to withdraw "Heritage" and enter it in the contest. But that was not his choice. Rather he was for leaving it with us at $40 and leaving it to us what more we could pay for the other poems. I explained what the Survey was; that in our Mexican number the Mexicans contributed gratis; how, as we are under no travel expense this time, we were making modest payments to contributors and what our page rate was. After which I said I thought perhaps we could pay him $10 in addition for such of the other poems as you chose to use. He fell in with that suggestion.[26]

Kellogg acted in the best interest of the issue by compromising, aware perhaps that as a White magazine, the *Survey Graphic* might be vulnerable to charges of exploitation if he mishandled this.

Locke was incensed. He believed that Cullen had gone behind his back and undermined his authority. He was right. Locke was not really in charge, and Kellogg was willing to allow an end run to be made by someone purportedly under Locke's charge. At the same time, had Cullen not circumvented Locke's position as "middleman," Cullen would not have received what he had previously stated was his price for "Heritage." Locke stopped corresponding with Cullen. "I am beginning to fear that you are very angry with me, and I am deeply concerned over your silence. Am I to lose another friend over a trifle?"[27] The other friend had been Langston Hughes, who had stopped corresponding with Cullen, according to Rampersad, because Cullen had revealed how intimate Hughes and Locke had been in Paris. Whatever doubt he had about the extent of Locke's anger was dispelled by Locke's response. "I have read, and worried over your letter to no slight degree," Cullen wrote on January 19. "Your language is decisive and beyond misinterpretation; still I will not accept the abrupt termination of a friendship which, from your own admission, has been no less acceptable to you than to me."[28]

This incident did not, however, end their relationship. In February, Locke invited Cullen to come to Washington to stay with him. Locke had fallen ill shortly after his letter to Cullen, a sign perhaps that the Cullen relationship meant more to him than he had imagined. It was not that Cullen was a love interest, but Cullen's potential as an artist helped Locke resist ending the relationship in 1925. Of all of the poets writing in 1925, Cullen was the one most capable of producing consistently beautiful poems that had universal appeal. His themes, of self-destruction, death, and ambivalence of identity also made him modern in a way that McKay was not. His technique was more controlled and finished than that of Hughes, despite the other's obvious brilliance with folk-inspired poems. Most important, Cullen's poems reached the universal by working through the emotion of race. To sever a relationship with him would have marginalized Locke and robbed him of influence on the poet who, from the perspective of the day, had the most potential for greatness. Once his anger cooled and his own neediness rose, Locke marshaled the necessary emotional resources to stay connected with Cullen. Although Cullen had exposed the weakness of Locke's position, it merely revealed what Locke already knew. Cullen had not withdrawn the poem, and the situation had not spilled out into a public controversy. This controversy demonstrated, however, the limits of his control over the publication, apart from the issues of its content.

The Cullen incident was not the only example of how working with the *Survey Graphic* had its limitations. Early in January 1925, Paul Kellogg proposed that the *Survey Graphic* host a special dinner as a send-off for the Harlem number. Such a dinner would be a landmark in that "like the number its approach would be the cultural renaissance of which Harlem is the stage; or at least the footlights. What would you think of it? Who would be the speakers? Would it not be possible as at the Du Bois dinner last fall to make it a meeting place for liberals of both races? How could we make it distinctive from that dinner so that it would strike a ringing note—make it another way an[d] avenue for the new Negro expressing himself? Perhaps we could get poets and playwrights and others to contribute as you did at that little Civic Club dinner which set the ball rolling for this number?"[29] One problem Kellogg voiced was that they needed to find a draw for the dinner. The obvious choice would be Roland Hayes, whose portrait, Locke would soon learn, would dominate the iconography of the issue. "But we could not of course recompense him," Locke wrote back enthusiastically. He outlined what he believed would be the choreography of the evening and volunteered to contact Hayes personally to secure his interest if not his participation.

But in February, Kellogg changed his mind. "After some prayer, canvassing the matter in the bosom of the family, and trying it out on a few people representing different points of view, we have decided against attempting a dinner in conjunction with the Harlem number." There were the normal excuses. "We have ahead of us a number of luncheon and dinner meetings ... in the next couple of months. . . . Also, Opportunity is planning a dinner in connection with their prize contest which will come possibly in April, and while Mr. Johnson was cordiality itself in offering to cooperate with us, still the two dinners would in a sense strike the same note."[30]

Even more remarkable than the decision not to hold the dinner was the racial rationale behind Kellogg's decision. "Aside from these practical considerations, a prejudice factor enters in; and that is, what effect such an inter-racial dinner here in New York might have, especially in the South, on the fortunes of the *Survey Graphic* as a whole. I hope, even sub-consciously, that this has not been the decisive factor with us. But we don't want to hamstring our ability to open men's minds and make for understanding by doing something which might close some of them up like a trap against us." An interracial dinner might sink the commercial success of the special issue. "If the fact that Negroes and whites sat down to dinner together should overshadow that [the *Survey* was taking a new approach to race] so far as newspaper publicity goes, what then? The whole thing might be hailed and damned merely as a gesture of social equality; discussion would be thrown back into the old rut; and the new approach would be lost sight of. This might not happen," Kellogg conceded. "But if it did the dinner would tend to defeat the purpose of the number and dinner alike and throw all the labor that had gone into the number as something affirmative, and nascent, differing from the old protest psychology, off the track."[31]

Kellogg's decision exemplified the failure of American modernism when it came to matters of race. An opening of "men's minds" to the "cultural renaissance of the Negro" had to be accompanied by an opening of their minds to greater social and political freedom, or the renaissance would be stillborn. Kellogg's decision also was a personal loss for Locke. At such a party, he could be thanked and praised as the man who deserved credit for advancing the New Negro. Now that would never happen. Perhaps that was fortunate. Given this decision and the logic behind it, he wasn't key. They had not even asked him to participate in the final discussion as to whether to hold the dinner. He was the odd man out, once again.

But that was the price of working within White modernism in the 1920s. In an ironic way, this was payback for Locke's elimination of McKay's "Mulatto" poem from the issue. Locke had cut the poem to make the New Negro more appealing to the White man. It did. But it also let White people off the hook from having to treat Black people equally or be critiqued. Locke quietly accepted Kellogg's decision. What else could he do? In shifting from Charles Johnson, the Black editor of *Opportunity*, to Paul Kellogg, the White editor of *Survey Graphic* Locke had lost the kind of leader who saw interracial commingling around literary success as critical to progress. Of course, Kellogg had to be concerned first of all with his magazine, which, though linked to liberal causes, was, like most Progressive-Era magazines, completely unwilling to challenge segregation. And there was the purely commercial angle. Kellogg had gone out on a limb to devote a huge percentage of its resources, both financial and labor, to a publication about Negroes. He did not want consorting with those Negroes in public to doom his publication.

That Whites felt most comfortable discussing Black issues without challenging their privileged position was again evident when Locke tried to edit the submission of a White contributor. In April 1924, Locke had asked Melville Herskovits to contribute an article on the "dilemma of social patterns" in Harlem, one that balanced "the Negro's acceptance of the American pattern—the barrier + his effort at duplication," on the one hand, with the Negro's internal "demand for a race pattern," or distinctive way of life, on the other.[32] Locke chose Herskovits because he wanted an anthropological rather than a sociological view of Harlem. American anthropology under Boas had pioneered looking at the lives of non-Western peoples as distinct cultural wholes with their own patterns of behavior. But Herskovits and Boas viewed America as one cultural pattern; and when they discussed ethnic and minority diversity in America, they tended to view it sociologically and insist that complete assimilation was the only way for immigrants and other fringe groups to succeed in America. Any failure to do so came close to justifying the arguments of racists that such groups could not assimilate because they were inferior. To his credit, Boas sympathized with the need of Blacks to build racial self-esteem through identification with an African heritage and had lobbied Andrew Carnegie and others to fund research on Africa and to train African Americans as anthropologists. Boas pursued a double enterprise: he encouraged the study of African heritage among Blacks, but argued that assimilation and disappearance of Black identity was the only solution to racism. The contradiction between these two positions was not explicit until the Locke-Herskovits controversy over his *Survey Graphic* article. Herskovits carried out the logic of the total assimilation argument, without balancing that against the presence of a separate ethnic identity among Black people. When Locke wrote to Herskovits asking him to address the question, "Has the Negro a Unique Social Pattern?" Herskovits instead attacked the notion that a unique racial culture was developing in Harlem.[33]

After considerable time spent in Harlem, Herskovits had concluded that Harlem was dominated by the same "churches and schools, clubhouses and lodge meeting-places, the library and the newspaper offices and the Y.M.C.A. and busy 135th Street and the hospitals and the social service agencies" of a middle-sized American town. Herskovits went on to attack the notion that a yearning for a separate culture existed among Harlem's Blacks and used as his evidence the comments of Black writers he had heard at the *Opportunity* dinner in 1924. "The proudest boast of the modern Negro writer is that he writes of humans, not of Negroes. His literary ideals are not the African folk-tale and conundrum, but the vivid expressionistic style of the day—he seeks to be a writer, not a Negro writer."[34] Herskovits preferred to ascribe any uniqueness in Harlem to regionalism—the remnants of a southern "peasant" culture that migrants had brought with them to the North. Nevertheless, Herskovits did admit in his discussion of the Negro singing of "the spirituals" that they exhibited an "emotional quality in the Negro, which is to be sensed rather than measured, [from which] comes the feeling that, though strongly acculturated to the prevalent pattern of behavior, the Negroes may, at the same time, influence it somewhat eventually through the appeal of that quality." But he refused to suggest that this quality had any connection to "African culture," of which he found "not a trace." He concluded that Negro activity in Harlem was "the same pattern" as Whites, "only a different shade."[35]

Herskovits's ending suggested he was mightily pleased with his essay. Locke was not. He seized on the admission that "the Negroes may, at the same time, influence" the "prevalent pattern" through their performance of the spirituals to suggest editorial changes that would do better justice to the complexity of the Harlem situation. These he sent, through the copyeditor, Geddes Smith, to Herskovits who, according to Smith, did not like the suggested revisions of his article. Herskovits claimed "that we have pushed him to positions which he cannot scientifically accept."[36] In doing so, Herskovits tried to use his position as a "scientist" to upstage and correct Locke, the humanist. Herskovits's resistance left Locke and the editors with a decision to either accept the article as it was or leave it out—a decision the editors left up to Locke. It was a tricky decision, because it might be politically dangerous to delete the article since Herskovits was an influential White man and a student of Franz Boas, whom Locke wanted to keep as an ally.

Locke decided to keep the article in, but to challenge its assertions in two ways. First, he appended a prefatory note to the article that critiqued its conclusion. "Looked at in its externals," Locke wrote, "Negro life, as reflected in Harlem registers a ready—almost a feverishly rapid—assimilation of American patterns, what Mr. Herskovits calls 'complete acculturation.' Internally, perhaps it is another matter. Does democracy require uniformity? If so, it threatens to be safe, but dull. Social standards must be more or less uniform, but social expressions may be different."[37] Second, Locke took another article by Konrad Bercovici, coupled it with Herskovits's article, and introduced it in the prefatory note as a "rebuttal" of Herskovits's article. "In the article which follows this Mr. Bercovici tells of finding, by intuition rather than research, something 'unique' in Harlem— back of the external conformity, a race-soul striving for social utterance." Bercovici observed "an awakened consciousness of race" in Harlem. "Backs are straightened out and heads are raised. Eyes look to their own level when they seek those of other people." Bercovici had toured the South, had witnessed postures of subservience associated with the Old Negro—the bent back, downcast eyes—developed because of violent enforcement of southern racial etiquette, and could see the northern New Negro posture's rejection of that pose. Bercovici's insight challenged Herskovits's claim that "they face much the same problems as those [other, immigrant] groups face," which ignored the specificity of southern racism and its unique impact on African American life and culture. Even more subtly, Bercovici noted, "I listened to the preachers in the churches of Harlem. I understood the language. But was there not something unsaid in the preachment? Was the preacher, the minister, not fashioning another God for himself and for his congregation while he spoke?" Here Bercovici confirmed Locke's sense that intuition could pick up that a unique system of meaning, style, and identity formation operated in Harlem beneath the radar of most White observers, even Columbia University–trained social scientists.[38]

Bercovici sensed Locke's argument that if the Negro aspired to nothing more than assimilation, there was really nothing transformative in the Harlems of America. "The feeling," Bercovici wrote, "is still one of being better than thou, but underneath that, it seemed to me, there was a striving for another culture that was not an imitative one." Further, he caught the distinction that "they are not inferiors. They do not have to strive for equality. They are different. Emphasizing that difference in their lives, in their culture, is what will give them and what should give them their value."[39] This "value" was part of the reason that Locke took the position he did against Herskovits. The Black community needed to be interested in forging a life that did more than simply imitate White middle-class life or there was no further purpose to the movement.

Remarkably, Locke's disagreement with Herskovits over his article did not end their relationship, but instead eventually transformed Herskovits's intellectual position on African American culture. Locke even facilitated Herskovits conducting research at Howard University. All the while he continued to pepper Herskovits with articles and insights about the uniqueness of African American culture and the possible role of African culture in fashioning that New World particularity. Intellectual historian Walter A. Jackson credits Herskovits's interaction with Locke and other Black intellectuals during the late 1920s as converting Herskovits to his mature position that African survivals existed in American Negro culture and made it distinctive from the rest of American culture. One can go even further and suggest that Locke's critique, and Herskovits's openness to it, laid the groundwork for a revolution in anthropological thinking within the

United States for it showed that anthropology as a science had to change in order to study racial diversity within modern society by abandoning the socio-logical model of assimilation and accepting the philosophical concept of cultural pluralism.

Locke's reaction to this power struggle with Herskovits and to the conflict with Cullen suggested growth on his part. Previously, Locke separated from people with whom he experienced painful or divisive conflict. Perhaps because he so loved managing a major publishing project, his ego was stronger, and he was able to remain involved with those who challenged his authority. His greater emotional flexibility may also have derived from the social dynamics of the *Survey Graphic* project. Despite differences of opinion on particular issues, the creative space of the *Survey Graphic* project enabled collaboration between him and the staff, even when their understandings of the race and ideological issues involved diverged. In that give and take, sometimes it was Locke who influenced a White intellectual, as in the case of Herskovits. At others, it was the staff at *Survey Graphic* who pushed Locke in a new direction from that which he would normally take.

A good example came with the debate over the cover to the number. Only weeks before the issue was to go to press, Paul Kellogg wired Locke a telegram for his approval to change the cover. "Sales and advertising experts say we can double sales of Harlem number if we use Reis[s's] marvelous head [of] Roland Hayes on Cover, [and] also inside. More sales more educational reach. More-over Hayes personifies youth[,] racial genius[,] New Negro as nothing else. Please wire him urging him grant this permission."[40] The original cover included broad blue borders of Reiss's modernist abstract pattern of gears, parallel lines, and circles that evoked both industrial machinery and African motifs, American art deco and primitivism. In the middle a White area served to background the title of the cover printed in bold letters. It was a nice but not startling design. Kellogg's suggestion, while economically driven, would result in the boldest cover of an American magazine to date.

Locke responded quickly that he did not like the idea, because the portrait and the design clashed. Kellogg was away when Locke's letter arrived, and in his absence, the editorial staff somehow concluded that he was leaving the decision up to Locke. One of the editorial assistants, Miss Merrill, sent Locke an engraver's proof of Hayes's portrait for his evaluation, and Locke continued to object to the combination. But Locke weakened his position by writing Kellogg that the final decision should be left up to Hayes, who would be forever associated with the issue. As was the case in the controversy over the "Mulatto" poem, Locke abdicated total responsibility for the decision, perhaps because he thought that Hayes would veto the idea or because he knew the decision would not rest on his opinion in the final analysis. But shifting the responsibility for the final approval to Hayes gave Kellogg the out they needed, for if Hayes gave his approval, they could go ahead.

While they awaited his decision, Kellogg continued to lobby Locke about the benefits of the new cover. "There is a lift, a lilt, a spirit to the portrait of Hayes which visualizes the gleam, which you have put into this cluster of manuscripts so admirably. It tells more than many words of the spirit of the thing."[41] Locke remained unconvinced and argued for a redesign if the portrait was used. In the end, Locke's objections were pointless, because Kellogg received a telegram from Hayes giving them a free hand and Kellogg decided to go with the bold design.

Locke's taste had failed him here. The cover and portrait clashed, but that clashing was the essence of modernism. Reiss's border mix of industrial and African design elements framed Hayes's head, situating African Americans in a new context—that of the urban, industrial civilization that African Americans entered through the Great Migration and owned because they brought their culture with them. The surrounding abstract design evoked a modern age of gear teeth and machinery. And Hayes's uplifting head with light shining on it from below anointed the Negro with a spiritual confidence that said, "We are unfazed by the challenge of such a new arena of struggle." More subtly, the jagged edges of the border suggested that the new urban context threatened as well as supported the New Negro, the cover nicely evoking the tension of the New Negro formulation, its promise and its dangers. The cover has endured as a symbol of the dynamic uncertainty of the New Negro moment in the mid-1920s.

Locke had lost another battle over control of the issue. But he probably did not fret over it, because the final decision had never been in his hands. That was also evident in another case where he wanted Reiss's abstract design "Dawn over Harlem" as the frontispiece of the issue. The *Survey Graphic* staff overruled that decision, because of their feeling that it was too modernistic to begin the issue. Kellogg's skill at magazine composition was surer than Locke's, obviously. Given that they had decided to put Hayes's head on the cover, it made sense to repeat that powerful symbol, without the modernist halo, inside because it was now the most powerful symbol of the New Negro. Having it on the cover and as the frontispiece created a rhythm that lifted the Reiss portraits from being illustrations to texts that drove the issue. In a sense, the prominence of the portraits and the designs switched the usual hierarchy of print and image in most Black magazines of the period.

Locke's voice, however, had not been ignored, simply overruled. And Locke seemed to have the self-knowledge and common sense not to challenge that position. After all, in countless other ways his insights were utilized throughout the *Survey Graphic*. A key example came shortly after the cover debate when Du Bois, perhaps realizing the growing significance of the *Survey Graphic* project and its documentation of Negro intelligentsia, decided to sit for a Reiss portrait. This coincided with Dr. Moton's decision also to sit for Reiss. By February 12, Kellogg was eyeing the commercial advantages of having these two portraits in the issue. "So far as the general public goes, it of course would have been a fine stroke to

Front cover, *Survey Graphic*, March 1, 1925. Reproduction courtesy of Black Classic Press.

have included these two portraits in the issue. But from the standpoint of the cultural front and the new approach of the issue, Hayes and Robeson were far more appropriate." Still, Kellogg wondered whether they might still "include one or both of them. What would you think?"[42] There was also the added pressure that Moton had called up the *Survey Graphic* and complained that the Hampton-Tuskegee nexus of Negro education had been left out of the issue.

Here Locke put his foot down. "Let's leave them out of this issue," he wrote on February 17. "There is no use bringing in through the back-door what we have so ceremoniously bowed out of the front. You see their very names raise the issue. Moton is in the heat of the Tuskegee-Hampton campaign with more hat-in-hand arguments than ever. Indeed he would be publicly embarrassed with our platform. Let's just stick to our original plan and put it over big." Kellogg agreed "that we ought to stick to our original last—a fresh one—and I have been staving off the pressure of the philanthropic-economic-education group who thought we were neglecting them."[43]

When the issue finally did appear on March 1, 1925, it was a stunning success. Some have claimed that the Harlem issue's popularity was largely due to advance purchase of copies by philanthropists. The *Survey Graphic* records tell a different story. While Albert Barnes ordered one thousand copies to distribute personally in Philadelphia, George Foster Peabody ordered one thousand copies to be sent out to his friends in the United States and abroad, and Amy and Joel Spingarn ordered another one thousand for Locke to distribute to Negro schools and universities, by the time those copies had been delivered, the first edition of twelve thousand copies had sold out. The *Survey Graphic* ordered second and third editions of twelve thousand copies each, and within two more months those were sold out. More than forty thousand copies were sold in the final tally, making it the largest sales ever for a *Survey Graphic* issue. The *Survey Graphic* received record numbers of requests for new subscriptions as a result of the Harlem number as well.

The Harlem number benefited from great timing, arriving on newsstands just in time to give a newly awakened public the most comprehensive introduction to the movement available. It caught the movement on its ascendance and accelerated it because of Locke's redefinition of the New Negro as a discursive sign of the future, an as-yet-unfinished subject that the readers of the magazine themselves could participate in constructing.

Also critical to its success was the collaboration between Locke and Kellogg. Locke had achieved something here that was unprecedented—to get a White mainstream journal to create the most powerful representation to date of Negro expression. The interaction among Locke, Kellogg, Reiss, and the staff, as well as the poets, sociologists, short-story writers and anthropologists, self-taught historians and degreed scholars was unique in American magazine history and resulted in an issue above and beyond what they could have done without that collaboration. The Harlem issue nicely embodied the central argument of the issue—that something transcendently beautiful emerged out of diversity, especially a diversity that went beyond simply the racial.

Perhaps, most remarkably, the issue seemed to speak to different, segregated audiences and elicit awe from almost all who picked it up and read it. Black people felt that it spoke for them, without committing them to any fixed position, by suggesting their untapped potential and Beauty. It reached a younger reading public that wanted a message of hope and possibility in a new century. By allowing the poetry, essays, and articles to be authored by Negroes, Kellogg allowed the voice of the New Negro to be expressed in a way that made a mainstream journal Black—if only temporarily. Indeed, Kellogg allowing Locke to foreground poetry and art in the issue reinforced the notion that what was important was the Negro voice, not the objectification of the Negro as a Negro problem. That resonated with White liberals and made the *Survey Graphic* hip in a way it had never been before.

And then Winold Reiss's pastel portraits and abstract designs translated the mood Locke wanted to communicate in the poetry and essays into something of powerful visual impact. The Reiss portraits translated "Negroness" into graphically intense and beautiful Italian Renaissance–like images of real people. African American eyes feasted on his portraits because nowhere could one find Black people visually represented as they appeared naturally. Like *Life* magazine, *Vanity Fair*, and dozens of other exciting picture magazines of the 1920s, the Harlem issue put the images up front and gave sympathetic or merely curious readers something they could engage without actually having to read it.

Here the cover was the key—a bold representation of the Negro as modern without equal in American publishing. Just carrying the Harlem number into a room drew attention to this bold Black face framed by a blue and white modern design. It was ironic that the *Survey Graphic* advertising people had forced Locke and the other editors to approve putting the face of a Negro on the cover for economic reasons. They were proved right, but American magazine editors subsequently have justified the paucity of Black people on covers with the homily that they would not sell to a predominantly White magazine-reading public. In the 1920s, the Negro was not only "finding beauty in oneself," but a significant portion of the American public also found beauty in the Negro. The Harlem number of the *Survey Graphic* gave a visually starved American public something visually satisfying about the Negro to look at. They continued to look and read in record numbers. Locke was again an American celebrity.

26

The New Negro and Howard

Less than four months after the spectacular Harlem issue of the *Survey Graphic* appeared, Locke, its guest editor, was out of a job. On June 16, 1925, Emmett Scott, Secretary-Treasurer of Howard University's Board of Trustees, wrote to Locke: "Voted: That, Alain LeRoy Locke, Professor of Philosophy, be not reemployed for the school year 1925–26." By way of explanation, Scott continued: "After very full discussion of the matter, in all its phases, your place, among others, it was decided, could be vacated and the work of the University not unduly suffer." That might seem surprising, for during the winter quarter, 1925, Locke had carried a heavy load of teaching, including Philosophy 2 Ethics, Philosophy 126 Modern Philosophy: Renaissance to the Present, Philosophy 129 Race Contacts (for graduate students), and Philosophy 130 Aesthetics and Literary Criticism.[1] Of course, on another level, Scott's comment reflected the low value placed on the teaching of philosophy, rather than religion, at Negro colleges and universities in the mid-1920s. As if to ensure that Locke did not feel unappreciated, Scott concluded: "I am directed to add an expression of the Executive Committee's appreciation on the behalf of the Board of Trustees of the services you have rendered since you have been connected with the University."[2]

How could the premier Negro institution of higher education in the United States fire its most-educated faculty member, especially after he had made history, again, by editing arguably the most important statement of Negro efficacy in 1925? The answer, while complex, came down to this: the New Negro was not a welcome attitude in all quarters of Negro America, especially among administrators of institutional Negro America who viewed the New Negro and its criticality of racial hegemony as a nuisance to be dismissed or, if that did not suffice, to be crushed.

Locke's problem was simple. He was not only the principal chronicler of the New Negro—he was a New Negro himself, an upstart rebel against the kind of paternalist control that had become the staple of Negro higher education. For years he had served as the secretary of the faculty committee peppering the board of trustees at Howard University with memoranda demanding better salaries for the faculty. As recently as January 1925, Locke, as secretary of the faculty committee on salaries, had penned a caustic letter to Jesse Moorland, chairman of the Budget Committee of the Howard Board of Trustees, challenging the board's statement in the press that most of the recent increase in salaries went to the teachers and not the staff.[3] Locke was the face of faculty rebellion against the board's obfuscations about faculty salaries. Locke had been able to keep his distance from this caldron of faculty rebellion against the board of trustees and Howard's White president by being away almost every other year and every summer since his mother's death in 1922; but that absenteeism inadvertently confirmed the university's judgment, coldly expressed by Scott, his campus nemesis, when he wrote that Locke's "place, among others, it was decided, could be vacated and the work of the University not unduly suffer." Locke's sexuality, his need to be away to live and love openly, his need to be abroad to find inspiration to reenter Black America with fresh ideas—all of that combined to make him expendable despite that he was again a household name in educated Negro America.

The tension between Locke and Howard revolved around different conceptions of the meaning of education. Declaring a Negro Renaissance in the *Survey Graphic* he edited, Locke neglected to mention that a broad transition in the notion of education had also accompanied the emergence of new art during the Italian Renaissance. Educated at Harvard under Irving Babbitt and Barrett Wendell, Locke imbibed the notion that the fifteenth century in Italy ushered in an educational revolution that consigned scholasticism to historical dustbins and launched humanism as the foundation of modern liberal arts and scientific education. This new education was as important as the new art in launching the new subjectivity of the Italian Renaissance and it was no different in the Negro Renaissance five hundred years later. Having struggled throughout his teaching career at Howard against what he believed was an outmoded form of education that suppressed the subjectivity of Negro students as well as Negro professors, Locke saw himself on the side of a renaissance generation, as was exemplified in his freshmen lecture, "The Ethics of Culture," making self-directed humanism the key to education at Howard. But Locke also did not mention in the *Survey Graphic* or *The New Negro: An Interpretation* that the earlier renaissance was also a period of intrigue, murder of leaders, abuse of power by patrons, and the fractured dismemberment of the city, Florence, that had birthed it. Silenced in Locke's utopic vision of renaissance was a dark side—colonialism, violence, exploitation, and the need to control the masses of the people so that the few, the gifted, and the anointed could pursue the life of art and humanities. The more contemporary Mexican Renaissance had as its wider goal destroying the vestiges of colonial thinking in its citizens through a revolutionary education system that would enable the "New Man" to emerge. But Locke had not wanted to announce publicly that for a real spiritual awakening to occur among American Negroes, there needed to be a fundamental change in the Negro world of education and the power relations that kept it conservative. His dismissal showed there were those intent on keeping such change from happening.

Most important, by downplaying the protest element in New Negro consciousness in the Harlem issue of the *Survey Graphic*, Locke silenced the strongest expressions of New Negro subjectivity in the mid-1920s—that of the Black student protest occurring on Negro university campuses! Just one month before the Harlem issue appeared, Fisk University, one of the oldest and most respected Negro universities in the United States, had erupted in a student rebellion against its White president, Fayette McKenzie, and his strict student codes of dress and conduct, and his suppression of student voices on campus. Stoked by the graduation speech a year earlier by none other than W. E. B. Du Bois criticizing the president for his dictatorial rule and questionable use of Black women students to sing at White men's clubs for money, students disrupted the campus on February 4, 1925. In response, McKenzie sent White Nashville police onto campus to arrest students in their dormitories. Formerly divided over McKenzie's tenure, because of his success in raising money, the Black community unified in its criticism of the president, forcing him to resign. Rebellion was endemic on the streets of Harlem, in working-class unions among the newly migrated, and in women's organizations to fight for the rights of laundresses. While Locke acknowledged such rebellion in "Youth Speaks," he downplayed its political significance in favor of the spiritual catharsis he favored. But the coming storm in his life would test both his spiritual poise and his avoidance of protest, since art could not save him.

Despite the popularity of the Harlem issue, various aspects of its new approach to Negro subjectivity angered some in the Black community. Clashes over how the *Survey Graphic* represented Black people and Harlem erupted immediately after its publication. James Weldon Johnson wrote to Locke on March 10 to complain about how Winthrop Lane's article, "The Grim Side of Harlem," had provided ammunition for unfavorable commentary about Harlem in the *New York World* and the *Savannah Morning News*. Johnson harangued that more White newspapers would use Lane's article to condemn the Negro in Harlem, judging it "a serious slip" to have published Lane's litany of Harlem's ills—the pervasiveness of policy-playing among poor Blacks, the exorbitant rents charged by Black real estate agents of poor Black migrants, the dozens of quack doctors, incompetent pharmacists, and various hustlers that took advantage, in Lane's language, of the "childlike" gullibility of the poor Negro migrant from the South—in the Harlem number. This was precisely the kind of mistake that the protest tradition's tendency to focus on White racism avoided—blaming the victim for the ills of the American social order.[4] Johnson, it seemed, wanted Negro beauty without Negro truth.

Locke handed the letter over to Kellogg, who responded with a serious rebuttal. He asserted that an objective view of Harlem had to include coverage of real problems, and that the right response was not to blame the messenger, but organize to help social workers and others on the scene eradicate the evils Lane documented. Kellogg welcomed Johnson and John Nail, the Black real estate developer, also incensed by the article, to help social workers deal with these problems, and even welcomed them to submit replies to Lane's assertions. Neither did, in part, perhaps, because Nail's real estate operation was accused of charging exorbitant rents, which some said fueled the need for unlawful sources of income. Neither took up Kellogg's suggestion to clean up Harlem. They were simply angry that Lane had outed Harlem and that progressive organizations like the NAACP were doing nothing to combat the day-to-day problems experienced by the masses of Black people in Harlem. Of course, such exposés as Lane's helped southern media suggest Blacks stay in the South, rather than risk the "immorality" of northern cities. New Negro "openness" was causing problems.[5]

Luckily, there was no rush of newspapers to join the *Savannah Morning News* in its indictment. But the deeper question remained: how true was Locke's forecast of a renaissance of a people in Harlem if the story of success was marred by serious social, economic, and moral failures? Even a Black New York newspaper questioned Locke's rosy view of Harlem's prospects. The *New York Age* argued Harlem was not a site of economic self-determination. Under the headline: "Survey of Business Development on Seventh Avenue," the *Age* reported, "colored men own 40 percent of business but whites operate the places that net the largest profits."[6] That challenged Locke's assertion that Harlem represented a new phase in Black-White power relations, since from a Marxian perspective, a cultural advance had to reflect a change in economic relations. It also undermined the renaissance analogy, since the *Age*'s statistics suggested that a true bourgeoisie had not emerged in Harlem. How could an economically marginal people produce beauty on a service worker's salary? Locke never accepted the defeatism implicit in the anomalies reported by Lane or the *Age*, but the arguments exposed the economic problem of Black cultural and educational advancement: part of why colleges and universities like Fisk had to have men like McKenzie as president was to beg enough money from philanthropic Whites to keep them afloat. Soon, this would also become an issue for Locke's aesthetic agenda as well.

More stinging critiques of Locke's leadership emerged, however, when at a meeting in Harlem, Paul Kellogg was asked by some residents why Locke, a nonresident, had been chosen as guest editor. Kellogg answered that question and received an ovation; but the implication lingered—Locke was barely known in Harlem. Other African Americans criticized some of Reiss's portraits, especially "Two Public Schoolteachers," which also appeared in the exhibition of Reiss's portraits organized by Ernestine Rose, the librarian at the Harlem branch of the New York Public Library. At a meeting, Elise McDougald wrote Locke, "One

Mr. Williams wondered if the whole art side of the issue were a 'piece of subtle propaganda to prejudice the white reader.' He told us that 'Should he meet those two schoolteachers in the street, he would be afraid of them.' It happened that one of them, Miss Price had come in late with me from another meeting. When an opportune moment arrived, she stood to express her regret that she would frighten him but claimed the portrait as a 'pretty good likeness.'"[7]

Locke reacted swiftly to the challenge made to his editorial authority in selecting Reiss to portray Harlem. Published in the May 1925 issue of *Opportunity*, "To Certain of Our Philistines," Locke called Reiss's critics "Philistines," who were not reacting out of an aesthetic judgment, but out of their own prejudice against the dark-skinned figures in the portraits. Their internal race prejudice "distorts all true artistic values," he wrote, "with the irrelevant social values of 'representative' and 'unrepresentative,' 'favorable' and 'unfavorable'—and threatens a truly racial art with the psychological bleach of 'lily-whitism.' This Philistinism cannot be tolerated." Defending Reiss's portrait of the teachers, he wrote: "It happens to be my particular choice among a group of thirty more or less divergently mannered sketches; and not for the reason that it is one of the most realistic but for the sheer poetry and intense symbolism back of it. I believe this drawing reflects in addition to good type portraiture of its sort, a professional ideal, that peculiar seriousness, that race redemption spirit, that professional earnestness and even sense of burden which I would be glad to think representative of both my profession and especially its racial aspects."[8] It did: both teachers clearly wore Phi Beta Kappa keys with an open magazine, perhaps *Opportunity*, in front of them. As usual, it was their skin color and their unassimilated Negro features that caused the bourgeoisie to recoil.

Being gay, Locke could see the bankruptcy of the Black bourgeoisie's conception of what and who is "representative" in a different light. A Black middle-class viewer of Reiss's portraits might perceive "A College Lad" as representative, because the very light-skinned, Anglo-looking man wearing a suit, and a serious pose, epitomized a Black Victorian ideal. But if this bourgeoisie knew that he was also sometimes a lover of Countee Cullen, then for most of them Harold Jackman would cease to be "representative." By contrast, the teachers, with their dark skin color, tired-looking faces, and relaxed clothing, were perhaps more "representative," on the basis of conventional heterosexual morality, than "A College Lad." Locke saw the irony of such categories and the inability of those who might seem representative in one set of values to live up to all of the criteria the aggressively assimilated imposed on those who "represented" them. The irony of the New Negro movement was that it was led by those like Locke, Cullen, Jackman, Hughes, and Walrond, to name only a few, who were "representative" only because they lived an open secret. Locke, who always hated skin color prejudice among Negroes, knew it was just another indication of the pressing need for a new vision of the ideal society for Black people.

Locke also dismissed the notion that a Negro American artist would have produced better portraits of the Negro. Since American society characterized Black people as lacking in beauty, "Negro artists, themselves victims of the academy-tradition," they tended to avoid serious artistic study of them. Instead, modern European artists, such as Reiss and Auguste Mambour, had developed "a new style or at least a fresh technique" in order to adequately portray a "new subject"—Africans and people of African descent. As a transnationalist, Locke realized that the outsider had something profound to contribute, especially to highly provincial societies. For Locke, that justified his decision to go with Reiss, for being from Europe and having grown up outside of American racial iconography gave him a unique perspective and access to European modernist traditions with which to depict a New Negro, one that transcended even American Negro aesthetic notions of "representativeness."

Beyond simply defending a particular drawing or his choice of Reiss, Locke made an ethical argument. He claimed that the emergence of the New Negro meant the birth of a new set of ideas. One of those was that African American life had moved away from aggressive emulation of White American values toward the search for an alternative, healthy, more self-accepting value system. Another was that the quest for a better life among Blacks was not exclusively racial, that Whites were part of this process, and that progressively minded allies existed among Whites who were critical to the unfolding of a new way of being Black in the world. Perhaps most profoundly, Locke was asserting that Black life and values themselves were going to have to change. The focus on the pigmentation of those who represented the Negro bourgeoisie (or whether they lived in their neighborhoods) had to give way to focus on whether their consciousness enhanced Negro identity and culture. What Locke was attempting with the New Negro was very subtle and perceived by some as dangerous—to stimulate an awakening among Black Americans to their unique cultural particularity, but also demand that that particularity lead to a broader universality and acceptance of internal and external difference than was common in provincial Black communities. National awakening could not be allowed to become knee-jerk essentialism.

The central philosophical dilemma was this: could an oppressed, or at least beleaguered, Black bourgeoisie adopt as its primary way of looking at itself and its community a revolutionary aesthetic perspective that foregrounded youth, rebellion, and the breaking down of self-protective defense mechanisms? Reiss had made an aesthetic breakthrough, but the Black middle class continued to view his work as a social document. Locke's position was that "Art must discover and reveal the beauty which prejudice and caricature have obscured and over-laid."[9] But it could only do so when the aesthetic value of the work was put first. Philistinism was not only a class ideology, but an epistemological predilection built up over years of dealing with White supremacy. While Locke might decry the criticism, the facts of the criticism, that the community felt entitled to critique and challenge its representation in an issue directed at Black people, was a positive. Locke had their attention. The question, as he said faced the New Negro generally, was what was he going to do with it?

The one thing Locke did not have to concern himself with too much was the criticism of Reiss. Reiss's portrait style, with their strong color delineation of Black faces against a white background, was almost immediately emulated by young African American artists, while his African-art inspired abstractions, called "imaginatives," became the design signature, really the visual brand, of the Negro Renaissance. Reiss expressed repeatedly in his interviews that the purpose of his portrait study was to interest a Negro artist in doing similar work. But there was no patron class in Harlem with the money and self-consciousness to keep alive a painter who rendered its image. Almost all of the outlets of African American publishing quickly commissioned Reiss to produce cover images and logos for them after the Harlem number appeared. For what the network of financially strapped, but exciting African American magazines, little journals, newspapers, and cultural events needed was easily reproduced images that communicated a modernist New Negro message. Reiss supplied it, even though he was White. Race was everywhere, even when Locke argued it did not matter.

But race was working for Locke, too. For even before the *Survey Graphic* hit the newsstands, Albert Boni had written to Paul Kellogg to express his interest in publishing a book based on the subject matter covered in the Harlem number. But as Kellogg conveyed to Locke, Boni did not want to "bring out the Harlem number in book form; but to use the materials as perhaps half of the contents of a much more formidable volume which would sell for $4.50 and which he hopes would be taken by every college and library in the country." Kellogg believed that "a volume such as Mr. Boni suggests...by its sheer handsomeness would be a pretty convincing exhibit of the caliber of the Negro Renaissance."[10] Boni's plan would "involve cutting down what would come from the Survey," which was fine with Kellogg, but which meant that there would be considerable more work editing the new material. Since he insisted that Locke be the sole editor, Kellogg encouraged him to think over the proposal carefully as it would involve considerable more work. Its benefits would be obvious. By transposing the Harlem issue into a nationally pivoted book, he would elude the criticism that he was not the most appropriate representative of Harlem. And in a book version, he would have the opportunity to include the work of several artists, perhaps "the work of a Negro artist in the new book," as Mrs. McDougald would later suggest to Kellogg.[11]

Locke leaped at the opportunity, because Boni's conception of the book matched his. "I am inclined to think," he wrote back to Kellogg, "that we have already so to speak had the popular edition with the Survey issues—and that the effective thing to do now is <u>document</u> even to a de luxe extent if Mr. Boni is willing to take the chances, The New Negro. And I quite agree with his desire for considerable new material:—I can immediately suggest the following:—enlarging Johnson's sketch to a full discussion of the economic situation in the larger city centers, 2. A chapter on The Negro in American Literature (I have the material already at hand for this) 3. A companion essay on The Spirituals to the Jazz article (material also in hand), 4. a chapter on Negro Leadership with a discussion of policies projected through personalities,—using the Reiss sketches...5. a chapter on Negro Education, and 6. enlarging Haynes article to discuss The Negro and Christianity."[12] While Locke did his thinking, the *Survey Graphic* sounded out other publishers and discovered that all of them turned down the project. Only Maxwell Perkins at Scribner's said he would be interested, but only if a single author wrote the book.[13] Boni was the only publisher who wanted to bring out a multi-authored anthology of the "cultural revival as a whole" and tap the same market primed by the *Survey Graphic*. That suited Locke just fine, and he encouraged Kellogg to finalize arrangements with Boni. With any luck, he opined, he could get the volume out soon, perhaps "before the middle of June, when I hope to get abroad again."[14]

Given that Locke assumed the book would be out in the summer, he made plans once again to fund his travel abroad with a Kahn Traveling Fellowship. Here again was the pattern that Howard University had observed but Locke had ignored. At every chance, he made plans to be away from the university, from Washington, either editing manuscripts in Harlem or planning yet another scheme to live off his journalistic writings globally. Of course, Locke was a master at rationalizing such schemes. The racial consciousness he had documented in Harlem was part of a transnational phenomenon, such that travel by a man of color to India, Japan, China, and the continent of Africa would open up their "representative leaders" to talk openly about race, nationalism, and the view of the West. Locke was aware that a broader, anti-European, anti-colonialist "renaissance" was taking place in Africa and Asia, hopefully with the same aspirations to find in art and culture an ethics for self-determination. Indeed, one could argue that Egypt, India, and Japan were constructing their own hyper-nationalist movements for liberation. Locke wanted to assess whether such movements were reactions to or attempts to transcend the racializing narratives of their oppressors. Locke also trotted out his notion of the "passport of color," that is, that "the mind of representative people in the Eastern continents is on the whole more open to a person obviously non-Nordic these days."[15]

Building on his successful working relationship with Kellogg, Locke asked him to write the letter nominating him for the fellowship. But Kellogg, exhibiting his usual perspicacious resourcefulness, also sent around a copy of his letter and Locke's proposal, to Elise McDougald, George Foster Peabody, and Albert Shaw—people whom Kellogg said might be better known to the Kahn people than he was. Though Kellogg recommended Locke enthusiastically, he also wrote Locke that it was a mistake for him to be abroad with so much going on in the

United States. It was an odd decision, on Locke's part, to desert America, and especially "Harlem," which, he had said himself was the most important Negro community in the world. With work on *The New Negro* at hand, and with the numerous other domestic opportunities to exploit it sure to follow its publication, why leave for India? Locke was establishing a pattern that his patron would later critique of escaping from the work he had begun. Most likely it was sex: he could better live the life of the homosexual gentleman of culture abroad than in New York. The Kahn people, however, turned down his fellowship. Documenting the "rising tide of color" of anti-Western consciousness was beyond what they wanted to be associated with, especially should it reach print.

As with the Harlem number, work on the book anthology went slower than expected. Apparently, by the second week of April, Boni had not made a definitive commitment to Reiss. Kellogg relayed to Locke that Reiss "had had some experiences with Mr. Boni and felt that one was not certain of him unless things were in black and white: he was a difficult man to deal with and rather inclined to gouge." This insight was particularly important, since Reiss had begun to feel a "bit disconsolate" over the lack of attention his work had garnered in the art establishment.[16] Reiss would receive a nice notice in the *New York Times*, but the major art reviews, galleries, and patrons ignored his work. The lack of a patron class in Harlem meant that there was no rush of sales; Reiss had sold only the portrait of Robert Moton, which had been purchased by George Foster Peabody, who intended to donate it to Hampton Institute. Locke did not want to lose the interest of Reiss at this crucial date, for he was committed to having Reiss's "sketches" in the volume. Fortunately, by the end of April, a firm contract with Locke, Reiss, and the *Survey Graphic* had been executed by Boni to produce *The New Negro: An Interpretation*.

Locke also responded favorably to Mrs. MacDougald's suggestion that he include the work of Negro visual artists in the book. Fortunately, in St. Louis, the young African American artist and future muralist Aaron Douglas had been so moved by the cover design of the Harlem issue of the *Survey Graphic* that he moved to New York to become one of Reiss's students. Douglas began to master the technique of using African design as the basis for an African American interpretive design based on African motifs. Douglas produced a half-dozen sketches for the book, showcasing the emergence of a fine artist from the race. Here was Locke again performing his signature role—taking criticism and turning it into a modus vivendi between contending camps—his that Reiss should illustrate the volume because he was the best artist to do it, others that a Negro renaissance ought to feature a Negro visual artist as well. Locke's approach made good political and commercial sense.

Including Douglas was only one of the moves Locke made to distinguish *The New Negro* from the *Survey Graphic*. He asked younger scholars to research new essays to document the wider context of the New Negro. Budding sociologist

E. Franklin Frazier gladly agreed to do an essay on the Black middle class in Durham, North Carolina, even though he knew little about the subject, because the request was one of the few opportunities for "self-expression" he had as a scholar "in the South."[17] Locke tapped Arthur Fauset to contribute an essay on one of the newest areas of research, Negro folklore, the subject of his doctorate at the University of Pennsylvania. And Locke asked his former colleague Montgomery Gregory to contribute on the "drama of Negro Life." Perhaps most interesting, Locke asked the sharp-witted critic, Heywood Broun, a regular of the Algonquin Round Table, to contribute an essay, though Broun begged off, because of a recent nervous breakdown. Documenting that the New Negro was a national phenomenon led Locke to attempt to suggest that it was a cosmopolitan one, as well. And Locke asked creative writers and poets like Eric Walrond, who had been left out of the *Survey Graphic*, to give him some of their latest writings. Given his desire for such new work, the inevitable resulted, and by the end of May, few of the new commissioned works had come in.

Not surprisingly, work on the new book gave Locke ample reason to spend more time up in Harlem that spring, which brought him considerable recognition there for the work he had done and continued to do. Ernestine Rose honored him with a reception at the library during the second week of April. Guests were a veritable who's who of the New York Black elite, and Locke was the featured speaker on an occasion that also prominently displayed Reiss's recent portrait of Locke. The next week Locke was again up in Harlem to deliver a speech on "The New Negro" at the "Big Meeting" at the YMCA Auditorium at 181 W. 135th Street. He was also a prominent participant on a program again at the library to mark the creation of the Department of Negro Literature and History based on the personal collection of Arthur Schomburg. But his greatest reward must have come when he attended the dinner for the *Opportunity* Awards, which he judged along with prominent White writers and cultural custodians Carl Van Doren, Zona Gale, Fannie Hurst, and Dorothy Scarborough. Locke had done something no other Black man had done: he had taken over a White publication and made it speak a Black message. Doing so, Locke showed Charles S. Johnson what he was capable of if he was paid for his work.[18]

Just as Locke was receiving all of this New York attention, events at Howard University returned his attention to Washington, D.C.—more than a month before he was fired. On May 7, students at Howard struck in protest against a rule by which "when a student has accumulated a total of twenty unexcused absences in physical education and ROTC combined, he shall be dropped from the college."[19] When the university suspended five students on May 5 for violation of the twenty-cut rule, the students organized a mass meeting and refused to attend classes until the students were reinstated and the rule changed. Students were already angry about the arbitrary system, supported by President Durkee, of recording and punishing students who did not attend chapel. But the May strike was less directed at the president and more at the faculty, especially the faculty of the Physical Education Department and the ROTC, who kept inadequate records of absences, sometimes suspended students who missed only a few classes, and wielded more power over the students than other academic faculty. Moreover, many students saw mandatory ROTC training as an anomaly in the aftermath of Black participation in the World War. Coupled with that sentiment against worthless military training was a rising desire for less demeaning treatment of students and the specific request that several "unproductive" White teachers be removed from the faculty and replaced with younger, "New Negro" Black teachers. The strike, therefore, embodied the themes of self-determination and racial leadership Locke had elucidated in the *Survey Graphic*, and not surprisingly, he was supportive of the student action.

Students brought education to a halt at Howard. A tumultuous meeting on May 10 outlined a path of reconciliation. Representing the students, a committee including Glenn Carrington, a former student and lifelong friend of Locke's, presented a list of demands, which included that no student participating in the strike be penalized, that no "cuts" be counted against students, and that no student be suspended over the twenty-cut rule. More broadly, students demanded that the administration review the policy of cuts for non-attendance at ROTC classes, reduce the number of years of physical education, in accord with other more "academic" requirements, and review the autumn schedule of physical education classes to make sure it did not prevent students from taking required academic classes to graduate. More fundamentally, students wanted a bigger role in planning and scheduling social and academic activities at Howard.[20]

Locke sympathized with the students' generational demand for more self-determination in their education. But strikingly, his was not the prevailing view among the faculty. Some, like finance professor Orlando Thompson, vehemently opposed the student position as a threat to faculty rights. Locke understood that the faculty, which was already feeling dominated by the administration, might not want to lose any remaining authority to the students. But Locke felt the faculty would gain more respect from students by trying to find a compromise, especially since he believed that such duties as ROTC training had to be self-imposed to be meaningful. At the meetings, Locke used his status as secretary of the faculty salaries committee, on the one hand, and his clout among students, on the other, to try to harmonize the values of faculty authority and student self-determination. Locke helped get the faculty to accept the principle that students should not be penalized for participating in the strike, and that the faculty would work with the administration to try and revise the rules on penalizing students for failure to participate in physical education classes. Meanwhile, students would be expected to continue to attend those classes without incident until the review was completed.

Despite Locke's role in resolving the strike, some in the administration felt that he was too sympathetic with the students and that, combined with his controversial advocacy for faculty raises, he was becoming a problem. Of the two issues, it appears that his role as committee secretary brought him the most negative attention from the board of trustees, who concluded that their continuing struggle with the faculty over salaries would be eased somewhat if he was not around. That same May 1924, Locke, along with several other faculty, signed a letter of petition to the board of trustees expressing that the faculty was regretful "that there is little resulting relief" from the board, which had refused to take action on their pleas to increase salaries to bring them in line with professors at similar institutions and the result was outmigration of talented faculty. The faculty acted because the administration had increased the academic incidental fee charged to students, and the faculty wanted a portion of that increase to go to their salary increase. The administration had other ideas and announced that all of the additional sum would go to removing the debt, which many of the faculty believed had accrued at least in part because of increases in the expenses of the administration. The faculty issued another memorandum criticizing the decision to spend all of the money on the debt. The board was getting tired of this constant haranguing, and Jesse E. Moorland, Locke's nemesis, hit upon a way to stop it.

At the board's June meeting, the board voted to appoint a special committee to study the issue of faculty salaries and make recommendations in October. At that October meeting, the committee, which included Moorland, recommended that the board allocate $15,100 to raising salaries, including those of the clerical staff. Also, the committee "recommends the employment of an Educational Expert to make a survey of the University operation of the Administrative and Academic Departments" to ascertain where cost-saving changes could be instituted. One of the members of the board raised the question as to whether the clerical staff raises were within the "construction of the vote taken . . . authorizing the Special Budget Committee." It was not, but the board decided that such a move was in the spirit of the earlier decision.

Needless to say, that decision left the faculty angry. Indeed, those on Locke's committee saw this as a deliberate attempt to humiliate the faculty. After meeting on the issue, the board received a "Communication dated January 8, 1925, from Dr. Locke, as Secretary of the Faculty Committee on Salaries, transmitting a request" to meet with the board. Instead, the board referred the matter to the budget committee. The board had effectively rid itself of having to deal with the faculty over salaries by referring all of its challenges to the budget committee, headed by Moorland. What the faculty did not see in this scenario was that Moorland and company had found in the "survey of the University operation" a means to get rid of the faculty it regarded as troublemakers.

Early in June, rumors of impending dismissals began to appear in the local Black newspaper, the *Washington Bee*. Locke confronted President Durkee about the rumors. He denied the rumors, then contradicted himself by saying that all such decisions were out of his hands. When the board met on June 15, 1925, the budget committee presented the results of the survey conducted by Dr. R. J. Leonard, of the Teachers College at Columbia University. It appears that the survey's only substantive recommendation was to eliminate the jobs of a few faculty who were associated with the salary effort. Kelly Miller was removed as dean of the College of Arts and Sciences; Dean Cook of the Finance Department was forced into retirement; and three professors, including Locke, were "discontinued." Emmett Scott, long an adversary of Locke's, must have enjoyed writing the June 14 letter that sent Locke packing.

Locke was furious. Suddenly, after thirteen years at Howard, he was fired for being a New Negro—standing up for the rights of Black scholars and intellectuals at Howard University. Here was the premier African American university in the nation firing its most educated faculty member, because he was too outspoken in a legitimate labor issue. Of course, such philosophical considerations were far from Locke's thoughts as he contemplated his next move. But Locke must have realized that he really had few options. Despite the plethora of institutions for the education of the race, where was a professor labeled as a troublemaker going to find work in the conservative world of Black higher education? Hampton and Tuskegee were not live options, given that Locke had rather high-handedly left them out of the *Survey Graphic*. Fisk was nearly under house arrest in the wake of its White president's forced resignation after months of student protests. While Fisk's Board of Trustees knew they had to go in a new direction, they were certainly not going to take a chance on a malcontent whose services were labeled as expendable.

Spending the last three years on sabbaticals to Europe did not help his case. Even when he was teaching, Locke was frequently off campus. In February 1924, President Durkee had written Locke inquiring how he had met his classes given that he had been observed giving a speech in Chicago during the middle of the week. Clearly, that was a warning sign, but Locke failed to heed it. He also failed to realize that Moorland was a powerful enemy. Moorland had developed a dislike for Locke in 1923 when he requested funding for his European-Africa research trip, which Moorland had turned down on the grounds that it was less important than the building of the medical school. Moorland was also a confidant of William Leo Hansberry, whom Locke had mistreated the previous year. Believing that Locke would undermine his attempt to get a course, "Negro Civilizations of Ancient Africa," adopted at the university, Hansberry carried out a campaign that lobbied Moorland to support his course and peppered Moorland with innuendo about the disloyalty and selfish interests of other members of the faculty. Hansberry even suggested that some faculty were eager to bring the various controversies over salaries and policies at Howard University to the press. Hansberry made it clear that he was on the side of the university in this matter, and work behind the scenes paid off. Ten days before Locke received his letter of dismissal, Howard announced that it would host Hansberry's "Symposium on Ancient African History." Locke had not just been blindsided, but cuckolded as well.[21]

But Locke's dismissal was also part of a larger maneuver by the Howard Board of Trustees to eliminate those professors who embodied and exemplified the New Negro criticality that Locke had announced in the *Survey Graphic*—a criticality that stemmed from a belief in their own intellectual independence. In addition to Locke, three other instructors were fired: Professor Alonzo H. Brown, Assistant Professor Metz T. P. Lochard, and Instructor Orlando C. Thornton. While Locke's dismissal was as unfair as it was unanticipated, it was also part of a broader challenge the New Negro had overcome to prove that philosophy as a course of study stood for something. Now he like the others was being tested as to whether his New Negro was merely rhetoric or a serious project that could win in a head-on confrontation with old Negro education's hegemony.

Locke's first response was to write back to Scott, saying that he had received the notice, but that his formal response would come later. He needed time to think, to consult with others, including Paul Kellogg, George Foster Peabody, and Jesse Jones—the latter two key players in the Fisk controversy—and compose a more comprehensive argument against the "discontinuance." He then wrote a more formal letter to Charles Brown, president of the board of trustees, protesting the action primarily on the grounds of procedures. The board of trustees had justified his "discontinuance" on the necessity of economic consolidation. But Locke argued that selecting who should be let go should be made in terms of "academic seniority, relative scholastic qualifications." Since he was a full professor and one of the most published faculty, Locke argued that others less senior should have been selected for dismissal. Moreover, this selection should have come "from my immediate academic superiors, the Deans," who historically had wielded considerable power at Howard. Locke also asserted that his dismissal violated his academic tenure and the normal expectation that an employee would be granted a personal hearing before the board.[22] As Locke would learn from lawyers he hired to examine his case, his contract with the university did not grant him tenure, even if he had been renewed yearly without evaluation. And the university was under no obligation to grant him a hearing, because the dismissal had not been based on any "specific" charges against him, but simply for economy, a rationale that took away redress.

Locke argued, further, that he should have been given the opportunity to propose other solutions to the demand to economize, such as his doubling up and teaching psychology or education, which he had done in the past. Here Locke hinted that he realized that William Nelson, a graduate of the Yale School of

Divinity, was being used to cover Locke's classes and render him unnecessary. An underlying thread of the action against Locke was to restore religion as the focal point of spiritual inquiry at Howard and erase what was an anomaly that Howard was the only Black college to teach philosophy, let alone to keep a full-time full professor of philosophy on its teaching staff. That Locke was a philosopher was also part of a larger perception that the board and Durkee may have had when deciding to fire him. The key phrase in the "discontinuance" letter was that "your place, among others, it was decided, could be vacated and the work of the University not unduly suffer." Locke, however, kept the focus of his letter on procedure: as a long-standing teacher, he ought to have been given an opportunity to challenge his dismissal. He ended his letter by petitioning for a "review and reconsideration of his case, with a personal hearing" before the board.

Brown responded that "as a university man, you" should know that all such decisions were the university president's and recommended that Locke see Durkee "regarding matters discussed." It was untrue. As Locke would point out in his reply, his decision to write Brown was based on his conference with Durkee, who had informed him that "these matters were 'entirely out of his hands' and had been placed by the Board in the hands of the Budget and Executive Committees, whose action would be issued by the Secretary-Treasurer." Locke had detected already that both the board and Durkee were trying to avoid responsibility for the decision to fire him.

Certainly, Durkee was an obvious suspect. He was a member of the board and had participated in its decision about Locke. And some of the other actions approved by the board when it dismissed Locke suggested that Durkee was at the least using the consolidation rationale to settle old scores and remove from leadership positions faculty who represented New Negro attitudes. Durkee had previously approved the creation of the College of Liberal Arts, which removed Kelly Miller as its dean, and had also supported closing the School of Finance, thereby forcing into retirement its dean, George William Cook, another of Locke's friends. When the Howard University Club of New York City adopted a resolution in June calling for Durkee's removal, it accused the president of demoting two faculty members from directing the Howard University Glee Club and Choral Society "for no other palpable reason than that at a recent convention in Washington, under conditions that were discriminatory, insulting and humiliating, the students of the Glee Club and Choral Society refused to sing, (and rightly so), and were supported in their praiseworthy stand by Professors Tibbs and Childers to the utter displeasure of the President of the University."[23] Durkee failed to understand the New Negro sentiment among African American students in the 1920s that opposed the singing of the spirituals before White folks to raise money for Black schools. Some Black students also felt that such performances made a spectacle of Black culture and fed White desires for a return to the rituals of deference developed under slavery. The Glee Club made the case that the president punished those who were New Negroes and who supported Black students' refusal to endure racial abuse from paternalistic Whites. The club concluded that Durkee used the dismissals and reassignments "to discipline those who" exemplified this New Negro spirit of racial pride, and that for that reason he had "outlived his usefulness at the University."

But Locke and Durkee's relationship had not been particularly contentious. Durkee had been quite forthcoming in granting Locke many leaves of absence, some of which included partial salary. He had also supported Locke's effort to establish a faculty and student research program in Africa and had written letters endorsing Locke's efforts to foreign scholars. It was true that Durkee had reprimanded Locke in 1920–1921 for failure to attend chapel; but that was four years earlier and a relatively minor infraction, committed by numerous other professors. By 1924, Durkee had conceded the rule was unenforceable. Interestingly, the incident about the students' singing of the spirituals was one of the few real conflicts between Locke and Durkee. On one occasion, Locke had discussed with students in his classroom the issue of whether singing the spirituals was objectionable, for which Durkee had reprimanded him. Neither of these incidents was enough to explain the decision to fire him.

On the other hand, Locke's constant challenging of the board over more money for the professors, along with his perceived sympathy for the student strike, did rise to the level of annoyance that would bring retaliation by the university. Locke's talent was also a problem for the board. His writing and expository skills helped make the faculty case over money issues against the administration more powerful and biting than it would have been otherwise. Unlike his cordial correspondence with Durkee, Locke's correspondence with Moorland was filled with tension. Durkee had supported the overall move against the professors, because it gave him an opportunity to punish noncompliants. But the action originated with a board member with considerable animus toward Locke, and was a board decision.

Regardless of who was most responsible for his dismissal, it was a crisis in Locke's life that forced him to change his approach to his public persona, to become, in a word, political in a way he had avoided in the past. To get his job back, he would have to make himself a public figure and project his struggle as more significant than his reinstatement. Only a campaign that brought a fundamental change in the administration, and the quality of life at Howard, would rationalize his retaliation against the administration as something higher than mere self-interest. Only then would his struggle become heroic. But the search for the hero in Locke would have to begin with a search for the villain who could be blamed not just for his dismissal, but for the general degradation of the educational mission of Howard.

Charles Brown gave Locke and his allies the villain they needed when he shifted onto Durkee the onus for the decision to dismiss Locke and the other professors. That act of bad faith on Brown's part created an opportunity for

Locke to link his personal loss to the desire of many other Negroes to use this conflict to bring New Negro leadership to Howard University. To make that connection, Locke would have to publicly identify his cause with the radical campaign of the Washington-based Howard alumni associations that had wanted to remove Durkee for some time. The dismissals and demotions gave these groups a cause célèbre around which to rally against Durkee. In their propaganda effort, the dismissals became evidence, as the historian Raymond Wolters points out, that Durkee was "punishing independent scholars" and had created an environment at Howard in which "servility has displaced scholarship and manhood." That rhetoric aroused the Black population.[24] The Student Council also characterized the dismissals as a campaign to remove those instructors who "refused to go along with the administration ... [and] as a warning to other members of the faculty that unless they think less of academic freedom and more of the administration's program, they, too, will be dismissed."[25] Such a narrative of disciplining and punishing academic freedom would have been difficult to explain away at a White college; but at a Black university, administered by a White president, the regime of domination translated into racial paternalism. The board's early unwillingness to take full responsibility for the dismissals effectively singled out a White man, Durkee, to be the scapegoat for a decision that had emanated from an interracial board of trustees. In effect, the board made the issue of the dismissals more racial than it really was and handed the enemies of the administration just the kind of justification they needed to fuel continued resistance to the decision. The moral challenge for Locke and the other opponents of the administration was how much to wage the battle overtly on racial grounds. If the opposition was made to Durkee purely on racial grounds, then Locke would lose the high moral ground of the openness of the New Negro movement to White participation that he had painstakingly argued.

Durkee complicated the racial situation with his bad judgment. In April 1925, he accepted a request from his alma mater to direct the Curry School of Expression in Boston, a school that barred African Americans as students. A firestorm of criticism emerged after the strike as students, faculty, and alumni questioned why a man who headed a university for Black education would consent to run a Whites-only school. Although Durkee resigned a few months after accepting the position, the damage to his reputation had been done. Durkee's desire for absolute control and his insensitivity to the politics of racial representation in America was read by Blacks as racial. Durkee, in turn, probably reacted to the resistance to his policies as resistance to him because he was White. That led him to be stubborn and monopolistic in his approach to the alumni associations that elected a secretary who represented the alumni's views to the administration. Durkee, however, decided to reject the secretary that the alumni associations proposed and "force," in the words of Arthur Mitchell, the president of the Howard Welfare League, "upon the Alumni a secretary of his own personal choice." That man, Emory Smith, took it upon himself to undermine the legiti-macy of the Washington-based alumni associations by arguing that their views were not representative of all of the alumni. In effect, Durkee was attempting to silence his New Negro critics. But that move backfired. By the end of the summer the Washington-based alumni carried out their own campaign and had the sup-port of fifteen different alumni associations for the removal of Durkee as presi-dent. In the final analysis, the issue that confronted Howard was not racial, but political: was Howard to be run as a democratic institution, responsible to the will of Black people, who were its most important constituency? Or was Howard to be an institution in which the board and its president dictated policy? That question would be answered in eight months.

Before publicly supporting this campaign to remove Durkee, Locke tried to work individually and privately to get his job back. At the end of his second letter to Brown, he confided that he had refrained from public protest in the newspa-pers, pending a private reconsideration of his case. As a Black Victorian, he had always prided himself on being on the right side of how things were supposed to be done and had used procedure against his enemies whenever he could. The questions that would inevitably be raised as to why he was chosen for dismissal had the potential of probing into his personal fitness for teaching and his barely cloaked homosexuality. While it is not clear that anyone in the administration knew for certain that he was gay, some at Howard did. It was generally known that he was unmarried, effeminate, and the subject, from time to time, of rumors and innuendos. Locke's sexual orientation was partly shielded by the plethora of Black scholars, such as Carter G. Woodson, who were confirmed, almost asexual, bachelors. Moreover, gentlemen and ladies on the faculty or in the administra-tion did not discuss homosexuality publicly, although they probably did pri-vately. As Locke planned his next move, he had to consider whether something would surface that could be used by the administration to discredit him if he criticized the university too forcefully. Locke would have tried to find out if the administration had any incriminating information or any disgruntled or accus-ing student, who might try to justify his dismissal on the grounds of public im-morality. No such information surfaced.

Locke could not completely rule out the possibility that questions about his personal relationships with students might have added some extra suspicion to the administration's view of him as a teacher. The attack on Locke could easily have been a clandestine way of suggesting that his tutelage of young men was morally as well as intellectually unsavory. Yet once it became clear to Locke that the board was not going to give him a private, individual opportunity to get his job back, he did not hesitate to fight, perhaps realizing that any hesitancy might draw attention to the sense that he might have something to hide. Even so, after he decided to fight his dismissal, Locke modulated his public statements early in the process to avoid becoming more of a target than he already was.

First, Locke canceled his trip to Europe. Without a sense of where his next check was to come from, Locke knew he could not waste any money on a vacation abroad. Second, work on *The New Negro* became even more important than before. He knew that his only chance for survival, especially if he refused to apply for other teaching work in order to keep the pressure on Howard, was to get the book out as quickly as possible, and use it as a basis for a lecture and speaking tour. Fortunately, that was well underway. Early in July, Reiss began work on the color plates for the book, and Locke obtained prints and etchings from Aaron Douglas. Getting the final manuscripts from his contributors was still a struggle. But the prospects for a late fall publication looked good in early July.

Almost as a relief, Locke elected to travel to Green Acre Baha'i School in Eliot, Maine, to attend the Baha'i Retreat meeting, the Seventeenth Annual Convention and Congress of the Baha'is of the United States and Canada. Taking place on a private estate, this large gathering of the faithful buoyed Locke's spirits. He spoke on July 5 on "The Dawn of Peace." Going to the Baha'i conference reinforced the side of Locke that was committed to universalism, to fostering a common ground among diverse peoples, despite the conflicts that divide them. But Locke's speech also reflected his realism. As he told the multiracial, multicultural, international audience assembled before him, "Today on this earth there are many souls who are the spreaders of peace and reconciliation and are longing for the realization of the oneness and unity of the world of man; but his intention needs a dynamic power so that it may become manifest in the world of being." That statement was almost an autobiographical transcript. Locke had been a harmonizing force in the arts, in the area of race relations, and in campus relations at Howard. But his dismissal was showing him that in order for a man of peace and reconciliation to prevail, he needed to harness his "dynamic power" to force change on those opposing it, when reconciliation and persuasion were not enough to carry the day. Locke was going to have to become much more of a participant in protest than in the past.

Locke returned from the peaceful universalism of Maine to confront his next step in his response to the dismissal. By late July there was no reply from Brown to his petition for a reconsideration and a personal hearing before the board. President Durkee had been studiously absent from Washington for much of the summer. The board and the president could simply ignore Locke, and eventually the public, even the Black public, would forget about him. If he wanted any chance of getting his job back, he would have to join the alumni clubs, especially Arthur Mitchell's Washington-based organization, and assist their campaign to remove Durkee from his position. Joining that campaign might not get his job back, but at least he would have the satisfaction of getting back at Durkee, whom Locke had identified as responsible for his dismissal. Locke did not know, it seems, that Durkee was not the main person responsible, but it was easier to focus on one individual, a White father figure, than to attack the entire board. Over the next six months, Locke would marshal all of his resources to undermine Durkee. In his mind, Durkee had fired him; now, he would fire Durkee.

Locke began to work aggressively with Arthur Mitchell to use his dismissal as a key indictment against Durkee. On August 8, Mitchell issued a press release that utilized information provided by Locke to blame Durkee for the turmoil at Howard University. Titled "The Case of the Howard Professors Decapitated by the Durkee Regime," Mitchell's press release claimed that "President Durkee worked to coerce heads of departments and deans into recommending the dismissal of certain men...and failing this, he presented the recommendation himself. In reply to their inquiries he informed them, it is alleged, that the immediate superiors of these men recommended that they be dropped, and that these men had been forewarned by complaints of their unsatisfactory work. Investigation shows, however, that these men had never received such complaints; and that on the contrary, some of them have been recently complimented on the efficiency of their work." This allegation against Durkee's lying about the consent of the deans derived from Locke's research and questioning of some of the trustees as to how he was selected to be dismissed. Since the Leonard Report had not identified which instructors ought to be let go in the cost-cutting move, the decision as to whom to fire was a board decision. The charge that "some of them have been recently complimented" was confirmed by Orlando Thornton, who had been praised by Durkee during the preceding semester as one of the most efficient professors on campus. Mitchell concluded: "President Durkee stands adjudged a prevaricator, despotically murdering educators because of some suspicion which may have arisen in his diseased mind. It is known that his mind feeds upon rumors, that almost anything will set him in action, and he acts without investigation."[26]

Mitchell's attack is noteworthy, because he avoided a racial attack on Durkee and instead caricatured him as a lunatic administrator. His publication also exposed that the university had made a public relations mistake by firing Locke. As Mitchell pointed out: "This drastic action becomes more apparent when one considers the type of men dismissed. One is a Rhodes Scholar, the only Negro who has ever attained such an honor; and he is a Doctor of Philosophy of Harvard University....If a man of such ripe scholarships as that of Dr. Locke cannot teach at Howard University, the administration cannot be endeavoring to run Howard as an institution of learning." The conclusion Mitchell led his readers to make, especially after he listed other Black scholars who had left the university in recent years because of conflicts with Durkee, was that "Howard was established as a university; to-day it is a political machine. It once had an educator at its head; it now has an elocutionary monstrosity." When Dean Brown issued a statement backing this "elocutionary monstrosity," the board's intransigence enraged the alumni and brought more supporters to Mitchell and his campaign.[27]

Even as Locke became more publicly involved in the attack on Durkee, he tried to remain in the background, coordinating the effort. Locke avoided the public outspokenness that Du Bois had adopted in his campaign against Fisk. On one level, that would not have made sense as a strategy if he wanted to get his job back. On another level, Locke's strategy reflected a Machiavellian view of conflict, that the high-mindedness of Howard's goals could only be realized—as he had stated at the Baha'i conference—by those willing to wield real power and force change.

Despite his reverence for reminding those in struggle to keep their attention on the higher ideals, Locke was a master tactician, a vicious in-fighter, who was willing to use all effective means at his disposal to bring down Durkee and those who had violated him. He saw educational conflict in America as a regime of power; and he believed that such regimes had to be opposed by alternative sources of power. But since he was relatively weak compared to the administration, he approached this conflict from a safe distance from which he could not be hurt. But he was also successfully using skills he had developed as a gay Black man, who often used hidden, secretive relationships, and a network of undercover alliances, to outmaneuver adversaries, apply pressure, and disseminate damaging information.

Locke's connections with students were particularly important in this regard, because they gave him another flank in his attack on the university. His student connections were particularly important because they were more focused on the reinstatement of their professors than were the alumni. As one student who wrote Locke put it: "The program of the students would be the restoration of our Professors. As to the removal of the President we are leaving to the alumni + others." Students also wanted to organize "leading business men" from the community to pressure the administration to restore the "school of finance + commerce" that had been the other significant action of the board at its June meeting. Whereas the alumni focused their attack primarily in the newspapers and public forums, the students and recent graduates privately planned acts of disruption in the fall and asked Locke's advice on strategy and tactics. Current students planned to picket the university, launch a publicity campaign drawing attention to the dismissals, hold mass meetings on campus in September, and communicate their criticisms to Congress, which largely funded Howard. At the same time, students sent representatives to congressional hearings on the budget to advocate for large appropriations for the school, as a way to combat the administration's "propaganda" in the newspapers that criticism of the administration was part of a campaign to destroy the university. Students led a fundraising campaign and communicated to Locke that many in the Black intelligentsia, such as Carter G. Woodson, A. Philip Randolph, and others had contributed money because they believed his treatment was fundamentally unjust. Students also asked Locke's advice on how to approach the faculty about a student strike in the fall, as they did not want to be diverted from their main goal—to get him and other faculty reinstated—by faculty resistance to yet another student-led disruption of classes. Rather than being a weakness, Locke's close relationships with his students were paying dividends. This sense of commitment to serve the larger community of Howard rather than simply their own self-aggrandizement was especially to be praised, from Locke's perspective, because it was a self-imposed, internally felt "duty" of young men, brought out by their "loyalty" to Locke.[28]

Yet, in order to be recognized as a leader in the struggle, Locke would have to publicly address those aspects of the Howard situation that went beyond simply his trying to get his job back. Locke was now a public intellectual, who had committed himself to attacking those elements in his community that stood in the way of the development of New Negro consciousness. But in both the Harlem number and especially in "Philistines," Locke's harshest criticism had been of Blacks as impediments to the New Negro consciousness. Now, whether he liked it or not, he had lent his name and reputation to a conflict that led directly to criticizing a White power structure in Negro education. In that sense, the Howard struggle had become a testing ground for the New Negro movement. Were the forces of White paternalist control of Negro institutions and Old Negro lackeyism going to carry the day at Howard and, by implication, at other Negro colleges? Or were the younger generations of Negro students and faculty strong enough to force the modernization of Black education in the 1920s?

Paul Kellogg had provided Locke with a perfect opportunity to address these issues before he was fired. When the Hampton people had contacted Kellogg to complain that they were left out of the Harlem number of the *Survey Graphic*, Locke and Kellogg had agreed that Locke would do a separate article on Negro education, with which Reiss's portraits of Moton and Du Bois might be illustrated. As early as March 11, Kellogg began to pepper Locke with requests to get going on the article, but working on *The New Negro* had kept this article on the back burner. Sensitive to the need to placate the industrial education wing of Negro education, Locke had accepted an invitation to speak at the commencement exercises of Hampton Institute, where he showcased the posture he had hoped to take in the article itself—that of a referee, again—between contending interpretations of Negro education. As reported in the newspapers, his speech was a model of Locke's role as a harmonizer of values, as he argued that the old divisiveness between collegiate and industrial education for the Negro had passed. In Locke's words, there was "a vision of common task behind a difference of program." This was a welcome message at Hampton, which, like Tuskegee, had received a large proportion of White philanthropy because of White feeling that training Negroes in the work of "the hands," as Locke put it, was most appropriate for a race of former slaves. But Hampton and Tuskegee were also stung by criticism that their educational systems were part of the Old Negro tradition;

and to have the messenger of the New Negro anoint their program as part of the "new movement" was gratifying to say the least.

Locke's tone of harmonious reconciliation between the liberal arts and the vocational wings of Negro higher education showcased in the Hampton speech became less relevant once he was dismissed from Howard. He was now considered a radical. As Locke began to draft his article, "Negro Education Bids for Par," to appear in the September "Education" issue of the *Survey Graphic*, his focus and orientation of the article changed. This was to be more of a statement of the philosophy of New Negro education, the second installment in "Enter the New Negro," than the conciliatory statement of a "referee."

Locke's article, "Negro Education Bids for Par," was a searching philosophical critique of how higher education in America was lived as a racial formation, a travesty of the democratic responsibility to educate citizens equally. "A recent appeal in the Tuskegee-Hampton endowment campaign estimates that the Negroes, constituting about one-tenth of the total population, receive less than 2 per cent of the billion dollars annually spent here for education; and of $875,000,000 spent annually on public schools, only a little more than one per cent is expended for Negroes."[29] For Locke, the battle was another double enterprise that had to be waged on two fronts—to pressure southern and other school districts to equalize funding and facilities in Negro education and view it as a public responsibility, not a private charity; and to develop a philosophy of Negro education that dealt with the reality that most Negro students were educated under segregated conditions "designed to demoralize the Negro at a particularly sensitive time in his personal and racial adolescence." Locke argued that Negro education had to be transformed to break the grip of deferential servitude perpetuated by "caste" education and fashion a new image of the Negro student as both competent and assertive. Locke wanted to foster for most college-bound Blacks the education for leadership he had received at Central High, Harvard, and Oxford in American Negro institutions of higher education.

Locke argued Negro liberal arts education needed to acknowledge its weaknesses and welcome a radical redefinition of its mission and its leadership. Negro liberal arts institutions had fallen behind Black vocational schools in the task to develop a Black leadership class because they were dominated by a conservative ideology of missionarism that strangled attempts at native leadership. It might seem odd that Locke used the term "missionarism" in an article ostensibly about Howard, which, though founded through the efforts of the American Missionary Association, was never under denominational control. But the missionary spirit still dominated at Howard, he argued, and at most other liberal arts institutions of Negro education, even though the need for post slavery tutelage had lapsed. Now, an outdated educational hegemony in the name of Christianity, fused with a politics of racial conservatism, crippled Negro higher education. Without mentioning Durkee, Locke made the point that White ministers often brought conservative racial and religious notions of education to such colleges. In the end, such minister-headed Black colleges and universities had not only failed to allow their constituents to "develop a modern emancipated spirituality of their own" but also had hampered the emergence of an independent-minded Black leadership class.[30]

No longer would young Negroes tolerate such paternalistic dictatorship of their educational livelihood, Locke declared. Frustrated by the paternalism White presidents had insinuated into campus policies and curricula, many of the students at Howard, Fisk, Morehouse, Atlanta, Wilberforce, Virginia Union, Johnson Smith, and Lincoln now demanded these colleges be governed by Blacks, even though most students believed their faculties should remain integrated. Locke supported this move. Locke did not want to say that only Black administrators could provide leadership in the current situation, but his article implied that that was probably the best choice. Only in a "family-like" atmosphere could the Negro liberal college begin to renew the spirit of race service that had really energized Negro education in the past and been its main rationale. That idealism was needed to stem the tide of rampant self-aggrandizement and escapism that Negro students, confronted with outdated religious proscriptions and disciplining, increasingly adopted. "If there is anything specially traditional and particularly needed in Negro education, it is the motive and ideal of group service. And though the loss of it in the more capably trained Negro of the present generation is partly due to the influence of the prevalent materialistic individualism of middle-class American life, a still larger loss is due to an inevitable and protective reaction against the present atmosphere of his education."[31]

Given that Negro education would remain segregated for the foreseeable future, it "ought to be free to develop its own racial interests and special aims for both positive and compensatory reasons." Locke's use of "positive reasons" is significant: once again, he signaled his commitment to Black aspirations that went beyond merely a reaction to racism. One such "positive reason" would be if Negro colleges and universities became centers for the study of race and Black culture. Here Locke had numerous analogies, from the Indian universities that made the study of Sanskrit and ancient Aryan texts their research specialty to Jewish universities that made the study of anti-Semitism and Judaism their special contribution. The Negro college should offer what other American colleges offered, but should also give students a course of study that integrated their desire for self-development with the "historic" ideal of "group service." A self-consciously New Negro administration would foster a different course of study, but also a different way to develop character in its students, such that students would emerge believing that success consisted of personal advancement and the advancement of the race.

"Negro Education Bids for Par" marked Locke's first public statement of protest against White domination of Negro life, delivered by a man more comfortable with private attacks on Whites. Here Locke was the most political and the most public he could be about White oppression because, in part, it hurt him personally for the second time in his life. That was the other way "Negro Education" was a watershed in signaling that Locke's fostering of White recognition for the New Negro movement had created opportunities for African Americans to criticize traditional "Negro" institutions (although as Locke's article suggested, they were not entirely "Negro" institutions). Mainstream Negroes and Negro institutions increasingly would view that aspect of the New Negro movement with profound ambivalence, since access to White publication gave leverage to rebel Negroes they lacked under traditional print segregation.

The article launched a new career for Locke as an educational philosopher with a lecturing campaign as an authority on Negro education and radicalism in the Black community. He used his new visibility to get paid speaking engagements about the new militancy in Black America. On September 22, he spoke before the National Conference on the Education of Colored Americans under the auspices of the National Sociological Society. His speech was titled "The Philosophical Basis of Education." He was still identified as Professor Alain Le Roy Locke, but instead of mentioning Howard, the lecture announcement referred to him as the "Winner of Rhodes Scholarship, Oxford University." Locke extended the critical analysis of his article that self-determination was the only logical philosophy of a separate Negro educational system. On November 10, he was giving a speech on "The Negro and Radicalism"—he identified as "Professor Alain Locke, formerly of Howard University"—at the Public Forum Meetings of the League for Industrial Democracy. No longer a harmonizer, he became a spokesperson for educational nationalism and a regular stump speaker in Washington, D.C., and New York to groups sympathetic to his plight.

Locke probably had not thought he would be giving lectures on education after the publication of the aesthetic Harlem issue of the *Survey Graphic*. As if to return to his first love, and defend his decision to utilize Reiss in the *Survey Graphic* and upcoming book anthology, Locke published two articles in the early fall of 1925 that documented the progressive portraiture done by European contemporary artists in *Opportunity* magazine. The articles, "The Art of Auguste Mambour" and "More of the Negro in Art," marked a reconciliation of sorts with Charles Johnson, whom Locke needed more urgently after being fired. More important, they engaged the space Locke had created for non-Blacks to contribute to the movement based on Negro themes. The articles advanced the notion that what mattered most was the quality of the work of and about the Negro, not simply that it was by a Negro. That the Europeans were advancing a portraiture superior to that of Americans was clearly evidenced in the stunning portrait of an African woman by Auguste Mambour that graced the cover of the issue in which the first article appeared. Mambour's study epitomized the contribution of the modern European artist to Black portraiture, for he had developed a portrait style that blended the cubist's fascination with cylindrical volumes with a soft pointillist shading faces and figures that made the figures appear almost three-dimensional. Although this style of depicting the human form was not exclusive to his Negro studies, it seemed to reach its epitome of emotional power with such subjects, perhaps because his style seemed to have derived from his collecting and studying of African sculpture. The portrait study on the cover synthesized best the twin goals of Mambour's technique—to render human form in terms of its volumes, and to depict Africans, especially women and children, as objects of beauty. Locke's article not only praised Mambour, but a whole generation of young European artists, presided over by Lucie Costurier, the godmother of the French African portraiture. It was she, he argued in "More of the Negro in Art," who had helped free contemporary European painting from the primitivist agenda. A new subject required a new form, and in this case, going outside of Europe for subject matter had opened up a new way of seeing and rendering form for these artists. If American artists, both White and Black, were willing to follow this modern European lead, a new American art lay before them.[32]

As a racial, sexual, and cultural transgressor—not to mention a Europhile—Locke was open to Whites whose transgressions into non-European culture opened up new possibilities for the Black aesthetic. By bringing examples of this new, invigorating European portraiture of the Negro to *Opportunity*, Locke was nimbly continuing to suggest that race was not the main reason for the limitations of Negro portraiture—it was the American approach to race that was the problem. Such an argument, when seen alongside his call for self-determination in Black education, opened Locke up to the charge of contradiction. How could he demand that Black institutions be headed by Black leaders, and yet welcome a White artist to illustrate a book that represented the aspirations of the Negro? Similarly, how could he eschew protest in the formulation of his New Negro philosophy only to embrace it in his campaign to get his job back at Howard? Despite his empowering nurture in White and European institutions, Locke knew that Howard did not empower the self-concept of Negroes, largely because its system of education was designed to contain Black assertiveness. When that system became abusive, protest—measured, reasoned, but impassioned—was legitimate. But just as important, when Whites made a bold attempt to break out of the paternalism and denigration of Negroes, Blacks should applaud the effort. That did not sit well with some essentialists whose dreams of self-determination allowed little room for the racial or sexual outsider. What saved Locke's argument—especially among those with no exposure to French or German artists—was the personal example of Reiss.

In the months following the publication of the *Survey Graphic*, Reiss had accepted criticism of his work graciously, had done numerous covers and broadsides for Black magazines and social events for very low fees, and had welcomed African American artists and intellectuals into his studio which, by the fall of

1925, had become an art crossroads for African American, Asian, and Mexican artists and their friends. Reiss crossed cultural lines without carrying with him the baggage of racial paternalism, while being personally open to the leadership of African Americans like Locke. As Reiss wrote to him after *The New Negro* was published, "I have to tell you again how much I liked to work with you and I only wish that we will have once an occasion in which we can prove just to all our ideals regardless of commercial people. It would make me very happy if my effort in helping your noble work would really be a small seed in the vast land that still has to be ploughed. Do not forget that you can always find me ready if you need help in your idealistic undertakings."[33]

Locke's idealistic coupling of Black leadership and interracial collaboration broke new ground. In aesthetic and educational politics, what mattered was less the color of one's skin than whether supporters were willing to allow Black intelligence to lead. While Locke asserted that race warped some Whites in his article on education—and those had to be opposed and removed where possible—his articles on European artists showed he understood that was not true of all. The New Negro had the self-confidence to be a "race man" and assert his or her right to head those institutions that catered predominantly to the race. But in one of the caveats that defined his intellectual career, Locke also asserted that race, while necessary, was not sufficient to determine allies and enemies. Working with Whites was as much a necessity for the New Negro as being able and willing to work alone. Now, for the first time in his adult life, he was really alone. He would be tested, like the New Negro he had declared newly born, to see if he could become an independent man.

27

The New Negro and *The Blacks*

An indelible scene defined Locke's life that fall of 1925. When Eric Walrond trudged up the three flights of stairs that led to the apartment on 144th Street in Harlem where Locke was living, finishing edits of materials for *The New Negro: An Interpretation*, he found a cheery Locke in a Victorian armchair, dozens of manuscripts sprawled on the low coffee table in front of him—reputedly with his feet in a tub of hot water beneath him. By October, unlike Washington, D.C., it was already cold in New York. Locke was huddled under a shawl but happy, as he was in Harlem to be closer to the writers whose contribution he sought for the anthology. While being fired might have made others forlorn, Locke appeared ebullient and full of energy. He waved Walrond over to the sideboard to pour the two of them small glasses of wine. Walrond was nervous because he was bringing his latest draft of "The Palm Porch," which Locke had requested for *The New Negro* but had forced him to revise repeatedly. Walrond hoped that Locke would accept this version and an additional short story by a gay friend of his. Walrond knew that Locke wanted to include writings from as many of the young Black gay community in Harlem; but he also knew that Locke demanded that that writing had to be the best. After about an hour filled with discussion about the writing, but also probably gossip about Jessie Fauset's demand that she be included in *The New Negro*, or rumors that Countee Cullen was considering marrying Yolanda Du Bois, Locke abruptly informed Walrond that he had another appointment.

Given that Walrond had written the most critical review of Fauset's *There Is Confusion*, he probably sided with Locke in the nastiest controversy of his editing of the anthology that had ensued that spring when Locke commissioned Arthur Fauset to contribute to the volume. Jessie informed Du Bois that she had not been asked to contribute to a book all of Black literary New York suspected would be a blockbuster. When Locke walked into the *Crisis* offices to pick up its editor's contribution to the book, Du Bois informed Locke that he would not participate in *The New Negro* unless Fauset was included. Unwilling to risk leaving out Du Bois, Locke agreed, but seethed at the imposition on his authority. That tense meeting reminded Locke of an earlier visit to Du Bois to get his article for the Harlem number. Locke recalled that on that occasion Du Bois tossed a group of essays at Locke to edit into a single essay for his contribution. Now that Locke's interpretation of the New Negro had become a success, Du Bois was using his clout to force Fauset's inclusion, yet another example from Locke's perspective of how Du Bois treated him condescendingly. Locke probably also believed that Du Bois's demand that Jessie be included was less a matter of critical judgment and more a need to placate his long-standing mistress. The most influential Black homosexual of the 1920s had to yield to the most influential Black heterosexist of the decade—and Locke did not like it. Tragically, Fauset's role in a movement she had helped start was by 1925 relegated to a conflict between two men.

When Jessie Fauset turned in her submission, "The Gift of Laughter," that summer, Locke waited until her summer idyll with Du Bois was concluded and then sent back her manuscript with an acerbic letter. "The 'Gift of Laughter' arrived and almost brought tears," he began. Surely, he asked, could she not see the genius in the work of such Black comedians as Bert Williams, whose mastery of pantomime, gesture, and body movement stood at the cutting edge of the modern theater? "Even DuBois—and I use 'even' because it is only his outward reputation, not his inner soul, that is regarded as 'stiff'—has written persuasively of the genius of black vaudeville. I shall never forget my first experience of seeing Bert Williams dance, and the ecstasy I experienced, and I consider myself an expert on European dance. Moreover, can't you see that humor has been a kind of saving grace for the Negro, and not simply a performance for whites?" Jessie, Locke was implying, *was stiff*, and typical of the Black bourgeoisie who condemned Black musical comedies for their performance of the laughing stereotype. Locke wanted a volume that celebrated the genius of Negro performance culture, even within its limitations, not a putdown of that culture by a Black Victorian. He was also aghast at her using her essay to critique Reiss. "I must object to your criticism of the Reiss portraits, but not over their substance. All of us have our opinions. But to publish such criticisms in a book for which Reiss's work provides the principal illustrations would be in terribly bad taste. Moreover, the point has no relation to the essay at hand. So let's just drop that, shall we, and reserve it for the review of the book." Interestingly, Jessie Fauset's objections did not extend to Reiss personally, since she appeared at parties he hosted in Greenwich Village.[1]

Locke's perspective is best apprehended in the foreword to *The New Negro* that he penned around the same time. "Of all the voluminous literature on the Negro...nine-tenths of it is about the Negro rather than of him, so that it is the Negro problem rather than the Negro that is known." To see "the Negro in his essential traits, in the full perspective of his achievement and possibilities," Locke continued, required the analyst to "seek the enlightenment of that self-portraiture which the present developments of Negro culture are offering."

Locke wanted Fauset to trace out the agency of "self-portraiture" that allowed even oppressed and overdetermined Black actors—and by inference any artist— to snatch bits and pieces of "self-expression from the jaws of unsympathetic patrons." Williams no less than Michelangelo had inscribed his genius within a traditional form that otherwise was banal. In that sense, Locke's struggle in *The New Negro* was to portray Negro art not as a concession to White power but as the struggle for self-determination through self-expression. "Without ignoring...that there are important interactions between the national and the race life, or that the attitude of America toward the Negro is as important a factor as the attitude of the Negro toward America, we have nevertheless concentrated upon self-expression and the forces and motives of self-determination." Locke appropriated self-determination, a rhetoric of national autonomy popularized by Woodrow Wilson, as well as Vladimir Lenin, as a rhetoric of individual and collective subjectivity for Negroes—and by implication all peoples. Bert Williams had the choice not to act; but if he did, he bore the responsibility to inscribe something of himself and his people's genius in his performance. And the responsibility of the New Negro cultural historian was to see the subjectivity, the individual self-determination, even in otherwise compromised performances that transcended, if only in a gesture, victimization. Not only did Locke want to transform how Whites looked at Negroes in the mass and as individuals but also how Black people viewed themselves. By insisting that being Negro did contribute to how the Black people, whether actor or artist or mechanic, saw themselves, Locke wanted Black researchers in *The New Negro* to investigate Black culture as a struggle for freedom, even through caricatured humor.

Once Locke read William Stanley Braithwaite's essay "The Negro in American Literature" and realized it made a similar point to Fauset's—that White authors had turned "the happy, care-free, humorous Negro" into "a fad"—Locke worried his book was becoming more an indictment of White misrepresentation than a statement of Black self-expression—the latter theme being the one that distinguished his book from other chronicles.[2] Tellingly, Locke would publish Braithwaite's essay almost as is, whereas he would not accept a similar argument from Fauset.

Nevertheless, Locke's editorial pressure seemed to pay off. Although earlier drafts of Jessie Fauset's essay have not survived to prove the point, it appears that the story of Black artistic agency surfaces in the published version of "The Gift of Laughter" in the book. "No matter how keenly he [the Negro] felt the insincerity of the presentation of his kind," she noted, "no matter how ridiculous and palpable a caricature such a presentation might be, the Negro auditor...was powerless to demand something better and truer....It was at this point in the eighteen-nineties that Ernest Hogan, pioneer comedian of the better type, changed the tradition of the merely funny, rather silly 'end-man' into a character with a definite plot in a rather loosely constructed but none the less well-outlined story. The method was still humorous, but less broadly, less exclusively."[3] Her essay was a more powerful statement of Black performativity than Montgomery Gregory's rather lackluster contribution, "The Drama of Negro Life," which merely restated the goals of the Howard University theater movement. Locke was achieving something distinctive after all—a book whose essays made visible how Blacks had assimilated even demeaning practices and revolutionized them to express something new through the mask of Negro laughter. Locke was applying what he had learned a year ago from Max Reinhardt—to focus on the genius of Black invention at the level of form as the basis for a new view of America; and where possible, as in his editing of the *Survey Graphic*, he forced contributors to advance his "interpretation" in their essays in *The New Negro*.

The Fauset incident highlights, though, the problem Locke faced in using a book anthology to advance the concept of the New Negro. Once the Harlem issue had exploded in popularity, everyone with a literary bent or Negro program wanted to be in the book. Feeling that he had to be representative of the collective progressive intelligence in the anthology, he yielded somewhat to the pressure to be inclusive, rather than exclusive. He could have dropped Du Bois's essay and thus saved himself from having to include Fauset's—although hers ended up being one of the better submissions to the book. Locke should have rejected other work, such as Albert Barnes's embarrassing "The Negro and Art" and Robert Moton's lifeless recapitulation of Hampton Institute's virtues. But Locke couldn't bring himself to do that. Locke was without a job. To antagonize potential allies—especially patrons and potential employers—was too risky. Plus, there were practical considerations. Including Barnes gave Locke access to the Barnes Foundation photographs of African art, while the Hampton essay allowed him to reproduce the stunning Reiss portrait of Moton in the volume. As time went on, the book ballooned toward a catalog. Locke knew that major Negroes would never forgive him if he excluded one of them from something as big as *The New Negro* promised to be. He couldn't afford their ire.

Despite its compromises, Locke found work on the book invigorating. No longer having his Howard post increased his investment in *The New Negro* as his book, even if he had to make concessions to ensure its success. Indeed, he spent his time in his Harlem garret shaping the book form along the lines Kellogg had shown him in work on the *Survey Graphic*, that of putting a variety of media—essays, photographs, broadsides—side by side in conversation with one another. The anthology strove to be even more multimedia than the *Survey Graphic* issue. Drawings by Winold Reiss, Aaron Douglas, and Miguel Covarrubias combined with photographs of African sculpture from the Barnes and other collections to make it a striking and unique volume in American literature. It was a graphic book. He also included a play, commentaries on African American music, and essays on Black institutions and local culture. The range in content was matched by more expansive claims about the "movement": New Negro artists were now to be found throughout the nation. As Locke wrote in the foreword:

> Enlarging this stage we are now presenting the New Negro in a national and even international scope. Although there are few centers that can be pointed out approximating Harlem's significance, the full signifi- cance of that even is a racial awakening on a national and perhaps even a world stage.[4]

Locke's enthusiasm and confidence is all the more remarkable when one remem- bers that Locke was compiling the book while he continued his struggle to regain his job at Howard. Locke's reverie of work on the book was interrupted by de- mands he be present in Washington to participate in strategy sessions as the leader of the group of professors fired by the board of trustees. The fight for his job, as he confided to Kellogg that fall, kept his life in turmoil.

Buoying his hopes of eventual return to Howard was an increasing army of activists who sought him out to assist them in their campaigns against the board. One of the most effective was George Parker, a Howard alumnus, who wrote Charles R. Brown, dean of the School of Divinity at Yale in September 1925, to ask whether the board of trustees had met or planned to meet before its next regularly scheduled meeting in February to deal with the turmoil at Howard. Parker's letter, a copy of which had been sent to Locke for his comments, was designed to trap Brown into declaring what action the board was planning to take to resolve the various controversies, and when Brown wrote back that no meeting had been held since June, Parker published the correspondence and suggested that the refusal to schedule a meeting before February showed that the board "evidently considers Negroes too ignorant to effect any serious trou- ble. Any agitation started, the Board seemingly thinks, can be easily stopped by the mere statement that the future existence of Howard is threaten[ed]. But if it [Howard] ceases to serve well the function for which it is entended[sic], we no longer need her and, therefore, do not want her. She is dedicated to a service from which she can not shirk and retain the support of the masses."[5]

In fact, the administration's propaganda campaign in Black newspapers was effective in convincing many African Americans that continued protest would destroy the university. White opponents of Congressional Appropriations for Howard were already issuing demands that the funding be held up until a full investigation could be completed, a threat that might close the institution. This argument found sympathetic ears not only among such African American educators as Dr. J. E. Shepard, the president of North Carolina College for Negroes (later North Carolina A&T) but also the militant *New York Age*, which in September was still not persuaded by the alumni's arguments against the Durkee administration. The *Age* conceded that the one thing that still needed to be explained by the administration was "the abrupt dismissal of four of its ablest and most efficient professors."

But the board refused to act. The Howard Alumni Association of St. Louis opened a new line of attack in October when it formed a "Committee to Investigate Conditions at Howard," chaired by L. S. Curtis, one of Locke's former students. That committee wrote Durkee demanding an explanation of his role in the dismissals. Realizing, belatedly, that his position as president was endangered by the continuing response to the dismissals, Durkee claimed that he was not responsible for them. Curtis forwarded the correspondence to Locke for his review and comment. Locke replied: "I am enclosing an official answer to your inquiries...which...you can use or follow as your judgment seems best. Dr. Durkee's avoidance of the responsibility for this action plays ultimately into our hands. How would the Budget and Executive Committee know whom to pick. I have the word of two members of that Committee that they acted only upon the President's recommendation, and one made inquiries as to whether we had had any intimation that our work was unsatisfactory, to which affirmative answer was given. This is contrary to fact in three of the four instances."[6] Locke worked with Curtis on how to frame the attack. Psychologically and politically, it was best that Durkee be the target of the attack about dismissals, since, as Locke revealed to Kellogg later on, "we really hope to remove the President whereas Boards of Trustees go on forever."[7] As Durkee probably realized too late, the board had set him up to take the fall, if somehow the attempt to remove the professors backfired.

Locke continued to press his case with his allies, such as Roscoe Conkling Bruce, to whom he suggested Durkee deliberately attacked Harvard men. "I think it will be effective to point out that one Harvard man after another has been allowed to leave the University, in fact urged to leave. There has been a break with the administration in every instance—Houston, Woodson, Gregory, Waring and Locke."[8] He also contacted Franz Boas, who wrote a letter to Professor A. O. Leuschner, president of the American Association of University Professors (AAUP), asking him to investigate the dismissals as violations of academic freedom. In Boas's letter, he noted that he had obtained his information "from the personal statement of one of the gentlemen concerned."[9] Action on the request was slow to materialize, in part because Leuschner was in Europe all fall.

That the administration stuck to its story that the dismissals were not based on teacher conduct or performance but on economic strictures kept Locke and other critics from being able to charge the administration with bias. Too strong an attack on Howard might damage Locke's chances of returning to alternative schools, should he not get his Howard job back. Psychologically and philosophically, Locke also had an aversion to being a firebrand. Thus, in all of his correspondence with the board and the public, Locke maintained that cultured demeanor his mother and her class had taught him should be maintained at all times in public, regardless of circumstances. It worked on one level: Brown replied to one of Locke's letters, for example, and thanked him for how cordial he had been. But the strategy cost Locke in that it kept him from releasing his anger and hurt, and the long-standing sense of shame and rejection he carried with him from his childhood, with anyone. Instead, he poured that anger into strategies behind the scenes designed to bring down the university.

Work on *The New Negro*, however, balanced Locke. There was the enticement of new poetry coming in, such as Lewis Alexander's haiku, "Enchantment." There was the strong short fiction, "Spunk," by Zora Neale Hurston, which had been awarded second prize in the *Opportunity* contest he had presided over, and which he was publishing for the first time in *The New Negro*. He already sensed that her work promised great things, because it linked so powerfully with another theme of the book: the folk inheritance. Here Arthur Fauset's "American Negro Folk Literature," but even more his collected stories "T'appin" and "Brer Buzzard" from interviews with Cugo Lewis, reputedly an African who had been brought to American in 1859, nailed Locke's point that the New Negro was part of a hidden cultural tradition in the folk heritage of Negroes. It also reinforced the narrative that the solution to the problem of the Black middle-class intellectual was to undertake an archaeological mission into the soul of his or her race, there to find a new vein of artistry and a new crop of artists who thought folk were nevertheless fine. This work made *The New Negro* a significant step forward in Black self-consciousness, far ahead of what he had achieved in the Harlem number.

But the delay in publication worried Locke, as he knew that every month that slipped by made it possible for another "mid-wife" to step forward and possibly steal his thunder. Always competitive, Locke realized that others were beginning to enter the field with statements that rivaled his own. In the *Los Angeles Times*, Du Bois had penned an article titled "A Negro Art Renaissance" that had appeared in June, lauding the work of Roland Hayes under a title that reminded Locke and a few other insiders that Du Bois had been the first to announce that a renaissance of Negro letters was on the horizon.[10] Locke knew from his contacts that V. F. Calverton's *Modern Quarterly* was slated to publish the *Crisis* editor's article, "The Social Origins of American Negro Art." Behind the curve of the burgeoning Negro art movement for some time, Du Bois was catching up. There were rumors as well that Charles Johnson was planning another special edition, or even a book on the movement he had created, but so far had not been adequately credited for. By October, Locke not only felt the heat of competitors on his back but also the increasing demand to be in Washington to coordinate with those leading the battle against the administration. Faced with this split personality, Locke spent more time—and more of his increasingly dwindling bank account—on the train.

Yet Locke had no alternative but to commit all of his creative resources to designing a cutting-edge anthology that in form and content would best its Negro competitors and set a new standard for American creative writing. The breakthrough quality of *The New Negro: An Interpretation* becomes apparent when compared to that other landmark 1920s literary anthology, Harold Stearns's *Civilization in the United States* (1922). There, Stearns was content to let experts comment on an American culture, but did not include contemporary imaginative literature speaking directly to the reader. By contrast, Locke designed his anthology to provide cogent, authoritative analysis, but also excerpts from the most arresting literature of the day—for example, "Carma" and "Fern" from Jean Toomer's *Cane*, excerpts of unimpeachable beauty that otherwise had been read by very few readers of the original publication. By varying fiction, poetry, essays, and broadsides of such historical milestones as Jupiter Hammon's "Address to the Negroes" and Madison Washington's slave narrative, Locke created a rhythm of interest that avoided tiring the reader. And all of that was held together by Reiss's artwork, not only the spectacular first-time publication of color photographs of portraits in an American book of literature but also his design signature throughout, on and inside the cover, such that the volume became as much a work of art as a commentary on the possibilities of art for group expression in America.

When *The New Negro* appeared in December 1925, it too benefited from excellent timing. It burst into American consciousness in the middle of the vogue of the Negro, just as urban Whites, breaking out of Victorian bounds in the roaring twenties were open to a new definition of what it meant to be urban in America. Unlike James Weldon Johnson's moribund *Book of American Negro Poetry* published just three years earlier, Locke could write as if the Black literary movement had entered advanced stages of development and launched a new identity, the New Negro, whose implications were broader and ran deeper than simply a new kind of literature on the American horizon. The term "New Negro" branded the new movement in a way that "book of American poetry" never would, for it suggested that new identity, a new way of being American, had emerged at the height of the Jazz Age, an alternative to the White-bread middle-class American who was not only Negro but a stylish originator of jazz, urbanity, and the poetry of modern life.

Plus, critical response to *The New Negro: An Interpretation* was also favorable. The *New York Times Book Review* saw it as "a book of surprises. No matter how well informed the reader, he will find here facts that he has not known about the progress of the Negro in America."[11] H. L. Mencken believed the book was evidence of "the American Negro's final emancipation from his inferiority complex, his bold decision to go it alone.... The Negroes who contribute to this dignified and impressive volume have very little to say about their race's wrongs: their attention is all upon its merits. They show no sign of being sorry that they are

Negroes. For the first time one hears clearly the imposing doctrine that, in more than one way, the Negro is superior to the white man."[12]

The striking color portraits by Reiss made that argument more persuasively than anything else in the volume. The writing in *The New Negro* almost became one long caption to the photographs of a new kind of American. Reiss painted striking brown faces and hands of his sitters while leaving their clothing white, as signifying how Black people who were proud of who they were and wore White culture as little more than a suit of clothes. Here were portraits of Black moderns, not primitives, who flourished in their vital aliveness, especially two—the portrait of Robert Moton, which showed he was a man with style, movement, and swagger altogether absent from thumbnail biographical sketches of him, and the portrait of Charles Johnson, leaning to the side, a brother maneuvering his way through life, despite having to negotiate with White power. There was consistent performativity to the Reiss portraits in *The New Negro*, which Locke sorted through the volume as single eruptions of color that broke the anthology into a series of visual wonders. While Locke dropped some of the *Survey Graphic* portraits Reiss had drawn of those from the streets of Harlem, he retained the most controversial portrait, "Two Public Schoolteachers," in *The New Negro*, thumbing his nose at its critics.[13] Its inclusion along with others of dark-skinned African Americans made a powerful visual statement. *The New Negro* decentered Whiteness by showing how Black people had absorbed all that America had thrown at them and become something more complex and interesting because of it.[14]

The book was also a paean to a new Black masculinity. The portraits were overwhelmingly of Black men and not Black women, in contrast to the *Crisis*, which featured photographs of Black women prominently. In *The New Negro*, while there were significant portraits of Black women, especially the hauntingly beautiful portrait of Elise Johnson McDougald, these were mainly interruptions to a narratology of Black male bodies that formed the homoerotic message of the book. The frontispiece, *Brown Madonna*, Locke's silent homage to his mother that opens the book, made the case even more powerfully: as in the Italian Renaissance paintings, the only way for women to enter the renaissance was as the mother of Christ, in this case, a Brown Madonna with a Brown baby put in this Black woman's arms by Reiss. The New Negro was always male in Locke's imaginary—the "changeling in their laps," in the lap of a Brown mother whose role was to birth and nurture but not epitomize the New Negro. The portraits reveal as well that other shift in emphasis from the *Survey Graphic* to *The New Negro*—a shift from the masses as the bearers and transformers of American culture to the homoerotic educated artists as the quintessential New Negroes of the American century. The deletion of the portraits from later editions of *The New Negro* to save production costs removes this essential component of Locke's innovation in volume.

The portraits also complicated the notion of race, for looking at them confused the reader as to who and what was Negro. While most of the artists, such as Paul Robeson, were dark-skinned men dressed in whited-out suits, others, such as Jean Toomer, appeared to be White, dressed in a black suit, with a ghost-like shroud seemingly pulsating around his body. Reproduced here as well was "Type Sketch: Ancestral," a portrait of an unnamed woman who looked more East Indian than Negro American, and whose draped body was posed against a background pattern more Native American than African. While Aaron Douglas's woodcut nicely suggested that a vibrant musical, dance, and religious culture anchored African American identity, Miguel Covarrubias's caricatures of con-temporary urban Black culture offered a more ironic interpretation. That Locke added his to *The New Negro*'s growing list of illustrations showed his willingness to risk further Black bourgeois condemnation in his pursuit of modernism, since Covarrubias's drawings were more scandalous than anything else in the book. Moreover, by including the work of a Mexican artist, Locke acknowledged not only the Mexican Renaissance but also reinforced the message that the American Negro possessed a multicultural inheritance. In that sense, Locke said that Covarrubias was also a New Negro.

The book was especially invigorating for young Negro thinkers and writers, who found inspiration in its pages. Decades later, Doxey Wilkerson, who would become a young communist in the 1930s, recalled the effect that reading *The New Negro* in the 1920s had on him. "The first thing I wrote for the University of Kansas newspaper, WAD I think was the newspaper's name, was a review of *The New Negro*. The book opened my eyes—excited me. [It showed] black folk doing things both in art and in terms of radicalism that I didn't know about."[15] It was not how the writing compared with that by Sinclair Lewis, for example, but that Negroes were writing poetry, fiction, and belles-lettres at all during the height of the Jim Crow era. *The New Negro* thus announced something that went beyond literature—that the Negro was capable to doing a number of spectacular things that most whites believed were impossible. The book thus expanded the range of the possible even for those who never contemplated picking up a pen to write a poem or a song.

But Locke scarcely had time to enjoy the publication or gauge its impact, be-cause just as it was published he was informed that he was due back at Howard University on December 10 for a meeting that promised to determine whether he would get his job back. Earlier, in October, Locke and his allies had discovered a chink in the board of trustees' armor. Technically, the dismissals were not final, because the budget committee had inadvertently violated Howard's charter in its rush to get rid of the professors. "The Charter invests the power of employ-ment and dismissal of teachers with the Board as such, the action of June 16th by a committee of said body can reasonably be regarded as not final, but as subject to either review and reconsideration or ratification." Without published minutes of the June 7 meeting to document that the entire board had voted to approve the budget committee recommendation, another meeting would be required for the entire board to certify the committee's recommendations.[16] Late in October, Locke was able to reach some of the trustees and pressure the board to consider the petitions for a reconsideration of the decision—and a vote publicly authorizing the budget committee's recommendation. The first to author and sign a letter requesting a meeting by the board were AME bishop John Hurst and Judge Stanton J. Peelle. Hurst left it up to Locke to try and obtain signatures from as many of the board members who lived in Washington, D.C., as possible before sending it off to Brown. Race was a part of the effort. As Hurst wrote to Locke: "I trust that you will try especially, to get Dr. Pierce and Thomas Jesse Jones (though he does not live there) also, to sign it. What I have in mind is, that the more of the white members we have to sign it, the less adverse criticism the movement will receive."[17] Ironically, even Black members of the board of trustees of a Negro university needed the support of White members to legitimate the "movement" to have the decision reconsidered by the full board.

The process had dragged through November, as Hurst sought but failed to get Jones's signature on the letter.[18] Eventually, the letter signed by five trustees—Justice Stanton J. Peelle, Dr. U. G. B. Pierce, Dr. C. Sumner Wormley, Gen. John H. Sherburne, and Bishop Hurst—forced Brown to hold "A Special Meeting of the Board of Trustees of Howard University" to consider the Alumni Association charges against Durkee and to officially vote on the recommendations of the budget and executive committees. When Emmett Scott informed Locke that such a meeting would be held on December 10, 1925, he did not specify whether Locke would be asked to speak. When he asked, a testy Scott informed him that it would be wise to make himself available in case he was asked to speak, but that Charles Brown had not issued any special invitation.

So pivotal was this upcoming presentation that Locke turned all of his attention toward preparing for his rendezvous with Howard's oligarchy rather than promoting his new book. He had to prepare himself emotionally to keep his feelings under wrap, while at the same time expressing forthrightly his indignation at the high-handed procedure of his dismissal. Accordingly, at 9 A.M. on a cold Thursday morning, as board members Charles Brown, Sara W. Brown, Role Cobleigh, Victor B. Deyber, Durkee, Albert Bushnell Hart (who directed Du Bois's PhD dissertation at Harvard), John R. Eawkins, M. O. Dumas, Thomas Jesse Jones (the man behind the Fisk University crisis), Moorland, James C. Napier, C. H. Pope, M. F. Wheatland, Peelle, Pierce, Sherburne, Wormley, and Scott filed into Library Hall, Locke and three other dismissed professors stood outside of Carnegie Library waiting to find out if they would be asked to speak. It was a considerable wait, because the first order of business was for the board members present to hear the eight charges brought by the Alumni Association against Durkee.[19]

Locke later characterized the meeting as a "court martial" affair, and it certainly was in terms of how the board and the Alumni Association approached it.

Benton Booth, dean of the law school, was the presiding judge, and there were attorneys representing the board and the Alumni Association, with a stenographer and witnesses.[20] Moreover, the defendants' presentation was meticulously planned by Thomas Dyett and others, who prepared the case, the witnesses, and the questions they would pose. The critics of the authority in charge did not have an opportunity to cross-examine Durkee, who had to sit through a meeting listening to a litany of criticisms of his presidency.

On one level, this was a performance, since nothing the alumni or professors said would result in a vote of no confidence in Durkee by the trustees. By allowing such a "performance," the board reassured Congress, White philanthropists, and their allies not only that Negro education was democratic but also that that education would never succeed in an attack on White control itself. But the board meeting was more than just a show for Whites: the board was multiracial and divided, because some of its Black members, except Moorland, felt that the treatment of Locke and the others had been unfair. Perhaps their earlier acquiescence to the dismissals had been purchased by assurances from Durkee that the professors' superiors had been consulted and had agreed with the decision. Now, however, the board had to deal with the mess that Moorland's maneuver had created for them—a litany of alumni charges against Durkee, mounting alumni agitation in Congress to hold up Howard's annual appropriation pending an investigation into the board's actions, building sentiment in the Black press that Durkee must go, and a clear belief among many that Locke and his colleagues had been dealt a dirty deal. The common front on the board was threatening to crack.

Dyett and his assistants brought forth professors, whose testimony matched the charges in the alumni memorandum and substantiated their claims against Durkee. Kelly Miller testified to being insulted by Durkee who called him a "contemptible cur," to agreeing not to discuss the incident publicly, and then to seeing Durkee's denials of the insult printed in Black newspapers. This suggested that Durkee was not only abusive, but a liar. Another witness, Turner, testified that Durkee grabbed him and physically pushed him violently out of his office during one of their conferences. Turner stated that only his concern that a suit against the president would hurt the university had kept him from seeking legal redress. In total, forty-five professors testified during the course of the inquiry, with Locke, Lochard, and Brown most likely being the last to be called.

Locke was the first of the fired professors to testify, coming before the board of trustees arrayed before him like a scene out of Jean Genet's play *The Blacks*.[21] In front and above him sat a group of men in masks—whether Black or White—men who claimed their only concern was the best interests of the university, who were in fact concerned now mainly with their own survival. Sitting in chairs upon on the stage from which ten years earlier he had given the first installment of lectures on imperialist race theory and practice in America, they were colonized subjects, overlords of Negro education fighting to keep control of a dying oligarchy. Instead of fighting for the right to teach race on campus, Locke was now performing in a farce—a reputed just proceeding to determine whether his dismissal was appropriate, even though he and the men arrayed above him knew nothing he said would reinstate him.

He must have been highly nervous, especially after spending most the morning outside wondering whether he would speak at all. Now, inside, he knew success would depend on his ability to be forthright but also dispassionate in his testimony. If he could remain controlled but persistent in questioning why he was selected for dismissal, he would find the path that would work best for him. He needed to keep the onus on the board to explain why he was let go.

Probably, Locke began with his surprise that after thirteen years of exemplary service to Howard University, he was let go so summarily. Since he could find no other evidence that he was unfit as a teacher, he was left to wonder whether his firing had anything to do with his previous conflicts with Durkee. Even this, he would have stated, was surprising, as he had copies of letters from Durkee in which he referred to Locke in very flattering language when Durkee promoted him to full professor, when he approved his leave of absences, and when he praised Locke for launching a research and teaching program for Howard faculty and students in Africa. This did not sound like the language of someone who believed that such a professor was inefficient or that his services could be severed from the university without unduly hurting its mission. Locke would also have reported that when he confronted Durkee in June about rumors of his dismissal, the president asserted they were unfounded. Here, Locke would have injected his concern with procedure, that after thirteen years of service, he deserved more advance notice of his impending dismissal, more specific charges of misconduct or inefficiency, and more of an opportunity to respond to either issue than the June decision to fire him had allowed. Probably, Locke would have concluded that if he had been notified earlier that the university did not value his services, he would have responded differently to the offer of a deanship and vice presidency of Wilberforce University.[22]

After Locke, Metz T. P. Lochard, former professor of French, and Alonzo H. Brown, former professor of Mathematics, had spoken, the board met in "Executive Session." Not surprisingly, it resolved that the charges against Durkee had not been proved and "ratified the action of the Executive Committee and the Budget Committee...in the matter of the discontinuance of certain teachers on June 15, 1925 as carrying out" the directions of the board of trustees in the matter of elimination, and contractions in conformity with the reorganization program of the university, as adopted June 2, 1925. But in what amounted to an admission to the unfairness of dismissing the professors on such short notice, the board stated in language that was as arcane as it was transparent:

That, inasmuch as the Executive Committee and the Budget Committee had no instructions extending beyond the action that they took with reference to the separation of certain professors on account of the consolidations and reductions incident to the reorganization program of the University, the Trustees hereby grant leave of absence to the following four persons, beginning July 1, 1925, for one year, full salaries to be paid at the same time and on the same terms as the regular academic salaries last received by them: Alain L. Locke, Alonzo H. Brown, Metz T. P. Lochard, and Orlando C. Thornton, Instructor in Finance and Business Organization. At the end of the year, June 20, 1926, all connections of these persons with the University shall cease.[23]

Locke's campaign had paid off, at least financially. It must have been particularly gratifying in that his action had also benefited the other professors dismissed, even Orlando C. Thornton, who had been a critic of the student strike and had refused to appear with the others at the board meeting. The question that remained was whether to take the money. Upon writing to Kellogg for advice, Locke stated that he did not want to do so if it appeared to absolve the board of any further responsibility for his dismissal. As one of Locke's colleagues put it, the offer of a year's salary was little more than hush money. But as Kellogg suggested, it made sense for Locke to take the money if it would not commit him to sign any such affidavit handing over his rights to continue the struggle against the administration. Caught between the need for the money and his principles, Locke almost cracked up, writing to Kellogg that he was emotionally exhausted from the "nervous strain," as he described it, of the whole proceeding. Eventually, Locke took the money.[24]

Returning to New York, Locke could once again settle in to managing the distribution and reception of his magnum opus, *The New Negro*. By early January, the most significant reviews of the book were in. Not surprisingly, most reviewers read the book in terms of their preconceived ideas about what was best for the Negro. Mary White Ovington, board member of the NAACP, believed the book was proof that the Negro was assimilating American values and lifestyle. "What is the New Negro? Read and see. You will find him, perhaps to your disappointment, very like his white neighbor."[25] But Black opinion on the issue was sharply divided. Whereas the *Pittsburgh Courier* alluded to the positive impact of *The New Negro* and Negro culture on Negro American self-esteem, the *Messenger* criticized the notion that Negro culture as such even existed. From a Black socialist perspective, Black people were merely "a product of machine civilization, just like the other people in the same environment," with "Negro literature" being a hoax perpetrated by the "two or three literary dictators of Aframerica."[26] Some White reviewers voiced similar reservations about the "New Negro" movement and were skeptical about how good the work was, how much of a "renaissance" the work constituted. According to Ernest Boyd of the *Independent*, "In 'The New Negro' are all the features to which, I, as a specialist in oppressed races, am accustomed. Every goose is a swan, and extravagant efforts are made to provide a tradition and prove America's indebtedness to it....But these records do not prove that there is a Beethoven or...a Leonardo da Vinci hiding in Harlem from illiterate Ku-Kluxers."[27] Before this, no one had known that Boyd was such a "specialist."

In a letter to Paul Kellogg, Locke responded to Boyd and other critics by challenging their shared notion that the movement needed to be "'taken down' an inch or two. Actually I think for what we are trying to put over, a certain self-assurance is necessary. The point I make about it is that it is self-confidence rather than exhibitionism....Take Boyd's quibble for instance. He says he doesn't see that we have discovered a Negro Leonardo da Vinci in Harlem. The best the Irish Renaissance could do was an E.A., a William Butler Yeats and Synge and Lady Gregory—not exactly Quatre cento-calibre—but significant and for these times and folk most invigorating."[28]

That renaissance Negro was precisely what some objected to in discussing the book. According to J. P. Whipple, the literary reviewer of the *Survey Graphic*:

> It is the art and gift of the old Negro that America loves. That art is vanishing faster than any other culture in America, even the dying ritualism of the Jew. The Negro came from the earth, Africa via Alabama. He is leaving the soil. He was naïve in passion and soul. He is becoming sophisticated. He lived in a tribe with folkways. He has come to live in a herd, regimented, machine-ridden, sapped of joy, like the rest of the herd....It would be God's blessing if the new Negro could sing us awake again. But he seems to me to pursue a paradox: he wants to live like a white man and sing like a Negro. He is talking art and meaning civil rights.[29]

Whipple said that the New Negro wanted it both ways, wanted to be a White man while at the same time being different and Black. He was right. That was the contradiction the New Negro was living out, a new way of being an American in which one assimilated all that America had to offer from White civilization and then one deployed it for one's own purposes. What the New Negro announced, therefore, was this new subjectivity that broke the old mold that was created by the European immigrant paradigm, that one either became 100 percent American or persisted in one's pre-American identity and refused to assimilate. Locke's New Negro advanced a new paradigm—that one was both assimilated and non-assimilated, culturally American, but psychologically Black; and thus, what that meant was that one was thoroughly modern in a complex way. One was inevitably both a White man and a Black man at one and the same time—

and that was a creative space, regardless of what this particular generation of artists and writers did with that space.

Even as Locke returned to the literary battlefield of New York, he did not stop his counter-attack on the university for his dismissal. With Franz Boas's support, he brought charges against Howard University through the AAUP for violating the accepted procedures of the treatment of tenured professors in America. Although Locke was not directly pressuring Congress to hold up Howard's annual appropriation, he assisted others who hounded the trustees. Perhaps one of the most interesting was the suit Arthur Mitchell filed against the officers of the Allied Industrial Finance Corporation, of which Emmett Scott was an officer, accusing it of fraud and mismanagement. Mitchell brought that suit to put pressure on the university, by accusing its officers of dishonesty that he claimed was responsible for the corporation filing for bankruptcy. This end run brought a vituperative response in the Black newspapers from Scott, who remarked: "the President of the so-called Howard Welfare League had inspired, aided and abetted the movement to embarrass the Howard University administration in every possible way." Eventually, early in February, the disagreement was resolved, and eventually Scott said that he would withdraw those remarks, in exchange for his hopes that Mitchell would work to get the suit settled out of court.[30] Clearly, the stakes were getting higher every day for Howard, for the counter-attack against the June decision was increasingly costly for the university, its officers, and its subsidiary interests.

Finally, in February 1926, came news to Locke from his lawyer Thomas Dyett that Durkee had decided to leave for another job.[31] Various factors were probably involved in the decision, not the least of which was the threat of Congress blocking Howard's appropriation. But personally Durkee must have known that his tenure at Howard was effectively over after the December meeting. Fully 30 percent of the faculty polled expressed a lack of confidence in the administration. Durkee also must have realized that the easiest way out of this impasse for the board and the university was to assign blame to him and force him to leave.

On March 25, 1926, a special meeting of the board of trustees was held "to consider the resignation of J. Stanley Durkee as President of Howard" and to look for a successor. Such a turn of events was certainly ironic. In granting Locke and the others a leave of absence, the board had stipulated that after June 20, 1926, "all connections of" Locke and the other professors "with the University shall cease." But now, because of the attack on him, "all connection" of Durkee with Howard would end after June 30, 1926. Locke had not gotten his job back, but in the history of Negro education he had done something more important: he had helped remove the last White man to run Howard University. But Durkee's resignation was a pyrrhic victory. He wasn't the man responsible for Locke's dismissal. It was Moorland. But because of the politics of race in Negro education, it was easier for Durkee to take the fall for a bad decision by the board of trustees, and Durkee realized that there was nothing he could do about it. In this case, Locke's blindness to the real cause of his dismissal removed a politically inept and educationally anachronistic administrator from stewardship of the institution. But Locke still did not have his job back.

With no assurance that he would ever get his job back, Locke had to reinvent himself and become a full-time promoter of the New Negro Renaissance. With his subsidy of a year's salary, Locke could afford to invest in this new career—to plunge into lecturing, writing, and spreading the movement's goals without worrying whether each lecture paid handsomely. Of course, being "excommunicated" from Howard had had the effect of repeating the cycle of isolation and loneliness, coupled with an intense desire for companionship, that he had experienced after his mother's death. Being cut off, while painful, already had been revitalizing.

But Locke must have felt incredibly alone. Since 1912, Howard had been his home, even if he was often away from it. He had been tethered to its larger mission of educating a new generation of college-prepared youth to take his place when he and others like him from the nineteenth century had passed on. Now, that mission was no longer his. Bereft of that larger sense of purpose, bereft really of the father Howard University had been for him—rigid, reproving, but nevertheless accepting—he was now the rejected son, again. But this time, unlike when he was a child, there was no cushioning mother at hand. He was really alone, an Odysseus headed out to journey on the sea of letters with little more than an oar. But that oar was a strong one—a volume titled *The New Negro: An Interpretation*. His very survival now depended on whether what he predicted in its pages was true, that a Negro of talent could survive on self-determination and a song—in his case, a song of beauty.

28

Beauty or Propaganda?

Sometime in the late 1920s or the early 1930s, Alain Locke and W. E. B. Du Bois entered a basement restaurant in Black Washington, D.C., where the future Black psychiatrist Charles Prudhomme was working as a waiter, and sat down for dinner. Each requested a glass of boiling water. Once the glasses arrived, Locke and Du Bois picked up their silverware and placed them in the boiling water.[1] That gesture reflected their opinion that Negro restaurants did not maintain the highest standards of cleanliness. Their concern for cleanliness was not unique. Booker T. Washington, more than a quarter of a century before, had made cleanliness the centerpiece of the civilizing mission of Tuskegee Institute.[2] Cleanliness not only anchored personal hygiene but also symbolized what Washington wanted instilled in the minds of ex-slaves—that their bodies, their selves, were worth preserving, worth investing in for the future, through self-care.

That Locke and Du Bois made such a gesture of self-protection suggests they doubted Washington's ethic of cleanliness had been adopted widely by the Black establishments that Jim Crow segregation forced them to eat in. Working-class, even entrepreneurial African Americans, had not yet, in the language of Washington, thrown off the negative conception of themselves that led them to maintain less than sterling standards of cleanliness in their restaurants. As these three-piece-suit wearing Europhile academics sat down in this modest Washington restaurant, Locke and Du Bois felt a sanitary gulf separated them from most other African Americans in the 1920s and 1930s. There was still work to be done, and their gesture suggests that all three men agreed on at least one thing—that art, science, business, politics, all education, really, had a dual purpose—to instill civilization in an uneducated people and to purify them, like those utensils, of the self-hate acquired in their sojourn in America. Indeed, so fatalistic was Locke about this process, it's a wonder he risked such a meal in a "Colored" establishment at all. Of the three, Locke was the extreme mysophobe, who often refused to shake hands, touch doorknobs, or otherwise make physical contact with dirt. Usually, instead of visiting such restaurants, Locke took his meals at Union Station, its restaurant the only "White" restaurant in Washington, D.C., that allowed Black people to dine in, since it was a federal facility. Locke too might need "purifying" of some of his accommodations to a White supremacist world.

Nevertheless, Locke had decided to join Du Bois for a dinner in the Black community on this occasion. With the smells of chicken frying, ribs boiling, and okra steaming filling the air around them, they talked for several hours. Prudhomme could not catch the conversation. But if it was in the late 1920s, it might very well have been on the subject on which both held strong and opposing opinions—the question of Black art and its role in the crisis of the Negro people. What was the goal of African American creative expression? Was it to defend Negroes against racism? Or uncover Beauty, especially among a people often thought of as lacking in Beauty? Later, Locke would pose this conflict of aspirations as a question of what the Negro wanted: "Art or Propaganda?"

Why was this an issue between two Harvard-educated Black intellectuals who agreed on much, such as the level of protection they needed from the lack of cleanliness in Black restaurants? Of course, both Locke and Du Bois believed in "art." Du Bois had defended the rights of artistic freedom for artists before the mid-1920s against "philistines" who tried to limit Negro artistic freedom. But when *The New Negro* was published in 1925, Du Bois reacted differently, for Locke went so far as to dethrone propaganda as the reigning raison d'être for Negro art and suggest that beauty was its highest goal. In his otherwise appreciative review in the *Crisis* in January 1926, Du Bois cautioned:

> With one point alone do I differ with the Editor. Mr. Locke has newly been seized with the idea that Beauty rather than Propaganda should be the object of Negro literature and art. His book proves the falseness of this thesis. This is a book filled and bursting with propaganda but it is propaganda for the most part beautifully and painstakingly done; and it is a grave question if ever in this world in any renaissance there can be a search for disembodied beauty which is not really a passionate effort to do something tangible, accompanied and illumined and made holy by the vision of eternal beauty. Of course this involves a controversy as old as the world and much too transcendental for practical purposes, and yet, if Mr. Locke's thesis is insisted on too much it is going to turn the Negro Renaissance into decadence. It is the fight for Life and Liberty that is giving birth to Negro literature and art today and when, turning from this fight or ignoring it, the young Negro tries to do pretty things or things that catch the passing fancy of the really unimportant critics and publishers about him, he will find that he has killed the soul of Beauty in his Art.[3]

Here was the most significant challenge to *The New Negro* Locke had to deal with in 1926 and 1927. While Locke had been extremely inclusive in *The New Negro* so as not to offend any established institutional gods of Negro America, Du Bois had sniffed out that the volume made Locke and his Negro aesthetic philosophy a threat to the Du Boisian view that Negro art was meaningful only as part of the political struggle for Negro freedom. Indeed, *The New Negro* displaced the NAACP agenda of protest art with a generational permission for Black artists to see themselves as artists first. "The elder generation," Locke wrote, "of Negro writers expressed itself in cautious moralism.... They felt art must fight social battles and compensate social wrongs.... The newer motive, then, in being racial is to be so purely for the sake of art."[4]

The phrase "for the sake of art" conjured for Du Bois the "art for art's sake" movement of late nineteenth-century Europe. One of its chief proponents, Walter Pater, narrated how humanity's authentic search for beauty culminated in a rejection of conventional morality—and conventional notions of social responsibility. Unlike Locke, Du Bois possessed a moralizing view of aesthetics: like Matthew Arnold, he believed the arts taught traditional moral values, and when they did not, they eroded those values, which led to decadence and sexual deviance. Protest art was, in fact, a kind of moral art, and Beauty was not so much an end, but a means to restoration of Black humanity. Locke's "Negro Youth Speaks" suggested the younger generation did not want to shoulder that burden, but to create art that might or might not advance the progressive race struggle. Locke believed protest art narrowed Black identity to always responding to White racism. For Locke, Negro subjectivity was richer and more various than anti-racism. To insist that all Negro artists be soldiers in a war against White racism denied them the right to be self-reflexive and human.

There was another issue between them: sex. A Negro art movement based on Beauty was a slippery slope to decadence and homosexuality, and Du Bois was having none of it. Although Du Bois engaged in serial adultery, that did not make him tolerant of prostitution, gambling, thugs, or homosexuality. When he discovered that his business manager had been arrested for same-sex soliciting in a public place, Du Bois fired him, although later he admitted that had been a mistake. Du Bois feared unleashed sexual desire as the defining identity of the Negro Renaissance. Locke, by contrast, had already come to terms with himself as an "Immoralist." To have a sexual life and continue to assert his right to be considered a "respectable Negro" required him to get past an impasse to self-representation that Du Bois still struggled with. Locke saw the Black Victorian tradition of self-control as part of the problem of the educated Negro and also part of his own problem with creative expression. Often he lamented that he was too "tightly wound" to allow his spirit to soar as a writer. In that sense, his

view of the Renaissance resonated with Du Bois's, but arrived at a different conclusion. The Negro Renaissance was a loosening of sexual restraint, and that was
a good thing. In that sense, he could be sympathetic to the desire for freedom
among the young artists, even if he wanted them to do something more with it
than simply celebrate their libido.

Du Bois's reaction to the new art shows the difference between him and
Locke, just as the dipping of silverware in hot water shows their similarity. Du
Bois was the Anglo-American, who saw art as an instrument of morality and
social change in a manner not too removed from the attitude of Matthew Arnold.
Culture should educate whether moralistically or racially. Locke, however, was
the European, who saw art as the highest product of civilization, to be revered
for its own sake, and to be loved like sex. Du Bois saw art as of instrumental
value in changing American racial practice; Locke extolled art as the eternal
search for the Beautiful. Du Bois was the Black Victorian, whose rigid sense of
the private and the public fueled his anger over how informal "at home" images
of Negroes were projected by the American media as the public identity of the
Negro. Locke was the Black Edwardian, who though horrified by how newspapers and some literature depicted Blacks, was also alienated by the provincial,
heterosexist, middle-class narrative that dominated literature written by Du
Bois, Jessie Fauset, and others like him.

Both Locke and Du Bois did eventually agree in later years that the Negro
Renaissance declined into decadence and wallowed in homosexual allusions. But
Locke claimed those were not his explicit goals for the New Negro Renaissance.
His movement did not exclude homosexuality, but was more a declaration of
freedom, that Negroes had the right to pursue art, as the ancients had, in the
search for Beauty as part of the Negro being human. If African Americans sacrificed that to the racists, the result, Locke argued, would be not only inferior art
but also the sacrifice of freedom and humanity.

Another question looms: were Du Bois and Locke talking about art or Locke's
dismissal from Howard when they visited that restaurant? Given that Prudhomme
could not recall the exact period of the visit, might it had occurred when Locke
was still unemployed? Or if later, might they have been discussing the continuing problems of Negro scholars in Negro higher education, something Du Bois
was concerned about for the rest of his career? Unlike Locke, Du Bois seemed
always to land on his feet, whether it was leaving Atlanta University in 1910 to
take the editorship of the *Crisis* at the NAACP or leaving the NAACP in 1934
after his dispute with its board and rejoining Atlanta University as a professor.
But not one major Black institution had come forward to offer Locke a job after
he was fired from Howard. Of course, Locke was not as eminent a Black intellectual as Du Bois; but arguably, he was the next after him. Neither the NAACP nor
the Urban League welcomed the second-best-educated Negro in America into its

operations. No Black journal or newspaper made him an editor, even though he had proven himself an exceptional editor of *Opportunity*, the Harlem number of the *Survey Graphic*, and *The New Negro*. But some of Locke's negatives were positives. "Howard has tried to hurt you," Hazel Harrison, a pianist and friend of Locke's, noted. "But they have actually pushed you forward. Many people who would not have known of you otherwise are talking about you and reading everything you write."[5]

Locke's dismissal had freed him to write more, lecture more, and nationalize his identity. It also enabled him to identify more with artists, most of whom also lacked institutional moorings. Locke knew that if he was to remain in the public eye, he would have to out-produce and outmaneuver other interpreters of the New Negro, men such as Walter White, Charles S. Johnson, James Weldon Johnson, George Schuyler, Carl Van Vechten, H. L. Mencken, and V. F. Calverton, and, of course, Du Bois, who enjoyed connections with institutions or publishers he lacked. To do so Locke anointed himself the "godfather" of the movement and took upon himself the responsibility to watch over the movement, to advance its artists, to define its goals, and to defend it from attacks. Locke threw himself into advocacy work so that no one could ignore him. The role gave him enormous energy. Without the distraction of teaching, Locke flooded the market with essays and articles that defined Negro Cultural Studies for the 1920s. He might sit down to dinner with Du Bois. But afterward, he would be up and running to get the next article in print or deliver the next speech to a paying crowd.

Locke wrote sympathetic, encouraging reviews of writers' first books, such as Countee Cullen's first book of poems, *Color*, in the January 1926 *Opportunity*. "Ladies and gentlemen! A genius!" Cullen was a great Negro poet because he possessed the "lyric gift" and wrote about universal subject matter as a Black man. "Pour into the vat all the Tennyson, Swinburne, Housman, Patmore, Teasdale you want, and add a dash of Pope for this strange modern skill of sparkling couplets,—and all these I daresay have been intellectually culled and added to the brew, and still there is another evident ingredient, fruit of the Negro inheritance and experience, that has stored up the tropic sun and ripened under the storm and stress of the American transplanting."[6] Some critics of *The New Negro* chided Locke for this kind of praise of new and untested poets whom Leon Whipple called average American writers. But Locke saw in Cullen a Negro talent surveying the field of human experience and giving it a spin that only Black youth could provide. Even when Cullen focused on the Negro predicament, he treated it with a freedom and subtlety lacking in others. "The paradoxes of Negro life and feeling that have been sad and plaintive and whimsical in the age of Dunbar and that were rhetorical and troubled, vibrant and accusatory with the Johnsons and MacKay [*sic*] now glow and shine and sing in this poetry of the youngest generation."[7]

In contrast to James Weldon Johnson, Locke also advanced Negro art as something more than Negro writers. Early in 1926, Locke wrote "The Negro Poets of the United States," for William Braithwaite's *Anthology of American Verse*, and made a distinction he returned to throughout the decade. "Negro poets and Negro poetry are two quite different things. Of the one, since Phyllis Wheatley, we have had a century and a half; of the other, since Dunbar, scarcely a generation. But the signification of the work of Negro poets will more and more be seen and valued retrospectively as the medium through which a poetry of Negro life and experience has gradually become possible."[8] In making Dunbar the beginning of the tradition of Negro poetry, Locke broke with Johnson, who had argued that contemporary Negro poetry was defined by its rejection of Dunbar and the twin emotions of humor and pathos in his poetry. Locke also distinguished himself from Du Bois, who evaluated literature in terms of its pragmatic utility in a war of representation with White racism. Locke announced that Negro art was a Black tradition of forms that existed even when Whites and race conflict were absent. The poetry of Dunbar showed that a Black voice transcended victimization and, when it did confront victimization, did so with irony, humor, and wisdom that short-circuited the dehumanization of racist discourses. To write poetry, Locke declared in 1926, meant to come out from under the shackle of racist discourses and write like a Black person whose experience was as rich and complex and rewarding as that of any other American's. His job was to sell the notion that one could write as a Black man or woman and say something compelling to all readers.

By February 1926, however, Du Bois could no longer suppress his critical feelings and extended his reservations about the philosophy of Beauty in *The New Negro: An Interpretation* into a "Symposium" in the *Crisis* that ran from February to July 1926. It was an extraordinary gesture, for it transformed Du Bois's reservations into a set of essays on the role of art in the representation of the Negro in American culture. Did writers, Black or White, and publishers, have an obligation to be representative, that is, to produce literature that not only embodied the literary taste of the day for stories and poems about working- and criminal-class urban culture but also told stories rooted in the lives of middle-class, stable, outwardly moral Black people? Was the popularity of certain characterizations of Negroes as criminals, pimps, and loose women not designed to discredit moral Black people? Was the willingness of publishers to disseminate stories with such characters and not those of moralistic middle-class Blacks a conspiracy to impede Black acceptance into the nation's mainstream? These questions not only had merit, they had weight.

Unfortunately for Du Bois, most of the contributors who wrote in to answer his questions rejected his position. Most thought the greater danger was censorship, especially self-censorship. Carl Van Vechten, whose racy novel, *Nigger*

Heaven, would be published later that year, argued that the main consequence of Du Bois's analysis was that it "might be effective in preventing many excellent Negro writers from speaking any truth which might be considered unpleasant."[9] DuBose Heyward, whose *Porgy* Du Bois referenced, responded that such middle-class lives "must be treated artistically. It destroys itself as soon as it is made a vehicle for propaganda."[10] Writer after writer responded that they valued their freedom over Du Bois's notion of their responsibility to the Negro—or any other—public. Almost all of the younger Negro writers, even those friendly to Du Bois, such as Countee Cullen and Langston Hughes, voted for the freedom of the artist and issued a truism: the artist should write what she or he felt. Most believed there was little causality between what they wrote and the actions of the larger, presumably White, community on racial issues. Among the young male writers, only Cullen agreed with Du Bois that a need existed for literary types that were "truly representative of us as a people," but even he admitted that he could not really endorse the "infringement of artistic freedom." The consensus was Du Bois was far out of step with contemporary writers, who found his critiques implausible.

But Du Bois had identified a real issue. The charge that the American media encouraged images of "twelve million Americans as prostitutes, thieves and fools" had merit. The history of Black minstrelsy suggested that White audiences of popular theater demanded Black actors perform caricatures of themselves. African Americans grew up in the early twentieth century bombarded with degrading and dehumanizing images in the popular press. Even Locke's Harlem issue of the *Survey Graphic* documented the impact of the racist discourse when Elise McDougald wrote that the Negro woman "realizes that the ideals of beauty, built up in the fine arts, exclude her almost entirely. Instead, the grotesque Aunt Jemimas of the street-car advertisements proclaim only an ability to serve, without grace or loveliness. Nor does the drama catch her finest spirit. She is most often used to provoke the mirthless laugh of ridicule; or to portray feminine viciousness or vulgarity not peculiar to Negroes. This is the shadow over her."[11] McDougald had documented how American advertising capitalism had fixed a racialized stereotype of servile labor into the minds of upwardly mobile American Whites without them being aware of it. Du Bois had perceived that art was class and racial advertisement and a weapon to redress the cultural if not the economic imbalance in America's representation of the Negro. But Locke believed one had to resist the temptation to utilize art in the same way as the oppressor did, because to do so reduced one's humanity to the low level of one's enemy.

Just as profound, Locke and Du Bois differed over the nature of racism and how racial images functioned in America. In a *Modern Quarterly* article, "The Social Origins of American Negro Art," Du Bois argued that negative racial images in American literature reinforced and sustained American racial practices. Published in October 1925, the article argued the constant and unrelenting dissemination of negative images of Black people by American literature forced the Negro American writer to counter this "propaganda" with a counterhegemonic literature. Racism, in other words, was propelled by an overwhelmingly racist American literature. Ever competitive, Locke answered Du Bois's argument in a *Modern Quarterly* article of his own soon afterward, "The American Literary Tradition and the Negro," where he argued American literature had not always disseminated wholly negative images of Black people. Applying his Marxian analysis of Race Contacts to American literature, Locke argued that the literary image of the Negro followed social practice toward the Negro, and changed over time in relation to the changing social and economic position of the Negro in American life. A docile Negro image, for example, had dominated when an economically thriving antebellum slavery regime needed to convince outside critics that Blacks were satisfied with slavery. After Reconstruction, when the ruling class of the South needed to discipline ex-slaves to work in the sharecropping regime, southern literature disseminated the image of the Negro as the animalistic brute, who was a threat to the social order and needed to be kept in line by the KKK. For Du Bois, race was a static, permanent phenomenon, while for Locke, it was fluid, varying in relation to changes in the demographic and economic calculus of American society. For Locke, the changeableness of the image of the Negro in literature showed that art was less of a propaganda tool and more of a barometer of race relations. The current New Negro image reflected a flexibility in the position of Negroes in modern American society being tapped by contemporary modernist Negro writers.

The art is propaganda argument was, in reality, a demand by Du Bois to constrain the Black literary awakening to producing positive, bourgeois images of the Negro to counter the debased representations emanating from racist American popular culture. He wanted Negro literature to generate more images of Black people as moral exemplars with a complexity all but absent from an American public imagery that confined Negro representation, usually, to negative, that is, lower-class, images of Blacks. Du Bois's problem was that serious American literature of the 1920s was decidedly anti-bourgeois. Such White writers as Sinclair Lewis and Sherwood Anderson depicted the middle class as buffoons, if not worse, and young Black writers would have marginalized themselves in American literature had they followed Du Bois's advice.

At root, Du Bois's argument was about sex. A notorious paramour, who sustained hot, sexually prolific relationships with dozens of women, such as Georgia Douglas Johnson and Jessie Fauset, while married, Du Bois was himself in the closet, unwilling to publicly support a literature movement that foregrounded sexual desire in its representation of the Negro. Added to this heterosexist contradiction was the homosexual one for Du Bois: he fired his business officer, Augustus Granville after Du Bois discovered he had been arrested for public solicitation. Later, Du Bois said he regretted it. But the message was clear: in an ideological war between the races, Du Bois could not afford to allow the reputation of that race, and the *Crisis*, to be damaged by public homosexual scandal.[12]

Du Bois's moralizing stand, therefore, helped Locke to advance himself as the writers' advocate, and the older man's critique of White publishers and playwrights created an opening for Locke to write for those White journals and launch a new argument that the most fertile field for the Negro Renaissance was in an integrated world of culture.

Even more, Locke exploited opportunities for magazine writing in fields ignored by Du Bois—art, music, and the theater—eager for articles on the implications of the Negro Renaissance. The field of Negro drama was particularly fertile and Locke published his first article on the Negro drama in a mainstream journal when "The Negro and the American Stage" appeared in the February issue of *Theatre Arts Monthly*. That article began a twenty-year association with its editor, Mrs. Edith Isaacs, whom Locke may have met through Paul Kellogg. That article also shifted his earlier emphasis from Negro playwrights to Negro actors as the most important element in contemporary Negro dramatic performance. Prior to this article, Locke had advocated that the Negro drama should be based in Negro universities, written by Negro playwrights, and acted by Negro actors. But in the year since the publication of "Max Rheinhardt Reads the Negro's Dramatic Horoscope," Locke embraced his analysis. "Welcome then as is the emergence of the Negro playwright and the drama of Negro life, the promise of the most vital contribution of our race to the theatre lies, in my opinion, in the deep and unemancipated resources of the Negro actor, and the folk arts of which he is as yet only a kind and hampered exponent."[13]

Having to survive in the literary marketplace without a university job helped Locke make an ideological shift—away from a nationalist notion of Black art as only appropriate in Black institutions to a notion of Black art as a kind of Trojan Horse intervention in White cultural spaces. His article also acknowledged that Black actors—Paul Robeson, Charles Gilpin, Rose McClendon, Opal Cooper, Inez Clough, Bert Williams, Florence Mills, Bill Robinson, Josephine Baker, Ethel Waters, and Abbie Mitchell—were having a bigger and more transformative impact on the American theater than was the African American playwright. He now made another logical leap: the ultimate value of a Negro drama would be to transform the American theater through dissemination of its "technical idioms and resources of the entire theatre" than in the segregated theater. Was Locke's optimism justified? Yes. Negro actors would transform by their performance plays written by White playwrights. Charles Gilpin, Locke's favorite as Brutus

Jones, had transformed *Emperor Jones* into a cerebral tour de force of a Black madman and given it an intellectual intensity absent from Eugene O'Neill's script. Most famously, actors in *Porgy* lifted a play of low life into a universal tragedy by their talent. Part of the reason was race: such performers as Leontyne Price starred in *Porgy* at a time when it was not possible for her to appear in an opera in America. Part of the reason was form: Black actors brought a technical facility to the performance of even flawed plays that lifted American drama onto a plane with the best of world drama.

In another article, "The Drama of Negro Life," in the October 1926 issue of *Theatre Arts Monthly*, Locke cleared a space for White participation in the New Negro movement. "A few illuminating plays, beginning with Edward Sheldon's *Nigger* and culminating for the present in O'Neill's *All God's Chillun Got Wings*, have already thrown into relief the higher possibilities of the Negro problem play. Similarly, beginning with Ridgeley Torrence's *Three Plays for a Negro Theatre* and culminating in *Emperor Jones* and *The No 'Count Boy*, realistic study of Negro folk-life and character has been begun, and with it the inauguration of the artistic Negro play."[14] While Locke continued to hope and work for the development of the Negro playwright and the Negro Theater, "the pioneer efforts have not always been those of the Negro playwright and in the list of the most noteworthy exponents of Negro drama, Sheldon, Torrence, O'Neill, Howard Culbertson, Paul Green, Burghardt Du Bois, Angelina Grimke, and Willis Richardson, only the last three are Negroes."[15]

Locke also used this article to begin his long answer to Du Bois's argument in the "Symposium" that Negro literature ought to provide answers to the charges of racists. "Propaganda, pro-Negro as well as anti-Negro, has scotched the dramatic potentialities of the subject. Especially for the few Negro playwrights has the propaganda motive worked havoc. In addition to the handicap of being out of actual touch with the theatre, they have had the dramatic motive deflected at its source. Race drama has appeared to them a matter of race vindication, and pathetically they have pushed forward their moralistic allegories or melodramatic protests as dramatic correctives and antidotes for race prejudice." Where Du Bois identified White playwrights as the enemy of a true Negro portrait, Locke argued White authors had written some of the most successful race problem plays of recent times. Their plays had succeeded because the race problem was, in some respects, the White man's problem. Willis Richardson had excelled so far at writing an alternative drama—a Negro "folk-drama" that would "grow in its own soil and cultivate its own intrinsic elements," as Dunbar's poetry had done. Locke preferred to see this interior view of Negro life on the stage. But both White and Black playwrights were co-constructing New Negro drama, drawing on their different strengths.

Locke held back from making the leap implied by his new approach to the Negro drama. If being a New Negro was only an attitude and a commitment to a beautiful portrayal of the Negro experience, then a White playwright was potentially as much a New Negro as a Black playwright or actor. The White artist acknowledged that there was something about the Negro experience that he needed to complete his identity as an American, whereas the Black actor in a White-authored play dialogued with the White side of his identity and in doing so reformulated African American identity. Locke was still a race man, though the trajectory of his articles and introductions redefined the Negro drama as an interracial dialogue. Locke was resurrecting Du Bois's earlier, more complicated notion of Negro identity, "double consciousness," as potentially a positive, not a debilitating divided self, but a dialogic American. The Negro drama must become a means of revelation and reconciliation of the two sides of Negro/American identity.

By 1926, Locke was acknowledging that if a Black impresario wanted a Negro drama to flourish, Negro drama needed White patronage, not to rely on Black colleges and universities. Locke's refashioning of Negro dramatic arts opened a new front in his continuing war with Black civil rights and service organizations, which he felt did not fully appreciate drama's cultural service. Locke hoped to pivot among these many cultural players, pit them against one another when necessary, stimulate creative energies of a Negro drama situated in the 1920s moment, and force Americans to speak to one another. If he could establish his own authority over such a drama, then he might, through criticism, bring White and Black playwrights toward a truly exciting conversation about race in America.

Locke's new approach in the drama and other arts paid dividends in expanded speaking opportunities. On May 12, he did one of the usual engagements, speaking to a Black, educated, lay audience in Washington. Anna J. Cooper's cheeky comment exposed a bit of Locke's self-inflation. "This is to remind you that we expect you Sunday May 16 . . . to tell us just what constitutes a race drama + how we may know it when we find it."[16] Paying opportunities came from White groups, such as the women's university club of Grand Rapids that invited Locke to speak that fall. "The club is particularly interested in the artistic side of the negro movement, and feels sure that you could give a very interesting talk on the subject."[17] Part of Locke's growing demand as a speaker in 1926 came from his ability to spice his presentations with witty, pithy statements. Lydia Gibson Miner teased Locke about one of his statements made at a visit to her school, namely: "'Statesmanship as distinguished from its counterfeits is the art of making progress without revolution.' A.L. Therefore:—Washington, Jefferson, John Adams, Samuel Adams, Cromwell, Massini, Lincoln, Frederick Douglass, Robespierre, Dante, Lenin, Stalin, Bukarin, Napoleon, and others—a few hundred—were counterfeit statesmen. Q.E.D."[18]

Locke's "statesmanship" used art to triangulate the positions of White supremacy and Black protest and allowed liberal Whites and conservative Blacks to re-engage in the discussion of race without having to take sides, for example, on the lynching bill before Congress. Part of the appeal of *The New Negro* was that it could be accepted by conservatives who read its call for self-determination as another form of self-help. "You will be interested to know," George Foster Peabody wrote to Locke, "that in a private letter from my very dear Friend, Honorable Newton D. Baker, he writes me as follows: 'Locke's The New Negro' is a genuinely significant and helpful book. If it is widely read among the Negros it ought to do much to stimulate the best thought of the race toward the achievement of a culture of their own and so divert much of their passion which is now worse than wasted in demands for recognition, as a matter of right, which, in the nature of the case, can only come when they are won by service—in this case when time has had a chance."[19]

Here was the risk of Locke's new approach: it gave fuel to conservative Whites, who saw art as a diversion of rightful protest into "achievement" and "service." Du Bois would make just this charge months later in "Criteria of Negro Art," his 1926 critique of Locke's position on Negro art, when he wrote: "there are others who feel a certain relief and are saying, 'After all it is rather satisfactory after all this talk about rights and fighting to sit and dream of something which leaves a nice taste in the mouth.'"[20] Locke's philosophy of aesthetics could be a mask that allowed White patrons to feel all he was advancing was a way for Whites to feel more comfortable that instead of rebelling, Blacks were satisfied to write poetry and worship Western civilization.

But these patrons were also at times shocked at what reading and studying led Blacks to understand—their agency in constructing civilization. On one occasion, Peabody was horrified to learn second-hand from one of Locke's students that the philosopher had advocated in one of his classes that the Nile was the birthplace of the Divine Being (perhaps a reflection of Locke's Coptic view that the ark had been removed from Jerusalem to Abyssinia). Peabody quickly corrected Locke that it was the Judea-Christian heritage located in Jerusalem that was the source of all faith in the one and only God! Such slips into what Peabody must have thought was paganism were dangerous for Locke because he was relying on Peabody in his continuing campaign to get his job back at Howard. Peabody had just glimpsed what was true—that Locke's attempt to restore the "proper" place of Africa within the history of civilization meant a radical displacement of the Judea-Christian heritage.[21]

Locke hid the revolution in global thinking implicit in a Black renaissance in order—and this is what Du Bois resented increasingly—to curry favor and get money from White patrons. But being unemployed, Locke was more vulnerable, more exposed to the market forces of unemployment in 1926, and more anxious that his writings serve a double purpose—to free the Negro and also to advance his own individual survival given that, as a Black homosexual, he was considered too toxic to be hired inside of Negro progressive institutions such as the NAACP and the National Urban League. Being an outsider to the Negro establishment drove Locke toward both a radical critique and a romance with the pillars of Whiteness. Without a job, Locke had to dissemble, bob and weave, and hope that he could advance a Black aesthetic without dashing his chance to get his Howard University position back because some trustee viewed him as a dangerous radical. Locke himself was looking for a renaissance in 1926.

Late in June that year, Locke left for Europe, having earned enough money from publishing and speaking to spend the summer abroad. He needed time in Europe to escape the quagmire of emotions that Black Washington had become for him. He wondered whether he should move permanently from Washington to New York, for in Harlem was developing a community of Black gay men who regularly saw one another in bars, cabarets, and nightclubs without the sense that they would be ostracized from the Literary Society. That sense of the private and the public also divided Locke from Du Bois, who could move easily between his professional life and spending evenings with a mistress, without fear of reproof if he was so discovered. For Locke, such freedom existed only abroad, in Paris or Berlin.

Locke also pursued other ambitions abroad. Through Helen Irvin Locke he learned that Dr. Mordecai Johnson, a Baptist minister, who was rumored to be on the short list of possible candidates for president of Howard University, was in Europe that summer. Irvin had known Johnson at the University of Chicago, thought well of him, and encouraged Locke to seek him out. Locke wanted to meet up with him on neutral ground to discuss his possible reinstatement. He managed to speak with him at length and was impressed by his intelligence, drive, and steely determination. Johnson's selection encouraged Locke that Howard was finally going to get the New Negro leadership it deserved.

Just as Locke left America, Du Bois was thundering to the NAACP convention in Chicago that "all art is propaganda and ever must be, despite the wailing of the purists . . . I do not care a damn for any art that is not used for propaganda."[22] Linked to Locke's growing frustration with Du Bois's position was his sense that Du Bois knew such narrowing of the range of Negro art appreciation was a lie. Du Bois, no less than Locke, loved the sonatas of Beethoven completely apart from any consideration of their representation of German humanity. They both loved the poetry of Goethe, Shelley, and Keats, without cataloging how the writings of each elevated their respective peoples in world renown. Locke knew that in Europe Du Bois walked under the same nocturnal foliage in the Bois de Boulogne, enjoyed cafes in the same neighborhoods, and attended similar concerts. Indeed, Locke might have felt a bit of pity for the great Du Bois who seemed to sacrifice appreciation for the sublime in the fight for the Negro's rights. Even in his Chicago declaration of all art is propaganda, Du Bois admitted that Beauty was something profoundly human that Negroes as well as all other humans had a right to.

> Such is Beauty. Its variety is infinite, its possibility is endless. In normal life all may have it and have it yet again. The world is full of it; and yet today the mass of human beings are choked away from it, and their lives distorted and made ugly. This is not only wrong, it is silly. Who shall right this well-nigh universal failing? Who shall let this world be beautiful? Who shall restore to men the glory of sunsets and the peace of quiet sleep?[23]

Locke's New Negro was a legitimate answer to these questions, as Locke knew that Du Bois loved the life of the cosmopolitan and its escape into art that was not political but somehow couldn't admit it from the helm of the *Crisis*. Was Du Bois just a bit jealous that the younger Harvard man had found an aesthetic philosophy more popular with the younger generation of Black writers than his? Locke had had the good sense not to respond to Du Bois's "Symposium" that February 1926, but when he returned to the United States he knew he would have to find a way to respond to what would become Du Bois's "Criteria of Negro Art" to keep his position as the defender of Negro youth. For he and Du Bois knew that the Negro artist was the best suited to answer these questions, to "right these wrongs." But Locke had few resources—he didn't even control a journal as Du Bois did—"to restore men the glory of sunsets and the peace of quiet sleep." Going abroad was a welcome escape from thinking about how tortured the American situation of race and beauty was for him.

When Locke's thought did turn to race and art that summer, it went back to Hughes and their walks together through Paris in 1924. Having not been abroad since that rendezvous, Locke may have found himself yearning to reconnect with his elusive friend. Possibly this interlude back in Paris catalyzed in Locke a desire to move closer to an active, mentoring relationship with Hughes, despite the earlier frustrations. In some respects, Hughes was all that was left of the original quartet of promising Black poets: Jean Toomer had left the race; McKay was about to be his enemy; and Cullen was too absorbed in his own flattering press to devote himself to the serious work of improving as a poet. Hughes, along with Hurston, might be the only ones willing to undertake what Locke preached—immersion in the Negro folk spirit to create great art. Perhaps there was still hope that a renaissance grounded in Blackness could emerge in an America generally alien to the pursuit of Beauty he enjoyed in quiet evenings abroad.

That all changed when Locke returned home in mid-September 1926. Controversy had broken out, in all places, in the *Nation*. George Schuyler, the puckish, iconoclastic contributing editor of the *Messenger*, had published an article, "The Negro Art-Hokum," that discounted not only the Black literary movement but also the notion that there was anything culturally distinctive about the Negro to express. A week later came a bombshell from Langston Hughes. "The Negro Artist and the Racial Mountain" was the young Negro artists' declaration of independence. "We younger Negro artists who create now intend to express our individual dark-skinned selves without fear or shame. If White people are pleased we are glad. If they are not, it doesn't matter. We know we are beautiful. And ugly too. ... If colored people are pleased we are glad. If not, their displeasure doesn't matter either." Hughes had also attacked Cullen, whose review of *The Weary Blues* had chided his rival for confining himself only to poems on Negro subjects. In a barely veiled reference, Hughes suggested that because Cullen wanted to be considered a poet, not a Negro poet, that Cullen wanted to be White. Such reductionism, so popular during the Black Arts Movement of the 1960s, suggested that only the poet who embraced race, regional, or national identity could become a great poet. Hughes's racial romanticism was compelling in 1926, because he linked it to an attack on the Black bourgeoisie, whom he argued so lived their lives for White approval that they distanced themselves from the "common people." Hughes included a critique of one of Locke's hang-ups, his distaste for jazz and the blues. "Let the blare of Negro jazz bands and the bellow-ing voice of Bessie Smith singing Blues penetrate the closed ears of the colored near-intellectuals until they listen and understand ... [and] ... catch a glimmer of their own beauty." He claimed his audience and sympathetic critics should em-brace these new forms as repositories of authentic Blackness.[24]

Locke had ignored "The Negro and the Racial Mountain," which was pub-lished just before his departure to Europe. But he could not ignore Hughes's challenge to transcend high aestheticism when he returned in September. In August, Carl Van Vechten, Hughes's patron, had published *Nigger Heaven*, which had become a commercial success, but also confirmed Du Bois's prediction that a focus on Beauty would lead the Negro Renaissance into decadence. Lurid, exotic, and erotic, *Nigger Heaven* not only had an insulting title but was also seen by many Black intellectuals as a slap in the face from a White author reputedly the Negro's friend. Although James Weldon Johnson and Hughes defended Van Vechten, the book and the controversy it spawned made its author a pariah in some circles. Locke refrained from publicly commenting on *Nigger Heaven* and used the fall publication of his review of *The Weary Blues* in the Black literary magazine *Palms* to defend Hughes's first book of poems from criticism by Black philistines. "There are lyrics in this volume which are such contributions to pure poetry that it makes little difference what substance of life and experience they were made of," Locke began, acknowledging the controversy over whether the work in *The Weary Blues* was really poetry. "Nor would I style Langston Hughes a race poet because he writes in many instances of Negro life"—which was also Locke's answer to Cullen's criticism. This was Negro poetry "because all his poetry seems saturated with the rhythms and moods of Negro folk life."[25]

That argument allowed Locke to confront the man whom he increasingly felt was a rival and bad influence on Hughes. "Taking these poems too much merely as the expressions of a personality, Carl Van Vechten in his debonair introduction wonders at what he calls 'their deceptive air of spontaneous improvisation.'"[26] In fact, there was an element of "deception" in that the poems were close transcriptions of blues Hughes had collected. Zora Neale Hurston put it bluntly in a letter to Cullen. "By the way, Hughes ought to stop publishing all those secular folk-songs as his poetry. Now when he got off the 'Weary Blues' (most of it a song I and most southerners have known all our lives) I said nothing for I knew I'd never be forgiven by certain people for crying down what the 'white folks had exalted', but when he gets off another 'Me and mah honey got two mo- days tu do de buck' I don't see how I can refrain from speaking. I am at least going to speak to Van Vechten."[27] Hughes mined a tradition, really two traditions, since his poems embodied "the rhythm of the secular ballad, but the imagery and diction of the spiritual." Locke's language of the "secular ballad" suggests he had still not embraced the jazz and blues traditions. But his sense of Hughes's ability to translate the Negro "spirit" into free verse allowed Locke to designate Hughes "spokesman" for the Negro masses. But haunting his approval was Locke's sense that Van Vechten, an aged homosexual spoiler of young Black men, victimized Hughes's work. Locke defended himself psychologically against any self-consciousness that he did the same thing.

When Locke left for Europe, Du Bois had delivered his "Criteria of Negro Art" speech at the NAACP convention in Chicago, which was published in October, a thinly veiled attack on Locke and the New Negro writers embodied in his declaration that "all art is propaganda, either for or against the race." Shortly after he returned, Locke was confronted with an explosive answer to "Criteria" that November in *Fire!!*, a collection of writing "devoted to the younger Negro artists," edited by St. Louis–born Wallace Thurman, a Black editor of the *Messenger*, who collaborated with Hughes, Zora Neale Hurston, Lewis Alexander, Aaron Douglas, and several others. When *Fire!!* appeared, it brought a bold Egyptian-inspired silhouette cover by Aaron Douglas, poetry by Hughes, a play by Zora Neale Hurston, and a homoerotic short story, plus contorted line drawings by Richard Bruce. *Fire!!* was an attack on the moralizing sensibilities of the Black bourgeoisie, an "art for art's sake" publication that used folk, working-class, and sexual innuendo to advance the credo of the romantic artist. Locke gave qualified praise to the effort in his review of the first issue in the *Survey Mid-Monthly* as "a gay and self-confident maneuver of artistic secession." Locke's reference to "secession" invoked the series of European rebellions by visual artists, some of which his friend Winold Reiss had participated in during the early twentieth century to hold exhibitions of work rejected by the art establishment. In this case, the Black "secession" was a rebellion against the sensibilities of the Black bourgeoisie. Ironically, in a magazine that Thurman wanted to be free of "Nordic" influence, it was a White man, Carl Van Vechten, who provided last-minute funding so that the magazine could be printed.

But Locke was somewhat critical of the quality of the work in the issue. "The churning eddies of the young Negro mind in the revolt from conservatism and convention have not permitted this to come clearly and smoothly to the surface," producing as yet "more of a drive than an arrival, more of an experiment than a discovery." Locke could also not pass without noting the "strong sex radicalism of many of the contributions" that he predicted would "shock many well-wishers and elate some of our adversaries." Here was Locke's limitation as a closeted gay critic: he did not support a literature that made sexual desire the explicit pivot of Black creativity. What Locke believed limited this work was generational rebellion for rebellion's sense. Locke hoped that in "subsequent issues, the younger Negro literary movement will establish its own base and with time gain a really distinctive and representative alignment."[28] But with poor sales, widespread Black condemnation, and a mysterious fire that consumed all the remaining copies of the first issue, no further issues of *Fire!!* appeared.

Nevertheless, by balancing his approval and critique, Locke found a way to give the magazine qualified praise and avoid alienating himself from the radical wing of the New Negroes. In doing so, he distanced himself further from Du Bois, who could not accept its foregrounding sexuality and amorality. But Locke began to have doubts about these young Black artists, who seemed committed to nothing beyond their own freedom. Privately, he worried that Thurman and his friends lacked a serious aesthetic philosophy and were motivated largely by a desire to give little more than a sexual identity to the Negro art movement, which he believed was reductionist.

More fireworks were in store for Locke. Hughes's second book of poems, *Fine Clothes for the Jew*, appeared in November and raised a storm of criticism from the Black press. The *Pittsburgh Courier* roasted Hughes for publishing a "vulgar" volume of poetry; the *Philadelphia Tribune* was repulsed by the "lecherous, lust-reeking characters that Hughes finds time to poeticize about." Given an opportunity to rebut the charges in the *Courier*, Hughes wrote "Those Bad New Negroes: A Critique on Critics," which was published in April 1927. "I have a right to portray any side of Negro life I wish to," Hughes wrote. By attacking the Black patronage class, rather than cultivating it, the "Young Turks" of the Negro Renaissance doomed the movement to either dependency on White patrons or an early death. Many of Hughes's critics blamed Carl Van Vechten for influencing him toward decadence. Locke also worried that Van Vechten was at least partly to blame for the superficiality of some of the artist's poems. But without the publishing contacts and associations of Van Vechten and Walter White, or the publishing outlet of Du Bois, Locke lacked the leverage to tilt Hughes or other artists toward the fundamental values he extolled.

While Locke began to have reservations about much of the writing coming out of the Renaissance in 1927, he decided that his public role was to defend the youthful writers against what he thought was hysterical condemnation by their critics. In "Our Little Renaissance," his first rebuttal to such critics, in his contribution to Charles S. Johnson's anthology, *Ebony and Topaz: A Collectanea*, Locke characterized the White critics of the movement as condescending. H. L. Mencken did not think the movement was Black enough, a "candle in the sunlight. It has kindled no great art." Heywood Broun, whom Locke had tried to get to contribute to *The New Negro*, allowed that the movement was "fairly successful, considering…the American atmosphere," and was "still full of promise-so it seems." Locke could not help "wonder what Mr. Pater would say. He might be even more skeptical…but one mistake he would never make—that of confusing the spirit with the vehicle, of confounding the artistic quality which Negro life is contributing with the Negro artist. Negro artists are just the by-product of the Negro Renaissance; its main accomplishment will be to infuse a new element into the stream of American culture."[29]

Locke's aesthetic idealism seems at first a sleight of hand. Given that Locke was beginning to feel that the artists so far had underperformed, he shifted the discussion to the idea of the Negro Renaissance, rather than its accomplishments. In doing so, he made a profound interpretation of the Italian Renaissance, suggesting that Michelangelo, da Vinci, and Botticelli were not the most important contributions of the "real" Renaissance, but its awakening of humanity to its own agency and creativity. Locke also took a shot at Du Bois. "We must divorce it in our minds from propaganda and politics. Otherwise, why call it a renaissance?" The revival of Humanism and Beauty within America through the art of the Negro experience was this renaissance's most important contribution to world history. The idea of a New Negro Renaissance was above all a call to recognize the redemptive force of African American literature and culture in Black lives.

Locke also sought some redemption. As early as his fall 1926 return to the United States, Locke had lobbied Arthur Mitchell to arrange a private meeting with Emmett Scott, who stated he was amenable to Locke's reinstatement. But Scott also shared with Mitchell "some particulars" of Locke's case that Mitchell thought should be shared with Locke only in person. What were those? Were they sexual accusations? Or rumors? Did Scott want Mitchell to obtain some assurances from Locke that his behavior would be above reproach before he was readmitted to Howard? We do not know. Even after those conferences, no action occurred. Locke's friend Metz T. P. Lochard, also fired, gave up hope and took a position with the *Chicago Defender*. Other options seem to close for Locke just as they opened up for the others. Locke had attempted to get a license to teach at a New York high school, but that hit a snag when two of the three doctors who examined Locke deemed him unfit for the rigors of teaching because of his heart. If that was not bad enough, Lewis Marks, the examiner, notified Locke that even if those difficulties could be cleared up, there was also the matter of a negative report given to the New York schools by Durkee, who referred to Locke as having been dismissed because he was an incompetent teacher. That retaliation required Locke to solicit from his former dean, Kelly Miller, a letter attesting that Locke had been an excellent teacher and that Durkee was a vindictive administrator with little or no knowledge of the abilities of the teachers at Howard University. As this struggle to win what was simply a demotion showed, the forces allied against Locke in early 1927 were formidable. As the winter deepened, he seemed to have no real prospect of getting his job back at Howard.

But in May 1927, something magical happened. W. E. B. Du Bois wrote to Jesse Moorland and stated: "I am interested in having Alain Locke reinstated at HU." He wrote to Moorland because "I have been told by disinterested parties that the chief objection to Locke is from you." Du Bois went on to make clear that he was not doing this out of some personal interest. "While I have known Mr. Locke for sometime, he is not a particularly close friend. I have not always agreed with him, and he knows nothing of this letter." Rather, Du Bois wrote because of two larger principles at issue in Locke's case:

> First there is the privilege of free speech and independent thinking in all Negro colleges. We have got to establish that, and the time must go when only men who say the proper things and walk the beaten track are allowed to teach our youth. Of course, there must be limits to this freedom, but the limits must be wide. In the second place, we must have cultured and well-trained men in our institutions. We have lamentably few. Locke is by long odds the best-trained man among the younger American Negroes. His place in the world is as a teacher of youth. And he ought to be at the largest Negro college, Howard. Nothing will discourage young men more from taking training, which is not nearly commercial and money making, than the fact that a man like Locke is not permitted to hold a position at Howard.[30]

Apparently, Du Bois's extraordinary act of generosity did the trick. The board of trustees reappointed Locke as professor of philosopher at Howard that summer. Ironically, this appointment came after Locke had been invited to spend the 1927–1928 academic year at Fisk University. In order not to penalize Fisk for its cordiality when he was desperate for a teaching job, Locke honored the Fisk appointment and began teaching at Howard University in the fall of 1928.

It is not certain Locke knew of Du Bois's intervention. Indeed, there is no proof that anyone informed Locke, least of all Du Bois. But that Du Bois knew that Moorland was the man blocking Locke—and others as well who had informed

Du Bois of this fact—created a crisis for Moorland that could only worsen and become public had Moorland not conceded. The Negro newspapers, still on Locke's side in the controversy, would have made scandal out of the news that a Negro educator blocked the reappointment of "the best-trained man among the younger American Negroes." Although Locke considered Du Bois his nemesis, the *Crisis* editor was actually his savior.

Why did Du Bois do it? As David Levering Lewis puts it, Du Bois and Locke were not friends. Du Bois never forgave Locke for trying, with Charles Johnson, in 1923, to get Beton to write an article critical of the Pan African Congress in *Opportunity* nor for trying to marginalize Jessie Fauset by excluding her from *The New Negro: An Interpretation*. Du Bois also appeared to disapprove of Locke because of his homosexuality. And yet, Du Bois wrote a letter that rescued Locke's professional career, shortly after Du Bois dismissed his business officer, Augustus Dill, ostensibly for public solicitation of another man. Was his letter to Moorland an act of unconscious atonement? Of course, in Du Bois's mind, the two cases were different for many reasons, not least of which that Locke was never arrested for any public display of his sexual orientation. Locke's "paralyzingly discreet" approach to his sexuality meant he was never an embarrassment "to the race," a critical issue for a race war general like Du Bois. But the possibility remains that Du Bois's act of simple justice was buttressed by a more complex internal balancing act, his emerging self-awareness of the cruelty of his own act of dismissing Dill and his compensation for that act by saving another of similar orientation.[31]

That intercession did not change their professional or personal relationship. Du Bois and Locke remained adversaries. Their conflict over art heated up again in 1928, just as Locke returned to Howard. That October, Du Bois turned over the attack to one of his younger minions—Allison Davis—who published "Our Negro Intellectuals" in the August 1928 issue of the *Crisis*. Davis attacked the entire group of New Negro writers for spreading filth as literature under the ideology of "sincerity" and artistic freedom. For Davis, "the plea of sincerity, of war against hypocrisy and sham, therefore, is no defence [sic] for the exhibitionism of Mr. George S. Schuyler and Mr. Eugene Gordon, nor for the sensationalism of such works as Dr. Rudolph Fisher's HIGH YALLER or Langston Hughes's FINE CLOTHES TO THE JEW." Davis charged that all were imitators and protégés of Carl Van Vechten and H. L. Mencken, that Black writers had bought into the "romantic delusion of 'racial literatures,'" and charged them with exploiting the desire for a distinctive Negro by "use of the Harlem cabaret and night life, and ... a return to the African jungles" in their poems and novels. Davis even hit at James Weldon Johnson for having felt the need to "yield to this jazz primitivism in choosing the title GOD'S TROMBONES for a work purporting to represent the Negro's religious fervor" and even "Mr. Miguel Covarrubias and Mr. Winold Reiss [who] did more than Mr. Aaron Douglas and Mr. Richard Bruce to represent the Negro as essentially bestialized by jazz and the cabaret." To make sure he did not leave out an attack on Locke's role, Davis attacked the "criticism" that had emerged with this movement as lacking "a vital grasp upon standards" to resist the temptation to praise what was only a "gushing forth of novelties."[32] As Van Vechten wrote to Hughes on August 2, 1928, "Allison Davis's article was both asinine and sophomoric. I'm glad you answered it, but what can you think of Du Bois printing such rubbish."[33] But that he did it reflected how angry Du Bois was with the "renaissance" he forecast in 1920.

Once Locke had gotten his job back, he felt more comfortable confronting the issue of propaganda out in the open. In an article, "Beauty Instead of Ashes," published in the *Nation* in April 1928, he argued that the art movement had been "a fresh boring through the rock and sand of racial misunderstanding and controversy" that had delivered to America a "living, well-spring of beauty."[34] Locke turned the criticism of current writers and their products into a larger question: could this opening be the beginning of something permanent, or would the attackers from the wings of racial controversy succeed in killing the "first products" of the renaissance and forcing Black self-expression to begin anew—all over again. Here, Locke built on his assertion in "The Drama of Negro Life" that the Negro Renaissance had advanced because of a "division of labor" between White and Black writers, and this time argued Blacks had excelled at poetry, while Whites had pioneered novel and playwriting. He sided with Hughes on *Nigger Heaven*, stating that while it was "studied," Van Vechten's was a "brilliant novel of manners"; similarly, he rebutted the criticism of White playwrights like Du Bose Heyward as a mistaken view that the modernist portrayal of the "folk-life" was racist when, in fact, in many cases, it was the "folk" to whom the White artist gained access. He ignored the power issues in such access, that the poor had few resources with which to defend or reshape their representation. It was hypocrisy for the Black elite to complain of their lack of portrayal by White writers and then deny those same writers access to its material.

Locke's only criticism came when he "hoped" that "the later art of the Negro will be true to original qualities of the folk temperament." The full promise of Negro literature remained in this arena, the site of an "inner vision" of what it means to be Negro. "That inner vision cannot be doubted or denied for a group temperament that, instead of souring under oppression and becoming materialistic and sordid under poverty, has almost invariably been able to give American honey for gall and create beauty out of the ashes."[35]

While Locke sympathized with Du Bois's demand for more balanced treatment, propaganda literature had failed. The Negro creative spirit had moved on, even if it incurred new demerits because of the sophomoric antics of the "young Negro artist." One could not create Beauty out of retaliatory anger or hypermoralism. The deeper philosophical point was that propaganda made Black expression dependent on the White man. Locke made precisely that point in "Art or Propaganda?" his last and most forthright answer to Du Bois, when it was published in *Harlem*, the second magazine edited by Wallace Thurman. Setting aside his misgivings about Thurman, Locke rose to the occasion one last time to defend his movement against Du Boisian prescriptions. "My chief objection to propaganda," he wrote, "apart from its besetting sin of monotony and dispro-portion, is that it perpetuates the position of the group inferiority even in crying out against it."[36] Locke wanted Black people to stop thinking of themselves as victims. He did not think as a victim, even though he was queer, Black, and un-employed much of 1926 and 1927. He might be marginalized by discourses of Whiteness and heterosexism, but his message was strong and unmistakable: move beyond Du Bois, and start thinking and acting like we own American literature. Negro art should subjectivize the Negro, make them powerful human beings, not repudiations of White racist stereotypes. Art should restore the "inner vision" of the Negro even in the midst of a debilitating American civilization.

African art offered the possibility of seeing Black people from the inside and not through the White lens of the Enlightenment. Building a foundation of art on the African traditions offered the opportunity to reveal the "true" identity or Idea of the Negro. That this was not yet evident was not evidence that it did not or could not exist. African art proved that Black people had created tens of thou-sands of objects of great beauty under different circumstances and (here came something of the aesthete) lived lives in which practical living, spirituality, and devotion to Beauty were intertwined inseparably. It could be expressed again if African Americans saw themselves as a modern people with ancient creative tra-ditions despite American circumstances.

Locke's vision remains a curious blend of pragmatism ("psalms will be more effective than sermons") in converting the heart of the oppressor to empathize with the oppressed, religious consciousness (a blend of Christianity and his Baha'i faith), mild Afrocentrism (a return to an African past as a non-Western basis of a Black modernism), and philosophical idealism. He aimed to modernize Black thought by sidestepping the hurt of the past.

That night in the mid- or late 1920s, when Locke and Du Bois finished their dinner in Washington, one wonders what they said as they prepared to part. Perhaps the traditionally tight-lipped Du Bois had little to say. Locke, proud and resentful of any demand for deference, probably could not bring himself to thank Du Bois if Locke knew of the older man's remarkable intervention in saving his academic career. Perhaps both could agree they hoped an artist would emerge who advanced the race as well as art. The controversy over art and propaganda had divided them, but not destroyed their cordiality. Their Black Victorian back-grounds, sense of manners, taste, and decorum, had served their relationship well. Unlike some of the younger writers coming after them, they believed that

Black intellectuals could not afford to self-destruct, even when they strongly disagreed.

"Now, Dr. Locke," Du Bois might have ventured to ask as they got up from their meal, "Who among the new young writers has the potential to write something beautiful?"

That question would have made Locke think a long time.

Chokwe Stool. Blondiau-Theatre Arts Collection. Private Collection.

29

Black Curator and White Momma

On Sunday, February 6, 1927, Locke walked up to the podium at the New Art Circle Gallery at 35 West 57th Street and prepared to deliver his remarks at the New York opening of the Blondiau-Theatre Arts Collection of "primitive African sculpture and craft art." Tired after years of fighting for his job back at Howard—Du Bois's letter to Moorland was still three months in the future—Locke had decided to become a curator and enter the business of collecting and exhibiting art and antiquities. During his trip the previous summer to Europe, Locke had carried out a mission for Edith Isaacs, editor of *Theatre Arts Monthly*, and purchased with her money a collection of African art from Belgian diplomat Roaul Blondiau, who had served for years in the Congo. After months of preparing this special exhibit, catalog copy, press releases, and promotional articles, Locke stood before a small audience principally of White women and men, who had come out on this cold Sunday afternoon to learn more about the craze for things African in New York.[1]

The year 1927 was an auspicious one to open this exhibit, as the *style negre* was everywhere in the modernist world. African designs adorned modern furniture, sets and plays for the theater, and art by Ferdinand Leger and Alberto Giacometti. The previous year, Locke had met Mrs. Isaacs in connection with an article he had written on the Negro in American theater that mentioned the rise of African themes. *Taboo*, a play by Mary Hoyt Wiborg, starring Paul Robeson, had been a minor hit in New York in 1922 largely because of its African theme and costumes. Eugene O'Neill, the famous author of *Emperor Jones* and *All God's Chillun Got Wings*, had a collection of African art. Locke had convinced Mrs. Isaacs to fund his trip to Europe during the summer of 1926 to purchase a collection of roughly one thousand works of Congo art—an example of Locke's resourcefulness in finding ways to fund his European trips while he was unemployed. After purchasing the collection, shipping it to New York, and finding a suitable gallery to exhibit it, Locke had also co-curated what was the first exhibit of African art at a commercial gallery in New York. And it was the first such exhibit of African art organized by an African American, who made sure the audience received a New Negro interpretation of its meaning and importance.

After acknowledging that European artists had brought aesthetic recognition to West African art, Locke reframed the meaning of African art in the history of world culture. "To possess African art permanently and not merely as a passing vogue we shall have to go beyond such reflected values and their exotic appeal and study it in its own context, link it up vitally with its own cultural background, and learn to appreciate it as an organic body of art." African sculpture not only revealed to contemporary culture a West African world but also "the importance of beauty in the ordinary. American art, especially with its current revival of interest in the decorative and craft arts, needs this message." As an American Negro, he was both proud that this message came from his ancestral heritage and also glad he had been able to bring this art to America so that Negro artists too could learn its lessons. African art was also an unexpected revelation for the American Negro, since "the arts of his ancestors" had been "crowded out of the slave ship." African art was now repossessed by its American heir.[2]

After concluding his remarks, Locke endured the crush of well-heeled Whites who rushed the lectern to get a closer look at the tiny, delicate, overly sophisticated New Negro who spoke so authoritatively about what guests assumed was his collection. But it was *Theatre Arts* editor Edith Isaacs's collection and it was for sale. If successful, the exhibit would transfer this African art to elite Whites who attended this midtown gallery opening, and its "art lessons" would be lost to the Negro artists Locke felt most needed them. If he were rich, of course, he would have bought the entire collection, opened a museum, and created an academy for artists to be inspired by this African art to create a new art. But Locke was not wealthy; he did not even have a job.

While Locke was packing up to leave, he became aware of an elderly White woman staring as if still listening to him. Relaxing her intimidating gaze, the seventy-two-year-old Charlotte Mason introduced herself. She was a widow of a wealthy psychiatrist with whom she shared a belief in the occult, spiritualism, and extrasensory perception. She had studied "primitive peoples," in which she included Indians, Africans, and even those African Americans unspoiled by Western civilization, since she was a young woman. She was interested in African art because of the power she believed it had to reconnect Western civilization to the spiritual values "primitives" had revered for centuries. She was moved by his remarks that Negroes such as himself were rising up to use their heritage to reform Western civilization. Locke nodded in agreement and calculated how to respond. He had a feeling of being uplifted, enhanced, and strengthened in Mason's presence. As they separated, Locke puckishly announced, "I am going to call up and ask to come and see you if I may."[3]

Mason did not wait for him to call. Three days later, she was back at the exhibit, and they had a long talk. Locke told her he planned to launch a committee to raise funds to purchase the collection and install it in a permanent museum.

Mason thought that a wonderful idea. Two days later, Locke left her a message about the committee and promised to call again. Before he did, she was back again at the exhibit, this time bringing her niece, Katherine Chapin, and purchasing a little man figure. Over the next month, she would make weekly, almost daily visits to the exhibit, often with friends, leading them on tours of the exhibit like Carl Van Vechten's uptown forays to Black speakeasies. But there was a difference. While it was not yet apparent to Locke, Mason was a cultural conservative, who saw the primitive as the harbinger of conservative religious and cultural revival, one diametrically opposed to the decadent urban modernism of Van Vechten.[4]

Something about Mason's enthusiasm led Locke to conclude that she would do more than simply help fund African art. He had put on the New Art Circle exhibition as a way to create interest and raise money through a subscription plan to purchase the collection from Isaacs for a museum in Harlem dedicated to the "art of the ancestors." Mason became a major player in that effort. But even more than a patron of African art, Mason, Locke perceived, was interested in something far grander—a multifaceted renaissance that could transform the landscape of African American culture for years to come. She already believed in what he had only dreamed of when he put together the exhibit at the New Art Circle gallery.

What if he could get Mason to do what other patrons had been unwilling to do—provide funds to free contemporary Black artists, such as the attractive Langston Hughes, from financial worry and allow them to concentrate on producing the great art Locke had claimed the Negro Renaissance was destined to produce? At a minimum, her opened purse would help him wrest power away from Van Vechten, whom he believed was ruining Langston Hughes, Eric Walrond, and others. And if Locke secured real financial support for Hughes, perhaps he might be enticed into a closer relationship with him. Accordingly, when Mason invited him to accompany her to a concert of the spirituals on February 16, Locke arrived early at her apartment at 399 Park Avenue to have tea before they went out. In a gesture that signaled she was courting him as well, Mason invited Locke to sit in her great-great-grandfather's chair. At the concert, Locke made his move. During the intermission, he sought out Hughes, probably by prior arrangement, and brought him over to meet Mason. After Hughes returned to his seat, Locke gauged her reaction and no doubt suggested that Hughes was the type of young man who could produce great art, if unburdened from niggling financial obligations.[5]

Aware that she was being courted, Mason peppered Locke with questions at their next meeting. What did he think of Carl Van Vechten, also at the concert? She had detected something vile in him. What did Locke think of the other "so-called Bohemian artists"? What did Locke believe the social status of Blacks should be in White society? Perhaps most important, what specific plans did he have for the Congo exhibit? Once he discussed his plans for a museum of African art in Harlem, she weighed in that such art should be planted in the "sub-soil" of Harlem to inspire all Negroes, especially young children, with the love of African civilization. It amazed him that they were thinking of the same thing. Listening to her was encouraging even when he disagreed with the particulars—which he of course kept quiet about now. Of course, Locke felt no need to keep quiet about his distaste for Van Vechten, his suspicions about the other White "Bohemians" interested in the Negro movement, or his enthusiasm for Roland Hayes, who had sung that night.[6]

Yet Mason was not yet convinced. She noted that Locke was an hour late to their next conference. Not satisfied to accept uncritically the proposal for the Harlem Museum of African Art he left at her home afterward, she called another meeting to discuss its particulars. Upon arriving, Locke, perhaps aware he was being scrutinized, "met her with open arms and a brush of the spirit," as Mason recalled. But Locke wanted to shift her attention from just African art to funding African American contemporary artists with her money. That next Saturday, February 26, he telephoned Mason and asked if he could bring Hughes up to her apartment to see her. She spoke with Hughes at length. She gave a somewhat bewildered Hughes a big dose of her fervent ideas, so much so that upon leaving, he asked Locke, "Who is this woman? How does she know so much about us?" He did not have to question the other gift she bestowed on him: a $50 bill pressed into his hand as he left.[7]

Hughes's question was a good one. Born Charlotte Van Der Quick on May 18, 1854, she was the great-great-great-granddaughter of a colonial Dutch immigrant, who received four thousand acres of land in Somerset, New Jersey, because of his friendship with King George III. The first American Van Der Quick was a farmer and a slave owner, although Charlotte quickly pointed out that her great-great-grandfather freed his slaves. By the time that Locke met her, Charlotte Mason was rich beyond imagination; and the resilience of her fortune during the Great Depression suggested that much of it still resided in landholdings. The only daughter in a family of three boys and a widowed father, she seemed to inherit the male side of the family's aggressiveness and self-confidence. Her aggressive approach to power was her defining characteristic. As Arthur Fauset recalled, "She was someone who let you know that if something was to be done, she was the one to do it."[8]

A strongly independent young woman, Charlotte had delayed getting married until she was thirty-four, spending her young adulthood in folkloric research among the Native Americans of the Southwest. From that she formed her sense that "primitive" peoples possessed a wisdom and connection to God unknown in Western civilization. She heard their critique of White man's destruction of their civilization and intuited their ability to communicate with one another beyond words, something that reinforced her sense of her own gift for psychic communication. Her psychic sensitivity was reinforced when she married Rufus Osgood Mason, a fifty-six-year-old psychiatrist, who studied hypnotism, ESP, and psychic phenomena as a regimen to liberate patients from suffering. After his death, Charlotte Mason devoted herself to funding projects, such as Natalie Curtis's *Indian Book* (1907), to bring attention to the neglected insights of primitive peoples. She believed the *Indian Book* embodied the true spirit of the American Indians and avoided prostituting that heritage for monetary or commercial gain. It is not clear she had had much contact with Negroes before meeting Locke in 1927, but she had surmised by analogy that Africans and African Americans possessed similar spiritual resources as the Native Americans and harbored similar resentments about the suppression of their ancestral culture. For her, African culture was still alive in America and ready to be revived in a counter-revolution against a soul-destroying Western civilization in America.[9]

This last aspect was key to Mason's vision—a reformation, really, more than a renaissance, was needed to save humanity—and she was the one to lead it. There was a war going on between the forces of Western materialism and primitive spiritualism, and the latter had to be protected from the false friends who would betray it for personal self-aggrandizement. Mason felt called to protect the vision of "primitive man" from the other Whites and those over-assimilated minorities who wanted to use primitive culture to fill their pocketbooks. That calling fueled her controlling personality. Primitive art had to be tightly controlled—along with the people involved in it—to keep it from being dissipated into egotism, the self-destructive individualism of Western man. This would be a slippery road to travel for Locke, who by his own admissions was an egotist and proud of it.

Less clear was that Mason was also a frustrated woman by 1927. At more than seventy-two years old, her body was wracked with pain from arthritis and other ailments that limited her mobility and made her dependent on a platoon of nieces and servants to survive. She was childless and facing death without having added to the powerful aristocratic legacy of her family or achieved anything that testified to her brilliance. Though a strong-minded woman of the upper class, she was reluctant to exert herself publicly as a leader of any movement. Throughout her relations with Locke and others, she always forbade any mention of her name. She had authored one article, "The Passing of a Prophet," about her husband, an indication that Mason felt more comfortable in public discourse paying homage to her husband, just as she always insisted on being referred to by her married name, Mrs. C. Osgood Mason, on all committee letterheads and other paraphernalia.[10] Beyond her desire to bring long-neglected peoples the attention they deserved existed another motivation for introducing herself to Alain Locke: she needed him and other Negroes to exert an influence on American culture that she could not effect herself. She was a mother without children; they, in turn, would become her "godchildren."

Just as Locke was closing in on Mason as a patron, another patron came roaring back into his life, a reminder that all such relationships were dangerous. A scathing review of Locke's New Art Circle Gallery exhibit appeared in the March 2 issue of the *Nation*, authored by Thomas Munro, a sycophant of Albert Barnes. Although Barnes later claimed he had nothing to do with the review, the article was part of Barnes's long history of planting negative reviews or defaming letters in magazines about exhibits or collections or individuals with whom he disagreed. Munro worked at the Barnes Foundation as an educational specialist and co-authored with Paul Guillaume *Primitive Negro Sculpture*, which was published by the Barnes Foundation. The *Nation* critique sought to discredit the quality and veracity of the Blondiau Collection, a project Barnes carried on against any collection of African art that might challenge his. Interestingly, Munro's review did not attack Locke personally—another Barnes tactic—but the quality of the collection. Munro asserted that it contained many unauthenticated, if not fake, artifacts, mostly craft rather than art objects, and being a collection of Congo art the collection was not representative of the best in West African art. As if that was not enough, Munro described the exhibit's design as old-fashioned, more in accord with the nineteenth-century ethnological rather than a modernist presentation of African art. The more modernist strategy was to exhibit fewer objects in large amounts of space to allow the visitor to study closely the plastic qualities of each piece of sculpture. Those were the qualities that had led Picasso, Modigliani, Brancusi, and other European artists to bring African art to world attention, the author of *Primitive Negro Sculpture* asserted, as exemplary of the African's aesthetic rather than anthropological genius.[11]

Locke counter-attacked immediately with a fierce letter to the editor of the *Nation*. It disputed Munro's arguments one by one, especially the notion that the collection contained more handicraft than art. If Munro was such an expert on African art, Locke asserted, then he should know that "the distinction did not exist in that culture itself." If such a distinction was "insisted upon," Locke quipped, then "more than half the plates of his [Munro's] own book on 'Primitive Negro Sculpture' would have to be eliminated." At least, Locke concluded, "The Blondiau Collection had not been accused of 'made in Paris' unless niches of anything in the Barnes Foundation collection automatically lifts it from its ordinary plane and canonizes it as 'fine art.'"[12]

West Africans, Locke argued, did not separate art and utility the way Westerners like Munro did. Of course, Locke still valued African art for its aesthetic qualities, but used this article to suggest that Barnes and Munro were actually misinformed outsiders to the African art traditions they wished to bend to what was already an outdated Western aesthetic. Boldly, Locke asserted that the truest meaning of African art was more than simply its inspiration of European cubists and abstract artists, but more its anchoring an entirely new conception of what art should do and be. It was this radical rejection of Western alienation of art from its context in the daily lives of the people that made African art truly inspirational. That shift from an art of the coterie to an art of the people was precisely what African art had to offer a visual arts renaissance among Negroes. Locke closed his letter with a telling counter to this orthodoxy. "Certainly it is at least as legitimate a modern use of African art to promote it as a key to African culture and as a stimulus to the development of Negro art as to promote it as a side exhibit to modernist painting and a stalking horse for a particular school of aesthetics."[13]

Munro's attack derived from Barnes's long-standing enmity toward Locke after he published "A Note on African Art," in the May 1924 *Opportunity*. Barnes believed Locke had stolen his ideas and published them as his own. But enmity had turned to white-hot hatred when Locke had had the audacity to write another essay on African art, "The Legacy of the Ancestral Arts," in *The New Negro: An Interpretation* that directly contradicted Barnes's essay "Negro Art and America," that Locke also published in the anthology. Locke had to include Barnes's essay in *The New Negro* because Locke needed Barnes's photographs of African art to illustrate the book. Barnes's article asserted that African art showed the "primitivism" of the African people had carried over into the contemporary American Negro. "The most important element to be considered is the psychological complexion of the Negro as he inherited it from his primitive ancestors and which he maintains to this day. The outstanding characteristics are his tremendous emotional endowment, his luxuriant and free imagination and a truly great power of individual expression."[14] This was too much for Locke, given his own independent study of African sculpture. He countered by arguing the Atlantic slave trade had resulted in transformations in Diaspora African cultures, such that the tone of American Negro culture was strikingly different from that of African art.

> The offshoot of the African spirit blended itself in with entirely different culture elements and blossomed in strange new forms. There was in this more than a change of art-forms and an exchange of cultural patterns; there was a curious reversal of emotional temper and attitude. The characteristic African art expressions are rigid, controlled, disciplined, abstract, heavily conventionalized; those of the Aframerican,— free, exuberant, emotional, sentimental and human. Only by the misinterpretation of the African spirit, can one claim any emotional kinship between them—for the spirit of the African expression, by and large, is disciplined, sophisticated, laconic and fatalistic.[15]

Locke's cheekiness was on display: instead of rejecting Barnes's essay, he published it in *The New Negro* along with his essay calling Barnes's argument a "misinterpretation," even riffing on Barnes's exact words in his critique. Locke even asserted that the typical American Negro experienced African art as foreign, strange, a "classic" tradition to be studied, like the Greek statuary that fueled the Italian Renaissance, to learn from it. That was the point of publishing Barnes's African art in *The New Negro* (a kind of exhibition itself) and then exhibiting another collection at the New Art Circle—to foment an encounter with a lost heritage to spark a renaissance among Negro visual artists in America. This was too much for the notoriously thin-skinned Barnes, who seized on Locke's exhibition in 1927 to mount a counter-attack.

The immediate effect of Munro's attack was to show Locke that Barnes would stop at nothing to discredit the Blondiau-Theatre Arts Collection. Locke arranged a national tour of the collection as a way to garner national media attention for the collection, to which his reputation was now tied. But the controversy also had the effect of pushing Locke further into a relationship with Mason as a kind of counterweight or protector to ward off attacks from Barnes. But Barnes did not attack again; and Locke would soon find that Mason held as problematical a set of notions about Negro primitivism as Barnes. And Locke's Oedipal defenses against the overweening Barnes would not protect him psychologically with Mason.

Actually, Locke had two White women patrons: Isaacs and Mason. On the surface, Isaacs had the most useful set of resources for a counter-attack on Barnes and Munro: she had money, connections, a major arts magazine, and now a collection. But Isaacs was unwilling to give Locke total control over the Blondiau Collection. By contrast, Mason was wealthier, more nurturing, and seemingly willing to make him the leader in whatever scheme he came up with to advance African art in America. Even after meeting Hughes at her apartment, Mason had returned to the exhibit that afternoon, this time with Roger Marian and Herbert Whitman. For her, the African spirit was the central issue: Hughes and any other contemporary Negro writer were *means* to a connection with that ancient but still living African presence. Most important, Mason, unlike Isaacs, saw the collecting of African art as something more than art—as a means to *subjectivize* the next generation of Black people. She envisioned a Harlem Museum of Art in which "little Negro children running in and out learning to respect themselves through the realization of those treasures" would be its focus. Isaacs, by contrast, merely wanted a collection of African art for its aesthetic value in stimulating contemporary arts, especially in the theater. Locke sensed that Mason needed Black people to realize a broader vision than that of Isaacs and that he could exploit that need to realize his agenda.

But Mason had not made any large financial commitment to the proposed Harlem Museum of African Art. With a committee that already included Franklin

Hopper of the New York Public Library, real estate agent John E. Nail, Mrs. Isaacs, George Foster Peabody, and a smattering of other influential Whites, Locke still lacked the kind of endowment needed to buy the collection, retrofit an appropriate building, and create a professional exhibition space and storage facility to permanently house the art.[16] Mason was as indefinite as Barnes had been about when or even if she would dispense some real cash.

As Locke was soon to learn, Mason was as full of surprises as Barnes. During a visit he made to her apartment on March 6, she suddenly announced that she was willing to help him go to Africa. She had a "mystical vision of a great bridge reaching from Harlem to the heart of Africa, across which the Negro world, that our White United States had done everything to annihilate, should see the flaming pathway . . . and recover the treasure their people had had in the beginning of African life on the earth." He was the bridge builder. Yet his choice of Abyssinia as the place at the end of the bridge that he would step into Africa was odd. Abyssinia did not have any West African sculpture. One wonders whether Mason knew how tentative his connection was to the Africa that had produced the Congo art she so loved. Locke chose Abyssinia for another reason: he hoped to entice young Langston Hughes to go with him, if funds for Hughes's accommodations could be raised. Mason had another surprise at that meeting. She was angry with him for having put her in "the ugly position of drawing the color line, which is the first time in my life this has ever happened" when he and Hughes came to her apartment.[17]

Here was an early symptom of Mason's psychopathology. Her remark made Locke, a Black man, responsible for her enacting a segregationist code in her own home. Perhaps a less eager seeker of patronage than Locke would have read this as a warning sign that Mason might be crazy. For her to welcome Blacks into her home and then blame them for her "drawing the color line" suggested a confused mind. But Locke was not daunted by this dressing down and returned two days later to deliver the African art pieces Mason had purchased from the Blondiau Collection. Locke accepted Mason's cruelty in order to keep her support, a support that so far had resulted in no financial endowment. She was not funding the Harlem of African Art the way that Mrs. Gardner had funded Barrett Wendell's projects. By contrast, Mason was ambivalent about the goals she said she shared with Locke.

Here was the rub in all of Locke's patronage schemes, whether projected on Barnes, Isaacs, or Mason: the full realization of Locke's aspirations would make Black people more powerful and independent of White influence than they were at present. Was that something these patrons really wanted to occur? Instead, most wanted such projects as a way to tie Black people to them, either as sycophants or minions. Mason no less than Barnes wanted a revolution that still required, ensured, really, the necessity of her! Mason bonded with Locke because it was clear he could not realize his goals without her; and yet she never gave him enough money and power to realize those goals. Mason thus empowered and disempowered him at the same time. Locke could not see this dirty little secret, because it had existed in his mother's empowering but limiting relationship with him. It even characterized his relationships with those less powerful young men under his sway. Mason became the White momma for a Black "boy" whose neurosis made him vulnerable to hers. The unanswered question was, could they accomplish anything with those neuroses together?

Four days later the two of them went together to open a bank safe deposit box into which to store the artifacts. On the way back, the two had a "tremendous talk along Riverside Drive." Mason advised Locke to write a book or long article on "Primitive Sexual Religion," a suggestion Locke certainly deflected, as he knew his take on sexuality would probably not coincide with Mason's.[18] But the general tone of their interchange had improved. She had returned to the realm of sweetness and nurture, giving him instructions on exercises for his back, head, and digestion, and enlarging his belief that care of his health was crucial because of the valuable role he was destined to play among his people.[19] Locke, in turn, shared with her his "great idea." First, he told her his suggestion to get Paul Robeson to sing a benefit concert for the Harlem Museum of African Art. This idea appealed to Mason, because, although she had already donated $500 to the fund, she, like many other White philanthropists, believed the people who benefited from their gifts ought to make the first and foremost contributions, however small, themselves. This was another classic example of the abusive relationship, often seen between physically abusive men and their wives, where the makeup time is one of almost ecstatic elation.

Given the considerable length of their car trip down Riverside Drive, it's possible something grander and more extensive than his "great idea" was discussed.[20] Perhaps Locke felt comfortable sharing with her his larger vision in which the benefit was merely the opening act of a more ambitious plan to transform how Negro art was produced in the twentieth century. The museum had always been to Locke a means to stimulate the production of contemporary art through contact with an African visual tradition. His persistence in bringing Hughes was only the leading edge of his plan to fund a phalanx of African American literary, visual, and musical artists who would flood the market with contemporary Negro art that he—and she—could be proud of as authentic and true.

What Locke envisioned was anything but primitive. It was a plan to modernize the art production by bringing the best of the Renaissance artists under a kind of modern Medici umbrella with her financial benefaction to turn out art that would revise permanently how the Negro was perceived culturally. Together, they would counterbalance the influence of the commercial market and employ New Negro artists to produce art that was beautiful, not simply commercially viable. By reaching as many of the talented and willing artists as possible, they could, together, produce novels, poetry, and books of folklore that would prove the legitimacy of African civilization in America, and confirm (he probably did not say this) his prediction that great art by Negroes would soon issue from the Negro Renaissance. By combining forces—her money and his contacts—they also could sponsor folklore research in Africa and America, train young diplomats and social scientists in African Studies, and improve upon *Opportunity* magazine's patronage by monitoring, regulating, rationalizing, and, most important, controlling what was produced. In a sense, Locke planned to take the production of Negro art out of the hands of the individual artist, whom Locke had already concluded was too weak to resist the temptations of easy money and cheap fame offered by the Van Vechtens, the commercial theater, and the enterprising publishing houses. Locke was imagining the transformation in production and convincing Mason that it was her idea. In doing so, he would have downplayed what this system really was: the modernization of art production on a scale never seen before in American art, let alone by Negroes.

After their thrilling car conversations, Mason began writing checks to fund the benefit concert, the first event to publicly connect a contemporary Negro artist, Robeson, with the Harlem Museum of African Art. Mason put up the money to secure the hall and piano, while Locke buttonholed Robeson and got his assent. As a rising star on the stage, Robeson had had to play a number of roles in which he tried to explore the theme of Africa on the legitimate stage. Robeson jumped at a chance not only to give something back to the Harlem community but also to make a statement for the serious study of things African. The Black bourgeoisie's ambivalence toward Africa made large-scale giving to the museum unlikely at the beginning, so the star's backing was a brilliant beginning to the campaign.

Collective work between Mason and Locke added to the increasing psychological intimacy of their relationship. Or so it seemed. As they moved forward to realize Locke's grand plan, a power struggle developed between them, ostensibly over Mason's ideology of primitivism but really over the authority and control of the wider operation. While Locke struggled to carve out his position in the system he constructed, his maneuvers were constrained by his powerlessness, that at any moment or over any disagreement, Mason could withdraw her money and the whole operation would collapse. Most difficult for him to finesse was that her notions of primitivism in the Black community were applied to him such that he, one of the most sophisticated people in America, was expected to embrace primitivism as his true personality.

Their discourse on this issue reached a head on March 18, when Mason wrote him a letter about his resistance to her ideas. She asked him whether his mother's teachings made him question Mason's ideas.[21] Little more than a month after they had met, Mason felt comfortable attacking the basis of his cultural identity, and Locke let her do it. On one level, it is easiest to understand this as simply something Locke had to put up with to continue his access to Mason's money. But without Mason having to tell him, Locke knew that the type of Culture his mother had inculcated in him during his youth was not the folk culture of the Black masses that Harlem Renaissance writers would celebrate in their writing. Increasingly in the literary debates of 1926 and 1927, Locke's lack of certainty about his support of working-class over bourgeoisie Black culture allowed a vagueness to creep into his critical writings that could not be resolved simply by arguing what was good or bad art. A fundamental realignment of what constituted culture was taking place in the literary and anthropological fields of Black expression in the mid-1920s. Although Locke gave lip service to folk culture, he knew that it was not really the culture he enjoyed as an aesthete. Schoenberg and Tchaikovsky were much more likely to be heard in his presence than anything resembling the blues.

What gave Mason's preference for folk culture some leverage with him was the larger shift in the definition of culture in the Black aesthetic—that others, not as wacky as Mason, were saying that folk culture was the basis of Black aesthetics in the twentieth century. Without some realignment in his taste or more openness to what Mason mistakenly called "primitive" Black culture, Locke was destined to fall increasingly behind the march of Black cultural discourse and be relegated to the position of a Du Bois or an Allison Davis, if he was not careful. It was not just Mason's money, but also the logic of cultural shift that gave her critique a bite he could not ignore. Mason was correct in perceiving that he still held on to his mother's ideas of Culture with a capital C; and in its most positive light, Mason's queries can be seen as starting a process of self-examination that, without her psychological—and especially her financial—pressure, would not have taken place. He needed to loosen the grip of Anglo-American cultural mores on his soul. But that loosening also took place under the relentless, cruel pressure of a maniacal mother surrogate, Charlotte Mason, whose goal was to break his dependency on his mother and shift it to her. Increasingly, it was Mason's emotional support that would be crucial in his life as much as or even more than her financial.[22]

But Mason was also acting in bad faith: Locke's mastery of Western civilization and elite knowledge was a key asset that not only fueled his success but also made him valuable to her. His working knowledge of the French language helped him increase the holdings of the Harlem Museum of African Art, as much of the available African art rested in French hands. His sophistication, decorum, and excellent manners made it possible for them to interact so easily. One suspects that what she really disliked was that he was someone already formed and thus had a limited ability to be remade by her. Part of the problem was the ambiguity of her use of the word *primitive*. At times, it meant childlike, naive, nature-loving, and pure; at other times, it meant focused, concentrated, and undistracted by modernity and its decentering sensibility. But if Locke had been more "primitive" in the latter sense, he would have had no need for Mrs. Mason. The former sense of *primitive* actually was what Locke found useful. He could perform the role of the loving child she never had more easily than being the entirely focused premodern. And that is what he began to do.[23]

Mason's attempt to supplant Mary Locke's place in his life was fraught with difficulties, however, as Mason would soon learn. His mother's domination of his life had produced resistance and subversion, not the least of which was his dandified homosexuality. Now, Mason would wrestle with his unique ability to combine dependency with subversive critique. A humorous example came after Locke and Hughes dined at Mason's on April 16. A comment overheard by someone—other than Mason, since she was deaf—reached her ears belatedly and caused her concern. In her notebook, she wrote that she planned to ask Locke about it when they next met. "When Langston & Alain were going away after dinner on April 16, Alain said 'Masque in one pocket and thick white envelope in another.' Alain, what was that?"[24] Actually, the comment's meaning was clear: another of Locke's infamous cutting witticisms, the remark "outed" the "hustle" of Hughes's new relationship in a moment of telling transparency. He revealed his true perspective on patronage. Locke's explanation must have been good, for the comment did not rupture their relationship. But the comment gave her pause, for it reinforced her persistent suspicion that she was just an old, rich, easily manipulated White woman who was being tapped for cash by Locke and his friends. She worried she was still a financial "touch," rather than the maternal, disciplining force she saw herself as being in his life. He was still the thief and the confidence man, who seemed to be saying to Hughes: "Get all you can and as much as you can, before this good thing ends." Locke's comment also punctured Hughes's later, carefully crafted pose in his autobiography, that he broke with Mason because he was not primitive enough for her. He was certainly primitive enough that night to get the "Masque" and the "envelope" from her. Locke was also reminding Hughes that he owed him for that envelope in his hands; only Hughes would think that he could benefit from Locke's intercession and not repay the favor eventually. In a sense, it was probably good that the comment got back to Mason, because Locke needed much more than a "thick white envelope" to fund the museum, let alone his great idea of revolutionizing patronage. Was she ever going to really commit her largesse to his plans?

Fortunately, April 1927 brought several opportunities for Locke to be away from Mason's constant prying and scrutiny, the price of the little money he was getting. He needed to earn some real money. First, he went to Louisville to give some public lectures, which gave him some much-needed cash, and then to

Nashville, where he gave a series of lectures at Fisk.[25] The latter were particularly important as Fisk's president wanted to hire Locke. After the lectures, the dinners, and the meetings with alumni, Locke would be offered a one-year temporary teaching position for the academic year 1927–1928.[26] Such an appointment, however, would mean living away from New York's artistic energy and Mason, and living in the South, not so easy for Locke.

Then, the Foreign Policy Association approved his grant to study and report on the African Mandates System of the League of Nations. Engineered by his one male patron, Paul Kellogg, with whom Locke never experienced conflict, the fellowship meant he could spend the summer and part of the fall in Europe, resurrecting his theorizing about European imperialism that had languished in his still-unpublished lectures on Race Contacts. Du Bois, among others, had demanded at Versailles that former German colonies be "liberated" by the Allies after the World War; but instead, the League of Nations had turned these colonies into wards to be "managed" by the Great War's victors according to "Mandates" about what their new colonizers—the English and the French—could do with the colonized. Raising armies from these former German colonies was verboten, but putting their inhabitants to work under conditions that veered into near-slavery was allowed. Locke suspected the English and French actually controlled and exploited these colonies through the League's Mandate system, especially as reports of starvation, widespread disease, and torture reached the news. If Locke could turn this stint observing deliberations about the future of these African colonies at the League headquarters in Geneva, Switzerland, into a crackerjack report, he might gain international reputation as a spokesperson and negotiator of African interests.

Overjoyed with the appointment, Locke brought the news to Mason. But she was not overly impressed and questioned what he could accomplish for primitive peoples through the League of Nations. She was also curious about his qualifications to do the job adequately and advised him to brush up on his French, since the League conducted business in that language. Locke countered he was fluent in French and was under contract to translate Rene Maran's Batouala into English. In the back of Locke's mind was the hope that if he did the job well, he might even receive some sort of diplomatic post and be able, finally, to live openly as a gay man in Europe.[27]

Still, Locke's major focus at mid-month was preparing the upcoming Paul Robeson benefit concert. Robeson and Lawrence Brown, his accompanist, agreed to do the benefit, and ticket sales were good. Mason provided the funds for all of the little things required to make it a success. That was another narcotic of their relationship—the drug of efficacy, of being able to get things done, an effectiveness that Locke associated with White people. But all patronage comes at a cost, and Locke would soon learn that.

As the date of the performance neared, Mason had a suggestion. Why not have Robeson don one of the African masks from the Blondiau Collection while he sang in the concert?[28] Of course, the program, which was Robeson's choosing, consisted mainly of spirituals and other African American folk music. Locke asked Robeson to do this, at a private meeting. Robeson refused. He knew that it was inappropriate to sing a program of African American folk music wearing an African mask. Some of the masks may have been sacred objects to be worn only by religious figures, who had the status to wear such things. It was inappropriate for anyone not from that community to wear those masks. Robeson was an African American, a blend of European, African, and perhaps Indian heritages, and a modern, who was light years removed from the culture and beliefs of the Congo that had produced the mask. Locke knew this request was absurd, but apparently he did not inform Mason of this. Instead, he carried the suggestion to Robeson and, after the rejection, had to explain what had happened. Here again, after the rejection, was an opportunity to dispel her likely reaction—that Robeson was a "White" Negro and thus did not want to do this act of identification with Africa because he was not primitive enough.[29] Locke knew anthropology well enough to explain to her that it was an act of disrespect to don other people's religious or ceremonial masks. Here was an opportunity to change his relationship with Mason forever and make her the student and him the teacher. Even if it took him a day or so, Locke had the time to compose a response. And Mason was not so dilettantish that she would not have understood the difference between a facile and a serious explanation. But he did not do it.

His subsequent acceptance of questionable and simply wrong assertions by Mason without contestation became a regular feature of their relationship. Something kept him from challenging her on this and other points crucial to the value of what her patronage could produce. Without realizing it, Locke had participated in a wake for himself as a New Negro of the 1920s. One of his assertions in The New Negro proved true in this incident. Locke had stated that the "younger generation" of Black voices was strong enough to oppose mindless White paternalism. In this instance, that voice had been Robeson's, not Locke's.

That Locke, a rather opinionated intellectual, would defer to the opinion of a rather unsophisticated devotee of the "primitive" is curious. He had been quite willing to infuriate Albert Barnes and his cockeyed notions about Black people, even when the reward for obsessive obeisance would have been money. That Barnes had been reluctant to give Locke money played some part in his attitude; but others, such as Thomas Munro, Aaron Douglas, Gwendolyn Bennett, and even Bertrand Russell, had been able to keep silent and deferential to Barnes's crass and overbearing authority long enough to receive some cash. Locke undermined that authority, almost as a matter of course, and had enjoyed doing so.

With Mason, he was different. She was no less crass, coarse, or brutal in her sweeping judgments of him and others; and yet the emotional chemistry between them elicited something rarely seen in him, a kind of fawning deference in her presence that allocated to her an unusual authority over him. Despite Locke's innate aggressiveness, his refined sensibilities, and his nuanced sense of decorum—indeed, his egotistical sense that he was always, even when neglected, the best and the brightest mind in the room—something in his armor had split in her presence, and the chink became wide enough that she could enter his inner sanctum and inhabit it in ways he had only experienced before with his mother.

Even Locke's relationship with his mother had been different. With Mary Locke he had the advantage of her in regards to education, breadth of culture, and cosmopolitan exposure—precisely those qualities she respected. With Mason, not only did she possess an insider's knowledge of aristocratic America, a knowledge he lacked, but she also respected the Western aesthetic culture he had mastered, even if his mastery of it went beyond hers. Mason was not a replacement for his actual mother, but more the idealized young Locke's fantasized mother, which no mother could completely embody. Part of the occasional meanness toward his real mother that surfaces in his correspondence with her is anger that she does not live up to this image of the omnipotent mother. Mason's psychological power in his life in 1927 comes from the fantasy, which she cultivated with all of her "godchildren," that she was the all-powerful mother, and she wielded her power over her "godchildren" because she found that place of weakness in their psyche that came from unresolved feelings for their own mothers. With Locke especially, Mason manipulated his dynamic need for a new, more powerful mother than his own and gained from it tremendous influence over him emotionally.[30]

And then there was the money. That such an emotional dependency would erupt in someone who had so confidently asserted the "self-determination" of the New Negro is perplexing until we realize that key to the fantasy of total self-determination was the fantasy of power and her money could bring him that. Locke was motivated by a desire, almost a craving, for power, authority, and control; in Mason, he saw those attributes, not only as her attributes but also something he could acquire through her financial resources. In 1927, he faced the reality that his own power, especially over the young Black writers and the Renaissance debates, generally, was waning. Mason became a way for Locke to exercise power over others he would not be able to control or influence on his own. That's why the all-powerful mother Mason represented herself to be was both emotionally and professionally intoxicating to him. He became weak around her, because he became in her presence the frightened little man desperately in need of love and nurture, a man running on empty five years after the death of the only person whom he was sure had really loved him.

Locke revived a persona with Mason—that of the "little boy." On one level, this persona was designed to win her confidence and secure her funding. But on another, it was not fake or manipulative. The phrase "little boy" or "your little boy" was exactly what he signed at the end of his letters to his mother. It would soon become evident that he gave his contact with Mason the same kind of valuation he reserved for his mother, since in the corpus of Locke's correspondence, the volume of Mason-Locke correspondence was only second to that which he maintained with his mother. Without perhaps completely realizing it at first, a kind of transference had occurred from Mary Locke to Charlotte Mason. What he did know was that he was desperate in 1927, and he could not do without this relationship. How desperate he was soon became clear.

A precipitous emotional slide for Locke into despair began after the concert was over. It had been a musical success, generating almost immediately talk as to when it might be repeated, perhaps on an annual basis. But Locke knew that one benefit concert was not enough to build a museum in New York. In a telephone conversation with Mason, Locke confided to her that what made him particularly despondent was a long, discouraging talk he had with Roland Hayes, who declined to contribute in a major way to the museum. It is not clear whether Hayes did not want to do a concert like Robeson or he did not want to give money outright to the project. Either way, his refusal of Locke's invitation was more than just another dead end, for Hayes was the man who had been the subject of one of Locke's first articles on the New Negro artist. That article had furthered Hayes's career, as had having his portrait by Winold Reiss on the cover of the Harlem issue of the *Survey Graphic*. Hayes had benefited from the work Locke had done for the movement, and yet he was not willing to help Locke in return for all he had given him. If the Black artists who were actually benefiting from the movement would not pour back into the movement some of the profits they were reaping, then where could Locke turn for such support? If Negroes of talent would not contribute to a Black arts institution, how could Locke expect Whites to do so? If this was the result of all of his hard work, what did he have to show for the five years since his mother's death that he had spent diverting the love he had had for her into an almost incessant promotional love for Negro artists?

Locke spent the next few days at Mrs. Mason's apartment, soaking up in eight-hour sessions with her whatever strength he could gain to go on. His conversation with Hayes had touched a deep well of pain. Hayes's rejection symbolized the broader failure of Locke's effort to create enduring Black institutions out of the Negro Renaissance.

Of course, in one sense, Black creativity would continue to flower without the kinds of institutions he wanted to create. But Locke correctly perceived that without a solid foothold in the "exhibitionary complex" of the art gallery, the art museum, the concert hall, the theater, and the university, Black artistic expression would remain a fitful expression of brilliance and lack the institutional structure to sustain such talent.[31] Hayes's reaction exposed that Locke was unable to convince the Black middle-class artists to think beyond the cult of individualism. But the setback also brought up Locke's deep-seated doubts about the ability of Negroes to work together to create something of permanent value. That feeling usually lurked under the public face of Alain Locke, unseen by most who knew him. But it was drawn out into the open by Hayes's reaction and was only beaten back by Mason. Locke was emotionally dependent on White patronage in large part because the Black bourgeoisie would not support his outsized dreams.

Ironically, as Locke was becoming more dependent on Mason, he felt more alive. She supported his projects, not the Black artists he had helped. That held a lesson for him that put into context all of those Black nationalists who called for a Black-only New Negro movement. Locke had tried that, first at Howard with the Howard Players, then in the streets and institutions of Harlem, Washington, and Philadelphia; and now Hayes's reaction suggested it would not work. The rejection by Hayes gave him permission to move in a direction he had always used effectively before—to build hopes of Black success, especially his success, on the interest of and support of largely White strangers.[32] Locke's move to Mason was predictable from the standpoint of the history of art institutionalization in America and a capitulation to the reality that a purely Black nationalist aesthetics had not succeeded among the very class of persons, the Black bourgeoisie, who were the natural patrons for such a movement. But as he was strengthened, he was simultaneously weakened as an independent subject. As Locke accepted Mason's support, he became increasingly subject to her pathological demands to stroke her, defer to her, and agree with her fantastical notions of Blackness and civilization. Receiving her psychological support required acquiescing to her intellectual dominance, which on some level was ridiculous.

Locke's dependency on Mason did not compel him to drop some of the most important masks he wore, however. On April 30, perhaps in response to his evasiveness after the Robeson-African "masque" episode, she noted in her diary that Locke "suffered" from a sense of protection "which slavery has created throughout the Negro race. Even with me, whom he trust(s) implicitly he is self-conscious in writing a letter."[33] Perhaps if Mason had been less willing to play the role of the master, he would have been less willing to be the trickster slave! Of course, that thought never crossed her mind. Her vicious maternalism created the conditions under which for his psychic survival, Locke felt he needed to keep some of those masks handy.

Most profoundly (and apparently successfully), Locke masked from her that he was gay. Apparently he fabricated a story of a pseudo-romantic relationship in order to explain to Mason why he never married. In a lengthy entry in Mason's diary, she chronicled Locke's story that he had a romantic relationship with Helen Irvin, his mother's friend, whom, according to the diary entry, he "never married because he could not have children on account of his heart."[34] Nowhere in the voluminous correspondence between Locke and his mother, or between Locke and Irvin, is there an inkling of a romantic feeling, let alone a courtship, between the two of them. It is true that an inclination of his heart did mean he did not have children, but it was the inclination of his heart not the weakness of it physiologically that caused their absence. His heart did periodically act up and forced him into a slower, almost sleepy regime, until the period passed. But that was the exception, rather than the rule, for the hyperactive hypochondriac. He was certainly capable of the physical exertion of sex, not to mention his exhausting travel and lecturing schedule. That Locke masked this central fact of his existence from Mason suggests why he was "self-conscious in writing a letter" to her. That Mason believed the story shows not only her gullibility but the intensity of her homophobic desire not to see the obvious if cloaked signs of Locke's homosexuality, not the least of which was his salivating pursuit of Langston Hughes.

That obsession doomed Locke's chance to have her finance a trip to Africa. Early in May, Mason drew up a list of "Reprimands," chief among them being that after hearing her comment about wanting to send him to Africa, he cultivated another patron's support "to carry him to Africa," as she put it. What he wanted was enough money from another patron to bring Hughes along! This was too much for Mason. It exemplified his "egotism."[35] But Locke was not interested in going to Africa in 1927 unless he could link it with the pursuit of Langston Hughes.

After writing about Locke's "egotism," Mason held her first meeting with Langston Hughes alone, an hours-long conference on May 22. Hughes's biographer suggests that meeting "consolidated" the relationship because Hughes accepted the emotional tone and personal requirements/expectations Mason imposed on him, specifically that he should call her "Godmother."[36] Hughes may have used that meeting also to confide perhaps that Locke's attentiveness made him uncomfortable. After the meeting, Hughes seemed to accept her conception of the primitive. He was the ideal child, someone she could mold, regardless of his chronological age, and retained the sense of wonder and creativity of the artistically gifted. Hughes seemed a better prospect to become this type of primitive—the child of "genius"—than the perpetually blocked and neurotic Locke. This comparison was not exclusive to Mason. Many of the "younger New Negroes," artists like Richard Bruce (Nugent), for instance, chafed under Locke's constant prattling conceit that the New Negro movement was his baby and that they, as the artists, ought to follow his prescriptions. Instead, "we felt that

Langston Hughes was much the better authority on the New Negro and a truer, more humble leader of the movement, as well."[37]

At that Sunday meeting, Mason very well may have asked Hughes whether he wanted to go to Abyssinia with Locke. Sitting one-on-one with her, Hughes had an opportunity to share with her his plans; he preferred to spend his summer going South, to Florida, to Cuba, in part because of his growing awareness of what Spanish-language poets were beginning to do in Cuba, and also his sense that the distinctive culture he had mined from Negro migrants in Washington, D.C., came from the South, not Africa. Hughes wanted to follow, in effect, the footsteps of those migrants back to the root of the culture they had transplanted north, the oral sources of a distinctively Black American tradition. What particular tradition Locke would be uncovering in Abyssinia remained hazy at best, especially for a poet like Hughes. The meeting alone with Mason, therefore, allowed Hughes to impress Mason with his own intellectual perspective, to assert his authority over his development as a poet, and to win her approval for those plans, thereby separating his career and relationship with her from Locke's.

Locke was losing authority with another poet as well. On June 4, 1927, Claude McKay did what he had threatened to do in October 1924—sever his relationship with Locke.[38] In the Harlem issue of *Survey Graphic*, Locke had changed the title of McKay's poem "White House" to "White Houses" and continued the new title in *The New Negro: An Interpretation* as well. Upon receiving his copy of the anthology, McKay had informed Locke that he had misrepresented the title of the poem. Then, once again, in 1927, Locke published the poem with "White Houses" as its title in *Four Negro Poets*, a short anthology of poetry by Toomer, Cullen, Hughes, and McKay. Dutifully, Locke brought the volume to Mrs. Mason, who loved it. But in June, McKay wrote a letter that attacked Locke's stated motivation for the change—that Locke did not wish to have the reading audience think that McKay was speaking about the residence of the American president—as weak-kneed and unnecessary. McKay no longer wanted Locke to represent or publish his work or consider him his friend. That Locke had continued to use the poem—which he could have simply not published in *Four Negro Poets*—shows something of Locke's sense of entitlement: he, representing and creating a market for their poetry, had a power superior to these "Negro Poets." The controversy shows, perhaps, how Mason's power over Locke prevailed. Her hegemony over him was another version of his over penniless authors like McKay.

Instead of going to Abyssinia, Locke left on June 21 for Europe, to spend most of that month trying to translate Rene Maran's *Batouala* into English and prepare for Geneva and the League of Nations conference he would be attending in September.[39] Locke forbade them to put his name on the ship's list, lest he be disturbed—a comment Mason liked, as it meant he would go into hiding, consistent with her belief that he needed to shield himself from distractions in order to work. But he also needed to shield himself from the emotional disappointments of the spring. At least in Europe he could reconnect with old lovers, dodge McKay, and try to forget Hughes. And he could escape for a while Mrs. Mason and her panopticonic gaze.[40]

Charlotte Mason. Photograph by Hollinger. Courtesy of the Moorland-Spingarn Research Center, Howard University.

30

Langston's Indian Summer

As Locke traveled to Europe during the summer of 1927, Mason's attention shifted to Langston Hughes, himself on the way south. After Hughes's second book of poems, *Fine Clothes for the Jew*, was almost universally attacked by the popular Black press (one newspaper writer declaring that he was "sickened by the 'lecherous, lust-reeking characters that Hughes finds time to poeticize about'"), Hughes retaliated with his article titled, "Those Bad New Negroes: A Critique on Critics," published in the April 14 issue of the *Pittsburgh Courier*. There he declared, "I have a right to portray any side of Negro life I wish to."[1] Shortly afterward a more serious condemnation of the entire Negro Renaissance appeared from the pen of Benjamin Brawley, an English Department colleague at Howard University. Unable to find a single quotable line in *Color*, Brawley argued that Cullen was overrated and singled out Hughes as the saddest case of the younger Negroes. He had talent, Brawley concluded, but "squandered it" under the influence of Carl Van Vechten. Although Van Vechten replied to Brawley's article privately, and Hughes wrote publicly disclaiming the influence of Van Vechten on his poetry, it was clear to Locke that the movement was losing support among educated Blacks in the North. And the stigma of association with Van Vechten was not helping Hughes. Such attacks gave ammunition to someone like Mason who believed that the condemnations were reactions to Van Vechten's influence, which she sought to replace with her own.

Touring the Deep South, beginning in New Orleans, which celebrated and feted him as a still-revered poet of the race, Hughes had the good fortune to run into Zora Neale Hurston, who was collecting research for Franz Boas at Columbia University, where she was a student. Hurston was already well known as an interpreter of the southern rural Negro, most famously for her short story "Spunk." Locke also had suggested Hurston as a potential recipient of Mason's funding, as he had liked Hurston since her student days at Howard University, where she was one of the outstanding students who participated in both the Howard Players and the *Stylus* literary magazine. Hughes also told Hurston about the white-haired, bespectacled, old benefactor who had so impressed him with her money and her conversation, and recommended that she contact Mason when she returned to New York that fall.

Hughes must have given Mason an itinerary of his trip, because periodically throughout his tour he received letters, money, and telepathic support from Mason, who was then spending her summer in Connecticut. Mason told him she was monitoring his progress spiritually and becoming more involved emotionally in his quest to collect and represent the culture of the southern Negro in his next work. With only one private meeting, Mason already felt comfortable telling him that "he must say nothing of his trip to his friends when he reached Manhattan, so that 'later when you are ready to use it the flame of it can burn away the *debris* that is rampant here.'"[2]

In that advice coalesced two aspects of Mason's anti-modernism. First, she possessed a conspiratorial, paranoiac opposition to "Western Civilization" and her desire to reclaim a spirituality she believed still resided in true heirs of "Primitive Man." Part of her insistence that people working with her isolate themselves from society came from her belief, shared by other reactionary modernists, that there was something profoundly destabilizing and maddening about life in the modern city. The true artist, in this narrative, was the heroic individual who transcended destabilization through a spiritual grasp of what was truly eternal.[3] Second, Mason, like some other modernists, ironically, believed a return to the past would recuperate a spirituality that was true and liberating only if it was based on discipline and control.[4] That's where her role came in: she was put on earth, it seemed, to inject this discipline in the heirs of "Primitive Man" to make sure they honored this heritage and were not themselves distracted by the false rewards offered by association with "Western Man." This discipline connected with her cruelty: like a mother chastising errant children, Mason's purpose was to force modernizing Blacks back into connection with a world of spiritualism Black migrants had left behind, according to Locke, when they came north to "modern America." Here was the deepest contradiction of Locke's courtship of Mason. She rejected the city, the world he had written about in the Harlem number as the liberation of the Negro. She was enlisting Hughes in a counter-revolution against the work, the voices, and the hedonistic lifestyle that his poetry had chronicled as the new Black way of living in the city in early twentieth-century America.

That Hughes did not immediately object to her presumptuousness in telling him with whom to discuss his findings suggests that he too possessed a psychological need that Mason perceived and capitalized on. Hughes was deeply alienated from his father, and in search of a lost mother to nurture his desire for a creative career rather than the business career his father had thought he was paying for when he sent his son to New York for an education. Hughes needed someone powerful to solve his financial needs—Mason eventually paid for his brother to attend school with payments made through Locke—but also his psychological need for support and reinforcement to make a go of it as a self-supporting Black writer. Hughes harbored many secrets—about sexual partners and proclivities, his whereabouts and travel plans, his inspiration for his poetry, and so forth—but also a latent conspiratorial attitude that he, like other rebellious Black artists, was engaged in a struggle to overcome the worst aspects of a Western civilization, some of which were disseminated by other Blacks. Mason exploited that attitude among Black creatives, as did Jean Toomer's mentor George Ivanovich Gurdjieff, who demanded secrecy of his charges to prevent "premature" airing of their ideas that might thwart the spiritual revolution they hoped to initiate.[5] Plus, secrecy would ensure that it would not be widely known Hughes was taking money from an old White woman to make a go of it as an independent Black writer.

When Hughes returned to New York that August, he hurried for a meeting alone with Mason. There he reported on his trip, including his travels with Hurston, and his plans for the future. Again, presumptuously, she told him that he ought to use the material to write a novel, a suggestion he was not enthused about. But Hughes did not reject her suggestion, just as he did not tell Van Vechten the year before that he had no interest in writing an autobiography. There was something in Hughes that allowed White patrons to press upon him suggestions they expected to be followed and that he refrained from squashing. Perhaps he expected them to forget or relinquish. He did not yet know that Mrs. Mason never forgot a demand. She also advised him to leave New York immediately. But he stayed in town, hanging out with friends in what was and still remained his natural atmosphere, the urban Black landscape he had helped to foster and celebrate in his poetry.[6]

Locke exhibited considerable resistance to her total control over his activities, which was one of the reasons Mason became increasingly involved with Hughes. A gap occurs in Locke's correspondence with her from June 21 to September 13, 1927, when he writes her on his birthday. Throughout July and August, Locke reputedly sequestered himself in France writing an English translation of *Batouala*. Yet the translation was never published. And later letters to the Nadal sisters employed by Rene Maran to do a translation suggest that if his translation survived it was so poor as to be unusable as a basis for their translation. What he may have been doing is hiding out in the *internationalisme noir*, Jane Nadal's telling phrase for the transnational community of Afro-Diaspora intellectuals in Paris, that included Jane Nadal, her sister Paulette, and Rene Maran, among others. Months later Jane Nadal would write Locke asking permission to translate *The New Negro* into French, as a way to open up the minds of the French to the Black consciousness movement outside of France. Locke agreed, even wanted to join in in the effort of translation, because by working collaboratively with the Nadal sisters, he might have produced a "transinterpretation" of the New Negro concept into new intellectual as well as geographical territory. Locke may have kept Mason in the dark to exclude her probing eyes from a different kind of family abroad, where he could experience the kind of peer production of new knowledge he had hoped for in the patronage scheme but not experienced so far.[7]

When Locke wrote Mason in September, he was ensconced in Geneva and facing the work that he was supposed to do, that of investigating the League of Nations' handling of the African Mandates System. "Dear Godmother: Your wireless birthday greeting reached me at 11 a.m. Already the air was full of ozone—an unusually beautiful day. Your words brought streams of strength and inspiration—as I can prove to you in a few minutes."[8] He wrote her passionately, linking her influence to that of his mother, and crediting her guidance for whatever he accomplished. But at the same time, he subverted her control. He did not send her a copy of his address before the League, as he had promised to do when he left. He did not give her up-to-date reports on his activities, which could have allowed her to intercede and direct them, but instead gave her after-the-fact summaries. And he pursued a schedule of activities at odds with her advice to focus on conducting research for the Mandates report and deemphasize other, scattering activities. His experiences negotiating the rituals of segregation as an African American at the League meetings was the focus of his thinking.

> It has become quite clear that the investigation of the League matters is the secondary matter. It has been the personal contacts that have counted—and the effect on the American colony here has been remarkable. Their first effort was an obvious effort to make an exonerating gesture here before European eyes. Gradually, I think the thing has taken a deeper hold on them—as today for example I am sure it has been due greatly to the fact that I have been reserved and have cut a few previous invitations. When Mr. McDonald kept me standing at the street corner while he finished a tea table conference (this was at an open sidewalk café) I eased out of his invitation to tea by asking him if he didn't want to continue the conference—I could just as well see him some other more convenient hour. So—today I was asked to the lunch for Locheur (Briand's right hand man) and put in a place evidently very carefully thought out—between Professor Holcombe of Harvard and Dean James of Northwestern. This afternoon still later Mrs. Grosvenor Clarkson had a tea for the Holcombes, myself and Ruth Pennybacher (of Galveston Texas) who you can see by the circular is an authority on "The Negro in Literature." I afterwards learned it was a "by request" affair—It was amusing. I wonder if they really think I can't see through it. It is good to learn how really sensitive they are before Europeans; and how easy it is to blackmail them into the reverse of their usual attitude.[9]

This was Oxford all over again, Locke performing Negro representation in a previously segregated global political space. What he did not see is that it was going to have a similar outcome. Instead, he reveled in employing poetry from Hughes and Cullen or from time to time "a perfectly frank statement about the situation in America (if a foreigner is present) to confound them completely." Locke was easily distracted. "Geneva is a whirl—and it isn't easy not to whirl with it. At times I have. But every once in a while I lay hold of your counsel and steady myself. And when I do—things just come to me. The scheme for African Studies at Howard—of which I have already told you, was one case in point. Another [was] Holcombes' volunteering today to get a grant from the Harvard research fund for preparing a young Negro in international government. The man whom I mentioned—Kirkland Jones—happened to have been one of Holcomb's former students—so I daresay that it will go through."[10] Of course, Mason had nothing to do with his African Studies suggestion, but Locke made every effort in his correspondence to Mason to attribute to her "counsel" any advance that he made to reinforce her feeling that she was essential to his success.

In Geneva, however, Locke was operating on his own. He met and impressed many Whites, especially the famous writer Romain Rolland, to whom Locke introduced the notion "that we too think to bring a unique cultural element into the world." Rolland promised to "think about it more—I will welcome it, if I can. I am not strong—but I must live to see a universal humanity dawn." Then, Locke rushed on to another event, another person to impress with his social skills or his connection to an African humanity only recently considered part of the universal community. Perhaps aware that the letter might disappoint Mason in that he was not doing what she counseled him to do in such situations, he closed on a flattering note. "It is due to your wisdom that I see a real vision ahead." Aware of her concern to see some fruits of her investments of money and counsel before her death, he hoped that "it only come quickly forward so that you may have the joy of seeing it and I the joy and help of sharing it with you. And today, Godmother, it isn't only I myself that thank you—it is mother, and father too,— who did all they could by way of parentage."[11] Clearly, Locke felt elated on his forty-second (though he represented to Mason as his forty-first) birthday. But Mason seemed more immediately impressed by the work being done by Hughes who, after all, was in the field actively collecting folklore with Hurston, rather than jetting around Geneva representing the race.

On September 20 Hurston met Mrs. Mason at her Fifth Avenue salon. Hurston was overwhelmed by a coincidence of her arrival at Mason's apartment—that Cordelia Chapin was arranging calla lilies when she entered, an image from a childhood dream that Hurston had carried with her from the South. Her meeting with Mason, therefore, fit her prophetic dream of entering a big house with two women—one old and one young—who welcomed her and culminated her "pilgrimage." Like Locke and Hughes, Hurston had a complicated relationship with a mother who superficially supported, but also limited, her abilities. Now, Hurston came face to face with a White woman who could be her all-powerful mother too and facilitate her dream to become an independent researcher and writer of fiction based on the life and culture of the rural Black poor. After the meeting, she confided to Hughes that she and Mason had gotten on very well and that she hoped Mason would take her up. Her own recent attempts to conduct the kind of folklore research she wanted to collect had left her depressed about future prospects without an infusion of cash and real concern. That was forthcoming.

But first Mason consolidated her position with Hughes. In October, she met with him again, alone, this time for seven hours, during which he found that he was never bored and that she was "entirely wonderful." No, he had not made progress on the novel, but she was not concerned about that. What she was concerned over was that his situation was so scattered and his money so thin that it was impossible for him to devote himself to such a project. Although they discussed the folk opera that Hurston had told Mason about during her meeting, Mason was more committed to funding his research. She was ready to make him an offer he could not refuse. In order to help give flight to his creative spirit, she would pay him $150 a month for a year, and his only obligation would be to report his expenditures fastidiously. The actual details of the payments she would arrange later in consultation with Locke. Although Hughes took a few days to decide, the decision was already made for him by his previous behavior: strapped for funds, unable to work at creditable jobs while he was still a student at Lincoln University, where he was dependent on Amy Spingarn to pay for his tuition and living expenses, Hughes could not help taking this old woman up on an offer that seemed based on who he was, not what he would produce.

Yet that erroneous impression resulted from Mason hiding her real intentions. The maternalism in which she wrapped her offer disguised the real basis of the relationship she proposed to Hughes. Actually, he was being paid to work, in an arrangement that resembled a retainer, but she did not reveal this. And Hughes, as an artist and a man, was seeking escape from the series of service jobs in restaurants, on the one hand, and the crushing assembly line work of the industrial world, on the other. In a sense, part of what attracted him to this arrangement was what attracted him to being an artist in the 1920s: it was an escape from the world of banal work his father reverenced as the essence of a modern Black identity, a world of work embraced by the Black proletariat whose lives fueled his poetry. Rather than becoming one of them, Hughes wanted to be their bard, to speak for their condition without living it. What he and others of the Harlem Renaissance sought was a freedom from the modernizing yet dehumanizing conditions that had made the Great Migration possible. What he did not yet realize was that freedom from this kind of work came at the price, in his case, of acquiescence to a premodern form of patronage.

Zora Neale Hurston was perhaps even more willing to take whatever supportive patronage Mason offered. In the 1920s Hurston lacked the plethora of sympathetic White friends that Hughes enjoyed. Hurston knew that Mason was her one good chance. For different reasons, Mason liked Hurston immensely—in part because of her performative genius, her ability to tell jokes to mimic others at parties, and to utilize the full range of her intellect to deconstruct the pretensions of Negroes of talent, whom she derisively termed the *niggerati*. There was also a touch of the macabre in Hurston, a sense of almost self-destructive exuberance in the face of danger, that allowed her to travel the highways of the rural South alone. She also understood that the renaissance was mainly a male movement dominated by gay Black men. She could not appeal to these men and gain their support by mastering the feminine ways of the Black Victorians. She was not a schoolteacher or a librarian. She was older than all of the other "younger Negroes" and lacked their finesse. But what she had was a dedication to the vocation of the folklore collector and creative writer. If she could get this old woman to believe in her and fund her work, she would do whatever it took to keep her interested. Moreover, genuine affection surfaced between them.

Also of importance to Mason was that Hurston was a woman and an anthropologist, given her own early career as a researcher among Native Americans. But Mason also saw her as somehow beneath Locke and Hughes—one was a world-renowned intellectual, regardless of his annoying sycophancy and Edwardian fussiness, the other a well-published and universally acclaimed poet, who was well supported by Mason's rivals in the Harlem Renaissance. Although she identified more with Hurston, Mason knew that Hurston was not yet a bona fide star; and, Mason knew she could cut a favorable deal with Hurston.

Thus, on December 8, 1927, Mason got Hurston's signature on an unusual contract—to employ (here the exchange character of the patronage relationship is made explicit) Hurston to go south during 1928 and collect southern Negro folklore that would hereafter become the property of Mrs. Mason. In a manner similar to that of Blondiau, who had collected and made the art of the Congo his property, Mason colonized the intellectual property of the Black southerner herself. The contract could be extended, she assured Hurston, if all went well, subject to review of her performance by Mason in consultation with Locke. It is difficult to tell whether the exploitative nature of the arrangement eluded Hurston or that she accepted it as inevitable.

The benefits of the arrangement must have seemed to Hurston straightforward: she would be freed of the academic oversight and inadequate funding she had labored under for some time. And Hurston probably felt that she was skillful enough as a manipulator to manage the problem implicit in the arrangement, that she would have no right to utilize the material she collected in her own work. In this, Hurston's reluctance to contest the terms of the contract had roots in her own complex relationship to the collection and utilization of folklore material in her own creative work. Part of her desire to sign the Mason contract was her desire to elude the kind of academic strictures on the use of folklore in anthropological scholarship. By accepting this contract, she thus gained freedom to pursue a potentially problematical overlap in her folklore collection and her creative writing, a problem of borrowing and using without attribution the cultural products of the subaltern. Because Hurston was Black, she had, as Locke would later put it, a "passport of color" that allowed her greater access to such material than Mrs. Mason would have had if she could have physically made the trip south. In 1928, the racial consciousness of most southern Blacks would not allow Mason the kind of access she had enjoyed earlier in the century among Indians. Employing Hurston to do this work was thus a shrewd move. Not only did Mason get the use of Hurston's body as a collecting subjectivity but also she encouraged Hurston to collude with her in the appropriation of another class's cultural production for the enjoyment and profit of them both. In that sense, what blinded Hurston no less than Hughes to the exploitative character of Mason's relationship to them was their own need to use the folk culture of the Black masses to launch and sustain their own creative projects as writers.

That Hughes and Hurston were Black did not fundamentally alter the class nature of their expropriation of the art of the subaltern to fund their careers as artists. No Black and unknown bards ever received a royalty check from the books published under Hughes's and Hurston's names. What smoothed over this type of appropriation was Hughes's and Hurston's genuine empathy with the Black poor, and their racial vocation to give authentic voice to the subaltern through their creative work. Shared with Mason was an essentialist belief that Black mining of African American folk culture was inherently better and more legitimate than White efforts.

All of this took place because of the initiative of Alain Locke, as Mason's frequent deferment of the details of future arrangements to him suggested. Indeed, this project was as much Locke's as Mason's idea, and he played a prominent role in its orchestration. After he returned from Geneva in late September, Mason consulted him before finalizing the arrangement with Hughes and the contract with Hurston. Thus, Locke was probably the source of Mason's view of Hurston as primarily a worker instead of an artist, a view that reflected her relative status and his generally negative view of women writers. At the same time, Hurston was the only woman he was recommending for a quite lucrative fellowship to conduct her research over three years. He was as engaged as the writers in the collusion to appropriate folk culture for Hughes and Hurston's purposes and accomplish his goal of advancing the scholarly and literary capital of the now-declining and increasingly disreputable Negro Renaissance.

After the contracts with Hughes and Hurston were finalized, Locke's role with Mason suddenly changed. Locke became overseer of the artists he had brought into her stable. A regular feature of her meetings with him would be answering her prepared questions about "Langston's financial situation," Zora's "academic status," their progress or lack of progress on their artistic and research projects, and any other personal item Mason thought crucial to their obligation to stay focused on the work for which they were being paid. Also, Locke was consistently recommending new protégés, such as Arthur Fauset and Aaron Douglas, and escorting Mason to exhibits, such as the Haiti pictures exhibit at the Ainslie Gallery in New York. For this he received sums of money as "gifts." Just as Locke was the first to be rewarded for his service to this system, he also was the first to feel the sting of Mason's condemnation and disapproval if he or they failed to follow all of her suggestions or keep her informed of all of their activities.

A crisis that erupted between November and December of 1927 exemplified the costs of his new intimacy with Mrs. Mason. Locke had become increasingly preoccupied with Zonia Baber and plans for the "Negro in Art" in Chicago, because Carson Perie Scott, the prestigious department store, suddenly reneged on its commitment to host the art exhibit in its galleries. Baber wrote to Locke almost hysterical over the prospect that the "Negro in Art Week" might collapse if they could not find a place to exhibit the visual art, the core of the project. She pressured him for ideas and for his commitment to bring the Harlem Museum of African Art to Chicago to anchor the show. Indeed, as her correspondence with the director of the Art Institute shows, it was the prospect of exhibiting Locke's African art collection that, in effect, persuaded the Art Institute director to find a place in the Children's Exhibition Hall for the whole art exhibit just weeks before the "Negro in Art Week" was scheduled to open. While Art Institute curators were not enthusiastic about the African American art in the show, they enthused about the African art, given its esteem by European modernists. Although Locke had sought to separate the significance of his collection from that influence, the African art's reputation in modernist circles helped secure the African American art exhibit at the Art Institute of Chicago.

All of this was also good for the Harlem Collection, for it proved the Blondiau-Theatre Arts Collection was very reputable in the art world. Mason, however, was not pleased. She thought it was a bad idea to try and tour the African art collection before establishing a permanent museum in Harlem. Her turn to financing Hughes's work was directly related to her sense that Locke was not serious enough in planning the Harlem Museum of African Art for her to continue to work diligently for its creation. She also was upset when he left for Chicago and did not tell her he would be gone as long as he was. On December 10, two days after she had arranged the contract with Zora, Mason attacked him for not giving her all of the information about his African Mandates speeches while he was abroad, failing to provide her advance copies of his speeches, and being so consumed with egotism that he played to the crowd in Chicago, instead of returning as soon as possible to New York.

The cheeky Locke hit back at her in a letter ostensibly expressing concern for her health, but ending with the hope that in her current illness she had regained full control of her mind. That infuriated her. "This is unbelievable that you could be so plain stupid. Nothing the matter with my mind only that physically I have to jump hurdles." Locke was not stupid, but vindictive, and unable to resist taking a shot like the one she had heard about after Hughes's first visit. In spite of himself, Locke could not avoid being subversive, even when it brought down more fury on him. By suggesting that she was going weak in the mind, he was demeaning her as an old woman and hence an intellectual inferior. She issued a lengthy reprimand and threat. "There is nothing the matter with my mind, Alain. It is my heart. You have shattered my belief—and you can not afford to lose it."[12] She was right. He could not afford to lose her support. All of his plans to advance the literary side of the declining Renaissance depended on her; and increasingly, even with the "Negro in Art Week" success, he was feeding her new visual artists as well. If he wanted to keep her support, he was going to have to find a way to keep her more satisfied, give up more authority to her in his decision-making, or at least appear to do her bidding, while he squirreled away opportunities and contacts that he kept only for himself. And if he failed in that maneuvering, he risked having the Negroes he introduced to her receive her money, power, and attention, without him.

Mason's maternalistic approach to her patronage of Black artists was working its magic. Like paternalism generally, Mason's caring for Locke and the artists came with an obligation to do her bidding exactly as she wished it or be dressed down like a child. Part of her power came from her ability to pit Locke and the artists against one another as if they were so many wayward children in need of discipline. Locke already had lost his prominence in her life, at least in part because of Hughes. As he sat in her parlor and listened to her reprimands, it could not escape him that she repeatedly compared his behavior to Hughes's and found him less grateful. He had to listen to how Hughes was less White than he was, that Hughes was less interested in public flattery, that Hughes's spirit was so delicate that she did not want Locke to disturb it by his attentions, the latter perhaps a veiled confidence to Mason from Hughes about Locke's continuing advances toward him. In addition to having to listen to her insults, he had to face the prospect of losing control of a patron he had discovered and set up. As he looked around for someone to blame, his attention focused increasingly on Hughes, whom Locke felt was not sufficiently grateful to *him* for having put Hughes into this arrangement. The scheme Locke had designed to enhance his power was being turned against him, in part because Hughes had created conditions of patronage favorable to him and not especially to Locke.

This turnabout points to a central fact of the patronage situation Locke had set up: Mason was in control. While his subversiveness was always available, she was too aware of what her money and emotional support meant to him and too insecure to allow him the kind of independence he enjoyed with other patrons. As the others would eventually learn, Mason was ready at a moment's notice to retract her money and support and abandon a too-independent Negro. Locke was going to have to do a better job of keeping her happy, while also keeping some of his autonomy. Finding that tricky balance was even more complicated with Hughes and Hurston in the equation. Now that she had Hughes, Mason dispensed with her earlier plans to fund the Harlem Museum of African Art and instead concentrated on a young Black male artist who was more attractive and more willing to be primitive than Locke. That was his real punishment for not having conducted the museum project as she had wished.

Locke was learning a powerful lesson. Mason was more adept than he at using people to get her way. Her money and her manipulative use of it allowed her emotional independence at the apex of her surrogate family. Her money allowed her to replace her godchildren when they were bad. Locke had been reduced from a potential director of a museum to an assistant to help keep Hughes's spirit from being clouded by details. Hurston had just landed a contract for $200 a month when he was still trying to negotiate to get his job back at Howard. As 1927 ended, Locke, a supreme manipulator, had been played.

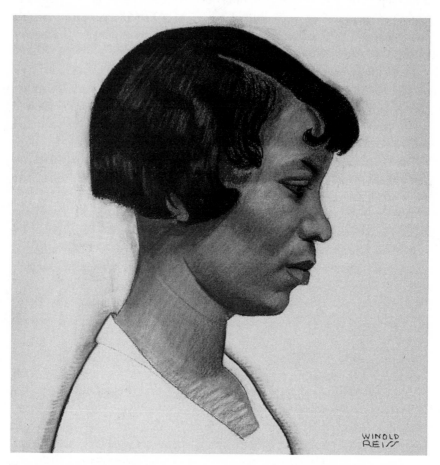

Zora Neale Hurston, 1925. Pastel on board. Winold Reiss. Photograph courtesy of the Reiss Archives. Copyright and permission to publish courtesy of Fisk University Galleries, Nashville, Tennessee.

31

The American Scholar

In "The American Scholar" in 1837, Ralph Waldo Emerson declared the American Mind ought to separate from European models of excellence and immerse itself in the daily life of the common people of America, the true source of its unique culture.[1] In 1928, Alain Locke struggled to find in the "common" culture of the Black folk a source for his modernist reinterpretation of American culture. Shortly after New Year's, he departed Washington on the Southern Railway for Nashville, Tennessee, where he would be teaching at Fisk for the winter quarter. Unlike Emerson, the African American scholar taking such a journey could not but help coming into contact with "the common," as accommodations below the Mason-Dixon line were always segregated. Riding in the dirty coach set aside for Negroes was a reminder to Locke that he was entering a southern world that still regarded Negroes as scum. As the train snaked around the West Virginia mountains, and he settled into the greasy seat shown him by the conductor, Locke may have remembered that a similar trip south had sparked W. E. B. Du Bois and Jean Toomer to write *Souls of Black Folk* and *Cane*, respectively. But Emerson never considered that the White "common," working- and lower-middle-class White Americans saw any elevation of the Black "common" as a threat. Locke must have recalled his earlier trip into the South in 1912 with Booker T. Washington, when angry Whites met him and the "great conciliator" at train stations with violence and even death toward anyone who tried to lift the lot of the Negro over theirs. As Locke settled into "Negro mode," that conditioning of himself to the segregated American life, he may have reflected on the series of events that had forced him so deep into the southern "common" once again—not by philosophical choice, as Emerson suggested, but by professional necessity. With no base in Harlem, no control of a Negro public institution, and no access to elite White institutions of higher education in America, Locke, like Emerson after the Divinity School address, was going to have to make his future on speaking, writing, and secular preaching to a "common," but one divided by hate, rivalry, and threats of death to any who tried to change the racial status quo in America. As Locke grimaced inside at the many little insults he endured as he entered the segregated South, he must have wondered at that future. Emerson never confronted the racial division in the American "common" or the racial sickness of the American Mind. But Locke was going to have to confront both in Nashville. Feelings of dread began to grow.

Locke's mood lifted temporarily upon his arrival in Nashville. He was welcomed like a king. Fisk's president invited him to dinner, provided him excellent faculty rooms on campus, and funded a stenographer to transcribe his lectures. The president actually hoped to persuade Locke to stay at Fisk, despite the recently tendered offer from Howard to return. The president's entreaties were flattering to Locke, but he could not seriously consider moving to Fisk permanently. It would force him to make a monthly trek between Nashville and New York if he wanted to keep anything like a national literary life or a love life alive. Moving to Fisk would push him further into a clandestine homosexual life, since Black Victorian strictures were even more dominant at Fisk than at Howard. Though he had been glad to escape New York and Mrs. Mason, Locke began to feel more vulnerable as an isolated Black northerner in Nashville. Suddenly, after two weeks at Fisk, he succumbed to a mysterious illness that sent him to bed. Soon, he wired Mrs. Mason about his condition. Sick, lonely, and second-guessing his decision to come, Locke stifled the urge to return immediately to the East with a catastrophic medical collapse as his excuse. Unwilling to give into the illness, Locke righted himself and sent a second telegram. "Do not worry. Nothing more serious it seems than Southern hookworm"—an apt metaphor, perhaps, for his reaction to the South—and to her.[2] He often rationalized about never vacationing in the South due to its heavily spiced food. Now, his ailment became a way for him to ensure that Mason's love was still focused on him. Her concerned replies convinced him that he was still her "little boy," while also convincing himself that he could survive the South at such distance from her.

First priority from January to March at Fisk were his two lecture courses—one on the Negro in American Literature and the other on Race Contacts and Inter-Racial Relations. On January 6, 1928, he gave his first lecture at Fisk on the image of the Negro in American Literature. Atrocious transcripts of this and other lectures given at Fisk do not do justice to the lectures. The transcription work was probably the onerous responsibility of a Fisk student, who seemed unable to hear Locke clearly, a sign, perhaps, too, that Locke had not yet emancipated himself from his whispering Bostonian accent. Mason hounded him to get rid of it. Still, what comes through was surprising—Locke saw racism as malleable, changeable, indeed, already changing under their very noses. Locke must have jolted his young audience in Nashville when he asserted that the African was originally a heroic figure in early English literature, only to be transformed by the emergence of Puritanism as the dominant force in American literature.

Locke used these literary lectures, along with another delivery of his 1916 Race Contacts lectures, to inspire Black students, to give them a sense that even the horrific negative stereotypes of the Negro in later American literature were not fixed, but able to change with the changing social and political prospects of the Negro. American race relations followed an arc he outlined in his lectures that reflected the changing calculus of power in American life. The inspirational part came with this issue of power. If race was nothing more than a symbol of a group's power and reputation, Locke hoped the generation maturing in college in the late 1920s would change the assessment of the race by becoming more powerful, by seizing the resources at hand to create art, culture, and social innovations that were still available to Negroes acting with free will even in the segregated South. A new subjectivity for Negroes was possible in the emerging present of the 1920s that could shape the foreseeable future if they approached their present with creative action and agency.

These lectures reminded Locke that he was an American scholar, not just an errand boy for a powerful benefactor. He wrote Montgomery Gregory that these lectures would "soon become books." Unfortunately, they did not. His schedule really did not permit it. With Nashville as a base, he traveled and lectured widely in the South. He also used his time in Nashville to make intellectual contacts his segregated appointment at Howard had not fostered. He was able, for example, to meet and speak with Edwin Mims, the celebrated southern literary historian of Vanderbilt University, although he was prevented by southern "custom" from actually visiting with him at Vanderbilt. Perhaps the still-rigid race lines in Tennessee played a role in his decision to return to teach in Washington, despite a lucrative offer that exceeded what Howard could pay him. But he did not have time to turn these lectures into books while he was negotiating the etiquette of segregation and of kowtowing to Mrs. Mason.

Even at Fisk, Locke maintained his obligations as the coordinator of a vast effort to realize projects he and Mason had agreed on. These latter projects often required much secret communication and maneuvering, leaving him little time for serious, scholarly study. On February 24, he wrote Hurston: "You have already heard I know from Godmother about the possible crossing of your lines by influences which she and I both agree should be kept entirely away not only from the project at hand but from this entire movement for the rediscovery of our folk material." Who the offending decadent was, the letter does not say. "The main thing...is to have C.L. [Cudjoe Lewis, a Hurston folk informant] entirely silenced. If the person undertakes to visit Mobile during my visit here, which unfortunately ends March 19, I will accompany him. If [it] looks as if it were best for me to cover the situation here, [I will] forego the pleasure I anticipated in spending some few days with you in your field work."[3]

In reality, Black research was suddenly hot and there was plenty of competition from White anthropologists who also saw the value of publishing "their" discoveries of "untarnished" Blackness. Mason was also protecting her investment, since she was paying for the research and owned the results as her "property." On a psychological level, Mason was a paranoid, often fearing that another, usually

White person, would not only steal the information from under them, but prostitute it by turning it into popular culture. Mason and Locke shared a bias against popular culture, and she intensified his hatred of it, telling him to make sure not to let Max Reinhardt "get his hands on this material." In that sense, working with Mason accentuated his suspiciousness, his deviousness, and his manipulation of other people's access to what was not really "our folk material." In this particular instance—since he did not go down to Mobile—the need for him to play this role cost him an opportunity to spend time with Hurston in fieldwork that might have opened his eyes to what "the folk" really were like and advanced him intellectually. But as a Black Victorian gay male, Locke was not that interested in visiting Hurston in Mobile for "field work."

His letters to Zora Neale Hurston show the power Locke gained from his relationship with Mason. Despite Hurston's pioneering scholarship and her courage, she still had to kowtow to Locke, especially when Mason backed up his opinion. "The more I think of it," he continued, "the more work becomes important, especially from the point of view of the possible survivals of African traits in the performance and action side of the games and stories. Do not let this side of the matter escape your attention." Here, his knowledge of Boasian anthropology and his exchanges in the mid-1920s with Melville Herskovits gave him some knowledge in the area of African survivals. Hurston must have gritted her teeth when she read this paean to Locke's authority. Did she need him to tell her the importance of her work? Locke treats Hurston here as a student and naif in folklore research, when just the opposite was the case. He concluded, "I know your work must be making you very happy and I am happy in the thought that it has come to you in the beautiful way that it has."[4] Hurston had to defer to those who have put her "in the field," though Locke's letter belies she is his intellectual superior in the arena of African American folk culture.

Beyond managing Hurston's and Mason's espionage work, Locke served as an agent for Rene Maran. Maran desperately needed funds and used Locke to represent his various manuscripts to American publishers in hopes of landing a lucrative contract. While not sanguine about the willingness of the Black middle class to purchase the exclusive edition of Maran's books, Locke remained enthusiastic about the White audience for book. "Our colored American friends...are more interested in dollars than in books." Unfortunately, Maran's latest more naturalistic contribution, *Kongo*, had not found a publisher. "The Boni's like it very much—but they feel that they cannot make it what we call a 'best seller' in its present form....They feel that a longer work on the *Kongo* with still more African material can be made a grand success. Do not think this is a characteristic American point of view towards your work. It is really their excessive interest that your novel should have even greater success than Batouala."

Locke's own work found a ready outlet in the literary and opinion magazines. With funds from Mason to buy a Dictaphone, and with a stenographer provided to him by Fisk University, Locke turned out a vast amount of quick writing—essays, reviews, and shorter expository pieces that he could finish off between classes. Locke completed an assessment of the "Newest Negroes" for poet Lewis Alexander's special Negro number of the *Carolina Magazine*, which carried his sparkling article on the "newest negro" poets to emerge since 1925. He argued that New Negro writers were beginning to document an alternative world of beauty already existing in the folk Black experience, laying the groundwork for a cosmopolitan transnational literature of beauty. In addition to "Beauty Instead of Ashes" in the *Nation*, he published a stinging review of Mary White Ovington's *Portraits in Color*, explaining that her book, like others written in reaction to racism, exaggerated its subjects. At the same time, he was encouraging Rene Maran to get out a popular novel of African culture and pressuring his publisher to follow up an earlier advance of $500 for Maran (which Locke had wrung from them) with more money for the fledgling French writer.

Once settled at Fisk, Locke exuded a kind of energy for lecturing, speaking, and proselytizing that would have humbled a less driven man. On February 10, 1928, he was in Jefferson City, Missouri, lecturing on "The African Background" to students at the "other" Lincoln University; two days later, he was speaking at an "Interracial Sunday" at Roberts Park Methodist Episcopal Church about "Recent Gains in Race Relations." In demand as a speaker before White audiences because of his upbeat message and his diminutive, non-threatening physique and manner, Locke grew in his ability to use Black culture to convert the fence-sitting liberals into outright supporters of race progress. "I had an invitation to give a talk at the Chapel Service of Scarret [sic] College. I got through the speech very well which was not easy—considering that it was a frank talk on The New Negro and the New South to an audience of 250 Southerners, mostly young women. I hope some of Langston's poetry (I too Sing America) and Lewis Alexander's Dark Brother did them good. At any rate they flocked around afterwards to shake hands, and did not say the usual thing about loving Negroes and knowing them better than anybody. Incidentally I told them they didn't know the Negro and never would until they opened up both their minds and hearts so that their eyes could really see and their ears really hear."[5] Locke found in the language of the Black church a means to advance himself as a Black ambassador to the White conscience. But such frenetic running from classroom to chapel service distracted Locke from a deeper fear that he was not any closer to producing his own major book that would be an intellectual sequel to *The New Negro: An Interpretation*.

Constant traveling did assuage Locke's loneliness and longing for romantic intimacy. A few new interesting young men had entered his life, principally from his trip in December to Chicago—Richmond Barthé, the young Art Institute painter, with his chiseled good looks—and Albert Dunham, the brilliant philosophy undergraduate at the University of Chicago, who opened a thoughtful, encouraging, and philosophically rich correspondence with Locke that spring.

But neither had declared any willingness to be Locke's lover, and both were still in Chicago, although Barthé planned to move to New York to jump-start his professional career. Locke was becoming desperate. How else to explain that in June he kept open the possibility of accepting a position at the Alexander Hamilton High School in Brooklyn?[6] New York continued to beckon as a place where he could live more openly as a gay man. Clearly, Locke longed for a permanent young love to fight off what was beginning to loom as a potential mid-life crisis.

Locke was not so busy that February that he could not check in with Hughes, whom he wrote from Lincoln. "I have not been as free from pressure as I had hoped. Lectures and still more lectures. However the two extension courses here promise to be the rough material of two books, one on the Negro in American Literature (not Negro literature, but the Negro in Literature) and the other on Race Contacts and Inter-Racial Relations, awfully academic but necessary. Godmother mighn't altogether approve—but certain subjects have to be treated to prevent them being worse treated," he confided, suggesting though, perhaps exaggerating, his independence from Mason's control. He then offered that he would be returning to "the Land of Freedom, March 20th—and hope to see you soon thereafter." Realizing that the hint might not be enough to compel Hughes to see him, Locke followed up the invitation to get together to report on the newest challenges to Hughes's supremacy—"You ought to read the proofs of McKay's new novel *Home to Harlem*. It is humanity stripped not to its underclothes but down to its underskin. It is powerfully done though. Its realism even staggered Bud Fisher—so you know"—and his visiting with the young poet Sterling Brown, who was teaching English at Lincoln. "I would love to meet you, Langston," Brown penned at the bottom of Locke's postcard. But the implication was clear; others were on the move in the very fields—Black novel writing and folk poetry composition—that were supposed to be Hughes's. At the end, Locke could not help including an almost pathetic beg: "Have you heard from Zora? Do write."[7] Hughes did not.

Perhaps the emptiness in Locke's personal life pushed him to focus on his professional activities, especially his activities as manager of the complex "empire" he had built with Mason. Even while at Fisk, he took almost full responsibility as "secretary" of the Harlem Museum of African Art for almost all aspects of operation, likely because it was becoming a major headache. Early in February, Mrs. Isaacs, the purchaser of the Blondiau-Theatre Arts Collection, and now a board member of the Harlem Museum of African Art, wrote him enraged because the Rochester Museum of Art had notified her that some items listed in the traveling exhibition, valued roughly at $1,000, were missing from the collection as delivered. While Isaacs and Locke had been close in the past, they had grown more distant as Locke's loyalties had shifted to Mason and her larger endowment of the museum. The loss in the traveling exhibition, therefore, opened a door for Isaacs to critique, indirectly, Locke's leadership of the museum, especially since some of the items missing still belonged to her. Locke engineered the recovery of the pieces, propped up the insurance for the show (about to lapse for nonpayment of the premium), and turned the incident to his advantage by removing most of her objects from the traveling collection—at her request—and then assuming full control over the remaining exhibit pieces. All the while, he was contracting for more sites for the exhibit (turning down a possible visit to Philadelphia because it would not be at the new Philadelphia Museum of Art), soliciting support from a Black group associated with the Karamu Theatre and the Cleveland Museum of Art, and negotiating the complicated terms of shipping, final payment, and insurance in transit to acquire more African art from European collectors for his museum. He took no chances after the debacle at Rochester: he pulled the strings, curated and even installed the shows, and built the collection, all with little money of his own.

Indeed, so complete was Locke's control over the museum by June that Isaacs, realizing she had been marginalized for her tirade, allowed objects from her private collection to be included when Locke installed the traveling exhibition at Howard University Gallery of Art. Perhaps his greatest achievement was to install sixty-five African art objects from the permanent collection in the 135th Street New York Public Library in Harlem. Locke was gaining a reputation as an auteur of the presentation of African art, not simply an expert on the artifacts. When Robert Abbott, the editor of the *Chicago Defender*, learned of a valuable collection of fine art from the Ivory Coast that was available, he contacted Locke, who right away fired off letters to the French owners of that collection, while working to keep Abbott silent about the prospect. In the course of those arrangements, Locke became a bonded importer of African art.

Locke was trying to become an American scholar by arguing that African art and African American literature should become the alternative center of a more authentic American culture. To affect that radical shift, Locke needed the help of others, especially the young writers of the Renaissance, to supply the raw material for his theorizing and produce texts that would legitimate his argument that the Negro artist was creating a renaissance for America. Those needs led to increased conflicts with the very writers whom he had brought into the patronage arrangement. Before meeting Mason, Hurston had written flattering letters to Locke, especially one in 1927 in which Hurston suggested that she, Hughes, and Locke—with the two artists on the bottom and Locke at the apex—would form an intellectual triangle that would transform Negro art. But as 1928 advanced and the lines of power hardened into arrangements, Mason made it clear that she would manage Hughes, who was now deep at work on the novel Mason commissioned him to write, even while he was at Lincoln University in Pennsylvania. Hurston would spend two years in the South collecting the material Mason had hired her to find. While in the South, her views of Locke, Mason, and Hughes would shift.

Zora began to feel that willingness to go into the rural South as she was doing, commit to close study of the people and their culture, and express that culture without fitting it to White or modernist expectations was the litmus test of who was an authentic interpreter of Negro culture. While at Fisk, Locke and Hurston had discussed and even planned that he would visit her in Mobile, Alabama. But once Locke shrunk back from joining her there, Hurston's evaluation of him began to dip.

In 1928, Locke became less sure of the road forward in theorizing about Black culture in the future. As he searched around for inspiration and direction, he tried to extract information he needed from Hurston. Resentful of his suggestions for how she should conduct her research, Hurston was reluctant to share her information readily with him and instead began to put her findings before Hughes, who became her confidant and often the real middleman between Mason and her. She distrusted Locke and felt he would steal her ideas if given a chance. "I had written to Dr. Locke at H.U. about March 6th," she informed Hughes. "I wonder if he ever got it. . . . I have come to five general laws, but I shall not mention them to Godmother or Locke until I have worked them out. Locke would hustle out a volume right away." Her willingness to put her body in harm's way had reaped intellectual dividends.

1. The Negro's outstanding characteristic is drama. That is why he appears so imitative. Drama is mimicry. Note gesture in place of words.
2. Negro is lacking in reverence. Note number of stories in which God, church, + heaven are treated lightly.
3. Angularity in everything, sculptures, drawing, abrupt storytelling
4. Redundance
5. Restrained ferocity in everything. There is a tense ferocity beneath the casual exterior that stirs the onlooker to hysteria. Note effect of Negro music, dancing, gestures on the staid Nordic.
6. Some laws in dialect. The same form is not always used.[8]

She shared these six insights with Hughes because she needed his advice and counsel to turn material into finished plays. Locke needed her for anthropological material, but she needed Hughes for literary structure. Her way of getting that was to propose that they produce the new "black theatre" together. "Did I tell you before I left about the new, the _real_ Negro art theatre I plan? Well, I shall or rather we shall act out the folk tales, however short, with the abrupt angularity and naiveté of the primitive 'bama nigger.' Just that with naïve settings. What do you think?" In the next letter, she enthused, "I _know_ it is going to be glorious! A really new departure in the drama."[9]

Hurston's insights were a really new departure in Black Cultural Studies, for unlike so many other commentators, she found that "Negro folk-lore is _still_ in the making, a new kind is crowding out the old." Locke might have been useful to her, for if the two of them had been able to collaborate, they could have produced an article or book that would have redefined the theory of Black culture.

Instead, her distrust of him and his insecurity about acknowledging her eminence as a great scholar of Negro folklore doomed the possibilities. As Hurston continued in her letter to Hughes, "I found another one of the original Africans, older than Cudjoe[,] about 200 miles upstate on Tombigbee River. She is most delightful, but no one will ever know about her but us," and the *us* did not include Locke.[10] Moreover, she also discovered self-taught visual artists on her trip, some of whom were sculptors, others portraitists who "draw better than Douglas." In an art movement that needed to de-individualize in order to become revolutionary, neither Locke nor his Black "workers" reflected on the way that Mason's patronage scheme was dividing them against one another.

Locke's greatest failure of this period was his inability to acknowledge Zora Neale Hurston as the preeminent American scholar of the 1920s. He had helped her and was continuing to help her. But it was not enough, for Locke never trusted Hurston as a fashioner of a new American Cultural Studies that transcended political/national borders. Had he made a way for her to enter into Howard University as a scholar, he might have realized his dream of making the school the center of African-based American scholarship. But Hurston was not the kind of woman he resonated with, not being willing to play the mother to him; and because she was a woman, she could not be a kind of object of desire, like Hughes, and lead Locke to move mountains to get her at Howard. So, she suffered gendered, class, and sexual marginality all her own. Thus, if her patron dumped her, she would not have the ability, as the highly middle-class Jessie Fauset would when Du Bois dumped her, to teach French at a Black high school. Indeed, in one of her last letters to Mrs. Mason, Hurston would state she was planning to try to make money by selling chicken soup based on her unique recipe! While many men of the Harlem Renaissance and after would see her as hysterically unbalanced, her class, gender, and racial vulnerability shaped powerfully her behavior. That is why she worked so hard to keep the patron she had despite Mason's dehumanizing maternalism.

What gave Hurston an advantage in dealing with Mason was that Hurston's concern and even paranoia about others stealing her material mirrored Mason's concerns and paranoia. As women, they perhaps shared a sense of how men, whom they believed were less intelligent and less resourceful than they, were taking advantage of them to anoint themselves as "American scholars." Over time, Mason began to side more and more with Hurston in a protective maternalism that lifted Hurston, eventually above both Locke and Hughes, because to Mason, Hurston was the true spirit—both because of her "primitiveness" and the laser-like insights of her mind. Hughes began to feel left behind in Hurston's plans. Sensitive to his concerns, Hurston worked hard in her second letter to Hughes to calm his worries.

Adding to Hughes's pecking order woes was artistic vulnerability: he had not written anything memorable since 1927, poetry based on the blues talk and lyrics of recent southern migrants. Yet critically for Hughes, he could not bring himself to return to ethnographic research to fuel his muse. He canceled his plans to join Hurston in the South that summer of 1928. Struggling to balance a professional writing career and college work, he gave as his excuse the need to finish strongly in his exams, although the real reason may have been his desire to avoid greater, possibly romantic, intimacy with Hurston. Saddened by his rejection, she became depressed. "I have been through one of those terrible periods when I can't make myself write," she wrote him by July. "But you understand, since you have 'em yourself." To keep herself going, she took to reading aloud Hughes's poetry at the turpentine camps she visited, to attract the attention of the local storytellers and promote herself as one of a few Black artists appreciative of folk culture. She found that Black workers in the rural South loved his poems, especially those in *Fine Clothes for the Jew*, filled as it was with raunchy rhymes and transplanted rhythms of the South. So successful was the act that she sold several copies, sent the money back from them to Hughes, and requested more. "I wanted to let your publishers know what a hit you are with the people you write about, but Godmother doesn't want me to say anything at present. But I shall do it as soon as this is over."[11]

Hughes also began to advise Hurston on how to manipulate Mason. Here, he did not so much usurp Locke's role as displace it, since Locke remained fiercely loyal to Mason. Hughes's rise as the schemer advising Hurston on how to handle Mason nevertheless undermined Locke's role as an effective middleman or broker in the patronage scheme. When combined with Locke's lack of scholarship in the field of Black folklore and his unwillingness to side with Hughes and Hurston against Mason, Locke was vulnerable. By 1929, Hurston would conclude, "Locke is intellectually dishonest. He always wants to be with the winner." His refusal to stand up to Mason had squeezed him into an unsatisfying role: he did not receive the deference from Hughes and Hurston that they showed Mason, because she had the money; and he did not receive the same respect from Mason they received, because they had the talent.

Without Hurston's help and intimate contact with African American folk culture, Locke could not really claim to be a scholar of the new Black culture emerging out of the South into northern consciousness. He needed such contact, because in the late 1920s and throughout the 1930s, the pioneers in the American search for culture were those digging up what they believed to be a usable past "on native grounds," to borrow Alfred Kazin's memorable title. The way of the future lay in collecting the culture produced by poor people, largely poor Black people. When fine art was not the goal, the Black folk were still the focal point, from the folk field recordings of Alan Lomax to the hundreds of Works Progress Administration (WPA) interviewers who would fan out over the South in the 1930s to capture the waning reminiscences of the last who lived under slavery. To keep step Locke had to be willing to do what Hurston did: put his body in the belly of the South, "with blood on its mouth," as Hughes put it, to speak with authority about the folk. But it was highly unlikely that a cane-toting, three-piece-suit wearing, fedora-hatted Alain Locke would be able descend into phosphate mines and railroad camps of Alabama and find culture.

Marooned in a quickly fading Black modernity, Locke turned down an offer from Eugene Kinckle Jones to take over editing *Opportunity*, when Charles Johnson resigned in March. Locke remained peeved that he had not been approached earlier, when he was unemployed. With a secure job at Howard, Locke could afford to snub the more demanding job of making *Opportunity* a go in the waning years of the Renaissance. Instead, he busied himself with his duties as a critic, including reviewing Du Bois's *Dark Princess* for the *New York Herald Tribune*. Locke made clear now how boring reading Du Bois's novel was when he closed a letter to Langston Hughes with the quip, "Unfortunately I must leave you for her." Other tasks were pure pleasure, such as unpacking and installing the traveling exhibition of the Harlem Museum of African Art in the art gallery at Howard. Locke still had to endure criticism from Mason about how he documented his use of her money: "I find that you do not touch Langston for rendering account. The difference is between a Negro who has never had anything and a gentleman of the world to the lady who keeps him." But that was in fact the reality: he was the gentleman of the world, though she wanted him to act like a Negro who never had anything! That he continued to put up with her shows how desperate his situation was emotionally, now that he had his job back.

Increasingly, Locke found the courage to protest. In one particular incident, Mason criticized him for a proposal to make back some of the cost of a traveling exhibition and lecture series by charging vendors expenses. Mason abhorred any scheme to "make money" on African or African American art, especially as she was already fronting him a considerable amount of money to conduct such activities. But this time he reacted angrily. "I have thought back carefully and find I have reported almost exactly and verbatim. There was no mention of 'making money' in the conversation. I think you must have misunderstood something as my voice flagged periodically—you know how it does! Perhaps it was this—I was mentioning that McKay, Du Bois and Pickens had all accepted money for their personal expenses." Mason thought that if she was covering most of his expenses that this should be enough to allow him to relinquish his usual tendency to think advocating Black art should pay.

But Mason was not giving him enough money to make a real go of the Harlem Museum of African Art. In fact, he was being paid for performing three or four jobs for her, without the time and leisure to develop the museum project into a real permanent institution. He bore some of the responsibility for his predicament. He allowed the relationship to be framed in terms of her "gifts" to him, which freed him from having to "earn" the money, as Hurston and Hughes were doing. But as the recipient of gifts, a degree of intimacy entered into their relationship that undermined his ability to request outright the kind of endowment he needed to make the museum sustainable.

Locke escaped to Europe again that summer of 1928. Before leaving, he had to tidy up a number of loose ends—closing down the Howard University Gallery of Art exhibition of the African Art traveling exhibition, writing letters to Frenchmen about visits he planned to examine their collections while in Europe, and communicating with the Mandates Commission of the League of Nations to announce his attendance at their September sessions as an observer. Adding to his frustration were the artists themselves, as he realized that Hughes was even more aloof than before Locke had introduced him to Mason. It must have dawned on him that Hughes was not attracted to him and also not attracted to the prospect of an open-closet public life. To become closer to Locke would have made Hughes homosexual by association. Indeed, few younger Black gay artists in the Renaissance were willing to chance living in any public way as gay men. Just before leaving that July, for example, he learned that Countee Cullen, his former if only occasional bed partner, was, incredibly, marrying Yolanda Du Bois, the daughter of W. E. B. Du Bois!

Du Bois decided to make a spectacle out of the wedding: at one point, he had planned to release doves in the church during the ceremony. Not only were more than 1,300 guests invited but also Yolanda had sixteen bridesmaids. Afterward, he wrote about his daughter's wedding in the Crisis. He described it as "the symbolic march of young black America. America, because there was Harvard, Columbia, Smith, Brown, Howard, Chicago, Syracuse, Penn and Cornell. But it was not simply conventional America—it had a dark and shimmering beauty all its own; a calm and high restraint and sense of new power; it was a new race; a new thought; a new thing rejoicing in a ceremony as old as the world."[12] Apparently, Locke had advised Cullen against the marriage, but Cullen went through with it anyway, presumably to remain part of a compromised Black bourgeois world. The marriage was the breaking point in their relationship. As he wrote to Cullen, "I can forgive you for refusing my advice, but I cannot forgive you for transgressing a law of your own nature—because nature herself will not forgive you."[13] Cullen's wedding would be followed by another irony— the marriage of painfully dark-skinned Wallace Thurman to the ravishingly light-complexioned Louise Thompson in September. Increasingly, it seemed, prominent gay New Negroes opted for the oldest of camouflages—the marriage of convenience—rather than live a transparently gay single life.

Such subterfuges of the "youngest Negroes" helped Locke deflect their criticisms of him. At least he had not tried to "pass" for heterosexual. Of course, Locke had his own masks to manage as he ventured to Europe that summer. He rationalized it as a trip to search for more collections of African art and to attend meetings of the Mandates Commission of the League of Nations of the treatment of Germany's former colonies in Africa. But what was uppermost on his mind was undertaking a regimen of self-care. Not long after giving an enthusiastic clarion call to brotherhood with Africans at the West African Studies Union in London, Locke hopped over to Paris to meet with collectors and then headed to Germany, where perhaps for the first time, with Mason's travel gift of usually $100–200, he had the finances to enroll for at least two weeks at the Nanheim Spa and Clinic in Germany and sample its expensive and experimental methods to rejuvenate his "tired heart."

Taking his rest cure around the restorative baths of the Nanheim resort, Locke could sit bundled up in sumptuous, white towels and gaze for hours at the glistening German bodies of the local well-heeled youths. Here were bodies that fit Locke's ideal—slender, athletic, disciplined, yet frolicking sinewy youth, whose freedom and energy spoke to Locke's loins. Safely out of view in Germany, Locke benefited from a kind of invisibility to move silently and unnoticed through the brothels and resorts of gay Germany without notice from Germans or vacationing Brits and Americans. If Hughes, the love of his life, was not going to reward Locke for providing him access to Mason's money, Locke was going to reward himself by living as a gentleman rake of the world, regardless of what Mason thought about it.

League of Nations meetings in Geneva paled by comparison. Indeed, it is not certain that Locke went to Geneva, since his attendance was not recorded in the official account of the League's deliberations, although that was not unusual; he was not an appointed member of the council. Certainly, he missed the October meetings of the Permanent Mandates Commission, as he had the preceding year, since to attend those would have made him late for the beginning of fall classes at Howard. A major reason he had had difficulty finishing the report in the year following his first trip to Geneva in 1927 was that he never actually attended the Mandates Commission session, and thus had no hard data on the operation of the Mandate System of oversight on former German and other European colonies in Africa and the Middle East. Most likely he stopped in briefly at the League of Nations meetings in September 1928 and witnessed debate of the League on one of the previous year's Mandate Report on South Africa. In this debate the League, while praising the report for recounting efforts at "local government," requested that next year's report detail more on efforts to stimulate "self-government" among the native population. In his written response, Jan Smut of South Africa expressed his chagrin. The notion that the Mandates opened up the possibility for African transition to self-government made it into Locke's eventual report.

Rushing home before October also denied Locke a golden opportunity to see Marcus Garvey, who delivered a speech on October 6 that might have helped Locke hone his skills as an inspirational speaker, and also as a reporter on the importance of the League's activities for the international Negro. Marcus Garvey addressed almost 1,600, mostly White listeners at the Theater of the Gaiete Rochechouart. It was Garvey's bid to enlist France as a partner to establish a country and government for the Negro in Africa. Garvey had recently filed a petition with the League demanding it provide the Negro an independent state in Africa. The speech, as well as the petition, showed Garvey's growing sophistication as a manipulator, since both sought to curry favor with the French by lauding

France as the only nation to treat Africans with dignity. But Garvey went on to threaten the international community with an uprising of the 11 million followers he believed still awaited his instructions back in the United States, if it did not act on the reputed "promises" President Wilson had made to "liberate the small nations of the world." Garvey's militant, if unlikely, demand for self-determination might have given Locke evidence for his report of a growing concern in the Black Diaspora with having a stake in the League's activities in Africa.[14]

But without making contact with Garvey, Locke had no such evidence, thin as that would have been, to argue to the Foreign Policy Association (FPA) that a groundswell of interest in the League had arisen among people of color outside of Africa. And having missed the Mandates meetings in June and October, he had little concrete evidence of how the Mandates Commission worked that could be put in his report, still unfinished when he returned home. "I can understand," Raymond Buell, the director of research at the FPA, wrote Locke, "the many delays to which you have been subjected, but I think that you too can appreciate the position we are in, and understand our desire to receive some return for the assistance which the Association placed at your disposal. Could you then send me something so that I may relieve the impression which the situation has created in the office and among the members of the Board of Directors?"[15] Locke's growing embarrassment had been caused in part because of the shift in his professional life since 1926. When he had engaged the Foreign Policy Association in the scheme, he had been unemployed with a relatively free calendar, no patron, and no obstacles to spending the kind of time in Europe needed to monitor the League activities. But once taking a position at Fisk and managing Mason's own Black empire, he lacked the freedom, the research, and the motivation to produce a detailed report.

While Locke struggled to finish the report, he began his fall teaching. Howard University was undergoing dramatic change. Not only did it have its first Black president, Mordecai Johnson, elected in June 1926 but the university also achieved its first milestone in financial stability when Congress passed a bill in December 1928 that authorized annual appropriations to Howard. Rather than haggling every year with southern members of Congress as to whether there would be support for the university, the president and his allies in Congress merely had to bicker over the size of the appropriation. Moreover, Johnson brought a zeal for transforming Howard into an elite university on a par with the best American universities. Toward that end, he began a rebuilding campaign that upgraded the faculties of the professional schools, and the faculty of the College of Liberal Arts.

Perhaps most important, Locke found in Johnson a president who was greatly enamored of him and very pleased he had not left for Fisk. In the spring Locke had resubmitted his old proposal for an African Studies Program to an enthusiastic, if cautious, Johnson. Over the next five years, Locke would become Johnson's trusted confidant, helping to identify and bring to Howard PhD-trained, leftist-oriented specialists in the social and human sciences, including political scientist Ralph

Bunche, sociologist E. Franklin Frazier, philosopher Albert Dunham, linguist Louis Achille, poet Sterling Brown, and historian Harold Lewis. To make space for these younger, progressive-minded scholars, Locke maneuvered behind the scenes to force out the "old guard" professors, some of whom had secretly supported his ouster in 1925. For the first time in his academic career, Locke felt Howard was home.[16]

After settling in at Howard, Locke turned his attention, once again, to projects he had undertaken with Mason's patronage. He unpacked and began to catalog the shipment of African art from the Ivory Coast he had purchased from Laporte in Paris. He wrote letters as secretary of the Harlem Museum of African Art to report on the sad financial state of the treasury for the projected museum, and begged Black intellectuals and artists to make contributions to a project that would enhance the standing and dignity of the Negro in America. Perilously few contributions had come in over the last six months, in part because Locke had been elsewhere and no one had been assigned to raise money in his absence. The weakness of the Harlem Museum of African Art project was plain from a business perspective: it was a one-man operation, with Locke, the jack of all trades, serving as the curator, the secretary, the exhibit designer and installer, the booking agent, and the fundraiser. He had found no one to take over the most important of these: fundraising. Mason lacked both the administrative knowledge and the financial will to hire the requisite staff to make the museum a functioning unit. Part of her reluctance was curious: she believed that "Negroes themselves" ought to endow this museum. If so, why was she involved at all?

Locke still functioned as a middleman between Mason and her cadre of Black artists and continued to collect artists at the same rate as he collected African art. In the fall of 1928, his latest catch was Richmond Barthé, the painter turned sculptor, who was leaving Chicago to come to New York for more training and wider recognition. Bringing Barthé to Mason was particularly important, because Barthé was a sculptor, enormously gifted, and willing to be flexible about bending his art practice to meet Mason's concerns. After bringing Barthé to her Park Avenue apartment, Locke had to answer many questions before she opened her pocketbook to Barthé. She wanted details on his ancestry, his nurture by Jesuit Catholic priests, and Locke's true estimate of his real talent. Eventually, Locke wore her down with persistence—a gift of *Jubilee Singer*, a cut-down sculpture, sweetened her temperament—in part because Locke was determined to get funding for Barthé.

Part of Locke's zeal was his attraction for Barthé. Although they were not lovers in any permanent way, Locke and Barthé were occasional sexual partners. Perhaps even more significant to Locke in 1928 was that Barthé, unlike other artists Locke helped, was always enormously appreciative of his help, even as Barthé sought endorsements, patronage, and even catalog introductions from other critics, such as Carl Van Vechten. Plus, as a sculptor, he was more amenable than many of the Black painters to the idea of using African art as an inspiration for contemporary art. Barthé even proposed in 1930 to go to Africa, instead of Europe, to study sculpture, a proposal that endeared him to Mason as well as to Locke.

Locke also sought to establish transatlantic business relationships between Black Americans and West Africans, through his friend King Amoah (Kwamina Tandoh/Amoah III) from Ghana. Locke had met Amoah sometime in 1925–1926, when the king had visited the United States.[17] At that time, Locke had written an article on Amoah for the *Survey Graphic*, accompanied by a stunning portrait of Amoah done by Winold Reiss, that detailed the enlightened leadership emerging in Africa and willing to forge relationships with African Americans. On and off over the next two years, Locke worked to try and set up some kind of economic relationship between American Negroes and Amoah, perhaps to begin importation of African raw materials—coffee, for example—directly into the United States. In a sense, this lay behind his efforts in the League of Nations—to use trips to Europe to meet and forge economic relationships with African elites and others from colonized peoples. Locke also was using Mason to create an umbrella for such efforts. But this relationship, like so many of the others he brokered with Mason's support, exposed the pitfalls of Locke's middleman role. In late January 1929, he reacted strongly against Mason's criticism, sharply delivered, about Negroes never getting anything done. "I note keenly what you say about dropped stitches," he wrote to Mason. "But I cannot be responsible for the failure of others to follow through. I have heard nothing from either Amoah or Dyett."[18]

The most fruitful outcome of Locke's curating African art, dabbling in global politics, reading African literature, and managing, at a distance, Zora Neale Hurston's pioneering research, was his article, "The Negro's Contribution to American Art and Literature," published in the *Annals of the American Academy of Political and Social Science* in November 1928. "There are two distinctive elements," he began this seminal essay, "in the cultural background of the American Negro: one, his primitive tropical heritage, however vague and clouded over that may be, and second the specific character of the Negro group experience in America." Influenced by Mason's Afrocentrism, and Hurston's view that Negro folk culture was a living, evolving, presence in American life, Locke advanced beyond the notion he had outlined in "The Legacy of the Ancestral Arts," in *The New Negro*, that African culture was a distant, forgotten tradition. Now he argued that the African cultural presence persisted as an important, if submerged, influence in African American culture even as the Negro had made a complete adaptation to European culture.

> Torn from his native culture and background, he [the Negro] was suddenly precipitated into a complex and very alien culture and civilization, and passed through the fierce crucible of rapid, but complete adaptation to its rudiments, the English language, Christianity, the labor production system, and Anglo-Saxon mores. His complete mental

and spiritual flexibility, his rapid assimilation of the essentials of this new culture, in most cases within the first generation is the outstanding feat of his group career and is almost without parallel in history. Costly as it was, it was complete and without reservations. And yet from the earliest efforts at crude self-expression, it was the African or racial temperament, creeping back in the overtones of his half-articulate speech and action, which gave to his life and ways the characteristic qualities instantly recognized as peculiarly and representatively his.[19]

Locke came perilously close to suggesting primitivism was "creeping back" into civilization because of the presence of Negroes. But Locke had something else in mind. For him, the success story of the American Negro cultural history was the complete and rapid assimilation of the European language, foodways, work rhythms, familial and social institutions by the Negro accompanied by the retention of a distinct intelligence or consciousness by which the Negro selected that from the smorgasbord of Anglo-American culture what to emphasize, stress, and style, such that the completely assimilated culture was then re-expressed, uniquely. This intelligence was best revealed in an aesthetic sensibility that allowed the Negro to create unique, composite forms out of what she or he found in America, producing a composite but distinct set of innovations that were more inventive and complex than those created by European migrants. This article broke new ground because here, for the first time, Locke made clear that what distinguished the Negro culturally in America was not the experience of racism, but the unique improvisation of form—in music, storytelling, dance, speech, and song—based on African principles. "The materials were all American," he concluded, "but the design and the pattern were different."[20]

By calling his article "The Negro's Contribution to American Art and Literature," Locke asserted himself as an American scholar and transcended the segregated frame in which Mason and Hurston celebrated African and Negro American folklore. Mason saw African culture as diluted and debased through contact with "Western forms," while Hurston sought to capture a Black folk culture that thrived under segregation, away from White people. Locke realized that too strong an emphasis on Negro culture as "different" would back the movement into the corner that Lothrop Stoddard had tried to position the Negro Renaissance in his published March debate with Locke, "Should the Negro Be Encouraged to Cultural Equality?" There Stoddard had argued that segregation was necessary not because the Negro was inferior but "different" from Whites. Du Bois, who had publicly debated Stoddard, had used the example of miscegenation to counter the notion that Whites wanted to be separate from Negroes. Locke went for a more nuanced rebuttal: it was not biological intermixing that rendered Black and White difference a chimera, but rather that the African American culture, which had been absorbed and mimicked by Whites, who grew up reading Brer

Rabbit tales and singing spirituals, actually suffused American popular culture. Assimilation was not a one-way street. Whites in America had imbibed and mimicked Black culture even as they remained racist. Once they recognized their debt, Locke believed, a cultural revolution must eventually follow that would recognize African culture as a transformative force in making American culture. A wholly European or White American culture was thus a fiction. The American Mind Emerson had pointed to in 1837 could now be recognized in 1928 as a racially formed Mind in which the African elements were predominant in the way popular American culture formed.

That America was an African culture was too much even for most Negroes to accept in 1928. Locke's bold prediction fell on deaf ears. Black and White commentators ignored his dialectical mapping of American consciousness as the product of an "Aframerican" culture. Locke still lacked the ability to speak directly to the American Mind when he had the mouthpiece of the *Nation* article and say unequivocally that American "Beauty" transcended America's racial "propaganda." His writings still reflected, perhaps inevitably, the segregated nature of his American mind.

But Locke's *Annals* article was a personal triumph, for he had found a way to put together the two aspects of culture—his mother's culture and that of the folk he had encountered more directly during his time in Nashville. By showing the two antagonistic views of Negro culture dialectically linked, Locke revealed "Afamerican" culture as far more complex than any other commentator had rendered it. Locke had harmonized divergent processes—the Negro completely assimilated Anglo-American values, the Negro had remained a separate cultural formation—and carved out the possibility of a new way of conceptualizing African American art in its relations to American culture. The article also allowed Locke to situate the New Negro awakening within a longer history of syncretic inventiveness, something he had announced but failed to explicate fully in *The New Negro*. Having found that synthesis, Locke gained confidence. Now, he could begin to separate from the Negro Renaissance and craft new critical personae without simply mimicking or stealing the ideas of other commentators like Hurston.

When Elmer Carter, the editor of *Opportunity*, asked Locke in December 1928 to begin a series of annual reviews of Negro literature, Locke seized the prospect to create a forum to clarify the mission of African American art and declare himself arbiter of that mission. Just as important, the reviews allowed him to revise his opinions about the Negro Renaissance and create a new identity—the African American critic as prognosticator. More than detailed criticism of individual books, Locke's "reviews" were prescriptive, prophetic commentary on what ailed the Negro and mappings of what direction healthy Negro literature should go.

Even before the stock market crash of October 1929, for example, Locke predicted in "1928: A Retrospective Review," the crash of the Negro fad in Harlem literature. Rather than despairing, he cheered the collapse as necessary to return Negro art to a sounder foundation as something pursued by artists devoted to its internal values and not those chasing the latest get-rich scheme on Broadway stages or in the Tin Pan Alley of pop fiction. Along the way, Locke praised Claude McKay's *Home to Harlem* as solid, vibrant realism and saw Rudolph Fisher's *Walls of Jericho* as proof that the Negro writer could write great satire. Interestingly, he reserved his greatest praise for a woman writer—Nella Larson. Her first novel, *Quicksand*, was "a living, moving picture of a type not often in the foreground of Negro fiction." Locke was evidently touched by its portrait of an alienated, educated, sensitive Black woman lost in the paternalism and patriarchy of early twentieth-century segregated America.

Once again, though, Locke's optimism trumped his desire to criticize and blame. After consigning Du Bois's novel, *Dark Princess*, to the dust heap of Negro propaganda, he applauded the promising explosion of little magazines in Boston, Washington, Chicago, and elsewhere, which showed the New Negro impulse to self-expression existed beyond showy Harlem. Deliberative, thoughtful, contemporary Negro culture had much work to do, he concluded, before it could begin to match the seriousness and profundity to be found in recent studies of the African, both ancestral and contemporary, such as Blaise Cendrar's anthology of African folklore, *The African Saga*: "Milton Staffer's symposium entitled *Thinking with Africa*, the publication of the new quarterly journal of the International Institute of African Languages and Culture...and very notably, I think J. W. Vandercook's *Black Majesty*." Perhaps the new seriousness in African research and fiction forecast a brighter future for Negro culture studies in America, for "even when the reaction comes that was predicted at the outset of this article, there will be a vast net gain that can be counted upon as a new artistic and cultural foundation for a superstructure which it really is the privilege and task of another generation than ours to rear."[21] Emerson would have recognized that a new man had emerged to take up the task he had passed on to another generation—and perhaps another race—to complete: to fashion a vibrant intellectual vision out of the cultures of America.

A profound personal transformation had begun under the veil of White patronage and reached fruition in Nashville. Through an arrangement to help artists find their way, Locke had found his way. With a new mother, Locke had begun to face aspects of his personality and Black culture that he had kept hidden in the past. Despite the pain and humiliation Mason had caused him, Locke was becoming stronger, more direct, and more confident as a thinker. Having left her bosom to enter the South's, he had found strength in his ability to survive segregation and connect more directly with the African American folk. Less of an aesthete, more than a cultural custodian, Locke was becoming a literary general, directing his ideas, like troops, over a wide landscape he could call his own: American culture.

Alain Locke, ca. 1929. Photograph by Harold Hone. Courtesy of the Moorland-Spingarn Research Center, Howard University.

32

On Maternalism

The year 1929 began on a sour note for Alain Locke. A couple of weeks before New Years, he had learned that the Foreign Policy Association, to which he had submitted a report, "The Mandate System: A New Code of Empire," in December, was so displeased with his report that it would not publish it in its current form, as had been planned previously. The rejection of this work hit Locke like a blow in the stomach, so unaccustomed was he to having his writing rejected outright, especially by influential White people. Worse, over the previous year, he had peppered the press with notices of his trips to Geneva conducting research for the report, fueling expectations that the finished project would appear in print. Now it would not, and its non-publication would heighten a perception he wanted to avoid—that as the heralded philosopher and promoter of the Negro Renaissance since 1925, when his epic anthology, *The New Negro: An Interpretation*, had appeared, he was now, four years later, slipping, having not published a book since *Four Negro Poets* in 1927. Worried, perhaps overly, about the potential fallout from this failure, he chose his usual weekend visit with Mrs. Charlotte Mason, his millionaire Park Avenue patron, to pour out his frustration and seek consolation from a major personal setback.

As this diminutive, hypochondriac professor of philosophy fidgeted nervously in the drawing room of his psychic, overbearing matron, Locke, a man of almost clairvoyant personal diplomacy skills, confessed he had sensed something bad was going to result from a foreign policy project he had started years earlier. Locke had submitted his report late, after months of nagging by Raymond Leslie Buell. Although Locke knew its members were upset about his tardiness, he had hoped the brilliance of his approach would impress them. Rather than detailing the abuses of the British and French in administering Germany's former colonies under the Mandates System, Locke had opted for a higher ground and a futuristic perspective. The Mandates System had been set up under the League of Nations, because of Woodrow Wilson's insistence in Article 22 of its charter that Germany's and Turkey's former African colonies should be administered with international oversight now that they belonged to the Allies after the World War. The article stated that "to those colonies and territories which as a consequence of the late war have ceased to be under the sovereignty of the States which formerly governed them and which are inhabited by people not yet able to stand by themselves under the strenuous conditions of the modern world, there should be applied the principle that the well-being and development of such peoples form a sacred trust of civilization and that securities for the performance of this trust should be embodied in this covenant."[1] This "trust" would be exercised by putting these colonies under the administration and control of "advanced nations"—the French and the British—who "by reason of their resources, their experience or their geographic position, can best undertake" to provide the required "tutelage" of "such peoples" as a "responsibility" or "Mandatories on behalf of the League."[2] Of course, the "people not yet able to stand by themselves" were the Africans, since, by contrast those other peoples who belonged to the "Turkish Empire" were deemed to "have reached a stage of development where their existence as independent nations can be provisionally recognized." From a social Darwinist perspective, "those of Central Africa are at such a stage that the Mandatory must be responsible for the administration of the territory" to ensure "freedom of conscience and religion" and "prohibition of abuses, such as the slave trade," among others.

As a philosopher, Locke had seized on Article 22 for its moral language—that the Mandatories had a "responsibility" for the "development of such peoples" toward a moment in the future when the existence even of the peoples of Central Africa "as independent nations" could "be provisionally recognized." Rather than attack its failure to live up to that "sacred trust," which the evidence of British and French Mandatories seem to suggest, Locke wanted to write a paper about the future—a vision of what the Mandates tended toward even in their imperfect iteration in 1919 as documents and in 1928 as practices. As he had put it in his proposal to the Foreign Policy Association for the study, "The administration of mandates in the spirit of international guardianship of the rights of the undeveloped peoples and their preparatory tutelage for participation in government and constructive *self-adjustment* is one of the most important and progressive aspects of the work of the League of Nations" (italics added).[3]

Locke had aimed for something higher than the Foreign Policy Association imagined he would produce—something more visionary than the typical foreign policy fact sheets that they were familiar with. Locke wanted to write something that spoke to a higher consciousness of what was possible in the world of foreign affairs that could be revealed only if the document and its promise were liberated from the maze of facts and claims that dogged discussions of the League of Nations. As a philosopher, Locke was committed to doing something more, something different, something high-minded rather than self-interested, as most foreign policy papers were—a New Negro approach that was more than simply acting out what would be an expected Black response to the system, that is, simply to blister the League of Nations project as handing over the destiny of

Germany's African nations to a patronizing band of thieves like the British and French imperialists after their victory in the World War. Something like that kind of "Black" indictment of the Mandates as a fig leaf of Western imperialism would be produced later by the Du Bois protégé Rayford W. Logan in *The Operation of the Mandate System in Africa, 1919–1927* (1942). And it meant producing something other than the liberal, empathetic, but largely acquiescent study of the Mandates System that Raymond Buell, the White director of the Research Department of the Foreign Policy Association, and an adjunct professor of international relations, had produced in his magnum opus, the two-volume study, *The Native Problem in Africa* in 1928.[4]

But Locke had had problems finding his legs in writing his report, in part because he was not immersed in current foreign-policy research, not trained in international relations, and not sure that his prescriptive, non-empirical thought-piece about colonialism in general and the plight of Germany's former colonies in particular would find sympathetic ears at the Foreign Policy Association. Like so many of the ventures that this nervous, brilliant, but opportunity-seeking philosopher produced after *The New Negro: An Interpretation*, the FPA report was not grounded in a firmly grasped intellectual trajectory that made sense to all those around him. He sought to uncover something embedded in the current situation, but unseen by the policymakers of the day. And like the New Negro positionality itself, the report, even when finished, was an unfinished statement that reflected the unfinished nature of the New Negro. The report was more than simply the latest iteration of race consciousness, but a new, more cosmopolitan, more transnational notion of Negro possibility—what African nations could become, not what they currently were. And that incompleteness had crept like a leprechaun into his writing of the report, such that a lack of firmness in where he was going stole some of the energy from the argument he was making.

Nevertheless, Locke's proposal was brilliant, for by advocating a "third way" neither completely condemnatory of the Mandates nor acquiescent to the exploitation that they had allowed, Locke proposed strengthening the Mandates to allow them to become a real process of education in self-government, economic self-development, and responsible leadership among the colonized. By holding back on enslaving, debasing, and raping the raw materials of colonies, the European powers might model a behavior that the colonized would adopt, that of enlightened use of natural and human resources for the benefit of the colonized people and thus create the conditions for a sustainable path to eventual freedom and a more harmonious postcolonial world. While Locke did detail some of the abuses of the Americans or the Europeans in creating exploitative "closed-door" colonial relationships through shady loans and pressured deals with the colonized, he was a pragmatist. He advocated strengthening the path to freedom by utilizing African American and international criticism and pressure to embarrass abuser nations and stimulate rational development in the colonies even while they still remained under domination. In his doctoral dissertation on value theory, Locke had argued that the key to valuing by humans was their ability to transcend acting simply in their own naked self-interest to do that which seemed designed to reach beyond the immediate gratifications of desire, to aim at what Aristotle called that for which other things are done.[5]

This aiming higher and laying the groundwork for a better future for the colonized was really the revolutionary aspect of his report. Taking Woodrow Wilson's insistence in Article 22 of the League of Nation's charter that set up the Mandates System as his text, Locke argued that a policy of international restraint on the naked exploitation of Germany's former African colonies was the beginning of a "new code" of empire. Article 22, Locke argued, established a new ethical principle for the West in its conduct toward Africa, to wit that the nations that seized the colonies of German, Turkish, and other Axis empires had to administer them as a "sacred trust of civilization." England, France, and even South Africa, which acquired South-West Africa, were not to enslave the populations, not exploit the land and natural resources to the point of ecological disasters, not to raise colonial armies for offensive military purposes, and most important, not to look upon these colonies as their permanent possessions. Rather, the Allies, Locke referenced Woodrow Wilson as declaring, should administer these colonies as a trusteeship that should help the inhabitants transition, eventually, to self-government. This was the core outcome of a world war to make the world "safe for democracy."

But the Foreign Policy Association did not like his report. Mrs. Moorhead dismissed it as inadequate. Locke did not know why. But it is not hard to guess. The committee had not wanted a high-minded "thought piece" from Locke, but a hard-nosed research and policy assessment in line with the Association's incredibly detailed, case-by-case examinations of decisions by agencies like the Mandates Commission. The Foreign Policy Association produced passionate exposes of domestic and international crises and detailed, incredibly boring "reports": both kinds of papers made it possible for the Foreign Policy Association to assert its liberalism, but do nothing radical or practical to change the conditions they exposed. By contrast, Locke's report spelled out a practical course of action for intervention. Even so, the report was weak: beyond its lack of detail of abuses, it even lacked specific recommendations as to how to increase interest and participation of Black Americans in the operation of the Mandates Commission. The latter, ostensibly, was the reason the FPA had enlisted Locke in the first place. The FPA was not interested in a Black intellectual's visionary reinterpretation of the Mandates possibilities for change. What they wanted was a detailed treatment of the current situation, with some tepid recommendations for European forbearance, which could be published, put in a drawer, and forgotten.

Locke was responsible in large part for their reaction. Had he turned the report in on time, the evaluation committee might have been less upset with its shortcomings and more willing to see it as a rushed, incomplete document that could still be shaped by their input. Under such circumstances they would have felt comfortable giving extensive suggestions for revisions. But his tardiness amplified that Locke was not suited for the type of work they wanted done. Indeed, he had really elbowed his way into this assignment, masqueraded as the right man for the job, and then refused to work more closely with Raymond Buell, the Harvard scholar enlisted by the FPA on such reports. Here, as elsewhere, Locke's desire for autonomy in his work hurt him, because it alienated allies who might have helped avoid catastrophe.

Mrs. Mason likely smirked while listening to Locke pour out his frustration. The African Mandates work had been a source of tension in their relationship, going back to his unwillingness to preview his first speech to the League of Nations in 1927 with her. She had sensed he did not want to share with her his thinking on the matter, perhaps because he knew that she was a strong supporter of General Smuts of South Africa, an apologist for apartheid and continued racial domination in South Africa, whom Locke did not want to laud in the report. She had also criticized him for not telling Paul Kellogg, one of the members of the research committee who had recommended Locke for this work, that her money had partially subsidized his trips to Geneva to do the research for the project. She suspected that Locke had wanted to do this work on his own, and by carving out this independent space, perhaps create a diplomatic career for himself as an international broker of African liberation—a dream he had harbored since Oxford. He could forget that now. But his failure in this instance resulted from a more fundamental life problem that Locke needed to face—he had too many irons in the fire that distracted him from the really important work he was destined to do: to write the history and culture of his people in such a way that it would enlighten and catalyze them to greatness.

Mason let him finish his story. He concluded by saying that the only person on the Research Committee of the FPA who spoke up for him was Paul Kellogg, who said perhaps there had been a misunderstanding between Locke and the committee as to what was wanted. Locke had written Kellogg thanking him and admitting that he was not good at the kind of report the FPA obviously had expected. He would try and make the report the basis for a curriculum in the African Studies Program he hoped to start at Howard. "So, thank God, I won't have to go back to Harvard myself for re-boring," he had ended his letter to Kellogg. "You see I think I know my role and appreciate its limitations—I'm a fairly good starting battery—not a magneto."[6] That Locke, now forty-three, even contemplated a return to graduate work, shows how much he had hoped this report would lead him out of his current life at Howard in Washington, D.C.

Interestingly, Mason seemed to grasp the situation better than Locke. The major fault, according to Mason, was his audience. "Extreme hostility" is all that they will like. Oddly, she had captured one of the dynamics of White patronage of Black people in connection with Black issues: in her opinion, the Foreign Policy

Association expected him to play the *nigger*—to attack the entire apparatus of colonial government and League of Nations sanction through the Mandates System. In that scenario, they would then be able to use the report to attack their enemies, while at the same time dismissing the report as hysterical and racially biased. In short, the report was not "Black enough." Whether this was true or not, Mason did perceive accurately his dilemma as an African American scholar working on this type of subject. "Alain, your not being ready to tell what you think is the exact truth about the Mandate is the matter with your paper. It is not, of course the <u>time</u> to do it." This was the deeper truth of his failure here and elsewhere in his professional life. Close reading of the report reveals Locke's cautiousness, tentativeness, and self-consciousness in putting across what was, at base, a brilliant strategy for using the existing international apparatus to create a roadmap to freedom for colonized Africans. Locke was too nuanced in his writing for an audience used to the harangue of a Marcus Garvey or a W. E. B. Du Bois. Mason concluded: "They think your opinion is the best balanced of any among Negroes and that you won't go to an extreme about anything. That was why they asked you to do it."[7]

Locke could feel the knife twisting in his stomach as he sat nodding his head nervously and frenetically in assent, as he heard his life reduced to a formula. That formula could best be described as maternalism, a set of reciprocal obligations and expectations that the Foreign Policy Association, and particularly, Mrs. Moorhead, believed Locke had violated by his comeuppance. Mason could analyze it accurately, because she was a master of it. The historian Eugene Genovese developed a theory of paternalism to describe the ideology plantation masters utilized to justify their exploitation of slaves—a series of mutual obligations that structured the relationship between people with different kinds of power. Masters saw themselves as obligated to take care of their slaves, in exchange for the slaves being obligated to give the master their labor. The enslaved simultaneously accommodated and resisted the male masters meeting but also evading their expectations.[8] Some one hundred years later, Locke had chosen to enter into a series of maternalist relationships with Mrs. Isaacs, Mrs. Mason, and now Mrs. Moorhead in the belief that he could enjoy a greater degree of autonomy under their protection than with such twentieth-century paternalist heirs as Barnes. Secretly, Locke had hoped to elude the encroaching power of Mason through serving the interests of Moorhead; but this episode showed that each of these maternalists wanted him not because of his intrinsic value—because of who he was, as had been the case with his first maternal guardian, his mother—but because of how he served their interests. When his attempts at resisting their program became obvious, they could simply discard him like yesterday's papers. And maternalism was always changing the expectations—having groomed himself for years to be the "safe Negro" for Whites, he was losing out now because he was not militant enough!

It no longer mattered that he had made sacrifices to finish the report, despite its shortcomings according to the FPA. Without the kind of subsidy that would have been appropriate to his commission, he had had to secure money from Mrs. Mason just to get to Geneva, let alone tour Africa to get the kind of on-the-ground information that the FPA seemed to want in the report. It was not what *this* particular mistress wanted. He had experienced an illusion of freedom under Moorhead's maternalism, had been able to show up in Geneva and disrupt the logic of segregation in the administration of African affairs by American diplomats, enjoy hanging out in Europe, only now to have his maternal patron in the Foreign Policy Association dismiss him for not being Black enough, not being detailed enough, not being more than simply another highly educated Uncle Tom she no longer needed. Here too was an inkling of what lay in store for him if he really ever disappointed Mason.

Maternalism was also a metaphor for Locke's subject matter, for the nomenclature of the "Mother Country" suffused colonial discourse. It was not accidental. The Mandates System was itself an exercise in maternalism, captured in the metaphor that the victors in the Great War had a "mandate" to "care" for the colonies of the vanquished Europeans. Of course, even Locke's cursory investigation revealed that abominations like slavery, forced labor, and raising of armies were present in the former German colonies now administrated by the English and the French. Since the United States had no African colonies, Wilson's idea was that America as the good mother or aunt would come in and counsel "good parenting" to those "Mother countries" in charge of even more Black colonies because of the war. Du Bois's analysis of "The African Roots of the War" had been borne out: the war had been a grab for more African colonies by warring European nations, and less a destruction of European right to empire, as Locke had predicted in "The Grand Disillusionment." Maternalism had one other important role in this situation: Locke's own proposal was a sympathetic maternalism on the ground, the idea that the European nations would prepare, through education and political-economic nurture, the African peoples for adulthood, maturity, that is, self-government. In effect, Locke's plan was an extension of the logic of the Mandates' "mothering" concept, except that, in reality, the Mandates System was a fig leaf to justify the continued extraction of economic and human resources from Africa for the benefit of England and France. Locke's proposal, though brilliant, and logically consistent, had no chance of realization, as it would have undermined the real purpose of the Mandates System, which was to keep the colonials dependent "children." The Foreign Policy Association and his difficult "mother" Mrs. Moorhead knew this. From her standpoint, he had wasted the Association's time and money theorizing some other outcome. And he and Mason knew it.

It did not matter that in January 1929, the gentlemanly Raymond Buell wrote to him cordially stating that the committee felt he had "discharged" his "obligation" to the Foundation for the funds he had received for the research, and that it further believed that there was valuable information in the report that should be published, if he was willing to revise the report. And if he were to commit to such a task and succeeded, the committee would offer an additional $100 compensation for that labor. But Locke declined.

As he walked out of Mason's apartment building onto Park Avenue, he was momentarily dazed. He could no longer dream of a life in Geneva, where he could hear one's Wagner without humiliation. His transnational freedom pass had been confiscated. He was stuck in an America that consistently devalued him. During a visit in Chicago to continue the momentum in Negro visual and theater arts started years ago in the 1927 "Negro in Art Week," the manager of the Hotel Potomac burst into Baber's dinner party to exclaim that the hotel did not allow seating of a Negro—Locke—in its dining room. Afterward, Zona Baber, his dinner host, wrote: "This condition grieves me more than any other fault or sin of our body social." Locke's reaction was muted: "Please do not mention even the disagreeable aspect of matters like that of Friday evening—I personally feel the thrill of battle in them, and only wish we had more crusading companions."[9] That was another lie—he gritted his teeth even thinking of situations in which he was denied access to elite spaces because someone complained that he was Black. Such incidents were an ever more frequent part of his segregated life in America. "I am today facing a similar issue with Mrs. Wilson-Green over a Wagner series of opera for which I have of course tickets, and my bank, I hope, the cancelled check to Mrs. Green." Locke was becoming increasingly pessimistic about serving as a "race-slave," as he described himself to Hughes.

So far, 1929 was less energetic, less energizing, and more mired in old ruts of race than his escape to Fisk had been just twelve months earlier. And yet dreaming international was more than simply soul survival for Locke; he continued to envision it as the American Negro's survival as well. Internationalism and Americanism were linked pairs for him, but also for the Negro, who had the most agency, Locke believed, when most African and international. For not only was White supremacy deeply international, but the praxis of racial advocacy by the Negro was inherently intertwined with the internationalist struggle against colonialism.

An instance of that arose that February when Locke was asked by Anson Phelps Stokes, the administrator of the Phelps Stokes Fund, to deliver remarks at the Harmon Foundation's ceremony at which it awarded a gold medal to sculptor May Howard Jackson—"an old family friend," Locke confided to Stokes—at Washington's Nineteenth Street Baptist Church. That stint led to an invitation to visit Stokes's home the afternoon of February 20 for a meeting with C. F. Andrews, a Scotsman and advisor to Gandhi, that included Howard University president Mordecai Johnson and several other official Negroes. "This afternoon," Locke recounted to Mason, who wanted to influence the Gandhi movement, "was this stiff, rather condescending conference. . . . Andrews asked direct questions as to the attitude of the American Negroes on equality, religion, active revolt, etc. The conservatives assured him that all is well, that the Negro could not hate and further realized that the odds were against him, and that the Negro would have to win his way by conciliation." Such talk irked Locke in the aftermath of the FPA debacle. "Mordecai Johnson was very wary—he said that the Negro's job in America and throughout the world was to convert the white man back to the essentials of his own religion." Locke contributed the core philosophy of the New Negro to the discussion: "I said the younger generation was interested in finding a point of view within themselves that could afford to ignore the white man's attitude toward them; but that they had not yet discovered it."[10] Of course, Locke believed they had—in the arts; but once again, he did not voice that, for fear in this setting that it could be used against him or against the cause of relating the Gandhi movement in India to the Negro movement in America. But the problem for Locke and those at the Stokes meeting was the inability to speak the truth about what should be the Black agenda. Paternalism in this case would not let them in 1929.

Locke's strength was his ability to keep going, even when he was running on empty. The pose of the literary cad bounding around Harlem sampling the latest literary wares hid an increasingly bitter and frustrated man, who was slipping into Mason's negative outlook, including her anti-Semitism. Writing to Hughes after a spate of writer's block, Locke sulked: "I am going up to New York this weekend to see God-mother, and to see what I can help [King] Amoah do. I'm having a time on this matter of the Jew. In Chicago it was of course the Rosenwalds. Mrs. Rosenfels, close friend of and relative of theirs, gave an elaborate buffet supper for thirty, and really did give us a fine send off last Sunday." Mason's anti-Semitism, part of her upper-class prejudice toward Jewish rivals in New York, was an ill-fitting cloak for Locke's sense of failure. The only White people other than Mason who engaged in social reform efforts for the Negro in the 1920s and would work with him were generally Jewish women. He had no real Black allies. His letter to Hughes sought also to deflect Mason's criticism. "Had a characteristic letter from Zora, Happy New Year, and all success on the last lap of the track. Barthe is coming East next week and will be staying sometime in Washington. Would you like to run down, and could you do it in fairness to your work? Of course, we would both be delighted if you could." Once again, Hughes could not spare time to spend with Locke and Barthé. Indeed he did not even bother to write.[11] The warmth and gratitude he received from young visual artists like Barthé compensated for the lack of courtesy from Hughes and Hurston.

Locke's unrequited love for Hughes was cooling in 1929. That coolness slipped into his letters to Hughes that now were mere reportage. "I spent a wonderful week end with Godmother. . . . Barthe is here since yesterday and we are enjoying life together very much except for our Negro society friends whom we have to meet and shake hands with at dinner. Why will they do it? Barthe is quite anxious to meet you as I am to have you meet him—however both of us understand the importance of your work at this juncture and the inconvenience of the trip."[12] As usual, Locke continued to throw himself into "race-slave" work as a distraction from loneliness.

The stint at the Nineteenth Street Baptist Church in Washington, D.C., to present the Harmon Award to Mary Howard Jackson was the kind of race work Locke excelled at. That event allowed Locke to introduce himself to the Harmon Foundation people, especially Mary Beattie Brady, its strong-willed director. The Harmon Foundation had started a national forum of annual exhibitions and cash prizes to Negro artists to stimulate production of quality work in the visual arts. Although not yet a serious platform for first-rate artists—many of the award recipients did not exhibit with the Harmon Foundation—the effort was gaining momentum. Locke's talk at the awards ceremony opened up a correspondence between him and Brady, who, with a well-organized and staffed Foundation, was interested in upgrading the Negro artists' effort. Here was another potential maternalist relationship for him. It was not clear that it would empower him more than Mason's or compensate him for his growing alienation from the young New Negro writers.

As Hurston put it in a letter to Hughes, "Locke is utterly disgusted at Wallie."[13] Wallace Thurman's play, *Harlem*, a burlesque comedy had opened on Broadway in March 1929 and was making a killing at the box office. When Locke saw the play, he was appalled that Thurman, who always posed as the serious artist of the movement, had written a cynical potboiler that made fun of working-class life in Harlem for no other purpose than to make money. For Locke, the play was the low watermark of the Negro Renaissance, although he refrained from writing about it publicly. Here again he echoed Mason's refrain: "You're not being willing to tell the truth" is the problem.

Locke began to pour out his feelings and woes to his friends, even some younger ones he had not known very long. One of them was Albert Dunham Jr., a brilliant young philosopher and brother of already-famed dancer and choreographer Katharine Dunham, whom Locke may have met through the "Negro in Art Week" festivities in 1927. After a year of casual correspondence about Dunham's prospects for graduate education and dangling the possibility that Dunham would join Locke in a new, revitalized Philosophy Department at Howard, Locke began to confide in Dunham his deepening paralysis.

> I just haven't been able somehow to write. When I mentioned my depression, I think you thought I was joking or at least tried to joke me out of it. As a matter of fact, in spite of all pleasant developments, including an unexpected raise of salary, I have been in a mild lotus-eaters

melancholy. Part of it is physical,—I have a spell of tired heart. But then, if I may borrow your mood of Easter night—"one cannot carry on indefinitely alone." And it is lonely if one insists on keeping company with even one or two ideals in this day of God-forsaking. Everyone it seems can be bought off so cheap. These young Negroes especially.[14]

He concluded the letter by saying he would rather see Dunham go to Europe for a year and then come to Howard than go to Harvard. To comfort himself, Locke had Richard Bruce stay overnight.

One uplifting development was that Hurston had enough research for a collection of stories. Over the coming months, Locke, Godmother, and Hughes would get to see what Hurston had collected. Publication was not her only plan. She wrote Hughes that she also wanted to buy some property she had located in Florida "to start A Negro art colony. . . . You, and Wallie, and Aaron Douglas and Bruce and me and all our crowd." Locke was not on the list. But before she could act on the property, she came down with a liver ailment in July and had to be hospitalized.[15] By October 1929, she had recovered and was ready to begin crafting entries for publication. "Godmother wants the dirty words cut out." Additionally, "Alain said that I was not definite enough about some of the religious cults of New Orleans so I am thinking of returning there shortly and correcting the errors and closing up the conjure volume too. He said I needed to clinch some of my statements by photostatic copies of documents plus some more definite information, which I had seemed to take for granted the reader would understand. I shall go in November for by that time I shall be about cleared up here."[16] Once Hurston had produced something tangible, Hughes wired her congratulations. "Well, honey, your wire did me <u>so much</u> good," she replied. "Gee, I felt forlorn. Too tired. Been walking two years without rest + behind that all my school life with no rest, no peace of mind. But the Bahamas trip did me a world of good. I got rested while working hard. Do you need some money?" Hurston was flush after a year and a half of receiving $200 from Mason. With money, success in her research, and attention from all of the members of the "family," Hurston was in a good mood as the year ended. Her letters oozed good feeling. "It is so good to have the counsel of both you and Alain," she wrote Hughes. "Well, I tell you Langston, I am nothing without you. That's no flattery either." Zora was coming home to New Jersey, where she and Hughes would share an apartment-work place and begin to move forward on collaborations.[17]

What was under slavery was also true of the patronage relationship between Mason and her young Negro writers in the twentieth century: the "workers" had some power to shape how the system operated through various forms of resistance and accommodation. As one of the "enslaved," Hurston had created her own hierarchy of whom she trusted and to whom she distributed trusted information. She confided to Hughes, "Dear Pal, I am glad that you saw the other material in New York for I was very eager to know what you thought about it. I am glad you like. About AL, he approves anything that has already been approved. I told him nothing but asked him about editing the material, and I only asked him that [because G. said she wanted me to be more cordial to him]. I have only written him about four times since I have been down. But thanks for the tip. I shall be even more reticent from now on. I'll keep my big mouf shut."[18]

Not only had Hurston decided that Locke was a kind of overseer and thus unreliable but also Hughes urged her not to confide her plans and discoveries to Locke, presumably because he told Godmother whatever they told him. In particular, Hughes sought to ensure that neither Locke nor Mason knew that Hughes was advising Hurston about how to manipulate the situation. "No, never would I speak of any of the things you tell me. I know they are for me only and I am most discreet. I know that you tell me things to guard my relations with G." Langston as the "enslaved" was strategizing to control the patronage relationship by keeping Mason pleased and believing that they completely followed her dictums and proposals, while he and Hurston pursued their own agenda. Hurston had concocted her own plan to use Hughes to advance some of her plans to Mason, since he was the one most in Mason's graces. Hurston figured he could propose potentially controversial ideas to Mason, such as her desire to write a magazine article on her research, because whenever she advanced such a topic it typically angered Mason.

Such strategies of resistance enabled Hurston to be more independent of "G" and more critical of Locke. "The trouble with Locke is that he is intellectually dishonest. He is too eager to be with the winner, if you get what I mean. He wants to autograph all successes, but is afraid to risk an opinion first hand."[19] Actually, this had not always been true—but it was increasingly true of Locke under the pressure of maternalism, increasingly fearful of uttering or supporting any idea that was not liable to win Mason's approval. Here was the ultimate sin of the American scholar—the sacrifice of intellectual independence for the illusion of maternal protection.

But the reality was more complex. Excited by the discoveries that Hurston was making in rural folklore that documented a separate, post slavery southern culture, Locke was also a confirmed modernist, convinced that Black people had to embrace change in order to become a modern people. Locke was looking for a synthesis that would validate the persistence of cultural forms and formation of an independent racial world view in Hurston's material, while also wanting her to approach that material as a scientist who documented how social forms ultimately changed and became modern over time. Locke was not simply a slave to Mason's racial essentialism. In fact, Mason relied on Locke's judgment as much as her own to point out places in Hurston's material that needed to be improved. Rather than merely "parroting" Mason's opinion, Mason was actually consulting Locke constantly about the written material she received from Hughes and

Hurston before she responded to the artists. Indeed, Mason's neurotic interruptions and interventions in their work signified that she was on uncertain ground, as they all were, in the pioneering business of documenting a culture unseen and unanalyzed because of the history of racial neglect by American scholars. Each was struggling to gain the most power from the "discovery" and representation of a culture that in the strictest sense belonged to none of them. Mason owned the material, but knew the least about it; Hurston and Hughes mined and refined it, but had no scholarly authority to advance it in the journals; and Locke was in the middle, half aware of its revolutionary importance, yet on uncertain ground unsure because he was not an anthropologist by training. Weaker than the others since he was neither a worker nor owner of the means of cultural production, Locke had the advantage of being a scholar whose forte was textual analysis and criticism.

In the midst of such conflicts, Locke soldiered on, serene if depressed about his permanent "bachelorhood," as he put it, and his alienation from meaningful work. To Albert Dunham, whom he was still hoping to woo, he confided: "Barthe has done a bust of me, which is really good. I would like you to see it,—to see if you agree that it has caught something that as yet cannot be told"[20] (see page 656). Dunham's response was informed and coy. "Can I have a photo of the Barthe bust? Dick is so versatile, I'm anxious to see if its Rodin or <u>Houdin</u>. For you, I think the latter suits much better."[21] In another gender direction, Locke allowed Sue Bailey, a young Black woman student activist, to arrange for him to speak at a summer Young Women's Christian Leadership Conference, an act of noblesse oblige for this gay Black man who usually disliked being surrounded by young women. Locke liked Bailey for her class and commitment to a student struggle at Black colleges that was all but forgotten in the late 1920s.

Locke was at ebb tide creatively. Few essays or articles flowed out of his pen as they had done the year before. Reviews of the literature that reached the public were perfunctory and bland. In "Heads or Tales on the Race Question!" published in the *Survey Graphic* in May, a review of *Black America* by Scott Nearing, and *What the Negro Thinks* by R. R. Moton, Locke saw the former as a superb history of Negro life, augmented by a consistent analysis of the need for a strong, solidified working class if the race was to excel, while the latter placed the blame for much of the ills of the race on Black people themselves. In "Both Sides of the Color Line," published the next month, Locke found *The Blacker the Berry* by Wallace Thurman more sensitive in its portrayal of Negro life than Jessie Fauset's *Plum Bun*. In another review, he praised White writer Julia Peterkin for her novel, *Scarlet Sister Mary*.[22]

Only in "Beauty and the Provinces," published in the June issue of the *Stylus*, a revived edition of the Howard University literary magazine, did Locke catch fire with the energy and vitality of his mid-1920s writing. Perhaps in the protected audience of the Howard literary community, Locke felt comfortable saying what he really felt. All of those critics who were charging that the Renaissance was not about Harlem, that it was happening everywhere there was a critical mass of Negroes, forgot their Italian Renaissance history and the art of Black creativity in recent American history. Capitals, he mused, had always been the centers of talent, the magnets that had drawn talent to them, nurtured them, and then spread their gifts back to the provinces. He chided that Negroes who were educated should not forget what it had been like to live in small-town Black America, which suffocated the artist with the kind of provincialism that strangled talent in White America as well. Even Philadelphia and Washington had starved artists. New York was America's cultural capital, and Harlem its Black capital, because it welcomed, nurtured, and valued artists for themselves, not as window dressing for Black philistine posturing. Beauty always left the provinces for more fertile ground, ironically but consistently, in the city.[23]

As Locke prepared for his usual summer European vacation, he even was drained of energy to escape. Wherever Locke went in the Western world, he now realized, he was still on a virtual plantation. He longed to escape, but where to? On May 22, Locke wrote Dunham:"I even played with the idea of staying home this summer, and asking if you could spend a large part of it with me writing. My mind has begun again on the old subject of values. But it was a question of the time, the place, and the [not readable]. I even discussed it with my dear mentor in New York, and for a day or so we were making inquiries about places on Long Island. But [it] is really an impossibility, either you must put up with a family or eat precarious food, and I cannot eat precarious food. Moreover, I had no word from you."[24] As the year of teaching came to a close, there was at least the good news that Stewart Nelson, the assistant professor of religion appointed by Durkee to displace Locke, was leaving the department, while Ralph Bunche had joined the faculty. "In a year or so the youngsters here will be a great bunch," and the stage would be set for Dunham's arrival. But that still felt far-off to Locke.

The persistent problem for Locke as a lover was, of course, that he was often attracted to men who were not homosexual or at least did not consider or iden-tify themselves as homosexual. Thus, often, they were surprised by the sudden revelation of the emotion he had for them. Because they did not pick up as quickly as those "in the know" that Locke was hitting on them, they sometimes did not respond quickly or appropriately enough for Locke to keep open the emotional door. Dunham wrote back June 1 that he was flattered by Locke's in-terest, but disappointed that Locke did not have the courage of his convictions. "You were a little too severe not to push the Long Island idea to the limit. Nothing could have been more to my liking for the summer; and I've got a fresh start in value theory that bids fair to bear sound fruit. This year, from a dozen quarters, has given me what seems to be happy background for something good in values. But it will keep, though I hope we can tap it soon. How do you feel about the value terrain, particularly as a pragmatic development?" Staying in

America did have some potential benefits for companionship. "Europe is simply out of reach," as Dunham was financially responsible for his sister Katherine, who had been just expensive enough to keep him in America. "And now Mother is failing."[25] He had hoped that Locke would come to Chicago, so that they could plan when he would come to Howard. For Locke, this prospect was doubly invigorating, since through Dunham, Locke was journeying back to his discipline, philosophy, inspired by the young "research assistant" he had told Mason he needed to inspire him in his work.

Albert Dunham was eager to come to Howard. "Not only do I want to see an application, but to talk rank, salary, collaboration, with all of that in mind as a definite alternative to foundation research. My fellowship, so far as I know, is good again. Harvard seems certain if I want it, and why not with Lewis, Elliot, . Whitehead, and Perry there? But I'm beginning to feel the spirit of what you, Just, and Johnson are doing at D.C. I see possibilities in a department that could five years hence take first place in value theory, aesthetics, and criticism. And still I realize that I'd be worth more to you after the discipline of a degree, and a year abroad a la Guggenheim." Aware perhaps of the subtext of Locke's interest in him, Dunham closed his letter with the tantalizing line, "Never more yours, Albert."[26]

Locke would not let slip a chance for a consummating trip to Europe without one more attempt to entice Dunham. Locke lingered stateside, perhaps deliberately, using his heart—the tired one—as an excuse. "Your letter was just right and came at the right time," he wrote Dunham on June 11. "And the reason that you hear from me from this side will somewhat explain why. In the exhaustion of over-work my heart began to cut up on you [sic] and I had to cancel a perfectly good sailing for the 11th. I am now indefinitely delayed, as you know what June sailings are. However, its up to me to be philosophical and that's what I am. Though I had to feed considerably on your letter." Locke was feeding on Dunham's provocative letter, because a relationship with Dunham at Howard promised to reignite his career, his sense of purpose, and his will to live. "One other thing the letter served,—as a reminder to put you vividly before Dr. Johnson, who now I believe after our last conference understands fully my attitude toward you in connection to the Howard proposition, and your attitude toward our new program. He said to me, after a long chat,—'I am happy to know this chap is interested in us,—by all means keep your hand on him, and let me know when he is ready to come.' I quite agree that both Harvard for the fall, and the camp for the Summer are the best of all possible things." Then, shifting to a more personal, confidential tone, Locke mused that "spells like I have recently had remind me of the precariousness of life. However folks of my sort live largely on enthusiasm and hope."[27]

Dunham was not going to take the bait and come to Europe, but he nevertheless gave Locke hope by planning to see him in September. Dunham had been a nimble game player as well. He had offered just enough to get Locke's support in front of President Johnson, but not so much as to be committed to anything more definite professionally or personally. And Dunham had found the one excuse that worked with Locke. As Locke wrote, "Don't think I do not appreciate your family attitude.... In fact I admire it. And I particularly understand and sympathize how you must feel about your mother. I do hope there will be improvement in this direction. Does she know of me, and will you give her my warm regards?"[28]

After a restful trip in Europe, much of it at Nanheim taking his rest cure in the special waters, Locke returned for the fall quarter at Howard and the divisive intrigue of Mason maternalism. Without a clear compass himself, he could allow himself to be directed by her and others, like Hughes and Hurston, whom he admitted had more of the creative force in them than he did. But increasingly, Hurston dismissed Locke's advice, even when it was wise and well intended. "Locke will be a great help too, but I am afraid he will not see it just as we do," she confided to Hughes in October. Nevertheless, she did return to New Orleans to firm up her research, acting on his advice that she needed more detail and documentation to prove her points. No one of them—Hurston, Hughes, Locke, Mason, or even Boas—was an expert on the folklore collection of the Black material that she was doing. What did work for Hurston was that she could consult with all of them for suggestions about how to present her material. Hurston was not alone in having produced something: at the end of 1929, Hughes had finished a draft of his novel and Mason asked Locke to begin editing what would become *Not Without Laughter*. "When the manuscript comes, I shall do my lovable best," he informed Hughes. There was no need of them getting together. "Work of this sort I can do alone. I am terribly handicapped however in my general work because of typing."[29]

Other than Hughes and Hurston, the New Negro creative movement was drained of vitality as 1930 dawned. The Stock Market Crash of 1929 had had almost an immediate effect of making irrelevant to critics, publishers, and readers the kind of heady farce literature that Carl Van Vechten and Wallace Thurman were producing in the late 1920s. With little of merit published in 1929 to justify a retrospective review, Locke realized he was going to have to broaden his field into sociological literature if he was going to maintain an authoritative voice in Negro cultural affairs. His review of a dry report, *The Negro in Richmond Virginia: Report of the Negro Welfare Survey Committee*, was telling. After nearly a decade of denigration of sociology in favor of imaginative literature as the lens through which to see the Negro situation, Locke lauded this report as indicative of the new progressive "social conscience" arising in the South. Rather than apology or statistical survey, it offered constructive recommendations for change. It symbolized too Locke's growing attraction to southern regionalism as the new paradigm for Negro studies. Why shouldn't he embrace the South and draw attention to what liberal southerners were doing if finally, after hundreds of years of ignoring, if not repudiating, the Negro contribution to the South, they were willing to recognize the Negro in a rational, quasi-scientific way? That meant embracing White writers and social scientists as legitimate and worthy contributors in the area of Negro studies.

Such a position ran counter to the essentialism of Mrs. Mason and Hurston, both of whom, in different ways, were dismissive of White artists and researchers in the Negro cultural arena. But the contradictions in their positions showed the weakness of their thinking in these areas and often required Locke to step in to resolve the conflicts. In the fall of 1928, he had come to Hurston's rescue when she improvidently reviewed a special issue on Negro folklore produced by White anthropologists associated with the University of North Carolina. In her review she dismissed the value of any research done by White social scientists. Allowing herself an ill-advised freedom in her letter to Mrs. Mason, Zora commented that the Indians had been correct, that no White person could be trusted to handle Negro materials with honesty and insight. She was surprised when Mason's feelings were hurt. Hurston hurriedly wrote Locke and Hughes explaining that she was the one surprised. "I had just been saying what Godmother says all the time. I just forgot to say 'Present company excepted.'"[30] But she still sent Franz Boas and others copies of her collected material for validation and advice (in secret because such sharing was explicitly ruled out in her contract with Mason), a sign she valued "white opinion." Of course, Hurston also denigrated other Blacks as authorities—not only Locke but also trained folklorists such as Arthur Fauset and writers like Helene Johnson. Mason and Hurston both said they preferred Black people and Black culture over that of the Whites, yet both held onto their White connections as firmly as Locke held to his Harvard accent and European tastes. Although both of them denigrated him, they relied on him to smooth over their conflicts. After some explanatory words from Locke, Mason seemed to forgive Hurston for calling her White and distrustful, and eventually the two resumed their easy familiarity in using racial categories to evaluate everyone—except themselves.[31]

Distrust was integral to the kind of patronage relationship Mason created because her maternalism was based on a contradiction: they were supposed to be her "godchildren," but unlike real "godchildren," Hurston and Hughes had to labor to keep her motherly love. Any suspicion that they were not faithful workers, like the slaves on the nineteenth-century plantations Genovese examined, would deem them ungrateful children! Such arrangements bred within them resistance to the master's control and in this case destruction of the patronage system Mason had so meticulously constructed.

The situation began to unravel after Mason decreed that Hurston and Hughes should live in Westfield, New Jersey, a safe distance away from the spiritually "distracting" influence of devil New York. In January 1930, Hurston took an apartment blocks away from where Langston Hughes was already living, waiting for the proofs of his novel, *Not Without Laughter*. Hughes had completed a draft in June and worked on several revisions, requested by Mason and Locke, before submitting the final version late in 1929. When Hurston arrived in Westfield, she was busy turning her collected material into a book that Mason was eager to get published. After Hurston and Mason met that spring to review material Hurston had collected, Locke reported to Hurston that "I thought it would cheer you at this critical stage of your work that she [Mason] really thinks you have done well and is eagerly looking forward to pushing the book. She thinks it would be a mistake even to have a scientific tone to the book, so soft pedal all notions of too specific documentation and let loose on the things that you are really best equipped to give—a vivid dramatizing of your material and the per-sonalities back of it." Hurston felt this was a snub, especially as she was (secretly) trying to get Franz Boas to inform her about the best scholarly interpretation of the material she had collected. Further, because Locke knew that Mason, a now elderly woman, was eager to see the research she had sponsored reach the public, Locke suggested Hurston make the changes straight away: "You can do this in a feverish two or three days and then it will be all over, but the shouting."[32] Locke would then be happy to edit the manuscript immediately, so that perhaps Hurston could present the final draft of the manuscript to Mason as a gift on her birthday on May 18. Feeling her control over the volume was threatened, Hurston began to stall. She wrote Locke that "it has been very hard to get the material in any shape at all,"[33] and she decided a more appropriate birthday gift was to write Mason a long, sweet, ingratiating letter. Here, Hurston was exhibiting the kind of resistance Locke had manifested when he had avoided turning in his report to Mrs. Moorhead a year and a half earlier.

Soon, Mason was furious with Hurston, although Hurston seemed not to understand why. Rampersad and Boyd, Hughes's and Hurston's biographers, re-spectively, believed that Locke told Mason that instead of working, Hurston and Hughes, along with Louise Thompson, whom Mason had hired as Hughes's ste-nographer, were having too much fun. Zora *was* spending much of her time with Hughes acting out stories she had collected in her two years of research, rather than working on the book. Once aware that Mason was displeased, Hurston tried to contact Godmother, but was rebuffed. As usual, she turned to Hughes, who tried to reach Godmother, but was also unsuccessful. He then wrote an apologetic letter to Mason, where he expressed his confusion about what had angered her. The incident is often portrayed as another sign of Mason's irration-ality, but in fact, there was a rational explanation.

Mason wanted them to finish expeditiously their work for which they were being well paid, and turn in finished manuscripts on a schedule that conformed to her specifications. Locke did not think such demands were unusual, since as a student of the Italian Renaissance he knew what patrons typically required and got for their money. Indeed, patrons regularly sued painters and other artists during that Renaissance when they failed to meet deadlines for submission of material, or veered from the patron's specifications of the kind of work to be produced. Patrons often dictated quality and schedule of work, without any racial motivation behind such demands. Perhaps because of her rhetoric of maternal love, these Black intellectuals could not see that they were in fact proletarians working for their patron. Eventually, Mason forgave her little "primitives," but they knew she was watching them closely now.

But instead of working feverishly on the projects Mason had assigned them, Hughes and Hurston set to work on a theater project dangerously close in focus to what Mason had specifically told them not to work on in January 1929. Here, again, Hurston and Hughes evidently believed that maternalism gave them the right to shape the patronage relationship toward their agenda. Hughes had been encouraged by a friend in the theater to come up with a folk comedy that might be easily and quickly produced. Hughes and Hurston began to work on a play, *Mule Bone*, about two men in the South who fight over which one killed a turkey. Based on a story, "The Bone of Contention," that Hurston had heard, the play took shape as Hurston acted out the parts, and Hughes altered the story, putting in additional elements that aided the dramatic presentation. Hurston may have delayed finishing the book project of her collected stories as an act of resistance, because the book, based on material Mason owned by contract, *was actually not Hurston's*. Work on the collected stories was alienated labor. The play would be hers. Plus, working with Hughes was a chance for her to do something that would realize her aspirations for the drama, which, in some respects, was closer to her heart. But after sailing along with Louise Thompson, typing as fast as they created, Hurston grew restless and left. Since Hurston did not specify at the time what caused her to become disenchanted, it remains a mystery. She left first for New York and then went south, reputedly to continue her research and finish work on Act 2 of the play.

Before Hughes could figure out what had happened, Hurston had abandoned the play altogether, reputedly because of jealousy toward the beautiful Louise Thompson. During the composition and typing of the manuscript, Hughes had hit on the idea of giving Thompson part authorship of the resultant play as part compensation for her labor beyond what she was being paid by Mason. That angered Hurston. Then, Hughes made another mistake. In May, Hughes told Mason he planned to go to Washington with his former fellow students at Lincoln for a weekend of conviviality. Mason thought he should stay in Westfield and write. Rebelling against her, Hughes decided to go without her approval. Mason exploded, dressing him down about how much he was costing her—$150 a month, plus $75 a month for Louise Thompson's typing services. Deeply hurt, Hughes carried himself to Washington and met with Locke—the first time in months that he had visited the man who had introduced him to Mason—and confided his frustrations and hurts. Suddenly, Hughes needed Locke, after having avoided close contact with him for years. When Hughes returned to New York, he went to Mason and asked her to end her payments to him. "The fault is mine. The darkness is mine," he confessed to her. He wanted to go back to the time when he had first met her and was not receiving money, a time he recalled as happier than now. He then returned some of the money she had given him, borrowed some from Van Vechten, and then socialized some more with his Lincoln University friends.

On June 7, Mason wrote back her answer to his request. She turned his critique of their relationship's pecuniary quality into a critique of him and his obsession with accounts. "Dear child, what a hideous spectre you have made for yourself of the dead thing money!"[34] This was a fiendish maneuver from a woman who had complained one November that in his "accounting of your expenses for October you have forgotten to put what is remaining in your Bank account. This leaves me a little uneasy about your expenses and need of money at this juncture." She had written this right after telling Locke he did not touch Hughes in his faithful accounting of the funds she gave him. "The dead thing money" was all-important to Mason as her way of controlling them and ensuring that they were worthy of her time. Hughes's attempt to free himself from the financial basis of their relationship showed his naiveté: he was loved because he worked, not asked to work because he was loved. Mason wielded a similar kind of power in her relationships with White artists. She concluded her letter by announcing that he was not bound to her, which carried with it an ominous subtext he had not anticipated—she was no longer bound to him either. "I therefore enclose in this letter a check for 250.00.... Hail to Alamari! Love and good hope to you as you seek the sea. Success for whatever plan you make for revivification."[35] When he wrote her two weeks later asking to confer with her about his plans, she sent a telegram telling him "under present conditions it is useless for me to undertake any more than I have promised."[36] Swiftly and unequivocally, he had been cut loose like a slave freed from the plantation, but with nowhere to go. But it was 1930, not 1865, and it was the second year of the Great Depression.

Just as paternalism was not the true nature of the slavery relationship, but an ideology that disguised its naked economic exploitation, so too maternalism disguised the true nature of this patronage relationship, which was little more than a capitalist system of production in which Hughes and Hurston—and other artists—labored to produce commodities on a schedule. Maternalism was still useful to Mason, who used its language to characterize Hughes as the materialist: he was the worker obsessed with money, rather than the "primitive" devoted to the true "higher things" mother asked him to create. That language handcuffed him emotionally, because it was what he had believed he was asked to do. He had rebelled against what his mother had asked him to do. Who, especially a sensitive Black male, could support that?

Apparently, not Locke. When Hughes next heard from Locke, the young artist realized that Locke was in agreement with Mason's decision. He congratulated Hughes on receiving his hefty farewell check and stated: "I am trying my best to cause her the least possible disillusionment," a swipe that suggested Hughes was responsible for whatever disillusion she now experienced.[37] Once Hughes realized that his desire for financial release meant he was emotionally discarded, he became ill, remaining in Westfield as his stomach knotted up with nausea. Publishing three poems in *Opportunity* focused on despair and death made his friends Joel and Amy Spingarn uneasy. Now, emotionally adrift without Mason's support, he became despondent. Even the publication of *Not Without Laughter* (1930) and its favorable reviews did not lift his spirits. Interestingly, Locke, who had edited *Not Without Laughter* extensively, seldom gets any credit for this work. He was in fact insisting on revisions past the point when Mason had any additional recommendations. Locke's involvement as an overseer in Mason's operation had reduced his esteem as a critic and intellectual. Once the book was out, Hughes's only use of Locke was to try and help him get back in Mason's good graces.

But Locke was not interested in helping Hughes. From Paris in July, Locke wrote casually mentioning that he had visited the old building where he had climbed the steps every morning and awakened Hughes when they were there in 1924. Curtly, Locke concluded by noting that he had nominated Hughes for a literary prize worth $400 to the winner; but if he did not want the involvement, he recommended Hughes write the people and decline the nomination. Perhaps if Locke had been a larger, more sympathetic leader of the Negro Renaissance, he would have mortgaged whatever capital he still had with Mason to help out Hughes. The departure of Hughes from Mason was an abrupt end to the Golden Era of the Negro Renaissance and Locke's dream of a Lorenzo-like stable of artists creating great works under patronage. But unlike Lorenzo de Medici, Locke did not have his own fortune and no control over the relationship he had spawned between Mason and Hughes. And now Hughes was gone.

Given the shenanigans Hughes had indulged in behind Locke's back, it's understandable why Locke no longer cared what happened to Hughes. For at least two years, Hughes had refused to respond regularly to Locke's letters, had refused to meet casually with him in Washington even with third parties, had undermined Locke's authority with Hurston, counseled Hurston not to confide in Locke information he probably wanted to have, and exulted in the knowledge that Locke had no authority over Hughes's relationship with Mason. That last fact was his undoing. Since Hughes was so confident he knew how to manage his White patron, why should Locke come to his rescue now? Locke could not think of a reason.

But Locke was responsible for bringing Hughes into the relationship, losing control of it, and then standing by paralyzed while it collapsed and burned everyone associated with it. That he could not feel enough responsibility to try and repair the breach—or head it off when he met with Hughes in Washington before the break—showed Locke's limitation as a steward of collaborations. He had unleashed racial and maternal feelings in the patronage scheme that he couldn't manage psychologically. While Hughes had been disloyal to him, he had been disloyal to Hughes and Hurston and the larger notion, implicit in *The New Negro*, that New Negroes should refuse to allow themselves to be dictated to by Whites. His failure to be loyal to that concept had fundamentally undermined his authority with Hughes and Hurston. Some humility about that would have helped.

There was one more thing. Locke never seemed to consider that perhaps his sexuality contributed to the collapse of the patronage relationship. Did his lusting after Hughes even after the younger man made clear he did not want a romantic relationship with Locke contribute to the breakdown of the triangle between Mason, Hughes, and Hurston? It seemed so. Locke's desire created a sense of threat in Hughes and the suspicion that the whole patronage scheme was really about sex, not the production of art. Getting the money for Hughes, taking care of him financially and psychologically, and then expecting some sexual favors made Hughes defensive and encouraged Hughes to undermine Locke's leverage over him. Locke did not want to face that pursuing a "midwife" relationship with the artists while trying to sleep with them might be a reason he was never as successful a mentor to them as he wanted to be. Even the Westfield blowup between Hughes and Hurston turned on the suspicion that sex was the underlying motivation for Hughes bringing Louise Thompson into the arrangement, an echo of Locke sexual politics. He sowed seeds of suspicion and sexual competition that ultimately taught his mentees to be as guarded and manipulative as he was. Since they were not the masters of it that he was, they inevitably stumbled and crashed. He could then feel superior as he stepped away and watched Hughes fall.

But Locke's stock fell as well. After Hughes's abrupt departure, Mason began to wash her hands of all of the Negro artists—and some non-artists—she was supporting upon Locke's recommendation. In September, Mason called in Louise Thompson and fired her, partly because she had not been producing any work in months. For her defense, it should be noted there was no work for her to produce: neither Hughes nor Hurston gave her any work to type after Hurston abruptly left Westfield. But that was around April; she had continued to cash the check Mason sent her until November. That may have been when Hurston fingered her as the reason why the collaboration in Westfield had collapsed.[38]

That November Hughes was in for another shock. In Cleveland with his mother, he visited his friends Russell and Rowena Jellife, who ran the Gilpin Players, Cleveland's famous Black drama group, and made a startling discovery. They were going to produce a play in February written by Zora Neale Hurston. It was *Mule Bone*, but without his name or contribution acknowledged. Hurston had submitted the play as solely her creation, although later she stated she had cut out all his additions and rewritten it to her own specifications after leaving Westfield.[39] *Mule Bone* was now a "bone of contention" between the two of them, fittingly enough. Once Hughes contacted Hurston and accused her of misrepresenting the work as her own alone, Hurston counter-attacked by bringing the whole thing to Mason and enlisting her support in defending her. Fortunately, Locke had not been involved in that work, since the work had gone on without Mason's or his explicit approval. Mason came to Hurston's support, believing her story that it was she who had been badly treated, rather than Hughes. And Locke supported Hurston's side in the conflict, no doubt feeling there was nothing to gain by supporting the now-departed Hughes. Plus, Hurston was on a tirade. "I wish you could get Langston and me together before you," she spewed venomously to Mason as the year 1930 ended. "Then I could prove that he is lying about what he contributed to my play."[40]

As the larger goals of the patronage system evaporated, Locke's relationship with Mason focused now on mentoring him rather than using him to manage others. She had pursued that goal all along when not distracted by managing the book production assembly line. As early as 1928, she had chided him for a lack of razor-like focus in his intellectual work. "Alain puts his mind on reading a book—intends to get what's in it but when he's read it he hasn't got anything of what I call the book—if its a valuable one—its running between his two ears....My whole relation with Alain is the life of a surgeon—mending broken relationships 'broken bones.'"[41] In 1929, she critiqued his approach to lecturing as unnecessarily obtuse. "Demand with might and manner that simplicity shall live and breathe and have its nests within my [your] Being. For example, in your yearning to attain simplicity of expression realize as you go down the street next time you are walking straight ahead one foot after the other. What would it be if you walked a step ahead then one foot over the fence? Can't you see that what happens to your boys in the audience is that they don't get your point—because it has so many pairs of trousers on it and keeps moving to the side and into the dark. Of course Langston's Survey is running up and down the College campus with nothing on!"[42]

While often vicious and unfair, there was some truth telling in Mason's criticism, as when she criticized Locke for not getting Hurston's book out in May 1930, but went on to chide him for his dismissive attitude toward Hurston.

> Alain, do you remember you promised me you would do everything in your power to help this work? Do not balk it or Zora. That Conjure book must be on the boards as soon as possible. Such a pity your tongue couldn't be hung front to back so you could preach to yourself and not to the world! I suppose you think you know your classes...my

boy...[but] you will never really know what is behind their faces till
you learn to think and not to chatter. You had a chance in your classes
to bring Zora out but you blockaded her and did not think she was
anything. When you're good you're very, very good but when you are
bad****![43]

It was unfair to blame him for Hurston not finishing her book, but Mason
correctly exposed here that Locke had refused to treat Hurston with the seriousness she deserved. For years, he could not see past Hurston's crude, unsophisticated, and anti-bourgeois exterior to value her as a powerful anthropological
thinker, who also was becoming a compelling writer. Mason saw those qualities
in Hurston and recognized Locke did not. He could have brought Hurston to lecture to his Howard University classes, a gesture that would have helped her psychologically and conferred on her the status of a peer. But he did not, because he
looked down on Hurston. Mason was not afraid to tell him he had much to learn
from Hurston, because he did.

Mason's goal in these "surgical" criticisms was to make him a more powerful
spokesperson. "My dear Boy, it seems terrible to have to write you this kind of
letter," she wrote in a particularly critical letter of his accepting yet another assignment from Howard University president Mordecai Johnson, "but what can I
do to help you in your growth. Your health and your message for your people if I
let you submerge the Alain whom I believe can be born...to transfigure before
[the] white race, what lies in the real Negro?"[44] Despite the viciousness of her
comments, Locke took them seriously.

As the Hughes-Hurston patronage scheme collapsed, Locke took his skills as
a producer of other people's work and applied them to the theater. In 1930 Locke
arranged for the Rochester production of Richard Bruce's *Sadhji*, which Locke
had co-produced by getting Mrs. Mason to pay William Grant Still to compose
and perform the music for this sensual African ballet by the homosexual rebel of
the Negro Renaissance. Unfortunately, Locke's cheapness spoiled some of the
pleasure seeing the performance would have brought him. He decided not to
attend the performance because he could not do so without stopping in New
York and bringing Bruce with him. "That would have entailed considerable expense," he wrote to Mrs. Mason, "as I would have had to buy him a suitable set of
clothes to attend, along with the fare for the train trip." Afterward, he regretted
not having attended. With the funds he received from Mason declining, as she
began to punish him for the many "missteps of the Negroes," Locke was being
more careful about how much money he expended for the sake of the New Negro.[45]

Fortunately for Locke, 1931 began with the possibility of his eventual freedom from Mason's often withering criticism and rituals of deference. In January,
he received a startling announcement. Forwarded from Cambridge, where it had
been sent to a "Dr. Alain Locke, Harvard University," the letter informed him

that an Englishman, Thomas Clarke, had died and left his estate of roughly 40,000 pounds sterling to Locke, a man he had never met. The case was complicated, however, because Clarke had given his estate to an unnamed "missionary" of God "for the furtherance of God's work," and named only Locke as that missionary in an unwitnessed codicil executed one day before Clarke died. The will instructed his "Trustees to send to God's missionary quickly after my death a moderate sum up to several thousand pounds on account." Unfortunately for Locke, the trustees held up payment in response to the family's challenge to the will and especially the codicil, claiming that Clarke was suffering from "testamentary incapacity," or temporary insanity, when he composed them both. While elated by the prospect of a windfall, Locke knew realistically it was a long shot. Yet, he could not help hoping, when he wrote to L. Hollingsworth Wood, whom Locke retained to represent him. "The whole matter hangs by a very slender threat.... I think I ought to make a desperate stab for it, don't you? Some of it would put the Harlem Museum account on its feet." He requested that Wood ask his London representative to intervene in the case, and then Locke, almost in an afterthought to his own reference to the Museum, asked: "How is the Treasury—or does it really wait on my legacy. I hope I'm not like the African girl—but this isn't the first fortune I've lost."[46] Surely tempting was the thought that with such a "legacy" he could become a patron rather than simply overseer for one.

Very depressing was the relative silence from former friends and artists. "I have heard almost nothing from New York," he confided again to Mason in 1930. He had begun to avoid going there, as witnessing the poverty and suffering of young artists who "continued to flock to New York like moths to the flame," became too much for him. Without Hughes in Mason's stable of artists, there were few he could call his charges. Relations with Hurston continued to deteriorate early in 1931 as she ratcheted up her criticism of Hughes. She wrote Mason claiming that Hughes had borrowed some of her words for *Not Without Laughter*. These attacks seemed more important to her than moving forward on work she was supposed to publish with Locke's involvement. She missed several meetings with him. Hurston was ducking him, while continuing to act like she still wanted his involvement. Mason was confused: "why is she doing this," she wrote in her notebook. Hurston wanted to appear available for consultations, so that she could continue to receive money and dodge interference. Mason continued to support her, but reduced her allowance to $100 a month by November.

Locke's self-confidence seemed to improve in 1931, perhaps because of the possibility of his English legacy. The tone of his letters to Mason began to change. He became less slavish, less confidential, and less pleading in his attempts to get her approval. Without Hughes and with less and less of Hurston, Mason seemed to be less needy of fawning attention she had required in the past. They still shared an abiding hatred of Van Vechten: "I have reports that Van Vechten has been hospitalized with blood poisoning. Why won't he simply die!!"[47] Locke turned to reporting gossip in the Black community over discussing how to manage shared projects because, in fact, there were not many. Artists like Aaron Douglas and Richmond Barthé still received a pittance, which was important as the Depression advanced and Locke continued to get money to distribute as he saw fit. But the sense was palpable of closing up the shop called Negro artistic idealism that he had opened up with her in 1927.

A more pressing concern emerged in his letters—Howard was under attack by members of Congress, who wanted to remove Mordecai Johnson from the presidency. Locke became a major organizer of the battle to save Johnson's presidency. Some members of Congress accused the president of harboring communists; some malcontents on the faculty and in the alumni accused Johnson of autocracy in removing the old guard and hiring new faculty. Orchestrating a behind-the-scenes defense of the president kept Locke in Washington more than usual, as late-night and weekend meetings mended fences and supplied the president's defenders on the board of trustees and in Congress with the ammunition to beat back the attacks. Hurston predicted Johnson would have to go in a May letter to Mason, claiming that Johnson was accused of the very abuses that had brought down Durkee. But Johnson's presidency was saved, in no small part because of the efforts of Locke and the younger generation of social science professors, such as Ralph Bunche, who came to his defense. The effort, while invigorating, exhausted Locke.

Locke welcomed his trip abroad to fight for the Clarke legacy. Once he arrived in England that July, however, Locke learned that all was lost: the judge in the case ruled the codicil invalid, since it had not been witnessed. Given that there was no "missionary of God" to accept the funds, they would revert to the family of Thomas Clarke. Although Locke had known that getting the money was unlikely, realizing that the money was lost sent him into a deep depression. He confided in his letters to Mason, "I had begun to think of what I could do with the money to help some of the deserving people and advance some of the many projects I have hoped for over the years." Mason, sensitive always when Locke was emotionally crushed, came to his aid by immediately wiring him some extra money. It helped; but it did not fundamentally change his mood. That became darker as he looked up Black artists in London and Paris and found them destitute, when he could find them at all. "The poverty here has been devastating." Suddenly, it all had come to an abrupt end—the hoped-for breakthrough in literature, the spreading of creativity abroad as well as throughout the United States, the prospect of publishing a wealth of literature that would permanently transform the image and valuation of the Negro in world civilization.

Locke fell into an intense depression. Mason was concerned, sent him money to pay off the lawyers, and tried to buoy his spirits. Here was the other side of her maternalism, care and support in moments of crisis that he still needed.

After a month or so wandering around Europe, Locke seemed to emerge from his dour mood. Something positive had happened to Locke in the process of coming so close to real financial independence and realizing he would still remain dependent on some kind of patronage in order to advance Negro subjectivity. Moreover, the disappearance of Hughes and the collapse of the patronage scheme was another death, another reason, along with the money that had just escaped from his hands, not to want to go on. All of his plans had come to naught.

Finally, after drifting around Europe in a kind of emotional daze, Locke came home renewed. Something about coming so close to getting that Legacy had transformed him. He—not Hughes, Hurston, or Mason—was the "missionary of God." Something about no longer being responsible for running Godmother's patronage system buoyed him as well. After a long period of separation after his mother's death, Locke's otherwise oppressive subservience to Mason had produced a kind of rapprochement, a refueling, that, ironically, had freed him to move forward on his own, without her constant support. Suddenly he was on his own, again, but with more power to act independently. He still checked back with Mason in times of stress; but it was different now: he was informing her of his plans, rather than having her plan his future.

The collapse of the patronage scheme had freed Locke. Maternalism was something more than a confusing ideology for Locke. He still had Mason's love and attention despite the collapse of her fellowship payment plan. There was, despite all the criticism and humiliation, a bond with Mason that was the closest thing Locke experienced to the kind of unconditional love he received from his mother. There were still some conditions; but it was close enough. After Hughes left, Locke enjoyed her undivided attention and less constraining control. Indeed, as would begin to happen, he would produce the books Mason longed to see born, not for money on an assembly line, but out of his self-fulfillment empowered by her.

Hughes's end was Locke's rebirth as her "loving boy," undistracted by side glances.

PART III

METAMORPHOSIS

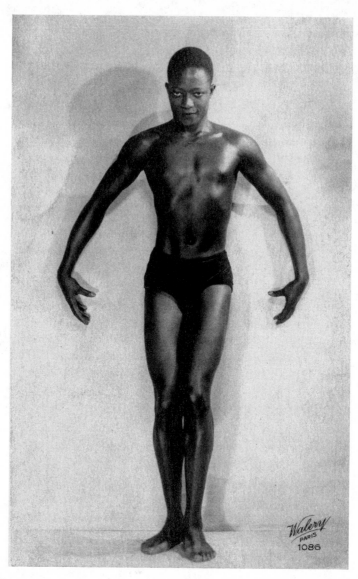

Feral Benga. Postcard. Courtesy of the Moorland-Spingarn Research Center, Howard University.

33

The Naked and the Nude

A metamorphosis in Locke's public role began to occur in 1931, putting another spin on the title, "Beauty Instead of Ashes," his declaration of independence from Du Boisian aesthetics in 1928. In the ashes of the collapse of the Hughes-Hurston-Locke triangle under Mrs. Mason's patronage lay an exquisite corpse waiting to be reborn—that of a more independent, self-sufficient, self-activating Locke who had been buried for the last four years while he squirmed under Mason's domination. In basketball language, a man who had depended on a dominant coach and a celebrated team was now going to have to get his own shot, with new, less experienced players. But that would be a blessing, a "saving grace," as Locke would put it one year later in his retrospective review of a different kind of crash—not the stock market—but the patronage scheme with Mason, Hughes, and soon Hurston.

Another catalyst of metamorphosis had emerged earlier in 1929. The underlying motivation for the Mason patronage scheme had always been desire: Locke's love of Langston Hughes. As that love withered and began to atrophy in 1929, another infatuation blossomed the same fall that brought the Stock Market Crash to America. Ralph Bunche, newly minted with an MA in government from Harvard, came to teach at Howard University, likely the result of Locke's maneuvering. Locke had been an unofficial advisor of Howard's new president, Mordecai Johnson, since 1927 when he rehired Locke and sought his advice on how to recast Howard as a leader in modern higher education. Locke wanted to build a powerhouse social science division, where Locke, uniquely in American higher education, had philosophy housed. Locke always saw philosophy as a science and wanted it to sit atop a social science division staffed with the top Negro scholars from prestigious White universities like Harvard. Bunche had already caused a stir at Harvard, so impressing his professors in government that they offered him a graduate fellowship to stay on campus. But a sixth sense in Bunche told him to come to Howard, the nation's most powerful Negro university, and join forces with Locke to remake the field of what today is called Black Studies.

For Locke, however, Bunche brought a different kind of grace: the devilishly handsome political scientist enabled Locke to put behind him the love of Langston Hughes and embark upon an intellectual revolution in Locke's thinking that would move toward a world systems class analysis of the plight of the Negro in the United States. There is no evidence of a romance between Locke and Bunche, but it is clear that Locke was quite taken with the brilliant, slender, and light-skinned young man from Los Angeles who was now a graduate of Harvard. It was not just how Bunche looked—it was that he was a brilliant and supremely well-mannered sophisticate—someone with all of the social intelligence that Locke had without the prickly negative energy that Locke also possessed. Bunche was easy on the eyes and on the social space he glided through so effortlessly that he put everyone else at ease—which is one of the reasons he became one of the most successful diplomats the United States produced in the twentieth century. Whether Locke and Bunche were ever lovers or not, it is clear that they were intimate, close friends, who traveled together, debated often, and worked to each other's benefit.

Most important, a pattern repeated with Bunche that had occurred with Langston Hughes: a romantic interest or at least an infatuation with an attractive man catalyzed an intellectual transformation for Locke. It had been the love of Hughes, after all, in Europe, that beget the New Negro in Locke's writing. Similarly, contact with and really learning from Bunche, a very opinionated Marxist political thinker in the early 1930s, began to move Locke off his single-minded focus on race to more recognition of the class and imperialist nature of American oppression. In a sense, Bunche helped Locke return to an earlier formation he had abandoned during much of the 1920s—the Marxist analysis of race contacts and interracial relations he had pioneered in his Howard lectures of 1915 and 1916. Bunche engendered a renaissance of the social scientist in Locke, precisely as Locke began to situate his thinking in the social science division at Howard in the 1930s.

Hired as a professor, and charged with starting a Political Science Department at Howard as part of his job, Bunche was nevertheless relatively poor and after getting married took on additional work as an assistant to Mordecai Johnson, work that Bunche found challenging because of Johnson's mercurial and bombastic personality—a personality type that Bunche struggled with throughout his long career. Locke too found much to dislike in Johnson, even though Johnson had been the one who had brought him back to Howard. But Johnson represented to Locke and Bunche the vagaries of the old-style Negro leadership, a leadership class that was disproportionately, in their minds, based in the Black church affiliations of those leaders, and the political connections to old-style Washington, where telling jokes to Whites, currying favor, and scooping up money were key parts of the game of Negro-White "liberalism."

In this context Bunche began to think seriously about what topic he would select for his doctoral dissertation at Harvard, and Locke played an important role. Locke suggested to Bunche that he take an African topic for his dissertation, one aligned with the research Locke had undertaken with Raymond Buell and the Foreign Policy Association. While the final topic came from Buell, the orientation toward Buell and the whole perspective of an African topic came from Locke.[1] In those early years of Bunche's residence as a professor at Howard, Locke mentored him as to how to negotiate his way through the sometimes hostile and intrigue-based academic politics at Howard.[2] In Bunche, Locke saw an earlier version of himself, a rebel against the notion that Negro intellectual thought should be confined to the small, the narrow, and the segregated American mindset, which Locke and Bunche saw as being co-constructed by Whites and Blacks in the American context. Africa allowed a way out of petty in-group Negro politics to globalism, a larger and more capacious context in which the calculus of race was changed because globally Black people were more of a majority, but also in need of modernizing intellects such as Locke's and Bunche's. A global dissertation opened doors for Bunche that Locke had wanted to open for himself in 1928, but which his limitations as a political scientist kept closed. Now, by putting Bunche in conversation with Buell, Locke achieved a kind of deliverance from the ghosts of his failed Foreign Policy Association paper, by bringing African American eyes, a lived experience of colonialism at home, into the conversation about the future of Africa and global affairs. The point of view of the Black American intellectuals was crucial not only because they were natural diplomats but also because they embodied by heritage and lived experience the discourse of racism.

But the road to approval of Bunche's final dissertation topic—"French Administration in Togoland and Dahomey"—would be a bumpy one, and Locke would help Bunche traverse it. In a letter to Howard University dean Davis in December 1930 requesting a leave of absence, Bunche stated the leave would be spent conducting research for a doctoral dissertation..."on 'The League of Nations and the Suppression of Slavery.'"[3] But the matter was not settled even though Bunche asserted in that letter that the topic had been approved. Some of his advisors at Harvard wanted him to do a dissertation on political activities of Blacks in West Virginia, a relatively narrow topic. Most important, his dissertation director, Professor A. N. Holcombe, favored another topic, a comparative study of race attitudes in Brazil and the United States.[4] There was also the implicit problem of a study of slavery in Africa: while the project naturally flowed out of the League of Nations' demand that under the Mandates System, the colonial powers would suppress slavery in Africa, investigation of such practices might expose Bunche to danger. Most important, Bunche did not want to disappoint Holcombe if the latter was set on having Bunche research Brazilian versus American racial attitudes. But a funny thing happened when Holcombe contacted

Edwin Embree, the so-called liberal president of the Julius Rosenwald Fund, one of the few foundations that would fund overseas research by a Negro, about the research project. Embree expressed reservations about an "American" doing a comparative study of race attitudes in Brazil and America. According to Holcombe, Embree opined, "The interracial conditions in Brazil are so different from those in this country that I wonder if much can be carried over from the experience in one country to that in the other. As I understand it, there is practically no racial discrimination as among the three bloods that comprise the population: Indian, Negro and Latin. Might there also be some danger that an American student would really be led astray by the position of Negroes in public affairs in Brazil? Indiscreet utterances and reports on the basis of Brazilian experience might really do harm in this country."[5]

As Bunche later confessed to Holcombe, Locke had known that the Foundation would not support such a study. "Your letter of February 17 is a very kindly one and has been of inestimable value in aiding me to map out a definitive course … for next year. The statement which you quoted from Mr. Embree's letter was a distinct surprise and somewhat of a shock to me. His statement is of no little significance in respect to the decision which I have made however. Dr. Locke in particular seems to feel that there is scant possibility of aid from the Rosenwald Fund for the Brazilian study. He thought so before he saw Mr. Embree's statement and is quite convinced of it now."[6]

Eventually, Bunche chose for his dissertation the study of the African Mandates, most likely at Locke's suggestion. After meeting with Raymond Buell about his thesis topic, also likely upon Locke's recommendation, Buell refined the topic and gave him a different focus, although still one on the subject of Africa and the Mandates. Rather than try to document the elusive and dangerous practice of slavery under the Mandates, why not do a comparative study of two colonies administered by one nation—France—in Africa to find out if the Mandates proscription to rule in the ex-German colonies under the Mandates was actually better than under traditional colonial rule. When Bunche informed Holcombe of this newly refined African Mandates topic and the dilemma of funding, Holcombe allowed Bunche to choose whichever topic he wished. In July 1931, Bunche received the good news that the Rosenwald Fund had approved financial support for his dissertation research in Africa.

The episode reveals not only Locke's close advisory relationship with Bunche but also his changing relationship to patronage. From 1924 to 1930, Locke had relied on patrons to finance his numerous projects; by 1931 he was preparing to tap institutional patrons by mastering the complexities and codes necessary to get corporations and non-profit organizations to provide the funds for his projects. While he still relied on Mrs. Mason—and other White women matriarchs—for emotional support and project opportunities, he was shifting funding procurement to institutional networks, governed by men, to garner the money for art and social science knowledge production. Locke adapted to the transformation from individual to institutional support for scholarly and cultural innovation that began before the Great Depression but accelerated during and because of it. As early as 1930, Locke was teaching Bunche how to navigate White institutional patronage, something Locke would soon show himself a master of by mid-decade.

Like the Locke-Hughes relationship, the Locke-Bunche relationship was dialogical. Bunche was a willing and apt student for the lessons Locke had to offer about how to survive in the racial order of American higher education and navigate the world of institutional patronage; but Bunche also taught Locke how to adapt to the 1930s by introducing the older man to the new Black take on class analysis of the Negro problem arising among young Black intellectuals. Indeed, for the next seven years, Locke and Bunche would regularly tussle over the merits of a class-based analysis of the Negro problems versus Locke's notion that race functioned like class in construction of the modern world. The deeper point was also evident: brilliant young men moved Locke out of his intellectual comfort zones to revise his conceptual frames and advance new ones. Locke's romantic interest in highly educated young men was a catalyst to move forward intellectually; but the process of intellectual transformation would not be easy for Locke; and it would remain largely clandestine.

That's because even suggesting the possibility of intimacy in many of Locke's relationships was explosive. If even the possibility of a romantic relationship between Locke and Bunche had been raised in the mid-twentieth century, it would have crippled Bunche's future—which included Bunche becoming the chief UN negotiator for the Arab-Israel conflict after World War II. Locke, and certainly Bunche, would understand this and do everything to avoid its consequences. Given this "guilt by association" dynamic, Locke's pariah status kept him from wielding the kind of power that the married and eminently respectable Ralph Bunche would have in the larger culture.

Despite claiming to friends not to be embarrassed by his homosexuality, Locke and those same friends found numerous occasions to conceal their overwhelming predicament. How were they to transform into neutral public monuments the psychological tensions arising from the fact that they were gay Black intellectuals in love with the male body as something erotic? As much as Locke struggled in the early 1930s to reconcile himself with a dramatic change in the dominant political philosophy, he also struggled with asking young visual artists to be open and revealing about their racial identity while concealing their sexual identities. Given that many of the artists Locke counseled, no less than some of the social scientists he mentored, were either queer or queer-friendly, the question remained for many of them, no less than Locke, how to assert a leadership role in the Black community while indulging in practices that many in that community viewed as disqualifying for its leaders. This explains, perhaps, why Locke remained attached to aesthetics as his main terrain of contestation even in the 1930s: the language of beauty allowed him to shape what many found physically and morally objectionable as uplifting and eternal.

The language of visual beauty helped reconcile two different discourses about the nature of loving men. For example, in his classic study of the nude in art, art critic and historian Kenneth Clark gives us some estimate of what the predicament must have been like. "The English language," Clark writes, "with its elaborate generosity, distinguishes between the naked and nude."[7] Nakedness was considered a form of deprivation, of diminishment, an impoverished human object, without clothing, a broken, "embarrassed" body. It was sexual hunger revealed. The nude, on the contrary, was pure, welcome, alive, a work of art to be admired and emulated. How was Locke, the leader of a new Black aesthetic, to lead this community, itself a kind of "embarrassed" body, to see its vulnerabilities, what mainstream American society viewed as moral transgressions, as crucial to the production of art? How could the Black body simultaneously be both naked and nude? Here is where Negro and gay identity coalesced into a problem of how to make the invisible visible and attractive to a wider audience while remaining true to one's love.

That reconciliation seemed more elusive for Locke as 1931 began. Locke continued to trek to New York to go to Small's Paradise, a gay community hang-out in Harlem. Inside, with its ornate mirrors, chrome tables, raised and intimate bandstand, Small's was the perfect environment for Locke and others to do their stealth cruising. But Locke's protégé and confidant, Professor Richard Long, rejects the idea that Small's anchored a gay community. "There was no gay community, there was a Black community, and we were in it. We frequented Small's just like everybody else."[8] What Locke and others found at Small's, no less than the rest of Harlem, was a welcoming space, where gay Black aesthetics, performativity, even laughter, took and shaped the social mix that was Renaissance Harlem. Since Negro gays had been the lion's share of contributors to the Negro Renaissance—Alain Locke, Countee Cullen, Langston Hughes, Wallace Thurman, Bruce Nugent, and others—there was a race celebrity attached to Black gays coming out of the 1920s. Promise of greater respect and inclusion in the Black community may have been part of the reason Locke was, at times, wildly optimistic about the potential of the Negro Renaissance to transform the place of the Negro in American life.

The previously mentioned Sadie T. Alexander, of the Black elite Mossell family of Philadelphia, waited until my formal interview was over, the tape recorder turned off, the questions about Locke's family's status—or lack of it—dispensed with, to confide in a hushed but firm voice, "He messed up a lot of young boys." She said no more, slowly shook her head, and repeated the same mantra, one that must have echoed in her class's estimation of who Locke was. Very likely she referred to Locke's relationship with Scholley Pace Alexander, whom Locke was intimate with while the former was an adolescent. Locke's practice of his homo-sexuality was viewed as a threat to middle-class standards of appropriate stan-dards of adult behavior. He violated Black Victorian values that she and other Philadelphians held dear. Yet Locke was unapologetic about what he considered love relationships.

> Yes—I will plead guilty when the bitter time comes "to corrupting the youth" —but there they are—as Socrates would have said—my spirit-ual children—Jean Toomer—Langston Hughes, Countee Cullen, Lewis Alexander, Richard Bruce—Donald Hayes—Albert Dunham there they are—can a bad tree bring forth good fruit?[9]

Socrates, the Greek allusion of homosexual philosopher, allowed for the naked, the "spoiler," to give birth to the "good fruit" of art, in other words, the nude. Yet Locke must have known of such sentiments as Sadie's in the Black intellectual communities of Philadelphia and Washington and limited his ability to be a leader of the Black community. Bruce Nugent alluded to the impact that such ostracism had on Locke rather ironically when he stated, "I never understood why Locke was so insecure. He came from the right family."[10] But Nugent knew all too well why such marginalization affected Locke: Nugent had changed his name to Richard Bruce once he became an out gay writer to protect the reputa-tion of his family from censure and derision.

Harlem was not so much a utopia as a hideout where the exiled could behave in ways unacceptable in Black Victorian circles farther south. The punishing winter of 1931 exposed how much Harlem was not a utopia, that Locke's predictions of its escape from the conditions that rendered other Black communities little more than slums were fanciful, in part, because of the sexual freedom he experi-enced there. The Great Depression exposed that Harlem was not a quilombo but an economic dependent of the rest of New York, especially White New York. Speakeasies closed; cabaret shuttered; and Whites stopped trekking up to Harlem to kick up their heels, a la Negre, to spend their non-existent weekly checks. Their hungry eyes and surplus capital were gone. Harlem was naked before the rapacious forces of capitalism, as Black unemployment quadrupled and death from cold, hunger, and illness staggered Harlem as it did the rest of America. On his trips there, Locke could see the unemployed all around him. The dimes he habitually handed out to beggars at bus stops hardly seemed adequate now. Those beggars were his friends, former artist protégés, and prospective New Negroes. Had he "messed up a lot of young boys" by making them think they could escape the hellhole of labor marginality by becoming poets instead of bellboys?

Just as Locke felt no compunction about sustaining himself with young lovers, he felt no remorse about his predictions of a new era of freedom in Harlem now that the Depression had dawned. Rather, in his "retrospective review" of the literature of 1930, published the following February, he called the first true year of the Great Depression "This Year of Grace" and portrayed the economic collapse of Harlem and the art movement as an act of providence that would help advance a sustainable renaissance.

> The much exploited Negro renaissance was after all a product of the expansive period we are now willing to call the period of inflation and overproduction; perhaps there was much in it that was unsound, and perhaps our aesthetic gods are turning their backs only a little more gracefully than the gods of the market-place. Are we then, in a period of cultural depression, verging on spiritual bankruptcy? Has the afflatus of Negro self-expression died down? Are we outliving the Negro fad? Has the Negro creative artist wandered into the ambush of the professional exploiters? By some signs and symptoms. Yes. But to anticipate my conclusion—"Let us rejoice and be exceedingly glad!" The second and truly sound phase of the cultural development of the Negro in American literature and art cannot begin without a collapse of the boom, a change to more responsible and devoted leadership, a revision of basic values, and along with a penitential purgation of the spirit, a wholesale expulsion of the money-changers from the temple of art.[11]

Expressed here was the pent-up frustration shared privately with Mrs. Mason for years about the cheap and sexualized sensationalism of late-1920s Negro art. Locke the Arnoldian moralist was ascendant in these remarks. There had been too much nakedness on stage. Where were the classical nudes of true art Locke wanted the Negro to produce in America? Unwilling to call out "money-changers" like Carl Van Vechten or "betrayers" like Wallace Thurman by name, Locke posed the problem as an identity politics: "I think the main fault of the movement thus far has been the lack of any deep realization of what was truly Negro, and what was merely superficially characteristic. It has been assumed that to be a Negro automatically put one in a position to know; and that any deviation on the part of a white writer from the trite stereotypes was a deeply revealing insight. Few indeed they are who know the folk-spirit whose claims they herald and proclaim."[12] Here was the part of Locke that the young radicals hated—his willingness to switch to a Du Boisian language of moral condemnation once the tide turned against the aesthetes and dandies. And that last line would be something that Zora Neale Hurston would have said applied to Locke as much as anyone else.

Locke adopted that language to cover up a sobering reality—Black artistic production had collapsed in the face of the economic depression. There was less "bad art" because there was less "art" overall. Producing less art never produced better art in the long run, at least in the history of the Western civilization he wanted Negroes to emulate. Nevertheless, Locke tried to make the best of it. "It is, therefore, significant that this year has witnessed a waning of creative expression and an increasing trend toward documentation of the Negro subject and objective analysis of the facts." He tried to utilize the metaphor of tempering to extract a progressive message from the situation. "And with all the improvement of fact and attitude, the true Negro is yet to be discovered and the purest values of the Negro spirit yet to be refined out from the alloys of our present cultural currency."[13] Whatever his pronouncements, the facts of weaker and lesser production came out in the structure of his "retrospective review" for that year, which included more reviews of White-authored books about Negroes and more sociological literature, such as James Weldon Johnson's *Black Manhattan*, which Locke enthusiastically reviewed. The reality was that of contraction and not refined expression on the creative side, something that he acknowledged, ironically, with a tepid review of Langston Hughes's *Not Without Laughter*. Despite his involvement in its production, he concluded: "As it is despite immaturity of narrative technique, this novel is one of the high-water marks of the Negro's self-depiction in prose."[14] Such a line could not have endeared him to Hughes or the other Negro authors who were once his raison d'être. The signal was clear. Locke was pivoting away from being the promoter of Negro literature to being its critic.

But Locke needed a new creative field to plow even as he included more and more social science literature in his reviews. He needed a new arena of aesthetic knowledge while he gradually redefined himself as a social scientist as well as a humanist and fine arts scholar. He found that opportunity in a calling—to advance contemporary art as the most important new terrain on which to turn sexuality into enduring aesthetic form. It came to him, once again, as a calling from a woman, an older White woman, as was usual in his life, but this time, a woman connected to a system of institutional patronage.

In January 1931, Mary Beattie Brady, the director of the Harmon Foundation, asked Locke to contribute an essay to a catalog that would accompany the Foundation's exhibition of contemporary Negro visual artists that year. Five years earlier the Foundation had started awarding prizes for exemplary achievement in scholarship and social reform by Negroes. This small, privately held and managed foundation had emerged from real-estate tycoon William E. Harmon's vision of providing opportunities for Negroes to develop Christian morals, habits of thrift, and assimilation of Western civilization. Aside from recognizing existing Negro artists, Harmon Foundation prizes stimulated the production of African American visual art as all manner of artistically inclined Black people sent in material to try and secure the cash prizes, which ranged from $100 to $400. In 1928, the Foundation took the next step and began putting the best art submitted on exhibition at the International House, a social service organization on Riverside Drive in New York. It gained higher visibility for the program when Brady got Alan Bement, a judge, to allow the Foundation to have its 1931 exhibition in the prestigious Art Center on the Upper East Side of New York. This reflected Brady's desire to become a major player in the Negro art world in New York and her sense that the Foundation's program would never be taken seriously unless it appeared in a museum-like setting.

While Negro literary activity declined precipitously after the Stock Market Crash of 1929, Black visual arts production accelerated, in part because of the Harmon Foundation's patronage, but also because other institutions, such as the Howard University's Fine Arts Department and the Harlem Arts Workshop, had nurtured young visual artists who had begun to emerge as the late-blooming flowers, as Locke put them, of the Negro Renaissance. Lois Mailou Jones, a graduate of the School of the Museum of Art in Boston, had won honorable mention at the Harmon Foundation awards exhibition in 1930 for *Negro Youth*. She had also been recruited the year before by James Herring at Howard to teach painting and design to a new generation of Negro art students. Archibald Motley, whom Locke met in Chicago along with Richmond Barthé, had won a Harmon Foundation prize in 1927; in 1929, he had a one-man show at the Ainslee Galleries in New York. Brady's invitation to Locke showed that she realized she needed a major Black intellectual to validate the Foundation's program if it was going to be taken seriously among the broader Negro art world.

Locke had harbored huge aspirations for a visual arts awakening as part of the Negro Renaissance. The visual arts were more conservative than the literary, Locke observed, with the result that painting was slower to move away from the domination of "caucasian idols" than poetry. But the visual arts were crucial to the movement because of the greater power of the visual to change Black self-conceptions of Beauty. Advances were not being made, though, in the 1920s, except through scattered works by European artists. Auguste Mambour, even more than Reiss, fused modernism, especially cubism, with a romantic image of the Black as subject. Mambour's canvasses throbbed with the allure, dignity, and mystery of the Black subject on its own terms—not as an answer to any White American discourse. Beauty in Blackness could only be achieved by artists detached enough from the White and the Black American discourses to ignore them.

That change in perspective seemed to be evident among younger contemporary Black artists emerging by the early 1930s who were producing a few works of genuine beauty. When Locke attended the Harmon Foundation exhibition held in January 1930, he was stunned by the artists and their recent work. There was Malvin Gray Johnson, whom Locke would later describe as the first true modernist Black painter, turning out gems, like his poignant study, *Meditations*. Locke liked the bold prints of his Howard University colleague, James Lesesne Wells; but Locke's most propitious discovery was the darkly handsome William H. Johnson, the most radically modernist artist of this younger generation of Black painters. Johnson channeled Van Gogh, Soutine, and even Picasso in "earthquake" landscapes and disturbingly off-kilter portraits whose underlying forms seemed to be alive and in constant motion. Held up in his Harlem loft for much of 1929 painting feverishly, he had headed back to his native birthplace, Florence, South Carolina, in the fall of 1930. There, he caused a public uproar by erecting an easel outside the local whorehouse and painting the house of ill repute in garishly brown and red colors in the middle of the day. Narrowly avoiding arrest—either for painting the bordello or for being a Negro painter—he came north and spent a few nights at Locke's apartment.

Most likely the stay did not result in the kind of romantic bliss Locke would have liked. The heterosexual Johnson was on his way back to Denmark and his Danish wife, Hokscha, whom he adored. The focus of this visit was not sexual, but economic. Having produced over a dozen canvases down South, Johnson wanted Locke to act as his agent and sell his work, for which Johnson expected to find a ready market in the wake of his having won the gold medal at the Harmon Foundation exhibition. Locke agreed and hid the small cache of paintings in his apartment. But he must have wondered to whom he was going to sell the wildly expressionistic paintings. It was one thing for bohemian judges in New York to see Johnson's work as brilliant and quite another to get the bourgeoisie, White or Black, of Washington to put one of these canvases up in their parlors. Fortuitously, Langston Hughes, with whom Locke was still friendly, had stopped by while Johnson was at Locke's apartment. As a gesture of admiration for Hughes's accomplishments, Johnson gave Hughes a painting. Suddenly Locke's apartment at 1326 R Street was beginning to seem like what he always wanted it to be—a crossroads of Black talent who met there, loved one another, and exchanged art and ideas because of him.

Thus, when Brady's invitation to write the catalog essay came early in 1931, Locke jumped at the chance. Her invitation was really a way to get Locke's help in curating the exhibition. Locke didn't mind; he threw himself into contacting and cajoling artists to submit their best work. While chagrined at Motley's refusal to send work, Locke believed he was too arrogant after he had had a one-man exhibition at a White gallery. Nevertheless, the effort netted some impressive work. Brady granted Locke's request to include some of the small African sculpture from the now-permanent location of the Harlem Museum of African Art at the 135th Street New York Public Library. That collection helped ground Locke's argument in the catalog that the contemporary Negro artist was a harbinger of an ancient and spectacular career as a visual artist in Africa, which Locke hoped would experience a rebirth among Black artists in contemporary America. Perhaps most gratifying was Locke's personal rewards from working with Brady. While more distant emotionally than Mason, Brady was more sophisticated about stroking Locke's ego. She named one of the prizes the Locke Portrait Prize, given that year to Edwin Harleston for "The Old Servant." As Locke noted to Brady when he received the catalog and learned of the honor, "I was in ignorance of the beautiful personal surprise tribute which it contained until a few hours ago. Imagine my surprise and pleasure. Really I know nothing that I would rather have had—for recognition so seldom comes so appropriately." Then, to deflect attention from himself, he added, "Of course, all of us down here [at Howard] are enormously pleased at the prize won by young Wells," a teacher in the Art Department at Howard.[15]

The exhibition was critical to Locke publishing the first article on contemporary Negro art in a mainstream art history journal, the *American Magazine of Art*, that September. The magazine had contacted Locke directly during his work as guest curator of the exhibition because it wanted an article on this "event" of the New York art world by the reigning interpreter of Negro aesthetics. Locke seized on the opportunity not only to cement his reputation as the voice of the Negro visual artist but also to re-narrate American cultural history from what Black people created out of their experience of it.

> The American Negro as an artist is completely different from his African prototype. In his homeland, his dominant arts were the decorative and craft arts—sculpture, metal-working, weaving...design, but in America, the emotional arts have been his chief forte...his chief artistic expression music, dance, and folk poetry. Why should this be? There is an historical reason. Slavery not only transplanted the Negro, it cut him off sharply from his cultural roots and his ancestral heritage, and reduced him to a cultural zero by taking away his patterns and substituting the crudest body labor with only the crudest tools. This slavery severed the trunk-nerve of the Negro's primitive skill and robbed him of his great ancestral gift of manual dexterity. Alexandre Jacovleff, the Russian artist...has well said of Africa—"A continent of beautiful hands." This fact is really a symbol—the hardships of cotton and rice-field labor, the crudities of the hoe, the axe, and the plow, reduced the typical Negro hand to a gnarled stump.[16]

Later, Black critics and artists would complain that Locke's characterization was inaccurate, but what Locke was doing was crafting a compelling mythology.

Locke had to convince a skeptical contemporary visual art audience to see paintings, sculpture, and drawings by Negroes as art. He did it by reversing the typical narrative of modernism: rather than the broken, decentered Western subject, who had entered a "wasteland" in modernity, Locke suggested no modern subject better epitomized the psychological breach with all that he knew, held true, and needed to anchor his identity than the Negro, the former African, the ex-slave. America's past was the Negro's "wasteland" and, through an almost alchemical renaissance, a new Black subject had put himself back together and reclaimed a lost facility—the visual arts. However fantastic the story, the evidence was in stunning black-and-white photographs of such appealing portraits as Edwin Harleston's "The Old Servant" and William H. Johnson's "Sonny," but also visualized in the decorative excellence and superb design of James Lesesne Wells's "The Wanderers" and such other Negro "modernists" as Hale Woodruff and Aaron Douglas.

What separated the New Negro contemporary artists from their White American fellow travelers was that the Negro modernist came bearing a racial gift from the African tradition. Locke's favorite from the Harmon show received his most loving notice in the article. "Sargent Johnson's bust *Chester* is particularly striking; it has the qualities of the African antique and recalls an old Baoule mask. It is a long stretch from an isolated Negro sculptor living and working in California to the classic antiques of bygone Africa, but here it is in the captivating naive bust for even the untutored eye to see."[17] Johnson's work perfectly exemplified Locke's renaissance aesthetic—that the New Negro artist was rewriting the contemporary history of modernism by reconnoitering with the past to bring forth a sustainable modernity in American culture. By making a compelling argument for the New Negro visual artist as a racial modernist, Locke also created a market for their work, not only among bourgeois Negroes but also still-liberal-leaning Whites. Getting the American elite to see these objects as high aesthetics was important to getting Negroes seen as artists; but characterizing race as a creative visual space was crucial to creating an uplifting mood for buying and displaying this art.

The downside of the exhibition and the article was that they led nowhere. The Harmon Foundation did not hold an exhibition the next year, and Brady did not offer Locke the opportunity to become a permanent curator of Negro art for the Foundation. As was so often the case throughout his career—whether at the *Survey Graphic*, *Opportunity* magazine, with Mason—no one allowed Locke to lead the initiative. Since most of the insiders of the racial improvement organizations knew he was gay, Locke was not respectable enough to front an operation such as the National Urban League, a conservative Black advocacy group. With the Harmon Foundation, Brady reserved for herself the role of director of Negro artists and the coordinator of exhibits. While it was quite likely Brady was a lesbian, it was quite another thing to hire a gay Negro in an all-White Christian benevolent institution. Like other organizations of the 1930s strapped for cash and operating on lean budgets, the Harmon Foundation felt there was little need to employ him full-time when they could obtain his services largely for free.

As 1932 dawned, Alain Locke was watching a literary movement he had helped create wither and die. Wallace Thurman, one of the bright lights of the movement, drank himself to death at the age of thirty-four. Thurman had been able to publish some fiction, but even here, like Locke, he was mostly an expository writer. Some blamed Thurman's death on his ebony skin color, or rather, his own personal revulsion at it; others on his revulsion at his homosexuality and his impossible desire for permanent cohabitation with a young, blond man; still others on his failure as a writer to live up to the unrealistic expectations he imposed on his work and that of others. But when Locke wrote Mason, whom he still confided in and leaned on, he attributed the movement's failures to its Black subjects: "Things seem to be at an awful ebb—but of course we drained our own pond long before the great ebb came along. In fact, it is rather a pity that we have the general depression as an alibi. I am challenged with that whenever I criticize the young Negroes who certainly had their chance."[18] Increasingly, despite his seeming cordiality toward Hughes, Cullen, and even Paul Robeson, Locke privately blamed them for not living up to the standards of ideal form he had sought to impose on their work as a critic and supporter.[19]

One of the remaining bright spots for Locke was Hurston. In the aftermath of the "Mule Bone" debacle, Hurston had disappeared for awhile, as she expressed to Mason, "to find out what I can do." What she could do was to come up with another play, really an opera, titled *The Great Day*, which also, promptly, found a company willing to produce it. Mason, though, still controlled the rights to the material Hurston had collected, which served as the story or stories upon which the play was based. Thus, Hurston came back to Mason and Locke to get permission and money to produce the play. Mason assigned Locke to manage Hurston's play and refused to allow her to use some parts of the material. As the play limped toward its opening in January 1932, Mason's grip on the production tightened. She rejected changes the director wished to make to the script and sent Locke to view the rehearsals. At one point, she dispatched Locke to Hurston's house where he delivered Godmother's "message straight and without emotion. The effect on her was immediate. It was like an electric shock that shook a drunken man out of his stupor. She realizes now the rightness of your vision; I set to work revising the program on her kitchen table, with her peering over my shoulder. It is much improved now and she agrees with the changes."[20] Most likely, given Locke's good literary taste, the program was sounder after his intervention. In another hour or so, he also wrote the notes for the opera that appeared in the program, which was probably left unfinished for fear it would not meet with Mason's approval. Here again Locke seemed unaware of the impact of his enormous intervention into Hurston's work. Eventually, Mason counseled him to stop insisting on additional changes because of the emotional strain on Hurston. Locke's perfectionism, a tendency toward endless revision, was given free rein because of Mason's leverage.

This perfectionism also hindered Locke's ability to become a published creative writer. The critic overwhelmed the voice that wished to sing its own song in poetry, prose, or drama. The literary and artistic training and exposure he had imbibed at Central High, Harvard, Oxford, Berlin, and avocational study among aesthetes on both continents had inculcated in him a higher level of aesthetic criticality than he could achieve creatively in his poetry or prose. Some of the anger he must have felt at that dilemma made its way into his often crushing critical attitude on the work of first-time Black writers. What he could not see was that his weddedness to the ideal form, the nude rather than the naked, made it more difficult for the artists he advised to grow under his tutelage. Locke's inability to let go as a writer might be connected to his struggle to accept his racial identity, as Mason seemed to suggest. But it also was related to his ambivalence about his own sexuality and his inability to publicly address it or support writers who openly confronted it. Locke could not allow himself to be naked in public.

In private, however, Locke could at times break through. In fragments of abandoned narratives in the papers he preserved and donated to Howard University, some of it is quite stunning in its psychological and sexual daring. "In a moment," one story narrates, its beginning having been torn away.

> It was done—He lay beneath the horse a great lump of mass with the print of the horses shoes on his forehead. Years later he could not understand why he feared to grasp tightly the thing he loved—why he could not picture pleasure without pain—why there was never the complete wedding of the spiritual + mental in the consummation of desire. He had heard his mother say—Yes—the Herndons are coming (dislikes white people)—done for a visit (cannot stand patronage-sulks) they will take the guest room, of course. R. will have to sleep with Herman— not with ___ with his grey-green eyes and yellow freckled body, red brown hair, but with H full of ___ bronze dark brown eyes with brows as heavy and coarse and black as a horse's mane—with phallus dark + lovely to look upon—he had overheard his sister tell another girl: "It is the most perfect one I've ever seen just like a brown dill pickle[.]" [T]oday he has an insatiable appetite for dill pickles (puts salt on grapefruit) (try ____ on it). He was in bed first—H came in turned on the light—" If the light bothers you Rich I'll undress in the dark." "No, no, it doesn't <u>bother</u> me at all (favorite phrases) I'm not sleeping anyway (I'm not hungry)." But he closed his eyes not too tightly (craftiness stealth) H was undressing—He watched him take off every garment.
>
> (Carson's effusive). He saw his body strong, slim + brown—while the older boy put on his pajamas he was caressing the fine arms of the smooth brown body (faster approach). H is now in bed—he sleeps very fitfully—he slides his legs in sleep over the younger boy is wide awake. He begins to snore. R caresses his thighs—then very stealthily he opened the pajama pants.[21]

In this writing Locke drew a scene of homoerotic intensity that captured his own stealthy approach to sexuality.

Locke's postmodernist prose unveils Black desire, one that prefers the Brown body over the White that Thurman and even Bruce Nugent obsessed over in

their lives and in their writings. While Locke had White lovers, his story reveals a desire to find in the Black body a kind of home, regardless of his ambivalence about Blackness and Black people. And Locke also longed for a future in
which the transgressive act of loving people of whatever race or color would be
accepted and even celebrated. But in the 1930s, the act of esteeming the Black
body as transcendently desirable was a courageous step made against the various and sundry racial and sexual discourses that made Whiteness the desired
object of Black affection. In some respects it is tragic that Locke could not write
such prose in books that could see the light of day in the 1930s. Not only would
it have cleared a space for him as a creative writer, but it would have cleared a
space for the homoerotic imagination to emerge in American literature rooted in
the Harvard aesthetes. Locke suppressed that creative voice in favor of the voice
of the critic, who would channel the anger of the unfulfilled creative writer into
critical reviews of others who also failed to tell the truth about themselves in
print, but dared to print something anyway.

That Locke continued to focus his attention on the racial dimensions of his
American experience rather than the sexual he explored in private or the class
basis that Bunche focused on came in part because the racial experience so painfully constrained Locke's public life—especially in his attempts to continue his
connection with Beauty and the ideal form in art. An incident in 1932 makes the
point powerfully. With the decline of the Harlem Renaissance, Locke was increasingly stuck in Washington, D.C., where his increasingly "long and unbroken
stay" brought on unbridled "stagnation." One way out of that stagnation was to
go to the theater; but in Washington, that was an impossibility because of segregation. Locke thought he found a way to combine the naked and the nude when
he went to see the play *Lysistrata*, "a successful, ribaldly pictured sex-strike of
the Greek women which forces the Athenians and Spartans to make peace and
recognize women's rights." But here again, it was the racial that structured Locke's
experience of the art. "I had a time seeing it at all. When I got in at Baltimore, I
telephoned a student friend, Dr. Bowman, now interning at the Negro hospital
there...[and they] took a cab to the Maryland Theatre. The Colored doorman
started to open our cab door as we drove up—but on noticing me desisted—my
first real intimation of what we were in for. Bowman is fair—I hadnt chosen him
for that—but instantly saw that I must use strategy—so I gave him the money
for the two tickets." Once they were inside, having selected the less challenging
mezzanine, an usher rushed up and told them to take their tickets to the box
office. "Why No answer." Then, the doorman joined them and encouraged them
to get their money back. When the dispute continued, the manager came up and
asked if they were "colored. Why certainly—we wouldnt be anything else. That
startled him." When he stated there were "certain restrictions," Locke challenged
him as to what he was going to do about it. In the end, the refusal to be segregated netted them two tickets in the balcony. Although the White couple they

were seated next to got up and moved, another came and took their place without self-consciousness or concern. Though Locke criticized this show as well—its "amateur troupe" was not up to the director's aspirations—and enjoyed the play's "paganism," the dominant narrative of his recounting to Mason was "just what an unnatural life being a Negro involves." Locke was the Black body in the mid-Atlantic states, not the nude.[22]

A welcome escape from America came that summer of 1932 when Locke went to Europe and told Mason he was taking with him Ralph Bunche, who was going to Geneva to conduct research for his dissertation. Also on the trip was Louis Achille, a French man of color, whom Locke had recruited to teach French at Howard, and Señor Eusebio Fuertes, a young Basque instructor in Spanish at Howard, who, according to Achille, had been "recruited by Dr. Spratlin on one of his trips to Europe."[23] Locke was so taken with Bunche that he confided to Mason that he was thinking of going on to Geneva with Bunche, if Mason thought it the right time (she had told him it was not the right time in 1927). On the way, the two of them spent some time in Paris, where Bunche spent considerable time in the archives of French colonial administration. Achille's photographs of Locke and Bunche at a Parisian cafe show them engaged in spirited discussions, although with Bunche largely listening to the lecturing Locke. Clearly, Locke as the man who had already traversed the terrain of Geneva and the League of Nations Mandate policy had much to share with the younger man.

Alain Locke, Ralph Bunche, and Señor Eusebio Fuertes at a sidewalk cafe on Place de la Sorbonne, Paris, July 1932. Photograph by Louis T. Achille. Courtesy of Louis T. Achille.

Bunche, Fuertes, and Locke at a sidewalk cafe on Place de la Sorbonne, Paris, July 1932. Photograph by Louis T. Achille. Courtesy of Louis T. Achille.

But there was another aspect to these photographs. Commenting on them in a letter, Achille described Locke's easy manner as in contrast to the photograph of him mounted in the reading room of the Moorland-Spingarn Research Center at Howard University—in the more formal photograph of Locke at Howard in dark suit and whitening hair. "The look on his face is interested and attentive, quite different from his relaxed smile, like Bunche's at the Parisian cafe. Unfortunately, this, his best photo, shows only his mask." But in the second photograph of Bunche reading a paper and Locke looking smilingly at the camera, Locke had dropped "the mask" and sat at ease as the Black dandy in Paris. Achille's comment, reminiscent of Dunbar's poem, "We Wear the Mask," shows Locke could drop the mask and be naked—a Black gay cosmopolitan intellectual at a cafe with Bunche, Achille, and Fuertes—abroad. Bunche's easy familiarity with Locke also suggests that he was dropping a mask, but also charting his own path with the older man's support.[24] Walking with Locke and Fuentes to his left in another photograph, Bunche is very much himself the Black dandy abroad, wearing his cocked white hat at an angle that is almost pimpish.

Such photographs show that Bunche was both with Locke and independent of him, on close terms and yet his own man. Bunche would not falter as Locke had five years earlier. Instead, Bunche would go on alone to Geneva and also to French Africa to do on-the-ground comparative research on French colonialism in Africa.

Bunche, Locke, and Fuertes on Place Edmond Rostand, where Boulevard St. Michel and Rue Soufflot meet. In the background is the Pantheon, Paris, July 1932. Photograph by Louis T. Achille. Courtesy of Louis T. Achille.

The resultant dissertation, "French Administration in Togoland and Dahomey" was a tour de force, thoroughly researched and powerfully written that won a prize for Bunche when finished in 1934. Some even argued it led to the establishment of the field of international studies at Harvard as an interdisciplinary area of inquiry and research. The success of the dissertation was due not only to his obvious competence as a political science scholar but also because Bunche brought a level of criticality to the study of colonialism that situated the particularities of the administration of Togoland and Dahomey in a larger narrative of the failure of imperialism. That had been lacking in Locke's Foreign Policy Association paper. At the same time, Bunche preserved the New Negro "third way" strategy of Locke's FPA report by avoiding simply a doomsday assessment of Africa's future. Rather, Bunche, like Locke, suggested that a way out could be on the horizon if Europeans approached Africa anew with a rational plan by which it too could partake of the democracy and self-determination that the West said was the self-evident right of all peoples. Bunche had succeeded also because he was the attractive ideal of the young handsome African American scholar, something that eased his way into the French archives and administrators as well as the hearts and minds of his Harvard professors. Bunche was the nude, rather than the naked, messenger of de-coloniality.

For Bunche produced something more nuanced than simply a typical Marxist analysis of colonialism. Perhaps because of Locke's influence, the dissertation shows that racial dehumanization of the victims distinguishes colonialism from other forms of capitalist greed, a key point in Locke's much earlier Race Contacts and Interracial Relations lectures. Something of that earlier document's acid critique of the racist self-deception, overt manipulation, and denigration of the African by the European echoes in Bunche's dissertation.[25] Indeed, the *self* in self-deception is perhaps Bunche's best arrow into the heart of imperialism. For Bunche shows how imperialism is a mix of motives, sometimes humanitarian, sometimes naked greed, but always self-interested and self-congratulatory, so that even when helping the African, the European is really writing the history of Europe's glory in the African's mind.

Bunche's dissertation, which Locke most likely read and commented on, stressed the point that Locke had struggled with personally throughout his education—that European arrogance was not simply economic exploitation, but a warping of African minds such that they found it difficult to properly value what was valuable in their own traditions after internalizing Europe's doctrines. This had been Locke's struggle from the days at Harvard when he trudged out to an African American church to try and accept the brilliance of Dunbar as central to a self-appreciative Negro literature. It was the struggle he had failed to take up when he declined to go south to study southern Negro culture with Zora Neale Hurston. Here, in a social science dissertation, was Locke's dilemma but also his message going forward after the tough tutelage he had received from Hughes, Hurston, and even Mason—that ridding this "miseducation," as Carter G. Woodson put it, was part of the necessary project of de-colonization of the Negro artists' mind.

Early in January 1933, Locke got his chance. Brady contacted Locke urgently requesting that he contribute an essay to that year's exhibition catalog of work by Black artists. After skipping the 1932 exhibition, the Harmon Foundation had decided to take another chance on exhibiting what was now a much larger group of competent Negro artists. Because the decision to hold the 1933 exhibition was made late in December 1932, Brady approached Locke at the last minute. "We would like you to do an essay on 'The Negro in Art' for the catalogue, which we realize is very short notice, but hope it will not be too difficult as you can revisit some of the positions you outlined in your Mount Holyoke paper." Brown even felt entitled to outline what Locke should say in the essay, telling him that they wished he would "link the creative work of the people here with that of the Cuban."[26] Locke did not to write extensively about the sculpture of Teodoro Ramos Blanco, although he had nothing against the Cuban artist whose work had come into the Foundation's purview through the advocacy of Arthur A. Schomburg. Locke saw himself in competition with other intellectuals like Schomburg or Cloyd L. Boykin, director of "The Primitive African Art Center" in New York, who were making advances in the field of contemporary African and African American exhibitionary practice where he, with the Harlem Museum of African Art, had failed. Boykin had gotten a Carnegie Corporation grant to fund the Primitive African Art Center, whereas Locke's own request for museum funding had been turned down. If he was to fend off competitors and assert his own dominance in the field of Negro visual arts, it would be by creating an intellectual rationale for why Negro artists were valuable *in the America of the 1930s*, not by serving merely as a collector or institution builder.

Sitting at Howard University, Locke hammered out a new statement of his critical position on contemporary Negro art in less than a week, jettisoning his old argument that Negro American art was mainly important as a twentieth-century continuation of the genius of African art. But in pivoting away from "the African," Locke was actually building on the notion implicit to a de-colonial view that contemporary Negro artists were so warped after internalizing European notions of White supremacy that they found it difficult to properly value what was valuable in their own traditions, especially the Black body itself. This time he drove that point home by exploiting a dichotomy that had always existed as a subtext in his visual and literary art criticism of Black cultural production in America—the distinction, first emphasized in 1926, between Negro art and Negro artists.[27] Locke ratcheted up the argument into a categorical imperative in 1933: without Negro art—a distinctive effort to represent the Negro (or Negroness) in art—there was little rationale for special attention to or exhibitions for the Negro artist. International modernism, through which African art had entered the American mind, was dead, buried in part by the anti-modernism unleashed by the Great Depression. Negro artists needed a new reason for Whites to think about their art, and to find that Locke decided to contradict Marc Connelly's comments in the 1931 catalog that Negro art as such did not exist. What Locke saw, despite being thoroughly grounded in the socially constructivist anthropological argument about race, was that the very need for a separate exhibit, put on by a philanthropic organization like Harmon, rather than a New York art gallery or American museum, to give Negro artists an adequate showing, showed that prejudice by Whites against Blacks in elite cultural spaces was a historical formation. American art was a racial formation. This was one reason such a separate show and a separate domain called Negro art existed. Exclusion of the Negro as artist was not because of talent, but because the Negro face and form—color, figure, and culture—were denigrated by the ruling majority as realities that Whites sought, perhaps unconsciously, to erase from the representation of the American. That marginalization had created a separate sphere of meaning, interpretation, and perception that crystallized into a distinctive form that Locke called Negro art. A victim of the segregated thinking in America about intellect and culture, Locke reasoned that such an art argued for a fundamentally cultural pluralist vision of America. This was true, in fact, of Connelly's work, the play *Green Pastures*, even if Connelly, perhaps a bit self-consciously, denied it. There was a distinctive Black culture in America, a system of speech, belief, gesture, and attitude that Connelly had portrayed, somewhat paternalistically, on stage. Was it not, therefore, the responsibility of the Negro artist to portray that reality visually in American art, and thus escape the negative cultural discourse about Negro-ness that even many Negro artists had internalized? Was there not a way for Negro artists to give meaning to their work by choosing to explore, develop, and reveal the beauty in the Black face and form that the culture of Whiteness sought to cover up? Locke thought so and said so in his catalog essay, "The Negro Artist Comes of Age."

Although Mary Beattie Brady published Locke's essay in that year's catalog, she did not agree with its analysis and said so when the two of them appeared on a radio broadcast designed to advertise the exhibition and the work of the Harmon Foundation. Locke started off the discussion by suggesting that he was going to be provocative and asserted that in essence the Negro artist was nothing without Negro art. Brady took the bait. "Well, it is all well and good to be provocative. But can you prove it?" Locke was ready. "I think that I can. . . . Indeed, I turn to the Harmon Foundation exhibitions themselves as my proof. Is it not the case that in prosecuting the prize awards and exhibitions sponsored by the Harmon Foundation, you discovered that you had to make propaganda for Negro art in order to stimulate and strengthen the Negro artist?" Brady conceded that that had been the case, "but I don't want the public to think we created the Negro artist." Locke retorted: "No one could think that from the historical record. . . . The occasional Negro artist is almost as old as American art itself. In the 1850s, Edmonia Lewis (a Boston Negro woman) was a recognized sculptor in Rome, and in the 1870s, Wm. Duncanson, a Negro mural painter who had won recognition in England, Scotland, and France, was decorating the mansions of the patrician families of Cincinnati,—the ancestral Tafts and Longworths." Yes, Brady concurred, and offered that they like other American artists, had to go abroad for training and recognition. "But more so," Locke continued, "in the case of the Negro artist. He not only went abroad for his start but stayed like Tanner, whenever he could, for the finish. Unfortunately, along with this went a disdain for the Negro subject. Many Negroes were so influenced by the after-effects of prejudice and handicap that they refused to paint Negro types."[28]

Here lay the heart of Locke's argument. Prejudice was internalized by its victims and then lived out in their avoidance of what prejudice taught them to despise—their own image. Suddenly, Brady agreed: "Why we even ran into that attitude with some of the younger Negro artists as late as 1927." Alon Bement, the director of the Art Center where the exhibit was held, also participated in the radio program, and tried to move discussion back to the American context Brady had outlined earlier. "After all, should we blame these Negro artists? American artists for a long while avoided the American Scene and native material." But Locke would not let them off the racial hook. "Yes, but for the Negro artist, there was a special reason. You see, no one, but especially an artist, likes to be pinned up in a ghetto, and as long as the Negro theme was expected of the Negro artist and imposed upon him by outside opinion, it was bound to seem a handicap rather than an opportunity—a ball and chain restriction instead of wings of inspiration."[29]

Fearing perhaps that Locke was dominating the entire program, Brady turned to the two artists also invited to participate for their comments. Romeyn Lippman from Boston spoke first. "I think the Negro artist should have the whole world of art for his pasture. I search for the paintable idea, whether it be the Negro subject or some other theme. In my opinion subject-matter depends upon the temperament of the individual artist, and the fundamental element in his success is the mastery, after years of experimentation, of the technical problems involved in saying in a masterful way whatever he wishes to say."[30] Allan Crite, another artist from Boston, commented, "I myself prefer the Negro subject, and have been specializing in depicting what hasn't yet been expressed,— the typical life of ordinary colored people today as I see it about me. I also think the Negro institutions, schools, churches, and the like, ought to sponsor art expressed in terms of our own racial traditions, using them both historically and symbolically."[31] Bement seemed to concur that Crite had utilized Negro themes persuasively, such as in his painting of a Negro church.

Then, Locke asked Bement directly what he noticed at the first exhibit of Negro artists assembled for the Harmon Prize competitions in 1927. "I went to this exhibition expecting to see the Negro through the eyes of the Negro artist. Not that I expected the Negro artist to limit himself entirely to the Negro theme, but after all any artist expresses best that which he knows best and most intimately. So I was quite disappointed at the scarceness of the Negro subject, the prevalence of the conventionally academic, and in many places an obvious strain of weak imitation."[32] Now, with the validation of White authority, Locke's views compelled Brady's assent: "We were all disappointed,—and surprised. From this first exhibit it looked as if the Negro had been made, in reaction to prejudice, half-ashamed of himself." With his point made by the Whites, Locke could return to crediting the Foundation for its work in advancing both the Negro artist and Negro art. "So that is why, I suppose, you have made it since then an objective of the Harmon Foundation's encouragement of Negro art to try to free the Negro artist from this handicapping idea as much as your other objective of developing more interest and better technique among Negroes in art."[33]

Bement chimed in. "Well, Miss Brady, I was surprised at the rapid success you had. It was your third Harmon show in 1931 that I noticed a decided change. Here the Negro subject and native materials predominated, and many new painters and sculptors seem to have sprung up overnight from the magic wand of racial expression. And it was amazing to see how the technical quality of the work improved as the Negro came to closer grips with his own subject matter." It went unsaid that Locke had been pivotal in locating much of that art that seemed to "have sprung up overnight" in the 1931 exhibit and convincing some reluctant Black artists to participate. "Yes I particularly remember the difference between Malvin Gray Johnson's first academic fishing-boats and his vibrant Virginia landscapes, later. And the difference between Wm. Johnson's cubistic Southern French landscapes and his remarkable portrait sketches of South Carolina folk types." Bement concluded: "Yes, the Negro artist has as much to gain by coming home spiritually as the American artist in general." He then allowed Locke his conclusion: "Of course it is the same movement, only the Negro's path has been longer and harder. Still is, I should say."[34]

After this debate, Brady, according to a later interview she gave in the 1970s, said she feared that Locke was advocating a form of "Black nationalism" in his essays for her catalogs and, presumably, in this debate. And Romeyn Lippman perhaps had a valid reason to react negatively to Locke creating a canon that would exclude the works of artists who avoided Negro subject matter. But what Locke outlined was profound—that art had been a psychological process by which the Negro artist became a subject by rendering himself or herself in pictures and sculpture. In doing so, Locke outlined an important theory of the artist's relationship to society. Unlike Du Bois who advocated that Black artists produce art propaganda against White propaganda, Locke argued a more subtle transformation that needed to occur for Black people, as well as White people, to see Beauty differently—and in new places.

Perhaps the most beautiful thing about the debate on the radio was how it marked a transformation in Locke, in how he had learned over the last four years, to deal with maternalism. No longer was he bowing and scraping before a know-it-all who happened to be White and female and in control of cultural capital—or real capital—that he needed. He seemed to have realized after the debacle of the Mason patronage scheme that he was as needed for these transracial interventions to succeed as the woman at the apex of maternalistic structures of patronage. His ideas were more correct, more deeply rooted in the psychology of liberation than theirs. And he was not going to keep quiet about them in front of other people as he had done so often in Mason's shadow. Finally, Locke had heard the famous admonition in 2 Corinthians of the King James Bible: "come out from among them, and be separate!"[35]

In his remarks to Brady about what happens to Negro artists who create Negro art, Locke revealed that a process of "purification" to remove the self-disgust and self-avoidance that American racism taught Negro artists when they looked at the Negro face and form had to be undertaken for the Negro artist to create great art. Bement confirmed that such had occurred over the course of the Harmon Foundation exhibitions. That disgust blocked artists' ability to be profoundly creative in whatever work they did as an artist. A catharsis, Locke argued, must start within, because much of the weakness of the work produced by Negro artists derived from failure to come to terms with themselves.[36] In the terminology that the art historian Kenneth Clark uses, it is to return to the Negro the capacity to look at himself or herself as a nude, as the ideal of human form, and not just the naked.

But Locke goes one step beyond Clark: through New Negro art, the image undergoes a transition not merely from the naked to the nude, but from an object alienated from its creator to a mirror of the artist's community. In that process, the elements of the entire culture are recombined, reconfigured, and made into something wholly new that can—if allowed—transform society. That's what Brady was instinctively afraid of—that a Negro art would destabilize the implicit hierarchy, or dethrone the "Caucasian ideals" inherent in the notion of beauty in the West. In Brady's racial imaginary, that would lead to "black nationalism." In Locke's imaginary, it would lead to a world of "beauty that included our racial own." Unconsciously, even while working for Negro artists, Brady maintained a sense that White artists create art that is beautiful and that Black artists need to rise to that standard, instead of a sense that the entire system in which White artists themselves operate needed to be changed to birth a world of beauty welcoming to all. In the end, art had to be a path to truth, a transforming truth of the person creating it, if art was going to do what was most necessary for humanity and especially the Negro: provide a path to subjectivity and a voice in a silencing world. Ultimately, the grander role of the Negro artist was to foment a process of radical liberation from the discourses of White supremacy in the wider population itself. That was his or her raison d'être.

What Locke aimed at came together better the day the Harmon Exhibition of Contemporary Negro Art officially opened in February 1933, when a moment of celebration was captured in a film made by the Harmon people. The moment occurred when Locke was reunited with Barthé in front of one of Barthé's sculptures. In the film, Locke and Barthé pose before a life-size plaster torso painted black.[37] The two men appear, smiling, shaking hands in front of the torso, a sculpture that went largely unnoticed by the judges and did not win a prize. Yet the posing, smiling gentlemen signal its specialness and its secret. Its specialness comes from the fact that it is one of a pair of sculptures: one, the ideal of a white torso, chunkier, stockier, more muscular; and, the second, the one in the Harmon show, the ideal Black physique, leaner, slenderer, svelte, and of course, Black. For Barthé and Locke, this torso represented an ideal toward which the Negro body tended, especially those young bodies they had known intimately themselves. Barthé's torso was a conversation about the multiple discourses of the beautiful that coursed through the ideal he had loved— the classical tradition of the Greek and Roman body—as well as the lessons of African sculpture, with the slightly elongated torso embodying African principles of design. Rather than an Afrocentric creation, Barthé's torso was a hybridic triumph, interweaving classical, ancient African, Italian Renaissance (Michelangelo), and modernist sculptural traditions and sexual insights into a thoroughly African American ideal. Moreover, his was not a decadent image, but a sculpture that visualized a new Black masculinity. That self-acceptance was part of a process not only of rebellion against the notion of self-disgust that the European had inserted into the African's mind, as Bunche narrated in his dissertation, but also a process of racial and sexual de-coloniality in the African American's mind.

The sculpture's secret was that under the cover of a Negro art Barthé had created an icon of Black homosexual desire, a sculpture whose beauty came also from the way that the body curled and shifted from the hips upward into a stance that was both Black and gay. Here was a love of the Black body rendered in plaster as a carnal ideal Locke and Barthé both recognized and celebrated. Through the nude, they had smuggled the naked into the Harmon Exhibition. Here, under the cover of Blackness, was another "return of the repressed," though unseen or unrecognized by most of the bourgeois Black and White visitors at the reception. And this Black body was exhibited under the auspices of a Harmon Foundation whose founder, William E. Harmon, had written his checks for the awards and prizes for, as he put it, "good darkies." Here, two "good darkies" stood in front of this body, rendered Black and beautiful and desirable for those who knew what they were looking at.

The sculpture was a triumph too for Barthé since five years earlier a similarly full-figured naked Negro had been rejected for an outdoor sculpture in Philadelphia. In the climate of the 1930s, with the head and legs removed, with the allusions to classicism strengthened, and yet with the homoerotic pose as prominent in the sculpture as ever, Barthé had created a sculpture that represented both Locke's Black and homosexual selves.

Locke had "midwifed" a Black visual arts that made visible his sexual orientation in ways that he never achieved in Black literature. That such nakedness could be expressed may have been in some small degree because Locke was working with Mary Beattie Brady, who herself may have been a lesbian. As the maternal mother, she was more like his mother in allowing him the freedom to express his sexuality, and he was able to do that, in a hidden, closeted, subterranean way, through Negro visual arts. In some ways, the Black visual artists were more successful in creating art that was about their fundamental concern. There was still the contradiction that Locke wanted them to be upfront and explicit about their race, but not their sexual orientation. But the form—the visual—was about revealing, and as revelation of the body, it engaged—at least here, the naked, Black sexuality. That also brings out why Locke was always insisting so much that Black artists had to reveal their race: it was a metaphor, a code, for their sex. He wanted to come out, but couldn't; so, if not sexually, he at least wanted them to come out as Negro. But art was like a mask behind which the institutions of art always wanted Black—and homosexual—artists to hide, who they really were, people defined as not human in the canon of Western art. Locke had turned his mask into a nude.

Male Torso by Richmond Barthé. Photograph by Gregory R. Staley. The Howard University Gallery of Art, Permanent Collection, Washington, D.C. Gift of Alain Locke.

Sculpture of Alain Locke by Richmond Barthé. Courtesy of the Moorland-Spingarn Research Center, Howard University.

34

The Saving Grace of Realism

When Locke stepped out of the Art Center after the reception for the 1933 Harmon Foundation exhibit that February, he reentered New York dominated by the Great Depression and the real suffering it was producing. While the election of Franklin Delano Roosevelt the previous November had buoyed America's hope that the Depression would soon be over, the nation had suffered through one of the cruelest winters leading up to the presidential swearing-in in March. All around him as he bounded from art exhibition to subway and Pennsylvania Station were signs of how far the city had fallen from the euphoria of a Renaissance he had predicted just eight years ago. Artists had been turned into beggars, veterans into apple sellers, and romantic versifiers into propaganda poets as the smell of death. Black-owned businesses in Harlem were suddenly, almost inexplicably bankrupt.

The art exhibit had been a success in two ways. Locke had succeeded in finding a Negro artist in Richmond Barthé who was comfortable with his homosexuality and adept at expressing it sinuously in sculpture. Barthé also had no difficulty seeing himself as a Negro artist, expressing himself in African-influenced forms, and yet keeping his eye on the goal of all artists to try and create eternal works of art. Locke had also found a new maternal patron in Mary Beattie Brady who, while overbearing and opinionated, allowed him to say what he wanted, without the pathological need to control and censor him in ways Mrs. Mason could not resist. But Brady was also not handing over any money or power to Locke, either. As successful as the exhibition had been, it did not lead anywhere, being the last that the Harmon Foundation would do in which he would play a dominant role. As the cold wind of the worst winter of the Great Depression hit his face, Locke still lacked access to the kind of leverage to foment broad-based cultural production in the early 1930s. So, alone now in a way he had not been in the recent past, Locke focused his attention on polishing his chops at the one thing he could do on his own: be a critic. That, in fact, was the saving grace of being on his own.

Locke still commanded a forum in the world of educated Black readers due to his popular annual retrospective reviews of Negro literature. Those retrospective reviews became the place where he recorded the change in Negro intellectual life and revised his social philosophy self-consciously in light of that change. Wedded publicly to the concept of race as the central metaphor of the Negro experience in America, Locke acknowledged the paradigm shift that had occurred, as a younger generation of writers and scholars matured in the early 1930s, studied at White elite universities, and now argued that class was more important to explaining the Negro's current desperate plight. This youthful energy was sparking a largely invisible "renaissance" of what he would later call the "Newest Negro" that was bubbling up even in the field of creative literature. As his retrospective reviews increasingly revealed, a plethora of little magazines, theater groups, and art "collectives" had been inspired by the brash intellectual energy that Marxism, with its method of dialectical materialism and its seemingly prophetic prediction of the collapse of capitalism, injected into the New York literary and art communities.

No one knew better than Locke that it was not the script that he had written. Although Locke was not the target of those younger thinkers who began to rail against Negro leadership for having "misled" the Negro in the past, it was a sign of his lack of significance that when the "Young Turks"—E. Franklin Frazier, Abram Harris, and Ralph Bunche—had met in January with the heads of the NAACP in Amenia, New York, and attacked Du Bois, James Weldon Johnson, and others for not embracing a class analysis of the Negro plight, Bunche had not even invited Locke to come along. Indeed, Locke was not even mentioned. This was what always happened in Locke's infatuations with young radicals— they drew upon his insight and support in private but dismissed him in public when around their younger radical friends. He was not even toxic in the social science division at Howard; it was worse—he was seen as irrelevant. Feeling the sting of being ignored, Locke used his retrospective reviews to insert himself into the discussion given that others were not going to do so. The very definition of a retrospective review became a tool for Locke to revise his own cultural philosophy in public and give his audience a consistent education in why looking backward was essential to moving forward.[1]

That December 1933, Locke would use the review, "The Saving Grace of Realism," to interpret the political sea change from Black liberalism to Black Marxism as a literary odyssey from Negro romanticism to realism.

> We can trust and encourage a literary philosophy that can sustain the devoted art of a Julia Peterkin, that can evoke from the liberal white South a book like The Tragedy of Lynching, that can transform gradually the superficial, caricaturist interest of the early Roark Bradford into the penetrating, carefully studied realism of his latest novel....And to the extent that James Weldon Johnson's autobiography represents a new and effective step in Negro biography, it can be attributed to the

sober, realistic restraint that dominates it in striking contrast to the flamboyant egotism and sentimentality of much of our previous biographical writing. So we must look to enlightened realism as the present hope of Negro art and literature, not merely because it is desirable for our art to be in step with the prevailing mode and trend of the art and literature of its time—important though that may be—but because both practical and aesthetic interests dictate truth as the basic desideratum in the portrayal of the Negro—and truth is the saving grace of realism.[2]

What was the *truth* of Locke's situation—the saving grace of a realist view of himself as a Black intellectual in 1933, the fourth year of a Great Depression that showed no signs of ending its assault on Black writers, artists, and thinkers, his natural constituency?

A realistic *self*-assessment would encompass that Locke's years, roughly from 1927 to 1932, spent embosomed in the maternalism of Mrs. Mason's patronage, had hurt him by alienating him from the forces of economic and social change that affected the masses of Black people in the Depression. Of course, the key factor in his remaining solvent was that he had a job—a professorship, no less, at Howard University. But the patronage scheme had given him extra money at a time most Black people lacked even the confidence of continued essential earnings, but even more—by running the patronage organization with Hughes, Hurston, and half a dozen other Black artists receiving coin from Mrs. Mason, Locke had been removed from the rest of the Black community's struggling to make it without such patronage. He had also been isolated by her maternalism, her domination of his psyche, her constant instructions to avoid other Negroes so that now, in 1933, he was alienated from other Negroes who might have been helpful to him. She was also more feeble by 1933, moving into a hospital to live, where she would stay for the next dozen years. Still writing her weekly, the volume and intensity of Locke's correspondence declined, but also her voice declined in his brain; and with it came a new freedom, but also abandonment, a lack of direction, a lack of surety. But the most important consequence of all that listening to her was a lack of listening to the lumpenproletariat of Black people in the first years of the Great Depression. What Mrs. Mason had never realized is that the urban African Americans who had transitioned through the Great Migration to the North were the greatest source of Black intelligence in America, and her maternalism had driven him away from that.

Now, in 1933, something new was on the scene. A new generation of young White writers was taking up pen and writing stories, novels, essays, and books on the Black reality in America. If Locke was going to survive the Black Literary Depression, he realized he was going to have to use his alienation as a plus, an openness, to what other Black critics were not considering—the writing on the

Negro done increasingly and sometimes more effectively by Whites. His saving grace was that he could write about Erskine Caldwell instead of Claude McKay and Jessie Fauset.

As the volume of Black poetry, novels, and nonfiction books plummeted in the Depression, Locke shifted to reviewing more White books of "Negro litera-ture" to establish his authority as their critic too. Of course, such spade work meant praising even modest efforts by White writers to transcend the blatantly racist literary characterization of the Negro in the past. Locke's own survival as a critic was dependent on separating himself from his past allegiances and form-ing new ones based on the race and class politics of the 1930s. Ever the "realist," he pivoted without a blink of an eye. But the pivot was not always as easy for Locke because now Whites felt they were authorities on the Black issue and were willing to assert that authority when it came to vetting Black writers who had had the field to themselves for years. While Locke might inhabit the position of the gatekeeper in his retrospective reviews of Negro creative literature, he was a supplicant to that power structure when, as a writer, he had to submit books for review and critique by others inside American publishing.

The same February in which he successfully challenged Brady's attempt to define Negro visual art he was fencing with the American Library Association about what qualified as acceptable Negro history. This gig—another one of Locke's assets as a minted "Negro authority"—was for him to write a pamphlet and recommend a course of readings on the Negro question for distribution throughout the nation's libraries. The project, "Reading with a Purpose," was designed to encourage the use of libraries for systematic self-motivated educa-tion, part of a wider effort of nonprofit educational or quasi-educational organ-izations in the 1930s to address the crisis in unemployment by making forms of adult education free and widely available. Locke contracted to write this pam-phlet on the American Negro to give it his own particular intellectual stamp. "I knew the thing would be done by some cowardly racialist if I didn't do it," he wrote Godmother. "It is put as straight from the shoulder as writing for such an organization will permit—remember it had to go South, North and West and to fit the white and the Negro reader."[3] By doing so, he would make a little money, but also extend his influence by utilizing the institutional reach and apparatus of the American library system.

The achievement did not come without a struggle. After submitting his man-uscript and book recommendations, Locke had to wait several weeks while the editor pored over his text and sent it out to anonymous critics who, in turn, tried to second-guess Locke's recommendations, especially in the field of his-tory. As his editor wrote, "Everyone agrees in admiring the manuscript but there is some difference in opinion about the selections of books. Of course I am aware of the fact that the titles you selected, or nearly all of them, were on the list we sent to you of books recommended by reader's advisement of the librarians. In spite of that fact the critics of your manuscript, who are better informed in this particular field, have offered criticisms which I think should be brought to your attention and I hope you will change one or two of the books at least." In particular, "Carter Woodson's book has been questioned by several. The critics say that it is written with a bias that makes it inadvisable to recommend. Would you be willing to substitute Brawley's Short History of the American Negro, which seems generally acceptable? Our sociologist calls it the best thing available." In addition, the critics wanted to substitute Countee Cullen's *Caroling Dusk* for V. F. Calverton's *Anthology of American Negro Literature*. They cited the "many purple pages" in Mary White Ovington's *Portraits in Color* and argued that something other than the special issue of the *Annals of the American Academy* devoted to the study of the Negro should be recommended because of the difficulty of the libraries stocking this rather specialized item.[4]

By 1933, cultural organizations like the ALA were determined to police the version of Black knowledge they would disseminate to the American public. The ALA had "our sociologist" who felt authoritative enough to declare that Brawley's *Short History* was better than Woodson's and confident enough of that authority to tell Locke, an eminent Black scholar, what to put on a reading list for largely Black readers. White academics were now in the game of Black Studies in a way that had not been the case in 1925, and they were reacting against Negro nationalist–based histories like Woodson's that reflected a sharper critique of White power in the history of the Negro. But Woodson enjoyed tremendous popularity in the Black community, by virtue of his Association for the Study of Negro Life and History conferences, teacher workshops, and directed marketing of books to Black readers, even if he was unpopular with White academics who saw the arc of African American studies going in a more socialist and integrationist direction in the 1930s. Such White authorities felt comfortable trying to marginalize Woodson's work as flawed by anti-White "bias," but Locke knew that if he wanted his series to resonate with the Black reading public, he had to have someone with Woodson's Black lumpen cache.

Locke wrote back to the editor: "After wrenches of change of mind, I find myself coming back to my original judgment about these books. The Brawley short history is too simple and orthodox, and I think we must consider that the younger generation today do not want their facts too highly glossed or watered down." Locke was educating the ALA that if it wanted to have any authenticity with the younger generation of Black readers, it would have to promote books that reflected their criticality toward America in the fourth decade of the twentieth century, especially given the Great Depression. Locke respected Woodson's fierce integrity in his histories that pulled no punches about the hypocrisy of American institutions and his promotion of self-determination as a legitimate Black response to living in a segregated America. As Locke explained to Miller, "I have felt I should thread through with a fairly systematic interpretation," because he was "conscious all along of the necessity for putting a rather chaotic house into some sort of intelligible order." That "order" was a Black cultural pluralist paradigm in which Black Studies was more than simply the record of successful assimilation of American "civilization" that Brawley narrated, but also a critique of the American project in light of the treatment of the Negro. Similarly, Locke wanted to keep the *Annals* collection with his own essay, "The Negro's Contribution to American Art and Literature," as well as *The New Negro*, to force recognition that Negroes possessed a unique culture and a unique history of resistance against complete acquiescence to White cultural supremacy.[5]

While a minor skirmish in Locke's biography, the tussle with ALA is important for two reasons. One, it exemplified Locke's new mood—willingness to stand up to White authority and risk losing a gig because of a philosophic principle of self-agency as a Black thinker who knew his mind and resources, and had been strengthened in standing up for himself by his work with Mrs. Mason. Despite all the abuse he took from her, something of her fierce strength had been migrated into his subjectivity, so that he was not going weak at the knees when confronted with White authority that had a bit of power behind it. But the second point is as important: Locke had picked up the new militant mood among unemployed, heartbroken Negro men and women, who had nowhere to turn for knowledge that explained their condition, something that had fallen back into the dungeon of pessimism about the future that the Negro Renaissance had temporarily interrupted. He had to find a way to connect with and hopefully rescue from total despair the mind of the still-thinking Negro who worked ten-hour days for a dollar and read books to keep his or her mind alive. He had to find a way to produce something in the 1930s that would resonate with all aspects of the thinking Black reading public like *The New Negro* had done in the mid-1920s. Having recommended *The New Negro* to be part of the Reading with a Purpose series, his publisher assured him that it would keep the book in print—perhaps longer than it would have done so otherwise, for an eight-year-old book selling for $5.00 in the depths of the Depression.

The larger literary problem for Locke—and the Negro Renaissance—was that the books from the 1920s and even those being published in 1933 were not destined to become the classics of American or even African American Studies. While McKay and certainly Fauset might see Locke's critical reviews of their books as an act of betrayal, the truth was that both *Banana Bottom* and *Comedy, American Style* reflected a moment that, politically at least, had passed with the Great Depression. Their themes, especially intra-racial conflicts around class, peasant versus bourgeois origins, color and Victorian ideology, did not command White attention by 1933. They enjoyed no vogue in the 1930s the way *Home to Harlem* and *There Is Confusion* had in the 1920s. As Locke was beginning to note in his retrospective reviews, the paradigmatic form of the 1930s was not poetry or fiction, but the documentary exposé.

Fauset was at the end of her creative writing life, a victim of the masculinist bias of the Harlem Renaissance. Just as important, she was imprisoned by the middle-class Black imagination that, so far, had failed to create a great work of literature. The Black middle class was so hemmed in by segregation that it produced fiction or poetry mainly about its marginality as a class. Fauset's cruel charge in her letter to Locke that he was a critic because he was a failure as a creative writer contained more than a crumb of truth. Both of them had been prepared by a middle class that was not a true middle class, not an owner of the means of the production, at least in Philadelphia and Washington, and thus were sons and daughters of a class that lacked the boldness to produce transformative writers.

Unlike Fauset, Locke was neither a creative writer, nor about to stop writing critical essays when Fauset stopped writing novels. But he was unable to move beyond writing the essay form, because he rarely slowed down enough to invest his intellect in a single, larger project. There also was the sexual problem: he was always running off to Europe each summer, hoping that it would produce a novel or substantial work, but it never did. He looked to Mason to give him the approval to avoid serious work. "I was much touched to hear that you thought I ought to go on with my usual vacation trip and the treatment" in Europe, he wrote to Godmother in May. He confessed that he remembered her earlier critique that by going to Europe he foreclosed the one opportunity he had all year to sit still and write something enduring. "I would really like to stay home and write, if conditions could ever be found for a decently healthful and relaxing atmosphere. I wonder if people ever stop to think what impossible conditions America imposes on Negroes who want to live and express themselves finely and creatively!" Once again, he voiced the bourgeois narrative of racial limits. "Of course, you have always known, and have in so many cases tried to help take the pressure off a few," although never to the extent of inviting Colored godchildren to spend the summer with her in Maine. That was now out of the question, as Mason's health had plummeted, she had been hospitalized, and Cornelia Chapin, one of her nieces, had taken over the reading of Locke's letters. While he made plans to sail on the *Bremen* on June 17, 1933, he returned to his familiar reportage with Mason, keeping her abreast of the latest accomplishments—and failures—of the New Negroes. "Aaron Douglas opened an exhibit today at the Cay-Delbos gallery. He has about twenty canvases, mostly still life vividly and strongly painted. There is no doubt of a maturing of his ability to say things on canvas." But Locke could not restrain his canonical view that the only true vocation for the Negro artist was to render Negroes. "As I told him, it seems that he has increased his power to say things but has forgotten the things he started out to say. The Negro things are weak and are echoes of his earlier work—not even as promising as those things were." That appeared to be a judgment Locke could have rendered on much of the artistic production of New Negroes in the 1930s.[6]

"I shall try to be a real Negro and improvise," he wrote to Mason in a bon voyage letter. "In fact, though suffering, that is just what is keeping Negroes alive these days—they have the art of day to day living—and while it has been a handicap in times past—today it is an advantage."[7] As usual, he kept up the barrage of bile against Hughes. "I have met one Ernestine Evans on the ship—a radical publisher's agent who knows Langston. She says he is returning to the States via Siberia and China—and that his book on the Russian treatment of minorities is coming out soon." That reminded Locke that in a "premature and unguarded talk I had years ago (you remember) with L. about our going to Russia" that he, Locke, had mentioned the idea of a book on the Soviet treatment of minorities. That resentment was temporarily relieved when Locke was noticed by a reporter on board the ship and asked for an interview, in which he said "among other things" that he was going abroad to "look into the question of the European treatment of minorities (especially in Germany)—as there was a deep connection between these world questions and our Negro problem."[8]

In fact, Locke was not undertaking a study of minorities in Europe, but attempting, finally, to get down to work on a long-delayed biography of Frederick Douglass, a project that Mason may have suggested. He had many notes from Douglass's papers with him in Europe, where he began to "dig in" and "digest it by elimination"—a curious anal metaphor. Before exposure to Mason's philosophy, he confided, he would have tried to write a biography of the entire life; but now, he realized that to write something that really lived required pruning away the dross. "I see now that I must simplify and clarify what I have before me, and if I should succeed, his life story will live again—and be influential in this and the next generation." What attracted him, and perhaps Mason, to Douglass was his "manliness," for as Locke observed, "we need manly Negroes above all else." Yet, Locke had seemed to view Douglass through a narrow notion of what his manly rebellion against racial convention consisted of. "I have been on the lookout for defects—but I find at least little egotism and no false pride in his earlier work. After emancipation, vanity and egotism do come in stronger, and I take it, that led to his second marriage and his loss of power." In a surprising way, Locke saw Douglass through a Black Nationalist lens uninformed by his own struggles with the problem of finding love within his own racial group. Mason may have been responsible for that tack. It was problematical, not only for understanding Douglass but also for fitting his thought with the intellectual tenor of the 1930s. Racial essentialism was increasingly out of step with the times, which tended toward interracialism, not only in the daily practice of Leftist organizations but also in the theory of social advancement being advanced by Marxists.

Being abroad did allow Locke to observe the spread of Nazism in Germany and Austria, and theorize about one of his favorite subjects, Europeans who shared Negro attributes. "You know, Godmother, Austrians are somewhat like Negroes—in their artistic fineness and nonchalance" and, in particular, for

Locke's way of thinking, the similarity to Negroes in that Austrians "have to endure so much at the hands of more practical cruder people. Just now, they are having a terrible time fighting off German propaganda to turn Austria Nazi—which of course means annexation." What Locke could not avoid seeing was the way in which Hitler had transformed Austria and the Germany he had come to know and love. "Almost every other day a border guard is shot from ambush—and with printed propaganda forbidden, the Germans are crowding the air with propaganda radio often on Austrian wave lengths that spoil their concert programs. Isn't that the height of devilry—I should say the depth?" The Austrians and the liberal-minded Germans became the minorities Locke was studying in Europe. He began to keep notebooks written in coded English to mail home to himself from Germany to keep them from being seized. From Berlin he exclaimed: "But what a world—you cannot wink an eyelid today or something startling has stolen up on you. The mad drama is going at such a reeling pace." Then, "what they say about Germany is all too true. They have loosed a hoodlum element and cannot leash it again—all sorts of violence are being perpetrated in Germany now—and the concentration camps of political enemies are unspeakable in their brutality. But what nation has clean enough hands to stop them and call a halt! Roosevelt should dare, and would, I think, if he hadn't already his hands full with the domestic situation. But Hitler has already twice reminded the United States, a propos of protests over the Jewish pogroms, about the United States treatment and lynching of Negroes."[9] Here, Locke voiced an idea that would later flower into his editing another issue of the *Survey Graphic* in 1942, "Color: The Unfinished Business of Democracy," in which he would revisit the notion that America's moral authority vis-á-vis Germany was crippled because of the propaganda weakness of America's own treatment of its minorities.

As Locke prepared to return to the United States, he waxed philosophic about the way in which the aristocracy in Austria and Germany had enabled the rise of Hitler. "Several people think that the monarchists and Junkers were using Hitler to offset the rising tide of socialism and communism, counting on keeping the power in their own hands behind the throne, but that the movement got out of their hands and the Hilarities by a coup took the reins themselves. They now secretly wish something would happen to unseat Hitler, but must carry through their gestures of support and approval."[10] Yet, remarkably, he wished to remain in Vienna. "Really I wish I had a quiet year here in which to write and think—rather than what faces me in a fortnight or so—the return to Hades. And yet in these uncertain times one perhaps ought to be thankful for bed and board in Hades." In that last line, "realism" was beginning to intrude on Locke's romantic attachment to Austria and things German. Even he realized that as bad as Howard University and Washington, D.C., were for his Eurocentric aesthetic self, the fantasy of a Black Austrian life of the mind was being interrupted—along with the radio broadcasts of Viennese concerts—by violence and terror.

Back home in October, he was once again disappointed with the quality of Black cultural productions. "I do want to see the Paul Robeson film of Emperor Jones," he confided to a bedridden Mason, for whom going to a movie theater with Locke was now out of the question. "A few discriminating critics call attention to his poor acting while praising his magnificent singing.... If successful they say Porgy will be filmed—and there with Rose McClendon we have a real actress, and one who deserves a chance. Her art should be captured for posterity—and the inspiration of another generation of Negro actors." Unfortunately, Locke was thoroughly disappointed by the Emperor Jones film. "How the critics can rave over it as they have is hard to understand—the photography is poor—and the acting not only overdone—but done almost completely from the outside. Gilpin played the character from the inside—with sincerity and genuine force. Paul barnstorms and poses—to me it is a very poor piece of work. This is all too bad—and is part of the times, I suppose." By contrast, Locke continued to praise women actors and singers who seemed to honor the aesthetic values of deliberative creativity. "Abbie Mitchell gave a recital to a packed house in the Howard University chapel. She was grand—she makes up in maturity and understanding for the loss of the early bloom in her voice—and whenever anything deeply dramatic or tragic is called for she registers as few American artists can. She sometimes recalls Schumann-Heink—however it is best to say she is herself—since she has a unique range and is true soprano in her upper register. I mention this because the prejudiced local newspaper gave her two-thirds of a column write-up and compared her with Schumann-Heink."[11]

Locke contrasted the way her performance honored the classical values of Black expression to the crass way in which the art of Black history was being promoted in America. Here his ambivalence toward Carter G. Woodson surfaced, but also his recognition that as a speaker he still struggled to connect with a mass Black public audience. Invited to give a lecture on African art for Woodson's ASNLH, Locke lamented the commercial way in which Black history and culture was sold. He was overwhelmed by a slew of meetings, handshaking, and meaningless talk. Of course, he liked his own talk on African art and thought it much better than the first one he had read to her in 1927 when they met. "And if I had dared put you in a front seat in my imagination, it would have been still better. But I could not after one glance at the audience—there was just too much dead wood there." Lacking the ability to set his audience on fire about African art, Locke fell back into a familiar tirade—blaming the Black rank and file for its lack of inspiration.[12]

More hopeful to Locke was the political news. "All we hear of the administration's policy toward both the Negro and the Indian is more favorable than any administration since Theodore Roosevelt's."[13] Later he went to hear President Roosevelt's address to the Twenty-fifth Anniversary meeting of the Federal Council of Churches and remarked on how inspiring it was. "His speech was as simply and beautifully phrased as one of Lincoln's, and his voice rang clear" without the occasional "false demagogic tone [that] has crept into his voice if I have detected aright from close listening to him on the radio." While inspired by Roosevelt's "3 sentences on lynching—but what a clear and strong stand"— Locke worried that "if Roosevelt fails—where shall we be—and most of what he is trying to save doesn't deserve to be saved."[14] Even more inspiring politically was the activities against segregation that Negroes themselves were launching in his own town.

> I got back to find that the younger element in Washington had organ- ized a New Negro Alliance and were beginning a real common-sense campaign for Negro self-help and employment. They have so far forced the A and P Grocery stores and a chain of drug stores to employ about a dozen Negro clerks after a house to house canvas of neighborhoods in the Negro section persuading people not to trade with these stores unless they did so. There is a new spirit stirring in the ranks—it is only our leadership that is bad and selfish. I was very impressed and touched by their selection of the New Negro slogan—Saturday I went to one of their meetings—and remained in the back row even though they in- sisted on a speech. I shall work with them quietly and with pride in their initiative and courage.[15]

Naming the New Negro Alliance after *The New Negro* was more than a compli- ment: it signaled that the awakening of criticality of the New Negro in the mid- 1920s had, in fact, blossomed into class and racial activism in the 1930s. *The New Negro: An Interpretation* had had a broader impact than Locke imagined, as Doxey Wilkerson, the young communist educator attested. "That book opened my eyes to that there were Negroes who were artists, who were poets, writers, who were somebody."[16] That "somebodyness" meant Negroes were subjects who were activists because they realized they too were citizens with power to reshape American life. The New Negro Alliance was a step forward in the argument that the Negro possessed a cultural citizenship that demanded change. John Davis, the young organizer of the movement, realized that the Negro as consumer was a powerful force and that the boycott was an effective weapon against racist seg- regationist policies of commercial establishments in Washington. This activist extension of Locke's idea of a New Negro was a compelling affirmation of the ability of the spirit of the New Negro to reinvent itself beyond aesthetics.

Yet that affirmation of his nomenclature did not move Locke to invest time and energy in the group. Shortly afterward, he was on the road again, closing out the year with a lecture trip "into the heart of the South—Atlanta. I hadn't seen for some six years," he confessed to Mason, "so I accepted the invitation.... It was so good to see the South—stricken as it is, and bristling with new possibilities of conflict between the races (over competition for jobs)—it was nevertheless a sense of belonging which came over me."[17] Here was something of a break-through for Locke, a man who had never before felt a sense of belonging in the South, around rank-and-file Black people. That did not mean that he really felt that he was one with them, although he tried.

> [This is] due, of course, to my new sense of being truly Negro and part of the real folk. How fine they are even in their depravity and almost hopeless backwardness—for after all they all have a genuine joy in living and a direct simplicity and sincerity. If only that could be kept along with education—and maybe that will in time be possible. Certainly there will have to be different leadership in the schools and colleges— but already they are shaking free of the missionary influences. The young students speak and act more naturally—and simply despise those of their teachers who are hypocrites.[18]

His condescension did not obliterate his sense that the New Negro was alive and growing. For "wherever there is a sincere intelligent young teacher[,] he has a group of bright youngsters around him—who protect his radicalism in most in-stances." He went on to document the emergence of these New Negro teachers: "For example—at Petersburg, Virginia when I spoke December 10th, about three such teachers quietly gathered some twenty-odd students in a fraternity room in the basement of the men's dormitory—and we talked back and forth for over three hours." Locke was being shown into a kind of "underground" where the students and younger faculty spoke "direct, frank—not over-optimistic, and their greatest hatred was for the hand-picked Negro leader who betrays those whom he is supposed to lead. That means much, I think, for the future." In par-ticular, it was "a welcome surprise" to find the same New Negro Alliance "spirit in the far South."[19]

Locke's challenge was clear: how was he going to connect with this New Negro Alliance spirit among the New Negro of the 1930s? Clearly, protest, the one ele-ment of the original New Negro conception he had exorcised from his anthology was back with power in the 1930s. It was #blacklivesmatter energy bubbling up from the youth of the 1930s to seize control of their lives no matter what the costs—and in some cases in the South that cost would be death. There was cour-age in the protests against the Scottsboro Boys in 1931 that had blossomed into an international movement for their freedom by 1933. But Locke had left him-self out of that, had been out of the Left as a whole. It was time to find a way back in to the source of Black intellectual fervent in America or die as a relevant Black intellectual, looking backward for Hughes, Hurston, and Mrs. Mason's advising.

That was the saving grace of realism Locke needed as he stumbled into 1934.

35

Bronze Booklets, Gold Art

Early in the 1930s, when Locke happened to be in Washington, D.C., on Saturday nights, sometimes he would stop in at his friend Ralph Bunche's house. As the historian Harold Lewis recalled many years later, a small group of young Black social scientists "tended to focus around Ralph Bunche" at Howard University, "not only because he was an attractive (that's not really the word) personality, but also because he was one of the few faculty members who lived on campus in one of the two houses that are long gone." Lewis recalled that "we used to gather there every Saturday night and I recall that Locke was rarely a visitor to the group, but Ralph Bunche, Abe Harris, the economist...several of the younger people, and [E. Franklin] when he came from Fisk was accepted as a member. It had such a different perspective on this whole matter of social change...we thought the future of mankind was tied up with some sort of Popular Front and it wasn't racial."[1]

Bunche *was* an "attractive personality," and a highly attractive man. What Lewis and others at those meetings did not know was how close Bunche and Locke were, even though Locke was "rarely" a participant in Bunche's Saturday night meetings. But that Locke dropped by at all suggested Locke realized what was brewing at Bunche's house on Saturdays—a new renaissance of thinking, this time launched by some of the finest young African American social scientists of the 1930s, whose discussions of political theory, sociological controversies, cultural politics, and the prospects for a global revolution were laying the groundwork of a 1930s awakening that would rival in a different way the one Locke had chronicled in the 1920s. After all, the New Negro literary awakening had been launched in fact in Washington, D.C., by Georgia Douglas Johnson, whose Saturday Nighters had featured Jean Toomer. Now, in the 1930s, another generation of radical-thinking young men, albeit educated in elite White universities, and immersed in Marxian economic and modern sociological theories, were convinced their thinking would lead to the liberation of Black people in ways older race theories could not. While other radical intellectuals were meeting and discussing these issues in the early 1930s, what distinguished these men, of course, was that they were African American, forced to teach at Howard University though possessing Ivy League PhDs, and convinced that the Black experience was at the center of capitalist exploitation in America. In particular, they believed that African Americans needed to eschew Black nationalism and race-only theorizing because such nationalist sentiments made it more difficult for the Black masses to do what was absolutely necessary in the historical moment: join with White workers in such progressive labor organizations as the Committee on Industrial Opportunity and challenge capitalism in a Popular Front.

Of course, economic determinism was not Locke's philosophy of social change, and he bruised easily in the rough-and-tumble tussling conversations that erupted on Bunche's Saturday night evenings—debates really between highly educated, self-confident, even arrogant young Black intellectuals who felt the future of the race depended on advancing the correct line on social change during the Depression. Abram Harris, the young economist, who would eventually be the first to leave Howard for the University of Chicago, was particularly critical of Locke and Du Bois, as well as others, for emphasizing race over class in their analyses of Negro progress. E. Franklin Frazier, the sociologist, regarded Locke as something of a dilettante since Frazier seemed to turn out a massive new tome on the Negro Family every couple of years, while Locke produced mainly magazine articles that did not even appear, generally, in scholarly journals.[2] Harris also recalled that Locke was a furtive, almost invisible figure around Howard in 1934, when the group around Bunche really started to articulate what would become a Black Radical critique of capitalism with the Black masses at the center of it. Most of them dismissed him as a real social thinker, having never been exposed to his Race Contacts lectures. But Harris noted they sensed that Locke had been a radical much earlier at Howard, but that he had been "burnt" by the experience.[3] They did not know he had been fired, but knew that he was protective, aloof, and, most often, alone.

Part of Locke's problem was that solitude did not really work for him creatively. His best writing was always done when husbanded by the creativity of young men around him. How could he reproduce that kind of collaboration of the 1920s in the current historical moment? He did not agree enough with the intellectual community around Bunche, and he seemed not to be able to generate a new one around himself. How could he tap the intellectual energy of this new scholarly Black community around Bunche without having to join in with their largely heterosexist, Black masculinist Marxian culture generating up out of their scholarly activism on Howard's campus?[4]

Where could Locke turn for a community to fire his muse, now that the old ones had turned against him or abandoned him in insanity? Early in 1933, Morse Cartwright, the director of the American Association for Adult Education, asked Locke to evaluate two "experimental" efforts in Negro adult education at the Harlem "Schomburg" library and Atlanta's Negro library. These efforts were administered by the AAAE and funded by the Carnegie Corporation. Locke had been in the hunt to secure funding for his projects from the Carnegie Corporation since 1928 when he contacted them about an African Studies Department at Howard University. He renewed his efforts in 1931 when seeking life support for the dying Harlem Museum of African Art. After Frederick Keppel, the Carnegie Corporation head, rejected that request, Locke realized that he would have to develop proposals that fit already-existing program initiatives of the Corporation. Corporate funding required outside evaluation, unlike his Mason projects. Locke acceded to a request from Cartwright to evaluate the Harlem and Atlanta projects, because he needed a nonprofit, nationally based, and professionally managed organization like the American Association for Adult Education to sanction his work for the corporate funder if he was ever to access Carnegie funds.

Locke entered AAAE as an evaluator but eventually transformed himself into a subcontractor of a program the AAAE sanctioned and the Carnegie Corporation funded. By gaining this institutional support, Locke showed his growing institutional competency in negotiating the sea change from personal to corporate patronage of the arts and education in mid-twentieth-century America. He was no stranger to adult education even if one considered it unusual, at first glance, that one of the most highly educated Black men in the nation would invest years of effort in a program to bring simplified knowledge to adult learners seemed a stretch. Adult education had roots in his own family history back in the nineteenth century when his grandfather and father, like other Black Victorians, had educated ex-slaves and their descendants through literary, historical, and church-based self-help associations as well as schools. As early as 1927, Locke had been attending local Negro adult-education meetings, learning the cast of characters who ran such initiatives in Harlem and Atlanta, and engaging them in discussions about what should be the nature of adult education for the Negro. When Morse Cartwright, the head of the AAAE, whom Locke had been courting for years, asked Locke to evaluate these projects for their renewal of their three-year grant from the Carnegie Corporation, Locke had his chance to define himself publicly as an authority on adult education.

Before Locke had completed his report, Cartwright asked him to present his preliminary findings in May 1933 at the American Association of Adult Education's annual convention in Amherst, Massachusetts. Locke used that platform to launch a bold idea. After noting that the Harlem and Atlanta adult-education projects had benefited from being located in libraries—especially the 135th Branch of the New York Public Library in Harlem "by virtue of its unusual equipment of the Schomburg Collection" of Negro history and art materials—Locke judiciously criticized the pervasive segregation of American education, the lack of basic skills of the adults who attended, but also the great hunger for knowledge of Negro history, politics, art, and economics that was voiced by the participants. Locke's "judiciousness" was especially noted. As Cartwright put it: "I should like to add my personal appreciation of the careful, scholarly way in which you described the Harlem Experiment and brought out the important implications which it has not only for Negro adult education, but for the problem of racial development. Mr. Bryson spoke for all of us when, during the panel discussion on Wednesday morning, he commended the philosophic temper and measured restraint of your paper."[5]

Locke's remarks convinced the AAAE leadership that he was a "safe Negro," something Mason had already informed him was one of the prerequisites of White people in power giving him power. He was not someone who would hurt them or embarrass the adult-education movement by throwing up in their faces the obvious—that segregation and racism was a crime against public education. But he also impressed them as the Renaissance man, with broad learning who had little or no political interests, but who only wanted to help those less fortunate and less educated than he. His conversation was sprinkled with references to Plato, John Dewey, Greek culture, classical music, and world literature, and he made them feel confident that in advancing adult education for Negroes he meant to open up the minds of poor Negroes to the worldly knowledge he possessed. Impeccably dressed, holding forth on pedagogy theory as easily as the realities of Negro education in the South, Locke impressed them as embodying the kind of enlightened inquiry they wished for Negro adult education even if it did not exemplify it yet in its programs. Locke had convinced them that he was a disinterested scholar who would steer the Negro adult-education movement away from what they regarded as "propaganda"—analyses that blamed all of the Negro's problems on White people and racism—and toward cultivating a desire for self-education and rewards of the life of the mind available to Negro adult learners albeit in a segregated library system.

Locke utilized this positive regard to make an even bolder suggestion: given the paucity of quality research guides for Negro adult learners, why not have the Carnegie Corporation fund the preparation of materials—easy-to-read syllabi or pamphlets—that answered the substantive questions the Harlem and Atlanta adult learners raised in their discussion sessions? He included that proposal as part of the list of recommendations in his report of how best to continue the "work for Negro centers in Adult Education." The first recommendation, of course, was to continue funding the two projects and perpetuate credible work done already, especially as both projects had excessive race propagandizing and overemphasis on practical knowledge. Second, Locke proposed that the key weakness of these programs—that they lacked adequate study materials for the population targeted—be overcome by allowing him to publish a series of "syllabi" on subjects of interest to the students. Over time, as he was asked to refine this idea in a series of memoranda, the syllabi evolved into "booklets" authored by professionally trained young Black scholars on topics such as Black politics, art, economics, music, literature, drama, and so forth, that had been established as desired areas of learning for these programs.

Perhaps the most challenging recommendation was the third one—to fund a young man or woman "of high scholastic equipment" to be a roving ambassador of adult education, who would visit the projects, consult with the librarians and clients about their needs, and stimulate the local chapters with strategies on how to get Black people to come and grow their minds. This ambassador would help start similar adult-education projects in communities that lacked them. Having such a trained person circulating nationally would counterbalance one of the weaknesses that Locke pointed out about the local adult-education advisory boards and committees, that they were far too often staffed by people with civic goodwill but no scholarly or higher educational training to make the programs anything more than perfunctory. Locke also recommended that Negro adult-education work be connected to some "permanently organized institution in the communities already catering to the cultural and social needs of the Negro group, such as a Negro college or University, branch public library." But the heart of the program from Locke's standpoint was the production of these "syllabi," for even alone they would raise the level of learning in these projects and bring the emerging criticality of modern Black humanities and social science to a lay public.[6]

Locke offered to pull together a group of scholars—here he had in mind the scholars arrayed around Ralph Bunche at those Saturday-night gatherings—to write the series of syllabi or pamphlets and sell these booklets to individuals, libraries, schools, and so on. As usual, with Locke, there was always a double motivation—his self-promotion as the one who would coordinate and benefit from the arrangement and the altruistic impact of distributing knowledge to people who lacked the opportunity to get a college or university education. Rather than provide the bare minimum of reading, arithmetical, and technical knowledge to Blacks in order for them to get a job and accept "their place" in a segregated society, Locke offered to deliver critical knowledge on art, literature, politics, economics, even education itself, in short, inexpensive pamphlets. He would call them the Bronze Booklets.

It might seem odd that Locke, one of the most educated men in the United States, and one of the most difficult professors for students to understand at Howard University, would choose to create an adult-education project to publish easy to understand pamphlets to the Black masses. But in some respects, he had little alternative. The usual avenues of advancement for a professor like Locke were blocked. Racism kept him at Howard University and away from those kind of research universities in his field of philosophy that would have allowed him to develop a complex expression of his views at the highest level of sophistication. His hopes to generate that kind of enlightenment at Howard University were dashed early in 1934 just after he returned from his New Year's break in New

York. One day his door burst open and an extremely agitated Albert Dunham, the junior philosopher in the department, entered, verbally abused Locke, and then abruptly left. As Locke confided to Mrs. Mason, "The next day I barely got off with a sound neck after a struggle in the office" as Dunham chased the much smaller Locke around his desk and into the hallway, where Locke called for help. Mercifully, other professors, secretaries, and students came quickly after hearing the noise and subdued the unhinged Dunham. Locke "arranged to have him committed for observation to Gallinger Hospital," but soon Dunham was transferred to St. Elizabeth's, Washington, D.C.'s renowned psychiatric hospital. Locke's friend, psychiatrist Dr. Benjamin Karpman, most likely took charge of the case. Diagnosed with "dementia praecox," or paranoid schizophrenia, it is known today that Dunham had suffered from this condition previously. He would never recover from this breakdown, never return to Howard University, and never fulfill his considerable promise.[7]

Dunham's breakdown shook Locke. "Of course after the struggle I went myself to our hospital—and after an examination just retreated to a private room for rest overnight—but nothing developed. "But you can imagine," he confided to Mrs. Mason, "that I have had to blank out everything like cutting an electric switch."[8] Dunham's illness was a tremendous professional loss for Locke, since Dunham was the most brilliant Black philosopher of his generation and also someone whom Locke hoped would inspire him to renew his interest in professional philosophy. The loss was deeply personal because of Locke's barely hidden attraction for Dunham. Since the collapse of his fantasy about a lover-muse relationship with Langston Hughes, Locke had searched for someone who would give his work—and his life—meaning. While there is no evidence Dunham was gay, Locke courted him, most likely had sex with him, as if he believed Dunham was open to a love affair. Is it possible that Dunham's attack on Locke was his reaction to Locke's having slept with him? Or was this attack, which followed a steady increase in the frequency and intensity of Dunham's breakdowns once he arrived at Howard, his reaction to the reality that after a brilliant career at the University of Chicago he had no alternative but to teach, perhaps forever, at a segregated school? Was Dunham increasingly frustrated that at Howard, his philosophy colleague was an aging gay philosopher known more for race propaganda than first-order philosophy? Surely, none of these stimuli alone would have been enough to produce the permanent psychotic break that Dunham experienced. Still, any of them could have been the final straw.

Dunham may have been in Locke's mind when he wrote an unpublished essay in 1937 titled "On Insanity," which he shared with Benjamin Karpman. In it Locke argues that brilliant minorities were especially prone to mental illness because society has no place for them—or rather only a place that suffocates their genius. Remarkably, Locke speculates—ever so briefly—on how homosexual and racial minorities are particularly vulnerable to psychic breakdowns because society deems them abnormal. Locke usually took a "tough-minded" view of any attempt to link psychological difficulties to racism, suggesting to friends and lovers that racism brought out the spiritual discipline in Negroes—or if it did not, they were lost. But "On Insanity" admitted such discipline crippled Negroes who internalized the "discipline" of segregation or homophobia. Gifted Negroes who tried to live a life of reason in an irrational segregated America faced a daily struggle with questions of what constituted sanity. Locke's hospitalization following Dunham's attack suggests that it touched Locke in ways he found difficult to handle.

At forty-nine years old, Locke was a respected middle-aged professor, but a peculiar one as well. Howard students giggled about his nervous tics, his peculiar habits, and his strange phobias. On one occasion, students who knew he never touched the doorknob first when the bell rang and the class emptied played a trick on him. All the students in class refused to exit before him. Locke became nervous, urging the students—"go on, go on out." After students refused and repeatedly said, "No, after you Dr. Locke," he took a handkerchief out of his pocket, grabbed the doorknob with it, and exited hurriedly.[9] Locke too had been a promising philosophy PhD expected to make a dent in his field of value theory, but he had not. Instead, he had adapted to the reality of segregation, had become a "Negro writer," a "Negro critic," and a "Negro leader," and then struggled to inject his philosophical acumen into "race work." Sitting in his office alone while his friend and erstwhile philosophical collaborator was incarcerated, Locke had to wonder if they were not both in straitjackets.

Two weeks after Dunham's collapse, a letter from Jessie Fauset delivered another blow that showed the road forward would probably not be through creative writers he could nurture as he had done in the early 1920s. Stewing over Locke's patronizing review of her novel, *Comedy, American Style*, the 1934 retrospective review, Fauset released a barrage of criticisms that summed up their tense, decade-long professional relationship. "I have always disliked your attitude toward my work dating from the time years ago when you went out of your way to tell my brother that the dinner given at the civic club for 'There Is Confusion' wasn't for me. I still remember the consummate cleverness with which you that night as toastmaster strove to keep speech and comment away from the person for whom the occasion was meant." She not only accused him of bias against her but also of rendering invisible other women writers of the New Negro movement who were co-creators of the literary frisson that led to the Harlem Renaissance awakening. "Incidentally," Fauset continued, "I may tell you now that that idea originated with Regina Anderson and Gwendolyn Bennett, both members of a little literary club with which I was then associated. How you and one or two others sought to distort the idea and veil its original graciousness I in common with one or two others have known for years."[10]

Unfortunately for Fauset, this women's literary group had not felt confident enough to advance this graciousness without enlisting Charles Johnson to help them pull it off. And Johnson, in turn, was not confident enough to run the event without turning to the precocious Alain Locke, who made the event about his male writers, many of whom were gay and viewed subsequently as the leading lights of New Negro fiction. The *Opportunity* dinner was the first salvo in an internecine war between Black gay men and Black women for much of the 1920s, and it came to a head in Fauset's letter in 1933. Fauset had a valid point: Locke had orchestrated a process that decentered women writers in his choice of whom to include in anthologies to review in his essays and to promote, and in doing so had advanced a male subjectivity as normative in the New Negro movement even though its original impetus had come from women writers.

From Locke's perspective, he was evaluating *Comedy, American Style* within the context of the 1930s and the necessity New Negro literature had to adapt to a new situation. By January 1934, Negro literature had "become a prominent and permanent strain in contemporary American literature" and no longer a minority preserve in which Negro writers could carry on in isolation or ignore the presence of White writers. With such books as *The Conjure Man Dies* by Rudolph Fisher, *The Southern Road* by Sterling Brown, and *Folk Culture on St. Helena Island* by Guy B. Johnson, "the typical Negro author is no longer propagandist...the average white author is now neither a hectic faddist nor a superficial or commercialized exploiter."[11] The dominant trend was away from the "moralizing Puritans" and toward social realism, with one prominent exception, Miss Fauset. "Lacking forceful style and handling," her novel, he charged, was too "mid-Victorian" to be relevant.[12] Social realism, a harbinger of socialist masculinity, marginalized women's voices and women's stories, no less than New Negro primitivism of the 1920s.

Rather than accuse him of misogyny, Fauset attacked Locke for being racially biased. "It has always both amused and annoyed me to read your writing....But today's article is positively the worst because in it you have shown yourself so clearly as a subscriber to that purely Negroid school whose motto is 'whatever is white is right.'" She claimed that in his reviews of White fiction writers, such as Julia Peterkin and Roard Bradford, he glided lightly over their faults, but when it came to her and Claude McKay, "our virtues are barely outlined, our faults greatly stressed and in my own case I am left without a leg to stand on, characterization, style, sentiment, treatment are all wrong. My art is 'slowly maturing'; my 'championship of upper and middle class Negro life' is not even 'singlehanded'; it is 'almost singlehanded.'" She concluded that he had misread the novel's main point—that it was not the "story of 'one dark child in a family'" but instead was "the story of a woman who was obsessed with the desire for whiteness."[13]

There was another element to their long enmity—Fauset seemed to object to the style of Locke's reviews, regardless of whether they approved of her work or not. She despised his style, because it was too gay, with its hypertrophy of form, its studied obscurity, and its persistent irony. Fauset asserted something similar in a letter she wrote to Locke asking him if he could not use his influence with Bruce Nugent to avoid "bad writing" even if he persisted in narrating salacious, that is, homoerotic, literary subject matter. Fauset's role as a literary broker had declined in the late 1920s in part because she could not represent overtly homoerotic Black writers. And Locke could not tolerate reading one more heternormative story about the tragic middle-class Black woman who had everything going for her except her race. Having created a space for queer artists of color, he could not create a space for heterosexist Black women as well.

Dunham's breakdown and Fauset's putdown strengthened Locke's resolve to do philosophy in a new way and build, rather than abandon, his new critical voice. He would produce in the Bronze Booklets a critical philosophy of the humanities and social sciences by tapping the young social scientists, humanists, and activists of the 1930s, and an extended version of *The New Negro*—but this time as a series of separate books, rather than one anthology, spliced up by short books written by him. Locke was laying the ground for a knowledge revolution later called Black Studies by bringing a form of social philosophy to the masses in Bronze Booklets distributed through libraries and community centers across a segregated nation.

As early as Plato's *Republic*, bronze was the designation given to workers, farmers, and proletarians in the fabled ideal society: their work was necessary so that the Gold people, the philosophers, could rule without distraction. Just as Plato moved from recording the philosophical insights of Socrates to creating a social system to realize those insights in the daily life of the people of Athens, Locke was moving from promoting the writers of the Negro Renaissance to institutionalizing their contributions in a distribution system he would call the Bronze Booklets. Rather than disseminate the Greek and Western philosophical tradition he so loved, Locke performed the role of a Black philosopher by disseminating a universal knowledge of how racism, classism, and power operate in the modern world. The Bronze Booklets reflected a pedagogical strategy to activate culture and critical thinking by teaching the Bronze people how the world worked from a critical Black scholarly perspective. In that sense, situating knowledge for the masses meant conveying to them a theoretically rigorous critique of how the fruits of the Western tradition were denied them and how Black people had created alternative structures of knowledge the Bronze Booklets made available to them. Rather than lowering the complexity of knowledge delivered to Black adults, Locke wanted to raise it. Such a stroke was radical in adult education. As was the case with much adult education directed at poor Whites, many agencies made the "obvious mistake of playing down to [the] disadvantaged condition" of poor people, as Locke put it.[14] What they needed was a system of adult education that raised their desire to learn by giving them knowledge that gave them power and understanding over their situation in the modern world.

But in spite of writing a historic proposal and several positive developments that spring, Locke's internal mood turned dark. When isolated, Locke wallowed in his regret and hostility toward those ungrateful for his help. "You will see from the enclosed clipping," Locke wrote to Mrs. Mason, "that Langston and Roland are working the same game in the same place. How tragic for them. I do not pity the victims [mainly White supporters]—that is the same crowd with whom Jean Toomer got off the track—and his residence at Carmel was responsible for his tragic marriage. How the moths will find the flame—even though it be miles away. It reminds me of a sight I saw at Salzburg this last summer—a searchlight on the hill-side—and a crew of men scooping in the moths and insects as they reeled against the scorching lenses." Once the excitement of a possible new venture cooled as he waited months for a reaction, he succumbed to self-pity. He comforted himself by getting more sleep, taking "brisk walks in the open—(rain or shine)—and an occasional pick-up of good music on the radio. Toscanini is back on the air and was he grand!"[15] Locke felt ignored and abandoned.

There were some bright spots, however. British socialite Nancy Cunard had assembled and edited the *Negro Anthology*, and included Locke's spirited essay celebrating Sterling Brown as the next great Black folk poet. It was one of Locke's best, most hopeful essays on Black literature since the late 1920s. Sterling Brown epitomized what Locke had wanted to see in the poetry of Langston Hughes and the short stories and novels of Zora Neale Hurston. Brown's *Southern Road* had distilled a wonderful cache of poems from his research into the folk speech and mentality of the working poor in Nashville, Tennessee. Sitting in on barbershops, drinking spots, and shacks of blues-singing, story-telling "folk" Negroes, Brown had translated their lyrical voices into powerful poetry. His poem, "Strong Men," became a kind of national Black workingman's anthem. That same year, Brown would join Howard's English Department, adding an ally on campus who believed in the kind of folk-based renaissance Locke now advocated as the future of the New Negro. No longer was he alone in his literary community as he had been in years past, with Brown in town. Aaron Douglas was commissioned to create four murals, titled *Aspects of Negro Life*, for the 135th Street Branch of the New York Public Library where the adult-education "experiments" were taking place, adding visual monumentality and African American nobility to many pieces from the Harlem Museum of African Art still on exhibit there. And the Harmon Foundation had established a traveling exhibition of Negro art in collaboration with the College Art Association, sending Negro artists' work around the country, albeit with no input from Locke.

Another bright spot was President Roosevelt, whom Locke applauded not only for the New Deal but also especially, at least to Godmother, for his new policy toward "the Indian. John Collier has gone west with a considerable staff of young men to consult the Indians themselves about the new program." Here was a connection to his pedagogical dreams. "I understand the old-time govern-ment schools are to be completely abandoned, and new reservation schools es-tablished.... The one unexpected is the quite unheard of expression of guilt and error on the part of the...under-secretary in charge and the new officials of the Indian Bureau." He was "itching to write an article about this—as a Negro—and the next time I am in New York I will talk with Paul Kellogg about it." After that bright suggestion went nowhere, probably because Kellogg reserved Locke for commentary on "Negro topics," Locke's mood turned dark again. "The other clip-ping [I enclose] is not so cheering—the latest blast from Langston." It was an article by Hughes questioning whether the Negro ought to fight in the next world war, given the continued exploitation of Blacks after the last one. Though expressing what was no doubt a widespread mood among Blacks in the 1930s, the article signaled to Locke that Hughes had self-appointed himself a Negro spokesman, which Locke thought ridiculous. "His megalomania grows to ridicu-lous proportions."[16] Rather than feeding off the energy of his possible new ven-ture in adult education, Locke continued to wallow in bitterness—at least when corresponding with Mason, which he kept up even though she was no longer giving him the funds she had in the past.

Indeed, Locke's letters to Mason in the 1930s served as a kind of confessional of regrets on a variety of topics, especially his alienation at Howard. "I never thought that I would ever think of my work as just a 'job'—and daily my resent-ment grows against those forces that have made it so. Although the students say 'your classes are so different,' I know they are not—in any very vital way—but what couldn't be done in a real school!" He noted that "two classes are really worth while—and those hours I find nourishing—but three other classes are like life-sucking leeches—and after them I am simply exhausted." As for the Howard University president, Mordecai Johnson, after he orchestrated Locke's return to Howard in 1927 and utilized him as a confidant, he had dropped Locke from his inner circle and Locke did not like it. In conclusion, Locke believed "the institution as a whole is drifting and becomes more and more of an open farce as the days go on."[17]

Good news did break in on Locke's mood on two occasions. The first came from Hurston, then teaching at the Florida school, "the first word in God knows when." Hurston praised Locke's appreciation of Sterling Brown as the New Negro poet of the 1930s. She clapped and applauded, perhaps glad that some new male poet had stolen the limelight from Langston Hughes, now also her nemesis. "Zora has several articles—on Negro speech, which is really genuine and good in the same anthology. All has not been wasted [and] I think—without making any apologies for her—that even in the ashes some fire will always burn—and flare out occasionally—whereas Langston is all clinkers and ashes."[18]

Locke also brightened up when he heard the news that Claude McKay had returned to Harlem from Europe. Surely, Locke thought, McKay would agree with the judgment that Black writers of the 1920s—McKay accepted, of course—had misinterpreted their mandate as New Negro writers and prostituted the Negro theme rather than seriously develop it. Locke hunted up news of McKay's whereabouts, but strangely could not find him, initially. McKay had not contacted Locke upon arriving in the States, although he knew Locke's address well and needed money. When Locke eventually found him, McKay was penniless in Harlem but unbowed, living off Max Eastman, his long-time friend, the editor of the *Liberator*, and sleeping in Arthur Schomburg's Harlem apartment. Locke thought McKay saw things as he did. But McKay blamed Locke and other bourgeois intellectuals like him for the failure of the New Negro Renaissance, especially their lack of courage in challenging the White establishment's norms of what constituted "good Negro writing." Often out of touch with how others regarded him, Locke could not imagine that McKay might see him as the one responsible for the failed promise of the New Negro, nor did McKay reveal his feelings in 1934. For now, he was friendly, because he needed money, and most likely Locke gave McKay all he could spare when they saw one another. Locke even dutifully brought McKay's predicament to Mrs. Mason's ears, although she declined to open her pocketbook this time.[19]

While Locke drifted in terms of the current Negro literary scene, he kept up pressure on Morse Cartwright, the president of the AAAE, about his Bronze Booklets proposal. When Locke sent in a second, more-detailed budget version of the report in March, the AAAE president referred it immediately to his internal board of directors. Cartwright also informed Locke that Charles S. Johnson, now chair of Fisk's Sociology Department, was also working on a series of syllabi for use in Negro secondary schools. Cartwright suggested that Locke get in touch with him and collaborate.[20] Locke had no desire to do so. Around the same time, Johnson wrote to Arthur Schomburg that he had heard Keppel was about to invest in the adult-education movement. "That explains why our friend has become interested in it," a reference to Locke. Once collaborators, Locke and Johnson were now competitors for funding from the Carnegie Foundation. But Locke had the inside position on the adult-education funding. He already had been paid $2,000 by the Corporation to produce the evaluation, a huge sum in the 1930s. If his proposal was funded, he would receive another $5,000 to produce the booklets.

But a problem surfaced in April, when Cartwright wrote back about the proposal with a different tone. He still loved the book publication project and wanted to continue funding the miniscule efforts at the Atlanta and Harlem libraries, but his board of directors had expressed reservations about the idea of a paid ambassador of Negro adult education. In his plan, Locke wanted to hire a young Black sociologist, Ira De Reid, already an expert on adult-education activities in Atlanta, to spread the good news about adult education among Negroes. But Cartwright balked. Under no circumstances was he willing to fund a proselytizing Black adult whose advocating for adult-education programs might mushroom into an effective—and controversial—educational program that might change the racial calculus in the South. As he wrote to Locke, "I have discussed your proposal with others, and there has been a rather strong reaction to the part of the proposal in which you advocate us creating a field secretary to stimulate adult education in the field. As someone had put it in the office, the Association has always relied on local efforts to stimulate adult education on its own, without stimulation from the national organization. And we feel that there is no reason why Negro adult education ought to be treated any differently from White adult education."[21]

This was a remarkable statement from a nationally aware educator, given that Cartwright knew the disparities in education for White and Black adults in segregated America. Locke had no way of dramatizing this issue with Cartwright and his board because Locke had studiously avoided a critique of segregation in his argument for the booklet proposal. Even so, the board was not fooled: they could see that this adult-education program, especially if guided by a northern activist intellectual, could undermine the logic of southern education and foster strong self-conscious Black thinkers whose existence would come to the attention of the authorities. And these authorities or a lynch posse might view adult education as "dangerous" and hold the AAAE responsible. Scared to run afoul of southern segregationists and threaten the educational status quo in the South, the AAAE refused to sponsor even one Black adult-education activist to go out in the field to interest adult Black learners in adult education under its auspices.

When the proposals were presented to Frederick Keppel, president of the Carnegie Corporation and founder of the national adult-education association, he concurred with the Association's view that appointing a field representative was dangerous. Keppel and Cartwright were clear that they did not see adult education as destabilizing the class structure in America, nor were they interested in it upending the educational etiquette of segregated America. The Rosenwald Foundation, also consulted about Locke's proposal, was skeptical of this element too, especially since its director had other plans for Mr. Reid. Both the Carnegie and Rosenwald Foundations believed in educating Negroes to fit within existing segregationist structures of learning, whether in the North or the South. They were prepared to fund Locke's proposal only if it was clear that no effort would be made to use such education to transform the racial social order.

Sensing the delicacy of the situation and the moment, Locke let Eugene Kinckle Jones, the former head of the National Urban League, and by 1934, working as an advisor on Negro affairs in the US Commerce Department, react to the gutting of the proposal's most activist element. As chairman of Locke's advisory committee, Jones fired off a letter to Cartwright expressing his strong disappointment with the funders and stated that the Association's refusal to fund the field representative was a tragic setback for the program, dooming it to be a passive rather than an activist pedagogical intervention. But when

Cartwright was unmoved, Locke did not press the issue. For one thing, Locke was not an activist, having studiously avoided grass-roots involvement throughout his career. That Locke proposed someone other than himself to be the roving ambassador had been telling. If he were that man, he would have to confront Deep South segregation on a daily basis and be exceedingly careful that his sexual orientation did not expose him to unwanted attention. He had already been kicked out of Howard University for the volatile mix of being a visible gay professor and activist leader of its Black faculty in its struggle with the school's White president. And if he could not hire someone else to do this kind of dangerous work in highly segregated Black communities, he would drop that part of the proposal. What also was sacrificed was the research and dialogical potentialities of the proposal, for without a field representative, the Bronze Booklets ambassador could not bring back to the project the reactions of those who were being educated to be poured into future book lists, learning strategies, and so on.

Locke turned this stumbling block to his advantage. While the funders were focused on the paid activist component of the proposal, he shifted the definition of what constituted a "syllabus" from an outline of topics to quite substantial little "booklets" to be written by the best Black scholars in the United States. He noted that, given the paucity of quality Black scholarship even in most of the libraries in America, the syllabi should include introductions to the subject matter that could stand alone. The pamphlets themselves would be powerful agents of consciousness-raising, by articulating a critical race history and politics for Black people. The booklets could give Black readers a sense of their destiny as a world historical people, who could transcend racism and make their own futures if they read the texts he presented them.

When Locke had updated his proposal to Cartwright in March, most of the authors he listed as "sub-editors" were professors at Howard, despite his telling Mason he needed to get away from that "prison of the mind." First among them was Bunche, who chose to write a theoretical treatise on the idea of race from a global perspective. Recommended for a booklet on the economics of the American race problem was University of Chicago–educated Abram Harris. Sterling Brown, fresh off the acclaim for Southern Road, volunteered to author two literary history books—one on Negro literature and the other on Negro drama, subjects one might expect Locke to tackle. Instead, Locke decided to pen two other books—one on Negro art and one on Negro music, both areas of which were close to his heart and new areas in which he could advance himself as an expert through these publications. Rounding out the controversial list were Du Bois, whom Locke would ask to do a critique of the Negro and the New Deal, and Carter G. Woodson.

The list was a marvelous mixture of political and erotic tension. Du Bois and Woodson were associates, barely friends, but often adversaries of Locke. Harris sparred with Locke at the Saturday-night meetings, with Harris rejecting Locke's aesthetic idealism in race relations. By contrast, Bunche and Brown had allowed

Locke to take them under his wing. The most intriguing relationship was with Bunche, who spent most of his life away from his wife and family, traveling for his career. It is hard to imagine that Locke would not have made a pass at Bunche, and Bunche's reaction was not one of disgust. Just as important to the success of their relationship and the Bronze Booklets was a change in Locke. He had finally learned he had to stop pushing a relationship with future stars beyond what they wanted if he wanted to reach his goals. Locke's other transformation was just as profound: he had moved away from the star system still ascendant in Black social sciences to a collaborative model in which, for once, he was not as obsessively critical of collaborators that they could not breathe, have their own thoughts and independence, and produce the work he was going to ask them to do. He had moved beyond the Du Bois model and that of Woodson too—less dictatorial and controlling, more willing to indulge and tolerate those who disagreed with him—even of those who held quite different opinions. What Locke proposed in the Bronze Booklets projects was a modern, corporate system of knowledge production in what would later be called Black Studies.

While Locke waited to hear the final decision of Keppel and the Adult Education Association on whether it would publish the Bronze Booklets, he spent April, as usual, casting around for a way to go abroad for the summer, albeit under more complicated world circumstances. His previous summer trip to Germany had been dicey enough, as the Nazis carried out a purge of homosexuality, closing "homophile" clubs in Berlin, burning the library of the Institute of Sexual Research, the intellectual center of gay Berlin, and arresting and sending homosexuals to concentration camps. In the spring of 1934, the idea that homosexuality was a threat to racial purity had gained traction. That June, when Hitler decided to eliminate his potential rivals in the Night of the Long Knives, he justified the murder of Ernst Rohm, the head of the feared SA, as necessary because his homosexuality was a threat to the German race. Locke knew his race and his homosexuality made him doubly a target in a race-obsessed, hyper-homophobic Germany. He wrote to Mason, "It will be very unwise...for me to go abroad this summer. Although of course I must get psychologically out of this prison of mind and soul I work in." He mentioned that if he could be in New York with periods to see her, "I would be in another healing and enriching world."[22] If Locke was fishing to have Mason set him up in New York, it did not work. Mason, by now, was living in a hospital, where she would remain for another decade. Of course, even New York did not offer the kind of complete sexual freedom that going abroad promised.

Locke settled on taking an Italian cruise through the Mediterranean to Athens, which he had never visited, Constantinople, and Russia, but difficulties rose even before he set foot on the boat.

When they discovered I was a Negro, they informed me they could not book me for shore excursions—unless I would agree to a special carriage or auto for "my exclusive use." I wrote saying I was experienced enough traveller to conduct my own shore excursions—and would unless they should discover that they could book me in the ordinary way. Am anxious to get their reaction to that. Isn't it childish! Later, if I do get on, I can see the green horns now trying to pick up information and guidance—and I expect to have to help some of them count their foreign money or ask a simple question. And I'll let them know what their tourist agency thinks.[23]

The world was a plantation wherever Locke went.

Indeed, Locke was increasingly faced with the disgusting specter of segregation in Washington, D.C., as he tried to attract more Negroes into the official national adult-education association. In May 1934, while preparing to leave for the Mediterranean, Locke had to deal with an ugly issue: how to interest Negroes in attending the AAAE's annual meeting in Washington, D.C., when the Hotel Shoreham, chosen by Cartwright for the meeting, refused, like all other major hotels in Washington, D.C., to allow Negro guests. Eventually the hotel's management conceded that African Americans could attend the Association's sessions held in the hotel, but not eat or stay overnight at the hotel. Cartwright turned to Locke, who secured dormitory accommodations at Howard University for speakers and visitors at the meeting. Once the meeting got underway, Locke played a prominent role, talking up the guests, smoothing ruffled feathers, and speaking at the discussion section on Negro Adult Education, where once again he provided his high-minded justifications and recommendations for the Harlem and Atlanta "experiments." He then participated at an evening session with the leaders of the adult-education movement, including Morse Cartwright and Franklin Hopper. As reward, Locke was elected vice president of the Association for 1934–1935.[24]

Mercifully, at the end of June, his summer escape began. The day of departure, Locke got to the *Roma* at 7:30 A.M. June 30, almost the first traveler on board. "Knew I had a difficult situation before me,—as a cruise is something more than a crossing—and I had already had a taste of reflected prejudice." By getting there early, "I knew I couldn't have any excuses of 'tables filled'—and wanted to see what they would do." Almost immediately, the chief steward started "using an eraser liberally as I left" on the table plan, "'moving' his clients. At lunch and dinner it turned out to be 'my table,'" at which he sat alone. As Locke confided to Mason, "You know I take these situations as challenges, and provided one can be vital and fresh enough, there is always an eventual victory." Self-possessed, Locke "went into the dining room with dignity, and paying no attention to anything—but with a smile—and I decided that smile wouldn't change if the situation kept up the 40 days I was to be on the boat. By the morning of the second day, there were two ladies at the table—who later spoke—my mere acknowledgement of their presence breaking the ice. Later still I found one to be a New York schoolteacher, the other, if you please, a supervisor of nurses from Florida."[25]

On "the third day I was invited to a neighboring table by a young university couple (Swedish extraction) from Chicago. I declined, explaining that I had a fixed philosophy of sitting tight and letting the situation change about me. I hoped they would understand." Then, "by the fourth day there were five at 'our table' and then I decided to accept the invitation to the next table for one meal—explaining my absence from the first table by going over there before taking a seat where I was guest." Locke was choreographing the situation.

> Now I daresay there isn't anyone who hasn't taken sides. I can feel it all around me—that the boat has been divided into two camps and that they are re-fighting the Civil War with the North winning as before. One definite reason for saying so is the guilty look on the faces of some with marked Southern accent, and this incident—a young girl's coming up under cover of late twilight as we were leaving Madeira, to comment first on the coast line, and then to say "I'm Mary Jo Norton from Birmingham—we'all are going to the Passion Play from our school."[26]

Between him and ship's segregationists, there was no contest. A different reality confronted him when Locke took shore leaves. "Why is it that these natural paradises are always filled with a misery stricken population on the verge of starvation! Beautiful eyes in pock-marked faces—wonderful hair over anemic skins—gay spirits in labor-broken bodies. Man is the cruelest where nature is kindest."[27] Even with this pause of self-consciousness, Locke never stopped to think that the kind of country-hopping excursions he participated in perpetuated the conditions of dependence and poverty he lamented in the Mediterranean.

Locke moved on to Egypt where he avoided the sun, and instead bathed himself in premodern spectacle. Stopping by the Cairo Museum, which he had visited a decade ago on the opening of Tutankhamen's tomb, Locke could report that the Egyptians had done a fabulous job of installing the exhibit of the artifacts taken out of the tomb—those not shipped off to the British Museum. "Such infinite care of craftsmanship—the coffin cases three of them enclosed one within the other have been beautifully mounted—with reflecting mirrors—so one can see both the top and the bottom—and of course, the bottom is just as elaborately worked in enamel inlay and incised gold as the top—and often in better taste—because not too heavily embossed. The archeologists cannot explain this orgy of prodigal care and display, nor the spurt of technical skill which made it possible."[28]

Angling to see the pyramids in the cooler evening, Locke positioned himself with the most attractive Egyptian tour guide he could find.

When I spoke to him...he agreed to come to take me out to the Pyramids that night—and by doing the decent thing I won his affection—I asked him to have dinner with me—and to choose the restaurant. So as soon as he got rid of his charges, he came around—we had dinner—and then went out by auto-bus to Mena....By moonlight these huge mounds were ghostly and almost dream shapes and they looked ethereal, and spiritual rather than ponderous and earthly. I am sure that most of the Egyptian ritual must have been centered around sunset—night worship and dawn. The only reason we didn't see dawn was a silly regulation of the reservation police—not even Suleiman's pleas could move them—and once we had asked, we dared not disobey.[29]

This interruption almost ruined an otherwise romantic night for Locke. Just as impressive to him was his visit to the Sphinx, a haunting sight at night. Locke could convey to Mason that a Harvard professor was excavating beneath its paws and upending years of misinformation about what the Sphinx symbolized for ancient Egypt. "In the moonlight the expression on the face was the serenest smile I have ever seen—a real benediction, Godmother, and you know whose name was in my mind and almost on my lips,—and together with mother's (it was her birthday anniversary) I thanked the stars for the great mothering love I have been lucky enough to experience."[30] Even when Locke no longer received money from Mason, he continued to laud her for the "mothering love" he continued to carry within his mind and heart.

Despite the heat and the disruptive police, Locke had a wonderful time in Egypt until it was time to depart. The *Roma* snaked its way along the coast northward, first to Odessa and then to Yalta. In 1934 both cities were part of the Soviet Union, affording Locke a chance to peek in on the Soviet experiment. Modern buses escorted Locke and the other passengers to camps and outlying areas, where worker communes were thriving. "We inspected a bread factory just opened with a capacity of 300,000 loaves of bread a day. To my mind—the original vision must have been a great one—but somehow class vengeance came in and fogged this vision." Locke had to tread lightly here since Mason was a fierce anti-Soviet, who repeatedly cautioned him against getting "tricked" by Russia. "They were careful," Locke confided to her, "to guard you every minute with two official guides to each party of fifteen." He peppered guides with semi-embarrassing questions, such as what happened to the people whose land was confiscated or where they got such new uniforms—learning, thereby, from one guide, that he had to give it back after the day's tour. Nevertheless, Locke was clearly smitten. "To me one thing seems certain—they are doing a good job with the children—never saw such hearty, wholesome, happy uninhibited things. But they are ruthlessly sacrificing everybody else—even their own party workers. In other words, they don't intend fixing anything in the immediate present—it is a gamble on the future—and an indirect but ruthless sacrifice of one and a half to two whole generations—and an indirect extermination of whole classes."[31] Despite Mason's caveats, Locke came away ecstatic about the Soviet experiment. What really impressed him was the way the revolution spoke to the Black situation; it had transformed the outlook and self-concept of the children in the ways he had hoped to do for Negro children with *The New Negro* and the Harlem Museum of African Art. The communist revolution triggered a type of transformed consciousness the Negro needed to fulfill its destiny.

From Russia, Locke headed for Greece, the object of desire for much of his adult life, certainly since he began reading the classics in high school. But what was the image of Greece that resonated so much in his soul that he confided to Hughes ten years earlier that he hated teaching philosophy and wished instead he could teach the classics? No doubt it was "Greek love," a synonym for homosexual love. Entering Athens was thus a way to consummate a love that had been a fantasy for much of his life. Finally, he was coming to a community where what he did, whom he loved, what made his life complete was celebrated and embraced. In that sense, entering Greece was akin to going home, a home he had never had, a community of fellow lovers of men he had never seen before. "Athens,—and the long-wished for sight of Greece have made me very happy," he wrote to Mason. "And though the heat is great, with care, I am experiencing a spirit-restoring time."[32]

Locke also embraced the Grecian sunlight, so important to him spiritually, as he had confided years earlier, now that Mason had given him permission to love the sun and not avoid it as his grandmother had cautioned. This light was a metaphor for something deeper—the light in his personality, the joy of a little man whose romance with the world was often suppressed by the burden of his Victorian strictures, neurotic tics, and obsessive preoccupations. In coming to Greece, Locke was seeking a refuge from the dark burden of racial representativeness he had shouldered for so long. In Greece, he was no longer Black, but some shade of bronze that reminded him of a different "god Locke"—the Greco-Egyptian god he imagined himself to be when bathed in the aura of positive primitivism. All of these factors—the quasi-religious, the sensual, the sexual, the bronzeness—released the mask of the academic race man he had brought with him abroad.

We can assume that Locke did not fail to sample the local community of beautiful young boys that even heterosexist observers like Henry Miller commented on when they wrote about Athens. But such escapades were silenced in his letters to Mrs. Mason, his main correspondent on this trip, who seemed to view his sexuality as a necessary evil. Since Mason did not view the Greeks as real "primitives," certainly not analogs to her beloved Indians, Locke's sojourn to the Greeks was doubly suspect—a "time-out" for wanton sex and a diversion from where he ought to have gone—to Africa, which Locke studiously avoided on this and other "Grand Tours" of primitivism. Locke replaced any reference to the "beautiful boys" with aesthetic patter about the landscape. He narrates beauty to her—and to himself—as a beautiful perspective. In Locke's letters to Mason he criticizes other tourists who obsess with visiting monuments instead of standing back and appreciating how the placement of monuments concretized a perspective on the landscape that only he and other aesthetes can see and appreciate. He searched in vain for a postcard among the hundreds available that captured this sophisticated conversation between building and landscape; finally, he found a photograph that shows the Acropolis with the crumbled landscape in front of it. "What impresses me most of all—more than the buildings is the art of choosing the right spot. Every temple has a view which is still standing—even though the temple is in ruins, to proclaim what the people saw and meant by their effort."[33]

Locke was searching for confirmation of his life mission by trying to see his world as the Greeks saw theirs. He was in Athens trying to become ancient Greek himself and see the landscape of the rest of his life as they saw theirs—and with that the silenced desire to love bodies as freely as the Greeks themselves, he imagines, did. Indeed, so obsessed was he in this search to embrace the ancient Greek perspective on the landscape and, by implication, on life that he told Mason he found himself unable to be fully comfortable with the modern Greeks. At an outdoor Greek play, he sat far away from the natives, because they laughed and joked during the performance instead of adopting the requisite reverential attitude toward the play. Here, Locke reproduced the same attitude toward the Greeks that he adopted in his attitude toward things African: he approached them with an attitude of reverence for that which was ancient about them, not their modern approximations. As his friend Azikiwe put it, "Locke loves things African, but I never see him with any Africans."

While young beautiful boys were available, Locke's primary attachment went in another direction, as a photograph that survives from this trip attests. Taken inside on one of the monuments, Locke appears—dapper in his summer outfit of dark jacket, white linen pants, white shirt and tie, with two other men, one unknown African man, dressed a bit more conservatively, and the other a White man, University of Chicago philosopher T. V. Smith, whom Locke met and bonded with in Athens. Of the two figures, Locke wrote only about the latter to Mason, telling her that Smith was a "real humanist," who was not "ego-mad" and intellectually arrogant as so many of his non-colleagues were in the profession. Locke and Smith had known each other from some previous connection, perhaps in Chicago at one of John Dewey's fêtes. Locke writes to Mason that he and the bi-curious Smith decide to visit sites, share transportation and dinner costs, and talk about the contemporary political situation back in New Deal America. Locke, faced with an opportunity to immerse himself in Greece, chose instead to sojourn with an American.[34]

Locke, T. V. Smith, and unidentified man, Greece, 1934. Courtesy of the Moorland-Spingarn Research Center, Howard University.

Smith was running for Congress and asked Locke to visit him back home to lend support to his campaign in the suddenly politically efficacious Black Chicago. Early in the fall, Locke obliged by traveling out to Chicago to give a number of speeches for Smith's candidacy. Locke also campaigned for Arthur Mitchell, his lawyer friend who came to his aid in his fight to get his job back at Howard, and who was running to become the first African American Democrat elected to Congress. Both Mitchell and Smith succeeded. Locke's sojourn in Greece ended in an unexpected destination—the taking up of Greek democracy in modern America and the possibility that Locke could have a political efficacy beyond the racial world.

Interestingly, Locke did not discuss Greek democracy in his ruminations to Mason. Having come to Greece ostensibly for its past, it was Greece's influence on American modernity that seized him. Having come to Greece presumably expecting a romp or two or several with Greek youth, Locke actually found satisfaction in bonding with a mature intellectual man, with whom he could achieve, if only briefly, an integration of his philosophical, aesthete, and political selves. Whether Locke realized it or not, the reason he was of use to T. V. Smith was because of the politics of race—Locke's usefulness in helping to deliver Black support for a White Democrat back home. Having come to Greece to escape race, he was retuned to racial representativeness with his American companion. Yet Locke got from Greece what he needed—a sense that the new modernism he was creating was more in conversation with the truth of ancient Greece. While ancient Greece was emotionally liberating, modern Greece was not, because, intuitively, Locke sensed that modern Greece was tending toward that modern form of decadence that was flowering in Nazism rather than Bronze modernism.

That reality was made plain to Locke when he arrived in Italy, the last nation on his cruise through southern Europe. "Here in Rome," he wrote to Mason, "but again under the shadow of tyranny—this isn't the sunshine of Greece—or even of the old Italy. True, it is infinitely cleaner, more modern, more efficient—but something has been drained out of the people—and they are no longer happy in spite of improved external conditions. They think they are happy—one never saw such arrogance—but one who has learned from Godmother sees through such things." Once again, the contemporary people have swerved away from the truth of their ancestors in the interest of "modern efficiency," seemingly a cautionary tale for Locke as to what can happen to the Negro in America if the pursuit of modernity required the sacrifice of the soul. "I thought you would appreciate seeing the modern motorcade Signor M"—Mussolini,—"constructed (or 'caused to be constructed' as the new Latin on the pillar-posts proclaims) right through the heart of the old Forum. The problem is to find the forum." Better to suffer the inconveniences of pre-civilization than to die in the clutches of mechanization that hid the very basis of Roman democracy. "For me, however, [give me] the old forgettable sunsets of Monte Pincio—and the sombre elegance of the pines of the Villa Borghese. I have spent three afternoons there and have fed deeply—because something tells me that this next year will be trying—and I am building up reserves to stand in store." Yet, this restorative moment came at a price in 1934. "My way has led through Italy because of a cheap railroad rate, 70% reduction in railway fare on one very interesting condition. You must go through Rome, stop off and see the 'exposition' of the Fascist Revolution—pass through fourteen rooms of clever pictorialized propaganda— go up a long flight of steps to have your special reduced ticket 'stamped and validated' and then pass out through an alley of bayonetted Black shirt guards. Well—I considered that I had earned the reduction after the ordeal—no other way round it—except shutting ones eyes—(which I did occasionally.)" Locke also indulged in a kind of dangerous protest. "I tried keeping my hat on as an experiment—was twice requested to remove it. Did so—innocently—and thought three might prove fatal." Mussolini's Italy sought to reclaim a grand classical past, but for something different from the aesthetic politics Locke had in mind— to anchor a modernist propaganda of the patriarchal ruler without a god. Locke found himself forced to bow down before Mussolini's rituals of deference or incur a most uncomfortable kind of attention.[35]

Despite that last-minute ominous reminder of the gathering storm in Europe, Locke returned ebullient to America that September, so much so that he bypassed trying to visit Godmother at her hospital bed when he landed in New York. That piqued her, as she later claimed that she saw the ship he sailed home on, as it made its way up New York harbor. He avoided seeing her initially to postpone the inevitable criticism that would be part of any extended conversation with her about the trip. Once again, he had escaped from working on his projects, she thought, for sex abroad. This time, even from a distance, Locke brought her good news. "On the boat, I have been drafting an article on Negro music, which I want to publish soon. Especially since I believe I'm going to get a chance to bring out a series of pamphlet courses in Negro music, art, literature, the economic side of the race problem under the auspices of the adult education movement.... For such an audience, I'll have to be simple and straight forward— so it ought to mean a decided change and improvement in style. The summer has done its part—so if I fail, I'll have no excuse or possible alibi."[36]

The summer had "done its part," because the article, "Towards a Critique of Negro Music," was really an important breakthrough. He spoke simply and directly to the Negro people to declare that Black people are superb cultural producers. But he chastised as well. They had created the original forms of Negro spirituals, blues, jazz—all original aesthetic forms—and yet consumed bad copies of these original works of art. Locke perceived that White musicians and composers were actually improvising these forms into more classically sophisticated forms for which Black people got no credit. He urged trained Black musicians to stop resting on their laurels, perfect their craft through study in Europe, and create the great symphonic music of the twentieth century.[37]

Critics of Locke's music reviews dismiss him for charting Negro musical development along the arc of European cultural development. But such criticism ignores the deeper questions Locke was raising. Is it a "Negro" thing to settle for the least aesthetically sophisticated and most commercially fluid iterations of these musical forms? The example of African art seems to contradict that. Or is it our accommodation to the low level of expectation in American popular culture that explains why we sometimes produce aesthetically vapid cultural products? Are critics subtly buying into the Western notion of the Negro artist as primitive when they eschew the demand that Negro artists be as trained as European or White American artists? Is the Negro artist excluded from the demand to create the most enduring, sophisticated works of art?

Locke was demanding that Negroes use their art to advance themselves as America's quintessential artists. He was trying to subjectivize the Negro musician to demand not just to be heard, but to be heard creating his best music, to be the steering force in a system of music production that his genius created and sustains. Locke wrote in the article "Towards a Critique of Negro Music":

> Things Negro have been and still are the victims of two vicious extremes—uncritical praise or calculated disparagement. Of no field is this more true than Negro music. I have read nearly all that has been written on the subject, and do not hesitate to rate most of it as platitudinous piffle—repetitious bosh; the pounds of praise being, if anything, more hurtful and damning than the ounces of disparagement. For from the enthusiasts about Negro music comes little else than extravagant superlatives and endless variations on certain half-true commonplaces about our inborn racial musicality, our supposed gift of spontaneous harmony, the uniqueness of our musical idioms and the infectious power and glory of our transmuted suffering. True—or half-true as these things undoubtedly are, the fact remains that it does Negro music no constructive service to have them endlessly repeated by dilletante [sic] enthusiasts, especially without the sound correctives of their complementary truths. The state of Negro music, and especially the state of mind of Negro musicians needs the bitter tonic of criticism more than unctuous praise and the soothing syrups of flattery. While the Negro musician sleeps on his much-extolled heritage, the commercial musical world, reveling in its prostitution, gets rich by exploiting it popularly.... The real damage of the popular vogue rests in the corruption and misguidance of the few rare talents that might otherwise make heroic and lasting contributions. For their sake and guidance, constructive criticism and discriminating appreciation must raise a standard far above the curb-stone values of the market-place and far more exacting than the easy favor of the multitude.[38]

Locke called for the Negro composer to push himself to a new, higher level of aesthetic production in Black music, just as Alain Locke anchored himself in a higher level of social science criticality through his association with the Young Turks of Bunche's Saturday Nighters to push himself to a higher level of criticality in his cultural writings. The connection to the community of scholars at Bunche's house was real, even if most of them could not see the cultural implications of their largely sociological and political science ruminations. But Locke could. Already well-versed in Marx and Marxist literary criticism coming out of the Soviet Union in the early 1920s, Locke made connections between what they argued about a class and economic analysis of the Negro's "situation" in America as a sub-proletarian class to the new Marxist analysis of literature, music, and art as tied to a cultural means of production. Those on the international Left suggested that the artist must become a self-critical being if he or she is not to be completely destroyed by what Walter Benjamin called the "mechanical means of reproduction."[39] In America, Locke was arguing, it was not just class, not just industrialization, not just economics, but the way that the system of cultural production was racial that made a huge difference—the system by which Whites could appropriate from Blacks the fruits of cultural labor and profit from them just as they did under the system of slavery.

Unfortunately, Locke lacked a solid enough foothold in the music industry to institutionalize the consciousness he recommended for Black musicians and composers, although some were appreciative. William Grant Still, a young, aspiring, Georgia-born Black composer, wrote to thank Locke not only for the line of appreciation in the article but also for the challenge to do great things as an artist. But few Black composers had access to independent cultural patronage to avoid catering to the codes of the "curb-stone of the market place" and lacked enough leverage in the commercial sector to become mainstream hits. Yet his deeper message still rang true: create sophisticated art or music out of your own tradition, not imitating the European or catering to the commercial rewards of playing to the cheap seats.

When Locke looked around, he saw one composer, one musician, one artist who epitomized all he said in this article—Duke Ellington. For it was during the 1930s that Ellington abandoned competing for purely commercial rewards with big bands like Tommy Dorsey's and Glenn Miller's and created enigmatic, complex compositions like *Symphony in Black* (1935) and *Black, Brown, and Beige: A Tone Parallel to the History of the American Negro* (1943), and the *Liberian Suite* (1947). Such compositions seemed as if Ellington was listening to Locke. "You may never be greatly appreciated in America," Locke was telling African American composers. "But you can be great—if you demand the best of yourself, regardless of what the white man thinks of it."

Bronze people could create a Gold art.

36

Warn a Brother

The 1934 trip to Greece rekindled Locke's love of philosophy by kindling his affection for a philosopher. We do not know if there was sex or even the promise of it. But Locke found something in T. V. Smith that quickened his desire, and he pursued Smith for several years. Smith could write on ethics, stump speech for Roosevelt, and stamp through the ruins of Athens with insight and aplomb. He was philosopher as sophisticated cosmopolitan, a bit like Locke, without being the original thinker Locke was. But he was warm in ways Locke never was and gave him a new sense that philosophy mattered and could enrich rather than clog his cultural criticism. As Horace Kallen put it after the 1935 conference both Smith and Kallen attended at Howard: "I have always liked Smith immensely as a person." So did Locke.[1]

Of course, philosophy had always been the invisible architecture in Locke's cultural criticism. But there was something about that trip to Greece that gave him the confidence to produce a more thoroughgoing philosophical critique in 1935. When he began writing the first drafts of his adult-education booklet, *The Negro and His Music*, finished later that year, he utilized his very sophisticated value theory from his dissertation to argue the Black experience held special potential for the development of fine-art music. Black folk music, he would argue, even from those unschooled in formal music theory, contained within it a "pre-aesthetic" quality that came from how Africans traditionally engaged their environment, their daily lives, in terms of the aesthetic, the music, the dance. Rather than a genetic disposition, Black people carried from Africa an aesthetic valuation that continued to survive despite the radical change in context.

Shortly after returning to the United States in the fall of 1934, Locke moved quickly to create an opportunity for him to reconnect with Smith and build on this new enthusiasm for philosophy by hosting a conference at Howard University titled "Philosophy and Problems of Minority Groups." Howard's Board of Trustees had reorganized the College of Letters and Sciences and created a new division, the Social Science Division, that included the Department of Philosophy; it also made Locke the first head of that division. This was no accident. Locke had insisted for years that philosophy belonged with the social sciences, not the humanities, as the meta-discipline of the human sciences. Remarkably, the board had acceded to his wish, put him in charge, and allowed him to drive the conversation about what that new division would examine in modern society. Jumping at the opportunity, Locke proposed and received $600 in funding for the conference, which allowed him to push philosophy to the forefront of the new division and bring his philosophy friends to campus. Such figures as William E. Hocking, the heir to Josiah Royce's social idealism at Harvard, came along with Kallen and Smith, who, as a congressman was already often in Washington. Planning for the conference took an enormous amount of Locke's time securing the other speakers. Locke had his hands full at Howard in ways he had not had in the past. But finally after years of thankless labor as a philosophy teacher at Howard he was now able to build an edifice for philosophical research and public comment—and provide a context to continue his relationship with Representative Smith.

In the meantime, Locke maintained himself with sex with philosophically in-clined young aesthetes with whom he had tense if rewarding romantic relation-ships. One of those was with Solomon Rosenfeld, a student at City College of New York, who in April had reported on his classes he was taking with public philosopher Harry Overstreet, the chairman of the Philosophy Department. Drawn to Overstreet's lectures, "almost entertaining," on "the question of free-dom of speech, violence, and isms as in quotation marks," Rosenfeld shared Locke's distaste for metaphysics. "Do you suppose that the aesthetic minded generally disliked metaphysics? Or do you think that I am just ignorant and gen-erally not interested in philosophy?"[2] After a difficult rendezvous in New York following Locke's return from Greece, the relationship, as was habitual of Locke's relationships with younger men, turned dark. "Was it not an air of finality about our last meeting? I felt so. At any rate I shall not be able to see you for sometime. Please do not misunderstand. I am just experimenting with many things in life. For instance, I have just joined a dance group to try to find expression in that art. I have not had time to get back to Plato; but if you need the book do not hesitate to ask for it and I shall send it to you."[3] The loaned book on Plato was perhaps a sign. Was Locke less tolerant of the emotional self-absorption of a young aes-thete with only Greek philosophical inclinations after experiencing the real thing with a mature philosopher in Greece? As much as Locke chased young aesthetes throughout his career, the longing for a peer romantic relationship grew as he rounded middle age. Locke was forty-nine in 1934. Was it now time to settle down? Smith was not ready. No one else was either.

Locke received an early Christmas present in 1934. On December 21, Morse Cartwright informed him that the Carnegie Corporation had decided to fund Locke's Negro adult-education project, the only project by a Black intellectual the Carnegie Corporation would fund during the 1930s. In addition to continu-ing the "experimental" adult-education centers in Harlem and Atlanta set up by the AAAE, the funding included $5,250 to go to Locke to prepare the "syllabi for use in the Negro adult groups."[4] The Carnegie Corporation award consummated a masterful campaign by Locke to match his desires with the goals of a corporation, but now the really difficult work began—to get the authors contracted and the books written.

Most important, the funding to create these "Bronze Booklets" furthered Locke's politics of collaboration with younger scholars and solidified his reputation as a new kind of minority intellectual. Locke sidestepped the rewards of intellectual individuality to knit together disparate scholars and artists to produce one powerful collective statement of the contemporary Negro mind. Deeding his talent to this group expression showed great maturity, but also brought great risk. Locke was an outsider to the group of younger scholars who formed the main body of authors.

Some were wary of Locke. As Harold Lewis recalled, "We had mixed feelings about him...the way in which Locke used to dress. I do have some visions of Locke wearing spats, carrying a cane and if I'm not mistaken wearing a pince-nez. The judgments that some of us made about Locke were judgments that took him out of his perspective and therefore was unfair. Now, they weren't malicious, but they were in a way presumptuous.... Here is an old man who doesn't exactly want to plunge into these fights in the way we do. I do recall some circumstances... some of us used to say this about him, that, maybe, Locke sometimes has a point that he wields a stiletto where we tend to result to the shillelagh."[5] Locke was the aging, dandified queer in the 1930s, and some were suspicious of his motives. But he offered them access to White money and the possibility to reach the Black masses with Black scholars, something no one else offered. His success would depend on whether he could close the deal—get the money from the Association and get the books published by an unpredictable group of young socialist intellectuals who would force him to change or fall back into irrelevance.

Others were downright undermining. In January 1935, Mary Beattie Brady wrote to Locke that James A. Porter, a lecturer in the Department of Art at Howard, had brought Robert Goldwater, a young PhD candidate at New York University where both studied art history, to the Harmon Foundation office looking for images to illustrate an article Goldwater was working on.[6] Locke had gotten the Foundation to photograph the African art he had deposited at the 135th Street New York Public Library, and Brady's letter in part requested more information from Locke on the pieces in order to compile detailed descriptions of them. Perhaps a survey or document of all the African art collections in this country could be produced. Perhaps Mr. Goldwater, already an expert on West African art, might be the one to produce it.

But the key here is that Porter, Locke's colleague, had brought Goldwater to the Harmon Foundation to obtain photographs of art that Locke had collected.

As Porter well knew, Locke was the man at the Harmon Foundation. Locke must have wondered why Porter had not spoken to him about this opportunity instead of going straight to Brady. Brady continued, "Mr. Goldwater has expressed some interest in our work, has looked at the pictures, and stated that he was writing an article on this subject, and if we would hold the pictures for illustration in any article that he could get published, he would be glad to cooperate by making the material available to me."[7] In other words, Goldwater wanted to reserve the photographs for his work, photographs that had been made at Locke's instigation and of Locke's collection. And Locke's Black colleague at Howard had engineered his access to and potential publication control of photographs of Locke's collection at the Harmon Foundation.

Given that Porter's portrait, "Woman with a Jug," had received a Harmon Foundation prize in 1933, when Locke had co-curated the exhibition, one might ask why Porter would not defer to Locke and ask him directly to help his friend. But Porter was a protégé of James Herring, who detested Locke and his theories on Negro art. Herring, for example, as director of the Howard University Art Gallery, had refused to put on an exhibition of the very same African artwork that Porter was interested in having used in Goldwater's articles. Both Porter and Herring disagreed with the argument Locke had made in the catalogue to the 1931 Harmon Foundation exhibition that American Negro artists should look to African art for inspiration, modeling European artists who had been inspired by the "art lessons" of African art to create modernism. Goldwater was working on a theory that modernist artists had misread ancient African art, and that visual modernism had emerged from Westerner's misguided notions of African "primitivism."[8] No doubt Goldwater and Porter had had conversations on the subject.

One might ask why Goldwater did not approach Locke directly. Goldwater needed Locke's help, because it was difficult to get photographs of African art collections in the United States, especially since the "peculiar Dr. Barnes," as Brady referred to him in her letter, refused to have anything to do with art historians. But Goldwater was a mentee of Meyer Schapiro, who had penned the critical article on Locke in the *New Masses*. Not only did Goldwater consult Schapiro extensively during the writing of his dissertation but also the two were close allies in the rough-and-tumble world of Trotskyite politics in New York. Interestingly enough, Robert Goldwater's father was Dr. Sigismund Schultz Goldwater, commissioner of the Department of Hospitals, who refused to meet with La Guardia's committee investigating the causes of the Harlem riot of 1935. Robert Goldwater was thus very familiar with Locke but no doubt viewed him, as did Schapiro, as an "ethnic chauvinist," whose attempt to inscribe the role of Black people in the fashioning of modernism was not only wrongheaded but also dangerous. Goldwater thus tried to bypass Locke to access a very valuable commodity in 1935—high-quality photographs of a major African art collection—because he felt he could do so without consequences.

Porter's and Goldwater's maneuver revealed an uncomfortable truth of Locke's scholarly career: pursuing multiple lines of entrepreneurship, one of which now was an adult-education publishing company, robbed Locke of the kind of focused concentration on one issue that established scholarly reputations. Locke had not established himself as an authority on African art by writing a major book on it. Time was running out on Locke. Even supporters like Miss Brady were antsy. She was game to give this young expert access to the photographs if he could give her accurate descriptions of them. But Brady also sensed the implications of Porter's ploy. "I had hoped that it would be possible for you to get out an article on the general subject of primitive African art in the art field, and have been holding these pictures for your use in that event. I know, however, how busy you are, and that there is a limit to your strength."[9] Unlike Porter, who also sensed Locke's limitations, Brady gently goaded him to publish. This is one reason why Locke trusted these older White women patrons: even when difficult, they protected his self-interest rather than undermined it. By contrast, James Porter, his young Howard colleague, and a Negro, whom one might think would "warn a brother," did not. This incident suggests the irony of the racial brotherhood ideology Locke continued to advance in Negro art despite its contradictions in his own experience.

Of course, Locke's main goal that February 1935 was to move the Bronze Booklets toward publication. He advanced that process with a Memorandum of Organization that informed Cartwright that Eugene Kinckle Jones would be chairman, Garnett Wilkerson treasurer, Locke secretary, and Lyman Bryson the second member of the editorial committee that contained Mary McLeod Bethune of the Bethune-Cookman College, A. J. Foster of the Chicago Urban League, and Mary Beattie Brady of the Harmon Foundation, among others. Interestingly, Locke chose to be the secretary of the project, a sign of how Locke chose a secondary administrative title in projects he developed to avoid garnering too much attention on his role in these almost secret operations. But there was nothing secret about who was in charge in his correspondence with the authors. He invited them to join "in a series of booklets for adult education groups—white as well as Negro—made possible by a grant of the Carnegie Corporation through the American Association for Adult Education. These booklets are to be prepared, however, under my general editor-ship and there is no restriction as to content,—and the sponsoring publication medium will be a committee styled:— Associates in Negro Folk Education,—who will administer the grant."[10]

Here was another contradiction: while Keppel and Cartwright, the Carnegie Corporation, and the AAAE always insisted these were booklets solely for Negro readership, Locke was conveying that this critical education in the history of America from the Black experience was intended for "White" readers as well. Indeed, after Locke promised each author would receive a $200 honorarium upon receipt and acceptance of the manuscripts, he expressed another opinion at odds with the AAAE adult-education agenda. "I look upon the venture how-ever as primarily an opportunity for legitimate academic publicity,—and as an opportunity also for gaining a much wider public than otherwise possible for competent scholarship on Negro life and culture."[11] Locke intended to use these "adult-education" booklets to create a market for Black scholarship outside the academy and upgrade contemporary Black public discourse by making Black scholars, rather than ministers, lawyers, schoolteachers, and so forth, the acces-sible stewards of policy and civic debate.

And yet the academy continued to distract him from a complete focus on the Bronze Booklet project. As he wrote Godmother, "At the university we have been doubly upset—there is prospect of a change of administration—President Johnson's egotism which you detected years ago is now apparent to everyone—and government (Department of Interior) investigator[s] have been on the grounds for the last two months."[12] The Interior Department investigators ar-rived, because the federal government had been subsidizing Howard since 1928, and with that came increased oversight of the president and the political lean-ings of Howard's professors. Johnson's securing of this long-term federal appro-priation at the beginning of his tenure in 1926 had been seen as an act of genius, ensuring Howard's financial future and its emergence as the preeminent Negro university in America. Now, it appeared as also an act of folly: as Congress re-viewed the appropriation every year, southern Congressmen, many of whom disliked congressional funding for a Black school in the first place, used the review process to carry out a witch hunt.

Johnson's personality did not help matters. He reacted to the constant ques-tioning and internal attacks that came with being president by returning fire with fire. He became distant toward and publicly critical of Howard's faculty after the alumni attacked him viciously in 1931. Suspicious of friends as poten-tial enemies, Johnson could also be petty. When Ralph Bunche, who had ac-cepted a job to be Johnson's assistant in 1931, took a leave of absence to go to Europe and Africa to complete his Harvard PhD dissertation on colonial admin-istration, Johnson publicly expressed his displeasure in front of the faculty by declaring, "Bunche is going all the way to Africa to find a problem."[13] When Bunche returned to Howard as a faculty member, he became one of Johnson's staunchest critics. He was also partly responsible for Locke's increasingly hostile attitude toward Johnson. On one occasion, students reported that when inter-rupted from lecturing by the mowing of the grass outside his classroom's window, Locke turned toward the window and said, "If Howard University had a president who was not a Baptist minister, it would be an infinitely better insti-tution of higher education!"[14] This attitude also reflected the change in Locke's relationship with the president. Early in his return to Howard, Locke had been one of Johnson's trusted advisors; after the conflict of 1931 with the alumni, Johnson drew the circle of trusted friends tighter, and Locke was left out.

Locke coped with the disappointments at Howard by giving lectures at other schools. One of his favorites was the "Bennett College for Women" in Greensboro, North Carolina, which he visited over one weekend in January 1935. In the southern comfort of overhanging trees and lush walkways on the small campus, Locke gave what had become his signature lecture of the early 1930s: the "Negro's Contribution to American Culture." As he related it to Mason, "The talk was sound, I think, especially since it admitted what we haven't done—and that statement seems to have paved the way for me to speak out in an article on 'Why the Negro Renaissance Failed.' An independent magazine has been started in New York called *The Metropolitan*. It isn't what it should be, but its under Negro management . . . it would be wrong to discuss this in any publication but a Negro journal." Here was another double bind. He was reluctant to air publicly his frustrations with Negro writers lest it become grist for the mill of White supremacy attacks on Negro cultural production as fundamentally inferior. In the end, the article would not be written, although elements of it would be sprinkled throughout his retrospective reviews of the 1930s and 1940s. "It does not seem the right moment for this, even if there were the right medium," he concluded. A public attack on former allies would risk criticism from inside the race and might backfire, drawing attention to how his predictions had not panned out. That sense of responsibility for what had not been realized gnawed at him. Locke knew his prediction, however well coached in defensible language, that a literary renaissance would free Negro subjectivity in America, had not only been far-fetched, but now seemed cruelly misleading. He felt pressure to say something about the movement's collapse "having been so intimately involved," as he phrased it to Mrs. Mason.[15] But even he knew that simply pointing the finger at others would not make for a coherent—or convincing—argument.

Howard University remained the key to whether the second phase of the Negro Renaissance would succeed by generating a lay audience for Black high aestheticism and critical social science, but Locke had trouble securing the writers he wanted for the Bronze Booklets. First, Eugene Kinckle Jones, executive director of the National Urban League, begged off writing the pamphlet on adult education as he was too busy with his new job at the Department of Commerce, especially during the Great Depression. Then came a rejection from Abram Harris, the most outspoken member of Howard's "Young Turks." A Trotskyite economist and fierce critic of Black progressivism's emphasis on race, Harris argued in his classic study, *The Black Worker* (1931), that a race focus did not help the Black worker, because it exacerbated conflict with the White working class. Harris and his coauthor, Sterling Spero, also soundly criticized independent Black business development, arguing it would never become big enough to change the material conditions of most Black workers.[16] Abram Harris and Ralph Bunche had even criticized the young student movement, the New Negro Alliance, that in 1933 began to stage boycotts of Washington, D.C., stores that refused to hire Negro workers, arguing that "Don't Buy Where You Can't Work" campaigns displaced White workers, caused a backlash, and failed to address the main problem causing unemployment: cyclical capitalism. Harris could hardly take seriously Locke's advocacy that the Negro Renaissance could mitigate the oppression of Negroes.[17] There was also considerable personal competitiveness between Locke and Harris. When Locke participated in the Saturday-night sessions at Ralph Bunche's house, sparks would fly between the two of them. On one occasion, Harris reputedly called Locke an "intellectual whore" for his willingness to shift positions in response to the changing times of the 1930s. Not surprisingly, when he received Locke's letter asking him to do a pamphlet on the economic situation of the Negro funded by money from the Carnegie Corporation, Harris declined to participate.

Being undermined, rejected, and criticized by Negroes at Howard did not stop Locke. As the winter of 1935 turned spring, he moved forward with the adult-education project, pulled together his conference, and responded to the challenge that Robert Goldwater posed to his control over African art. Once he got his wake-up call from Brady, Locke moved to get an article with Miss Griffiths's photographs of African art published in the *Magazine of Art*, the same magazine in which he had published his pivotal article on American Negro artists in 1931. After writing, calling, and leaving messages for its elderly editor, Mr. Whiting, for two weeks, Locke learned that Whiting had turned the magazine over to his son. The younger Whiting demurred about having Locke write an article with Griffiths's photographs, but did need a review of the first exhibition of African art at a major American museum, the Museum of Modern Art. Preparations were already causing a stir that first week of March as the museum closed to the public while more than six hundred works of African art were installed on four floors. The curator had spent months in Europe and the United States tracking down the best examples of African art in collections and may have been helped by Locke to secure some pieces he had collected for Mrs. Edith Isaacs for this exhibition. Thanked in the catalog by Sweeney, Locke was recognized as a curator by this exhibit, but not really as an intellectual authority on African art. Nevertheless, Locke hustled up to see the exhibition, trying to coordinate his visit so that he could see it with Sweeney; when that failed, he took Miss Brady and Miss Brown to the exhibition, letting Sweeney know that he had brought influential members from the Harmon Foundation through it.[18] Locke wanted to get photographs made of the exhibition, so that he could use them in the article he was preparing for the *Magazine of Art*. Sweeney secured permission from the museum director, and got Locke the photographs, which became the stunning focus of Locke's article. Sweeney even gave Locke an interview about the exhibit, also featured in the article, "African Art: Classic Style," that appeared in the May 1935 issue.

Locke's article gushed over the exhibit for documenting African art as embodying a civilization devoted to high aesthetics long before the European

Renaissance. He applauded the beauty of the artworks discovered, including a beautiful mask, made by the "lost wax process," whose backstory was that it was exemplary of "Benin, the chief city of one of the great Negro empires" with "cultural arts as early as the tenth century," a monumental city of avenues "seven or eight times wider than the main street of Amsterdam," and with a "royal palace that was said to be as large as the whole city of Harlem." Locke applauded how MOMA exploited the brilliant show. A thousand schoolchildren from Manhattan and the Bronx toured the exhibit one Saturday after Easter in 1935 and marveled at "the amusing, delicately designed, tiny bronze weights for measuring gold dust, and the textiles...in which the harsh fibre has been refined by the hand of the weaver almost to the softness of velvet." Dramatizing the exhibit for the children, a museum press release related how these fine designs were "created in the jungles of the Congo before white men had penetrated them." Here on 53rd Street was the vision of African civilization Locke had hoped to generate among Black schoolchildren on 135th.[19]

But Goldwater capitalized on the exhibit too, getting an article in the MOMA brochure with photographs of the exhibit shot by the up-and-coming Walker Evans. More substantively, the article for which Goldwater had wanted the Griffiths photographs also came out that fall. Published in an obscure art historical journal, *Parnassus*, "An Approach to African Sculpture" signaled a major shift to close, formal analysis of the plastic achievements of African art with a priority on ethnological examination of individual art objects and whole traditions within their social and cultural—often religious—contexts. Goldwater was moving African art interpretation away from evaluating it in terms of taste, as a connoisseur, and also away from analogous assessment, such as European nomenclature like "classic," Locke used in his article, to describe African art.

Modern art and African art, Goldwater contended, should be studied as independent traditions, because they emerged from different societies that became interrelated only because of the way Europeans and Americans had come to know African art—through modernism. Goldwater argued that African art could not have really germinated modern art because their forms and use of forms were quite different.

Revelatory as this analysis was, it diminished the world historical work done by African art in launching European modernism. Ironically, Goldwater's preference for an ethnological analysis of African art effectively covered up that African art had opened the doorway to abstraction, cubism, and even conceptual art for modern European artists, regardless of whatever mistakes they made in understanding it. Much of art history has been driven by misinterpretations of earlier formal traditions, as Locke pointed out in his review of the MOMA show, when he noted the Italian Renaissance's "misreading" of Greek sculpture. Goldwater's cultural reading of African art marginalized how artists used African art—to open up the doorway to post-representational art of the twentieth century. Reading African art "on its own terms" severed that art from the circulation of ideas and forms that constituted world modernism, a circulation African art had participated in and shaped.

But Locke could not attend to this debate in 1935. While Locke wrote his African art article, he wrestled with getting people lined up for his conference held over two weekends—April 4–6 and April 11–13. Two problems dogged him. First, many of the prominent people he sought to include simply could not make it. His first choices of speakers reflected his strategy to bring in powerful New Deal figures to discuss minority problems and to insert himself into the discourse and communities of knowledge of the New Deal. Unlike Bunche's conference planned for May, Locke wanted to mine the New Deal for strategies that could advance minorities. Many of those prominent New Deal figures were simply already booked. Locke's second problem was more revealing. The people he selected were a curious mix. Some were quite old, like Raymond Leslie Buell, his sometime friend at the Foreign Policy Association, or William Ernest Hocking, Locke's former professor at Harvard—not John Dewey, the more contemporary philosopher who begged off. Then, there were the young rebels like Bunche, Frazier, and Benjamin E. Mays—the latter the newly minted dean of the School of Religion at Howard University. The assortment of people and perspectives exemplified Locke's role as harmonizer of divergent values, disciplines, positions, and people, who often brought together profoundly antagonistic intellectuals and scholars to find common ground. But it also showed the split between the two sides of Locke—the conservative, old-world approach to policy and philosophy versus the radical, new-critical approach predominantly academic and social science based. Even if the effort was not a success, Locke tried to bridge the racial divide in American higher education and start an intergenerational conversation about the direction of minority progressivism in the 1930s.

A global perspective also distinguished Locke's choices. The conference opened with a lecture by Marvin Lowenthal of New York University titled "The Plight of Minorities in the Present Day World." He argued that contemporary attacks on Jews in Germany, to be formalized in the Nuremburg Laws that fall, were analogous to the Jim Crow laws of segregation in the United States. Right after Lowethal's stirring keynote, Locke slotted in a discussion of the New Deal's policy on the Indian, by John Collier, the New Deal commissioner of Indian Affairs, and Ernest Gruening, director of the US Division of Territories and Insular Possessions—a rather remarkable follow-through on his correspondence the year before with Mason on how he wished to do something on the Indian question for the *Survey Graphic*. The next day's "discussion conference" featured Leifer Magnusson, director of the International Labor Office, speaking on the politics of assimilation, with Bunche giving his insights from his research on the African Mandates system and "indirect" colonial domination outside of the Americas. E. Franklin Frazier, who was working on his theory of the assimilation of American Negroes of Anglo-American family and social mores, spoke on the politics of bi-racialism.

Most provocatively, Locke chose Raymond Buell to deliver a key lecture on Friday evening titled, "Autonomy vs. Assimilation: A Comparative View," with Bunche following with a talk on the "new politics of imperialism." That Locke invited Buell, given his involvement with the Foreign Policy Association that had rejected Locke's African Mandates report six years earlier, speaks volumes about Locke's ability to put past mistakes—or hurts—behind him to resurrect a relationship he might need in the future. Buell gave an amazing talk: after discussing the racial problem globally, Buell argued that "the American Negro, while not abandoning his quest for equal rights, would make further progress if he supported the principle of Negro autonomy and group representation in certain areas of the country." For example, Buell argued that the "Bankhead bill creating the Farm Tenant Homes Corporation" was a "real opportunity" to increase "domestic purchasing power" if it was used by Negroes effectively despite its defects. Rather than sell land to individuals alone, the bill should be augmented to "organize cooperative farm communities" and "earmark part of the funds for the establishment of Negro farming communities. So long as full discretion as to the allotment of these funds is left in the hands of the administration, grave danger of discrimination against the Negroes exists." But if "half of the Bankhead fund should be used to develop Negro cooperative farming communities—in other words, to develop a kind of Negro TVA...it would help those 'many Negro families' who were 'utterly landless.'" Buell even went so far as to suggest that "the Negroes should carefully consider the wisdom of advocating the adoption in certain states of the idea of racial representation" and of fighting for the right to elect, say, "a certain proportion of the members of the state legislature" to "take part in the state legislature upon a complete basis of equality."[20] In having Bunche follow Buell, Locke set up an ironic debate between a White man advocating a form of Black power and a Black man advocating that only class analysis and solidarity with the White working class could transform the colonial situation of minorities, at home or abroad.

Racial and generational debates continued in another session, "Minority Tactics and Techniques of Minority Assertion." There, Locke set up a discussion among Rabbi Jacob Weinstein, W. E. B. Du Bois, and Howard president Mordecai Johnson, who was included here to discuss nonviolent tactics by Black activists. Here again, Locke put aside his personal distaste for Johnson to have him participate meaningfully in a discussion of the militant versus nonviolent tactics of forcing change by young Blacks—some of whom were Howard University students. Du Bois spoke on two sessions, the second one resonating with Buell's address—that Blacks ought to embrace self-segregation to build economic power at a time when even the New Deal was not really helping them. Here too, some of Locke's burgeoning interest in the Soviet Union bore fruit in a talk by the *New Masses* editor, Joshua Kunitz, on "The Soviet Policy and Program for Minorities."

Most important for Locke's future as a philosopher, the conference had panels on philosophy and social change, which brought friends T. V. Smith and Horace Kallen to the conference. That paid off almost immediately. Smith invited Locke to do an article for the *International Journal of Ethics*, where Smith was associate editor.[21] In the process of developing that article, Locke began reading the *Journal* closely, especially its articles on value theory, which brought him back into sync with contemporary moral philosophy and gave him a new context in which to place his musings on the philosophy of value. Kallen followed up his presentation with an invitation of his own—for Locke to write an essay for a volume on contemporary philosophy that he and Sidney Hook were editing.[22] The volume, *American Philosophy Today and Tomorrow*, included essays by Harry Overstreet, Harry Costello, Paul Weiss, Irwin Edman, Will Durant, as well as Kallen and Smith. Ultimately, Locke would publish an essay in Kallen's anthology and not in Smith's *Journal*.

Even before the conference, Kallen had helped Locke with suggestions of speakers, such as Lowenthal, a protégé of Kallen, and Hocking, his former colleague at Harvard. At the final session of the conference, titled, "Cultural Reciprocity," with Locke chairing, Kallen articulated his philosophy that ethnic pluralism was the essence of American democracy. Their reconnection through the conference would initiate Kallen's insertion of Locke in professional philosophy circles. He would look out for him, bring opportunities to him, and promote Locke as a serious Black philosopher in the White American philosophical world at a time when the "Black philosopher" was an oxymoron in mainstream American philosophy.

Two other speakers at the conference played an important role in Locke's future intellectual production. Locke used the opportunity of including W. E. B. Du Bois, always a draw as a prominent Black intellectual, in the conference to invite him to do one of the booklets, titled, "The Negro and Social Reconstruction," a study of the Negro during the Great Depression, for the adult-education series. Du Bois's second talk, an evening critique of the New Deal administration's approach to the Negro and the impoverishment caused by the Great Depression, prefigured his analysis in his booklet. The other key participant was Bernhard Stern, a Columbia University professor of education, who spoke on "Religion as a Separatist Force," with whom Locke would later collaborate. Even the contentious E. Franklin Frazier must have been pleased with the conference, as Locke brought Frazier's mentor, the dean of the Chicago School of Sociology, Robert Park, to lecture on his theory of the relationship of race and culture.

Locke could not, however, bask in the positive aura of the conference, because even during its planning, a nasty conflict emerged with Carter G. Woodson. Locke thought he had a verbal assurance from Woodson to write the booklet on

Negro history for the Bronze Booklets. But when Locke wrote at the beginning of April to say that he had secured funding and expected Woodson to contribute the book, Woodson balked and claimed he had never agreed to such a proposal. One aspect of Locke's letter undoubtedly irritated Woodson: Locke coupled his request with begging off his own writing commitment to Woodson. Earlier that year, Woodson had written to Locke, "Not long ago you promised to prepare a biography of Frederick Douglass. There is a demand for such a book. We should like very much to publish it at once. Kindly let us know when we may have the manuscript. If you do not intend to write the work, kindly be frank about it for it is necessary to have such a work produced by some one in the near future."[23] Locke's answer was not an apology for failing to meet his writing obligation, an admission that he had reached a mental block in writing the biography as he confided to Mason, but his claim to have stopped writing because Benjamin Brawley, the series editor, had told him that the project had been discontinued. The other irritation for Woodson was that Locke had secured funding from the Carnegie Corporation that he would have liked. "I am now in a position to take up formally your appreciated verbal acceptance of a commission to do a pamphlet for the Adult Education Series on Negro History." Locke continued:

> There will be nine of these booklets, Negro Music, Negro Art, the Negro in American Fiction and Drama, Negro Poetry, the History of the Negro, The Negro and Economic Imperialism, Economic Reconstruction and the Negro and Economic Aspects of the Race Question. These booklets will be approximately 96 to 112 pages and will be published under the grant given by the Carnegie Corporation through the American Association of Adult Education. I have assurance in writing that there will be "no restriction as to content," and I know very definitely,—since your name was mentioned in all discussions of the project that you would be as welcome a collaborator to the Committee and the sponsorship as you are to us.... The topics might very well follow the general outline of your The Negro in Our History.[24]

Woodson replied that he could not possibly write such a booklet for Locke's series, unless Locke let Woodson publish the entire series under his Associated Publishers. The request stunned Locke, but it shouldn't have. After all, Woodson was the head of an association that had been doing public history programming for almost a decade. He invented the Negro History Week celebration in 1926, along with annual meetings to stimulate the study and appreciation of Negro history among the public and among Negro teachers and self-trained scholars. Woodson had even supported some of Locke's proposals to research African art, had hired Locke to teach African art in his correspondence courses, and even created a publishing firm to print and distribute his and other books on Negro history. As Woodson put it to Locke, "The only way for me to cooperate with you would be to serve as the publisher of the entire series. This firm will gladly welcome the opportunity to bring out this series in keeping with its policy to stimulate adult education as it has done through the Association for the Study of Negro Life and History. You cannot expect the undersigned to join with others to duplicate what he is already doing."[25] Locke was proposing to create a publishing firm in Negro Adult Education to compete with Woodson's own efforts in this area, even if his did not bear the official title of adult education.

Not surprisingly, Locke was unwilling to deed over to Woodson the publishing of the booklets, since Locke had secured the funding to publish them himself. Locke accused Woodson of reneging on his previous commitment but then somewhat disingenuously suggested that "the matter of publication is as you may imagine entirely in the hands of our Committee," which might be more inclined to have Woodson publish the series if he was to contribute a book. But that was really not going to happen, as Locke made clear in the rest of the letter. "I am sure, for one thing, that few would agree with you in the rather monopolistic interpretation you make concerning this general field of work. I, myself, thought of this pamphlet as a friendly way of recognizing the work that you and your association have done in this field, and of making through this primer considerable publicity for The Negro in Our History and other of your publications."[26] Woodson's reply barely contained his fury: "You refer to a verbal agreement which I have never made. You must be using your imagination. When you talked to me about the affair I replied in the negative. I said in the first place that I would not write such a work for less than $500, and I advised you not to mention my name to your committee." Then, going to the heart of the matter between them, Woodson used the race card to hide the fact that they were now, in fact, competitors: "As to my 'monopolistic interpretation' I shall say only that Negroes need to cooperate in presenting their case to the world rather than serve those who for the last four centuries have been doing this for them in a distorted attitude."[27]

There was a kernel of truth in Woodson's charge, but at core he resented Locke for succeeding where he had failed in getting funding from the Carnegie Corporation to fund a publishing project. Indeed, despite his critique of Locke for "serving" the White people, Woodson himself had sought and received $25,000, paid in installments of $5,000 a year for five years—from the very same Carnegie Corporation in 1921 when starting the ASNLH.[28] The image that Woodson sought to convey—that his was a completely independent Black agency aloof from seeking support and funding from White folks—was an illusion, although he did not have to work under the American Association of Adult Education, a fact that would be important soon. As recently as 1927, Woodson had been pressuring Keppel to give him a substantial grant. Rejection of his grant request came because of an assessment in the Carnegie Corporation that

Woodson was difficult and irascible; by contrast, Locke was perceived as someone they could work with. Plus Locke had presented his proposals within the nomenclature of Adult Education, a Carnegie initiative with AAAE oversight. Locke had trumped Woodson in getting the Carnegie money, and Woodson was not happy about it.

Before the adult-education publication project mushroomed into another crisis, Locke had his own publication to finish. Kallen had been serious about having Locke contribute to the volume of American philosophy, and Locke's first opportunity to publish philosophy was due July 1. The article was a real struggle for him emotionally, but he found writing an essay on pure philosophy a welcome escape from the problems of being a Negro intellectual in Depression-era America. Even though Kallen pushed Locke to include something on his racial politics as a Negro in this article, Locke resisted, except in the autobiographical statement that accompanied the article. The essay he contributed, "Values and Imperatives," dealt with issues of diversity and group conflict raised at his conference but he posed them as a problem of values rather than a problem of race. In doing so, Locke formulated a new voice for himself speaking to American culture about its fundamental ethical confusions. So nervous was Locke about whether the article accomplished its goals that he submitted a draft of it to Smith to review before turning it over to Kallen. "Now I wonder if I could really impose on good friendship. Here is a copy of the paper for Kallen's anthology. I have asked him...if it deserves the mortuary's lap. But he just might be too embarrassed to do it. So will you please give me the benefit of your usual long-sighted sort of friendship? With the travails [?] of the fatiguing year, no local consultation available, I have been at a complete loss; and it is maybe a fizzler. Could you let me have your reactions rather promptly?"[29] Smith's reactions were swift. "Between legislative committees I have read your piece, and with no little enjoyment. To answer all questions at once, I say this: If Kallen declares the morg for your article, then I will be happy to immortalize it by publishing it in the Journal. I think it just that good." Kallen published it in *American Philosophy Today and Tomorrow*, well situating Locke's maiden philosophical publication in a broad community of contemporary philosophers.[30]

Indeed, the essay probably made Locke uneasy because of its boldness: it takes that community to task for abdicating its responsibility to construct a common ethics of the twentieth century after Nietzsche's declaration that God is dead and William James's declaration that all values were pragmatic. Universal values had also received a different kind of blow from Franz Boas, who taught that diverse peoples viewed and valued the world quite differently. But Locke challenged American philosophers to avoid succumbing to value anomie even while recognizing all values were contextual. He criticized American philosophers for their bad faith in not confronting the problem posed by twentieth-century revolutions in knowledge—how to develop and promote a system of values that is inclusive of difference and promotes a new global consciousness of tolerance without undermining the power of values to order our world. "Though they have at times discussed the problems of value, they have usually avoided their normative aspects, which has led them into a bloodless behaviorism as arid as the intellectualism they have abandoned or else resulted in a completely individualistic and anarchic relativism which has rightly been characterized recently as 'philosophic Nihilism.' In de-throning our absolutes, we must take care not to exile our imperatives, for after all, we live by them."[31] Values might be relative, but they were necessary.

Relativism, Locke argued, could not answer the fundamental question of the twentieth century: how do we construct a shared understanding of what we value in life? Pragmatism and positivism largely wished it away by saying values as such did not exist, which, as he brilliantly observed, is itself a value statement. "By waiving the question of the validity of value ultimates as 'absolutes,' we do not escape the problem of their functional categorical character as imperatives of action and as norms of preference and choice."[32] It is better to face the reality that we live making value judgments all the time even as we as yet have no philosophically adequate rationale as to why our values are superior. Instead of an intellectual critique of "realms of value," Locke shifts the focus to our "modes or kinds of *valuing*."[33]

Strikingly, the essay does not fit easily into any familiar philosophical camps, being less a pragmatic philosophical statement than a psychological one. Locke directly repudiates John Dewey, arguing that relegating values to the "logico-experimental slant" makes "truth too exclusively a matter of the correct anticipation of experience, of the confirmation of fact. Yet truth may also sometimes be the sustaining of an attitude, the satisfaction of a way of feeling, the corroboration of a value. To the poet, beauty is truth; to the religious devotee, God is truth; to the enthused moralist, what ought-to-be overtops factual reality."[34] This reveals a bit about why this essay appeared in 1935 while Locke was wrestling with the thorny questions of how to continue to promote poetry, the arts, and especially performance, as forms of knowledge at a time when knowledge seems increasingly sequestered to the scientific. The psychological perspective on values was his way out of the cul-de-sac the philosophical community heads backed itself into with its attention to the experimental approach to truth. Unlike the lions of pragmatism, Locke puts the feeling subject at the center of any discussion of value.

Locke's recurring phrase—a "functional analysis of value norms"—grounds any theory of value in the experience of the feeling subject, whether accessed through Gestalt theory or Jungian symbolism, both of which Locke references, to uncover the nuanced feelings, aesthetic-like reactions, to our experience that becomes over time our values. That's why they are often expressed in poetry and religion and politics, not simply in scientific or philosophical arguments. "For every value transformed by change of logical pre-suppositions, scores are switched by a radical transformation of the feeling-attitude. We are forced to conclude that the feeling-quality, irrespective of content, makes a value of a given kind."[35]

Putting feeling at the center of value creation also places the artist at the center of understanding not only about how values emerge but also how they change and acquire meanings from our experience. "The artist may feel duty towards his calling, obligation toward his unrealized idea.... Instead of the repose or ecstasy of contemplation or the exuberant flow of creative expression, he feels the tension and pull of an unrealized situation, and feeling obligation and conflict, senses along with that a moral quality. The changed feeling-attitude creates a new value; and the type-form of the attitude brings with it its appropriate value category. These modes co-assert their own relevant norms; each sets up a categorical imperative of its own, not of the Kantian sort with rationalized universality and objectivity, but instead the psychological urgency (shall we say necessity) to construe the situation as a particular qualitative form character. It is this that we term a function categorical factor, since it operates in and through feeling."[36] Like James's earlier work, Locke is tracing the formation of value consciousness and charting how it works and moves as a consciousness, not constructing an argument about the best way to test the truth of values. More than a statement about what is reality, valuing is a feeling with which we structure the reality we have.

Centering feeling in value theory also connected Locke's philosophical musings of 1935 with his adult-education interests. Values should not be deemed as valid only when they came from *rational* subjects, that is, educated philosophers. The common person values as much as the intellectual, and his or her tendency to be nonreflective and nonreflexive about his or her values is a key to what values are—a set of feelings about what is the good, the beautiful, and the just that we live by and are fiercely attached to. "The common man, in both his individual and group behavior...sets up personal and private and group norms as standards and principles, and rightly or wrongly hypostasizes them as universals, for all conditions, all times and all men."[37]

The deeper question, then, of the 1930s, was how to keep these commonly held "universals" from leading to a kind of conflict that could, if unchecked, destroy the world? What was the antidote to "Nordicism and other rampant racialisms" that seemed on the rise throughout the world? Locke's answer to this problem was that even White supremacy and anti-Semitism "might achieve historical sanity or at least prudential common-sense to halt at the natural frontiers of genuinely shared loyalties and not so their own eventual downfall through forced loyalties and the counter-reactions which they inevitably breed." Here, Locke reached back to his philosophy professor at Harvard, Josiah Royce, and his principle of "loyalty to loyalty" for the idea that those who fiercely held to their values could see the value in value loyalty. In a Kantian way, if they saw this kind of loyalty as a categorical good, as something good for all peoples, then the loyalty of other peoples to their values was a good and something to be upheld and defended despite our disagreement with them. It was analogous to the defense of free speech as a good even when I disagree with what others have to say. How can we have and celebrate our values without needing to deny to others their right to their values, their cultural preferences, their way of organizing space, their love of their way of doing things? That was the larger moral question facing the world in 1935, and Locke's essay answered it by posing a "principle of maximizing values" as the most likely to curb their excesses.

Locke's strength could be perceived as a weakness, since his tentative answer, loyalty to loyalty, and "maximizing values" did not outline any new path to get racists, imperialists, or fascists to stop imposing their will through violence on those who disagreed with "their values." What if the source of conflict was not over different values but the desire for the same value, the desire for monopoly? What if the conflict that led to a world war, a race riot, or a general strike was really that different groups or peoples wanted more of the same thing—such as power, or decent living conditions, or money? Indeed, as brilliant as Locke's analysis was, it skirted a burning issue—the issue of power, and how the powerful could impose their values, and keep more of what they valued for themselves and away from the weak, despite calls for tolerance. Tolerance itself needed to be backed by power to compel the more powerful to refrain from crushing the different or weak. Power, it seems, was the one key that Locke did not have an answer for, yet.

Loyalty to loyalty was not particularly useful for Locke in his own personal career when dealing with conflicts with others. During the conference, Locke had asked W. E. B. Du Bois to do a book for the Bronze Booklets series, which Du Bois agreed to immediately. Du Bois pumped out his booklet in record time and turned in the complete manuscript by June 1935, before anyone else. And it was a well-written and sharp critique of the New Deal approach to a "reconstruction" of the Negro. It was ideological, a plain but sharply worded statement of his conversion to nationalism in the 1930s. It was nationalistic rationalism in the face of segregation that said that Black folk needed to self-organize and follow in the footsteps of other immigrant groups who economically and politically fed their own. Initially, Locke seemed enthusiastic about Du Bois's submission. "I received yesterday our first manuscript,—that on Social Reconstruction and the Negro, from Dr. Du Bois. It is a very interesting piece of work of 108 pages"—the exact length that Locke had specified for the manuscripts and most other writers exceeded it.[38] Locke decided to send Du Bois one-half of the honorarium, plus $40 in secretarial typing expenses that Du Bois also requested, with the balance of $100.00 to be sent upon editorial revision and acceptance of the manuscript. But Locke became more cautious once he had read the manuscript thoroughly. It became clear that Du Bois's manuscript essentially critiqued all White intervention in Black social problems. Self-determination was the only solution to such problems. While sympathetic to this argument, Locke edited the manuscript with an eye to cleave off those arguments that might draw attention from the AAAE liberals whom he was producing, in an adult-education series, a radical adult-education critique of Americanism. Locke revised Du Bois's paragraphs to tone down his anger. As for Du Bois's alarming summary, "A Creed," that made explicit the rejection of White assistance and the embrace of Black self-determination, Locke jettisoned that completely in favor of having Du Bois conform to the format of including study questions at the end of each of the short chapters.

But Du Bois would not cooperate. He accepted a few changes and was open to others Locke might find or point out in his manuscript as "errors of taste" or "problems of fact." But he would not compromise on interpretation. He also resisted the idea of eliminating "A Creed." At that point, Locke elected not to challenge Du Bois. He could have replied with a simple statement that explained he could not accept the manuscript without the changes. Instead, he seemed to accept that Du Bois could only be moved so far. He had the manuscript typed up with some of the changes reversed and wrote the editor's preface that appeared at the beginning of each of the pamphlets. This preface introduced the author and rather deliberately encouraged the reader to "make up one's own mind" about the proposals Du Bois made. Locke still held back on publishing "A Creed," which was, quite frankly, a clear attempt by Du Bois to use the adult-education book as a propaganda advertisement for his program of Black self-organization.

Then Locke sent the manuscript to Lyman Bryson, whose role was to ensure that the series was written in the kind of simple language that would reach marginal readers in the adult-education target audience. However, form was not what Bryson was most interested in. Throughout his comments on this and other manuscripts, Bryson's eye most often fell on content. In the most important exercise of his "co-editor" role, Bryson apparently expressed extreme dislike for the manuscript turned in by W. E. B. Du Bois—and not because of its style. Locke countered Bryson's critique of Du Bois's manuscript by defending the right of the series to be "controversial." No letter from Bryson showing what he objected to in the Du Bois manuscript survives in the Alain Locke Papers at Howard, although he must have written Locke about the manuscript. He also must have made a stand on the Du Bois manuscript, and his threat was real, since if he alerted the Association that something untenable was being published under their auspices, they could end the whole series, with only part of the money having been dispensed.

The controversy threatened to bring an end to the whole Bronze Booklets publishing venture. Locke made that clear in a letter he wrote to Bryson:

> I am concerned about your reaction to the manuscript, not so much because of the manuscript itself, but because of the principle that it

raises. I had already considered the possibility that we would not publish the manuscript when I sent the first installment of the honorarium to Dr. Du Bois, believing that considering the extensive amount of time and effort he put into it, he should receive at least some of the honorarium. But the issue goes beyond simply the manuscript. Actually, I had considered that Du Bois might have a strident attitude in his manuscript on the racialist side, but believed that publishing his along with Bunche's more Marxist manuscript, would have the effect of boxing the compass of prevailing attitudes in the black community. As I stated in the proposal, I did not want to publish or believe that it would be successful to publish simply staid sociological studies of the Negro situation, but that for the series to succeed with the reading black public, it would have to be controversial or at least engage the controversial issues of the day. If this principle cannot be adhered to, then I would rather be done with the whole project than to put out a series of pedestrian pamphlets.[39]

This perhaps explains why Locke had not elected simply to write a big book that covered all of the subjects recommended in the series, for he could not express the radical views that needed to be expressed in order to connect with the radical temper of the 1930s. Instead, he had to let others write, because they could express his own opinions more sharply than he could and therefore establish him as a harmonizer of divergent values. But now those opinions, Du Bois's especially, together with Bryson's reaction to them, threatened his middleman position.

Locke was not committed to publishing Du Bois's manuscript at all costs. But as he had earlier expressed to Woodson, "I have assurance in writing that there will be 'no restriction as to content.'"[40] Du Bois was a lightning rod, but that was part of his appeal, and Locke needed his pamphlet to gain national, public attention for the series, to counterbalance some of the more tame booklets. If Locke could still publish the Du Bois manuscript in the first batch of booklets, the series might be an intellectual and political blockbuster and elevate Locke as publisher into the kind of impresario of contemporary Black Studies.

But Bryson was unrelenting. He suggested that the matter be put to a committee. Initially, Locke objected to this idea, recognizing that such a procedure would undermine his position as editor. But Locke's position was already undermined as editor. It is not clear that if challenged, Bryson would have gone to the Carnegie officials and won such a confrontation, since it would have been risky for Cartwright to shut down Locke's operation with the possibility of a public scandal over White censorship of Black thought through a supposedly liberal and democratic adult-education program. Yet Locke did not challenge Bryson.

Rather, he scheduled a meeting of the editorial committee to consider three issues: (1) what should be done about the Du Bois manuscript; (2) whether, in principle, the series should publish controversial books; and (3) what kind of disclaimer should be appended to each pamphlet to absolve the Association from responsibility for the views expressed by the authors to address Bryson's concerns. No notes survive from that meeting, but it is clear that the committee affirmed Locke's interpretation that the series should publish controversial books. A subcommittee was formed to consider the Du Bois manuscript and a statement was approved to absolve the AAAE of responsibility for the views expressed in the Bronze Booklets.

In the end, however, Locke did not publish Du Bois's manuscript in the series.

Not publishing his book was especially devastating to Du Bois, who was almost unemployed in 1935. Locke did remit to Du Bois the second half of payment for the book, bringing the total to the $200 promised. Afterward, Du Bois would tell friends that one could not trust Locke, and in fact, he was right. Locke would not sacrifice the adult-education project for Du Bois. This feeling of the betrayal of one Black intellectual by another lingers, even though Du Bois's stubbornness in the matter of publishing his creed made it more difficult for Locke to stick with him. Loyalty to another Black intellectual who, despite his irascibility, had come to Locke's aid in the conference was not enough for Locke to put loyalty to another Black scholar ahead of his own self-interest. Once again, something of his weakness as a leader was reflected in his choosing, albeit faced with a difficult decision, to ally with the powerful White people in his public politics.

The controversy delayed the publication of the first batch of Bronze Booklets for a year. Finally, at the very end of 1936, the Bronze Booklets appeared with Ralph Bunche's *A World View of Race* as his first signature publication in the four booklets that launched the series. By dumping Du Bois and foregrounding Bunche, whose Marxist take on race was in sync with thinking of the day, Locke gave his series an immediate currency it would not have had otherwise. This decision marked a turning point for Locke. He had turned his back on old-style Black nationalist proposals of social change and embraced, if only tentatively, the new, younger politics of Marxist criticism. Ralph Bunche had become something Locke needed: a muse. Locke's two booklets were written with a verve and clarity unseen in the rest of his writings. Teetering throughout the project on the brink of falling in love with Bunche, Locke absorbed not only Bunche's beauty and grace but also his strength of mind into his prose. Ironically, by rejecting Du Bois's manuscript, Bryson had helped Locke distance himself from the frankly nationalist, and increasingly dated, Du Bois, something that Locke would not have been strong enough to do on his own. Despite their conflicts, Du Bois had been a forerunner, someone who, since *Souls of Black Folk* had appeared in 1903, had been writing the books that

Locke wanted to write. Now, in a stunning move, Locke kept Du Bois from publishing his book, at least temporarily, and published two of his own instead—*The Negro and His Music* and *Negro Art: Past and Present*. These were short booklets, to be sure, but milestones in his own career, his first solo-authored books in a long career as a writer.

W. E. B. Du Bois went ahead and published his booklet, *The Social Reconstruction of the Negro*, privately. He then poured his efforts into getting his *Encyclopedia of the Negro*, a massive compendium of all knowledge about Black people, written and published. He had the support of Anson Phelps Stokes, who believed he could convince the General Education Board to fund the encyclopedia to the amount of roughly $130,000 if they could secure matching funds for the multi-volume project. That was a lot of money in 1937. By 1937, Locke had produced a much more modest set of eight booklets for $5,000. Locke had already published books by some of the Young Turk scholars at Howard that Du Bois was trying to get to work on the *Encyclopedia*, but they were rebuffing Du Bois because he had, in the words of E. Franklin Frazier, too many "politicians and not scholars" lined up to contribute. But Du Bois paid that no mind. He charged forward with the support of another Howard professor, Rayford Logan, also a critic of Locke, to try and get the GEB funding and to get Frederick Keppel to accept his proposal for the Carnegie Corporation to fund the *Encyclopedia*.

So convinced was Du Bois that his project would finally be funded that he invited Logan to wait with him for the telephone call on April 7, 1938, that he had been promised immediately following the GEB trustees meeting expecting confirmation that Stokes would call with news that his *Encyclopedia* would be funded. A bottle of vintage champagne sat chilling on Du Bois's desk in a fine bucket. The phone never rang. Months later Du Bois would learn that the Carnegie Corporation also would not fund the *Encyclopedia*. Du Bois biographer David Levering Lewis notes that a group of "foundation WASPs" had determined that Du Bois was a propagandist and not "objective."[41] Certainly, Lyman Bryson had reached that conclusion. There was no chance that the Carnegie Corporation was going to fund Du Bois's *Encyclopedia* after Bryson had rejected Du Bois's manuscript for the Bronze Booklets. Du Bois apparently never knew that it was the White representative of Carnegie who blocked his booklet's publication. Locke surely did not want to admit that the White man on his board held the ultimate power.

A photograph of the group of people Du Bois had assembled to contribute to the *Encyclopedia* tells the story (see page 716). Locke is off to the right of the picture, his tiny body wrapped in a silver-gray double-breasted suit, quite content. Du Bois is in the center, unmistakably facing away from Locke whom he believes is a backstabber. Keppel should never have let Du Bois think he had a chance to get the Corporation's funding for the *Encyclopedia*, and Locke probably would have told Du Bois that if he had asked. But as in many of these

Contributors to the *Encyclopedia Africana*, ca. 1938.

competitive struggles for White money among Black intellectuals, there was no chance of solidarity, or that one would "warn a brother" that he was about to be disappointed. In the end, this was the purpose of patronage in the larger struggle of Black intellectual self-determination in the mid-twentieth century. It was designed to divide and conquer. As with Mrs. Mason before, it succeeded.

37

The Riot and the Ride

Two days before Alain Locke trekked to the Museum of Modern Art in midtown Manhattan on March 21, 1935, to enthuse over Benin bronzes and Ife masks, Negroes ninety blocks northward had smashed plate-glass windows, fought police, and looted the trinkets of another decadent civilization. Two Black acts—the visit and the riot—with apparently nothing in common proceeded almost simultaneously. Locke, a professor, returned repeatedly to the temple of high modernism trying to claim an art tradition all but destroyed by European colonialism, then hijacked by European modernists, and now claimed as the intellectual property of American curators and art historians like James Sweeney and Robert Goldwater, while Harlem's African American residents destroyed $2 million worth of property after it massed outside of a Kress's Five-and-Ten because of rumors a young Puerto Rican thief had been mercilessly beaten by store clerks. Moving like a ragtag army, the unemployed—and underemployed—hurled rocks, broke through storefronts, and burned everything they did not take on 125th Street. So often dark and depressing in the evenings of the Great Depression in comparison to well-lit mid-Manhattan, Harlem lit up like New Orleans during Mardi Gras. Yet this was one party Locke missed. No mention of it disturbs his correspondence. No commentary exudes from this usually loquacious cultural critic as to why Negroes living at starvation levels with no exposure to high aestheticism were destroying every symbol of White commodity civilization in A-train New York.

The irony was tragic, but also comic, as Locke's concerns would have seemed ridiculous to the poor Black people exiting Kress Five-and-Ten Store windows with hot combs, lightening cream, and pen knives. Not only poor, Black unemployed, but also highly employed White aesthetes would ask Locke, why bother? Or as Irving Howe famously said to Ralph Ellison, the "Negro is not metaphysical." Locke, however, had tried to establish a Harlem Museum of African Art in the 1920s to no effect to show the Negro that she and he were heirs of a great civilization and thus subjects of the world. But he had failed precisely because neither Negroes nor Whites saw African art and high aestheticism as a means for Black people to rise up again. Instead, the riot dominated the front pages of New

York newspapers and cast the Negro as something else—a poor, hungry, but suddenly angry product of American civilization, now bent on tearing it down if she or he could not find justice within it. Unable to confront the contradiction head-on, Locke avoided the burned-out stores, the broken plate-glass windows, and the disheveled people stumbling around aimlessly yet angrily on 125th Street, Black people who knew they had been misused by New York and now decided to burn it down. Historians say the riot marked the end of the renaissance he had announced ten years earlier. Negro art was threatening to become little more than an exquisite corpse, an archived artifact seen only by White people in a mid-Manhattan museum.

It is worth taking a moment to see what Locke saw when he visited the Museum of Modern Art. He entered a spare exhibition space that from the first room taught the lesson he was trying to teach the world and Negroes with African art, that a dialogue existed between art and the Black subject in such spaces, when the horrific historical cacophony of colonialism, racism, and decline through Western contact was silenced. In a bright, white-walled space, a sculpture of a thin, angular, but powerfully armed African stood on one side of the twenty-five-foot-square room. The figure was the famous iron Dahomey Gu (war god). Opposite this spectacular figure was the most aesthetically radical representation of a human head in the show, a huge mask (tsesah) from the

Installation view of the exhibition, African Negro Art, March 18, 1935, through May 19, 1935. The Museum of Modern Art, New York. Digital image © The Museum of Modern Art/Licensed by SCALA/Art Resource, NY.

Bamileke people of late nineteenth-century Bamendjo, Cameroon, that showed why European modernists seeking a doorway to conceptual art seized on African art in the early twentieth century. For this mask contradicted all of the Renaissance notions of how to represent the head, turning eye sockets into bullets and topping off the head with an uplifting fan-like structure that seemed part antennae, part crown. Yet here, too, was the face, the visage, of a man, who was imbued with the Spirit—and joyful. He was not sad. He was in control of his world even as he acknowledged the control of the Spirit. He was alive with possibility, not beaten down by others' oppression. He was free, the creation, one could imagine, of the free, warrior-like figure on the opposite side of the room, facing his destiny with confidence and hope. Here was the dialogic relationship Locke had hoped to create in the Harlem Museum of African Art—and perhaps forestall the descent into darkness the 1935 riot represented to him—by allowing the twentieth-century Negro to gaze on the ancient Negro and the conceptual art mask he had created.

But Harlem Negroes were not in the room with Locke. They were picking up glass and the remnants of their tattered lives seventy blocks north of this museum, where a White man, James Sweeney, had brought to life Locke's message of a self-sufficient African manhood. That message would be mainly consumed by White not Black Manhattan, since Locke had failed in his attempts to teach the masses of Blacks to think aesthetically about their environment, about their possibilities. Where Locke felt free in this White block of aestheticism, he was sociologically incarcerated in Harlem, where the reality of the failure of the Negro Renaissance was scrawled on the now-boarded up and heavily policed built environment. But there was a message up there for Locke as well. In the messy, broken-glass environment of riot-torn Harlem, the Negro of the twentieth century was at least in dialogue with her environment, speaking back through violence to a built environment s/he had not built, but was now oppressed by despite the vision of the Black metropolis Locke had created in "Harlem." The riot was just as creative an act of exhibition as MOMA's, except it was the "ashes" response to oppression rather than the beauty he wanted. Yet so addicted was Locke to the vision of African identity represented in this exhibit that he could hardly tear himself away to trek back up to Harlem to stay at the YMCA, where he was allowed to stop in New York overnight. Locke could not escape the new reality: his vision of an aestheticized New Negro who turned anger into art was no longer widely credible. Up to 1935, Locke had acted as if he did not have to account for the "left behinds." Beauty mattered, not the ashes.

Now, however, in March 1935, a Black subaltern people no longer accepted being silent sufferers. Stripped of the right to picket stores that took their money but refused to hire them as employees, stymied by bureaucratic red tape from receiving decent health and social services, a rebellion had erupted with such a clear sense of outrage at the living conditions of Harlem that even *Time* magazine called a protest. But protest was something Locke instinctively avoided. Feeling that protest created the most degraded forms of art possible, he had eschewed and criticized the trend toward "protest" and "proletarian" art in the early 1930s. He continued to argue that art was an alternative to protest, and the only true art was that which refused to voice the harangue of the mob. But as he soon would learn, protest—even violence—against the injustices of Black life did matter, and they mattered more in the 1930s than they ever had. Protest, violence, and rebellion were things he had not yet accounted for, nor the possibility that they could, if he were not careful, derail his entire cultural strategy and make it—and him—irrelevant.[1]

It was not the case that Locke was unaware of the sociological, economic, and political dynamics that produced and sustained the African American ghetto. As early as his Race Contacts lectures in 1915–1916, Locke had developed one of the most sophisticated theories of race and space in American intellectual history, one that outlined how "restricted status," as Locke had put it, was marked in American society by assigning minorities, such as the Negro and the American Indian, to "separate" spaces—the ghetto for the Negro, because his labor was needed close at hand by White society, the reservation for the Indian, because his labor was not needed. That was another reason why Locke had grouped the two at the Minority Problems Conference in 1935; they were linked by the "separate sphere" spatial ideology that defined how they were controlled under what amounted to American "imperialism." Although the papers on "nonviolent" and "militant" activism presented at the conference are now lost, it seems likely that some mention of the recent Harlem riot would have been made.

The problem for Locke was that he could not put together, yet, the sociological and the aesthetic analyses of race when it came to something like the postmodern phenomenon of a rebellion against the commodities of mid-twentieth-century America out of reach of the Black poor in Harlem in 1935. More broadly, Locke could admit that social conditions were important and crucial, but he could not allow them to invade and distort the true purpose of art, which was beauty. That was the crux of his dilemma. How could he relate the pursuit of beauty to the pursuit of justice in Black America without reducing the former to the latter?

From 1930 to 1935, Locke had refused to give in to the pressures to make that kind of reductionism in his literary and cultural criticism. In that sense, his advocacy of the New Negro so far was bracketed by two reductionist approaches to art—what might be called the Queer Black aesthetic of the late 1920s and the proletarian art and literature of the 1930s. The shift from the 1920s emphasis on the beautiful Black subject to the 1930s championing of the angry Black subject was disturbing for Locke. But in fact the two had much in common, something Locke ultimately vehemently opposed. They started from the premise that art should represent its subjects according to some ideal, usually connected to the agenda of shocking or dethroning or destroying the hegemony of the bourgeoisie. Even during the 1920s, Locke reacted against what Bruce Nugent, Wallace Thurman, and Langston Hughes were doing—shackling, in Locke's mind, the agenda of a young Black art production to celebration of the "strength of the black gay spirit" rather than the production of great art. Locke's commitment to art as the embodiment of the diversity of Black humanity made him wince at attempts to achieve revolutionary solidarity through art, the direction in which the arts of the 1920s were headed. That seemed more like dogma than art to Locke, even though at times these movements produced exceptions that transcended such dogma.

By the mid-1930s, the poetry of Sterling Brown, Richard Wright, and Frank Marshall Davis, the plays of Samuel Raphaelson, and the newly militant writing of Langston Hughes in Scottsboro, Ltd. began to interpret the Great Depression and the disproportionate suffering of Blacks under it as evidence that the American capitalist system had to be overturned if Blacks were to achieve freedom and justice in America. Locke, however, was not very enthusiastic: "some of the younger Negro writers and artists see this situation in terms of what is crystallizing in America and throughout the world as 'proletarian literature.' What is inevitable is, to that extent at least, right. There will be a quick broadening of the base of Negro art in terms of the literature of class protest and proletarian realism. My disagreement is merely in terms of a long-term view and ultimate values. To my thinking, the approaching proletarian phase is not the hoped-for sea but the inescapable delta. I even grant its practical role as a suddenly looming middle passage, but still these difficult and trying shoals of propagandist realism are not, never can be, the oceanic depths of universal art."[2]

Locke was not free of bias in these judgments. He had adopted the strategy of art as a means of social change in the 1920s as an alternative to protest. He resented protest literature, as if it was a contradiction in terms. In addition, Locke was ambivalent about the Black masses and any literature that focused too exclusively on the anger of those Black masses. Fundamental to his approach to literature prior to 1936 was an elitist conception of Afro-American culture that was created by a cultivated "Talented Tenth" of Black writers who mined the folk and blues traditions to create what was inevitably "fine art." But the folk that Locke loved were the romanticized and aestheticized folk of the Harlem novels—not the angry, society-destroying Black masses of 1930s agitprop literature. For Locke, Afro-American cultural strategy in the 1920s was about being used to bring harmony between the races and providing an opportunity for gradual reform of American attitudes. By the 1930s, literature carried as subtext a confrontational approach to social change in America—something Locke could not stand.

Subtly, slowly, Locke began to ameliorate his antipathy to protest art after the 1935 riot. Interestingly, Godmother, a fierce anti-communist, suggested he get tickets to see two new plays by Leftist playwright Clifford Odets at the Longacre Theatre. That she sent him to these radical plays gave him maternal sanction to temporarily shed his usual class antipathies and begin to refashion his views as a critic of the new American aesthetics. "John [Mason's Black chauffeur] drove me over to the theatre," he wrote her. "The audience was small—but over-enthusiastic—not entirely from the normal reaction to the plays—but because they were partisans of one or another left-wing movements. It had the effect of a claque, and set me leaning backwards in the other direction." Yet Locke was open to what happened on stage, even if he was not as "enthusiastic" as the crowd. "Odets is a coming force in American drama and our social life—but he is over-anxious about his effects, packs them in too thick, and gets melodramatic on the slightest provocation.... There is vital new material here—and a living purpose beyond the stale ones of amusement or sophisticated analysis...an invigorating slap in the face of our bigots and charlatans and exploiters."[3]

To the first play, Odets's *Till the Day I Die*, Locke reacted in his typical way to 1930s agitprop theater: it was in too much of a hurry to convey its message and not focused enough on how accurately or how well it conveyed such messages. "I wish Odetts [sic] knew his Germany better—his Nazi types are grim caricatures...the hand chopping was too premeditated—(Odets wanted the audience to know it was coming so as not to miss it) as if they could? And things like that all through. Still, I wonder who could be neutral about Hitler and his gang after seeing the play—they ought to be sentenced to see it themselves." Key to his critique was his continuing opposition to the way that such plays did not pay attention to what made art interesting—the style, energy, and deliverance of the message. He had heard that "*Till the Day I Die* had been played once recently by a radical but amateur Negro players' group under Rex Ingraham (who played Stevedore) and that Odets had said 'They made a new play of it.' Of course, what they added was conviction, naturalness and spontaneity."[4] They had put soul in an otherwise soulless play.

Odets's other play, *Waiting for Lefty*, touched Locke more. "To me the most effective scene was one where the superintendent of the hospital is trying to wash his hands like Pilate over the intrusion of politics into his hospital and the loss of a patient in an operation because a relative of a higher-up must get this chance to enhance his reputation. This is real drama, because with the operation off stage, it leaves something for your imagination to do. Other scenes are too packed with realism and the actual message—so they either go preachy or melodramatic." The play narrated his struggle to accept the legitimacy of protest. But Locke was quick to add, perhaps mindful that Mason had recommended these performances to him, "Mind you, I am not belittling these plays—they are worth a score of Broadway successes and stale formula dramas. Only Odets and his theatre must grow up—and if they grow up unspoiled and uncommercialized they will be the American theatre of the future."[5]

"Leaning backwards in the other direction" was the memorable phrase from his letter to Mason, and it captures the whole problem. The art of the 1930s demanded that he engage with the reality of those suffering more than him. Confrontational aesthetics existed because the audience had to be shaken in order to break out of the blinders that bourgeois status imposed on the middle. For some time, he knew he had to come to terms with this art, with the dramatically changed reality of Black life outside of his Howard citadel, outside of his imagination of Harlem as a Mecca, as his attempt to provide a balanced assessment in this letter to Mason shows. He opined that once the art "grew up," it would become "the American theatre of the future." But it was Locke who had to "grow up" and create a more adult version and less romanticized view of Black social reality in the Great Depression. Locke had to change his orientation, but he had been unable or unwilling to do it.

Locke realized instinctively that the riot opened up a new racial landscape of interest and commitment of resources by the White establishment. By destroying property, rather than attacking White people directly, Blacks had brilliantly seized upon the one thing that had valuation in capitalism. The riot that destroyed a chunk of New York real estate brought Black people to the attention of Mayor Fiorello La Guardia, no less than President Roosevelt, and Locke had in his desk drawer a proposal for something they could do to address the situation and perhaps keep Black people from doing that again.

Prior to the riot, Locke had penned a brief proposal for an art center under which to house Negro visual and performing art activities, both creative and educational, in Harlem. Aware that in the aftermath of the riot, New York mayor La Guardia had set up a commission to study the conditions behind the riot and that E. Franklin Frazier, his Howard University colleague, headed up the research team, Locke updated his proposal for a Harlem Cultural Center as one way the city could try and make beauty out of the ashes of the Harlem race riot. In May 1935, he sent to Brady a brief "memorandum" for "A Harlem Center of Culture" to be installed in the YMCA building on the southeast corner of Lenox Avenue and 124th Street—one block from the center of the rioting. Interestingly, Locke made no direct mention of the riot in the proposal, but pitched it instead as a response to the "lack" of "facilities for art, music, drama, and adult education" in the "Harlem community" even though there was "much latent talent" there that needed "only favorable opportunity for expression."[6]

Aware that the riot was being interpreted as a violent expression of discontent, Locke alluded to the events merely by stating the obvious: "The development of this talent will add to the happiness of the people." Here, the idea offered the palliative that was often recommended in the aftermath of urban riots: "Such a center would be a spiritual force of the community" and allow "the best efforts of its gifted members" to be "displayed for the encouragement and inspiration of all." Such a sacred space would germinate a "'vision splendid' to encourage and stimulate the best in the community" and "congregate those who have distinguished themselves by praiseworthy achievements in the arts to encourage and inspire greater numbers of their fellow citizens." In such a center, the "master spirits of the Negro" would "inspire" the rest of the Negroes to "noble endeavor" and become "what Athens was to Greece, what Paris and Vienna are to Europe—greater centers of racial culture, racial aspiration and racial achievement." Not surprisingly, Locke recommended that the "director or Executive Director" of the Center be a Negro, selected by the board of education "because of his sympathy and vision to see the illimilable [sic] possibilities of the project and ability to conduct the center effectively." Clearly, Locke saw himself as such a person. Just as clearly, Locke articulated the older, cathartic view of art that he had proposed for much of his career as a Black aesthete and not the more militant view of art as a weapon of social upheaval as articulated by Augusta Savage, Romare Bearden, and Charles Alston.[7]

Tellingly, when a Mr. Rivers in the mayor's office suggested having hearings as part of bringing the proposal before the commission, Locke demurred. "I think this ill-advised," Locke wrote to Brady, "unless it is absolutely necessary. A committee of representatives ought to take the matter either straight to the Mayor, knowing in advance that the Investigating Committee will favor it; or the plan should come through as one of the Committee's recommendations reached in their deliberations. Why not let the Committee have the credit! Getting the idea across is the main thing." Locke urged Rivers to take the "scheme" to the "Investigating Commission chairman." Locke even spoke directly to "two members of the Committee" and suggested a "remedial finding urging immediate prosecution of a W.P.A. housing scheme for Harlem" that might include the cultural center as an elevating and humanizing part of the overall redevelopment of Harlem.[8] For years, Locke had been quietly feuding with Augusta Savage over her and other Harlem artists' control of art educational efforts in Harlem. He had been frustrated, along with Miss Brady, with art-education activities controlled by Ernestine Rose, the White librarian at the 135th Street Branch of the New York Public Library in Harlem. Locke did not want a public hearing where competitors like Savage or Rose could weigh in as being the legitimate custodians of such an effort in their veritable backyards.

Indeed, Rose had offered her own proposal to develop a "program of the extension of the library plant" to take advantage of the attention the riot had focused on the anger of the Black masses in Harlem and to suggest that art education might be a way to ameliorate local tensions. When the perspicacious Locke learned of her plan, he conceded that Rose's annex "could very well be housed in one end of the Community Center, although the management ought to be distinct." In other words, her project could be "housed" in his center if the "management" of the two entities was kept "distinct," because he and Mary Beattie Brady had already crossed swords with Rose. In order to establish his center and his appointment as its director, Locke would have to displace those arts managers resident in Harlem, and he did not want them getting wind of it before it was a fait accompli.

The committee headed by the rigorous, and critical, E. Franklin Frazier did not decide that a "Harlem Center of Culture" should be one of its main recommendations to address the systemic problems of poverty, unemployment, chronic and rampant disease, dirt, filth, and crowding in housing that plagued the area. And as Locke tired of struggling to advance his version of aesthetic education in an inhospitable climate after the riot, he longed to escape to Europe. Right after offering his proposal to the Harlem Commission in June 1935 and having it tabled, he left on a six-week tour of Paris, Brussels, Zurich, and Vienna, returning from what had happened over the summer in Harlem.

There was the rub. As a transnational, trans-urban cultural worker, Locke lived everywhere and nowhere. Of course, there was the upside to that kind of cultural mobility—in the Harlem Renaissance, he had brought together the German artist Winold Reiss, the West Indian writers Eric Walrond and Claude McKay, the French colonial critic Rene Maran, and other "most gifted" citizens of their respective cities and nations, to make Harlem into a symbol of the "vision splendid." But like other transnationals, Locke was not deeply inserted in the local. Locke's imaginary was diasporic, and in his letters to Mason that spring, it was the Italian-Ethiopian War and its threat to the Ethiopian homeland of Black Christianity, not Harlem, that consumed him. Mason chastised him for his need to escape Europe in ways he said "hurt." He admitted, "I must be made to realize that someday I must seize the courage to get a favorable place to work on my own ideas during the one free period in the year I have." He needed to finish his Bronze Booklets and advance his center idea at home. But his double bind reasserted itself every summer. "The only way of being reasonably comfortable would be to find a small cottage somewhere—and then the trouble of companionship would begin. The resorts for Negroes are entirely impossible—privacy is out of the question."[9] There was no place in America where he could be both Negro and queer—except, perhaps, in Harlem, if he could establish his center and some permanent income there. But that didn't happen, in part because Locke was not embedded in the daily living conditions of the community he wanted to resuscitate.

Returning home, however, Locke discovered his center idea might be in play again. Paul Kellogg, the editor at *Survey Graphic*, came to Locke with a proposal. Frazier had finished a preliminary report while Locke was in Europe and submitted it to Mayor La Guardia for comment, approval, and publication. La Guardia demurred. Kellogg then became involved when Oswald Garrison Villard, the perennial Leftist and commission member, had offered an article on the report's conclusions to *Survey Graphic*, and then withdrawn it when Kellogg circulated the draft through city departments for review prior to publication. Kellogg needed someone to write a "balanced" article on the subject and repeatedly asked Locke to do it. Rather than hire Frazier to do the article presenting the report's findings to the public, Kellogg wrote to Locke in January 1936 asking if he would be willing to study the report the Commission had made, meet with city commissioners criticized by the report, and write an article for a popular audience that would set the record straight.[10] Locke demurred, citing the pressure of work, which included trying to get the first set of Bronze Booklets published. But Locke inquired whether the mayor might be interested in creating the Harlem Cultural Center he had earlier proposed. If the mayor did create such a center, Locke could have a place where he could plant all of his efforts to make Negro literary, visual, and theater arts an engine of change for the Black community in Harlem.

But in March, a challenge emerged to Locke's whole philosophy of racial renaissance when Meyer Schapiro, a fiery, Jewish, Trotskyite professor of art at Columbia University, published an article, "Race, Nationality, and Art," in the March 1936 issue of *Art Front*, the radical monthly journal of the Artists' Union. In that article, he stated: "There are Negro liberals who teach that the American Negro artist should cultivate the old African styles, that his real racial genius has emerged most powerfully in those styles, and that he must give up his effort to paint and carve like a white man. This view is acceptable to white reactionaries, who desire . . . to keep the Negro from assimilating the highest forms of culture of Europe and America. . . . But observed more closely, it terminates in the segregation of the Negro from modern culture."[11]

A year earlier, Locke had been going to MOMA in part to encourage Black artists to seize on African art as inspiration. Locke was not alone. Several such artists, such as Romare Bearden and Norman Lewis, were also going to MOMA, although without acknowledging Locke as their source of inspiration. Now Locke had a White radical intellectual criticizing his views—without mentioning him by name—suggesting that such advice was tantamount to self-segregation. More devastating, this critic repudiated the notion that something like a racial art tradition existed at all.

Schapiro was the most spectacularly original and brilliant young art historian in America. "Race, Nationality, and Art" was mainly an attack on the German art historical tradition that used race and nationality to characterize world art as falling into neat national or racial traditions that embodied the particular psychologies of those nations or peoples. Schapiro argued that what were thought of as enduring psychological traits in national traditions were mere conventions of how art history had been studied and lacked any scientific basis. He claimed such notions of national or racial proclivities in art inevitably led to Nazism, a view confirmed, it seemed, by German art historians' support of the Nazis when they came to power in Germany. Schapiro was building an alternative approach to art history—that of analyzing art in terms of its social basis in its own time and suggesting that great art usually emerged from class and other conflicts in a society or civilization, such that the tensions, disconnects, and discontinuities of a social order erupted in a work of art and gave it its distinctive style. Schapiro was dismissive of all trans-historical factors in shaping a work of art, and he categorized race as one of those factors, a dangerous myth and analytical anachronism that had no place in a "scientific" art history of modern art.

Schapiro's attack on Locke was part of Schapiro's broader reaction to the changing landscape of American Marxism. For years, American Marxists had argued that if Black artists produced a racial art, they were ethnic chauvinists driving a wedge between White and Black workers and undermining socialists' efforts to foster class-consciousness among American workers. But building on his theory of socialist culture in his 1925 speech, "The Political Tasks of the University," Stalin encouraged ethnic nationalism within the Soviet Union and ethnic cultures in the union republics in the 1930s as not contradictory to socialism. Stalin's form of Soviet cultural pluralism captured in the line "socialist in content, national in form," however, was anathema to Schapiro and other Trotskyites in the United States, who wanted to keep Soviet cultural pluralism out of US socialism. But it was already happening, to his chagrin. By 1935, faced with the rise of Hitler in Germany as a threat to the Soviet Union, the International Seventh Congress of the Comintern declared a "People's Front Against Fascism," in which communists would enlist liberals and progressives in alliances with communists in the fight against fascism. These two developments—the acceptance of cultural pluralism and the welcoming of liberals into the Radical Left circles of culture in the mid-1930s—led the Communist Party USA to welcome "Negro liberals," as Schapiro called them, into its summer camps, to lower criticism of their racial arguments, and to make celebration of African American culture a key part of the "revolutionary" education for workers in the Party. Suddenly, the ideological control that Schapiro and others like him had had over the socialist art movement in the United States by claiming that any assertion of a distinctive culture produced by Blacks in America was tantamount to "chauvinism." In coming down on Locke, Schapiro saw himself as turning the White and Black proletariat away from the worship of false idols, such as race, and directing them toward the monotheism of Marxism as the one true and new religion—despite that that "religion" had evolved into something quite different in the Soviet Union.

Locke's argument was actually subtler than Schapiro's would allow. As Locke had argued in "Harlem" in the 1925 *Survey Graphic*, the New Negro was not a fixed identity, but a work in progress being constructed by modernity. "Hitherto, it must be admitted that American Negroes have been a race more in name than in fact, or to be exact, more in sentiment than in experience. The chief bond between them has been a common condition rather than a common consciousness; a problem in common rather than a life in common"—a "body-in-pieces" that needed a "fiction," the New Negro, an invented "I" to pull its pieces together into a coherent, mature identity.[12] The function of literature, art, the theater, and so on was to complete the process of self-integration through visual and literary art and produce a Black subjectivity that could become the agent of a cultural and social revolution in America. Promoting the study of African art was not his attempt to take the modern African American back to a pre-American romantic past, but to anchor a progressive "transformation that takes place in the subject when he assumes an image," as Jacque Lacan put it, teaching the "child race," as Locke once put it, that it was the modern heir of a great tradition. Modern Black art would do something that ancient African art never had to do—synthesize a disparate body-in-pieces of the Negro race, drawn by the African slave trade, the Diaspora and slavery, and modern segregation into a new whole. And to do that required a Moses—a role that Booker T. Washington, W. E. B. Du Bois, and Marcus Garvey had each seen himself as performing, but that Locke saw himself taking up through art, not economics or protest politics. Blacks needed to form a stronger identity in order to join any larger collectivity called the American working class, but some on the Left in the 1930s viewed that stronger racial identity as a threat.

Harold Cruse characterized this type of conflict as intrinsic to how Jewish intellectuals treated African American cultural production during the 1930s.[13] But not all Jewish intellectuals and even art historians approached Negro culture and African art as Schapiro did. Another Jewish art historian, born a year after Schapiro, was Viktor Lowenfeld, who fled to the United States two years after Schapiro's article was published and accepted a position teaching art at the Hampton Institute, the Negro college in Virginia, in 1939. Unlike Schapiro, Lowenfeld encouraged his art students to develop an art that reflected the particularities of the Black experience in the South and the urban North. In part because of his firsthand experience of Nazi terror, John Biggers, his most famous student, recalled seeing Lowenfeld break down in tears when he learned his family had been massacred by the Nazis—and theorized that Lowenfeld's own experience with suffering and oppression conditioned him to encourage his students to use their art to confront how Blacks lived and coped with American oppression, rather than run away from it in their art. According to art historian Alvia Wardlaw, "Lowenfeld actively used Hampton's collection of art from Africa and other cultures. It was the African works that most sparked Biggers' imagination. He recalls that the first time he saw these sculptures he was repulsed and could not understand why Lowenfeld 'wanted us to look at that ugly stuff!' "[14] At the time Biggers could not fully appreciate the bridge to African heritage that former Hampton student William Sheppard had hoped to build by donating Juba and Central Kongo art to Hampton.

But Lowenfeld insisted on exposing his students to these objects, believing that in studying them they would discover a direct and palpable link with their

African heritage. As he expressed his art philosophy in the *Hampton Bulletin of 1943*, "Culture has never developed without unity of life and art. [Teaching art is only justified] if it makes a definite contribution to Negro life and culture, in spreading art into community life, homes, and schools, and in making the campus art conscious."[15] While Locke and Lowenfeld would not meet until the 1940s, they were kindred spirits despite differences of heritage because both believed in the psychological healing of deep explorations of heritage and identity.

Lowenfeld's perspective developed out of a direct experience of the Holocaust. Schapiro's attitude emerged out of his experience of America as a reformed Jewish immigrant boy, who attended Columbia during his adolescence and found in art history, and especially Marxism, a way to escape what many of his generation felt was a stifling Jewish ghetto in America. Schapiro found in Trotsky communism a space for the reformation of ethnic identity into a higher identity, a kind of cosmopolitan equality antithetical to religious or ethnic heritage. Even Ralph Bunche, like Schapiro, believed that a Marxist revolution based on class would wash away racism and the need for counter-identities such as Locke promoted. Marxism and modern art were signs of freedom; race and religion signs of backwardness. Why would anyone want to go back to that, Schapiro must have thought.

But while Trotskyite and even Communist Party cells, camps, and parties were freer, more diverse, and more sexually open than conservative or liberal political communities, a racial intellectual division of labor also existed in Communist USA circles. Jokes like "You bring the schwartzes, I'll bring the booze" reveal a sense that Blacks were the bodies needed to authenticate the enterprise, not the minds who would guide or refine the enterprise of creating this new world of post-capitalist America.[16] As the historian of African art Ladislas Segy pointed out during a visit to his gallery in New York, all three of the architects of modernism were Jewish—Karl Marx, Sigmund Freud, and Albert Einstein.[17] Blacks, in other words, were latecomers to modernism—the intellectual proletariat to follow in the footsteps of the new Moses.

A generational revolution was also undermining Locke's program in the 1930s as much as ethnic competition between two oppressed minorities. Two months after Schapiro's article appeared, Locke received a mimeographed manifesto from the Harlem Artists Guild announcing a policy of "non-cooperation" with the Harmon Foundation. The Texas Centennial Exposition had planned an exhibition of work by Negro visual artists and had asked the Harmon Foundation to help organize the event. The Harlem Artists Guild was also invited to participate. But when the Guild circulated its memorandum of "non-cooperation" with the Harmon Foundation, it dashed the Foundation's plans to "organize" the Negro exhibition. Locke was livid. To Miss Brady, he wrote:

> I was going to write you that I could give some time, while in New York proofreading, to your plans for an art show and to the scenario of the

movie. But when you read the enclosed memorandum of the Harlem Artists Guild, which I just received in this morning's mail, you will, I think, join me in a reaction of protest and disgust. I really don't see much use in putting out time and energy disinterestedly in behalf of folks with so little sense of appreciation and gratitude. All the more so, I imagine, in your case. I had no wind of this, though I am not terribly surprised. I had a casual talk, recently with Augusta Savage, who was soliciting my interest in her forthcoming art festival week. She gave no indications of this attitude or I would have rebuked her. You may still consider going on, but I really don't see how a show could be very successful in the face of such a group boycott. To me, the main motive seems to be new-found independence because of the W.P.A.'s support. That would be alright if they had discharged their obligations to the foundation and admitted the helpfulness of the past. I don't want to be too cynical, but I would wager that three months after the government stopped its gratuities, most of them would be knocking at your doors again with their hands out as usual. I would challenge their position publicly, but they don't fight fair, and I am too tired and disillusioned to take them on.[18]

The Guild's memorandum was an artistic declaration of independence that stated:

> The Guild, comprising the majority of Negro artists in Greater New York and numbering in its ranks some of the foremost Negro artists of the country, is convinced that the Harmon Foundation does not serve the best interests of the Negro artist. We feel that the Harmon Foundation's past efforts to advance Negro art have served the opposite purpose by virtue of their coddling rather than professional attitude toward the Negro as an artist. Basic in the ill direction of the Harmon Foundation's efforts has been the fact that they are not a recognized art agency and, possibly for this reason, have presented Negro art from the sociological standpoint rather than from the aesthetic. The selection of the Harmon Foundation as entrepreneur for the Negro artists in the instance of the Texas Centennial Exposition is a clear example of how insidiously the Foundation has become an arbiter of the Negro artist's fate through the mere fact of its original, perhaps well-intentioned, philanthropy on the part of an organization which is incompetent to judge art except on a racial basis that we take this occasion to announce our reasons for not cooperating with the Harmon Foundation in this particular instance.[19]

Eleven years earlier, Locke had written in *The New Negro: An Interpretation*, "Tutelage of any sort is rejected in favor of the New Negro wanting to go it alone." Now, he was angry because the Harlem Artists Guild rejected the Harmon

Foundation's tutelage. But he saw this as a swipe at him as "an arbiter of the Negro artist's fate," since for several years he had served as a guest curator and judge of art in the Harmon Foundation exhibitions. Brady seemed less upset, out of weariness perhaps, with the memorandum and less convinced that it was the work of Savage. "Frankly I do not know who the malcontents are definitely as they do not come out in the open. I have been under the impression that Miss Savage had a very co-operative feeling, also Mr. Alston and Mr. Aaron Douglas. None of them have ever come out and told us to our faces that they don't like us. In fact Miss Brown has been a connecting link and she has had very definitely the feeling that they were very friendly disposed."[20]

But the Foundation should have seen this rebellion coming. When Brown had visited a Mrs. Pollak, who had control of many of Augusta Savage's and other young Black artists' artwork to coordinate exhibiting in Texas, Pollak informed her that the WPA would do its own installation at the Dallas Centennial and would not lend any of Augusta Savage's art to the Harmon Foundation. When Miss Brown expressed surprise, she was told to meet with Holger Cahill, the director of the Federal Art Project, in Washington, D.C. When she did so, Brown found "Mr. Cahill was exceedingly indifferent and finally stated that the real reason behind their unwillingness to cooperate with us was that the artists themselves did not like to exhibit through the Harmon Foundation." The memorandum from the Guild merely concretized a brewing attitude of self-determination by Black visual artists who were tired of having to go through Brady and Locke and the Foundation to get their work seen. Brady must have known of these rumblings of dissent before the Guild letter arrived, and if she did not, she was a quite a bit less astute in this area than she showed herself to be in others. Nonetheless, Brady was not in a mood to fight. "I dislike argument of an unnecessary nature and I certainly do not want to undertake anything that is not helpful," Brady confided to Locke.[21]

Locke was correct about one thing: the emergence of the W.P.A., founded that April 1935 with Holger Cahill as the director of the Federal Art Project, made "non-cooperation" with the Harmon Foundation possible. Cahill had moved aggressively to make the WPA a player in the American art world, especially by employing African American artists, some of whom, like seasoned artists Charles Alston and Archibald Motley, received employment checks for work as artists for the first time in their lives. And in Harlem, artist-entrepreneurs like Augusta Savage seized on the WPA to secure employment for her favorite artists and to lobby Cahill and others to create what local artists had wanted for years—a Harlem Community Center run by artists. With that new lease on government money, Harlem visual artists were independent of the kind of private patronage the Harmon Foundation offered. That independence extended to subject matter, as the WPA allowed a wide range of freedom to artists to explore political themes like lynching, poverty, urban decay, rural decline, and working-class life, more politically edgy work than the Harmon Foundation favored. And the WPA allowed a degree of integration the Harmon's segregated shows did not foster, bringing together Black artists to work with and study with more established White artists who also needed a WPA paycheck to live. Clearly, the WPA was a better patron, despite Locke's belief in loyalty to the Foundation that had secured earlier recognition for Black visual artists. There was little loyalty to loyalty in the 1930s.

Locke and Brady refused to acknowledge, though, the simmering resentment that had existed for years toward the Foundation. While the Harlem Artists Guild exaggerated how much Black artists had to "bow and scrape" to get the support of the Harmon Foundation, some like William H. Johnson felt the Foundation was not aggressive in selling his work (something frankly they were ill-equipped to do) and that the Harmon Foundation was cheap. It charged unemployed artists to frame their work and refused to return it to them until they reimbursed the Foundation even though the framing was only done to exhibit the work for the Harmon Foundation! Harmon was losing position to the WPA, because the Foundation refused to employ artists, again, something it was not equipped to do on a large scale. But that was what Black artists needed—not tepid exhibitions that sold no work. Even Locke was never employed by the Foundation for his labor. The Foundation embodied the old Christian benevolent idea that Blacks were so downtrodden, they should be grateful for any assistance; but that attitude was rapidly disappearing among "New Negro" visual artists of the 1930s, even if Locke did not like their criticality toward his allies.

An intriguing subtext also existed to this "rebellion" that Brady revealed in her letter to Locke.

> Mr. Schomburg was in the office the other day and he volunteered the suggestion that several years ago when a young man named Bearden wrote an article for Opportunity on the disadvantages of Negro artists associating with the Harmon Foundation, that it was his understanding that Claude McKay had written the article. I always find it difficult, as you know, to get Mr. Schomburg right down to the actual point.... He said he would get his ear to the ground and give us the advantage of any information he was able to dig up.[22]

That article had been written by Romare Bearden in 1934 to complain about the Harmon Foundation not being a legitimate art institution and putting on shows that contained very weak art by Negroes alongside the more sophisticated. It had been the first public rebuke of the Harmon Foundation by a Black artist and had contributed, perhaps, to Brady's decision to back away from hosting expensive exhibitions for "ungrateful" Black artists. Interestingly, Brady did not readily believe that McKay had been behind the Bearden article, because McKay "had received a recognition from the Harmon Foundation a number of years ago, later applied to us for a grant to continue his research and study in some foreign country.... We gave him all the helpful suggestions we could." But they did not give him any money! Here again was the Harmon conceit—penniless artists like McKay ought to be grateful for "helpful suggestions" when what they needed was cash. "It has always been my understanding that as far as he [McKay] thought of us at all it was in a very friendly way." Obviously, Brady was unfamiliar with McKay, who castigated even those who gave him money, let alone those who only gave "helpful suggestions."[23]

Locke did not respond directly to Brady about Schomburg's confidence, but he would not have missed its significance. That McKay, a closeted Black nationalist, might be behind the Harlem Artists' Guild's declaration of independence signaled that this awakening was very different than Meyer Schapiro's. The Harlem rebellion was a radical movement of artists who were committed to a Black Nationalist notion of art and community. Locke would have read the insertion of McKay into this challenge to the Harmon Foundation as a sign he might be as much an enemy as a friend.

As the summer of 1935 approached, Locke faced three challenges to his aesthetic leadership—Black rioters, whose protest in the streets diminished the importance of high aestheticism projects like his; a White-led radical art movement that attacked Black aesthetic nationalism as racist; and a Black-led activist insurgency that was deeply critical of the White institutional patrons he had allied with after Mason. Underlying each was a challenge to a quietist racial politics in which art was aligned with palliative measures in the Black community that did not fundamentally challenge segregation and its system of psychological degradation of Black people to maintain power and resources for Whites in America. Locke's theory of art awakening was designed to awaken and sustain Black subjectivity without confronting—or dismantling—institutional racism, a program that was increasingly ineffectual and old-fashioned in the militant 1930s.

The American Association of Adult Education would highlight this problem. It again held its annual meeting in Virginia, without anticipating that the hotel it selected had Jim Crow policies that refused to give rooms to Black presenters and members—the very participants that the organization said it was most eager to attract to make adult education a national imperative. Cartwright sought to find "alternative" sleeping arrangements for the Negroes, rather than pull out and take the financial hit of having to hold the conference elsewhere. Plus, as an organization with national aspirations, ruling out the South as a site of the meetings would mean conceding that its adult-education agenda could not be fulfilled without desegregation, a topic the leadership studiously avoided. This time some Black members balked at Cartwright's "arrangements," setting up a potential confrontation with the hotel at the annual meeting.

Once again the Association turned to Locke to solve its problem. He was tired of it. Morse Cartwright was surprised. "I have just had a letter from Professor Cooper at Hampton Institute who shared your feeling with regard to the meeting. He plans to come only on Thursday and since he is to be in Washington, or Baltimore at that time anyhow, the attendance is made fairly easy."[24] But "Miss Hawes" was coming and declaring she would force integrating the Sky Lodge meeting. As usual, Black women were in the vanguard of contesting segregation's vicious humiliations, as Locke wrote Cartwright:

> I have made extensive inquiry about the policies of some of the other liberal organizations on this matter of discrimination. Such definite public announcements and comments have been made on the position of the Women's League for Peace and Freedom, the National Conference of Social Work and the Y.W.C.A. that I am surprised to find that they have no express legislation on the matter. In each case it is an agreed policy on the part of the officers and executives of these organizations, and that they have refused to make arrangements for several years for meetings anywhere there is likely to be discrimination. Their executive officers announce such a policy to convention hotels and authorities of host cities and to delegates or agents seeking the selection of a city as a convention meeting place, and receive assurances in writing about the absence or waiving of discriminatory practices in all usual accomodations [sic] for official delegates and members of these associations.[25]

Locke stated that he regretted the situation had developed, but he was actually glad, for it forced the Association to take a stand on segregation at meetings, which it should have done when it first decided to get into the "Negro business." Cartwright was forced to decide never to schedule meetings at hotels that did not explicitly state a nondiscriminatory policy and had Lyman Bryson draw something up.

As Locke wrestled with the implications of the Harlem Artists Guild rebellion and the limitations of the American Association for Adult Education as a progressive organization, a door to a more independent base of operations seemed to open. The *Survey Graphic* still wanted to do an article on the Harlem race riot. Rather than hire Frazier to present the riot commission report findings to the public, Kellogg continued to pressure Locke to write the article on the Harlem report. By May, the ever-resourceful Kellogg had gotten the mayor to allow Locke to read the confidential report in the mayor's offices and to meet with the city commissioners to discuss its findings. When Kellogg supported Locke's private recommendations to the mayor that an art center be built in Harlem, Locke agreed to do the report.

Since Locke planned to go abroad at the end of June 1936, he had little time to produce such a report. Nevertheless, he swung into action. He made several trips to New York to read the report and collect data, much of it from the commissioners who were the target of the report's criticisms. Within record time, Locke came up with his main line of attack on the problem—to argue that the new social reality in Harlem of abject pervasive poverty and city-wide discrimination was a powder keg ready to explode and destroy Harlem—and perhaps the rest of New York—if immediate improvement of conditions was not made. Locke the harmonizer also asserted that such improvement was already occurring in large part because the La Guardia administration was moving quickly to correct the grosser hospital, education, and sanitation inadequacies of Harlem, even though he believed something more fundamental and enduring needed to happen if the soul of Harlem was to be saved. Locke was confident that his Harlem article had done what it needed to do—expose the toxic situation in Harlem, but create support for renewed progressive investment in Harlem.

Locke enthusiastically greeted his time away that summer, which took him to the Soviet Union and exposure to its program for cultural and racial minorities. The immediate rationale for going there was that the Soviet Union had refurbished its spas on the Black and Caspian Seas to cater to the traveling elite who now avoided Hitler's Germany. Kislovodsk—Russian for sour waters—was famous for mineral springs like those at Nanheim. Ringed by gorgeous mountains, Kislovodsk was so breathtaking that Locke could only tolerate its beauty in stretches. "I have been up in the hills three times since I last wrote you—just often enough for it is really too grand for a daily experience. Of course, as in all mountain neighborhoods, you have to keep your eyes on the sky—clouds come up at short notice and pour down occasionally—but always with quick clearings and gorgeous sun-bursts afterwards." But the most important aspect of the trip was the opportunity to see the blossoming of a new consciousness issuing forth from the Soviet regime:

> The more I see of this regime, the more it impresses me. A striking example was today's celebration in honor of the Soviet aviators who broke the world's record. They were received in Moscow and decorated—but their first official visit was to the factory which had turned out their motor—aviators, designers and engineers went to the factory and thanked the workman who had built the plane—there is a wonderful sense of national unity and the interest in the progress of the regime is so great that long queues of people stand twice daily at the newspaper booths to get the newspapers—and then if there is a shortage, they form in small groups while some volunteer reads the paper aloud from start to finish.[26]

In Kislovodsk, even Asia's nomadic peoples seemed to embrace Soviet modernism, marked by "clean hands and face,—the inevitable sign of the new influence." Even while looking down from his pince-nez at the naive efforts of the local theater, he realized something singular was happening in the Soviet Union. "Naturally, like children, they [the Soviet players] want to show us all they have at once." But "there is no theatre like it in the world. Each one of these minorities (Gypsies, Serbians) enjoys a state theatrical troupe on government subsidy." The plays conveyed the stories of the people with a realism and truthfulness not imaginable in racist America, where "such things are impossible under present conditions for the Negro," even under the Federal Theatre Project. "The Russians are the only nation treating racial and national minorities honestly and decently through and through."[27]

So enthusiastic was Locke about the Soviet cultural renaissance he was witnessing that he sent Mrs. Mason, an avid anti-communist, an excerpt from the radio talk he delivered once he reached Moscow:

> The Soviet Theatre is becoming a federation of many national and minority cultures, each with its place of attention and recognition. This unusual program was clearly evident in the opening festival performance of the Theatre of Peoples' Art. Here we saw excellent performances by amateurs of the folk arts of more than a score of the Russian nationalities, including minority groups that but a few years back under the old regime were not only politically oppressed and exploited, but also culturally despised and discouraged. Now with state support, their popular art is recognized and their formal art encouraged. This Theatre of People's Art, though recently established, represents a new program of deepest significance.[28]

Locke witnessed in this theater a new subjectivity emerging. As an experienced skeptic, Locke knew the Soviets manufactured situations and staged spectacles of Soviet euphoria to sway visitors. And yet something in the people was indelibly different from any other oppressed minority he had observed. A disrespected people—some had always referred to the Russians as the "niggers of Europe"—had been transformed. He wanted to see that visualized in the faces of Negroes in the United States, something he glimpsed in the precolonial African faces in the MOMA exhibit, but could see nowhere else in Black America. Of course, what Locke did not see was the kind of violent revolutionary upheaval that had been necessary to make these peasant people subjects. Nowhere did Locke call for the social revolution that had upended the prior Russian society and erected a different one in its place. Rather, he wanted the revolution to be imagistic, cerebral, and symbolic. Yet he believed the Soviets had achieved something that was indelible and important to America, not only to Negroes.

Upon his return to the United States, Locke was bubbling over with enthusiasm for Russia, as recorded by the staff of *Survey Graphic*, who wrote Paul Kellogg, "Alain Locke was here this afternoon on the chance that he could talk to you about Russia. He wondered if you contemplate bringing out a special number on Russia. He seems convinced that the Soviet has solved the problem of economic security permanently and not merely while in the process of building."[29] Locke's reaction resembles that of other American intellectuals who traveled to Russia in the 1930s, especially after disillusioning experiences with American reform. Not surprisingly, Kellogg ignored Locke's suggestion to have him write an article about the Soviet "revolution." Kellogg had had specifically Negro work for Locke to do, and from Kellogg's perspective, Locke had already done that quite well.

Locke's article on the riot, "Harlem: Dark Weather Vane," had been published by the *Survey Graphic* in August while he was still in the Soviet Union and had been lauded generally by Kellogg and the liberal New York establishment. It had taken on added political significance when it appeared and afterward because La Guardia refused to publish the commission's report. In essence, Locke's article became the official report on the riot from the standpoint of the New York press, eclipsing and eliding the commission's report authored by his colleague at Howard, sociologist E. Franklin Frazier. Frazier's more critical report reflected the new mood among young Black social scientists of the 1930s, who not only criticized American society for its racism but also for the class and structural inequalities they believed caused the Great Depression. Not surprisingly, Kellogg was pleased with the article and wrote La Guardia shortly after it had appeared: "I should like you to know how altogether happy I am at the outcome of Dr. Locke's appraisal of the Harlem findings. I had a cordial note from him during the summer and am sure that, from your angle, you too must have felt that my confidence in his execution of this delicate commission was not misplaced."[30]

A different reaction awaited Locke when he returned to campus. Frazier asked Locke to go for a ride with him. According to Harold Lewis, a friend of theirs: "Frazier was so furious that he got Locke, I don't know how he got him in his car, but Frazier had an old Packard what we used to call coupe, you know a two-seater, and he said later that he drove Locke all over the city telling him what he thought of him. Not only did he [Locke] get it [Frazier's report] and published it without information, but he tended to water it down."[31] A year later, Frazier was still angry. Locke wrote Kellogg, "The social work set-up at Howard is in charge of Franklin Frazier—and there is still enough personal estrangement to make suggestions from me unwelcome in that quarter."[32]

This reaction did not surprise Kellogg. When Locke had completed a draft of his article, Kellogg had circulated it among the city commissioners whom Frazier's report had criticized to give them a chance to certify whether Locke's article was accurate. They took full advantage of that opportunity to insist that the specific indictments of the Frazier report were no longer accurate, because the numbers had changed and most of the specific problems had been addressed in the year since the riot. But when Kellogg circulated the report to Frazier, he was livid. He wrote to the *Survey Graphic* and termed Locke's article as "an attempt, first, to relieve the present administration in New York City of all responsibility for conditions in Harlem and, second, to give the impression to the public that many sections of the report will be out of date because of recent improvements. Of course, as a social scientist, you can understand why I would not be supportive of such conclusions."[33]

Adding personal pain to Locke's professional embarrassment, the city-funded Harlem Art Center he had proposed never opened. While the mayor met with Locke a few times to discuss it, in the end, he failed to act. Unfortunately, the only place the mayor found to house the center was a building controlled by the city's Department of Education, which did not want to release it to be devoted to art activities. Then, too, the mayor may have decided that such a city-run center was no longer needed. In 1937, the WPA opened a Harlem Community Art Center, funded by federal dollars, and headed by Augusta Savage. If the federal government was funding art activities in Harlem, headed by a known art teacher and firebrand, why should the mayor open a competing center run by an outsider? The shift in cultural power from the local to the federal level, and Locke's lack of influence in the WPA–Harlem Artists' Guild collaboration meant, in effect, that he had no leverage. He had helped the mayor out of a difficult spot, yet had nothing, in the end, to show for it, and meanwhile he had damaged relations with a valuable colleague back at home at Howard.

Locke had been played. He had been repeatedly assured that the commission's report would be published soon; but when the report was not published and Locke's more optimistic article appeared, it seemed to be a cover-up. Locke had also tricked himself—lured by the prospect of a Harlem Art Center and a possible permanent position in New York, something he had wanted for years. The line that drew Frazier's particular ire was "in some senses the report is out of date because many of the abuses mentioned in the report have been corrected." When the draft of Locke's article was circulated to Oswald Garrison Villard, a member of Frazier's commission, he drew attention to it in his otherwise favorable review of the article. "Mr. Locke has done a masterful job of summing up what we have labored to communicate in much longer prose. But there is one place where he is absolutely wrong—in the matter of the abuses now having been cleared up. They have not."[34] Locke and Kellogg knew what they were doing. In all of the editing of Locke's article that assertion remained.

Locke appears to have been taken in by the civility of his relations with both the mayor and the city administrators, who, in addition to bombarding him with statistics citing a few more Black nurses were working at Harlem Hospital than the report had claimed, wrote courteous letters that seemed to draw Locke in.

Locke's "cordial note" to Kellogg after the embarrassment of the article's repudiation by his Howard colleague suggests how civility had to be maintained with Whites at all costs. Locke's civility had undermined him in this situation, and his article had permanently harmed his relationship with a respected Howard colleague.

While Locke was technically correct that some of the more egregious practices of New York City administration in Harlem were changed once exposed by Frazier's report, Harlem life was not improving. The ride in Frazier's Packard was a wake-up call. Frazier presented a problem Locke could not navigate around without consequences. The Young Turks on Howard's campus, the Leftist rebels in his own Social Science Division, knew that he had betrayed the larger truth of the Black situation in Harlem by pushing himself into a situation where he was not the expert. He was delegitimized in their eyes. And he could hardly be thought of more positively by the Black artists and cultural activists in Harlem, who had another piece of evidence that when a clear decision had to be made in terms of racial loyalty, Locke would side with the Whites over the Black working poor. That was not completely true; his article had made some forthright and clarion calls for action. But without any power to force La Guardia to even release the original report, let alone to commit any of his limited political capital to reforming city administration in Harlem, Locke had no compensation for having let La Guardia and his administration off the hook from having to bring real change to Harlem.

Locke did not like violence—the Harlem riot kind or the fiercely expressed harangue of Frazier in a Packard coupe. But Frazier had done something that was critical to Locke's political self-consciousness in forcing him to listen to Black anger that would be turned on him if he did not recognize its legitimacy. Frazier's attack on Locke had shown that he was not sufficiently identified with the advancing political consciousness of the 1930s Negro radical to represent it adequately in his public discourse. Before he got in Frazier's Packard, Kellogg and the mayor of New York, Miss Brady and Morse Cartwright had already been taking Locke for a ride—to serve their interests; and that ride was leading to his demise as a relevant Black thinker.

As the end of 1936 approached, Locke could take heart that three of the Bronze Booklets were finally published, while the fourth, Ralph Bunche's *A World View of Race*, would be out early in 1937. But Locke knew that was not enough. He had to find a way to reposition himself and his views of art's efficacy as an enabler of the radical politics of the 1930s or become little more than an exquisite corpse—beautiful, nice to look at, with its many limbs, but dead as the Harlem Museum of Art and its cousin, the city-funded Harlem Art Center.

38

Transformation

A different Locke appeared on the stage of the pearly white Metropolitan Opera House at Broad Street in Philadelphia on October 19, 1937, to speak for the first time to a meeting of the National Negro Congress, a communist-front organization. The difference was in the location as well as the man. Locke had for years traveled thousands of miles to hear opera sung from stages like the one he was standing on in 1937, in the wonderfully ornate former Philadelphia Opera House that when built in 1908 symbolized Philadelphia's cultural coming of age. But now, in the late years of the Great Depression, the building was rented out to any quack radical element that could pay the rental fees—an analogy to what had become of Locke himself, now that his grand vision of a Negro Renaissance of the 1920s lay in tatters. Hard times had hit the Metropolitan and Locke, for America was no longer interested in, nor able to afford, Culture with a capital C. Both the Metropolitan and Locke were struggling to reinvent themselves in times inhospitable to their original ideas, their founding missions.

Invited by John P. Davis, national secretary of the organization, to appear at the second meeting of the National Negro Congress, Locke was not on completely unfamiliar ground. The organization had been started by two of his close friends, Ralph Bunche and Arthur Fauset. But Locke would nevertheless be in unfamiliar company. A. Philip Randolph, the NNC president and head of the Sleeping Car Porters Union, was a union organizer turned intellectual who would later go on to originate the idea of the March on Washington in 1941. Davis was the firebrand organizer of the New Negro Alliance that protested discrimination in hiring in five-and-ten cent stores in Washington, D.C. The NNC also included James Ford of the Communist Party and was in the midst of a power struggle over the extent to which it would follow the line of the Communist Party USA. All of these men were activists in ways Locke usually found repugnant. And yet, here he was, answering Davis's call to "serve as Discussion Leader of the sub-session on 'Cultural Problems of the Negro.' The subject of the discussion at this time will be 'Traditions and Cultural Problems of Negro Artists.'"[1] But Locke used his talk to do something more powerful: to transform himself into a Black radical cultural critic of the 1930s.

If Locke arrived on Friday, October 17, to the meeting, he would have heard NNC president, A. Philip Randolph, argue from the stage of the Metropolitan Opera auditorium that "while it [the NNC] does not seek, as its primary program, to organize the Negro People into trade unions and civil rights organizations, it does plan to integrate and coordinate the existing Negro organizations into one federated and collective agency so as to develop greater and more effective power. The Congress does not stress or espouse any political faith or religious creed, but seeks to formulate a minimum political, economic and social program which all Negro groups can endorse and for which they can work and fight." "True liberation," Randolph announced, "can be acquired and maintained only when the Negro people possess power; and power is the product and flower of organization—organization of the masses, the masses in the mills and mines, on the farms, in the factories, in churches, in fraternal organizations, in homes, colleges, women's clubs, student groups, trade unions, tenants' leagues, in cooperative guilds, political organizations and civil rights associations."

Randolph was reinventing the NNC as well. From now on, he declared, the NNC would be less concerned with union organizing and promoting working-class unity between the races and more committed to Negro socialist self-determination, an argument that fit the agenda of Locke's speech. Davis was eager to have Locke, "the unanimous choice of our committee," to buttress the argument that the NNC was itself a kind of Popular Front organization, with a broad program of race advancement grounded in Negro culture and a broad appeal to progressive-minded Negro intellectuals of the late 1930s. Here was a perfect opportunity for Locke to launch his new cultural analysis—that the New Negro's racial self-determination in the arts of the 1920s laid the foundation for a workers' literature of the 1930s that would actually reach the Black masses.

When it came time for Locke to speak that Sunday, he argued that the core idea of the New Negro movement all along was to express a folk culture rooted in the Black masses; but the self-indulgent writers of the 1920s had squandered the opportunity to achieve that goal. In a nimble rationalization, Locke contended that the core of the New Negro movement was a proletarian voice that now was heard in social realist literature. He did not mention Beauty once in his speech. Rather, Locke suggested that his experience with the preceding generation gave him the perspective to counsel the coming generation not to become "dogmatic or too inflexible, because the common aim of all good art is truth through a formula and not a formula at the expense of truth." Locke, too, was looking ahead. Perhaps if he could string together a number of presentations that inserted proletarian literature in the canon of Negro literature, he could announce himself as the critical advisor for a new generation of writers who heretofore had been enemies of the New Negro he represented in the past.[2]

Arthur Fauset, vice president of the NNC, may have suggested Locke to Davis to help Locke win friends and build a new sympathetic audience for his views among the young radicals who were the driving force in the NNC. Fauset was again in Locke's good graces, after Fauset confided he was leaving the Communist Party and divorcing his wife, Crystal Bird, whom Locke hated. While the divorce did not materialize until 1944, Locke and Fauset became sufficiently reconciled for Locke to feel comfortable coming to serve as "discussion leader" at the Philadelphia meeting of an umbrella left-wing organization of Black socialists that was Fauset's latest attempt to forge a Black radical identity as a closeted homosexual.

Locke had to distract his new audience from that he had all but erased the rebellious New Negro working-class and the radical Black socialist intellectuals of the 1920s from his version of the New Negro in *The New Negro: An Interpretation*. But here he was reinventing the New Negro as a Black working-class subject, whose racial self-consciousness was the inevitable forerunner of the class consciousness of the Black proletarians of the 1930s. "The contemporary generation of our artists must not overlook, however, the considerable harmony there is between the cultural racialism of the art philosophy of the 1920's and the class proletarian art creed of today's younger generation. In the expression of Negro folk life, they have a common denominator, as the work of Langston Hughes and Sterling Brown, who belong to both generations, clearly proves."[3] The race consciousness of the 1920s New Negro had prepared the ground for the class-conscious New Negro of the 1930s, whose essence, like the trope of the New Negro itself, was the capacity to begin again despite past tragedies.

Crediting race consciousness as part of the formation of Negro workers' self-consciousness elicited a reaction from Loren Miller, a young Black lawyer, who lit into him during the question-and-answer period. Miller had met Locke on the ill-fated Russian film trip in 1933 and evidently had retained a dislike for him. On this occasion, Miller challenged Locke's racial consciousness argument from a traditional Marxist point of view. He recounted how recent anthropology had determined race to be a myth and a dangerous one at that. How could Locke advocate that a new, progressive organization like the NNC wed itself to such a discredited concept or the writings of those who had created a counter-myth to Black racialism in *The New Negro*?[4]

Locke seemed ready for this attack. "Mr. Miller" was quite right that anthropology had discredited and rightly so, race as a biological concept. *The New Negro* had specifically repudiated such outworn ideas, except in those sections written by Albert Barnes, W. E. B. Du Bois, and James Weldon Johnson that contained the notions Miller cited. "In the editorial sections of the book such assumptions were explicitly ruled out, particularly in the sections on Negro music and art, where cultural factors were advanced as the correct explanations of characteristic traits and qualities to be found in the Negro or in Negro art." *The New Negro* remained progressive and relevant in the 1930s because its "cultural racialism" advanced the right of artists to mine their ethnic and social heritage. Having already drawn a parallel between the Negro and the Irish Renaissance, Locke returned to it here with a vengeance, suggesting that no one could reasonably argue that W. B. Yeats was racist. "Dr. Locke cited the irrelevance of a question as to how much more Irish blood Yeats, Lady Gregory and Synge had than Bernard Shaw or George Moore. It was simply that Shaw and Moore had chosen to express themselves in the mainstream of traditional English culture and the adherents of the Irish Renaissance in terms of the revival of the folk-traditions and idioms of their Irish ancestors." The Negro artist in the 1930s had the right to the same choice, "some deciding to take the one, some the other cultural platform for his art. The New Negro movement was based on the deliberate choice for emphasis of the folk values and a reconstructed racial tradition."[5] That answer handcuffed Miller, since his friend Langston Hughes was more a poet like W. B. Yeats, who chose the "emphasis of folk values" in his poems before detouring into proletarian poetry.

Adult education was Locke's other foil against his communist critics: he was creating a literature of liberation for the masses, something acknowledged even at the National Negro Congress meeting. "The speaker [Locke] expressed appreciation for Mr. Miller's favorable mention of the Bronze Booklet series issued by the Association in Negro Folk Education of Washington, D.C. for its effort to bring materials on Negro life and culture and problems involved in Negro life before the public at popular prices."[6] The problem was not Locke's reluctance to endorse proletarian or agitprop art, but his continuing loyalty to racial self-consciousness as a revolutionary force in modern life.

Locke's adult-education series gave him cover at the October meeting of the National Negro Congress, because the first batch of four Bronze Booklets had come out a month earlier. Miller referenced the Bronze Booklets as a very positive accomplishment, largely because it included Ralph Bunche's *A World View of Race*. Bunche held to Miller's view that race was little more than a wedge driven between White and Black workers. But the Bunche booklet had given Locke a lot of trouble. Bunche had taken the Boasian scientific view of race in the same direction that Miller did at the conference—that race was wholly socially constructed and should be dispensed with conceptually by all right-thinking people, especially Blacks. After Locke had received the first draft of Bunche's manuscript, he had provided extensive editorial changes to eliminate what even Lyman Bryson called its "doctrinaire tone." As Bryson commented in June 1936, "Evidently the young man has listened to your sage advice....I think Bunche is badly mistaken in his principal idea...that there will be no race problem in a 'class-less society.' But no one who has given the subject much thought can deny that 'race' is a bogey raised by those who want economic advantages."[7] The series had been delayed almost six months while Bunche completed revisions that Locke insisted on.[8] Nevertheless, the publication of Bunche's booklet in the series helped Locke gain credit as a closet Marxist editor publishing the radical criticality of this younger generation of social scientists and aligning his work with theirs—since the first batch of four included two works by him.

Turning against former friends and allies was the second strategy Locke employed to shed his old skin as a leader of the Negro Renaissance and become the critic of the 1930s school of radical thinking. As early as his January 1937 Retrospective Review, "God Save Reality!" Locke began that process of separation by attacking Charles S. Johnson for *A Preface to Racial Understanding*: "that this book is obviously a primer for the great unenlightened does not excuse Dr. Johnson's...obvious lapse from the advanced position of last year's book, *The Collapse of Cotton Tenancy*, to the 'coaxing school' of moralistic gradualism and sentimental missionary appeal."[9] In the same issue, Locke praised his younger Howard University colleague, Marxist economist Abram Harris, for his critical study, *The Negro as Capitalist*.

More interesting was Locke's public turn against Claude McKay, whose travelogue autobiography, *A Long Way from Home*, outed Locke as an intellectual old fogey precisely at the moment that he was trying to invent himself as a radical. McKay's autobiography contained devastating thumbnail sketches of former friends like Locke, whom McKay skewered by publishing Locke's preference for the statues of the Prussian kings in the Tiergarten that the radical German artist George Grosz had described as "the sugar-candy art of Germany." McKay also revealed that Locke was repulsed by the drawings of George Grosz. Posing Locke against Grosz made Locke hopelessly old-fashioned in the late 1930s and revived the notion, most recently argued by Schapiro, that all racial nationalism ultimately devolved into the rabid nationalism epitomized by the Nazis. Even more tellingly, McKay described Locke as "a perfect symbol of the Aframerican rococo," whose "metamorphosis" into "doing his utmost to appreciate the new Negro that he had uncovered" was "interesting," but whose introduction to *The New Negro* was a kind of literary soufflé—all puffed up but with nothing really substantial to say.

Of course, there was some truth to McKay's claims, which is why they hurt. Locke's taste in German art was decidedly old-fashioned, while Locke had agonized over *The New Negro* introduction as failing to say what he wanted to say. But these claims were also payback for Locke's high-handedness in changing the title of McKay's poem, "White House," to "White Houses," in *The New Negro* and for Locke not highlighting McKay's poetry in the Harlem issue of the *Survey Graphic* or *The New Negro* the way he did Countee Cullen's and Langston Hughes's. Even so, Locke thought he had done McKay some critical service by praising in print McKay's breakthrough novel, *Home to Harlem*, with its revolutionary theme of cross-class, intra-racial dialogue, despite his private reservations about it. Locke had also given the perennially destitute McKay gobs of money over the years. But Locke he had not praised McKay's later novels perhaps as much as

McKay expected Locke should. As if to rub it in, McKay invited Locke to a book launch party at Sardi's restaurant in New York in March 1937 as one of "those Mr. McKay would most like to be there."[10] It is not clear whether Locke attended the event, but he must have been hurt by the publication of *A Long Way from Home*. Locke always felt McKay—a bisexual confidant since the early 1920s—accepted him, but he now realized that was not true.

Locke got his chance to respond when *New Challenge*, a New York–based Black literary journal edited by the young communist writer Richard Wright, asked him to review McKay's autobiography. Locke began with a philosophical question. What were the spiritual values exemplified by McKay's memoir? Locke answered "Spiritual Truancy." It was a devastating metaphor for a man lacking in any moral responsibility to speak for the communities that had embraced him.

> Although now back on the American scene and obviously attached to Harlem by literary adoption, this undoubted talent is still spiritually unmoored, and by the testimony of this latest book, is a longer way from home than ever. A critical reader would know this without his own confession; but Mr. McKay, exposing others, succeeds by chronic habit in exposing himself and paints an apt spiritual portrait in two sentences when he says: "I had wandered far and away until I had grown into a truant by nature and undomesticated in the blood"—and later, "I am so intensely subjective as a poet, that I was not aware, at the moment of writing, that I was transformed into a medium to express a mass movement."[11]

McKay had consistently encouraged others to think of him as a representative of a group—first Jamaicans, then Marxists, then New Negroes—only to repudiate them once they made any demands on him to serve the cause. "If out of a half dozen movements to which there could have been some deep loyalty of attachment, none has claimed McKay's whole-hearted support, then surely this career is not one of cosmopolitan experiment or even innocent vagabondage, but, as I have already implied, one of chronic and perverse truancy."[12]

"McKay, exposing others, succeeds by chronic habit in exposing himself" was Locke's telling line. McKay outed others sexually but outed himself. McKay let a succession of sponsors, friends, agents, and editors think he agreed with their politics only to abandon them and their politics when they no longer suited him. "Basic and essential... [to] real spokesmanship and representative character in the 'Negro Renaissance,'—or for that matter any movement, social or cultural [is] the acceptance of some group loyalty and the intent, as well as the ability, to express mass sentiment." The New Negro literary movement's purpose, Locke rationalized, was not simply to integrate individual Black writers into the Western canon of literature but to transform the writer into the voice of a community. Loyalty to a community was the litmus test of authenticity. "Even a fascinating style and the naivest egotism cannot cloak such inconsistency or condone such lack of common loyalty. One may not dictate a man's loyalties, but must, at all events, expect him to have some."[13]

A new clarity suddenly emerged in Locke's sentences. Combat strengthened his writing. In his critique of McKay as disloyal to any community, Locke also answered criticisms of himself, most recently delivered by Frazier, that Locke's Harlem article had been disloyal to the Black community. In attacking McKay, Locke defined a revolutionary ethics: whether racial or class-based, revolutionary art had to embed itself in a community and embody the lived experience of a people—some people—if it was to have any social meaning at all. In the process of attacking McKay, moreover, Locke defined his own calling going forward—to find a way to embed himself in the emerging new Black radical community of thinkers who, like it or not, were willing to close ranks and fight for what they believed in for a larger Black community in America. Speaking almost to himself, Locke concluded "Spiritual Truancy" with the imperative that "New Negro writers must become truer sons of the people, more loyal providers of spiritual bread and less aesthetic wastrels and truants of the streets."

Locke accepted this as his new mission when, in "Jingo, Counter-Jingo and Us," he took on Benjamin Stolberg's criticism of Black aspirational and celebratory history. In the October 23 issue of the *Nation*, Stolberg, a well-known journalistic firebrand, had termed inspirational histories of Black success nothing more than "minority jingo." Stolberg wrote a caustic review of Benjamin Brawley's *Negro Builders and Heroes* stating that such segregated histories of Negro achievement did more harm than good by making Black people feel better about themselves rather than critiquing race and class divisions that kept Black people confined to second-class citizenship. That December, Locke answered these charges by transforming his annual retrospective review into a powerful defense of the dialectical nature of Black intellectual work. He reminded Stolberg and other commentators that, in attacking the "minority jingo," such critics forgot to mention the original cause of such literature—"majority jingo." An industry of popular and scholarly publication has inundated the national mind with advertisements of White accomplishment and the claim that only Whites had been successful. That discourse had to be opposed somehow. While minority jingo was a weak antidote, it did save the Negro mind from being defeated. "Thus," Locke concluded, "we must not load all [of] the onus and (ridicule) upon the pathetic compensations of the harassed minority, though I grant it is a real disservice not to chastise both unsound and ineffective counter argument. The Negro has a right to state his side of the case (or even to have it stated for him)."[14]

But instead of just attacking Stolberg, Locke attacked Brawley as well for selling "Pollyanna optimism." Black people needed critical, scientific, and sound inspiration for what serious, thoughtful, and wise marshaling of their resources could accomplish. In critiquing Brawley's old-fashioned Black popular history, Locke laid the groundwork for his Bronze Booklet series without naming it as the antidote to racial brainwashing.

> As I see it, then, there is the chaff and there is the wheat. A Negro, or anyone, who writes African history inaccurately or in distorted perspective should be scorned as a "black chauvinist," but he can also be scotched as a tyro. A minority apologist who overcompensates or turns to quackish demagoguery should be exposed, but the front trench of controversy, which he allowed to become a dangerous salient must be re-manned with sturdier stuff and saner strategy. Or the racialist to whom group egotism is more precious than truth or who parades in the tawdry trappings of adolescent exhibitionism is, likewise, to be silenced and laughed off stage.... I merely want to point out that minority expression has its healthy as well as its unhealthy growths, and that the same garden of which jingo and counter-jingo are the vexations and even dangerous weeds has its wholesome grains and vegetables, its precious fruits and flowers.[15]

Here was the new Locke of the retrospective reviews—chastising radical and unsympathetic, White critics and slamming groveling Black allies whose work embarrassed him and the race. His prose had new life—an incisive, pulsing energy with sentences pulsating with rhythm and the telling metaphor. By critiquing Stolberg for his "wholesale plowing-under or burning over" of all Negro advocacy, Locke not only put him in his place, but defined himself as the interracial arbiter both Negro culture and Marxist apologetics needed—someone who could deliver "intelligent refereeing instead of ex-cathedra outlawing." Locke shouldered the responsibility for embodying the Negro intellectual praxis of "criticizing" and "correcting" White and Black excesses rather than dismissing Negro intellectual projects.

Locke's review also announced the third way Locke reinvented himself in the late 1930s by showing he was beginning to change his attitude toward protest literature or what he called "propaganda." Before the review, art and propaganda were opposites in his writing; in this review, he connected them as part of a continuum. "Just as sure as revolution is successful treason and treason is unsuccessful revolution, minority jingo is good when it succeeds in offsetting either the effects or the habits of majority jingo and bad when it re-infects the minority with the majority disease. Similarly, while we are on fundamentals, good art is sound and honest propaganda, while obvious and dishonest propaganda are bad art."[16] Here, Locke finally accepted protest literature as art. What he had still to accept was that protest art was not simply a means by which the oppressed expressed pain and suffering caused by oppression, but that such art was also a tool of change. But he was moving toward a deeper, more political notion of the work that art could do.

To make that pivot, Locke weaponized his language. In 1937–1938, the military metaphor recurs throughout his writing. "The front trench of controversy which he [Brawley] allowed to become a dangerous salient must be re-manned with sturdier stuff and saner strategy." Black intellectuals are engaged in a war with the White discourse, with themselves, with the weaker parts of their body politic, who could not "man" the flanks well enough for the main assault on White supremacy to be successful. Locke himself was "manning" up to match the level of combat inherent to left-wing politics of the decade. One way Locke ingratiated himself with the Young Turks was to take on their masculinist style in his critique.

Brawley was not the only former friend Locke attacked in a gendered critique to curry favor with the newer generation of Black (and male) thinkers. In the same issue, he took a swipe at Zora Neale Hurston's epic novel, *Their Eyes Were Watching God*, suggesting that it was not sufficiently grounded in the folk consciousness it claimed to represent. He decried the tendency of Hurston to produce "folkloric fiction" that ignored the political critiques of the wider social context of the 1930s. Failing to recognize that *Their Eyes Were Watching God* was a breakthrough in making the subjectivity of Black women central to a late New Negro Renaissance novel, Locke vented in the review his frustration over Hurston's refusal to remain "true" to the documentary folk methodology that Mrs. Mason had supported financially. But he also joined the cacophony of the new Black masculinist radicals like his Howard colleague Sterling Brown and his new acquaintance, Richard Wright, who were slamming Hurston for not dealing overtly with southern racism and Marxian notions of class struggle in her novels. To them, Hurston was part of the tradition of writing as if racism did not matter to Black people's social consciousness.

But in critiquing *Their Eyes Were Watching God*, Locke was making public his misogynist project of the early days of the Negro Renaissance. Part of his queer project of becoming "the man" of Negro literary criticism in the 1920s had been to marginalize Black women's critical agency. When he invited Hurston, a queer curious if not clearly queer Black woman rebel, into the patronage quadrangle of the late 1920s, he had found the perfect woman with whom to parry the argument that his New Negro movement was merely a mechanism for promoting the careers of young Black men. By the late 1930s, increasingly bitter because he believed Hurston and Hughes had "betrayed" him and Mason, Locke was willing to slam Hurston precisely at the moment when she created Janie, the one iconic female subject of the New Negro Renaissance. This was no accident. Part of the self-fashioning Locke did in the late 1930s was to refashion his identity as a hyper-masculine subjectivity, an aggressive male persona. Having abandoned a nurturing, read mothering, presence in his writing, Locke recast himself as the literary general who would lead the Black male assault on the citadel of White Marxism, Jewish male socialist hegemony, and anyone else—certainly Hurston—who stood in the way of his becoming relevant again.

Hurston was quick to respond. Writing to Elmer Carter, the editor of *Opportunity* magazine, she asserted she would "send my toenails to debate Alain Locke on the nature of the folk!" She accompanied the "toenails" challenge with a demand that the editor publish her remarks and set up a real opportunity for her to debate Locke publicly on what constituted the folk and its authentic representation in literature. Locke was glad that Carter did not take Hurston's suggestions seriously. The episode pointed out that dissing his former friends in print could backfire in a way he might not be able to handle. Interestingly, only the women—Fauset and Hurston—who were on the receiving end of his attacks in the retrospective reviews of this period had the gumption and courage to write back and challenge his right to criticize their work.

Hurston's counter-attack exposed that Locke was still not believable as the legitimate voice of the Black radical tradition of the 1930s. Yes, he had succeeded in his talk before the 1937 meeting of the National Negro Congress in presenting himself as a harmonizer of generational values by proposing a synthesis of the New Negro and proletarian literatures. The evolutionary metaphor was a bit weak, however, despite his persuasive argument that Black proletarian literature was the logical continuation of the New Negro radicalism of the 1920s. But he still recoiled from a complete endorsement of the new literature. Even his endorsement of Richard Wright in "Jingo, Counter-Jingo and Us" was made in the old language. He described the prose of Wright as having the salty tang of the peasant, suggesting that Locke still could only accept the working class through the language of primitivism. The year before Locke had chastised Charles S. Johnson for misreading the situation of the southern folk as that of the peasant instead of what it was: the quintessential American proletariat. But face-to-face with working-class anger, Locke fell back himself into the language of primitivism. He still struggled in 1937 and 1938 with an aesthete's working-class bias that southern folk had to be "picturesque" for him to appreciate them.

More successfully, Locke evolved his own conception of the function of art for an oppressed people in the late 1930s. Rather than remaining wedded to the notion that art mainly functioned as an emotion-releasing catharsis for the oppressed, Locke expressed a new position in his July contribution to the *Crisis*, "Freedom Through Art," written on the seventy-fifth anniversary of the Emancipation Proclamation. Locke had been searching for a new raison d'être for art to rationalize why it still mattered in a world where the oppressed Negro faced starvation during the Great Depression and a fate worst than starvation of a lifetime of racialized class conflict that Richard Wright chronicled in his short stories. Instead of providing a distraction from the tragedy of racism in Black lives, the real function of Negro art was "self-emancipation" Locke now argued.

Art no longer could be asked to take our minds away from the carcass of American democracy lining the streets of Black urban and rural communities. Now, "the proper and peculiar function of a minority literature and art" was to teach us how to liberate ourselves and Black humanity from the nightmare of American racism.

"Every oppressed group is under the necessity, both after and before its physical emancipation from the shackles of slavery,—be that slavery chattel or wage—of establishing a spiritual freedom of the mind and spirit. This cultural emancipation must needs be self-emancipation and is the proper and peculiar function of a minority literature and art. It gives unusual social significance to all forms of art expression among minorities often shading them unduly with propaganda or semi-propaganda and for whole period inflicting them also with an unusual degree of self-consciousness and self-vindication....But for these faults and dangers we have compensation in the more vital role and more representative character of artistic self-expression among the 'disinherited;' they cannot afford the luxury, or shall we say the vice, of a literature and art of pure entertainment."[17]

Locke's new position parried the thrusts of such younger writers as John A. Davis, Richard Wright, Sterling Brown, and Ulysses Lee, who in a variety of essays critiqued the New Negro movement for its optimistic faith in the healing power of art. Indeed, "Freedom Through Art" was a direct answer to Richard Wright's article "Blueprint for Negro Writing," for Wright had argued that the Black writer should speak for the Black masses and avoid serving as an "artistic Ambassador" to Whites. When John A. Davis's "We Win the Right to Fight for Jobs" (1938) had attacked the New Negro strategy of using art to improve race relations, Locke provided another answer to these critiques in his end-of-the-year retrospective review "The Negro: 'New' or Newer," that recast his New Negro writings as a prologue to the 1930s rebellion. In "The Negro: 'New' or Newer," Locke finally was able to synthesize conflicting aesthetic philosophies and values, and move from the theory of art as catharsis to a theory of art as revolutionary praxis. It still needed to be beautiful; but it had another purpose—to transform the Negro mind and transform the world. Indeed, his new position reflected his new role: he was now the critic, rather than promoter, of art and thus did apologize for weak art. Now, he was insisting that Negro artists meet the hardest tests—to be both superb artists in terms of form, and also revolutionary in terms of content. It was a tall order, but one, he argued, the Negro artist, whether literary or visual or dramatic, could no longer avoid. He could not avoid it either.

Locke's new vision led to new speaking opportunities. He was invited in the summer of 1938 to address a retreat held by the Communist Party, in which he lobbied for a positive view of Black culture as essential to working-class unity. Indeed, the Party during the Popular Front era adopted, at least implicitly,

Locke's New Negro strategy—the social uses of Black art and culture—partly to attract "fellow travelers" like Locke, but also to combat White chauvinism in the Party. One of Locke's points was that African American culture humanized; that was in fact what the Party was looking for as it wrestled with the White racism of some of its proletarians. In effect, the Party needed Locke's old theory—that Negro art was a form of catharsis for the soul wounded by racism—as much as it needed his new ideology of art as a weapon of class and racial liberation. The more muscular second part of his philosophy allowed the Party and other radicals to embrace the earlier, more cathartic role that had always been his strong suit. In effect, Locke was coming around to radical aesthetics, but the radicals, especially the White radicals of the Popular Front era, were coming around to him, as well.

But the personal advance for Locke was his ability to amend his aesthetic taste and accept protest in literature, to accept a literature of the masses, and to redefine the mission of African American literature as militant mental liberation. Seeing such plays as *Waiting for Lefty* by Clifford Odets had helped. But no artist helped Locke move in this new direction more than Richard Wright, a fiction writer whose angry Black realism was far from the kind of "poetic realism" Locke favored. Locke had given qualified praise to some of Wright's poetry in "Propaganda—or Poetry?" but had remained skeptical of this young writer's work until in "Jingo, Counter-Jingo and Us" he lauded Wright's short story, "Big Boy Leaves Home," as "the strongest note yet struck by one of our own writers in the staccato protest realism of the rising school of 'proletarian fiction.'"[18] All along, Locke's main complaint was that proletarian writing had not produced a great writer. By January 1938, Locke had begun to believe he had found one.

The fiction of Richard Wright had seduced Locke. Something in Wright's autobiographical vignette, "Living Jim Crow," and the short story, "Big Boy Leaves Home," touched him. Also, Locke had interacted personally with Wright, who was the editor of the issue of *New Challenge*, where Locke's review of *A Long Way from Home* appeared. Never really friends, there was just a whiff of sexual compatibility. But the real attraction for Locke was Wright's powerful prose, its searing, cutting, angry attack on the whole system of silences that hid the extreme social and physical violence that underlay Jim Crow in Black lives. Reading "Big Boy Leaves Home" convinced Locke that Wright had found the way to create convincing characters whose struggle to maintain an ounce of self-respect in a crushing system was believable and moving. Wright's short stories gave flesh and blood feeling to the larger social structure and mechanism of race and class oppression Black southerners lived under. Locke paid Wright the highest compliment he could when he suggested Wright's relationship to the proletarian literary movement was akin to that of Jean Toomer to the Negro Renaissance: both had shown that the Black experience of America could sing in prose when narrated by a supremely gifted writer. After Locke's review was published, Wright won the *Story Magazine* first prize in the WPA Writer's Project contest for his short story, "Fire and Cloud." Locke had external confirmation of his assessment that "Richard Wright has found a key to mass interpretation through symbolic individual instances which many have been fumbling for this long while. With this, our Negro fiction of social interpretation comes of age."[19]

Then, in his 1941 retrospective review, "Of Native Sons," Locke defended Richard Wright's *Native Son* and completed the process of reinventing himself as the critic of the new literature. Against Black and White critics of the novel who claimed it was unrepresentative, Locke argued Wright's effort was an American *J'Accuse*, an exposé in prose of the horrific consequences of Jim Crow segregation and placed it within the context of the work of such other realists as Erskine Caldwell and William Faulkner.

> It is to Richard Wright's everlasting credit to have hung the portrait of Bigger Thomas alongside in this gallery of stark contemporary realism. There was artistic courage and integrity of the first order in his decision to ignore both the squeamishness of the Negro minority and the deprecating bias of the prejudiced majority, full knowing that one side would like to ignore the fact that there are any Negroes like Bigger and the other like to think that Bigger is the prototype of all. Eventually, of course, this must involve the clarifying recognition that there is no one type of Negro, and that Bigger's type has the right to its day in the literary calendar, not only for what it might add in his own right to Negro portraiture, but for what it could say about America. In fact, Wright's portrait of Bigger Thomas says more about America than it does about the Negro, for he is the native son of the black city ghetto, with its tensions, frustrations, and resentments. The brunt of the action and the tragedy involves social forces rather than persons; it is in the first instance a *Zolaesque J'Accuse* pointing to the danger symptoms of a self-frustrating democracy.[20]

Wright's character of Bigger Thomas was certainly not an exquisite portrait of who and what the Negro was. But the death of Black Beauty yielded a new Black sublime, in which Black literature attained significance as a purveyor of truth and justice more important in the moment than traditional notions of the beautiful.

That same year he wrote so approvingly of Richard Wright's literary breakthrough, Locke found another artist whose painterly portrait of the Black experience confronted as unflinchingly as Wright the agony and triumph of Black segregated life in America. In 1941, Jacob Lawrence, a dark-skinned product of the Great Migration, produced a sixty-panel tribute to the Great Migration that Locke had stated in 1925 was the key to the revolution he titled the New Negro.

An artist birthed by that movement had matured in the Harlem of the 1930s, studied at the Harlem Art Center, and been employed by the WPA, but had escaped the handicapping formulas of either WPA American Scene celebrationism or the crippling formulas of social realism. Lawrence's diminutive panels of scenes from the life of Black migrants exuded a strange new beauty, abstractly rendered but narratively accessible and powerful, a moving window on how life was lived and changed by the poorest of African Americans. Locke had followed Lawrence's career for several years, had helped him get a Rosenwald grant to do the Migration Series, but nevertheless was stunned at Lawrence's achievement in this series, for he had found a way to move beyond visual biography to translate social history into cinema-like paintings. Lawrence had distilled the African advice Locke had seen ignored by dozens of African American artists into a uniquely African American abstract expressionism that was not copied from the African but informed and enhanced by it. It confirmed what Locke had seen exemplified at the MOMA exhibit—that African abstraction could be used to portray a living proletarian movement, the Great Migration.

Wright and Lawrence had put back in the New Negro art the anger Locke had left out of the *Survey Graphic*—both the 1925 Harlem issue and the 1935 riot review—anger that was needed to convey the truth of the experience of Blackness in the North. On his own, Locke had not been able to see, let alone embrace, the violence of American life as lived by Black people—without help. Now, after Frazier's challenge and Wright's and Lawrence's examples, Locke could see that protest was not inimical to art, but one of its highest forms. For their art revealed the ugly beauty of America that had to be embodied by Black aesthetics if freedom through art was to have any meaning at all for the oppressed.

Locke had accomplished a great deal in finding these two artists who embodied the promise announced from the stage of the Metropolitan in 1937 that a rapprochement between the race consciousness of New Negro folk movement and the criticality of the proletarian movement would yield a more authentic radical art and literature. He had crafted a new philosophy of culture that announced art was now a means and an end of freedom for the oppressed. And Locke had shed his skin as an apologist of a failed New Negro aestheticism and redefined the New Negro as a dialectical subjectivity constructed now by proletarian artists. And lest we forget, his most satisfying accomplishment was perhaps personal. Despite all his detractors, Locke had reinvented himself as an arbiter of radical Negro thinking on art and culture in the 1930s and become a force to be reckoned with in print.

Jacob Lawrence (1917–2000). One of the largest race riots occurred in East St. Louis. 1940–1941. Panel 52 from *The Migration Series*. Tempera on gesso on composition board, 12″ × 18″. Gift of Mrs. David M. Levy. The Museum of Modern Art. Jacob Lawrence © 2017 The Jacob and Gwendolyn Knight Lawrence Foundation, Seattle / ARS, New York.

39

Two Trains Running

Two trains were running in Locke's life, running parallel to his political transformation in the late 1930s. Alongside the public race man, the private Locke was running strong.

Locke had another life, a hidden life of cruising, signaling, and nonverbal communications that constituted a hidden code of communication between him and likely prospects that, more often than not, ended in success, but also disappointment. Locke was always hunting men, but always doing so with a protection system in place to hide his intentions from those not in "the life." Robert Martin, a professor of political science at Howard University, whom Locke recruited as a young man to manage the printing and distribution operation of the Bronze Booklets produced by the Associates of Negro Folk Education, remarked about Locke's "system." Of course, Martin insisted, he was not one of Locke's lovers. But he related how Locke tried to recruit him. "I was working at a local theatre in the 1930s, and we used to be required to wear these bright red uniforms, and after I had gotten to know Locke and was working distributing the Bronze Booklets, he told me that he had seen me working at that theater, and that he had made a signal to me that I would only recognize and react to if I was one of them. Of course, I had no recollection of having seen him."[1]

Martin, though, was intimately involved in Locke's affairs given that he was Locke's only assistant handling the day-to-day operation beginning in the spring of 1937. He visited the post office box for the associates and processed the orders for books from bookstores, libraries, benevolent societies, social movement organizations, individuals, and even prisons. A trickle of requests in 1937 swelled to a flood by 1939, creating constant work answering queries, binding up books, mailing them out, and keeping track of the accounts. Meanwhile, Locke advertised, promoted, and sold the books to libraries, schools, bookstores, and anyone who would buy them. Martin's disclaimer may have been a response to Locke's will being published in the Washington Black newspaper. Robert Fennell, one of Locke's students and close friends, remarked that after that, "He called me up and told me all about how he knew all of Locke's associates, but that he wasn't one of them, etc. I didn't ask for that information. Really, he gave himself away with that." Locke completely dominated Martin's life on campus. "Martin could be seen carrying Locke's books and bags all over campus."[2]

Locke collected Black men as well as he collected the African art that bedecked his mantle at home. He mentored them and he loved them. Those, like Hercules Armstrong, came and went, often in response to their desire, usually unrealized, to become a famous writer or artist. He would gather them in, read their work, give them his honest, often searing critical opinion, and have sex with them. Sometimes Locke would try to get them jobs or place their work in publications. Sometimes that did not happen, and then they would begin to hit him up for money, usually by asking for loans. A rather awkward dance would ensue, in which Locke would know that continued access to these beautiful young men required his financial contribution to their lives, lives that were often constrained their limited talent, as well as by structural racism, chronic unemployment, and career confusion. Eventually, the sex would dry up, the touch for money would become too excruciating for the penurious Locke, and they disappeared from his life.

One of the tensions in such relationships was Locke's criticality, especially his criticism of them if they failed. One such lover confided that Locke became upset with him when he had flunked a French exam. That was intolerable to Locke. Too many of such failures ended Locke's interest in a young man. Of course, Locke himself had failed, disastrously at Oxford, and lied about it to keep the fiction of his uninterrupted success inviolate. Locke's failure made his policing of other young, gay men's failures more intense than it would have been otherwise. But its deeper root was that educational success was essential to Black Victorian identity, as Du Bois described it in "Of Our Spiritual Strivings." After being rejected by a young White girl in a school exchange of cards and realizing he was shut out of their world, Du Bois "lived above it in a region of blue sky.... That sky was bluest when I could beat my mates at examination time."[3] Beating the White man was essential to one's self-respect as a Black Victorian, and Locke imposed its "discipline," as he would probably have called it, on his young lovers, even though, existentially, as a strategy, it was failure regardless of how well one did as an academic. As Locke's colleague in the Howard University Department of Philosophy put it, "No matter what are your credentials, a black intellectual is not accepted as an authentic man."[4] Locke insisted that young Black moderns of the 1920s and 1930s adopt his approach to the profound bitterness of this predicament, even though when those moderns saw through the tactic and realized they were condemned to be Black in a disrespectful world regardless of whether they passed their French exam or not.

Sex, however, with men added another way for Locke to keep his sky blue. They were another classroom, as he educated them on all he had learned about how to survive not only as a thoughtful Black person but also as a queer man in a world that hated queers almost as much as Negroes. They also were important in another way—they were Beauty personified, works of art themselves, their gorgeousness anchoring his love of art that featured the Black body. Something of his love for Black men explains the tenacity with which he held on to the notion that a Negro art existed from the race of the artist who rendered it. The beauty and love of these men's bodies shaped his aesthetic taste that preferred portraits and sculpture that featured the body. That love allowed this elite White-educated misanthrope to sustain a loyalty to Black people, because beautiful Black men anchored his belief in the beauty of the Black experience. No matter what the White folks said, he knew he loved these men, and loving them was another form of resistance against the discourse of Black male inferiority America taught him and them.

But these men also served another purpose for Locke. Part of the reason Locke demanded his lovers be brilliant was that better men catalyzed his creativity. Locke's most important intellectual breakthroughs seemed to occur at those points in his life when he desired spectacular men. At Harvard, it had been Locke's relationship with Carl Dickerman that had helped lead him to appreciate Paul Laurence Dunbar's achievement, when everything in his Black Victorian taste led Locke in the opposite direction. Love of Langston Hughes had turned him from a worldly aesthete into a New Negro. Smith had stimulated an important return to Locke's earlier love affair with philosophy. Locke advanced in his intellectual life when he was intimate with really brilliant men; and he stalled and stumbled when he had to make due with less intelligent lovers. While Locke claimed his sexual raiding of young men was justified by his mentoring them into great artists, the truth was that his most important insights required catalytic men who provided alternative pathways to his typical reactions and transformed the cultural production of his life. Fundamentally, Locke was a dialogical thinker whose desired subjects shaped what he thought and did.

Bunche and brilliant young radicals had accelerated Locke's desire to create a knowledge system that educated the masses with critical Black knowledge. And remarkably, the nonprofit publishing company Locke created to do so was thriving by 1938. Locke rented a warehouse to store the books, secured a post office box as its official mailing address, and after spending the summer of 1937 hassling authors to get the remaining books finished, had a second batch of four Bronze Booklets out by the end of the year. Sterling Brown, a poet, friend, and faculty member at Howard, did two of them. Locke had anointed Brown the best Negro folk poet in Nancy Cunard's *Negro Anthology*, to Zora Neale Hurston's chagrin, and after helping to bring him to Howard in 1929 had peppered Brown with requests to complete two Bronze Booklets until Brown finished *Negro Poetry and Fiction* and *Negro Drama*. Those two books quickly became the most popular Bronze Booklets, because they carried forward the kind of criticality that the Black reading audience hungered for and that Locke's retrospective reviews prepared the White reading public for. When Locke sent copies of these books to Mrs. Mason, he gloated that they were essentially carrying forward his analysis of literature, which on one level was true—a Cultural Studies reading of literature as a bellwether of the mind of people was his innovation of the 1920s. But as he also admitted to her, Brown's books were almost violent critiques of the American literary tradition, especially the southern literary tradition, for its treatment of the Negro in print, much more forceful than Locke would have dared to write. There was bound to be a reaction. "But let them," Locke concluded, knowing full well that the brunt of the reaction would be borne by Brown, not him. The other great seller was *The Economic Reconstruction and the Negro* by T. Arnold Hill, the sociologist of race relations in Chicago, who had been engaged with the National Urban League in the 1930s in pressing FDR for the inclusion of Negroes in the National Industrial Recovery Act. While his booklet was not the fire-breathing tome that Du Bois had penned, it was, in fact, a solid economic critique based on experience innovating for the Negro within the New Deal.

The Associates in Negro Folk Education reached many adult Black readers, because it operated outside of segregated public education in America. It even reached White readers, who purchased, borrowed, or stole the books from bookstores, libraries, or friends and imbibed its radical critical knowledge of America in the late 1930s. How many books sold is remarkable. By the end of November 1938, Locke had sold 1,144 copies, with Brown's *Fiction* selling the most at 251, and Reid's earlier *Adult Education and the Negro* selling the least at 93. But another 2,542 books were sold by the end of February 1939. Hill's *Economic Reconstruction* sold 382 paperbacks and 63 hardbacks in three months.

By 1940, Locke was almost out of the bestselling books by Brown and Hill, and stock of his own two booklets was nearly exhausted. He prepared to ask the Association of Adult Education for more money to reprint those for further distribution, because, given that the cost of the booklets was 50¢ each, their sale price barely met production expenses. Such success is especially remarkable given that he ran his publishing company out of a professor's office and a warehouse with Martin, part-time. Orders flew in from the Frederick Douglass Bookstore in New York and an Arab bookstore in London, from segregated libraries all across the South, even from penitentiaries, let alone hundreds of individual buyers, who showered Locke with letters of thanks for the intellectual food these booklets brought them despite the intellectual isolation of Jim Crow America.

That Locke was able to keep this publishing company going while maintaining a full teaching schedule and authoring other books and dozens of articles and essays is astounding, but also a testament to his organizational and marketing skills. Locke created an advertising and distribution system by which Black working- and middle-class people throughout the country came into libraries to access the knowledge that other Black intellectuals wrote about but could not deliver in cheaply available texts. Locke accomplished this because the Bronze Booklets were part of an interlocking system—whenever he gave a lecture, helped organize an exhibition, and brought visitors to the university, he made sure he displayed the Bronze Booklets, advertised and distributed them through the Harmon Foundation, and made them visible at every venue he knew. Those lectures and later exhibitions made Associates in Negro Folk Education like a university extension course—since most of the books were authored by Howard professors—and made those who purchased them, literally, associates of folk education. But it was folk in Locke's terminology, because it was not really folk knowledge but a sophisticated system of scholarly knowledge production that disseminated Black criticality far away from Howard University where most of its authors taught. Bronze Booklets announced that Black folk education had taken Negro middle-class anger at systemic racism of the knowledge industry in America and turned it into material for the reading masses.

His queerness shaped all aspects of this project, from the way that he moved secretly to garner the funding to finance the project, to his taking the title of "secretary" rather than "president" of the nonprofit organization, which allowed him to run it invisibly. Indeed the entire enterprise is largely invisible in American intellectual history and educational history, in part because he wanted it to be. It was radical knowledge in the closet. This critique of American and global White supremacy was hidden in an educational Trojan Horse—adult education—that would transform what even Whites are able to read about the Negro if they went into a library and looked up "Negro" in the finding aid. Because eventually, their thumb would come to rest on *Negro Poetry and Fiction* or *Negro Art: Past and Present*, and they would be subjected to an alternative point of view, one that argued the Negro was not crushed by the degradations of Negro-haters, but continually pushing forward, creating culture, and defining the terms of what it meant to be an American from the bottom.[5] "And a queer man of color created the book you are holding in your hands," Locke might have told them, "you just don't know it, because I am not letting you know it."

Yet that was not enough.

Despite Locke's public intellectual innovations and his well-oiled engine of private promiscuity, a pain ate away at Locke's soul in the late 1930s, as he struggled with a life without love. Of course, he had regular conquests of men and resumed contacts with those around for years. Collins George, from the 1920s, would cycle back into intimacy every so many years. There was Jimmy Daniels, the cabaret singer, who always appreciated Locke's help, especially when he got him a job at the Los Angeles *Sentinel*. There were new ones, like

Bili Bond a wonderfully lighthearted presence who always cheered Locke up with his joie de vivre. But Bili was a very intermittent presence, as all of them were, because Locke could not compel a lifelong love commitment from any of them.

Sometimes, Locke blamed it on Washington. Even as a relatively secure professor at a major university, with a lovely home, he felt he could not risk using either to create a platform for long-term intimacy. The first time Robert Fennell visited Locke at home he noticed that Locke was paranoid.

> You know Locke's house was the first apartment I ever visited that had a buzzer, an intercom. I was 19 years old and I came up to his house and pushed the buzzer. And he would answer, "hello?" And I would say "Fennell here," and he would say, "Oh Fennell, come on up." He would then ring that buzzer. But you know he would not come down to that door himself. No! He was one of the most cautious, really paranoid men that I ever met. He would change the names on his mailbox. You'd come by there and the name would be Dick Jones [Laughter] on the box; next time it would be Charles Smith. Paranoid. He never had Alain Locke on that box. And he wouldn't open that door unless he knew who you were.[6]

Fennell recalled that one time Locke was furious when a friend of his brought someone to the house that Locke did not already know. Extreme cautiousness was needed to avoid life-changing scandal, but it is interesting that Fennell used the word *paranoid* even while being an intimate of Locke sexually. His program of survival resulted in psychological damage that imprisoned him. That prison meant that there was no chance that Locke could sustain the kind of intimacy in Washington that might lead to love.

Even more fundamentally, Locke suspected that those who slept with him did so only because of what he could do for them, not because of any love of him. He could not escape the feeling that his doorbell rang because a sexual partner wanted something from him, rather than wanting him. The story he heard from these young lovers was always the same. Their landlady was about to kick the young man out for non-payment of rent; the young man had not eaten in days and was on the verge of starvation; his clothes were in the cleaners and he needed to get them out to survive the freezing New York winter—not lies, but truths he was not responsible for that were deployed to tap the old man for money. Even when Locke helped these desperate "friends," there was little return for his gifts, often not even thanks. And afterward, they disparaged him. Bruce Nugent contacted him in the mid-1930s after many years to ask for help getting a job on the WPA. Locke became engaged in trying to secure the job. Lacking the influence to secure such a position, Locke probably gave Nugent some money to make up for the paltry sums he received from relief. But Locke's willingness to try and help Nugent in his desperate hours did not affect Nugent's assessment of Locke. After Locke was dead, Nugent would tell anyone who would listen that Locke was inept in bed and unrespected by the fierce radicals like himself, Hughes, and Wallace Thurman.[7]

Even professional success could be interpreted as failure, as Locke would learn when he picked up the May issue of *Art Front* and discovered that that other train was not running so well in 1937 after all. His Howard University colleague, James Porter, had published an acid review of Locke's *Negro Art: Past and Present* in that issue. "This little pamphlet," Porter wrote, "is one of the greatest dangers to the Negro artist to arise in recent years. It contains a narrow racialist point of view.... Dr. Locke supports the defeatist philosophy of the 'Segregationist.'" Porter deftly twisted Locke's notions that the Negro artist should study African art and see himself as part of a Negro modernism in the arts into a position that confined the Negro artist to an artistic "ghetto." The "pamphlet," as Porter dismissively called Locke's book, was "dangerous" because it threatened to keep the Negro artist from exercising the freedom that the "modern" situation afforded to paint, draw, and sculpt about any subject he wanted. Porter ventriloquized a critique coming out of Howard University's Art Department begun by his mentor, James V. Herring, who, queer himself, was incensed by what he considered Locke's traversing that department's exclusive territory. Herring hated that Locke critiqued his idol, Henry O. Tanner, for moving to France and refusing to lead a visual arts movement among Negroes at home or abroad. Tanner was a symbol of success to academic Negro artists like Herring, whose refusal to do "racial art" made him a "pure" artist in their eyes. Such criticism was blasphemy, especially in the year of Tanner's death. Porter delivered a blow in return.

The review's venom was all Porter. It attacked all of Locke's signature ideas—the notion that the Negro artist was a racial subjectivity, that Negro art existed as a dialectical formation within the world art, and that the Negro artist should be inspired by African art. Porter utilized Robert Goldwater's argument to assert there was no connection between African art and modern art, adding his particular emphasis that there was no way that contemporary Negro artists could create art based on ancient African aesthetic principles. Interestingly, Porter also critiqued Locke's use of Winold Reiss to illustrate *The New Negro: An Interpretation*, arguing that it was self-contradictory to employ an "Austrian" [*sic*] artist in an anthology devoted to a Negro arts movement. In Porter's mind Negro art was only art created by Negro artists, not a way of rendering the world aesthetically that anyone could learn. Finally, Porter noted that Locke failed to mention protest art that had been engendered by the civil rights struggles of the 1930s. Here was a powerful charge, one that resonated with the likes of Romare Bearden and Augusta Savage, whose work

Locke had not yet embraced. The bottom line was that Porter and his clique were aghast that having gotten the Negro artist into American art, Locke would demand they paint as racial subjects, as representatives of communities that were still outside.

Locke was quick to reply in a letter to the *Art Front* editor that was printed. He quoted passages from the booklet to justify his position rather than take the argument to Porter. The interesting part of the quote was its assertion that no vital breakthrough could come from Negro artists as long as their art avoided confronting the internalized prejudice, which was the price of living under White supremacy. Coincidentally, Locke had felt something quite similar to Porter's anger thirty years earlier when "the race" seized on Locke as a "representative" and "role model" when he won the Rhodes Scholarship. But, in 1937, Porter's cry for artistic freedom seemed to Locke a way to hide in a different kind of closet— the mask of the artist who through abstract or other nonrepresentative art, remain anonymous. Negro art could be great only if it connected to the lived experience of the Negro artist through "a very real and vital racialism. But such an adoption of the course of Negro art does not, it must always be remembered, commit us to an artistic ghetto or a restricted art province. . . . It binds the Negro artist only to express himself in originality and unhampered sincerity, and opens for him a relatively undeveloped field in which he has certain naturally intimate contacts and interests."[8]

Nevertheless, Locke's letter to the editor was weak. Something about Porter's attack handcuffed Locke. Porter himself was revising his MA dissertation on Negro artists into a book and wanted to knock Locke off his perch as the reigning voice in Negro art criticism. Porter's charge that Locke's loyalty was not to the artists but to a racialized notion of their subjectivity problematized his reputation as their best spokesperson. There was some truth to that. For Locke, there was little that was unique about the ascendancy of Negro artists into the art world unless it was connected to the arc of the Negro subject and African aesthetic form in the Western world.

More cynically, Locke knew that most of the artists like Porter were not great artists. When Locke looked at their art as a pure aesthete, he knew that it would not have lasting significance without being in dialogue with something larger than itself. Locke proposed visual artists follow his lead and give world historical significance to their individual struggles for recognition. Even if Black people did not have the most power and were divided because of their colonial-like position in the world order, they still could behave as a cohesive group and give themselves the swagger that Europeans displayed in their art. But Locke did not dare say that in his letter to the editor.

After Porter's hostile review and Locke's response, Howard University became a virtual battleground, as Lois Mailou Jones, an instructor in art, and John Biggers, a student at Hampton, recalled. Biggers was shocked at the level of animosity in the Art Department toward Alain Locke, who was a kind of an intellectual hero at Hampton. As Biggers put it, "At Howard, you had to choose—between following them, Porter and Herring, or Locke. I didn't like the situation, so I got out of there."[9] Lois Jones confirmed that hostility but found a way around it to develop essentially two sides of her artistic oeuvre. "Professor Herring recruited me in 1929 because of my design work and my French Impressionist studies, not because of my Negro things."[10] But Jones recalled that when she would run into Locke on campus, he would encourage her to "do something of your own people." She was already developing a renaissance design iconography in the early 1930s, and in 1934, had taken a step toward the kind of portraiture Locke liked in her wonderful *Negro Musician*. Lois Jones was assimilating the design of African masks into her portraiture, using volume and mass to give three-dimensionality and emotional depth to her portraits. She depicted the emergence of a new subjectivity in the Black community, the intense and race-proud musician whom Locke was documenting in his other pamphlet, *The Negro and His Music*. Clearly, Locke still had his adherents.

Negro Musician (Composer) by Löis Mailou Jones, 1934. Charcoal on paper, 23 11/16″ × 18 5/8″. Museum of Fine Arts, Boston. Gift of the Löis Mailou Jones Pierre-Noël Trust. Photograph © 2006 Museum of Fine Arts, Boston.

But the review had exposed some blind spots for Locke. In 1937, he still had a problem appreciating the value of the protest art of the 1930s that moved many Negro artists to paint and sculpt. And he failed to see African art from the perspective of many working Negro artists. Despite the enthusiasm of European modernists for African art, most American Negro artists still viewed African art as "primitive" and opposed to their own definition of "modern" Negro art. Plus, African art had fallen out of favor in the 1930s among the White American art people—the WPA administrators, gallery owners, collectors, and artists whose taste ran now to "folk art"—with roughly rendered face jugs from South Carolina preferred, rather than the finely wrought sculptures from Benin. To many young Black artists on the make, African and American Negro art occupied two distinct spaces in the American art world.

Fortunately for Locke, there were a number of young artists, such as Lois Jones, Elton Fax, Bob Blackburn, Roy De Carava, and Jacob Lawrence, who saw making art and making contribution to the larger racial consciousness movement as synonymous and were not afraid of acknowledging African art as an influence in their work. But those artists were located in New York and most employed on the WPA's Federal Art Project working on the Harlem Hospital murals and participating in the activities of the Harlem Artists Guild. Henry Bannarn had taken over from Charles Alston as the teacher on the Harlem Hospital mural project, and he shared Locke's sensibility that art had an educational role to play in the Black community if it was not merely propagandistic. Locke, by contrast, was stuck in Washington with an increasingly hostile Howard University Art Department. Of course, his major motivation in wanting to go to New York was its more tolerant sexual atmosphere; but just as important was the other train in his life: his lifelong attempt to reconcile the career of art with the arc of the race. Most of the artists who shared that intersectional view of Negro art were located in New York. Locke was marooned at Howard.

Then, Locke learned that the Harlem Art Center that he had labored so long for with New York mayor La Guardia finally was opening its doors in 1937, but with Augusta Savage as its director. The Harlem Artists Guild working with Cahill persuaded Joseph Sheehan, superintendent of the New York City schools, to allow one of its buildings to be turned into a local art center with WPA funding. Locke had again been outmaneuvered by the introduction of federal funding into local arts education in the New Deal era. When assistant director and poet Gwendolyn Bennett, who seemed genuinely to like and respect Locke, asked him to attend the grand opening in December 1937 at 290 Lenox Avenue, with the likes of A. Philip Randolph and James Weldon Johnson giving speeches, Locke accompanied Bennett to the event. Afterward, she gushed about how much she enjoyed being there with him. It was a bittersweet moment for Locke. All of the compromises he had made and all of the alienation he had endured in trying to create a center for the arts had come to naught.

Locke became despondent as the spring of 1938 turned into summer. At first it had seemed promising, romantically. Arthur Fauset had circled back into Locke's life once again, as Locke had written Mrs. Mason in May. Locke gushed that Fauset had "written a real Negro book—clean, clear and true—the life of Sojourner Truth. I am sending you a copy—and think you will get its spirit at a glance." Locke also announced that he and Fauset might spend the summer together, but by July, there was no sign of Fauset in Locke's life. As was the case with many of the men that Locke was attracted to, Fauset was bisexual and unwilling to identify himself as gay by spending a romantic summer with Locke.[11]

There was more depressing news. After dental surgery, Arthur Schomburg had died that June, leaving unfinished what had become their collaboration in writing the Negro history book for the Bronze Booklets. Locke would have to write it alone, but the fire was gone, along with his Puerto Rican friend. "I have the Schomburg Outlines of Negro History to finish for the last of the Bronze Booklets—since his death—about which I wrote you in early June. It is particularly difficult to write something that has to go under some one else's name; and do justice at the same time . . . to him and the subject. However since we are in this sad dilemma it must be gone through with. Strange how often I get into situations like this."[12] Actually, Mason probably thought it was not strange at all. She had chastised him for years about how he had wasted his energies on being an agent of other people's subjectivity. Fashioning opportunities for others as the publisher of a Negro studies series instead of writing and publishing those books himself had pushed him back into an old role, that of the midwife, even as pursuing it had catalyzed him to publish two books of his own. Locke mysteriously was unable to complete the volume, even though two chapters of the proposed book, obviously written by Locke, survive in his papers.

Having been energized by the founding of the Bronze Booklets in 1935, Locke had run out of creative gas by 1938. That same summer Locke probably realized he could not finish his biography of Frederick Douglass, which, at various times in the past, he had informed Mason was almost finished. Locke had hoped living with Fauset might help him complete this biography as Fauset had just completed the biography of Sojourner Truth. A midwife and sexual companionship might have helped Locke launch his own late adulthood renaissance.

Faced with another summer in steamy Washington, shut out of Berlin by Hitler, and confronting the reality that his views were out of favor on campus, Locke dreamed of a permanent move to New York, teased by the sudden death of James Weldon Johnson in a car accident and the prospect that he might replace him as a New York University teacher of Negro literature. Bryson and other White friends, such as Hugh Mearns, from his Philadelphia School of Pedagogy days, were working on that, having put his name forward. Not until the fall would Locke learn that door was blocked by another nemesis, Carl Van Vechten.

Teased by the prospect of escape to New York, Locke wrote a letter to his old Sinhalese friend, Lionel de Fonseka. In his reply, de Fonseka tried to counsel Locke in this crisis. De Fonseka, a queer aesthete who was now married and living in France, was the perfect audience for Locke's story of woe. De Fonseka sensed the homosexual longing and frustration at the base of Locke's desire to escape Black Washington. But de Fonseka was skeptical that a permanent move to New York was the cure.

> Scrutinize the plan a little further…at New York, on your way here, you gather on the spot all the available information about all the posts available. Then here from the solitudes of Thorenc you survey the prospects of Washington + New York alike with an impartial eye, choose one or reject both—in favor of Ceylon or the Himalayas, the advantage of which will be presented to you by me personally.[13]

De Fonseka had some self-interest in luring Locke to France—Locke's friend was working on a "second book" and wanted Locke to "midwife" this one as he had his earlier one. De Fonseka recommended that Locke come immediately to Europe and stay with him and his wife—traveling from New York to Cannes, bus to Thorenc, Alpes Maritimes, France. Later, he could accompany Locke back to Cannes, spend a few weeks with him there, and then Locke could return to New York on the *Rex*. In a sense, de Fonseka was offering the best of both worlds—a rest in a patriarchal household abroad in which the wife would minister to Locke's emotional needs for maternal nurturing, while allowing the two men to have more romantic rewards. De Fonseka commented that he could not decide whether Locke was just tired out after having spent "two consecutive years in America," or undergoing a real "spiritual crisis, which most men go through between 40 + 50—the men(t)opause of the males."[14] If the latter, de Fonseka believed a "spiritual adjustment" was needed rather than a "physical displacement" to New York.[15]

Unlike de Fonseka, Locke had no home where he could be productive and have an open sexual life. His friend had made a compromise that Locke could not make, having married a woman who not only was comfortable with de Fonseka's sexuality but also with Locke. She too wanted Locke to come live with them, a kind of invitation to permanent expatriation that Locke would get from friends throughout his life. And yet that was also a step Locke couldn't take. He could not give up the side of himself that was hardwired to do battle in the race wars of America even as he trekked off every summer to gay Europe.

Some more fundamental change in the calculus of Locke's life was necessary if he was to find real peace, as de Fonseka recognized.

The sage of Thorenc...is inclined to hold to the Eastern wisdom that at 40 (in Europe + America 50) each man should cease to be a householder (translate—citizen, bread-winner, or professor...as you like) & should adopt the homeless life in the forest...leave Washington if you like but not to become a householder elsewhere. Every house in this sense that you may try to establish now will be divided against itself; so flee houses,—there is no other remedy.[16]

Householder was an apt term for Locke's crisis. At fifty-three, he could not unite a house divided between the gay man of the night and the race man of the day. He could not abandon America, because he wanted others to look up to him as a leader to follow into the promised land of Negro self-fulfillment. He wanted the attention, the adulation, of Negro (and White) audiences that he went before and spoke as the representative Negro, with the authority and recognition of the race. And yet he could not live a life of personal satisfaction. Becoming another Black aesthete expatriate would cut off half of his now-mature personality. He could not perform his art—the queer Black impresario—as an expatriate, and he knew it.

Locke did not go to Europe that summer, but instead went to speak at a Harlem Communist Party summer camp in 1938. Doxey Wilkerson, a Communist Party member at the time, recalled that the Party would rent cabins for a week-end, host a variety of recreational activities, a cultural discussion, and almost inevitably a musical program in which someone sang "Negro songs." This was the third train running in Locke's life, hidden from view or knowledge of most who thought they knew him—his role as a closet radical. After his speech before the National Negro Congress in Philadelphia the year before, Locke had become the chosen speaker for socialists and communists, especially on the Black Left, who wanted someone to fulfill the cultural mandate of the Popular Front era to celebrate Negro culture.

Although the transcript of Locke's remarks has not been located, most likely he spoke on the historical and cultural importance of the spirituals, and on Frederick Douglass. Douglass represented the hero Locke could not be, the hyper-masculine answer to the discourse of subservience to White male power under and after slavery, and the hero Locke could not write about sustainably. And yet there was something in Douglass's predicament that attracted Locke, that fascinated him, a man whose courage resembled that of Locke's father, and whose weaknesses reminded him of his father's and his own—the egotism that Mason had accused him of, which kept him from identifying completely with Douglass. What became apparent to Locke was that Douglass was de-tached from the rest of the free Black population, leading Douglass to look down on other Blacks because they had not faced the challenge of the hero as he had faced it and lived to tell about it in his own words. Douglass's triumph had been so singular—to escape slavery and to write his autobiography as a man born into slavery in his own language, and with that singularity had come arrogance that allowed for no real intimacy with other Black people who were merely free.

To have written Douglass's biography would have required Locke to face himself and the tragedy that Black specialness and arrogance created in his personality as well. Locke could learn, however, from Douglass's mistake of Olympian self-absorption—the refusal to bond with those who were different and less able than him, to transcend the segregation of exemplary personality to find common cause with those who could help the superlative Black individual escape the irrelevance that befell Douglass in the post–Civil War period. If Locke had written a biography that made that visible, that kind of dialogue between biography and autobiography would have been extraordinary.

Locke hated camping, the bugs, the dirt, and the uncleanliness of the food. But he went anyway—to speak about Black people's culture and its continued relevance to a revolutionary imaginary that seemed only occasionally to include Negroes. Again, he was in vogue, mostly among younger Black communists, and Locke noticed that that summer of 1938. He would befriend people who were unlike him, heterosexuals frolicking at a communist retreat, weak-kneed White liberals who cared only to use the Negro to further their agenda, and Black radicals too young to realize the interracial revolution they imagined was not coming anytime soon.

By staying in America, by suppressing his desire to escape to Europe, and by committing to a revolutionary imaginary that barely included him, Locke did something even de Fonseka could not imagine: he sacrificed himself for the possibility of a larger good. And he did that by believing that he could be a race man and a queer man, one very much out front in racial battles while the other Locke thrived under wraps. It was a painful pragmatism. Opposed even by other queers like James Herring, attacked by haughty heterosexual queens like James Porter whose career he had advanced in the past, increasingly alone as the older generation of race men like Schomburg and James Weldon Johnson died off, Locke also could not find long-term companionship with the young blood of sexually ambivalent men like Arthur Fauset or flamboyant homosexuals like Bruce Nugent. Locke tried to turn the divisiveness of doubleness into an asset, to be a race man who loved other men, to merge his double self into a better and truer self. His goal was that he "simply wishes to make it possible for a man to be both... without being cursed and spit upon by his fellows, without having the doors of opportunity closed roughly in his face," as Du Bois had put it in the *Souls of Black Folk*.[17] His life proved that that resolution was possible, even if the price was a life of paranoia, nervous ticks, destabilizing habits, and a perennially broken heart.

Locke decided to believe in a positive double consciousness—that he could will himself to be both queer and race conscious in America, and succeed. Interestingly, Locke began to find new acceptance among those he had felt most alienated from—radical-minded Whites and Blacks who tolerated, perhaps even welcomed, his homosexuality. It had always been among the bohemian Whites that he had felt most comfortable. Now, under the umbrella of international Communism, he did again.

Alain Locke. Courtesy of the Moorland-Spingarn Research Center, Howard University.

40

The Queer Toussaint

Rather than escaping during the summer of 1938, Locke accepted the challenge to make American culture what he wanted it to be. He now undertook this work with a kind of military zeal. Black people could only be freed if their avant garde, intellectually weaponized Black artists followed him into battle against the notion that Black people should not be proud to be Black in a discursively White America. His sense of destiny now matched his ability to fulfill his calling without the help of any one person. No longer a lieutenant of someone else's agenda, Locke fulfilled his own agenda believing it was the last best hope for a world historical Black race.

Locke applied himself to what was in front of him—the coming conference on Negro adult education that he himself had put into motion during the spring. Since this adult-education meeting was held at Hampton Institute, housing was not an issue. By holding the conference at a Negro college, Locke not only solved the problem of Jim Crow hotels by putting attendees in Black college dormitories but also made a larger point—that adult education was part of higher education. He also pulled in the White authorities on adult education into the bosom of Black education and forced them to see Negro education as American education, and vice versa.

Still, there were hassles in the run-up to the conference, as Locke, the go-between of establishment adult education and Black grass-roots adult education, had to balance the conflicting agendas. At the last minute, the delicate balance of bringing large numbers of White administrators into conversation with Black ones was threatened when Morse Cartwright, director of the American Association for Adult Education, insisted the conference change its dates so that the Secretary of Education could speak. But the star speaker at the conference was Locke, who delivered one of his powerful speeches on a subject that transcended the factions and elites he brought together—and defined what Negro adult education had to teach American adult education. In a rare moment when he acknowledged the reality of segregation, Locke cast it as an opportunity for American education to reinvent itself. Mainstream American adult educators could learn something from how Negro adult educators engaged communities displaced from the American dream by teaching them to think critically about what lifelong education really meant. It meant the teaching of people to think for themselves. If American education could embrace that notion, it would not only have learned something from Negroes, it would have learned something about how to transform America.

Of course, after the conference, Locke was exhausted, his heart taxed by the networking, chitchatting, and hand shaking that Locke usually avoided. But the conference had renewed his faith in his interracial diplomacy if for no other reason than he had brought together in the same college auditorium people who never saw one another and made them interact. Once he had recovered his strength and regained traction in teaching that fall quarter's classes, Locke took a chance. He wrote to "Papa Keppel," as he called the head of the Carnegie Corporation, with a powerful proposal. He wanted to produce a portfolio of images of Negro art that would be a companion to his Bronze Booklet, *Negro Art: Past and Present*, and present the argument of that booklet in a large format. The new art book would include photographs of African art, art by Negro artists, and art of the Negro subject by White artists. Most of the artwork already had been located during the research for the Bronze Booklet. He needed a Carnegie subvention to shoulder the costs of getting high-quality plates made of artwork and to price the book low enough to reach Negro artists, Negro college students, and the Negro lower middle class.

But the radicalism of the proposal did not escape the notice of the art experts Keppel consulted for a recommendation. "We are interested in anything you think well of," Keppel wrote back in a month, "but our advisers believe there is a mistake in principle about this whole enterprise and, under the circumstances, I am inclined not to take it up formally with my Board, but to wait, if you agree, for the next suggestion that will come from your fertile mind."[1] Not willing to simply accept the rejection, Locke used his reply to make a stronger counterargument even as he accepted Keppel's decision not to bring the proposal before the Carnegie Board of Trustees. He knew well the advisor's objections, but also believed he had an answer for them.

> Oddly enough had the project been framed merely as a record of the work of Negro artists, the major dilemma would have been resolved. But as in the little booklet on "Negro Art" I am committed to the less established position of emphasizing the Negro subject as an art theme rather than the more chauvinistic position of merely playing up the work of Negro artists. The position that it is wrong to emphasize the color line in art is logically sound and seems to take the high moral ground. But it is a Pharisaical virtue. It denies us as a group already the victims of an enforced cultural separatism the positive incentives and residual advantages of a situation which isn't cured by partially

ignoring it. The work of the Negro artist needs documentation and is maturing to a point where it deserves it. Yet this emphasis in my judgment would be chauvinistic and reactionary if it were not threaded into the broader theme of the development of the art of the Negro subject, and in a way to show the collaboration of the white artist in an ever-increasing penetration into the Negro types as subject matter for American art.[2]

The Black body, that he loved, had to be the centerpiece of a book on Negro art that enabled Black subjectivity—the "less established position of emphasizing the Negro subject." Although Locke did not say so in his letter to Keppel, putting the work of African artists and European artists in the same book with African American artists would also be radical—and break down the racial segregation of canonical art history. The proposal also rejected the notion that Black art could be studied in isolation, as not always in conversation with, reaction against, revision of the work of White artists and European and American art histories. Locke's book would reveal that the White artist had had a love affair with the very same Blackness that Western society routinely demonized. It had had no chance of being recommended by Keppel's experts.

Instead of sulking, Locke advanced his approach to Negro art through a curatorial strategy even in major Black exhibitions he did not control. As he wrote Mason in January 1939, "There is to be a grand show of the work of Negro artists at new Baltimore Museum of Art—opening February 3rd. I have helped make contacts and in return they are asking me to be guest speaker at the opening-night—8:30 pm." In the process, he circumvented his opposition through connections to White museums that relied on his judgment and aesthetic taste to make their curatorial decisions in the Negro art field. When the trustees of the Baltimore Museum of Art, and a local committee of African Americans, headed by Sarah Fernandis, expressed the desire to recognize recent activity among African American artists in some way, Locke and Brady had convinced the museum to do the show.[3] Neither Keppel's "experts" nor Howard University Art Department teachers were influential with that class.

Indeed, the leadership of the Howard University Art Department had to welcome Locke when the Baltimore curator selecting the work for the exhibition contacted Locke to accompany him on a studio visit to Howard University, but an awkward situation emerged. "Friday afternoon he [Rogers] came over," Locke wrote to Brady, "and as he asked me to make the arrangements with Herring, etc., there had to be a sacred truce, which went off all right as far as I was concerned." Being asked to do studio visits with the Baltimore curator provided Locke some sweet satisfaction. "There were some terribly ironic moments; among them a visit to Porter's home and my having to help un-pack Miss Jones's canvases. Mr. Rogers took only one thing of Miss Jones's—a watercolor;

nothing of Porter's—whose work he criticized very objectively but firmly. I discreetly left the room during most of this, but had to participate in the beginning as Mr. Rogers cross-examined me to get concurrence on certain points." Lois Jones, influenced by Locke, was selected to be in the show, while Porter was not. And Herring dared not block Locke's access to artists in the Howard University Art Department given that he accompanied a White curator.

> The local Howard art people have been very nasty and non-cooperative—
> although I ignored their previous attitude to take the curator around
> their studios. But he took almost nothing—criticized them frankly—
> and now I have earned their greater enmity. I took Mrs. Biddle to our
> lovely little University gallery—she enjoyed it—but did not realize that
> the director [James Herring] scarcely speaks to me—regarding me an
> intruder into "his" field. He himself cannot write a clear sentence and is
> vain as a mangy peacock. This isn't spleen—its just truth.[4]

Herring dared not block Locke's access to the Howard University Gallery of Art when Mrs. Biddle visited. She was the wife of the Attorney General of the United States, and it might have cost him his job.

Not surprisingly, Locke was pleased with the experience. "I am really quite impressed with Mr. Roger's interest and sincerity. He is evidently deeply interested in Negro artists and their work; obviously more so than when he began. But he feels that they need criticism and that double standards or conventional ones either will do them more harm than good."[5] It was thrilling to have a White man with unimpeachable art credentials reinforce his recommendations. Lois Jones was the only artist in the Howard University Department of Art to have something selected by the curator of the show, and she was the only faculty member who followed Locke's ideas. The "Contemporary Negro Art" exhibit showed the depth of Locke's influence in the art world: a White curator of a major American museum of modern art was putting together an exhibit based on Locke's ideas, selecting art Locke's taste had shaped, and doing the work his writings had said needed to be done.

Locke's newfound prominence alienated some former allies. Mary Beattie Brady had always had a tense relationship with Locke. Later in her retirement, Brady would confide to David Driskell in an extensive interview that she always was skeptical of Locke's "Negro nationalism" and attempts to create a race-based program in Negro art. Richard Long, a Locke protégé and confidant, recalled a different reason for Brady's late career animus toward Locke. It was not ideological. Reputedly, while discussing the prospects for the Contemporary Negro Art exhibit with Adelyn Breeskin, the chief curator of the Baltimore Museum of Art, she suggested that what the museum intended was something akin to the Harmon Foundation exhibits. Locke's retort told his side of the story. "Oh,

I think we can do better than that."[6] Somehow, that comment got back to Brady to her chagrin.

Nevertheless, Locke's influence on the exhibit worked to the Harmon Foundation's advantage. Locke encouraged Richmond Barthé and Jacob Lawrence to bring their artwork to the Harmon Foundation offices, which served as an entrepôt for the New York–based artists to have their work catalogued for shipment to Baltimore. Brady seized on this opportunity to heighten the drama of the historic exhibition, by having James Allen photograph Barthé presenting a sculpture, *Stevedore*, to a White registrar, while next to him stands Lawrence with a box containing paintings of the Toussaint L'Ouverture series. Strikingly, the photograph registers the racial/sexual politics of Locke's exhibitionary politics, and how Barthé adapted to the Zeitgeist of the 1930s, since his bulbous, hyper-masculine working-class *Stevedore* diverged sharply from the lean, classically beautiful Black nude he had submitted to the Harmon exhibition in 1933. Locke and Brady lobbied the Baltimore Museum of Art to devote an entire room to exhibiting Lawrence's multi-panel series visualizing the Haitian Revolution of 1804 on its own, making it the artistic hit of the exhibition.

So influential was Locke in the staging of this exhibit that the Baltimore leadership gave him a prominent role in the printed materials and public rollout of the exhibition. Ever the queer strategist, Locke wanted to ensure that such a speaking role would not compromise his leading-from-behind strategy in steering the exhibition. As he wrote Brady early in 1939, "Professor Boas has asked me to do a foreword for the catalogue, which I will try to make justify your expectations. This especially since your suggestion must have started it. The suggestion has also been made that I give a brief talk opening night. I will discuss it further in Baltimore on Wednesday—as I am anxious to avoid the suspicion of putting myself forward. However, it looks like a hot campaign anyway; so why retreat?" Once again, the military metaphor announced a war for Negro art and against those enemy forces that would hold it back. "Negro art must go forward; and we seem to be critically challenged. I think I should accept it. Of course if I had realized this earlier I would have scouted around even more widely for available material."[7]

While no photograph survives of Locke giving the opening-night speech at the "Contemporary Negro Art" exhibition, an indelible image does show us what Locke achieved with the exhibition. It is a photograph of two young children looking up at a large, mask-like sculpture by Ronald Moody, a Jamaican artist based in Paris (see page 776). The pre–Columbian looking Afro-Indian sculpture is huge, even more so in contrast to the little children gazing from below. Instead of the challenges of segregated life in the Great Depression, these young children display hope, optimism, and wonder at the huge possibilities before them. This photograph captures Locke's purpose—to generate an art that would uplift the gaze of the young Negroes by filling them with a sense of pride, style, and wonder at what they could achieve if they believed.

Locke's opening remarks that evening, printed in the foreword to the catalog, showed his willingness to change his message in order to reach that new generation. "Art in a democracy should above all else be democratic, which is to say that it must be truly representative." Negro art had come into the center of the

Boys and sculpture, Contemporary Negro Art exhibition, The Baltimore Museum of Art, 1939. Photograph Collection, Archives and Manuscripts Collection, The Baltimore Museum of Art. AN6.40.

cultural democracy that those in WPA circles referenced as the raison d'être of cultural public art to build a new, more representative democracy for the future. Government support of the arts was breaking the elitist stranglehold that the gallery system and private patronage had exercised on American art. Speaking more directly to the Baltimore Museum's intervention, Locke announced it exemplifying "changing the role of the museum from that of a treasure storehouse of the past to that of a clearing house for the contemporary artist," a vision that Locke had communicated to the Baltimore museum in recommending the exhibit in the first place. Their staff's receptiveness signaled a corner had been turned in "our now generally accepted objective to have American art fully document American life and experience, and thus more adequately reflect America."[8] Here was another new position: Negro art was justified as the logical outgrowth of the demand for cultural democracy in the 1930s, in which all of America's constituencies should be represented in American art. Having pined for so long in the fields of an African-centered argument for American Negro art, Locke found traction in that long-ago developed argument of cultural pluralism.

Perhaps as significant as who was included in the Baltimore Museum of Art exhibit was who was not. No Harmon Foundation critics from the Harlem Artists Guild such as Augusta Savage or Romare Bearden had work in this February 1939 exhibition. But Harlem Guild Artists still enjoyed the advantage of location in New York. Augusta Savage had scored a personal triumph when those planning the New York World's Fair commissioned her in 1938 to do a sculpture to commemorate the African American contribution to American culture. Unfortunately, Savage was not able to restart her career as a sculptor with that commission: her huge sculpture, *Lift Every Voice and Sing*, was roundly criticized as amateurish and poorly executed, by "experts," though it was extremely popular with Black visitors to the Fair.

Indeed, the New York World's Fair gave Locke an argument to anchor an article in *Opportunity* about his debate with the ideological perspective of the Harlem Art Guild. The New York World's Fair exhibit arguably trumped the Baltimore Museum exhibit in that works like Savage's were exhibited in the American pavilion rather than an all-Negro show. In the run-up to the exhibit, Locke heard New York's Negro artists debating whether the Negro artists should exhibit in the American or international pavilion, with the latter venue including African art.[9] Rumor circulated that the Harlem group turned down the international opportunity and chose the American gallery partly in reaction to being segregated with "primitive" African art. Locke seized on this debate to write his most incendiary essay on African American art to date, boiling over with his frustration with what he saw as the lack of strategic vision on the part of Negro visual artists.

Titled "Advance on the Art Front," the article sparkled. "The recent advances in contemporary Negro art remind me of nothing so much as a courageous cavalry move over difficult ground in the face of obstacles worse than powder and shell—silence and uncertainty." With telling use of the military metaphor, Locke sold the notion that Negro art represented a world historical subjectivity, whose fate hinged on its courage, clarity, and unity in the face of White disdain and racist dismissal of the worth of Negro art. "I have read only one book of military strategy, and remember only one or two sentences.... One said, 'It's not the ground you gain but the ground you hold that counts'; the other, 'Even retreat, organized, is safer than disorganized advance'."[10]

Victory would not be possible for Negro art unless it went beyond a few individual or even collective successes on the exhibitionary level to "consolidate our art gains" with a coordinated strategy. Referencing the success of Marian Anderson, who, once prevented from singing in Constitution Hall by the Daughters of the American Revolution, sang to an even more memorable effect on the steps of the Lincoln Memorial, Locke snapped: "But why should we wait upon a mismaneuver of the enemy or hang precariously on a fumble of our opposition? The essence of strategy is planned action and the tactics of intentionally organized resources. Imagine the educative public effect of a permanently organized traveling exhibit of the work of contemporary Negro artists? Or visualize the social dividends on such a representative collection as part of the Golden Gate Exposition or the New York World's Fair?" But that had not happened at the New York World's Fair because of internal dissent over whether to include their work in a national or international exhibition. Locke went on to argue against the rejection of identification with African art by saying one could not pry away from South Africa or any of the European nations the African art they put on display. Almost every nation in the World's Fair was double billing—showing in the international hall but also mounting a national show to advertise their agency in art to gain attention, while the Negro fumbled the opportunity by forcing upon itself a "consistency [that] was the enforced virtue of the disinherited." Black artists exhibiting at the fair thought of themselves only as representatives of the American nation when America did not even consider them citizens.

What made Locke unique is that he could hold such fierce Black nationalist opinions while at the same time working the White people in his camp to garner all of the power he could get. It was a revolutionary dialogic nationalism, and some of them could see it. When he wrote Mary Beattie Brady after the article's publication saying that it had said some harsh things, but "Negro art must go forward," she was silent about the article, no doubt, disturbed by its fierce nationalism, but dependent on his discursive power to defend her presence in the domain of Negro art where she had no real aesthetic authority. But she had a taste in her selection of art to promote, a more mixed-race notion of new world art than Locke had, and she also had an institutional structure that could make Negro art more than a local, community phenomena. If there were to be a "permanent traveling exhibition of contemporary Negro art," the only entity that could mount such a campaign was the Harmon Foundation, especially once conservative right-wing congressmen began dismantling the WPA in 1939. Suddenly, the Harlem Artists Guild's WPA "leverage" was disappearing and such Black artists like Charles Alston, Augusta Savage, and Gwendolyn Bennett would have to fend for themselves without government patronage. While artists saw being an educator as a step down, Locke saw education—as his parents had seen it—as a step up for the Negro.

Jacob Lawrence knew he needed a strategy for survival as an artist, which is why he eased out from under the collapsing Harlem Artists Guild umbrella and into the more sustainable patronage opportunities available from working with Locke and Brady. A member of the Haitian governmental ministry visited the Baltimore show and expressed a desire for the Haitian government to acquire the L'Ouverture series for display back home. Locke immediately communicated this information to Lawrence, who was enthusiastic. When it became clear that the Haitian government lacked the funds to purchase the series, Lawrence was not concerned. "It means much more to an artist to have people like and enjoy his work, than it does to have a few individuals purchase his work, and it not have the interest of the masses. As I told you when you were here, selling these things was the last thing I thought of when I conceived them."[11] But Locke cautioned him against letting his work go for free, since he knew that the Negro artist had to profit from such work in a capitalist world of art if he or she was to have a sustainable career. Sensing that Locke and Brady had his long-term interest at heart, Lawrence would stay in constant contact with them in the coming months, letting Brady hold onto the L'Ouverture series while he traveled and worked on the John Brown series, later the Harriet Tubman series, and then the monumental Migration series that would cement his reputation.[12]

Coming artists like Lawrence, Elton Fax, Ronald Moody, and even the venerable Barthé scored through their association with Locke. Barthé's sculpture, *The Mother*, retitled *Mother and Son* at the New York World's Fair, was given considerable attention in "Advance on the Art Front." *The Mother* epitomized Locke's program—to foster art by Negroes that served multiple agendas but remained devoted to the central goal to create beautiful and subtle works of art. "Here is a subject racial to the core—a Negro peasant woman kneeling and mournfully cradling in her arms the limp, broken-necked body of her lynched son. But striking enough to be more potent anti-lynching propaganda than an armful of pamphlets, this statue group is properly, as a work of art, universalized," because it used Michelangelo's famous sculpture of the death of Jesus as the lens through which to capture the poignancy of an American experience.

Such art had to stand on its own as quintessential modern art even as it advanced a politics of revelation about what and who the Negro was. This came out forcefully in correspondence Locke had with a young man, Hercules Armstrong, whom Locke met at the exhibition. Recruiting Locke as a patron and a lover, Armstrong sent Locke some of his poems already published in radical journals. His poetry was fierce and white-hot with unadulterated Black anger. Locke wrote back sternly if affectionately that, in his opinion, Armstrong needed to do more work crafting his poetry before sending it out. Mere expression of harsh if heartfelt anger at the situation of the Negro was not poetry. Poetry required the crafted utterance, the subtle phrase, the ability to say something without saying it, so that the protest burned through the page and forced the reader to return to the poem again and again. Here was the quality that Jacob Lawrence's paintings had that Locke wanted Armstrong's poems to embody and become sophisticated and unexpected renderings of their subject matter. Armstrong was stung a bit by Locke's harsh words, but also knew that this is what Locke stood for. In the 1930s, when all art had to be propaganda to be relevant, Locke still held that the best propaganda was great art, and great art was the best propaganda.

The day after "Advance on the Art Front" appeared in *Opportunity*, a very welcome letter from Morse Cartwright, director of the American Association of Adult Education, appeared in Locke's mailbox.

> While officially I must be as dumb and silent as the Sphinx in the matter, personally I am glad to be able to tell you that there is a ray of hope with respect to the Negro art portfolio. After our conversation of the other day I wrote a memorandum for Mr. Keppel in which I recommended that the Corporation make, through this Association, a supplemental grant to the Associates in Negro Folk Education, on account of the Bronze Booklet Series. Mr. Keppel has responded by giving me permission to poll my Board with respect to their willingness to recommend the utilization of a $2,000 balance remaining in the adult education experimental fund for the current year. If we should get favorable action on the part of our Board members, Mr. Keppel would be prepared to put up to his Trustees a proposal to match that sum, thus making a total of $4,000 available to the Associates for the further development of the Bronze Booklet Series. This would give you funds with which to go ahead with the Negro art portfolio.[13]

How did it happen that Locke's proposal found such favor with Cartwright that he would come up with this plan to fund the Negro Art portfolio over Keppel's objections? The answer is simple. The financial success of Locke's Bronze Booklets brought very positive buzz to the AAAE, which otherwise had little to show for its intervention in Negro adult education. And the booklets countered whatever negative discourse existed within the AAAE about funding Negro adult education. Locke had run a cost-effective operation that was enormously successful in getting books to market, without causing any trouble with the segregated educational establishment. Black people were buying radical books with a class as well as a racial critique of America's problems, and Locke was delivering that knowledge without eliciting a congressional investigation. Locke had effectively run an adult-education project that served the AAAE agenda and a subversive Black agenda at the same time.

Cartwright was careful, however, not to embarrass Keppel in rewarding Locke for the overall success of the Associates of Negro Folk Education.

> If this plan goes through and the portfolio is finally issued, then I think we should be sure to protect Mr. Keppel in his relations with his arts advisers by omitting from the volume any reference to the fact that its publication was made possible by funds provided by the Carnegie Corporation. The book will thus merely stand as a publication paid for out of receipts from the Bronze Booklet Series, which, of course, in effect is a true statement, in that this supplemental grant from the Carnegie Corporation, if and when made, is for the purpose of covering manufacturing and other costs relating to the presentation of the series as a whole.[14]

Locke agreed. Cartwright's letter explains the mystery of who funded *The Negro in Art*, since nowhere in the book does it reference the Carnegie or AAAE subvention.[15]

Locke confided to Mrs. Mason that he had had to go to a meeting of the Adult Education Association in order to seal the deal for funding the Negro Art portfolio. Here again was a lesson. Going to these meetings with liberal Whites, listening to their ideas and opinions about what Negroes needed to learn, and bringing a few Black experts into the AAAE fold helped both the Negro educators and the AAAE leadership more effectively converse with one another. This harmonizer role created the conditions for Cartwright to value Locke enough to work around the obstacle of the funder's restrictions to fund completion of Locke's portfolio. Here, Locke's insight that he needed a third party—the AAAE—to sanction his projects to obtain the funding from a patron, the Carnegie Corporation, had an unexpected benefit: the AAAE acted independently to secure funding for the book without his having to change its controversial argument.

Such funding was not the only opportunity to come to Locke through Morse Cartwright. While Locke was busy hunting down photographs to finalize the Negro art portfolio, Morse Cartwright told Claude Barnett, the founder of the Associated Negro Press, located in Chicago, to ask Locke and Mary Beattie Brady to assist him in arranging for a real Negro art presence at the American Negro Exposition, projected to open in July 1940. Barnett had taken over planning for the exposition, a flailing project he was trying to save from problems generated by its earlier mismanagement. Barnett saw the American Negro Exposition as a way to bring attention to the Negro entrepreneurial and cultural awakening in Chicago. He needed someone to arrange an exhibit of African art for the exposition, but also to manage a juried selection process to exhibit the best Negro American art in America at the exposition. Locke's network of Cartwright and Brady brought Locke's name to Barnett's attention; and Barnett also became part of Locke's network. In Barnett, Locke found a similarly competent—and a similarly dapper—Negro man who shared his desire to advance Negro agency in the twentieth century. While working as a postal worker after graduation from Tuskegee, Barnett began sending out photographs of famous Black people, creating a profitable mail-order business. Then, in 1919, he created the Associated Negro Press to supply news content for the fledging Black newspapers across the country and established a media network. Barnett exemplified the Black renaissance's westward shift due to the Negro middle class's greater entrepreneurial success in Chicago than in New York, and as such, Barnett provided Locke with a new base of operations away from the East Coast.

In April 1940, Barnett traveled to Washington, D.C., to win federal financial support for the Chicago Exposition. Not only did he secure the federal financial support, but the Labor, Agricultural, and Interior Departments also agreed to send representatives to the exposition, elevating it from a regional to a national celebration of the Negro's coming of age. Despite meeting with Herring, Barnett chose Locke to be the unofficial coordinator of the art exhibits at the exposition. "Reaffirming our conversation, our idea is roughly that we will be guided by the suggestions of you and Miss Brady. Mr. Herring has been good enough to outline some very useful suggestions which I passed on to Miss Brady and which she evidently has approved."[16] Barnett had to include Brady as she had the storage facility, the administrative apparatus, and the financial resources for shipping, installing, and arranging art in space. Barnett divided invitations to artists regionally, with one group from New York and Washington, another from Chicago, the third from Atlanta. Key to the selection was Locke's point that major art world critics and art museum players should be on the selection committees. Barnett planned to design the gallery space to accommodate African sculpture and contemporary sculpture by Negroes, following the logic of Locke's portfolio. Barnett hoped he would be able to sell the portfolio and Bronze Booklets at the Exposition.

Locke also wanted a favor in return. The annual meetings of the Association for Adult Education were being held on May 20–24, in Astor, New York, and Locke asked if Barnett could take part. If Barnett could not attend, Locke asked if he would be willing to send a paper, "The Negro Press and Negro Mass Education," to be read at the conference, which he did.

Locke would prove critical to the success of the art side of the exposition. He even provided a list of judges and contacted his friend, Peter Pollack, who was launching the Chicago Community Art Center, for help in securing the best artwork for the exposition. "Your suggestions … are invaluable," Barnett wrote to Locke in April. "So clear and worthwhile are they that I am confident they can serve as the basis of our plans for the Art Exhibit. Our program calls for the carrying out immediately of the various steps which you outline."[17]

By July 3, on the eve of the exposition's opening, everything was in place, according to Locke. As he wrote to Brady: "You need have no concern about the exhibit. It will be very, very good. The Western material was rich and plenteous, and the jury worked professionally on it. Even so, over a hundred items were passed. It was an enthusiastic jury. Mr. Rich of the Art Institute expressed himself as 'amazed.'"[18] Part of the reason she did not need to worry is that Locke was overseeing every aspect of the evaluation and installation of the art.

> I sat with the jury, and after they had completed the jury pieces, took the liberty of asking their advisory opinion on the Harmon items. They went carefully through them all, which gave us the benefit of a check up criticism. They weeded out some pieces to the advantage, I think, of the showing. They liked Malvin Gray particularly, but thought his show would be better if about six or seven items were left out. The same with Albert Smith. . . . They omitted Waring's Mother and Daughter, which I like because of subject matter, but must admit is very "flat." . . . They also took out Aaron Douglas, but I saw that Power Plant was restored. They like the large William Johnsons. They were very fond of the later Palmer Haydens.[19]

Perhaps most important was Locke's role in the actual installation of the galleries. Locke had recommended Barnett use Alonzo Aden, the Howard University Gallery of Art curator, to install the galleries. It was an example of Locke's power that he got the spectacularly handsome Aden the job of installing the exhibit galleries rather than the "peacock," Herring. Aden got needed experience, according to Locke, who helped him lay out and hang some of the galleries. The result was a tremendous success. "Barnett was very pleased," Locke wrote Brady. Certainly, he had to be pleased that, with Locke's participation, the exposition had the full support of people like Daniel Rich of the Art Institute, who even headed the prize jury that also, not surprisingly, included Locke. One wonders if Brady needed to be told that Locke would be making the keynote speech.

But even when someone else headed the jury selection, the prize-winning art epitomized Locke's deeper message that Negro art exemplified Black power. The prizewinners mixed the modern, social realist urgency of the Great Depression with a powerful visual narrative of the Black body. Winning first prize at the American Negro Exposition, Charles White's "There were no crops to share" was both social critique and powerful Negro art. Frederick Flemister's "Artist with a Brush" redrew Italian Renaissance portraits with a Black subject as the artist.

Despite the objections of those like James Porter, James Herring, and Romare Bearden that the Negro artists should not be confined to Negro subjects, the art that succeeded at the American Negro Exposition, judged by White and Black artists and critics, was an art of the Negro subject.

The American Negro Exposition in Chicago capped Locke's remarkable journey over the last two years from intellectual outcast to the most influential force in African American art. Barnett had valued him for what he had become in the 1930s—a curator, an author, and a publisher whose system of cultural production allied the American Association of Adult Education, the Harmon Foundation, and the Carnegie Corporation, with artists, critics, and curators, Negro and White. Locke's array of talent and influence had transformed the exposition's exhibition from an also-ran sideshow into a major statement of the city's—and the Negro's—artistic coming of age. The American Negro Exposition was as much a renaissance for Locke as for the Windy City.

A photograph does survive of Locke giving the opening remarks at this art exhibition, a sign of Locke's efficacy. Shot from the back, a tiny man is speaking to a small crowd garbed in their Sunday best, hanging on the words of this dapper presenter whose face is hidden from view. At the opening festivities of the American Negro Exposition in Chicago, Locke projected a larger-than-life-persona from a diminutive Black body barely noticeable in a crowd. Richard Long told the story of a woman appearing at an informal gathering asking to meet Dr. Locke, only to have to be steered away from a commanding presence in the room toward the tiny man standing isolated in the corner. Here, no one needed to be told who was the famous Dr. Locke: he was there, right in front in 1940, the dominant curator of Negro art in America.

41

The Invisible Locke

Locke was a chameleon who changed constantly to adapt to his context, because he feared becoming outdated, irrelevant, forgotten, a kind of living death he feared more than actual death. Because of that fear, he could never be satisfied with one avenue of success, one voice, one triumph, even those he achieved at the Baltimore Museum of Art or the American Negro Exposition. Despite legions of critics and biographers calling Locke an "aesthete," the truth was that he was so much more—a renaissance man in the finest sense of being a man of sociology, art, philosophy, diplomacy, and the Black radical tradition—though these competencies were often invisible. But he kept feeding them, because he was afraid that art would never be enough for him to be remembered for making a difference in the lives of his fellow men and women, something he hungered to be recognized for throughout his life.

A hidden dimension of this quest for immortality occurred in January 1939, just days before his speech at the opening of the Baltimore Museum of Art exhibition. Locke answered a call from Thyra Edwards, the young Black woman internationalist who organized the American Medical Bureau in Spain during the Spanish Civil War. She was writing to ask him to speak at a meeting about race, war, and the Black role in the fight against fascism. At the Conference on the Relation of the Present Struggle in Spain to Democracy and Its Meaning to the Negro People at the Lincoln Congregational Tabernacle in Washington, in early January, Locke also volunteered to say "a strong word about the relevance of the Jewish issue" to the present struggle. Here was a Black organized radical meeting where, though again an outsider, he could greet old acquaintances like Paul Robeson and William Pickens, the latter having just returned from Spain from a fact-finding mission, and Mary Bethune, his long-time ally and friend.

In deciding to speak at the meeting, Locke was helping Edwards, an acquaintance, the kind of strong, engaged, whip-smart Black woman Locke respected. She was herself embattled with American White communists who did not think the Black contribution to the fight against fascism in Spain was that significant. Edwards had tried earlier to hold the forum on the Negro and Spanish fascism as part of the annual meeting of the League of Peace and Democracy, but the

League's leadership had refused, forcing her to put on a separate meeting to link the discussion of the persecution of Jews in Germany to the issues of Ethiopia, Spain, China, and the campaign against lynching in America. She had spent months in Spain organizing the relief effort for injured soldiers. Robeson had gone to Spain and sung, with both Franco's fascist and Republican forces stopping fighting for a brief time to listen him. Edwards and her allies were linking their struggles for democracy in America to the democratic struggle against fascism around the world.

Locke's reflections from the Lincoln Congregational Tabernacle provide a glimpse into what really mattered to him. After the meeting, he wrote to Mrs. Mason about listening to "Dr. Donawa, the former Howard dental man, who was dental surgeon for 18 months at the Spanish front."[1] After being forced out of his deanship by Howard president Mordecai Johnson, Dr. Arnold B. Donawa had returned to private practice and in 1938 went to tend to the injured in Spain, specializing in treating those who had had their jaws blown apart. Locke wrote touchingly about this "magnificently quiet man" who had "the courage of his convictions" to risk death in Spain because of his feeling that the fight for freedom halfway around the world meant something to Negroes. "They report over 300 American Negro volunteers in Spain before the recent evacuations," Locke informed Mason.[2] Donawa had done something Locke had been unable to do: leave the bosom of Howard to chart a heroic life on the real battlefield.

There were others. Salaria Kea became the first and only Negro nurse to work at the front in the Spanish Civil War. She had trained at Harlem Hospital and led a protest in 1933 against the discriminatory conditions for Black nurses perpetuated by Dr. Goldwater. Upon graduation, she realized she would be barred by segregation from working as a nurse among White Americans. So, she took her talents to Spain, where as a member of the American Medical Unit, Salaria tended the injured and the dying. Like Thyra Edwards, her mentor, Kea believed that what was happening in Spain was tied to what had happened to Ethiopia when Italy invaded it in 1935 and to what was continuing to happen in the United States to Negroes. African American radical activists like Edwards and Kea were key players in a leftist attempt to link the consequences of racism and fascism together in what could be called a Black internationalism.[3]

Their courage was one of the reasons Locke was less enamored of the strictly rhetorical anger coming out of the "Newest Negro," as he called the radical proletarian militant writers of the late 1930s. In January, Locke also published his retrospective reviews in which he articulated a defense of the New Negro concept as still relevant to an understanding of the 1930s social protest movement in the arts and social sciences. Richard Wright critiqued the Negro Renaissance writers for being little more than ambassadors seeking the approval of Whites, and John A. Davis, who had organized boycotts of stores discriminating against Negroes in Washington, claimed the Negro Renaissance had failed because it had promised art would solve all the Negro's problems. In "The Negro: New or Newer?" Locke countered that the New Negro not only did not promise any such thing but also that the New Negro was an evolving subjectivity that changed in dialogue with its context. Taking up their challenge, Locke revised his conception of the New Negro once again, this time as being a subject that took different identities as it worked out the right balance between the social reality of Negro life, with all of its limitations and sordidness, and the aesthetic transcendence of Negro life in its literary and other expressive forms. The New Negro had always included two voices, Locke now proclaimed, one social and critical, the other aesthetic and empathetic. While admitting the Harlem writers had abandoned representing the real in their later writings, Locke suggested that, instead of attacking one another, the Newest Negroes should stand on the shoulders of earlier New Negroes who had won the right for Negro writers to speak and act without fear. Real courage was sacrificing the glory of being the latest literary celebrity and going to Spain to fight for universal freedom.

Locke no doubt sensed, too, that part of the attack of these "bright young people" was an attack on him as the New Negro Renaissance's homosexual leader, since the portrait drawn by Wright and Davis was a homophobic caricature of his role in the movement. Wright labeled Negro writers as "ambassadors of art" begging for recognition of the Negro's essential humanity from Whites as weak and effeminate seekers of favors. He dismissively characterized earlier writers as lacking in courage. True masculinity and patriarchy were things American society always held just out of reach of Black men under slavery and segregation, as almost all of Richard Wright's short stories and novels of the late 1930s and early 1940s substantiated. Part of the way John A. Davis and the activists of Washington, D.C., dealt with the pressure was to prove the masculinity of Negro men by taking it to the streets, in direct action through nonviolent demonstrations and boycotts of stores that refused to hire Black people, yet profited from their patronage.

Even with the rhetorical genius Locke displayed in "The Negro: New or Newer?" Locke realized he needed a new approach to the role of Negro epistemologies in American culture. For the criticism of these younger writers, artists, and social science intellectuals exposed the weaknesses in how Locke had formulated the argument for his cultural anthropology of the Negro people. His earlier anthropology, narrated in a series of articles in the 1920s, showed that America was in essence a Black nation from a folk and popular-culture standpoint. But younger Black Marxist intellectuals, like Ralph Bunche, Doxey Wilkerson, and Abram Harris dismissed the "Negro contributions" formula as hackneyed and unscientific. Not only did it reduce Blackness to a series of object-like gifts but it also ignored the structural nature of racism and class oppression that prevailed even after individual Whites recognized the nation's debt to the artistic genius of Negroes. This required that Locke do more than simply expand his taste by including the struggle through protest literature, but create an updated and complex sociology of race and power on a global platform of knowledge.

If Locke was going to maintain the serious position he and other Black queer intellectuals had carved out in the 1920s—that an intervention in the discursive world of Black representation by Black artists made a difference—he was going to have to place art, literature, even Negro nationalism in a fiercer intellectual context, that of a counter-imperialist uprising challenging colonialism in theory and practice around the world. Locke was forced to recover his earlier world-systems analysis of race in his Race Contacts and Interracial Relations lectures at Howard in 1915 and 1916 in order to update his argument that culture mattered in the late 1930s. Locke would have to expand on what he did in the foreword to the catalog for the Contemporary Negro Art exhibition at the Baltimore Museum of Art: move away from simply emphasizing the African contribution to American culture to suggest that America was a crucible of world culture flows in which the Black remained pivotal.

That is precisely what *When Peoples Meet* did. The thinking behind this transformational text began in 1938 while Richard Wright and the South Side writers were composing "Blueprint for Negro Writing" to critique him and his kind as weak and irrelevant to the social realist attack on systemic racism. While they attacked him, he was preparing a discursive answer to his militant critics that in complexity and scope went beyond what they proposed. That fall of 1938, he crafted the first of several proposals to the Progressive Education Association to edit and publish a scholarly version of the Race Contacts lectures he had delivered as a young radical Black sociologist. Locke's theory had argued in those lectures that race was the worldwide pivot of modern life in the way that Marx had treated class. That argument would be fully realized in *When Peoples Meet*, an anthology that offered a Black radical world systems analysis of how global racism functions as the theory and the practice of imperialism.

What made *When Peoples Meet* unique was the way it integrated two voices in one text. First, there was its sustained argument that while race had been dethroned as a legitimate scientific concept, it remained a powerful public discourse in the West that justified the imperialist rape of the resources of Africa and Asia. But it also documented how radicalized minorities answered—by developing practices and strategies of resistance that contained and even thwarted the brainwashing effects of the other discourse in the mind of the oppressed. Locke showed that race was not only a fig leaf for economic exploitation but also a consciousness by which communities of color built solidarity and resistance to their dehumanization at the hands of the West.

Compiled by Locke and Bernhard Stern, a radical sociologist and educator working at Columbia University, the book contained authoritative writings by experts in anthropology, sociology, and international affairs, on how difference based on color and caste operated throughout Africa, British India, and East

Asia. Not only about Black Americans, it showed how race kept Africans, Asians, Latin Americans, and others under the thumb of Western nations. For example, Locke and Stern reprinted an excerpt from *Half-Caste* (1937) by Cedric Dover, an example of the *Newest Negro* consciousness except that he was Indian. Dover's entry stated: "The dominance of color prejudice in the social scene must be attributed primarily to the unmoral economic relations between technically advanced and backward groups, and not to ethnic differences which are deliberately used to rationalize aggression."[4] Dover argued that the English were genetically as related to the population of Northern India as to the Welsh, yet the racial antagonism of the English toward the Indian far outstripped that manifested against the Welsh.

Here was the new criticality—using anthropological analysis to demystify racist explanations for imperialist behavior, yet focused clearly on the persistence of those myths and the exploitations they justify. The key to understanding race practice was to see its economic origins, as Locke had argued in Race Contacts and as Dover pointed out in linking anti-Indian feeling in England to Indian boycotts against British goods. This 1930s generation of new radical thinkers understood that the oppressed had as their only defense a counter-hatred for those who hated them.

When Peoples Meet brought together a new generation of African American, Asian, and Hispanic intellectuals who constituted a new renaissance. By emphasizing their scientific, sociological, and political revelations, Locke demonstrated an anti-colonialist awakening around the globe. *When Peoples Meet* revises the notion of what the renaissance really is—the awakening of humanity, including the Black, Brown, and Asian people excluded from the European renaissance, to their collective humanity through critique of the imperialist project.

How did Locke get such a radical book published in the early 1940s by an organization like the Progressive Education Association? It appears that Locke first began recruiting the Progressive Education Association (PEA) after 1932, when this rather sleepy progressive education advocacy group shifted its agenda toward seeing teachers as change agents to be armed with the latest "scientific" information about social conflict. Locke first proposed *When Peoples Meet* as an "intercultural" sourcebook that would help educators understand what happened when different cultures "met" and how to manage the conflict that almost inevitably resulted. This less volatile discourse of cultural pluralism allowed the book to be seen and promoted as a manual of how race conflicts could be managed rationally without any fundamental change in how the West behaved. But buried within its later sections was clearly documented evidence that, without a radical economic and political change, Western nations were not going to have an easy time continuing the imperialist mindset of the past. Locke's radicalism had been—and to some extent remained—invisible in a text that otherwise seemed like a primer for cosmopolitanism.

Of course, to produce this text, Locke wanted to get paid, and the PEA had very little money. But it did have a close and trusted relationship with the General Education Board (GEB), which had been endowed by John D. Rockefeller. As he had earlier with Carnegie and the American Association for Adult Education, Locke realized early that he would have to triangulate the PEA and the GEB and another "expert" if he wanted to get *When Peoples Meet* funded.

But Locke was not the only dog in the hunt. Charles Johnson, at Fisk, was also seeking funds for his path-breaking but relatively conservative studies of southern segregation. The NAACP was also seeking funds from the GEB; but it was refused, because board members thought it had harmed more than helped the situation of the Negro in the South. Carter G. Woodson was also in the chase for GEB funding, but was turned down because he was "too independent" and his public-education projects, such as Negro history week publications, were not perceived as in line with the board's agenda to fund "scholarly" projects. Locke succeeded where Woodson failed because he had invested years in building up relationships with the key players in the Progressive Education Association, tailored his request to the mindset of those players, and reflected the higher-education orientation of the General Education Board to publish "sourcebooks" of scholarship for teachers. By pitching his book as a resource on global intercultural problems for teachers, Locke persuaded the PEA to bring *his* knowledge of global thinking and practices about race to the White educators' audience. Here was a clue to why Locke kept his radical voice largely invisible to his public persona. Instead of developing a new theory of how race and class reinforced one another in Western imperialism in the pages of *Opportunity* and the *Crisis*, or publishing a scholarly tome on the subject, Locke chose a relatively obscure venue to fund his trenchant contribution to the Black radical tradition and, because of his invisibility as a radical, and a Black nationalist, he could also get paid.

Even so, the going was slow until 1938, when Locke felt he had built enough trust with the PEA leadership to propose a book on intercultural education. His idea immediately elicited objections from Henry Lasswell, a Yale University political scientist and social science theorist, who argued that such a book on how to advance intercultural understanding between diverse peoples would have to start as a research project. Not wanting to undertake that kind of academic heavy lifting, Locke offered to put together a sourcebook of writings already penned by authorities in anthropology, sociology, and political science on the theory and practice of race around the world aimed at teachers at the high school and college level. He would write the introduction and the substantial headnotes to each section of readings. Because he lacked the time and expertise to read such a voluminous literature, he needed a partner to select the individual essays to be included in the sourcebook. George Counts, who had set the PEA in its new direction, had been a professor at Columbia University, which led to the PEA's sea change, so it was socially competent for Locke to get somebody from there to serve as his co-editor and thereby legitimate the project. That Locke had tilted toward the radical is revealed by his choice of Bernhard Stern. There were many social scientists he could have chosen, but he selected someone not only deeply involved in the Columbia school of progressive thinking but also a fierce critic of anti-communists.

Locke's proposed that he and Stern be paid to take sabbaticals from their regular teaching duties to write the book, a rare practice in the 1930s. This would serve several purposes at once: buy Locke time away from teaching to work on all of his projects, including this one; leave Washington and Howard University for Columbia, where his entrée in a community of White radical scholars might help advance his career; and access a small, but well-established audience of upper-middle-class White teachers at the secondary and college level as a new market for his ideas. Locke submitted the proposal in November 1938 for $5,000, part of which would be in the form of payment for Locke and Stern to run summer workshops based on the readings for teachers and the rest to replace part of their normal teaching salary. Barely a month after Locke attended the conference on the Negro's role in the fight against fascism in Europe, the GEB would fund the intellectual explanation of how fascism was part of a larger global struggle against minorities around the world.[5]

During the summer of 1939, Locke and Stern received $500 each to conduct the summer workshops on race at Sarah Lawrence College, to be followed by another set of such workshops at other universities, including the University of Chicago, the next summer. These workshops allowed the PEA to show that the funding was being used to immediately educate teachers in this new global area of race. But the workshops were also part of a complex process of review, response, and revision, as the PEA required Locke to submit drafts of the book to various stakeholders in the field, including Ruth Benedict, the heir apparent to Franz Boas, and anthropologist Melville Herskovits. The constant work of revising the table of contents and consulting with experts slowed the process of assembling the manuscript.

A letter to Miss Brady reveals that all the while Locke was compiling the first draft of *When Peoples Meet*, he was attending and managing conferences, as well as searching for materials for *The Negro in Art*. In essence, he was working on both book projects, but because he was being paid by the GEB, *The Negro in Art* was on the backburner. "I was out of town," he notified Brady, "at Tuskegee for three days—our second annual conference on Adult Education among Negroes," a seemingly biannual obligation to keep up contacts with those he represented in publishing the Bronze Booklets. From there he jumped over to Georgia and spent "a day and a half at Atlanta, getting final materials from there for the portfolio," presumably plates of the Hale Woodruff Amistad panels that would be in the spectacular color insert of *The Negro in Art*. He lamented, "It should have been done before, but I just turned in with Stern a 1260 page manuscript to Progressive Education Assoc[iation] (the General Education Board project.)"[6]

Shortly after Locke turned in the first draft of *When Peoples Meet* to the PEA, he ducked into the Hotel Annapolis on L Street in Washington, D.C., on March 2, 1940, for the Fourth Annual Conference of the American Committee for the Protection of Foreign Born, a communist front organization that nevertheless had a long progressive and inclusive history. Founded in 1933 by Roger Baldwin of the ACLU to focus on defending immigrants seeking refuge in the United States after fleeing European fascism, the group helped the foreign-born to become citizens, fought anti-immigrant legislation, and raised awareness about immigrant discrimination in the United States. While President Franklin D. Roosevelt sent a welcoming telegram to the conference, the major backer of the organization was the Communist Party USA, especially its International Labor Defense Fund, the CP legal arm that had defended the Scottsboro Boys and now shielded immigrants from deportation who were part of radical unions or sympathetic to the Soviet Union.

Locke was not there on his own initiative, but as a representative of the League of American Writers, another communist front organization, which had asked Locke to write a report on the proceedings and get himself elected to its board of directors. There is no other evidence that Locke was even a member of the League of American Writers, so invisible was his relationship to them. His report reveals that the meeting was run almost entirely by Black intellectuals from Howard University. Max Yergen, the Black radical activist and president of the National Negro Congress was supposed to preside but did not attend. William Hastie, the dean of the Howard University Law School, substituted for him. Charles Houston, the subsequent dean of Howard's Law School, delivered a report urging the education of all American citizens about the value of tolerance toward the foreign born. An organization founded to defend the civil rights of the "foreign born" was being steered by leftist Black intellectuals. That they had such a prominent role may explain why Locke was sent on this mission, but also why he was interested in going—to hear radical-thinking Black intellectuals direct an integrated radical organization that linked the issues of refugees fleeing fascism to Negroes fighting racism in America.[7]

Refugees from fascism, ironically, were seeking solace in the belly of American racism. That last fact became clear when the assembled members voted to send a letter of protest to the District of Columbia council, the House of Representatives, and the US Senate protesting that the hotel management had refused to allow the head of the Caribbean labor union attending the conference to ride in the hotel elevator. As Locke noted in his report, a "wit" stated, "Confucius say it is not news that a Negro is discriminated in a District of Columbia hotel, but it is 'news' when a white organization sends a letter of protest about it to the newspapers and US government agencies." That wit was probably none other than Alain Locke.[8]

This meeting shows that Black intellectuals were using communist front organizations to advance a progressive agenda that made Negro civil rights an internationalist issue on the eve of US entry into World War II. They were suggesting that the foreign born, whether communist or not, had to be linked to the cause to eradicate racism in America if they wanted the support of Black thinkers to help eradicate xenophobia and anti-immigrant laws in America.

So, what at first appears as an oddity for Locke is actually the opposite—the natural progression in his political education, as his pursuit of approval from and allegiance with the Newest Negroes of the 1930s forced him toward a post-essentialist notion of the role Negro leadership could play in a global war against fascism. Despite his occasional anti-Semitic remarks to Mason, who engendered and expected them from her Blacks, Locke was pro-Jewish, believing, as many of his friends testified, that Black people needed to be more like Jews in many ways, but especially in their international solidarity. He was comfortable supporting their domestic struggle to find acceptance in America, and representing the League of American Writers, because he was representing writers and defending their human right to write and have their writings about their experience of fascism read. Fascism brought a man who avoided radicalism into the lines of communists and other radicals who would have been ignored in less threatening times.

Locke's biracialism in 1940 was consistent with a move toward a post-essentialist advocacy of racial enlightenment. It was not that Locke was an essentialist—his notion of Negro identity was always based on the notion that to be Negro, especially a New Negro, was derived from a dialogue with Whiteness and Africa—as *The Negro in Art* would soon show. By including Asian and Latin American discourses, *When Peoples Meet* liberated his critique from having to bear a "Black only" burden. Attending the meeting of the American Committee on the Foreign Born added Eastern Europeans and European Jews to a mix that was now transracial, transnational, and anti-fascist.

Despite this new affinity with radicals, Locke's aesthetic voice remained his primary voice in 1940. When he attended the meeting of the American Foreign Born, Locke was putting the finishing touches on the premier concert stage performance of *And They Lynched Him on a Tree*, a choral work by William Grant Still accompanying a poem by Katherine Graham Chapin, Godmother's niece, also known as Mrs. Biddle, that Locke had midwifed.[9] Back in 1939, Locke had attended a musical performance of *Lament* by Katherine Graham Chapin, who had hit upon the idea of putting her poetry to music. Locke, always the critic, expressed to Mason after the performance that he was disappointed in the music. Perhaps Biddle could rework *Lament* into a more powerful statement on a topic dear to Mason's heart, the scourge of lynching in America. Chapin had what Locke was looking for in a poet of protest—poise, restraint, and irony when taking on an emotionally charged subject—plus the courage to attack it as a White woman. Locke also had a recommendation as to who should set the poem to music—William Grant Still, his favorite classically trained New Negro composer.

When Locke proposed it to Mason, she embraced the idea and Chapin jumped at the chance for a unique collaboration. Indeed, Chapin was so enthusiastic she not only dashed off the new poem in a month but also flew out to Los Angeles to meet the reclusive Still, to ensure they would be in harmony in creating the new work of art.

Unlike Locke's earlier collaborations sponsored by Mason, there is no evidence that Mason interfered this time. She asked Locke to send her Still's name in writing, as that would facilitate her sending him telepathic messages of support "wirelessly," while he struggled in January with the complex composition. Key to Chapin's poem was that it contained two voices—represented by Still by two choruses, one White, one Black, that sing contesting responses to the lynching. Chapin's brilliant insight was that lynching in essence reflected two different views of America, one that endorsed the brutal and public murder of Black people outside the law as just, and the other appalled and enraged by the White mobs' desecration of Black bodies. This tension was embodied in the choral composition.

At Locke's and Mason's urging, Still finished the composition in May 1940 and was contacted immediately by Artur Rodzinski to perform the work on a program in Lewisohn Stadium, Philadelphia. Locke's and Mason's attempts to secure Marian Anderson failed, despite numerous attempts by Locke; but an able substitute, Luis Burge, agreed to sing the mother's lament. Also important, Chapin insisted on a Negro chorus to sing in the maiden performance of the piece.[10]

All went well until the conductor read the poem carefully and panicked thinking that the final two lines

> Talk of justice and take your stand,
> But a long dark shadow will fall across your land

would cause a strong negative reaction to the performance and those associated with it. Still and Chapin conferred, and agreed to make a change, but that introduced musical challenges for Still, since the music was scored exactly to match the words. Locke weighed in because he knew that changing the words and the music also threatened the takeaway from the performance by the audience, since the mood of righteous indignation had to be balanced by a sense of pity, irony, and compassion achieved in the original ending. Three different versions were still in play by the evening of the performance. While the program printed the less-inflammatory version, the chorus sang the original lines on June 25, 1940, to thirteen thousand in attendance, a packed house largely because Paul Robeson was also performing *Ballad for Americans* on the same night.

During the negotiations with the conductor, Locke, Chapin, and Still realized that Rodzinski was concerned about the possibility that the critique of the United States as a land that would pay a price for lynching might elicit a backlash from the government and affect the status of his sister, who was trapped in Poland attempting to immigrate to the United States. His objection to those lines was muted after Chapin got her husband, Francis Biddle, United States Solicitor General, to use his influence to secure a visa for the conductor's sister to come to the United States on the first boat leaving. This issue also suggests another possible reason Locke was at the meeting of the American Foreign Born in March. Increasingly, the future of African American aesthetics was bound up with the plight of the foreign born.[11]

Truth could speak the language of beauty, as Locke put it when he came to write "Ballad for Democracy" about the performance *And They Lynched Him on a Tree* "under the baton of Artur Rodzinski."[12] The evening was an enduring contribution to serious American music, according to Locke, because it was art—even as it made a political statement to the conscience of America. Unlike so many other reactions to Scottsboro and the continuing horror of lynching in America, its art was perfectly synchronized with its message. It was tough to express the emotions engendered by lynching musically without becoming shrill, but Still had risen to the challenge. That two choruses, one Black, one White, sang about lynching on the same stage in Philadelphia, was a metaphor for the two voices of America, being put into conversation on this brutal subject in an unprecedented way. The resolution of the musical composition—the two choruses had become one at the end—was a prophetic metaphor of where the nation would arrive, eventually, Locke, Still, and Chapin hoped, on the subject of lynching: one united voice for democracy. That a major classical music performance could be done based on the experience of lynching was a breakthrough because it was aimed at that ruling political class in America during debate in Congress over an anti-lynching bill.

"Ballad for Democracy" showed that Locke's aesthetic voice commingled with his radical internationalist voice when he wrote about this rarefied concert in 1940. Forced, perhaps, to justify why a poem on lynching was important as art, Locke quickly moved from saying that Chapin's poem, unlike so many others, made this American tragedy into true art, to making a very powerful statement of the international importance of lynching and America's star-crossed democracy now that the world was at war. Like the double chorus of *And They Lynched Him on a Tree*, Locke's two voices as a critic were united in this essay, as an intellectual whose social criticality and international political consciousness were in sync with his aesthetic judgment. Locke had found his true voice.

What really distinguished this new vision of democracy was the Black world systems perspective that Locke imported into an article on a choral classical music concert from *When Peoples Meet*. When discussing the violations of American civil rights under American democracy, he declared, "democracy is sick," and the cure, he said, is not found only domestically.

Let us glance at a stock list of our negative social symptoms. Britain has, here in the Caribbean, in Africa and India, indeed the world over, the critical problems of her colonial holdings. The United States has her perennial holdover problem of the Negro, her oriental exclusion dilemma, her Indian and other minority problems. France not only has her segment of the problem of empire but the ironic paradox of her yet unliberated colonial children safeguarding a democratic patrimony otherwise lost. Holland has her colonial problems, too, which in the chastisement of recent loss, she seems to be facing with clarified vision.

India, in turn has grievous internal problems of caste and her Hindu-Muslim mistrusts; Central Europe, the hard puzzle of reconciling her fanatical rationalism with the welfare of her minorities. Palestine has known its sad feud of Jew and Arab; while many of the American Republics to the south of us, have the problems of their Indian peasantry, their labor serfdom and the need for their progressive incorporation in the mainstream of the national life. Last but not least, in almost all our countries there looms up, to varying degrees, the disturbing undemocratic phenomenon of anti-Semitism.

Worst irony of all, observe the same undemocratic behaviour, venting itself in a Southern lynching or a mid-western race riot, boomeranged back at American democracy in mocking and insidious Japanese propaganda.[13]

Taken directly from *When Peoples Meet* was the notion that racism was not color prejudice, but the use of difference to create hierarchies of privilege and power that, in the face of world war, threatened the very existence of democracy. "These are no longer domestic affairs," he concluded.

Mason wrote Locke after receiving a copy of "Ballad for Democracy" that she loved the article, and in that missive laid a deeper message about the fusion of his double voice. The achievement of a more powerful single voice was the fulfillment of her vision. As a White woman in love with power, she had always wanted him to deal with the Black situation as she imagined she would deal with it, with the kind of certitude of authority, criticality, and power that he had now displayed in "Ballad for Democracy." The review marked a powerful resolution of their relationship. She had worked her criticality on Locke to fulfill her own needs for dominance, but also toward a higher end, at least in her mind, and his—to awaken a similarly powerful criticality to make him a stronger voice for liberation, which he now was.

On September 13, 1940, Locke wrote Mason thanking her for the letter of praise that reached him on his birthday. Receiving it "now is like *a new birth*. And indeed, Godmother, I hope it will be a new birth. Late as it is, with this crisis in the world, I hope to be of some real service to my people, and to the principles involved. To have been led all these years, so patiently by you to the point where I can hear, see and speak truth is a great thing."[14] The real truth was that that resolution had occurred largely because of work he had done outside the orbit of her influence. It was actually his moving away from her, his odyssey into the hotbed radicalism of the 1930s that had catalyzed a renaissance of earlier Race Contacts criticality in him and helped bring it forward into conversation with the enduring aesthete.

And They Lynched Him on a Tree also marked the year when Locke was at his collaborative best. Not only was he putting himself in dialogue with people he would have avoided before but also he was putting people like Chapin and Still in collaboration with one another, people who would never have met, let alone worked together, to create a unique racial collaboration on lynching, without him. Locke was a stronger and more effective harmonizer of divergent values, communities, and people in 1940 than he had been in the 1920s when such efforts often had resulted in disappointment and hurt feelings.

That year Locke also helped repair a breech between the gifted but star-crossed artist, Charles Sebree, and Countee Cullen. Early in 1940, the destitute Sebree contacted Locke for help. Sebree was well known in Chicago Black arts circles as a brilliant artist whose odd, curiously enigmatic drawings almost always sold where other, more realist renderings by the Chicago group of visual artists did not. Sebree's paintings did not read as Negro, but fused Arab, Middle Eastern, and Byzantium influences into a unique aesthetic, with faces large, distorted, heavily outlined, and overly expressive, especially in his treatment of eyes, which seemed like spiritual orbs in his compositions.

By March 1940, Sebree had alienated friends and supporters by being ingratiating and vulnerable sometimes and vicious and vindictive at others. He also was a braggart and unrepentant liar, who consistently invented stories about himself to fight off the psychological costs of going without food. Locke weighed in on this particular feature of his personality when he wrote to Sebree in April and chastised him for spreading "rumors of prosperity." Locke opined, "this 'make-believe' is one of the roots of your trouble, not that we should wear our hearts on our sleeves for daws [sic] to peek at but at the same time, one should I think not indulge in this inflation game, if we expect to be true artists, or do the Negro cause any good."[15] This letter suggests that Locke used racial discourse to instill a higher sense of responsibility in the artists and encourage them to view their art and themselves as serious enough to avoid triviality. Sebree was hitting Locke up to purchase some of his artwork, but Locke wanted to focus Sebree's attention on the work to be done, especially his outstanding commitment to illustrate Countee Cullen's book, an offer that seems to have been rescinded by Cullen because of Sebree's unstable behavior. Locke recommended that Sebree allow him to try and repair the breach and get Sebree to New York to work on the book with Cullen. As always, Locke accompanied his offer of help with a dose of

criticism: "Surely, you have in mind getting out of your rut of Dantesque adolescents, for much as I and other sophisticates like them, that isn't painting up to
today's outlook, and represents an over-worked vein in your work, in technique
and theme."[16]

Sebree acknowledged Locke's criticism. "In so many words Chicago has really
defeated me and my purpose. If I can go back to New York and work[,] Co[u]ntee
Cullen will make arrangements for all of my meals and all that I lack is a small
room and materials enough to prepare for a show of next late fall." He felt he had
"curbed a personality that has been in my way" and offered that, despite his
having disappointed many of his friends, some people still had faith in his ability
to "carry on from where I really started in new directions or approaches. As for
functional form of the mind the image will follow the free bent of desire[; it]
wont be so vigorously repressed here in the east. Mr. Locke if I can free myself
from mental misery, much watching and at times much crime."[17] The mangled
reference to "free bent of desire" seemed to reference his sexual orientation as a
queer Black man and his sense that some of his art as an "out" homosexual was
considered too offensive for the Chicago Negro art scene. He hoped, in other
words, that if he could get to New York, and especially Harlem, he could "free"
himself from the tendency to respond to repression by acting out, stealing, and
embarrassing himself and his friends. Locke was buoyed by the sense that Sebree
was ready to mend his ways, the first sign of which was that he accepted what
Locke had to say to him.

Why was Locke so willing to help Sebree? "He really is a genius," Locke wrote
to Mary Beattie Brady, whom he was trying to get interested in Sebree, "pitifully
naïve and helpless on one side, and willful and cunning on the other; a real
double personality. I think he knows it and plays it. However, he deserves help,
but I am all the more impressed as to the wisdom of my initial advice, to help
him with materials and living facilities rather than cash. He probably will never
learn how to dole out cash." Unlike Sebree, Locke was not naive: he was calculat-
ing to a fault and always disciplined, a sign to him of being a cultured person. For
example, Locke had a reputation for instructing young people how to sip rather
than guzzle wine at his apartment, while he also instructed them on how to get
control of their lives. Sebree was the ideal child for Locke to mentor, since he
took pride in bringing order to people who were personally out of order. And it
suggests the balance that working with artists must have brought to Locke
psychologically. Their craziness provided a way out of his obsessive desire for
control that stifled his own creativity.

Realizing that his future depended on Locke's help, Sebree gave him complete
control over his affairs, agreed not to talk to his friends about the plans before
or after arriving in New York, and allowed Locke to act on his behalf in patching
up the relationship with Cullen. In a sense, Locke's demands in exchange for
helping Sebree were remarkably similar to those Mason imposed on Langston

Hughes. Locke was mirroring her as he mentored Sebree. "Shall see Countee Thursday or Friday in New York. If he and I can arrive at some understanding your problem may be solved. I urge you not to write him in the meantime, however, and hope you will trust my judgment on this."[18] Here was another motivation for mentoring Sebree—the younger man's very helplessness gave Locke the kind of power he liked to wield in relationships. "But you must let me handle it in my own way. I shall write you immediately afterward, and hold your fingers crossed until then. Of course, if you want to write me in greater detail re your contacts with Countee, all the better, but that is left to your judgment. And now good cheer and better spirits. Tell me in detail your present resources, down to the last dime."[19] Once again, Locke the mother was in charge.

Evidently, the meeting was successful. Key to that success was that Locke provided the money for Sebree to find a room and pay for his living expenses while he worked with Cullen to finish the illustrations for The Lost Zoo. Toward the end of April, Cullen could write to Locke, "Sebree arrived, located a place, seems happy and full of enthusiasm and purpose. I think we are doing the right thing."[20] Not only was Sebree happy, but he had almost completed drawings for Cullen's book on cats. With Locke paying for Sebree and Sebree applying himself to the project, "Countee has been very helpful and fed me so well."[21] The results were worth it, at least to Cullen. By the end of 1940, his book, The Lost Zoo, appeared with Sebree's unique drawings of the animals that had not been allowed onto Noah's Ark.[22]

The book's title could be an epitaph of Locke's failed collaborations with writers and lovers of the 1920s; but this time, the outcomes were different. Locke had broken with Cullen over his marriage to Yolanda Du Bois and had had a rather critical and distanced relationship to him since the 1920s. Locke was able to keep himself out of the minutiae of The Lost Zoo project—again, much like Mason—and allow the project to move forward on its own once its internal obstacles had been removed. Locke was wiser now about what he could and should do in collaborative work and what he should leave to the principals to work out, so that art would emerge from his ability to put people in positive synergy with one another to produce art.

Part of the reason the aesthetic voice, unalloyed with radical sociology, remained dominant in Locke's life was that it was more often tied to sex. At one time or another, most likely Cullen and Sebree were lovers. That seems unlikely with Stern and the When Peoples Meet project. But the difference in attraction of these disparate projects went deeper than that. In America, the aesthetic voice of the Negro was always more rewarded than the Black world systems voice. That Locke had been able to fuse these voices temporarily in "Ballad for Democracy" that August did not mean they were no longer separately rewarded in the marketplace. As George Bernard Shaw quipped to Paul Robeson after he complained of reactions to his increasingly political commentary at his concerts, "Just sing

'Ol Man River.'" Shortly after Locke and Stern completed another set of summer workshops for the Progressive Education Association to whet the appetite of teachers, they learned that the publisher the Association had selected had rejected it. PEA president Frederick Redefer suggested one possible explanation for the publisher rejecting the project was that in the midst of the Depression, the book did not have as defined an audience as Stern's other publications had had. It was also possible that the work upon close reading raised some political concerns. Just as Rodzinski had worried that too critical a view of America in *And They Lynched Him* might result in a backlash, so too a social policy publisher might think the text that put American racism under the same umbrella as British and French imperialism might be too controversial.

The benefit, therefore, of having more than one voice meant that Locke was never stuck when a particular project stalled because it did not find the kind of support it deserved. The downside was that the critical edge the Black radical voice could bring to his aesthetic endeavors was muted and the aesthetic voicing of his sociological insights remained silent. He had to speak to separate communities of listeners in different voices to remain successful. That meant that the composite, complex, sociologist behind his aesthetic judgment—think of the sociology behind "Harlem" in the 1925 *Survey Graphic*—remained largely invisible.

To Locke, of course, the benefits outweighed the negatives. The separation, if not segregation of his aesthetic and sociological projects, meant that they had autonomous streams of support; and when one dried up, usually, another was flowing again. For example, when Keppel's "experts" stalled *The Negro in Art* in 1938, Locke adeptly shifted to proposals for the intercultural sourcebook and had it fund his summers in 1939 and 1940 running teacher-education workshops. But as *When Peoples Meet* stalled because it could not find a publisher, Locke shifted back to working full-time on pulling together *The Negro in Art*. But such segregation of knowledges also meant that no single magnum opus reflected the range, power, and deeper interconnections of his mind.

Shifting his focus to getting *The Negro in Art* out by his self-imposed publication date of December 15, 1940, Locke dove into collecting the last group of plates. In retrospect, it is hard to appreciate the amount of work that went into creating *The Negro in Art*. First, there simply was no single repository in the United States that contained all of the images by "White artists," meaning American, English, French, Spanish, German, and Dutch artists since the fifteenth century who had rendered the Negro form in drawing, painting, or sculpture. For years, Locke had been clipping pictures out of art history books and corresponding with museums, galleries, and private collectors whose names were listed in these books to try and obtain high-quality prints for the book of European, American, and Latin American art. Next, he was hunting down images of art by the young New Negro artists, many of whose work was not in galleries, museums, or private collections. Locke had to visit numerous galleries looking for that work, but also look for work that had been photographed and then cajole the photographer to provide a print at cost. The expressionist images of Norman Lewis were obtained this way after a visit to his New York studio. In other cases, it was even more mysterious. Georgette Powell stated that she had no idea how Locke obtained a print of her work and only knew he was interested in it when she discovered the image in the published book. Here, again, was another sense in which Locke was invisible—he moved secretly behind the scene to achieve his goals unseen by those who should have at least had a glance at what he was doing.

In other cases, Locke relied on the continued generosity of Mary Beattie Brady and the Harmon Foundation, as well as the Baltimore Museum of Art, which had photographed a great deal of art for their exhibitions. Similarly, the last section of the book, the African Art section, required hunting through catalogs, flyers, and making requests of the Museum of Modern Art to obtain those images, perhaps the rarest of all. The work was laborious, but also a labor of love. It was successful only because Locke spent years working as a curator and called on connections he had established over the years to make last-minute requests as he hurried the publication to press.

After Locke had secured color prints of the Hale Woodruff Amistad mural for the centerfold of the book, he sent off a late request to Sargent Johnson, the San Francisco–based sculptor and painter for an image dear to his heart—a modernist, almost primitive, painting of a mother and child done in brown and cream color. Because the request was so last minute, coming literally in October 1940, the frontispiece had to be printed separately from the rest of the book and inserted into each book. Selecting Johnson's image rather than Winold Reiss's imagery to open *The Negro in Art* suggested the journey Locke had taken in the fifteen years since *The New Negro*. *The Negro in Art* was a powerful continuation of the argument of the earlier book, but also a step beyond, for instead of a Brown mother and child done in a modernist pose reminiscent of the Italian Renaissance, the new mother and son was folklorist and ultramodernist, a formal emblem of a distinct Black aesthetic from the newest generation of Black visual artists. This book was compiled and written by him alone, and thus he could personalize it with a dedication that encapsulated his life: "To mother, who gave me a sense of beauty that included our racial own." When the book appeared in December, Locke rushed one of the first copies to Mrs. Mason, who gushed over it. She not only liked the book itself but she also liked the dedication to his mother and, without saying it, his mentioning her own name in the acknowledgments as one of the prime supporters on the project.

Unfortunately, the art book sales were worrisomely slow in January and February 1941. Locke had developed a sophisticated marketing plan for the book, which included preparation of folders that contained information on the book and a handful of illustrations from it to go out to bookshops, libraries, and adult-education groups. He was helped enormously by Mary Beattie Brady and Miss Brown, who forwarded those folders to their contacts and publicized the book through their network. Locke meticulously recorded each bookshop, each local southern public library, and each Negro reading group that ordered the book, and then tracked the payments for those books and where they ended up. Eventually, those records show, *The Negro in Art* became the most successful of the publications of the Associates of Negro Folk Education. It reached into diverse pockets of interest throughout the United States. Prison systems, to take one example, frequently requested the book, because of the large Black prison population in 1940 and the presence among such prisoners of artists who would be inspired by Negro art across the centuries. So many ordered the book—including sororities and fraternities, local women's clubs, the Frederick Douglass bookshop, the Memphis Public Library, the Museum of Modern Art, the Metropolitan Museum of Art, the Cleveland Museum of Art, and on and on—that by the end of 1941, the book was a hit.

The Negro in Art was not only a hit with the public. Reviewers, especially art critics, a notoriously dismissive group when it came to art by Negro artists, were overwhelmingly enthusiastic. Walter Pach perhaps summed it up best, "I approached this book with some trepidation, as I expected it to be filled with poorly executed art and with special pleading. Instead, I was pleasantly surprised by the quality of work." Locke had wisely begun the book with the European artists, making the point that the work of Negro artists that followed was part of a tradition of rendering the Negro face and form in art spanning centuries and continents, producing some of the finest art the world had. That was exactly the opposite tack of his work in the 1920s, which had prominently linked Negro artists to the African tradition. That tradition was smuggled into the last section of the book, but it suggested that this was a world tradition of announcing Negro subjectivity through art regardless of the color of the artists' skin.

Even James Porter had to give Locke credit for the book in his otherwise nit-picky, negative review in Carter G. Woodson's *Journal of Negro History*.[23] As usual, Porter criticized the linkage to the African tradition, disliked that White artists were the focal point of the book's beginning, and complained that a focus on the Negro image took away from the freedom of Negro artists to render whatever they felt was their destiny as artists. But even Porter was astounded that Locke had found all of these images, since, as he claimed in his MA dissertation, his work had been limited by his lack of ready access to the images he needed for his analysis. Although Locke's book did not stress analysis of the artwork, what Locke achieved was showing that Negro artists were part of a European tradition as much as or more than an African one.

Publication was linked to his role as an impresario of New Negro consciousness, a linchpin that justified the work he did creating events, hosting events, or appearing to say a few words at an event, which placed him in the company of people who acclaimed and affirmed his self-worth. Leftists were still the main people organizing these events in 1940. In May, Locke had been in Chicago to attend a meeting arranged around his visit to "encourage interest and develop action around some of the contributions and problems of Negro culture and its advancement." St. Clair Drake, Ishmael Flory, and Bernard Goss sought to broaden out from the arts to include people from education and the sciences, and Locke was the only person who brought these groups together.[24] On September 6, he was in New York to chair a program at which Richard Wright and Paul Robeson would speak, organized by Theodore Ward and the Negro Peoples' Theatre.[25] A kind of incessant energy drove Locke to accept almost every invitation he received lest he become a prisoner of a lonely life.

One welcome invitation came from Louis R. Finkelstein to become a founding member of a new organization of "scientists, philosophers and theologians" that included sociologist Robert M. MacIver and historian Harry J. Carman, both from Columbia; University of Chicago philosopher Mortimer J. Adler; Northwestern University biologist Edwin Conklin; French philosopher Jacques Maritan; and several others who wished to meet regularly to discuss "the preservation of democracy." This was not linked to the radical wing operative at Columbia, since Finkelstein was a conservative Jewish rabbi and Talmudic scholar. Lyman Bryson, Locke's long-time ally on the board of the Associates of Negro Folk Education, probably engineered the invitation, since he would serve as the organization's vice president. The format would combine serious discussions of the thorny issues and challenges to democracy in closed executive sessions for which papers would be circulated prior to meetings, with open debate in public meetings where participants would summarize papers followed by discussions from the floor. The first meeting in September would discuss a paper by Albert Einstein; unfortunately, Locke could not attend. But afterward, he became a regular and eager participant in this unique opportunity—to exchange ideas with the best and the brightest among mainstream intellectuals in positions of power in the American academy. Indeed, the group, later called the Conference on Science, Philosophy, and Religion and Their Relation to the Democratic Way of Life, Inc., would catalyze Locke to produce some of his best writing on cultural relativism and ideological peace, and strengthen the voice of universalism in Locke, already heard in *When Peoples Meet* and "Ballad for Democracy." Locke's thinking as a philosopher would be bolstered by dialogue with philosophers and scientists concerned with why democracy was in danger. Locke would be among the very few in that group who could actually explain why that was.

Locke's notion of universalism was exemplified that December in the seventy-fifth anniversary of the 13th Amendment celebration held at the Library of Congress. Enlisted at the last minute that fall of 1940 by the newly appointed

Librarian of Congress, the radical poet Archibald MacLeish, Locke helped plan the musical program and curated the art exhibit. Relying once again on Mary Beattie Brady for help pulling together a credible art exhibit, Locke was mainly invested in the musical program, especially since he was featured on the program to lecture on the significance of the spirituals, with musical accompaniment by the Golden Gate Quartet. In the storied Coolidge auditorium that had never hosted an event on Negroes, let alone had them speak from the podium, Locke defined for his upper-middle-class White listeners how to read America through the lens of emancipation. "Nothing so subtly or so characteristically expresses a people's group character as its folk music. And so we turn to that music to discover if we can grasp the essence of what is Negro or, if we cannot do that, at least to try to sample the best of the Negro's racial experience."[26]

His opening sentences on the spirituals laid down their meaning as something formed by the Negro's racial experience of America. America was a pluralistic universe, because that had been the experience of the Negro in America. The American character was formed by race and the yearnings for freedom, both physical and cultural, that the spirituals embodied in song. The spirituals, therefore, embodied the highest wisdom of the Negro racial experience. "For the spirituals are, even when lively in rhythm and folkish in imagination, always religious in mood and conception...always the voice of a naïve, unshaken faith, for which the things of the spirit are as real as the things of flesh. This naïve and spirit-saving acceptance of Christianity is the hall-mark of the true spiritual."[27] Recognizing that the Negro had no power to change these things in this world, the enslaved developed the fervent belief that there must be a higher power. Their experience of the holy—that "the things of the spirit are as real as the things of flesh"—was "spirit-saving," since it meant that God recognized the Negro's essential humanity even though other Americans did not. This experience of the holy, which the rapture of the spirituals expressed, was a universality tied to the Negro's racial experience.

Locke tried, unsuccessfully, to get *And They Lynched Him on a Tree* performed as part of the program. But to William Grant Still, Locke confided that Mrs. Whitehall, of the George Whitehall Foundation that put up the money for the event, demanded that Roland Hayes and Dorothy Maynor sing on the program, along with the Budapest Quartet, effectively gutting the budget for anyone else. Locke was terribly disappointed that the choral poem was not performed. Most likely, Mrs. Whitehall did not want her money to fund a choral poem about lynching in a Library of Congress program with her name attached to it. Better to insist on celebrity performers, who were safe. Locke did arrange a performance of Chapin and Still's work at Howard, which a "small but appreciative audience" attended.

The challenge that eluded Locke so far was to ground his aesthetic politics in a particular local community. Washington would never feel like home for Locke with its Black bourgeois homophobia, its southern devotion to segregation in public spaces, and its clique of Negro artists around James Porter and James Herring who avoided race consciousness in art. Their philosophy of Negro art found its fullest expression in the tiny Barnett Aden Gallery begun in Herring's home, where Herring and Aden exhibited and patronized international as well as African American artists for decades. Its doors would open to Washington-area artists of all races in 1943, but would not be welcoming to Locke, though he most likely attended some openings. As in New York, he could visit, but never join its community. His heart would always belong to Harlem, but the combination of Augusta Savage and Romare Bearden holding forth in Harlem's art circles meant that they would never allow Locke to ground his aesthetic leadership there. Some broader opportunities for community activism did emerge late in 1940, when the American Association of Adult Education finally gave him a $3,500 grant to hire a roving proselytizer of Negro adult education in the South. While certainly a stimulus to the sale of the Bronze Booklets and *The Negro in Art*, it was too late to be the basis of a robust investment of Locke's time in grass-roots literacy organizing. By 1941, most of the second batch of Bronze Booklets was out of print, and prospects for funding a third edition were dim.

Locke longed for a city in the North where he could feel at home and develop a core of artists, patrons, and tastemakers who embraced his vision of a New Negro art movement of the late 1930s. Locke's trips to Chicago to curate the art exhibits at the American Negro Exposition in 1940 had reacquainted him with the burgeoning and more accessible visual arts scene there. Collecting work for the Western art exhibit for Barnett had revealed that some of the freshest art of the Negro—the powerful social realist drawings of working-class bodies by Charles White, the elongated modernism of Eldzier Cortor, and the Picassoesque work of Charles Sebree—was coming out of Chicago. There was a vibrant group of local Black women activists pushing for a cultural renaissance in their city, a White aesthete whom Locke could coordinate with, Peter Pollack, and an emerging Black entrepreneurial class whose capital, along with federal funding, might make his contribution pay. Added to that, Locke spent part of the summers of 1939 and 1940 in Chicago running the workshops for the Progressive Education Association/General Education grant. Several of the members of the Science, Religion, and Philosophy conferences were also located at the University of Chicago. The city began to look like a place where he could integrate his voices and become a new base of operations for him.

Of course, Chicago already had a long tradition of Negro artistic production and recognition beginning at least with the Negro Art Week in 1928. But according to Margaret Burroughs, a young radical artist, local artists had no permanent place to congregate, discuss art, and exhibit what they produced.[28] A key change occurred when the Federal Art Project (FAP) decided to invest in that community by organizing events to create a real bricks-and-mortar community art center, part of the ideology of art for democracy that suffused the artistic projects of the WPA. Spearheading that Federal Arts Project community art center campaign was Peter Pollack, a liberal, Jewish photographer and gallery owner, who was tapped because his was the only downtown Chicago gallery that had exhibited the work of local Black artists. As he put it in an interview later, he exhibited their work not because they were Negroes, but because their artwork was good, which resonated quite well with Locke's views.[29]

Following a pattern of philanthropy popularized by Julius Rosenwald, the Federal Art Project sponsored a community art center if the local communities raised the funding to secure a permanent site. The FAP would supply a director, staff, and technical assistance to run the center, especially its signature feature, art classes that brought art to the masses and provided employment for the artists who taught them. In Chicago, the fundraising effort brought together disparate parts of the Negro community, as the Negro upper class organized several fundraising events such as the Artists and Models Balls. Local Chicago artists innovated more grass-roots fundraising strategies such as the "Mile of Dimes" campaign in which Burroughs recalled standing on 39th Street collecting dimes from passersby until she raised $100.[30]

Peter Pollack gave hundreds of speeches to diverse groups, White and Black, selling them on the intrinsic value of such a community center in Black Chicago. After one such stretch of proselytizing, he wrote Locke somewhat perplexedly that his audiences were barely interested when he sold the idea as bringing art to the community, but were wildly enthusiastic and contributed funding when the idea of art was pitched as a means of racial progress, both uplifting the Negroes, and creating a dialogue between Whites and Blacks to advance racial understanding. "What do you make of that?" he queried Locke.[31]

This remark says something about Peter Pollack's idealism and naiveté.

> The center movement...was to us the most essential thing because it was bringing art into the communities. It was bringing art into communities that never saw art. You had dedicated, altruistic people in those days. None of us took any money at the center. We organized the people. We talked, we came with open hands.... "'Here, build yourself a building. We'll supply you with exhibitions and artists who will teach. We will supply you with a director, we will supply you with a staff of people who will run this thing for you. It's your structure and it's your property. You own it. But you must feel that you want it. We can't go and build it for you, or pay rent for you.'"[32]

But an arts community had already formed in Chicago around the artist George Neal, who had taught art classes at the South Side Settlement House, Jane Addams's social reform institution in the Black community, where such artists as Charles White, Eldzier Cortor, Charles Sebree, Bernard Goss, and Margaret Burroughs had become powerful, accomplished artists. An informal community art center already met in people's homes, raising money to send people to the Art Institute for art classes, which is one of the reasons that the fundraising effort of the FAP in Black Chicago succeeded. This local grass-roots effort was driven by the idea that "art was an instrument of social change." Neal was the unsung hero of this movement, someone Charles White recalled "made us conscious of the beauty of Black people," who got artists to focus on depicting the local community, its space, housing, and "shacks."[33]

While Peter Pollack is usually given the credit for the idea of the community art center in Chicago, even by such art informants as Margaret Burroughs, records from the period suggest that the original idea came from five Black women Chicago activists, "Pauline Kligh Reed, Frankie Singleton, Susan Morris, Marie Moore, and Grace Carter Cole," who "brought the idea to Peter Pollack, then director of the Federal Arts Project in Illinois and owner of a downtown gallery."[34] A cadre of middle-class Black women activists approached Pollack, who then brought the largesse and institutional power of the FAP to their project and helped them make history. After years of fundraising, in 1940, the committee had raised $8,000 to purchase the former mansion commonly noted as the former home of Charles Comiskey, the owner of the White Sox, on Michigan Avenue, a street and a house abandoned by White flight to Black criminal elements. Once purchased, the Federal Arts Project brought in workmen who restored completely the "rat-infested" house and created an exhibition and teaching community center on the South Side of Chicago.

It could not have been lost on Locke that these Black bourgeois Chicagoans had been able to purchase a building as an art center, while Harlem had been unable to do that to create the Harlem Museum of African Art. Chicago had an entrepreneurial economic base of Black-owned beauty shops, barber shops, funeral homes, hair preparations factories, Pullman porters with disposable income, and newspapermen and newspaperwomen, who, even in the midst of the Great Depression, could buy a building and create the kind of art space he dreamed of.

Peter Pollack was essential in bringing the connections to the New Deal hierarchy that added national legitimacy to the effort. This was notably on display when he secured Mrs. Eleanor Roosevelt to speak at the dedication of the South Side Community Art Center in May 1941. That commitment sealed the deal for Locke to attend as well. As Locke wrote to Pollack on March 22, 1941, "Congratulations on having landed Mrs. R. I wasn't going to miss it anyway, but doubly so now, as I have had several contacts with her and know she is interested in this matter.... She has a copy of the book [*The Negro in Art*] and was much interested in the Library of Congress show."[35] Once Locke had committed along with Mrs. Roosevelt, Pollack arranged to have their remarks broadcast nationally over the radio. Pollack's efforts to make the dedication into a powerful spectacle paid off.

Newspaper coverage of the event reveals that there were multiple non-artistic motivations for Mrs. Roosevelt to attend the official opening of an art center in the Black ghetto area of Chicago. In the *Chicago Defender*, arguably the nation's most important Negro newspaper, the photographs of Roosevelt's visit to the art center were part of a collage of photographs of "Mrs. R" at several other several sites of Negro preparedness for the war that everyone knew America would be entering soon.

"First Lady Spends Busy Three Hours in Chicago," May 17, 1941. *Chicago Defender*. Reproduction courtesy of South Side Community Art Center. Courtesy of the *Chicago Defender*.

The headline, "First Lady Spends Busy Three Hours in Chicago," announced that Mrs. Roosevelt "crowded into three hours, the inspection of the Household Training center at 2720 Prairie avenue, the dedication of the South Side Community Art Center, 3831 Michigan avenue, a brief visit to the Ida B. Wells homes, low-rent housing project, and attendance at the art center dedicatory banquet at the Parkway ballroom." Key to the turnout at the center, for which crowds lined up for blocks, of course, was that she was there. "Hundreds of persons unable to secure admission, stood outside the recently opened art center (No. 1) to catch a glimpse of the First Lady. At the banquet (No. 2) Mrs. Roosevelt was presented a painting by Charles Davis by Peter Pollack, director of the new center.... Left to right (No. 6) just before broadcast are Dr. Alain Locke, professor of philosophy, Howard university, who participated in the radio broadcast; Howard S. Drew, state administrator, Works Projects Administration; Mrs. Pauline Kigh Reed, president of the art center; Atty. Patrick B. Prescott, chairman, board of directors of the center; Mrs. Roosevelt and Mrs. Annabelle Carey Prescott, chairman of the planning committee for the dedication."[36]

In his remarks, Locke said that what made this center unique was that "for the first time, at least on such a scale with prospects of permanency, a practicing group of Negro artists has acquired a well-equipped working base and a chance to grow roots in its own community soil." The idea here was that the artist was the expression of the community's soil and soul, and that the community found its expression through the artists.

Other aspects of the photographs and the *Defender* story suggest that art was important, but mainly as a symbol for Roosevelt and the New Deal of Black incorporation into a discourse of American nationalism, even though Locke wanted it to be a symbol of community self-determination through art. Some photographs show Roosevelt meeting with Black women in the WPA Household Training Center and African American honor guard from the local American Legion (No. 3 & 4) marking the impending transition from the New Deal to America's impending entry into World War II when Black bodies would be important for national mobilization. Standing in uniform with Mrs. Roosevelt performed loyalty to a national mobilization for a global war for Four Freedoms Black citizens did not enjoy at home. The irony of the photographs anticipated the saluting African soldier (No. 5) on the cover of *Paris Match* that Roland Barthes analyzed as "an exemplary figure of French imperiality." [37] Locke hints at a similar irony in his address, where he says that there is a double mission here of national affirmation and racial affirmation in the dedication of the South Side Community Art Center. The center affirms the democratic ideal in American art by including the Negro, and it affirms the self-organization of the Negro by having an art center in the middle of the ghetto in Chicago. This double voice is being spoken in the center dedication, which is created out of a democratic impulse of openness to all people, and yet because of the spatial and social segregation of Chicago is really only about Black people. It is shackled by the spatiality of race in Chicago, and yet it is empowered by that structure, because segregation has forced these Black people to pool their talent into one space.

That Peter Pollack was photographed giving a painting by Black artist Charles Davis to Roosevelt, as the guiding hand behind this dedication, is critical to this discourse. Pollack was head of the Federal Arts Project in Illinois and the person who pooled federal resources for the center, which had actually been in meager operation since 1938, when a local group of Black artists and citizens formed the center out of an "art committee." Pollack got federal dollars to support an art school through the center, which was successful in attracting students long before 1941. He was likely the one who realized that this kind of kickoff event was needed to propel such a center into some kind of notoriety that might give it a chance to survive as the war approached.

A photograph from the event exudes tension: it features Mrs. Pauline Kigh Reed, president of the art center, who was the real director of the center, not Pollack, along with Mrs. Annabelle Carey Prescott, chairman of the planning committee for the dedication, on the other side of Mrs. Roosevelt.

Eleanor Roosevelt and Peter Pollack, May 17, 1941. *Chicago Defender*. Reproduction courtesy of South Side Community Art Center. Courtesy of the *Chicago Defender*.

Roosevelt at the Household Training Center and American Legion Post, May 17, 1941. *Chicago Defender*. Reproduction courtesy of South Side Community Art Center. Courtesy of the *Chicago Defender*.

Cover of *Paris Match* magazine, no. 326, June 25–July 2, 1955. ©Izis/Paris Match Archive/Getty Images.

of the First Lady. At the banquet (No. 2) Mrs. Roosevelt was presented with a painting by Charles Davis by Peter Pollack, director of the new center. Immaculately attired in their snow white uniforms, staff members and students at Household Training center line up (No. 3) to hear brief message from distinguished visitor. Honor guard from Giles Post, No. 87, American Legion, under command of Senior Vice Commander Stephens, greeted First Lady (No. 4) upon arrival at training center. (No. 5) Striking view of First Lady during address at banquet. Left to right (No. 6), just before broadcast are Dr. Alain Locke, professor of philosophy, Howard university, who participated in radio broadcast; Howard S. Drew, state administrator, Works Projects Administration; Mrs. Pauline Kigh Reed, president of the art center; Atty. Patrick B. Prescott, chairman, board of directors of center; Mrs. Roosevelt and Mrs. Annabelle Carey Prescott, chairman of the planning committee for the dedication.—Photos by James Gushiniere and Clynell Jackson, Defender staff photographers.

Alain Locke, Howard S. Drew, Peter Pollack, Pauline Kigh Reed, Patrick B. Prescott, Eleanor Roosevelt, and Annabelle Carey Prescott, May 17, 1941. *Chicago Defender.* Reproduction courtesy of South Side Community Art Center. Courtesy of the *Chicago Defender.*

A conflict between Locke and the Black women of the center emerged, although its nature is perhaps now lost. Perhaps it was about whether the artists were going to be foregrounded in this discourse or the bourgeois community, who put their money, time, and connections into making this event and the center a success. Perhaps Locke was mad that his friends—the artists—were standing outside the center, while the community, especially the bourgeois fundraising community, was inside. While the center was in many respects the perfect realization of all that he had been working for, he could not build on it. As in the Harlem Art Center, it was commandeered and controlled by local Black women deeply rooted in the local community, bourgeois Black women married to powerful local men. Locke was brought in to sanctify the event, but his presence was reduced to that of a gadfly. Even so, Locke was not about to pass up an opportunity to crack a joke, now lost, and crack up Ethel Waters and other artists there with whom he had a closer feeling.

But Locke hinted at the irony of his marginality and his possible alienation from bourgeois Black cultural politics when he summed up the significance of the center in his remarks:

> Proportionate recognition and gratitude should go to the pioneers of
> the effort; to the Citizen's Sponsoring Committee, through whose

Ethel Waters, Locke, Eleanor Roosevelt, and unidentified woman. Courtesy of the
Moorland-Spingarn Research Center, Howard University.

labors the property was acquired; to the Federal Art Program of the
Work Projects Administration and the Illinois Art Project, that salvaged
and sustained the younger generation talent through the depression,
enabling many of them to attain maturity in their art; to directing officers of the project, Holger Cahill, George Thorp, Norman MacLeish,
Peter Pollack, and others who have given, in excess of their official
responsibilities, private time, energy and counsel to the venture; and
above all perhaps, to the artists themselves, whose collective zeal has
inspired the community concern and effort in their behalf and whose
creative work, as convincingly displayed by this exhibition, vindicates
that effort and concern.[38]

"Proportionate" stands out as a rich term in his remarks, of his withholding
credit from the president of the art center and relegating her and others to a
"Citizen's Sponsoring Committee." He decided not to call the women's names
over the radio nationally, although he did those of the White "fathers" of the
effort. Perhaps most tellingly, he ended by drawing attention back to the artists,
without whom there would be nothing for the bourgeoisie of the community to

celebrate—even though most of them are standing outside. Once again, Locke sided with the artists, the bohemians, and not the bourgeoisie.

Right after the Chicago South Side Community Art Center dedication, Locke received a most welcome letter from Frederick Redefer that a publisher was interested in *When Peoples Meet*. After a quick update of the table of contents, Locke and Stern submitted the complete manuscript and it was scheduled for publication early in 1942. Suddenly, there seemed to be a market among college educators for a book that explained to them the coming world conflict in racial terms. Hitler's Germany was killing Jews, justifying it with racist propaganda, and was on the move to take over England's and France's colonial empire in Africa. Suddenly, Locke's Black internationalist voice was in fashion.

The squelching of his Black aesthetic voice would become even more explicit six months later, when Locke would be on hand for the Downtown Gallery opening in New York on December 7, 1941, of an exhibition of work by African American artists. But when the Japanese bombed Pearl Harbor that day, all of the brilliant plans of Edith Halpert, the Jewish gallery director, who planned to use the exhibition to introduce Negro artists to the New York art world and persuade the owners of other New York art galleries to invite at least one Black artist into each of their stables, came to naught. Few would come to the impressive exhibit, which included sixty panels of Jacob Lawrence's Migration series that chronicled in small, beautiful, abstract renderings the history of the Great Migration that launched the New Negro.

It was Locke's book, *The Negro in Art*, that had given Halpert the idea to mount a show of Negro American art in her gallery. It was Locke who had written letters of recommendation for the funding that made it possible for Lawrence to paint the series. It was Locke who showed Halpert the Migration series, most likely at the Harlem Community Art Center. And it was Locke who counseled Lawrence to accept a unique purchase of his series in which the Phillips Collection and the Museum of Modern Art divided the panels between them.

Superb art was not enough to save the Downtown Gallery show from invisibility. America's entry into World War II meant Halpert's show closed with a fraction of the total attendance it would have garnered otherwise. The attack on Pearl Harbor allowed New York galleries to avoid integrating their galleries racially, and the war meant the decline in popularity of art of social realism and the social criticism of 1930s art.

No longer would Negro art be the voice of American cultural transformation as it had promised in the 1930s. Never again would Locke enjoy the national platform he had shared with Eleanor Roosevelt on May 7, 1941. Negro artists were for a brief moment featured as exemplars of national reconciliation through Black self-determination at the South Side Community Art Center that day when Mrs. Roosevelt visited Black Chicago for three hours and spent one of them with Alain Locke.

42

FBI, Haiti, and Diasporic Democracy

On February 20, 1942, Locke walked quickly through downtown Washington, D.C., into the Federal Triangle, the landmark of federal government buildings. As perhaps the shortest adult visitor to the Department of Justice building, the setting overwhelmed Locke physically and psychologically. It was not merely the building's incongruous blend of Greek revival and Art Deco architecture that made him shudder, but also the irony of the message chiseled into the building: "Justice is founded in the rights bestowed by nature upon man. Liberty is maintained in security of justice." Locke probably wondered if his liberty was about to be taken from him. He was on his way to the FBI headquarters upstairs, as he had received notice his presence was required to answer questions in regard to information about him that had come to the FBI's attention. He was anxious to face, if not his accusers, at least their accusations and put to rest, if only temporarily, the extreme worries that had come over him since he received the notice. He knew the FBI had targeted others at Howard University, ever since the 77th Congress had passed Public Law 135 that empowered the FBI to investigate people employed by the federal government suspected of being disloyal to the government. Most of those were known communists. He was not. He also shouldered an additional burden. As a gay man employed at Howard University, he might be considered a security risk because of his sexual orientation. This meeting might out him as a closeted homosexual just as it might charge him with being a traitor. Indeed, in the minds of most Americans, the two were synonymous. An ordinarily nervous man, Locke was beset with more tics and twitching than usual all week. His paranoia in not letting people he did not know into his apartment and changing the name on his doorplate every few weeks had been neurotic preparation for this very day.

Once inside FBI headquarters, Locke learned of the "information" about his "alleged activities" that had been communicated to the Bureau. He was told, "in order that your statement may have particular credence, you will be placed under oath."[1] Then, he was then asked if he had "any objection to" speaking under oath. "No," Locke answered. "I would rather affirm. There is a Quaker streak in my ancestry." With a quip Locke had announced that he was not intimidated.

He was then asked whether he was now or ever had been a member of the Washington Committee for Democratic Action. "No sir," he replied. "I don't even know of the organization. Can you tell me about the Committee? What is it?" The interviewer, a "Mr. King," was a bit surprised by Locke issuing the questions. "I am no authority on the organization. It was formed here in Washington, I believe, several years ago." Locke replied again, "I don't even know of it." When pressed as to whether he really did not know about it, Locke expanded on his answer.

> That's why I asked you what it is all about. I get a great many circulars from Liberal and radical organizations, and some of them go into the wastebasket. Usually it is a request to write your Congressman about something that is up before Congress. My name is on a number of mailing lists, but I don't even identify the organization.

The interviewer then tried to draw Locke into a conclusion he had not made. "If your name was used as a sponsor for this organization, it was used without your permission and authority?"

> I would have to see the list before I would definitely—you see, I am under oath and I have to be very careful therefor [sic].

The interviewer continued: "Mr. Locke, are you now, or have you ever been, a member of the National Federation for Constitutional Liberties?" He denied being a member or having attended meetings of the organization. Again, Locke suggested that in such interviews, it would be best to have information, perhaps letterheads, of the organizations referenced. "You have no idea what stacks of mail one gets from one organization or another. I remember in the case of the Spanish Aid I got so mixed up I didn't know which organization was what. There were some four or five repeatedly sending to me."

Here, then, clearly, was Locke's main line of defense. Overwhelmed by radical mailings, he may have inadvertently associated with some who were considered subversive by the FBI. There were some, however, that he could not deny he was associated with, such as the National Negro Congress. When asked about it, Locke admitted he had spoken before them on two occasions, "attended their meetings," but was not "formally a member of the National Negro Congress."

> Mr. Locke, are you at the present time, or have you ever been, a member of any organization which you have reason to believe is dominated by the Communist Party of the United States of America, or may be controlled, or its policies dictated by any foreign government?

Locke's response showed he was fully alert. "Will you repeat that?" The interviewer then stated, "Are you at the present time a member of any organization which you have reason to believe is dominated by..." Locke's answer showed his acumen.

No, absolutely not. Not at the present time. The reason, Mr. King, I asked you to repeat that was that I didn't know the tense, "at the present time." You see, I caught that when you repeated it. I asked you particularly because of this case. I was interested in and a subscriber to about three of the Spanish Aid societies. There was one of them that I have reason to believe was Communist-controlled. I did not know it at the time, but I became one of the sponsors. When I suspected that it was—incidentally, that was through Mrs. ROOSEVELT's resigning from the Board....I investigated the Washington office, and was reassured that it was not. I therefore did not remove my name from the sponsors' list. About three weeks after that, an issue which came out further confirmed my suspicions, and then I did withdraw, and have a carbon copy of the letter which I wrote to the National secretary.

The interviewer thought Locke was being evasive. "Mr. LOCKE, the question I did ask you was, 'Are you at the present time, or have you ever been.' Locke pulled him up short. "In the second reading, you didn't say, 'Have you ever been.'"

Mr. King was getting a taste of what it was like to try and match wits with Locke. He had to admit he had misspoken (and perhaps misled) Locke when he repeated the question. With the caveat of this one organization, Locke said that he had never knowingly joined such an organization that was communist controlled and had never advocated the overthrow of the government. Suddenly, the interview was over. When asked if he wanted to make a statement, he declined—except to ask: "If there have been specific charges—I am sure there have been—but if there have been specific charges, it seems fair, without divulging the source, to be informed of the nature of the charges."

Locke's question was pertinent—why was he being interviewed if it was not illegal to be associated with or a member of the Communist Party? The interviewer hurried to state that Locke wasn't being charged with a crime, but was responding to information the Bureau had received about him. That left hanging two unasked questions—what exactly was that information and who had provided it?

As Locke left the Department of Justice, he must have wondered if he was being investigated because his name appeared on the letterhead of these organizations, or if someone had informed on him and perhaps included other information on his activities that he had not been questioned about. The FBI, led by J. Edgar Hoover, had been empowered at the beginning of the war to investigate anyone suspected of being a member of a subversive organization or advocating the overthrow of the federal government. The latter claim was ridiculous; even the first seemed preposterous, since Locke saw himself as merely a progressive advocating what was in the best interest of the United States.

Locke had been so careful. The FBI review of arrest records showed he had never been arrested for any crime. Yet it was common knowledge in the Black community that Locke was gay; and now the FBI knew that he had attended meetings, sponsored, and cavorted with organizations that were communist or at least considered subversive by the US government. From now on, he realized, he would be under intensified surveillance: FBI agents would interview his neighbors about him, a copy of the report would be submitted to Howard University, and on one occasion, the FBI entered his apartment and took samples from his typewriter to check whether he had typed certain letters that came into its possession. Now, he would have to be even more careful.

From a sexual standpoint, the surveillance could not have come at a worse time. For the first time in years, Locke had found someone, a young Black man, whom he was really fond of, and the relationship held promise as the long-term love he had been seeking for years. Handsome, lean, and light-medium-brown skinned, Maurice V. Russell was a young man in his late teens when Locke met him, probably on one of his trips to Philadelphia, where Maurice lived with his mother in the early 1940s. Maurice would go on to earn a PhD in social work from Columbia University, work at Columbia, become the director of the Social Service Department and professor of clinical social work at New York University Medical Center, and be an innovator of mental health services in New York. But as a young man, he was sexually ambivalent, lacking in confidence, and needy for a mature male presence in his life. Russell was enormously impressed with Locke. The relationship grew slowly in part because of the enormous age difference and Russell's ambivalence about identifying himself as gay. Locke had mentored Russell for a couple of years, and it could be said that his educational and professional success were in part due to Locke's influence. Their relationship was a secret, of course, when Locke began to write the nineteen-year-old. But now the system protecting that secret would be tested more than ever before.

Just four days after Locke's interview with the FBI, he was penning a letter to this young man. That Russell lived in Philadelphia made it a bit less risky to carry on the relationship, given that the FBI seemed to be tracking his activities in Washington and New York rather closely. Locke could stop off in Philadelphia, on the train between the other two cities, and perhaps not attract the FBI's attention. Part of Russell's attraction to Locke, of course, was that he was enormously attached to his mother, a single parent after Russell's father was killed in a car accident when the boy was seven. Russell's first letter, a response to Locke's initial inquiry about Russell's education plans, outlined this relationship. "I do not believe that I shall get back to school any time soon. You see my mother is partially dependent on me so I have made it my business to support her."[2]

Locke replied, "I have nothing but admiration for your manly assumption of a responsibility which came first in my life and should come first in any man's. Again let me suggest, as soon as you can get adjusted [Maurice had taken a civil service job at the Philadelphia Navy Yard], your taking even just a course or two in evening hours to keep on the track. Training is imperative for everyone nowadays, particularly for the younger Negro. Philadelphia youth haven't seemed to realize this as realistically as they should. The town is full of nice, untrained but complacent people."[3] The point was still clear: for Locke to be involved with Russell on any serious level, Russell would have to step up and commit himself to educational self-advancement like the older man. Russell did; he began attending night school at Temple after Locke's encouragement.

Unlike so many of the other young men Locke knew, Russell possessed an inner calm, a personal sophistication without formal training. That sophistication came through in his early letters to Locke that suggested Russell was pursuing Locke as much as the other way around. "I know how you detest praise," Russell had written in his first letter to Locke, though the letter was a testimonial to how he had admired Locke for years.[4] He knew full well that Locke craved praise. At the same time, Russell wanted something from Locke—access to a world of culture, beauty, and "luxury" that he heard in the classical music records that he played before he met Locke. Russell wrote to Locke after an outing together:

> Last weekend was truly a memorable one for me! Every moment was well-spent and this knowledge gave me a wonderful feeling when I returned to Philadelphia. Need I describe the thrill of the dinner aboard train or the luxury of the train? Do you think that I shall soon forget the gripping, emotional, grotesque, humorous <u>Porgy</u>? Such acting ability as displayed by the members of our race. How proud we should be of them!
>
> My meeting with Todd Duncan should be recorded—it was the fulfillment of wish of long standing. Thank you so very much!!
>
> What a pleasant surprise to get to see the [Katherine Dunham] dance films.... The beautiful captivating haunting music of the various dance sequences blending the graceful beauty of the dance added the necessary ingredients for complete pleasure....
>
> The Museum of Modern Art, with its aspect of luxury, aroused any amount of compliments from my limited vocabulary but I was confronted and bothered [by] the question: Do I understand all of this? Do I get the fullest possible appreciation from all of this?[5]

Russell possessed a hunger for education, culture, self-improvement, and mentoring that he recognized Locke could bring him. That made him an ideal "youth" for Locke, a person he could craft in his own image, and who offered a soul in sync with his own.

Russell was, however, nearly forty years his junior, and like most young men, enmeshed in a circle of friends with whom he shared a life of frivolity and queer merriment quite different from what he had with Locke. That circle of friends could cause problems for Locke. Russell's initial letter to Locke mentioned that he and "Eddie" might be down in Washington sometime soon. Locke's response noted that "Eddie Atkinson" had visited the following weekend without Russell. "Barged in with his usual court train, and without previous notice. I was busy on the second installment of my retrospective reviews and just couldn't stop to entertain them properly." Having just met with the FBI, Locke was not in the mood to entertain them at all. He was in no humor to hold court with a train of strangers with Atkinson, an over-the-top gay man from Philadelphia, down in Washington to kick up his heels. The queer Victorian rules Locke operated by—prior announcement of a visit being one of them, no strangers brought to the house without asking first being another— protected him from sexual exposure. Russell picked up the hint. Nevertheless, the deeper challenge was Atkinson and his circle of friends, who were at least a generation removed from Locke's and interested in something other than a "refined evening." Another member of the "gang" that Locke knew even better was Owen Dodson, another Philadelphia young man, whom Locke had courted. Even after the "elevated" evening with Locke in Philadelphia, Russell had stopped off at Eddie's where Owen Dodson was visiting. "This meeting with Owen gave me a chance to observe him at least and I feel that he has an intellect that should carry him far. He seems to think a great deal of <u>Owen</u> which perhaps might be justifiable?"[6] Locke would make it possible for Owen to study theater at Howard University.

From Locke's standpoint, the point of his relationship with Russell was to move his focus from this younger group of merrymakers and conceits to deep immersion in culture. Russell agreed with that agenda as well and also seemed to recognize that for some reason, Locke wanted to rendezvous in Philadelphia or New York. Russell helped move that along in 1942 by sending Locke the program for the "Robin Hood Dell concerts," a summer series of concerts by the world-famous Philadelphia Orchestra in Fairmount Park, in a letter that Russell signed for the first time with only his first name. Locke was positively impressed, viewing this as a sign of greater intimacy. He sent a check for half of the program, though he knew he would be able to make no more than "two or three of them in your good company," suggesting using the others for "Lenwood [Morris] or some other friend of yours." He said the programs that "interest me most;— Rubinstein, Anderson, Robeson, the All Tchaikovsky [sic] and the 3 B's, are special." Locke clearly appreciated Russell's gesture, and it prompted an unusual meditation on the frustrations of his life as a Black aesthete and his affection for

Jews. "You see youth is my hobby. But the sad thing is the increasing paucity of serious minded and really refined youth."[7]

Locke noted that years ago he had had to go to classical music concerts with a young Jew because of his appreciation and reliability. "I used to have two tickets to all the concert series in Washington, but would often have a vacant seat to put my hat and coat on through some student or colleague backing out at the last moment (dance or just carelessness or lateness)." Here is the loneliness of Locke. Refinement like his was generally not of much interest among young Blacks, Locke believed, because of racial prejudice. Russell agreed that "racial prejudice [w]as a possible discouragement to our mutual friends. I feel that it is most definitely a factor that should be listed as a cause of non-interest or lack of initiative." But this was not an inevitable response, according to Locke, because for him, culture was always a choice, and aesthetics was not just transcendence of a colonial mentality, but a way to reconstruct one's identity in ways that eluded the erosions of racism. Locke and Russell agreed that "the Jewish boy or girl is never perturbed about such distinctions and in forging ahead so steadily manages to up hold his entire race as well as making a definite niche for himself in this present struggle for the 'survival of the fittest.'" Locke relayed how he had bumped into a young German friend of his with whom he had attended concerts in Berlin and who had come to New York penniless a year ago. This German friend now had a house and a well-paying job. "These Jews," Locke exclaimed, out of envy at the resourcefulness of those he knew who created their own personal renaissance in America after fleeing the Holocaust. In this comparison, however, Locke seemed to forget that newly arrived Jews in America did not face the same kind of "racial prejudice" as an obstacle to advancement that he had just been discussing or grown up with a narrative of their inferiority in their own country. For Locke still saw the race problem through his own experience of race in America, as an obstacle to be overcome.

Locke preferred to forge an aesthetic companionship with an African American. The ideal still burned in his breast to find the young Black man who would believe, like him, that loving art not only bypassed racism, but contained the possibility for a new social contract in America. Going to concerts was a start. Locke ended his letter by saying that he would discuss details later, perhaps "en route to New York. I have to shuttle back and forth all through the summer on account of editorial work there."[8]

That editorial work was for a new special edition of the *Survey Graphic* that Paul Kellogg had asked him to do in response to the issue of race, Negroes, and the American war mobilization. FDR had articulated the ideology for the war even before the country entered it, in his January 1941 State of the Union Address. Almost as soon as the president laid out the Four Freedoms—Freedom of speech, Freedom of worship, Freedom from want, and Freedom from fear— for which the war would be fought, African Americans made it known that for them these rights were unattainable in America. A. Philip Randolph, having left the National Negro Congress, proposed in 1941 a march on Washington to demand desegregation of the armed forces, elimination of discrimination in hiring, and equal opportunity for Negroes in federal government contracts as the price of full-throated Black support for the war effort. FDR avoided that embarrassing protest in the nation's capital by issuing Executive Order 8802 that banned discrimination in the hiring in wartime jobs, the awarding of contracts, and established the toothless but symbolically valuable Federal Employment Practices Commission (FEPC), but the *Chicago Defender* kept the pressure on by announcing a "Double V" campaign—victory in Europe and victory in America—to tie the loyalty of Negroes in war to an expected transformation of American race relations in peace.

Kellogg's invitation to do this special issue could not have come at a better time for Locke, coinciding with his visit to the FBI. Editing an issue on the race issue in 1942 for a timidly social, reform-minded journal like *Survey Graphic* gave him a welcome opportunity to show his early 1940s thinking was the logical outgrowth of a New Deal mentality toward race and gave him cover for radical associations that might be considered evidence of his disloyalty. The issue was "safe" in that almost every liberal press outlet was publishing something on the obvious contradictions of America waging a global war in the name of freedom, while restricting the freedom of Negroes to serve in the military only in segregated units. But the contradictions went much deeper than that. Randolph's threatened march highlighted that while the war was a welcome opportunity to most Americans to escape the Great Depression's still-lingering unemployment, Negroes were not being hired. Kellogg's desire to weigh in on this issue reflected his need for the *Survey Graphic* to be part of the radical conversation about the contradiction of asking African Americans to participate in a war for the "Four Freedoms" when they lacked at least three of those freedoms—freedom of speech, freedom from want, and freedom from fear—in America, especially in the South. The proposed issue also made common sense. Kellogg dared not concede this area of impassioned public debate to his competitors if he wanted his "Calling America" series to be taken seriously as a forum on the burning issues "calling" on America for its attention. Happily, Locke would be reunited with the German artist Winold Reiss to use modernist design to anchor the new debate about race in the 1940s.

Here was an opportunity for Locke to establish his credibility as an American moralist. His lead article set a high literary metaphoric tone for the entire issue. "All of us by now are aware of the way in which this global war has altered the geography of our lives." Geography, of course, was the key issue of the war as Germany, Italy, and Japan were attempting to take over all the geography of Europe and Asia. Geography also was key to the Negro—when masses took the Great Migration to come north and seize opportunity. Locke was no longer speaking for the Negro, but for America by asking it to make a similar mental shift from "medieval to modern America" in its conception of what freedom really meant. "Americans are reminded enough of that with our armed forces dispersed over five continents and the seven seas and speeding to every compass point of the sky. But even more revolutionary changes are due to take place in the geography of our hearts and minds." Often, wars produced internal revolution, as World War I led to the Russian Revolution. In America, Locke hints, the roots of revolution were already planted in that mental geography, a "foreshortening" of "cultural and social distance" between Blacks and Whites, but also between goals and practices, because this was a war of inclusion and economic and social integration.

Locke predicted a cultural outcome of the war—a retreat for the forces and ideologies of difference, even those he had championed, and an advance for the logic of integration. Total war would render the strategy of separate racial agendas archaic for both America and Locke, forcing both to try to forge one comprehensive voice. "New forces for unification are closing in on that great divide of color which so long and so tragically has separated not only East and West, but two thirds of mankind from the other third."[9]

Was not this issue supposed to be about America's race problem? In the midst of organizing an issue to speak to how America's obsession with race prejudice contradicted the Four Freedoms, Locke shifted the analysis to a global context—East and West and the exploitation through separation of "two thirds of mankind from the other third." This larger perspective shaped how Locke organized the entire issue. "Part I: Negroes, U.S.A. 1942" contained articles, charts, paintings, photographs, and poems on the "Negro in the War" and the "Negro in America"; but "Part II: The Challenge of Color" offered a similar combination of media to show "color" was a challenge in the "New World" of the Caribbean and Latin America as well as the "Old World" of Africa, India, and the Pacific Rim. Certainly, when John Becker, whom Paul Kellogg credited with suggesting the idea for the issue, had imagined a *Survey Graphic* intervention on this topic, he did not imagine as its focus the large canvas Locke painted for the issue—"Color: Unfinished Business of Democracy"—a discussion of race from an anti-imperialist, anti-colonialist perspective. Maybe this issue was not such a good cover for his radicalizing theories after all.

To fully appreciate how radical Locke's intervention was, one only has to compare its global perspective with Gunnar Myrdal's Carnegie Corporation–financed two-volume tome, *An American Dilemma*, published two years later. Whereas Myrdal framed the "dilemma" as a conflict between America's "creed"—as embodied in the Declaration of Independence phrase "all men are created equal, with an equal right to life, liberty and the pursuit of happiness"—and American's practices of racial segregation and discrimination, Locke posed the question in terms of a global issue of the "Colored" people around the globe coming to the

aid of self-described "White" democracies about to be overrun by an Axis of racists. In places like French West Africa, it was the African colonial who still was
fighting for universal freedom in 1942, while the French in Europe had "accepted
defeat and submission to Germany," as Egon Kaskeline wrote in his article, "Felix
Eboué and the Fighting French." By including this article on a French West
African freedom fighter, Felix Eboué, Locke made visible the deeper irony of
World War II—that it was the people of color, the formerly enslaved, the currently colonized, who were fighting to free the White people who had enslaved
and colonized them for almost a century. Colored peoples' freedom around the
globe was what the war was really about, not the freedom of their overlords to
continue the same policies, outlook, and biases that led the world to war in the
first place. One would not find that argument in Myrdal's two-volume excavation of America's racial schizophrenia.

Also distinctive was that "Color: Unfinished Business of Democracy" foregrounded the subjectivity of the oppressed rather than seeing them as "the
problem" to be resolved as Myrdal and others did in his strictly sociological lens.
That is because Locke continued his earlier Harlem issue interdisciplinarity by
integrating poems, essays, and photographs of people of color from around the
world in a compelling montage. "Sorrow Home," a poem by Margaret Walker, a
member of Richard Wright's Chicago South Side Writers group; "Eternal," a sculpture by Ramon Banco, the Cuban sculptor introduced to Locke by Mary Beattie
Brady; a compelling standing sculpture by Richmond Barthé; and poem from James
Weldon Johnson were "much more than the plea of the Negro to America; they
speak symbolically for the non-white peoples in a world become circumscribed
and interdependent."[10] Perhaps the most telling and humorous part of "Color"
was supplied by Sterling Brown, whose collection of Negro comments about the
war attested to Black criticality toward US war propaganda: "Man, those Japs
really do jump, don't they? And it looks like everytime they jump, they land."[11]

In the intervening years, Locke had learned that the subjectivity he had announced earlier in 1925 was a worldwide phenomenon. In 1925, the global perspective was in the margins, but now it was out front. He had also learned that it was in
his interest to allow the criticality of the oppressed to be heard in such forums. Its
charts, graphs, and powerful poems and images made visible to the *Survey Graphic*
reader of 1942 that a new world of critically conscious people of color was still
coming and that America must deal with them if America was to be saved.

Photographs of Black workers in the war industry gave a compelling sense of
the tragic irony of compelling people to work for a democracy that excluded
them from its main benefits. And aesthetics allowed Locke to frame the frustration of such a predicament within the same prospect for a willingness to join in
the work of democracy despite earlier treatment. The poem "Boy in the Ghetto"
by Hercules Armstrong suggested the racially oppressed were willing to abandon
their self-destructive behaviors if welcomed into the work of civilization building.

Boy burning with anger—
Shake the violence from your eyes:
Throw that knife in the gutter!
Step where men fight to free
Your world, your dreams.[12]

The Winold Reiss–designed cover conveyed powerfully Locke's message that the road forward was through Colored heads brought together by a common world-transforming purpose. This powerful multicolored image of humanity against the backdrop of a world map centered on Africa suggested a global perspective should circumscribe Americans' subjectivities moving forward. While Locke highlighted the demographic challenge to America's race biases with dozens of charts, graphics, and photographs, he also showed that color was America's opportunity. If America got its racial house in order and deployed its democratic values honestly for world citizenship, it could dominate the world. Locke had gleaned what the Roosevelt agenda really was.

This New Deal imperialist argument allowed Locke to slip in his critical mode without eliciting more negative attention from the prying eyes of the FBI. It did not challenge democracy itself as one of the main agents for the perpetration of racism in America and abroad. Under surveillance, contained by the period's discourse of "win the war first," Locke was not going to deepen his criticality in the face of a nation that felt the Negro ought to help out. Locke would have to tread carefully in the wake of *Color*'s success not to elicit further interest from the FBI as being a threat to the American war effort. Remaining invisible was tougher now.

No matter how successful "Color: The Unfinished Business" was at repackaging Black internationalist critique as pressing domestic agenda, it did not make the splash of his 1925 Harlem *Survey Graphic*. Using the war to leverage greater civil rights as benighted citizen soldiers was quite a different strategy than declaring a New Negro had arisen in 1925. Plus, the *Survey Graphic* was no longer the vehicle for radical intervention it had been. Well meaning, necessary, and well distributed as this journal was, this twenty-five-year-old Progressive-Era journal had been eclipsed by more radical contemporary magazines raising ire about the Negro's anomalous position in the war. When the Schomburg Library in Harlem, now headed by Lawrence Reddick, invited Locke and Kellogg to speak about their issue in 1942—a repeat of a similar library forum for the Harlem issue of *Survey Graphic* in 1925—several other magazines, notably the *New Masses*, were also presented to speak about their coverage of the same topic. Other people had adopted Locke's earlier critiques, almost rendering his intervention outdated, especially since his was not connected to a full-throated call for activism. A discourse of democratic inclusion was triumphant, as also evident in James Porter's *Modern Negro Art*, published that same year, with its aggressive declaration that Negro art should be nothing more than a province of American art. Locke's cultural pluralist views were too nuanced for these times.

Nevertheless, Locke kept building his intellectual platform to achieve in 1943 a monumental, if largely hidden, intellectual breakthrough far away from New York. In Port-au-Prince, Haiti, as an official visitor of the Haitian government, Locke articulated an altogether new Black diasporic perspective that redefined his concept of race. The thinking behind his new approach to the Negro probably began with his relationship with Eric Williams, which began sometime in the late 1930s, most likely through his Oxford connections or simply through his desire to secure a job at Howard University. Locke tapped this elegant radical to supply what had been missing from the Bronze Booklets series all along—a book on the diasporic nature of the Black New World experience that would explain the relationship of social processes worldwide that created a Black Caribbean and a West Indian migration to the United States. After agreeing to do the Bronze Booklet, Williams took a trip to Cuba in 1940 to work in the archives there, as his specialty was the British and French West Indies, not the Spanish Caribbean.

The Negro in the Caribbean appeared as the last Bronze Booklet in 1942. Its central argument was a Marxist explanation of the economic issues that determined the course of slavery and its after-effects in the Caribbean. Locke also included an article on the Caribbean by Williams in the "Color" issue of the *Survey Graphic* that condensed *The Negro in the Caribbean* into a pithy contribution to Locke's global approach to race in America. When published in 1944 in the book *Capitalism and Slavery*, Williams's insights would overturn the historiography of slavery, for he would argue that economic considerations, not moral conscience, led Britain—even its abolitionists—to end the slave trade. England's suppression of slavery was competitive—to crush its rivals in France, Spain, Holland, and of course America, still dependent on agricultural production by slave laborers. Locke's editorial work with Bronze Booklet scholars to shorten, simplify, and sharpen their writing may have helped Williams to transition from his cautious Oxford dissertation to the boldest presentation of his unique thesis. Also important was the impact of working with Williams on Locke. Under Williams's influence, Locke thought through how different hemispheric slavery regimes resulted in different post slavery Negro social formations, a diversity of Negro subjectivity in what Locke would later call the "Three Americas." Fortunately for Locke, one of those "Three Americas" was calling him.

Locke may have begun planning the lecture trip to Haiti as early as 1939, perhaps an outgrowth of that Haitian minister's interest in Haiti obtaining Jacob Lawrence's Toussaint L'Ouverture series when it was exhibited at the Baltimore Museum of Art. That year Haiti organized its national library, the Bibliothèque Nationale d'Haïti, a symbol of growing national pride and self-consciousness about Haiti's literary and cultural contributions to world culture. Although the purchase of Lawrence's series never took place, the Lawrence discussions may have led to conversations with Locke's long-time friend, Dantès Bellegarde, the dandyish Haitian intellectual and foreign minister to Washington, who encouraged increased intellectual contacts and exchanges between Haitian and African American intellectuals. When Élie Lescot was elected in 1941 as president of Haiti, the invitation materialized as part of Lescot's agenda to heighten the country's national and international prominence by inviting cultural leaders to talk up its cultural significance. Locke seized on this opportunity to develop a unique theory of the cultural nature of the African Diaspora in the "Three Americas."

Most Diaspora thinkers focused on how oppression had driven a people from their homeland into satellite communities linked by their common origin and argued salvation through a return to a holy land—either Palestine in the Jewish Diaspora or Africa in Marcus Garvey's imaginary. But a unique notion of the Diaspora had been implicit to Locke's thinking ever since 1925 and his Harlem article in the *Survey Graphic*. There, Locke posed Harlem as the reversal of the historic forced migration of the Atlantic slave trade by choice to found a New Jerusalem in a new place, where the main effects of the forced Diaspora could be reversed and the race reborn. "Hitherto, it must be admitted that American Negroes have been a race more in name than in fact, or to be exact, more in sentiment than in experience. The chief bond between them has been a common condition rather than a common consciousness; a problem in common rather than a life in common." In Harlem, the dismembered parts of the African body came together in "the first concentration in history of so many diverse elements of Negro life."[13] Harlem was a magneto drawing dispersed people together, rather than apart, into a new future, a reintegration as a race, ironically not in the Caribbean or other diasporic peripheries, but at the center of New World capitalism, New York.

Locke believed the healing process, which is what the New Negro represented psychologically, was started by coming to Harlem, but required a racially conscious art to complete it. Locke knew that the effort to mirror a fully sutured self in the Negro Renaissance literature had also failed. Partly, it was the weakness of the artists. Partly, it was the Great Depression that had prematurely shortened the Harlem Renaissance. But partly it was America, whose powerful counterforce to racial self-determination—Whiteness—created a desire to assimilate into the body of America without reservations. In various ways, Locke had struggled to define the alternative—a separate Black body, an appendage, an American body that was essentially Black, and so on. Although Locke had made that a transnational body through his own "practice of diaspora" to Black Europe, working with the Nadal sisters and others, for example, to translate *The New Negro* into French, or through his associations in Africa with trips to Egypt and with King Amoah, he had avoided until now the opportunity to extend it to the Caribbean, except for his brief sojourn with his mother to the Bermuda.

Locke began to gravitate toward a hemispheric diasporic perspective in the 1940s, following an intellectual path charted by African American women artists, especially Zora Neale Hurston, Katherine Dunham, and Lois Jones, who visited and even moved, in some cases, to Haiti and other Caribbean nations to develop artwork based in Africanisms stronger there than in the United States. For these artists, Diaspora was both a cultural strategy to connect with Africa and a way to reinvigorate African American cultural formations by connecting them with Caribbean aesthetic and religious traditions where Africanisms flourished. These artists innovated a second notion of Diaspora, not the flow of bodies, but the flow of ideas, northward. For them, Diaspora was both resource and muse. Hurston, for example, completed writing *Their Eyes Were Watching God* in Haiti.

Howard University's transformation from an institution to train students in liberal arts education to an institution for the production of critical knowledge was another important influence. Ralph Bunche, E. Franklin Frazier, Sterling Brown, Abram Harris, and now Eric Williams had made research on the African Diaspora more important than it had been in the past, even if that was not their main focus. This second generation of social scientists and artists were "integrationist scholars," to be sure, but their excavation of the political, sociological, and economic processes undergirding Black life instinctively tied the study of African Americans to worlds beyond the United States. Ralph Bunche's Harvard doctoral dissertation was on the African mandates system, the one Locke had studied ineptly in 1928. Frazier advanced the theory that the survival of Africanisms in African American life was minimal, but in the course of his running debate with Melville Herskovits on this issue, he won a research grant to study African survivals in Brazil. And Eric Williams brought a global systems approach to Diaspora and Caribbean thinking—a criticality toward Latin America, its race and economic structures, and the suffering experienced by people even under the "Latin code" of race relations, as it was termed, south of the American border. Howard's emphasis on political and sociological analysis of the differences and similarities among North America, the Caribbean, and Latin America suggested that the sociologist in Locke could find ample materials for a more global theory of the New Negro by developing a diasporic theory of his own in his Haiti lectures.

Locke almost did not get the opportunity to give the lectures. Invited originally to give the lectures in Haiti in 1942, the federal government refused to issue him a passport when he requested it early in the year. Haiti had become strategically important, as Eric Williams mentioned in his Bronze Booklet, when a rumor circulated that Hitler had plans to invade America by seizing the Caribbean with his U-boats. Although it was later clear that such a plan was preposterous, that did not stop *Life* magazine from publishing a series of maps in March 1942 that outlined how the enemy might force its way into the Western

Hemisphere through the Caribbean and enter the southern United States by way of the Gulf of Mexico.[14] The federal government not only took that threat seriously but had also already intervened in Haiti's internal affairs in 1941 to pressure its president to resign to make the way for Elie Lescot, whom US officials believed was more likely to advocate economic policies to help American wartime interests. The expectations of help turned into policy that the heirs of the slave trade and colonialism ought to assist America and its war allies remain, ironically, free to determine the political and economic destiny of the unfree. The federal government also was serious about Locke as a security threat. After all, Locke had made numerous trips to Germany even after the Nazi takeover in 1934. He was accused of being on the boards of known communist-front organizations. Could he be going to Haiti on a mission other than cultural exchange? By the fall of 1942, Locke had cancelled his request for the passport, as it was not going to be granted that year. In early 1943, he made another request, perhaps after some indication from the government that it might allow him to go after all. After some maneuvering, he was able to get Haiti to invite him again and obtain another leave of absence from Howard for the spring quarter of 1943. Mercifully, the US government issued his passport.

Fortunately, Locke had been working on the lectures, having produced an outline as early as October 1941. There was then the matter of having them translated into French. At first Louis Achille started translating them, but Locke then had to seek out another translator to finish the job. The six lectures documented the contribution of the Negro to the various societies of what Locke called the "Three Americas"—North, South, and Caribbean societies shaped by slavery. He suggested that the pivot of democracy, as he had argued in "Color," was each society's treatment—legal, political, and social—of the Negro in its post slavery formations. His first innovation of the lectures was to chart a new direction for Diaspora as a dialogue among societies shaped by the Atlantic slave trade and the Negro, a dialogue over differences as well as similarities among those societies, with an emphasis on what was distinct in each and what each could learn from the other. The co-sponsors of the trip prompted this diasporic adventure, as Locke acknowledged in characteristically ironic voice, when he noted:

> Your [American] Committee [for Inter-American Artistic and Intellectual Relations] has saddled me with a difficult task. I was sorely tempted to buck off half the load on the plea that the Negro problem of the United States was back-breaking in itself. However, on conscientious thought, I discovered underneath my feeling of protest the incorrigible human trait of habit: I was sniffing at familiar cats and pulling toward the accustomed stall. But the more I reflected on the matter, the more welcome the subject became in the wider perspective of the original assignment. In discussing the Negro in terms of both North and South

and Central America, we not only have the benefit of certain important but little discussed contrasts, but can use the wide-angle comparison as a more scientific gauge and a more objective yardstick for measuring both the historical and the contemporary issues of the American race question.[15]

The assignment had forced Locke to develop a more nuanced theory of Negro identity formation as a global dialogue than he otherwise would have done. That spoke to the larger reality of Locke in the 1940s—despite the hurts, the frustrations, the disappointments of his life, he still possessed the capacity to react to his experience and turn its challenges into new ideas.

Locke developed a contrastive analysis of the New World societies that had emerged out of the Latin or the Anglo code of race relations in his lectures and deployed a new set of insights of how different norms of interracial relations under slavery had produced positive and negative consequences for Negro social formations in slavery's wake. Each system had its benefits; and Locke dispelled the notion that coming up slave or free under the Latin code was more humane than living under the English. Instead, using E. Franklin Frazier's analysis of South American race relations, Locke argued that the Latin code transferred to color and class conflict internal to the Negro group what had remained as racial and external conflict with Whites in the North American society.[16] The bane of the North American system was its rigid insistence that one drop of Negro blood rendered the bearer Black and relegated to the most intense of segregationist systems of exclusion and penalty to those so labeled. But the bane of the Latin was that it granted mulatto descendants of the interracial unions a special status below that of Whites but above Blacks. Over time, this mulatto class became an elite sphere of influence that refused to see itself as connected to or representative of the Blacks as in the United States. Racism English-style had been the cruelest form of New World social relations but had its unforeseen benefit: the educated, the talented, and the favored, and the pure Negro and mixed-race, penalized equally in the law, became a powerful political and cultural voice of the Negro community as a whole.

Locke showed his modernity by taking an airplane to Haiti. In 1943, flying on an airplane was something not many people would choose to do, as Mrs. Mason acknowledged when she wrote him later, "My brave boy flying on wings of truth to Haiti!" It was also wise from Locke's perspective, for as he quipped in a letter to a friend, "I didn't want to become shark's bait because of Hitler's U boats!" Locke landed safely in Port-au-Prince on May 1, and was whisked to the Hotel Oloffson, the most sumptuous hotel in town.[17]

But on arrival, Locke got wind that there might be trouble. He was informed that his analysis of racial formation in the Western Hemisphere might discomfort the main audience of his lectures, President Lescot and the Haitian government.

Lescot had staffed that government largely with friends and acquaintances from his own mulatto class, and he emphasized that Haiti's future success depended on it being led by an elite drawn exclusively from that class. His Haitian benefactors expected Locke to provide the kind of paean to Haiti and its African retentions and status as a resource that other African American artists had mined for their art. Certainly, Locke acknowledged that African Americans had much to learn from Haiti and that a dialogic approach to Diaspora meant a much longer list of Black writers, artists, and playwrights from which to make his Negro contributions to American cultures. But by the 1940s, the sociological voice, the voice of Black criticality, had led him to ground his cultural analysis in commentary on the social contradictions under which diasporic cultures breathed and lived. This line of analysis exposed that people living in Caribbean nations favored by the Latin code were crushed by a color and class oligarchy that made Blackness a badge of internal oppression in so-called postcolonial nations.

As he wrote to Maurice Russell, at the opening reception all of the "Haitian and American dignitaries [were] present and all the critics keen for the occasion, you can imagine it isn't easy even for a veteran."[18] The assembled Haitian elite would not be pleased to hear their country's current political direction and social conflict aired as dirty laundry in his lectures. Hurriedly, as he confided to another friend, Arthur Wright, Locke rewrote his lectures "when I sensed the situation." He then contracted with a local translator to retranslate them before each lecture. Locke was nervous not only because he treaded on delicate territory in his lectures but also because he delivered his remarks in translated French. More than eight hundred people came to hear his first lecture, graced by the "dramatic entrance of the President and staff and a click heel presentation before and after the [United States] Ambassador and staff [entered]. [I]t was enough to make me nervous, even outwardly so." That was not surprising. A verbal slip or a wrong phrase could offend a listener and cause an international incident. What Locke had imagined as a welcome vacation from teaching had turned into a trying assignment to speak truthfully about the diasporic situation of the Negro without alienating his listeners so much that he could not be heard—or leave unharmed by the experience.[19]

Locke was up to the challenge. After years of fine-tuning his controversial messages to White American audiences, Locke possessed the rhetorical strategies to convey his points without his audience often noticing how devastating they were to their subject position. Evidently, President Lescot was pleased, hosting a lavish dinner for Locke on Palm Sunday and arranging for Locke to fly by military airplane to the citadel at Christophe. Lescot got what he wanted out of Locke's visit, part of what one critic later called Lescot's strategy of inviting distinguished lecturers to the country during World War II, wining and dining them, and conferring on them honors—Locke was awarded the nation's Legion of Merit at the final ceremony—to get their assent for his government that maintained "low living standards for the masses, bitter poverty for the peasants, puppet politicians, color and class divisions, which help the foreign exploiter, and a 'cultural crusade' to hide the hideousness which lurks behind the cultivated facade of its mulatto elite."[20]

Locke seemed to realize that he was being used. But there were unexpected benefits. Visited by disaffected Haitian students, who had heard the hidden criticality of his message, they shared with Locke "private memoranda on color prejudice between the upper class mulattos and the black peasantry, which in my judgment was more of a tribute than the decoration which the President gave me."[21] Such students would be the major force in launching a student strike and a series of street demonstrations in 1946 that eventually deposed Lescot and installed a Black cabinet.[22]

Locke's dialogic theory of Diaspora was itself an attempt to teach the Haitian nation how to become modern. Lescot could not see that, using Locke to legitimate what he was already doing, instead of viewing him as an opportunity to collaborate on rethinking the social direction of the Haitian nation. In proposing an inter-American diasporic dialogue, Locke was asking whether the life of the people in one particular country can be improved "by borrowing from each other what is working to improve democracy" in the other country. Influenced by Ralph Bunche, Locke suggested the diasporic Negro could gain from invoking the Anglo-American notion of fair and proportional representation as key to democratic legitimacy, something that if acted upon in Haiti would have led Lescot to democratize his cabinet without needing the revolution of 1946 to depose him. Here, without mentioning Eric Williams by name or his critique of the treatment of agricultural laborers and the poor in the Caribbean, Locke suggested that a dialectical relationship must be insisted on between cultural and social democracy, or an anomaly would result. The struggle for political and cultural representation in the Western Hemispheric imaginary, he contended, should be the rationale for a postwar consciousness movement in the Three Americas.

The most revolutionary part of Locke's Haiti lectures was not the most controversial. Indeed, it went completely unnoticed in the charged atmosphere about the caste and color issues of which he argued that a new kind of America was possible in the Western Hemisphere based on Diaspora. Diaspora, in other words, was the key to a new internationalism. Equality between nations, races, and cultures was the next necessary step in the evolution toward diasporic democracy that would not become real at the political level in a satisfactory manner, Locke argued, until spiritual and moral convictions could be used to govern just and lasting relations between different human groups. Implicit was a call for the Negro in the new diasporic conversation to transcend both race and nationalism.

Locke's dialectical pragmatism allowed him to advance race consciousness, at the early stage of his lectures, as a benefit to the North American Negro's sense of community, but then argue later that even that stage must be transcended if the true realization of democracy as a shared inheritance was to erupt in the Three Americas. Transcending race meant transcending provincialism and national identification. True diasporic consciousness could only develop through the transformation of those provincialisms, deeply rooted in these various cultures, into something that moved beyond race and kinship loyalties as the basis of community. Those provincialisms created proud feelings of exclusivity and superiority, but they also led to degrading some other subjectivity or excluding some other people from a larger diasporic perspective.

Locke argued that a truly diasporic view of the Caribbean required the Negro to take into account the large "Indian population" and the "large East Indian or Hindu populations" that were also part of the Caribbean. A real inter-American dialogue about race and culture must take into account the indigenous peoples of the Caribbean displaced by colonization and acknowledge that the African was not the only Diaspora to the Caribbean. Although Locke did not detail the history in his lecture, he was clearly referencing that "large East Indian or Hindu populations" existed in Trinidad and Tobago, Jamaica, and other Caribbean nations because of their forced migration to the Caribbean by British capitalists, who needed cheap labor for the sugar plantations after slavery was outlawed in 1833. While not technically slaves, they endured similar conditions of forced labor, malnutrition, and early death, and now constituted a "large population" in some Caribbean islands. A dialogic approach to social formation in the Caribbean had to appreciate the "polyracial character of our Continent as more crucial and critical in our inter-Continental life and its progressive development than in even our respective national societies."[23]

This was the stroke of genius in his diasporic theory of community formation: if Diaspora was the basis of our notion of community, then all of those who had migrated into the inter-American theater of culture and society or been displaced by such migrations must be included in the dialogue about the future. Such inclusive thinking means acknowledging and facing the differences in our histories and experiences as well as learning from our shared realities. Those displaced by diasporas (the native inhabitants) and those who have come through other diasporas (the East Indians) must be part of the inter-American conversation in order to avoid reproducing the same provincialisms that spawned the existing racial nightmare. This is what the North American attitude had to learn from the "polyracial" nature of the Caribbean.

This universalism came from a capacity found in African Diaspora art, Locke naturally argued. The spirituals had always been fundamentally universal; they just had to be labeled and promoted as Black art because under the Anglo code of race, the official culture denied Negroes any humanity or pride in their cultural fecundity. He and others had had to advance African-derived cultural products as racial armor, but the spirituals expressed the yearnings of all people for deliverance from suffering regardless of race or national origin. Such art was a gift to the world from the inevitable mixing of cultures that the Diaspora produced. Negro culture possessed within it a diasporic universalism that could become the basis for the disparate countries of the Western Hemisphere to write.

Perhaps a twentieth-century global consciousness could begin with the Negro. What Locke suggests is that the diasporic peoples of color begin to form an international federation, a kind of United States of the Americas, by beginning the practice of mutual exchange and positive regard of one another, and create the conditions to welcome others, Whites, into that. Some steps in the direction of a racially self-conscious Latin American formation had occurred already in Brazil, which had witnessed the emergence of a *Frente Negra Brasileira* (Brazilian Black Front) in 1931. What Locke was advocating was to extend the notion of community he had first announced in Harlem in terms of the New Negro into a New Diaspora—a new subjectivity and a new sense of community that allowed Black, Indian, Hindu, and others to enter into conversation about their experiences of colonialism, White supremacy, and new-world diasporic migrations, and lay the groundwork for a new inter-nation collaboration. A new diasporic community might emerge with a unique sense of hemispheric culture and democracy without limitation of country of origin or present residence.

This was heady stuff that most likely went over the heads of Lescot and his Haitian government cronies and even the people at the Guggenheim Fellowship and the State Department, to whom Locke had to report after returning to the United States. But few in America, let alone in largely impoverished locations in the Black hemispheric Diaspora, could enact what Locke recommended. That was brought home to him dramatically that summer of 1943 when, during a brief stay over in New York, he walked out of the Hotel Theresa and right into the Harlem Race Riot of 1943.

Unlike the 1935 Harlem riot, Locke experienced this one live, as Black people ran, smashed store windows, stole goods, screamed and laughed hysterically, and set buildings on fire. Locke feared physical violence and, even though these were Black people wreaking havoc mostly on White businesses, it roused in him first fear and then confusion, as if he could not believe his eyes. Suddenly, all of his theories about the historic patience of the Negro with all manner of racial and economic degradation in America, or about art as a catharsis to alleviate the centuries of pain, were rendered irrelevant as he witnessed the violent self-destruction of the very community, Harlem, he had so celebrated for almost twenty years.

Of course, this Harlem was a different Harlem from that of 1925. It was beset with continuing economic unemployment despite Executive Order 8802. It was struggling with more decrepit housing scarcity than in the 1920s. It had limped through the worst depression in American history. And, it was angry Black men and women being sent to fight the Germans, the Italians, and the Japanese, while those on the home front still endured crushing poverty and discrimination. Locke realized the rioters were a far cry from the self-conscious race-proud New Negroes he had worshipped in print eighteen years earlier. Or were they? Were these rioters not self-conscious and cognizant that the only way to get the attention of New York and the nation was to destroy their neighborhoods and the businesses that regularly overcharged them, in an act of liberation? Locke was confused about what this riot meant, having realized, painfully, how inept his earlier understanding of the 1935 riot had been. Harlem's catastrophic decline finally sunk in, as he experienced a deep sense of loss that horrific night.

The riot, coming so soon on the heels of Locke's forecast of the possibilities for what could be called a Diasporic Renaissance in the Western Hemisphere, confounded him. His social theorizing never adequately addressed the powerful pull toward anomic rebellion in the lower- and working-class urban communities of the North. A contradiction persisted between his conception of what that updated Renaissance might look like and the quality of life actually experienced by the Black masses. This highlighted the tension between the purely discursive and often brilliant innovations of Black intellectuals and artists and the still soul-destroying social and economic conditions under which rank-and-file Black people suffered despite those brilliant innovations. Locke's democratic and diasporic theorizing flourished, but the people he theorized about languished.

The violence of the Harlem riot thrust Locke into a deep depression. Weeks later, after conveying his experience to Kellogg, the editor had asked Locke if he would write up his impressions for a sequel to his 1936 article, "Harlem, Dark Weather Vane." But this time the vane was too dark. Locke tried to write something, but in the fall of 1943 confessed to the editor that he was too deeply disturbed to write about it professionally. He had nothing to say. Or perhaps he could not say what he felt to a public fed on his optimistic, concluding sentences. Words could not capture his disappointment at where the material conditions had led the Negro—and that there was no uplifting catharsis on the horizon, only horror.

When three years later, Locke heard the news of the military coup in Haiti that deposed his benefactor, he must again have been saddened. He had tried to tell the self-congratulatory president of Haiti that a major change was required to keep legitimate power, but Elié Lescot had not listened, just as American leaders had not listened when he wrote in the 1942 *Survey Graphic* that America was at the breaking point since its democratic values were so plainly contradicted by its racist war mobilization. The streets of Harlem no less than the streets of Port-au-Prince were crowded with hapless Black boys and girls without a place to go in the national imaginary. In that sense, the inter-American diasporic conversation Locke had forecasted in his lectures was taking place. But it was saying something much darker and destructive than anything he could bring himself to say.

Bili Bond, unidentified man, and Locke, November 7, 1947. Courtesy of the
Moorland-Spingarn Research Center, Howard University.

43

Wisdom *de Profundis*

It was as welcome as it was unexpected.

In the spring of 1945, Locke received a note from a mere acquaintance, Max C. Otto, a philosopher at the University of Wisconsin, with an invitation. "Those of us here at the University wondered whether you would be available to come to Wisconsin for a year as a visiting professor. My inquiry is not official since we don't have authorization yet. But I wanted to inquire whether this might be a possibility."

Where did this come from? Locke's visibility as a philosopher had steadily increased since the publication of "Values and Imperatives" in 1936, especially in the early 1940s, after he was invited to join Finkelstein's conference. Locke had taken participation in that annual conference seriously, presenting two papers that allowed him to redefine pragmatism and cultural pluralism. Of the two, "Cultural Relativism and Ideological Peace," had been the most innovative in charting his answer to the question highlighted by World War II: to what extent were values relative in the face of fascism? Pluralism allowed people who looked at the world through different eyes to move through stages of consciousness in holding together opposites and difference, yet at the same time recognized that some things, such as the value of human life, were nonnegotiable. His mature, careful, and unique approach to the philosophical problem of unity and diversity had caught the attention of the fellow participants in the conference. Evidently, it caught the attention of Max Otto as well, as this liberal social philosopher decided his department ought to break with the segregated tradition of institutional philosophy in America. On June 11, 1945, Otto wrote formally inviting Locke to come as visiting professor the spring semester, January to June 1946, for $2,500. That was twice the salary of the assistant professors at Wisconsin. Still, Locke took six months to accept the invitation in writing, perhaps because of financial considerations. While the salary offered by Wisconsin was considerable, Locke had to take a pay cut to teach at the White university, because Howard's administration insisted on a full two-quarter leave dating from December 31, even though he still conducted departmental registration through January. But once a front-page article appeared in the Sunday edition of the local paper announcing the historic visiting professorship of Dr. Locke to the university, Locke hurried off his formal acceptance to Otto.[1]

For Locke, the invitation could not have come at a better time. He was exhausted with teaching at Howard, where he felt its students and its administration did not fully appreciate him. Philosophy had remained an anomaly at Howard despite his being able to hire some assistants like Eugene Holmes, the Marxist social philosopher, and William McAllister, an able ethics philosopher. The truth was that few students were interested in philosophy as a major, and most students took his large introductory classes because Locke was a celebrity on campus, whose international reputation as a scholar and rumors about his sexuality made him a draw. But Locke wanted students who would study his works, listen to his philosophizing about contemporary issues, and take philosophy seriously. On a White midwestern campus, he would be followed, be the center of attention, and might attract large numbers of students who took philosophy seriously.

From Howard's standpoint, Locke being on leave was a kind of blessing. Someone would pay his salary, one of the highest on campus, and his absence would mean there was less of a chance he might cause a sexually embarrassing scandal. But the issue was larger than Locke. In 1945, Abram Harris accepted the invitation of the Economics Department at the University of Chicago to join its permanent faculty. Reputedly despondent about the cause of Negro liberation, as well as teaching at Howard University, Harris was glad to be one of the first, if not the first, Black professors to be hired to a permanent position at a White research university in the United States. Ralph Bunche had already left Howard at the outbreak of World War II, having been recruited by the Office of Strategic Services, the forerunner to the Central Intelligence Agency, to work as an analyst of colonial affairs. From OSS he went to the State Department in 1943, becoming an associate director under Alger Hiss and a major player in planning the United Nations in 1945. Howard had nurtured a generation of African American scholars who were able to take advantage of the changing racial climate to serve in mainstream institutions of higher education after the war. Could Locke, the elder statesman of the group, take full advantage of the opportunities that a rapidly desegregating system of higher education offered him?

Going to Wisconsin showed Locke was willing to try. As his letters to friends and lovers attest, he had a fabulous time at the White university. "I am delighted to be able to tell you," he wrote Horace Kallen, "that things continue to go well out here at Madison. I think and hope dear Max is satisfied, and have tried my darndest to have it so. The contrast both in student reaction, colleague's friendliness, and, of course, administration situation has been damning in Howard's disfavor."[2] Locke also made an impression outside of the university. In February, he wrote Kallen that he had "just come in from a talk on 'The Price of Democracy' to The Lions Club at the Park Hotel. Mentioned this because they took it and seemed to like it and got it foursquare with only indirect reference to the Negro end of it." Here, Locke was reprising arguments he had made in the "Color" issue of *Survey Graphic*, that America could not continue to promote itself as a world-changing democracy without paying the price of confronting its domestic contradictions. Here he was at the Lions Club telling White people they had to change their ways if they wanted to survive in the postwar world and they applauded him for saying it. While he had expected a positive student and faculty reaction, he was more than pleased with the "cordial community reaction after three weeks." It was "quite something to be proud of, and thankful for, because it vindicates Max Otto—that being the main point."[3] Locke did not mention that such a lecture before White folks in a prestigious hotel would have been unthinkable in still rigidly segregated Washington, D.C. One wonders if Locke would have been tempted by a permanent offer, but one never came.

For the first time, Locke had students he believed were genuinely interested in him as a philosopher. His undergraduate lecture course on the Philosophy of the Arts enrolled a whopping 156 students, an undergraduate seminar on Elementary Logic drew 29, and a graduate seminar in Theory of Value attracted 8. Coming two years after his pioneering lectures in Haiti on the revolutionary universalism of Negro aesthetics, and just after he had signed a contract with Random House to write his magnum opus on *The Negro Contribution to American Culture*, his lectures suggested Locke was on the verge of a fuller statement of his theory of how aesthetics—art, music, and literature—could be a process of healing. But referencing Freud in his lectures showed that Locke was willing to broach two subjects that other Black public intellectuals never addressed: sex and desire.

As an active homosexual in his sixties, Locke's sexual life was a kind of victory over the Victorian tradition of repression so endemic to his upbringing as a Black Philadelphian. And it was the embrace of the life of art advocacy, the mentoring of young artists to accept their sexual identities—or even to define them—that had been a major part of his mothering the various iterations of the New Negro artist. Freud had stunned the world of psychiatry with such outrageous notions at the time that children had sexual lives. By bringing up Freud in a course on aesthetics in 1946, Locke was telling his White students that they too had to acknowledge the unacknowledged—racial and sexual—sources of their own potential creativity, and the creativity of artists. That he seemingly felt comfortable discussing this aspect of art formation at the University of Wisconsin suggested another aspect of desire—the desire of a Black intellectual such as him to be able to enter White spaces of learning that had been walled off from Black subjectivity with controversial knowledge.

Here was the crux of the career of Alain Locke. He narrated inclusion, self-determination, universalism, and pluralism as characteristics of the world and the discourse of the New Negro. But they also were about him. He was the Black aesthetic nationalist escaping Black education by taking a job in a White institution of higher education. His public lectures in Madison exemplified that the major part of his life as a public intellectual was lecturing to audiences of sympathetic if uninformed White people. At the University of Wisconsin, two sides of his career, his academic labor as a teacher of young students and his public intellectual career as a teacher of adults, came together—as an advocate for the enlightenment of liberal-minded White people. More deeply, what Wisconsin represented was something he had written about profoundly in his 1915–1916 Race Contacts lectures—that segregation contained the seeds of its downfall because it created desire—for those walled off from each other by segregation to break through those walls. He and dozens of other Black intellectuals were getting a taste of White academic life, and the students, no less than the people who showed up at the Lions Club, were getting a taste of a Black academic subjectivity they had heard about but never experienced before. It was not simply that White students at the University of Wisconsin were more interested in philosophy than those at Howard, but that they were interested in him. And he liked that.

Locke's experience at Wisconsin was a metaphor of the 1940s New Negro—the talented if alienated Black artist and intellectual, who, after decades of preparation in segregated spaces and European venues, suddenly was attractive to elite cultural institutions. Locke had documented this trend two years earlier in "The Negro Contribution to American Culture," published in the *New Masses*, where he noted the 1940s trend of desire for the New Negro. Broadway, for example, had mounted *Othello*, starring Paul Robeson, in the first major American production that starred a Black man in the lead role. Locke was able to hobnob with Robeson in Madison while the actor visited the parental home of Uta Hagen, Desdemona in the production and now Robeson's mistress.

But inclusion came at a price, just as democracy did. Inclusion meant the New Negro had to pursue opportunity as an individual divorced from the larger politics of community taken up in the 1930s or rhetorically invoked by Locke in the 1920s. When Paul Robeson refused simply to enjoy the sexual and celebrity freedom America granted him and started critiquing cold war hysteria and attacks on working-class movements, the State Department turned him into a pariah in his own community. Also suppressed by inclusive discourses of the 1940s were radical nationalist discourses. The publication of Gunnar Myrdal's *An American Dilemma* in 1944 dominated the postwar national discussion of race without any involvement by Locke, Du Bois, or Woodson. Myrdal utilized Ralph Bunche and E. Franklin Frazier—younger, specialist trained, and aggressively assimilationist thinkers to make his argument that Black nationalist discourses in religion, politics, and culture were part of the problem for an America committed to the notion that "all men are created equal." Scholars like Locke were old and antiquated from Myrdal's perspective. Even though Locke's essays in the 1940s proclaimed the democratic necessity of acceptance of the Negro by the American mainstream, his cultural pluralism demand that difference be acknowledged in that process put him at odds with the terms of incorporation, which were complete worship of mainstream American culture.

The intellectual sea change of the 1940s brought a double irony—it adopted Locke's notion that the Negro had made special contributions to American culture and then removed support from those voices that were considered "too Black" or "too nationalist" that had made that argument all along. Similarly, in art circles Locke found himself decentered, as his argument that Negro artists had had a special contribution to make to American art was widely adopted but without any discussion or support for articulating what exactly was special about that contribution. After the University of North Carolina Press published *Modern Negro Art* by James A. Porter in 1942, the book became the bible of the younger Negro artists like Romare Bearden and Norman Lewis, who had always chafed against Locke's prescriptions that they mine the African tradition for inspiration or create art that would advance Black subjectivity. Porter's argument synchronized perfectly with the ideology of assimilationist inclusion of the 1940s that also made political art, especially racially self-conscious art by Negroes, unpopular. The tide in America had turned away from social-activist notions of aesthetics and toward new ideas made explicit by abstract expressionism—that all true art did not reflect its social milieu. Major art critics like Clement Greenberg would argue vociferously that artists needed to divorce themselves from the dirty business of trying to foment social change through art if they wanted to be originals. Ironically, such trend and market-value-determining critics refused to recognize Norman Lewis as a true participant in abstract expressionism even though he voiced its aesthetic ideology.[4]

Locke responded as best he could. When the Albany Institute of History and Art asked him to write a catalog introduction to its 1944 exhibition of Negro artists, Locke emphasized that their exhibit showed "the happy and almost complete integration of the Negro artist with the trends, styles and standards of present-day American art."[5] He applauded that the younger Negro artist now had freedom to take part in all of the trends of American art and do so without any sense of betrayal of the Negro cause in art. But having been so publicly identified with the notion of the Negro artist as a racial subject, Locke could not pivot quickly enough to claim leadership of the new color-blind Negro art, nor did he really want to. He had created, largely through his writings and work with the Harmon and other race-based institutions, the conditions for the absorption of the Negro artist into the mainstream, but without bringing Black aesthetic politics into that mainstream.

There were other ironies as well. In 1945, the American Association of Adult Education elected him president. This was largely a ceremonial position as the director held the real power in the organization. Locke was pleased with the appointment and the recognition that came with it. But becoming president did not mean he could launch a revolution in adult education based on theories he had lectured about to the organization for more than a decade. And it was that same organization that decided not to reprint any of the Bronze Booklets. A separate Black intellectual formation like the Bronze Booklets now smacked of segregation, even as the system of segregation in school-age and adult education continued unabated. As president Locke did not have the authority to develop what he had hinted at for years—a series of Bronze Booklets for the White people that would reveal their "true history." Instead of taking the lessons from Black educational marginality and allowing him to develop a critical history of American history, adult education, no less than scholarly history, inserted the Negro subject in an American history that remained largely the same, as was done by John Hope Franklin when he published his breakthrough *From Slavery to Freedom* in 1947. That book immediately put in its shadow all of the publications Carter G. Woodson had been pumping out from the Association for the Study of Negro Life and History for decades. Locke praised Franklin's book for that, even as he realized its ambition made that of his Bronze Booklets series seem small. Indeed, during the 1940s sales of the books—with the exception of Bunche's *The World View of Race*—fell off dramatically. In 1945, he ordered more copies of *The Negro in Art* printed without the expensive color insert, thinking he could find funds to bind them once the war ended. But at the war's end, there was no funding to bind and sell his major art book, even though he was president of the AAAE. Certainly, there was no reason for Locke to try and finish the moribund African-centered history of the Negro that Arthur Schomburg had started: he couldn't even move unsold copies of *Adult Education and the Negro* and *The Negro in the Caribbean.*

Locke's personal irony epitomized the plight of the New Negro. Wanting self-determination, and yet working inside White institutions like the AAAE, Locke and the New Negro were boxed in by superficial inclusion. The New Negro had changed the way America talked about itself, renegotiated the spheres of segregated culture by mid-century, and announced a Negro subjectivity in the arts, letters, and social sciences. But it had failed to give the Negro power to reconfigure American education with the insights of the Black experience. Without real institutional power, it—and Locke—could do little but persist in old Negro segregated institutions or accept honorific appointments in liberal White institutions that could not become revolutionary despite his enlivening presence.

Nonetheless, invitations kept coming from White institutions and opened up opportunities he had never enjoyed before. In March 1946, Horace Kallen wrote him with "an unofficial inquiry. Would you be available as Visiting Professor in the Graduate Faculty of the New School for the spring term of 1947?" Kallen was offering Locke $2,000 to $2,500 to come for one semester as "an American philosopher."[6] Locke hurried off a positive reply, "Terribly pleased at your usual but ever surprising friendly concern in my behalf." Locke was definitely interested in the chance to be close to New York and to Kallen. The difficulty was that Howard was on the quarter system. He inquired whether he could give courses in the evening beginning on Thursday so that he could teach at both schools in winter quarter and then take the spring quarter off from Howard. He hoped especially that it would work out because he "had to take a financial loss" going to Wisconsin. "But, of course, it has been more than worth while." It made sense that Locke was resigned to sticking to his post at Howard "with only five more years before retirement and the possibilities of working out from there as a base on such welcome assignments as these, which, incidentally increase my prestige and potential influence at Howard itself."[7] Then, after his successful visit at the New School that spring of 1947, invitation came from the City College of the City University of New York, to be visiting professor in 1948. He took this position, in part, because it allowed him to teach in New York Thursday evenings and all day Friday, while still keeping his post at Howard.

The invitation from Kallen and the New School was significant. Teaching in New York would realize a long-held dream—one that had begun during his stay in Harlem compiling *The New Negro: An Interpretation* and whetted by his hankering after James Weldon Johnson's NYU post and his struggle to direct a cultural center in the 1930s. Locke took the money he had squirreled away from years of projects outside of his job at Howard University to buy a house at 12 Grove Street, a stunning red-brick three-story walk-up in Greenwich Village on October 31, 1946. He bought the house from a Rae Lechner by taking out a mortgage for $11,775.00.[8] The three-story flat already had tenants on the second and third floor, allowing Locke to secure the ground-floor apartment for his own use. Being able to stay over in his own apartment rather than Hotel Theresa made it financially feasible for the now-elderly Locke to teach part-time in New York. Such a purchase contextualizes Locke's assertion that he took a "financial loss" when he went to the University of Wisconsin. It is possible, since Arthur Fauset claimed that Locke borrowed $6,000 from him to make the down payment. In return, Locke let Fauset live in the first-floor apartment when Locke was not in New York, with Fauset decamping to his home in Philadelphia when Locke needed the apartment.[9] Unfortunately, six months earlier, his "Godmother," Charlotte Mason had died, removing another person with whom he could have visited more easily from his new perch in Greenwich Village. He had not visited her since 1944; but if she had been alive, there would have been the chance to have one last rapprochement, without having to run to catch the train or hole up at the Hotel Theresa afterward.

That Locke purchased his New York residence in Greenwich Village, rather than Harlem, was significant. Race took a back seat to sexuality, it appears, since Greenwich Village already had a gay-friendly reputation by the late 1940s. Under the cover of an appointment at the New School, Locke avoided Harlem, where he would have faced more scrutiny of his comings and goings. Then too, Harlem in the late 1940s was a scourge of heroin drug addiction, reeling under an epidemic that put the last nail in the coffin of whatever it was that could be called a renaissance. Harlem might have been too depressing, given the failed dreams that still haunted its streets for him. Perhaps the logic of inclusion was also doing its work on Locke; teaching at a White institution of higher education, Locke sought inclusion in a White bohemian space in Greenwich Village. That did not mean he could avoid the problem of race. Locke revealed to Fauset that upon his first arrival at the house someone had laid the body of a dead rat on its doorstep.[10]

All of these opportunities—to work in an enabling White institution of higher education where being a Negro philosopher made him a celebrity, to work in an environment with peer philosophers who rekindled his zeal to develop a new theory of aesthetics, and to get a book contract from a major publisher to bring all of his insights together—were coming too late for him to take full advantage of them. It was probably too late for him to have made the move to Wisconsin and abandon his East Coast contacts and lovers, but a permanent offer from a university in New York would have allowed him to live and work in the city he loved. But no such offer was forthcoming.

Another invitation was quite welcome. In 1947, Locke was asked to resurrect his annual retrospective reviews of Negro literature for a new publication, *Phylon*, a journal started by W. E. B. Du Bois in 1944. In an article, "Phylon: Science or Propaganda?" Du Bois took on those who denigrated Black intellectual practices that did not adhere to the Myrdal color-blind ideology ascendant during the 1940s.[11] In contrast to Locke, Du Bois was a vigorous seventy-six years old in 1944, capable of reinventing himself by creating in *Phylon* a new *Crisis*-like vehicle for Black intellectual assertion. Once again, Du Bois's boldness created the opportunity for Locke to continue his work of charting the direction of African American literature when other journals believed no such separate intellectual agenda was worthy. That Locke began again in 1947 to chronicle the particular literary trajectory of Negro writing in the postwar period suggests that his intellectual strategy was similar to his academic one—to reverse the postwar practice of Negro inclusion inside White institutions, by including, as of old, reviews of White-authored novels in new retrospective reviews in a Black media institution. Nevertheless, these new retrospective reviews kept alive the notion that Black literature and culture should be discussed separately from the mainstream of American literature. But the double consciousness along with the double burden of teaching two jobs a year was beginning to take its toll.

Then, in 1948, according to his confidant Robert Fennell, an incident took place at Howard that must have shaken Locke. As Fennell noted:

> A man, or a boy really, at the school, accused Locke—the boy was a homosexual prostitute. And he attempted to blackmail Locke, not for

money but for a grade. A meeting was called of a committee consisting
of—let me see, Mordecai Johnson, I believe, Sterling Brown, maybe
Robert Martin, one or two other friends of Locke. The boy was around
20 years old and was attempting to blackmail Locke. Well that boy
didn't know what he was doing. They switched it around on him so they
made him the subject of the inquiry. They said to him, "We have reports
that you are in and out of the men's dormitories, which you are a homosexual prostitute, and we don't want anyone like you in this school."
That boy was a fool—you don't bring a charge like that against a prominent man like that. I saw the man again in 1958. He was a derelict, his
hair falling out. It was remarkable, the change. But the point is you
couldn't track Locke when it came to the homosexual thing. He was
very discreet.[12]

It is not known whether the young man's accusations were true or not, but
having to go before a committee of friends and allies to defend himself against a
student must have been disturbing, especially as Locke was under surveillance
by the FBI. Nevertheless, Locke was able to use his institutional power to crush
an adversary. Instead of the adversary being Jessie Fauset, Albert Barnes,
J. Stanley Durkee, or W. E. B. Du Bois, it was a student, and a homosexual one at
that, who felt the sting of Locke's counter-attack. Notably, in Fennell's recollection there is no concern with whether the accusation of Locke's impropriety was
true or not, merely that "you don't bring a charge like that against a prominent
man like that." But that the younger man had had gumption to bring such a
charge must have shaken Locke, even though he escaped without a public scandal.

Working two jobs, traveling regularly to New York, and increasing threats to
his livelihood in Washington created incredible physical and psychological strain
on Locke. He awoke in the middle of the night on November 21, 1948, gasping
for air and clutching at his chest. He was sweating profusely, as the tightening
in his chest became excruciating. In the dark, a sense of panic overtook him as
he realized that the biggest heart attack of his late adulthood was upon him.
Fortunately, that night, a young intern who answered the phone at the Frederick
Douglass Hospital on Howard University's campus knew exactly who Dr. Locke
was and what to do next. Quickly dispatching an ambulance to 1326 R Street, he
jumped in to accompany the orderlies to Locke's apartment. Ringing the doorbell to the bottom apartment, he woke the landlady, who got the master set of
keys to the building. Upon entering the second-floor apartment, they saw Locke
passed out. The intern carried him down the steps and folded him delicately into
the back of the hearse. This time it would not be carrying him to his grave, but to
the hospital. It was a narrow escape.[13]

Locke had heart attacks throughout his life, even though sometimes it was
difficult to determine whether some of them were real or convenient excuses for

not showing up at engagements or responsibilities he did not wish to honor. But this one was different. A massive collapse of the major artery going into the right aorta required considerable doses of medication to stabilize the heart and eliminate the arrhythmia. Three days later, it was still not certain he would survive. This heart attack was different because at age sixty-three, Locke was far weaker than he had been in 1937 when his last massive attack had come. His health had been poor of late, as the combination of advancing age, overwork, nervous tension, and demanding schedule had begun to make him look and feel older than his years. Given that Locke had suffered from a weakened heart valve from infancy, it was remarkable he had made it to his sixties at all. But Locke's entire life had been a victory of will over physical limitations. Locke, ever sensitive to signs, could see that this heart attack was one of them. He now had to face a burning question: what did he wish to do with his final years? And, relatedly, what would be his legacy?

Locke was the eternal optimist. He believed he could manage the new constraints on his energy imposed by this latest heart attack, and still continue teaching, socializing, and writing, albeit at a slower pace, that he had planned for his active retirement. Perhaps this belief that he could continue to juggle a dozen commitments a week was his undoing. He refused to give up his life to finish his magnum opus, *The Negro in American Culture*. From 1948 to 1954, he continually cited its significance to him. Letters from 1951 to John Rhoden and Richmond Barthé were typical. In the first, he apologized for not seeing Rhoden and Barthé off to Jamaica because of work on the book, "and that is all important right now as all of us know." He recognized that the book was his best chance to ensure his legacy, his own place in history, for as he remarked to Barthé, Locke felt he "must stick to the book: it's an awful bother, but must turn out up to expectation in the long run." But what was Locke ready to sacrifice in order to produce it? Locke did cut back on some of his obligations. In 1948 alone, he declined invitations to attend the Adult Education Conference in Michigan, to serve on the Baha'i planning committee, to participate in a forum on race progress held by the Congress on Racial Equality, and to travel across the country to rescue friends, such as Jimmy Daniels, from the consequences of their own actions. But most of these were obligations he would just as soon abandon in any case. When it came to more visible and long-standing obligations, he tended to fit them in.

Some of these were significant, such as his annual retrospective reviews of literature for *Phylon* magazine. In January 1949, the editor Hill wrote to inquire whether Locke would be able to produce that year's two-part retrospective, as he had already missed the usual end-of-the-year deadline, and hence the usual publication of the reviews in the January and February numbers. Hill even suggested that if Locke's health prevented him from doing the reviews, he was willing to give the responsibility to Lawrence Reddick. But Locke refused to relinquish it; with some obligatory griping about the work—"I have to review Walter White's *A Man Called White*, which nauseates me"—he penned the two segments, submitting the reviews in time for them to appear in March and April issues, respectively. This was understandable. His reviews of particular books had declined; his ability to agent or represent books to publishers had diminished, and his direct influence on writers had shifted from prepublication reading and commentary to guiding their careers through inspirational and personal advice. It made sense to hang on to the retrospective reviews because by the end of the 1940s, they were the main way in which he exerted any critical opinion over African American literature.

Locke used those reviews to produce something profound. His retrospective review for 1949 appeared in 1950 under the provocative title, "Wisdom De Profundis." Using the title of Oscar Wilde's postmortem on his love affair with Alfred Douglas to head his review of the "literature of the Negro," Locke noted that the most powerful literature of the year, from Alan Paton's *Cry, the Beloved Country* to William Faulkner's *Intruder in the Dust*, was written in a gloomy, depressive tone that was found in Wilde's confessions. Here was a brilliant example of Locke using gay literature to inform and subtly critique Black literature. In a sense, Locke made the same point about African American literature, or at least literature about African Americans and Black Africans, at mid-century as Wilde had. It was not the best, but it was the most truthful.

The title of the review, however, signified Locke's own love affair with a much younger man. Maurice Russell was the cause of trouble for Locke, although not the kind that Alfred Douglas posed for Wilde. Not long after his heart attack in 1948, Russell, his long-time lover, abandoned Locke to go live with another man. Locke learned, once again, he could not trust a young man with his heart. As was his tendency, he turned to other men, even fantasizing about relationships with younger men who were not really available, like Arthur Wright. Suddenly alone, impaired, and beleaguered, Locke recommitted himself to writing, although without the zeal that writing with a loved one in mind gave him. The relationship crisis highlighted a wisdom de profundis of his own, that he needed to exhibit some of the passion that Wilde had manifested in his last years to write his opus. He needed to open up, be vulnerable, and risk writing a kind of intellectual confessional if he was to communicate the imaginative possibilities of Negro creativity to the American people.

What had Locke learned over four decades of commitment to the cause of Negro intellectual liberation? A full rebellion against caution was needed to create a conversation-changing book that would answer that question and suggest why his service as the Black Moses of art made a difference. Somewhere in that narrative, subtle subtext, or merely hidden, he needed to hint that the art movement was a product of the homosexual revolution of the 1920s. Yet, as always, the moment he tried to do that in his writing, he found himself checked by being unwilling—or unable—to reveal himself in print, just as he felt checked in revealing himself in the bedroom, according to informants like Owen Dodson and Bruce Nugent.

As seemed always to happen, a person with special qualities emerged once again in Locke's life with whom he could reveal himself privately even when he struggled to reveal himself in print publicly. That person was a vibrant, precocious young man named Douglas Stafford, who may have been an undergraduate or graduate student at Harvard University during the late 1940s and early 1950s when the two became especially close. It is not clear that Locke loved Stafford. Indeed, he probably did not, but his spectacular mind and aggressive sense of confidence in being gay was liberating, and also a welcome contrast to Russell's hesitant ambivalence toward his sexual identity. Where Russell was still questioning in the late 1940s whether he wanted to live "the life," Stafford had no such reservations. In one of his early letters to Locke, Stafford related that Locke's intuition that he, Stafford, was perhaps about to be outed by his classmates, came to fruition. Realizing that rumors about his sexual orientation were circulating, Stafford seized on an opportunity to publicly humiliate a young, effeminate, possibly gay member of a class he was taking, doing it brutally and forcefully as a heterosexist critique, in order to deflect, he hoped permanently, aspersions about his own sexual orientation. Hesitant at first that Locke was being critical of this maneuver to ensure the survival of his subjectivity in a homophobic environment, he was relieved to find that Locke approved. This revealed the inner Locke, the fierce survivor who, at various times over his career, had crushed competitors or destabilized adversaries in a variety of areas, not merely sexual, as part of his practice of subjective sustainability. Yet, faced with that moment of de profundis, that he had had to be, from time to time, both racially and sexually, a kind of monster to survive, what did that mean for a study of what it meant to be Negro in a homophobic, racist America?

Locke revealed life insights on long walks with Stafford when he would circle through Washington during the late 1940s—walks on which the older man advised this up-and-coming gay Black man on how to survive under oppression, as Stafford well knew, but also how to preserve the reason for surviving: to enjoy art, to practice the true purpose of friendship, to value companionship, and to help others who would not destroy one's own life. As was the case with all the others, Locke shared with Stafford his love of classical music, introducing him to less well-known composers, buying records for him—although requiring Stafford to pay him back for them on time—and encouraging the brilliant young man to value education as an end in itself not just a means to a higher-paying job. This mentorship role was the essence of his relationship with all of his young charges in the Black, gay world, from Russell, to Arthur Wright, to Bili Bond and to the up-and-coming Richard Long, perhaps the most gifted of Locke's young mentees, already teaching in the late 1940s at Morgan State in Baltimore. The attention of these other young men helped Locke screw up his courage, heal his broken heart, and recommit himself to writing his book in 1949.

But Locke lacked the brilliant young dialogic partner in the late 1940s and early 1950s to stimulate him to a new formulation for the mid-century. Russell was an intelligent young man who went on to make an outstanding career in New York mental health social services, in part because of mentorship by Locke. But he was no Langston Hughes, no Ralph Bunche, and no Eric Williams, whose conversations with Locke and the last Bronze Booklet, *The Negro in the Caribbean*, might have pricked Locke to address the absence of a hemispheric perspective in his theory of race and culture with an original theory of the Diaspora in his Haiti lectures. Desire for young, original, male thinkers provided a sexual-psychological vitality to make intellectual breakthroughs. But in his later years, he could not find the generative thinker who could teach him how to move in a new direction. Here was Locke's wisdom de profundis that resonated with Wilde's—the quality of one's lovers determines the quality of one's life.

Nevertheless, welcome invitations from his other lovers—institutions— appeared, this one from his beloved Harvard, which invited him, some might say finally, to teach American philosophy for six weeks in the summer of 1950 in Salzburg, Austria, as part of its Salzburg Seminar in American Studies. Interestingly, the invitation hailed not from the philosophy faculty per se, but from an institution started by three Harvard students, who started the seminar in response to the cold war during which they desired to introduce postwar Europe to American civilization. Held in the "Schloss Leopoldskron, a rococo palace built in 1744 by the Archbishop of Salzburg,"[14] the seminar was taught, fittingly, by Margaret Mead and the gay English professor and chronicler of the American Renaissance, F. O. Matthiessen. Locke already knew Matthiessen, who tragically committed suicide the year Locke went to the Salzburg Seminar, a testament to the reality that even being at Harvard, "where these things are understood," as Locke put it in a letter to a young man, did not ensure survival for the gay American intellectual. Matthiessen may even have had a hand in Locke's invitation, because, importantly, the seminar was led by major figures in American Studies, not philosophers, per se. While he was to teach American philosophy that summer, the real focus was on his work charting the influence of the Negro in American civilization. Nonetheless, recognition by Harvard was welcome. It gave Locke an opportunity to put forward in one venue his views on values and cultural pluralism, international peace and foreign policy, and the role of race in creating a unique American culture under the auspices of Harvard, the one institution he had dreamed of teaching at his whole life. Taking place in Salzburg was also sweet. One can imagine Locke holding court in the Schloss Leopoldskron in a city he had visited almost every trip to Europe in August to listen to music at the Salzburg Summer Music Festival. There, two halves of his life—the racial chronicler of the Negro in American culture and the lover of European high aesthetics—came together one beautiful summer in 1950.

While preparing to leave for the trip, Stafford sent him a request. He needed a loan of $200 to help him and his mother over a particularly difficult stretch. A day or two passed before Locke wrote and said no, even though he had helped Stafford in the past with loans, always with Locke's usual proscription that if one paid him back on time, he was always good for another loan. But this time, Locke said no, claiming that because of his weakened medical condition, he had to take an unusual amount of money abroad with him to Salzburg, in case he had a flare-up while in Europe. Of course, this explanation made sense. But, at the same time, given that Locke now owned 12 Grove Street, he should have had financial reserves from years of teaching at two universities. So, it is hard to believe that a $200 loan would have broken him. The reality was that money was also a talisman of power in his relationship with these "bright young men," and Locke was in some respects disappointed, perhaps, in Stafford. Here, too, was a continuing problem for Locke: he could not really trust them. The request for money came out of the blue, after several months of Locke not hearing from Stafford.

After a blissful summer in Austria and a grueling schedule of teaching in the fall, Locke entered 1951 with a sense of renewed commitment to his book. But after a productive spring and summer, a struggle with nervous tension dominated his fall of 1951. Such a bout with nerves was not unusual to Locke; but because of his heart's weakened condition, it was more serious this time. Only by strictly following his doctor's orders for four to five weeks of uninterrupted rest in Washington, D.C.—and no travel—during December and January did he keep this assault from triggering another heart attack. His desire to travel to New York was emotional not financial: Maurice Russell was back in Locke's life and Locke was eager to keep tabs on him, if at all possible, to avoid losing him again. Locke endured a forced diet of love starvation and submerged anxiety precisely when the holiday season freed him to be away from Howard.

Locke's health was increasingly frustrating. In one respect, he was as mentally alert as ever and, with his newfound maturity, even better prepared to do the work he still planned to do. But his nerves and his body were fragile. Always dependent on a seemingly inexhaustible supply of nervous energy to keep numerous projects afloat, that nervous energy now flagged, leaving him perennially tired, or worse, the victim of epileptic-like attacks when his body seemingly turned against him. Of course, the underlying cause was his heart: over the years, he had carefully managed his heart with cures, rest periods, but most important, by pushing his heart, almost exercising and thus strengthening it with constant work. Now, that regime no longer produced positive results, but rather exhaustion and dissipation.

In such moments of lethargy and frustration with his body, the one thing that continued to bring Locke joy and a smile to his face was Russell. Russell had a smooth, gracious manner that was not fake or hysterical, like that of Douglas Stafford. Russell was calming and sublime, a balm in this late winter of Locke's affections. Somehow Locke rallied toward the end of January 1952 to resume teaching the winter and spring quarters. He met his classes regularly, with only a few more unannounced absences than usual. And he found that interacting with his youthful students at Howard University was more stimulating than usual, in part because the restrictions on his travel and speaking engagements meant he spent more time and energy around Howard and in Washington. Yet even such minimal exertion took its toll. Shortly after the end of the spring quarter, once the summer heat and humidity of Washington was upon him, his heart collapsed.

Turning deathly ill in June, Locke was rescued from almost certain death by the intercession of friends. Horace Kallen, hearing from others at the New School that Locke was very ill, contacted a friend, Dr. Wolffe, at the Valley Forge Heart Hospital in Fairview Village, Pennsylvania, and got Locke admitted. Another friend, Margaret Just Butcher, played just as critical a role. As Robert Fennell described it, Butcher rushed in shortly after he was forced to bed, came to his house everyday, made all of the arrangements, and took Locke to Valley Forge Hospital herself. "She was a take-charge sort of woman, who would cuss you out in a minute, but who got things done."[15] Once at the hospital, Locke stayed there the entire summer. In the hands of a heart specialist, he received "the most expert care and a somewhat fresh diagnosis" of his condition, which included an assessment that he suffered from a hyperthyroid condition. Wolffe prescribed the unorthodox treatment of isotope iodine treatments to stabilize the thyroid condition that he felt was aggravating the heart condition. As the result of this treatment and thorough rest away from all the distractions of New York and the heat and humidity of Washington, Locke rallied—once again. Once back at home, Margaret Butcher again came to his aid, visiting him daily, cooking his meals, and encouraging him not to take on any responsibilities. He could write with pride in October to William Cooper, secretary treasurer of the National Conference on Adult Education and the Negro, that while unable to attend the upcoming meeting, "I am back on my feet with prospects for staying so (with care, of course) indefinitely." Nevertheless, he planned to "definitely" retire from teaching next year.

Locke's improved health that fall of 1952 allowed him to devote more time to his book, *The Negro in American Culture*, which was overdue. He had renewed enthusiasm for the project because Butcher, sensing that work on the book was his main source of anxiety, volunteered to help him complete the book. How exactly this commitment came about and what its actual terms were remain a mystery. From several undated letters from Butcher to Locke, it appears that Locke volunteered to pay her to help him with the book. In 1952 and 1953, Locke signed several notes for her, presumably for loans. Perhaps, as a way to thank or reward him for that support, Margaret promised to work on the book.

Such support was crucial if Locke was going to finish the book. He was still teaching full-time, and in his spare time, he had to rest lest he have a relapse. As he confided to Barthé in November, "I just find the chores which I used to do for myself most wearying now, they take such a toll of time and energy." Consequently, he found he had little energy left over to work on the book, despite his best intentions. Aside from an introductory chapter, which had been published in the anthology *New American Writing*, Locke had not completed any of the other chapters of the book by the fall of 1952. Indeed, Butcher later claimed that she penned that essay from Locke's fragmentary notes. What is clear is that by September or October, Butcher had begun to work on the book. "I have 'pulled' the folder, (just the one) on <u>Negro in Am. Drama</u> to take home to work on. My feeling is that I might best be able to 'attack' Chapters 4,6,7,8, as indicated on the revised outline. As you say, I certainly can't 'write like Locke' (I wish I could!) but I can assemble and you can polish." Locke's comment that she couldn't "write like Locke" suggests that there was some tension in the relationship, and further, that she may have been the one who suggested that she write the book as a way to work off the money he had loaned her. Her idea, however, was that if she could pen a first draft based on his notes, he could then edit them into his own voice and not have to expend his limited energy on organizing the material. It also appears from his comment their arrangement was she would ghostwrite the book. Unfortunately for Locke, it appears that Butcher did not finish any drafts that fall.

Despite his restricted regime, Locke continued to get out occasionally to see local performances. "I saw the Bali dancers here," he continued to Barthé. "They are wonderful, and again were a vindication of a culture and a climate that knows how to live and take life beautifully whatever comes." This was one of the beliefs he hoped to foreground in his book. Racism, he still believed, like other social evils, did not prevent anyone, even the Negro, from living a life of beauty. But one of his frustrations, and a factor perhaps in his difficulty writing the book, was that "the Negro" in the early 1950s seemed to Locke uninterested in living a life of beauty in spite of social evils. Indeed, the dominant trend of the current generation of Negroes, as he had opined in "Wisdom *De Profundis*" was away from beauty and retention of ancestral forms of expression. This was as true in Barthé's Diaspora home as in the United States. "I hope," he continued in his letter to Barthé, that "the new hotels [in Jamaica] won't intrude too much on your paradise, and especially that there will be a few unspoiled people left" in the face of the "civilizing process," the White tourism business that was actually making Jamaica economically viable for the first time since slavery.

Barthé recalled years later that during 1952 he begged Locke to give up his position at Howard and the strain of living a closeted life in Washington, D.C., to come and live with him in Jamaica. Locke refused. He wished to make one final run at finishing his magnum opus. Only by finishing the book would he avoid the judgment of his many enemies—and perhaps his own conscience—that he had failed to produce a single major statement of his theory of the Negro in American culture.

The book was not the only or even the main reason Locke did not take up Barthé's offer. Of course, there were many reasons why Locke was not ready to abandon the lifestyle of the single, closeted, Black academic in Washington for Jamaica. For one thing, it would mean the end of his professional career as a prominent Black academic, something he seemed to believe he could continue in what he envisioned was an "active" retirement of writing and lecturing. For another, Locke had medical needs that he believed could only be met within striking distance of major American hospitals. Barthé, however, believed that if Locke could have gotten away from the tensions of the academic life, his heart problems would have dissipated. And Locke did admit that such a change might do him much good. As he noted to de Fonseka, "As soon as I safely can plan either to come abroad where a cheaper currency will make life more easy or to Jamaica where a close friend—Barthé the sculptor[—]has a nice place on the North shore of the island with all the salubriousness one could wish except the expert medical care I immediately need."[16]

But there was another important reason for Locke not to go to Jamaica: he was still in love with Maurice Russell. One week after his letter to Barthé, Locke would go to New York to spend the evening with Russell, as indicated in Locke's cryptic itinerary for the eighth of November. "MVS 9:30–12:30 p.m. [*sic*] Double Irony—discussion of REC celeste give-away Tis not a pity he's a whore." The next day was spent with Russell again, and while similarly intriguing—"[MVR woke REC—one hour late. Reference to MHL—new, Dinner: Athens Chop House"— the sum total of the experience was pleasure. "6:30 train to DC Home—in time 4 Blissful sleep." In his closeted Washington-to-New York romance, Locke had much more of what he longed for here than in Jamaica.

Locke's rekindling his romance with Russell did not mean that Locke was not pursuing other lovers. A monogamous gay relationship, a kind of middle-class marriage between men, was not Locke's ideal. Locke desired an intense emotional relationship with a special person over a long period of time, but also the freedom to sleep with other people at the same time. A case in point was his pursuit of R.E.C., or Robert E. Claybrooks, on his November 8 trip to New York, while Locke was romantically involved with Russell. A month and a half later, Locke received a letter from Claybrooks, which confirmed Locke was still in the game. As usual, Locke had tried to mentor Claybrooks by suggesting that he read a Nathaniel Hawthorne short story.

> <u>David Swann</u> has now been read. It is easy to see how much the premonitory instinct and the element of chance of this story have influenced your life. Naturally, I can see only too clearly where the crux of

the tale may easily apply to me now, and where it might, or might not
have in the past. In being called David; does it presuppose too much on
my part, or on yours?

Claybrooks was intrigued, but also wary. He found himself "old enough and ex-
perienced-wise so that I'm on the qui vive, but there lurks in my thinking the
thought that there is much I cannot encompass." Claybrooks's problem was not
the intellectual challenge of dealing with Locke's formidable mind. "What I am
trying to say, Alain, is that you excite me in every other area but a sexual one.
It has nothing to do with the differences in ages. Of that I'm certain. Perhaps
physical contact was precipitated too soon—I don't know. But I do know, and
this I have withheld until now, an intense feeling of nausea accompanied me
after the initial affair, and I know it would be repeated each time, if such were to
happen again, until I would be estranged, eaten up with hostility."[17] Once again,
Locke had carried a relationship "a step further" than his young friend was
"emotionally equipped to take." The result, once again, was rejection.

Of course, such rebuffs did not deter Locke in the past and did not now. But
the reality could not have been lost on Locke. His ability to get and keep lovers
was declining. Russell, a strikingly handsome man, may very well have recruited
Claybrooks for Locke. The pattern of recruiting, training, and emotionally tor-
turing new assistants, and then inducting them into his sexual menagerie, was
not working as effectively as before.

But instead of spending whatever time Locke had alone without Claybooks
getting deeper into the writing of his book, Locke instead found, at sixty-seven,
that he had little interest in this book. Locke's involvement with the race issue
had been pragmatic, a means to advance himself—to gain recognition, to be esteemed, and ultimately to be loved by the people. But now, as the rewards from
proselytizing the race were remote, Locke showed declining interest in a book
whose rationale was tied to racial recognition. While "REC" closed his letter with
the hope that "some zip has returned to your prose, and that you've regained
some measure of fluidity," the reality was that whatever "zip" Locke had regained, he had applied to the game of love. He was turning away from the kind
of death-embalming aestheticism that led Marcel Proust to cloister himself in
his bedroom for years to write at all hours of the night and day, refusing to see
friends or even to leave his house. By contrast, Locke hit the streets whenever
his wounded heart would let him. Claybrooks hoped the book was "rapidly as-
suming larger and larger status, or should be, within your mind." But was it?
Notecards and correspondence from the last two years of his life lack any sustained or even fleeting reflections on race and culture, but are jammed with
notes of rendezvouses and escapades. Even after his rejection of Locke's sexual
advances, Claybrooks wrote that he was "ever eager that it [the book] should be
a final testimony (in the sense of a probable last, major work) to your intellect

and genius."[18] But the book was not enough to make Claybrooks sleep with him. The book, therefore, became a sign of Locke's decline, his diminished appeal, the face of death. No wonder he avoided it.

A hint at a new message surfaced in one of Locke's shortest and little noticed articles published by *Phylon* in 1950. "Self-Criticism, the Third Dimension in Culture" was written to sum up a special symposium devoted to Black literature by contemporary young African American literary critics, a symposium that, significantly, Locke had not been asked to contribute to as a participant. The articles by J. Saunders Redding, Hugh Gloster, Lawrence Reddick, and others represented the passing of the torch to younger scholars, and yet Locke did not react defensively or competitively as he had done sometimes in the past. He took the theme of the symposium—criticism of Negro literature by Negro critics—and turned it into a more universal concept: that self-criticism within was the necessary step to cultural maturity of any movement. He applauded the main thrust of the "new criticism," that Negro literature had been too mired in protest, self-justification, and plaintive calls for racial justice camouflaged—barely—in short story and novelistic forms. The first dimension was to assert one's right to self-expression, something he had promoted Negro writers doing in 1925; and the second dimension was to "social discoveries of common denominator human universals between Negro situations and others," which made, as the critics in that volume asserted, Negro literature "sounder and more objective." But it was "self-criticism" itself that was really needed and the willingness to direct such "self-criticism" back into self-expression to open up areas of creative exploration off-limits to Negro literature so far.[19]

Here, Locke spoke of the secrets avoided by Negro writers. "I will venture to speak even more plainly on my own responsibility." There were several "taboos of Puritanism, Philistinism and falsely conceived notions of 'race respectability'" in the Negro community that were powerful "repressions" that brought great harm to Negro literature. Negro writers needed to express that "we are all basically and inevitably human" and that being Negro did not eliminate the full range of human emotions from being expressed in Negro life.[20]

> Why then this protective silence about the ambivalence of the Negro upper classes, about the dilemmas of intra-group prejudice and rivalry, about the dramatic inner paradoxes of mixed heritage...or the tragic breach between the Negro elite or the conflict between integration and vested-interest separatism in the present day life of the Negro? These, among others, are the great themes, but they moulder in closed closets like family skeletons rather than shine like the Aladdin's lamps that they really are.[21]

That last line revealed the great, undeveloped theme in Negro literature—the plight and experience of the Negro homosexual in the Black community, caught in a unique "Third Dimension," between alienation from the White community because of race and alienation from the Black community because of sexual orientation. Here was one of the "closed closets like family skeletons" that even Locke had not been able to explore in print or accept enough "consciously and unconsciously" about himself to be able to fire his muse. Here, Locke was approaching the kind of voice that James Baldwin would use to talk about what lay in America's "closets" after the publication in 1956 of the first explicitly homosexual novel by an African American writer, Baldwin.

Perhaps Locke's difficulty finishing his book was that it was not the book he needed to write. He could not continue to write in the closet in 1950 as he had for most of his life. "Self-Criticism" was perhaps Locke's way of rendering publicly his own "self-criticism" for not facing his homosexuality in print. Obviously, the Knopf book was to be a kind of intellectual autobiography; yet, a key issue that had defined his career, his homosexuality, could not be part of the story. Of course, given FBI surveillance of him and the charge brought against him by the student, Locke felt he had even less opportunity to do that than earlier in his career. But if he could have been frank in public, Locke would have admitted that what had stifled the Negro Renaissance was that he and others criticized in this special issue of *Phylon* had not written about what mattered most to them for fear—legitimate fear—that such writings would be used to destroy them. Locke, no less than Negro literature, had been blocked tragically by self-silencing. Locke could pursue sex to the end of his life, but not write about it openly; and that lack of openness to others and perhaps to himself now made him unable to write about himself at all.

At such times of sterility in the past, what helped Locke was to turn to that which was most unlike himself and thereby gain perspective through difference. A case in point was his revision of his earlier dismissive attitude toward the work of the artist Horace Pippin. Locke had known of Pippin's work ever since his inclusion in the Museum of Modern Art show of "folk" artists in 1938, and his purchase of some of Pippin's work from the one-man gallery opening in Philadelphia. But when asked to recommend Pippin for a Guggenheim in 1944, Locke made an ambiguous assessment of what the rewards would be of sending Pippin south to do paintings of Negro life. "I'm not sure what it would produce. It might produce great art. It might fizzle." Locke was uncomfortable with the "primitivism" and "folk" quality of Pippin's art, feeling perhaps that it was so internally focused as to be unnameable to outside influences. But later, when asked to write an essay for a retrospective on the late Pippin's work in 1948, Locke had changed his mind. He suggested that Pippin had achieved a new synthesis, and become a new kind of contemporary artist for "combining folk quality with artistic maturity so uniquely as almost to defy classification."[22] Locke was able to get beyond his own middle-class distaste for "folk" art and realize he needed to develop a new paradigm for what was unique about Pippin's art, and, by extension, what was unique about contemporary Negro art—as it combined the experimental, the new, with the old, the revered, and the traditional, such that a new kind of art emerged from the universal particularity of the Negro experience of America. "Pippin became a blend of the folk-artist and the sophisticated stylist, the 'primitive' and the technical experimenter, the genre-painter and the abstractionist, the negro historical folklorist as in the John Brown series and a Blakeian religious mystic as in *The Holy Mountain* and other symbolic paintings."[23] By meditating self-critically on Pippin, Locke became an "experimenter," a new kind of cultural critic able to escape, if only for one essay, the "closed closets" of Negro elite thinking about art.

Self-criticism was the third dimension in culture in one last sense. If Negro literature became great, it would have to transcend the kind of narrowness of vision that hampered the larger reach of identity-politics formations. Whether focused on working-class culture, queer aesthetics, or Black consciousness poetry, artists of all stripes had to find a way to tell the story of a particular people in a language that touched the souls of all others. This did not mean avoiding the people's experience of racism, sexism, homophobia, and class oppression but to render it in its "universalized particularity." How could those writing about the Negro experience do so in such a way that it became emblematic of the American experience? How could Black writers make the language of the Negro reality convey how tied to the Black experience every American life was? Here, buried in "Self-Criticism, the Third Dimension of Culture," lay an argument about the "universal particularity" of minority discourse in America that could have energized the Random House book.

Locke reached for something of that universal vision when he came to write a review of his Harvard professor's book, *Domination and Powers*, in *Key Reporter*, the journal of the Phi Beta Kappa honor society. This assignment came as part of a broader request to submit regular reviews in the area of "Philosophy, Religion, and Education" to the journal of Phi Beta Kappa, which had inducted him in 1907 after he was at Oxford. Now, with the perspective of more than forty years spent in the field of race scholarship, Locke returned in this article to his first love—the kind of aesthetically informed philosophy of living that Santayana embodied and was able to express in his writings. Santayana embodied Harvard aestheticism and left the United States to settle in Europe, a move Locke had contemplated many times in his past. *Dominations and Powers* was the kind of book Locke needed to write—less a summing up and more a burrowing into new territory with a vision strengthened by years of reflection. Locke noted that Santayana had produced a testament to what the life of reason now confronted— a world of hate, suspicion, and unreason as the price the West was paying for "domination" at mid-century. Santayana confronted contemporary readers with the contradictions no less than ironies embedded in the modern world, and modeled, perhaps too late, a way out of the quagmire of nationalism—that of "calm and urbane historical and cultural detachment" toward the crisis of the postwar era. Locke too was speaking out against the threats to freedom of speech and inquiry of a McCarthy-era America in meetings with other philosophers and intellectuals in the early 1950s.

But while Locke welcomed the "wisdom" of Santayana's book, his review registered there were obvious weaknesses to it. "In spite of the reasonableness of his general position, many readers will find themselves in sharp disagreement with some of Santayana's obviously temperamental quips and biases."[24] Locke's challenge to Santayana was similar if more subtle to that he registered against McKay's life of detachment in *A Long Way from Home*. Commitment to transform the West was more laudable than detached judgment about it. The review, therefore, registered how far Locke had advanced beyond Santayana even if Locke had not produced the corpus of writings his former teacher had. Locke had not followed Santayana's path, had not adopted aloofness as his response to modernity, but instead had plunged into the conflicts at the center of the West's industrial societies in a philosophical practice of engagement rather than detachment. A real breakthrough would have resulted if Locke had been able to take Santayana's *Domination and Powers* as a text to react against and written a book for Alfred Knopf that detailed how wrestling with the West's race question for nearly half a century defined a new role for the American philosopher. Unfortunately, it was too late for that.

The *Key Reporter* assignment also synchronized with a request from Howard University to help its effort to win approval for a Phi Beta Kappa chapter at Howard. Locke threw himself in work for the chapter, coordinating the on-site visit of Brown University's William Hastings and the Phi Beta Kappa committee to campus to interview campus officials and faculty members of Phi Beta Kappa, according to historian Rayford Logan.[25] The effort was successful: on April 8, 1953, in a ceremony in Rankin Chapel at which Ralph Bunche returned to Howard to speak on the occasion, the Gamma Chapter of Phi Beta Kappa was installed. It was a moment of deep consolidation of Locke's four decades of effort to bring the highest standards of scholarly endeavor to Howard University.

But in the period from 1951 to 1953, such service and continued teaching took its toll on the energy Locke had to devote to trying to finish his book, which he would not simply put down and was unable to take up in a sustained way. Locke found that the only effective time for writing was in the mornings. He rose later than usual, predictably after 9, sometimes close to 10. After a light breakfast, he usually had an hour or two of writing—on days he did not teach—before noontime interruptions and the daily search for suitable lunch options began. Since Washington was still rigidly segregated in 1952, the only place Locke found to eat that was suitable to his palate and stomach was Union Station, a bus ride away from his home. After the bus ride home he would take a nap, from which he would awake around 4 P.M. Visitors would normally begin to arrive around 5 or 5:30 P.M. He had only episodic help from Margaret Butcher, whose mother became mentally unstable, limiting how much time Margaret, an administrator in the D.C. public school system, could devote to him. Even more, Margaret may have had some reservations about writing a book for which she might receive no public credit. Locke had, of course, given Margaret money, and it seems that the expectation that she would write the book had been tied to his financial support. Ironically, Locke, who had enlisted a patron to pay Black writers in the Harlem Renaissance who failed, in his mind, to earn the money his patron had paid them, faced a similar situation in 1952: he was a patron anxiously awaiting someone else to produce work he could not produce himself.

Nevertheless, Margaret did make a renewed commitment to the book project in January 1953, aided by an additional assistance Locke provided her. "Stenographer here working on chapter. Will call you Wednesday night or you wire me where you want material sent."[26] Her promise derived from her willingness, she said, to scale back other commitments. "I'm cutting out any extra activities (aside from teaching Mondays, Wednesdays, and Fridays)....If you can outline what other chapters I can do, and give me either references or materials, I'll divide the working days. There's no nonsense on this. It's now or never."[27] Butcher had finished the first draft of her own dissertation and thus felt comfortable with a schedule that involved teaching three days a week, revising her dissertation, and drafting Locke's chapters. But what does not surface from the correspondence is what arrangement the two of them had agreed to whereby she drafted the chapters of his book. If the arrangement was still that she was ghost-writing the book that might explain why she did not make any progress on it. After all, the contract for the book was given to Locke alone, and it was a good contract, according to Locke, because "after publication in hard back form by Knopf, the text is to be reprinted in these new popular paper backs in the Mentor New American Library Series, and to be distributed widely they tell me." Yet he could not write the book, and, apparently, neither could she. Despite her assurances to work on the project, little if any real writing took place that winter and spring of 1953.

Having decided to retire in 1953, after the Phi Beta Kappa chapter was established, Locke got an unexpected reward in his final year at Howard. The university decided to confer upon him an honorary Doctorate of Humane Letters. That warmed Locke's heart and helped him to feel that his years teaching at America's premier Black university had not been a waste. Indeed, the award helped him to separate from an institution that had anchored him, for better or worse, for forty years. Graduation also meant packing up and moving north to take up full-time residence at 12 Grove Street. In anticipation of the move, Arthur Fauset graciously moved into his own apartment on the second floor and left the entire ground-floor apartment for Locke alone. Robert Martin, Locke's loyal "Boy Friday" on campus, volunteered to pack up Locke's office, as well as his apartment, and helped arrange the shipping of artifacts and personal effects to New York. But, as Locke remarked to Barthé, no one could help with the psychological strain. The weather, however, miraculously did help. Just three weeks before he moved on June 13, the humidity that hung over Washington, D.C., lifted and cooler weather descended on the usually steamy city. That made sorting, shipping, and moving more bearable than he had hoped.

But Washington was not done with him, yet. In January 1953, the FBI had reopened its investigation of Locke and on May 21 hauled him back into FBI headquarters to interview him. Seriously ill, withered, and frail, Locke neverthe-less was ready for the questions, giving himself a spirited defense while admit-ting he had belonged to some of the organizations cited by the US Attorney General, the House Un-American Activities Committee (HUAC), or the California Committee on Un-American Activities. The list of organizations that the FBI presented him this time was much longer, but Locke's answers were more to the point, stating repeatedly that he had not knowingly joined or remained in any organization that advocated the overthrow of the government.

The FBI was especially interested in Locke's participation in a series of Black radical organizations begun or headed by Paul Robeson, William Hunton, or Max Yergen. According to FBI transcripts of the interview:

> Locke continued that he had been a board member of the Council on African Affairs at the invitation of the executive secretary by the name of [William] Hunton who was formerly a Howard University professor and a member of the National Negro Congress.[28]

Locke told them he had met "an old friend of his named Max Yergen" who told him the Council was being launched to promote the study of "African culture and arts." The FBI seemed to garble its transcript of the interview, for it recorded Locke as saying that he was "quite disappointed when Ralph Bunche was placed on the board of the council . . . and was quite pleased at a later time to be included as a member of this organization." But apparently things turned sour when a struggle for control of the Council erupted between Yergen and Paul Robeson, leading Locke eventually to resign from the organization. Similarly, Locke claimed he had resigned from the National Negro Congress after the defection of A. Philip Randolph, who claimed communists had infiltrated the organization. He admitted to being an honorary member of the Southern Negro Congress, because he supported its "professed principles of getting intelligent youthful voters to strive for civic and economic equality" and had given lectures at the George Washington Carver School in New York at the "request of Miss Gwendolyn Bennett," formerly a colleague at Howard University. His lectures at the Carver School took place in the fall term of 1943, after his return from Haiti, and led to lectures at the Philadelphia School of Social Science and Art in 1945. But Locke asserted that he "separated all of his connections with" such schools once he realized they were "Communistically inclined."[29] They were so listed by the Attorney General of the United States.

Clearly, Locke had not been cowed by the scrutiny. He had continued to participate in Leftist organizations and educational ventures after his interview with the FBI in 1942. The month before his second interview Locke had been quoted in the *Washington Post* as being highly critical of the campaign, launched by Illinois senator William E. Jenner and Wisconsin senator Joseph McCarthy, to "probe into what students should be taught in" college. "How are we as teachers going to face issues of the contemporary world when we are not completely free to give our students any guidance?" Locke might be unafraid, but the FBI was closely monitoring public activities.

Locke's defense of academic freedom and his associations with radical organizations were not the only and may not have been the real cause of his being interviewed a second time in May 1953. The reopening of the investigation of Alain Locke may have occurred because someone in Baltimore, Maryland, whose name was blacked out in FBI documents, had accused Locke of being a homosexual. Locke did not know that, but he would not have been surprised. Baltimore was hardly a better environment for Black gay men than Washington. His friend Richard Long wrote Locke that the president of the Baltimore Black college at Morgan State suspected every unmarried male teacher might be gay. That last interview at FBI headquarters must have confirmed for Locke it was time to leave Washington, D.C., and its environs for safer ground in New York.

This informant contextualizes Locke's decision not to allow Douglas Stafford to room with him while the latter was stationed in military school in Washington, D.C. Stafford wrote that he would not be in Locke's way, not be a bother, nor cramp his older friend's freedom or lifestyle. But Locke wrote back quickly to state that it was out of the question. Not only would it have been complicated, given that Margaret was still taking care of Locke on a weekly basis, but Locke could also not risk having his gay lifestyle marked by a living arrangement with another man in Washington. Once again, what might have been a satisfying companionship with one of the brightest of the young men he knew was squashed by at least the threat of it being used against him.

On June 8, 1953, the Monday before Locke moved out of his forty-year residence on 1326 R Street, NW, Washington restaurants began to desegregate their dining rooms. Three African Americans, who had been forced to leave a Washington restaurant, sued the restaurant for violation of their civil rights; and their lawyers discovered that a neglected 1873 District law still on the books required any "licensed restaurant, eating house, barroom, sample room, ice cream saloon, or soda fountain room" to serve "any well-behaved and respectable person." The action brought an end to the racial barriers at all of Washington's better restaurants, but too late to do Locke any good. "I found it quite an irony," he wrote Mrs.

Biddle, "that Washington became more livable just ten days before I left. What many hours and energy were lost in trips twice daily to Union Station for meals during over twenty five of those years is both hard to imagine and contemplate."[30] Regardless of the long-standing ties to the nation's capital, it was good for Locke to leave behind its legacy of racism and its sexual constriction.

Locke's arrival in New York was filled with optimism. Once Locke moved in he turned the first-floor apartment into a shrine to the new, more modern Alain Locke. Stafford, after a visit, confirmed as much, "I much prefer Grove Street. While the R Street location was fine given that it certainly reflected you, I found the object spatial ratio overwhelming at R Street. Now, at Grove Street, I come away with clear impressions of the art objects and can appreciate it more than I ever could on R Street."[31]

After getting settled, Locke spent July and August back at Valley Forge Hospital under Dr. Wolffe's care. Consequently, Locke faced the fall with renewed health, but not enough for the kind of "active retirement" he had envisioned. Even in New York, Locke found the daily grind of work on his book strenuous, while Margaret Butcher was further away and swamped with responsibilities. The book lay fallow.

Living in New York gave him freedom and time to do "some of the things that gave him joy," as Arthur Fauset recalled. He continued to go to Small's Paradise "on Friday nights," which Fauset called a "Bohemian retreat," and would relate "some of the stories" and "laugh about what had taken place that evening" with Fauset. Thus, "no matter how ill he was he could usually get a great deal out of the hours that he would spend in a place like that." Small's Paradise was his home away from home in the fall of 1953 and the winter of 1954, where he could mix openly with his gay friends and laugh with younger folk about the foibles of life behind his particular "veil."

On June 4, 1954, Locke's doctor at Mt. Sinai Hospital requested he come in for a checkup. Fauset recalled:

> I walked with him through the street, through Grove Street and to 8th Avenue where the subway was.... It was in the day time and we, well of course, we had to walk. We had to take the bus or the train at 8th Avenue in order to get to the hospital. And I remember how sad I felt because I realized that Locke perhaps would not make that walk again. And, he was not in shape to make the walk then. But, there was no transportation, at least no transportation in that direction, we, [had to walk] from our home on Grove Street slowly but not with too great difficulty, to the subway or bus. And we went on then of course down 50th Street there where Mt. Sinai is and we then went into the hospital.[32]

Locke did not want to go to the hospital. After the initial examination, a younger doctor was ready to release Locke to go home. But because of his youth, he had to get clearance from the senior doctor on staff. When that doctor examined Locke, he stated, "Oh, I didn't know that this man was as ill as he is. I didn't know his condition had deteriorated. We can't release him." Locke was very upset because he wanted to get out of the hospital and had told Fauset he was coming home. According to Fauset, "the next time I saw him—I went up to where they were going to bed him and stayed a few minutes and left—after he was in the hospital . . . he was fixed in a way that nothing else that I have seen affects me. It reflects my thought that he was tied down in a hospital." Remarkably, even though Locke was very ill, he had been able to "navigate himself and more or less do everything that the average person does" at home.[33] Now he was trapped in the hospital and unable to return home.

Fauset thought that if he could get Locke admitted back at the Valley Forge Hospital, where the radical treatment of Dr. Wolffe had saved Locke before, that maybe he could survive. Fauset reached Dr. Wolffe, who agreed to take him. But by then it was too late. On June 9, five days after he was admitted to Mt. Sinai, Locke was dead.

Until the end, Locke was optimistic and looking forward to future projects, and wanting most of all to live.

44

The New Negro Lives

Shortly after his death that summer of 1954, visitors filed in singly or in small groups to Benta's Funeral Home at 157 West 132nd Street in Harlem to view Locke's body lying in the parlor. It seemed incongruous that this tiny Black man, who was perpetually in motion, suddenly lay still in a plain wooden box. Thirty-two years after his mother's wake, at least Alain was not sitting up in his home. Arthur Fauset made sure the arrangements at Benta's were proper and top-notch. More important than the funeral were the people there. There was W. E. B. Du Bois and his wife, Shirley Graham Du Bois, Mrs. Paul Robeson, Charles Johnson—luminaries of Black intellectual culture—alongside Bili Bond Locke's sometime lover, Maurice Russell, the love of Locke's life, sculptor Richmond Barthé, and Mary Beattie Brady, his best ally in the work of promoting African American visual arts—a community that was diverse sexually, socially, racially, and class-wise, but a community nonetheless created by the man now lying in peace in Harlem. He had been the one alienated from Black folks' usual congregations, and kept on the outside by hatred of his kind. He had empowered gay aesthetics to change the discourse of the Negro in America and shifted the image of the Negro from that of a social science object to be pitied, to be seen, at least by the elite thinkers of the nation, as the originator of the only superlative culture America had yet given to the world. He had pulled together these people who did not know one another into a kind of family for himself and other Black queers. Negro art had made this community, and now its architect was gone.

But Locke's work was not done. Locke had formed that community with a higher purpose—to subjectivize the Negro, to spur the Negro to become a shaper of the world around him or her with unflinching confidence and supreme competence to change the climate of hate and defeat. Though he critiqued the language of propaganda his wake minister Du Bois had used, Locke had weaponized art to weaponize Negroes to give them the consciousness that their role was to transform the race through their brilliance.

While Du Bois gave one of his most poignant and powerful eulogies about his old enemy that decried America for not letting Alain Locke be a philosopher without the burden of race, others in the small crowd slipped away to 12 Grove

Street, to Locke's first-floor apartment, where they entered the beautiful, modernist sanctuary that they had visited when Locke was alive. Gripped by grief or more likely greed, they took objects of art they had eyed while talking with the old man. They had listened to him lecture them for hours about art and the meaning it had, to show the world that Negroes were a great race, but they had not really understood. Instead, his friends took pieces of him to their homes (or maybe to the pawn shop) to admire or profit from. They took for themselves what he intended for the community and proved yet again that his work was not finished.

Fortunately, not everything of value in Locke's large art collection was on display at his home; most of it was tucked away safely in a warehouse in New York. When asked about the theft, Arthur Fauset, whose responsibility it was to handle the funeral arrangements and execute his estate, blamed the loss on Myron O'Higgins, the other executor named in Locke's will, because Locke had given O'Higgins the responsibility to arrange for the collection to be shipped to Howard University. Fauset claimed that O'Higgins took a long time to make the trip from Chicago to New York to take control of the collection. "What was one to do?" Fauset replied weakly. "Put it in storage?"[1]

Others were less kind. "That fool Arthur Fauset" was what Robert Fennell called him. The intermittent theft went on for weeks, apparently, while Fauset waited for O'Higgins to travel to New York. Did Fauset resent that Locke had chosen another person, perhaps a closer friend, to handle the most valuable part of his estate? Why did O'Higgins delay coming to New York to handle what he must have realized was a priceless collection of art? Fennell may have provided a clue. He noted that someone, who was not a friend of Locke's or his close associates, got a copy of Locke's will and published it in the Baltimore Black newspaper, the *AFRO*. Fennell emphasized that such a publication was not welcomed by those listed in it, including Fauset, O'Higgins, William McAllister, the Howard University philosophy professor who had witnessed the will, and others, for such public association with Locke outed them. As Fauset and O'Higgins, so this reasoning goes, worried about how connection with Locke's public passing colored their reputations, others less concerned about their reputations stole from that estate with impunity. One could characterize this as the problem of homosexual succession, for without a family Locke's legacy was dependent on the competency of those who suddenly wanted as little public connection as possible with this queer Black intellectual.

Locke's will was a magnificent act of generosity. He left half of 12 Grove Street to Howard University, the other half to Arthur Fauset. To Howard University he donated his art collection to be mounted in a special permanent exhibition in the university's Fine Arts building. The rest of his net worth, including two houses he owned in Philadelphia, several US saving bonds, retirement and liability insurance policies, plus approximately $5,000 in cash, were deeded to his estate, to be used to ensure the transfer of his library, papers, and effects to Howard University and set up in a separate collection. Whatever funds remained were to be used for the processing and publication of such papers as his executors, each receiving $500, and Howard University, deemed appropriate. Certainly, this was one of the most generous donations of a professor's wealth to Howard University. Thomas Dyett, Locke's long-time lawyer, moved quickly to process Locke's will in order that Howard could receive this largesse, contacting and working closely with George E. C. Hayes, general counsel for Howard University.[2]

Just as quickly the process encountered difficulties. First, Locke's will was in a safety deposit box in a Washington, D.C., bank, requiring a court order to transfer it to New York. Once the will was filed, more drama emerged from Arthur Fauset. The will stipulated that Fauset could live in the house on Grove Street for five years, but he was ready to help Howard sell the property and allow half of the proceeds to go to Howard quickly. But there was a rub. Fauset presented to Dyett a note for $6,500 dollars, which he said Locke borrowed from him for the house's down payment. As it turned out, the safety deposit box also contained a note that Fauset owed Locke (and now his estate) $2,000. Anxious, perhaps, not to have to come up with that amount from his own finances, Fauset proposed that the two amounts be allowed to cancel each other out—an "exceedingly generous offer," as Dyett noted. As Dyett also noted, there was no proof that Locke still owed Fauset this money, now that "one of the parties is dead." But, as Fauset claimed, the two of them were to settle up this amount, but never got around to it because Locke to the very end believed he would not die.[3]

All of these negotiations and transfers lasted into 1956, when Fauset brought another problem to the attention of Dyett and the chief counsel of Howard University, who were collectively trying to liquidate Locke's assets and bring them to Howard. Not long after Locke passed away and Myron O'Higgins had finally removed his apartment's remaining art objects, Fauset rented it out to Michelle Dougherty, a White woman. Dougherty complained to Fauset that the door to her apartment was difficult to open and needed repair, but he did not attend to it. One day, Dougherty claimed, coming home with groceries, she struggled with the door and when pushing it, it gave way, and she fell to the ground. Afterward, she informed Fauset of her injuries, as he relayed the story to Dyett, and demanded financial compensation. These demands grew until Fauset had to bring them to the attention of Dyett and Hayes, especially since Dougherty refused to accept the $500 Fauset offered and threatened to sue. The complication emerged that this suit could be made against Howard University, as co-owner of 12 Grove Street, because Fauset had neglected to renew the liability insurance on the house after Locke had died. Fauset claimed that a transfer of the policy and the departure of the original insurance agent were responsible for a bill not being sent to the house. But as Hayes noted, it was most "unfortunate" that Fauset had been so neglectful, especially when one considered that Fauset was a "real estate" man. As executor of the estate and co-owner of the property, his first responsibility was to keep it free and clear.

Fauset quickly sought buyers for the 12 Grove Street property, but as late as 1960, Dougherty was still living there and still was set on getting a large compensation, especially once she learned Howard University owned the property. Although Fauset assured them she would not be a problem, and even Hayes believed that Howard could not be sued, Miss Dougherty brought suit in the United States District Court in Washington, D.C., for $50,000 in damages—against Howard University and Fauset, six years after Locke's death. Fauset was doing a good job confirming Fennell's assessment that he was a "fool."[4]

A deeper irony pervaded the whole struggle between Dougherty, Howard, and Fauset. Fennell remarked that Locke had only rented out apartments in 12 Grove Street to Whites. "Niggers will break things up," Fennell recalled Locke's quip. But what Locke could not have foreseen was that a White person threatened the transfer of his wealth to those at Howard whom Locke wanted to benefit from a life of paid lectures and wealth accumulation. In reality, Whites and African Americans were no different when it came to wanting to be rewarded for the stupidity of landowners.[5]

Irony continued to dog Locke's legacy. Once his art collection arrived at Howard, James Porter rushed to put the stunning collection of African art on view. An exhibition in 1960 brought attention to the gift precisely at a time when international attention was focused on the emergence of African nations from European colonialism. While the collection was beautifully hung, it was not secured. A beautiful collection of African ivories disappeared. After this temporary exhibition and the fiasco of lost treasures, Locke's art collection was locked away. Nevertheless, a priceless African staff disappeared. A few university administrators cruised through the collection of African American–centered art and selected a piece to adorn their offices. Upon their retirement, sometimes the piece could not be found. Queen-like aesthetes James Porter, as an art historian, and James Herring, as director of the Howard Gallery of Art of the Art Department, had made careers out of dismissing the importance of Locke's African-centered philosophies of art and bore the responsibility for this loss of art, since they were the campus authorities on art. Their bias against Locke and the African art that predominated in his collection may have made it difficult for them to take seriously the securing of Locke's collection. Yet Howard's rank and file acquired his art because of its spiritual value to them. Theft, whether in Harlem or in Washington, D.C., showed Locke had not been wrong. Art spoke to the people; and when given a chance to have it, to hold it, to display it in their personal space, they did, and incorporated its subject-enhancing power into their lives.

A different type of disappearance occurred with regard to the collection of Locke's personal effects. A rumor circulated that amid the hundreds of boxes of correspondence, unpublished essays, and drafts of speeches, a curious box was found by the head of the Moorland-Spingarn Research Center, Dorothy Porter, James Porter's wife. In that box, reputedly, Locke had collected semen samples from those with whom he had had sex. It was his way of proving to himself—and perhaps to others whom he showed the box and its contents—that he had slept with men who denied it afterward. An interview with Porter late in her life confirmed that she had thrown the box out, in an effort to protect him—and especially the university—from scandal. Other items, such as photographs, graphic material, and explicit items were discarded as well, in an understandable act of concern for how such information could be used against him and Howard University. But irreplaceable information about Locke's lovers and his habits, information that could prove or disprove rumors and innuendoes, vanished. Mrs. Porter also did not realize the dream of Locke's will to have a room devoted to his collection like the one given to Jesse Moorland and Arthur Spingarn. Instead, Porter dispersed his books throughout the library's regular circulating collection, perhaps believing they would be more accessible to students that way.

Fauset, however, had the most difficulty of anyone in fulfilling the mandate Locke gave him. That extended even to the question of what to do with Locke's ashes after he was cremated. Apparently, Locke did not want his body to be buried. Margaret Butcher, who had clashed with others around Locke in the past, traveled to New York for the funeral and stated she thought that Locke's ashes should be buried in Philadelphia.[6] Butcher fulfilled her commitment to Locke in another way, publishing a book based on Locke's writings and her own work with him in his last years, titled *The Negro in American Culture*, two years after his death. But Fauset, claiming authority from Locke to handle this part of his passing, refused to let her have Locke buried. Perhaps Fauset, another Black Philadelphian, worried that a burial in Philadelphia would draw unwanted attention to Locke as a gay man. That Fauset was defensive about this aspect of Locke's identity was revealed when he described homosexuality as a disease, and thus of very little importance in a biography of Locke.[7] The struggle for power between Locke's homosexual business partner and his heterosexual pseudo-god daughter represented a power struggle between traditional patriarchy and a gay fraternity laying to rest the most out member of its community.

Butcher and Fauset wrangled back and forth, apparently for days, over the proper burial site for Locke's ashes. Eventually, Butcher gave up and left New York to return to Washington. Fauset, unable to make a firm decision, kept the ashes with him. In a repeat of what had occurred thirty years earlier when Locke kept the ashes of his mother on the mantle in 1326 R Street, Fauset kept Locke's ashes in his residences until, in 1983, he passed away. Fauset's niece, Conchita Porter Morison, kept the ashes but later gave them to Reverend Sadie Mitchell, associate at St. Thomas Church, who put them in a bag on which was written the inscription, "Cremains given to Locke's friend, Dr. Arthur Huff Fauset. Arthur is deceased." She kept the remains intending to give them to Howard, but never did.[8]

Instead, Locke's ashes languished in her possession until sometime in the 1990s when J. Weldon Norris, a musician and later historian of music at Howard, visited St. Thomas in connection with a concert. He was eating dinner with friends when a lady walked up to him and said, "Dr. Norris, could you please do me a favor?" When Norris heard she wanted to give him the philosopher's remains, "all our forks stopped in midair," he said. Norris transported the ashes to Howard University, where Locke's papers reside in the manuscript division of the Moorland-Spingarn Research Center.[9]

By then, Howard University had recovered from the shock of receiving materials that it thought might embarrass the institution. Dorothy Porter, deceased by the 1990s, had acted responsibly in beginning the processing of Locke's papers in the early 1960s, when a new generation of young people imbued with a sense of racial self-consciousness as a positive attribute of their identity emerged at Howard and on college campuses demanding an education relevant to their Blackness. Race, African art, and African consciousness were suddenly revived and thriving among Black youth in America, and Locke's constellation of interests—African art, African Diaspora consciousness, Black literature—were in vogue again, even if the students knew nothing about Locke's homosexuality. This new youth movement was angry, curious, and, though frequently homophobic, looked back to the generation of the 1920s as their forerunners.

Several publishers took advantage of this new interest in identity by reissuing Locke's book, *The New Negro*, in paperback, which gained a new audience in the Black Studies courses that proliferated through American colleges and universities during the late 1960s and early 1970s. Even Bronze Booklets from his moribund Associates of Negro Folk Education were rediscovered, republished, and reread. Locke's publishing enterprise made visible to a new generation that it had a self-conscious aesthetic and intellectual history. A unitary system of knowledge that included art, poetry, fiction, social criticism, music, and history existed that race-conscious intellectuals in the past had created for what became known as the Black consciousness movement in the 1960s. When Michael Winston and Thomas Battle took over leadership of Moorland-Spingarn Research Center, they featured Locke's writings and papers as the nearly invisible forerunner of this movement.

Even some enemies became converts. James Porter applied for a grant to travel through Africa, where he became energized by his intimate exposure to African art. When he returned to the United States, his art began to reflect a more abstract approach to the figure based on such African principles of design as elongation and simplification of forms. Porter never acknowledged that Locke's theory had been borne out in his own practice—that exposure to African art could reinvigorate a moribund Negro American artist. But he did not have to. As he relinquished the chairmanship of the Howard University Art Department in the 1960s, the Black Arts Movement shaped the aesthetic vision of those who came after him at Howard, including Ed Love and Jeff Donaldson, the latter who launched with others the AfriCoba Movement. Under their leadership, the Art Department moved away from the assimilationist orientation that success for the Black artist meant insertion into the American mainstream and toward a global African Diasporic perspective on aesthetics. Donaldson went to Africa and brought back beautiful works of African art. Artists and art teachers at Howard gathered together Locke's donation of African art to Howard, secured them, and beautifully displayed them along with Donaldson's pieces from Africa in a permanent exhibition in the Fine Arts Department at Howard University. Locke's African art had found a home.

But where was Locke? Until recent years, no one knew. A White Rhodes Scholar, Jack Zoeller, and a Black Rhodes Scholar, George Keys, visited the Alain Locke Papers and discovered Locke's ashes in the Moorland-Spingarn Research Center manuscript division. They sensed an anomaly: Locke's remains stood on a shelf in a library and not interred. After a fundraising effort among several Black Rhodes Scholars (John Edgar Wideman, the writer, and J. Stanley Sanders, the lawyer, the first two Black Rhodes Scholars after Locke in 1963), Keys and Zoeller worked with Kurt Schmoke, the former Baltimore mayor, and Howard University to bring Locke's remains to the Congressional Cemetery in Washington, D.C. Alain Locke was finally buried on September 13, 2014. Oxford and Howard, two institutional lovers Locke was most ambivalent about during his life, provided a final resting place for his remains.

But did Locke want to be buried? No evidence suggests that he did. Indeed, the evidence suggests that he preferred not to be interred. Robert Fennell stated that Locke and Fauset had a pact that whoever died first, the other would handle the deceased's funeral arrangements. Fauset had resisted Margaret Butcher's attempt to bury Locke in Philadelphia. Was Fauset resistant to Butcher's desire to have Locke buried in Philadelphia because Fauset did not want Locke buried in Philadelphia or buried at all? It seems the latter, since Fauset, who easily could have buried Locke in New York or Washington, kept possession of the ashes until his death. Part of Locke's decision to cremate his mother was to keep her remains close to him, not hidden away underground to be forgotten. In asking Fauset to cremate him, Locke may have wanted to remain above ground, in the midst of living beings, an influence. Locke knew he would be dead, but he did not want to be buried. But Howard, by now the mature spouse Locke never had, stepped in and did the right thing. As E. Ethelbert Miller put it, "We can't have Dr. Locke up on the shelf." Appropriately interred in a dignified ceremony, Locke, the lifelong vagabond, finally came to rest.[10]

Toward the end, Locke could not see actually what he had done. He had made the discourse over Black aesthetics central to intellectual discussion of Black politics in ways it had never been before. He had nurtured two generations of Black writers, had birthed a discourse of the necessity of Black visual artists that

ensured their visibility and created an interdisciplinary space for Black literature, art, theater, and dance that made each critical to the humanities and
American Studies, by exposing the criticality, epistemologies, and social implications of Black art creativity in his essays and exhibition catalogs. He had launched
a new cultural anthropology of modernity in his Harlem issue of *Survey Graphic*
and *The New Negro: An Interpretation*, by showing how Black people assimilated
White culture through migration north, but put the acquired cultures to their
own uses. In the process, Locke defined the relevance of cultural pluralism to an
understanding of how difference was lived inside of America, rather than as a
project of "primitive" peoples outside of it. Perhaps most profoundly, he defined
identity as constructed in response to space, becoming a philosopher of spatial
analysis as much as cultural pluralism, because he made visible how African
Americans redefine urban space through a unique approach to assimilation.
Locke found something other observers like Melville Herskovits had missed but
learned—that Black migrants to Harlem in the 1920s not only assimilated
mainstream American popular culture but directed it toward their own racial
purposes, because they had the aesthetic facility to stylize mainstream culture
in their own way—wear commercial White clothing in a Black style, to play
standard American tunes and create jazz, that is, be independent aesthetic in-
novators on the level of form wherever they went in the United States and
throughout the "Three Americas."

Survival in the American social order had forced him to abandon some of
these insights in favor of others to remain afloat. Nonetheless, in the concept
of the New Negro, he put his finger on the often ignored but absolutely crucial
feature of the African American experience—the capacity of an oppressed
people to reinvent itself time and again in the most mean circumstances one
could imagine. Even more than identifying it in the Black experience, he embodied that principle in his own intellectual life, reinventing himself almost every
half-decade with a new voice, a new set of concerns, and a new array of insights
into the American character as well as the African American experience. In that
sense, his theory of culture is confirmed by all that came after it—the bebop
jazz era, the Black abstractionism of Norman Lewis, Alma Thomas, and Mark
Bradford, cool jazz, rhythm and blues, hip-hop—even if he was not sympathetic
to those movements on the level of taste. He realized that Black creativity
erupted every ten years or less in new iterations of formal inventiveness. He
found such creativity alive on the streets of Harlem, where nestled in the capital
of capitalism, New York welcomed artists who refused to succumb to its soul-
defeating logic.

Locke's failure was his success. Although Harlem never lived up to his prog-
nostications, his idea that Black aesthetics was alive on the streets of urban
communities of the American North and could be tapped to vitalize those communities remains pregnant with possibilities. His innovation of starting art

centers jump-started community renewal by giving artists work through the WPA and bringing art instruction to beleaguered children and adults. In the twenty-first century, his theory that aesthetics could catalyze a social, economic, and even political renaissance of Black communities is not so much wrong as untested. Art could interrupt the logic of internalized self-destruction if that is desired. The question Locke never faced is, is it desired? If the answer is yes, his formula has a chance of success. Locke was naive in many ways about the workings of racism, how it structured not only African American life but also his life, his opportunities, and his failures. But what he refused to do as so many others had done when facing the "racial mountain," as Hughes memorably put it, was be defeated by it.

Locke learned an inconvenient truth—that the New Negro could not achieve his or her goals without White resources. He underwent a painful journey to learn how to gain White patronage without succumbing to its psychopathologies. With his relationship with Mrs. Mason, he gave up the independence the New Negro was supposed to have in order to acquire some of the power that she had—with disastrous consequences. But Locke became one of the most innovative nonprofit entrepreneurs of culture in the twentieth century by transitioning to institutional from individual patronage and advocating for Black intellectual agency without abandoning the need to dialogue with White administrators and their institutional agendas.

Locke's psychosocial skill as a harmonizer of divergent interests, perhaps gained as a young child from a household of strong-minded, disagreeing parents, became a way to create collaboration across difference that moved the ball forward in adult education and progressive community education. That skill allowed Locke to go outside of academia and find support for elite, trained, Black radical scholarship to reach a wider public, a still unrealized aspect of Black Studies today. Dying a few days after the *Brown v. Board of Education* Supreme Court decision desegregating American education, Locke perhaps passed away believing that segregation would end and his racial adult-education efforts would no longer be necessary. But sixty years later, a transracial educational system still is needed to deliver accessible scholarly knowledge to segregated adults.

Hidden to those who filed in to pay their last respects to Locke was that lying there was a radical philosopher, who tied his aesthetic theorizing to a radical critique of race and class in modern society. His original theory of how race is shaped by economic and demographic flows of modern society remains an underdeveloped theory of the sociology of modern life in the West. That theory allowed him to accommodate and improve the theorizing of Black Marxists in the 1930s like Ralph Bunche and Richard Wright, and to join with others, like Arthur Fauset, John P. Davis, Doxey Wilkerson, and Thyra Edwards more radical than he, to knit Black aesthetics to calls for revolution.

Locke evolved from seeing art as an alternative to politics to seeing art as a space of political imagination and a path to revolutionary freedom. His participation in numerous anti-fascist and pro-communist spaces in the 1930s and 1940s, and even in the last years of his life, drew the FBI's attention and harassment. This was particularly frightful given that Locke was a closeted homosexual and vulnerable to threats to his career and livelihood from the FBI. But he did not run and hide. Instead, he fenced with the FBI to the very end of his life and refused to stop associating with known radicals and their organizations. In the end, the most profound product of the Harlem Renaissance was not the books, poems, or short stories, but people like Locke, the New Negroes themselves.

Locke and an unidentified group of friends at a nightclub, New York, ca. 1953.
Courtesy of the Moorland-Spingarn Research Center, Howard University.

Epilogue

"Beauty. Its variety is infinite, its possibility is endless," as W. E. B. Du Bois wrote in 1926. He went on to note, however, that beauty is denied the "mass of human beings" who are "choked away from it, and their lives distorted and made ugly." The charge to humanity was a challenge to all of us. "Who shall right this well-nigh universal failing? Who shall let this world be beautiful? Who shall restore to men the glory of sunsets and the peace of quiet sleep?"[1]

Alain Locke provided one powerful answer to these questions, by asserting something quite radical in the 1920s, something radical today—that Black people are charged with righting this universal failing, by demanding the right to beauty in their own lives, lives distorted in the public discourse of race relations, and demeaned for not measuring up to standards mistakenly described as White. What Locke demanded is the right of African Americans to beauty, to speak of and write about, and carve out realms of beauty unnoticed by most of America because that America itself was lacking in, denied the benefit of, seeing its life as beautiful, ground down daily by a labor unrewarding as much as it is blinded to beauty around us. America was supposed to be the promised land, the place where this "universal failing" of fallen man was righted, where the "glory of sunsets" was to be restored, but instead had become, by 1925, and even more by 2017, a place of unquiet sleep.

That Locke would site beauty in a people routinely described as ugly, as recent descendants of apes, as appendages of various animal types, was so profound that it took even Du Bois by surprise, especially as it was connected to another equally radical conception—that Black people could pursue this beauty without reference to White people or the state of race relations at all. This latter concept—seeking and exploring and developing one's deeper connections to beauty, to Africa, to an independent humanity, without reference to the ongoing bitter struggle over White supremacy and its debilitating effects, was too much for Du Bois and legions of Black pundits and public intellectuals for years after *The New Negro: An Interpretation* appeared in 1925. But it should not have been that surprising a notion that Black people had a history, a culture, a being in the world, that a philosopher like Locke would call an ontology, that existed and flourished regardless of whomever they were dropped off with or denigrated by in whatever century one considered. A *people*, an often used but seldom understood concept, is just that—an unwavering sense of destiny among a group of humans who, for whatever reason, started out together in a place, developed a history, and used that history to create a future out of its present. Black people had that history, that shared set of experiences, and managed challenges wherever they went—and demanded to be taken on face value, to be appreciated, seen as beautiful despite the ugliness of lives in America, and did so regardless of what anyone else thought.

Locke demanded that artists be able to carve a beauty out of that mean experience without having to reference continually the struggle in the streets for citizenship rights seemingly always denied them. He wished for art that transcended the need, however valuable, to generate propaganda to fight the good fight for America. Black people, in other words, were more than simply civil rights—they were a people with a right to all of humanity, and Locke saw himself as the one to right that "universal failing" in this one crucial instance.

As it turned out, Locke was an imperfect messenger of this message. Despite his argument for what today would be described as an autonomous Blackness, he was rife with doubt about Black people, continually trying to escape close contact with Africans even as he theorized about Africa, and perpetually leaving America for Europe, in part because he was gay, but also because he could not rid his mind of the image of European excellence his Black Victorian upbringing had bestowed on him. The terms of survival for educated Negroes from the nineteenth century to now was to look askance at oneself because of what Cornel West called the "white normative gaze" that taught us to see ourselves in a judging mirror of what we had not done that White people had. This mirror was internalized in Locke himself, a man who struggled throughout his life with a sense of his own ugliness though he was the most beautiful of men, a gay man constantly attracting admiring attention from men and women, but who was systematically cruel to women like Jessie Fauset who might find him attractive in that way. Curiously, this man who sought to repulse too close an intimacy with Black people and independent Black women was enormously attracted to motherly women of all races, because he himself could not for most of his life separate himself from his mother or her surrogates.

But here was another of Locke's revealing ironies. While the typical psychoanalytic model is separation from the mother as the critical necessity of independence, Locke pioneered another psychic strategy—to use mother figures as fueling stations throughout his life for independent action, in large part, to craft a life of propulsive accomplishment. In many respects, his attachment to his mother was analogous to his recommendation that Negro artists attach themselves to the African tradition—a mother of the creativity African Americans exemplified over and over again by developing original forms such as the blues, jazz, hip-hop, or slave narratives, in a stream of inspiration that had no analogy in the rest of America fleeing beauty. As such, Locke became an exemplar of the New Negro he wanted the rest of African America to become—an independent-acting tornado who, though conflicted, tore through one project after another to build knowledge, beauty, and most important, efficacy wherever he went. In a sense, Locke acted as he wished a Black nation to act—and as the American nation had behaved right after its successful revolution: take no prisoners, act in your own interest, make alliances with anyone, but break those alliances when it serves your interest, act with impunity knowing you represent a people who are beautiful and destined to right this universal failing, not just for Black people, but for all people around the world.

There was another surprise: being gay, homosexual, queer, whichever nomen-clature works, actually helped Locke see unseen possibilities and craft a movement on something other than protest in the Harlem Renaissance of the 1920s. Something about the heteronormativity of Progressive-Era civil rights repulsed him and led him to explore what one theorist today calls the "quiet" dimensions of Black humanity. Being gay meant he couldn't hang out in the marriage- and mistress-driven male culture of the NAACP dominated by Du Bois and his extra-marital affairs. Being gay screened Locke from certain kinds of couplings and opened up others—deeper resources of how one could effect change more subtly, more indirectly, for his closeted politics for it opened the door to what else was in the Black closet—a whole range of feelings, loves, triumphs, and epiphanies routinely hidden by the need to keep one's life one-dimensional to fight the racists to the death. Locke saw that the warping effect of living in the closet in America was also a metaphor for the warping effect of living one's life as propaganda for the race struggle. A race relation's perspective on one's art and life was as narrowing as a heteronormative one. And in creating the New Negro of 1925 in his own image, he infused that concept with the sexual complexity that was the life of many of those artists who were the most important artists of the Black twenties.

Something about the hidden nature of Locke's desire allowed him to see into the hidden dimensions of the Black experience and write in such a way that the rococo curves and moves of his writing gave permission to other gay writers, artists, dancers, and dramatists to go forward like scouts of a queer nation in Black and create worlds of signification that went beyond Blackness. Locke let the gay out in his prose and his praise for Countee Cullen, Langston Hughes, Wallace Thurman, Bruce Nugent, Nella Larsen, Jean Toomer, and Zora Neale Hurston, and gave the New Negro a freedom to explore sexuality in all its variety, such that later artists, such as Luther Vandross, Michael Jackson, and Prince, could make sexual ambiguity as much an attraction as race. Locke's New Negro was not simply gay, but sexually open, unfixed, transsexual, capacious rather than exclusive. His New Negro was never simply Black, but undetermined, a pos-sibility, unrealized, yes, but a gift, his gift of openness to us and our future. The New Negro was the new man.

The New Negro was also sexist, relentlessly self-promoting of a male hegemony in the arts justified by same-sex love. Yet perhaps the most innovative writer in American literature, Zora Neale Hurston, was his friend, though she relentlessly criticized him; she too was a New Negro, sexually ambiguous, constantly reinvented, and transdisciplinary in a way that Locke could never be because he could never escape the Black Victorian closet to write compelling poetry or prose. In the end, she was the artist he most respected, though he could never publicly admit it. The irony of his life is that it was with women and through women that he was most successful, and yet he felt he had to destroy women because he saw them as competitors. Locke was an imperfect messenger of that message that beauty was everywhere, as perhaps we all are.

Locke's most important conceptualization is that a New Negro is always in us. Hidden, perhaps, clouded over by trauma, travesty, and travail, but there waiting for us to address and revive. A spirit lurks in the shadows of America that, if summoned, can launch a renaissance of our shared humanity. That is his most profound gift to us. To African Americans, his gift is also to attend to what Black people have actually done—to constantly reinvent ourselves over decades and centuries, creating new forms of art and life, despite the current state of race. However limited that notion is today in an era of recognition of the systemic nature of racism and its structural shackles on our lives, there is something empowering about the notion that each of us can pick up a brush, a pen, some clay, a computer, an app, and create something new, like those in the decrepit 1970s who picked up a turntable and turned it into a music industry. A New Negro is in all of us—not just African Americans, but every American who embraces this capacity for reinvention through African forms, because those forms are in them too, waiting, like the rest of us, to be released to soar.

NOTES

Chapter 1

1. *The Washington (D.C.) Evening* Star, April 23, 1922.
2. *The Washington (D.C.) Evening Star*, April 25, 1922. Copy of death notice, General Correspondence, Alain Locke Papers, Unprocessed, Manuscript Division, The Moorland-Spingarn Research Center, Howard University; hereafter cited as ALP.
3. Interview with Mae Miller Sullivan, April 4, 1976, Washington, D.C.
4. Ibid.
5. Douglas K. Stafford, "Alain Locke: The Child, the Man, and the People," *Journal of Negro Education* 30, no. 1 (Winter 1961): 25–34, 29.
6. Interview with Metz T. P. Lochard, June 13, 1975, Chicago, Ill.
7. *Crisis* 24, no. 3 (July 1922): 127.
8. Langston Hughes, "Mother to Son." *The Norton Anthology of African American Literature*, ed. Henry Louis Gates Jr. and Nellie Y. McKay (New York: Norton, 1997), 1254–1255.
9. *Crisis* 24, no. 3 (July 1922): 127–128.
10. Ibid.
11. Ibid.
12. Alain Locke, "Hail Philadelphia," *Opals* 1 (Spring 1927): 3.

Chapter 2

1. Although Alain Locke gave September 13, 1886, as his birthday, it certainly was 1885; no Alain or Alan Locke was recorded born in Philadelphia in 1886, but an Arthur Locke was born in 1885. See birth certificate, "Arthur Locke," Department of Records, Vital Statistics, Philadelphia, Pa.; and "Personal Astrology," envelope. ALP.
2. W. E. B. Du Bois, *The Philadelphia Negro* (Philadelphia: University of Pennsylvania Press, 1899), 61–62.
3. Wm. F. Miller et al. to Ishmael Locke, December 5, 1844, Ishmael Locke Folder. ALP.
4. Philip S. Foner and George E. Walker, eds., *The Proceedings of the Black State Conventions, 1840–1865*, vol. 2. *Proceedings and Address of the Coloured Citizens of N.J. Convened at Trenton, August 21st and 22nd, 1849 for the Purpose of Taking the Initiatory Measures for Obtaining the Right of Suffrage in this Our Native State* (Philadelphia: Temple University Press, 1980).
5. Martin Green, *Children of the Sun: A Narrative of "Decadence in England after 1918"* (New York: Basic, 1976), 27.
6. Christopher J. Perry, "Pencil Pusher's Points: A Brief Sketch of Pliny I. Locke, One of the Brainiest Men of His Day and Time," *The Philadelphia Tribune*, 1905.
7. Ibid.
8. Pliny Locke (PL) to Mary Locke (ML), July 29, 1878. ALP.

9. Ibid.
10. PL to ML, January 15, 1869. ALP.
11. PL to ML, February 22, 1869. ALP.
12. PL to ML, December 15, 1872. ALP.
13. PL to ML, October 13, 1875. ALP.
14. PL to ML, May 19, 1872. ALP.
15. Notes, Box 93. ALP.
16. PL to ML, December 22, 1876. ALP.
17. Perry, "Pencil Pusher's Points."
18. Autobiographical Sketch, n.d. ALP.
19. Ibid.
20. Toni Morrison, *Song of Solomon* (New York: Vintage International, 1977), 132.
21. Interview with Arthur Davis, April 4, 1975, Washington, D.C.
22. Biographical Memo: Alain (LeRoy) Locke, n.d. ALP.
23. Ibid.
24. Ibid.
25. Autobiographical Sketch, n.d. ALP.
26. Ibid.
27. Douglas K. Stafford, "Alain Locke: The Child, the Man, and the People," *Journal of Negro Education* 30, no. 1 (Winter 1961): 28.
28. Ibid.
29. Biographical Memo.

Chapter 3

1. Robert E. Fennell interview, April 11, 1987, Washington, D.C.
2. My reference to Locke as "child god" and Sartre as a "child King" comes from Annie Cohen-Solal, *Jean-Paul Sartre: A Life*, trans. Anna Cancogni (New York: New Press, 2005), 27.
3. See Rayford Logan, *The Betrayal of the Negro, from Rutherford B. Hayes to Woodrow Wilson* (New York: Collier, 1965).
4. Henry Turner, "The American Negro and His Fatherland" (speech given at the Congress of Africa in Atlanta, December 13–15, 1985). Later published in *Africa and the American Negro: Addresses and Proceedings of the Congress on Africa of Gammon Theological Seminary in Connection with the Cotton States and International Exposition*, ed. J. W. E. Bowen (Atlanta: Gammon Theological Seminary, 1896), 195–198.
5. Robert E. Fennell interview.
6. Emma Lapansky, "'Since They Got Those Separate Churches': Afro-Americans and Racism in Jacksonian Philadelphia," *American Quarterly* 32, no. 1 (Spring 1980): 54–78.
7. Mary Locke (ML) to Alain Locke (AL), May 22, 1905. ALP.
8. ML to AL, n.d. [possibly October 1904]. ALP.
9. ML to AL, n.d. ALP.
10. I am inspired here by Martin Green's superb study, *The Problem of Boston* (New York: Norton, 1966), especially chapter 1: "The Problem of Culture." Of course, I realize that Philadelphia was not Boston, and never focused as much of its resources on creating a society that fostered great literature as Boston did. But Philadelphia was no literary slouch, either, and was able to claim, for example, Benjamin Franklin, Edgar Allan Poe, Mark Twain, and Walt Whitman, even if Philadelphia never fully embraced Whitman, and some substantial publishing concerns such as the Curtis Publishing Company that published, among other things, the *Ladies Home Journal*. My point here is that Philadelphia educated and nurtured in Locke a high-minded notion of culture, taste, and standards that prepared him to enter Harvard and the world of the Boston aesthetes as a peer.
11. ML to AL, May 7, 1906. ALP.
12. Interview with Sadie Alexander, April 30, 1983, Philadelphia, Pa.
13. Douglas K. Stafford, "Alain Locke: The Child, the Man, and the People," *Journal of Negro Education* 30, no. 1 (Winter 1961): 28.

14. Ibid., 29.

15. Ibid., 30.

16. Ibid., 31.

17. Ibid., 31–32.

18. *Handbook of the Central High School* (Philadelphia, 1922), 15.

19. Ibid., 9, 13–18.

20. Interview with William Banner, April 10, 1982, Washington, D.C.; School of Pedagogy Reports; in Robert Thompson to Hart, May 17, 1904, L folder. HA.

21. Hughes Mearns to AL, December 21, 1925. ALP.

22. Albert Rowland to AL, n.d. ALP.

23. Phil Boyer (PB) to AL, n.d. ALP.

24. AL to PB, n.d. ALP.

25. PB to AL, n.d. ALP.

26. AL to HM, August 20, 1904. ALP.

27. Martin Green, *Children of the Sun: Narrative of Decadence in England After 1918* (London: Pimlico, 1992).

28. Locke's essay written at the School of Pedagogy on American drama, ca. 1903.

29. AL to PB, n.d. ALP.

30. AL to ML, n.d. ALP.

31. AL to PB, March 29, 1949. ALP.

Chapter 4

1. Alain Locke (AL) to Mary Locke (ML), September [n.d.,] 1904. ALP.

2. Ibid.

3. Ibid.

4. Ibid.

5. Rollo Brown, *Harvard in the Golden Age* (New York: Current, 1948) 17.

6. AL to ML, October 10, 1904. ALP.

7. Autobiographical Memoir, n.d. ALP.

8. ML to AL, n.d. (noted as her third letter to Locke at Harvard, Wed. 2 P.M. 1904). ALP.

9. ML to AL, September 22, 1904. ALP.

10. AL to ML, September 21, 1904 (noted as Monday evening). ALP.

11. AL to ML, September 23, 1904. ALP.

12. Ibid.

13. AL to ML, September 26, 1904. ALP.

14. W. E. B. Du Bois, "A Negro Student at Harvard," *Massachusetts Review* 1 (May 1960): 439.

15. AL to ML, September 21, 1904. ALP. Note: Page 6, on which the reference to "coons" appears, is missing from folder 25, Box 164-47.

16. AL to ML, October 4, 1904. ALP.

17. AL to ML, October 17, 1904. ALP.

18. Ibid.

19. AL to ML, October 6, 1904. ALP.

20. Ibid.

21. Ibid.

22. ML to AL, n.d. ALP.

23. AL to ML, October 13, 1904. ALP.

24. AL to ML, November 17, 1904. ALP.

25. AL to ML, November 27, 1904. ALP.

26. Ibid.

27. AL to ML, December 2, 1904. ALP.

28. AL to ML, November 30, 1904. ALP.

29. AL to ML, September 27, 1904. ALP.

30. AL to ML, n.d. ALP.

31. Ibid.

32. AL to ML, March 7, 1905. ALP.
33. Ibid.
34. AL to ML, October 21, 1904 (noted as Friday). ALP.
35. Bruce Kuklick, *The Rise of the American Philosophy: Cambridge, Massachusetts, 1860–1930* (New Haven: Yale University Press, 1979), 139.
36. AL to ML, n.d. ALP.
37. Ibid.
38. AL to ML, February 17, 1905. ALP.
39. AL to ML, September [n.d.,] 1906. ALP.
40. AL to ML, January 10, 1906. ALP.
41. AL to ML, December 9, 1905. ALP.
42. AL to ML, [Spring (n.d.), 1906]. ALP.
43. Ibid.
44. AL to ML, April 2, 1905. ALP.
45. AL to ML, n.d. (ca. 1905). ALP.
46. Ibid.
47. AL to ML, February 19, 1906. ALP.
48. AL to ML, May 3, 1906. ALP.
49. AL to ML, October 24, 1905. ALP.
50. Martin Green, *The Problem of Boston* (New York: Norton, 1966), 23.
51. AL to ML, December 9, 1905. ALP.
52. Ibid.
53. Ibid.
54. "Secretary's Third Report: Harvard Class of 1906. Biographical Sketch by James Arthur Harley" (Crimson Printing Co., 1906), 178.

Chapter 5

1. Notes written on "The Romantic Movement as Expressed by John Keats," January 1905. ALP.
2. Ibid.
3. English 46 class notes. ALP.
4. Alain Locke, "The Prometheus Myth: A Study in Literary Tradition" (essay submitted for the 1905 Bowdoin Prize competition).
5. Ibid.
6. Alain Locke, "Art as a Catharsis" (submitted in 1905 for Dr. D. H. Maynadier's course on English Literature).
7. Ibid.
8. Ibid.
9. Ibid.
10. Matthew Arnold, *Culture and Anarchy* (London: Smith, Elder & Company, 1869).
11. Edwin H. Abbot, Albert Matthews, and Paul E. More, who judged the winning essay.
12. Alain Locke, "Tennyson and His Literary Heritage," June 4, 1907: 1. Harvard Library, HU 89.165.692.
13. Ibid., 3.
14. Ibid., 4.
15. Marcellus Blount, "The Preacherly Text: African American Poetry and Vernacular Performance," *PMLA* 107, no. 3, Special Topic: Performance (May 1992): 582–593.
16. AL to ML, n.d. ALP.
17. Ibid.
18. The Dunbar lecture. ALP.
19. Ibid.
20. Ibid.
21. Ibid.
22. See W. B. Yeats, "The Young Ireland League," in *W. B. Yeats: Early Articles and Reviews: Uncollected Articles and Reviews Written Between 1886–1900*, ed. by John P. Frayne and Madeeine Marchaterre (New York: Scribner, 2004), 146–148.

23. Alain Locke (AL) to Mary Locke (ML), February 12, 1907. ALP.
24. ML to AL, February 25, 1907. ALP.
25. AL to ML, April 19, 1907. ALP.
26. Ibid.

Chapter 6

1. R. F. Scholz and S. K. Hornbeck, *Oxford and the Rhodes Scholarships* (London: Leopold Classic Library, 1907), 40.
2. Lord Rosebery to Parkin, March 17, 1903, Sir George R. Parkin Papers, Archives Branch, Public Archives, Canada.
3. See Brian Roberts, *Cecil Rhodes: Flawed Colossus* (London: Thistle, 2015).
4. Alain Locke (AL) to Mary Locke (ML), May 10, 1906. ALP.
5. AL to ML, September [n.d.,] 1906. ALP.
6. George Santayana to Horace Meyer Kallen, November 10, 1913, MS, Horace Kallen Papers, American Jewish Archives. Cincinnati, Ohio.
7. Sarah Schmidt interviews with Horace Kallen (1971). HKP.
8. Horace Meyer Kallen, "Alain Locke and Cultural Pluralism," *Journal of Philosophy* 54, no. 5 (February 1957): 119–127.
9. AL to ML, January 14, 1907. ALP.
10. Charles T. Copeland comments written on Alain Locke's essay, "Impressions of Dante," January 1907. ALP.
11. Ibid.
12. Copeland's comments on Locke's book review of Wells's *Future in America*, 1907. ALP.
13. AL to ML, February 10, 1907. ALP.
14. AL to ML, February 28, 1907. ALP.
15. AL to ML, March 3, 1907. ALP.
16. Barrett Wendell to Horace Kallen, n.d. HKP.
17. AL to ML, March 2, 1907. ALP. This letter suggests that Mary communicated to him that her "prophecies" weren't "favorable" for him getting the Rhodes.
18. The minutes of John Haas, March 9, 1907. ALP.
19. Arthur Fauset, *For Freedom: A Biographical Study of the American Negro* (Philadelphia: Franklin Publishing and Supply Co., 1934), 175.
20. Dean L. B. B. Briggs, Dean of Faculty of Arts and Sciences, Harvard to Provost Harrison, March 6, 1907. ALP.
21. George R. Parkin, "Appointment of a Negro Scholar," Special Report (1907), Rhodes Scholarship Trust Records, Microfilm, Canada Archives.
22. Quoted in a letter from C. Boyd to Rosebery, April 6, 1907. (RST).
23. Parkin, Postscript, "Negro Scholar." (RST).
24. Sir Francis Wylie, "The Rhodes Scholars and Oxford, 1902–1931," in *The First Fifty Years of the Rhodes Scholarships, 1903–1953*, ed. Lord Elton (London: Oxford, 1956), 99.
25. AL to Sir Francis Wylie (SFW), May [n.d.,] 1907. ALP.
26. "The First Colored Man to Go on the Rhodes Foundation," the *American Missionary* 61, no. 8 (October 1907): 247.
27. AL to ML, March 23, 1907. ALP.
28. AL to Duty, quoted in AL to ML, n.d. ALP.
29. S. T. Bivins to AL, March 29, 1907. ALP.
30. ML to AL, n.d. (ca. March 17, 1907). ALP.
31. Ibid.
32. AL to ML, March 23, 1907. ALP.
33. Ibid.
34. See *Harrisburg Telegraph* from Harrisburg, Pennsylvania, and the *Danville Morning News* from Danville, Pennsylvania (Monday, April 15, 1907 issues): 1.
35. AL to ML, n.d. ALP.
36. Ibid.
37. AL to ML, April 1907. ALP.

38. Ibid.
39. AL to ML, July 15, 1907. ALP.
40. AL to ML, May 10, 1907. ALP.
41. Ibid.
42. AL to ML, June 3, 1907. ALP.
43. Ibid.
44. ML to AL, June 7, 1907. ALP.
45. Ibid.
46. "Fewer Lynchings: Record for 20 Years in the Last Six Months" (remarks by President Eliot), *Boston Globe*, March 12, 1907, 5.
47. AL to ML, July 15, 1907. ALP.

Chapter 7

1. Alain Locke (AL) to Mary Locke (ML), September 24, 1907. ALP.
2. Ibid.
3. AL to ML, September 30, 1907. ALP.
4. AL to ML, October 23, 1907. ALP.
5. Ibid.
6. Ibid.
7. Ibid.
8. Ibid.
9. AL to ML, October 7, 1907. ALP.
10. George Parkin to President Benjamin Wheeler, October 8, 1908. (RST).
11. AL to ML, October 7, 1907. ALP.
12. AL to ML, October 23, 1907. ALP.
13. Horace Kallen's diary, October 18, 1907. (HKP).
14. HK to Barrett Wendell, October 22, 1907. (HKP).
15. Written on back of letter: Elinor Dicey to AL, October 24, 1907. ALP.
16. AL to ML, December 1, 1907. ALP.
17. Ibid.
18. Appointment card: AL meeting with F. S. Wylie, October 21, 1907. ALP.
19. AL to ML, November 1, 1907. ALP.
20. Horace Kallen, "Alain Locke and Cultural Pluralism," *Journal of Philosophy* 54 (February 28, 1957): 122.
21. AL to ML, December 1, 1907. ALP.
22. Ibid.
23. Ibid.
24. Douglas Stafford, "Alain Locke: The Child, the Man, and the People," *Journal of Negro Education* 25 (Winter 1961): 28.
25. Horace Meyer Kallen, "Alain Locke and Cultural Pluralism," *Journal of Philosophy* 54, no. 5 (February 1957): 122–123. HKP.
26. Ibid.
27. Ibid.
28. Ibid.
29. Ibid.
30. AL to anonymous friend. n.d. ALP.
31. AL to ML, December 1, 1907. ALP.
32. Ibid.
33. Ibid.

Chapter 8

1. Alain Locke (AL) to Mary Locke (ML), December 5, 1908. ALP.
2. AL to ML, January 3, 1908. ALP.

3. Ibid.

4. Ibid.

5. Ibid.

6. AL to ML, January 9, 1908. ALP.

7. ML to AL, January 21, 1908. ALP.

8. AL to ML, n.d. 1908. ALP.

9. Horace Kallen to AL, January 17, 1908. ALP.

10. AL to ML, January 18, 1908. ALP.

11. Ibid.

12. Notes written on back of invitation to visit Cairds of Balliol College, February 19, 1908. ALP.

13. AL to ML, n.d. 1908. ALP.

14. Dr. Collier's examination notes. n.d. ALP.

15. AL to ML, n.d. 1908. ALP.

16. AL to ML, n.d. 1908. ALP.

17. AL to ML, March 14, 1908. ALP.

18. Isaka Seme (IS) to Booker T. Washington, April 15, 1908. ALP.

19. AL to ML, March 17, 1908. ALP.

20. Ibid.

21. Ibid.

22. Ibid.

23. AL to ML, n.d. ALP.

24. Ibid.

25. AL to ML, n.d. ALP.

26. Ibid.

27. Ibid.

28. IS invitation. ALP.

29. Alain Leroy Locke, "Oxford Contrasts," *The Independent* 67 (July–December 1909): 139.

30. Edward Burnett Tylor, *Primitive Culture: Researches into the Development of Mythology, Philosophy, Religion, Art and Custom* (London: John Murray, 1871).

31. Thomas Babington Macaulay, "Minute of 2 February 1835 on Indian Education," *Macaulay, Prose and Poetry,* selected by G. M. Young (Cambridge, Mass.: Harvard University Press, 1957), 721–724, 729.

32. Alain Locke, "Epilogue," *The Oxford Cosmopolitan*, 1908.

33. Ibid.

34. Ibid.

35. Ibid.

36. Alain Locke, "Harlem," *Survey Graphic* (March 1, 1925): 630.

37. AL to ML, June 18, 1908. ALP.

38. AL to ML, May 27, 1908. ALP.

39. Ibid.

40. AL to ML, n.d. ALP.

Chapter 9

1. Alain Locke (AL) to Mary Locke (ML), September 16, 1908. ALP.

2. Ibid.

3. ML to AL, n.d. 1908. ALP.

4. AL to ML, n.d. 1908. ALP.

5. AL to ML, October 31, 1908. ALP.

6. Hamid El Alaily, "Modern Egypt," *The Oxford Cosmopolitan* 1 (November 1908): 22.

7. Moustafa Kamel Pasha as cited in Alaily, "Modern Egypt."

8. Malcolm X, James Baldwin-Malcolm X Debate, April 25, 1961, in *James Baldwin: The Poet You Produced* in *Voices of Pacifica* (1961) Part III, April 25, 1961, audiotape. https://www.youtube.com/watch?v=usFsXNCoYzc.

9. AL to ML, n.d. ALP.

10. Har Dayal, "Obstacles to Cosmopolitanism," *The Oxford Cosmopolitan* 1 (October 1908): 27–35.
11. Ibid.
12. [Proposal] AL to Assistant Registrar of Oxford University, n.d. ALP; Minutes of Education Committee, Hertford College, January 16, 1909. HCA; AL to ML, November [n.d.]. ALP.
13. Ibid.
14. Ibid.
15. AL to ML, December 19, 1908. ALP.
16. Ibid.
17. Sydney Franklin (SF) to AL, June 2, 1909. ALP.
18. Ibid.
19. AL to SF, n.d. ALP.
20. SF to AL, January 31, 1909. ALP.
21. AL to ML, December 15, 1908. ALP.
22. W. Boyd notes, Hertford governing board minutes, January 16, 1909.
23. AL to ML, February 10, 1909. ALP.
24. AL to ML, n.d. [1909]. ALP.
25. Locke, "Notes April 1909, Southern Rhodes Scholars vs. English Tory Allies." ALP.

Chapter 10

1. Alain Locke (AL) to Mary Locke (ML), March 15, 1909. ALP.
2. Ibid.
3. Ibid.
4. Ibid.
5. AL to ML, March 22, 1909. ALP.
6. AL to ML, April 3, 1909. ALP.
7. AL to ML, April 12, 1909. ALP.
8. AL to ML, April 18, 1909. ALP.
9. AL to ML, April 28, 1909. ALP.
10. Ibid.
11. AL to ML, April 27, 1909. ALP.
12. AL to ML, April 12, 1909. ALP. The book, which was not "bosh," was Wilbur Urban's *Valuation: Its Nature and Laws, Being an Introduction to the General Theory of Value* (1909).
13. AL to ML, May 5, 1909. ALP.
14. Ibid.
15. Ibid.
16. Ibid.
17. Ibid.
18. ML diary. July 31, 1914. ALP.
19. ML diary. August 23, 1914. ALP.
20. Alain Locke, "The American Temperament," *North American Review* 1914 (August 1911): 262–270. In Jeffrey C. Stewart's *The Critical Temper of Alain Locke: A Selection of His Essays on Art and Culture* (New York: Garland, 1983), 399.
21. Locke, "The American Temperament," 400.
22. AL to ML, March 3, 1910. ALP.
23. AL Cable to Booker T. Washington (BTW), March 12, 1910. ALP.
24. BTW to Locke, Telegram, April 18, 1910. ALP.
25. ML to AL, April 20, 1910. ALP.

Chapter 11

1. Chancellor Court Record, June 3, 1910, University Archives, Bodleian Library, Oxford University.
2. Henry Boyd, Hertford College Board Meeting Notes, May 31, 1910. HCA.

3. Booker T. Washington, letter of recommendation for Alain Locke to Lawrence Abbott, editor of the *Outlook*. ALP.

4. Alain Locke (AL) to Booker T. Washington (BTW), June 15, 1910. ALP.

5. Ibid.

6. BTW to AL, July 7, 1910. ALP.

7. Sydney Franklin to AL, July 12, 1910. ALP.

8. ML to AL, July 11, 1910. ALP.

9. ML to AL, July 12, 1910. ALP.

10. ML to AL, August 4, 1910. ALP.

11. J. Bush to AL, August 21, 1910. ALP.

12. Frederich von Voss (FV) to AL, August 19, 1910. ALP.

13. Ibid.

14. FV to AL, Spring 1911. ALP.

15. Ibid.

16. Ibid.

17. Locke's Thesis, "The Concept of Value," 124–125. ALP.

18. Ibid.

19. Ibid.

20. Ibid.

21. Hugo Munsterberg to AL, January 11, 1911. ALP.

22. "Meeting of the Board Holders," minutes of *Literae Humaniores* board decision 3:17, February 8, 1911.

23. Ibid.

24. Notes by H. Boyd the Principal, Herford College Munisments 4/2/6, March 10, 1910, Bodleian Library, Oxford.

25. ML to AL, April 2, 1910. ALP.

26. Ibid.

27. ML to AL, April 11, 1910. ALP.

Chapter 12

1. Lionel de Fonseka to AL, April 7, 1911. ALP.

2. Alain Locke, "Some Aspects of Modernism," 1911. ALP.

3. Ibid.

4. Ibid.

5. Jayston Edwards to AL, April 24, 1911. ALP.

6. See Robert Gooding-Williams's *In the Shadow of Du Bois* (Cambridge, Mass.: Harvard University Press, 2009), 57–60.

7. Lee Harry Liebersohn, *Fate and Utopia in German Sociology, 1870–1923* (Cambridge, Mass.: MIT Press, 1990).

8. Lionel de Fonseka (LdF) to AL, June 28, 1911. ALP.

9. Ibid.

10. Ibid.

11. Ibid.

12. Alfred Fouillee, "Race from the Sociological Point of View," First International Races Congress (July 26, 1911), First Session titled *Fundamental Considerations*.

13. Franz Boas, "The Instability of Human Types," First International Races Congress (July 26, 1911), Second Session titled *The Conditions of Progress: General Problems*.

14. Ibid.

15. Ibid.

16. Israel Zangwill, "The Jewish Race," First International Races Congress (July 28, 1911), Fifth Session titled *The Modern Conscience*.

17. Ibid.

18. Ibid.

19. *The London Times* (July 29, 1911), 4.

20. Louis Lochner, *Always the Unexpected* (New York: Macmillan, 1956), 39.

21. ML to AL, August 3, 1911. ALP.

22. Ibid.

23. Ibid.

24. Locke, typescript note, ca. 1932. ALP.

Chapter 13

1. Alain Locke (AL) to Mary Locke (ML), November 2, 1911. ALP.

2. Alain Locke, "The Negro and a Race Tradition" (speech, Yonkers Negro Society for Historical Research in New York, December 12, 1911). ALP.

3. Ibid.

4. W. E. B. Du Bois, "Of the Training of Men," in *The Souls of Black Folk* (1903), published in *W.E.B. Du Bois: Writings, The Library of America* (Cambridge: Cambridge University, 1986), 438.

5. Ibid.

6. John Bruce (JB) to John Cromwell (JC), December 11, 1911. ALP.

7. AL to ML, n.d. ALP.

8. Ibid.

9. JB to JC, October 15, 1917. ALP.

10. AL to ML, February 17, 1912. ALP.

11. JB to JC, February 8, 1912. ALP.

12. JB to JC, December 11, 1911. ALP.

13. Booker T. Washington (BTW) to AL, January 8, 1912. ALP.

14. BTW to S. G. Elbert (SGE), February 26, 1912. ALP.

15. AL to ML, n.d. ALP.

16. "Immense Crowd Hears Dr. Booker Washington Speak," *Pensacola Journal*, March 2, 1912, 7.

17. AL to ML, March 2, 1912. ALP.

18. AL to ML, March 8, 1912. ALP.

19. AL to ML, n.d. ALP.

20. Al to ML, March 18, 1912. ALP.

21. Carl Diton (CD) to AL, March 12, 1912. ALP.

22. CD to AL, March 24, 1912. ALP.

23. ML to AL, Fall 1911. ALP.

24. AL to BTW, July 1912. ALP.

25. Telegram from Lewis Moore to AL, September 14, 1912. ALP.

26. AL to BTW, September 1912, Booker T. Washington Papers, Library of Congress.

27. Alain Locke, "Cosmopolitanism and Culture," unpublished manuscript. ALP.

28. Ibid.

29. Ibid.

30. Ibid.

31. Ibid.

32. Ibid.

Chapter 14

1. Mary Locke (ML) to Alain Locke (AL), September 24, 1912. ALP.

2. Bishop Levi Coppin to AL, October 23, 1911. ALP.

3. AL to Booker T. Washington (BTW), September 16, 1912. BTW.

4. AL report to Dean Moore, 1915. ALP.

5. Ibid.

6. Christian Fleetwood to AL, February 20, 2012, ALP.

7. AL to ML, January 1913. ALP.

8. AL to ML, February 16, 1913. ALP.

9. Ibid.

10. Lionel de Fonseka (LdF) to AL, March 18, 1913. ALP.

11. AL to ML, February 27, 1913. ALP.

12. Alexander Walters (AW) to AL, April 9, 1913. ALP.

13. Charles F. Kellogg, *NAACP: A History of the NAACP*, vol. 1, *1909–1920* (Baltimore: John Hopkins University Press, 1967), 159–166.

14. Alexander Walters (AW) to AL, September 3, 1913. ALP.

15. AL to ML, January 15, 1914. ALP.

16. Ibid.

17. See Mabel O. Wilson, *Negro Building: Black Americans in the World of Fairs and Museums* (Berkeley: University of California Press, 2012), 147–149.

18. ML to Varick, August 4, 1914. ALP.

19. ML Diary, July 31, 1914. ALP.

20. ML to Varick, August 4, 1914. ALP.

21. Ibid.

22. "Gerard Bringing Refugees: His Special with 400 Americans Goes to Rotterdam," *New York Times*, August 14, 1914, 4.

23. Gilchrist Stewart telegraph to AL, October 13, 1914. ALP.

24. Handwritten notes on the telegraph.

25. August 12, diary, Kemper Harreld, in possession of Josephine Harreld Love.

26. ML to AL, n.d. 1911. ALP.

27. Alain Locke, "The Great Disillusionment," September 26, 1914, in *Race Contacts and Interracial Relations: Alain LeRoy Locke*, ed. Jeffrey C. Stewart (Washington, D.C.: Howard University Press, 1992), 107.

28. Ibid.

29. "Europe at Armageddon," *The North American Review* 1142 (September 2014): 321–322.

30. Locke, "The Great Disillusionment," 108.

31. Ibid., 110.

32. Ibid., 106.

33. Ibid., 108.

34. AL to ML, October 28, 1914. ALP.

35. Ibid.

36. AL to ML, November 19, 1914. ALP.

37. AL to Booker T. Washington, April 29, 1915. BTW.

38. AL to ML, February 8, 1915. ALP.

39. "My dear Dr. Newman, I have been thinking for sometime over the new Course on Racial Contact proposed by Professor Locke and recommended by the Faculty of the Teachers' College of Howard University. That matter was presented to our Trustees some time ago and I think it was referred back to you and the Executive Committee for further consideration. I visited Columbia University this summer and my vision was very much enlarged. There were over a hundred colored students among the plus six thousand whites ... I thought of 'Dear Old Howard' and was proud that she was represented by our Professor Gregory and our Professor Locke. I am sending you a clipping from the Catalogue and would call your special attention to the paragraph marked and under the heading, 'Missions.' This shows that Columbia is 'stealing' the thunder of Howard. This Course inaugurated this summer at Columbia is practically the same as that proposed by Professor Locke at Howard. Howard, I think, can justly claim priority in this field, which apparently is being rapidly developed at several other Universities." William Sinclair to Rev. S. M. Newman, September 18, 1915. ALP.

40. W. E. B. Du Bois, *The Conservation of the Races*. Occasional Papers, 2. The American Negro Academy, 1897.

41. Alain Locke, lecture 5, "Race Progress and Race Adjustment," in *Race Contacts and Interracial Relations*, 100.

42. AL to ML, March 28, 1916. ALP.

43. AL to ML, April 9, 1916. ALP.

44. Alain Locke, *Race Contacts and Interracial Relations*.

Chapter 15

1. Alain Locke (AL) to Mary Locke (ML), n.d. (summer 1916). ALP.
2. Ibid.
3. ML to AL, June 28, 1916. ALP.
4. William Stanley Braithwaite, *Anthology of Magazine Verse* (1916): xiii–xiv.
5. AL to Archibald Grimke, n.d. [March 1916]. Archibald Grimke Papers, Moorland-Spingarn Research Center, Howard University.
6. Ibid.
7. See Kevin Quashie's book, *The Sovereignty of Quiet: Beyond Resistance in Black Culture* (New Brunswick: Rutgers University Press, 2012) for a superb discussion of the art versus propaganda debate that has greatly informed my own understanding of the losses that a purely activist notion of Black identity exacts. I thank Monife Love Asante for bringing this wonderful book to my attention.
8. W. E. B. Du Bois, "Criteria of Negro Art," *Crisis* 32 (October 1926): 290–297. http://www.webdubois.org/dbCriteriaNArt.html, accessed May 17, 2017.
9. Alain Locke, "A Criticism of the Bosanquetian Doctrine of Judgment Forms," turned in January 8, 1917, to Alfred Hoernle's Logical Theory course. ALP.
10. Alfred Hoernle's comment to paper. ALP.
11. Ralph Barton Perry, "The Definition of Value," *Journal of Philosophy, Psychology and Scientific Methods* 11 (March 12, 1914): 150.
12. Alain Locke, "The Problem of Classification in the Theory of Value: Or an Outline of a Genetic System of Values" (PhD diss., Harvard University, 1918).
13. Alain Locke, scribble on back of Hoernle's invitation, February 23, 1917. ALP.
14. Alain Locke, scribble on the back of CHS club meeting invitation, January 18, 1917. ALP.
15. Meta Warrick Fuller to ML, January 23, 1917. ALP; C. Henry Dickerman to AL, September 28, 1917. ALP; Plenyano Gbe Wolo to AL, November 3, 1917, May 9, 1919, June 3, 1921. ALP; Moco McCaulay, "The Remarkable Untold Story of Plenyono Gbe Wolo, Harvard's First African Graduate," *The Liberian Echo* (January 27, 2016). http://liberianecho.com/the-remarkable-untold-story-of-plenyono-gbe-wolo-harvards-first-african-graduate/, accessed May 22, 2017.
16. Alain Locke, "Emile Verhaeren," in *The Critical Temper of Alain Locke*, 35.
17. Ibid.
18. Locke, "Emile Verhaeren," in *The Critical Temper of Alain Locke*, 36.
19. Locke, "The Problem of Classification."
20. AL to Arthur Schomburg, n.d. ALP.
21. Alain Locke's written tribute to Bishop Walters. ALP.
22. Ibid.
23. Ibid.

Chapter 16

1. R. R. Thompson to Alain Locke (AL), July 15, 1917. ALP.
2. Ibid.
3. Ibid.
4. Montgomery Gregory (MG) to AL, August [n.d.,] 1917. ALP.
5. Ibid.
6. MG to AL, April 1, 1918. ALP.
7. MG to AL, April 23, 1918. ALP.
8. Ibid.
9. AL to Ralph Barton Perry, Fall 1917. ALP.
10. Ibid.
11. Ralph Barton Perry, *The Present Conflict of Ideals: A Study of the Philosophical Background of the World War* (New York: Longmans, Green, 1918).
12. Alain Locke presentation, later published as "The Role of the Talented Tenth," *Howard University Record* 12 (December 7, 1918): 15–18.

13. Alain Locke, "Howard Univ. in the War—A Record of Patriotic Service," *Howard University Record* 13 (1919): 169.

14. Jeffrey C. Stewart, ed., *Race Contacts and Interracial Relations: Alain LeRoy Locke* (Washington, D.C.: Howard University Press, 1992), 53.

15. William Stanley Braithwaite (WSB) to AL, July 27, 1919. ALP.

16. Ibid.

17. Ibid.

18. AL to Langston Hughes (LH), n.d. (circa April 1923). ALP.

19. "Theatrical Notes," *The New York Times*, November 2, 1920, 26.

20. W. E. B. Du Bois (WEBDB) to AL and Montgomery Gregory (MG), April 4, 1919. ALP.

21. Ibid.

22. *The New York Times*, November 2, 1920.

23. Lincoln Johnson to AL, March 14, 1919. ALP.

24. Georgia Douglas Johnson, *Bronze: A Book of Verse* (New York: Books for Libraries Press, 1922; 1971).

25. Georgia Douglas Johnson to AL, August 10, 1920. ALP.

26. Nathan Pinchback Toomer to AL, November [n.d.,] 1919. ALP.

Chapter 17

1. Alain Locke (AL) to Sir Francis Wylie, n.d. 1921. ALP.

2. Jean Toomer (JL) to AL, January 26, 1921. ALP.

3. Ibid.

4. JT to AL, November 8, 1921. ALP.

5. Helen Irvin to AL, February [n.d.,] 1922. ALP.

6. William Crusor George to AL, n.d. ALP.

7. Helen Irvin to Miss Hunt, February [n.d.,] 1922. ALP.

8. Isabella Claphan to Locke, n.d., [1922]. ALP.

9. William George (WG) to AL, n.d., [1922]. ALP.

10. Scribbled notes on a letter. ALP.

11. WG to AL, n.d. ALP.

12. WG to AL, May 7, 1922. ALP.

13. WG to AL, May 17, 1922. ALP.

14. AL to WG's parents, n.d. (ca. May 28, 1922). ALP.

15. WG to AL, n.d. (June 1922). ALP.

16. AL to WG, July 4, 1922. ALP.

17. Ibid.

18. Ibid.

19. Ibid.

20. W. E. B. Du Bois, *The Souls of the Black Folk* (Boston: Bedford, 1903; 1997), 38.

21. Ibid., 39.

22. Handwritten, "Homo Ball" at "<u>Madeline</u> till 12:15." ALP.

23. Alain Locke, "Steps Toward the Negro Theatre," *Crisis* (December 1922): 66.

24. Ibid.

25. "Hinkemann" (1922). ALP. *Hinkemann* is a German expressionist play by the left-wing playwright Ernst Toller. Performances of the play were attacked by national socialists in 1924. See https://de.wikipedia.org/wiki/Hinkemann, accessed May 17, 2017.

26. Stephen Spender, *World Within World: The Autobiography of Stephen Spender* (London: Hamish Hamilton, 1951), 97.

27. Otto Friedrich, *Before the Deluge: A Portrait of Berlin in the 1920s* (New York: Harper & Row, 1995), 11.

28. Moco McCaulay, "The Remarkable Untold Story of Plenyono Gbe Wolo, Harvard's First African Graduate," *The Liberian Echo* (January 27, 2016). http://liberianecho.com/the-remarkable-untold-story-of-plenyono-gbe-wolo-harvards-first-african-graduate/, accessed May 22, 2017.

Chapter 18

1. Jean Toomer (JT) to Alain Locke (AL), August 1923. ALP.
2. JT to Georgia Douglas Johnson, January 7, 1920. ALP.
3. JT to AL, August 1923. ALP.
4. Countee Cullen (CC) to AL, September 24, 1922. ALP.
5. Ibid.
6. CC to AL, January 12, 1923. ALP.
7. CC to AL, January 29, 1923. ALP.
8. Ibid.
9. AL to CC, n.d. (ca. February/March) 1923. ALP.
10. CC to AL, March 3, 1923. ALP.
11. Ibid.
12. CC to AL, April 4, 1923. ALP.
13. Ibid.
14. CC to AL, May 1923. ALP.
15. Helen Irvin to AL, February 13, 1923. ALP.
16. AL to CC, February 3, 1923. ALP.
17. Ibid.
18. CC to AL, January 20, 1923. ALP.
19. AL to Langston Hughes (LH), January 17, 1923. ALP.
20. LH to AL, February 19, 1923. ALP.
21. Ibid.
22. Charles Spurgeon Johnson (CSJ) to AL, January 4, 1923. ALP.
23. Alain Locke, *Goat Alley*, *Opportunity* 1, no. 2 (February 1923): 30.
24. CSJ to AL, February 1923. ALP.
25. Alain Locke, "Public Opinion in War and Peace," *Opportunity* 1, no. 7 (July 1923): 223.
26. CSJ to AL, June 6, 1923. ALP.
27. Ibid.
28. Eugene Kinckle Jones to AL, July 6, 1923. ALP.
29. LH to AL, April 6, 1923. ALP.
30. Ibid.
31. AL to LH, n.d. LHP.
32. Ibid.
33. LH to AL, [May 1923]. ALP.
34. AL to LH, n.d. LHP.
35. LH to AL, Thursday [May 1923]. ALP.
36. CC to AL, April 13, 1923. ALP.
37. CC to LH, n.d. LHP.
38. AL to CC, n.d. CCP.
39. CC to AL, June 8, 1923. ALP.
40. CC to AL, August 26, 1923. ALP.
41. CC to AL, August 23, 1923. ALP.

Chapter 19

1. Helen Irvin (HI) to Alain Locke (AL), June 28, 1923. ALP.
2. Roscoe Conkling Bruce to AL, October 22, 1923. ALP.
3. CSJ to AL, ca. 1923. ALP.
4. Melville Herskovits to AL, September 1923. ALP.
5. Alain Locke, "The Problem of Race Classification," *Opportunity* 1, no. 9 (September 1923): 261.
6. Ibid., 262.
7. Alain Locke, "The Colonial Literature of France," *Opportunity* 1, no. 11 (November 1923): 331.
8. Ibid.
9. Ibid., 334.

10. Herbert Marcuse, *The Aesthetic Dimension* (Boston: Beacon, 1977).

11. Alain Locke, "The Black Watch on the Rhine," *Opportunity* 2, no. 13 (January 1924): 7.

12. Ibid.

13. Locke, "The Black Watch," 6.

14. Ibid., 9.

15. Ibid.

16. René Maran, "French Colonial Policy: Open Letter to Prof. Locke," *Opportunity* 2, no. 21 (September 1924): 261; also appeared in *Les Continents* of June 15, 1924.

17. Aimé Césaire, "Discourse on Colonialism," trans. Joan Pinkham, *Monthly Review Press* (1972): 1; originally published as *"Discours sur le colonialisme"* by Editions Presence Africaine (1955): 1. http://www.rlwclarke.net/theory/SourcesPrimary/CesaireDiscourseonColonialism.pdf, accessed September 20, 2016.

18. Claude McKay to AL, August 1923. ALP.

19. Claude McKay, *A Long Way from Home* (New York: Arno, 1969 [1937]), 312–313.

20. Helen Irvin to AL, November 1923. ALP.

21. Alain Locke, "Roland Hayes, An Appreciation," *Opportunity* 1, no. 12 (December 1923): 356.

22. Ibid.

23. Ibid.

24. Ibid.

25. Ralph Ellison, "The Little Man at Chehaw Station: The American Artist and His Audience," *The American Scholar* 47, no. 1 (Winter 1978): 26.

26. Locke, "Roland Hayes," 358.

27. Ibid.

28. Roland Hayes (RH) to AL, December 1, 1923. ALP.

29. Ibid.

30. RH to AL, October 4, 1924. ALP.

31. Ibid.

32. AL to HI, 1923. ALP.

33. Alain Locke, "Impressions of Luxor," *Howard Alumnus* 2, no. 4 (May 1924): 74–78.

Chapter 20

1. Alain Locke, "Impressions of Haifa," *Bahái World* 2 (1928): 125.

2. Alain Locke (AL) to Ms. Parsons, n.d. 1928. ALP.

3. Locke, "Impressions," 125.

4. Ibid.

5. Jon Woodson, *To Make a New Race: Gurdjieff, Toomer and the Harlem Renaissance* (Jackson: University Press of Mississippi, 1999).

6. Charles Mason Remey, "The Universal Consciousness of the Baha'i Revelation: A Brief Treatise Introductory to the Study of the Baha'i Religion" (New York: Baha'i Publishing Committee, 1925).

7. Alain Locke, "Apropos of Africa," *Opportunity* 2, no. 14 (February 1924): 37.

8. Alain Locke, "Impressions of Luxor," *Howard Alumnus* 2, no. 4 (May 1924): 74–78.

9. AL to Montgomery Gregory (MG), n.d. 1924. ALP.

10. AL to Kamal Hamdy, n.d. 1924. ALP.

11. Locke, "Apropos," 40.

12. Ibid., 39–40.

13. Ibid.

14. Ibid.

15. Ibid.

16. Locke's Cairo guidebook. ALP.

17. AL to MG, n.d. ALP.

18. Ibid.

19. Locke, "Impressions of Luxor," 74–78.

20. George Foucart to AL, January 19, 1924. ALP.

21. Locke, "Impressions of Luxor," 74–78.
22. Ibid.

Chapter 21

1. Card from the *Tyrrhenia*. ALP.
2. Alain Locke, "Apropos of Africa," *Opportunity* 2, no. 14 (February 1924): 37.
3. Ibid.
4. Ibid., 38.
6. Ibid.
7. Ibid.
8. Ibid.
9. Ibid., 39.
10. J. Stanley Durkee to George Foucart, September [n.d.,] 1924. ALP.
11. Alain Locke, "Max Rheinhardt Reads the Negro's Dramatic Horoscope," *Opportunity* 2 (May 1924): 145; (*Critical Temper*, 77). Locke (or the typesetter) misspelled Reinhardt as Rheinhardt.
12. Ibid., 145–146.
13. Ibid., 146.
14. The Studio Theatre: *The Millennium Project: Part One. Waiting for Godot* (Washington, D.C.: 1998), 5.
15. See http://www.playbill.com/article/dc-studio-begins-millennium-project-with-godot-sept-2-com-77154, accessed May 11, 2017.
16. Locke, "Max Rheinhardt," 146.
17. AL to Walter White (WW), January 24, 1924. ALP.
18. WW to Herman Lieber, February 3, 1924. ALP.
19. WW to AL, February 6, 1924. ALP.
20. Ibid.
21. "American Institute of Negro Letters, Music and Art," ca. February 1924. ALP.
22. Ibid.

Chapter 22

1. Charles S. Johnson (CSJ) to Alain Locke (AL), March 4, 1924. ALP.
2. CSJ to AL, March 1924. ALP.
3. Ibid.
4. CSJ to AL, January 10, 1924. ALP.
5. CSJ to AL, March 7, 1924. ALP.
6. Gwendolyn Bennett to AL, March 21, 1924. ALP.
7. CSJ to AL, March 19, 1924. ALP.
8. Alain Locke lecture to the Civic Club, March 12, 1924. ALP.
9. Ibid.
10. "The Debut of the Younger School of Negro Writers," *Opportunity* 2, no. 17 (May 1924): 143.
11. Carl Van Doren, "The Younger Generation of Negro Writers," *Opportunity* 2, no. 17 (May 1924): 144.
12. Locke, "The Debut," 143.
13. Van Doren, "The Younger Generation," 144.
14. Interview with Arthur Fauset, December 27, 1980, Philadelphia, Pa.
15. Barnes to Dewey, March 22, 1924. ALP.
16. Jessie Fauset to AL, January 9, 1934 [erroneously dated 1933]. ALP.
17. David Levering Lewis, *When Harlem Was in Vogue* (New York: Penguin repr., 1997); Arnold Rampersad, *The Life of Langston Hughes*, vol. 6, *1902–1941: I, Too, Sing America (Life of Langston Hughes, 1902–1941)*, 2nd ed. (New York: Oxford University Press, 2002); and Thadious Davis, *Nella Larsen, Novelist of the Harlem Renaissance: A Woman's Life Unveiled* (Baton Rouge: Louisiana State University Press, 1996).

18. "Young Writers Group Dinner to Fellow Member at Civic Club," *The New York Age*, March 29, 1924, 8.

Chapter 23

1. Albert Barnes (AB) to Howard University, January 25, 1924. ALP.
2. Ibid.
3. Bertrand Russell, *Autobiography* (London: Routledge, 1991), 463.
4. According to Arthur Fauset, Locke and Johnson were rivals as well as colleagues in the effort to secure access to African art. Interview with Arthur Fauset, December 27, 1980. Philadelphia, Pa.
5. Marianna Torgovnick, *Gone Primitive: Savage Intellects, Modern Lives* (Chicago: University of Chicago Press, 1991).
6. AB to Alain Locke (AL), January 25, 1924. ALP.
7. AB to AL, March 3, 1924. ALP.
8. Copy of letter from Walter White (WW) to AB, March 24, 1924. ALP. "I am rather thrilled at my good fortune in meeting and talking with you at the dinner last Friday night. I find that much of that good fortune is due to the kindness of our mutual friend, Mr. Locke, who arranged that we should sit together."
9. Copy of AB to WW, March 25, 1924. ALP.
10. Ibid.
11. AB to AL, March 25, 1924.
12. AB to WW, March 27, 1924.
13. Interview with Arthur Fauset, December 27, 1980, Philadelphia, Pa.
14. Copy of Charles S. Johnson (CSJ) to AB, April 7, 1924. ALP.
15. CJ to AL, May 1924. ALP.
16. Albert Barnes, "The Temple," *Opportunity* 2, no. 17 (May 1924): 139.
17. AB to AL, May 7, 1924. ALP.
18. AL to Belata Heroui, March 23, 1924. ALP.

Chapter 24

1. Claude McKay to Alain Locke (AL), May 1, 1924. ALP.
2. Eric Walrond to AL, June 4, 1924. ALP.
3. Langston Hughes (LH) telegram to AL, February 2, 1924. ALP.
4. LH to AL, February 4, 1924. ALP.
5. AL to LH, May 22, 1924. LHP.
6. Jessie Fauset to LH. LHP.
7. LH to Harold Jackman. LHP.
8. Paul Kellogg (PK) to AL, April 7, 1924. ALP.
9. PK to AL, May 10, 1924. ALP.
10. PK to Albert Barnes, May 28, 1924. Barnes Foundation.
11. PK to AL, May 10, 1924. ALP.
12. AL to LH, 1924. ALP.
13. PK to AL, June 17, 1924. ALP.
14. Arnold Rampersad, *The Life of Langston Hughes*, vol. 6, *1902–1941: I, Too, Sing America (Life of Langston Hughes, 1902–1941)*, 2nd ed. (New York: Oxford University Press, 2002), 91.
15. LH to Countee Cullen, July 1924. LHP.
16. AL to LH, August 10, 1924. ALP.
17. LH to AL, 1924. ALP.
18. AL to LH, 1924. ALP.
19. Ibid.
20. Rampersad, *The Life of Langston Hughes*, 93–94.
21. Langston Hughes, *The Big Sea: An Autobiography* (New York: Hill and Wang, 1940), xx.
22. Rampersad, *The Life of Langston Hughes*, 94.

23. CJ to AL, August 8, 1924. ALP.
24. Ibid.
25. René Maran's Open Letter to Prof. Locke appeared in *Les Continents* of June 15, 1924. Republished in "French Colonial Policy: Open Letters," *Opportunity* 2, no. 21 (September 1924): 261. Although Johnson also published Locke's reply to the letter, Locke's response deferred to Maran's greater knowledge of French colonialism in a somewhat awkward and embarrassed concessionary missive.
26. J. P. Gee and J. Green, "Discourse Analysis, Learning, and Social Practice: A Methodological Study," *Review of Research in Education* 23 (ed. E. W. Gordon), American Educational Research Association, Washington, D.C.: 119–169.
27. AL to PK, n.d., Paul Kellogg Papers, Social Welfare Archives, University of Minnesota.
28. Alain Locke, "The New Negro," n.d. ALP.
29. Ibid.
30. Alain Locke, "The Negro Mind," Survey Graphic Folder. ALP.
31. Alain Locke, "Harlem," *Survey Graphic* 53, no. 11 (March 1, 1925): 630.
32. Ibid.
33. Previous version of "Harlem," titled "The New Setting." ALP.
34. Alain Locke, "Harlem," 629.
35. Locke, "The New Negro," n.d. ALP.

Chapter 25

1. Claude McKay (CK) to Alain Locke (AL), September 22, 1924. ALP.
2. Paul Kellogg to AL, September 26, 1924. ALP.
3. Alain Locke, "Harlem," *Survey Graphic* 53 (March 1, 1925): 630.
4. CK to AL, October 7, 1924. ALP.
5. Ibid.
6. AL to CK, October 7, 1924. ALP.
7. PK to Kelly Miller, October 27, 1924. ALP.
8. Cornel West, "The New Cultural Politics of Difference," *October* 53 (1990): 93–109.
9. Interview with William Banner, April 10, 1982, Washington, D.C.
10. AL to PK, n.d. ALP.
11. Claude McKay, "Like a Strong Tree," *Survey Graphic* 53 (March 1, 1925): 662.
12. Anne Spencer, "Lady, Lady," *Survey Graphic* 53 (March 1, 1925): 661.
13. Elise J. McDougald to AL, November 17, 1924. ALP.
14. Countee Cullen (CC) to AL, October 27, 1924. ALP.
15. Locke, "Harlem," 630.
16. Arthur A. Schomburg, "The Negro Digs Up His Past," *Survey Graphic* 53 (March 1, 1925): 670.
17. J. A. Rogers to AL, March 7, 1925. ALP.
18. J. A. Rogers, "Jazz at Home," *Survey Graphic* 53 (March 1, 1925): 712.
19. Locke, "*Enter the New Negro*," *Survey Graphic* 53 (March 1, 1925): 631.
20. Geddes Smith (GS) to AL, January 23, 1925. ALP.
21. CC to AL, October 17, 1924. ALP.
22. CC to AL, October 31, 1924. ALP.
23. CC to AL, November 28, 1924. ALP.
24. CC to AL, December 9, 1924. ALP.
25. CC to AL, December 20, 1924. ALP.
26. PK to AL, December 23, 1924. ALP.
27. CC to AL, 1925. ALP.
28. CC to AL, January 19, 1925. ALP.
29. CC to AL, January 1925. ALP.
30. CC to AL, February 1925. ALP.
31. Ibid.
32. AL to Melville Herskovits, April 24, 1924. ALP.

33. See Walter A. Jackson, "Melville Herskovits and the Search for Afro-American Culture," in *Malinowski, Rivers Benedict and Others*, ed. George W. Stocking Jr. (Madison: University of Wisconsin Press, 1986), 98–101.
34. Melville J. Herskovits, "The Dilemma of Social Pattern," *Survey Graphic* 51 (March 1, 1925): 677.
35. Ibid., 678.
36. GS to AL, January 26, 1925. ALP.
37. Locke, prefatory notes to Herskovits, "The Dilemma," 676.
38. Konrad Bercovici, "The Rhythm of Harlem," *Survey Graphic* 51 (March 1, 1925): 679.
39. Ibid.
40. PK to AL, February 5, 1925. ALP.
41. PK to AL, February 12, 1925. ALP.
42. Ibid.
43. PK to AL, February 17, 1925. ALP.

Chapter 26

1. Howard University Catalogue, 1923–1926 [January 1924], Washington, D.C., Founders Library.
2. Emmett Scott to Alain Locke (AL), June 16, 1925. ALP.
3. Locke to Jesse Moorland, January 1925, ALP. Also, see the "Memorial of the Teachers of the Academic Faculty to the Board of Trustees," Howard University, November 25, 1924. ALP.
4. James Weldon Johnson (JWJ) to AL, March 10, 1925. ALP.
5. Kellogg to JWJ, n.d. ALP.
6. "New Negro is only an integral part in Seventh Ave. Business. Survey of Business Development on Seventh Avenue," *New York Age*, March 28, 1925, 1.
7. Elise McDougald to AL, n.d. ALP.
8. Alain Locke, "To Certain of Our Philistines," *Opportunity* 3 (May 1925): 156; also in *The Critical Temper of Alain Locke: A Selection of His Essays on Art and Culture*, ed. Jeffrey C. Stewart (New York: Garland, 1983), 162.
9. Locke, "To Certain," 155.
10. Paul Kellogg (PK) to AL, March 20, 1925. ALP.
11. PK to AL, May 21, 1925. ALP.
12. AL to PK, March 24, 1925. SWArchives.
13. Maxwell Perkins to Kenderdine, March 19, 1925. ALP.
14. AL to PK, March 24, 1925. SWArchives.
15. PK to Kahn Fellowship, n.d. ALP.
16. PK to AL, April 8, 1925. ALP. As Kellogg wrote, "Yesterday, we had a little gathering of reins at the Library. All of us felt that yours is one of the least satisfactory of the portraits; but the gallery is certainly stunning. None of the art critics have visited it, and no downtown gallery has made overtures to display the pictures, so that Mr. Reiss is a little bit disconsolate. But that is the price of pioneering. We were really all of us breaking new ground in this Harlem number." Because of dissatisfaction with the first portrait, Reiss did a second portrait of Locke, which was published in *The New Negro: An Interpretation* (1925) and appears on the cover of this book.
17. E. Franklin Frazier (EFF) to AL, May 26, 1925. ALP.
18. EFF to AL, May 1, 1925. ALP.
19. Raymond Wolters, *The New Negro on Campus: Black College Rebellions of the 1920s* (Princeton: Princeton University Press, 1975), 113.
20. Rayford W. Logan, *Howard University: The First Hundred Years, 1867–1967* (New York: New York University Press, 2004), 220–222.
21. William Hansberry to Jesse Moorland, June 1924. JMP.
22. AL to Charles R. Brown, June 1924. ALP.
23. HU Club of New York City Resolution, June 17, 1925. ALP.
24. Wolters, *The New Negro on Campus*, 108.
25. Ibid., 109.

26. A. W. Mitchell, "The Case of the Howard Professors Decapitated by the Durkee Regime," The Howard Welfare League, Washington D.C. August 8, 1925. W. E. B. Du Bois Papers (MS 312). Special Collections and University Archives, University of Massachusetts Amherst Libraries.

27. Ibid.

28. Such sophistication in student planning reflected a level of personal commitment Locke had been urging on students for the last ten years. Locke had urged students to find in service to the race, the finest opportunity for their individual fulfillment. Now he was seeing it manifested, ironically, in the area of protest, which he had disparaged before, but now an area made more to him because it was protest for his reinstatement. As one of his former students put it: "I have decided to remain here [in Washington, after his graduation] because I now feel that it would be unloyal for me to desert old H. in its bitterest moments. I should cast my lot & be willing to fight too. I feel also that I would be unworthy of your friendship if I would not be willing to sacrifice something since you have been forced to suffer for our welfare. At first I thought that I could not tolerate going up there anymore after the harsh actions of the trustees but now I feel that it is my duty to help reestablish normalcy and bring justice to the ones that are humiliated."

29. Alain Locke, "Negro Education Bids for Par," *Survey Graphic* 54 (September 1925): 567.

30. Ibid., 570.

31. Ibid.

32. Alain Locke, "More of the Negro in Art," *Opportunity* 3 (1925). Reprinted in *The Critical Temper of Alain Locke: A Selection of Essays on Art and Culture*, ed. Jeffrey C. Stewart (New York: Garland), 1983.

33. Winold Reiss to AL, December 31, 1925. ALP.

Chapter 27

1. Alain Locke (AL) to Jessie Fauset, n.d. [August 1925]. ALP.

2. William Braithwaite, "The Negro in American Literature," in *The New Negro: An Interpretation*, ed. Alain Locke (New York: Albert and Charles Boni, 1925), 31.

3. Jessie Redmon Fauset, "The Gift of Laughter," in *The New Negro: An Interpretation*, ed. Alain Locke (New York: Albert and Charles Boni, 1925), 162.

4. Alain Locke, foreword to *The New Negro: An Interpretation*, ed. Alain Locke (New York: Albert and Charles Boni, 1925), ix.

5. George Parker to Charles R. Brown, September 16, 1925. ALP.

6. AL to L. S. Curtis, n.d. 1925. ALP.

7. AL to Paul Kellogg (PK), n.d. 1925. ALP.

8. AL to Roscoe Conkling Bruce, n.d. 1925. ALP.

9. Franz Boas to A. O. Leuschner, n.d. 1925. ALP.

10. W. E. B. Du Bois, "A Negro Art Renaissance," *Los Angeles Times*, June 14, 1925.

11. *The New York Times Book Review*, December 30, 1926.

12. H. L. Mencken, for *American Mercury* (February 1926). Review excerpt in Box 710. PKP.

13. I am indebted to Martha Nadell for first pointing this out to me. See her *Enter the New Negroes: Images of Race in American Culture* (Cambridge, Mass.: Harvard University Press, 2004) and her discussion of the "inartistic." It was rational to eliminate many of these portraits of "Harlem Types" as the book's purpose was to represent the national New Negro movement.

14. See Michel Foucault, "Foucault Maurice Florence," in *Aesthetics, Method, and Epistemology*, ed. James D. Faubion (New York: New Press, 1998), 459–477.

15. Interview with Doxey Wilkerson, May 6, 1982, Washington, D.C.

16. Unfortunately for Locke and Parker, as of September 1925, African American opinion was divided on the issue of whether a change in administration was needed at Howard. The administration increasingly utilized its allies to carry out a propaganda campaign in the Black newspapers to make the argument that the current protest by the alumni and its allies was destined to destroy the university. This argument found sympathetic ears among those who agreed with racial conservatives that the progress already made by the race in institutions like Howard was too precious to threaten with "rioting, lawlessness, disorders, strikes." Dr. J. E. Shepard,

the Black president of North Carolina College for Negroes (later North Carolina A&T) made this argument in a September issue of the *New York Age*; and in an editorial that accompanied Shepard's statement, the *Age*'s editors argued that the alumni associations had yet to make a persuasive case against the Durkee administration, because most of the charges were too vague. But even here, the *Age* argued that the only action that seemed to "require explanation or defence[*sic*], is the abrupt dismissal of four of its ablest and most efficient professors." Locke's case, therefore, and those of his fellow professors, remained the most effective challenge to the legitimacy and rationality of Durkee and the current administration.

17. John Hurst (JH) to AL, October 28, 1925. ALP.

18. JH to AL, November 13, 1925. ALP.

19. "1. His educational policies have been erratic, ill-advised and productive of sudden, arbitrary and disrupting changes in the organization and management of the university. 2. He has ignored the regular channels and customs of the university, especially in the appointment and dismissal of faculty members without the advice, recommendation and knowledge of the deans and heads of the departments. 3. By reason of personal disagreement with Dr. Durkee, the university has lost a number of the most scholarly members of the teaching force, some of whom had national and international reputations. 4. He had pursued an arbitrary and dictatorial policy, supported by a system of espionage and intimidation, and has established a reputation of personal suspicion, unreliability, reliance upon rumor without investigation, and personal animus and bias. 5. He has disregarded and antagonized the officials of the alumni association...by imposing upon this body an alumni secretary of his personal choice.... He has insulted and violently handled faculty members, particularly Dr. Thomas W. Turner, whom he forcibly ejected from his office, and Dean Kelly Miller, whom he called a 'contemptible cur.' He diverted approximately 50 percent of the sum of $15,000 provided by the trustees for increases of salaries of academic teachers to the employment of new teachers, all of whom he preferentially retained in June 1925 when his so-called retrenchment program went into effect. He has been arbitrary and vindictive in his recommendations of promotions, increases of salary and other executive action with reference to the teaching force. His influence has been irreparably impaired by his open affront and insult to the Race in his acceptance of the presidency of the Curry School of Expression." List taken from Raymond Wolters, *The New Negro on Campus: Black College Rebellions of the 1920s* (Princeton: Princeton University Press, 1975): 125–126.

20. Wolters, *The New Negro on Campus*, 126–127.

21. Jean Genet, *The Blacks: A Clown Show*, trans. Bernard Frechtman (New York: Grove, 1994).

22. These conjectures about Locke's testimony are taken from a "Memorandum: Alain Leroy Locke: Howard University. 1925." ALP.

23. Executive Committee and the Budget Committee, June 15, 1925.

24. PK to AL, December 14, 1925. ALP; AL to Charles Brown, January 30, 1926. ALP.

25. Mary White Ovington, "The Negro's Gifts," *The Bookman* (March 1926): 98.

26. *Pittsburgh Courier*, December 19, 1925; George Schuyler, "Shafts and Darts," *The Messenger* 8 (January 1926): 9.

27. Ernest Boyd, "Review of The New Negro," *The Independent* (January 16, 1926). Review copy in Box 710. PKP.

28. AL to PK, February 23, 1926, Box 710. PKP.

29. J. P. Whipple, "Can the Negro Save His Act," *Survey Graphic* (January 1, 1926): 114.

30. Emmett J. Scott to Arthur Mitchell, 1232 U Street, NW, 4 Feb. 1926 on Allied Industrial Finance Corporation stationary. ALP.

31. Thomas Dyett to AL, February 10, 1926. ALP.

Chapter 28

1. Interview with Charles Prudhomme, April 11, 1976. Washington, D.C.

2. Booker T. Washington, *Up from Slavery* (1901), "Making Their Beds Before They Could Lie on Them." http://xroads.virginia.edu/~hyper/washington/ch11.html, accessed November 28, 2016.

3. W. E. B. Du Bois, "Review," *Crisis* 31 (January 1926): 140–141.

4. Alain Locke, "Negro Youth Speaks," *The New Negro: An Interpretation*, ed. Alain Locke (New York: Albert and Charles Boni, 1925), 50–51.

5. Hazel Harrison to Alain Locke (AL), n.d. 1926. ALP.

6. Alain Locke, "Color—A Review," *Opportunity* 4, no. 36 (January 1926): 14.

7. Ibid.

8. Alain Locke, "The Negro Poets of the United States," in *Anthology of Magazine Verse for 1926 and Yearbook of American Poetry*, ed. William Braithwaite (Boston: B. J. Brimmer Co., 1926), 143; Jeffrey C. Stewart, *The Critical Temper of Alain Locke: A Selection of His Essays on Art and Culture* (New York: Garland, 1983), 43.

9. *Crisis* 31 (February 1926): 165.

10. *Crisis* 31 (March 1926): 219.

11. Elise Johnson McDougald, "The Double Task: The Struggle of Negro Women for Sex and Race Emancipation," *Survey Graphic* 53 (March 1, 1925): 689.

12. David Levering Lewis, *W. E. B. Du Bois: The First for Equality and the American Century, 1919–1963* (New York: Henry Holt, 2000), 204–205.

13. Alain Locke, "The Negro and the American Stage," *Theatre Arts Monthly* 10 (February 1926): 113; Stewart, *The Critical Temper of Alain Locke*, 80.

14. Alain Locke, "The Drama of Negro Life," *Theatre Arts Monthly* (October 1926): 701–702; Stewart, *The Critical Temper*, 87–88.

15. Ibid, 88.

16. Anna J. Cooper to AL, May 12, 1926. ALP.

17. Ibid.

18. Lydia Gibson Miner to AL, January 1, 1926. ALP.

19. George Foster Peabody (GFP) to AL, February 11, 1926. ALP.

20. W. E. B. Du Bois, "Criteria of Negro Art," *Crisis* 32 (October 1926): 290. http://www.webdubois.org/dbCriteriaNArt.html, accessed May 20, 2016.

21. GFP to AL, February 13, 1926. ALP.

22. W. E. B. Du Bois, "Criteria of Negro Art," *Crisis* 32 (October 1926): 290. http://www.webdubois.org/dbCriteriaNArt.html, accessed May 20, 2016.

23. Ibid.

24. Langston Hughes, "The Negro Artist and the Racial Mountain," *The Nation* (June 23, 1926). http://www.english.illinois.edu/maps/poets/g_l/hughes/mountain.htm.

25. Alain Locke, review of "The Weary Blues," by Langston Hughes, *Palms* 4, no. 1 (October 1926): 25–29.

26. Ibid.

27. Zora Neal Hurston to Countee Cullen (CC), March 11, [1926], Countee Cullen Papers, Manuscript Division, Library of Congress.

28. Alain Locke, "Fire: A Negro Magazine," review of *Fire!! Survey Graphic* 15 (September 1927): 563.

29. Alain Locke, "Our Little Renaissance," *Ebony and Topaz*, ed. Charles S. Johnson (New York: National Urban League, 1927), 117; *The Critical Temper of Alain Locke*, 21.

30. W. E. B. Du Bois (WEBDB) to Jesse Moorland, May 5, 1927. WEBDP.

31. Lewis, *W. E. B. Du Bois*, 162.

32. Allison Davis, "Our Negro Intellectuals," *Crisis* 35 (August 1928): 268–269.

33. Carl Van Vechten to Langston Hughes (LH), August 2, 1928. Langston Hughes Papers, Yale.

34. Alain Locke, "Beauty Instead of Ashes," *The Nation* 126 (April 18, 1928): 432. Reprinted in *The Critical Temper of Alain Locke*, 23.

35. Locke, "Beauty Instead of Ashes," 434.

36. Alain Locke, "Art or Propaganda?" *Harlem* 1 (November 1928): 12; *The Critical Temper of Alain Locke*, 27.

Chapter 29

1. Edith Isaacs to Alain Locke (AL), August 18, 1926. ALP.

2. Alain Locke, "Art Lessons from the Congo," *Survey Graphic* 57 (February 1, 1927): 587; *The Critical Temper of Alain Locke: A Selection of His Essays on Art and Culture* (New York: Garland, 1983), 137.

3. Charlotte Mason diary entry, March 6, 1927, Mason Notebooks. ALP.

4. Ibid.

5. Ibid.

6. Mason diary entry, February 20–21, 1927; edited August 11, 1927. ALP.

7. Mason diary entry, March 6, 1927. ALP.

8. Ardie Sue Myers, "Relations of a Godmother: Patronage During the Harlem Renaissance" (MA thesis, George Washington University, 1981); interview with Arthur Huff Fauset, December 27, 1980, Philadelphia, Pa.

9. Jeffrey Stewart, "A Biography of Alain Locke: Philosopher of the Harlem Renaissance" (PhD diss., Yale University, 1979).

10. Charlotte Osgood Mason, "The Passing of a Prophet: A True Narrative of Death and Life," *The North American Review* 185, no. 621 (August 16, 1907): 869–879.

11. Thomas Munro, "Art: Good and Bad Negro Art," *The Nation* 2 (March 2, 1927): 242.

12. Alain Locke, "African Art in America," *The Nation* 124, no. 3219 (March 16, 1927): 29.

13. Ibid.

14. Alain Locke, *The New Negro: An Interpretation* (1925; New York: Albert and Charles Boni, 1927), 19.

15. Ibid., 254.

16. AL to Arthur Spingarn, February 25, 1927. Arthur Spingarn Papers, MSRC, HU.

17. Mason diary entry, March 6, 1927. ALP.

18. Mason diary entry, March 10, 1927. ALP.

19. Ibid.

20. Charlotte Mason (CM) to AL, March 17/27, 1927. ALP.

21. Mason diary entry, March 10, 1927; edited August 10, 1927. ALP.

22. Mason diary entry, March 18, 1927. ALP.

23. Mason diary entry, March 18, 1927; edited August 10, 1927. ALP.

24. Mason diary entry, April 16, 1927. ALP.

25. Mason diary entry, May 1, 1927. Mason Notebooks.

26. Ibid.

27. Mason diary entry, April 19, 1927. ALP.

28. Mason diary entry, March 10, 1927. ALP.

29. Mason diary entry, April 24, 1927. ALP.

30. For a discussion of the "lost mother," see Claudia Tate, *Psychoanalysis and Black Novels: Desire and the Protocols of Race* (New York: Oxford University Press, 1998), 46, 56–58.

31. See Tony Bennett, "The Exhibitionary Complex," *New Formations* 4 (Spring 1988): 73–102.

32. E. Franklin Frazier, *The Black Bourgeoisie: The Book That Brought the Shock of Self-Revelation to Middle-Class Blacks in America* (New York: Simon & Schuster, 1997).

33. Mason diary entry, April 30, 1927. ALP.

34. Mason diary entry, May 1, 1927. ALP.

35. Mason diary entry, May 21, 1927. ALP.

36. Rampersad, *Life of Langston Hughes*, 148.

37. Interview with Richard Bruce Nugent, ca. 1985, Hoboken, N.J.

38. Claude McKay (CM) to AL, June 4, 1927. ALP.

39. Lewis S. Baer to AL, August 1, 1927. ALP.

40. Michel Foucault, *Discipline and Punish: The Birth of the Prison*, trans. Alan Sheridan (New York: Vintage, 1995), 195–228.

Chapter 30

1. Langston Hughes, "Those Bad New Negroes: A Critique on Critics," *Pittsburgh Courier*, April 14, 1927.

2. See Arthur Rampersad, *The Life of Langston Hughes*, vol. 6, *1902–1941*, 2nd ed., *I, Too, Sing America (Life of Langston Hughes, 1902–1941)* (New York: Oxford University Press, 2002), 152.

3. Richard Sheppard, *Modernism—Dada—Postmodernism* (Evanston, Ill.: Northwestern University Press, 2000), 13–19.

4. See Michael Hardt and Antonio Negri, *Empire* (Cambridge, Mass.: Harvard University Press, 2000), 73–92.

5. See Jon Woodson's *To Make a New Race: Gurdjieff, Toomer, and the Harlem Renaissance* (Jackson: University of Mississippi Press, 1999). Some of the artists who came under Toomer's teachings of Gurdjieff's doctrines included George Schuyler, Wallace Thurman, Dorothy Peterson, Nella Larsen, Aaron Douglas, Arna Bontemps, Harold Jackman, Rudolph Fisher, and Zora Neale Hurston. Woodson argues that one evidence of the secret reference to Gurdjieff was to place coded references to his name and beliefs throughout the works of these artists so that the initiated could recognize them and the uninitiated would not.

6. See Rampersad, *The Life of Langston Hughes*, 153.

7. See Brent Hayes Edwards, *The Practice of Diaspora: Literature, Translation, and the Rise of Black Internationalism* (Cambridge, Mass.: Harvard University Press, 2003), 16–23. "Transinterpretation" comes from a presentation by Chela Sandoval on May 2, 2017, at UC Santa Barbara.

8. Alain Locke (AL) to Charlotte Mason (CM), September 13, 1927. ALP.

9. Ibid.

10. Ibid.

11. Ibid.

12. CM to AL, September 20, 1927. ALP.

Chapter 31

1. "That which had been negligently trodden under foot by those who were harnessing and provisioning themselves for long journeys into far countries is suddenly found to be richer than all foreign parts," had mused Emerson (Ralph Waldo Emerson, "The American Scholar," a speech given on August 31, 1837, to the Phi Beta Kappa Society at the First Parish in Cambridge in Cambridge, Massachusetts).

2. Telegram, Alain Locke (AL) to Charlotte Mason (CM), January 15, 1928. ALP.

3. AL to Zora Neale Hurston (ZNH), February 24, 1928. ALP.

4. Ibid.

5. AL to CM, February 19, 1928. ALP.

6. "I very much appreciate your inquiry as to my availability for assignment to your school.... My commitments now make it impossible for me to be available before February 1929. I shall hope, however, to keep in touch with appointments situation in the interim." AL to Gilbert J. Raynor, principal, Alexander Hamilton High School, Brooklyn, New York, June 2, 1928. ALP.

7. AL to CM, February 22, 1928. LHP.

8. ZNH to Langston Hughes (LH), April 12, 1928. LHP.

9. ZNH to LH, May 1, 1928. LHP.

10. Ibid.

11. Hurston wrote to Hughes specifically recommending that he tour the South reading his poetry, "not in auditoriums, but in camps, and water-fronts and the like. You are the poet of the people and your subjects are crazy about you. Why not? There never has been a poet [that] has been acceptable to His Majesty, the man in the gutter before, and laugh if you will, but that man in the gutter is the god-maker, the creator of everything that lasts." ZNH to LH, November 22, 1928. Yale.

12. W. E. B. Du Bois, "So the Girl Marries," *Crisis* (June 1928): 202.

13. Locke, "From Letter to Countee Cullen," n.d. ALP.

14. "Report of Speech by Marcus Garvey," *The Marcus Garvey and UNIA Papers* (vol. 3): 278–279. (Originally published in the *Chicago Tribune*, Paris edition, ca. October 6, 1928.)

15. Raymond Buell to AL, October 16, 1928. ALP.

16. Interview with Arthur Davis, April 4, 1975, Washington, D.C.; Rayford W. Logan, *Howard University: The First Hundred Years, 1867–1967* (New York: New York University Press, 1969), 258–269.

17. See Jeffrey Green, "Kwamina Tandoh/Amoah III, Ghanaian." http://www.jeffreygreen.co.uk/ 126-kwamina-tandohamoah-iii-ghanaian-leader-in-early-20th-century-britain, accessed November 30, 2016.

18. AL to CM, January [n.d.,] 1929. ALP.

19. Alain Locke, "The Negro's Contribution to American Art and Literature," *Annals* 140 (1928): 234.

20. Ibid.

21. Alain Locke, "1928: A Retrospective Review," *Opportunity* 7, no. 1 (January 1929): 11.

Chapter 32

1. From a typed copy of Article 22, located in the ALP.

2. Ibid.

3. "Memorandum: FOREIGN POLICY ASSOCIATION; Alain Locke re African Mandates Study Project," May 26, 1927. ALP.

4. Rayford Logan, *The Operation of the Mandate System in Africa, 1919–1927* (Washington, D.C.: Foundation, 1942); Raymond Buell, *The Native Problem in Africa*, 2 vols. (New York: Macmillan, 1928).

5. See Rose Cherubin, "Culture and the *Kalos*: Inquiry, Justice, and Value in Locke and Aristotle," in *Philosophic Values and World Citizenship*, ed. Jacoby Adeshei Carter and Leonard Harris (Lanham, Md.: Rowman & Littlefield, 2010), 7–19.

6. AL to Paul Kellogg (PK), January [n.d.,] 1929. ALP.

7. Charlotte Mason (CM) to AL, January [n.d.,] 1929. ALP.

8. Eugene D. Genovese, *Roll Jordan Roll: The World the Slaves Made* (New York: Vintage, 1976).

9. Zonia Baber to AL, January 23, 1929; January 24, 1929. ALP.

10. AL to CM, February 20, 1929. ALP.

11. AL to Langston Hughes (LH), January 23, 1929. ALP.

12. Ibid.

13. Zora Neale Hurston (ZNH) to LH, July 23, 1929. Yale.

14. AL to Albert Dunham, April 20, 1929. ALP.

15. ZNH to LH, July 23, 1929. Yale.

16. ZNH to LH, October 15, 1929. Yale.

17. ZNH to LH, December 10, 1929. Yale.

18. Ibid.

19. Ibid.

20. AL to AD, May 22, 1929. ALP.

21. Albert Dunham (AD) to AL, June 1, 1929. ALP.

22. Wallace Thurman, "Both Sides of the Color Line," *Survey Graphic* 62 (June 1, 1929): 325–326; Julia Peterkin, "Review of Scarlet Sister Mary," *Opportunity* 7, no. 6 (June 1929): 190–191.

23. Alain Locke, "Beauty and the Provinces," *The Stylus* 2 (June 1929): 3–4.

24. AL to AD, May 22, 1929. ALP.

25. Ibid.

26. AD to AL, June 1, 1929. ALP.

27. AL to AD, June 11, 1929. ALP.

28. Ibid.

29. AL to LH, December 6, 1929. ALP.

30. ZNH to AL and LH, June 14, 1928. ALP.

31. Locke came to Hurston's rescue several times from 1928 to 1930. In May 1928, after he had smoothed Mason's racial sensitivities after Hurston's "white folks can't be trusted" blunder, Locke again had to help smooth over Mason's anger at Hurston's publication of "How It Feels to Be Colored Me" in *The World Tomorrow*. Locke had to vouch for the fact that Hurston had written and submitted that article before Hurston and Mason met, and thus it was not covered by the contractual agreement that specified Hurston not publish any of her material collected during Mason's financial support.

32. See Valerie Boyd, *Wrapped in Rainbows: The Life of Zora Neale Hurston* (New York: Scribner, 2003), 195.
33. Ibid.
34. CM to LH, June 6, 1930. LHP.
35. Ibid.
36. CM to LH, Telegram, June 17, 1930. LHP.
37. AL to LH, n.d. LHP.
38. Interview with Louise Patterson, March 17, 1987. Oakland, Calif.
39. Hurston discussed her reputed rewriting of *Mule Bone* to her own specifications without any of Hughes interventions and suggestions in her January 20, 1931, letter to Mrs. Mason. ALP.
40. Hurston to Mason, January 20, 1928. ALP.
41. CM to AL, January 15, 1928. ALP.
42. CM to AL, April 20, 1929. ALP.
43. CM to AL, May 21, 1930. ALP.
44. CM to AL, July 12, 1929. ALP.
45. AL to CM, May 24, 1931. ALP.
46. Locke to L. Hollingsworth Wood, May 13, 1931. ALP.
47. AL to CM, March 29, 1931. ALP.

Chapter 33

1. Charles P. Henry, *Ralph Bunche: Model Negro or American Other?* (New York: New York University Press, 1999).
2. Pearl T. Robinson, "Ralph Bunche the Africanist: Revisiting Paradigms Lost," in *Trustee for the Human Community: Ralph J. Bunche, the United Nations, and the Decolonization of Africa*, ed. Robert A. Hill and Edmond J. Keller (Athens: Ohio University Press, 2010), 73.
3. Ralph Bunche (RB) to Dean E. P. Davis at Howard University, December 22, 1930, Ralph Bunche Papers, Collection Number 2051, Department of Special Collections, Charles E. Young Research Library. UCLA.
4. A. N. Holcombe (ANH) to RB, August 7, 1930, Ralph Bunche Papers, Collection Number 2051, Department of Special Collections, Charles E. Young Research Library. UCLA.
5. ANH to RB, December 11, 1930, Ralph Bunche Papers, Collection Number 2051, Department of Special Collections, Charles E. Young Research Library. UCLA.
6. RB to ANH, Department of Government, Harvard University, February 28, 1931, Ralph Bunche Papers, Collection Number 2051, Department of Special Collections, Charles E. Young Research Library. UCLA.
7. Bill Jay, *Views on Nudes* (London: Focal, 1972), 92.
8. Interview with Richard Long, March 3, 2012, Atlanta, Ga.
9. Fragment in Locke's handwriting, n.d. ALP.
10. Interview with Richard Bruce Nugent, December 11, 1982, Hoboken, N.J.
11. Alain Locke, "This Year of Grace: Outstanding Books of the Year in Negro Literature," *Opportunity* 9 (February 1931): 48.
12. Ibid.
13. Ibid.
14. Ibid., 49.
15. AL to Mary Brady (MB), February 24, 1931. ALP.
16. Alain Locke, "The American Negro as Artist," *The American Magazine of Art* 23 (September 1931): 210. Reproduced in Jeffrey C. Stewart, *The Critical Temper of Alain Locke: A Selection of His Essays on Art and Culture* (New York: Garland, 1983), 171.
17. Locke, "The American Negro," 217.
18. AL to Charlotte Mason (CM), November 10, 1932. ALP.
19. AL to CM, February 8, 1932. ALP.
20. AL to CM, n.d. ALP.
21. Locke fragment, n.d. ALP.
22. AL to CM, January 28, 1932. ALP.

23. Louis T. Achille, Lyon, France, to author, March 16, 1992.
24. Ibid.
25. For example, in chapter 4, Bunche writes: "The organized and official partition of Africa occurred... [and]... no single motive is applicable of course, but it is a safe assumption to make in a capitalistic, industrial world, the economic motive was the dominating one. The justification was easy to find. In the first place it was pointed out that no people have the right to isolate themselves (and their riches) from the rest of the world, while the world on the other hand has a superior right to take what it needs. (Footnote a. Girault, Principes de Colonization). The creed of imperialism paraded economic necessity as adequate justification, which was simple enough—the raw materials of the 'backward regions' were necessary for a hungry and overpopulated world." P. 75. "French Administration in Togoland and Dahomey," 1934, Ralph Bunche Papers, Collection Number 2051, Department of Special Collections, Charles E. Young Research Library. UCLA.
26. MB to AL, January 28, 1933. ALP.
27. See, for example, Locke's articles, "To Certain of Our Philistines," "The Negro Poets of the United States," and "The Drama of Negro Life," in Stewart, *The Critical Temper of Alain Locke*, 161–162, 43–46, 91.
28. Synopsis of radio Broadcast with Alain Locke, Mary Brady, and Alan Bement in connection with Harmon exhibition of contemporary Negro art. 1933. ALP.
29. Ibid.
30. Ibid.
31. Ibid.
32. Ibid.
33. Ibid.
34. Ibid.
35. 2 Corinthians 6:17, King James Bible.
36. Ibid.
37. This sculpture is now part of the Howard University Gallery of Arts collection, left to Howard by Locke in his will.

Chapter 34

1. See James Young, *Black Writers of the Thirties* (Baton Rouge: Louisiana State University Press, 1973).
2. Alain Locke, "The Saving Grace of Realism: Retrospective Review of the Negro Literature of 1933," *Opportunity* 13 (January 1934): 8–9; reprinted in Jeffrey C. Stewart, *The Critical Temper of Alain Locke: A Selection of His Essays on Art and Culture* (New York: Garland, 1983), 221–222.
3. Alain Locke (AL) to Charlotte Mason (CM), May 20, 1933. ALP.
4. Emily Miller (EM) to AL, February 20, 1933. ALP.
5. AL to EM, March 30 1933. ALP.
6. AL to CM, May 20, 1933. ALP.
7. AL to CM, June 19, 1933. ALP.
8. Ibid.
9. AL to CM, August 30, 1933. ALP.
10. AL to CM, August 18, 1933. ALP.
11. AL to CM, October 25, 1933. ALP.
12. AL to CM, November 5, 1933. ALP.
13. AL to CM, November 13, 1933. ALP.
14. AL to CM, December 12, 1933. ALP.
15. Ibid.
16. Interview with Doxey Wilkerson, May 6, 1982, Washington, D.C.
17. AL to CM, December 21, 1933. ALP.
18. Ibid.
19. Ibid.

Chapter 35

1. Interview with Harold Lewis, April 17, 1982, Washington, D.C.
2. See Jonathan Holloway, *Confronting the Veil: Abram Harris Jr., E. Franklin Frazier, and Ralph Bunche, 1919–1941* (Chapel Hill: University of North Carolina Press, 2002).
3. Interview with Harold Lewis, April 17, 1982, Washington, D.C.
4. The strategy referenced here is taken from Gayatri Chakravorty Spivak, *An Aesthetic Education in the Era of Globalization* (Cambridge, Mass.: Harvard University Press, 2012), 3.
5. Morse Cartwright (MC) to Alain Locke (AL), May 28, 1933. ALP.
6. Locke, Memorandum on Adult Education Among Negroes, February 26, 1934. ALP.
7. AL to Charlotte Mason (CM), January 11, 1934. ALP. Dunham was not the only brilliant casualty of 1934. Rudolph Fisher, the physician, novelist, and the best short-story writer of the Renaissance, expired that December of intestinal cancer, brought on by overexposure to X-rays in his own laboratory. That same month, Wallace Thurman died of tuberculosis, although most of his friends believed he really died of alcoholism—and his paralyzing self-consciousness. For Locke, both were already dead before their actual passing. As he told Mrs. Mason, they were, in his opinion, consumed by "egotism."
8. Ibid.
9. Interview with Robert E. Fennell, April 11, 1987, Washington, D.C.
10. Jessie Fauset to AL, January 9, 1933 [actually 1934]. ALP.
11. Alain Locke, "The Saving Grace of Realism: Retrospective Review of the Negro Literature of 1933," *Opportunity* 13 (January 1934): 8.
12. Ibid., 9.
13. Jessie Fauset (JF) to AL, January 9, 1933 [actually 1934]. ALP.
14. Locke, Memorandum on Adult Education Among Negroes, February 26, 1934. ALP.
15. AL to CM, January 21, 1934. ALP.
16. Ibid.
17. Ibid.
18. AL to CM, April 2, 1934. ALP.
19. AL to CM, April 14, 1934. ALP.
20. Morse Cartwright (MC) to AL, March 28, 1934. ALP.
21. MC to AL, April 19, 1934. ALP.
22. AL to CM, June 7, 1934. ALP.
23. AL to CM, June 30, 1934. ALP.
24. MC to AL, May 28, 1934. ALP.
25. AL to CM, July 5, 1934. ALP.
26. Ibid.
27. Ibid.
28. AL to CM, July 26, 1934. ALP.
29. Ibid.
30. Ibid.
31. AL to CM, August 10, 1934. ALP.
32. Ibid.
33. Ibid.
34. AL to CM, August 18, 1934. ALP.
35. AL to CM, August 27, 1934. ALP.
36. AL to CM, September 10, 1934. ALP.
37. Ibid.
38. Alain Locke, "Towards a Critique of Negro Music," *Opportunity* 12 (November 1934): 328. Reprinted in Jeffrey C. Stewart, *The Critical Temper of Alain Locke: A Selection of His Essays on Art and Culture* (New York: Garland, 1983), 109.
39. Walter Benjamin, *The Work of Art in the Age of Mechanical Reproduction*, ed. Hannah Arendt; transcribed, Andy Blunden (1936; New York: Schocken/Random House, 1998; proof and correct, 2005). https://www.marxists.org/reference/subject/philosophy/works/ge/benjamin.htm.

Chapter 36

1. Alain Locke (AL) to T. V. Smith (TVS), August 26, 1951. ALP. For Locke's work in helping Smith with his campaign, see AL to TVS, January 24, 1935. ALP.
2. Solomon Rosenfeld (SR) to AL, April 4, 1934. ALP.
3. SR to AL, December 12, 1934. ALP.
4. Morse Cartwright to AL, December 21, 1934. ALP.
5. Interview with Harold Lewis, April 17, 1982, Washington, D.C.
6. Mary Beattie Brady (MB) to AL, January 15, 1935. ALP.
7. Interview with Harold Lewis.
8. See Robert Goldwater, *Primitivism in Modern Painting* (1938; New York, London: Harper & Brothers, 1967).
9. MB to AL, January 15, 1935. ALP.
10. AL to "Colleagues," February 1, 1935. ALP.
11. Ibid.
12. AL to Charlotte Mason (CM), January 13, 1935. ALP.
13. See Brian Urquhart, *Ralph Bunche: An American Life* (New York: W.W. Norton), 45.
14. Interview with Harold Lewis, April 17, 1982, Washington, D.C.
15. AL to CM, January 13, 1935. ALP.
16. Sterling Denhard Spero and Abram Lincoln Harris, *The Black Worker: The Negro and the Labor Movement* (New York: Columbia University Press, 1931).
17. Ibid.
18. James Johnson Sweeney to Locke, May 11, 1935. ALP.
19. Alain Locke, "African Art: Classic Style," *American Magazine of Art* 28 (May 1935): 271–278.
20. Raymond Buell, "Autonomy vs. Assimilation: A Comparative View" (lecture delivered at the Minorities Conference held at Howard University, April 5, 1935).
21. TVS to AL, June 5, 1935. ALP.
22. Horace Kallen to AL, May 9, 1935. ALP.
23. Carter G. Woodson (CGW) to AL, April 4, 1935. ALP.
24. AL to CGW, April 2, 1935. ALP.
25. CGW to AL, April 9, 1935. ALP.
26. AL to CGW, April 8, 1935. ALP.
27. CGW to AL, April 1935. ALP.
28. Jacqueline Goggin, *Carter G. Woodson: A Life in Black History* (Baton Rouge: Louisiana State University Press, 1997): payments from Carnegie Corporation in 1921 for ASNLH.
29. AL to TVS, June 20, 1935. ALP.
30. TVS to AL, June 24, 1935. ALP.
31. Alain Locke, "Values and Imperatives," in L. Harris, ed., *The Philosophy of Alain Locke: Harlem Renaissance and Beyond* (Philadelphia: Temple University Press, 1991), 34.
32. Ibid., 35.
33. Ibid., 38.
34. Ibid., 37.
35. Ibid., 40.
36. Ibid., 41.
37. Ibid., 35.
38. AL to CGW, June 1935. ALP.
39. AL to Lyman Bryson, June 8, 1936. ALP.
40. AL to CGW, April 2, 1935. ALP.
41. David Levering Lewis, *W. E. B. Du Bois: The Fight for Equality and the American Century, 1919–1963* (New York: Henry Holt, 2000), 445–447.

Chapter 37

1. "Mischief Out of Misery," *Time* 25, no. 13 (April 1935): 13.
2. Alain Locke, "Deep River: Deeper Sea: Retrospective Review of the Literature of the Negro for 1935," *Opportunity* 14, no. 1 (January 1936): 8.

3. Alain Locke (AL) to Charlotte Mason (CM), June 30, 1935. ALP.
4. Ibid.
5. Ibid.
6. "A Harlem Center of Culture," memorandum AL to MB, n.d., ca. 1935. ALP.
7. Ibid.
8. Ibid.
9. AL to CM, April 4, 1935. ALP.
10. PK to AL, January 17, 1936. PKP.
11. Meyer Schapiro, "Race, Nationality, and Art," *Art Front* 2, no. 4 (March 1936): 10.
12. Alain Locke, "Harlem: Mecca of the New Negro," *Survey Graphic* 3 (March 1925): 630.
13. Harold Cruse, *The Crisis of the Negro Intellectual: A Historical Analysis of the Failure of Black Leadership* (1967; New York Review Books Classics, 2005).
14. Alvia J. Wardlaw, *The Art of John Biggers: View from the Upper Room* (New York: Harry N. Abrams, in association with the Museum of Fine Arts, Houston, 1995), 28.
15. Viktor Lowenfeld, *Hampton Bulletin of 1943*, 27.
16. Interview with Daniel Aaron, October 15, 2011, Cambridge, Mass.
17. Interview with Ladislas Segy, June 15, 1982, New York.
18. AL to Mary Beattie Brady (MB), May 27, 1936. ALP.
19. Memorandum titled, "THE HARLEM ARTISTS' GUILD," in AL to MB, May 27, 1936. ALP.
20. MB to AL, May 29, 1936. ALP.
21. Ibid.
22. Ibid.
23. Ibid.
24. Morse Cartwright (MC) to AL, May 3, 1936. ALP.
25. AL to MC, May 4, 1936. ALP.
26. AL to Paul Kellogg (PK), n.d. 1936. ALP.
27. Ibid.
28. AL to CM, September 11, 1936. ALP.
29. Janet Sabloff to PK, October 14, 1936. PKP.
30. PK to Fiorello H. La Guardia, September 11, 1936. New York Municipal Archives.
31. Interview with Harold Lewis, April 17, 1982, Washington, D.C.
32. AL to PK, September 4, 1937. PKP.
33. E. Franklin Frazier to Victor Weybright, July 3, 1936. PKP.
34. Oswald Garrison Villard review of Locke's article, n.d., unpublished. ALP.

Chapter 38

1. John P. Davis (JD) to Alain Locke (AL), September 30, 1937. ALP.
2. "Resume of Talk and Discussion: Alain Locke Sunday Afternoon Session: National Negro Congress," n.d. [1937]. ALP.
3. Ibid.
4. Ibid.
5. Ibid.
6. Ibid.
7. Lyman Bryson to AL, June 23, 1936. ALP.
8. AL to Beals, March 9, 1937; LB to AL, June 23, 1936. ALP.
9. Alain Locke, "God Save Reality! A Retrospective Review of the Literature of the Negro: 1936," in *The Critical Temper of Alain Locke: A Selection of His Essays on Art and Culture*, ed. Jeffrey C. Stewart (New York: Garland, 1983), 252; originally published in *Opportunity* 15, no. 2 (February 1937): 8–13, 40–44.
10. Ruth Raphael to Locke, April 27, 1937. ALP.
11. Alain Locke, "Spiritual Truancy," *New Challenge* 2 (Fall 1937): 81.
12. Ibid.
13. Locke, "Spiritual Truancy," 83.
14. Alain Locke, "Jingo, Counter-Jingo and Us—Part 1. Retrospective Review of the Literature of the Negro: 1937," *Opportunity* 16, no. 1 (January 1938): 8.

15. Ibid.
16. Ibid.
17. Locke, *Critical Temper*, 269.
18. Locke, "Jingo," 11.
19. Alain Locke, "The Negro: 'New' or Newer," *Opportunity* 17 (January 1939): 5.
20. Alain Locke, "Of Native Sons: Real and Otherwise," *Opportunity* 19 (January–February 1941): 299.

Chapter 39

1. Interview with Robert Martin, August 8, 1982, Washington, D.C.
2. Interview with Robert E. Fennell, April 11, 1987, Washington, D.C.
3. W. E. B. Du Bois, *W.E.B. Du Bois: Writings, The Library of America* (Cambridge: University of Cambridge, 1986), 364.
4. Interview with Dr. William Banner, April 10, 1982, Washington, D.C.
5. Alain Locke, *Negro Poetry and Fiction* or *Negro Art: Past and Present*. Bronze Booklet (1942).
6. Interview with Robert E. Fennell.
7. Interview with Richard Bruce Nugent, December 11, 1982, Hoboken, N.J.
8. Alain Locke, letter to the editor, *Art Front* (October 1937): 19–20.
9. Interview with John Biggers, January 17, 1990. Dallas, Tex.
10. One of the latter, *Negro Youth*, a study of one of her students at Palmer Institute, had won honorable mention at the 1930 Harmon Foundation exhibition.
11. Alain Locke (AL) to Charlotte Mason (CM), May 1938. ALP.
12. AL to CM, July 21, 1938. ALP.
13. Lionel de Fonseka (LdF) to AL, July 28, 1938. ALP.
14. Ibid.
15. Ibid.
16. Ibid.
17. W. E. B. Du Bois, *Souls of the Black Folk* (Boston: Bedford, 1903; 1997), 2–3.

Chapter 40

1. Frederick P. Keppel (FPK) to Alain Locke (AL), December 13, 1938.
2. AL to FPK, December 20, 1938. ALP.
3. Romare Bearden and Harry Henderson, *A History of African-American Artists from 1792 to the Present* (New York: Pantheon, 1993), 240–241.
4. AL to Mary Beattie Brady (MB), January 25, 1939. ALP.
5. Ibid.
6. Interview with Richard Long, March 3, 2012, Atlanta, Ga.
7. AL to MB, January 25, 1939. ALP.
8. Alain Locke, foreword to *Contemporary Negro Art*. The Baltimore Museum of Art. Exhibition of February 3–19, 1939, and accompanying catalog.
9. Margaret Vendryes, *Expression and Repression of Identity: Race, Religion and Sexuality in the Art of American Sculptor Richmond Barthé* (PhD diss., Princeton University, UMI Press, 1997).
10. Alain Locke, "Advance on the Art Front," *Opportunity* 17, no. 5 (May 1939): 132.
11. Jacob Lawrence to AL, ca. June 1939. ALP.
12. Bearden and Henderson, *A History of African-American Artists*.
13. Confidential to AL from Morse A. Cartwright, May 1, 1939. ALP.
14. Ibid.
15. Morse A. Cartwright (MAC) to AL, May 31, 1939. ALP.
16. Claude Barnett (CB) to AL, April 20, 1940. ALP.
17. CB to AL, May 14, 1940. ALP.
18. AL to MB, ca. July 3, 1940. ALP.
19. Ibid.

Chapter 41

1. Alain Locke (AL) to Charlotte Mason (CM), January 15, 1939. ALP.
2. Ibid.
3. Mark Naison, *Communists in Harlem during the Depression* (Urbana-Champaign: University of Illinois Press, 2005).
4. Cedric Dover, *Half-Caste* (London: Secker & Warburg, 1937).
5. Frederick Redefer to AL, telegram, February 22, 1939. ALP.
6. AL to Mary Beattie Brady (MB), n.d. ALP.
7. Franklin Folson to Alain Locke, March 21, 1940. ALP.
8. Alain Locke, "To the League of American Writers on the Fourth Annual Conference" (report given to the American Committee for the Protection of Foreign Born. Hotel Annapolis, Washington, D.C., March 2–3, 1940).
9. Wayne D. Shirley, "William Grant Still's Choral Ballad and They Lynched Him on a Tree," *American Music* 12, no. 4:425–461.
10. William Grant Still, "And They Lynched Him from a Tree," choral ballad first performed as radio broadcast, October 1939.
11. Ibid.
12. Alain Locke, "Ballad for Democracy," *Opportunity* 18, no. 8 (August 1940): 228.
13. Alain Locke and Bernhard J. Stern, eds., *When Peoples Meet: A Study in Race and Culture Contacts* (New York: Progressive Education Association, 1942).
14. AL to CM, September 13, 1940. ALP.
15. AL to Charles Sebree (CS), April 6, 1940. ALP.
16. Ibid.
17. CS to AL, n.d. 1940. ALP.
18. CS to AL, April 10, 1940. ALP.
19. AL to CS, April [n.d.,] 1940. ALP.
20. Countee Cullen (CC) to AL, April 25, 1940. ALP.
21. CS to AL, April 22, 1940. ALP.
22. Countee Cullen and Sebree Charles, *The Lost Zoo*: A Rhyme for the Young, but Not Too Young (New York: Harper & Bros., 1940).
23. Woodson was so thrilled with Porter's generally critical review that Woodson chose it as the best review of 1940. Refusing to let his animus toward Locke having the gall to create his own—and now quite successful—adult-education publishing series, Woodson was determined to find every opportunity to publicly dismiss the products of Locke's press. Certainly, criticality toward the book was warranted. But that it was motivated by a sense of unnecessary rivalry speaks to the sad legacy of this period of Black intellectual history, when a handful of Harvard-educated Black intellectuals found competition a more appropriate use of their meager resources than collaboration.
24. Ishmael P. Flory to AL, May 13, 1940. ALP.
25. Theodore Ward to AL, n.d. ALP.
26. Alain Locke, "Spirituals," in Jeffrey C. Stewart, *The Critical Temper of Alain Locke* (New York: Garland, 1983).
27. Alain Locke speech as part of "Program of Negro Folk Song with Commentary Emancipation Celebration," December 20, 1940.
28. Margaret T. G. Burroughs, quoted in George J. Mavigliano and Richard A. Lawson, *The Federal Art Project in Illinois, 1935–1943* (Carbondale: Southern Illinois University Press, 1990), 67.
29. Peter Pollack (PP) to AL, n.d. ALP.
30. Burroughs in *The Federal Art Project*, 67.
31. PP to AL, n.d. ALP.
32. Ibid.
33. Charles White quoted in *The Federal Art Project in Illinois*, 72.
34. Erin P. Cohn, "Art Fronts: Visual Culture and Race Politics in Mid-Twentieth Century United States, 2010," *Publicly Accessible Penn Dissertations*: 107.
35. AL to PP, May 7, 1941. PPP.

36. Eleanor Roosevelt's trip to Chicago, *Chicago Defender*, May 8, 1941.
37. See Peter J. Bloom, *French Colonial Documentary: Mythologies of Humanitarianism* (Ann Arbor: University of Michigan Press, 2008), 35–37.
38. Alain Locke, "Chicago's New Southside Art Center," *Magazine of Art* 34, no. 7 (August–September 1941): 370.

Chapter 42

1. "Washington, D.C. February 20, 1942, Typescript of stenographer's transcription of FBI interview with Alain Leroy Locke," FBI files. All further references to this interview are from this same source.
2. Maurice V. Russell (MVR) to Alain Locke (AL), February 10, 1942. ALP.
3. AL to MVR, February 24, 1942. ALP.
4. MVR to AL, February 10, 1942. ALP.
5. MVR to AL, August 25, 1942. ALP.
6. Ibid.
7. AL to MVR, June 14, 1942. ALP.
8. Ibid.
9. Alain Locke, "The Unfinished Business of Democracy," *Survey Graphic* 31, no. 11 (November 1942): 455.
10. Locke, "The Unfinished Business," 454.
11. Sterling Brown, "Out of Their Mouths," loc. cit., 482.
12. D. Hercules Armstrong, "Boy in the Ghetto" loc. cit., 542.
13. Alain Locke, "Harlem: Mecca of the New Negro," *Survey Graphic* 6, no. 6 (March 1925): 629–634.
14. "Six Ways to Invade U.S.," *Life Magazine* 12, no. 9 (March 2, 1942).
15. Alain Locke, "The Negro in the Two Americas," typescript. ALP.
16. Ibid.
17. CM to AL, September 23 1943. ALP.
18. AL to Maurice V. Russell (MVR), n.d. [1943]. ALP.
19. Ibid.
20. Max L. Hudicourt, *Haiti Faces Tomorrow's Peace*, trans. Anita Weinstein (New York: L'Association Democratique Haitienne, 1945).
21. AL to CM, September 13, 1943. ALP.
22. See http://www.globalsecurity.org/military/world/haiti/history-13.htm, accessed December 31, 2014.
23. Alain Locke, "The Negro in the Three Americas," *Journal of Negro Education* (Winter 1944): 7–8.

Chapter 43

1. Letter from Department of Philosophy, University of Wisconsin, to author, 1977.
2. Alain Locke (AL) to Horace Kallen (HK), March 8, 1946. ALP.
3. AL to HK, February 12, 1946. ALP.
4. See Jeffrey C. Stewart, "Beyond Category: Before Afro-Futurism There Was Norman Lewis," in *Procession: The Art of Norman Lewis* (Philadelphia: Pennsylvania Academy of Fine Arts, 2015), 161–191.
5. Alain Locke, introduction to *The Negro Artist Comes of Age: A National Survey of Contemporary American Artists* (Albany, N.Y.: Albany Institute of History and Art, 1945).
6. Horace Kallen (HK) to AL, March 5, 1946. ALP.
7. Ibid.
8. Purchase of 12 Grove Street, Greenwich Village.
9. Interview with Arthur Fauset, December 27, 1980, Philadelphia, Pa.
10. Ibid.
11. See http://nedstuckeyfrench.com/essays-in-america/phylon-science-or-propaganda-by-w-e-b-du-bois/, accessed January 24, 2015.
12. Interview with Robert Fennell, April 11, 1987, Washington, D.C.

13. Ibid.
14. "The Salzburg Seminar in American Studies—Celebrating 50 Years in 1997," http://www .americansc.org.uk/online/salzburg.html, accessed January 1, 2017.
15. Interview with Robert Fennell.
16. AL to Lionel de Fonseka (LdF), n.d. ALP.
17. Robert E. Claybrooks to AL, December 19, 1952, ALP.
18. Ibid.
19. Alain Locke, "Self-Criticism: The Third Dimension in Culture," *Phylon* 11 (4th Quarter, 1950): 391–394.
20. Ibid., 393–394.
21. Ibid., 394.
22. Alain Locke, "Horace Pippin." In Horace Pippin Memorial Exhibition, The Art Alliance, April 8–May 4, 1947. Philadelphia, Pa.
23. Ibid.
24. Alain Locke, "Santayana," *The Key Reporter* 16, no. 4 (Autumn 1951): 4.
25. Rayford W. Logan, *Howard University: The First Hundred Years, 1867–1967* (New York: New York University Press, 2004), 434.
26. Margaret Butcher (MB) to AL, January 27, 1953. ALP.
27. MB to AL, January 30, 1953. ALP.
28. Transcript of interview with FBI. FBI.
29. Ibid.
30. AL to Mrs. Biddle, January 4, 1954. ALP.
31. Douglas Stafford to AL, n.d. [1954]. ALP.
32. Interview with Arthur Fauset, December 27, 1980, Philadelphia, Pa.
33. Ibid.

Chapter 44

1. Interview with Arthur Fauset, December 27, 1980, Philadelphia, Pa.
2. Thomas Dyett (TD) to George E. C. Hayes (GECH), June 17, 1954. ALP.
3. TD to GECH, January 24, 1956. ALP.
4. TD to J. B. Clarke (JBC), January 28, 1957; Arthur Huff Fauset to JBC, February 7, 1957; JBC to TD, February 5, 1957; JBC to TD, March 20, 1958; JBC to GECH, January 6, 1959; Earl H. Davis to Luther W. Youngdahl, May 7, 1959. ALP.
5. See David Roediger, *The Wages of Whiteness: Race and the Making of the American Working Class* (New York: Verso, 2007) for a powerful explication of this sense of entitlement. Clearly, Ms. Dougherty was victimized by Fauset's negligence. But the way she hung in and ballooned her requests to $50,000 shows her greediness to try and exploit the accidental fact that the house was now owned by a Black university subsidized by the federal government and reveals her sense of entitlement. That Locke announced even in jest that Whites were better tenants than Blacks becomes ironic and revealing of the limits of his Black consciousness.
6. Interview with Robert Fennell. April 11, 1987. Washington, D.C.
7. Interview with Arthur Fauset.
8. Frances Stead Sellers, "The 60 Year Journey of the Ashes of Alain Locke, Father of the Harlem Renaissance," *Washington Post Magazine* (September 12, 2014), http://www.washingtonpost .com/lifestyle/magazine/the-60-year-journey-of-the-ashes-of-alain-locke-father-of-the-harlem-renaissance/2014/09/11/2ea31ccc-2878-11e4-86ca-6f03cbd15c1a_story.html, accessed November 14, 2016.
9. Ibid.
10. Interview with Robert Fennell.

Epilogue

1. W. E. B. Du Bois, "Criteria of Negro Art," *Crisis* 32 (October 1926), 290. http://www. webdubois.org/dbCriteriaNArt.html, accessed September 5, 2016.

SELECT BIBLIOGRAPHY

Manuscript Collections

Alain Locke Papers. Moorland-Spingarn Research Center. Howard University. Washington, D.C. (ALP).

Archibald Grimke Papers, Moorland-Spingarn Research Center. Howard University. (AGP).

Arthur Spingarn Papers. Moorland-Spingarn Research Center. Howard University. (ASP).

Booker T. Washington Papers. Library of Congress. (BTW).

Claude A. Barnett Papers. Chicago History Museum. (CBP).

Countee Cullen Papers. Amistad Research Center. Tulane University. (CC).

Countee Cullen Papers. Manuscript Division. Library of Congress.

Harmon Foundation Papers. Library of Congress. (HFP).

Hertford College Archives. Oxford. (HCA).

Horace Kallen Papers. American Jewish Archives, Cincinnati, Ohio. (HKP).

Jesse Moorland Papers. Moorland-Spingarn Research Center. Howard University. (JMP).

Josephine Harreld Love Papers. Private Collection.

Langston Hughes Papers. James Weldon Johnson Collection, Beinecke Library, Yale. (LHP).

League of American Writers Archives. Bancroft Library, University of California, Berkeley. (LAW).

New York Municipal Archives. New York City. (NMA).

Paul Kellogg Papers. Archives of Social Welfare History. University of Minnesota. Minneapolis, Minn. (PKP).

Peter Pollack Papers. Archives of American Art, Smithsonian Institution. (PPP).

Ralph Bunche Papers. Department of Special Collections, Charles E. Young Research Library. UCLA. (RBP).

Rhodes Scholarship Trust Records. Microfilm, Canada Archives. (RST).

Sir George R. Parkin Papers. Archives Branch, Public Archives, Canada. (GPP).

Southside Community Art Center Archives. Chicago, Ill. (SCAAC).

United States Department of Justice. Federal Bureau of Investigation File #218,903 Alain Leroy Locke. (FBI).

W. E. B. Du Bois Papers. Special Collections and University Archives, University of Massachusetts Amherst Libraries. (WEBDP).

Interviews

Aaron, Daniel. October 15, 2011. Cambridge, Mass.

Achille, Louis. February 6, 1992. Paris, France.

Alexander, Sadie. April 30, 1983. Philadelphia, Pa.

Banner, William. April 10, 1982. Washington, D.C.

Biggers, John. January 17, 1990. Dallas, Tex.

Davis, Arthur. April 4, 1975. Washington, D.C.
Fauset, Arthur. December 27, 1980. Philadelphia, Pa.
Fennell, Robert E. April 11, 1987. Washington, D.C.
Jones, Lois Mailou. May 15, 1988. Washington, D.C.
Lewis, Harold. April 17, 1982. Washington, D.C.
Lochard, Metz T. P. June 13, 1975. Chicago, Ill.
Long, Richard. March 3, 2012. Atlanta, Ga.
Martin, Robert. August 8, 1982. Washington, D.C.
Nugent, Richard Bruce. December 11, 1982. Hoboken, N.J.
Patterson, Louise. March 17, 1987. Oakland, Calif.
Prudhomme, Charles. April 11, 1976. Washington, D.C.
Segy, Ladislas. June 15, 1982. New York, N.Y.
Sullivan, Mae Miller. April 4, 1976. Washington, D.C.
Wilkerson, Doxey. May 6, 1982. Washington, D.C.

INDEX

Figures and notes are indicated by f and n following the page numbers.